RDA

RESOURCE DESCRIPTION & ACCESS

2014 REVISION

Includes changes and updates through April 2014

Developed in a collaborative process led by the
Joint Steering Committee for Development of RDA (JSC), representing

The American Library Association

The Australian Committee on Cataloguing

The British Library

The Canadian Committee on Cataloguing

CILIP: Chartered Institute of Library and Information Professionals

Deutsche Nationalbibliothek

The Library of Congress

AMERICAN LIBRARY ASSOCIATION, CHICAGO
CANADIAN LIBRARY ASSOCIATION, OTTAWA
CILIP: CHARTERED INSTITUTE OF LIBRARY AND INFORMATION PROFESSIONALS, LONDON

PUBLISHED 2014 BY

American Library Association
50 East Huron Street
Chicago, Illinois 60611

ISBN: 978-0-8389-1293-5

Canadian Library Association
1150 Morrison Drive, Suite 400
Ottawa, ON K2H 8S9

ISBN: 978-0-88802-344-5

CILIP: Chartered Institute of Library and Information Professionals
7 Ridgmount Street
London WC1E 7AE
ISBN: 978-1-78330-042-6

The Library of Congress has cataloged the earlier version as follows:

Resource description & access : RDA / developed in a collaborative process led by the Joint Steering Committee for Development of RDA (JSC).
v. (loose-leaf) cm.
Resource description and access
RDA
Also available online as part of the RDA toolkit.
Includes index.
Based on prepublication information from ALA Publishing.
ISBN-13: 978-0-8389-1093-1 (loose-leaf : alk. paper)
ISBN-10: 0-8389-1093-9 (loose-leaf : alk. paper) 1. Descriptive cataloging--Standards. I. Joint Steering Committee for Development of RDA. II. Title: Resource description and access. III. Title: RDA.
Z694.15.R47 R47
025.3'2 22

2010038434

Library and Archives Canada has cataloged the earlier version as follows:

RDA : resource description and access / developed in a collaborative process led by the Joint Steering Committee for Development of RDA (JSC) representing the American Library Association ... [et. al.].

Co-published by: Canadian Library Association, CILIP : Chartered Institute of Library and Information Professionals.
Includes index.
ISBN 978-0-8389-1093-1 (American Library Association).--ISBN 978-0-88802-335-3 (Canadian Library Association).--ISBN 978-1-85604-749-4 (Chartered Institute of Library and Information Professionals)

1. Resource description & access. 2. Descriptive cataloging--Standards. I. Joint Steering Committee for Development of RDA II. Canadian Library Association III. Chartered Institute of Library and Information Professionals IV. Title: Resource description and access.

Z694.15.R47R43 2010 025.3'2 C2010-906792-4

A catalogue record is also available from the British Library.

∞ This paper meets the requirements of ANSI/NISO Z39.48-1992 (Permanence of Paper).

POD2014-1

Content Development for RDA: Resource Description and Access

The Joint Steering Committee for Development of RDA (JSC), working with the RDA Editor, is responsible for developing the content of RDA. The JSC consists of representatives from seven major cataloguing communities, including the American Library Association (ALA), the Australian Committee on Cataloguing (ACOC), the British Library (BL), the Canadian Committee on Cataloguing (CCC), the Chartered Institute of Library and Information Professionals (CILIP), Deutsche Nationalbibliothek, and the Library of Congress (LC).

The JSC reports to the Committee of Principals (CoP), whose members are the directors (or directors' representatives) of the Canadian, UK, and US professional library associations, the British Library, Library and Archives Canada, the Library of Congress, and the National Library of Australia.

Other groups involved in the preparation of RDA include the Appendices Working Group (revising the appendices on capitalization, abbreviations, and initial articles) and two RDA Examples Groups (reviewing and updating examples for inclusion in RDA).

For detailed information about the JSC and the RDA content development process, including

- the JSC membership rosters, 1974–present;
- a brief history of the process;
- the procedure for submitting comments and proposals for revision of RDA;
- working documents;
- historical documents; and
- JSC and RDA news,

see the JSC website, www.rda-jsc.org.

Preface to the 2014 Revision

The 2014 Revision of *RDA: Resource Description and Access* represents a reissue of the base volume of *RDA*. Since its initial publication in 2010, *RDA* has undergone three types of revision—annual RDA Updates, periodic Fast Track changes, and a one-time rewording. The 2013 Revision of *RDA* included the one-time rewording and RDA Updates from 2012 and 2013, as well as all Fast Track changes between 2010 and July 2013. This new revision updates the 2013 Revision. RDA Toolkit subscribers receive all revisions automatically as part of their subscription.

The Joint Steering Committee for Development of RDA issued updates to the content of RDA in April 2014. This annual RDA Update contains approved proposals from the JSC meeting held in November of 2013. The details of the changes that the JSC made to RDA are available for RDA Toolkit subscribers through the RDA Update History section found at the bottom of the RDA tab in RDA Toolkit. Those changes are also available in the "Sec final" versions of the proposals posted on the JSC web site (www.rda-jsc.org). The 2014 Revision includes the complete 2014 RDA Update.

Fast Track changes are minor changes and corrections of typographical errors that have been reviewed by the JSC Secretary. Fast Track changes are made to RDA whenever there is a new release of RDA Toolkit. Complete lists of all Fast Track changes can be found on the JSC website in the Secretary Document Series. The 2014 Revision includes all Fast Track changes from July 2013 through April 2014.

RDA Co-Publishers, September 2014

RDA TABLE OF CONTENTS

SECTION 4: RECORDING ATTRIBUTES OF CONCEPT, OBJECT, EVENT, AND PLACE

SECTION 5: RECORDING PRIMARY RELATIONSHIPS BETWEEN WORK, EXPRESSION, MANIFESTATION, AND ITEM

SECTION 6: RECORDING RELATIONSHIPS TO PERSONS, FAMILIES, AND CORPORATE BODIES

SECTION 7: RECORDING RELATIONSHIPS TO CONCEPTS, OBJECTS, EVENTS, AND PLACES

SECTION 8: RECORDING RELATIONSHIPS BETWEEN WORKS, EXPRESSIONS, MANIFESTATIONS, AND ITEMS

SECTION 9: RECORDING RELATIONSHIPS BETWEEN PERSONS, FAMILIES, AND CORPORATE BODIES

SECTION 10: RECORDING RELATIONSHIPS BETWEEN CONCEPTS, OBJECTS, EVENTS, AND PLACES

0

INTRODUCTION

0.0 Purpose and Scope

RDA provides a set of guidelines and instructions on recording data to support resource discovery.

The data created using RDA to describe a resource are designed to assist users performing the following tasks:[1]

find—i.e., to find resources that correspond to the user's stated search criteria

identify—i.e., to confirm that the resource described corresponds to the resource sought, or to distinguish between two or more resources with similar characteristics

select—i.e., to select a resource that is appropriate to the user's needs

obtain—i.e., to acquire or access the resource described.

The data created using RDA to describe an entity associated with a resource (a person, family, corporate body, concept, etc.) are designed to assist users performing the following tasks:[2]

find—i.e., to find information on that entity and on resources associated with the entity

identify—i.e., to confirm that the entity described corresponds to the entity sought, or to distinguish between two or more entities with similar names, etc.

clarify—i.e., to clarify the relationship between two or more such entities, or to clarify the relationship between the entity described and a name by which that entity is known

understand—i.e., to understand why a particular name or title, or form of name or title, has been chosen as the preferred name or title for the entity.

RDA provides a comprehensive set of guidelines and instructions covering all types of content and media.

---

1. Based on the user tasks defined in IFLA Study Group on the Functional Requirements for Bibliographic Records, *Functional Requirements for Bibliographic Records: Final Report* (München: K.G. Saur, 1998), 82. Available online at: http://archive.ifla.org/VII/s13/frbr/frbr.pdf.
2. Based on the user tasks defined in IFLA Working Group on Functional Requirements and Numbering of Authority Records (FRANAR), *Functional Requirements for Authority Data: A Conceptual Model*, edited by Glenn E. Patton (München: K.G. Saur, 2009).

0.1 Key Features

RDA provides a flexible and extensible framework for the description of resources produced and disseminated using digital technologies while also serving the needs of agencies organizing resources produced in non-digital formats.

RDA is designed to take advantage of the efficiencies and flexibility in data capture, storage, retrieval, and display made possible with new database technologies. RDA is also designed to be compatible with the legacy technologies still used in many resource discovery applications.[3]

In RDA, there is a clear line of separation between the guidelines and instructions on recording data and those on the presentation of data. This separation has been established in order to optimize flexibility in the storage and display of the data produced using RDA. Guidelines and instructions on recording data are covered in chapters **1** through **37**; those on the presentation of data are covered in appendices **D** and **E**.

---

3. For an outline of how RDA data might be stored in a relational or object oriented database structure or in the legacy database structures still used in many library applications, see *RDA Database Implementation Scenarios*, http://www.rda-jsc.org/docs/5editor2rev.pdf

0.2 Relationship to Other Standards for Resource Description and Access

RDA is built on foundations established by the *Anglo-American Cataloguing Rules* (AACR) and the cataloguing traditions on which it was based.[4] [5] [6] [7]

Instructions derived from AACR have been reworked to produce a standard that will be easier to use, more adaptable, and more cost-efficient in its application. A key factor in the design of RDA has been the need to integrate data produced using RDA into existing databases developed using AACR and related standards.

Other key standards used in developing RDA include the *International Standard Bibliographic Description (ISBD),* [8] the *MARC 21 Format for Bibliographic Data,* [9] and the *MARC 21 Format for Authority Data.* [10]

The RDA element set is compatible with ISBD, MARC 21, and Dublin Core.[11] For mappings of the RDA element set to ISBD and MARC 21, see appendices **D** and **E**.

RDA also conforms to the *RDA/ONIX Framework for Resource Categorization.*[12]

The metadata standards used in other communities (archives, museums, publishers, semantic web, etc.) were taken into consideration in the design of RDA. The goal was to attain an effective level of interoperability between those standards and RDA.

---

4. Charles A. Cutter, *Rules for a Dictionary Catalog,* 4th ed., rewritten (Washington, D.C.: Government Printing Office, 1904).
5. International Conference on Cataloguing Principles, *Report* (London: International Federation of Library Associations, 1963), 91–96.
6. Seymour Lubetzky, *Principles of Cataloging: Final Report: Phase I: Descriptive Cataloging* (Los Angeles, Calif.: University of California, Institute of Library Research, 1969).
7. Antonio Panizzi, "Rules for the Compilation of the Catalogue," in *The Catalogue of Printed Books in the British Museum,* vol. 1 (London, 1841), [v]–ix.
8. *International Standard Bibliographic Description (ISBD),* preliminary consolidated ed. (München: K.G. Saur, 2007).
9. *MARC 21 Format for Bibliographic Data,* 1999 ed. (Washington: Library of Congress, 1999–).
10. *MARC 21 Format for Authority Data,* 1999 ed. (Washington: Library of Congress, 1999–).
11. *Dublin Core Metadata Element Set,* version 1.1 ([Dublin, Ohio]: Dublin Core Metadata Initiative, 2006), http://dublincore.org/documents/dces/.
12. *RDA/ONIX Framework for Resource Categorization,* version 1.0 (Released August 1, 2006), http://www.rda-jsc.org/docs/5chair10.pdf.

0.3 Conceptual Models Underlying RDA

0.3.1 General

A key element in the design of RDA is its alignment with the conceptual models for bibliographic and authority data developed by the International Federation of Library Associations and Institutions (IFLA):

Functional Requirements for Bibliographic Records (FRBR)[13]

Functional Requirements for Authority Data (FRAD).[14]

The FRBR and FRAD models provide RDA with an underlying framework that has the scope needed to support:

a) comprehensive coverage of all types of content and media

b) the flexibility and extensibility needed to accommodate newly emerging resource characteristics

c) the adaptability needed for the data produced to function within a wide range of technological environments.

---

13. IFLA Study Group on the Functional Requirements for Bibliographic Records, *Functional Requirements for Bibliographic Records: Final Report* (München: K.G. Saur, 1998). Available online at http://archive.ifla.org/VII/s13/frbr/frbr.pdf.

14. IFLA Working Group on Functional Requirements and Numbering of Authority Records (FRANAR), *Functional Requirements for Authority Data: A Conceptual Model,* edited by Glenn E. Patton (München: K.G. Saur, 2009).

0.3.2 Alignment with FRBR

The RDA data elements for describing a resource generally reflect the attributes and relationships associated with the entities work, expression, manifestation, and item, as defined in FRBR.[15] Those entities are defined in RDA as follows:

work—a distinct intellectual or artistic creation (i.e., the intellectual or artistic content)

expression—the intellectual or artistic realization of a work in the form of alpha-numeric, musical or choreographic notation, sound, image, object, movement, etc., or any combination of such forms

manifestation—the physical embodiment of an expression of a work

item—a single exemplar or instance of a manifestation.

In future releases, the scope of RDA may be extended to cover additional attributes and relationships that are associated with these four entities and support resource discovery, but are not currently defined in FRBR.

Attributes and relationships currently out of scope. Attributes and relationships associated with these four entities whose primary function is to support user tasks related to resource management (e.g., acquisition, preservation) are currently out of scope.

---

15. See the attributes defined in sections 4.2–4.5 and the relationships defined in sections 5.2–5.3 of *FRBR*. For details on the correspondence between RDA elements and FRBR attributes and relationships, see *RDA to FRBR Mapping*, http://www.rda-jsc.org/docs/5rda-rdafrbrmappingrev2.pdf.

0.3.3 Alignment with FRAD

The RDA data elements for describing entities associated with a resource generally reflect the attributes and relationships associated with the entities person, family, corporate body, and place, as defined in FRAD.[16] Those entities are defined in RDA as follows:

person—an individual or an identity established by an individual (either alone or in collaboration with one or more other individuals)

family—two or more persons related by birth, marriage, adoption, civil union, or similar legal status, or who otherwise present themselves as a family

corporate body—an organization or group of persons and/or organizations that is identified by a particular name and that acts, or may act, as a unit

place—a location identified by a name.

RDA also covers additional attributes of the entity work that are defined in FRAD but are not included in FRBR.

Attributes associated with the entities name, identifier, controlled access point, and rules, as defined in FRAD, are covered selectively.

In future releases, the scope of RDA may be extended to cover additional attributes and relationships (associated with the entities person, family, corporate body, place, work, expression, name, identifier, controlled access point, and rules) that support resource discovery, but are not currently defined in FRAD.

Attributes and relationships currently out of scope. The following attributes and relationships are currently out of scope:

- attributes and relationships associated with the entities concept, object, and event, as defined in FRAD
- relationships between controlled access points, as defined in FRAD
- attributes and relationships (associated with the entities person, family, corporate body, work, and expression) whose primary function is to support user tasks related to rights management.

---

16. See the attributes defined in sections 4.1–4.7 and the relationships defined in sections 5.3–5.4 of *FRAD.* For details on the correspondence between RDA elements and FRAD attributes and relationships, see *RDA to FRAD Mapping*, http://www.rda-jsc.org/docs/5rda-rdafradmappingrev.pdf.

0.4 Objectives and Principles Governing Resource Description and Access

0.4.1 General

RDA guidelines and instructions have been designed in accordance with the objectives and principles set out at **0.4.2–0.4.3**.

The IFLA *Statement of International Cataloguing Principles* [17] informs the cataloguing principles used throughout RDA.

While the statement of objectives and principles serves to provide overall guidance for the development of RDA, trade-offs sometimes have to be made between one principle and another.

---

17. *Statement of International Cataloguing Principles* (2009), http://www.ifla.org/files/cataloguing/icp/icp_2009-en.pdf.

0.4.2 Objectives

0.4.2.1 Responsiveness to User Needs

The data should enable the user to:

- *find* resources that correspond to the user's stated search criteria
- *find* all resources that embody a particular work or a particular expression of that work
- *find* all resources associated with a particular person, family, or corporate body
- *find* all resources on a given subject
- *find* works, expressions, manifestations, and items that are related to those retrieved in response to the user's search
- *find* persons, families, and corporate bodies that correspond to the user's stated search criteria
- *find* persons, families, or corporate bodies that are related to the person, family, or corporate body represented by the data retrieved in response to the user's search
- *identify* the resource described (i.e., confirm that the resource described corresponds to the resource sought, or distinguish between two or more resources with the same or similar characteristics)
- *identify* the person, family, or corporate body represented by the data (i.e., confirm that the entity described corresponds to the entity sought, or distinguish between two or more entities with the same or similar names, etc.)
- *select* a resource that is appropriate to the user's requirements with respect to the physical characteristics of the carrier and the formatting and encoding of information stored on the carrier
- *select* a resource appropriate to the user's requirements with respect to the content characteristics of the work or expression (e.g., form, intended audience, language)

obtain a resource (i.e., acquire a resource through purchase, loan, etc., or access a resource electronically through an online connection to a remote computer)

understand the relationship between two or more entities

understand the relationship between the entity described and a name by which that entity is known (e.g., a different language form of the name)

understand why a particular name or title has been chosen as the preferred name or title for the entity.

0.4.2.2 Cost Efficiency

The data should meet functional requirements for the support of user tasks in a cost-efficient manner.

0.4.2.3 Flexibility

The data should function independently of the format, medium, or system used to store or communicate the data. They should be amenable to use in a variety of environments.

0.4.2.4 Continuity

The data should be amenable to integration into existing databases (particularly those developed using AACR and related standards).

0.4.3 Principles

0.4.3.1 Differentiation

The data describing a resource should differentiate that resource from other resources.

The data describing an entity associated with a resource should differentiate that entity from other entities, and from other identities used by the same entity.

0.4.3.2 Sufficiency

The data describing a resource should be sufficient to meet the needs of the user with respect to selection of an appropriate resource.

0.4.3.3 Relationships

The data describing a resource should indicate significant relationships between the resource described and other resources.

The data describing an entity associated with a resource should reflect all significant bibliographic relationships between that entity and other such entities.

0.4.3.4 Representation

The data describing a resource should reflect the resource's representation of itself.

The name or form of name chosen as the preferred name for a person, family, or corporate body should be:

a) the name or form of name most commonly found in resources associated with that person, family, or corporate body
or

b) a well-accepted name or form of name in a language and script preferred by the agency creating the data.

Other names and other forms of the name should be recorded as variant names:

names found in resources associated with the person, family, or corporate body

names found in reference sources

names that the user might be expected to use when conducting a search.

The title or form of title chosen as the preferred title for a work should be:

a) the title most frequently found in resources embodying the work in its original language
or

b) the title as found in reference sources

or

c) the title most frequently found in resources embodying the work.

Other titles and other forms of the title should be recorded as variant titles:

titles found in resources embodying the work

titles found in reference sources

titles that the user might be expected to use when conducting a search.

0.4.3.5 Accuracy

The data describing a resource should provide supplementary information to correct or clarify ambiguous, unintelligible, or misleading representations made on sources of information forming part of the resource itself.

0.4.3.6 Attribution

The data recording relationships between a resource and a person, family, or corporate body associated with that resource should reflect attributions of responsibility, whether these attributions are accurate or not. Attributions of responsibility can be found either in the resource itself or in reference sources.

0.4.3.7 Common Usage or Practice

Data that are not transcribed from the resource itself should reflect common usage in the language and script chosen for recording the data. The agency creating the data may prefer one or more languages and scripts.

When there is more than one part in the name of a person or family, the part chosen as the first element of the preferred name should reflect the usage or practice in the country and language most closely associated with that person or family.

0.4.3.8 Uniformity

The appendices on capitalization, abbreviations, order of elements, punctuation, etc., should serve to promote uniformity in the presentation of data describing a resource or an entity associated with a resource.

0.5 Structure

RDA is divided into ten sections: sections 1–4 cover elements corresponding to the entity attributes defined in FRBR and FRAD; sections 5–10 cover elements corresponding to the relationships defined in FRBR and FRAD.[18]

The initial chapter in each section sets out the functional objectives and principles underlying the guidelines and instructions in that section, and specifies core elements to support those functional objectives.

Subsequent chapters within each section cover attributes or relationships that support a specific user task as follows:[19]

Attributes

Section 1 covers the attributes of manifestations and items that are most commonly used to identify a resource (chapter **2**), to select a resource appropriate to the user's requirements with respect to format and encoding (chapter **3**), and to obtain a resource (chapter **4**).

Section 2 covers the attributes of works and expressions that are most commonly used to identify a work or expression (chapter **6**), and to select a work or expression appropriate to the user's requirements with respect to content (chapter **7**).

Section 3 covers the attributes of persons (chapter **9**), families (chapter **10**), and corporate bodies (chapter **11**) that are most commonly used to identify those entities.

Section 4 covers the attributes of concepts (chapter **13***[19]), objects (chapter **14***[19]), events (chapter **15***[19]), and places (chapter **16**) that are most commonly used to identify those entities.

Relationships

Section 5 covers the primary relationships between a work, expression, manifestation, and item (chapter **17**).

Section 6 covers the relationships that are used to find works (chapter **19**), expressions (chapter **20**), manifestations (chapter **21**), and items (chapter **22**) associated with a particular person, family, or corporate body.

Section 7 covers the relationships that are used to find works on a particular subject (chapter **23***[19]).

Section 8 covers the relationships that are used to find related works (chapter **25**), related expressions (chapter **26**), related manifestations (chapter **27**), and related items (chapter **28**).

Section 9 covers the relationships that are used to find related persons (chapter **30**), related families (chapter **31**), and related corporate bodies (chapter **32**).

Section 10 covers the relationships that are used to find related concepts (chapter **34***[19]), objects (chapter **35***[19]), events (chapter **36***[19]), and places (chapter **37***).

Supplementary guidelines and instructions are provided in appendices as follows:[20]

Appendix A provides guidelines on capitalization for English and a selected number of other languages. The appendix includes guidelines that apply to elements that require transcription and to elements that are recorded.

Appendix B provides instructions on the use of abbreviations when recording specified elements and on using symbols instead of abbreviations, when appropriate. It includes lists of abbreviations in English and a selected number of other languages.

Appendix C lists articles to be omitted when applying the alternative instructions for titles for works and names of persons, corporate bodies, and places. The initial articles are listed by language.

Appendix D provides mappings of RDA data elements used to describe a resource to a selected number of related metadata schemes for encoding or presentation of resource description data (e.g., ISBD, MARC 21).

Appendix E provides mappings of RDA data elements used to describe an entity associated with a resource to a selected number of related metadata schemes for encoding or presentation of access point and authority data (e.g., AACR2, MARC 21).

Appendix F provides instructions on choosing and recording names of persons in a number of specific languages, supplementing the general guidelines and instructions in chapter **9**.

Appendix G provides information on titles of nobility, terms of rank, etc., used in a number of specific jurisdictions.

Appendix H provides information on recording dates in the Christian calendar.

Appendix I lists terms used as designators to indicate the nature of a relationship between a resource and a person, family, or corporate body associated with that resource. The relationship designators define the relationship more specifically than the relationship element by itself. The appendix provides definitions for terms used as relationship designators and instructions on their use.

Appendix J lists terms used as designators to indicate the nature of a relationship between works, expressions, manifestations, and items. The relationship designators define the relationship more specifically than the relationship element by itself. The appendix provides definitions for terms used as relationship designators and instructions on their use.

Appendix K lists terms used as designators to indicate the nature of a relationship between persons, families, and corporate bodies. The relationship designators define the relationship more specifically than the relationship element by itself. The appendix provides definitions for terms used as relationship designators and instructions on their use.

*Appendix L** lists terms used as designators to indicate the nature of a relationship between concepts, objects, events, and places. The relationship designators define the relationship more specifically than the relationship element by itself. The appendix provides definitions for terms used as relationship designators and instructions on their use.

---

18. Sections and chapters covering the attributes of *concept, object,* and *event* defined in FRAD, and the "subject" relationship defined in FRBR will not be developed until after the initial release of RDA.
19. Chapters marked with an asterisk will not be developed until after the initial release of RDA.
20. Appendices marked with an asterisk will not be developed until after the initial release of RDA.

0.6 Core Elements

0.6.1 General

Certain elements in RDA are identified as core elements.

The RDA core elements for describing resources were selected according to the FRBR assessment of the value of each attribute and relationship in supporting the following user tasks:[21]

identify and *select* a manifestation

identify works and expressions embodied in a manifestation

identify the creator or creators of a work.

The RDA core elements for describing entities associated with resources were selected according to the FRAD assessment of the value of each attribute and relationship in supporting the following user tasks:[22]

find a person, family, or corporate body associated with a resource

identify a person, family, or corporate body.

The elements identified in RDA as core elements are listed at **0.6.2–0.6.9**. Only one instance of a core element is required. Subsequent instances are optional.

As a minimum, a resource description for a work, expression, manifestation, or item should include all the core elements that are applicable and readily ascertainable. The description should also include any additional elements that are required in a particular case to differentiate the resource from one or more other resources with similar identifying information.

A description of an entity associated with a resource should include all the core elements that are applicable and readily ascertainable. The description should also include any additional elements that are required in a particular case to differentiate the entity from one or more other entities with the same name or title.

The inclusion of other specific elements or subsequent instances of these elements is optional. The agency responsible for creating the data may choose:

a) to establish policies and guidelines on levels of description and authority control to be applied either generally or to specific categories of resources and other entities

or

b) to leave decisions on the level of detail to the judgment of the cataloguer or the individual creating the data.

---

21. See FRBR, chapter 6.
22. See FRAD, chapter 6.

0.6.2 Section 1: Recording Attributes of Manifestation and Item

When recording data identifying and describing a manifestation or item, include as a minimum all the following elements that are applicable and readily ascertainable.

Title

Title Proper

Statement of Responsibility

Statement of responsibility relating to title proper (if more than one, only the first recorded is required)

Edition statement

Designation of edition

Designation of a named revision of an edition

Numbering of serials

Numeric and/or alphabetic designation of first issue or part of sequence (for first or only sequence)

Chronological designation of first issue or part of sequence (for first or only sequence)

Numeric and/or alphabetic designation of last issue or part of sequence (for last or only sequence)

Chronological designation of last issue or part of sequence (for last or only sequence)

Production statement

Date of production (for a resource in an unpublished form)

Publication statement

Place of publication (if more than one, only the first recorded is required)

Publisher's name (if more than one, only the first recorded is required)

Date of publication

Distribution statement

Place of distribution (for a published resource, if place of publication not identified; if more than one, only the first recorded is required)

Distributor's name (for a published resource, if publisher not identified; if more than one, only the first recorded is required)

Date of distribution (for a published resource, if date of publication not identified)

Manufacture statement

Place of manufacture (for a published resource, if neither place of publication nor place of distribution identified; if more than one, only the first recorded is required)

Manufacturer's name (for a published resource, if neither publisher nor distributor identified; if more than one, only the first recorded is required)

Date of manufacture (for a published resource, if neither date of publication, date of distribution, nor copyright date identified)

Copyright date

Copyright date (if neither date of publication nor date of distribution identified)

Series statement

Title proper of series

Numbering within series

Title proper of subseries

Numbering within subseries

Identifier for the manifestation

Identifier for the manifestation (if more than one, prefer an internationally recognized identifier if applicable)

Carrier type

Carrier type

Extent

Extent (only if the resource is complete or if the total extent is known)

0.6.3 Section 2: Recording Attributes of Work and Expression

When recording data identifying a work, include as a minimum the following elements that are applicable and readily ascertainable.

Preferred title for the work

Identifier for the work

The preferred title is the basis for the authorized access point representing the work. When constructing that access point, precede the preferred title, if appropriate, by the authorized access point representing the person, family, or corporate body responsible for the work (see **6.27.1**).

If the preferred title for a work is the same as or similar to a title for a different work, or to a name for a person, family, or corporate body, differentiate them by recording as many of the additional identifying elements in the following list as necessary. Record these elements as separate elements, as parts of the access point representing the work, or as both.

Form of work

Date of work

Place of origin of the work

Other distinguishing characteristic of the work

When identifying a musical work with a title that is not distinctive, record as many of the following elements as are applicable. For musical works with distinctive titles, record as many of the following elements as necessary to differentiate the work from others with the same title. Record the elements as separate elements, as parts of the access point representing the work, or as both.

Medium of performance

Numeric designation of a musical work

Key

When recording data identifying an expression, include as a minimum the following elements that are applicable to that expression. Record the elements as separate elements, as parts of the access point representing the expression, or as both.

Identifier for the expression

Content type

Language of expression

Record as many of the additional identifying elements in the following list as necessary to differentiate one expression of a work from another. Record the elements as separate elements, as parts of the access point representing the expression, or as both.

Date of expression

Other distinguishing characteristic of the expression

When describing a cartographic expression, include as a minimum the following additional elements that are applicable to that expression.

Horizontal scale of cartographic content

Vertical scale of cartographic content

0.6.4 Section 3: Recording Attributes of Person, Family, and Corporate Body

When recording data identifying a person, family, or corporate body, include as a minimum the following elements that are applicable and readily ascertainable. Record the elements as separate elements, as parts of the authorized access point representing the person, family, or corporate body, or as both.

Preferred name for the person

Title of the person (a word or phrase indicative of royalty, nobility, ecclesiastical rank or office; a term of address for a person of religious vocation)

Date of birth

Date of death

Other designation associated with the person (for a Christian saint, a spirit, a person named in a sacred scripture or an apocryphal book, a fictitious or legendary person, or a real non-human entity)

Profession or occupation (for a person whose name consists of a phrase or appellation not conveying the idea of a person)

Identifier for the person

Preferred name for the family

Type of family

Date associated with the family

Identifier for the family

Preferred name for the corporate body

Location of conference, etc.

Date of conference, etc.

Associated institution (for conferences, etc., if the institution's name provides better identification than the local place name or if the local place name is unknown or cannot be readily determined)

Number of a conference, etc.

Type of corporate body (for a body whose name does not convey the idea of a corporate body)

Identifier for the corporate body

If the preferred name for the person, family, or corporate body is the same as or similar to a name by which another person, family, or corporate body is known, differentiate them by recording as many of the additional identifying elements in the following list as necessary. Record these elements as separate elements, as parts of the authorized access point representing the person, family, or corporate body, or as both.

Title of the person (another term indicative of rank, honour, or office)

Fuller form of name

Profession or occupation

Period of activity of the person

Other designation associated with the person

Place associated with the family

Prominent member of the family

Location of headquarters

Date of establishment

Date of termination

Period of activity of the corporate body

Associated institution

Other designation associated with the corporate body

0.6.5 Section 5: Recording Primary Relationships between Work, Expression, Manifestation, and Item

When recording primary relationships between a work, expression, manifestation, and item, include as a minimum the work manifested. If there is more than one expression of the work, record the expression manifested.

If more than one work is embodied in the manifestation, only the predominant or first-named work manifested is required.

If more than one expression is embodied in the manifestation, only the predominant or first-named expression manifested is required.

0.6.6 Section 6: Recording Relationships to Persons, Families, and Corporate Bodies Associated with a Resource

When recording relationships between a resource and persons, families, and corporate bodies associated with that resource, include as a minimum the following elements that are applicable and readily ascertainable.

Creator (if more than one, only the creator having principal responsibility named first in resources embodying the work or in reference sources is required; if principal responsibility is not indicated, only the first-named creator is required)

Other person, family, or corporate body associated with a work (if the authorized access point representing that person, family, or corporate body is used to construct the authorized access point representing the work)

0.6.7 Section 7: Recording Subject Relationships

When recording relationships between a work and an entity that is the subject of that work, include as a minimum at least one subject relationship element.[23]

---

23. When using an access point to represent the subject entity, the access point can be constructed by using either the preferred name, title, or term for the entity, or a classification number representing the entity. Construct the access point representing the subject entity following the standards for subject access points and classification numbers used by the agency creating the data.

0.6.8 Section 8: Recording Relationships between Works, Expressions, Manifestations, and Items

The recording of relationships between related works, expressions, manifestations, and items is not required. For the primary relationships, see **0.6.5**.

0.6.9 Section 9: Recording Relationships between Persons, Families, and Corporate Bodies

The recording of relationships between persons, families, and corporate bodies is not required.

0.7 Access Points

RDA provides instructions on the construction of authorized and variant access points representing works, expressions, persons, families, and corporate bodies.

RDA also provides instructions on the use of authorized access points to record the following types of relationships:

primary relationship between a manifestation and a work or expression embodied in the manifestation

relationships between a resource and persons, families, and corporate bodies associated with that resource

relationships between works, expressions, manifestations, and items

relationships between persons, families, and corporate bodies.

In addition, RDA provides guidance on the use of titles (title proper, parallel title, variant title, etc.) as access points.

RDA does not provide guidance on the use of other data elements as access points. Agencies using RDA data may determine which additional elements are to be indexed based on the needs of their users and the capabilities of their data management systems.

0.8 Alternatives and Options

RDA includes a number of guidelines and instructions that are labelled as alternatives or as options.

Alternative guidelines and instructions provide an alternative to what is specified in the immediately preceding guideline or instruction.

Optional instructions provide for:

either

a) the *optional addition* of data that supplement what is called for in the immediately preceding instruction

or

b) the *optional omission* of specific data called for in the immediately preceding instruction.

The agency responsible for creating the data may choose:

a) to establish policies and guidelines on the application of alternatives and options

or

b) to leave decisions on the use of alternatives and options to the judgment of the cataloguer or the individual creating the data.

0.9 Exceptions

RDA includes a number of instructions that are labelled as exceptions.

An exception is an instruction that takes precedence over the immediately preceding instruction and applies to a specific type of resource, condition, etc.

0.10 Examples

The examples in RDA illustrate the application of the specific instruction at which they appear. They illustrate only the data that are addressed by that instruction.

If data in another element is directly relevant to the element being illustrated, the related element is generally referred to in an explanatory note. For example, at an instruction on recording other title information, the example illustrates other title information and includes an explanatory note indicating the form recorded as the title proper:

> Applesoft command editor
> *Title proper:* A.C.E.

Examples normally do not show the preceding or enclosing punctuation that is required for an ISBD presentation. (Guidelines on the presentation of data according to ISBD specifications, including ISBD punctuation, are in **appendix D**.)

However, ISBD punctuation is shown in examples that illustrate a structured description of a related resource. For example, at an instruction on recording a relationship to a related manifestation, the structured description of the related resource is displayed with ISBD punctuation between the elements:

> *Reproduced as:* Lacey, WA : OCLC Preservation Service Center on behalf of University of Washington Libraries, 2005. — 1 microfilm reel ; 10 cm, 35 mm. — On reel with other titles

ISBD punctuation is also shown in explanatory notes that include two or more data elements. For example, at an instruction on constructing the authorized access point to represent an arrangement, transcription, etc., of a musical work, the note is displayed with ISBD punctuation:

> Berlioz, Hector, 1803–1869. Corsaire; arranged
> *Resource described:* The corsaire : overture for concert band / transcribed by Gunther Schuller. *Originally for orchestra*

Examples illustrating the construction of authorized and variant access points use the punctuation specified in AACR2 (see **appendix E**).

Smith, John, 1832–1911

Catholic Church. Pope (1978–2005 : John Paul II)

When using an authorized access point or structured description to record a relationship to a related work, expression, manifestation, or item, the examples illustrate the use of relationship designators. The authorized access point or structured description is preceded by an introductory phrase paralleling the applicable relationship designator (see **Appendix J**).

Parody of: Tolkien, J. R. R. (John Ronald Reuel), 1892–1973. Lord of the rings

Systematic transliterations used in examples follow the schemes chosen jointly by the American Library Association, the Canadian Library Association, and the Library of Congress, available on the Library of Congress website at http://hdl.loc.gov/loc.standards/docs.roman.

All examples illustrate elements as they would be recorded by an agency whose preferred language is English.

0.11 Internationalization

0.11.1 General

RDA is designed for use in an international context.

RDA includes the following guidelines to support use in an international context:

language and script (see **0.11.2**)

numerals (see **0.11.3**)

dates (see **0.11.4**)

units of measurement (see **0.11.5**).

0.11.2 Language and Script

When the instructions for an element specify transcription, data are transcribed in the language and script in which they appear on the source of information from which the data are taken. However, allowance is made for recording the data in a transliterated form if they cannot be recorded in the script used on the source from which they are taken. Allowance is also made for recording the data in a transliterated form in addition to the form in the original script.

Other elements are generally recorded in a language and script preferred by the agency creating the data.

However, there are a number of instructions that specify the use of an English-language term (e.g., *publisher not identified*) or provide a controlled list of terms in English (e.g., the terms used for media type, carrier type, base material). Agencies creating data for use in a different language or script context will modify such instructions to reflect their own language or script preferences and replace the English-language terms specified in RDA with terms appropriate for use in their context. Authorized translations of RDA will do likewise.

0.11.3 Numerals

When the instructions for an element specify transcription, numerals are transcribed in the form in which they appear on the source of information from which the data are taken. When recording numerals, allowance is made for recording the data in the form preferred by the agency creating the data, either as a substitute for or in addition to recording the data on the source.

Numerals appearing in certain other specified elements are also generally recorded in the form in which they appear on the source of information from which the data are taken. However, allowance is made for substituting or adding equivalent numerals in a script preferred by the agency creating the data.

0.11.4 Dates

When the instructions for an element specify transcription, dates are transcribed in the form in which they appear on the source of information from which the data are taken. When recording dates, allowance is made for recording the data in the form preferred by the agency creating the data, either as a substitute for or in addition to the data in the original form.

Dates appearing in certain other specified elements are also generally recorded in the form in which they appear on the source of information from which the data are taken. However, allowance is made for substituting equivalent numerals in a script preferred by the agency creating the data. Allowance is also made for adding dates in the Gregorian or Julian calendar if the data on the source of information are not in that form.

Information on recording dates in the Christian calendar is provided in **appendix H**.

0.11.5 Units of Measurement

When the instructions for an element specify transcription, units of measurement are transcribed in the form in which they appear on the source of information from which the data are taken.

Dimensions of carriers and containers are recorded using metric units of measurement. However, allowance is made for recording dimensions in the system of measurement preferred by the agency creating the data.

Playing speeds are generally recorded either in metric units (e.g., metres per second) or in terms of revolutions per minute, frames per second, etc. However, allowance is made for recording playing speeds for analog tapes in inches per second.

0.12 Encoding RDA Data

RDA has been designed for use with a variety of encoding schemes typically used in library applications. Appendices **D** and **E** provide mappings of RDA elements to the MARC 21 formats for bibliographic and authority data.

For certain elements, the RDA instructions refer to an external ***vocabulary encoding scheme*** (e.g., the instruction on recording the script or scripts used to express the language content of a resource directs the cataloguer to the terms listed in ISO 15924).

For certain elements, the RDA instructions include a vocabulary encoding scheme that is internal to RDA (i.e., a controlled list of terms defined specifically for use with RDA). For those elements, data may be encoded using a substitute vocabulary encoding scheme, provided the encoding scheme is identified.

When RDA instructions specify recording a name or a term in an element, the data may be recorded using a substitute vocabulary encoding scheme (e.g., a country code from ISO 3166 for a place), provided the scheme is identified.

1

GENERAL GUIDELINES ON RECORDING ATTRIBUTES OF MANIFESTATIONS AND ITEMS

1.0 Scope

This chapter provides background information to support the application of guidelines and instructions in chapters **2–4** on recording attributes of manifestations and items. It includes:

a) an explanation of key terms (see **1.1**)

b) the functional objectives and principles underlying the guidelines and instructions in chapters **2–4** (see **1.2**)

c) the core elements for the description of manifestations and items (see **1.3**)

d) guidelines and instructions that apply to various elements in chapters **2–4**:

  i. language and script (see **1.4**)

  ii. transcription (see **1.7**)

  iii. numbers expressed as numerals or as words (see **1.8**)

  iv. dates (see **1.9**)

  v. notes (see **1.10**)

e) general guidelines on description:

  i. type of description (see **1.5**)

  ii. changes requiring a new description (see **1.6**)

  iii. facsimiles and reproductions (see **1.11**).

1.1 Terminology

1.1.1 Explanation of Key Terms

There are a number of terms used in this chapter and in chapters **2–4** that have meanings specific to their use in RDA. Some of these terms are explained at **1.1.2–1.1.5**.

Terms used as data element names in chapters **2–4** are defined at the beginning of the instructions for the specific element. In addition, all terms used in those chapters with a specific technical meaning are defined in the glossary.

1.1.2 Resource

The term ***resource*** is used in chapters **2–4** to refer to a manifestation or item (see **1.1.5**).

For most elements covered in chapters **2–4**, the term *resource* normally refers to a manifestation. However, for some elements in those chapters, the term *resource* refers to an item (e.g., custodial history of item, immediate source of acquisition of item).

The term *resource*, depending on what is being described, can refer to:

a) an individual entity (e.g., a single videodisc)
or

b) an aggregate of entities (e.g., three sheet maps)

or

c) a component of an entity (e.g., a single slide issued as part of a set of twenty, an article in an issue of a scholarly journal).

The term *resource* can refer either to a tangible entity (e.g., an audiocassette) or to an intangible entity (e.g., a website).

1.1.3 Mode of Issuance

Mode of issuance is a categorization reflecting whether a resource is issued in one or more parts, the way it is updated, and its intended termination.

Some guidelines and instructions in chapters **2–4** refer specifically to resources with a particular mode of issuance.

The term ***single unit*** refers to a resource that is issued either as a single physical unit (e.g., as a single-volume monograph) or, in the case of an intangible resource, as a single logical unit (e.g., as a PDF file mounted on the web).

The term ***multipart monograph*** refers to a resource issued in two or more parts (either simultaneously or successively) that is complete or intended to be completed within a finite number of parts (e.g., a dictionary in two volumes, three audiocassettes issued as a set).

The term ***serial*** refers to a resource issued in successive parts, usually having numbering, that has no predetermined conclusion (e.g., a periodical, a monographic series, a newspaper).

The term ***integrating resource*** refers to a resource that is added to or changed by means of updates that do not remain discrete but are integrated into the whole (e.g., a loose-leaf manual that is updated by means of replacement pages, a website that is updated continuously).

Guidelines and instructions in chapters **2–4** that apply to serials also apply to:

a) resources that exhibit characteristics of serials, such as successive issues, numbering, and frequency, but whose duration is limited (e.g., newsletters of events)

and

b) reproductions of serials.

1.1.4 Comprehensive, Analytical, and Hierarchical Description

Some guidelines and instructions in chapters **2–4** refer to specific ways of describing a resource (see **1.5**).

The term ***comprehensive description*** refers to a description that describes the resource as a whole (e.g., a map, a periodical, a collection of posters assembled by a library, a kit consisting of a filmstrip, an audiotape, and a teacher's manual).

The term ***analytical description*** refers to a description that describes a part of a larger resource (e.g., a single volume of a three-volume biography, a single map forming part of a map series).

The term ***hierarchical description*** refers to a description that combines a comprehensive description of the whole resource with analytical descriptions of one or more of its parts.

1.1.5 Work, Expression, Manifestation, and Item

The terms *work, expression, manifestation,* and *item* are used as follows:

The term ***work*** refers to a distinct intellectual or artistic creation (i.e., the intellectual or artistic content).

The term ***expression*** refers to the intellectual or artistic realization of a work in the form of alpha-numeric, musical, or choreographic notation, sound, image, object, movement, etc., or any combination of such forms.

The term ***manifestation*** refers to the physical embodiment of an expression of a work.

The term ***item*** refers to a single exemplar or instance of a manifestation.

Each of these terms, depending on what is being described, can refer to individual entities, aggregates, or components of these entities (e.g., the term *work* can refer to an individual work, an aggregate work, or a component of a work).

1.2 Functional Objectives and Principles

The data describing a manifestation or item should enable the user to:

a) *find* manifestations and items that correspond to the user's stated search criteria

b) *identify* the resource described (i.e., confirm that the resource described corresponds to the resource sought, or distinguish between two or more resources with the same or similar characteristics)

c) *select* a resource that is appropriate to the user's requirements with respect to the physical characteristics of the carrier and the formatting and encoding of information stored on the carrier

d) *obtain* a resource (i.e., acquire a resource through purchase, loan, etc., or access a resource electronically through an online connection to a remote computer).

To ensure that the data created using RDA meet those functional objectives, the guidelines and instructions in chapters **1–4** were designed according to the following principles:

Differentiation. The data should serve to differentiate the resource described from other resources.

Sufficiency. The data should be sufficient to meet the needs of the user with respect to selection of an appropriate resource.

Representation. The data should reflect the resource's representation of itself.

Accuracy. The data should provide supplementary information to correct or clarify ambiguous, unintelligible, or misleading representations made on sources of information forming part of the resource itself.

Common usage. Data that is not transcribed from the resource itself should reflect common usage.

In RDA, transcription of data from the source ensures that, where applicable, the data reflects the resource's representation of itself. Transcription can also function as a means of differentiating one resource from another.

1.3 Core Elements

When recording data identifying and describing a manifestation or item, include as a minimum all of the following elements that are applicable and readily ascertainable.

Title

Title proper

Statement of responsibility

Statement of responsibility relating to title proper (if more than one, only the first recorded is required)

Edition statement

Designation of edition

Designation of a named revision of an edition

Numbering of serials

Numeric and/or alphabetic designation of first issue or part of sequence (for first or only sequence)

Chronological designation of first issue or part of sequence (for first or only sequence)

Numeric and/or alphabetic designation of last issue or part of sequence (for last or only sequence)

Chronological designation of last issue or part of sequence (for last or only sequence)

Production statement

Date of production (for a resource in an unpublished form)

Publication statement

Place of publication (if more than one, only the first recorded is required)

Publisher's name (if more than one, only the first recorded is required)

Date of publication

Distribution statement

Place of distribution (for a published resource, if place of publication not identified; if more than one, only the first recorded is required)

Distributor's name (for a published resource, if publisher not identified; if more than one, only the first recorded is required)

Date of distribution (for a published resource, if date of publication not identified)

Manufacture statement

Place of manufacture (for a published resource, if neither place of publication nor place of distribution identified; if more than one, only the first recorded is required)

Manufacturer's name (for a published resource, if neither publisher nor distributor identified; if more than one, only the first recorded is required)

Date of manufacture (for a published resource, if neither date of publication, date of distribution, nor copyright date identified)

Copyright date

Copyright date (if neither date of publication nor date of distribution identified)

Series statement

Title proper of series

Numbering within series

Title proper of subseries

Numbering within subseries

Identifier for the manifestation

Identifier for the manifestation (if more than one, prefer an internationally recognized identifier if applicable)

Carrier type

Carrier type

Extent

Extent (only if the resource is complete or if the total extent is known)

Include any additional elements that are required in a particular case to differentiate the manifestation or item from one or more other manifestations or items with similar identifying information.

1.4 Language and Script

Record the following elements in the language and script in which they appear on the sources from which they are taken:

Title

Title proper

Parallel title proper

Other title information

Parallel other title information

Variant title

Earlier title proper

Later title proper

- Key title
- Abbreviated title

Statement of responsibility

- Statement of responsibility relating to title proper
- Parallel statement of responsibility relating to title proper

Edition statement

- Designation of edition
- Parallel designation of edition
- Statement of responsibility relating to the edition
- Parallel statement of responsibility relating to the edition
- Designation of a named revision of an edition
- Parallel designation of a named revision of an edition
- Statement of responsibility relating to a named revision of an edition
- Parallel statement of responsibility relating to a named revision of an edition

Numbering of serials

- Numeric and/or alphabetic designation of first issue or part of sequence
- Chronological designation of first issue or part of sequence
- Numeric and/or alphabetic designation of last issue or part of sequence
- Chronological designation of last issue or part of sequence
- Alternative numeric and/or alphabetic designation of first issue or part of sequence
- Alternative chronological designation of first issue or part of sequence
- Alternative numeric and/or alphabetic designation of last issue or part of sequence
- Alternative chronological designation of last issue or part of sequence

Production statement

- Place of production
- Parallel place of production
- Producer's name
- Parallel producer's name
- Date of production

Publication statement

- Place of publication
- Parallel place of publication
- Publisher's name
- Parallel publisher's name
- Date of publication

Distribution statement

- Place of distribution
- Parallel place of distribution
- Distributor's name
- Parallel distributor's name
- Date of distribution

Manufacture statement

- Place of manufacture
- Parallel place of manufacture
- Manufacturer's name

Parallel manufacturer's name

Date of manufacture

Series statement

Title proper of series

Parallel title proper of series

Other title information of series

Parallel other title information of series

Statement of responsibility relating to series

Parallel statement of responsibility relating to series

Numbering within series

Title proper of subseries

Parallel title proper of subseries

Other title information of subseries

Parallel other title information of subseries

Statement of responsibility relating to subseries

Parallel statement of responsibility relating to subseries

Numbering within subseries

Alternative

If an element in this list cannot be recorded in the script used on the source from which it is taken, record the element in a transliterated form.

Optional Addition

Record an element listed at **1.4** in a transliterated form in addition to the form recorded in the script used on the source.

When adding data within an element listed at **1.4**, record the added data in the language and script of the other data in the element unless the instructions for a specific element indicate otherwise.

When information is supplied in an element listed at **1.4**, record the supplied information in the most appropriate language and script.

Record all other elements (including notes) in a language and script, or languages and scripts, preferred by the agency creating the data.

Exception

Names, titles, or quotations in notes. Record a name, title, or quotation incorporated into a note in the language and script in which it appears on the source from which it is taken.

Alternative

Record a name, title, or quotation incorporated into a note in a transliterated form.

1.5 Type of Description

1.5.1 Different Ways of Describing a Resource

There are three different ways of describing a resource. Choose the way that is applicable for the type of resource and is appropriate to the purpose of the description:

a) a comprehensive description (see **1.5.2**)

b) an analytical description (see **1.5.3**)

c) a hierarchical description (see **1.5.4**).

1.5.2 Comprehensive Description

A comprehensive description is used to describe the resource as a whole. It can be used to describe any of the following types of resources:

a) a resource issued as a single unit (e.g., a single audio disc, a PDF document)

b) a multipart monograph (e.g., three videocassettes issued as a set, a kit consisting of a digital videodisc, a model, and an instruction booklet)

c) a serial (e.g., a magazine published in monthly issues, an online journal)

d) an integrating resource (e.g., an updating loose-leaf, a website that is updated on a periodic basis)

e) a collection of two or more units assembled by a private collector, a dealer, a library, an archive, etc. (e.g., a private collection of printed theatre programs, a database of digital images compiled by a museum, an archive of personal papers).

When using a comprehensive description for a resource that has more than one part, record details about the parts of the resource in any of the following ways that are applicable:

a) as part of the description of the carrier (see **3.1.4**)

b) as a relationship to a related work (see **25.1**)

c) as a relationship to a related manifestation (see **27.1**).

1.5.3 Analytical Description

An analytical description is used to describe a part of a larger resource. It can be used to describe any of the following types of parts:

a) a part contained within a larger resource issued as a single unit (e.g., the music for a single song printed as part of a volume containing music for twelve songs, one remote-sensing image in a database containing three hundred images)

b) a part of a multipart monograph (e.g., a filmstrip issued as part of a kit containing the filmstrip, an audiotape, and a pamphlet)

c) a part of a serial (e.g., a single volume of a series, a single issue of a periodical, an article in a magazine or online journal)

d) a part of an integrating resource (e.g., one chapter in an administrative manual issued as an updating loose-leaf volume, a discussion paper on a regularly updated website)

e) a part of a collection assembled by a private collector, a dealer, a library, an archive, etc. (e.g., a set of lithographs in a collection of art prints, a digital recording of a performance in a database compiled by a repertory theatre).

It is possible to prepare separate analytical descriptions for any number of parts of a larger resource (i.e., for one part only, for two or more selected parts, or for all parts of the resource).

When using an analytical description, record details about the larger resource or about the other parts of the resource in any of the following ways that are applicable:

a) as a series statement (see **2.12**)

b) as a relationship to a related work (see **25.1**)

c) as a relationship to a related manifestation (see **27.1**).

1.5.4 Hierarchical Description

A hierarchical description is used to describe a resource consisting of two or more parts. It combines both a comprehensive description of the whole and analytical descriptions of one or more of the parts. If parts of the resource are further subdivided into their own parts, analytical descriptions can be created for those further subdivisions.

For guidelines on presenting a hierarchical description according to ISBD specifications for multilevel descriptions, see appendix **D** (**D.1.3**).

For instructions on recording relationships between works, expressions, manifestations, and items, see chapters **24**–**28**.

1.6 Changes Requiring a New Description

1.6.1 Multipart Monographs

1.6.1.1 Change in Mode of Issuance of a Multipart Monograph

Create a new description if a multipart monograph changes to a serial or an integrating resource (see **2.13**).

Create a new description if a serial or integrating resource changes to a multipart monograph (see **2.13**).

1.6.1.2 Change in Media Type of a Multipart Monograph

Create a new description if there is a change in the media type (see **3.2**) of a multipart monograph.

1.6.2 Serials

1.6.2.1 Change in Mode of Issuance of a Serial

Create a new description if a serial changes to a multipart monograph or an integrating resource (see **2.13**).

Create a new description if a multipart monograph or integrating resource changes to a serial (see **2.13**).

1.6.2.2 Change in Carrier Characteristics of a Serial

Create a new description if there is a change in the media type (see **3.2**) of a serial.

If:

the carrier type (**3.3**) of a serial changes to *online resource* from another computer carrier

or

changes from *online resource* to another computer carrier

then:

create a new description (see **3.1.6.1**).

1.6.2.3 Major Change in the Title Proper of a Serial

Create a new description if there is a major change in the title proper of a serial (see **2.3.2.12.2**).

1.6.2.4 Change in Responsibility for a Serial

Create a new description if there is a change in responsibility that requires a change in the identification of the serial as a work (see **6.1.3.2**).

1.6.2.5 Change in Edition Statement

Create a new description when there is a change in an edition statement indicating a significant change to the scope or coverage of a serial.

1.6.3 Integrating Resources

1.6.3.1 Change in Mode of Issuance of an Integrating Resource

Create a new description if an integrating resource changes to a multipart monograph or serial (see **2.13**).

Create a new description if a multipart monograph or serial changes to an integrating resource (see **2.13**).

1.6.3.2 Change in Media Type of an Integrating Resource

Create a new description if there is a change in the media type (see **3.2**) of an integrating resource.

1.6.3.3 Re-basing of an Integrating Resource

Create a new description for an integrating resource if a new set of base volumes is issued for an updating loose-leaf.

1.6.3.4 Change in Edition Statement

Create a new description when there is a change in an edition statement indicating a significant change to the scope or coverage of an integrating resource.

1.7 Transcription

1.7.1 General Guidelines on Transcription

The instructions in chapters **2–4** specify transcription of certain elements as they appear on the source of information. When transcribing, apply the following general guidelines:

capitalization (see **1.7.2**)
punctuation (see **1.7.3**)
diacritical marks (see **1.7.4**)
symbols (see **1.7.5**)
spacing of initials and acronyms (see **1.7.6**)
letters or words intended to be read more than once (see **1.7.7**)
abbreviations (see **1.7.8**)
inaccuracies (see **1.7.9**).

When these guidelines refer to an appendix, apply the additional instructions in that appendix, as applicable to the element being transcribed.

> ***Alternatives***
>
> The agency creating the data may establish in-house guidelines for capitalization, punctuation, numerals, symbols, abbreviations, etc., or choose a published style manual, etc., as its preferred guide (e.g., *The Chicago Manual of Style*). In such situations, use those guidelines or that style manual instead of the instructions at **1.7.2–1.7.9** and in the appendices.
>
> Accept data without modification if:
>
> a) using a description created by another agency
> *or*
> b) using data derived from a digital source of information by automated scanning, copying, or downloading process (e.g., by harvesting embedded metadata or automatically generating metadata).

For instructions on transcribing numbers expressed as numerals or as words, see **1.8.1**.

1.7.2 Capitalization

Apply the instructions on capitalization in appendix **A**.

1.7.3 Punctuation

Transcribe punctuation as it appears on the source.

...and then there were none

What is it?...what is it not?

Vessels on the Northwest coast between Alaska and California -- 1543–1811

I don't do dishes!

»... dass der Mensch was lernen muss.«

Exceptions

Punctuation separating different elements. Omit punctuation that separates data to be recorded as one element from data to be recorded as a different element.

DDC 21

Title appears on the source of information with punctuation separating it from the other title information: DDC 21: international perspectives

Vanderbilt University

Publisher's name appears on the source of information with punctuation separating it from the place of publication: Vanderbilt University, Nashville

Punctuation separating instances of the same element. Omit punctuation that separates data to be recorded as one element from data recorded as a second or subsequent instance of the same element.

Dakar

Place of publication appears on the source of information with punctuation separating each place: Ottawa – Dakar – Montevideo – Nairobi – New Delhi – Singapore

Add punctuation, as necessary, for clarity.

Travaillez mieux, vivez mieux

Title appears on the source of information with each word on a separate line. Comma added for clarity

by Louis Henkin (University Professor Emeritus and Special Service Professor, Columbia University), Gerald L. Neuman (Herbert Wechsler Professor of Federal Jurisprudence, Columbia Law School), Diane F. Orentlicher (Professor of Law, Washington College of Law, American University), David W. Leebron (Dean and Lucy G. Moses Professor of Law, Columbia Law School)

Statement of responsibility appears on the source of information with each name, academic title, and affiliation on a separate line. Commas and parentheses added for clarity

For instructions on the use of punctuation for the display of descriptive data according to ISBD specifications, see appendix **D** (**D.1.2**).

1.7.4 Diacritical Marks

Transcribe diacritical marks such as accents as they appear on the source of information.

Optional Addition

Add diacritical marks that are not present on the source of information in accordance with standard usage for the language of the data.

Les misérables

Source of information reads: LES MISERABLES

1.7.5 Symbols

Replace symbols and other characters, etc., that cannot be reproduced by the facilities available, with a description of the symbol. Indicate that this description was taken from a source outside the resource itself (see **2.2.4**).

> Robust H [proportional to] stabilization of stochastic hybrid systems with Wiener process
> *Symbol for "proportional to" appears on source of information*
>
> My name is Brain [crossed out] Brian
> *The word "Brain" appears with an X through it on source of information*

Make an explanatory note if necessary (see **2.17**).

Ignore typographical devices that are used as separators, etc.

1.7.6 Spacing of Initials and Acronyms

If separate letters or initials appear on the source of information without full stops between them, transcribe the letters without spaces between them, regardless of spacing on the source.

> ALA rules for filing catalog cards
>
> prepared by members of the AIAA Technical Committees on Space Systems and Space Atmosphere Physics

If such letters or initials have full stops between them, omit any internal spaces.

> T.U.E.I. occasional papers in industrial relations
>
> The most of S.J. Perelman
>
> edited by P.C. Wason and P.N. Johnson-Laird
>
> W.W. Norton & Company
> *Publisher's name*

1.7.7 Letters or Words Intended to Be Read More Than Once

If a letter or word appears only once but the design of the source of information makes it clear that it is intended to be read more than once, repeat the letter or word.

> Canadian citations
> Citations canadiennes
> *Source of information reads:* Canadian CITATIONS canadiennes. *Intended readings recorded separately as title proper and parallel title proper*

1.7.8 Abbreviations

Apply the instructions on the use of abbreviations in transcribed elements in appendix **B** (**B.4**).

1.7.9 Inaccuracies

When instructed to transcribe an element as it appears on the source, transcribe an inaccuracy or a misspelled word unless the instructions for a specific element indicate otherwise (e.g., exception at **2.3.1.4**).

> The wolrd of television
>
> A comprehensive law book on proceedings under every statute/ordinance with upt-to-date case law by superior courts

Make a note correcting the inaccuracy if considered important for identification or access (see **2.17**).

If the inaccuracy appears in a title and a corrected form of the title is considered important for identification or access, record a corrected form of the title as a variant title (see **2.3.6**).

1.8 Numbers Expressed as Numerals or as Words

1.8.1 General Guidelines

When recording numbers expressed as numerals or words, apply the following guidelines:

form of numerals (see **1.8.2**)
numbers expressed as words (see **1.8.3**)
inclusive numbers (see **1.8.4**)
ordinal numbers (see **1.8.5**).

The guidelines at **1.8.2–1.8.5** apply when recording numbers expressed as numerals or as words in the following elements:

Numeric and/or alphabetic designation of first issue or part of sequence
Chronological designation of first issue or part of sequence
Numeric and/or alphabetic designation of last issue or part of sequence
Chronological designation of last issue or part of sequence
Alternative numeric and/or alphabetic designation of first issue or part of sequence
Alternative chronological designation of first issue or part of sequence
Alternative numeric and/or alphabetic designation of last issue or part of sequence
Alternative chronological designation of last issue or part of sequence

Date of production

Date of publication

Date of distribution

Date of manufacture

Copyright date

Numbering within series
Numbering within subseries

Year degree granted

Alternative

Early printed resources. For early printed resources, transcribe numbers expressed as numerals or as words in the form in which they appear on the source of information in the following elements:

numbering of serials
date of production
date of publication
date of distribution
date of manufacture.

When recording numbers expressed as numerals or as words in a transcribed element, transcribe them in the form in which they appear on the source of information. Apply the general guidelines on transcription (see **1.7**), as applicable.

Fifty key literary theorists
Title proper

55 places to discover your favourite tea
Other title information

1.8.2 Form of Numerals

Record numerals in the form preferred by the agency creating the data, unless the substitution would make the numbering less clear.

tome 3
Numbering within series on source of information reads: tome III

Alternatives

Record numerals in the form in which they appear on the source of information.

tome III
Numbering within series

Record the numerals in the form in which they appear on the source. Add the equivalent numerals in the form preferred by the agency creating the data. Indicate that the information was taken from a source outside the resource itself (see **2.2.4**).

tome III [3]
Numbering within series on source of information reads: tome III

1.8.3 Numbers Expressed as Words

Substitute numerals for numbers expressed as words.

1.8.4 Inclusive Numbers

When recording inclusive dates and other inclusive numbers, record both the first and last number in full.

1967–1972
Source of information reads: 1967–72

1.8.5 Ordinal Numbers

When recording ordinal numbers (expressed either as numerals or as words), record them as numerals and indicate that they are ordinal numbers following standard usage for the language:

English language source. When recording ordinal numbers from an English-language source, record them as numerals in the form *1st*, *2nd*, *3rd*, *4th*, etc.

Chinese, Japanese, or Korean language source. When recording ordinal numerals from a source in Chinese, Japanese, or Korean, record them as numerals accompanied by the character indicating that the numeral is ordinal.

第 8
8th in Chinese

Source in a language other than English, Chinese, Japanese, or Korean. When recording ordinal numerals from a source in another language, record them as numerals and indicate that they are ordinal numbers following the usage of the language, if ascertainable.[1]

1er, 1re, 2^{e}, 3^{e}, etc.
French

1., 2., 3., etc.
German

1°, 1^{a}, 2°, 2^{a}, 3°, 3^{a}, etc.
Italian

If the usage of a language cannot be ascertained, use the form *1., 2., 3.*, etc.

---

1. A useful source for the form of ordinal numerals in European languages is: C.G. Allen, *A Manual of European Languages for Librarians,* 2nd ed. (London; New Providence, NJ: Bowker-Saur, ©1999).

1.9 Dates

1.9.1 General Guidelines

When recording dates appearing on the source of information, apply the guidelines at **1.8**.

Apply the instructions at **1.9.2** when recording a supplied date for any of the following elements:

a) date of production (see **2.7.6.6–2.7.6.7**)

b) date of publication (see **2.8.6.6**)

c) date of distribution (see **2.9.6.6**)

d) date of manufacture (see **2.10.6.6**).

For additional instructions on recording dates in the Christian calendar, see appendix **H**.

1.9.2 Supplied Dates

Record a supplied date or dates as instructed at **1.9.2.1–1.9.2.5**, as applicable. Indicate that the date was taken from a source outside the resource itself (see **2.2.4**).

1.9.2.1 Actual Year Known

If the actual year is known, record the year.

[2003]

1.9.2.2 Either One of Two Consecutive Years

If the date is known to be either one of two consecutive years, record both years separated by *or.*

[1971 or 1972]

1.9.2.3 Probable Year

If the probable year is known, record the year followed by a question mark.

> [1969?]

1.9.2.4 Probable Range of Years

If the probable date falls within a range of years, record the range. Record *between*, followed by the earliest probable year, then *and* and the latest probable year, followed by a question mark.

> [between 1846 and 1853?]
> [between 1800 and 1899?]
> [between 1970 and 1979?]
> [between 1400 and 1600?]

1.9.2.5 Earliest and/or Latest Possible Date Known

If the earliest possible date is known, record *not before* followed by the date.

If the latest possible date is known, record *not after* followed by the date.

> [not after August 21, 1492]

If both the earliest possible and latest possible dates are known, record *between* followed by the earliest possible date, then *and* and the latest possible date.

> [between August 12, 1899 and March 2, 1900]

1.10 Notes

1.10.1 General Guidelines on Notes

When the instructions in chapters **2–7** specify making a note, apply the following general guidelines:

capitalization (see **1.10.2**)

quotations (see **1.10.3**)

references (see **1.10.4**)

applicability of the information recorded in a note (see **1.10.5**).

1.10.2 Capitalization

Apply the instructions on the capitalization of notes in appendix **A** (**A.8**).

> *Alternatives*
>
> The agency creating the data may establish in-house guidelines for capitalization, punctuation, numerals, symbols, abbreviations, etc., or choose a published style manual, etc., (e.g., *The Chicago Manual of Style*) as its preferred guide. In such situations, use those guidelines or that style manual instead of appendix **A**.
>
> Do not modify the capitalization of information used in a note if it is derived from a digital source using an automated scanning, copying, or downloading process (e.g., by harvesting embedded metadata or automatically generating metadata).

1.10.3 Quotations

Record quotations from the resource or from other sources in quotation marks. Follow the quotation by an indication of its source, unless that source is the preferred source of information for the identification of the resource (see **2.2.2**).

"Published for the Royal Institute of Public Administration"

"A textbook for 6th form students"—Preface

"Generally considered to be by William Langland"—Oxford companion to English literature

1.10.4 References

Refer to passages in the resource, or in other sources, if:

a) the references support assertions made in the description
or
b) the references save repetition of information readily available from other sources

Introduction (page xxix) refutes attribution to John Bodenham

1.10.5 Applicability of the Information Recorded in a Note

If it is known that the note does not apply to the entire resource, identify the applicable part or iteration.

1.11 Facsimiles and Reproductions

When describing a facsimile or reproduction, record the data relating to the facsimile or reproduction in the appropriate element. Record any data relating to the original manifestation as an element of a related work or related manifestation, as applicable.

2

IDENTIFYING MANIFESTATIONS AND ITEMS

2.0 Purpose and Scope

This chapter provides general guidelines and instructions on recording the attributes of manifestations and items that are most often used to identify a resource. These attributes are recorded using the elements covered in this chapter.

The elements in chapter 2 reflect the information typically used by the producers of resources to identify their products (e.g., title, statement of responsibility, edition statement). The user generally relies on these same elements:

a) to determine whether the resource described is the one sought

b) to distinguish between resources with similar identifying information.

Not all of the elements covered in this chapter will be applicable to the description of a particular resource. For those elements that are applicable, the description of the resource should include at least those that are identified as core elements (see **1.3**). If the core elements are not sufficient to differentiate the resource from others with similar identifying information, include additional elements, as necessary, from:

this chapter

or

chapter **3** (Describing Carriers)

or

chapter **4** (Providing Acquisition and Access Information).

2.1 Basis for Identification of the Resource

2.1.1 General Guidelines

Choose an appropriate source of information as the basis for identification of the resource.

Choose a source of information that is appropriate to:

a) the type of description that will be created (see **1.5**)
and
b) the mode of issuance of the resource (see **1.1.3**).

Use the guidelines applicable for the type of description:

comprehensive description (see **2.1.2**)

or

analytical description (see **2.1.3**).

2.1.2 Comprehensive Description

2.1.2.1 General Guidelines

When preparing a comprehensive description, choose a source of information appropriate to the mode of issuance:

single unit (see **2.1.2.2**)

or

more than one part (see **2.1.2.3**)

or

integrating resource (see **2.1.2.4**).

2.1.2.2 Resource Issued as a Single Unit

When preparing a comprehensive description for a resource issued as a single unit (e.g., a textbook in one volume, an audio recording) that is not an integrating resource (see **2.1.2.4**), choose a source of information identifying the resource as a whole (e.g., a source with a collective title). If the resource embodies multiple works (e.g., a compact disc embodying multiple works), prefer a source that has a collective title.

If there is no source of information identifying the resource as a whole, but one source has a title identifying a main or predominant work or content (e.g., a single videodisc containing a feature film along with trailers, outtakes, interviews, or other material related to the feature film), consider that source to identify the resource as a whole.

If there is no source of information identifying the resource as a whole and no source has a title identifying a main or predominant work or content (e.g., a single videodisc containing multiple feature films but with no source of information identifying the resource as a whole), treat the sources of information identifying its individual contents as a collective source of information for the resource as a whole.

2.1.2.3 Resource Issued in More Than One Part

When preparing a comprehensive description for a resource issued in more than one part (e.g., a series of scientific treatises, a periodical, a compact disc set) that is not an integrating resource (see **2.1.2.4**), choose one of the following, as appropriate, as the basis for identifying the resource as a whole:

a) If the resource is issued as a set that is unnumbered, or if the numbering does not help to establish an order (e.g., a compact disc set containing an opera, a kit), choose a source of information identifying the resource as a whole, preferring a source that has a collective title. See categories d) or e) if there is no source of information identifying the resource as a whole.

b) If the resource has sequentially numbered issues or parts, choose a source of information identifying the lowest numbered issue or part available.

c) If the resource has unnumbered issues or parts, or if it has numbering that does not help to establish an order, choose a source of information identifying the issue or part with the earliest date of issue.

d) If there is no source of information identifying the resource as a whole, but one source has a title identifying a main or predominant work or content, consider that source to identify the resource as a whole.

e) If there is no source of information identifying the resource as a whole and no source has a title identifying a main or predominant work or content (e.g., a videodisc set containing multiple feature films but with no source of information identifying the resource as a whole), treat the sources identifying the individual parts as a collective source of information for the resource as a whole.

If the identification of a resource with ordered parts is not based on the first issue or part, make a note identifying the issue or part used as the basis for identification of the resource (see **2.17.13.3**).

For sources of information for numbering identifying the last issue or part of a serial (or the first or last issue in a separate sequence of numbering), see **2.6.1.2**.

For sources of information for the date of production, publication, distribution, and/or manufacture of the last issue or part of a multipart monograph or serial, see:

date of production (**2.7.6.2**)

date of publication (**2.8.6.2**)

date of distribution (**2.9.6.2**)

and/or

date of manufacture (**2.10.6.2**).

2.1.2.4 Integrating Resource

When preparing a comprehensive description for an integrating resource (e.g., an updating website), choose a source of information identifying the current iteration of the resource as a whole.

If there is no source of information identifying the current iteration of the integrating resource as a whole, treat the sources of information identifying its individual contents as a collective source of information for the whole.

Make a note identifying the latest iteration consulted in making the description (see **2.17.13.4**).

For sources of information for the date of production, publication, distribution, and/or manufacture of the first iteration of an integrating resource, see:

date of production (**2.7.6.2**)

date of publication (**2.8.6.2**)

date of distribution (**2.9.6.2**)

and/or

date of manufacture (**2.10.6.2**).

2.1.3 Analytical Description

2.1.3.1 General Guidelines

When preparing an analytical description, choose a source of information appropriate to the mode of issuance of the part or parts being described:

single unit (see **2.1.3.2**)

or

more than one part (see **2.1.3.3**)

or

integrating resource (see **2.1.3.4**).

2.1.3.2 Single Part

When preparing an analytical description for a single part of a resource (e.g., an article in a journal, one volume of a multivolume history, a separately titled issue of a professional journal) that is not an integrating resource (see **2.1.3.4**), choose a source of information identifying the particular part being described.

2.1.3.3 More Than One Part

When preparing an analytical description for more than one part of a resource (e.g., two volumes covering Renaissance plays in a multivolume monograph on English theatre, a serial update accompanying a monograph) that is not an integrating resource (see **2.1.3.4**), choose a source of information as instructed at **2.1.2.3**, as applicable to the parts being described.

2.1.3.4 Integrating Resource

When preparing an analytical description for a part or parts issued as an integrating resource (e.g., one volume of a multivolume set issued as an updating loose-leaf, one section of a website with multiple updating sections), choose a source or sources of information identifying the current iteration of the particular part or parts being described.

2.2 Sources of Information

2.2.1 Application

Apply the instructions at **2.2.2–2.2.4** when choosing a source of information. Apply for all elements covered in chapter 2 unless the instructions on sources of information for the element specify otherwise.

2.2.2 Preferred Source of Information

2.2.2.1 General Guidelines

Use as the preferred source of information a source forming part of the resource itself that is appropriate to:

a) the type of description (see 2.1)
and
b) the presentation format of the resource (see 2.2.2.2–2.2.2.4).

When choosing a preferred source of information, treat as part of the resource itself:

a) the storage medium (e.g., paper, tape, film)
and
b) any housing that is an integral part of the resource (e.g., a cassette, a cartridge).

When describing the resource as a whole using a comprehensive description, treat accompanying material as part of the resource itself.

When preparing an analytical description of one or more components of a resource, treat accompanying material as a source outside the resource itself (i.e., as a related resource).

Treat a container issued with the resource (e.g., a box in which a game or kit is issued, a clamshell box containing compact discs in individual jewel cases or cardboard sleeves) as part of the resource itself. Treat a container that is not issued with the resource (e.g., a box or case made by the owner) as a source outside the resource itself.

If there is more than one source of information that qualifies as the preferred source of information for the resource (as specified at 2.2.2.2–2.2.2.4), apply the additional instructions at 2.2.3 (more than one preferred source of information).

If information required for the identification of the resource is not available from a source forming part of the resource itself, take it from another source as instructed at 2.2.4.

2.2.2.2 Resources Consisting of One or More Pages, Leaves, Sheets, or Cards (or Images of One or More Pages, Leaves, Sheets, or Cards)

If the resource consists of:
one or more pages, leaves, sheets, or cards (e.g., a book, an issue of a periodical, a poster, a series of sheet maps, a set of flashcards)
or
images of one or more pages, leaves, sheets, or cards (e.g., a microform reproduction of a musical score, a PDF file of a text, microform reproductions of a set of sheet maps, a JPEG image of a photograph)
then:
use the title page, title sheet, or title card (or an image of it) as the preferred source of information.

> *Alternative*
>
> If the resource consists of microform or computer images of one or more pages, leaves, sheets, or cards, use an eye-readable label with the title instead of the image of the title page, title sheet, or title card. The label must be permanently printed on or affixed to the resource.

If the resource lacks a title page, title sheet, or title card (or an image of it), use as the preferred source of information the first of the following sources that has a title:

a) a cover or jacket issued with the resource (or an image of a cover or jacket)

b) a caption (or an image of a caption)

c) a masthead (or an image of a masthead)

d) a colophon (or an image of a colophon).

Exception

Early printed resources. If an early printed resource (or a reproduction of it) lacks a title page, title sheet, or title card (or an image of it), use as the preferred source of information the first of the following sources that has a title:

a) a colophon (or an image of a colophon).

b) a cover or jacket issued with the resource (or an image of a cover or jacket)

c) a caption (or an image of a caption)

If none of these sources has a title, use as the preferred source of information another source within the resource that has a title. Give preference to a source in which the information is formally presented.

If the resource does not contain a colophon, cover, or caption (or an image of one of them), use as the preferred source of information another source forming part of the resource itself. Give preference to sources in which the information is formally presented.

2.2.2.3 Resources Consisting of Moving Images

If the resource consists of moving images (e.g., a film reel, a videodisc, a video game, an MPEG video file), use the title frame or frames, or title screen or screens, as the preferred source of information. If the title frames or title screens only list the titles of the individual contents and another source forming part of the resource has a formally-presented collective title, use as the preferred source of information the first applicable source with a formally-presented collective title.

Alternative

Use a label with a title that is permanently printed on or affixed to the resource in preference to the title frame or frames, or title screen or screens. This alternative does not apply to labels on accompanying textual material or a container.

If the resource does not contain a title frame or title screen, apply the following guidelines for tangible or online resources to choose the preferred source of information.

2.2.2.3.1 Tangible Resources

Use as the preferred source of information the first of the following with a title:

a) a label that is permanently printed on or affixed to the resource, excluding accompanying textual material or a container (e.g., a label on a videodisc)

b) for a comprehensive description, a container or accompanying material issued with the resource

c) an internal source forming part of a tangible digital resource (e.g., a disc menu).

If none of these sources has a title, use as the preferred source of information another source forming part of the resource itself, giving preference to sources in which the information is formally presented.

2.2.2.3.2 Online Resources

Use as the preferred source of information the first of the following with a title:

a) textual content

b) embedded metadata in textual form that contains a title (e.g., metadata embedded in an MPEG video file).

If none of these sources has a title, use as the preferred source of information another source forming part of the resource itself, giving preference to sources in which the information is formally presented.

2.2.2.4 Other Resources

For a resource that is not covered at **2.2.2.2–2.2.2.3**, apply the following guidelines for tangible or online resources to choose the preferred source of information. If a source of information only lists the titles of the individual contents and another source forming part of the resource has a formally-presented collective title, use as the preferred source of information the first applicable source with a formally-presented collective title.

2.2.2.4.1 Tangible Resources

Use as the preferred source of information the first of the following with a title:

a) a textual source on the resource itself (e.g., a slide) or a label that is permanently printed on or affixed to the resource, excluding accompanying textual material or a container (e.g., a label on an audio CD or a model)

b) an internal source, such as a title screen, whose textual content formally presents the title

c) for a comprehensive description, a container or accompanying material issued with the resource.

If none of these sources has a title, use as the preferred source of information another source forming part of the resource itself, giving preference to sources in which the information is formally presented.

2.2.2.4.2 Online Resources

Use as the preferred source of information the first of the following with a title:

a) textual content

b) embedded metadata in textual form that contains a title (e.g., metadata embedded in an MP3 audio file).

If none of the sources has a title, use as the preferred source of information another source forming part of the resource itself, giving preference to sources in which the information is formally presented.

2.2.3 More Than One Preferred Source of Information

If there is more than one source of information that qualifies as the preferred source of information for the resource (as specified at **2.2.2**), use the first occurring of these sources, unless one of these conditions applies:

different languages or scripts (see **2.2.3.1**)
different dates (see **2.2.3.2**)
sources of information for the reproduction and the original (see **2.2.3.3**).

2.2.3.1 Preferred Sources of Information in Different Languages or Scripts

If the resource contains preferred sources of information in more than one language or script, use as the preferred source of information (in this order of preference):

a) the source in the language or script that corresponds to the language or script of the content of the resource

b) the source in the language or script that corresponds to the predominant language or script of the content of the resource

c) the source in the language or script of translation, if the resource contains the same work in more than one language or script and translation is known to be the purpose of the resource

d) the source in the original language or script of the content, if the resource contains the same content in more than one language or script and the original language or script can be identified

e) the first occurring of the sources

f) the source in the language or script preferred by the agency preparing the description, if the resource is formatted *tête-bêche*, as a head-to-head bound monograph, or as a head-to-tail bound monograph.

If none of the categories is applicable, choose one of the sources of information as the preferred source.

2.2.3.2 Preferred Sources of Information With Different Dates

If:

a resource is not a multipart monograph or serial

and

the resource contains preferred sources of information with different dates

then:

use as the preferred source of information the source with the later or latest date.

2.2.3.3 Preferred Sources of Information for the Reproduction and the Original

If:

the resource is a facsimile or reproduction of an original resource

and

the resource contains a preferred source of information for the reproduction as well as a preferred source of information for the original

then:

use the source for the reproduction as the preferred source of information.

2.2.4 Other Sources of Information

If information required to identify the resource does not appear on a source forming part of the resource itself (see **2.2.2.1**), take it from one of the following sources (in order of preference):

a) accompanying material (e.g., a leaflet, an "about" file) that is not treated as part of the resource itself as described in **2.2.2.1**

b) other published descriptions of the resource

c) a container that is not issued with the resource itself (e.g., a box or case made by the owner)

d) any other available source (e.g., a reference source).

When instructions specify transcription, indicate that the information is supplied from a source outside the resource itself:

by means of a note (see **2.17**)

or

by some other means (e.g., through coding or the use of square brackets).

Indicate that information is supplied for any of the following transcribed elements:

Title

Title proper

Parallel title proper

Other title information

Parallel other title information

Statement of responsibility

Statement of responsibility relating to title proper

Parallel statement of responsibility relating to title proper

Edition statement
- Designation of edition
- Parallel designation of edition
- Statement of responsibility relating to the edition
- Parallel statement of responsibility relating to the edition
- Designation of a named revision of an edition
- Parallel designation of a named revision of an edition
- Statement of responsibility relating to a named revision of an edition
- Parallel statement of responsibility relating to a named revision of an edition

Numbering of serials
- Numeric and/or alphabetic designation of first issue or part of sequence
- Chronological designation of first issue or part of sequence
- Numeric and/or alphabetic designation of last issue or part of sequence
- Chronological designation of last issue or part of sequence
- Alternative numeric and/or alphabetic designation of first issue or part of sequence
- Alternative chronological designation of first issue or part of sequence
- Alternative numeric and/or alphabetic designation of last issue or part of sequence
- Alternative chronological designation of last issue or part of sequence

Production statement
- Place of production
- Parallel place of production
- Producer's name
- Parallel producer's name
- Date of production

Publication statement
- Place of publication
- Parallel place of publication
- Publisher's name
- Parallel publisher's name
- Date of publication

Distribution statement
- Place of distribution
- Parallel place of distribution
- Distributor's name
- Parallel distributor's name
- Date of distribution

Manufacture statement
- Place of manufacture
- Parallel place of manufacture
- Manufacturer's name
- Parallel manufacturer's name
- Date of manufacture

Series statement
- Title proper of series
- Parallel title proper of series

Other title information of series
Parallel other title information of series
Statement of responsibility relating to series
Parallel statement of responsibility relating to series
ISSN of series
Numbering within series
Title proper of subseries
Parallel title proper of subseries
Other title information of subseries
Parallel other title information of subseries
Statement of responsibility relating to subseries
Parallel statement of responsibility relating to subseries
ISSN of subseries
Numbering within subseries

Exception

Do not indicate that the information was taken from a source outside the resource itself if the resource is of a type that does not normally carry identifying information (e.g., a photograph, a naturally occurring object, a collection).

ATTRIBUTES OF THE MANIFESTATION

2.3 Title

CORE ELEMENT

The title proper is a core element. Other titles are optional.

2.3.1 Basic Instructions on Recording Titles

2.3.1.1 Scope

A ***title*** is a word, character, or group of words and/or characters that names a resource or a work contained in it.

It is possible for more than one title to appear:

in sources of information (e.g., on a title page, title frame; as a caption title, running title; on a cover, spine; on a title bar)

or

on a jacket, sleeve, container, etc.

or

in material accompanying the resource.

It is also possible for a resource to have one or more titles associated with it:

through reference sources

or

through assignment by a registration agency (e.g., a key title)

or

by an agency preparing a description of the resource (e.g., a cataloguer's translation of the title).

For purposes of resource description, titles are categorized as follows:

a) title proper (see **2.3.2**)

b) parallel title proper (see **2.3.3**)

c) other title information (see **2.3.4**)

d) parallel other title information (see **2.3.5**)

e) variant title (see **2.3.6**)

f) earlier title proper (see **2.3.7**)

g) later title proper (see **2.3.8**)

h) key title (see **2.3.9**)

i) abbreviated title (see **2.3.10**).

2.3.1.2 Sources of Information

For guidance on choosing sources of information for titles, see the instructions for specific types of titles as follows:

a) For title proper, see **2.3.2.2**.

b) For parallel title proper, see **2.3.3.2**.

c) For other title information, see **2.3.4.2**.

d) For parallel other title information, see **2.3.5.2**.

e) For variant title, see **2.3.6.2**.

f) For earlier title proper, see **2.3.7.2**.

g) For later title proper, see **2.3.8.2**.

h) For key title, see **2.3.9.2**.

i) For abbreviated title, see **2.3.10.2**.

2.3.1.3 Facsimiles and Reproductions

When a facsimile or reproduction has a title or titles relating to the original manifestation as well as to the facsimile or reproduction, record the title or titles of the facsimile or reproduction. Record any title relating to the original manifestation as a title of a related manifestation (see **27.1**).

> *Exception*
>
> If the title of the original manifestation appears on the same source of information as the title of the facsimile or reproduction, apply the instructions at **2.3.2.3**.

2.3.1.4 Recording Titles

Transcribe a title as it appears on the source of information (see **1.7**).

StarOffice

The 1919/1920 Breasted Expedition to the Far East

Sechs Partiten für Flöte

Drawing a blank, or, How I tried to solve a mystery, end a feud, and land the girl of my dreams

Instructor's guide and key for The American economy

IV informe de gobierno

4.50 from Paddington

I due Foscari

When Frank was four

Visitrend + visiplot

Tables of the error function and its derivative, [reproduction of equations for the functions]

The most of P.G. Wodehouse

Heirarchy in organizations
Title misspelled and should read: Hierarchy in organizations

new translations, interpretive notes, backgrounds, commentaries
Other title information

an encyclopedia of domestic architectural detail
Other title information

Optional Omission

Abridge a long title only if it can be abridged without loss of essential information. Use a mark of omission (...) to indicate such an omission. Never omit any of the first five words.

BWV 29, Ratswahl-Kantate, für Soli SATB, Chor SATB und Orchester ...
Abridged other title information. Source of information reads: Wir danken dir, Gott, wir danken dir, BWV 29, Ratswahl-Kantate, für Soli SATB, Chor SATB und Orchester: 3 Trombe, Timpani, 2 Oboi, Violino solo, Organo obligato, 2 Violini, Viola e Basso continuo

A booke of cookerie and the order of meates to bee serued to the table ...
Source of information reads: A booke of cookerie and the order of meates to bee serued to the table, both for flesh and fish dayes, with many excellent wayes for the dressing of all vsuall sortes of meates, both bak't, boyld or rosted, of flesh, fish, fowle, or others, with their proper sawces, as also many rare inuentions in cookery for made dishes, with most notable preserue of sundry sorts of fruits, likewise for making many precious waters, with diuers approved medicines for grieuous diseases, with certaine points of husbandry how to order oxen, horses, sheepe, hogges, &c., with many other necessary points for husbandmen to know

Exceptions

Introductory words. For instructions on introductory words not intended to be part of the title, see **2.3.1.6**.

Inaccuracies. For a serial or an integrating resource, correct obvious typographic errors in the title proper. Make a note recording the title as it appears on the source of information (see **2.17.2.4**). In case of doubt about whether the spelling of a word is incorrect, transcribe the spelling as found. Record as a variant title (see **2.3.6**) the title of a serial or an integrating resource as it appears on the source of information, if considered important for access.

Housing starts
Source of information on v. 1, no. 1 reads: Housing sarts

Date, name, number, etc., that varies from issue to issue. If a title of a serial includes a date, name, number, etc., that varies from issue to issue, omit this date, name, number, etc. Use a mark of omission (...) to indicate such an omission.

Report on the … Conference on Development Objectives and Strategy
Source of information reads: Report on the 4th Conference on Development Objectives and Strategy

Supply estimates for the year ending …
Source of information reads: Supply estimates for the year ending 1997

Frommer's Washington, D.C. on $… a day
Source of information reads: Frommer's Washington, D.C. on $35 a day

The annual report of Governor …
Source of information reads: The annual report of Governor Rhodes. *The name of the governor changes with each specific term of office*

… annual report
Source of information reads: 1st annual report

Earlier title, etc. For a serial or an integrating resource, do not transcribe any statement that mentions an earlier title, title absorbed, etc., as part of the title. Do not transcribe such statements even if they are grammatically linked to the rest of the title. Do not use a mark of omission (…) to indicate such an omission. Record the earlier title, title absorbed, etc., as the title of a related work (see **25.1**).

International gas report
Source of information reads: International gas report, including World gas report

2.3.1.5 Names of Persons, Families, and Corporate Bodies

If a title consists solely of the name of a person, family, or corporate body, record the name as the title.

Georges Brassens

Conference on Industrial Development in the Arab Countries

Woody Guthrie

If:
the title includes a name that would normally be treated either as part of a statement of responsibility or as the name of a publisher, distributor, etc.
and
the name is an integral part of the title (e.g., connected by a case ending)
then:
record the name as part of the title.

Marlowe's plays

Eileen Ford's a more beautiful you in 21 days

Ernst Günther läser Balzac

La route Shell

Larousse's French-English dictionary

a selection of the bitter definitions of Ambrose Bierce
Other title information

proceedings of the Robert Owen Bicentennial Conference, Thrall Opera House, New Harmony, Indiana, October 15 and 16, 1971
Other title information

official scientific journal of the European Society of Agricultural Engineers
Other title information

2.3.1.6 Introductory Words, Etc.

Do not transcribe words that serve as an introduction and are not intended to be part of the title.

Sleeping Beauty
Source of information reads: Disney presents Sleeping Beauty

Selections from The desert song
Source of information reads: Decca Records presents selections from The desert song

Southern mountain guitar
Source of information reads: Mel Bay presents Southern mountain guitar

Oklahoma's official web site
Source of information reads: Welcome to Oklahoma's official web site

Optional Addition

Variant title. If considered important for identification or access, record the form in which the title appears on the source of information as a variant title (see **2.3.6**).

2.3.1.7 Titles of Parts, Sections, and Supplements

If the title of a separately issued part, section, or supplement appears on the source of information without the title that is common to all parts or sections, record the title of the part, section, or supplement as the title.

British journal of applied physics
Title of part recorded as title proper. Common title, which does not appear on the same source, recorded as title proper of series: Journal of physics

When a common title is not recorded with the title of a part, section, or supplement, record it in any of the following ways that are applicable:

a) as part of the series statement (see **2.12**)

b) as the title of a related work (see **25.1**).

If the title of a separately issued part, section, or supplement appears on the source of information with the title that is common to all parts or sections, apply these instructions, as applicable:

title of part, section, or supplement insufficient to identify the resource (see **2.3.1.7.1**)

title of part, section, or supplement sufficient to identify the resource (see **2.3.1.7.2**).

2.3.1.7.1 Title of Part, Section, or Supplement Insufficient to Identify the Resource

If:

the title of the separately issued part, section, or supplement appears on the same source of information with the title common to all parts or sections (or the title of the larger resource)

and

the title of the part, section, or supplement alone is insufficient to identify the resource

then:
record the common title followed by the title of the part, section, or supplement.

Advanced calculus. Student handbook

Acta Universitatis Carolinae. Philologica

Key abstracts. Industrial power and control systems

Journal of the American Leather Chemists' Association. Supplement

Études et documents tchadiens. Série B

If the title of the part, section, or supplement has an enumeration or alphabetic designation, record (in this order):

a) the common title

b) the enumeration or designation of the part, section or supplement

c) the title of the part, section, or supplement.

Journal of polymer science. Part A, General papers

Progress in nuclear energy. Series II, Reactors

Der Ring des Nibelungen. Zweiter Tag, Siegfried

Treat a phrase such as *new series*, *second series*, etc., that appears on the same source of information with the title proper of an unnumbered monographic series as the title of a part, section, or supplement. If such a phrase differentiates a new sequence of numbering of a numbered monographic series or serial, treat it as part of numbering within the series (see **2.12.9.6**) or numbering within the serial (see **2.6.2.3**).

Cambridge studies in international and comparative law. New series
Title of part and common title recorded as title proper of an unnumbered monographic series

2.3.1.7.2 Title of Part, Section, or Supplement Sufficient to Identify the Resource

If:
the title of a separately issued part, section, or supplement appears on the same source of information with the title common to all parts or sections (or the title of the larger resource)
and
the title of the part, section, or supplement alone is sufficient to identify the resource
then:
record the title of the part, section, or supplement as the title.

Structured settlements
Title of part recorded as title proper. Common title recorded as title proper of series: Art of advocacy

Chuckles bites the dust
Title of part recorded as title proper. Common title recorded as title proper of series: Mary Tyler Moore

Exception

Serials and integrating resources . For serials and integrating resources, record the common title followed by the title of the part, section, or supplement even if the title of the part, section, or supplement alone is sufficient to identify the resource.

> Key abstracts. Industrial power and control systems

2.3.2 Title Proper

CORE ELEMENT

2.3.2.1 Scope

The ***title proper*** is the chief name of a resource (i.e., the title normally used when citing the resource).

An alternative title is treated as part of the title proper.

The title proper does not include:

parallel titles proper (see **2.3.3**)
other title information (see **2.3.4**)
parallel other title information (see **2.3.5**).

A file name or data set name is not considered a title proper unless it is the only title appearing in the resource.

2.3.2.2 Sources of Information

Take the title proper from the preferred source of information as specified at **2.2.2–2.2.3**.

If there is no title provided within the resource itself, take the title proper from one of the sources specified at **2.2.4**.

Make a note on the source of the title proper, if required (see **2.17.2.3**).

CHOOSING THE TITLE PROPER

2.3.2.3 Facsimiles and Reproductions

When the title of a facsimile or reproduction is different from the title of the original manifestation, choose the title of the facsimile or reproduction as the title proper.

> Pugin's ecclesiastical ornament
> *Title of facsimile recorded as title proper. Title of original manifestation:* Glossary of ecclesiastical ornament and costume

If the title of the original manifestation appears on the same source of information as the title of the facsimile or reproduction, record it:

either
a) as a parallel title proper, if it is in a language or script different from the title of the facsimile (see **2.3.3**)
or
b) as other title information (see **2.3.4**)
or
c) as the title of a related manifestation (see **27.1**).

If the title of the original manifestation appears elsewhere in the resource, record it as the title of a related manifestation (see **27.1**).

2.3.2.4 Title in More Than One Language or Script

If:

the content of the resource is written, spoken, or sung

and

the source of information for the title proper has a title in more than one language or script

then:

choose as the title proper the title in the language or script of the main content of the resource.

If:

the content is not written, spoken, or sung,

or

there is no main content in a single language

then:

choose the title proper on the basis of the sequence, layout, or typography of the titles on the source of information.

2.3.2.5 Title in More Than One Form

If:

the source of information for the title proper has a title in more than one form

and

the titles are in the same language and script

then:

choose the title proper on the basis of the sequence, layout, or typography of the titles on the source of information.

If the sequence, layout, and typography do not provide the basis for a clear choice, choose the most comprehensive title.

MapEasy's guidemap to Philadelphia

Two forms of title on source of information: MapEasy's guidemap to Philadelphia *and* Welcome to Philadelphia. *First form chosen as title proper based on layout on the source of information.*

> ***Exception***
>
> ***Serials and integrating resources.*** If the title of a serial or integrating resource appears on the source of information for the title proper in full as well as in the form of an acronym or initialism, choose the full form as the title proper.
>
> Linguistics and language behavior abstracts
>
> *Title appears on source of information in full and as* LLBA

If the other title or titles are considered important for identification or access, record them:

either

a) as other title information (see **2.3.4**)

or

b) as variant titles (see **2.3.6**).

2.3.2.6 Collective Title and Titles of Individual Contents

Record collective titles and titles of individual contents as appropriate to the type of description:

comprehensive description (see **2.3.2.6.1**)

or

analytical description (see **2.3.2.6.2**).

2.3.2.6.1 Comprehensive Description

If:

the type of description chosen for the resource is a comprehensive description (see **1.5.2**)

and

the resource has a source of information for the title proper with both a collective title and the titles of individual contents within the resource

then:

record the collective title as the title proper.

> Three notable stories
>
> *Source of information also has the titles of the three stories contained in the resource:* Love and peril *by the Marquis of Lorne;* To be or not to be *by Mrs. Alexander; and* The melancholy hussar *by Thomas Hardy*
>
> Six Renoir drawings
>
> *Source of information also has the titles of the six drawings contained in the resource:* La danse à la campagne*;* Les deux baigneuses*;* Pierre Renoir*;* Enfants jouant à la balle*;* Baigneuse assise*; and* Étude d'une enfant

Optional Addition

Record the titles of the individual contents as titles of related works (see **25.1**).

2.3.2.6.2 Analytical Description

If:

the type of description chosen for the resource is an analytical description (see **1.5.3**)

and

the resource has a source of information for the title proper with both the title of the content being described and a collective title for the larger resource

then:

record the title of the content being described as the title proper.

> English history, 1914–1945
>
> *Source of information also has the series title:* The Oxford history of England
>
> Miss Mapp
>
> *Source of information also has the collective title for the larger work:* All about Lucia

Record the collective title for the larger resource as a series title (see **2.12.2**).

Optional Addition

Record the collective title for the larger resource as the title of a related work (see **25.1**).

Exception

If the title of the individual content being described is insufficient to identify the manifestation, record the collective title for the larger resource, followed by the title of the content being described (see **2.3.1.7**).

RECORDING THE TITLE PROPER

2.3.2.7 Recording the Title Proper

Record the title proper by applying the basic instructions at **2.3.1**.

Speedball technique charts

Supplement to The conquest of Peru and Mexico

Why a duck?

Digital shaded-relief image of Alaska

Sunday school edition of New songs of the gospel

Lost by a hare on my terra pin pin

λ-calculus and computer theory

Fourteen hours

U-boat operations of the Second World War

Records of the Socialist Labor Party of America

L'éducation 25 ans plus tard! Et après?

4 days in the Queen Charlottes

Revised Washington State flood damage reduction plan

Listening to popular music, or, How I learned to stop worrying and love Led Zeppelin

WorldVitalRecords.com

Record an alternative title as part of the title proper.

2.3.2.8 Other Elements Recorded as Part of the Title Proper

Record these other elements as part of the title proper, as applicable:

type of composition, medium of performance, key, etc. (see **2.3.2.8.1**)

scale (see **2.3.2.8.2**).

2.3.2.8.1 Type of Composition, Medium of Performance, Key, Etc.

If a music title consists only of:

a) the name or names of one or more types of composition

or

b) the name or names of one or more types of composition and one or more of the following:

i. medium of performance

ii. key

iii. date of composition

iv. number

treat all the elements together (in the order in which they appear on the source of information) as the title proper.

Rhapsody

Songs & dances

Piano concertos 1 & 2

Sonate en ré majeur, op. 3, no. IX, pour flûte traversière (ou hautbois, ou violon) et basse continue

Scherzo for two pianos, four hands

Symphony no. 3, A minor, opus 56

Zwei Praeludien und Fugen für Orgel, op. posth. 7

Musik für Saiteninstrumente, Schlagzeug, und Celesta

Sinfonia I (1970)

VIII. Symphonie c-Moll

In all other cases, treat statements of medium of performance, key, date of composition, and/or number as other title information (see **2.3.4**).

Fugue on Hey diddle diddle
Other title information: for SATB unaccompanied

Sinfonia mazedonia
Other title information: Nr. 4 für grosses Orchester

In case of doubt, treat statements of medium of performance, key, date of composition, and number as part of the title proper.

2.3.2.8.2 Scale

If the title proper of a cartographic resource includes a statement of the scale, include that statement as part of the title proper.

Topographic 1:500,000 low flying chart

New "half-inch" cycling road maps of England and Wales

2.3.2.9 Resource Lacking a Collective Title

If:

the type of description chosen for the resource is a comprehensive description

and

the resource lacks a collective title

then:

record the titles proper of the parts as they appear on the source of information for the resource as a whole.

Lord Macaulay's essays ; and, Lays of ancient Rome

En famille ; Deux amis ; et La ficelle

If the sources of information identifying the individual parts are being treated as a collective source of information for the resource as a whole (see **2.1.2**), record the titles proper of the parts in the order in which they appear in the resource.

Clock symphony
Surprise symphony

Saudades do Brasil
Le carnival de Londres
Trois rag-caprices

Henry Esmond
Bleak House

The Wilson papers
The Cole-Hatt papers

London pageant
Concertante for three wind instruments and orchestra
Suite from "Tamara"
Cathaleen-ni-Hollihan

Alternative

Devise a collective title by applying the instructions at **2.3.2.11**. If considered important for identification or access, record the titles of individual parts as the titles proper of related manifestations (see **27.1**).

2.3.2.10 Resource with No Title

If there is no title in the resource itself, record as the title proper:

either
a) a title taken from another source (see **2.2.4**)
or
b) a devised title (see **2.3.2.11**).

Make a note to indicate the source of the title proper (see **2.17.2.3**).

2.3.2.11 Recording Devised Titles

If:
the resource itself has no title (see **2.3.2.10**)
and
a title cannot be found in any of the other sources of information specified at **2.2.4**
then:
devise a brief descriptive title that indicates *either*:

a) the nature of the resource (e.g., map, literary manuscript, diary, advertisement)
or
b) its subject (e.g., names of persons, corporate bodies, objects, activities, events, geographical area and dates)
or
c) a combination of the two, as appropriate.

Use the language and script appropriate to the content of the resource being described, except where instructed to use specific terminology.

Anarchist bombing, Union Square, New York City, March 1908

Pleasure boat on the Murray River, Mildura, Victoria

Sydney Bicycle Club badge

Dance poster collection

Posters of World War I

Portrait of General Emiliano Zapata and his staff, Puebla, Mexico

Letters from Don Banks to Suzanne Gleeson

Alternative

Devise a title in a language and script preferred by the agency preparing the description.

If the resource is a type that would normally have identifying information (e.g., a published book), make a note to indicate that the title has been devised (see **2.17.2.3**).

Apply these additional instructions for special types of resources, as applicable:

music (see **2.3.2.11.1**)

cartographic resources (see **2.3.2.11.2**)

moving image resources (see **2.3.2.11.3**)

archival resources and collections (see **2.3.2.11.4**).

2.3.2.11.1 Devised Titles for Music

In a devised title for music, include as applicable: medium of performance, numeric designation (e.g., serial number, opus number), key, and/or other distinguishing characteristic.

Trio for piano and strings, no. 2, op. 66, C minor

Sämmtliche Lieder, Balladen und Romanzen, 4. Heft. Erster Verlust

2.3.2.11.2 Devised Titles for Cartographic Resources

In a devised title for a cartographic resource, always include the name or an identification of the area covered and, if applicable, the subject portrayed.

Gravity anomaly map of Canada

Relief model of California showing vegetation

Lunar globe

Ontario county and district maps colour series

Nautical chart of the coast of Maine from Cape Elizabeth to Monhegan Island

Street maps of the incorporated cities and towns of Maryland

2.3.2.11.3 Devised Titles for Moving Image Resources

In a devised title for a short advertising film or video, include the name or an identification of the product, service, etc., advertised, and the word *advertisement.*

Manikin cigar advertisement

Road safety campaign advertisement

In a devised title for unedited moving image material, stock shots, or news film, include all the major elements present in the resource in order of their occurrence (e.g., place, date of event, date of shooting (if different), personalities, and subjects).

Phantom jet landing at R.A.F. Leuchars, July 1971

Alternative

Record a description of the action and length of each shot as a related manifestation (see **27.1**).

2.3.2.11.4 Devised Titles for Archival Resources and Collections

In a devised title for an archival resource or a collection, include the name of the creator, collector, or source, if appropriate.

Bessye B. Bearden papers

St. Paul African Methodist Episcopal Zion Church records

William Gedney photographs and writings

The Jascha Heifetz collection

Daniel Murray Collection of W.E.B. Du Bois photographs displayed at the International Exposition in Paris, 1900

Photograph of Theodore Roosevelt

CHANGE IN THE TITLE PROPER

2.3.2.12 Recording Changes in the Title Proper

Record a change in title proper as appropriate to the mode of issuance of the resource:

multipart monographs (see **2.3.2.12.1**)

serials (see **2.3.2.12.2**)

integrating resources (see **2.3.2.12.3**).

2.3.2.12.1 Multipart Monographs

If there is a change in the title proper on a subsequent part of a multipart monograph, and the change is considered important for identification or access, record the subsequent title as a later title proper (see **2.3.8**).

2.3.2.12.2 Serials

If there is a major change (as defined at **2.3.2.13.1**) in the title proper on a subsequent issue or part of a serial, make a new description for the issues or parts appearing under the new title.

Treat the two descriptions as descriptions for related works (see **25.1**).

If the change is a minor change (as defined in **2.3.2.13.2**) but is considered important for identification or access, record the later title as a later title proper (see **2.3.8**).

2.3.2.12.3 Integrating Resources

Change the title proper to reflect the current iteration of an integrating resource if there is a change of title proper on a subsequent iteration.

Record the earlier title as an earlier title proper (see **2.3.7**) if the change is considered important for identification or access.

2.3.2.13 Major and Minor Changes in the Title Proper of Serials

Differentiate between major and minor changes in the title proper of a serial by applying these instructions:

major changes (**2.3.2.13.1**)
minor changes (**2.3.2.13.2**).

2.3.2.13.1 Major Changes

In general, consider the following to be major changes in a title proper:

a) the addition, deletion, change, or reordering of any of the first five words (the first six words if the title begins with an article) unless the change belongs to one or more of the categories listed as minor changes (see **2.3.2.13.2**)

b) the addition, deletion, or change of any word after the first five words (the first six words if the title begins with an article) that changes the meaning of the title or indicates a different subject matter

c) a change of name for a corporate body included anywhere in the title if the changed name is for a different corporate body.

2.3.2.13.2 Minor Changes

In general, consider the following to be minor changes in a title proper:

a) a difference in the representation of a word or words anywhere in the title (e.g., one spelling vs. another; abbreviated word or sign or symbol vs. spelled-out form; arabic numeral vs. roman numeral; number or date vs. spelled-out form; hyphenated word vs. unhyphenated word; one-word compound vs. two-word compound, whether hyphenated or not; an acronym or initialism vs. full form; or a change in grammatical form (e.g., singular vs. plural))

b) the addition, deletion, or change of articles, prepositions, or conjunctions anywhere in the title

c) a difference involving the name of the same corporate body and elements of its hierarchy or their grammatical connection anywhere in the title (e.g., the addition, deletion, or rearrangement of the name of the same corporate body, the substitution of a variant form)

d) the addition, deletion, or change of punctuation, including initialisms and letters with separating punctuation vs. those without separating punctuation, anywhere in the title

e) a different order of titles when the title is given in more than one language on the source of information, provided that the title chosen as title proper still appears as a parallel title proper

f) the addition, deletion, or change of words anywhere in the title that link the title to the numbering

g) two or more titles proper used on different issues of a serial according to a regular pattern

h) the addition to, deletion from, or change in the order of words in a list anywhere in the title, provided that there is no significant change in the subject matter

i) the addition, deletion, or rearrangement anywhere in the title of words that indicate the type of resource, such as "magazine," "journal," or "newsletter" or their equivalent in other languages.

In case of doubt, consider the change to be a minor change.

2.3.3 Parallel Title Proper

2.3.3.1 Scope

A ***parallel title proper*** is the title proper in another language and/or script.

An alternative title in another language and/or script is treated as part of the parallel title proper.

Treat an original title in a language different from that of the title proper as a parallel title proper if it is presented as the equivalent of the title proper.

2.3.3.2 Sources of Information

Take parallel titles proper from any source within the resource. If the title proper is taken from outside the resource, take parallel titles proper from the same source.

2.3.3.3 Recording Parallel Titles Proper

Record a parallel title proper by applying the basic instructions on recording titles at **2.3.1**.

> Les Cris des forêts
> *Title proper:* Wood Cree
>
> Introduction to the morphology of blood
> *Title proper:* Einführung in die Blutmorphologie

Record an alternative parallel title proper as part of the parallel title proper.

If there is more than one parallel title proper, record the titles in the order indicated by the sequence, layout, or typography of the titles on the source or sources of information.

> Carte routière de la Suisse
> Road map of Switzerland
> *Title proper:* Strassenkarte der Schweiz

If:
an original title is in a language different from that of the title proper
and
the title is presented as an equivalent to the title proper
then:
record it as a parallel title proper.

> 20 poemas de amor y una canción desesperada
> *Title proper:* Twenty love poems and a song of despair
>
> À bout de souffle
> *Title proper:* Breathless

If a parallel title proper is taken from a different source than the title proper, and that fact is considered important for identification, make a note on the source (see **2.17.2.3**).

2.3.3.4 Medium of Performance, Key, Etc.

If:
the source of information includes statements of medium of performance, key, date of composition, and/or number that are treated as part of the title proper (see **2.3.2.8.1**)
and
these statements are in more than one language or script
then:
record such statements as part of the parallel title proper. Record them in the order in which they appear on the source of information.

D major, for horn and orchestra
ré majeur, pour cor et orchestre
Title proper: Concerto, D-Dur, für Horn und Orchester

2.3.3.5 Recording Changes in Parallel Titles Proper

Record a change in a parallel title proper as appropriate to the mode of issuance of the resource:

multipart monographs (see **2.3.3.5.1**)

serials (see **2.3.3.5.2**)

integrating resources (see **2.3.3.5.3**).

2.3.3.5.1 Multipart Monographs

Variant title. Record an added or changed parallel title proper as a variant title (see **2.3.6**), if considered important for identification or access.

If a parallel title proper is deleted on a subsequent part, make a note on the deletion if considered important for identification or access (see **2.17.2.4**).

2.3.3.5.2 Serials

Variant title. Record an added or changed parallel title proper as a variant title (see **2.3.6**), if considered important for identification or access.

If a parallel title proper is deleted on a subsequent issue or part, make a note on the deletion if considered important for identification or access (see **2.17.2.4**).

2.3.3.5.3 Integrating Resources

Record an added or changed parallel title proper to reflect the current iteration.

Variant title. Record the earlier parallel title proper as a variant title (see **2.3.6**), if considered important for identification or access.

If a parallel title proper is deleted on a subsequent iteration, delete the parallel title proper to reflect the current iteration.

Variant title. Record a deleted parallel title proper as a variant title (see **2.3.6**), if considered important for identification or access.

2.3.4 Other Title Information

2.3.4.1 Scope

Other title information is information that appears in conjunction with, and is subordinate to, the title proper of a resource.

Other title information can include any phrase appearing with a title proper that is indicative of:

the character, contents, etc., of the resource

or

the motives for, or occasion of, its production, publication, etc.

Other title information includes subtitles, etc. It does not include variations on the title proper such as spine titles, sleeve titles, etc. (see **2.3.6**) or designations and/or names of parts, sections, or supplements (see **2.3.1.7**).

In general, do not supply other title information. Other title information can be supplied for:

cartographic resources (see **2.3.4.5**)

moving image resources (see **2.3.4.6**).

2.3.4.2 Sources of Information

Take other title information from the same source as the title proper (see **2.3.2.2**).

2.3.4.3 Recording Other Title Information

Record other title information that appears on the same source of information as the title proper. Apply the basic instructions on recording titles at **2.3.1**.

analyzing the communication environment
Title proper: A.C.E.

works from the Phillips Collection
Title proper: A collection in the making

the maple sugar paintings of Eastman Johnson
Title proper: Sugaring off

the definitive biography
Title proper: Kerouac

for SATB unaccompanied
Title proper: Fugue on Hey diddle diddle

a new edition of Tokyo up-to-date
Title proper: A complete map of Tokyo

Nr. 4 für grosses Orchester
Title proper: Sinfonia mazedonia

the fourteenth exhibition of the Council of Europe
Title proper: The age of neo-classicism

newsletter of the Somerset and Dorset Family History Society
Title proper: The greenwood tree

LLBA
Title proper: Linguistics and language behavior abstracts

Exception

Serials and integrating resources. Record information about the currency of the contents or the frequency of updating as frequency (see **2.14**).

If there is more than one element of other title information, record the elements in the order indicated by the sequence, layout, or typography of the elements on the source of information.

acute care of at-risk newborns
a resource and learning tool for health care professionals
Title proper: ACoRN

If an original title appears on the same source of information as the title proper, and it is in the same language as the title proper, record it as other title information.

L'anima del filosofo
Source of information has original title in addition to title proper: Orfeo ed Euridice

> Cantates françaises à voix seule, mêlées de symphonies, oeuvre cinquième
> *Source of information has original title in addition to title proper:* Les quatre saisons

2.3.4.4 Other Title Information in More Than One Language or Script

If other title information appears in more than one language or script, record the other title information that is in the language or script of the title proper. If this criterion does not apply, record the other title information that appears first.

> for piano solo and woodwind choir
> *Title proper:* Variations on a Czech love song. *Other title information also appears in French*

2.3.4.5 Supplying Other Title Information for Cartographic Resources

If:

the title proper of a cartographic resource does not include an indication of the geographic area covered and/or the subject portrayed

and

the other title information does not include such an indication or there is no other title information

then:

supply as other title information a word or brief phrase indicating the geographic area covered and, if applicable, the subject portrayed. Indicate that the information was taken from a source outside the resource itself (see **2.2.4**).

Indicate that the information was taken from a source outside the resource itself (see **2.2.4**).

> [in Botswana]
> *Title proper:* Vegetation

2.3.4.6 Supplying Other Title Information for Moving Image Resources

If:

the resource is a trailer containing extracts from a larger moving image resource

and

the title proper does not indicate this

then:

supply *trailer* as other title information. Indicate that the information was taken from a source outside the resource itself (see **2.2.4**).

Indicate that the information was taken from a source outside the resource itself (see **2.2.4**).

> [trailer]
> *Title proper:* Annie Hall

2.3.4.7 Recording Changes in Other Title Information

Record a change in other title information as appropriate to the mode of issuance of the resource:

multipart monographs (see **2.3.4.7.1**)

serials (see **2.3.4.7.2**)

integrating resources (see **2.3.4.7.3**).

2.3.4.7.1 Multipart Monographs

Variant title. Record added or changed other title information as a variant title (see **2.3.6**), if considered important for identification or access.

If other title information that was recorded is then deleted on a subsequent part, make a note on the deletion (see **2.17.2.4**).

2.3.4.7.2 Serials

Variant title. Record added or changed other title information as a variant title (see **2.3.6**), if considered important for identification or access.

If other title information that was recorded is then deleted on a subsequent issue or part, make a note on the deletion (see **2.17.2.4**).

2.3.4.7.3 Integrating Resources

Record added other title information to reflect the current iteration of an integrating resource if the addition is considered important for identification or access.

Change other title information to reflect the current iteration of an integrating resource, if the changes are considered important for identification or access.

If the changed other title information is not considered important for identification or access, delete the other title information.

Variant title. Record earlier other title information as a variant title (see **2.3.6**), if considered important for identification or access.

If other title information that was recorded is then deleted on a subsequent iteration, delete the recorded other title information to reflect the current iteration.

Variant title. Record deleted other title information as a variant title (see **2.3.6**), if considered important for identification or access.

2.3.5 Parallel Other Title Information

2.3.5.1 Scope

Parallel other title information is other title information in a language and/or script that differs from that recorded in the other title information element.

2.3.5.2 Sources of Information

Take parallel other title information from the same source as the corresponding parallel title proper (see **2.3.3.2**).

If there is no corresponding parallel title proper, take parallel other title information from the same source as the title proper (see **2.3.2.2**).

2.3.5.3 Recording Parallel Other Title Information

Record parallel other title information in the same order as the parallel titles proper to which the information corresponds. Apply the basic instructions on recording titles at **2.3.1**.

> Eskimo women's music of Povungnituk
> musique des Esquimaudes de Povungnituk
>
> *Title proper in Inuktitut:* Arnait puvirnitumiut katutjatut amalu qanirpalutut. *Parallel titles proper in English:* Inuit throat and harp songs, *and in French:* Chants inuit-gorge et guibarde
>
> Meisterwerke der botanischen Illustration
> masterpieces of botanical illustration
> chefs-d'œuvre
>
> *Title proper in German:* Ein Garten Eden. *Parallel titles proper in English:* Garden Eden, *and in French:* Un jardin d'Eden

If:

there are no parallel titles proper

and

other title information appears in one or more languages or scripts that are different from that of the title proper

then:

record the other title information that appears first as other title information (see **2.3.4.4**). Record the other title information in other languages as parallel other title information.

> pour piano soliste et ensemble de bois
>
> *Title proper in English. No parallel title proper. Other title information in English recorded as other title information*

2.3.5.4 Recording Changes in Parallel Other Title Information

Record a change in parallel other title information as appropriate to the mode of issuance of the resource:

multipart monographs (see **2.3.5.4.1**)

serials (see **2.3.5.4.2**)

integrating resources (see **2.3.5.4.3**).

2.3.5.4.1 Multipart Monographs

Variant title. Record added or changed parallel other title information as a variant title (see **2.3.6**) if considered important for identification or access.

If parallel other title information that was recorded is then deleted on a subsequent part, make a note on the deletion (see **2.17.2.4**).

2.3.5.4.2 Serials

Variant title. Record added or changed parallel other title information as a variant title (see **2.3.6**) if considered important for identification or access.

If parallel other title information that was recorded is then deleted on a subsequent issue or part, make a note on the deletion (see **2.17.2.4**).

2.3.5.4.3 Integrating Resources

Record added parallel other title information to reflect the current iteration of an integrating resource, if considered important for identification or access.

Change parallel other title information to reflect the current iteration of an integrating resource, if considered important for identification or access.

Variant title. Record earlier parallel other title information as a variant title (see **2.3.6**), if considered important for identification or access.

If the changed parallel other title information is not considered important for identification or access, delete the parallel other title information.

If parallel other title information that was recorded is then deleted on a subsequent iteration, delete the recorded parallel other title information to reflect the current iteration.

Variant title. Record deleted parallel other title information as a variant title (see **2.3.6**), if considered important for identification or access.

2.3.6 Variant Title

2.3.6.1 Scope

A ***variant title*** is a title associated with a resource that differs from a title recorded as the title proper, a parallel title proper, other title information, parallel other title information, earlier title proper, later title proper, key title, or abbreviated title.

Variant titles include the following:

a) those that appear in the resource itself (e.g., on a title page, title frame, title screen; as a caption title, running title; on a cover, spine), on a jacket, sleeve, container, etc., or in accompanying material

b) those associated with a resource through reference sources

c) those assigned by an agency registering or preparing a description of the resource (e.g., a title assigned by a repository, a cataloguer's translation or transliteration of the title)

d) those assigned by the creator or by previous owners or custodians of the resource, etc.

e) corrections to titles that appear in the resource in an incorrect form

f) part of a title (e.g., an alternative title or a section title recorded as part of the title proper)

g) variations in parallel titles proper, other title information, or parallel other title information appearing on an earlier iteration of an integrating resource or on a later issue or part of a multipart monograph or serial.

Variations in the title proper appearing on an earlier iteration of an integrating resource are treated as earlier titles proper (see **2.3.7**).

Variations in the title proper appearing on a later issue or part of a multipart monograph or serial are treated as later titles proper (see **2.3.8**).

2.3.6.2 Sources of Information

Take variant titles from any source.

2.3.6.3 Recording Variant Titles

Record variant titles that are considered important for identification or access by applying the basic instructions on recording titles at **2.3.1**.

Good mousekeeping
Title proper recorded as: Little Roquefort in Good mousekeeping

The world of television
Title proper recorded as: The wolrd of television

Arranging and describing archives and manuscripts
Title proper recorded as: Arranging & describing archives & manuscripts

National Football League rocks
Title proper recorded as: NFL rocks

Aging in the Americas into the twenty-first century
Title proper recorded as: Aging in the Americas into the XXI century

Quatre danses de Terpischore
Title proper recorded as: 4 danses de Terpischore

Sechs kleine Stücke für Anfänger
Six easy pieces for beginners
Title proper recorded as: 6 kleine Stücke für Anfänger. *Parallel title proper recorded as:* 6 easy pieces for beginners

Strategic sustainable planning
Title on cover. Title proper recorded as: SSP, a civil defense manual for cultural survival

How I learned to stop worrying and love Led Zeppelin
Alternative title. Title proper recorded as: Listening to popular music, or, How I learned to stop worrying and love Led Zeppelin

We're still standing
Title on container. Title proper recorded as: Four the moment

Law & strategy for businesses and corporations
Earlier other title information on iterations from 1997–2000. Other title information on current iteration: Business transactions and Brownfield redevelopment

Site du Web des noms géographiques officiels du Canada
Earlier parallel title proper appearing on iterations from 1995–2000?

An online guide for amphibians in the United States and Canada
Earlier other title information viewed August 11, 1998. Other title information on current iteration: An online guide for the identification of amphibians in North America north of Mexico

Glossario del Banco Mundial
Later parallel title proper also appearing on volume 2. Title proper: The World Bank glossary. *French parallel title proper on volume 1:* Glossaire de la Banque mondiale

Meisterwerke der Makonde
Later parallel title proper appearing on volumes 2–3. Title proper: Masterpieces of the Makonde. *No parallel title proper on volume 1*

Inter-American review of bibliography
Later parallel title proper appearing on issues from 1952 on

Studies in educational administration
Later other title information appearing on issues from vol. 1, no. 3 on

Make a note on the source or basis for the variant title (see **2.17.2.3**) if considered important for identification or access.

2.3.6.4 Translations or Transliterations of the Title Proper

Record as a variant title a translation or transliterated form of the title proper created by the agency preparing the description. Apply the basic instructions on recording titles at **2.3.1**.

Plant physiology
Translation of Russian title proper

2.3.7 Earlier Title Proper

2.3.7.1 Scope

An ***earlier title proper*** is a title proper appearing on an earlier iteration of an integrating resource that differs from that on the current iteration.

2.3.7.2 Sources of Information

Take earlier titles proper from sources in earlier iterations of an integrating resource, using the source specified for the title proper (see **2.3.2.2**).

2.3.7.3 Recording Earlier Titles Proper

For changes in the title proper of an integrating resource, apply the instructions at **2.3.2.12.3**.

Record a title proper no longer present on the current iteration of an integrating resource as an earlier title proper, if considered important for identification or access. Apply the basic instructions on recording titles at **2.3.1**.

Taxation of intangible assets

Earlier title proper appearing on iterations from 1997–1998. Current title proper: Federal income taxation of intellectual properties and intangible assets

Washington newspapers database

Earlier title proper viewed October 6, 1999. Current title proper: Washington state newsstand

Environmental liability

Earlier title proper appearing on iterations from 1990–2001. Current title proper: Managing environmental liability

Euroinfo international

Earlier title proper viewed May 10, 1998. Current title proper: Infobel world telephone directories

Telephone directories international

Earlier title proper viewed September 9, 1999. Current title proper: Infobel world telephone directories

Make a note on the publication dates to which the earlier title proper applies (see **2.17.2.3**). For online resources, instead of a note on publication dates, make a note on the date the earlier title proper was viewed (see **2.17.13.5**).

Alternative

If the changes have been numerous, make a general note (see **2.17.2.4**).

2.3.8 Later Title Proper

2.3.8.1 Scope

A *later title proper* is a title proper appearing on a later issue or part of a multipart monograph or serial that differs from that on the first or earliest issue or part.

2.3.8.2 Sources of Information

Take later titles proper from sources in later issues or parts of a multipart monograph or serial, using the source specified for the title proper at **2.3.2.2**.

2.3.8.3 Recording Later Titles Proper

For changes in the title proper, see the instructions appropriate to the mode of issuance:

multipart monographs (**2.3.2.12.1**)

serials (**2.3.2.12.2**).

Record a later title proper in these cases, if considered important for identification or access:

if there is a change in the title proper on a later part of a multipart monograph

or

if there is a minor change in the title proper on a later issue or part of a serial.

Apply the basic instructions on recording titles at **2.3.1**.

Annual report on pipeline safety

Later title proper appearing in issues from 1999. Title proper recorded as: Annual report of pipeline safety

Eminent Indian mathematicians of the twentieth century

Later title proper appearing from volume 5 of multipart monograph. Title proper recorded as: Some eminent Indian mathematicians of the twentieth century

Dictionnaire des églises de France, Belgique, Luxembourg, Suisse

Later title proper appearing on volume 2 of multipart monograph. Title proper recorded as: Histoire générale des églises de France, Belgique, Luxembourg, Suisse

Dictionnaire des églises de France

Later title proper appearing on volumes 3–5 of multipart monograph. Title proper recorded as: Histoire générale des églises de France, Belgique, Luxembourg, Suisse

The magazine antiques

Later title proper appearing in issues of serial from January 1928–July 1952; March 1971. Title proper recorded as: Antiques

Make a note on the numbering or publication dates to which the change in the title proper applies (see **2.17.2.3**).

> *Alternative*
>
> If the changes have been numerous, make a general note (see **2.17.2.4**).

2.3.9 Key Title

2.3.9.1 Scope

A ***key title*** is the unique name assigned to a resource by an ISSN registration agency.

2.3.9.2 Sources of Information

Take the key title from the following sources (in order of preference):

a) the ISSN Register

b) a source within the resource itself

c) any other source.

2.3.9.3 Recording Key Titles

Record a key title as it appears on the source.

IFLA journal

Volunteer (Washington)

British Library Bibliographic Services Division newsletter

Image (Niagara ed.)

2.3.10 Abbreviated Title

2.3.10.1 Scope

An ***abbreviated title*** is a title that has been abbreviated for purposes of indexing or identification.

An abbreviated title is created either by the agency preparing the description or by another agency (e.g., an ISSN registration agency, an abstracting or indexing service).

2.3.10.2 Sources of Information

Take abbreviated titles from any source.

2.3.10.3 Recording Abbreviated Titles

Record an abbreviated title as it appears on the source.

Can. j. infect. dis. med. microbiol.

2.4 Statement of Responsibility

CORE ELEMENT

Statement of responsibility relating to title proper is a core element (if more than one, only the first recorded is required). Other statements of responsibility are optional.

2.4.1 Basic Instructions on Recording Statements of Responsibility

2.4.1.1 Scope

A ***statement of responsibility*** is a statement relating to the identification and/or function of any persons, families, or corporate bodies responsible for the creation of, or contributing to the realization of, the intellectual or artistic content of a resource.

A statement of responsibility sometimes includes words or phrases that are neither names nor linking words.

Statements of responsibility may occur in association with:

a title proper (see **2.4.2–2.4.3**)
a designation of edition (see **2.5.4–2.5.5**)
a designation of a named revision of an edition (see **2.5.8–2.5.9**)
the title of a series (see **2.12.6–2.12.7**)
the title of a subseries (see **2.12.14–2.12.15**).

For statements identifying performers of music whose participation is limited to performance, execution, or interpretation, see **7.23**.

For statements identifying performers, narrators, and/or presenters, see **7.23**.

For statements identifying persons who have contributed to the artistic and/or technical production of a resource, see **7.24**.

For statements identifying persons, families, or corporate bodies responsible for:

the production of a resource, see **2.7.4–2.7.5**
the publication of a resource, see **2.8.4–2.8.5**
the distribution of a resource, see **2.9.4–2.9.5**
the manufacture of a resource, see **2.10.4–2.10.5**.

2.4.1.2 Sources of Information

For guidance on choosing sources of information for statements of responsibility, see the instructions for specific types of statements of responsibility as follows:

a) For statement of responsibility relating to title proper, see **2.4.2.2**.

b) For parallel statement of responsibility relating to title proper, see **2.4.3.2**.

c) For statement of responsibility relating to the edition, see **2.5.4.2**.

d) For parallel statement of responsibility relating to the edition, see **2.5.5.2**.

e) For statement of responsibility relating to a named revision of an edition, see **2.5.8.2**.

f) For parallel statement of responsibility relating to a named revision of an edition, see **2.5.9.2**.

g) For statement of responsibility relating to series, see **2.12.6.2**.

h) For parallel statement of responsibility relating to series, see **2.12.7.2**.

i) For statement of responsibility relating to subseries, see 2.12.14.2.

j) For parallel statement of responsibility relating to subseries, see 2.12.15.2.

2.4.1.3 Facsimiles and Reproductions

When a facsimile or reproduction has a statement or statements of responsibility relating to the original manifestation as well as to the facsimile or reproduction, record the statement or statements of responsibility relating to the facsimile or reproduction. Record any statement of responsibility relating to the original manifestation as a statement of responsibility of a related manifestation (see 27.1).

2.4.1.4 Recording Statements of Responsibility

Transcribe a statement of responsibility as it appears on the source of information (see 1.7).

by Walter de la Mare

Fats Waller

by Dr. Johnson

by Sir Richard Acland

by Alfred, Lord Tennyson

by a Lady of Quality

par Charles M. Schultz

directed and produced by the Beatles

af Martin A. Hansen

edited and introduced by Mrs. C.F. Leyel

created by the fourth grade class of Washington Elementary School, Berkeley, CA

authorized by the United Lutheran Church of America

by [E.B.C.]
Creator's initials represented by musical notes on source of information

chosen for this edition by the author
Title proper: Selected poetry of W.H. Auden

text, translation, inroduction and commentary by Joseph Rabbinowitz
Third word misspelled and should read: introduction

Optional Omission

Abridge a statement of responsibility only if this can be done without loss of essential information. Do not use a mark of omission (...) to indicate such an omission. Always record the first name appearing in the statement. When omitting names from a statement of responsibility naming more than one person, etc., apply the instructions at 2.4.1.5.

by Harry Smith
Source of information reads: by Dr. Harry Smith

Charles F. Hoban, Jr.
Source of information reads: Charles F. Hoban, Jr., Special Assistant, Division of Visual Education, Philadelphia Public Schools

sponsored by the Library Association

Source of information reads: sponsored by the Library Association (founded 1877)

Exception

Serials. Record a statement of responsibility identifying an editor of a serial only if the name of the editor is considered an important means of identifying the serial (e.g., if a particular person edited the serial for all or most of its existence; if the person's name is likely to be better known than the title of the serial).

editor: Wyndham Lewis

founded, edited, and published by Jean-Paul Sartre

compiled and edited by Richard L. Coulton with the assistance of voluntary aid

2.4.1.5 Statement Naming More Than One Person, Etc.

Record a statement of responsibility naming more than one person, family, or corporate body as a single statement whether those persons, etc., perform the same function or different functions.

edited by P.C. Wason and P.N. Johnson-Laird

compiled from the best authorities of both languages by Professors De Lolme and Wallace, and Henry Bridgeman

prepared for the Ethical Union by Mass-Observation

Jane Austen and another lady

developed by Dale Kahn with Laurie Fenster

Duke Ellington and his orchestra

compiled and edited by Richard L. Coulton with the assistance of voluntary aid

L.H. Booth, P. Fisher, V. Heppelthwaite, and C.T. Eason

Ellen Goodman, Patricia O'Brien

Optional Omission

If a single statement of responsibility names more than three persons, families, or corporate bodies performing the same function (or with the same degree of responsibility), omit any but the first of each group of such persons, families, or bodies. Indicate the omission by summarizing what has been omitted in a language and script preferred by the agency preparing the description. Indicate that the summary was taken from a source outside the resource itself (see **2.2.4**).

Roger Colbourne [and six others]

Source of information reads: Roger Colbourne, Suzanne Bassett, Tony Billing, Helen McCormick, John McLennan, Andrew Nelson and Hugh Robertson

Raymond Queneau, Jacques Jouet [and 4 others]

Source of information reads: by Raymond Queneau, Italo Calvino, Paul Fournel, Jacques Jouet, Claude Berge & Harry Mathews

If the members of a group, ensemble, company, etc., are named as well as the group, etc., omit the names of the members from the statement of responsibility. If they are considered important for identification, access, or selection, record them in a statement identifying performers, narrators, and/or presenters (see **7.23**).

> Gerry Mulligan Quartet
> *Members of the group are also named on the source of information:* Gerry Mulligan, baritone; Chet Baker, trumpet; Henry Grimes, bass; Dave Bailey, drums

2.4.1.6 More Than One Statement of Responsibility

If there is more than one statement of responsibility, record the statements in the order indicated by the sequence, layout, or typography of the source of information from which the corresponding title, edition, or series information is taken.

> by F. Scott and Zelda Fitzgerald
> selected by Scottie Fitzgerald Smith and Matthew J.Bruccoli
> with a foreword by Scottie Fitzgerald Smith
>
> prepared by members of the AIAA Technical Committees on Space Systems and Space Atmosphere Physics
> edited by Arthur Henderson, Jr., and Jerry Grey
>
> ABC News
> producer and writer, James Benjamin
> director, Al Niggemeyer
> director, Dan Bessie
> writer, Phyllis Harvey
> animation, B. Davis
> editor, I. Dryer
>
> Raymond C. Kammerer and Carl R. Steinbecker
> made by Creative Sights & Sounds

If the sequence, layout, and typography are ambiguous or insufficient to determine the order, record the statements in the order that makes the most sense.

If statements of responsibility appear in sources other than the source from which the corresponding title, edition, or series information is taken, record them in the order that makes the most sense.

2.4.1.7 Clarification of Role

Add a word or short phrase if necessary to clarify the role of a person, family, or corporate body named in a statement of responsibility.

Indicate that the information was taken from a source outside the resource itself (see **2.2.4**).

> [collected by] Chet Williams
> *Title proper:* Baijun ballads
>
> **but**
>
> Charles Dickens
> *Title proper:* Bleak House
>
> National Gallery of Art
> *Title proper:* Brief guide

the Rolling Stones
Title proper: Beggars banquet

2.4.1.8 Noun Phrases Occurring with a Statement of Responsibility

If a noun or noun phrase occurs with a statement of responsibility, treat the noun or noun phrase as part of the statement of responsibility.

research and text by Colin Barham
Title proper: Roman Britain

dramatised adaptations by Barry Campbell
Title proper: Characters from Dickens

2.4.1.9 No Person, Family, or Corporate Body Named in the Statement of Responsibility

Record a statement of responsibility even if no person, family, or corporate body is named in that statement.

by a group of students with a Korean resource person

with a spoken commentary by the artist

2.4.1.10 Recording Changes in Statements of Responsibility

Record a change in a statement of responsibility as appropriate to the mode of issuance of the resource:

multipart monographs (see **2.4.1.10.1**)
serials (see **2.4.1.10.2**)
integrating resources (see **2.4.1.10.3**).

2.4.1.10.1 Multipart Monographs

Make a note (see **2.17.3.6.1**) if:

a statement of responsibility is added, deleted, or changed on a subsequent part of a multipart monograph

and

the addition, deletion, or change is considered important for identification or access.

2.4.1.10.2 Serials

Make a note (see **2.17.3.6.2**) if:

a statement of responsibility is added, deleted, or changed on a subsequent issue or part of a serial

and

the addition, deletion, or change does not require a new description (see **1.6.2**)

and

the change is considered important for identification or access.

2.4.1.10.3 Integrating Resources

Revise the statement of responsibility to reflect the current iteration of an integrating resource if a statement of responsibility is added or changed on a subsequent iteration.

Make a note giving the earlier statement of responsibility (see **2.17.3.6.3**) if the earlier statement is considered important for identification or access.

If a statement of responsibility is deleted on a subsequent iteration, delete the statement of responsibility to reflect the current iteration. Make a note on the deletion if considered important for identification or access (see **2.17.3.6.3**).

2.4.2 Statement of Responsibility Relating to Title Proper

CORE ELEMENT

If more than one statement of responsibility relating to title proper appears on the source of information, only the first recorded is required.

2.4.2.1 Scope

A ***statement of responsibility relating to title proper*** is a statement associated with the title proper of a resource that relates to the identification and/or function of any persons, families, or corporate bodies responsible for the creation of, or contributing to the realization of, the intellectual or artistic content of the resource.

2.4.2.2 Sources of Information

Take statements of responsibility relating to title proper from the following sources (in order of preference):

a) the same source as the title proper (see **2.3.2.2**)

b) another source within the resource itself (see **2.2.2**)

c) one of the other sources of information specified at **2.2.4**.

2.4.2.3 Recording Statements of Responsibility Relating to Title Proper

Record statements of responsibility relating to title proper by applying the basic instructions at **2.4.1**.

by James Clavell

edited, with an introduction, by Royal A. Gettmann

by Mrs. Charles H. Gibson

Jacques Offenbach
music adapted and arranged by Ronald Hanmer
new book and lyrics by Phil Park

University of London Audio Visual Centre
produced, directed, and edited by N.C. Collins

by Miss Read

by the late T.A. Rennard

prólogo del Excmo. Sr. D. Manuel Fraga Iribarne

translated from the German by Carolyn Gammon

[edited by] John Paxton
Title proper: Everyman's dictionary of abbreviations

by John Malo
Title proper: Malo's complete guide to canoeing and canoe-camping. *Name of creator appears separately on the source of information as well as in the title proper*

herausgegeben in dem Ministerium der Geistlichen, Unterrichts- und Medizinal-Angelegenheiten

If not all statements of responsibility appearing on the source or sources of information are being recorded, give preference to those identifying creators of the intellectual or artistic content. In case of doubt, record the first statement.

2.4.2.4 Statement of Responsibility Relating to Title Proper in More Than One Language or Script

If a statement of responsibility relating to title proper appears on the source of information in more than one language or script, record the statement in the language or script of the title proper. If this criterion does not apply, record the statement that appears first.

> International Tin Council
> *Title proper:* Tin prices. *Statement of responsibility appears in English, French, Spanish, and Russian*
>
> edited by Dr. Zoltán Pipics
> *Title proper:* Dictionarium bibliothecarii practicum. *Statement of responsibility appears in English and German*

2.4.3 Parallel Statement of Responsibility Relating to Title Proper

2.4.3.1 Scope

A ***parallel statement of responsibility relating to title proper*** is a statement of responsibility relating to title proper in a language and/or script that differs from that recorded in the statement of responsibility relating to title proper element.

2.4.3.2 Sources of Information

Take parallel statements of responsibility relating to title proper from the same source as the corresponding parallel title proper (see **2.3.3.2**).

If there is no corresponding parallel title proper, take parallel statements of responsibility relating to title proper from the same source as the title proper (see **2.3.2.2**).

2.4.3.3 Recording Parallel Statements of Responsibility Relating to Title Proper

Record parallel statements of responsibility relating to title proper by applying the basic instructions at **2.4.1**.

> Mary E. Bond, rédactrice et réviseure
> *Statement of responsibility relating to title proper:* Mary E. Bond, compiler and editor

If there is more than one parallel statement of responsibility relating to title proper, record the statements in the same order as the parallel titles proper to which they correspond; if that is not applicable, record them in the order found on the resource.

> Conseil international de l 'etain
> Consejo Internacional del Estaño
> Международный совет по олову
> *Statement of responsibility relating to title proper:* International Tin Council

2.5 Edition Statement

CORE ELEMENT

Designation of edition and designation of a named revision of an edition are core elements. Other sub-elements of edition statements are optional.

2.5.1 Basic Instructions on Recording Edition Statements

2.5.1.1 Scope

An ***edition statement*** is a statement identifying the edition to which a resource belongs.

An edition statement sometimes includes a designation of a named revision of an edition.

An edition statement sometimes includes a statement or statements of responsibility relating to the edition and/or to a named revision of an edition.

For resources in an unpublished form, statements indicating the version of the work contained in the resource are treated as edition statements. Some examples of a resource in an unpublished form are manuscript drafts or videorecordings that have not been commercially released or broadcast.

2.5.1.2 Sources of Information

For guidance on choosing sources of information for edition statements, see the instructions for specific sub-elements of an edition statement as follows:

a) For designation of edition, see **2.5.2.2**.

b) For parallel designation of edition, see **2.5.3.2**.

c) For statement of responsibility relating to the edition, see **2.5.4.2**.

d) For parallel statement of responsibility relating to the edition, see **2.5.5.2**.

e) For designation of a named revision of an edition, see **2.5.6.2**.

f) For parallel designation of a named revision of an edition, see **2.5.7.2**.

g) For statement of responsibility relating to a named revision of an edition, see **2.5.8.2**.

h) For parallel statement of responsibility relating to a named revision of an edition, see **2.5.9.2**.

2.5.1.3 Facsimiles and Reproductions

When a facsimile or reproduction has an edition statement or statements relating to the original manifestation as well as to the facsimile or reproduction, record the edition statement or statements relating to the facsimile or reproduction. Record any edition statement relating to the original as an edition statement of a related manifestation (see **27.1**).

2.5.1.4 Recording Edition Statements

Transcribe an edition statement as it appears on the source of information (see **1.7**).

Draft

Interactive version

Household ed.

Facsim. ed.

Neue Aufl.

Deuxième edition revue et augmentée

Rev. et corr.

Nouvelle édition

World's classics ed., New ed. rev.

1st standard ed.

Wyd. 2-gie

6. Aufl.

2e éd. du recueil noté

Second edition

52nd edition

Director's cut

Editio secunda auctior et correctior

Optional Addition

If a resource lacks an edition statement but is known to contain significant changes from other editions, supply an edition statement, if considered important for identification or access. Indicate that the information was taken from a source outside the resource itself (see **2.2.4**).

[Hand-coloured and corrected edition]

F major edition
Note on edition statement reads: Edition statement from publisher's catalog

2.5.1.5 Edition Statements Relating to Issues or Parts

If:
the resource consists of multiple issues or parts, including accompanying material,
and
there are edition statements relating to the whole as well as to parts
then:
record only the edition statements relating to the whole resource.

Make a note giving edition statements relating to issues or parts if considered important for identification (see **2.17.4.3**).

2.5.1.6 Recording Changes in Edition Statements

Record a change in an edition statement as appropriate to the mode of issuance of the resource:

multipart monographs (see **2.5.1.6.1**)
serials (see **2.5.1.6.2**)
integrating resources (see **2.5.1.6.3**).

2.5.1.6.1 Multipart Monographs

Make a note (see **2.17.4.5.1**) if:

edition statements differ from one part of a multipart monograph to another

and

the difference is considered important for identification or access.

2.5.1.6.2 Serials

Make a note (see **2.17.4.5.2**) if:

an edition statement is added, deleted, or changed on a subsequent issue or part of a serial

and

the change is considered important for identification or access.

2.5.1.6.3 Integrating Resources

Change the edition statement to reflect the current iteration if:

an edition statement is added, deleted, or changed on a subsequent iteration of an integrating resource

and

the change does not require a new description (see **1.6.3.4**).

If the earlier edition statement is considered important for identification or access, make a note giving the earlier statement (see **2.17.4.5.3**).

2.5.2 Designation of Edition

CORE ELEMENT

2.5.2.1 Scope

A ***designation of edition*** is a word, character, or group of words and/or characters, identifying the edition to which a resource belongs.

Note that in some languages the same term or terms can be used to indicate both edition and printing. A statement detailing the number of copies printed is not a designation of edition.

In case of doubt about whether a statement is a designation of edition, consider the presence of these words or statements as evidence that it is a designation of edition:

a) a word such as *edition, issue, release, level, state*, or *update* (or its equivalent in another language)
or
b) a statement indicating:

i. a difference in content

ii. a difference in geographic coverage

iii. a difference in language

iv. a difference in audience

v. a particular format or physical presentation

vi. a different date associated with the content

vii. a particular voice range or format for notated music.

2.5.2.2 Sources of Information

Take designations of edition from the following sources (in order of preference):

a) the same source as the title proper (see **2.3.2.2**)

b) another source within the resource itself (see **2.2.2**)

c) one of the other sources of information specified at **2.2.4**.

2.5.2.3 Recording Designations of Edition

Record a designation of edition by applying the basic instructions at **2.5.1**.

Ny udgave

1st ed.

New ed., rev. and enl.

1st American ed.

Urtextausg.

NORC test ed.

Rev. ed. 10/2/82

*** ed.

Somerset ed.

World Cup ed.

Abridged

Corr. 2nd print.

Draft, May 2000

Version 2.5

Northern ed.

Éd. pour le médecin

New edition

Second college edition

Troisième édition revue et augmentée

Canadian edition

Widescreen version

Nunc primum in lucem aedita

Full score

Vollständiger Klavierauszug

Klavierauszug zu 2 Händen mit Singstimme und Text

If a designation of edition consists of a letter or letters and/or a number or numbers (expressed either as numerals or as words) without accompanying words, add an appropriate word. Indicate that the information was taken from a source outside the resource itself (see **2.2.4**).

3e [édition]

[State] B

[Version] 1.1

First [edition]

If there is more than one designation of edition, record the statements in the order indicated by the sequence, layout, or typography of the statements on the source of information.

1. Auflage
Partitur, zugleich Orgelstimme

1. vyd.
partitura a hlasy

2.5.2.4 Designation of Edition in More Than One Language or Script

If a designation of edition appears on the source of information in more than one language or script, record the statement in the language and/or script of the title proper. If this criterion does not apply, record the statement that appears first.

> 6th revised and enlarged edition
> *Title proper in Latin. Designation of edition appears in English and German*
>
> 4th edition
> *Title proper in English. Designation of edition appears in English and French*

2.5.2.5 Statements Indicating Regular Revision or Numbering

For serials and integrating resources, record statements indicating regular revision as a note on frequency (see **2.17.12**) (e.g., *Revised edition issued every 6 months*, *Frequently updated*).

For serials, record statements indicating numbering as numbering (see **2.6**) (e.g., *First edition*, *2010 edition*).

2.5.2.6 Designation of Edition Integral to Title Proper, Etc.

If:

a designation of edition is an integral part of the title proper, other title information, or statement of responsibility

or

the designation is grammatically linked to any of these elements

then:

record the designation of edition as part of the element to which it is integrated or linked. Do not record it again as a designation of edition.

> The compact edition of the Oxford English dictionary
> *Designation of edition integral to title proper. No designation of edition recorded*
>
> Tenth anniversary edition of Economic justice for all
> *Designation of edition integral to title proper. No designation of edition recorded*
>
> Bullarum diplomatum et privilegiorum sanctorum Romanorum pontificum Taurinensis editio
> *Designation of edition integral to title proper. No designation of edition recorded*
>
> a revised and augmented edition of the Glossary of biotechnology and genetic engineering
> *Designation of edition integral to other title information. No designation of edition recorded*
>
> édition française revue par Germaine Meyer-Noire
> *Designation of edition integral to statement of responsibility. No designation of edition recorded*

2.5.3 Parallel Designation of Edition

2.5.3.1 Scope

A ***parallel designation of edition*** is a designation of edition in a language and/or script that differs from that recorded in the designation of edition element.

2.5.3.2 Sources of Information

Take parallel designations of edition from the following sources (in order of preference):

a) the same source as the designation of edition (see **2.5.2.2**)

b) another source within the resource itself (see **2.2.2**)

c) one of the other sources of information specified at **2.2.4**.

2.5.3.3 Recording Parallel Designations of Edition

Record parallel designations of edition by applying the basic instructions at **2.5.1**.

> Révision 1980
> *Designation of edition:* Rev. 1980
>
> 2e éd., rev. et corr.
> *Designation of edition:* 2de herziene en verb. uitg.
>
> Éd. canadienne
> *Designation of edition:* Canadian ed.
>
> 6. verbesserte und erweiterte Auflage
> *Designation of edition:* 6th revised and enlarged edition

If there is more than one parallel designation of edition, record the statements in the order indicated by the sequence, layout, or typography of the statements on the source or sources of information.

> 2^{a} edizione
> 2. Auflage
> *Designation of edition:* 2e édition

2.5.4 Statement of Responsibility Relating to the Edition

2.5.4.1 Scope

A ***statement of responsibility relating to the edition*** is a statement relating to the identification of any persons, families, or corporate bodies responsible for the edition being described but not to all editions.

2.5.4.2 Sources of Information

Take statements of responsibility relating to the edition from the same source as the designation of edition (see **2.5.2.2**).

2.5.4.3 Recording Statements of Responsibility Relating to the Edition

Record statements of responsibility relating to the edition by applying the basic instructions at **2.4.1**.

> revised collectively by the Peking Opera Troupe of Peking
> *Designation of edition:* May 1970 script
>
> introduction by J. Hillis Miller
> notes by Edward Mendelson
> *Designation of edition:* New Wessex ed.
>
> edited by J.S. Sykes
> *Designation of edition:* Seventh edition
>
> revised and updated by Alan Powers
> *Designation of edition:* New edition
>
> with maps redrawn by N. Manley
> *Designation of edition:* 3rd ed.
>
> arrangement by Otto Singer
> *Designation of edition:* Vocal score

> by the composer
> *Designation of edition:* Piano/vocal score

If:

there is doubt about whether a statement of responsibility applies to all editions or only to some

or

there is no designation of edition

then:

record the statement of responsibility as a statement of responsibility relating to title proper (see **2.4.2**). When describing the first edition, record all statements of responsibility as statements of responsibility relating to title proper (see **2.4.2**).

2.5.4.4 Statement of Responsibility Relating to the Edition in More Than One Language or Script

If a statement of responsibility relating to the edition appears on the source of information in more than one language or script, record the statement in the language or script of the title proper. If this criterion does not apply, record the statement that appears first.

> reviderade og udvidet af David Hohnen
> *Title proper:* Høst's Engelsk-Danske og Dansk-Engelske lommeordbog. *Designation of edition:* 14. opl.
> *Statement of responsibility relating to the edition also appears in English*

2.5.5 Parallel Statement of Responsibility Relating to the Edition

2.5.5.1 Scope

A ***parallel statement of responsibility relating to the edition*** is a statement of responsibility relating to the edition in a language and/or script that differs from that recorded in the statement of responsibility relating to the edition element.

2.5.5.2 Sources of Information

Take parallel statements of responsibility relating to the edition from the same source as the corresponding parallel designation of edition (see **2.5.3.2**).

If there is no corresponding parallel designation of edition, take parallel statements of responsibility relating to the edition from the same source as the designation of edition (see **2.5.2.2**).

2.5.5.3 Recording Parallel Statements of Responsibility Relating to the Edition

Record parallel statements of responsibility relating to the edition by applying the basic instructions at **2.4.1**.

> rédigé par Larry C. Lewis
> *Statement of responsibility relating to the edition:* edited by Larry C. Lewis
>
> revised and enlarged by David Hohnen
> *Statement of responsibility relating to the edition:* reviderade og udvidet af David Hohnen

If there is more than one parallel statement of responsibility relating to the edition, record the statements in the same order as the parallel designations of edition to which they correspond; if that is not applicable, record them in the order found on the resource.

2.5.6 Designation of a Named Revision of an Edition

CORE ELEMENT

2.5.6.1 Scope

A ***designation of a named revision of an edition*** is a word, character, or group of words and/or characters, identifying a particular revision of a named edition.

2.5.6.2 Sources of Information

Take designations of a named revision of an edition from the following sources (in order of preference):

a) the same source as the designation of edition (see **2.5.2.2**)

b) another source within the resource itself (see **2.2.2**)

c) one of the other sources of information specified at **2.2.4**.

2.5.6.3 Recording Designations of a Named Revision of an Edition

If the source of information has a statement indicating a revision of an edition (e.g., a named reissue of a particular edition containing changes from that edition), record that statement. Apply the instructions on recording designations of edition (see **2.5.2.3**).

> reprinted with corrections
> *Designation of edition:* 4th ed.
>
> new edition, revised, reset, and illustrated
> *Designation of edition:* World's classics edition
>
> 2nd (corr.) impression
> *Designation of edition:* 3rd ed.
>
> Roads revised
> *Designation of edition:* 4th ed.
>
> OSIRIS IV version
> *Designation of edition:* ICPSR ed.

Do not record statements relating to a reissue of an edition that contains no changes unless the resource is considered to be of particular importance to the agency preparing the description.

2.5.6.4 Designation of a Named Revision of an Edition in More Than One Language or Script

If a designation of a named revision of an edition appears on the source of information in more than one language or script, record the statement in the language or script of the title proper. If this criterion does not apply, record the statement that appears first.

> 3rd corr. impression
> *Title proper in English. Designation of named revision of edition also appears in French*

2.5.7 Parallel Designation of a Named Revision of an Edition

2.5.7.1 Scope

A ***parallel designation of a named revision of an edition*** is a designation of a named revision of an edition in a language and/or script that differs from that recorded in the designation of a named revision of an edition element.

2.5.7.2 Sources of Information

Take parallel designations of a named revision of an edition from the following sources (in order of preference):

a) the same source as the designation of a named revision of an edition (see **2.5.6.2**)

b) another source within the resource itself (see **2.2.2**)

c) one of the other sources of information specified at **2.2.4**.

2.5.7.3 Recording Parallel Designations of a Named Revision of an Edition

Record parallel designations of a named revision of an edition by applying the basic instructions at **2.5.1**.

> 3e réimpr. corr.
> *Designation of named revision of edition:* 3rd corr. impression

If there is more than one parallel designation of a named revision of an edition, record the parallel statements in the order indicated by the sequence, layout, or typography of the statements on the source or sources of information.

2.5.8 Statement of Responsibility Relating to a Named Revision of an Edition

2.5.8.1 Scope

A ***statement of responsibility relating to a named revision of an edition*** is a statement relating to the identification of any persons, families, or corporate bodies responsible for a named revision of an edition.

2.5.8.2 Sources of Information

Take statements of responsibility relating to a named revision of an edition from the same source as the designation of a named revision of an edition (see **2.5.6.2**).

2.5.8.3 Recording Statements of Responsibility Relating to a Named Revision of an Edition

Record statements of responsibility relating to one or more named revisions of an edition by applying the basic instructions at **2.4.1**.

> with the assistance of Eleanor Gould Packard
> *Designation of edition:* Rev. ed. *Statement of responsibility relating to the edition:* with revisions, an introduction, and a chapter on writing by E.B. White. *Designation of a named revision of an edition:* 2nd ed.
>
> programmed by W.G. Toepfer
> *Designation of edition:* 3rd ed. *Designation of a named revision of an edition:* Version 1.2

2.5.8.4 Statement of Responsibility Relating to a Named Revision of an Edition in More Than One Language or Script

If a statement of responsibility relating to a named revision of an edition appears on the source of information in more than one language or script, record the statement in the language or script of the title proper. If this criterion does not apply, record the statement that appears first.

> by N. Schmidt
> *Title proper in English. Statement of responsibility related to named revision of edition also appears in German*

2.5.9 Parallel Statement of Responsibility Relating to a Named Revision of an Edition

2.5.9.1 Scope

A ***parallel statement of responsibility relating to a named revision of an edition*** is a statement of responsibility relating to a named revision of an edition in a language and/or script that differs from that recorded in the statement of responsibility relating to a named revision of an edition element.

2.5.9.2 Sources of Information

Take parallel statements of responsibility relating to a named revision of an edition from the same source as the corresponding parallel designation of a named revision of an edition (see **2.5.7.2**).

If there is no corresponding parallel designation of a named revision of an edition, take parallel statements of responsibility relating to a named revision of an edition from the same source as the designation of a named revision of an edition (see **2.5.6.2**).

2.5.9.3 Recording Parallel Statements of Responsibility Relating to a Named Revision of an Edition

Record parallel statements of responsibility relating to a named revision of an edition by applying the basic instructions at **2.4.1**.

> af N. Schmidt
> *Statement of responsibility relating to named revision of an edition:* by N. Schmidt

If there is more than one parallel statement of responsibility relating to a named revision of an edition, record the statements in the same order as the parallel designations of a named revision of an edition to which they correspond.

2.6 Numbering of Serials

CORE ELEMENT

Core elements are numeric and/or alphabetic designation of first issue or part of sequence, chronological designation of first issue or part of sequence, numeric and/or alphabetic designation of last issue or part of sequence, and chronological designation of last issue or part of sequence. Other numbering is optional.

2.6.1 Basic Instructions on Recording Numbering of Serials

2.6.1.1 Scope

Numbering of serials is the identification of each of the issues or parts of a serial.

Numbering of serials may include:

a) a numeral, a letter, any other character, or a combination of these (with or without a caption (volume, number, etc.))
and/or
b) a chronological designation.

A serial sometimes has more than one sequence of numbering. A new sequence generally begins when a new system of numeric and/or alphabetic designations begins.

A serial sometimes has more than one concurrent system of numeric and/or alphabetic designations.

For numbering within series, see **2.12.9**. For numbering within subseries, see **2.12.17**.

2.6.1.2 Sources of Information

For guidance on choosing sources of information for numbering of serials, see the instructions for specific sub-elements of numbering of serials as follows:

a) For numeric and/or alphabetic designation of first issue or part of sequence, see **2.6.2.2**.

b) For chronological designation of first issue or part of sequence, see **2.6.3.2**.

c) For numeric and/or alphabetic designation of last issue or part of sequence, see **2.6.4.2**.

d) For chronological designation of last issue or part of sequence, see **2.6.5.2**.

e) For alternative numeric and/or alphabetic designation of first issue or part of sequence, see **2.6.6.2**.

f) For alternative chronological designation of first issue or part of sequence, see **2.6.7.2**.

g) For alternative numeric and/or alphabetic designation of last issue or part of sequence, see **2.6.8.2**.

h) For alternative chronological and/or alphabetic designation of last issue or part of sequence, see **2.6.9.2**.

2.6.1.3 Facsimiles and Reproductions

When a facsimile or reproduction has numbering relating to the original manifestation as well as to the facsimile or reproduction, record the numbering relating to the facsimile or reproduction. Record the numbering relating to the original manifestation as numbering of a related manifestation (see **27.1**).

2.6.1.4 Recording Numbering of Serials

Record numbers expressed as numerals or as words by applying the general guidelines at **1.8**.

Transcribe other words, characters, or groups of words and/or characters as they appear on the source of information by applying the general guidelines at **1.7**.

July/August 2005

1

Vol. 1, no. 1

summer 1978

4th issue

Exception

Substitute a slash for a hyphen, as necessary, for clarity.

1961/1962

Designation appears on issue as 1961–2

1999/2000

Designation appears on issue as 1999–2000

Record the numbering for the first issue or part (see **2.6.2–2.6.3**).

When describing a serial that has ceased publication, record the numbering for the last issue or part (see **2.6.4–2.6.5**).

> Vol. 3, no. 6
> *Numeric designation of first issue*
>
> Aug./Sept. 1970
> *Chronological designation of first issue*
>
> volume 5, number 3
> *Numeric designation of last issue*
>
> Mar. 1972
> *Chronological designation of last issue*

If the numbering starts a new sequence with a different system, record:

the numbering of the first issue or part of each sequence (see **2.6.2–2.6.3**)

and

the numbering of the last issue or part of each sequence (see **2.6.4–2.6.5**).

Record each sequence of numbering in the order in which they occur.

> Vol. 1, no. 1
> *Numeric designation of first issue of first sequence*
>
> November 1943
> *Chronological designation of first issue of first sequence*
>
> volume 10, number 12
> *Numeric designation of last issue of first sequence*
>
> June 1953
> *Chronological designation of last issue of first sequence*
>
> number 1
> *Numeric designation of first issue of new sequence*
>
> July 1974
> *Chronological designation of first issue of new sequence*

Makes notes on variations in designations (see **2.17.5.4**) if:

there are variations in designations that do not constitute a new sequence

and

the variations are considered important for identification.

If a serial has more than one concurrent system of numbering, record the second or subsequent systems as alternative numbering (see **2.6.5–2.6.9**). Record them in the order in which they are presented.

> Vol. 3, no. 7
> *First system of numeric designation of first issue of sequence*
>
> No. 31
> *Alternate system of numeric designation of first issue of sequence*

2.6.2 Numeric and/or Alphabetic Designation of First Issue or Part of Sequence

CORE ELEMENT

Numeric and/or alphabetic designation of first issue or part of sequence for the first or only sequence is a core element.

2.6.2.1 Scope

Numeric and/or alphabetic designation of first issue or part of sequence is numbering (see **2.6.1.1**) presented in numeric and/or alphabetic form on the first issue or part of a sequence of numbering for a serial.

2.6.2.2 Sources of Information

Take the numeric and/or alphabetic designation of the first issue or part of a sequence from the following sources (in order of preference):

a) the source on the first issue or part of that sequence that has the title proper (see **2.3.2.2**)

b) another source within the first issue or part of that sequence (see **2.2.2**)

c) one of the other sources of information specified at **2.2.4**.

2.6.2.3 Recording Numeric and/or Alphabetic Designation of First Issue or Part of Sequence

If the first issue or part of a sequence of a serial is identified by a numeric and/or alphabetic designation, record the designation by applying the basic instructions at **2.6.1**.

Number 1

Issue no. 1

Pt. 1

#01

Volume 1, issue 1

RP 1

First edition

If the designation consists of a year and a number that is a division of the year, record the year before the number.

97-1
Designation appears on part as: 1–97

1998-1
Designation appears on issue as: 1-1998

In some cases, the sequence of numeric and/or alphabetic designation is continued from a previous serial. When this occurs, record the numeric and/or alphabetic designation of the first issue or part of the serial represented by the new description, continuing the numbering from the previous serial.

Vol. 1, no. 6
Designation appears on last issue of previous serial as: vol. 1, no. 5

If a second or subsequent sequence of numbering is accompanied by wording to differentiate the sequence, such as *new series*, include this wording.

new series, v. 1, no. 1

If a new sequence with the same system as before is not accompanied by wording such as *new series*, supply *new series* or another appropriate term. Indicate that the information was taken from a source outside the resource itself (see **2.2.4**).

[new series], no. 1

[3rd series], no. 1
Previous sequence: [new series] no. 1–no. 3

[2nd series], number 1
Previous sequence: number 1–number 6. *Subsequent sequences:* 3rd series, 4th series

If:
the first issue or part of a sequence has no numeric and/or alphabetic designations
and
subsequent issues or parts define a numeric and/or alphabetic designation pattern for the sequence
then:
supply a numeric and/or alphabetic designation for the first issue or part of the sequence based on the pattern. Indicate that the information was taken from a source outside the resource itself (see **2.2.4**).

[Part 1]
Subsequent issues numbered: Part 2, Part 3, *etc.*

If:
the identification of the resource is based on an issue or part other than the first of a sequence
and
a numeric and/or alphabetic designation for the first issue or part of the sequence can be readily ascertained
then:
supply a numeric and/or alphabetic designation for the first issue or part. Indicate that the information was taken from a source outside the resource itself (see **2.2.4**).

Alternative
Make a note on the numbering of the first issue or part of the sequence (see **2.17.5.3**).

2.6.2.4 Numeric and/or Alphabetic Designation of First Issue or Part of Sequence in More Than One Language or Script

If the numeric and/or alphabetic designation of the first issue or part of a sequence appears on the source of information in more than one language or script, record the designation that is in the language or script of the title proper. If this criterion does not apply, record the designation that appears first.

Band 1
Title proper in German. Designation also appears in English

2.6.3 Chronological Designation of First Issue or Part of Sequence

CORE ELEMENT

Chronological designation of first issue or part of sequence for the first or only sequence is a core element.

2.6.3.1 Scope

Chronological designation of first issue or part of sequence is numbering (see **2.6.1.1**) presented in the form of a date (e.g., a year; year and month; month, day, and year) on the first issue or part of a sequence of numbering for a serial.

For a designation consisting of a year and a number that is a division of the year, see **2.6.2.3**.

2.6.3.2 Sources of Information

Take the chronological designation of the first issue or part of a sequence from the following sources (in order of preference):

a) the source on the first issue or part of the sequence that has the title proper (see **2.3.2.2**)

b) another source within the first issue or part of the sequence (see **2.2.2**)

c) one of the other sources of information specified at **2.2.4**.

2.6.3.3 Recording Chronological Designation of First Issue or Part of Sequence

If the first issue or part of a sequence of a serial is identified by a chronological designation, record the designation by applying the basic instructions at **2.6.1**.

1975

Jan./Feb. 1964

September 2003

spring 2004

2010 edition

Optional Addition

If the chronological designation includes dates not of the Gregorian or Julian calendar, add the corresponding dates of the Gregorian or Julian calendar. Indicate that the information was taken from a source outside the resource itself (see **2.2.4**).

If:

the first issue or part of a sequence has no chronological designation

and

subsequent issues or parts define a chronological designation pattern for the sequence

then:

supply a chronological designation for the first issue or part based on the pattern. Indicate that the information was taken from a source outside the resource itself (see **2.2.4**).

> [novembre 2006]
> *Designation appears on issue as:* Vol. 01, no 01; *subsequent issues include chronological designation*

If:
the identification of the resource is based on an issue or part other than the first of a sequence
and
a chronological designation for the first issue or part of the sequence can be readily ascertained
then:
supply a chronological designation for the first issue or part. Indicate that the information was taken from a source outside the resource itself (see **2.2.4**).

> *Alternative*
> Make a note on the numbering of the first issue or part of the sequence (see **2.17.5.3**).

2.6.3.4 Chronological Designation of First Issue or Part of Sequence in More Than One Language or Script

If the chronological designation of the first issue or part of a sequence appears on the source of information in more than one language or script, record the designation that is in the language or script of the title proper. If this criterion does not apply, record the designation that appears first.

> May 1977
> *Title proper in English. Chronological designation also appears in French*

2.6.4 Numeric and/or Alphabetic Designation of Last Issue or Part of Sequence

CORE ELEMENT

Numeric and/or alphabetic designation of last issue or part of sequence for the last or only sequence is a core element.

2.6.4.1 Scope

Numeric and/or alphabetic designation of last issue or part of sequence is numbering (see **2.6.1.1**) presented in numeric and/or alphabetic form on the last issue or part of a sequence of numbering for a serial.

2.6.4.2 Sources of Information

Take the numeric and/or alphabetic designation of the last issue or part of a sequence from the following sources (in order of preference):

a) the source on the last issue or part of the sequence that has the title proper (see **2.3.2.2**)

b) another source within the last issue or part of the sequence (see **2.2.2**)

c) one of the other sources of information specified at **2.2.4**.

2.6.4.3 Recording Numeric and/or Alphabetic Designation of Last Issue or Part of Sequence

If the last issue or part of a sequence of a serial is identified by a numeric and/or alphabetic designation, record the designation by applying the basic instructions at **2.6.1**.

no. 10

volume 10, number 12

v. 4, no. 12

If the designation consists of a year and a number that is a division of the year, record the year before the number.

If:

the last issue or part of a sequence has no numeric and/or alphabetic designations

and

previous issues or parts define a numeric and/or alphabetic designation pattern for the sequence

then:

supply a numeric and/or alphabetic designation for the last issue or part based on the pattern. Indicate that the information was taken from a source outside the resource itself (see **2.2.4**).

[issue 12]

No numeric and/or alphabetic designation on last issue of sequence. Designation on previous issue: issue 11

If:

the identification of the resource is based on an issue or part other than the last of a sequence

and

a numeric and/or alphabetic designation for the last issue or part of the sequence can be readily ascertained

then:

supply a numeric and/or alphabetic designation for the last issue or part. Indicate that the information was taken from a source outside the resource itself (see **2.2.4**).

Alternative

Make a note on the numbering of the last issue or part of the sequence (see **2.17.5.3**).

2.6.4.4 Numeric and/or Alphabetic Designation of Last Issue or Part of Sequence in More Than One Language or Script

If the numeric and/or alphabetic designation of the last issue or part of a sequence appears on the source of information in more than one language or script, record the designation that is in the language or script of the title proper. If this criterion does not apply, record the designation that appears first.

Band 162

Title proper in German. Designation also appears in English

2.6.5 Chronological Designation of Last Issue or Part of Sequence

CORE ELEMENT

Chronological designation of last issue or part of sequence for the last or only sequence is a core element.

2.6.5.1 Scope

Chronological designation of last issue or part of sequence is numbering (see **2.6.1.1**) presented in the form of a date (e.g., a year; year and month; month, day, and year) on the last issue or part of a sequence of numbering for a serial.

2.6.5.2 Sources of Information

Take the chronological designation of the last issue or part of a sequence from the following sources (in order of preference):

a) the source on the last issue or part of the sequence that has the title proper (see **2.3.2.2**)

b) another source within the last issue or part of the sequence (see **2.2.2**)

c) one of the other sources of information specified at **2.2.4**.

2.6.5.3 Recording Chronological Designation of Last Issue or Part of Sequence

If the last issue or part of a sequence of a serial is identified by a chronological designation, record the designation by applying the basic instructions at **2.6.1**.

Dec. 31, 1999

Optional Addition

If the chronological designation includes dates not of the Gregorian or Julian calendar, add the corresponding dates of the Gregorian or Julian calendar. Indicate that the information was taken from a source outside the resource itself (see **2.2.4**).

If:

the last issue or part of a sequence has no chronological designation

and

previous issues or parts define a chronological designation pattern for the sequence

then:

supply a chronological designation for the last issue or part based on the pattern. Indicate that the information was taken from a source outside the resource itself (see **2.2.4**).

[2005]

No chronological designation on last issue of sequence. Designation on previous issue: 2004

If:

the identification of the resource is based on an issue or part other than the last of a sequence

and

a chronological designation for the last issue or part of the sequence can be readily ascertained

then:

supply a chronological designation for the last issue or part. Indicate that the information was taken from a source outside the resource itself (see **2.2.4**).

Alternative

Make a note on the numbering of the last issue or part of the sequence (see **2.17.5.3**).

2.6.5.4 Chronological Designation of Last Issue or Part of Sequence in More Than One Language or Script

If the chronological designation of the last issue or part of a sequence appears on the source of information in more than one language or script, record the designation that is in the language or script of the title proper. If this criterion does not apply, record the designation that appears first.

January 1978
Title proper in English. Chronological designation also appears in French

2.6.6 Alternative Numeric and/or Alphabetic Designation of First Issue or Part of Sequence

2.6.6.1 Scope

Alternative numeric and/or alphabetic designation of first issue or part of sequence is a second or subsequent system of numbering (see **2.6.1.1**) presented in numeric and/or alphabetic form on the first issue or part of a sequence of numbering for a serial.

2.6.6.2 Sources of Information

Take the alternative numeric and/or alphabetic designation of the first issue or part of a sequence from the following sources (in order of preference):

a) the source on the first issue or part of the sequence that has the title proper (see **2.3.2.2**)

b) another source within the first issue or part of the sequence (see **2.2.2**)

c) one of the other sources of information specified at **2.2.4**.

2.6.6.3 Recording Alternative Numeric and/or Alphabetic Designation of First Issue or Part of Sequence

If the first issue or part of a sequence of a serial is identified by an alternative numeric and/or alphabetic designation, record the designation by applying the basic instructions at **2.6.1**.

85
Issue # 156

2.6.6.4 Alternative Numeric and/or Alphabetic Designation of First Issue or Part of Sequence in More Than One Language or Script

If an alternative numeric and/or alphabetic designation of the first issue or part of a sequence appears on the source of information in more than one language or script, record the designation that is in the language or script of the title proper. If this criterion does not apply, record the designation that appears first.

2.6.7 Alternative Chronological Designation of First Issue or Part of Sequence

2.6.7.1 Scope

Alternative chronological designation of first issue or part of sequence is a second or subsequent system of numbering (see **2.6.1.1**) presented in the form of a date (e.g., a year; year and month; month, day, and year) on the first issue or part of a sequence of numbering for a serial.

An alternative chronological designation may include a date in a different calendar.

2.6.7.2 Sources of Information

Take the alternative chronological designation of the first issue or part of a sequence from the following sources (in order of preference):

a) the source on the first issue or part of the sequence that has the title proper (see **2.3.2.2**)

b) another source within the first issue or part of the sequence (see **2.2.2**)

c) one of the other sources of information specified at **2.2.4**.

2.6.7.3 Recording Alternative Chronological Designation of First Issue or Part of Sequence

If the first issue or part of a sequence of a serial is identified by an alternative chronological designation, record the designation by applying the basic instructions at **2.6.1**.

> *Optional Addition*
>
> If the chronological designation includes dates not of the Gregorian or Julian calendar, add the corresponding dates of the Gregorian or Julian calendar. Indicate that the information was taken from a source outside the resource itself (see **2.2.4**).

2.6.7.4 Alternative Chronological Designation of First Issue or Part of Sequence in More Than One Language or Script

If an alternative chronological designation of the first issue or part of a sequence appears on the source of information in more than one language or script, record the designation that is in the language or script of the title proper. If this criterion does not apply, record the designation that appears first.

2.6.8 Alternative Numeric and/or Alphabetic Designation of Last Issue or Part of Sequence

2.6.8.1 Scope

Alternative numeric and/or alphabetic designation of last issue or part of sequence is a second or subsequent system of numbering (see **2.6.1.1**) presented in numeric and/or alphabetic form on the last issue or part of a sequence of numbering for a serial.

2.6.8.2 Sources of Information

Take the alternative numeric and/or alphabetic designation of the last issue or part of a sequence from the following sources (in order of preference):

a) the source on the last issue or part of the sequence that has the title proper (see **2.3.2.2**)

b) another source within the last issue or part of the sequence (see **2.2.2**)

c) one of the other sources of information specified at **2.2.4**.

2.6.8.3 Recording Alternative Numeric and/or Alphabetic Designation of Last Issue or Part of Sequence

If the last issue or part of a sequence of a serial is identified by an alternative numeric and/or alphabetic designation, record the designation by applying the basic instructions at **2.6.1**.

number 57

2.6.8.4 Alternative Numeric and/or Alphabetic Designation of Last Issue or Part of Sequence in More Than One Language or Script

If an alternative numeric and/or alphabetic designation of the last issue or part of a sequence appears on the source of information in more than one language or script, record the designation that is in the language or script of the title proper. If this criterion does not apply, record the designation that appears first.

2.6.9 Alternative Chronological Designation of Last Issue or Part of Sequence

2.6.9.1 Scope

Alternative chronological designation of last issue or part of sequence is a second or subsequent system of numbering (see **2.6.1.1**) presented in the form of a date (e.g., a year; year and month; month, day, and year) on the last issue or part of a sequence of numbering for a serial.

An alternative chronological designation may include a date in a different calendar.

2.6.9.2 Sources of Information

Take the alternative chronological designation of the last issue or part of a sequence from the following sources (in order of preference):

a) the source on the last issue or part of the sequence that has the title proper (see **2.3.2.2**)

b) another source within the last issue or part of the sequence (see **2.2.2**)

c) one of the other sources of information specified at **2.2.4**.

2.6.9.3 Recording Alternative Chronological Designation of Last Issue or Part of Sequence

If the last issue or part of a sequence of a serial is identified by an alternative chronological designation, record that designation by applying the basic instructions at **2.6.1**.

> *Optional Addition*
>
> If the chronological designation includes dates not of the Gregorian or Julian calendar, add the corresponding dates of the Gregorian or Julian calendar. Indicate that the information was taken from a source outside the resource itself (see **2.2.4**).

2.6.9.4 Alternative Chronological Designation of Last Issue or Part of Sequence in More Than One Language or Script

If an alternative chronological designation of the last issue or part of a sequence appears on the source of information in more than one language or script, record the designation that is in the language or script of the title proper. If this criterion does not apply, record the designation that appears first.

2.7 Production Statement

CORE ELEMENT

Date of production is a core element for resources issued in an unpublished form. Other sub-elements of production statements are optional.

2.7.1 Basic Instructions on Recording Production Statements

2.7.1.1 Scope

A ***production statement*** is a statement identifying the place or places of production, producer or producers, and date or dates of production of a resource in an unpublished form.

Production statements include statements relating to the inscription, fabrication, construction, etc., of a resource in an unpublished form.

2.7.1.2 Sources of Information

For guidance on choosing sources of information for production statements, see the instructions for specific sub-elements of a production statement as follows:

a) For place of production, see **2.7.2.2**.

b) For parallel place of production, see **2.7.3.2**.

c) For producer's name, see **2.7.4.2**.

d) For parallel producer's name, see **2.7.5.2**.

e) For date of production, see **2.7.6.2**

2.7.1.3 Facsimiles and Reproductions

When a facsimile or reproduction has a production statement or statements relating to the original manifestation as well as to the facsimile or reproduction, record the production statement or statements relating to the facsimile or reproduction. Record any production statement relating to the original as a production statement of a related manifestation (see **27.1**).

2.7.1.4 Recording Production Statements

Record a production statement or statements for a resource that is in an unpublished form (e.g., a manuscript, a painting, a sculpture, a locally made recording).

Transcribe places of production and producers' names as they appear on the source of information (see **1.7**).

Record dates of production as they appear on the source of information. Apply the general guidelines on transcription for words that are not numbers (see **1.7**). Apply the general guidelines on numbers expressed as numerals or as words (see **1.8**).

2.7.1.5 Recording Changes in Production Statements

Record a change in a production statement as appropriate to the mode of issuance of the resource:

multipart monographs (see **2.7.1.5.1**)
serials (see **2.7.1.5.2**)
integrating resources (see **2.7.1.5.3**).

2.7.1.5.1 Multipart Monographs

Make a note (see **2.17.6.4.1**) if:

the place of production changes on a subsequent part of a multipart monograph

and

the change is considered important for identification or access.

If the change is only in the presentation of the place name, make a note if the change is considered important for identification.

> *Alternative*
> If the changes have been numerous, make a general note (see **2.17.6.4.1**).

Make a note (see **2.17.6.4.1**) if:

a producer's name changes or a different producer is named on a subsequent part of a multipart monograph

and

the change is considered important for identification or access.

If the change is only in the presentation of the name, make a note if the change is considered important for identification.

> *Alternative*
> If the changes have been numerous, make a general note (see **2.17.6.4.1**).

2.7.1.5.2 Serials

Make a note (see **2.17.6.4.2**) if:

the place of production changes on a later issue or part of a serial

and

the change is considered important for identification or access.

If the change is only in the presentation of the place name, make a note if the change is considered important for identification.

> *Alternative*
>
> If the changes have been numerous, make a general note (see **2.17.6.4.2**).

Make a note (see **2.17.6.4.2**) if:

a producer's name changes or a different producer is named on a later issue or part of a serial

and

the change is considered important for identification or access.

If the change is only in the presentation of the name, make a note if the change is considered important for identification.

> *Alternative*
>
> If the changes have been numerous, make a general note (see **2.17.6.4.2**).

2.7.1.5.3 Integrating Resources

Change the place of production to reflect the current iteration of an integrating resource. Make a note on the earlier place if considered important for identification or access (see **2.17.6.4.3**).

Change the producer's name to reflect the current iteration of an integrating resource. Make a note on any earlier name if considered important for identification or access (see **2.17.6.4.3**).

> *Alternative*
>
> If the changes have been numerous, make a general note (see **2.17.6.4.3**).

2.7.2 Place of Production

2.7.2.1 Scope

A ***place of production*** is a place associated with the inscription, fabrication, construction, etc., of a resource in an unpublished form.

2.7.2.2 Sources of Information

Take places of production from the following sources (in order of preference):

a) the same source as the producer's name (see **2.7.4.2**)

b) another source within the resource itself (see **2.2.2**)

c) one of the other sources of information specified at **2.2.4**.

2.7.2.3 Recording Place of Production

Record the place of production by applying the basic instructions at **2.7.1**.

Include both the local place name (city, town, etc.) and the name of the larger jurisdiction or jurisdictions (state, province, etc., and/or country) if present on the source of information.

> *Optional Additions*
>
> Include the full address as part of the local place name, if considered important for identification or access.
>
> Supply the name of the larger jurisdiction (state, province, etc., and/or country) as part of the local place name if considered important for identification or access. Indicate that the information was taken from a source outside the resource itself (see **2.2.4**).

Include any preposition appearing with the place name that is required to make sense of the statement.

If the place name as transcribed is known to be fictitious, or requires clarification, make a note giving the actual place name, etc. (see **2.17.6.3**).

2.7.2.4 More Than One Place of Production

If more than one place of production is named on the source of information, record the place names in the order indicated by the sequence, layout, or typography of the names on the source of information.

If:
there are two or more producers
and
there are two or more places associated with one or more of the producers
then:
record the place names associated with each producer in the order indicated by the sequence, layout, or typography of the place names on the source of information.

2.7.2.5 Place of Production in More Than One Language or Script

If the place of production appears on the source of information in more than one language or script, record the form that is in the language or script of the title proper. If this criterion does not apply, record the place name in the language or script that appears first.

2.7.2.6 Place of Production Not Identified in the Resource

If the place of production is not identified in the resource, supply the place of production or probable place of production. Apply the instructions in this order of preference:

a) known place (see **2.7.2.6.1**)

b) probable place (see **2.7.2.6.2**)

c) known country, state, province, etc. (see **2.7.2.6.3**)

d) probable country, state, province, etc. (see **2.7.2.6.4**).

Indicate that the information was taken from a source outside the resource itself (see **2.2.4**).

Record *Place of production not identified* if neither a known nor a probable local place or country, state, province, etc., of production can be determined. Indicate that the information was taken from a source outside the resource itself (see **2.2.4**).

2.7.2.6.1 Known Place of Production

If the place of production is known, supply the local place name (city, town, etc.). Include the name of the larger jurisdiction if necessary for identification.

> [Salem, Massachusetts]

2.7.2.6.2 Probable Place of Production

If the place of production is uncertain, supply the name of the probable local place of production. Include the name of the larger jurisdiction if necessary for identification.

If only the local place name is supplied, follow it with a question mark.

If:
the name of the larger jurisdiction is supplied
and
the place of production is known to be within that jurisdiction
and
the locality within that jurisdiction is uncertain
then:
add a question mark following the name of the probable local place.

If:

the name of the larger jurisdiction is supplied

and

it is not known if the place of production is in that larger jurisdiction

then:

add a question mark following the name of the larger jurisdiction.

> [Port Alberni, British Columbia?]

2.7.2.6.3 Known Country, State, Province, Etc., of Production

If the probable local place is unknown, supply the name of the country, state, province, etc., of production.

> [Denmark]

2.7.2.6.4 Probable Country, State, Province, Etc., of Production

If the country, state, province, etc., of production is uncertain, supply the name of the probable country, state, province, etc., of production followed by a question mark.

> [France?]

2.7.2.7 Change in Place of Production

For instructions on recording a change in place of production, see 2.7.1.5.

2.7.3 Parallel Place of Production

2.7.3.1 Scope

A ***parallel place of production*** is a place of production in a language and/or script that differs from that recorded in the place of production element.

2.7.3.2 Sources of Information

Take parallel places of production from the following sources (in order of preference):

a) the same source as the place of production (see 2.7.2.2)

b) another source within the resource itself (see 2.2.2)

c) one of the other sources of information specified at 2.2.4.

2.7.3.3 Recording Parallel Places of Production

Record parallel places of production by applying the basic instructions at 2.7.1.

If there is more than one parallel place of production, record the names in the order indicated by the sequence, layout, or typography of the names on the source or sources of information.

2.7.4 Producer's Name

2.7.4.1 Scope

A ***producer's name*** is the name of a person, family, or corporate body responsible for inscribing, fabricating, constructing, etc., a resource in an unpublished form.

A producer's name may be represented by a characterizing word or phrase.

2.7.4.2 Sources of Information

Take producers' names from the following sources (in order of preference):

a) the same source as the title proper (see **2.3.2.2**)

b) another source within the resource itself (see **2.2.2**)

c) one of the other sources of information specified at **2.2.4**.

2.7.4.3 Recording Producers' Names

Record the producer's name by applying the basic instructions at **2.7.1**.

> *Optional Omission*
>
> Omit levels in a corporate hierarchy that are not required to identify the producer. Do not use a mark of omission (...) to indicate such an omission.

If the name as transcribed is known to be fictitious, or requires clarification, make a note giving the actual name, etc. (see **2.17.6.3**).

For instructions on recording the relationship to the producer of an unpublished resource, see **21.2**.

2.7.4.4 Statement of Function

Record words or phrases indicating the function performed by a person, family, or corporate body as they appear on the source of information.

> *Optional Addition*
>
> If the function of a person, family, or corporate body recorded in the producer's name sub-element is not explicit or clear, add a term indicating the function. Indicate that the information was taken from a source outside the resource itself (see **2.2.4**).

2.7.4.5 More Than One Producer

If more than one person, family, or corporate body is named as a producer of the resource, record the producers' names in the order indicated by the sequence, layout, or typography of the names on the source of information.

2.7.4.6 Producer's Name in More Than One Language or Script

If the name of a producer appears on the source of information in more than one language or script, record the form that is in the language or script of the title proper. If this criterion does not apply, record the name in the language or script that appears first.

2.7.4.7 No Producer Identified

Record *producer not identified* if:

no producer is named within the resource itself

and

the producer cannot be identified from other sources (see **2.2.4**).

Indicate that the information was taken from a source outside the resource itself (see **2.2.4**).

2.7.4.8 Change in Producer's Name

For instructions on recording a change in producer's name, see **2.7.1.5**.

2.7.5 Parallel Producer's Name

2.7.5.1 Scope

A ***parallel producer's name*** is a producer's name in a language and/or script that differs from that recorded in the producer's name element.

2.7.5.2 Sources of Information

Take parallel producers' names from the following sources (in order of preference):

a) the same source as the producer's name (see **2.7.4.2**)

b) another source within the resource itself (see **2.2.2**)

c) one of the other sources of information specified at **2.2.4**.

2.7.5.3 Recording Parallel Producers' Names

Record parallel producers' names by applying the basic instructions at **2.7.1**.

If there is more than one parallel producer's name, record the names in the order indicated by the sequence, layout, or typography of the names on the source or sources of information.

2.7.6 Date of Production

CORE ELEMENT

Date of production is a core element for resources issued in an unpublished form. If the date of production appears on the source of information in more than one calendar, only the date in the calendar preferred by the agency preparing the description is required.

2.7.6.1 Scope

A ***date of production*** is a date associated with the inscription, fabrication, construction, etc., of a resource in an unpublished form.

For an archival resource, the date of production is:

the date the resource was produced

or

the date or dates of record-keeping activity.

For a collection (i.e., one assembled by a private collector, a dealer, a library, etc.), the date of production is:

the date of production of the unpublished resources contained in the collection

or

the date of publication of the published resources contained in the collection.

2.7.6.2 Sources of Information

Take dates of production from any source.

2.7.6.3 Recording Date of Production

Record the date of production by applying the basic instructions at **2.7.1**.

2006

Optional Addition

If the date as it appears in the resource is not of the Gregorian or Julian calendar, add the corresponding date or dates of the Gregorian or Julian calendar. Indicate that the information was taken from a source outside the resource itself (see **2.2.4**).

If the date as it appears on the resource is represented in different calendars, record the dates in the order indicated by the sequence, layout, or typography of the dates on the source of information.

If the date as it appears in the resource is known to be fictitious or incorrect, make a note giving the actual date (see **2.17.6.3**).

2.7.6.4 Chronograms

If the date of production as it appears on the source of information is in the form of a chronogram, transcribe the chronogram as it appears.

Optional Addition

Add the date in numerals (in a script and calendar preferred by the agency preparing the description). Indicate that the information was taken from a source outside the resource itself (see **2.2.4**).

Alternative

In place of the chronogram, supply the date in numerals (in a script and calendar preferred by the agency preparing the description). Indicate that the information was taken from a source outside the resource itself (see **2.2.4**).

Make a note giving the chronogram if considered important for identification (see **2.17.6.3**).

2.7.6.5 Multipart Monographs, Serials, and Integrating Resources

If the first issue, part, or iteration of a multipart monograph, serial, or integrating resource is available, record the date of production of that issue, part, or iteration, followed by a hyphen.

1999–

If:
production of the resource has ceased or is complete
and
the first and last issues, parts, or iterations are available
then:
record the dates of production of the first and last issues, parts, or iterations, separated by a hyphen.

1982–2001

If:
production of the resource has ceased or is complete
and
the last issue, part, or iteration is available, but not the first
then:
record the production date of the last issue, part, or iteration, preceded by a hyphen.

–2002

For an integrating resource, supply the date of the last update, if considered important for identification.

If the date of production is the same for all issues, parts, or iterations, record only that date as the single date.

1967

If the first and/or last issue, part, or iteration is not available, supply an approximate date or dates by applying the instructions at **1.9.2**.

If the date or dates cannot be approximated for a multipart monograph, serial, or integrating resource, do not record a date of production.

2.7.6.6 Date of Production Not Identified in a Single-Part Resource

If the date of production is not identified in a single-part resource, supply the date or approximate date of production (see **1.9.2**).

If the date or an approximate date of production for a single-part resource cannot reasonably be determined, record *date of production not identified.* Indicate that the information was taken from a source outside the resource itself (see **2.2.4**).

2.7.6.7 Archival Resources and Collections

If the date of production of an archival resource or collection occurs within a single year, record the year, or record a specific date within that year.

For a single archival resource, record the exact date or dates.

1906 March 17

If the archival resource or collection spans a period of time, record as the inclusive dates:

the earliest and latest dates of production of the resource

or

the earliest and latest dates of the record-keeping activity.

1849–1851

Optional Addition

If the majority of the items in the resource have dates of production that differ significantly from the inclusive dates, record the inclusive dates followed by the predominant or bulk dates. Precede the bulk dates with an explanatory term, such as *bulk.*

1785–1960, bulk 1916–1958

If no date can be found in the resource or determined from any other source, supply the date or approximate date of production (see **1.9.2**). If applicable, indicate that the information was taken from a source outside the resource itself (see **2.2.4**).

1867?

between 1952 and 1978

not after 1866

If it is misleading to record an approximate date, record *date of production not identified.* Indicate that the information was taken from a source outside the resource itself (see **2.2.4**).

2.8 Publication Statement

CORE ELEMENT

Place of publication, publisher's name, and date of publication are core elements for published resources. Other sub-elements of publication statements are optional.

2.8.1 Basic Instructions on Recording Publication Statements

2.8.1.1 Scope

A ***publication statement*** is a statement identifying the place or places of publication, publisher or publishers, and date or dates of publication of a resource.

Publication statements include statements relating to the publication, release, or issuing of a resource.

Consider all online resources to be published.

For statements relating to the production of resources in an unpublished form, see **2.7**.

2.8.1.2 Sources of Information

For guidance on choosing sources of information for publication statements, see the instructions for specific sub-elements of a publication statement as follows:

a) For place of publication, see **2.8.2.2**.

b) For parallel place of publication, see **2.8.3.2**.

c) For publisher's name, see **2.8.4.2**.

d) For parallel publisher's name, see **2.8.5.2**.

e) For date of publication, see **2.8.6.2**.

2.8.1.3 Facsimiles and Reproductions

When a facsimile or reproduction has a publication statement or statements relating to the original manifestation as well as to the facsimile or reproduction, record the publication statement or statements relating to the facsimile or reproduction. Record any publication statement relating to the original as a publication statement of a related manifestation (see **27.1**).

2.8.1.4 Recording Publication Statements

Record a publication statement or statements for a published resource.

Transcribe places of publication and publishers' names as they appear on the source of information (see **1.7**).

Record dates of publication as they appear on the source of information. Apply the general guidelines on transcription for words that are not numbers (see **1.7**). Apply the general guidelines on numbers expressed as numerals or as words (see **1.8**).

2.8.1.5 Recording Changes in Publication Statements

Record a change in a publication statement as appropriate to the mode of issuance of the resource:

multipart monographs (see **2.8.1.5.1**)
serials (see **2.8.1.5.2**)
integrating resources (see **2.8.1.5.3**).

2.8.1.5.1 Multipart Monographs

Make a note (see **2.17.7.5.1**) if:

the place of publication changes on a subsequent part of a multipart monograph

and

the change is considered important for identification or access.

If the change is only in the presentation of the place name, make a note if the change is considered important for identification.

> *Alternative*
> If the changes have been numerous, make a general note (see **2.17.7.5.1**).

Make a note (see **2.17.7.5.1**) if:

a publisher's name changes, or if a different publisher is named on a subsequent part of a multipart monograph

and

the change is considered important for identification or access.

If the change is only in the presentation of the name, make a note if the change is considered important for identification.

> *Alternative*
> If the changes have been numerous, make a general note (see **2.17.7.5.1**).

2.8.1.5.2 Serials

Make a note (see **2.17.7.5.2**) if:

the place of publication changes on a later issue or part of a serial

and

the change is considered important for identification or access.

If the change is only in the presentation of the place name, make a note if the change is considered important for identification.

> *Alternative*
> If the changes have been numerous, make a general note (see **2.17.7.5.2**).

Make a note (see **2.17.7.5.2**) if:

a publisher's name changes, or if a different publisher is named on a later issue or part of a serial

and

the change is considered important for identification or access.

If the change is only in the presentation of the name, make a note if the change is considered important for identification.

> *Alternative*
> If the changes have been numerous, make a general note (see **2.17.7.5.2**).

2.8.1.5.3 Integrating Resources

Change the place of publication to reflect the current iteration of an integrating resource. Make a note on the earlier place if considered important for identification or access (see **2.17.7.5.3**).

Change the publisher's name to reflect the current iteration of an integrating resource. Make a note on any earlier name if considered important for identification or access (see **2.17.7.5.3**).

> *Alternative*
> If the changes have been numerous, make a general note (see **2.17.7.5.3**).

2.8.2 Place of Publication

CORE ELEMENT

If more than one place of publication appears on the source of information, only the first recorded is required.

2.8.2.1 Scope

A ***place of publication*** is a place associated with the publication, release, or issuing of a resource.

2.8.2.2 Sources of Information

Take places of publication from the following sources (in order of preference):

a) the same source as the publisher's name (see **2.8.4.2**)

b) another source within the resource itself (see **2.2.2**)

c) one of the other sources of information specified at **2.2.4**.

2.8.2.3 Recording Place of Publication

Record the place of publication by applying the basic instructions at **2.8.1**.

Include both the local place name (city, town, etc.) and the name of the larger jurisdiction or jurisdictions (state, province, etc., and/or country) if present on the source of information.

Köln
Westport, Connecticut
Lugduni Batavorum
Wellington, New Zealand
Tolworth, England
Carbondale, Ill.
Den Haag
Taunton, Somerset
Christiania
Mpls
Santiago
Aldershot, Hampshire, England
Burlington, VT, USA

Optional Additions

Include the full address as part of the local place name, if considered important for identification or access.

6 Ludgate Hill, London

Supply the name of the larger jurisdiction (state, province, etc., and/or country) as part of the local place name if considered important for identification or access. Indicate that the information was taken from a source outside the resource itself (see **2.2.4**).

Dublin [Ireland]
Dublin [Ohio]

Include any preposition appearing with the place name that is required to make sense of the statement.

V Praze

If the place name as transcribed is known to be fictitious, or requires clarification, make a note giving the actual place name, etc. (see **2.17.7.3**).

2.8.2.4 More Than One Place of Publication

If more than one place of publication is named on the source of information, record the place names in the order indicated by the sequence, layout, or typography of the names on the source of information.

> Ann Arbor, Mich.
> Tylers Green, Buckinghamshire
>
> Toronto
> Buffalo
> London
>
> Lanham, Maryland
> Toronto
> Oxford
>
> London, UK
> Lawrence, KS, USA
>
> Kassel
> Basel
> London
> New York
> Prag
>
> Toronto
> Montréal
> *Source of information reads:* Montréal, Toronto. *Toronto given prominence by typography*
>
> London
> New York
> Sydney
> *Source of information reads:* New York, London, Sydney. *London given prominence by typography*

If:
there are two or more publishers
and
there are two or more places associated with one or more of the publishers
then:
record the place names associated with each publisher in the order indicated by the sequence, layout, or typography of the place names on the source of information.

2.8.2.5 Place of Publication in More Than One Language or Script

If the place of publication appears on the source of information in more than one language or script, record the form that is in the language or script of the title proper. If this criterion does not apply, record the place name in the language or script that appears first.

> Genf
> *Title proper in German. Place of publication also appears as:* Genève

2.8.2.6 Place of Publication Not Identified in the Resource

If the place of publication is not identified in the resource, supply the place of publication or probable place of publication. Apply the instructions in this order of preference:

a) known place (see **2.8.2.6.1**)

b) probable place (see **2.8.2.6.2**)

c) known country, state, province, etc. (see **2.8.2.6.3**)

d) probable country, state, province, etc. (see **2.8.2.6.4**).

Indicate that the information was taken from a source outside the resource itself (see **2.2.4**).

Record *Place of publication not identified* if neither a known nor a probable local place or country, state, province, etc., of publication can be determined. Indicate that the information was taken from a source outside the resource itself (see **2.2.4**).

2.8.2.6.1 Known Place of Publication

If the place of publication is known, supply the local place name (city, town, etc.). Include the name of the larger jurisdiction if necessary for identification.

[Toronto]

2.8.2.6.2 Probable Place of Publication

If the place of publication is uncertain, supply the name of the probable local place of publication. Include the name of the larger jurisdiction if necessary for identification.

If only the local place name is supplied, follow it with a question mark.

[Munich?]

If:
the name of the larger jurisdiction is supplied
and
the place of publication is known to be within that jurisdiction
and
the locality within that jurisdiction is uncertain
then:
add a question mark following the name of the probable local place.

[Lake Placid?, New York]

If:
the name of the larger jurisdiction is supplied
and
it is not known if the place of publication is in that larger jurisdiction
then:
add a question mark following the name of the larger jurisdiction.

[Sofia, Bulgaria?]

2.8.2.6.3 Known Country, State, Province, Etc., of Publication

If the probable local place is unknown, supply the name of the country, state, province, etc., of publication.

[Canada]

2.8.2.6.4 Probable Country, State, Province, Etc., of Publication

If the country, state, province, etc., of publication is uncertain, supply the name of the probable country, state, province, etc., of publication followed by a question mark.

> [Spain?]

2.8.2.7 Change in Place of Publication

For instructions on recording a change in place of publication, see **2.8.1.5**.

2.8.3 Parallel Place of Publication

2.8.3.1 Scope

A ***parallel place of publication*** is a place of publication in a language and/or script that differs from that recorded in the place of publication element.

2.8.3.2 Sources of Information

Take parallel places of publication from the following sources (in order of preference):

a) the same source as the place of publication (see **2.8.2.2**)

b) another source within the resource itself (see **2.2.2**)

c) one of the other sources of information specified at **2.2.4**.

2.8.3.3 Recording Parallel Places of Publication

Record parallel places of publication by applying the basic instructions at **2.8.1**.

> Genève
> *Place of publication:* Genf

If there is more than one parallel place of publication, record the names in the order indicated by the sequence, layout, or typography of the names on the source or sources of information.

2.8.4 Publisher's Name

CORE ELEMENT

If more than one publisher's name appears on the source of information, only the first recorded is required.

2.8.4.1 Scope

A ***publisher's name*** is the name of a person, family, or corporate body responsible for publishing, releasing, or issuing a resource.

A publisher's name may be represented by a characterizing word or phrase.

For early printed resources, printers and booksellers are treated as publishers.

2.8.4.2 Sources of Information

Take publishers' names from the following sources (in order of preference):

a) the same source as the title proper (see **2.3.2.2**)

b) another source within the resource itself (see **2.2.2**)

c) one of the other sources of information specified at **2.2.4**.

2.8.4.3 Recording Publishers' Names

Record the publisher's name by applying the basic instructions at **2.8.1**.

> Oxford University Press
>
> World Health Organization
>
> University of Leeds, Dept. of Spanish
> Dept. *is abbreviated on the source*
>
> Universal Edition
>
> University of Toronto Press
>
> Penguin Books
>
> McGraw-Hill
>
> Grolier
>
> Bridge Records, Inc.
>
> H.M.S.O.
>
> John Lane, the Bodley Head
>
> Institut géographique international
>
> A. Hébert
>
> Supraphon
>
> Tactus
>
> Educational Productions
>
> Public Works and Government Services Canada

Optional Omission

Omit levels in a corporate hierarchy that are not required to identify the publisher. Do not use a mark of omission (…) to indicate such an omission.

If the name as transcribed is known to be fictitious, or requires clarification, make a note giving the actual name, etc. (see **2.17.7.3**).

For instructions on recording the relationship to the publisher, see **21.3**.

2.8.4.4 Statement of Function

Record words or phrases indicating the function (other than solely publishing) performed by a person, family, or corporate body as they appear on the source of information.

> SAGE Publications on behalf of McGill University
> *Source of information reads:* Published by SAGE Publications on behalf of McGill University
>
> In Kommission bei Otto Harrassowitz

Optional Addition

If the function of a person, family, or corporate body recorded in the publisher's name sub-element is not explicit or clear, add a term indicating the function. Indicate that the information was taken from a source outside the resource itself (see **2.2.4**).

2.8.4.5 More Than One Publisher

If more than one person, family, or corporate body is named as a publisher of the resource, record the publishers' names in the order indicated by the sequence, layout, or typography of the names on the source of information.

> McClelland and Stewart
> World Crafts Council
>
> Gauthier-Villars
> University of Chicago Press
>
> Dutton
> Clarke, Irwin
>
> Baedeker
> Allen & Unwin

2.8.4.6 Publisher's Name in More Than One Language or Script

If the name of a publisher appears on the source of information in more than one language or script, record the form that is in the language or script of the title proper. If this criterion does not apply, record the name in the language or script that appears first.

> Éditions du peuple
> *Title proper in French. Publisher's name also appears in English*
>
> Health Canada, Pest Management Regulatory Agency
> *Title proper in English. Publisher's name also appears in French*

2.8.4.7 No Publisher Identified

Record *publisher not identified* if:

no publisher is named within the resource itself

and

the publisher cannot be identified from other sources (see **2.2.4**).

Indicate that the information was taken from a source outside the resource itself (see **2.2.4**).

2.8.4.8 Change in Publisher's Name

For instructions on recording a change in publisher's name, see **2.8.1.5**.

2.8.5 Parallel Publisher's Name

2.8.5.1 Scope

A ***parallel publisher's name*** is a publisher's name in a language and/or script that differs from that recorded in the publisher's name element.

2.8.5.2 Sources of Information

Take parallel publishers' names from the following sources (in order of preference):

a) the same source as the publisher's name (see **2.8.4.2**)

b) another source within the resource itself (see **2.2.2**)

c) one of the other sources of information specified at **2.2.4**.

2.8.5.3 Recording Parallel Publishers' Names

Record parallel publishers' names by applying the basic instructions at **2.8.1**.

> Commoner's Publishing
> *Publisher's name recorded as:* Éditions du peuple
>
> Santé Canada, Agence de réglementation de la lutte antiparasitaire
> *Publisher's name recorded as:* Health Canada, Pest Management Regulatory Agency

If there is more than one parallel publisher's name, record the names in the order indicated by the sequence, layout, or typography of the names on the source or sources of information.

2.8.6 Date of Publication

CORE ELEMENT

If the date of publication appears on the source of information in more than one calendar, only the date in the calendar preferred by the agency preparing the description is required.

2.8.6.1 Scope

A ***date of publication*** is a date associated with the publication, release, or issuing of a resource.

2.8.6.2 Sources of Information

Take dates of publication from the following sources (in order of preference):

a) the same source as the title proper (see **2.3.2.2**)

b) another source within the resource itself (see **2.2.2**)

c) one of the other sources of information specified at **2.2.4**.

For multipart monographs and serials, take the beginning and/or ending date of publication from the first and/or last released issue or part, or from another source.

For integrating resources, take the beginning and/or ending date of publication from the first and/or last iteration, or from another source.

2.8.6.3 Recording Date of Publication

Record the date of publication by applying the basic instructions at **2.8.1**.

> 1975
>
> May 2000
>
> 1733
> *Source of information reads:* MDCCXXXIII

> *Optional Addition*
> If the date as it appears in the resource is not of the Gregorian or Julian calendar, add the corresponding date or dates of the Gregorian or Julian calendar. Indicate that the information was taken from a source outside the resource itself (see **2.2.4**).

4308 [1975]

Minguo 28 [1939]

5730 [1969 or 1970]

Heisei 1 [1989]

anno 18 [1939]

If the date as it appears on the resource is represented in different calendars, record the dates in the order indicated by the sequence, layout, or typography of the dates on the source of information.

5772
2012

Date of publication appears in both the Jewish and Gregorian calendars

1377 H.Sh.
1419 H.Q.

Date of publication appears in both the Hijri Shamsi (solar) and Hijri Qamari (lunar) calendars. Source of information reads: 1377 H.Sh. 1419 H.Q.

2485 BE
1942

Date of publication appears in both the Thai (Buddhist Era) and Gregorian calendars. Source of information reads: 2485 BE, 1942

If the date as it appears in the resource is known to be fictitious or incorrect, make a note giving the actual date (see **2.17.7.3**).

2.8.6.4 Chronograms

If the date of publication as it appears on the source of information is in the form of a chronogram, transcribe the chronogram as it appears.

Ipso anno tertIo saeCVLarI typographIae DIVIno aVXILIo a gerManIs InVentae

Optional Addition

Add the date in numerals (in a script and calendar preferred by the agency preparing the description). Indicate that the information was taken from a source outside the resource itself (see **2.2.4**).

Ipso anno tertIo saeCVLarI typographIae DIVIno aVXILIo a gerManIs InVentae [1740]

Alternative

In place of the chronogram, supply the date in numerals (in a script and calendar preferred by the agency preparing the description). Indicate that the information was taken from a source outside the resource itself (see **2.2.4**).

[1740]

Make a note giving the chronogram, if considered important for identification (see **2.17.7.3**).

2.8.6.5 Multipart Monographs, Serials, and Integrating Resources

If the first issue, part, or iteration of a multipart monograph, serial, or integrating resource is available, record the date of publication of the first issue, part, or iteration, followed by a hyphen.

1988–

If:
publication of the resource has ceased or is complete
and
the first and last issues, parts, or iterations are available
then:
record the dates of publication of the first and last issues, parts, or iterations, separated by a hyphen.

1968–1973

If:
publication of the resource has ceased or is complete
and
the last issue, part, or iteration is available, but not the first
then:
record the publication date of the last issue, part, or iteration, preceded by a hyphen.

–1997

For an integrating resource, supply the date of the last update, if considered important for identification.

1995–1998 [updated 1999]
First and last published iterations of an updating loose-leaf available; date of last update known

If the date of publication is the same for all issues, parts, or iterations, record only that date as the single date.

1997

If the first and/or last issue, part, or iteration is not available, supply an approximate date or dates by applying the instructions at **1.9.2**.

[1998]–
Earliest issue available: v. 1, no. 3, July 1998

1997–[2000]
Last part not available but information about ending date known

[1988–1991]
First and last issues not available but information about beginning and ending dates known

If the date or dates cannot be approximated for a multipart monograph, serial, or integrating resource, do not record a date of publication.

2.8.6.6 Date of Publication Not Identified in a Single-Part Resource

If the date of publication is not identified in a single-part resource, supply the date or approximate date of publication (see **1.9.2**).

[2004?]
Date supplied based on statement in colophon: Dépôt légal: octobre 2004, N^{O} 41576-2 (073109)

If an approximate date of publication for a single-part resource cannot reasonably be determined, record *date of publication not identified*. Indicate that the information was taken from a source outside the resource itself (see **2.2.4**).

2.9 Distribution Statement

CORE ELEMENT

Place of distribution is a core element for a resource in a published form if the place of publication is not identified. Distributor's name is a core element for a resource in a published form if the publisher is not identified. Date of distribution is a core element for a resource in a published form if the date of publication is not identified. Other sub-elements of distribution statements are optional.

2.9.1 Basic Instructions on Recording Distribution Statements

2.9.1.1 Scope

A ***distribution statement*** is a statement identifying the place or places of distribution, distributor or distributors, and date or dates of distribution of a resource in a published form.

2.9.1.2 Sources of Information

For guidance on choosing sources of information for distribution statements, see the instructions for specific sub-elements of a distribution statement as follows:

a) For place of distribution, see **2.9.2.2**.

b) For parallel place of distribution, see **2.9.3.2**.

c) For distributor's name, see **2.9.4.2**.

d) For parallel distributor's name, see **2.9.5.2**.

e) For date of distribution, see **2.9.6.2**.

2.9.1.3 Facsimiles and Reproductions

When a facsimile or reproduction has a distribution statement or statements relating to the original manifestation as well as to the facsimile or reproduction, record the distribution statement or statements relating to the facsimile or reproduction. Record any distribution statement relating to the original as a distribution statement of a related manifestation (see **27.1**).

2.9.1.4 Recording Distribution Statements

Record a distribution statement or statements for a published resource.

Transcribe places of distribution and distributors' names as they appear on the source of information (see **1.7**).

Record dates of distribution as they appear on the source of information. Apply the general guidelines on transcription for words that are not numbers (see **1.7**). Apply the general guidelines on numbers expressed as numerals or as words (see **1.8**).

2.9.1.5 Recording Changes in Distribution Statements

Record a change in a distribution statement as appropriate to the mode of issuance of the resource:

multipart monographs (see **2.9.1.5.1**)

serials (see **2.9.1.5.2**)

integrating resources (see **2.9.1.5.3**).

2.9.1.5.1 Multipart Monographs

Make a note (see **2.17.8.4.1**) if:

the place of distribution changes on a subsequent part of a multipart monograph

and

the change is considered important for identification or access.

If the change is only in the presentation of the place name, make a note if the change is considered important for identification.

> *Alternative*
>
> If the changes have been numerous, make a general note (see **2.17.8.4.1**).

Make a note (see **2.17.8.4.1**) if:

a distributor's name changes, or if a different distributor is named on a subsequent part of a multipart monograph

and

the change is considered important for identification or access.

If the change is only in the presentation of the name, make a note if the change is considered important for identification.

> *Alternative*
>
> If the changes have been numerous, make a general note (see **2.17.8.4.1**).

2.9.1.5.2 Serials

Make a note (see **2.17.8.4.2**) if:

the place of distribution changes on a later issue or part of a serial

and

the change is considered important for identification or access.

If the change is only in the presentation of the place name, make a note if the change is considered important for identification.

> *Alternative*
>
> If the changes have been numerous, make a general note (see **2.17.8.4.2**).

Make a note (see **2.17.8.4.2**) if:

a distributor's name changes, or if a different distributor is named on a later issue or part of a serial

and

the change is considered important for identification or access.

If the change is only in the presentation of the name, make a note if the change is considered important for identification.

> *Alternative*
>
> If the changes have been numerous, make a general note (see **2.17.8.4.2**).

2.9.1.5.3 Integrating Resources

Change the place of distribution to reflect the current iteration of an integrating resource. Make a note on the earlier place if considered important for identification or access (see **2.17.8.4.3**).

Change the distributor's name to reflect the current iteration of an integrating resource. Make a note on any earlier name if considered important for identification or access (see **2.17.8.4.3**).

> *Alternative*
>
> If the changes have been numerous, make a general note (see **2.17.8.4.3**).

2.9.2 Place of Distribution

CORE ELEMENT

Place of distribution is a core element for a resource in a published form if the place of publication is not identified. If more than one place of distribution appears on the source of information, only the first recorded is required.

2.9.2.1 Scope

A ***place of distribution*** is a place associated with the distribution of a resource in a published form.

2.9.2.2 Sources of Information

Take places of distribution from the following sources (in order of preference):

a) the same source as the distributor's name (see **2.9.4.2**)

b) another source within the resource itself (see **2.2.2**)

c) one of the other sources of information specified at **2.2.4**.

2.9.2.3 Recording Place of Distribution

Record the place of distribution by applying the basic instructions at **2.9.1**.

Include both the local place name (city, town, etc.) and the name of the larger jurisdiction or jurisdictions (state, province, etc., and/or country) if present on the source of information.

> Oshawa, Ontario

> *Optional Additions*
>
> Include the full address as part of the local place name, if considered important for identification or access.
>
> Supply the name of the larger jurisdiction (state, province, etc., and/or country) as part of the local place name if considered important for identification or access. Indicate that the information was taken from a source outside the resource itself (see **2.2.4**).

Include any preposition appearing with the place name that is required to make sense of the statement.

If the place name as transcribed is known to be fictitious, or requires clarification, make a note giving the actual place name, etc. (see **2.17.8.3**).

2.9.2.4 More Than One Place of Distribution

If more than one place of distribution is named on the source of information, record the place names in the order indicated by the sequence, layout, or typography of the names on the source of information.

> Frederick, MD, USA
> Letchworth, Herts, United Kingdom
> *Place of publication:* The Hague, The Netherlands

If:
there are two or more distributors
and
there are two or more places associated with one or more of the distributors
then:
record the place names associated with each distributor in the order indicated by the sequence, layout, or typography of the place names on the source of information.

2.9.2.5 Place of Distribution in More Than One Language or Script

If the place of distribution appears on the source of information in more than one language or script, record the form that is in the language or script of the title proper. If this criterion does not apply, record the place name in the language or script that appears first.

2.9.2.6 Place of Distribution Not Identified in the Resource

If the place of distribution is not identified in the resource, supply the place of distribution or probable place of distribution. Apply the instructions in this order of preference:

a) known place (see **2.9.2.6.1**)

b) probable place (see **2.9.2.6.2**)

c) known country, state, province, etc. (see**2.9.2.6.3**)

d) probable country, state, province, etc. (see **2.9.2.6.4**).

Indicate that the information was taken from a source outside the resource itself (see **2.2.4**).

Record *Place of distribution not identified* if neither a known nor a probable local place or country, state, province, etc., of distribution can be determined. Indicate that the information was taken from a source outside the resource itself (see **2.2.4**).

2.9.2.6.1 Known Place of Distribution

If the place of distribution is known, supply the local place name (city, town, etc.). Include the name of the larger jurisdiction if necessary for identification.

> [Berlin]

2.9.2.6.2 Probable Place of Distribution

If the place of distribution is uncertain, supply the name of the probable local place of distribution. Include the name of the larger jurisdiction if necessary for identification.

If only the local place name is supplied, follow it with a question mark.

[Chicago?]

If:
the name of the larger jurisdiction is supplied
and
the place of distribution is known to be within that jurisdiction
and
the locality within that jurisdiction is uncertain
then:
add a question mark following the name of the probable local place.
If:
the name of the larger jurisdiction is supplied
and
it is not known if the place of distribution is in that larger jurisdiction
then:
add a question mark following the name of the larger jurisdiction.

2.9.2.6.3 Known Country, State, Province, Etc., of Distribution

If the probable local place is unknown, supply the name of the country, state, province, etc., of distribution.

[Prince Edward Island]

2.9.2.6.4 Probable Country, State, Province, Etc., of Distribution

If the country, state, province, etc., of distribution is uncertain, supply the name of the probable country, state, province, etc., of distribution followed by a question mark.

[Netherlands?]

2.9.2.7 Change in Place of Distribution

For instructions on recording a change in place of distribution, see **2.9.1.5**.

2.9.3 Parallel Place of Distribution

2.9.3.1 Scope

A ***parallel place of distribution*** is a place of distribution in a language and/or script that differs from that recorded in the place of distribution element.

2.9.3.2 Sources of Information

Take parallel places of distribution from the following sources (in order of preference):

a) the same source as the place of distribution (see **2.9.2.2**)

b) another source within the resource itself (see **2.2.2**)

c) one of the other sources of information specified at **2.2.4**.

2.9.3.3 Recording Parallel Places of Distribution

Record parallel places of distribution by applying the basic instructions at **2.9.1**.

If there is more than one parallel place of distribution, record the names in the order indicated by the sequence, layout, or typography of the names on the source or sources of information.

2.9.4 Distributor's Name

CORE ELEMENT

A distributor's name is a core element for a resource in a published form if the publisher's name is not identified. If more than one distributor's name appears on the source of information, only the first recorded is required.

2.9.4.1 Scope

A ***distributor's name*** is the name of a person, family, or corporate body responsible for distributing a resource in a published form.

A distributor's name may be represented by a characterizing word or phrase.

2.9.4.2 Sources of Information

Take distributors' names from the following sources (in order of preference):

a) the same source as the title proper (see **2.3.2.2**)

b) another source within the resource itself (see **2.2.2**)

c) one of the other sources of information specified at **2.2.4**.

2.9.4.3 Recording Distributors' Names

Record the distributor's name by applying the basic instructions at **2.9.1**.

Hachette

Columbia University Press

Diffusion Interlivres

Optional Omission

Omit levels in a corporate hierarchy that are not required to identify the distributor. Do not use a mark of omission (...) to indicate such an omission.

If the name as transcribed is known to be fictitious, or requires clarification, make a note giving the actual name, etc. (see **2.17.8.3**).

For instructions on recording the relationship to the distributor, see **21.4**.

2.9.4.4 Statement of Function

Record words or phrases indicating the function performed by a person, family, or corporate body as they appear on the source of information.

Distributed by New York Graphic Society

Sold by Longman

Distributed by Independent Publishers Group

Distribution by: MapArt Publishing Corporation

Distributed by Coach House Records Ltd.

Optional Addition

If the function of a person, family, or corporate body recorded in the distributor's name sub-element is not explicit or clear, add a term indicating the function. Indicate that the information was taken from a source outside the resource itself (see **2.2.4**).

> Guild Sound and Vision [distributor]
>
> Voluntary Committee on Overseas Aid & Development [distributor]

2.9.4.5 More Than One Distributor

If more than one person, family, or corporate body is named as a distributor of the resource, record the distributor's names in the order indicated by the sequence, layout, or typography of the names on the source of information.

> Sold and distributed in North, Central and South America by: Aspen Publishers, Inc.
> Sold and distributed in all other countries by: Extenza-Turpin Distribution Services
> *Publisher's name:* Kluwer Law International

2.9.4.6 Distributor's Name in More Than One Language or Script

If the name of a distributor appears on the source of information in more than one language or script, record the form that is in the language or script of the title proper. If this criterion does not apply, record the name in the language or script that appears first.

2.9.4.7 No Distributor Identified

Record *distributor not identified* if:

no distributor is named within the resource itself

and

the distributor cannot be identified from other sources (see **2.2.4**).

Indicate that the information was taken from a source outside the resource itself (see **2.2.4**).

2.9.4.8 Change in Distributor's Name

For instructions on recording a change in distributor's name, see **2.9.1.5**.

2.9.5 Parallel Distributor's Name

2.9.5.1 Scope

A ***parallel distributor's name*** is a distributor's name in a language and/or script that differs from that recorded in the distributor's name element.

2.9.5.2 Sources of Information

Take parallel distributors' names from the following sources (in order of preference):

a) the same source as the distributor's name (see **2.9.4.2**)

b) another source within the resource itself (see **2.2.2**)

c) one of the other sources of information specified at **2.2.4**.

2.9.5.3 Recording Parallel Distributors' Names

Record parallel distributors' names by applying the basic instructions at **2.9.1**.

If there is more than one parallel distributor's name, record the names in the order indicated by the sequence, layout, or typography of the names on the source or sources of information.

2.9.6 Date of Distribution

CORE ELEMENT

Date of distribution is a core element for a resource in a published form if the date of publication is not identified. If the date of distribution appears on the source of information in more than one calendar, only the date in the calendar preferred by the agency preparing the description is required.

2.9.6.1 Scope

A ***date of distribution*** is a date associated with the distribution of a resource in a published form.

2.9.6.2 Sources of Information

Take dates of distribution from the following sources (in order of preference):

a) the same source as the title proper (see **2.3.2.2**)

b) another source within the resource itself (see **2.2.2**)

c) one of the other sources of information specified at **2.2.4**.

For multipart monographs and serials, take the beginning and/or ending date of distribution from the first and/or last released issue or part, or from another source.

For integrating resources, take the beginning and/or ending date of distribution from the first and/or last iteration, or from another source.

2.9.6.3 Recording Date of Distribution

Record the date of distribution if:

the date of distribution differs from the date of publication

and

the date of distribution is considered important for identification.

Apply the basic instructions at **2.9.1**.

1973
Date of publication: 1971

Optional Addition

If the date as it appears in the resource is not of the Gregorian or Julian calendar, add the corresponding date or dates of the Gregorian or Julian calendar. Indicate that the information was taken from a source outside the resource itself (see **2.2.4**).

If the date as it appears on the resource is represented in different calendars, record the dates in the order indicated by the sequence, layout, or typography of the dates on the source of information.

If the date as it appears in the resource is known to be fictitious or incorrect, make a note giving the actual date (see **2.17.8.3**).

2.9.6.4 Chronograms

If the date of distribution as it appears on the source of information is in the form of a chronogram, transcribe the chronogram as it appears.

Optional Addition

Add the date in numerals (in a script and calendar preferred by the agency preparing the description). Indicate that the information was taken from a source outside the resource itself (see 2.2.4).

Alternative

In place of the chronogram, supply the date in numerals (in a script and calendar preferred by the agency preparing the description). Indicate that the information was taken from a source outside the resource itself (see **2.2.4**).

Make a note giving the chronogram, if considered important for identification (see **2.17.8.3**).

2.9.6.5 Multipart Monographs, Serials, and Integrating Resources

If the first issue, part, or iteration of a multipart monograph, serial, or integrating resource is available, record the date of distribution of the first issue, part, or iteration, followed by a hyphen.

If:

distribution of the resource has ceased or is complete

and

the first and last issues, parts, or iterations are available

then:

record the dates of distribution of the first and last issues, parts, or iterations, separated by a hyphen.

If:

distribution of the resource has ceased or is complete

and

the last issue, part, or iteration is available, but not the first

then:

record the distribution date of the last issue, part, or iteration, preceded by a hyphen.

For an integrating resource, supply the date of the last update, if considered important for identification.

If the date of distribution is the same for all issues, parts, or iterations, record only that date as the single date.

If the first and/or last issue, part, or iteration is not available, supply an approximate date or dates by applying the instructions at **1.9.2**.

If the date or dates cannot be approximated for a multipart monograph, serial, or integrating resource, do not record a date of distribution.

2.9.6.6 Date of Distribution Not Identified in a Single-Part Resource

If the date of distribution is not identified in a single-part resource, supply the date or an approximate date of distribution (see **1.9.2**).

If an approximate date of distribution for a single-part resource cannot reasonably be determined, record *date of distribution not identified*. Indicate that the information was taken from a source outside the resource itself (see **2.2.4**).

2.10 Manufacture Statement

CORE ELEMENT

Place of manufacture is a core element for a resource in a published form if neither a place of publication nor a place of distribution is identified. Manufacturer's name is a core element for a resource in a published form if neither a publisher nor a distributor is identified. Date of manufacture is a core element for a resource in a published form if neither the date of publication, the date of distribution, nor the copyright date is identified. Other sub-elements of manufacture statements are optional.

2.10.1 Basic Instructions on Recording Manufacture Statements

2.10.1.1 Scope

A ***manufacture statement*** is a statement identifying the place or places of manufacture, manufacturer or manufacturers, and date or dates of manufacture of a resource in a published form.

Manufacture statements include statements relating to the printing, duplicating, casting, etc., of a resource in a published form.

2.10.1.2 Sources of Information

For guidance on choosing sources of information for manufacture statements, see the instructions for specific sub-elements of a manufacture statement as follows:

a) For place of manufacture, see **2.10.2.2**.

b) For parallel place of manufacture, see **2.10.3.2**.

c) For manufacturer's name, see **2.10.4.2**.

d) For parallel manufacturer's name, see **2.10.5.2**.

e) For date of manufacture, see **2.10.6.2**.

2.10.1.3 Facsimiles and Reproductions

When a facsimile or reproduction has a manufacture statement or statements relating to the original manifestation as well as to the facsimile or reproduction, record the manufacture statement or statements relating to the facsimile or reproduction. Record any manufacture statement relating to the original as a manufacture statement of a related manifestation (see **27.1**).

2.10.1.4 Recording Manufacture Statements

Record a manufacture statement or statements for a published resource.

Transcribe places of manufacture and manufacturers' names as they appear on the source of information (see **1.7**).

Record dates of manufacture as they appear on the source of information. Apply the general guidelines on transcription for words that are not numbers (see **1.7**). Apply the general guidelines on numbers expressed as numerals or as words (see **1.8**).

2.10.1.5 Recording Changes in Manufacture Statements

Record a change in a manufacture statement as appropriate to the mode of issuance of the resource:

multipart monographs (see **2.10.1.5.1**)
serials (see **2.10.1.5.2**)
integrating resources (see **2.10.1.5.3**).

2.10.1.5.1 Multipart Monographs

Make a note (see **2.17.9.4.1**) if:

the place of manufacture changes on a subsequent part of a multipart monograph

and

the change is considered important for identification or access.

If the change is only in the presentation of the place name, make a note if the change is considered important for identification.

> *Alternative*
> If the changes have been numerous, make a general note (see **2.17.9.4.1**).

Make a note (see **2.17.9.4.1**) if:

a manufacturer's name changes, or if a different manufacturer is named on a subsequent part of a multipart monograph

and

the change is considered important for identification or access.

If the change is only in the presentation of the name, make a note if the change is considered important for identification.

> *Alternative*
> If the changes have been numerous, make a general note (see **2.17.9.4.1**).

2.10.1.5.2 Serials

Make a note (see **2.17.9.4.2**) if:

the place of manufacture changes on a later issue or part of a serial

and

the change is considered important for identification or access.

If the change is only in the presentation of the place name, make a note if the change is considered important for identification.

> *Alternative*
> If the changes have been numerous, make a general note (see **2.17.9.4.2**).

Make a note (see **2.17.9.4.2**) if:

a manufacturer's name changes, or if a different manufacturer is named on a later issue or part of a serial

and

the change is considered important for identification or access.

If the change is only in the presentation of the name, make a note if the change is considered important for identification.

> *Alternative*
> If the changes have been numerous, make a general note (see **2.17.9.4.2**).

2.10.1.5.3 Integrating Resources

Change the place of manufacture to reflect the current iteration of an integrating resource. Make a note on the earlier place if considered important for identification or access (see **2.17.9.4.3**).

Change the manufacturer's name to reflect the current iteration of an integrating resource. Make a note on any earlier name if considered important for identification or access (see **2.17.9.4.3**).

> *Alternative*
> If the changes have been numerous, make a general note (see **2.17.9.4.3**).

2.10.2 Place of Manufacture

CORE ELEMENT

Place of manufacture is a core element for a resource in a published form if neither a place of publication nor a place of distribution is identified. If more than one place of manufacture appears on the source of information, only the first recorded is required.

2.10.2.1 Scope

A ***place of manufacture*** is a place associated with the printing, duplicating, casting, etc., of a resource in a published form.

2.10.2.2 Sources of Information

Take places of manufacture from the following sources (in order of preference):

a) the same source as the manufacturer's name (see **2.10.4.2**)

b) another source within the resource itself (see **2.2.2**)

c) one of the other sources of information specified at **2.2.4**.

2.10.2.3 Recording Place of Manufacture

Record the place of manufacture by applying the basic instructions at **2.10.1**.

Include both the local place name (city, town, etc.) and the name of the larger jurisdiction or jurisdictions (state, province, etc., and/or country) if present on the source of information.

> Twickenham
>
> Long Beach Island
>
> West Hill, Ont.

Optional Additions

Include the full address as part of the local place name, if considered important for identification or access.

Supply the name of the larger jurisdiction (state, province, etc., and/or country) as part of the local place name if considered important for identification or access. Indicate that the information was taken from a source outside the resource itself (see **2.2.4**).

Include any preposition appearing with the place name that is required to make sense of the statement.

If the place name as transcribed is known to be fictitious, or requires clarification, make a note giving the actual place name, etc. (see **2.17.9.3**).

2.10.2.4 More Than One Place of Manufacture

If more than one place of manufacture is named on the source of information, record the place names in the order indicated by the sequence, layout, or typography of the names on the source of information.

If:
there are two or more manufacturers
and
there are two or more places associated with one or more of the manufacturers
then:
record the place names associated with each manufacturer in the order indicated by the sequence, layout, or typography of the place names on the source of information.

2.10.2.5 Place of Manufacture in More Than One Language or Script

If the place of manufacture appears on the source of information in more than one language or script, record the form that is in the language or script of the title proper. If this criterion does not apply, record the place name in the language or script that appears first.

2.10.2.6 Place of Manufacture Not Identified in the Resource

If the place of manufacture is not identified in the resource, supply the place of manufacture or probable place of manufacture. Apply the instructions in this order of preference:

a) known place (see **2.10.2.6.1**)

b) probable place (see **2.10.2.6.2**)

c) known country, state, province, etc. (see**2.10.2.6.3**)

d) probable country, state, province, etc. (see **2.10.2.6.4**).

Indicate that the information was taken from a source outside the resource itself (see **2.2.4**).

Record *Place of manufacture not identified* if neither a known nor a probable local place or country, state, province, etc., of manufacture can be determined. Indicate that the information was taken from a source outside the resource itself (see **2.2.4**).

2.10.2.6.1 Known Place of Manufacture

If the place of manufacture is known, supply the local place name (city, town, etc.). Include the name of the larger jurisdiction if necessary for identification.

> [Brisbane, Queensland]

2.10.2.6.2 Probable Place of Manufacture

If the place of manufacture is uncertain, supply the name of the probable local place of manufacture. Include the name of the larger jurisdiction if necessary for identification.

If only the local place name is supplied, follow it with a question mark.

If:
  the name of the larger jurisdiction is supplied
  and
  the place of manufacture is known to be within that jurisdiction
  and
  the locality within that jurisdiction is uncertain
then:
  add a question mark following the name of the probable local place.

If:
  the name of the larger jurisdiction is supplied
  and
  it is not known if the place of distribution is in that larger jurisdiction
then:
  add a question mark following the name of the larger jurisdiction.

> [San Diego, California?]

2.10.2.6.3 Known Country, State, Province, Etc., of Manufacture

If the probable local place is unknown, supply the name of the country, state, province, etc., of manufacture.

> [China]

2.10.2.6.4 Probable Country, State, Province, Etc., of Manufacture

If the country, state, province, etc., of manufacture is uncertain, supply the name of the probable country, state, province, etc., of manufacture followed by a question mark.

> [Italy?]

2.10.2.7 Change in Place of Manufacture

For instructions on recording a change in place of manufacture, see **2.10.1.5**.

2.10.3 Parallel Place of Manufacture

2.10.3.1 Scope

A ***parallel place of manufacture*** is a place of manufacture in a language and/or script that differs from that recorded in the place of manufacture element.

2.10.3.2 Sources of Information

Take parallel places of manufacture from the following sources (in order of preference):

a) the same source as the place of manufacture (see **2.10.2.2**)

b) another source within the resource itself (see **2.2.2**)

c) one of the other sources of information specified at **2.2.4**.

2.10.3.3 Recording Parallel Places of Manufacture

Record parallel places of manufacture by applying the basic instructions at **2.10.1**.

If there is more than one parallel place of manufacture, record the names in the order indicated by the sequence, layout, or typography of the names on the source or sources of information.

2.10.4 Manufacturer's Name

CORE ELEMENT

Manufacturer's name is a core element for a resource in a published form if neither a publisher nor a distributor is identified. If more than one manufacturer's name appears on the source of information, only the first recorded is required.

2.10.4.1 Scope

A ***manufacturer's name*** is the name of a person, family, or corporate body responsible for printing, duplicating, casting, etc., a resource in a published form.

A manufacturer's name may be represented by a characterizing word or phrase.

2.10.4.2 Sources of Information

Take manufacturers' names from the following sources (in order of preference):

a) the same source as the title proper (see **2.3.2.2**)

b) another source within the resource itself (see **2.2.2**)

c) one of the other sources of information specified at **2.2.4**.

2.10.4.3 Recording Manufacturers' Names

Record the manufacturer's name by applying the basic instructions at **2.10.1**.

CTD Printers

Tip. de las Huérfanos

UDO (Litho)

Optional Omission

Omit levels in a corporate hierarchy that are not required to identify the manufacturer. Do not use a mark of omission (...) to indicate such an omission.

If the name as transcribed is known to be fictitious, or requires clarification, make a note giving the actual name, etc. (see **2.17.9.3**).

For instructions on recording the relationship to the manufacturer, see **21.5**.

2.10.4.4 Statement of Function

Record words or phrases indicating the function performed by a person, family, or corporate body as they appear on the source of information.

> Manufactured and marketed by PolyGram Video, a division of PolyGram Records, Inc.

Optional Addition

If the function of a person, family, or corporate body recorded in the manufacturer's name sub-element is not explicit or clear, add a term indicating the function. Indicate that the information was taken from a source outside the resource itself (see **2.2.4**).

2.10.4.5 More Than One Manufacturer

If more than one person, family, or corporate body is named as a manufacturer of the resource, record the manufacturers' names in the order indicated by the sequence, layout, or typography of the names on the source of information.

2.10.4.6 Manufacturer's Name in More Than One Language or Script

If the name of a manufacturer appears on the source of information in more than one language or script, record the form that is in the language or script of the title proper. If this criterion does not apply, record the name in the language or script that appears first.

2.10.4.7 No Manufacturer Identified

Record *manufacturer not identified* if:

no manufacturer is named within the resource itself

and

the manufacturer cannot be identified from other sources (see **2.2.4**).

Indicate that the information was taken from a source outside the resource itself (see **2.2.4**).

2.10.4.8 Change in Manufacturer's Name

For instructions on recording a change in manufacturer's name, see **2.10.1.5**.

2.10.5 Parallel Manufacturer's Name

2.10.5.1 Scope

A ***parallel manufacturer's name*** is a manufacturer's name in a language and/or script that differs from that recorded in the manufacturer's name element.

2.10.5.2 Sources of Information

Take parallel manufacturers' names from the following sources (in order of preference):

a) the same source as the manufacturer's name (see **2.10.4.2**)

b) another source within the resource itself (see **2.2.2**)

c) one of the other sources of information specified at **2.2.4**.

2.10.5.3 Recording Parallel Manufacturers' Names

Record parallel manufacturers' names by applying the basic instructions at **2.10.1**.

If there is more than one parallel manufacturer's name, record the names in the order indicated by the sequence, layout, or typography of the names on the source or sources of information.

2.10.6 Date of Manufacture

CORE ELEMENT

Date of manufacture is a core element for a resource in a published form if neither the date of publication, the date of distribution, nor the copyright date is identified. If the date of manufacture appears on the source of information in more than one calendar, only the date in the calendar preferred by the agency preparing the description is required.

2.10.6.1 Scope

A ***date of manufacture*** is a date associated with the printing, duplicating, casting, etc., of a resource in a published form.

2.10.6.2 Sources of Information

Take dates of manufacture from any source.

2.10.6.3 Recording Date of Manufacture

Record the date of manufacture by applying the basic instructions at **2.10.1**.

> 2006

> *Optional Addition*
>
> If the date as it appears in the resource is not of the Gregorian or Julian calendar, add the corresponding date or dates of the Gregorian or Julian calendar. Indicate that the information was taken from a source outside the resource itself (see **2.2.4**).

If the date as it appears on the resource is represented in different calendars, record the dates in the order indicated by the sequence, layout, or typography of the dates on the source of information.

If the date as it appears in the resource is known to be fictitious or incorrect, make a note giving the actual date (see **2.17.9.3**).

2.10.6.4 Chronograms

If the date of manufacture as it appears on the source of information is in the form of a chronogram, transcribe the chronogram as it appears.

> *Optional Addition*
>
> Add the date in numerals (in a script and calendar preferred by the agency preparing the description). Indicate that the information was taken from a source outside the resource itself (see **2.2.4**).

> *Alternative*
>
> In place of the chronogram, supply the date in numerals (in a script and calendar preferred by the agency preparing the description). Indicate that the information was taken from a source outside the resource itself (see **2.2.4**).
>
> Make a note giving the chronogram, if considered important for identification (see **2.17.9.3**).

2.10.6.5 Multipart Monographs, Serials, and Integrating Resources

If the first issue, part, or iteration of a multipart monograph, serial, or integrating resource is available, record the date of manufacture of the first issue, part, or iteration, followed by a hyphen.

> 1999–

If:
manufacture of the resource has ceased or is complete
and
the first and last issues, parts, or iterations are available
then:
record the dates of manufacture of the first and last issues, parts, or iterations, separated by a hyphen.

1982–2001

If:

manufacture of the resource has ceased or is complete

and

the last issue, part, or iteration is available, but not the first

then:

record the manufacture date of the last issue, part, or iteration, preceded by a hyphen.

–2002

For an integrating resource, supply the date of the last update, if considered important for identification.

If the date of manufacture is the same for all issues, parts, or iterations, record only that date as the single date.

1967

If the first and/or last issue, part, or iteration is not available, supply an approximate date or dates by applying the instructions at **1.9.2**.

If the date or dates cannot be approximated for a multipart monograph, serial, or integrating resource, do not record a date of manufacture.

2.10.6.6 Date of Manufacture Not Identified in a Single-Part Resource

If the date of manufacture is not identified in a single-part resource, supply the date or an approximate date of manufacture (see **1.9.2**).

If an approximate date of manufacture for a single-part resource cannot reasonably be determined, record *date of manufacture not identified.* Indicate that the information was taken from a source outside the resource itself (see **2.2.4**).

2.11 Copyright Date

CORE ELEMENT

Copyright date is a core element if neither the date of publication nor the date of distribution is identified. If the copyright date appears on the source of information in more than one calendar, only the date in the calendar preferred by the agency preparing the description is required.

2.11.1 Basic Instructions on Recording Copyright Dates

2.11.1.1 Scope

A ***copyright date*** is a date associated with a claim of protection under copyright or a similar regime.

Copyright dates include phonogram dates (i.e., dates associated with claims of protection for audio recordings).

2.11.1.2 Sources of Information

Take information on copyright dates from any source.

2.11.1.3 Recording Copyright Dates

Record copyright dates by applying the general guidelines on numbers expressed as numerals or as words (see **1.8**).

Precede the date by the copyright symbol (©) or the phonogram copyright symbol (℗). If the appropriate symbol cannot be reproduced, precede the date by *copyright* or *phonogram copyright.*

©2002

copyright 2005

℗1983

phonogram copyright 1993

> *Optional Addition*
>
> If the date as it appears in the resource is not of the Gregorian or Julian calendar, add the corresponding date or dates of the Gregorian or Julian calendar. Indicate that the information was taken from a source outside the resource itself (see **2.2.4**).
>
> ©2556 [2013]
>
> *Copyright date appears in Buddhist calendar on the source of information*

If the date as it appears on the resource is represented in different calendars, record the dates in the order indicated by the sequence, layout, or typography of the dates on the source of information.

If the resource has multiple copyright dates that apply to various aspects (e.g., text, sound, graphics), record any that are considered important for identification or selection.

℗2009
©2010
Source of information reads: ©2010, disc ℗2009

If the resource has multiple copyright dates that apply to a single aspect (e.g., text, sound, or graphics), record only the latest copyright date.

> *Optional Addition*
>
> Make a note giving the other copyright dates (see **2.17.10.3**) or record the other dates as copyright dates of related manifestations (see **27.1**).

2.12 Series Statement

CORE ELEMENT

Core elements are title proper of series, numbering within series, title proper of subseries, and numbering within subseries. Other sub-elements of series statements are optional.

2.12.1 Basic Instructions on Recording Series Statements

2.12.1.1 Scope

A ***series statement*** is a statement identifying a series to which a resource belongs and the numbering of the resource within the series.

A series statement sometimes includes information identifying one or more subseries to which the resource belongs.

Series statements sometimes include statements of responsibility relating to a series or subseries.

The information relating to one series, or one series and one or more subseries, constitutes one series statement.

For instructions on recording a series or subseries as a related work, see 25.1.

2.12.1.2 Sources of Information

For guidance on choosing sources of information for series statements, see the instructions for specific sub-elements of a series statement as follows:

a) For title proper of series, see 2.12.2.2.

b) For parallel title proper of series, see 2.12.3.2.

c) For other title information of series, see 2.12.4.2.

d) For parallel other title information of series, see 2.12.5.2.

e) For statement of responsibility relating to series, see 2.12.6.2.

f) For parallel statement of responsibility relating to series, see 2.12.7.2.

g) For ISSN of series, see 2.12.8.2.

h) For numbering within series, see 2.12.9.2.

i) For title proper of subseries, see 2.12.10.2.

j) For parallel title proper of subseries, see 2.12.11.2.

k) For other title information of subseries, see 2.12.12.2.

l) For parallel other title information of subseries, see 2.12.13.2.

m) For statement of responsibility relating to subseries, see 2.12.14.2.

n) For parallel statement of responsibility relating to subseries, see 2.12.15.2.

o) For ISSN of subseries, see 2.12.16.2.

p) For numbering within subseries, see 2.12.17.2.

2.12.1.3 Facsimiles and Reproductions

When a facsimile or reproduction has a series statement or statements relating to the original manifestation as well as to the facsimile or reproduction, record the series statement or statements relating to the facsimile or reproduction. Record any series statement relating to the original manifestation as a series statement of a related manifestation (see 27.1).

2.12.1.4 Recording Series Statements

Transcribe the sub-elements of a series statement as they appear on the source of information (see 1.7).

For additional instructions on transcribing numbering within series and numbering within subseries, see 2.12.9 and 2.12.17, respectively.

2.12.1.5 Resource in More Than One Series

If:

the resource belongs to more than one series
and/or
the resource belongs to more than one series and subseries

then:

record each series statement separately by applying the instructions at 2.12.2–2.12.17.

> Video marvels
> *Title proper of first series*
>
> no. 33
> *Numbering within first series*
>
> Educational progress series
> *Title proper of second series*
>
> no. 3
> *Numbering within second series*

If:
parts of the resource belong to different series
and
the relationship between parts of the resource and different series cannot be stated clearly in the series statement
then:
make a note giving details of the series (see **2.17.11.3**).

2.12.1.6 Recording Changes in Series Statements

Record a change in series statements as appropriate to the mode of issuance of the resource:

multipart monographs and serials (see **2.12.1.6.1**)
integrating resources (see **2.12.1.6.2**).

For changes indicating that the resource belongs to more than one series, apply the instructions at **2.12.1.5**.

2.12.1.6.1 Multipart Monographs and Serials

Make a note (see **2.17.11.5.1**) if:

a series statement is added, deleted, or changed on a subsequent issue or part of a multipart monograph or serial

and
this change cannot be stated clearly in the series statement

and
the change is considered important for identification or access.

2.12.1.6.2 Integrating Resources

Change the series statement to reflect the current iteration of an integrating resource if a series statement is added, deleted, or changed on a subsequent iteration.

Make a note if the change is considered important for identification or access (see **2.17.11.5.2**).

2.12.2 Title Proper of Series

CORE ELEMENT

2.12.2.1 Scope

The ***title proper of series*** is the chief name of a series (i.e., the title normally used when citing the series).

An alternative series title is treated as part of the title proper of series.

2.12.2.2 Sources of Information

Take the title proper of a series from the following sources (in order of preference):

a) the series title page

b) another source within the resource itself (see **2.2.2**)

c) one of the other sources of information specified at **2.2.4**.

2.12.2.3 Recording Title Proper of Series

Record the title proper of the series by applying the basic instructions on recording titles at **2.3.1**.

Bartholomew world travel series

Great sacred choruses

Allstate simulation film library

Sahitya Akademi archives of Indian literature film series

Listening, looking, and feeling

An anthology of South-East Asian music

Practicorp no-nonsense software

PCMI collection

How the health are you?

H.C.

Journal of physics

The Oxford history of England

A1 street atlas series

Record an alternative title proper of series as part of the title proper of series.

If the title proper of the series includes numbering as an integral part of the title, transcribe the numbering as part of the title proper of the series.

Publication #122 of the Social Science Education Consortium

The twenty-sixth L. Ray Buckendale lecture

Cuaderno número G del instituto

Exception

If:

the resource being described consists of two or more issues or parts

and

numbering that is an integral part of the title proper of the series differs from issue to issue or part to part

then:

omit the numbering from the title proper of the series. Use a mark of omission (…) to indicate such an omission. Record the numbering as numbering within the series (see **2.12.9**).

Publication … of the Indiana University Research Center in Anthropology, Folklore, and Linguistics

2.12.2.4 Title of Series in More Than One Language or Script

If the source of information for the title proper of the series has a title in more than one language or script, see **2.3.2.4**.

> Mercury series
> *Title of series also appears as:* Collection Mercure. *Resource is in English*

2.12.2.5 Title of Series in More Than One Form

If the source of information for the title proper of the series has a title in more than one form and both or all of the titles are in the same language and script, see **2.3.2.5**.

> Collection "À pleine vie"
> *Title of series also appears as:* À pleine vie

2.12.3 Parallel Title Proper of Series

2.12.3.1 Scope

A ***parallel title proper of series*** is the title proper of a series in another language and/or script.

2.12.3.2 Sources of Information

Take parallel titles proper of series from any source within the resource.

2.12.3.3 Recording Parallel Titles Proper of Series

Record parallel titles proper of series by applying the instructions on recording parallel titles proper at 2.3.3.3.

> Regional development series
> *Title proper of series:* Série sur le développement régional
>
> Statistiques de la Suisse
> *Title proper of series:* Statistische Quellenwerke der Schweiz

2.12.4 Other Title Information of Series

2.12.4.1 Scope

Other title information of series is information that appears in conjunction with, and is subordinate to, the title proper of a series.

2.12.4.2 Sources of Information

Take other title information of series from the same source as the title proper of the series.

2.12.4.3 Recording Other Title Information of Series

Record other title information of a series only if considered necessary for the identification of the series.

When recording other title information of a series, apply the instructions on recording other title information at **2.3.4.3**.

> a collection of facsimile reprints
> *Title proper of series:* English linguistics, 1500–1750

their origin, use, and spelling
Title proper of series: Words

2.12.4.4 Other Title Information of Series in More Than One Language or Script

If other title information of series appears on the source of information in more than one language or script, record the information that is in the language or script of the title proper of the series. If this criterion does not apply, record the other title information that appears first.

2.12.5 Parallel Other Title Information of Series

2.12.5.1 Scope

Parallel other title information of series is other title information of a series in a language and/or script that differs from that recorded in the other title information of series element.

2.12.5.2 Sources of Information

Take parallel other title information of the series from the same source as the corresponding parallel title proper of the series (see **2.12.3.2**).

If there is no corresponding parallel title proper of the series, take parallel other title information of the series from the same source as the title proper of the series (see **2.12.2.2**).

2.12.5.3 Recording Parallel Other Title Information of Series

Record parallel other title information of series by applying the instructions on recording parallel other title information at **2.3.5.3**.

2.12.6 Statement of Responsibility Relating to Series

2.12.6.1 Scope

A ***statement of responsibility relating to series*** is a statement relating to the identification of any persons, families, or corporate bodies responsible for a series.

2.12.6.2 Sources of Information

Take statements of responsibility relating to a series from the same source as the title proper of the series (see **2.12.2.2**).

2.12.6.3 Recording Statements of Responsibility Relating to Series

Record statements of responsibility associated with the series title only if considered necessary for identification of the series.

When recording a statement of responsibility relating to a series, apply the basic instructions on recording statements of responsibility at **2.4.1**.

Association of American Geographers
Title proper of series: Map supplement

Beach Erosion Board
Title proper of series: Technical memorandum

Thomas Mann
Title proper of series: Sämtliche Werke

Maurice Le Lannou
Title proper of series: Nouvelle collection

University of Sussex Centre for Continuing Education
Title proper of series: Occasional papers

Universidad de Chile, Departamento de Geologia
Title proper of series: Publicación

2.12.6.4 Statement of Responsibility Relating to Series in More Than One Language or Script

If a statement of responsibility relating to series appears on the source of information in more than one language or script, record the statement in the language or script of the title proper of the series. If this criterion does not apply, record the statement that appears first.

2.12.7 Parallel Statement of Responsibility Relating to Series

2.12.7.1 Scope

A ***parallel statement of responsibility relating to series*** is a statement of responsibility relating to series in a language and/or script that differs from that recorded in the statement of responsibility relating to series element.

2.12.7.2 Sources of Information

Take parallel statements of responsibility relating to a series from the same source as the corresponding parallel title proper of the series (see **2.12.3.2**).

If there is no corresponding parallel title proper of the series, take parallel statements of responsibility relating to series from the same source as the title proper of the series (see **2.12.2.2**).

2.12.7.3 Recording Parallel Statements of Responsibility Relating to Series

Record parallel statements of responsibility relating to series by applying the basic instructions on recording statements of responsibility at **2.4.1**.

If there is more than one parallel statement of responsibility relating to series, record the statements in the same order as the parallel titles proper relating to series to which they correspond.

2.12.8 ISSN of Series

2.12.8.1 Scope

An ***ISSN (International Standard Serial Number) of a series*** is the identifier assigned to a series by an ISSN registration agency.

2.12.8.2 Sources of Information

Take the ISSN of a series from the following sources (in order of preference):

a) the series title page

b) another source within the resource itself (see **2.2.2**)

c) one of the other sources of information specified at **2.2.4**.

2.12.8.3 Recording the ISSN of a Series

Transcribe the ISSN (International Standard Serial Number) of a series as it appears on the source of information.

ISSN 0317-3127

Optional Omission

If the ISSN of a subseries appears on the source of information (see **2.12.16.2**), omit the ISSN of the main series.

2.12.9 Numbering within Series

CORE ELEMENT

2.12.9.1 Scope

Numbering within series is a designation of the sequencing of a part or parts within a series.

Numbering within series can include a numeral, a letter, any other character, or the combination of these. Numbering is often accompanied by a caption (*volume*, *number*, etc.) and/or a chronological designation.

2.12.9.2 Sources of Information

Take the numbering within a series from any source within the resource.

2.12.9.3 Recording Numbering within Series

Record the numbering of the resource within the series as it appears on the source of information. Apply the general guidelines on transcription (see **1.7**) and the general guidelines on numbers expressed as numerals or as words (see **1.8**).

no. 8

v. 12

4

63-2

tome 3, partie 2

v. 12, part 3, fasc. 1–2

Exception

If necessary for clarity, substitute a slash for a hyphen.

For a term that is part of the series numbering, apply the instructions on capitalization appropriate to the language of the term (see appendix **A**).

Capitalize other words and alphabetic devices used as part of a numbering system according to the usage in the resource.

set 1

reel A-4

imleabhar 11

Bd. 8

May 1996

album 15

A

Parts in this series are numbered A, B, C, D, *etc.*

NSRDS-NBS 5

MCE 329

1245A

L-510

If the numbering consists of a year and a number that is a division of the year, record the year before the number (see **2.6.2.3**).

2000, no. 3
Numbering appears on the source of information as: no. 3, 2000; *numbering restarts each year*

When the numbering is grammatically integrated with the series title, apply the instructions at **2.12.2.3**.

If the numbering that appears on the source of information is known to be incorrect, transcribe it as it appears. Make a note giving the correct numbering (see **2.17.11.4**).

Bd. 24
Numbering should read: Bd. 25

2.12.9.4 Chronological Designation

If the resource has both a numeric and/or alphabetic designation and a chronological designation (see **2.6.3.3**), record both. Do not treat a date of production, publication, distribution, or manufacture as a chronological designation.

v. 3, no. 2
Sept. 1981

2.12.9.5 Numbering in More Than One Language or Script

If the numbering appears on the source of information in more than one language or script, record the numbering that is in the language or script of the title proper of the series. If this criterion does not apply, record the numbering that appears first.

2.12.9.6 New Sequence of Numbering

Include wording intended to differentiate a new sequence of numbering (wording such as *new series*).

new series, v. 3

4th series, 30

Supply *new series* or another appropriate term if:

a new sequence of numbering has the same numbering as an earlier sequence

and

the new sequence of numbering is not accompanied by wording such as *new series*.

Indicate that the information was taken from a source outside the resource itself (see **2.2.4**).

> [new series], no. 1
>
> [neue Folge], Heft 1

2.12.9.7 Alternative Numbering Systems

If the series has more than one separate system of numbering, record the systems in the order in which they are presented.

> 1
> 235
> *When series changed title, publisher began a new system with* 1 *and continued the system from the earlier title with* 235

2.12.9.8 Separately Numbered Issues or Parts

When describing a resource consisting of two or more issues or parts, record numbering within series as appropriate to the mode of issuance of the resource:

multipart monographs (see **2.12.9.8.1**)

serials (see **2.12.9.8.2**).

2.12.9.8.1 Multipart Monographs

Record the first and the last numbers, separated by a hyphen if:

parts of a multipart monograph are separately numbered within a series

and

the numbering is continuous.

> v. 11–15
>
> disc 3–4

If the numbering is not continuous, record all the numbers.

> v. 131, 145, 152

2.12.9.8.2 Serials

Record the numbering within a series only if all issues or parts of the serial have the same series number.

> no. 1124
> *Each issue of the serial has the same series number*

2.12.10 Title Proper of Subseries

CORE ELEMENT

2.12.10.1 Scope

The ***title proper of subseries*** is the chief name of a subseries (i.e., the title normally used when citing the subseries).

2.12.10.2 Sources of Information

Take the title proper of a subseries from the following sources (in order of preference):

a) the series title page

b) another source within the resource itself (see **2.2.2**)

c) one of the other sources of information specified at **2.2.4**.

2.12.10.3 Recording Title Proper of Subseries

Record the title proper of the subseries by applying the instructions on recording titles proper of the series at **2.12.2**.

> East Asian and Pacific series
> *Title proper of main series:* Department of State publication
>
> Stockholm studies in the history of literature
> *Title proper of main series:* Acta Universitatis Stockholmiensis
>
> Trains
> *Title proper of main series:* Standard radio super sound effects
>
> English, 1642–1700
> *Title proper of main series:* Three centuries of drama

2.12.10.4 "New Series," "Second Series," Etc.

If a phrase such as *new series, second series,* etc., appears with an unnumbered series on the source of information, record such a phrase as a subseries title.

> New series
> *Title proper of subseries*
> *Title proper of unnumbered main series:* Cambridge studies in international and comparative law

If a phrase such as *new series, second series,* etc., appears with a numbered series, record the phrase as part of the numbering of the series (see **2.12.9.6**).

2.12.10.5 Subseries or Separate Series

In case of doubt about whether a series title is a subseries or a separate series, treat it as a separate series (see **2.12.1.5**).

2.12.10.6 Numeric and/or Alphabetic Designation of Subseries

If the subseries has a numeric and/or alphabetic designation and no title, record the designation as the subseries title.

> Series 2
> *Title proper of main series:* Music for today

If the subseries has a title as well as a designation, record the title following the designation.

> 4, Physics
> *Title proper of main series:* Viewmaster science series
>
> Series D, Geophysical bulletin
> *Title proper of main series:* Communications of the Dublin Institute for Advanced Studies

2.12.11 Parallel Title Proper of Subseries

2.12.11.1 Scope

A ***parallel title proper of subseries*** is the title proper of a subseries in another language and/or script.

2.12.11.2 Sources of Information

Take parallel titles proper of subseries from any source within the resource.

2.12.11.3 Recording Parallel Titles Proper of Subseries

Record parallel titles proper of subseries by applying the instructions on recording parallel titles proper at 2.3.3.3.

> La France d'aujourd'hui
> *Title proper of subseries:* France today
> *Title proper of main series:* World films
>
> Série C, Bibliographies
> *Title proper of subseries:* Series C, Bibliographies
> *Title proper of main series:* Papers and documents of the I.C.I.
> *Parallel title proper of main series:* Travaux et documents de l'I.C.I.

2.12.12 Other Title Information of Subseries

2.12.12.1 Scope

Other title information of subseries is information that appears in conjunction with, and is subordinate to, the title proper of a subseries.

2.12.12.2 Sources of Information

Take other title information of subseries from the same source as the title proper of the subseries.

2.12.12.3 Recording Other Title Information of Subseries

Record other title information of a subseries by applying the instructions on recording other title information of series at **2.12.4**.

2.12.13 Parallel Other Title Information of Subseries

2.12.13.1 Scope

Parallel other title information of subseries is other title information of a subseries in a language and/or script that differs from that recorded in the other title information of subseries element.

2.12.13.2 Sources of Information

Take parallel other title information of the subseries from the same source as the corresponding parallel title proper of the subseries (see **2.12.3.2**).

If there is no corresponding parallel title proper of the subseries, take parallel other title information of the subseries from the same source as the title proper of the subseries (see **2.12.10.2**).

2.12.13.3 Recording Parallel Other Title Information of Subseries

Record parallel other title information of a subseries by applying the instructions on recording parallel other title information at **2.3.5.3**.

2.12.14 Statement of Responsibility Relating to Subseries

2.12.14.1 Scope

A ***statement of responsibility relating to subseries*** is a statement relating to the identification of any persons, families, or corporate bodies responsible for a subseries.

2.12.14.2 Sources of Information

Take statements of responsibility relating to a subseries from the same source as the title proper of the subseries (see **2.12.10.2**).

2.12.14.3 Recording Statements of Responsibility Relating to Subseries

Record statements of responsibility associated with the title of a subseries only if considered necessary for identification of the subseries.

When recording a statement of responsibility relating to a subseries, apply the basic instructions on recording statements of responsibility at **2.4.1**.

2.12.14.4 Statement of Responsibility Relating to Subseries in More Than One Language or Script

If a statement of responsibility relating to a subseries appears on the source of information in more than one language or script, record the statement in the language or script of the title proper of the subseries. If this criterion does not apply, record the statement that appears first.

2.12.15 Parallel Statement of Responsibility Relating to Subseries

2.12.15.1 Scope

A ***parallel statement of responsibility relating to subseries*** is a statement of responsibility relating to a subseries in a language and/or script that differs from that recorded in the statement of responsibility relating to subseries element.

2.12.15.2 Sources of Information

Take parallel statements of responsibility relating to a subseries from the same source as the corresponding parallel title proper of the subseries (see **2.12.11.2**).

If there is no corresponding parallel title proper of the subseries, take parallel statements of responsibility relating to subseries from the same source as the title proper of the subseries (see **2.12.10.2**).

2.12.15.3 Recording Parallel Statements of Responsibility Relating to Subseries

Record parallel statements of responsibility relating to subseries by applying the basic instructions on recording statements of responsibility at **2.4.1**.

If there is more than one parallel statement of responsibility relating to subseries, record the statements in the same order as the parallel titles proper relating to subseries to which they correspond.

2.12.16 ISSN of Subseries

2.12.16.1 Scope

An ***ISSN (International Standard Serial Number) of a subseries*** is the identifier assigned to a subseries by an ISSN registration agency.

2.12.16.2 Sources of Information

Take the ISSN of a subseries from the following sources (in order of preference):

a) the series title page

b) another source within the resource itself (see **2.2.2**)

c) one of the other sources of information specified at **2.2.4**.

2.12.16.3 Recording the ISSN of a Subseries

Transcribe the ISSN (International Standard Serial Number) of a subseries as it appears on the source of information.

> ISSN 0319-9470

Optional Omission

When recording the ISSN of a subseries, omit the ISSN of the main series.

> ISSN 0826-6875
> *ISSN of main series (0316-1854) not recorded*

2.12.17 Numbering within Subseries

CORE ELEMENT

2.12.17.1 Scope

Numbering within subseries is a designation of the sequencing of a part or parts within a subseries.

Numbering within subseries can include a numeral, a letter, any other character, or the combination of these. Numbering is often accompanied by a caption (*volume*, *number*, etc.) and/or a chronological designation.

2.12.17.2 Sources of Information

Take the numbering within a subseries from any source within the resource.

2.12.17.3 Recording Numbering within Subseries

Record the numbering within a subseries by applying the instructions on numbering within series at **2.12.9**.

> TSP 1
> *Title proper of subseries:* Physics
> *Title proper of main series:* Sciences
>
> 1
> *Title proper of subseries:* Artes aplicadas
> *Title proper of main series:* Biblioteca de arte hispánico. *Numbering of main series:* 8

2.13 Mode of Issuance

2.13.1 Basic Instructions on Recording Modes of Issuance

2.13.1.1 Scope

Mode of issuance is a categorization reflecting whether a resource is issued in one or more parts, the way it is updated, and its intended termination.

2.13.1.2 Sources of Information

Use evidence presented by the resource itself (or on any accompanying material or container) as the basis for determining the mode of issuance of the resource. Take additional evidence from any source.

2.13.1.3 Recording Modes of Issuance

Record the mode of issuance of the resource using one or more of the terms listed in table 2.1. Record as many terms as are applicable to the resource being described.

TABLE 2.1

single unit	A resource that is issued either as a single physical unit (e.g., as a single-volume monograph) or, in the case of an intangible resource, as a single logical unit (e.g., as a PDF file mounted on the web).
multipart monograph	A resource issued in two or more parts (either simultaneously or successively) that is complete or intended to be completed within a finite number of parts (e.g., a dictionary in two volumes, three audiocassettes issued as a set).
serial	A resource issued in successive parts, usually with numbering, that has no predetermined conclusion (e.g., a periodical, a monographic series, a newspaper). Includes resources that exhibit characteristics of serials, such as successive issues, numbering, and frequency, but whose duration is limited (e.g., newsletters of events) and reproductions of serials.
integrating resource	A resource that is added to or changed by means of updates that do not remain discrete but are integrated into the whole (e.g., a loose-leaf manual that is updated by means of replacement pages, a website that is updated continuously).

2.14 Frequency

2.14.1 Basic Instructions on Recording Frequency

2.14.1.1 Scope

Frequency is the intervals at which the issues or parts of a serial or the updates to an integrating resource are issued.

2.14.1.2 Sources of Information

Take information on frequency from any source.

2.14.1.3 Recording Frequency

Record the frequency of release of issues or parts of a serial or the frequency of updates to an integrating resource, if known. Use an appropriate term from the following list:

daily
three times a week
biweekly
weekly
semiweekly
three times a month

bimonthly
monthly
semimonthly
quarterly
three times a year
semiannual
annual
biennial
triennial
irregular

If none of the terms in the list is appropriate or sufficiently specific, make a note giving details of the frequency (see **2.17.12.3**).

2.14.1.4 Recording Changes in Frequency

Make a note on a change in frequency (see **2.17.12.4**).

2.15 Identifier for the Manifestation

CORE ELEMENT

If there is more than one identifier for the manifestation, prefer an internationally recognized identifier, if applicable. Additional identifiers for the manifestation are optional.

2.15.1 Basic Instructions on Recording Identifiers for the Manifestation

2.15.1.1 Scope

An ***identifier for the manifestation*** is a character string associated with a manifestation that serves to differentiate that manifestation from other manifestations.

Identifiers for manifestations include:

registered identifiers from internationally recognized schemes (e.g., ISBN, ISSN, URN)
other identifiers assigned by publishers, distributors, government publications agencies, document clearinghouses, archives, etc., following their internally devised schemes
"fingerprints" (i.e., identifiers constructed by combining groups of characters from specified pages of an early printed resource)
music publishers' numbers (see **2.15.2**) and plate numbers (see **2.15.3**).

For identifiers intended to provide online access to a resource using a standard Internet browser, see **4.6**.

2.15.1.2 Sources of Information

Take identifiers for the manifestation from any source.

2.15.1.3 Facsimiles and Reproductions

When a facsimile or reproduction has an identifier or identifiers associated with the original manifestation as well as with the facsimile or reproduction, record the identifier associated with the facsimile or reproduction. Record any identifier associated with the original manifestation as an identifier for a related manifestation (see **27.1**).

2.15.1.4 Recording Identifiers for Manifestations

If there is a specified display format for the identifier for the manifestation (e.g., ISBN, ISSN, URN), record it using that format.

ISBN 0-552-67587-3

ISBN 978-90-70002-34-3

ISSN 0046-225X

ISMN M-705015-05-8

ISBN 978 1 85604 693 0

doi:10.3133/of2007-1047
Digital Object Identifier for: U.S. Geological Survey open-file report 2007-1047

urn:nbn:de:gbv:089-3321752945
Uniform Resource Name for: Oliver Schmachtenberg's online dissertation Nitric oxide in the olfactory epithelium

doi:10.1145/1462198.1462199
Digital Object Identifier for: Marko A. Rodriguez, Johan Bollen, and Herbert Van de Sompel. Automatic metadata generation using associative networks. In: ACM transactions on information systems. February 2009, volume 27, issue 2

If there is no specified display format for the identifier, record it as it appears on the source. Precede the identifier with a trade name or the name of the agency, etc., responsible for assigning the identifier, if readily ascertainable.

Supt. of Docs. no.: I 19.16:818

Warner Bros.: K56151

Tamla Motown: STMA 8007

Island: ILPS 9281

Nimbus: NI 5114-NI 5148

European Commission: CA-23-99-031-EN-C

UPC: 093228062929

National Library of Australia: nla.pic-an21464324
Persistent identifier for: Wolfgang Sievers' The gears

2.15.1.5 More Than One Identifier for the Manifestation

If:
describing a resource consisting of two or more parts
and
there is an identifier for the resource as a whole as well as identifiers for the individual parts
then:
record the identifier for the resource as a whole.

ISBN 0-7887-1649-2 (set)
Consists of a set of 5 audiocassettes and accompanying book. The book also has a separate ISBN

When describing only a single part, record the identifier for that part.

Optional Addition

Record both the identifier for the resource as a whole and any identifiers for individual parts. Add a qualification to each identifier by applying the instructions at **2.15.1.7**.

ISBN 0-379-00550-6 (set)
ISBN 0-379-00551-4 (v. 1)

ISBN 1-887744-11-8 (video)
ISBN 1-887744-12-6 (student text)
ISBN 1-887744-46-0 (teacher guide)

Alternative

If there are more than three identifiers for individual parts, record only the first identifier and the last identifier.

If the identifiers are consecutive, separate them by a hyphen.

If the identifiers are not consecutive, separate them by a diagonal slash.

2.15.1.6 Incorrect Identifiers

If an identifier is known to be incorrectly represented in the resource, record the number as it appears. Indicate that the number is incorrect, cancelled, or invalid, as appropriate.

ISBN 0-87068-430-2 (invalid)

ISSN 0018-5811 (incorrect)

2.15.1.7 Qualification

If the resource has more than one identifier of the same type, record a brief qualification after the identifier.

ISBN 0-435-91660-2 (cased)
ISBN 0-435-91661-0 (pbk.)
Qualifier is abbreviated on the source of information

ISBN 0-387-08266-2 (U.S.)
ISBN 3-540-08266-2 (Germany)
Qualifier is abbreviated on the source of information

ISBN 978-1-4094-4206-6 (hbk)
ISBN 978-1-4094-4207-3 (ebk – PDF)
ISBN 978-1-4094-0374-5 (ebk – ePUB)
Qualifiers are abbreviated on the source of information

If the resource has only one identifier, record the type of binding or format, if considered important for identification.

ISBN 978-1-107-66485-2 (paperback)

For updating loose-leafs, add the qualification *(loose-leaf)* to the identifier.

ISBN 0-86325-016-5 (loose-leaf)

If identifiers for parts of the resource are recorded (see **2.15.1.5**), follow each identifier with the designation of the part to which it applies.

ISBN 0-08-019856-2 (v. 1)

ISBN 0-901212-04-0 (v. 38)

ISMN M-001-11270-3 (partition)

2.15.2 Publisher's Number for Music

2.15.2.1 Scope

A ***publisher's number for music*** is a numbering designation assigned to a resource by a music publisher. This number normally appears only on the title page, the cover, and/or the first page of music.

A publisher's number sometimes includes initials, abbreviations, or words identifying the publisher.

2.15.2.2 Sources of Information

Take publishers' numbers for music from any source.

2.15.2.3 Recording Publishers' Numbers for Music

Record publishers' numbers for music. If a publisher's number is preceded by an abbreviation, word, or phrase identifying a publisher, include that abbreviation, word, or phrase as part of the number.

6139

6201/9935
The complete set of numbers is 6201, 6654, 7006, 7212, 7635, 7788, 8847, 9158, 9664, 9935

2.15.3 Plate Number for Music

2.15.3.1 Scope

A ***plate number for music*** is a numbering designation assigned to a resource by a music publisher. The number is usually printed at the bottom of each page, and sometimes also appears on the title page.

A plate number sometimes includes initials, abbreviations, or words identifying a publisher. It is sometimes followed by a number corresponding to the number of pages or plates.

2.15.3.2 Sources of Information

Take plate numbers for music from any source.

2.15.3.3 Recording Plate Numbers for Music

Record plate numbers for music. If a plate number is preceded by an abbreviation, word, or phrase identifying a publisher, include that abbreviation, word, or phrase as part of the number.

S. & B. 4081

UE 19541-UE 19543

> 9674 H.L.-9676 H.L.
>
> R.10150E.-R.10155E.

2.16 Preferred Citation

2.16.1 Basic Instructions on Recording Preferred Citations

2.16.1.1 Scope

A ***preferred citation*** is a citation for a resource in the form preferred by a creator, publisher, custodian, indexing or abstracting service, etc.

2.16.1.2 Sources of Information

Take preferred citations from any source.

2.16.1.3 Recording Preferred Citations

Record a preferred citation in the form as it appears on the source.

> Janus Press Archive, Rare Book and Special Collections Division, Library of Congress
>
> W. G. Alma conjuring collection. Photographs
>
> Michelle L. Kaarst-Brown, Scott Nicholson, Gisela M. von Dran, and Jeffrey M. Stanton, School of Information Studies, Syracuse University, Syracuse, NY 13244 LIBRARY TRENDS, Vol. 53, No. 1, Summer 2004 ("Organizational Development and Leadership," edited by Keith Russell and Denise Stephens), pages 33–53
>
> PROV, VA 672 Premier's Office, VPRS 1163/P1 Inwards Correspondence Files, Unit 744, 1883/291 letter re. remedy for pauperism.
>
> Fletcher, P.R., (2004) PhD Thesis - How Tertiary Level Physics Students Learn and Conceptualise Quantum Mechanics (School of Physics, University of Sydney)
>
> http://nla.gov.au/nla.pic-vn3579894

NOTES

2.17 Note on Manifestation

2.17.1 Basic Instructions on Making Notes on Manifestations

2.17.1.1 Scope

A ***note on manifestation*** is a note providing information on attributes of the manifestation.

For notes on describing carriers, see **3.21**.

2.17.1.2 Sources of Information

Take information for notes on manifestation from any source.

2.17.1.3 Making Notes on Manifestation

Make a note on manifestation by applying the general guidelines at **1.10**.

2.17.2 Note on Title

2.17.2.1 Scope

A ***note on title*** is a note providing information on:

the source from which a title was taken

the date the title was viewed

variations in titles

inaccuracies, deletions, etc.

or

other information relating to a title.

2.17.2.2 Sources of Information

Take information for use in a note on a title from any source.

2.17.2.3 Title Source

Make a note on the source from which the title proper is taken if it is not one of these sources:

a) the title page, title sheet, or title card (or image of it) of a resource consisting of multiple pages, leaves, sheets, or cards (or images of them) (see **2.2.2.2**)

b) the title frame or title screen of a resource consisting of moving images (see **2.2.2.3**).

Title from container

Title from PDF cover page

Title from descriptive insert

Caption title

Title from publisher's catalogue

Title devised by cataloguer

Title from title screen

Title from menu

Title from codebook

Title from home page

Title from colophon

Optional Omission

If the resource has only a single title and the title appears on the resource itself, do not record the source from which the title proper is taken.

If a parallel title proper is taken from a different source than the title proper, make a note on the source of the parallel title proper if considered important for identification or access.

French title from cover

If considered important for identification or access, make a note on the source or basis for:

a variant title (see **2.3.6.3**)

an earlier title proper (see **2.3.7.3**)

a later title proper (see **2.3.8.3**).

Title on CD-ROM label: Student CD-ROM to accompany Fundamentals of operations management

Title on cover: Strategic sustainable planning
Title proper recorded as: SSP, a civil defense manual for cultural survival

Translated title: Plant physiology
Translation of Russian title recorded as title proper

Spine title: Rocque's map of Shropshire

Title on container: We're still standing

Running title: Economic atlas of Quebec

File name: CC.RIDER

Earlier title proper: Taxation of intangible assets, 1997–1998

Earlier other title information: Law & strategy for businesses and corporations, 1997–2000

Former French title, 1995–2000?: Site du Web des noms géographiques officiels du Canada

Issues for 1999– have title: Annual report on pipeline safety
Title proper recorded as: Annual report of pipeline safety

Issues for January 1928–July 1952; March 1971– have title: The magazine antiques

Vol. 1, no. 3– has subtitle: Studies in educational administration

German title also appears on v. 2–3: Meisterwerke der Makonde
Title proper recorded as: Masterpieces of the Makonde. *No parallel title proper on v. 1*

English title varies: Inter-American review of bibliography, 1952–

Volumes 5– have title: Eminent Indian mathematicians of the twentieth century
Title proper recorded as: Some eminent Indian mathematicians of the twentieth century

Volume 2 has title: Dictionnaire des églises de France, Belgique, Luxembourg, Suisse; volumes 3–5 have title: Dictionnaire des églises de France
Title proper recorded as: Histoire générale des églises de France, Belgique, Luxembourg, Suisse

For online resources, make a separate note indicating the date the resource was viewed (see **2.17.13.5**).

2.17.2.4 Title Variations, Inaccuracies, and Deletions

In some cases, scattered issues or parts, or occasional iterations of a resource have different titles proper, parallel titles proper, other title information, or parallel other title information. If the differences are not considered important for identification or access, make a general note indicating that the title, etc., varies.

Title varies slightly

Title on containers of parts 3 and 5–6 varies slightly

Subtitle varies

If an inaccuracy in a title has been transcribed as it appears on the source of information, make a note giving the corrected form of the title, if considered important for identification or access.

Title should read: Hierarchy in organizations
Title proper recorded as: Heirarchy in organizations

If an obvious typographic error has been corrected when transcribing the title of a serial or integrating resource (see **2.3.1.4**), make a note giving the title as it appears on the source of information.

> Title appears on v. 1, no. 1 as: Housing sarts
> *Title proper recorded as:* Housing starts

For multipart monographs and serials, make notes on the following deletions, if considered important for identification or access:

parallel titles proper (see **2.3.3.5**)

other title information (see **2.3.4.7**)

parallel other title information (see **2.3.5.4**).

Indicate the numbering or publication dates to which the deletion applies.

> Title in French not present on issues after 1998

2.17.2.5 Other Information Relating to a Title

Make notes on other details relating to a title if considered important for identification or access.

> Symbol for "proportional to" appears in title
> *Title proper recorded as:* Robust H [proportional to] stabilization of stochastic hybrid systems with wiener process
>
> The word "Brain" in the title appears with an X through it
> *Title proper recorded as:* My name is Brain [crossed out] Brian

2.17.3 Note on Statement of Responsibility

2.17.3.1 Scope

A ***note on statement of responsibility*** is a note providing information on:

a person, family, or corporate body not named in a statement of responsibility to whom responsibility for the intellectual or artistic content of the resource has been attributed

variant forms of names appearing in the resource

changes in statements of responsibility

or

other details relating to a statement of responsibility.

2.17.3.2 Sources of Information

Take information for use in a note on a statement of responsibility from any source.

2.17.3.3 Attribution

If:

responsibility for the intellectual or artistic content of the resource has been attributed to persons, families or corporate bodies

and

these persons, families, or corporate bodies are not named in a statement of responsibility

then:

make notes about the attributed relationship of these persons, families, or corporate bodies to the resource.

> Formerly attributed to J.S. Bach
>
> Sometimes attributed to Thomas Dekker, but more probably by Robert Tofte

2.17.3.4 Variant Forms of Names

Make notes on variant forms of names if:

the names of persons, families, or corporate bodies appear in the resource in forms that are different from those recorded in the statement of responsibility

and

the different forms are considered important for identification.

> Issued by: Abortion Law Reform Association
> *Statement of responsibility:* Alra
>
> Author's initials represented by musical notes

2.17.3.5 Other Information Relating to a Statement of Responsibility

Make notes on other details relating to a statement of responsibility, if considered important for identification or access.

> Dictated to Clare Wheeler
>
> Collection made by P.M. Townshend
>
> Additional contributors to program: Eric Rosenfeld, Debra Spencer
>
> At head of title: Arctic Biological Station

2.17.3.6 Change in Statement of Responsibility

Make notes on changes in a statement of responsibility as appropriate to the mode of issuance of the resource:

multipart monographs (see **2.17.3.6.1**)

serials (see **2.17.3.6.2**)

integrating resources (see **2.17.3.6.3**).

2.17.3.6.1 Multipart Monographs

Make notes on differences in statements of responsibility that occur on a subsequent part of a multipart monograph, if considered important for identification or access.

> Volumes 15–26 edited by W.B. Willcox; volume 27 edited by C.A. Lopez; volumes 28–35 edited by Barbara B. Oberg; volumes 36–39 edited by Ellen R. Cohn

2.17.3.6.2 Serials

Make notes on changes in statements of responsibility that occur after the first/earliest issue or part of a serial, if considered important for identification or access.

Issued by: Dept. of Health and Welfare, Bureau of Vital Statistics, 1964–1977; by: Dept. of Health and Human Services, Bureau of Vital Records, 1978–

Editors: 1975–1984, Howard Johnson; 1985– , G.L. Jones

Alternative

If the changes have been numerous, make a general note.

2.17.3.6.3 Integrating Resources

Make notes on statements of responsibility no longer present on the current iteration of an integrating resource or that appeared in a different form on earlier iterations, if considered important for identification or access.

Compiled and edited by: Dan Hill and Malcolm Evans, 1977–July 1980

Alternative

If the changes have been numerous, make a general note.

Editor varies

2.17.4 Note on Edition Statement

2.17.4.1 Scope

A ***note on edition statement*** is a note providing information on:

the source of an edition statement

edition statements relating to issues, parts, etc.

changes in edition statements

or

other information relating to an edition statement.

2.17.4.2 Sources of Information

Take information for use in a note on edition statement from any source.

2.17.4.3 Edition Statements Relating to Issues, Parts, Etc.

Make notes on edition statements relating to issues, parts, etc. that differ from the edition statement relating to the resource as a whole (see **2.5.1.5**).

2.17.4.4 Other Information Relating to an Edition Statement

Make notes on other details relating to an edition statement, if considered important for identification or access.

Edition statement on colophon varies: Shohan

Edition statement from jacket

2.17.4.5 Change in Edition Statement

Make notes on changes in edition statements as appropriate to the mode of issuance of the resource:

multipart monographs (see 2.17.4.5.1)

serials (see 2.17.4.5.2)

integrating resources (see 2.17.4.5.3).

2.17.4.5.1 Multipart Monographs

Make notes on differences in edition statements from one part of a multipart monograph to another (see 2.5.1.6.1), if considered important for identification.

> Volume 2 does not have an edition statement

Alternative

If the changes have been numerous, make a general note.

2.17.4.5.2 Serials

Make notes on changes in edition statements that occur after the first/earliest issue or part of a serial (see 2.5.1.6.2), if considered important for identification.

> Edition statement varies: International ed., 1998–
> *Edition statement prior to 1998:* International ed. in English

Alternative

If the changes have been numerous, make a general note.

2.17.4.5.3 Integrating Resources

Make notes on edition statements no longer present on the current iteration of an integrating resource or that appeared in a different form on earlier iterations (see 2.5.1.6.3), if considered important for identification.

Alternative

If the changes have been numerous, make a general note.

> Replacement title pages carry successive edition statements, e.g., replacement title page received with June 1985 supplementation carries the statement "1985 edition"

2.17.5 Note on Numbering of Serials

2.17.5.1 Scope

A ***note on numbering of serials*** is a note providing information on:

the numbering of the first and/or last issue or part

complex or irregular numbering (including numbering errors)

or

the period covered by a volume, issue, part, etc.

2.17.5.2 Sources of Information

Take information for use in a note on numbering of a serial from any source.

2.17.5.3 Numbering of First Issue or Part and/or Last Issue or Part

Make a note giving the numbering of the first issue or part and/or of the last issue or part if this information is not recorded as part of the numbering of serials element (see 2.6).

Began with volume 1, no. 1 in 2006

Ceased with no. 25

Began with May 2007 issue

Began with June 15, 1998 issue; ceased with issue for July 2007

Began in 2001

2.17.5.4 Complex or Irregular Numbering

Make notes on complex or irregular numbering of a serial, or numbering errors, if:

the information is not already specified in the numbering of serials element

and

it is considered important for identification.

Issues for Aug. 1973–Dec. 1974 also called v. 1, no. 7–v. 2, no. 12

Volume numbering irregular: v. 15–18 omitted, v. 20–21 repeated

Numbering begins each year with v. 1

Numbering irregular; some numbers repeated or omitted

Successive articles are uniquely identified by a manuscript number and date

Issues for 1996 are only available as individual articles, organized topically

Articles are continually added to each annual volume

2.17.5.5 Period Covered

Make a note on the period covered by a volume, issue, part, etc., of a serial if:

the serial is issued annually or less frequently

and

the period covered by the volume, etc., is other than a calendar year.

Report year ends June 30

Report year varies

Each issue covers: Apr. 1–Mar. 31

Each issue covers: Every two years since 1961–1962

2.17.6 Note on Production Statement

2.17.6.1 Scope

A ***note on production statement*** is a note providing information on:

details of the place of production, producer, or date of production

or

changes in the place of production, producer, or producer's name.

2.17.6.2 Sources of Information

Take information for use in a note on a production statement from any source.

2.17.6.3 Details Relating to Production Statement

Make notes on details relating to place of production, producer, or date of production not recorded in the production statement element, if considered important for identification or access.

2.17.6.4 Change in Production Statement

Make notes on changes in place of production and/or the producer's name as appropriate to the mode of issuance of the resource:

multipart monographs (see **2.17.6.4.1**)

serials (see **2.17.6.4.2**)

integrating resources (see **2.17.6.4.3**).

2.17.6.4.1 Multipart Monographs

Make notes on differences in place of production and/or producers' names from one part of a multipart monograph to another (see **2.7.1.5.1**), if considered important for identification or access.

> *Alternative*
>
> If the changes have been numerous, make a general note.

2.17.6.4.2 Serials

Make notes on changes in place of production and/or producers' names that occur after the first/earliest issue or part of a serial (see **2.7.1.5.2**), if considered important for identification or access.

> *Alternative*
>
> If the changes have been numerous, make a general note.

2.17.6.4.3 Integrating Resources

Make notes on place of production and/or producers' names no longer present on the current iteration of an integrating resource, or that appeared in a different form on earlier iterations (see **2.7.1.5.3**), if considered important for identification or access.

> *Alternative*
>
> If the changes have been numerous, make a general note.

2.17.7 Note on Publication Statement

2.17.7.1 Scope

A ***note on publication statement*** is a note providing information on:

details of the place of publication, publisher, or date of publication

or

changes in the place of publication, publisher, or publisher's name

or

suspension of publication.

2.17.7.2 Sources of Information

Take information for use in a note on a publication statement from any source.

2.17.7.3 Details Relating to Publication Statement

Make notes on details relating to place of publication, publisher, or date of publication not recorded in the publication statement element, if considered important for identification or access.

> Actually published by Moens
>
> *Publisher's name as transcribed from source:* Impr. Vincent

Published in London or Manchester

Actually published in Dublin
Place of publication as transcribed from source: Belfast

Published in Liverpool
Place of publication as transcribed from source: Lerpwl

Published in Oslo
Place of publication as transcribed from source: Christiania. *Oslo is the later name of Christiania*

Published in Rio de Janeiro
Place of publication as transcribed from source: Rio

Published in Trier
Place of publication as transcribed from source: Augustae Treverorum

Published in London, Ontario
Place of publication as transcribed from source: London

Original imprint covered by labels: on label Odeon, on container EMI Records
Publisher's name as transcribed from source: Odeon

Publication statement reads: Impressi per me Wilhelmum de Machlinia in opulentissima civitate Londonarium iuxta pontem qui vulgariter dicitur Flete Brigge
Publisher's name as transcribed from source: Impressi per me Wilhelmum de Machlinia

Probable year of publication based on date range in which the publisher was active
Date of publication recorded as: [1969?]

Make notes on the beginning and ending date of publication if the identification of the resource is based on an issue or part other than the first and/or last.

Began in 1996
First published issue not available but information about beginning date is known; resource still being published

Began in 1988; ceased in 1991
First and last published issues not available but information about beginning and ending dates known

Ceased publication in 1999
Description not based on either first or last issue, part, or iteration; ending publication date known

2.17.7.4 Suspension of Publication

If a multipart monograph, serial, or an integrating resource suspends publication with the intention of resuming at a later date, make a note indicating the suspension. If the resource resumes publication, include the dates or designations of the period of suspension.

Suspended with v. 11

No updates issued from 1999 to 2001

Suspended with v. 6, no. 2 (July 1992); resumed with v. 7, no. 1 (January 1995)

2.17.7.5 Change in Publication Statement

Make notes on changes in place of publication and/or the publisher's name as appropriate to the mode of issuance of the resource:

multipart monographs (see **2.17.7.5.1**)

serials (see **2.17.7.5.2**)

integrating resources (see **2.17.7.5.3**).

2.17.7.5.1 Multipart Monographs

Make notes on differences in place of publication and/or publishers' names from one part of a multipart monograph to another (see **2.8.1.5.1**), if considered important for identification or access.

> Volume 2 has variant publisher statement: Printed and published by T.P. Low
> *Publisher statement on volume 1:* Published by E. Low

> *Alternative*
>
> If the changes have been numerous, make a general note.

2.17.7.5.2 Serials

Make notes on changes in place of publication and/or publishers' names that occur after the first/earliest issue or part of a serial (see **2.8.1.5.2**), if considered important for identification or access.

> Published: Denver, 1995–1997; Boston, 1998–
> *Place of publication recorded as:* Dallas
>
> Published by: F. Angeli, 1987–1990; G. Mondadori, 1991–
>
> Presentation of publisher's name varies: William Cooke
> *Publisher's name recorded as:* B. Cook

> *Alternative*
>
> If the changes have been numerous, make a general note.
>
> > Name of publisher varies

2.17.7.5.3 Integrating Resources

Make notes on place of publication and/or publishers' names no longer present on the current iteration of an integrating resource, or that appeared in a different form on earlier iterations (see **2.8.1.5.3**), if considered important for identification or access.

> Published: New York, 1974–1975; South Hackensack, N.J., 1976–1978
> *Place of publication recorded as:* Colorado Springs, Colo.
>
> Published by Architext Software, 1994–1997
> *Name of publisher recorded as:* Excite, Inc. *Excite, Inc. became publisher in 1998*

> *Alternative*
>
> If the changes have been numerous, make a general note.

2.17.8 Note on Distribution Statement

2.17.8.1 Scope

A ***note on distribution statement*** is a note providing information on:

details of the place of distribution, distributor, or date of distribution

or

changes in the place of distribution, distributor, or distributor's name.

2.17.8.2 Sources of Information

Take information for use in a note on a distribution statement from any source.

2.17.8.3 Details Relating to Distribution Statement

Make notes on details relating to place of distribution, distributor, or date of distribution not recorded in the distribution statement element, if considered important for identification or access.

Distributed in the U.K. by: EAV Ltd

2.17.8.4 Change in Distribution Statement

Make notes on changes in place of distribution and/or the distributor's name as appropriate to the mode of issuance of the resource:

multipart monographs (see **2.17.8.4.1**)

serials (see **2.17.8.4.2**)

integrating resources (see **2.17.8.4.3**).

2.17.8.4.1 Multipart Monographs

Make notes on differences in place of distribution and/or distributors' names from one part of a multipart monograph to another (see **2.9.1.5.1**), if considered important for identification or access.

> ***Alternative***
> If the changes have been numerous, make a general note.

2.17.8.4.2 Serials

Make notes on changes in place of distribution and/or distributors' names that occur after the first/earliest issue or part of a serial (see **2.9.1.5.2**), if considered important for identification or access.

> ***Alternative***
> If the changes have been numerous, make a general note.

2.17.8.4.3 Integrating Resources

Make notes on place of distribution and/or distributors' names no longer present on the current iteration of an integrating resource, or that appeared in a different form on earlier iterations (see **2.9.1.5.3**), if considered important for identification or access.

> ***Alternative***
> If the changes have been numerous, make a general note.

2.17.9 Note on Manufacture Statement

2.17.9.1 Scope

A ***note on manufacture statement*** is a note providing information on:

details of the place of manufacture, manufacturer, or date of manufacture

or

changes in the place of manufacture, manufacturer, or manufacturer's name.

2.17.9.2 Sources of Information

Take information for use in a note on a manufacture statement from any source.

2.17.9.3 Details Relating to Manufacture Statement

Make notes on details relating to place of manufacture, manufacturer, or date of manufacture not recorded in the manufacture statement element, if considered important for identification or access.

2.17.9.4 Change in Manufacture Statement

Make notes on changes in place of manufacture and/or the manufacturer's name as appropriate to the mode of issuance of the resource:

multipart monographs (see **2.17.9.4.1**)

serials (see **2.17.9.4.2**)

integrating resources (see **2.17.9.4.3**).

2.17.9.4.1 Multipart Monographs

Make notes on differences in place of manufacture and/or manufacturers' names from one part of a multipart monograph to another (see **2.10.1.5.1**), if considered important for identification or access.

> *Alternative*
>
> If the changes have been numerous, make a general note.

2.17.9.4.2 Serials

Make notes on changes in place of manufacture and/or manufacturers' names that occur after the first/earliest issue or part of a serial (see **2.10.1.5.2**) if considered important for identification or access.

> *Alternative*
>
> If the changes have been numerous, make a general note.

2.17.9.4.3 Integrating Resources

Make notes on place of manufacture and/or manufacturers' names no longer present on the current iteration of an integrating resource, or that appeared in a different form on earlier iterations (see **2.10.1.5.3**), if considered important for identification or access.

> *Alternative*
>
> If the changes have been numerous, make a general note.

2.17.10 Note on Copyright Date

2.17.10.1 Scope

A ***note on copyright date*** is a note providing information on copyright dates not recorded as part of the copyright date element.

2.17.10.2 Sources of Information

Take information for notes on copyright dates from any source.

2.17.10.3 Details Relating to Copyright Dates

Record details on copyright dates not recorded as part of the copyright date element (see **2.11.1.3**).

> CD-ROM is copyright 2001
>
> *Copyright date recorded as:* 2002
>
> French language edition ©1982
>
> *Copyright date recorded as:* copyright 1987. *Resource described is a translation of the French language edition.*

2.17.11 Note on Series Statement

2.17.11.1 Scope

A ***note on series statement*** is a note providing information on:

complex series statements

incorrect numbering within series

or

changes in series statements.

2.17.11.2 Sources of Information

Take information for notes on series statements from any source.

2.17.11.3 Complex Series Statements

Make a note on information relating to series that is too complex to be recorded in a series statement.

> Pts. 1 and 2 in series: African perspective. Pts. 3 and 4 in series: Third World series. Pt. 5 in both series

2.17.11.4 Incorrect Numbering within Series

Make a note giving the correct numbering within a series or subseries if the numbering transcribed from the source of information is known to be incorrect (see **2.12.9.3**).

> Series numbering should read: Bd. 25
> *Numbering transcribed from source:* Bd. 24

2.17.11.5 Change in Series Statements

Make notes on changes in series statements as appropriate to the mode of issuance of the resource:

multipart monographs and serials (see **2.17.11.5.1**)

integrating resources (see **2.17.11.5.2**).

2.17.11.5.1 Multipart Monographs and Serials

Make notes on changes in series information that occur after the first/earliest part of a multipart monograph or serial if:

the changes are not already recorded as part of the series statement (see **2.12.1.6.1**)

and

the changes are considered important for identification or access.

Alternative

If the changes have been numerous, make a general note.

> Subtitle of series varies

2.17.11.5.2 Integrating Resources

Make notes on series information no longer present on the current iteration of an integrating resource (see **2.12.1.6.2**), if the deletions are considered important for identification or access.

Series title, 1991–1996: Client representation workbooks
Current iteration has series title: Special tax topics workbooks

If a series statement is added on a later iteration, make a note about the publication date of that iteration.

Series title began 1997
Resource began in 1995 without a series title

Alternative
If the changes have been numerous, make a general note.

2.17.12 Note on Frequency

2.17.12.1 Scope

A ***note on frequency*** is a note providing details on:

the frequency of release of issues or parts of a serial
the frequency of updates to an integrating resource
the currency of the contents

or

changes in frequency.

2.17.12.2 Sources of Information

Take information for notes on frequency from any source.

2.17.12.3 Details on Frequency of Updating or Currency of the Contents

Make notes providing details on the following:

a) the frequency of release of issues or parts of a serial

b) the frequency of updates to an integrating resource

c) the currency of the contents.

Monthly (except Aug.)
Monthly (during school year)
Several times a week
Six issues yearly
Revised edition issued every 4 months
Updated daily, except weekends
Continually updated
Includes amendments through order of December 5, 1983, effective April 1, 1984

2.17.12.4 Change in Frequency

Make notes on changes in frequency, stating the frequencies and their respective dates in chronological order.

Bimonthly, Nov./Dec. 1980–Mar./Apr. 1992; monthly, May 1992–

Alternative

If the changes have been numerous, make a general note.

Frequency varies

Frequency of updates varies

2.17.13 Note on Issue, Part, or Iteration Used as the Basis for Identification of the Resource

2.17.13.1 Scope

A ***note on issue, part, or iteration used as the basis for identification of the resource*** is a note identifying what was used to identify the resource:

the issue or part of a multipart monograph or serial

or

the iteration of an integrating resource.

For an online resource, the note on issue, part, or iteration used as the basis for identification can also include the date on which the resource was viewed for description.

2.17.13.2 Sources of Information

Take information for notes on the issue, part, or iteration used as the basis for the identification of the resource from any source.

2.17.13.3 Issue or Part Used as the Basis for the Identification of a Multipart Monograph or Serial

In some cases, the identification of a multipart monograph or a serial is not based on the first released issue or part (see **2.1.2.3**). When this occurs, make a note identifying the issue or part used as the basis for the identification.

Apply these additional instructions, as applicable:

numbered serials (see **2.17.13.3.1**)
unnumbered serials (see **2.17.13.3.2**)
multipart monographs (see **2.17.13.3.3**).

Identification of the resource based on: part 2, published 1998

Identification of the resource based on: Vol. 1, no. 3 (Aug. 1999)

Latest issue consulted: 1999/10

2.17.13.3.1 Numbered Serials

If more than one issue or part has been consulted, make a separate note identifying the latest issue or part consulted in preparing the description.

> Identification of the resource based on: no. 8 (Jan./June 1997)
> Latest issue consulted: no. 12 (Jan./June 1999)
>
> Latest issue consulted: 2001/3
> *Description based on 1991/1, the first issue*

Do not make a note of earliest and/or latest issues or parts consulted if they are the same as those recorded in the numbering of serials element (see **2.6**).

2.17.13.3.2 Unnumbered Serials

Make a note identifying the earliest issue or part consulted and its date of publication. If other issues or parts have also been consulted, make a separate note identifying the latest issue or part consulted and its date.

> Identification of the resource based on: Labor and economic reforms in Latin America and the Caribbean, 1995
>
> Identification of the resource based on: The wood demon / by Anton Pavlovich Chekhov; translated by Nicholas Saunders and Frank Dwyer, 1993
> Latest issue consulted: Ibsen : four major plays / translated by Rick Davis and Brian Johnson, 1995

2.17.13.3.3 Multipart Monographs

Make a note identifying the part of a multipart monograph on which the identification of the resource is based and/or its number or publication date, as appropriate. If more than one part has been consulted, make a separate note identifying the latest part consulted in making the description.

2.17.13.4 Iteration Used as the Basis for the Identification of an Integrating Resource

Make a note identifying the latest iteration of an integrating resource consulted in preparing the description.

> Identification of the resource based on: 1994 ed. through update 10
>
> Identification of the resource based on version consulted: Oct. 26, 2000

2.17.13.5 Date of Viewing of an Online Resource

For online resources, make a note identifying the date on which the resource was viewed for description.

> Identification of the resource based on contents viewed on October 21, 1999
>
> Viewed on January 13, 2000
>
> Former title (as viewed October 6, 1999): Washington newspapers database
>
> Former subtitle (viewed on August 11, 1998): An online guide for amphibians in the United States and Canada
> *Other title information on current iteration:* An online guide for the identification of amphibians in North America north of Mexico

ATTRIBUTES OF THE ITEM

2.18 Custodial History of Item

2.18.1 Basic Instructions on Recording Custodial History of Item

2.18.1.1 Scope

Custodial history of item is a record of previous ownership or custodianship of an item.

2.18.1.2 Sources of Information

Take information on custodial history of the item from any source.

2.18.1.3 Recording Custodial History of Item

Record transfers of ownership, responsibility, or custody or control of the resource. Record the name of a previous owner or owners. Add the years of ownership after the name.

> Previously owned by L. McGarry, 1951–1963

2.19 Immediate Source of Acquisition of Item

2.19.1 Basic Instructions on Recording Immediate Source of Acquisition of Item

2.19.1.1 Scope

Immediate source of acquisition of item is the source from which the agency directly acquired an item and the circumstances under which it was received.

2.19.1.2 Sources of Information

Take information on immediate source of acquisition of the item from any source.

2.19.1.3 Recording Immediate Source of Acquisition

Record the source from which the item was acquired, the date of acquisition, and the method of acquisition, if this information is not confidential.

> Gift of Jascha Heifetz, Feb. 4, 1952
>
> Purchased from Sotheby's, London, May 26, 2000
>
> Received from Charles Edward Eaton, Chapel Hill, N.C., in a number of installments beginning in 1977

2.20 Identifier for the Item

2.20.1 Basic Instructions on Recording Identifiers for the Item

2.20.1.1 Scope

An *identifier for the item* is a character string associated with an item that serves to differentiate that item from other items.

2.20.1.2 Sources of Information

Take identifiers for the item from any source.

2.20.1.3 Facsimiles and Reproductions

When a facsimile or reproduction has an identifier or identifiers associated with the original item as well as with the facsimile or reproduction, record the identifier associated with the facsimile or reproduction (see identifier for the manifestation, **2.15**). Record any identifier associated with the original item as an identifier for a related item (see **28.1**).

2.20.1.4 Recording Identifiers for the Item

If there is a specified display format for the identifier for the item, record it using that format.

If there is no specified display format for the identifier, record it as it appears on the source. Precede the identifier with the name of the agency, etc., responsible for assigning the identifier, if readily ascertainable.

> National Library of Australia MS 1
> *Identifier for the item:* Journal of the H.M.S. Endeavour, 1768–1771

2.20.1.5 Incorrect Identifiers

If an identifier is known to be incorrectly represented in the resource, record the number as it appears. Indicate that the number is incorrect, cancelled, or invalid, as appropriate.

2.21 Note on Item

2.21.1 Basic Instructions on Making Notes on Items

2.21.1.1 Scope

A ***note on item*** is a note providing information on attributes of the item.

For notes on describing item-specific carrier characteristics, see **3.22**.

2.21.1.2 Sources of Information

Take information for notes on item from any source.

2.21.1.3 Making Notes on Item

Make a note on item by applying the general guidelines at **1.10**.

3

DESCRIBING CARRIERS

3.0 Purpose and Scope

This chapter provides general guidelines and instructions on recording the attributes of the carrier of the resource. These attributes or characteristics are recorded using the elements covered in this chapter.

The elements in chapter 3 are typically used to select a resource that meets the user's needs in terms of:

a) the physical characteristics of the carrier

b) the formatting and encoding of the information contained in or stored on the carrier.

These elements are also used to identify a resource (i.e., to distinguish between resources with similar characteristics).

Not all of the elements covered in this chapter will be applicable to the description of a particular resource. For those elements that are applicable, the description of the resource should include at least those that are identified as core elements (see **1.3**).

3.1 General Guidelines on Describing Carriers

3.1.1 Sources of Information

Base the description of the carrier or carriers on evidence presented by the resource itself, or on any accompanying material or container. If additional information is considered important for identification or selection, take additional evidence from any source.

3.1.2 Manifestations Available in Different Formats

Manifestations of a work are sometimes available in different formats (e.g., as printed text and microfilm; as an audio disc and audiocassette). Record the elements that apply to the carrier of the manifestation being described.

For instructions on recording relationships to other available formats, see **27.1** (related manifestation).

3.1.3 Facsimiles and Reproductions

When describing a facsimile or reproduction, record the elements describing the carrier of the facsimile or reproduction.

For instructions on recording a relationship to the original manifestation, see **27.1** (related manifestation).

3.1.4 Resources Consisting of More Than One Carrier Type

When preparing a comprehensive description for a resource consisting of more than one carrier type, apply the method that is appropriate to the nature of the resource and the purpose of the description:

a) record only carrier type and extent of each carrier (see **3.1.4.1**)
or
b) record carrier type, extent, and other characteristics of each carrier (see **3.1.4.2**)
or
c) record the predominant carrier type and extent in general terms (see **3.1.4.3**).

Record additional characteristics of particular carriers if considered important for identification or selection (see **3.6–3.20**).

For instructions on recording information about the carrier of accompanying material, see **27.1** (related manifestation).

For instructions on recording extent for a comprehensive description of a collection, see **3.4.1.11**.

3.1.4.1 Recording Only Carrier Type and Extent of Each Carrier

If a detailed description of the characteristics of the carriers is not considered necessary, record only

a) the applicable carrier type or types (see **3.3**)
and
b) the extent of each type of carrier (see **3.4**).

computer disc
audio disc
sheet
Carrier types for a resource consisting of a computer disc, an audio disc, study prints, and a folded sheet

1 computer disc
1 audio disc
4 study prints
1 folded sheet
Extent of the same resource

Optional Addition

If the carriers are in a container, name the container and record its dimensions (see **3.5.1.5**).

slide
audiocassette
sheet
Carrier types for a resource consisting of slides, an audiocassette, and a map, all in a container

12 slides
1 audiocassette
1 map
Extent of the same resource

box 16 × 30 × 20 cm
Name and dimensions of the container of the same resource

3.1.4.2 Recording Carrier Type, Extent, and Other Characteristics of Each Carrier

If a detailed description of the characteristics of each carrier is considered important for identification or selection, record:

a) the applicable carrier type (see **3.3**)
and
b) the extent of each carrier (see **3.4**)
and
c) other characteristics of each carrier (see **3.5–3.19**).

slide
46 slides
5 × 5 cm
Carrier type, extent, and dimensions for the slides in a resource consisting of slides and an audiocassette

audiocassette
1 audiocassette
10 × 7 cm, 4 mm tape
analog

mono
Carrier type, extent, dimensions, type of recording, and configuration of playback channels for the audiocassette in the same resource

Optional Addition

If the carriers are in a container, name the container and record its dimensions (**3.5.1.5**).

audiocassette
1 audiocassette
10 × 7 cm, 4 mm tape
analog
4.75 cm/s
Carrier type, extent, dimensions, type of recording, and playing speed for the audiocassette in a resource consisting of an audiocassette and a leaflet in a container

volume
24 pages
15 cm
Carrier type, extent, and dimensions for the leaflet in the same resource

container 18 × 12 × 2 cm
Name and dimensions of the container of the same resource

3.1.4.3 Recording Predominant Carrier Type and Extent in General Terms

For a resource consisting of many different types of carriers, record:

a) the predominant carrier type (**3.3**)
and
b) the extent of the resource as a whole, describing the units as *various pieces* (see **3.4.1.5**).

Record details of the pieces in a note if considered important for identification or selection (see **3.21.2.3**).

sheet
27 various pieces
Predominant carrier type and extent recorded using a general term

Optional Omission

If the number of units cannot be readily ascertained or approximated, omit the number.

sheet
various pieces
Predominant carrier type and extent recorded using a general term, omitting the number of pieces

Optional Addition

If the carriers are in a container, name the container and record its dimensions (see **3.5.1.5**).

sheet
42 various pieces
Predominant carrier type and extent recorded using a general term

box 20 × 12 × 6 cm
Dimensions of the container

For instructions on recording extent for a comprehensive description of a collection, see **3.4.1.11**.

3.1.5 Online Resources

Record *online resource* as the carrier type for all online resources (see **3.3**).

For an online resource that is complete (or if the total extent is known), record the extent (see **3.4**).

1 online resource (1 image file)

1 online resource (75 pages)

Record other characteristics of the carrier, as applicable, if considered important for identification or selection (see **3.6–3.20**).

TIFF
Encoding format for an online resource

If:
the online resource consists of more than one file
and
a description of the characteristics of each file is considered important for identification or selection
then:
record the characteristics of each file (see **3.19**).

text file
RTF
73 KB
File type, encoding format, and file size for a text file in an online resource

audio file
WAV
18 MB
File type, encoding format, and file size for an audio file in the same online resource

3.1.6 Change in Carrier Characteristics

Record changes in carrier characteristics as appropriate to the mode of issuance of the resource:

multipart monographs and serials (see **3.1.6.1**)

integrating resources (see **3.1.6.2**).

These instructions apply to changes in the carrier characteristics of the resource being described. For instructions on describing manifestations in different formats, see **3.1.2**.

3.1.6.1 Multipart Monographs and Serials

If there is a change in the media type (**3.2**) in a subsequent issue or part of a multipart monograph or serial, create a new description (see **1.6**).

If there is a change in dimensions, apply the instructions at **3.5.1.8.1**.

If:

the carrier type (**3.3**) or other characteristics of the carrier (**3.6–3.20**) are changed in a subsequent issue or part

or

new carrier characteristics are introduced

then:

record the changed (or new) characteristics as instructed for those elements. Make a note if the change is considered important for identification or selection (see **3.21.4.3.1**).

> ***Exception***
>
> ***Serials***
>
> *If:*
>
> the carrier type (**3.3**) of a serial changes to *online resource* from another computer carrier
>
> *or*
>
> changes from *online resource* to another computer carrier
>
> *then:*
>
> create a new description (see **1.6.2.2**).

3.1.6.2 Integrating Resources

If there is a change in the media type (**3.2**) in a subsequent iteration of an integrating resource, create a new description (see **1.6**).

If there is a change in dimensions, apply the instructions at **3.5.1.8.2**.

If:

the carrier type (see **3.3**) or other characteristics of the carrier (see **3.6–3.20**) are changed in a subsequent iteration

or

new characteristics are introduced

then:

change the carrier description to reflect the current iteration. Make a note on the earlier characteristics if the change is considered important for identification (see **3.21.4.3.2**).

ATTRIBUTES OF THE MANIFESTATION

3.2 Media Type

3.2.1 Basic Instructions on Recording Media Type

3.2.1.1 Scope

Media type is a categorization reflecting the general type of intermediation device required to view, play, run, etc., the content of a resource.

3.2.1.2 Sources of Information

Use evidence presented by the resource itself (or on any accompanying material or container) as the basis for recording media type. Take additional evidence from any source.

3.2.1.3 Recording Media Type

Record the media type using one or more of the terms listed in table 3.1.

> ***Alternative***
>
> If the resource being described consists of more than one media type, record only:

a) the media type that applies to the predominant part of the resource (if there is a predominant part)

or

b) the media types that apply to the most substantial parts of the resource (including the predominant part, if there is one).

Use one or more of the terms listed in table 3.1, as appropriate.

TABLE 3.1

audio	Media used to store recorded sound, designed for use with a playback device such as a turntable, audiocassette player, CD player, or MP3 player. Includes media used to store digitally encoded as well as analog sound.
computer	Media used to store electronic files, designed for use with a computer. Includes media that are accessed remotely through file servers as well as direct-access media such as computer tapes and discs.
microform	Media used to store reduced-size images not readable to the human eye, designed for use with a device such as a microfilm or microfiche reader. Includes both transparent and opaque micrographic media.
microscopic	Media used to store minute objects, designed for use with a device such as a microscope to reveal details invisible to the naked eye.
projected	Media used to store moving or still images, designed for use with a projection device such as a motion picture film projector, slide projector, or overhead projector. Includes media designed to project both two-dimensional and three-dimensional images.
stereographic	Media used to store pairs of still images, designed for use with a device such as a stereoscope or stereograph viewer to give the effect of three dimensions.
unmediated	Media used to store content designed to be perceived directly through one or more of the human senses without the aid of an intermediating device. Includes media containing visual and/or tactile content produced using processes such as printing, engraving, lithography, etc., embossing, texturing, etc., or by means of handwriting, drawing, painting, etc. Also includes media used to convey three-dimensional forms such as sculptures, models, etc.
video	Media used to store moving or still images, designed for use with a playback device such as a videocassette player or DVD player. Includes media used to store digitally encoded as well as analog images.

If none of the terms listed in table 3.1 apply to the carrier of the resource being described, record *other*.

If the media type or types applicable to the resource being described cannot be readily ascertained, record *unspecified*.

3.3 Carrier Type

CORE ELEMENT

3.3.1 Basic Instructions on Recording Carrier Type

3.3.1.1 Scope

Carrier type is a categorization reflecting the format of the storage medium and housing of a carrier in combination with the type of intermediation device required to view, play, run, etc., the content of a resource.

3.3.1.2 Sources of Information

Use evidence presented by the resource itself (or on any accompanying material or container) as the basis for recording carrier type. Take additional evidence from any source.

3.3.1.3 Recording Carrier Type

Record the carrier type using one or more of the terms in the following list.

> *Alternative*
>
> If the resource being described consists of more than one carrier type, record only:
>
> a) the carrier type that applies to the predominant part of the resource (if there is a predominant part)
>
> *or*
>
> b) the carrier types that apply to the most substantial parts of the resource (including the predominant part, if there is one).
>
> Use one or more of the terms from the following list, as appropriate.

Audio carriers

audio cartridge
audio cylinder
audio disc
audio roll
audiocassette
audiotape reel
sound-track reel

Computer carriers

computer card
computer chip cartridge
computer disc
computer disc cartridge
computer tape cartridge
computer tape cassette
computer tape reel
online resource

Microform carriers

aperture card
microfiche
microfiche cassette
microfilm cartridge

microfilm cassette
microfilm reel
microfilm roll
microfilm slip
microopaque

Microscopic carriers

microscope slide

Projected image carriers

film cartridge
film cassette
film reel
film roll
filmslip
filmstrip
filmstrip cartridge
overhead transparency
slide

Stereographic carriers

stereograph card
stereograph disc

Unmediated carriers

card
flipchart
object
roll
sheet
volume

Video carriers

video cartridge
videocassette
videodisc
videotape reel

If none of the terms in the list apply to the carrier or carriers of the resource being described, record *other.*

If the carrier type or types applicable to the resource being described cannot be readily ascertained, record *unspecified.*

3.4 Extent

CORE ELEMENT

Extent is a core element only if the resource is complete or if the total extent is known. Record subunits only if readily ascertainable and considered important for identification or selection.

3.4.1 Basic Instructions on Recording Extent

3.4.1.1 Scope

Extent is the number and type of units and/or subunits making up a resource.

A *unit* is a physical or logical constituent of a resource (e.g., a volume, audiocassette, film reel, a map, a digital file).

A *subunit* is a physical or logical subdivision of a unit (e.g., a page of a volume, a frame of a microfiche, a record in a digital file).

For instructions on recording duration (i.e., playing time, running time, performance time, etc.), see **7.22**.

3.4.1.2 Sources of Information

Use evidence presented by the resource itself (or on any accompanying material or container) as the basis for recording the extent of the resource. Take additional evidence from any source.

3.4.1.3 Recording Extent

Record the extent of the resource by giving the number of units and the type of unit. For the type of unit, use an appropriate term from the list of carrier types at **3.3.1.3**. Record the term in the singular or plural, as applicable.

If:
the resource consists of more than one carrier type
and
information about the different carrier types is considered important for identification or selection
then:
record the extent by giving the number of units and the term for each carrier type.

Specify the number of subunits, if applicable (see **3.4.1.7–3.4.1.9**).

1 microfilm cassette

100 slides

2 audiotape reels

1 film reel

1 video cartridge

1 computer disc

1 online resource

3 microfiches

Alternative

Use a term in common usage (including a trade name, if applicable) to indicate the type of unit:

a) if the carrier is not in the list at **3.3.1.3**
or
b) as an alternative to a term listed at **3.3.1.3**, if preferred by the agency preparing the description.

audio slide

USB flash drive

If an applicable trade name or other similar specification is not used as the term for the type of unit, record that information as instructed at **3.20.1.3**.

Exceptions

Cartographic resources. For a printed, manuscript, graphic, or three-dimensional resource consisting of cartographic content (with or without accompanying text and/or illustrations), see **3.4.2**.

Notated music. For a printed or manuscript resource consisting of notated music (with or without accompanying text and/or illustrations), see **3.4.3**.

Still images. For drawings, paintings, prints, photographs, etc., see **3.4.4**.

Text. For resources consisting of printed or manuscript text (with or without accompanying illustrations), see **3.4.5**.

Three-dimensional forms. For resources consisting of one or more three-dimensional forms, see **3.4.6**.

For a resource that is part of a larger resource, see **3.4.1.12**.

For resources consisting of more than one type of carrier, see **3.1.4**.

3.4.1.4 Exact Number of Units Not Readily Ascertainable

If the exact number of units cannot be readily ascertained, record an approximate number preceded by *approximately*.

> approximately 600 slides

Optional Omission

If the number of units cannot be readily approximated, omit the number.

> slides

3.4.1.5 Units Cannot Be Named Concisely

If the units cannot be named concisely, record the number of physical units and describe them as *various pieces*. Record the details of the pieces in a note if considered important for identification or selection (see **3.21.2.3**).

> 48 various pieces

Optional Omission

If the number of units cannot be readily ascertained or approximated, omit the number.

> various pieces

3.4.1.6 Units and Sets of Units with Identical Content

If the units of the resource have identical content, add *identical* before the term indicating the type of unit.

> 30 identical microscope slides

If:

the resource consists of multiple sets of units

and

each set has identical content

then:

record the number of sets and the number of units in each set in the form *20 identical sets of 12 microscope slides*, etc.

> 24 identical sets of 2 computer discs

3.4.1.7 Number of Subunits

Specify the number of subunits (see **3.4.1.7.1–3.4.1.7.8**), if readily ascertainable and considered important for identification or selection. Record the number of subunits, in parentheses, following the term for the type of unit.

3.4.1.7.1 Computer Discs, Cartridges, Etc.

In some cases, a resource consists of one or more files in a format that parallels a print, manuscript, or graphic counterpart (e.g., PDF). When this occurs, specify the number of subunits by applying the instructions for extent of the appropriate parallel counterpart:

cartographic resources (see **3.4.2**)

notated music (see **3.4.3**)

still images (see **3.4.4**)

and/or

text (see **3.4.5**).

> 1 computer disc (184 remote-sensing images)
>
> 1 computer disc (xv pages, 150 maps)

For other types of files (e.g., audio files, video files, data files), specify the number of files. Use one or more terms listed at **3.19.2.3** to indicate the file type.

> 1 computer disc (8 audio files)
>
> 1 computer tape (3 data files)
>
> 1 computer disc (1 audio file, 3 video files)

Optional Addition

For a resource consisting of one or more program files and/or data files, add the number of statements and/or records, as appropriate.

> 1 computer tape (3 data files: 100, 460, 550 records)

If the number of subunits cannot be stated succinctly, record the details in a note if considered important for identification or selection (see **3.21.2.10**).

3.4.1.7.2 Filmstrips and Filmslips

Specify the number of frames or double frames.

1 filmstrip (28 frames)

1 filmstrip (10 double frames)

3.4.1.7.3 Flipcharts

Specify the number of sheets.

1 flipchart (8 sheets)

3.4.1.7.4 Microfiches and Microfilm

In some cases, a resource is in a format that parallels a print, manuscript, or graphic counterpart. When this occurs, specify the number of subunits by applying the instructions for extent of the appropriate parallel counterpart:

cartographic resources (see **3.4.2**)

notated music (see **3.4.3**)

still images (see **3.4.4**)

and/or

text (see **3.4.5**).

3 microfiches (1 score (118 pages))

1 microfilm reel (255 pages)

For other microfiche and microfilm resources, specify the number of frames.

1 microfiche (120 frames)

3.4.1.7.5 Online Resources

In some cases, a resource consists of one or more files in a format that parallels a print, manuscript, or graphic counterpart (e.g., PDF). When this occurs, specify the number of subunits by applying the instructions for extent of the appropriate parallel counterpart:

cartographic resources (see **3.4.2**)

notated music (see **3.4.3**)

still images (see **3.4.4**)

and/or

text (see **3.4.5**).

1 online resource (68 pages)

1 online resource (3 scores)

1 online resource (36 photographs)

For other types of files (e.g., audio files, video files, data files), specify the number of files. Use one or more terms listed at **3.19.2.3** to indicate the file type.

1 online resource (2 video files)

1 online resource (1 program file)

1 online resource (2 audio files, 1 video file)

Optional Addition

For a resource consisting of one or more program files and/or data files, add the number of statements and/or records, as appropriate.

1 online resource (1 program file: 96 statements)

If the number of subunits cannot be stated succinctly, record the details in a note if considered important for identification or selection (see **3.21.2.10**).

3.4.1.7.6 Overhead Transparencies

Specify the number of overlays or attached overlays.

1 overhead transparency (5 overlays)

1 overhead transparency (5 attached overlays)

3.4.1.7.7 Stereographs

Specify the number of pairs of frames.

1 stereograph disc (7 pairs of frames)

3.4.1.7.8 Videodiscs

For a videodisc that contains only still images, record the number of frames.

1 videodisc (45,876 frames)

3.4.1.8 Exact Number of Subunits Not Readily Ascertainable

If the subunits are unnumbered and their number cannot be readily ascertained, record an approximate number preceded by *approximately*.

1 filmstrip (approximately 100 frames)

3.4.1.9 Subunits in Resources Consisting of More Than One Unit

If:

the resource consists of more than one unit

and

each unit contains the same number of subunits

then:

specify the number of subunits in each unit as instructed at **3.4.1.7**, followed by *each*.

4 filmstrips (50 double frames each)

2 flipcharts (30 sheets each)

3 microfiches (120 frames each)

If the number of subunits in each unit is approximately the same, specify the approximate number of subunits in each unit. Apply the instructions at **3.4.1.8**, followed by *each*.

3 overhead transparencies (approximately 10 overlays each)

If the number of subunits in each unit is not the same (or approximately the same), apply one of these instructions, as applicable:

a) specify the total number of subunits (see **3.4.1.7**)
or
b) record an approximate total number of subunits (see **3.4.1.8**).

2 overhead transparencies (20 overlays)

2 microfiches (147 frames)

Optional Omission

Omit the total number of subunits and record only the number of units.

4 filmslips

3.4.1.10 Incomplete Resource

When preparing a comprehensive description for a resource that is not yet complete, record the term indicating the type of unit without the number. Apply also for a resource when the total number of units issued is unknown.

microscope slides

volumes

volumes (loose-leaf)

Alternative

Do not record extent for a resource that is not yet complete (or if the total number of units issued is unknown).

If:
the resource was planned to be in more than one unit, but not all have been issued
and
it appears that the resource will not be continued
then:
describe the incomplete set by recording the number of units issued. Make a note that no more units have been issued (see **3.21.2.4**).

3.4.1.11 Comprehensive Description of a Collection

When describing a collection as a whole, record the extent by using a method appropriate to the nature of the collection and the purpose of the description:

a) number of items, containers, or volumes (see **3.4.1.11.1**)
or
b) storage space (see **3.4.1.11.2**)
or
c) number and type of unit (see **3.4.1.11.3**).

3.4.1.11.1 Number of Items, Containers, or Volumes

Record the extent by giving the number or approximate number of items, or the number of containers or volumes.

> 123 items
>
> approximately 400 items
>
> 6 volumes
>
> 6 boxes

Optional Addition

If the number of volumes or containers is recorded, specify the number or approximate number of items.

> 3 volumes (183 items)
>
> 60 folders (1564 items)

3.4.1.11.2 Storage Space

Record the extent by giving the amount of storage space occupied by the collection in metric measurements and use the metric symbol *cm*, *m*, cm^3, or m^3, as appropriate.

> 10 m
>
> 1 m^3

Alternative

Record the amount of storage space occupied by the collection in the system of measurement preferred by the agency preparing the description. Use symbols or abbreviate terms for units of measurement as instructed in appendix B (**B.5.2**), as applicable.

> 40 linear ft.
>
> 10 cubic ft.

Optional Addition

Specify the number or approximate number of containers or volumes and/or items.

10 m (approximately 2250 items)

1.8 m (75 volumes)

3.6 m (2,400 folders)

1.5 m (30 items bound, 37 items unbound)

0.6 m (approximately 70 items, 12 bound)

3 m (12 boxes)

4.5 m (12 boxes, approximately 1000 items)

26.7 m (150 boxes, 109 oversize folders)

10 cm (1 box, 1 oversize folder)

3.4.1.11.3 Number and Type of Unit

Record the extent of each type of resource in the collection by giving the number of units and an appropriate term for each type.

68 photographs
16 architectural drawings

400 postcards

3.4.1.12 Analytical Description of a Part

When describing a resource that is part of a larger resource, record the extent of the part by applying one of these instructions:

a) number of units and/or subunits in the part (see **3.4.1.12.1**)
or
b) location of the part within the larger resource (see **3.4.1.12.2**).

3.4.1.12.1 Number of Units and/or Subunits in the Part

Record the extent of the part by giving the number of units and/or number of subunits, as appropriate. Apply the instructions at **3.4.1.3–3.4.1.10**.

310 pages

68 frames

3.4.1.12.2 Location of the Part within the Larger Resource

If the unit or subunit is numbered as part of a continuous sequence of numbering for the larger resource, record the position of the part within the larger resource. Indicate the specific unit or subunit in which the part is located.

pages 210–450

leaves 51–71

on side 1 of 1 audio disc

on reel 1 of 2 film reels

on cassette 3 of 4 microfilm cassettes

on side 2 of 1 videodisc

3.4.2 Extent of Cartographic Resource

CORE ELEMENT

Extent is a core element for cartographic resources only if the resource is complete or if the total extent is known.

3.4.2.1 Application

For a printed, manuscript, graphic, or three-dimensional resource consisting of cartographic content, record the extent by applying the instructions at **3.4.2.2–3.4.2.5**.

For resources consisting of cartographic content in other media (e.g., microforms), apply the basic instructions at **3.4.1**.

3.4.2.2 Recording Extent of a Cartographic Resource

Record the extent of the resource by giving the number of units and an appropriate term from the following list. Record the term in the singular or plural, as applicable.

atlas
diagram
globe
map
model
profile
remote-sensing image
section
view

If the resource consists of more than one type of unit, record the number of each applicable type.

1 map

3 diagrams

1 globe

1 model

If the exact number of units is not readily ascertainable, record an estimated number preceded by *approximately*.

approximately 800 maps

If none of the terms in the list is appropriate, use another concise term or terms to indicate the type of unit. Use terms from the lists for still images (**3.4.4.2**) or three-dimensional forms (**3.4.6.2**), if applicable.

7 wall charts

52 playing cards

Apply these additional basic instructions, as applicable:

units or sets of units with identical content (see **3.4.1.6**)

incomplete resources (see **3.4.1.10**)

comprehensive description of a collection (see **3.4.1.11**)

analytical description of a part (see **3.4.1.12**).

3.4.2.3 More Than One Cartographic Unit on One or More Sheets

If:
the resource consists of two or more sheets
and
each sheet contains a single cartographic unit
then:
record the extent as instructed at **3.4.2.2**.

If:
the resource consists of more than one cartographic unit on one or more sheets
and
the number of cartographic units differs from the number of sheets
then:
record the number of cartographic units and specify the number of sheets.

6 maps on 1 sheet

8 sections on 3 sheets

3.4.2.4 Cartographic Unit Presented in More Than One Segment

If:
the cartographic unit is presented in more than one segment designed to fit together to form one or more cartographic units
and
all the segments are on a single sheet
then:
record the number of complete cartographic units followed by *in* and the number of segments.

1 section in 4 segments

2 views in 6 segments

If the segments are not all on one sheet, record the number of complete cartographic units followed by *on* and the number of sheets.

1 map on 4 sheets

3.4.2.5 Atlases

Specify the number of volumes and/or pages, etc., in an atlas (see **3.4.5**). Record this information in parentheses following the term *atlas*.

1 atlas (3 volumes)

1 atlas (xvii, 37 pages, 74 leaves of plates)

1 atlas (1 volume (various pagings))

3.4.3 Extent of Notated Music

CORE ELEMENT

Extent is a core element for notated music resources only if the resource is complete or if the total extent is known.

3.4.3.1 Application

For a printed or manuscript resource consisting of notated music (with or without accompanying text and/or illustrations), record the extent by applying the instructions at **3.4.3.2**.

For resources consisting of notated music in other media (e.g., microforms), apply the basic instructions at 3.4.1.

3.4.3.2 Recording Extent of Notated Music

Record the extent of the resource by giving the number of units and an appropriate term for the format of notated music from the list at **7.20.1.3** .

If the resource consists of more than one type of unit, record the number of each applicable type in the order specified at **7.20.1.3**.

Record the term in the singular or plural, as applicable.

Specify the number of volumes and/or pages, leaves, or columns as instructed at **3.4.5**. Record this information in parentheses, following the term for the format of notated music.

1 score (38 leaves)

1 vocal score (x, 190 pages)

1 condensed score (2 volumes)

1 score (23 pages)
1 piano conductor part (8 pages)

1 choir book (240 pages)

1 table book (50 unnumbered pages)

Exceptions

Resource containing a set of parts. If the resource contains a set of parts, record the number of parts but omit the number of volumes and/or pages, leaves, or columns applicable to the parts.

1 score (viii, 278 pages)
24 parts

Resource consisting of a score and one or more parts in a single physical unit. If the resource consists of both a score and one or more parts in a single physical unit, record the extent in the form: *1 score and 4 parts*, etc., followed by the number of pages, leaves, or columns, in parentheses.

1 score and 1 part (5 pages)
Part printed on page 5

1 score and 3 parts (19 pages)
Parts printed on pages 11–19

Apply these additional basic instructions, as applicable:

units or sets of units with identical content (see **3.4.1.6**)
incomplete resources (see **3.4.1.10**)
comprehensive description of a collection (see **3.4.1.11**)
analytical description of a part (see **3.4.1.12**).

3.4.4 Extent of Still Image

CORE ELEMENT

Extent is a core element for still image resources only if the resource is complete or if the total extent is known.

3.4.4.1 Application

For a resource consisting of one or more still images in the form of drawings, paintings, prints, photographs, etc., record the extent by applying the instructions at **3.4.4.2–3.4.4.5**.

For resources consisting of still images in other media (e.g., slides, transparencies), apply the basic instructions at **3.4.1**.

For cartographic content in the form of still images, see **3.4.2**.

3.4.4.2 Recording Extent of Still Images

Record the extent of a resource consisting of one or more still images by giving the number of units and an appropriate term from the following list. Record the term in the singular or plural, as applicable.

activity card
chart
collage
drawing
flash card
icon
painting
photograph
picture
postcard
poster
print
radiograph
study print
technical drawing
wall chart

If the resource consists of more than one type of unit, record the number of each applicable type.

1 drawing
3 wall charts

If the exact number of units is not readily ascertainable, record an estimated number preceded by *approximately*.

approximately 1,000 photographs

If none of the terms in the list is appropriate, use another concise term or terms to indicate the type of unit.

7 flannel board pieces

Apply these additional basic instructions, as applicable:

units or sets of units with identical content (see **3.4.1.6**)
incomplete resources (see **3.4.1.10**)
comprehensive description of a collection (see **3.4.1.11**)
analytical description of a part (see **3.4.1.12**).

3.4.4.3 More Than One Image on One or More Carriers

If:
the resource consists of two or more carriers
and
each carrier contains a single image
then:
record the extent as instructed at **3.4.4.2**.

If:
the resource consists of two or more images on one or more carriers
and
the number of images differs from the number of carriers
then:
record the number of images and specify the number of carriers.

2 drawings on 1 sheet

3.4.4.4 One Image Spanning More Than One Carrier

If the resource consists of one image spanning more than one carrier, record *1 drawing*, etc., and specify the number of carriers.

1 print on 24 sheets

3.4.4.5 Albums, Portfolios, Etc.

For a resource consisting of one or more albums, portfolios, cases, etc., containing drawings, prints, photographs, etc., record the extent by giving the number of units and an appropriate term for the type of unit.

1 portfolio

2 sketchbooks

Optional Addition

Specify the number of drawings, etc., and use one or more appropriate terms from the list at **3.4.4.2**. Record this information in parentheses following the term for the container.

1 portfolio (40 prints)

3.4.5 Extent of Text

CORE ELEMENT

Extent is a core element for text resources only if the resource is complete or if the total extent is known.

3.4.5.1 Application

For a printed or manuscript resource consisting of text (with or without illustrations), record the extent by applying the instructions at **3.4.5.2–3.4.5.22**. These instructions apply to text resources in volumes, sheets, portfolios or cases.

Also apply the instructions at **3.4.5.2–3.4.5.22** to subunits in an atlas (see **3.4.2.5**) or in a resource consisting of notated music (see **3.4.3.2**).

For resources consisting of text in other media (e.g., microforms), apply the basic instructions at **3.4.1**.

RESOURCE CONSISTING OF A SINGLE UNIT

3.4.5.2 Single Volume with Numbered Pages, Leaves, or Columns

For a resource consisting of a single volume, record the extent in terms of pages, leaves, or columns according to the type of sequence used in the resource. Apply the following general guidelines:

a) If the volume is numbered in terms of pages, record the number of pages.

b) If the volume is numbered in terms of leaves, record the number of leaves.

c) If the volume consists of pages with more than one column to a page and is numbered in columns, record the number of columns.

d) If the volume consists of sequences of leaves and pages, or pages and numbered columns, or leaves and numbered columns, record each sequence.[1]

If the volume is numbered as leaves but has text on both sides, see **3.4.5.5** or make an explanatory note (see **3.21.2.11**).

Exceptions

Early printed resources. For early printed resources, record each sequence of leaves, pages, or columns in the terms and form presented. If the resource is printed in pages but numbered as leaves, record the numbering as leaves.

If required for identification or selection, record more precise information about pagination, blank leaves, or other aspects of collation: either expand the extent (if this can be done succinctly) or make a note (see **3.21.2.9**).

Updating loose-leafs. If the resource is an updating loose-leaf, record *1 volume* followed by *loose-leaf,* in parentheses.

1 volume (loose-leaf)

Serials. See also **3.4.5.16**.

Record the number of pages, leaves, or columns in terms of the numbered or lettered sequences in the resource. Record the last numbered page, leaf, or column in each sequence and follow it with the appropriate term.

327 pages

321 leaves

381 columns

xvii, 323 pages

27 pages, 300 leaves

Exception

For complicated or irregular paging, etc., see **3.4.5.8**.

Record pages, etc., that are lettered inclusively in the form *A–K pages*, *a–d leaves*, etc.

A–Z pages
Pages lettered: A–Z

Record pages, etc., that are numbered in words by giving the numeric equivalent.

32 pages
Pages numbered in words

Apply the additional instructions at **3.4.5.3–3.4.5.13** as applicable to the resource being described.

1. A sequence of pages or leaves is: (1) a separately numbered group of pages, leaves, etc.; (2) an unnumbered group of pages, etc., that stands apart from other groups in the publication; or (3) a number of pages or leaves of plates distributed throughout the publication.

3.4.5.3 Single Volume with Unnumbered Pages, Leaves, or Columns

If the resource consists entirely of unnumbered pages, leaves, or columns, record the number of pages, leaves, or columns using one of the following methods:

a) Record the exact number of pages, leaves, or columns, if readily ascertainable.

93 unnumbered pages

b) If the number is not readily ascertainable, record an estimated number of pages, leaves, or columns preceded by *approximately*.

approximately 600 pages

c) Record *1 volume (unpaged)*.

1 volume (unpaged)

When recording the number or estimated number of unnumbered pages or leaves, apply the following guidelines:

a) If the leaves are printed or written on both sides, record the extent in terms of pages.

b) If the leaves are printed or written on one side, record the extent in terms of leaves.

3.4.5.3.1 Numbered and Unnumbered Sequences

If the resource consists of both numbered and unnumbered sequences of pages, leaves, or columns, disregard the unnumbered sequences, unless:

a) an unnumbered sequence constitutes a substantial part of the resource (see also **3.4.5.8**)
or
b) an unnumbered sequence includes pages, etc., that are referred to in a note.

Exception

Early printed resources. For early printed resources, record unnumbered sequences of pages, leaves, or columns.

12 unnumbered pages, 72 pages, 10 unnumbered pages, 48 pages, 6 unnumbered pages, 228 pages, 16 unnumbered pages

91 leaves, 1 unnumbered leaf
Last leaf blank

When recording a sequence of unnumbered pages, etc., record:

either
a) the exact number (if the number is readily ascertainable) followed by *unnumbered pages*, etc.
or
b) an estimated number preceded by *approximately*
or
c) *unnumbered sequence of pages*, etc.

33 leaves, 31 unnumbered leaves
Unnumbered sequence constitutes substantial part; exact number of leaves ascertainable

8, vii, approximately 300, 73 pages
Unnumbered sequence constitutes substantial part; number of pages estimated

27 pages, unnumbered sequence of leaves
Numbered pages and a sequence of unnumbered leaves

8 unnumbered pages, 155 pages
Bibliography referred to in a note appears on 6th preliminary page

3.4.5.3.2 Inessential Matter

Disregard unnumbered sequences of inessential matter (advertising, blank pages, etc.).

Exception

Early printed resources. For early printed resources, record pages containing advertisements (when this can be done succinctly) if those pages are:

a) included in the same pagination sequence as the text
or
b) printed on the pages of an initial or final gathering also containing leaves or pages of text
or
c) printed on a separate gathering in a resource that is continuously signed.

40 leaves, 8 unnumbered pages

Otherwise, make a note (see **3.21.2.9**).

3.4.5.4 Change in Form of Numbering within a Sequence

If the form of numbering within a sequence changes (e.g., from roman to arabic numerals), ignore the numbering of the first part of the sequence.

176 pages
Pages numbered: i–xii, 13–176

Exception

Early printed resources. For early printed resources, record the numbering in the form presented.

xii pages, 1 unnumbered page, 14–176 pages
First twelve pages of the sequence numbered in lowercase roman numerals, followed by one unnumbered page, followed by remainder of the sequence numbered in arabic numerals

3.4.5.5 Misleading Numbering

In some cases, the numbering on the last page, leaf, or column of a sequence does not represent the total number in that sequence. When this occurs, do not correct it unless it gives a completely false impression of the extent of the resource (e.g., when only alternate pages are numbered or when the number on the last page, leaf, or column of the sequence is misprinted).

When correcting misleading numbering, record the numbering as it appears on the last page or leaf followed by *that is* and the correct number.

48 leaves, that is, 96 pages
Numbered leaves with text on both sides

329, that is, 392 pages

3.4.5.6 Incomplete Volume

If:
the last part of the volume is missing
and
the extent of the complete volume cannot be ascertained
then:
record the number of the last numbered page, leaf, or column using the appropriate term and add *(incomplete).*

xxiv, 179 pages (incomplete)

Record this imperfection as a note on item-specific carrier characteristic (see **3.22.1**).

If:
pages or leaves appear to be missing from both the first and last part of the volume
and
the extent of the complete volume cannot be ascertained
then:
record the first and last numbers of the pages, leaves, or columns preceded by the appropriate term.

leaves 81–149

Record this imperfection as a note on item-specific carrier characteristic (see **3.22.1**).

3.4.5.7 Pages, Etc., Numbered as Part of a Larger Sequence

If the pages, etc., are numbered as part of a larger sequence (e.g., as part of the continuous paging for a multivolume resource), record the first and last numbers of the pages, etc., preceded by the appropriate term.

pages 713–797

If the resource has pagination of its own as well as pagination forming part of a larger sequence, record the pagination for the individual resource. Make a note on pagination forming part of the larger sequence (see **3.21.2.6**).

328 pages
Pages also numbered as part of larger resource: 501–828

3.4.5.8 Complicated or Irregular Paging, Etc.

If the resource has complicated or irregular paging, etc., record the number of pages, leaves, or columns by using one of the following methods:

a) Record the total number of pages, leaves, or columns (excluding those that are blank or contain advertising or other inessential matter) followed by *in various pagings*, *in various foliations*, or *in various numberings*, as appropriate.

> 1000 pages in various pagings
>
> 256 leaves in various foliations
>
> 1283 columns in various numberings

b) Record the number of pages, leaves, or columns in the main sequences of the pagination and add the total number of the remaining variously numbered or unnumbered sequences.

> 560, 223 pages, 217 variously numbered pages
> *Resource with 1000 pages in various pagings*
>
> 366, 98 pages, 99 unnumbered pages

c) Record *1 volume (various pagings).*

> 1 volume (various pagings)
> *Resource with 1000 pages in various pagings*

Exception

Early printed resources. For early printed resources, record the paging, etc., in the form and sequence presented.

> 12 unnumbered leaves, 74 leaves, 32 unnumbered leaves, 62 columns, 9 unnumbered pages

3.4.5.9 Leaves or Pages of Plates

If the leaves or pages of plates in a resource are not included in the numbering for a sequence or sequences of pages or leaves of text, etc., record the number of leaves or pages of plates at the end of the sequence or sequences of pagination, etc. Record the number of leaves or pages of plates after the pagination, etc., whether the plates are found together or distributed throughout the resource.

> 246 pages, 32 pages of plates
>
> x, 32, 73 pages, 1 leaf of plates

If the resource contains both leaves and pages of plates, record the number in terms of whichever is predominant.

> 323 pages, 19 unnumbered pages of plates
> *Contains 16 pages and 3 leaves of plates*

If the numbering of the leaves or pages of plates is complex or irregular, see **3.4.5.8**.

Exception

Early printed resources. For early printed resources, if the leaves and pages of plates are numbered, or if there are both numbered and unnumbered plates, record each sequence of leaves and pages of plates in the appropriate terms.

246 pages, 38 leaves of plates, 24 pages of plates

Disregard unnumbered sequences of plates, unless:

a) an unnumbered sequence of plates forms a substantial part of the resource (see also **3.4.5.8**)
or
b) an unnumbered sequence includes plates that are referred to in a note.

xii, 24 pages, 212 leaves of plates, 43 unnumbered leaves of plates
Unnumbered sequence constitutes substantial part

xvi, 249 pages, 12 unnumbered leaves of plates
Unnumbered sequence includes a plate referred to in a note

3.4.5.10 Folded Leaves

If leaves are folded, record that they are folded.

122 folded leaves

230 pages, 25 leaves of plates (some folded)

25 folded leaves of plates

3.4.5.11 Double Leaves

If numbered pages, leaves, or columns are presented on a double leaf (e.g., books in the traditional East Asian style), record them as pages, leaves, or columns according to their numbering. If they are unnumbered, count each double leaf as two pages.

Make a note to explain the format (see **3.21.2.11**).

3.4.5.12 Duplicated Paging, Etc.

If the paging is duplicated (e.g., in some books with parallel texts), record both pagings and make an explanatory note (see **3.21.2.7**).

xii, 35, 35 pages

xi, EN185, FR189 pages
Bilingual dictionary with English to French terms followed by French to English terms separately paged. EN and FR appear on the resource

3.4.5.13 Pages Numbered in Opposite Directions

If the resource has groups of pages numbered in opposite directions (e.g., in some books with texts in two languages), record all the pagings. Record the pagings of the various groups in order, starting from the title page selected for the description.

iv, 127, 135, vii pages

Text in English and French on inverted pages; English title page selected

ix, 155, 126, x pages

Text in English and Hebrew; English title page selected

3.4.5.14 Single Sheet

Record the extent of a resource consisting of a single sheet as *1 sheet.*

1 sheet

If the sheet is designed to be read in pages when folded, record the extent as *1 folded sheet* followed by the number of pages laid out on the sheet, in parentheses.

1 folded sheet (8 pages)

Exception

Early printed resources. If an early printed resource consists of a single sheet designed to be used unfolded (whether issued folded or unfolded), include a count of the number of pages printed. Do not count blank pages. Record the number of pages in parentheses following the term *1 sheet.*

If a single sheet is folded into multiple panels and designed to be used folded, include a count of the number of physical panels on one side of the sheet when unfolded. Count both blank panels and panels containing text, illustrations, etc. Record the number of panels in parentheses following the term *1 folded sheet.*

1 folded sheet (16 panels)

Provide details of the sheet's layout (including the numbering of the panels) in a note if considered important for identification or selection (see **3.21.2.9**).

3.4.5.15 Single Portfolio or Case

For a resource consisting of one or more sheets, etc., housed in a single portfolio or case, record the extent as *1 portfolio* or *1 case*, as appropriate.

1 portfolio

Optional Addition

Specify the number and type of subunits (e.g., pages, leaves, columns, sheets, volumes) in parentheses following the term *1 portfolio* or *1 case*, as appropriate.

1 portfolio (24 sheets)

1 case (30 pages, 2 sheets)

For cases consisting of two or more volumes, see **3.4.5.16**.

RESOURCE CONSISTING OF MORE THAN ONE UNIT

3.4.5.16 More Than One Volume

If the resource consists of more than one volume, record the extent by giving the number of volumes and the term *volumes*.

3 volumes

Exceptions

Completed serials. For serials, record the extent by giving the number of bibliographic volumes as reflected in the numbering of the serial (see **2.6**) instead of the number of physical volumes.

Incomplete resources. If the resource is not yet complete (or if the total number of volumes to be issued is unknown), apply the instructions at **3.4.1.10**.

3.4.5.17 Continuously Paged Volumes

If the volumes are continuously paged, specify the number of pages, leaves, or columns (see **3.4.5.2–3.4.5.13**) in parentheses, following the term for the type of unit. Ignore separately paged sequences of preliminary matter in volumes other than the first.

2 volumes (xxxxi, 999 pages)

3 volumes (xx, 800 pages)
Pages numbered: i–xx, 1–201; i–xx, 202–513; i–xxi, 514–800

Optional Omission

For multipart monographs and serials, omit the number of pages, etc. See also **3.4.1.10**.

3.4.5.18 Individually Paged Volumes

If the volumes are individually paged, record the number of volumes and omit the pagination.

Optional Addition

Specify the number of pages, leaves, or columns in each volume (see **3.4.5.2–3.4.5.13**). Record this information in parentheses, following the term for the type of unit.

2 volumes (xvi, 329; xx, 412 pages)

3.4.5.19 Updating Loose-Leafs

If the resource is an updating loose-leaf, record the number of volumes followed by *loose-leaf*, in parentheses. For incomplete resources, see also **3.4.1.10**.

3 volumes (loose-leaf)

3.4.5.20 More Than One Sheet

If the resource consists of more than one sheet, record the extent by giving the number of sheets and the term *sheets*.

3 sheets

For sheets contained in a portfolio or case, see **3.4.5.15** or **3.4.5.21**.

3.4.5.21 More Than One Portfolio or Case

If the resource consists of more than one portfolio or case, record the extent by giving the number of units and *portfolios* or *cases*, as appropriate.

4 cases

Optional Addition

Specify the number and type of subunits (e.g., pages, leaves, columns, sheets, volumes) in each portfolio or case. Record this information in parentheses, following the term for the type of unit.

2 cases (iv pages, 16 leaves; iii pages, 20 leaves)

3.4.5.22 Units and Sets of Units with Identical Content

For a resource consisting of units or sets of units with identical content, apply the basic instructions at **3.4.1.6**.

3.4.6 Extent of Three-Dimensional Form

CORE ELEMENT

Extent is a core element for three-dimensional resources only if the resource is complete or if the total extent is known.

3.4.6.1 Application

For a resource consisting of one or more three-dimensional forms, record the extent by applying the instructions at **3.4.6.2–3.4.6.3**.

For globes and other cartographic resources in three-dimensional form, see **3.4.2**.

3.4.6.2 Recording Extent of Three-Dimensional Forms

Record the extent of a resource consisting of one or more three-dimensional forms by giving the number of units and an appropriate term from the following list. Record the term in the singular or plural, as applicable.

coin
diorama
exhibit
game
jigsaw puzzle
medal
mock-up
model
sculpture
specimen
toy

If the resource consists of more than one type of unit, record the number of each applicable type.

If the exact number of units is not readily ascertainable, record an estimated number preceded by *approximately*.

approximately 400 specimens

If none of the terms in the list is appropriate, use another concise term or terms to indicate the type of unit.

2 feather headbands
1 pair beaded moccasins

3 quilts

Apply these additional basic instructions, as applicable:

units or sets of units with identical content (see **3.4.1.6**)

incomplete resources (see **3.4.1.10**)

comprehensive description of a collection (see **3.4.1.11**)

analytical description of a part (see **3.4.1.12**).

3.4.6.3 Number of Subunits

When appropriate, specify the number and type or types of the component pieces, in parentheses, following the term for the type of unit.

1 jigsaw puzzle (1,000 pieces)

1 game (1 board, 50 cards, 5 role cards, 2 dice)

If the pieces cannot be named concisely or if their number cannot be readily ascertained, record *various pieces*.

2 games (various pieces)

Record the details of the pieces in a note (see **3.21.2.3**) if they are not recorded as part of the extent but are considered important for identification or selection.

3.5 Dimensions

3.5.1 Basic Instructions on Recording Dimensions

3.5.1.1 Scope

Dimensions are the measurements of the carrier or carriers and/or the container of a resource.

Dimensions include measurements of height, width, depth, length, gauge, and diameter.

For maps, etc., and still images, the dimensions can be:

a) the dimensions of the face of the map, etc., (see **3.5.2**) or of the pictorial area (see **3.5.3**)
and/or

b) the dimensions of the carrier.

3.5.1.2 Sources of Information

Use evidence presented by the resource itself (or on any accompanying material or container) as the basis for recording the dimensions of the resource. Take additional evidence from any source.

3.5.1.3 Recording Dimensions

Unless instructed otherwise, record dimensions in centimetres to the next whole centimetre up and use the metric symbol *cm* (e.g., if the height measures 17.2 centimetres, record *18 cm*).

Alternative

Record dimensions in the system of measurement preferred by the agency preparing the description. Use symbols or abbreviate terms for units of measurement as instructed in appendix B (**B.5.1**), as applicable.

3.5.1.4 Dimensions of Carrier

Record the dimensions of a carrier as instructed at **3.5.1.4.1–3.5.1.4.14**, as applicable. Unless instructed otherwise, record measurements as instructed at **3.5.1.3**.

3.5.1.4.1 Cards

Record the height × width of the card.

28 × 10 cm
Dimensions of a flash card

9 × 19 cm
Dimensions of an aperture card

8 × 13 cm
Dimensions of a microopaque

9 × 6 cm
Dimensions of a computer card

3.5.1.4.2 Cartridges

Audio cartridges. For audio cartridges, record the length × height of the face of the cartridge in centimetres followed by the width of the tape in millimetres. Record the width of the tape and use the metric symbol *mm*. Use a comma to separate the width of the tape from the dimensions of the cartridge.

14 × 10 cm, 7 mm tape

Computer cartridges. For computer cartridges, record the length of the side of the cartridge that is to be inserted into the machine.

10 cm
Dimensions of a computer chip cartridge

Film, filmstrip, and video cartridges. For film, filmstrip, and video cartridges, record the gauge (i.e., width) of the film or tape in millimetres and use the metric symbol *mm*. For 8 mm film, indicate whether the gauge is single, standard, super, or Maurer. Make a note on the length of the film or tape if considered important for identification or selection (see **3.21.3.3**).

standard 8 mm
Gauge of film in a film cartridge

35 mm
Gauge of film in a filmstrip cartridge

13 mm
Gauge of tape in a video cartridge

Microfilm cartridges. For microfilm cartridges, record the width of the film in millimetres and use the metric symbol *mm*.

35 mm
Width of film in a microfilm cartridge

3.5.1.4.3 Cassettes

Audiocassettes. For audiocassettes, record the length × height of the face of the cassette in centimetres followed by the width of the tape in millimetres. Record the width of the tape and use the metric symbol *mm*. Use a comma to separate the width of the tape from the dimensions of the cassette.

10 × 7 cm, 4 mm tape

Computer cassettes. For computer cassettes, record the length × height of the face of the cassette.

10 × 7 cm

Film and videocassettes. For film and videocassettes, record the gauge (i.e., width) of the film or tape in millimetres and use the metric symbol *mm*. For 8 mm film, indicate whether the gauge is single, standard, super, or Maurer. Make a note on the length of the film or tape if considered important for identification or selection (see **3.21.3.3**).

16 mm
Gauge of film in a film cassette

standard 8 mm
Gauge of tape in a videocassette

13 mm
Gauge of tape in a VHS videocassette

Microfiche cassettes. For microfiche cassettes, record the length × height of the face of the cassette.

Microfilm cassettes. For microfilm cassettes, record the width of the film in millimetres and use the metric symbol *mm*.

16 mm
Width of film in a microfilm cassette

3.5.1.4.4 Discs

Record the diameter of the disc.

> 30 cm
> *Diameter of an analog audio disc*
>
> 12 cm
> *Diameter of a digital audio disc*
>
> 21 cm
> *Diameter of a videodisc*
>
> 12 cm
> *Diameter of a computer disc*

3.5.1.4.5 Filmstrips and Filmslips

Record the gauge (i.e., width) of the film in millimetres and use the metric symbol *mm.*

> 35 mm

3.5.1.4.6 Flipcharts

Record the height × width of the flipchart.

> 23 × 18 cm

3.5.1.4.7 Microfiches

Record the height × width of the fiche.

> 11 × 15 cm

3.5.1.4.8 Overhead Transparencies

Record the height × width of the transparency, excluding any frame or mount. If applicable, make a note on the size as framed or mounted (see **3.21.3.3**).

> 26 × 22 cm

3.5.1.4.9 Reels

Audiotape reels. For audiotape reels, record the diameter of the reel in centimetres followed by the width of the tape in millimetres. Record the width of the tape and use the metric symbol *mm.* Use a comma to separate the width of the tape from the diameter of the reel.

> 18 cm, 13 mm tape

Computer tape reels. For computer tape reels, record the diameter of the reel in centimetres followed by the width of the tape in millimetres. Record the width of the tape and use the metric symbol *mm.* Use a comma to separate the width of the tape from the diameter of the reel.

31 cm, 13 mm tape

Film and videotape reels. For film and videotape reels, record the diameter of the reel in centimetres followed by the gauge (i.e., width) of the film or tape in millimetres and use the metric symbol *mm.* Use a comma to separate the gauge of the film or tape from the diameter of the reel. For 8 mm film, indicate whether the gauge is single, standard, super, or Maurer. Make a note on the length of the film or tape if considered important for identification or selection (see **3.21.3.3**).

18 cm, 25.4 mm
Videotape reel

Microfilm reels. For microfilm reels, record the diameter of the reel in centimetres followed by the width of the film in millimetres. Use the metric symbols *cm* and *mm*, respectively. Use a comma to separate the width of the film from the diameter of the reel.

11 cm, 25.4 mm

3.5.1.4.10 Rolls

Film and microfilm rolls. For film and microfilm rolls, record the gauge (i.e., width) of the film in millimetres and use the metric symbol *mm.* For 8 mm film, indicate whether the gauge is single, standard, super, or Maurer. Make a note on the length of the film if considered important for identification or selection (see **3.21.3.3**).

35 mm
Gauge of film in a filmstrip roll

super 8 mm
Gauge of film in a filmstrip roll

105 mm
Width of film in a microfilm roll

3.5.1.4.11 Sheets

Record the height × width of the sheet, excluding any frame or mount. If applicable, make a note on the size as framed or mounted (see **3.21.3.3**).

28 × 22 cm
Dimensions of a sheet of text

If the sheet is designed to be read in pages when folded, record only the height of the sheet when folded.

For other folded sheets, record the height × width when extended followed by the height × width when folded.

48 × 30 cm folded to 24 × 15 cm
Dimensions of a manuscript sheet

For scrolls, record the height × width of the unrolled scroll, followed by the height × diameter of the rolled scroll. Indicate that the dimensions are for an unrolled and rolled scroll.

> 27 × 471 cm rolled to 27 × 7 cm in diameter
> *Dimensions of a manuscript scroll*

Exceptions

Maps, etc. For maps, etc., see **3.5.2**.

Still images. For still images, see **3.5.3**.

3.5.1.4.12 Slides

Record the height × width of the slide.

> 5 × 5 cm
> *Dimensions of a photographic slide*
>
> 3 × 8 cm
> *Dimensions of a microscope slide*

3.5.1.4.13 Three-Dimensional Forms

For globes, record the diameter and indicate that it is the diameter.

> 12 cm in diameter

Other three-dimensional forms. For other three-dimensional forms, record the dimensions of the form itself. If necessary, add a word to indicate which dimension is being given. If multiple dimensions are given, record them as height × width × depth.

> 110 cm high
> *Dimensions of a sculpture*

Optional Omission

If the form is in a container, omit the dimensions of the form itself and record the dimensions of the container (see **3.5.1.5**).

3.5.1.4.14 Volumes

Record the height of the volume. If the volume measures less than 10 centimetres, record the height in millimetres and use the metric symbol *mm*.

> 22 cm
>
> 75 mm

Exceptions

If the width of the volume is either less than half the height or greater than the height, record the height × width.

20 × 8 cm

20 × 32 cm

If there is a significant difference between the height and/or width of the binding and the text block, and this difference is considered important for identification or selection, record (in this order):

a) the height (or height × width) of the text block

b) the height (or height × width) of the binding.

Indicate which dimension is being given.

22 cm in binding 24 cm

20 × 8 cm in binding 22 × 12 cm

If the volume contains separate text blocks of varying dimensions, record the height (or height × width) of the binding only. Make a note on the dimensions of the text blocks if considered important for identification or selection (see **3.21.3.3** or **3.22.3.3**, as applicable).

If the volume contains tactile text and is smaller or larger than the standard A3 size, record the height × width.

If the binding is known to be a replacement binding or one that was applied after the resource was issued, make a note indicating that fact (see **3.22.1.3**).

3.5.1.5 Dimensions of Container

If the resource is in a container, name the container. Record the dimensions of the container (height × width × depth) if considered important for identification or selection:

either

a) in addition to the dimensions of the carrier or carriers

or

b) as the only dimensions.

Unless instructed otherwise, record measurements as instructed at **3.5.1.3**.

16 × 32 × 3 cm
case 17 × 34 × 6 cm
Dimensions of a model and its container

box 30 × 25 × 13 cm
Dimensions of the container for a diorama; dimensions of the diorama not recorded

3.5.1.6 Resources Consisting of More Than One Carrier

If the resource consists of more than one carrier, and the carriers are all of the same type and size, record the dimensions of a single carrier (see **3.5.1.4**).

3 × 8 cm

Dimensions of a microscope slide in a resource consisting of 8 microscope slides all of the same size

24 cm

Dimensions of a volume in a resource consisting of 3 volumes all of the same size

Exception

Unbound sheets of text. For resources consisting of two or more unbound sheets of text, apply the instructions on recording the dimensions of a volume (see **3.5.1.4.14**). If the sheets are kept folded, add the dimensions when folded.

20 cm folded to 10 × 12 cm

35 × 66 cm, folded to 10 × 19 cm

If the carriers are of the same type but differ in size, record the dimensions of the smallest or smaller and the largest or larger size.

24–28 cm

Dimensions of the smallest and largest volumes in a resource consisting of 6 volumes of differing height

150 to 210 cm high

Dimensions of the smallest and largest sculptures in a resource consisting of 3 sculptures of differing height

11 × 15 cm–12 × 17 cm

Dimensions of the smaller and larger microfiches in a resource consisting of 2 microfiches of differing height and width

Alternative

If the carriers are all of two sizes, record both. If they are of more than two sizes, record the dimensions of the largest followed by *or smaller*.

8 × 13 cm and 10 × 15 cm

Dimensions of the smaller and larger cards in a resource consisting of cards of two sizes

26 × 21 cm or smaller

Dimensions reflecting the dimensions of the largest photographs in a collection containing photographs of more than two sizes

Exception

Notated music. For notated music, if the resource consists of more than one carrier of differing sizes, record the dimensions of each carrier containing a different type of unit. Record them in the order in which the units are listed at **7.20.1.3**.

> 20 cm
> 32 cm
> *Score measures 20 cm; parts measure 32 cm*

For a resource consisting of more than one type of carrier, record the dimensions of the carriers by applying the instructions at **3.1.4.2**.

3.5.1.7 Resources in More Than One Container

If the resource is in more than one container, and the containers are all of the same size, record the dimensions of a single container (see **3.5.1.5**).

> boxes 27 × 40 × 50 cm
> *Dimensions of the boxes in a collection consisting of 12 boxes all of the same size*

If the containers differ in size, record the dimensions of the smallest or smaller and the largest or larger size.

> boxes 20 × 30 × 5 cm–26 × 35 × 6 cm
> *Dimensions of the smaller and larger boxes in a collection consisting of boxes of two sizes*
>
> containers 14 × 26 × 8 cm to 16 × 38 × 22 cm
> *Dimensions of the smallest and largest containers in a collection consisting of containers of more than two sizes*

3.5.1.8 Change in Dimensions

If there is a change in dimensions, apply the instructions appropriate to the mode of issuance of the resource:

multipart monographs and serials (see **3.5.1.8.1**)

integrating resources (see **3.5.1.8.2**).

3.5.1.8.1 Multipart Monographs and Serials

If the dimensions of a multipart monograph or serial change, record the dimensions by applying the instructions on resources consisting of more than one carrier at **3.5.1.6**.

> 27–32 cm
> *Dimensions of the smallest and largest volumes of a serial*

Make a note on the details of the change if considered important for identification or selection (see **3.21.3.4.1**).

3.5.1.8.2 Integrating Resources

If the dimensions of an integrating resource change, change the dimensions to reflect the current iteration. Make a note if the change is considered important for identification or selection (see **3.21.3.4.2**).

3.5.2 Dimensions of Map, Etc.

3.5.2.1 Application

For a resource consisting of one or more sheets that contain one or more maps, diagrams, views, profiles, sections, etc., record the dimensions by applying the instructions at **3.5.2.2–3.5.2.7**.

In addition, apply the basic instructions on recording dimensions at **3.5.1** as applicable.

3.5.2.2 Recording Dimensions of Maps, Etc.

Record the dimensions of each map, etc., by giving the measurements of the face of the map, etc., measured within the neat line. Record the height × width or diameter, as appropriate. When recording diameter, indicate that it is the diameter.

> 25 × 35 cm
>
> 45 cm in diameter

Alternative

For early printed and manuscript sheet maps, etc., record the dimensions to the next tenth of a centimetre and use the metric symbol *cm*.

> 123.5 × 152.4 cm

Record the greater or greatest dimensions of the map, etc., itself, if the map:

a) is irregularly shaped,
or
b) has no neat line
or
c) bleeds off the edge.

In some cases, it is difficult to determine the points for measuring the height and width of the map, etc., itself (e.g., when the shape is extremely irregular, or when it was printed without one or more of its borders). When this occurs, record the height × width of the sheet. Indicate that the dimensions are for the sheet.

> sheet 45 × 33 cm

If appropriate, record more than one set of dimensions and indicate specifically the area to which each set of dimensions applies. Separate each set of dimensions by a comma.

3.5.2.3 Map, Etc., on More Than One Sheet of Differing Sizes

If the map, etc., is on sheets of two sizes, record both sets of sheet dimensions.

> sheets 25 × 35 cm and 30 × 35 cm

If the map, etc., is on sheets of more than two sizes, record the greatest height of any of the sheets followed by the greatest width of any of them, followed by *or smaller*.

> sheets 30 × 40 cm or smaller

3.5.2.4 Map, Etc., in Segments Designed to Fit Together

If:

the map, etc., is on one or more sheets

and

the map is in two or more segments designed to fit together to form one map, etc.

then:

record the dimensions of the complete map, etc., followed by the dimensions of the sheet or sheets. Separate the dimensions by a comma and precede the sheet dimensions with *on sheets* or *in sheets*, as appropriate, unless the number of sheets is recorded in the extent (see **3.4.2.4**).

> 10 × 60 cm, on sheet 25 × 35 cm
>
> 264 × 375 cm, sheets 96 × 142 cm
> *Extent recorded as:* 1 map on 9 sheets

If the segments have been assembled and mounted together, record the dimensions of the whole map, etc., alone.

> 120 × 276 cm
> *Mounted map created from several segments*

In some cases, it is difficult to determine the points for measuring the height and width of a complete map, etc., that is in segments, or to assemble the map, etc., for measuring. When this occurs, record only the height × width of the sheet or sheets. Indicate that the dimensions are for the sheet or sheets.

> sheets 30 × 40 cm
>
> sheets 60 × 60 cm or smaller

3.5.2.5 Dimensions of Map, Etc., in Relation to Dimensions of Sheet

If:

the measurement of either dimension of the map, etc., is less than half the measurement of the same dimension of the sheet on which it is presented

or

there is substantial additional information on the sheet (e.g., text)

then:

record the dimensions of the map, etc., followed by the dimensions of the sheet. Separate the dimensions by a comma and precede the dimensions of the sheet by *on sheet*.

> 20 × 31 cm, on sheet 42 × 50 cm

3.5.2.6 Map, Etc., on Folded Sheet

If:

the map, etc., is presented with an outer cover within which it is intended to be folded

or

the sheet itself contains a panel or section designed to appear on the outside when the sheet is folded

then:

record the dimensions of the map, etc., and add the dimensions of the sheet in folded form, preceded by a comma.

80 × 57 cm, folded to 21 × 10 cm

9 × 20 cm, on sheet 40 × 60 cm, folded in cover 21 × 10 cm

3.5.2.7 Map, Etc., Presented on Both Sides of a Sheet

If the map, etc., is presented on both sides of a sheet at a consistent scale, record the dimensions of the map, etc., as a whole. Add the dimensions of the sheet, separated by a comma and preceded by *on sheet.* If it is difficult to measure such a map, etc., record the dimensions of the sheet alone.

45 × 80 cm, on sheet 50 × 44 cm
Printed on both sides of sheet with line for joining indicated

on sheet 45 × 30 cm
Printed on both sides of sheet

3.5.3 Dimensions of Still Image

3.5.3.1 Application

For a resource consisting of one or more sheets that contain one or more still images in the form of drawings, paintings, prints, photographs, etc., record the dimensions by applying the instructions at **3.5.3.2–3.5.3.3**.

In addition, apply the basic instructions on recording dimensions at **3.5.1** as applicable.

For resources consisting of still images in other media (e.g., slides, transparencies), apply the basic instructions at **3.5.1**.

For sheets containing maps, etc., see **3.5.2**.

3.5.3.2 Recording Dimensions of Still Images

Record the dimensions of a still image by using the measurements of the pictorial area. Record the height × width, diameter, or other dimensions, as appropriate, and give the dimensions with reference to the position in which the image is intended to be viewed. When recording dimensions other than height × width of a rectangle, indicate what is being measured.

33 × 25 cm

6 cm in diameter

7 × 5 cm oval

41 × 36 cm irregular pentagon

244 × 26 cm, folded to 30 × 26 cm
Dimensions of a wall chart

Alternative

Record the dimensions to the next tenth of a centimetre and use the metric symbol *cm.*

32.2 × 22.4 cm

If appropriate, record more than one set of dimensions and indicate specifically the area to which each set of dimensions applies. Separate each set of dimensions by a comma.

6 cm in diameter, plate mark 8 × 7 cm

3.5.3.3 Dimensions of Image in Relation to Dimensions of Sheet

If:

the measurement of either dimension of the image is less than half the measurement of the same dimension of the sheet on which it is presented

or

there is substantial additional information on the sheet (e.g., text)

then:

record the dimensions of the image followed by the dimensions of the sheet (exclusive of any frame or mounting). Separate the dimensions by a comma and precede the dimensions of the sheet by *on sheet.*

20 × 31 cm, on sheet 42 × 50 cm

6 cm in diameter, plate mark 8 × 7 cm, on sheet 24 × 17 cm

3.6 Base Material

3.6.1 Basic Instructions on Recording Base Materials

3.6.1.1 Scope

Base material is the underlying physical material of a resource.

3.6.1.2 Sources of Information

Use evidence presented by the resource itself (or on any accompanying material or container) as the basis for recording the base material of the resource. Take additional evidence from any source.

3.6.1.3 Recording Base Materials

Record the base material of the resource if considered important for identification or selection. Use one or more appropriate terms from the following list:

Bristol board
canvas
cardboard
ceramic
glass
hardboard
illustration board
ivory
leather
metal
paper
parchment
plaster
plastic
porcelain
shellac
skin
stone

synthetic
textile
vellum
vinyl
wax
wood

vellum
Base material for a vellum manuscript

wood
Base material for a globe

plastic
Base material for a microscope slide

glass
Base material for a painting

synthetic
Base material for an acrylic model

wood
plaster
Base materials for a diorama

Exception

Microfilm, microfiche, photographic film, and motion picture film. For microfilm, microfiche, photographic film, and motion picture film, see **3.6.2**.

If none of the terms in the list is appropriate or sufficiently specific, use another concise term or terms to indicate the base material.

silk
Base material for a map

papier mâché
Base material for a model

Record details of base materials as instructed at **3.6.1.4**.

3.6.1.4 Details of Base Materials

Record details of the base materials if considered important for identification or selection.

Paper watermarked: KS and a crown

Image printed on thick gold paper
Details of base material for an art print

On green laid paper
Details of base material for a drawing

Recorded on paper tape
Details of base material for an audio recording

3.6.2 Base Material for Microfilm, Microfiche, Photographic Film, and Motion Picture Film

3.6.2.1 Scope

Base material for microfilm, microfiche, photographic film, and motion picture film is the underlying physical material of a microfilm, microfiche, photographic film, or motion picture film resource.

3.6.2.2 Sources of Information

Use evidence presented by the resource itself (or on any accompanying material or container) as the basis for recording the base material for microfilm, microfiche, photographic film, and motion picture film. Take additional evidence from any source.

3.6.2.3 Recording Base Materials for Microfilm, Microfiche, Photographic Film, and Motion Picture Film

For a microfilm, microfiche, photographic film, or motion picture film, record the base material using one or more appropriate terms from the following list:

acetate
diacetate
nitrate
polyester
safety base
triacetate

Apply the terms listed as follows:

a) Record *acetate* when it cannot be determined whether the film base is diacetate or triacetate.

b) Record *safety base* when the specific type of safety base cannot be determined.

nitrate
Base material for a motion picture film

Record details of base materials for microfilm, microfiche, photographic film, or motion picture film as instructed at **3.6.2.4**.

3.6.2.4 Details of Base Materials for Microfilm, Microfiche, Photographic Film, and Motion Picture Film

Record details of the base materials for a microfilm, microfiche, photographic film, or motion picture film if considered important for identification or selection.

3.7 Applied Material

3.7.1 Basic Instructions on Recording Applied Materials

3.7.1.1 Scope

Applied material is a physical or chemical substance applied to a base material of a resource.

3.7.1.2 Sources of Information

Use evidence presented by the resource itself (or on any accompanying material or container) as the basis for recording the applied material used in the resource. Take additional evidence from any source.

3.7.1.3 Recording Applied Materials

Record the applied material used in the resource if considered important for identification or selection. If there is more than one applied material and one material predominates, record the term for the predominant material first. Use one or more appropriate terms from the following list:

acrylic paint
chalk
charcoal
crayon
dye
gouache
graphite
ink
oil paint
pastel
plaster
tempera
watercolour

ink
Applied material for a hand-drawn map

oil paint
Applied material for a painting

watercolour
gouache
ink
pencil
Applied materials for a mixed media artwork

Exception

Microfilm and microfiche. Record the emulsion on the film for microfilm and microfiche as instructed at **3.7.2**.

If none of the terms in the list is appropriate or sufficiently specific, use another concise term or terms to indicate the applied material.

mother of pearl
Applied material for a sewing box

If multiple materials are known to have been applied, but not all can be readily identified, record *mixed materials*.

Record details of applied materials as instructed at **3.7.1.4**.

3.7.1.4 Details of Applied Materials

Record details of applied material if considered important for identification or selection.

Egg tempera paint with tooled gold-leaf halos

Silverpoint with white chalk highlighting

Collage of photographic prints, newspaper clippings, and paint

Watercolour, gouache, and pen and brown ink over pencil with gum arabic and scraping out

3.7.2 Emulsion on Microfilm and Microfiche

3.7.2.1 Scope

Emulsion on microfilm and microfiche is a suspension of light-sensitive chemicals used as a coating on a microfilm or microfiche (e.g., silver halide).

3.7.2.2 Sources of Information

Use evidence presented by the resource itself (or on any accompanying material or container) as the basis for recording the emulsion on microfilm and microfiche. Take additional evidence from any source.

3.7.2.3 Recording Emulsion on Microfilm and Microfiche

For a microfilm or microfiche, record the emulsion using one or more appropriate terms from the following list:

diazo
mixed
silver halide
vesicular

diazo
Emulsion on a microfiche

If none of the terms in the list is appropriate or sufficiently specific, use another concise term or terms to indicate the emulsion.

Record details of emulsion on microfilm or microfiche as instructed at **3.7.2.4**.

3.7.2.4 Details of Emulsion on Microfilm and Microform

Record details of the emulsion on a microfilm or microfiche if considered important for identification or selection.

3.8 Mount

3.8.1 Basic Instructions on Recording Mounts

3.8.1.1 Scope

Mount is the physical material used for the support or backing to which the base material of a resource has been attached.

3.8.1.2 Sources of Information

Use evidence presented by the resource itself (or on any accompanying material or container) as the basis for recording the material used to mount the resource. Take additional evidence from any source.

3.8.1.3 Recording Mounts

Record the material used to mount the resource if considered important for identification or selection. Use one or more appropriate terms from the list at **3.6.1.3**.

Bristol board
Mount for a print

wood
Mount for a printed map

If none of the terms in the list at **3.6.1.3** is appropriate or sufficiently specific, use another concise term or terms to indicate the material used to mount the resource.

granite
Mount material for a sculpture

Record details of the material on which the resource is mounted as instructed at **3.8.1.4**.

3.8.1.4 Details of Mount

Record details of the material on which the resource is mounted if considered important for identification or selection.

Mounted on starched linen

On brass stand

3.9 Production Method

3.9.1 Basic Instructions on Recording Production Methods

3.9.1.1 Scope

Production method is the process used to produce a resource.

3.9.1.2 Sources of Information

Use evidence presented by the resource itself (or on any accompanying material or container) as the basis for recording the method used to produce the resource. Take additional evidence from any source.

3.9.1.3 Recording Production Methods

Record the production method if considered important for identification or selection. Use one or more appropriate terms from the following list:

blueline
blueprint
collotype
daguerreotype
engraving
etching
lithograph
photocopy
photoengraving
photogravure
print

white print
woodcut

engraving
Production method for an art print

Exceptions

Manuscripts. For the method of production for manuscripts, see **3.9.2**.

Tactile resources. For the method of production for tactile resources, see **3.9.3**.

If none of the terms in the list is appropriate or sufficiently specific, use another concise term or terms to indicate the production method.

chromolithograph
Production method for a print

Record details of production method as instructed at **3.9.1.4**.

3.9.1.4 Details of Production Method

Record details of production method if considered important for identification or selection.

Finished using a gray wash technique

3.9.2 Production Method for Manuscript

3.9.2.1 Scope

Production method for manuscript is the process used to produce an original manuscript or a copy.

3.9.2.2 Sources of Information

Use evidence presented by the resource itself (or on any accompanying material or container) as the basis for recording the method used to produce a manuscript. Take additional evidence from any source.

3.9.2.3 Recording Production Method for Manuscript

For a manuscript, record the production method using an appropriate term from the following list:

holograph
manuscript
printout
typescript

Apply the terms listed as follows:

a) Record *holograph* for a manuscript handwritten by the person or persons responsible for the work or works contained in that manuscript.

b) Record *manuscript* for any handwritten manuscript other than a holograph.

holograph
Production method for a letter

manuscript
Production method for a score

typescript
Production method for a thesis

If none of the terms in the list is appropriate or sufficiently specific, use another concise term to indicate the production method for the manuscript.

If the manuscript or manuscripts are copies, add, in parentheses, *carbon copy, photocopy,* or *transcript.* Add *handwritten, typewritten,* or *printout* to *transcript.* If none of those terms is appropriate, use another concise term to indicate the type of copy.

holograph (carbon copy)

manuscript (photocopy)

manuscript (transcript, handwritten)

typescript (photocopy)

If the manuscripts are not all of the same type, add wording in parentheses to indicate this.

manuscript (some photocopy)

manuscript (transcript, handwritten, and photocopy)

Record details of production method for a manuscript as instructed at **3.9.2.4**.

3.9.2.4 Details of Production Method for Manuscript

Record details of production method for a manuscript if considered important for identification or selection.

3.9.3 Production Method for Tactile Resource

3.9.3.1 Scope

Production method for tactile resource is the process used to produce a tactile resource (e.g., embossing, thermoform).

3.9.3.2 Sources of Information

Use evidence presented by the resource itself (or on any accompanying material or container) as the basis for recording the method used to produce a tactile resource. Take additional evidence from any source.

3.9.3.3 Recording Production Method for Tactile Resources

For a tactile resource, record the production method using an appropriate term from the following list:

embossed
solid dot
swell paper
thermoform

If none of the terms in the list is appropriate or sufficiently specific, use another concise term to indicate the production method for a tactile resource.

tactile silk screen print
Production method for a tactile plan

collage, wood on wood
Production method for a tactile plan

raised ceramic outline
Production method for a tactile plan

Record details of production method for a tactile resource as instructed at **3.9.3.4**.

3.9.3.4 Details of Production Method for Tactile Resource

Record details of production method for a tactile resource if considered important for identification or selection.

3.10 Generation

3.10.1 Basic Instructions on Recording Generation

3.10.1.1 Scope

Generation is the relationship between an original carrier and the carrier of a reproduction made from the original (e.g., a first generation camera master, a second generation printing master).

3.10.1.2 Sources of Information

Use evidence presented by the resource itself (or on any accompanying material or container) as the basis for recording the generation of the resource. Take additional evidence from any source.

3.10.1.3 Recording Generation

Record the generation of the resource by applying these instructions, as applicable:

audio recordings (see **3.10.2**)
digital resources (see **3.10.3**)
microforms (see **3.10.4**)
motion picture films (see **3.10.5**)
videotapes (see **3.10.6**).

3.10.2 Generation of Audio Recording

3.10.2.1 Scope

Generation of audio recording is the relationship between an original audio carrier and the carrier of a reproduction made from the original (e.g., a tape duplication master, a test pressing).

3.10.2.2 Sources of Information

Use evidence presented by the resource itself (or on any accompanying material or container) as the basis for recording the generation of an audio recording. Take additional evidence from any source.

3.10.2.3 Recording Generation of Audio Recordings

Record the generation of an audio recording if considered important for identification or selection. Use an appropriate term from the following list:

master tape
tape duplication master
disc master
mother

stamper

test pressing

tape duplication master
Generation of an audiotape

If none of the terms in the list is appropriate or sufficiently specific, use another concise term to indicate the generation of an audio recording.

Record details of generation of an audio recording as instructed at **3.10.2.4**.

3.10.2.4 Details of Generation of Audio Recording

Record details of generation of an audio recording if considered important for identification or selection.

3.10.3 Generation of Digital Resource

3.10.3.1 Scope

Generation of digital resource is the relationship between an original carrier of a digital resource and the carrier of a reproduction from the original (e.g., a derivative master).

3.10.3.2 Sources of Information

Use evidence presented by the resource itself (or on any accompanying material or container) as the basis for recording the generation of a digital resource. Take additional evidence from any source.

3.10.3.3 Recording Generation of Digital Resources

Record the generation of a digital resource if considered important for identification or selection. Use an appropriate term from the following list:

original

master

derivative master

If none of the terms in the list is appropriate or sufficiently specific, use another concise term to indicate the generation of a digital resource.

Record details of generation of a digital resource as instructed at **3.10.3.4**.

3.10.3.4 Details of Generation of Digital Resource

Record details of generation of a digital resource if considered important for identification or selection.

3.10.4 Generation of Microform

3.10.4.1 Scope

Generation of microform is the relationship between an original microform carrier and the carrier of a reproduction made from the original (e.g., a printing master).

3.10.4.2 Sources of Information

Use evidence presented by the resource itself (or on any accompanying material or container) as the basis for recording the generation of a microform. Take additional evidence from any source.

3.10.4.3 Recording Generation of Microforms

Record the generation of a microform if considered important for identification or selection. Use an appropriate term from the following list:

first generation

printing master

service copy
mixed generation

printing master
Generation of a microfilm

If none of the terms in the list is appropriate or sufficiently specific, use another concise term to indicate the generation of a microform.

Record details of generation of a microform as instructed at **3.10.4.4**.

3.10.4.4 Details of Generation of Microform

Record details of generation of a microform if considered important for identification or selection.

3.10.5 Generation of Motion Picture Film

3.10.5.1 Scope

Generation of motion picture film is the relationship between an original carrier of a motion picture film resource and the carrier of a reproduction made from the original (e.g., a reference print).

3.10.5.2 Sources of Information

Use evidence presented by the resource itself (or on any accompanying material or container) as the basis for recording the generation of a motion picture film. Take additional evidence from any source.

3.10.5.3 Recording Generation of Motion Picture Films

Record the generation of a motion picture film if considered important for identification or selection. Use an appropriate term from the following list:

original
master
duplicate
reference print
viewing copy

original
Generation of a motion picture film

If none of the terms in the list is appropriate or sufficiently specific, use another concise term to indicate the generation of a motion picture film.

Record details of generation of a motion picture film as instructed at **3.10.5.4**.

3.10.5.4 Details of Generation of Motion Picture Film

Record details of generation of a motion picture film if considered important for identification or selection.

3.10.6 Generation of Videotape

3.10.6.1 Scope

Generation of videotape is the relationship between an original carrier of a videotape resource and the carrier of a reproduction made from the original (e.g., a show copy).

3.10.6.2 Sources of Information

Use evidence presented by the resource itself (or on any accompanying material or container) as the basis for recording the generation of a videotape. Take additional evidence from any source.

3.10.6.3 Recording Generation of Videotapes

Record the generation of a videotape if considered important for identification or selection. Use an appropriate term from the following list:

first generation
second generation, master copy
second generation, show copy

> second generation, master copy
> *Generation of a videotape*

If none of the terms in the list is appropriate or sufficiently specific, use another concise term to indicate the generation of a videotape.

Record details of generation of a videotape as instructed at **3.10.6.4**.

3.10.6.4 Details of Generation of Videotape

Record details of generation of a videotape if considered important for identification or selection.

3.11 Layout

3.11.1 Basic Instructions on Recording Layout

3.11.1.1 Scope

Layout is the arrangement of text, images, tactile notation, etc., in a resource.

3.11.1.2 Sources of Information

Use evidence presented by the resource itself (or on any accompanying material or container) as the basis for recording the layout of the resource. Take additional evidence from any source.

3.11.1.3 Recording Layout

Record the layout of the resource if considered important for identification or selection. Use one or more terms from the following list:

Cartographic images

both sides
back to back

Sheets

double sided
single sided

Tactile music notation

bar by bar
bar over bar
line by line
line over line
melody chord system
open score
outline
paragraph
section by section
short form scoring

single line
vertical score

Tactile text

double sided
single sided
double line spacing

both sides
Layout of a single manuscript map on both sides of the sheet

both sides
Layout of 3 maps printed on both sides of a single sheet

back to back
Layout of the same map printed on each side of a single sheet in a different language

double sided
Layout of a flip chart on double-sided sheets

double sided
Layout of a double-sided chart

bar by bar
Layout of tactile piano music for four hands

bar over bar
open score
Layout of a tactile vocal score

single sided
Layout of a tactile activity card

double sided
double line spacing
Layout of a volume of braille text showing double line spacing and double sided

single sided
Layout of a volume of braille text

If none of the terms in the list is appropriate or sufficiently specific, use another concise term to indicate the layout.

Record details of layout as instructed at **3.11.1.4**.

3.11.1.4 Details of Layout

Record details of layout if considered important for identification or selection.

Alternate pages blank

Images placed in frame both horizontally and vertically

Alternate leaves of print and braille

3.12 Book Format

3.12.1 Basic Instructions on Recording Book Formats

3.12.1.1 Scope

Book format is the result of folding a printed sheet to form a gathering of leaves (e.g., a sheet folded once to form a folio, twice to form a quarto, three times to form an octavo).

3.12.1.2 Sources of Information

Use evidence presented by the resource itself (or on any accompanying material or container) as the basis for recording the book format. Take additional evidence from any source.

3.12.1.3 Recording Book Formats

For an early printed book, etc., record the book format using an appropriate term from the following list:

folio
4to
8vo
12mo
16mo
24mo
32mo
48mo
64mo

4to

8vo

folio

Record details of book format as instructed at **3.12.1.4**.

3.12.1.4 Details of Book Format

Record details of the book format if considered important for identification or selection.

3.13 Font Size

3.13.1 Basic Instructions on Recording Font Size

3.13.1.1 Scope

Font size is the size of the type used to represent the characters and symbols in a resource.

For resources designed for persons with visual impairments, font size can be expressed either in general terms (e.g., large print), or in specific terms by adding the dimensions of the type measured in points (e.g., 20 point).

For resources designed for persons with visual and tactile impairments and for those learning braille, font size may also be used to represent the size and/or spacing of the raised dots representing characters and symbols (e.g., jumbo braille).

3.13.1.2 Sources of Information

Use evidence presented by the resource itself (or on any accompanying material or container) as the basis for recording font size. Take additional evidence from any source.

3.13.1.3 Recording Font Size

For resources with text in a font size designed for persons with visual impairments, record the font size using an appropriate term from the following list:

giant print
large print
jumbo braille

Optional Addition

Specify the dimensions of the type measured in points. Add the dimensions, in parentheses, following the font size.

giant print (36 point)

If none of the terms in the list is appropriate or sufficiently specific, use another concise term to indicate the font size.

Record details of font size as instructed at **3.13.1.4**.

3.13.1.4 Details of Font Size

For a resource designed for persons with visual impairments, record details of font size if considered important for identification or selection.

Font size varies from 18 point to 20 point

3.14 Polarity

3.14.1 Basic Instructions on Recording Polarity

3.14.1.1 Scope

Polarity is the relationship of the colours and tones in an image to the colours and tones of the object reproduced (e.g., positive, negative).

3.14.1.2 Sources of Information

Use evidence presented by the resource itself (or on any accompanying material or container) as the basis for recording the polarity of the resource. Take additional evidence from any source.

3.14.1.3 Recording Polarity

For a photograph, motion picture film, or microform, record the polarity if considered important for identification or selection. Use an appropriate term from the following list:

positive
negative
mixed polarity

negative
Polarity for a photographic negative

negative
Polarity for a microfilm

Record details of polarity as instructed at **3.14.1.4**.

3.14.1.4 Details of Polarity

Record details of polarity if considered important for identification or selection.

For motion picture films, record the form of print (e.g., negative, positive, reversal, reversal internegative, internegative, interpositive, colour separation, duplicate, fine grain duplicating positive, fine grain duplicating negative). For master material held in checkerboard cutting form, state if A, B, C, etc., roll.

3.15 Reduction Ratio

3.15.1 Basic Instructions on Recording Reduction Ratio

3.15.1.1 Scope

Reduction ratio is the size of a micro-image in relation to the original from which it was produced.

3.15.1.2 Sources of Information

Use evidence presented by the resource itself (or on any accompanying material or container) as the basis for recording the reduction ratio of the resource. Take additional evidence from any source.

3.15.1.3 Recording Reduction Ratios

For a microform, record the reduction ratio if considered important for identification or selection. Use one or more appropriate terms from the following list:

low reduction
normal reduction
high reduction
very high reduction
ultra high reduction

Apply the terms listed as follows:

a) Record *low reduction* for ratios of less than 16×.

b) Record *normal reduction* for ratios between 16× and 30×.

c) Record *high reduction* for ratios between 31× and 60×.

d) Record *very high reduction* for ratios between 61× and 90×.

e) Record *ultra high reduction* for ratios over 90×.

> low reduction
> *Reduction ratio of a microfilm*
>
> very high reduction
> *Reduction ratio of a microfiche*

If the reduction ratio is ultra high (i.e., greater than 90×), specify the ratio, in parentheses, following *ultra high reduction*.

> ultra high reduction (150×)

Record details of reduction ratio as instructed at **3.15.1.4**.

3.15.1.4 Details of Reduction Ratio

Record details of reduction ratio if considered important for identification or selection.

Reduction ratio varies

3.16 Sound Characteristic

3.16.1 Basic Instructions on Recording Sound Characteristics

3.16.1.1 Scope

A ***sound characteristic*** is a technical specification relating to the encoding of sound in a resource.

Sound characteristics include type of recording, recording medium, playing speed, groove characteristics, track configuration, tape configuration, configuration of playback channels, and special playback characteristics.

For instructions on recording additional characteristics of digitally encoded sound (e.g., audio encoding formats such as MP3), see **3.19**.

3.16.1.2 Sources of Information

Use evidence presented by the resource itself (or on any accompanying material or container) as the basis for recording the sound characteristics of the resource. Take additional evidence from any source.

3.16.1.3 Recording Sound Characteristics

For resources consisting primarily of recorded sound, record sound characteristics if considered important for identification or selection. Record the following sound characteristics, as applicable:

a) type of recording (see **3.16.2.3**)

b) recording medium (see **3.16.3.3**)

c) playing speed (see **3.16.4.3**)

d) groove characteristic (see **3.16.5.3**)

e) track configuration (see **3.16.6.3**)

f) tape configuration (see **3.16.7.3**)

g) configuration of playback channels (see **3.16.8.3**)

h) special playback characteristics (see **3.16.9.3**).

> *Optional Addition*
>
> For resources that do not consist primarily of recorded sound, record sound characteristics if considered important for identification or selection.

Record details of sound characteristics as instructed at **3.16.1.4**.

3.16.1.4 Details of Sound Characteristic

Record details of sound characteristics if considered important for identification or selection.

For details of any special equipment requirements for the playback of sound, see **3.20.1.3**.

3.16.2 Type of Recording

3.16.2.1 Scope

Type of recording is the method used to encode audio content for playback (e.g., analog, digital).

For instructions on recording the encoding format, etc., for digitally encoded sound, see **3.19.3.3**.

3.16.2.2 Sources of Information

Use evidence presented by the resource itself (or on any accompanying material or container) as the basis for recording the type of recording. Take additional evidence from any source.

3.16.2.3 Recording Type of Recording

Record the type of recording using an appropriate term from the following list:

analog
digital

> digital
> *Type of recording for sound encoded digitally on an audio disc*

If neither of the terms in the list is appropriate or sufficiently specific, use another concise term to indicate the type of recording.

Record details of the type of recording as instructed at **3.16.2.4**.

3.16.2.4 Details of Type of Recording

Record details of the type of recording if considered important for identification or selection.

> Made from an analog original
> *Type of recording recorded as:* digital

3.16.3 Recording Medium

3.16.3.1 Scope

Recording medium is the type of medium used to record sound on an audio carrier (e.g., magnetic, optical).

3.16.3.2 Sources of Information

Use evidence presented by the resource itself (or on any accompanying material or container) as the basis for recording the recording medium. Take additional evidence from any source.

3.16.3.3 Recording Recording Medium

Record the recording medium using an appropriate term from the following list:

magnetic
magneto-optical
optical

If none of the terms in the list is appropriate or sufficiently specific, use another concise term to indicate the recording medium.

Record details of the recording medium as instructed at **3.16.3.4**.

3.16.3.4 Details of Recording Medium

Record details of the recording medium if considered important for identification or selection.

3.16.4 Playing Speed

3.16.4.1 Scope

Playing speed is the speed at which an audio carrier must be operated to produce the sound intended.

For instructions on recording the encoded bitrate of an online sound file (e.g., streaming audio), see **3.19.7.3**.

3.16.4.2 Sources of Information

Use evidence presented by the resource itself (or on any accompanying material or container) as the basis for recording the playing speed. Take additional evidence from any source.

3.16.4.3 Recording Playing Speed

Record the playing speed of an audio recording if considered important for identification or selection. Use a measurement of speed appropriate to the type of recording.

For an analog disc, record the playing speed in revolutions per minute (*rpm*).

33 1/3 rpm

78 rpm

33 1/3 rpm
45 rpm
Different playing speeds on each side of an analog disc

For a digital disc, record the playing speed in metres per second (*m/s*).

1.4 m/s

For an analog tape, record the playing speed in centimetres per second (*cm/s*).

4.75 cm/s

9.5 cm/s

19 cm/s

Alternative

For an analog tape, record the playing speed in inches per second (*ips*).

1 7/8 ips

3 3/4 ips

7 1/2 ips

For a sound-track film, record the playing speed in frames per second (*fps*).

24 fps

Record details of the playing speed as instructed at **3.16.4.4**.

3.16.4.4 Details of Playing Speed

Record details of the playing speed if considered important for identification or selection.

3.16.5 Groove Characteristic

3.16.5.1 Scope

Groove characteristic is the groove width of an analog disc or the groove pitch of an analog cylinder.

3.16.5.2 Sources of Information

Use evidence presented by the resource itself (or on any accompanying material or container) as the basis for recording groove characteristics. Take additional evidence from any source.

3.16.5.3 Recording Groove Characteristics

For an analog disc, record the groove width if considered important for identification or selection. Use an appropriate term from the following list:

coarse groove
microgroove

> coarse groove
> *Groove width of an audio disc*

For an analog cylinder, record the groove pitch if considered important for identification or selection. Use an appropriate term from the following list:

fine
standard

> fine
> *Groove pitch of an analog cylinder*

If none of the terms in the lists is appropriate or sufficiently specific, use another concise term to indicate the groove characteristics.

Record details of groove characteristics as instructed at **3.16.5.4**.

3.16.5.4 Details of Groove Characteristic

Record details of groove characteristics if considered important for identification or selection.

> Vertically cut from inside outward

3.16.6 Track Configuration

3.16.6.1 Scope

Track configuration is the configuration of the audio track on a sound-track film (e.g., centre track).

3.16.6.2 Sources of Information

Use evidence presented by the resource itself (or on any accompanying material or container) as the basis for recording the track configuration. Take additional evidence from any source.

3.16.6.3 Recording Track Configuration

For sound-track films, record the track configuration using an appropriate term from the following list:

centre track
edge track

> centre track
> *Track configuration of a sound track film reel*

Record details of the track configuration as instructed at **3.16.6.4**.

3.16.6.4 Details of Track Configuration

Record details of the track configuration if considered important for identification or selection.

> Magnetic sound track

3.16.7 Tape Configuration

3.16.7.1 Scope

Tape configuration is the number of tracks on an audiotape.

3.16.7.2 Sources of Information

Use evidence presented by the resource itself (or on any accompanying material or container) as the basis for recording the tape configuration. Take additional evidence from any source.

3.16.7.3 Recording Tape Configuration

For tape cartridges, cassettes, and reels, record the tape configuration (i.e., the number of tracks on the tape) if considered important for identification or selection.

> 12 track

Record details of the tape configuration as instructed at **3.16.7.4**.

3.16.7.4 Details of Tape Configuration

Record details of the tape configuration if considered important for identification or selection.

3.16.8 Configuration of Playback Channels

3.16.8.1 Scope

Configuration of playback channels is the number of sound channels used to make a recording (e.g., one channel for a monophonic recording, two channels for a stereophonic recording).

3.16.8.2 Sources of Information

Use evidence presented by the resource itself (or on any accompanying material or container) as the basis for recording the configuration of playback channels. Take additional evidence from any source.

3.16.8.3 Recording Configuration of Playback Channels

Record the configuration of playback channels if the information is readily ascertainable. Use one or more appropriate terms from the following list:

mono
stereo
quadraphonic
surround

> stereo
> *Playback channels of an audiocassette*
>
> mono
> *Playback channels of an audio disc*
>
> mono
> stereo
> *Playback channels of an audio disc*

If none of the terms in the list is appropriate or sufficiently specific, use another concise term or terms to indicate the configuration of playback channels.

Record details of the configuration of playback channels as instructed at **3.16.8.4**.

3.16.8.4 Details of Configuration of Playback Channels

Record details of the configuration of playback channels if considered important for identification or selection.

3.16.9 Special Playback Characteristic

3.16.9.1 Scope

A ***special playback characteristic*** is an equalization system, noise reduction system, etc., used in making an audio recording.

3.16.9.2 Sources of Information

Use evidence presented by the resource itself (or on any accompanying material or container) as the basis for recording special playback characteristics. Take additional evidence from any source.

3.16.9.3 Recording Special Playback Characteristics

Record special playback characteristics if considered important for identification or selection. Use one or more appropriate terms from the following list:

CCIR standard
CX encoded
dbx encoded
Dolby
Dolby-A encoded
Dolby-B encoded
Dolby-C encoded
LPCM
NAB standard

> Dolby-B encoded
> *Playback characteristic of an audiocassette*

If none of the terms in the list is appropriate or sufficiently specific, use another concise term or terms to indicate the special playback characteristics.

Record details of special playback characteristics as instructed at **3.16.9.4**.

3.16.9.4 Details of Special Playback Characteristic

Record details of the special playback characteristics if considered important for identification or selection.

3.17 Projection Characteristic of Motion Picture Film

3.17.1 Basic Instructions on Recording Projection Characteristics of Motion Picture Film

3.17.1.1 Scope

A ***projection characteristic of motion picture film*** is a technical specification relating to the projection of a motion picture film.

Projection characteristics of motion picture film include presentation format and projection speed.

For instructions on recording the aspect ratio of a motion picture film, see **7.19**.

For instructions on recording the colour characteristics of a motion picture film, see **7.17**.

For instructions on recording the sound characteristics of a motion picture film, see **3.16** and **7.18**.

3.17.1.2 Sources of Information

Use evidence presented by the resource itself (or on any accompanying material or container) as the basis for recording the projection characteristics of a motion picture film. Take additional evidence from any source.

3.17.1.3 Recording Projection Characteristics of Motion Picture Film

Record projection characteristics if considered important for identification or selection. Record the following characteristics, as applicable:

a) presentation format (see **3.17.2**)

b) projection speed (see **3.17.3**).

Record details of projection characteristics of motion picture film as instructed at **3.17.1.4**.

3.17.1.4 Details of Projection Characteristic of Motion Picture Film

Record details of projection characteristics of a motion picture film if considered important for identification or selection.

For details of any special equipment requirements for projection, see **3.20.1.3**.

3.17.2 Presentation Format

3.17.2.1 Scope

Presentation format is the format used in the production of a projected image (e.g., Cinerama, IMAX).

3.17.2.2 Sources of Information

Use evidence presented by the resource itself (or on any accompanying material or container) as the basis for recording the presentation format. Take additional evidence from any source.

3.17.2.3 Recording Presentation Format

Record the presentation format of a motion picture film if considered important for identification or selection. Use one or more appropriate terms from the following list:

Cinerama
Cinemiracle
Circarama
IMAX
multiprojector
multiscreen
Panavision
standard silent aperture

standard sound aperture
stereoscopic
techniscope
3D

> Panavision
> *Presentation format of a motion picture film*

If none of the terms in the list is appropriate or sufficiently specific, use another concise term or terms to indicate the presentation format.

> Disney Digital 3-D

Record details of the presentation format as instructed at **3.17.2.4**.

3.17.2.4 Details of Presentation Format

Record details of the presentation format if considered important for identification or selection.

3.17.3 Projection Speed

3.17.3.1 Scope

Projection speed is the speed at which a projected carrier must be operated to produce the moving image intended.

3.17.3.2 Sources of Information

Use evidence presented by the resource itself (or on any accompanying material or container) as the basis for recording the projection speed. Take additional evidence from any source.

3.17.3.3 Recording Projection Speed

Record the projection speed of a motion picture film in frames per second (*fps*) if considered important for identification or selection.

> 20 fps

Record details of the projection speed as instructed at **3.17.3.4**.

3.17.3.4 Details of Projection Speed

Record details of the projection speed if considered important for identification or selection.

3.18 Video Characteristic

3.18.1 Basic Instructions on Recording Video Characteristics

3.18.1.1 Scope

A ***video characteristic*** is a technical specification relating to the encoding of video images in a resource.

Video characteristics include video format, broadcast standard, resolution, and bandwidth.

For instructions on recording the aspect ratio of a video, see **7.19**.

For instructions on recording the colour characteristics of a video, see **7.17**.

For instructions on recording the sound characteristics of a video, see **3.16**.

For instructions on recording additional characteristics of digitally encoded video, see **3.19**.

3.18.1.2 Sources of Information

Use evidence presented by the resource itself (or on any accompanying material or container) as the basis for recording the video characteristics of the resource. Take additional evidence from any source.

3.18.1.3 Recording Video Characteristics

Record video characteristics if considered important for identification or selection. Record the following characteristics, as applicable:

a) video format (see **3.18.2**)

b) broadcast standard (see **3.18.3**).

Record details of video characteristics as instructed at **3.18.1.4**.

3.18.1.4 Details of Video Characteristic

Record details of video characteristics (e.g., resolution (number of lines and frame rates), bandwidth, and other details), if considered important for identification or selection.

> Resolution: 1080i
>
> Standard: 405 lines, 50 fields, high band
>
> One side CAV, one side CLV

For details of any special equipment requirements for video playback, see **3.20.1.3**.

3.18.2 Video Format

3.18.2.1 Scope

Video format is a standard, etc., used to encode the analog video content of a resource.

For instructions on recording the format of digitally encoded video, see **3.19.3**.

3.18.2.2 Sources of Information

Use evidence presented by the resource itself (or on any accompanying material or container) as the basis for recording the video format. Take additional evidence from any source.

3.18.2.3 Recording Video Format

Record the video format of the resource if considered important for identification or selection. Use an appropriate term from the following list:

Beta
Betacam
Betacam SP
CED
D-2
EIAJ
8 mm
Hi-8 mm
Laser optical
M-II
Quadruplex
Super-VHS
Type C

U-matic

VHS

> Beta
> *Video format of a videocassette*
>
> CED
> *Video format of a videodisc*

If none of the terms in the list is appropriate or sufficiently specific, use another concise term to indicate the video format.

> LaserVision CAV
>
> VHS Hi-fi

Record details of the video format as instructed at **3.18.2.4**.

3.18.2.4 Details of Video Format

Record details of the video format if considered important for identification or selection.

For instructions on recording the encoding format, etc., for digitally encoded video, see **3.19.3.3**.

3.18.3 Broadcast Standard

3.18.3.1 Scope

Broadcast standard is a system used to format a video resource for television broadcast.

3.18.3.2 Sources of Information

Use evidence presented by the resource itself (or on any accompanying material or container) as the basis for recording the broadcast standard. Take additional evidence from any source.

3.18.3.3 Recording Broadcast Standard

Record the broadcast standard of the resource if considered important for identification or selection. Use an appropriate term from the following list:

HDTV

NTSC

PAL

SECAM

> PAL
> *Broadcast standard of a videotape*

If none of the terms in the list is appropriate or sufficiently specific, use another concise term to indicate the broadcast standard.

Record details of the broadcast standard as instructed at **3.18.3.4**.

3.18.3.4 Details of Broadcast Standard

Record details of the broadcast standard if considered important for identification or selection.

3.19 Digital File Characteristic

3.19.1 Basic Instructions on Recording Digital File Characteristics

3.19.1.1 Scope

A ***digital file characteristic*** is a technical specification relating to the digital encoding of text, image, audio, video, and other types of data in a resource.

Digital file characteristics include file type, encoding format, file size, resolution, regional encoding, encoded bitrate, data type, object type, number of objects, density, sectoring, etc.

For instructions on recording the colour characteristics of a digital file, see **7.17**.

For instructions on recording other sound characteristics of a digital file, see **3.16**.

For instructions on recording other video characteristics of a digital file, see **3.18**.

3.19.1.2 Sources of Information

Use evidence presented by the resource itself (or on any accompanying material or container) as the basis for recording the digital file characteristics of the resource. Take additional evidence from any source.

3.19.1.3 Recording Digital File Characteristics

Record digital file characteristics if considered important for identification or selection. Record the following characteristics, as applicable:

a) file type (see **3.19.2**)

b) encoding format (see **3.19.3**)

c) file size (see **3.19.4**)

d) resolution (see **3.19.5**)

e) regional encoding (see **3.19.6**)

f) encoded bitrate (see **3.19.7**).

For digitally encoded cartographic content, also record data type, object type, and number of objects (see **3.19.8**).

Record details of digital file characteristics as instructed at **3.19.1.4**.

3.19.1.4 Details of Digital File Characteristic

Record details of digital file characteristics (e.g., recording density, sectoring), if considered important for identification or selection.

> Single density
>
> Soft sectored
>
> 6,250 bpi
>
> Distributed as a Zip file
>
> Topology level 2
>
> Not copy-protected
>
> Hierarchical file structure
>
> Number of variables: 960

> Window media version streams at 700 kbps; Real Media version streams at 225 kbps
> Full audio structured by chapter

For details of any special equipment requirements, see **3.20.1.3**.

3.19.2 File Type

3.19.2.1 Scope

File type is a general type of data content encoded in a computer file.

3.19.2.2 Sources of Information

Use evidence presented by the resource itself (or on any accompanying material or container) as the basis for recording the file type. Take additional evidence from any source.

3.19.2.3 Recording File Type

Record the file type if it can be readily ascertained and is considered important for identification or selection. Use one or more appropriate terms from the following list:

audio file
data file
image file
program file
text file
video file

> image file
> *File type for an online resource containing images*
>
> audio file
> text file
> *File types for a resource containing both audio and text files*

If none of the terms in the list is appropriate or sufficiently specific, use another concise term or terms to indicate the file type.

Record details of file type as instructed at **3.19.2.4**.

3.19.2.4 Details of File Type

Record details of file type if considered important for identification or selection.

> Streaming video file

3.19.3 Encoding Format

3.19.3.1 Scope

Encoding format is a schema, standard, etc., used to encode the digital content of a resource.

3.19.3.2 Sources of Information

Use evidence presented by the resource itself (or on any accompanying material or container) as the basis for recording the encoding format. Take additional evidence from any source.

3.19.3.3 Recording Encoding Format

Record the encoding format if it can be readily ascertained and is considered important for identification or selection. Some formats (e.g., XML) apply to more than one category. Use one or more appropriate terms from the following list:

Audio encoding formats

CD audio
DAISY
DVD audio
MP3
RealAudio
SACD
WAV

Data encoding formats

Access
Excel
Lotus
XML

Image encoding formats

BMP
GIF
JPEG
JPEG2000
PNG
TIFF

Spatial data encoding formats

ArcInfo
BIL
BSQ
CAD
DEM
E00
MID/MIF

Text encoding formats

ASCII
HTML
Megadots
MS Word
PDF
RTF
SGML
TeX
Word Perfect
XHTML
XML

Video encoding formats

Blu-ray
DVD video
HD-DVD
MPEG-4
QuickTime
RealVideo
SVCD
VCD
Windows media

TIFF
Encoding format of a digital image

HTML
GIF
Encoding formats of an online resource with text and images

If none of the terms in the list is appropriate or sufficiently specific, use another concise term or terms to indicate the encoding format.

Mozart

PowerPoint

Record the version of the encoding format if it affects or restricts the use of the resource.

DAISY 3.0

Record details of the encoding format as instructed at **3.19.3.4**.

3.19.3.4 Details of Encoding Format

Record details of the encoding format if considered important for identification or selection.

3.19.4 File Size

3.19.4.1 Scope

File size is the number of bytes in a digital file.

3.19.4.2 Sources of Information

Use evidence presented by the resource itself (or on any accompanying material or container) as the basis for recording the file size. Take additional evidence from any source.

3.19.4.3 Recording File Size

Record the file size if it can be readily ascertained and is considered important for identification or selection. Record the file size in bytes, kilobytes (*KB*), megabytes (*MB*), or gigabytes (*GB*), as appropriate.

182 KB

6.6 MB

3.19.5 Resolution

3.19.5.1 Scope

Resolution is the clarity or fineness of detail in a digital image, expressed by the measurement of the image in pixels, etc.

3.19.5.2 Sources of Information

Use evidence presented by the resource itself (or on any accompanying material or container) as the basis for recording the resolution. Take additional evidence from any source.

3.19.5.3 Recording Resolution

Record the resolution if it can be readily ascertained and is considered important for identification or selection. Record the resolution by giving the measurement of the image in pixels.

> 2048×1536 pixels
>
> 3.1 megapixels

3.19.6 Regional Encoding

3.19.6.1 Scope

Regional encoding is a code identifying the region of the world for which a videodisc has been encoded and preventing the disc from being played on a player sold in a different region.

3.19.6.2 Sources of Information

Use evidence presented by the resource itself (or on any accompanying material or container) as the basis for recording the regional encoding. Take additional evidence from any source.

3.19.6.3 Recording Regional Encoding

Record the regional encoding if considered important for identification or selection.

> region 4
>
> all regions

3.19.7 Encoded Bitrate

3.19.7.1 Scope

Encoded bitrate is the speed at which streaming audio, video, etc., is designed to play.

3.19.7.2 Sources of Information

Use evidence presented by the resource itself, including embedded metadata, (or on any accompanying material or container) as the basis for recording the encoded bitrate. Take additional evidence from any source.

3.19.7.3 Recording Encoded Bitrate

Record the encoded bitrate of the file, if it can be readily ascertained and is considered important for identification or selection (e.g., for streaming audio or video).

> 32 kbps
>
> 7.17 Mbps

12.52 Mbit/s
Encoded bitrate recorded using the metric symbol

3.19.8 Digital Representation of Cartographic Content

3.19.8.1 Scope

Digital representation of cartographic content is a set of technical details relating to the encoding of geospatial information in a cartographic resource.

3.19.8.2 Sources of Information

Use evidence presented by the resource itself (or on any accompanying material or container) as the basis for recording the digital representation of cartographic content. Take additional evidence from any source.

3.19.8.3 Recording Digital Representation of Cartographic Content

For digitally encoded cartographic content, record the following information if it can be readily ascertained and is considered important for identification or selection:

a) data type (i.e., *raster*, *vector*, or *point*)

b) object type (e.g., *point*, *line*, *polygon*, *pixel*)

c) number of objects used to represent spatial information.

point
Data type

point
Object type

raster
Data type

pixel
Object type

5,000 × 5,000
Number of objects

vector
Data type

points, lines and polygons
Object type

vector
Data type

network chains
Object type

vector
Data type

point
Object type

13671
Number of objects

string
Object type

20171
Number of objects

GT-polygon composed of chains
Object type

13672
Number of objects

Record details of the digital representation of cartographic content as instructed at **3.19.8.4**.

3.19.8.4 Details of Digital Representation of Cartographic Content

Record details of the digital representation of cartographic content (e.g., topology level, compression) if considered important for identification or selection.

3.20 Equipment or System Requirement

3.20.1 Basic Instructions on Equipment or System Requirements

3.20.1.1 Scope

An ***equipment or system requirement*** is the equipment or system required for use, playback, etc., of an analog, digital, etc., resource.

3.20.1.2 Sources of Information

Use evidence presented by the resource itself (or on any accompanying material or container) as the basis for recording the equipment or system requirements of the resource. Take additional evidence from any source.

3.20.1.3 Recording Equipment or System Requirements

Record any equipment or system requirements beyond what is normal and obvious for the type of carrier or type of file. Record requirements such as the make and model of equipment or hardware, the operating system, the amount of memory, programming language, other necessary software, any plug-ins or peripherals required to play, view, or run the resource, etc.

For Information Design reader

For 65-note player piano

Filmslip mounted in rigid format for use with Phono-viewer

Requires PC with AudibleManager, or a portable device with AudiblePlayer, Audible Download Manager, AudibleAir, Windows Media Player, or Apple iTunes

Playaway, a dedicated audio media player

Requires RTI Series 500 CD-ROM DataDrive

Requires IBM PC AT or XT and CD-ROM player and drive

System requirements: IBM PC; 64K; colour card; 2 disk drives

System requirements: Adobe Acrobat Reader

System requirements: IBM-compatible PC with a Pentium processor or higher; 128MB of RAM; Windows 98, 2000, or XP; 11MB of available hard disk space; Windows-based word processing program

Requires: Windows: 98SE/2K/XP (preferred) PC, 400 MHZ PII or higher recommended, 64 MB RAM, 14X CD-ROM drive, 800x600, 16 bit color (thousands of colors), Microsoft DirectX5.2 or OpenGL (recommended)

Requires: Macintosh: power Macintosh/Power PC, OS9.1, OSX, 32 MB RAM, 14x CD-ROM drive

Alternative

Record the equipment or system requirements as they are presented on the resource.

System requirements: Windows XP SP2, 256 MB; Vista, 512 MB; 1.0 GHz; 15 GB hard drive; 56.6 kbps or better for Internet play; DirectX 9 hardware compatibility and audio card with speakers and/or headphones; DirectX 9.0c compliant video card with 32mb of ram and support for hardware transformation and lighting

NOTES

3.21 Note on Carrier

3.21.1 Basic Instructions on Making Notes on Carriers

3.21.1.1 Scope

A ***note on carrier*** is a note providing information on attributes of the carrier or carriers of the manifestation.

For notes on identifying manifestation attributes other than those describing carriers, see **2.17**.

3.21.1.2 Sources of Information

Take information for notes on carrier from any source.

3.21.1.3 Making Notes on Carrier

Make a note on carrier by applying the general guidelines at **1.10**.

3.21.2 Note on Extent of Manifestation

3.21.2.1 Scope

A ***note on extent of manifestation*** is a note providing information on the extent of a manifestation that is not recorded as part of the extent element.

3.21.2.2 Sources of Information

Use evidence presented by the resource itself (or on any accompanying material or container) as the basis for making notes on the extent of the manifestation. Take additional evidence from any source.

3.21.2.3 Describing Various Pieces

When applying the instructions at **3.1.4.3**, **3.4.1.5**, and **3.4.6.3**, the extent of a resource can be recorded as *various pieces*. In such cases, make a note providing details of the pieces if considered important for identification or selection.

Includes headdress, beaded shirt, trousers, and moccasins

Contains 1 small stage, 5 foreground transparencies, 2 backgrounds, 5 story sheets, and 1 easel

3.21.2.4 Resource Issued in More Than One Unit Not to Be Continued

If:

a resource is issued in more than one unit

and

not all the units have been issued

and

it appears that the resource will not be continued (see **3.4.1.10**)

then:

make a note that no more units have been issued.

No more published

3.21.2.5 Score and Parts in a Single Physical Unit

Make a note giving the number of parts included in a single physical unit with a score if this information is:

not recorded as part of the extent element (the exception at **3.4.3.2** is not applied)

and

considered important for identification or selection.

Includes 4 parts

3.21.2.6 Pagination Forming Part of a Larger Sequence

If:

a volume has pagination of its own as well as pagination forming part of a larger sequence

and

the pagination for the individual volume, etc., is recorded in the extent element (see **3.4.5.7**)

then:

make a note on pagination forming part of the larger sequence.

Pages also numbered 501–828

3.21.2.7 Duplicated Paging

Make a note explaining duplicated paging recorded in the extent element (see **3.4.5.12**).

Opposite pages have duplicate numbering

English to French terms followed by French to English terms separately paged

3.21.2.8 Number of Bibliographic Volumes Differing from Number of Physical Volumes

If the number of bibliographic volumes differs from the number of physical volumes, make a note indicating the number of bibliographic volumes.

8 bibliographic volumes in 5 physical volumes
Extent recorded as 5 volumes

Exception

Serials. The extent of a serial is recorded as the number of bibliographic volumes (see **3.4.5.16**). In general, do not record the number of physical volumes. If considered important for identification or selection, make a note on the number of physical volumes in the item being described. Record this information as an item-specific carrier characteristic (see **3.22**).

3.21.2.9 Early Printed Resources

For early printed resources, make notes about details of the extent of the manifestation (e.g., details of pagination, aspects of collation, the layout of sheets) if these details are:

not recorded as part of the extent element (see **3.4.5.2–3.4.5.13**)

and

considered important for identification or selection.

Signatures: A–Z^8, ^{2}A–M^8

Signatures: a–v^8 x^6

Make notes on the number of columns or lines, type measurements, frame measurements, etc., if considered important for identification or selection.

24 line; type 24G

Within single border (23.0×16.3 cm); text in 11 vertical lines

3.21.2.10 Resource Containing Both Text, Still Images, Etc., and Sound and/or Moving Images

For a resource containing text, still images, etc., as well as sound and/or moving images, record the extent of the text or still images in a note on extent of manifestation.

2400 frames of still images
Frames of still images on a videodisc that also contains moving images

See also **7.22.1.6** for instructions on recording the duration of the sound and/or moving images.

3.21.2.11 Other Details of Extent

Make notes providing other details of the extent of the manifestation if these details are:

not recorded as part of the extent element

and

considered important for identification or selection.

Numbers 263–267 are repeated in foliation

Numbers 237–238 are omitted from foliation

Leaves are joined end to end and folded accordion style

Leaves are printed on both sides

Numbered leaves are printed on both sides

3.21.3 Note on Dimensions of Manifestation

3.21.3.1 Scope

A ***note on dimensions of manifestation*** is a note providing information on the dimensions of a manifestation that is not recorded as part of the dimensions element.

3.21.3.2 Sources of Information

Use evidence presented by the resource itself (or on any accompanying material or container) as the basis for making notes on the dimensions of the manifestation. Take additional evidence from any source.

3.21.3.3 Details of Dimensions of Manifestation

Make notes providing additional information on the dimensions of the manifestation if this information is:

not recorded as part of the dimensions element

and

considered important for identification or selection.

Record dimensions as instructed at **3.5.1.3**.

Printed area measures 30 × 46 cm

Impressed on rectangular surface 20 × 20 cm

When making a note on the length of a motion picture film, give the length from first frame to last.

When making a note about the length of a videotape, give the length from first programme signal to last.

Record the length of a motion picture or videotape in metres to the nearest tenth of a metre and use the metric symbol *m*.

Film length: 4241.7 m

3.21.3.4 Change in Dimensions of Manifestation

Make notes on changes in dimensions of the manifestation as appropriate to the mode of issuance of the resource:

multipart monographs and serials (see **3.21.3.4.1**)

integrating resources (see **3.21.3.4.2**).

Record dimensions as instructed at **3.5.1.4**.

3.21.3.4.1 Multipart Monographs and Serials

Make notes on changes in dimensions of a subsequent issue or part of a multipart monograph or serial if considered important for identification or selection.

> Size varies: September 1891–September 1893: 18 × 26 cm; October 1893-December 1894, 18 × 27 cm

If the changes have been numerous, make a general statement instead.

3.21.3.4.2 Integrating Resources

Make notes on changes in dimensions from earlier iterations of an integrating resource if considered important for identification or selection.

If the changes have been numerous, make a general statement instead.

3.21.4 Note on Changes in Carrier Characteristics

3.21.4.1 Scope

A ***note on changes in carrier characteristics*** is a note on changes in the characteristics of the carrier that occur in subsequent issues or parts of a resource issued in successive parts or between iterations of an integrating resource.

3.21.4.2 Sources of Information

Use evidence presented by the resource itself (or on any accompanying material or container) as the basis for making notes on changes in carrier characteristics. Take additional evidence from any source.

3.21.4.3 Change in Carrier Characteristics

Make notes on changes in carrier characteristics as appropriate to the mode of issuance of the resource:

multipart monographs and serials (see **3.21.4.3.1**)
integrating resources (see **3.21.4.3.2**).

3.21.4.3.1 Multipart Monographs and Serials

Make notes on changes in carrier type or other carrier characteristics in a subsequent issue or part of a multipart monograph or serial if considered important for identification or selection.

> Some issues have audiocassette supplements, 1984–1997; compact disc supplements, 1998-

If the changes have been numerous, make a general statement instead.

3.21.4.3.2 Integrating Resources

Make notes on carrier characteristics no longer present on the current iteration if the change is considered important for identification or selection.

If the changes have been numerous, make a general statement instead.

ATTRIBUTES OF THE ITEM

3.22 Note on Item-Specific Carrier Characteristic

3.22.1 Basic Instructions on Making Notes on Item-Specific Carrier Characteristics

3.22.1.1 Scope

A ***note on item-specific carrier characteristic*** is a note providing additional information about carrier characteristics that are specific to the item being described and are assumed not to apply to other items exemplifying the same manifestation.

For notes on identifying item-specific characteristics other than those describing carriers, see **2.21**.

3.22.1.2 Sources of Information

Take information for notes on item-specific carrier characteristics from any source.

3.22.1.3 Making Notes on Item-Specific Carrier Characteristics

Make notes on item-specific carrier characteristics by applying the general guidelines at **1.10**.

Make a note about carrier characteristics of the specific item being described if considered important for identification or selection.

> Numerous wormholes throughout with some loss of text
>
> Library has copy number 38 of 50; signed by the artist
>
> Library's copy has errata sheets inserted
>
> Notes by author on endpapers

Record details of the library's holdings of a multipart monograph, serial, or integrating resource if those holdings are incomplete.

> Library set lacks slides 7–9

Also apply the following instructions, as applicable:

note on item-specific carrier characteristics for an early printed resource (see **3.22.1.4**)

note on extent of item (see **3.22.2**)

note on dimensions of item (see **3.22.3**).

3.22.1.4 Making Notes on Item-Specific Carrier Characteristics for an Early Printed Resource

For early printed resources, make a note about special features of the specific item being described (e.g., rubrication, illumination, binding).

Also make a note about other item-specific carrier characteristics as instructed at **3.22.1.3**.

> Pages 1–16 misbound after page 84
>
> Imperfect: wanting leaves 12 and 13 (b6 and c1); also the blank last leaf (S8)
>
> On vellum. Illustrations and part of borders hand coloured. With illuminated initials. Rubricated in red and blue
>
> Contemporary doeskin over boards; clasp. Stamp: Château de La Roche Guyon, Bibliothèque
>
> Blind stamped pigskin binding (1644) with initials C.S.A.C.
>
> Inscription on inside of front cover: Theodorinis ab Engelsberg
>
> Signed: Alex. Pope
>
> Original, signed by John Hancock
>
> Marginalia by Robert Graves

NOTES

3.22.2 Note on Extent of Item

3.22.2.1 Scope

A ***note on extent of item*** is a note providing information on the extent of the specific item being described that is not recorded as part of the extent element.

3.22.2.2 Sources of Information

Use evidence presented by the resource itself (or on any accompanying material or container) as the basis for making notes on the extent of the item. Take additional evidence from any source.

3.22.2.3 Making Notes on Extent of Item

Make notes providing additional information on the extent of the item if these details are:

not recorded as part of the extent element

and

considered important for identification or selection.

Library's copy lacks appendices, pages 245–260

Library's copy imperfect: leaves preceding leaf 81 and leaves after leaf 149 are lacking
Extent recorded as: leaves 81-149

Library's copy lacks pages after 179
Extent recorded as: xxiv, 179 (incomplete)

3.22.3 Note on Dimensions of Item

3.22.3.1 Scope

A ***note on dimensions of item*** is a note providing information on the dimensions of the specific item being described that is not recorded as part of the dimensions element.

3.22.3.2 Sources of Information

Use evidence presented by the resource itself (or on any accompanying material or container) as the basis for making notes on the dimensions of the item. Take additional evidence from any source.

3.22.3.3 Making Notes on Dimensions of Item

Make a note providing additional information on the dimensions of the item if these details are:

not recorded as part of the dimensions element

and

considered important for identification or selection.

Record dimensions as instructed at **3.5.1.3**.

Size when framed: 40 × 35 cm

Size as mounted 36 × 32 cm

4

PROVIDING ACQUISITION AND ACCESS INFORMATION

4.0 Purpose and Scope

This chapter provides general guidelines and instructions on recording the attributes of manifestations and items that are most often used to support acquisition and access. These attributes are recorded using the elements covered in this chapter.

The elements in chapter 4 are those used to obtain or access a resource (e.g., terms of availability, contact information, restrictions on access).

4.1 General Guidelines on Acquisition and Access

4.1.1 Sources of Information

Take acquisition and access information from any source.

4.2 Terms of Availability

4.2.1 Basic Instructions on Recording Terms of Availability

4.2.1.1 Scope

Terms of availability are the conditions under which the publisher, distributor, etc., will normally supply a resource or the price of a resource.

4.2.1.2 Sources of Information

Take information on terms of availability from any source.

4.2.1.3 Recording Terms of Availability

Record the terms on which the resource is available. These terms consist of:

the price (recorded in numerals with standard symbols) if the resource is for sale

or

a brief statement of other terms if the resource is not for sale.

£8.99

£6.99/$11.99

Free to students of the college

For hire

£0.50 per issue

$6.45 per year

Not for sale, for promotion only

Rental material

Optional Addition

When the terms of availability need qualification, record qualifying information briefly, in parentheses, following the terms of availability.

£10.00 (£5.00 to members)

$25.00 ($12.50 to students)

$30.00 per year ($25.00 to association members)

£3.00 to individuals (£8.40 to libraries)

$30.00 a year ($40.00 a year for Canada and all other countries)

$48.50 per annum, individuals ($112 libraries and institutions; $37.50 students)

4.3 Contact Information

4.3.1 Basic Instructions on Recording Contact Information

4.3.1.1 Scope

Contact information is information about an organization, etc., from which a resource may be obtained.

For published resources, contact information typically includes the name, address, etc., of the publisher, distributor, etc., of the resource.

For archival resources and collections, contact information typically includes the name, address, etc., of the archival repository that holds the resource.

4.3.1.2 Sources of Information

Take contact information from any source.

4.3.1.3 Recording Contact Information for Published Resources

Record contact information for a publisher, distributor, etc., if considered important for acquisition or access.

Diffusion Inter-Livres, 1701, rue Belleville, Lemoyne, Québec J4P 3M2

http://www.HaworthPress.com

http://www.loc.gov/cds

4.3.1.4 Recording Contact Information for Archival Resources and Collections

For archival resources and collections, record the name and location of the repository that holds the resource. Record the name of the repository, including any parent bodies. Include the mailing address and other contact information if considered important for access.

Alabama Department of Archives and History. 624 Washington Avenue, Montgomery, AL 36130-0100

4.4 Restrictions on Access

4.4.1 Basic Instructions on Recording Restrictions on Access

4.4.1.1 Scope

Restrictions on access are limitations placed on access to a resource.

4.4.1.2 Sources of Information

Take information on restrictions on access from any source.

4.4.1.3 Recording Restrictions on Access

Record all restrictions on access to the resource as specifically as possible. Include the nature and duration of the restriction.

> Accessible after 2008
>
> Open to researchers under library restrictions
>
> "Embargoed until 10:30 a.m. Friday 19 November, 2004"
>
> Access restricted to subscribers via a username and password or IP address authentication
>
> Restricted to institutions with a subscription
>
> Access is restricted; consult repository for details
>
> Restricted access according to signed release form and related notes
>
> Originals not available; consult repository for details

If information affirming the absence of restrictions is considered important for access, record that there are no restrictions on access.

4.5 Restrictions on Use

4.5.1 Basic Instructions on Recording Restrictions on Use

4.5.1.1 Scope

Restrictions on use are limitations placed on uses such as reproduction, publication, exhibition, etc.

4.5.1.2 Sources of Information

Take information on restrictions on use from any source.

4.5.1.3 Recording Restrictions on Use

Record all restrictions on use of the resource as specifically as possible. Include the nature and duration of the restriction.

> Written permission required for both reproduction and public use during the lifetime of the interviewee
>
> Reproduction and use in any form requires written permission of the donor
>
> Copyright retained by the donor during her lifetime, at which point it will revert to the Regents of the University of California
>
> Donor permission is required for public screening of films in this collection
>
> Permission of the collector is required to cite, quote, or reproduce
>
> Certain restrictions on use or copying of materials may apply
>
> This film is restricted to classroom use
>
> Films in off-site storage; advance notice is required for access

For a resource in unpublished form, the literary rights are sometimes reserved for a specified period or are dedicated to the public. If a document is available that states the literary rights, record *Information on literary rights available.*

4.6 Uniform Resource Locator

4.6.1 Basic Instructions on Recording Uniform Resource Locators

4.6.1.1 Scope

A ***Uniform Resource Locator***, or URL, is the address of a remote access resource.

Uniform Resource Locators include all resource identifiers intended to provide online access to a resource using a standard Internet browser.

4.6.1.2 Sources of Information

Take information on Uniform Resource Locators from any source.

4.6.1.3 Recording Uniform Resource Locators

Record the Uniform Resource Locator for the online resource being described.

> http://www.lemonde.fr/
>
> http://hdl.loc.gov/loc.rbc/jeff.16823
>
> http://nla.gov.au/nla.pic-an12766477
>
> http://dx.doi.org/10.3133/of2007-1047
> *Uniform Resource Locator for:* U.S. Geological Survey open-file report 2007-1047
>
> http://nbn-resolving.de/urn:nbn:de:gbv:089-3321752945
> *Uniform Resource Locator for:* Oliver Schmachtenberg's online dissertation Nitric oxide in the olfactory epithelium

If there is more than one Uniform Resource Locator for the resource, record one or more according to the policy of the agency preparing the description.

Record a Uniform Resource Locator for a related resource as part of the description of the related manifestation (see **27.1**).

4.6.1.4 Changes Requiring the Addition, Revision, or Deletion of a Uniform Resource Locator

If a Uniform Resource Locator is added or changed, add or revise the Uniform Resource Locator as appropriate.

If a Uniform Resource Locator no longer provides access to the online resource, add *(incorrect)* or *(invalid)* to it, as appropriate. Record a Uniform Resource Locator that does provide access to the resource, if readily ascertainable.

5

GENERAL GUIDELINES ON RECORDING ATTRIBUTES OF WORKS AND EXPRESSIONS

5.0 Scope

This chapter provides background information to support the application of guidelines and instructions in chapters 6–7 on recording attributes of works and expressions. It includes:

a) an explanation of key terms (see **5.1**)

b) the functional objectives and principles underlying the guidelines and instructions in chapters **6** and **7** (see **5.2**)

c) the core elements for the identification and description of works and expressions (see **5.3**)

d) guidelines on language and script that apply to elements in chapters **6** and **7** (see **5.4**)

e) general guidelines and instructions on constructing authorized access points representing works and expressions (see **5.5**)

f) general guidelines and instructions on constructing variant access points representing works and expressions (see **5.6**)

g) instructions on recording elements that provide clarification or justification for the data recorded to identify works and expressions:

   i. status of identification to indicate the reliability of the data identifying a work or expression (see **5.7**)

   ii. source consulted to cite sources used in determining titles and other information identifying a work or expression (see **5.8**)

   iii. cataloguer's note to assist in the use or revision of the data (see **5.9**).

5.1 Terminology

5.1.1 Explanation of Key Terms

There are a number of terms used in this chapter and in chapters **6** and **7** that have meanings specific to their use in RDA. Some of these terms are explained at **5.1.2–5.1.4**.

Terms used as data element names in chapters **6** and **7** are defined at the beginning of the instructions for the specific element. In addition, all terms used in those chapters with a specific technical meaning are defined in the glossary.

5.1.2 Work and Expression

The terms *work* and *expression* are used as follows:

The term ***work*** refers to a distinct intellectual or artistic creation (i.e., the intellectual or artistic content).

The term ***expression*** refers to the intellectual or artistic realization of a work in the form of alpha-numeric, musical or choreographic notation, sound, image, object, movement, etc., or any combination of such forms.

The terms *work* and *expression* can refer to individual entities, aggregates, or components of these entities (e.g., the term *work* can refer to an individual work, an aggregate work, or a component of a work).

5.1.3 Title

The terms *title of the work, preferred title,* and *variant title* are used as follows:

The term ***title of the work*** refers to a word, character, or group of words and/or characters by which a work is known.

The term ***preferred title for the work*** refers to the title or form of title chosen to identify the work. The preferred title is also the basis for the authorized access point representing that work.

The term ***variant title for the work*** refers to a title or form of title by which a work is known that differs from the title or form of title chosen as the preferred title for that work.

5.1.4 Access Point

The terms *access point, authorized access point,* and *variant access point* are used as follows:

The term ***access point*** refers to a name, term, code, etc., representing a specific work or expression. Access points include both authorized and variant access points.

The term ***authorized access point*** refers to the standardized access point representing an entity.

The authorized access point representing a work or expression is constructed by combining (in this order):

a) the authorized access point representing a person, family, or corporate body responsible for the work, if appropriate

b) the preferred title for the work

c) other elements as instructed at **6.27–6.31**.

The term ***variant access point*** refers to an alternative to the authorized access point representing an entity.

A variant access point representing a work or expression is constructed by combining (in this order):

a) the authorized access point representing a person, family, or corporate body responsible for the work, if appropriate

b) the variant title for the work

c) other elements as instructed at **6.27–6.31**.

5.2 Functional Objectives and Principles

The data recorded to reflect the attributes of a work or expression should enable the user to:

a) *find* works and expressions that correspond to the user's stated search criteria

b) *identify* the work or expression represented by the data (i.e., confirm that the work or expression represented is the one sought, or distinguish between two or more works or expressions with the same or similar titles)

c) *understand* the relationship between the title used to represent the work and another title by which that work is known (e.g., a different language form of the title)

d) *understand* why a particular title has been recorded as a preferred or variant title

e) *select* a work or expression that is appropriate to the user's requirements with respect to the content characteristics (e.g., form, intended audience, language).

To ensure that the data created using RDA meet those functional objectives, the guidelines and instructions in chapters **6** and **7** were designed according to the following principles:

Differentiation. The data should serve to differentiate the work or expression represented from other works and expressions, or other entities.

Representation. The title or form of title chosen as the preferred title for a work should be:

a) the title most frequently found in resources embodying the work in its original language
or
b) the title as found in reference sources
or
c) the title most frequently found in resources embodying the work.

Other titles and other forms of the title should be recorded as variant titles:

titles found in resources embodying the work

titles found in reference sources

titles that the user might be expected to use when conducting a search.

5.3 Core Elements

When recording data identifying a work, include as a minimum the following elements that are applicable and readily ascertainable.

Preferred title for the work

Identifier for the work

The preferred title is the basis for the authorized access point representing the work. When constructing that access point, precede the preferred title, if appropriate, by the authorized access point representing the person, family, or corporate body responsible for the work (see **6.27.1**).

If the preferred title for a work is the same as or similar to a title for a different work, or to a name for a person, family, or corporate body, differentiate them by recording as many of the additional identifying elements in the following list as necessary. Record these elements as separate elements, as parts of the access point representing the work, or as both.

Form of work

Date of work

Place of origin of the work

Other distinguishing characteristic of the work

When identifying a musical work with a title that is not distinctive, record as many of the following elements as are applicable. For musical works with distinctive titles, record as many of the following elements as necessary to differentiate the work from others with the same title. Record these elements as separate elements, as parts of the access point representing the work, or as both.

Medium of performance

Numeric designation

Key

When recording data identifying an expression, include as a minimum the following elements that are applicable to that expression. Record the elements as separate elements, as parts of the access point representing the expression, or as both.

Identifier for the expression

Content type

Language of expression

Record as many of the additional identifying elements in the following list as necessary to differentiate one expression of a work from another. Record these elements as separate elements, as parts of the access point representing the expression, or as both.

Date of expression

Other distinguishing characteristic of the expression

When describing a cartographic expression, include as a minimum the following additional elements that are applicable to that expression.

Horizontal scale of cartographic content

Vertical scale of cartographic content

Include additional elements covered in this chapter and in chapters **6** and **7** according to the policy of the agency creating the data, or according to the judgment of the cataloguer.

5.4 Language and Script

Record titles for works in the language and script in which they appear on the sources from which they are taken.

> *Alternative*
> Record a transliterated form of the title either as a substitute for, or in addition to, the form that appears on the source.

Record other identifying attributes of a work or expression in the language and script specified in the applicable instructions in chapter **6**.

Record the descriptive attributes of a work or expression covered in chapter **7** in a language and script preferred by the agency creating the data.

5.5 Authorized Access Points Representing Works and Expressions

When constructing an authorized access point to represent a work or expression, use the preferred title for the work (see **6.2.2**) as the basis for the access point.

Construct the authorized access point representing the work by combining (in this order):

a) the authorized access point for the person, family, or corporate body responsible for the work (see **6.27.1.2–6.27.1.8**), if applicable

b) the preferred title for the work (see **6.2.2**).

If two or more works are represented by the same or similar access points, include one or more additional identifying elements in the access point representing the work (such as form of work, date, place of origin, or other distinguishing term). For specific instructions on additions to access points representing works, see **6.27.1.9**.

When constructing an authorized access point to represent a part or parts of a work, apply the instructions at **6.27.2**.

When constructing an authorized access point to represent a particular expression of a work (or of a part or parts of a work), use the authorized access point representing the work and add one or more elements identifying the expression (see **6.27.3**).

Some changes affect the identification of a work issued as a multipart monograph, serial, or integrating resource and require the construction of an authorized access point representing a new work. For changes affecting the identification of a work, see **6.1.3**.

5.6 Variant Access Points Representing Works and Expressions

When constructing a variant access point to represent a work or expression, use a variant title for the work (see **6.2.3**) as the basis for the access point.

If the authorized access point for the work has been constructed using the authorized access point for a person, family, or corporate body followed by the preferred title for the work (see **6.27.1.2–6.27.1.8**), construct the variant access point by combining (in this order):

a) the authorized access point representing that person, family, or corporate body

b) the variant title for the work.

Make additions to the access point, if considered important for identification. Apply the following instructions on making additions, as applicable:

additions to access points representing works (see **6.27.1.9**)

authorized access points representing expressions (see **6.27.3**).

Construct a variant access point to represent a part or parts of a work by applying the instructions at **6.27.4.3**.

Construct a variant access point to represent a compilation of works by applying the instructions at **6.27.4.4**.

Construct a variant access point to represent an expression of a work by applying the instructions at **6.27.4.5**.

5.7 Status of Identification

5.7.1 Basic Instructions on Recording the Status of Identification

5.7.1.1 Scope

The ***status of identification*** is an indication of the level of authentication of the data identifying a work or expression.

5.7.1.2 Sources of Information

Take information on the status of identification from any source.

5.7.1.3 Recording the Status of Identification

Record the status of identification using an appropriate term from the following list:

fully established
provisional
preliminary

Apply the terms listed as follows:

a) Record *fully established* if the data is sufficient to establish fully an authorized access point representing the work or expression.

b) Record *provisional* if the data is insufficient to establish satisfactorily an authorized access point representing the work or expression.

c) Record *preliminary* if the data is taken from the description of a resource when the resource is not available.

fully established

5.8 Source Consulted

5.8.1 Basic Instructions on Recording Sources Consulted

5.8.1.1 Scope

A ***source consulted*** is a resource used in determining the title or other identifying attributes of a work or expression.

5.8.1.2 Sources of Information

Take information on sources consulted from any source.

5.8.1.3 Recording Sources Consulted

Cite sources used to determine a preferred or variant title, followed by a brief statement of the information found. Identify the specific location within the source where the information was found.

> An Act to Improve the International Commerce Transportation System of the United States, 1984: page 1 (citation title: Shipping Act of 1984)
>
> Pacheco, Cristina. La luz de México, 1988 series title page: Autores de Guanajuato; title page verso: Colección Autores de Guanajuato
>
> Wikipedia, viewed on December 7, 2007 Ginza Rba (in Mandaic, which translates into The Great Treasure) or Siddra Rba (The Great Book) is one of many holy scriptures of the Mandaean religion. It is also referred to as The Book of Adam

When appropriate, indicate the source where the information for other identifying attributes was found (for a work, see **6.3–6.8**; for an expression, see **6.9–6.13**).

> Premacanda. The gift of a cow, 1987: title page (translation of the Hindi novel, Godaan)
>
> Grove music online, viewed March 27, 2006: Sonata, vc, pf, 1991; also Sonata, vc, pf, 1972–3, rev. 2001
>
> Internet movie database, January 31, 2007 (Beowulf; film released in 2007; directed by Robert Zemeckis; lists one other film with same name, released in 1999)
>
> Flam, Jack D. Matisse : The dance, 1993: page 10, etc. (Dance I, 1909, oil on canvas, Museum of Modern Art, New York; Dance II, 1909–1910, oil on canvas, commissioned by Shchukin, Hermitage Museum, St. Petersburg; Unfinished dance mural, 1931, Musée d'art moderne de la ville de Paris; the Merion dance mural, 1932–1933, Barnes Foundation, Merion, Pa.; Paris Dance Mural, 1933, Musée d'art moderne de la ville de Paris)
>
> L'histoire de Barlaam et Josaphat, 1973 title page (L'histoire de Barlaam et Josaphat; version champenoise, from Bibliotheca Apostolica Vaticana ms. Reg. lat. 660) pages 8–9 (the version champenoise exists in 40 manuscripts in various European libraries; the term "version champenoise" given to the group by Paul Meyer, has stuck in spite of its inexactness)
>
> Bloch, Augustyn. Dialogi, [between 1980 and 1989?]: (label: Gilgamesz, ballet music in the concert version; container: written 1969, a shortened version of ballet of 1968)
>
> New Catholic encyclopedia, [2003], ©2003: volume 2, page 366 (B. and A. Elzevir introduced their second edition of the New Testament (1633) as the textus receptus, "the text received" by all; represents the official text of the Greek Church)

Cite other sources that were consulted but provided no useful information for establishing the preferred title. Record *No information found* following the citation for the source consulted.

> Anonymous classics : a list of uniform headings for European literatures, 2004 (No information found)
>
> Grove music online, searched December 8, 2007 (No information found)
>
> Encyclopaedia Britannica, 15th ed. (No information found)
> Academic American encyclopedia, ©1998 (No information found)
> The Oxford classical dictionary, 1996 (No information found)

5.9 Cataloguer's Note

5.9.1 Basic Instructions on Making Cataloguer's Notes

5.9.1.1 Scope

A ***cataloguer's note*** is an annotation that might be helpful to those using or revising the authorized access point representing a work or expression, or creating an authorized access point representing a related work or expression.

5.9.1.2 Sources of Information

Take information for use in cataloguer's notes from any source.

5.9.1.3 Making Cataloguer's Notes

Make the following notes, if considered important for clarification or justification:

a) notes on the specific instructions applied in creating the authorized access point

b) notes justifying the choice of preferred title, the form of the access point, etc.

c) notes limiting the use of the access point

d) notes differentiating works with similar titles.

> Preferred title chosen as Don Giovanni per 6.14.2.3, better known title in the same language
>
> Commonly known in film reference sources under title Mon oncle
>
> Not the same as FAO animal production and health paper
>
> Consider this and Polska for 2 vc, pf (1977) independent works
>
> Title could also be read as: Institution of Chemical Engineers symposium series
>
> Do not confuse with orchestral accompaniment version
>
> Not to be confused with the quarterly journal of the same title issued by the same publisher

Make any other notes that might be helpful to a cataloguer using or revising the authorized access point, or creating an authorized access point for a related work or expression.

> There are five Matisse paintings called Dance (Danse), which are frequently given sobriquets to distinguish them
>
> For earlier volumes, series statement may have appeared on back covers of paperback editions which were discarded before binding
>
> Sometimes published as AAPG studies in geology series
>
> Series issued also in Catalan
>
> Title fluctuates between Geological Survey professional paper and U.S. Geological Survey professional paper but as of 1300 is more consistently given in latter form; 1299 chosen as cut-off in consultation with the U.S. Department of the Interior Library

6

IDENTIFYING WORKS AND EXPRESSIONS

6.0 Purpose and Scope

This chapter provides general guidelines and instructions on:

a) choosing preferred titles for works (see **6.2.2**)

b) recording preferred and variant titles for works (see **6.2**)

c) recording other identifying attributes of the work or expression (see **6.3–6.13**)

d) constructing authorized access points representing the work or expression (see **6.27.1–6.27.3**)

e) constructing variant access points representing the work or expression (see **6.27.4**).

The chapter provides guidelines on recording titles and other identifying attributes as separate elements, as parts of access points, or as both.

In addition to the general guidelines, the chapter provides instructions on recording preferred and variant titles and other identifying attributes for special types of works and their expressions:

musical works (see **6.14–6.18**)
legal works (see **6.19–6.22**)
religious works (see **6.23–6.25**)
official communications (see **6.26**).

The preferred title for the work is used to construct the authorized access point. The variant title or titles for the work are used to construct variant access points. Other identifying attributes of the work and/or expression may also be included in the access point (see **6.27**).

Authorized access points representing works and expressions can be used for different purposes. They provide the means for:

a) bringing together all descriptions of resources embodying a work when various manifestations have appeared under various titles

b) identifying a work when the title by which it is known differs from the title proper of the resource being described

c) differentiating between two or more works with the same title

d) organizing hierarchical displays of descriptions for resources embodying different expressions of a work

e) recording a relationship to a related work (see chapter **25**) or a related expression (see chapter **26**).

In addition to the general guidelines, the chapter provides instructions on constructing authorized and variant access points for special types of works and expressions:

musical works and expressions (see **6.28**)
legal works and expressions (see **6.29**)
religious works and expressions (see **6.30**)
official communications (see **6.31**).

6.1 General Guidelines on Identifying Works and Expressions

6.1.1 Sources of Information

Take the title or titles of the work from any source.

For additional guidance on sources of information for the preferred title for the work, see **6.2.2.2**.

Take information on other identifying attributes of works and expressions from any source.

6.1.2 Using Access Points to Represent Works and Expressions

An authorized access point is one of the techniques used to represent:

a work or expression embodied in a manifestation (see **17.4.2**)

or

a related work (see **25.1**)

or

a related expression (see **26.1**).

When constructing authorized access points, apply the guidelines at **6.27.1–6.27.3**.

When constructing variant access points, apply the guidelines at **6.27.4**.

6.1.3 Changes Affecting the Identification of a Work

6.1.3.1 Works Issued as Multipart Monographs

For works issued as multipart monographs:

If:
a new description is created as the result of a change in mode of issuance or media type (see **1.6.1**)
and
there is also a change in responsibility for the work
then:
construct the authorized access point for the work to reflect responsibility for the work as represented in the part used as the basis for the new description (see **2.1**).

Consider changes in responsibility requiring the construction of an authorized access point representing a new work to include the following:

a) a change affecting the authorized access point representing a person, family, or corporate body that is used in constructing the authorized access point representing the work (see **6.27.1.1–6.27.1.8**)

b) a change affecting the name of a person, family, or corporate body used as an addition to the authorized access point representing the work (see **6.27.1.9**).

6.1.3.2 Works Issued as Serials

For works issued as serials:

If:
there is a change in responsibility (see **6.1.3.2.1**)
or
there is a major change in title proper (**6.1.3.2.2**).
then:
construct the authorized access point to represent a new work.

6.1.3.2.1 Change in Responsibility for the Work

If there is a change in responsibility, construct the authorized access point representing the work to reflect responsibility for the work as represented in the issue or part of the serial used as the basis for the new description (see **2.1**).

Consider changes in responsibility affecting the construction of the authorized access point for the work to include the following:

a) a change affecting the authorized access point representing a person, family, or corporate body that is used in constructing the authorized access point representing the work (see **6.27.1.1–6.27.1.8**)

b) a change affecting the name of a person, family, or corporate body used as an addition to the authorized access point representing the work (see **6.27.1.9**).

6.1.3.2.2 Major Change in the Title Proper

If there is a major change in the title proper (see **2.3.2.13.1**), construct the authorized access point representing the work to reflect the title as represented in the issue or part of the serial used as the basis for the new description (see **2.1**).

6.1.3.3 Works Issued as Integrating Resources

For works issued as integrating resources:

If:

there is a change in responsibility (see **6.1.3.3.1**)

or

there is a change in title proper (**6.1.3.3.2**).

then:

revise the authorized access point representing the work to reflect the latest iteration.

6.1.3.3.1 Change in Responsibility for the Work

If there is a change in responsibility, revise the authorized access point representing the work to reflect responsibility for the work as represented in the later iteration (see **2.1**). Use the former authorized access point as a variant access point representing the work.

Consider changes in responsibility affecting the construction of the authorized access point representing the work to include the following:

a) a change affecting the authorized access point representing a person, family, or corporate body that is used in constructing the authorized access point representing the work (see **6.27.1.1–6.27.1.8**)

b) a change affecting the name of a person, family, or corporate body used as an addition to the authorized access point representing the work (see **6.27.1.9**).

6.1.3.3.2 Change in the Title Proper

If there is any change in the title proper, revise the authorized access point representing the work to reflect the title as represented in the later iteration (see **2.1.2.4**). Use the former authorized access point as a variant access point representing the work.

6.2 Title of the Work

CORE ELEMENT

Preferred title for the work is a core element. Variant titles for the work are optional.

6.2.1 Basic Instructions on Recording Titles of Works

6.2.1.1 Scope

A ***title of the work*** is a word, character, or group of words and/or characters by which a work is known.

When identifying works, there are two categories of titles:

a) preferred title for the work (see **6.2.2**)

b) variant title for the work (see **6.2.3**).

6.2.1.2 Sources of Information

Take the title or titles of the work from any source.

For additional guidance on sources of information for the preferred title for the work, see **6.2.2.2**.

6.2.1.3 General Guidelines on Recording Titles of Works

When recording a title of a work, apply the guidelines on capitalization, numbers, diacritical marks, initial articles, spacing of initials and acronyms, and abbreviations, at **6.2.1.4–6.2.1.9**. When those guidelines refer to an appendix, apply the additional instructions in that appendix, as applicable.

6.2.1.4 Capitalization

Apply the instructions in appendix A (**A.3**) on the capitalization of titles of works.

6.2.1.5 Numbers Expressed as Numerals or as Words

When recording a title for a work, record numbers expressed as numerals or as words in the form in which they appear on the source of information.

For instructions on recording numerals used to identify particular parts of a work, see **6.2.2.9**.

> 10 things I hate about you
>
> Three threes and one make ten
>
> 3:10 to Yuma

6.2.1.6 Diacritical Marks

Record diacritical marks such as accents appearing in a title for a work as they appear on the source of information.

> *Optional Addition*
>
> Add diacritical marks such as accents that are not present on the source of information. Follow the standard usage for the language of the data.
>
> Études juives
> *Title of first two volumes of series appears without diacritical mark*
>
> Sur l'état du système des timars des XVIIe–XVIIIe ss.
> *Title appears in uppercase letters without diacritical marks*

6.2.1.7 Initial Articles

When recording the title, include an initial article, if present.

> The invisible man
>
> Der seidene Faden
>
> Eine kleine Nachtmusik
>
> La vida plena
>
> The most of P.G. Wodehouse

Alternative

Omit an initial article (see appendix C) unless the title for a work is to be accessed under that article (e.g., a title that begins with the name of a person or place).

Taming of the shrew
not The taming of the shrew

Ángeles borrachos y otros cuentos
not Los ángeles borrachos y otros cuentos

Enfant et les sortilèges
not L'enfant et les sortilèges

but

Los Angeles street map

L'Enfant and Washington, 1791–1792

Le Corbusier et l'architecture sacrée

El Salvador y su desarrollo urbano en el contexto centroamericano

La Niña and its impacts

6.2.1.8 Spacing of Initials and Acronyms

When recording a title for a work:

a) Do not leave a space between a full stop and an initial following it.

b) If separate letters or initials appear on the source of information without full stops between them, record the letters without spaces between them.

T.S. Eliot memorial lectures

Variationen und Fuge über ein Thema von J.S. Bach

ABC of practical astronomy
Title appears as: A B C of practical astronomy

6.2.1.9 Abbreviations

Use only the following abbreviations in titles of works:

a) those that are integral parts of the title

b) *etc.* in the title *Laws, etc.* (see **6.19.2.5**).

Letter to Joseph Hume, Esq., M.P.

Memoirs of Mrs. Abigail Bailey

Speech in the High Court of Parliament in Scotland spoken Novemb. 4, 1641

Konzert über ein Thema von Joh. Seb. Bach

Tech. bull.

Lund studies in geography. Ser. B, Human geography

TITLE

6.2.2 Preferred Title for the Work

CORE ELEMENT

6.2.2.1 Scope

The ***preferred title for the work*** is the title or form of title chosen to identify the work. The preferred title is also the basis for the authorized access point representing that work.

6.2.2.2 Sources of Information

Determine the title to be used as the preferred title for a work created after 1500 from resources embodying the work or from reference sources.

Determine the title to be used as the preferred title for a work created before 1501 from modern reference sources. If the evidence of modern reference sources is inconclusive, use (in this order of preference):

a) modern editions

b) early editions

c) manuscript copies.

CHOOSING THE PREFERRED TITLE

6.2.2.3 General Guidelines on Choosing the Preferred Title

Choose the preferred title for a work by applying the instructions at **6.2.2.4–6.2.2.7**.

For instructions on choosing the preferred title for special types of works, see:

musical works (**6.14.2**)
legal works (**6.19.2**)
religious works (**6.23.2**)
official communications (**6.26.2**).

6.2.2.4 Works Created after 1500

For works created after 1500, choose as the preferred title the title in the original language by which the work has become known either through use in resources embodying the work or in reference sources.

Martin Chuzzlewit

Preferred title for work by Dickens published under various titles: The life and adventures of Martin Chuzzlewit; Martin Chuzzlewit's life and adventures; *and others*

Whitaker's almanack

Preferred title for work first published under the title: An almanack for the year of Our Lord ...

Sun also rises

Preferred title for work by Hemingway also published under the title: Fiesta

Hamlet

Preferred title for work by Shakespeare first published under the title: The tragicall historie of Hamlet, Prince of Denmarke

American scholar

Preferred title for work by Emerson first published under the title: An oration delivered before the Phi Beta Kappa Society, at Cambridge, August 31, 1837

Gulliver's travels

Preferred title for work by Swift first published under the title: Travels into several remote nations of the world / by Lemuel Gulliver

> Trial of treasure
> *Preferred title for work first published under the title:* A new and mery interlude called the Triall of treasure

If:

there is no title in the original language established as the one by which the work is best known

or

in case of doubt

then:

choose the title proper of the original edition (see **2.3.2**) as the preferred title.

Do not include an alternative title as part of the preferred title.

> Pre-Raphaelite tragedy
> *Preferred title for work by William Gaunt later published under the title:* The Pre-Raphaelite dream
>
> Criminal
> *Preferred title for work issued in the United Kingdom as:* The criminal. *Later issued in the United States as:* The concrete jungle
>
> Little acorn
> *Preferred title for work by Christa Kauble that has only one expression and only one manifestation. The manifestation was published under the title:* The little acorn
>
> Listening to popular music
> *Preferred title for work by Theodore Gracyk published as:* Listening to popular music, or, How I learned to stop worrying and love Led Zeppelin

If the work is published simultaneously in different languages and the original language cannot be determined, choose the title proper of the first resource received as the preferred title. If the language editions are in the same resource (e.g., a work issued with the same text in French and English), choose the title proper named on the preferred source of information as the preferred title.

If the work is published simultaneously in the same language under different titles, choose the title proper of the first resource received as the preferred title.

> Rats in the larder
> *Preferred title for work by Joachim Joesten for use in an access point, based on the title of the edition published in New York:* Rats in the larder : the story of Nazi influence in Denmark. *Simultaneously published in London under the title:* Denmark's day of doom. *The resource published in New York is the first received*

For manuscripts and manuscript groups, apply the additional instructions at **6.2.2.7**, as applicable.

6.2.2.5 Works Created before 1501

For works created before 1501, choose as the preferred title the title or form of title in the original language by which the work is identified in modern reference sources. If the evidence of modern reference sources is inconclusive, choose (in this order of preference) the title most frequently found in:

a) modern editions

b) early editions

c) manuscript copies.

Dānishnāmah-ʾi ʿAlāʾī
Preferred title for work by Avicenna

Beowulf

De bello Gallico
Preferred title for work by Julius Caesar

Chanson de Roland

Pardoner's tale
Preferred title for work by Chaucer

Nibelungenlied

Edictum Theodorici

Exceptions

Classical and Byzantine Greek Works.

If:
a work is originally written in classical Greek
or
a work is created by a Greek church father or other Byzantine writer before 1453
then:
choose as the preferred title a well-established title in a language preferred by the agency creating the data.

Birds
not Ornithes
Preferred title for work by Aristophanes

Alexiad
not Alexias
Preferred title for work by Anna Comnena

Ecclesiastical history
not Ekklēsiastikē historia
Preferred title for work by Bishop Eusebius of Caesarea

Iliad
not Ilias
Preferred title for work by Homer

Odyssey
not Odysseia
Preferred title for work by Homer

Republic
not Politeia
Preferred title for work by Plato

Battle of the frogs and mice
not Batrachomyomachia

If there is no well-established title in a language preferred by the agency creating the data, choose the Latin title.

Argonautica
not Argonautika
Preferred title for work by Apollonius Rhodius

Meteorologica
not Meteōrologika
Preferred title for work by Aristotle

Contra Celsum
not Kata Kelsou
Preferred title for work by Origen

Theaetetus
not Theaitētos
Preferred title for work by Plato

If there is neither a well-established title in a language preferred by the agency creating the data nor a Latin title, choose the Greek title.

Synopsis historikē
Preferred title for work by Constantine Manasses

Geōrgos
Preferred title for work by Menander of Athens

Perikeiromenē
Preferred title for work by Menander of Athens

Katomyomachia
Preferred title for work by Theodore Prodromus

Anonymous Works Written Neither in Greek nor in a Preferred Script of the Agency.

If:
the work is an anonymous work created before 1501
and
the work is written neither in Greek nor in a preferred script of the agency creating the data
then:
choose as the preferred title an established title in a language preferred by the agency, if there is such a title.

Arabian nights

Book of the dead

Code of Hammurabi

but

Slovo o polku Igoreve
Published in English under several titles including Igor's tale, The campaign of Igor, *and* The tale of the campaign of Igor

For manuscripts and manuscript groups, apply the additional instructions at **6.2.2.7**, as applicable.

6.2.2.6 Cycles and Stories with Many Versions

A cycle is a collection of independent early poems, romances, etc., in the same language centered on a certain person, event, object, etc. Choose as the preferred title the generally accepted title for the cycle.

> Guillaume d'Orange
> *Resource described:* Guillaume d'Orange : chansons de geste des XIe et XIIe siècles. *Contains:* Li coronemens Looys. Li charrois de Nymes. La prise d'Orenge. Li covenans Vivien. La bataille d'Aleschans

If:
the cycle is identified only by a descriptive phrase (e.g., "the Arthurian romances," "the Grail legends," "the St. Francis legends")
or
the cycle has no established title
then:
use the title proper (see **2.3.2**) of the first resource received as the preferred title.

Do not include an alternative title as part of the preferred title.

> Légende arthurienne
> *First resource received:* La légende arthurienne : études et documents ... les plus anciens textes

For a basic story found in many versions, choose as the preferred title the title that is established in reference sources in a language preferred by the agency creating the data.

> Reynard the Fox
>
> Amis et Amiles

6.2.2.7 Manuscripts and Manuscript Groups

For works contained in a manuscript or manuscripts (including manuscript groups), choose the preferred title by applying the instructions appropriate for the work at **6.2.2.4–6.2.2.6**. If these instructions do not apply, choose one of these options as the preferred title (in this order of preference):

a) a title that has been assigned to the work subsequent to its creation or compilation

> Domesday book
> Cancionero musical de palacio
> Codex Amiatinus

b) the name of the manuscript or manuscript group if the work is identified only by that name

> Book of Lismore
> Dead Sea scrolls
> Tell-el Amarna tablets

c) a devised title. Use the authorized access point representing the repository (see **11.13.1**) followed by *Manuscript*. Add the repository's designation for the manuscript or manuscript group. If the manuscript is a single item within a collection, add the foliation, if known.

> British Library. Manuscript. Arundel 384
> Yale University. Music Library. Manuscript. LM 4708
> Herzog August Bibliothek. Manuscript. Helmstedt 628, folio 185–192

Variant titles. If the preferred title is chosen by applying a) or b) in this instruction and the manuscript or manuscript group has a repository designation, record a devised title as a variant title (see **6.2.3.5**). Construct the devised title by applying c) in this instruction.

RECORDING THE PREFERRED TITLE

6.2.2.8 Recording the Preferred Title for a Work

This instruction applies to single works and to compilations of works by different persons, families, and corporate bodies.

Record the title chosen as the preferred title for a work by applying the basic instructions at **6.2.1**.

When recording the preferred title for part of a work, see the additional instructions at **6.2.2.9**.

When recording the preferred title for a compilation of works by one person, family or corporate body, see the additional instructions at **6.2.2.10**.

When recording the preferred title for special types of works, see these additional instructions, as applicable:

musical works (**6.14.2**)
legal works (**6.19.2**)
religious works (**6.23.2**).

For instructions on using the preferred title to construct the authorized access point representing a work, see **6.27.1**.

6.2.2.9 Recording the Preferred Title for a Part or Parts of a Work

Record the preferred title for a part or parts of a work by applying the instructions at **6.2.2.9.1–6.2.2.9.2**, as applicable.

Exceptions

For parts of musical works, apply instead the instructions at **6.14.2.7**.

For parts of religious works, apply instead the instructions at **6.23.2.9–6.23.2.20**.

For instructions on constructing the authorized access point representing a part or parts of a work, see **6.27.2**.

6.2.2.9.1 One Part

Record the preferred title for the part by applying the basic instructions at **6.2.1**.

Two towers
Preferred title for a part of J.R.R. Tolkien's The lord of the rings

Du côté de chez Swann
Preferred title for a part of Marcel Proust's À la recherche du temps perdu

Come like shadows
Preferred title for a part of Simon Raven's Alms for oblivion

Sindbad the sailor
Preferred title for a part of The Arabian nights

Studia musicologica Upsaliensia
Preferred title for a part of Acta Universitatis Upsaliensis

Executive summary
Preferred title for a part of Annual report on carcinogens

King of the hill
Preferred title for a part of the television program The Simpsons

If the part is identified only by a general term with or without a numeric or alphabetic designation (e.g., Preface; Book 1; Band 3), record the designation of the part as the preferred title for the part. Record the numeric designation as a numeral.

Book 1
Preferred title for a part of Homer's Iliad

1. Theil
Preferred title for a part of Johann Wolfgang von Goethe's Faust

Supplement
Preferred title for a part of Raffles bulletin of zoology

A
Preferred title for a part of Emergency health series

Reeks B
Preferred title for a part of Annale van die Uniwersiteit van Stellenbosch

Season 6
Preferred title for a part of the television program Buffy, the vampire slayer

1946-03-10
Preferred title for a part of the radio program Jack Benny program

Exception

Serials and integrating resources. If the part is identified by both a designation and a title, record the designation first, followed by the title. Use a comma to separate the designation from the title.

> 2e partie, Sciences biologiques, industries alimentaires, agriculture
> *Preferred title for a part of* Bulletin analytique
>
> Series C, Traditional skills and practices
> *Preferred title for a part of* Marshallese culture and history

6.2.2.9.2 Two or More Parts

Consecutively numbered parts identified only by a general term and a number. When identifying a sequence of two or more consecutively numbered parts of a work, each of which is identified only by a general term and a number, record the designation of the parts as the preferred title. Record the general term in the singular followed by the inclusive numbers of the parts. Record the numeric designations as numerals.

> Book 1–6
> *Preferred title for the first six books of Homer's* Iliad
>
> Chapitre 6–7
> *Preferred title for chapters 6–7 of Henri Rollin's* L'apocalypse de notre temps

Unnumbered or non-consecutively numbered parts. When identifying two or more unnumbered or non-consecutively numbered parts of a work, record the preferred title for each of the parts. Apply the instructions at **6.2.2.9.1**.

> Purgatorio
> *Preferred title for a part of Dante Alighieri's* Divina commedia *in a compilation also comprising the part* Paradiso
>
> Paradiso
> *Preferred title for a part of Dante Alighieri's* Divina commedia *in a compilation also comprising the part* Purgatorio
>
> Book 1
> *Preferred title for a part of Homer's* Iliad *in a compilation also comprising book 6*
>
> Book 6
> *Preferred title for a part of Homer's* Iliad *in a compilation also comprising book 1*

Alternative

When identifying two or more unnumbered or non-consecutively numbered parts of a work, identify the parts collectively. Record the conventional collective title *Selections* as the preferred title for the parts. Apply this instruction instead of or in addition to recording the preferred title for each of the parts.

> Selections
> *Preferred title for the parts of the work in a compilation comprising books 1 and 6 of Homer's* Iliad
>
> Selections
> Book 1

Book 6

Preferred titles for the parts of the work in a compilation comprising books 1 and 6 of Homer's Iliad. The parts are identified collectively and individually

Selections

Preferred title for the parts of the work in a compilation comprising four episodes of the television program The Simpsons *originally broadcast between 1990 and 2001*

6.2.2.10 Recording the Preferred Title for a Compilation of Works of One Person, Family, or Corporate Body

If a compilation of works is known by a title that is used in resources embodying that compilation or in reference sources, apply the instructions at **6.2.2.4–6.2.2.5**.

For other compilations, apply the instructions at **6.2.2.10.1–6.2.2.10.3**, as applicable.

6.2.2.10.1 Complete Works

Record the conventional collective title *Works* as the preferred title for a compilation of works that consists of, or purports to be, the complete works of a person, family, or corporate body. Consider complete works to include all works that are complete at the time of publication.

6.2.2.10.2 Complete Works in a Single Form

Record one of the following conventional collective titles as the preferred title for a compilation of works that consists of, or purports to be, the complete works of a person, family, or corporate body, in one particular form:

Correspondence

Essays

Librettos

Lyrics

Novels

Plays

Poems

Prose works

Short stories

Speeches

If none of these terms is appropriate, record an appropriate specific collective title.

Posters

Fragments

Encyclicals

Do not apply to compilations of musical works (see **6.14.2.8**).

If the compilation consists of two or more but not all the works of one person, family, or corporate body in a particular form, apply the instructions at **6.2.2.10.3**

6.2.2.10.3 Other Compilations of Two or More Works

Record the preferred title for each of the works in a compilation that consists of:

a) two or more but not all the works of one person, family, or corporate body, in a particular form
or
b) two or more but not all the works of one person, family, or corporate body, in various forms.

Apply the basic instructions on recording titles of works at **6.2.1**.

> Dirk Gently's Holistic Detective Agency
> *First work in a compilation also containing Douglas Adams's* Long dark tea-time of the soul
>
> Long dark tea-time of the soul
> *Second work by Douglas Adams in the same compilation*

Alternative

When identifying two or more works in a compilation, identify the parts collectively by recording a conventional collective title (see **6.2.2.10.1** or **6.2.2.10.2**), as applicable, followed by *Selections*. Apply this instruction instead of or in addition to recording the preferred title for each of the works in the compilation.

> Novels. Selections

Exceptions

For compilations of musical works by a single composer, apply instead the instructions at **6.14.2.8**.
For compilations of laws, etc., apply instead the instructions at **6.19.2.5.1**.

6.2.3 Variant Title for the Work

6.2.3.1 Scope

A ***variant title for the work*** is a title or form of title by which a work is known that differs from the title or form of title chosen as the preferred title for the work.

6.2.3.2 Sources of Information

Take variant titles for a work from any source.

6.2.3.3 General Guidelines on Recording Variant Titles for Works

Record variant titles for works by applying the basic instructions at **6.2.1**.

Record a variant title for the work when it is different from the title recorded as the preferred title. Record as a variant title:

a title or form of title under which the work has been issued or cited in reference sources

or

a title resulting from a different transliteration of the title.

Exception

Record a title appearing on a manifestation of the work as a variant title for the work only in the following case:

if the title appearing on the manifestation differs significantly from the preferred title

and

if the work itself might reasonably be searched by that title.

For instructions on recording the title proper and other titles appearing on the manifestation, see **2.3**.

Apply the specific instructions at **6.2.3.4–6.2.3.5**, as applicable. Apply instructions in preceding sections of chapter 6, as applicable.

For instructions on using a variant title for the work to construct a variant access point representing a work, see **6.27.4**.

6.2.3.4 Alternative Linguistic Form of Title for the Work

If the title recorded as the preferred title for a work has one or more alternative linguistic forms, record them as variant titles for the work.

Different Language Form

Aisōpou mythoi
Fabulae Aesopi
English language form recorded as preferred title: Aesop's fables

Roland
Rolandslied
Song of Roland
French language form recorded as preferred title: Chanson de Roland

Hamlet
Russian language form for a 1964 motion picture recorded as preferred title: Gamlet

Leabhar an Leasa Mhóir
Leabhar Mhic Cárthaigh Riabhaigh
English language form recorded as preferred title: Book of Lismore

Liang nong zu zhi jia xu sheng chan he wei sheng cong shu
Loạt sách về chăn nuôi thú y của FAO
English language form recorded as preferred title: FAO animal production and health series

Annals of the University of Stellenbosch. Section B
Afrikaans language form recorded as preferred title: Annale van die Uniwersiteit van Stellenbosch. Reeks B

Dunhuang xie ben
English language form recorded as preferred title: Dunhuang manuscripts

Ḳodeḳs Vilnah 262
English language form recorded as preferred title: Vilnius codex 262

Different Script

大藏經
Chinese transliterated form recorded as preferred title: Da zang jing

Первые на луне
Russian transliterated form recorded as preferred title: Pervye na lune

טעוויע דער מילכיקער
טביה דער מילכיקער
Yiddish transliterated form recorded as preferred title: Ṭevye der milkhiḳer

ألف ليلة وليلة
كتاب ألف ليلة وليلة
English language form recorded as preferred title: Arabian nights

מגילות ים המלח
מגילות מדבר יהודה
מגילות פון ים המלח
死海文書
사해문서
ม้วนหนังสือแห่งทะเลสาบเดดซี
Χειρόγραφα της Νεκράς Θάλασσας
Кумранские рукописи
English language form recorded as preferred title: Dead Sea scrolls

粮农组织家畜生产和卫生丛书
English language form recorded as preferred title: FAO animal production and health series

Manuscript. Волоколамское собрание no. 630
Russian transliterated form recorded in preferred title: Manuscript. Volokolamskoe sobranie no. 630. *A manuscript in the collection of the Rossiĭskai͡a nat͡sional′nai͡a biblioteka*

敦煌寫本
English language form recorded as preferred title: Dunhuang manuscripts

Different Spelling

Eastward ho
Preferred title recorded as: Eastward hoe

Ṭevyeh der milkhiḳer
Preferred title recorded as: Ṭevye der milkhiḳer

Doomsday book
Preferred title recorded as: Domesday book

Cronycles of Englond
Preferred title recorded as: Chronicles of England

Annale van die Universiteit van Stellenbosch. Reeks B
Preferred title recorded as: Annale van die Uniwersiteit van Stellenbosch. Reeks B

Different Transliteration

Ta tsang ching
Preferred title recorded as: Da zang jing

Anyuta
Preferred title recorded as: Ani͡uta

Tun-huang manuscripts
Preferred title recorded as: Dunhuang manuscripts

6.2.3.5 Other Variant Title for the Work

Record other variant titles and variant forms of the title not covered by **6.2.3.4**.

Personal history of David Copperfield
Preferred title recorded as: David Copperfield

Encyclopædia Britannica Films presents Historical America in song
Preferred title recorded as: Historical America in song

2 towers
Lord of the rings. Two towers
Preferred title recorded as: Two towers

Three men and a baby
Preferred title recorded as: 3 men and a baby

Book of Mac Carthy Reagh
Book of Mac Cárthaigh Riabhach
Lismore, Book of
Preferred title recorded as: Book of Lismore

Dead Sea scrolls. 11QT
Dead Sea scrolls. Temple scroll
Preferred title recorded as: Temple scroll

Codex Egerton 2895
Codex Sánchez Solís
Codex Waecker Götter
Codice Zapoteco
Preferred title recorded as: Manuscript. Egerton 2895. *A manuscript in the collection of the British Library*

Cronycles of the londe of Englōd
Cronycles of the londe of Englond
Preferred title recorded as: Chronicles of England

Here begynneth a lytell treatyse for to lerne Englysshe and Frensshe
Here is a good boke to lerne to speke French
Preferred title recorded as: Lytell treatyse for to lerne Englysshe and Frensshe

Collected papers of Albert Einstein
Gesammelte Schriften Albert Einstein
Preferred title recorded as: Works

Selected plays of Lady Gregory
Short plays of Lady Gregory
Seven short plays
Preferred title recorded as: Plays. Selections

OTHER IDENTIFYING ATTRIBUTES OF WORKS

6.3 Form of Work

CORE ELEMENT

Form of work is a core element when needed to differentiate a work from another work with the same title or from the name of a person, family, or corporate body.

6.3.1 Basic Instructions on Recording Form of Work

6.3.1.1 Scope

Form of work is a class or genre to which a work belongs.

6.3.1.2 Sources of Information

Take information on form of work from any source.

6.3.1.3 Recording Form of Work

Record the form of the work.

Record form of work as a separate element, as part of an access point, or as both. For instructions on recording form of work as part of the authorized access point, see **6.27.1.9**.

> Play
> *Form of work of:* Charlemagne
>
> Tapestry
> *Form of work of:* Charlemagne
>
> Choreographic work
> *Form of work of:* The nutcracker
>
> Computer file
> *Form of work of:* NuTCRACKER
>
> Motion picture
> *Form of work of:* Ocean's eleven. *A film released in 1960*
>
> Motion picture
> *Form of work of:* Ocean's eleven. *A film released in 2001*
>
> Radio program
> *Form of work of:* War of the worlds
>
> Television program
> *Form of work of:* War of the worlds
>
> Chanson de geste
> *Form of work of:* Guillaume
>
> Series
> *Form of work of:* Scottish History Society
>
> Poem
> *Form of work of:* Chanson de Roland

6.4 Date of Work

CORE ELEMENT

Date of work is a core element to identify a treaty. Date of work is also a core element when needed to differentiate a work from another work with the same title or from the name of a person, family, or corporate body.

6.4.1 Basic Instructions on Recording Date of Work

6.4.1.1 Scope

Date of work is the earliest date associated with a work.

If no specific date can be identified as the date the work was created, treat the date of the earliest manifestation embodying the work as the date of work.

For instructions on date of promulgation of a law, etc., see **6.20.2**.

For instructions on date of a treaty, see **6.20.3**.

6.4.1.2 Sources of Information

Take information on date of work from any source.

6.4.1.3 Recording Date of Work

Record the date of the work in terms of the calendar preferred by the agency creating the data.

For works other than treaties, generally record the date of the work by giving the year or years alone.

For treaties, generally record the date of the work by giving the year, month, and day (see **6.20.3.3**).

For details on recording dates according to the Christian calendar, see appendix **H**.

Record date of work as a separate element, as part of an access point, or as both. For instructions on recording date of work as part of the authorized access point, see **6.27.1.9**.

For instructions on recording date of work as part of authorized access points representing special types of works, see additional instructions:

musical works (**6.28.1.9**–**6.28.1.10**)
legal works (**6.29.1.29**–**6.29.1.30**).

1631
Date of creation of a work by Rembrandt Harmenszoon van Rijn with title Adoration of the shepherds

1654
Date of creation of another work by Rembrandt Harmenszoon van Rijn with title Adoration of the shepherds

1960
Date of release of a motion picture titled Ocean's eleven

2001
Date of release of another motion picture titled Ocean's eleven

1762
Date of first publication of a periodical titled Dublin magazine

1965
Date of first publication of another periodical titled Dublin magazine

1987–1989
Date of creation of the motion picture Paris is burning. *Film was copyrighted in 1990 and shown at festivals that same year, but not released commercially until 1991*

1983
Date of creation of the Stephen Sondheim musical Sunday in the park with George

2004
Date of release of the motion picture Harry Potter and the prisoner of Azkaban

Indicate the source of information by applying the instructions at **5.8.1.3**.

6.5 Place of Origin of the Work

CORE ELEMENT

Place of origin of the work is a core element when needed to differentiate a work from another work with the same title or from the name of a person, family, or corporate body.

6.5.1 Basic Instructions on Recording Place of Origin of the Work

6.5.1.1 Scope

Place of origin of the work is the country or other territorial jurisdiction from which a work originated.

6.5.1.2 Sources of Information

Take information on place of origin of the work from any source.

6.5.1.3 Recording Place of Origin of the Work

Record the place of origin of the work. Record the place name as instructed in chapter **16**. Abbreviate the names of countries, states, provinces, territories, etc., as instructed in Appendix B (**B.11**), as applicable.

Record the place of origin as a separate element, as part of an access point, or as both. For instructions on recording the place of origin as part of the authorized access point, see **6.27.1.9**.

For instructions on recording place of origin as part of authorized access points representing musical works, see additional instructions at **6.28.1.9–6.28.1.10**.

Boise, Idaho
Place of origin of the monthly The advocate

Nairobi, Kenya
Place of origin of the quarterly The advocate

Australia
Place of origin of a television program titled Big brother

Netherlands
Place of origin of a television program titled Big brother

Geneva, Switzerland
Place of origin of the monographic series Collection "Passé et présent"

Indicate the source of information by applying the instructions at **5.8.1.3**.

6.6 Other Distinguishing Characteristic of the Work

CORE ELEMENT

Other distinguishing characteristic of the work is a core element when needed to differentiate a work from another work with the same title or from the name of a person, family, or corporate body.

6.6.1 Basic Instructions on Recording Other Distinguishing Characteristics of Works

6.6.1.1 Scope

Other distinguishing characteristic of the work is a characteristic other than form of work, date of work, or place of origin of the work. It serves to differentiate a work from another work with the same title or from the name of a person, family, or corporate body.

For instructions on recording other distinguishing characteristics of a legal work, see **6.21**.

6.6.1.2 Sources of Information

Take information on other distinguishing characteristics of the work from any source.

6.6.1.3 Recording Other Distinguishing Characteristics of Works

Record other distinguishing characteristics of the work.

Record other distinguishing characteristics of the work as separate elements, as parts of access points, or as both. For instructions on recording other distinguishing characteristics of the work as part of the authorized access point, see **6.27.1.9**.

For instructions on recording other distinguishing characteristics of the work as part of authorized access points representing special types of works, see additional instructions:

musical works (**6.28.1.9–6.28.1.10**)

legal works (**6.29.1.29–6.29.1.30**).

Geological Survey (South Africa)
Issuing body of a work titled Bulletin

New York State Museum
Issuing body of a different work titled Bulletin

New Zealand. Ministry of Education. Research and Statistics Division
Issuing body of a different work titled Bulletin

Anglo-Saxon poem
Other distinguishing characteristic of a work titled Genesis

Middle High German poem
Other distinguishing characteristic of a different work titled Genesis

Old Saxon poem
Other distinguishing characteristic of a different work titled Genesis

Galleria sabauda (Turin, Italy)
Owner of a Jan van Eyck painting titled Saint Francis receiving the stigmata

Philadelphia Museum of Art
Owner of a different Jan van Eyck painting titled Saint Francis receiving the stigmata

Douglas
Surname of the director of a 1965 motion picture titled Harlow

Segal
Surname of the director of a different 1965 motion picture titled Harlow

Canadian Broadcasting Corporation
Production company of a 1963 television program titled Othello

WOR-TV (Television station : New York, N.Y.)
Production company of a different 1963 television program titled Othello

Unnumbered
Other distinguishing characteristic of a work titled Caribbean writers series

Indicate the source of information by applying the instructions at **5.8.1.3**.

6.7 History of the Work

6.7.1 Basic Instructions on Recording the History of the Work

6.7.1.1 Scope

History of the work is information about the history of a work.

6.7.1.2 Sources of Information

Take information on the history of the work from any source.

6.7.1.3 Recording the History of the Work

Record information about the history of the work.

Record the history of the work as a separate element. History of the work is not recorded as part of the access point.

Originally written as a serial and published in 19 issues over 20 months from March 1836 to October 1837. There was no issue in May 1837 as Dickens was in mourning for his sister-in-law

History of Charles Dickens's Pickwick papers

Originally released as a motion picture in 1941 under title All that money can buy; re-released later that year as The Devil and Daniel Webster; re-issued in 1952 in a shortened version as Daniel and the Devil. Based on Stephen Vincent Benét's short story The Devil and Daniel Webster

History of the motion picture The Devil and Daniel Webster

Numbers 1–24 of the Manuscript report series were issued from 1964–1972 by Canada's Marine Sciences Branch. Numbers 25–54 were issued from 1972–1979 by the Marine Sciences Directorate. Since 1980, numbers 55 and on have been issued by the Marine Sciences and Information Directorate

History of the monographic series Manuscript report series

Book of the dead is the common name for an ancient Egyptian collection of funerary texts made up of spells or magic formulas, placed in tombs and believed to protect and aid the deceased in the hereafter. Probably compiled and re-edited during the 16th century B.C., the collection included Coffin texts dating from approximately 2000 B.C., Pyramid texts dating from approximately 2400 B.C., and other writings. Later compilations included hymns to Re, the sun god. Numerous authors, compilers, and sources contributed to the work. Scribes copied the texts on rolls of papyrus, often colourfully illustrated, and sold them to individuals for burial use. Many copies of the book have been found in Egyptian tombs, but none contains all of the approximately 200 known chapters. The collection, literally titled "The Chapters of Coming-Forth-by-Day," received its present name from Karl Richard Lepsius, German Egyptologist who published the first collection of the texts in 1842. The Papyrus of Ani is a well-known manuscript embodying this work

History of the Book of the dead

As appropriate, incorporate information associated with specific identifying elements (see **6.2.3–6.6**) into a history of the work element.

Indicate the source of information by applying the instructions at **5.8.1.3**.

6.8 Identifier for the Work

CORE ELEMENT

6.8.1 Basic Instructions on Recording Identifiers for Works

6.8.1.1 Scope

An ***identifier for the work*** is a character string uniquely associated with a work, or with a surrogate for a work (e.g., an authority record). The identifier serves to differentiate that work from other works.

6.8.1.2 Sources of Information

Take information on identifiers for works from any source.

6.8.1.3 Recording Identifiers for Works

Record an identifier for the work. Precede the identifier with the name or an identification of the agency, etc., responsible for assigning the identifier, if readily ascertainable.

ISWC: T-072.106.546-8

International Standard Musical Work Code for Cole Porter's I love Paris

National Library of Australia: anbd.aut-an35237496
Australian National Bibliographic Database permalink for Peter Carey's Oscar and Lucinda

Library of Congress control number: n 79046204
Identifier for the sacred work The Qur'an

Library and Archives Canada control number: 0053E3950E
Identifier for the sacred work The Qur'an

MOHAI 83.10.5,989
Identifier for a photographic image in the Museum of History and Industry

OTHER IDENTIFYING ATTRIBUTES OF EXPRESSIONS

6.9 Content Type

CORE ELEMENT

6.9.1 Basic Instructions on Recording Content Type

6.9.1.1 Scope

Content type is a categorization reflecting the fundamental form of communication in which the content is expressed and the human sense through which it is intended to be perceived. For content expressed in the form of an image or images, content type also reflects the number of spatial dimensions in which the content is intended to be perceived and the perceived presence or absence of movement.

6.9.1.2 Sources of Information

Take information on content type from any source.

6.9.1.3 Recording Content Type

Record the type of content contained in the resource using one or more of the terms listed in **table 6.1** . Record as many terms as are applicable to the resource being described.

Record content type as a separate element, as part of an access point, or as both. For additional instructions on recording content type as part of the authorized access point, see **6.27.3**.

Alternative

If the resource being described consists of more than one content type, record only

a) the content type that applies to the predominant part of the resource (if there is a predominant part)
or
b) the content types that apply to the most substantial parts of the resource (including the predominant part, if there is one).

Use one or more of the terms listed in in table 6.1, as appropriate.

TABLE 6.1

cartographic dataset	Cartographic content expressed through a digitally encoded dataset intended to be processed by a computer. For cartographic data intended to be perceived in the form of an image or three-dimensional form, see *cartographic image, cartographic moving image, cartographic tactile image, cartographic tactile*

	three-dimensional form, and *cartographic three-dimensional form.*
cartographic image	Cartographic content expressed through line, shape, shading, etc., intended to be perceived visually as a still image or images in two dimensions. Includes maps, views, atlases, remote-sensing images, etc.
cartographic moving image	Cartographic content expressed through images intended to be perceived as moving, in two dimensions. Includes satellite images of the Earth or other celestial bodies in motion.
cartographic tactile image	Cartographic content expressed through line, shape, and/or other forms, intended to be perceived through touch as a still image in two dimensions.
cartographic tactile three-dimensional form	Cartographic content expressed through a form or forms intended to be perceived through touch as a three-dimensional form or forms.
cartographic three-dimensional form	Cartographic content expressed through a form or forms intended to be perceived visually in three-dimensions. Includes globes, relief models, etc.
computer dataset	Content expressed through a digitally encoded dataset intended to be processed by a computer. Includes numeric data, environmental data, etc., used by applications software to calculate averages, correlations, etc., or to produce models, etc., but not normally displayed in its raw form. For data intended to be perceived visually in the form of notation, image, or three-dimensional form, see *notated movement, notated music, still image, text, three-dimensional form, three-dimensional moving image,* and *two-dimensional moving image.* For data intended to be perceived in an audible form, see *performed music, sounds,* and *spoken word.* For cartographic data see *cartographic dataset.*
computer program	Content expressed through digitally encoded instructions intended to be processed and performed by a computer. Includes operating systems, applications software, etc.
notated movement	Content expressed through a form of notation for movement intended to be perceived visually. Includes all forms of movement notation other than those intended to be perceived through touch (see *tactile notated movement*).
notated music	Content expressed through a form of musical notation intended to be perceived visually. Includes all forms of musical notation other than those intended to be perceived through touch (see *tactile notated music*).
performed music	Content expressed through music in an audible form. Includes recorded performances of music, computer-generated music, etc.

sounds	Content other than language or music, expressed in an audible form. Includes natural sounds, artificially produced sounds, etc.
spoken word	Content expressed through language in an audible form. Includes recorded readings, recitations, speeches, interviews, oral histories, etc., computer-generated speech, etc.
still image	Content expressed through line, shape, shading, etc., intended to be perceived visually as a still image or images in two dimensions. Includes drawings, paintings, diagrams, photographic images (stills), etc. For cartographic content intended to be perceived as a two-dimensional image, see *cartographic image.* For images intended to be perceived through touch, see *tactile image.*
tactile image	Content expressed through line, shape, and/or other forms, intended to be perceived through touch as a still image in two dimensions.
tactile notated movement	Content expressed through a form of notation for movement intended to be perceived through touch.
tactile notated music	Content expressed through a form of musical notation intended to be perceived through touch. Includes braille music and other tactile forms of musical notation.
tactile text	Content expressed through a form of notation for language intended to be perceived through touch. Includes braille text and other tactile forms of language notation.
tactile three-dimensional form	Content expressed through a form or forms intended to be perceived through touch as a three-dimensional form or forms.
text	Content expressed through a form of notation for language intended to be perceived visually. Includes all forms of language notation other than those intended to be perceived through touch (see *tactile text*).
three-dimensional form	Content expressed through a form or forms intended to be perceived visually in three-dimensions. Includes sculptures, models, naturally occurring objects and specimens, holograms, etc. For cartographic content intended to be perceived as a three-dimensional form, see *cartographic three-dimensional form.* For three-dimensional forms intended to be perceived through touch, see *tactile three-dimensional form.*
three-dimensional moving image	Content expressed through images intended to be perceived as moving, in three dimensions. Includes 3-D motion pictures (using live action and/or animation), 3-D video games, etc. Three-dimensional moving images may or may not be accompanied by sound.
two-dimensional moving image	Content expressed through images intended to be perceived as moving, in two dimensions. Includes

motion pictures (using live action and/or animation), film and video recordings of performances, events, etc., video games, etc., other than those intended to be perceived in three dimensions (see *three-dimensional moving image*). Moving images may or may not be accompanied by sound. For cartographic content intended to be perceived as a two-dimensional moving image, see *cartographic moving image.*

If none of the terms listed in **table 6.1** apply to the content of the resource being described, record *other.*

If the content type applicable to the resource being described cannot be readily ascertained, record *unspecified.*

6.10 Date of Expression

CORE ELEMENT

Date of expression is a core element when needed to differentiate an expression of a work from another expression of the same work.

6.10.1 Basic Instructions on Recording Date of Expression

6.10.1.1 Scope

Date of expression is the earliest date associated with an expression.

The date of expression may represent the date a text was written, the date of final editing of a moving image work, the date of first broadcast for a television or radio program, the date of notation for a score, the date of the recording of an event, etc.

If no specific date can be identified as the date of expression, treat the date of the earliest manifestation embodying the expression as the date of expression.

For additional instructions on date of expression of religious works, see **6.24**.

6.10.1.2 Sources of Information

Take information on date of expression from any source.

6.10.1.3 Recording Date of Expression

Record the date of the expression in terms of the calendar preferred by the agency creating the data. For details on recording dates according to the Christian calendar, see appendix **H**.

Record the date of the expression by giving the year or years alone unless a more specific date is needed to distinguish one expression from another expression.

Record date of expression as a separate element, as part of an access point, or as both. For instructions on recording date of expression as part of the authorized access point, see **6.27.3**.

For instructions on recording date of expression as part of the authorized access point representing an expression of the Bible, see instructions at **6.30.3.2**.

2000

Resource described: The complete works of Oscar Wilde / general editors, Russell Jackson and Ian Small. — Oxford ; New York : Oxford University Press, 2000–

1948

Resource described: The works of Oscar Wilde / edited, with an introduction, by G.F. Maine. — New collected edition. — London : Collins, 1948

1940

Resource described: Babar and his children / Jean de Brunhoff. — [United States] : Decca, [1940]. *An audio recording of an English translation of Jean de Brunhoff's children's story Babar en famille, narrated by Frank Luther with instrumental accompaniment. Recorded in New York City on October 28, 1940*

1992

Resource described: Blade runner / a Ladd Company release in association with Sir Run Run Shaw thru Warner Bros. ; Jerry Perenchio and Bud Yorkin present a Michael Deeley-Ridley Scott production ; produced by Michael Deeley ; screenplay by Hampton Fancher and David Peoples ; directed by Ridley Scott. — Director's cut, Widescreen version. *A revised version of the 1982 motion picture*

6.11 Language of Expression

CORE ELEMENT

6.11.1 Basic Instructions on Recording Language of Expression

6.11.1.1 Scope

Language of expression is a language in which a work is expressed.

6.11.1.2 Sources of Information

Take information on language of expression from any source.

6.11.1.3 Recording Language of Expression

Record the language or languages of the expression using an appropriate term or terms in a language preferred by the agency creating the data. Select terms from a standard list of names of languages, if available.

Record language of expression as a separate element, as part of an access point, or as both. For instructions on recording language of expression as part of the authorized access point, see **6.27.3**.

For instructions on recording language of expression as part of authorized access points representing expressions of special types of works, see additional instructions:

expressions of musical works (**6.28.3.6**)

expressions of religious works (**6.30.3.1**–**6.30.3.3**).

English

Resource described: The Zemganno brothers / by Edmond de Goncourt. *An English translation of a French novel*

Indonesian

Resource described: Ada apa dengan Cinta? / Miles Productions mempersembahkan ; sebuah film dari Rudi Soedjarwo ; produser, Mira Lesmana, Riri Riza ; skenario, Jujur Prananto. *The original motion picture in Indonesian*

Spanish

Resource described: Obras completas / W. Somerset Maugham. *A Spanish translation of the author's works*

English

Resource described: Colloid journal of the Russian Academy of Sciences. *An English translation of a Russian serial*

Hebrew

Resource described: Mosheh ṿe-Aharon : operah be-shalosh maʻarakhot / Arnold Shenberg ; tirgem Yiśra'el Eliraz. *A Hebrew translation of the libretto to Schoenberg's opera Moses und Aron*

Russian

Resource described: 27 ukradennykh p͡otseluev. *A Georgian motion picture dubbed into Russian*

Chinese

Resource described: Handel's Messiah in Chinese. *An audio recording of a performance of a Chinese translation of the oratorio*

If the expression involves more than one language, apply the additional instructions at **6.11.1.4**.

For guidelines on recording details about the language of expression, apply the instructions for language of the content at **7.12**.

6.11.1.4 Expressions Involving More Than One Language

If a single expression of a work involves more than one language, record each of the languages.

English
German
Russian

Resource described: Defiance / Paramount Vantage presents a Grosvenor Park/Bedford Falls production ; an Edward Zwick film ; executive producer, Marshall Herskovitz ; produced by Edward Zwick, Pieter Jan Brugge ; director of photography, Eduardo Serra ; screenplay by Clayton Frohman & Edward Zwick ; directed by Edward Zwick. *A motion picture with some dialogue in English, some dialogue in German, and some dialogue in Russian.*

English
Dutch
French
German
Italian
Spanish
Portuguese

Resource described: Joan Blaeu Atlas maior of 1665 / introduction and texts by Peter van der Krogt ; based on the copy in the Österreichische Nationalbibliothek, Wien ; with a selection of original texts by Joan Blaeu ; directed and produced by Benedikt Taschen. *An atlas in six volumes; each volume includes text in English and two of the other languages*

6.12 Other Distinguishing Characteristic of the Expression

CORE ELEMENT

Other distinguishing characteristic of the expression is a core element when needed to differentiate an expression of a work from another expression of the same work.

6.12.1 Basic Instructions on Recording Other Distinguishing Characteristics of the Expression

6.12.1.1 Scope

Other distinguishing characteristic of the expression is a characteristic other than content type, language of expression, or date of expression. It serves to differentiate an expression from another expression of the same work.

For additional instructions on other distinguishing characteristics of expressions of musical works, see **6.18**.

For additional instructions on other distinguishing characteristics of expressions of religious works, see **6.25**.

6.12.1.2 Sources of Information

Take information on other distinguishing characteristics of the expression from any source.

6.12.1.3 Recording Other Distinguishing Characteristics of the Expression

Record other distinguishing characteristics of the expression.

Record other distinguishing characteristics of the expression as separate elements, as parts of access points, or as both. For instructions on recording other distinguishing characteristics of the expression as part of the authorized access point, see **6.27.3**.

Buriat version
An expression of the epic poem Gesar

Mongolian version
Another expression of the epic poem Gesar

1st version
The first of three versions of Johann Gottlieb Fichte's Wissenschaftslehre 1804

2nd version
The second of three versions of Johann Gottlieb Fichte's Wissenschaftslehre 1804

A-text
The earliest version of William Langland's narrative poem Piers Plowman

B-text
A later version of William Langland's narrative poem Piers Plowman

C-text
An even later version of William Langland's narrative poem Piers Plowman

Beck
An English translation by Tom Beck of Aleksandr Pushkin's Evgeniĭ Onegin

Elton
An English translation by Oliver Elton of Aleksandr Pushkin's Evgeniĭ Onegin

Director's cut
The 1992 revised version of the 1982 motion picture Blade runner

Final cut
The 2007 revised version of the 1982 motion picture Blade runner

Baryshnikov
A version of the choreographic work The nutcracker *choreographed by Mikhail Baryshnikov in 1976*

Lynn and Uthoff
A version of the choreographic work The nutcracker *choreographed by Enid Lynn and Michael Uthoff in 1974*

Nureyev, after Vaĭnonen
A version of the choreographic work The nutcracker *choreographed by Rudolf Nureyev in 1967 and derived from Vasiliĭ Vaĭnonen's 1934 version*

Nelson Thornes
An expression of Shakespeare's complete works published in 2003 by Nelson Thornes

Yale University Press
Another expression of Shakespeare's complete works published in 2003 by Yale University Press

Dussollier
An audio recording of Victor Hugo's Notre-Dame de Paris *narrated by André Dussollier*

Huber
Another audio recording of Victor Hugo's Notre-Dame de Paris *narrated by Élodie Huber*

Indicate the source of information by applying the instructions at **5.8.1.3**.

6.13 Identifier for the Expression

CORE ELEMENT

6.13.1 Basic Instructions on Recording Identifiers for Expressions

6.13.1.1 Scope

An ***identifier for the expression*** is a character string uniquely associated with an expression, or with a surrogate for an expression (e.g., an authority record). The identifier serves to differentiate that expression from other expressions.

6.13.1.2 Sources of Information

Take information on identifiers for expressions from any source.

6.13.1.3 Recording Identifiers for Expressions

Record an identifier for the expression. Precede the identifier with the name or an identification of the agency, etc., responsible for assigning the identifier, if readily ascertainable.

> ISRC BR-BMG-03-00729
> *International Standard Recording Code for a recording of the song* Enquanto houver sol *by the musical group Titãs*
>
> National Library of Australia: anbd.aut-an35359434
> *Australian National Bibliographic Database permalink for Italian translations of Peter Carey's* Oscar and Lucinda
>
> Library and Archives Canada control number: 0018A4143E
> *Identifier for English translations of* Beowulf
>
> Library of Congress control number: no 96031405
> *Identifier for arrangements of Nicolò Paganini's* Caprices, violin, M.S. 25
>
> Library of Congress control number: n 00024915
> *Identifier for an expression of Oscar Wilde's complete works*
>
> Wolfgang's Vault ID: 20049774|1647
> *Identifier for a David Bowie concert recorded March 23, 1976*

ADDITIONAL INSTRUCTIONS FOR MUSICAL WORKS

6.14 Title of a Musical Work

CORE ELEMENT

Preferred title for the work is a core element. Variant titles for the work are optional.

6.14.1 Basic Instructions on Recording Titles of Musical Works

6.14.1.1 Scope

A ***title of a musical work*** is a word, character, or group of words and/or characters by which a musical work is known.

When identifying musical works, there are two categories of titles:

a) preferred title for a musical work (see **6.14.2**)

b) variant title for a musical work (see **6.14.3**).

6.14.1.2 Sources of Information

Take the title or titles of a musical work from any source.

For additional guidance on sources of information for the preferred title for the work, see **6.14.2.2**.

6.14.1.3 General Guidelines on Recording Titles of Musical Works

When recording a title of a musical work, apply the guidelines on capitalization, numbers, diacritical marks, initial articles, spacing of initials and acronyms, and abbreviations, at **6.2.1**. When those guidelines refer to an appendix, apply the additional instructions in that appendix, as applicable.

6.14.2 Preferred Title for a Musical Work

CORE ELEMENT

6.14.2.1 Scope

The ***preferred title for a musical work*** is the title or form of title chosen to identify the musical work. It is also the basis for the authorized access point representing that work.

6.14.2.2 Sources of Information

Determine the title to be used as the preferred title for a musical work created after 1500 from resources embodying the work or reference sources.

Determine the title to be used as the preferred title for a musical work created before 1501 from modern sources. If the evidence of modern reference sources is inconclusive, use (in this order of preference):

a) modern editions

b) early editions

c) manuscript copies.

6.14.2.3 Choosing the Preferred Title for a Musical Work

Choose as the preferred title for a musical work the composer's original title in the language in which it was presented.

Meistersinger von Nürnberg
Resource described: The mastersingers of Nuremberg

Damnation de Faust
Resource described: Fausts Verdammung

Tous les garçons et les filles
Resource described: Todos los chicos y chicas

Zolotoĭ petushok
Resource described: The golden cockerel

Präludium und Fuge
Resource described: Präludium und Fuge, D-Dur für Orgel ...

Rondo with fugato
Resource described: Rondo with fugato ...

Introduction et allegro
Resource described: Introduction et allegro ...

Exceptions

Better known title in the same language. If the work has become better known by another title in the same language, choose it as the preferred title (see also **6.2.2.4–6.2.2.5**).

> Don Giovanni
> *Resource described:* Il dissoluto punito, ossia, Il don Giovanni
>
> Nabucco
> *Resource described:* Nabucodonosor

Long titles. If the title is very long, choose (in this order of preference):

a) a brief title by which the work is commonly identified in reference sources

> Historia der Auferstehung Jesu Christi
> *Resource described:* Historia der frölichen und siegreichen Auferstehung unsers einigen Erlösers und Seligmachers Jesu Christi

b) a brief title devised by the cataloguer.

> St. John Passion
> *Resource described:* Historia des Leidens und Sterbens unsers Herrn und Heylandes Jesu Christi, nach dem Evangelisten St. Johannem

Numbered sequence.

If:

a work has a distinctive title that includes the name of a type of composition

and

all of the composer's works of that type are also cited as a numbered sequence of compositions of that type

then:

choose the name of the type as the preferred title.

> Sinfonia
> *Resource described:* Sinfonia eroica / composta da Luigi van Beethoven. *Also cited in lists of the composer's symphonies as no. 3. English language and plural form recorded as preferred title:* Symphonies

RECORDING THE PREFERRED TITLE

6.14.2.4 Recording the Preferred Title for a Musical Work

Record the title chosen as the preferred title for a musical work by applying the basic instructions at **6.2.1**.

When recording the title chosen according to **6.14.2.3**, omit from the title:

a) a statement of medium of performance (even if such a statement is part of a compound word, provided that the resulting word or words is the name of a type of composition)

b) key

c) serial, opus, and thematic index numbers

d) numbers (unless they are an integral part of the title)

e) date of composition

f) adjectives and epithets not part of the original title of the work.

In the following examples, the preferred title as defined in this instruction is in italics.

String *quartet*
Streich*quartett*
Symphonie no. 40
Clavierübung
Kammersymphonie
Symphonie fantastique
Carnaval op. 9
Concerto in A minor, op. 54
12 *sonatas*
Nocturne in F sharp minor, op. 15, no. 2
6 *Stücke* für Orchester
Fünf Orchester*stücke*
Four orchestral *pieces*
Five *little pieces* for piano
Drei *Gesänge*
Vier Orchester*lieder*, op. 22
Les *deux journées*
The *Ten commandments*
The *seventh trumpet*
Troisième *nocturne*
Mozart's favorite *minuet*
Célebre *serenata española*
Grandes études (So named by the composer)
Die *Zauberflöte*
War requiem

6.14.2.5 Preferred Title Consisting Solely of the Name of One Type of Composition

If the application of **6.14.2.3–6.14.2.4** results in a preferred title consisting solely of the name of one type of composition, apply the following instructions, as applicable:

choice of language (see **6.14.2.5.1**)

singular or plural form (see **6.14.2.5.2**).

6.14.2.5.1 Choice of Language

Record the accepted form of the name of the type of composition in a language preferred by the agency creating the data if:

the name has a cognate form in that language

or

the same name is used in that language.

Otherwise, record the form of the name of the type of composition in the language of the preferred title chosen according to **6.14.2.3**.

Quartet
Resource described: Quatuor pour 2 hautbois et 2 bassons. *English language form recorded by an English-language agency in Canada because it is a cognate to the French title*

Concerti grossi

Resource described: Six concerti grossi for 2 violins, viola, and violoncello soli with strings and harpsichord. *The same name for the type of composition is used in Italian and English*

Pieces

Resource described: Deux pièces pour hautbois et piano, op. 35. *English language form recorded by an agency in the United States because it is a cognate to the French title*

but

Stücke

Resource described: Vier Stücke Opus 5 für Klarinette und Klavier = Four pieces op. 5 for clarinet and piano. *German language form recorded by an agency in Australia because there is no English cognate*

Exception

For works intended for concert performance called *étude*, *fantasia*, or *sinfonia concertante* or their cognates, record the form of the name of the type of composition in the language of the preferred title chosen according to **6.14.2.3**.

Études

Resource described: Studies. *Composer's original title:* Études

6.14.2.5.2 Singular or Plural Form

Record the accepted form of the name of the type of composition in the singular form unless the composer wrote more than one work of that type with the same title.

Concerto

Resource described: Violinkonzert / Alban Berg. *The composer wrote only one concerto*

Quintets

Resource described: Quintetto VI in sol maggiore

Ballades

Resource described: Ballade for solo piano

Sonatas

Resource described: Sonata a viola da gamba e basso

Divertimenti

Resource described: Divertimento for bass trombone and piano

Symphonies

Resource described: Sinfonia eroica

6.14.2.6 Duets

Record *Duets* for works variously titled duos, duets, etc.

Duets

Resource described: Trois duos

PARTS OF MUSICAL WORKS

6.14.2.7 Recording the Preferred Title for a Part or Parts of a Musical Work

Record the preferred title for a part or parts of a musical work by applying the instructions at **6.14.2.7.1**–**6.14.2.7.2**, as applicable.

For instructions on constructing the authorized access point representing a part or parts of a musical work, see **6.28.2**.

6.14.2.7.1 One Part

Record the preferred title for a part of a musical work by applying the instructions at **6.14.2.4**. Apply the additional instructions at **6.14.2.7.1.1**–**6.14.2.7.1.5**, as applicable.

6.14.2.7.1.1 Part Identified Only by a Number

If each of the parts is identified only by a number, record the number of the part.

Nr. 5
Preferred title for a part of Johannes Brahms's Ungarische Tänze

6.14.2.7.1.2 Part Identified Only by a Title or Other Verbal Designation

If each of the parts is identified only by a title or other verbal designation, record the title or other verbal designation of the part.

Celeste Aïda
Preferred title for a part of Giuseppe Verdi's Aïda

Seasons of love
Preferred title for a part of Jonathan Larson's Rent

Andante cantabile con moto
Preferred title for a part of Ludwig van Beethoven's Symphony, no. 1, op. 21, in C major

6.14.2.7.1.3 Part Identified Both by a Number and by a Title or Other Verbal Designation

If:
each of the parts is identified by a number
and
each of the parts is identified by its own title or a verbal designation
then:
record the title or other verbal designation of the part.

Come scoglio
Preferred title for a part of Wolfgang Amadeus Mozart's Così fan tutte. *Each aria has a number (e.g.,* No. 14 *for* Come scoglio*) as well as a title*

If:
each of the parts is identified by a number
and
the parts are identified by the same title or other verbal designation
then:
record the number of the part.

N. 8
Preferred title for a part of Antonio Vivaldi's Estro armonico. *Each part has the title* Concerto *as well as a number*

6.14.2.7.1.4 Each Part Identified by a Number and Some Parts also Identified by a Title or Other Verbal Designation

If:
each of the parts is identified by a number
and
some of the parts are also identified by a title or other verbal designation
then:
record the number of the part followed by a comma and the title or other designation if there is one.

Nr. 30
Preferred title for a part of Robert Schumann's Album für die Jugend

Nr. 2, Soldatenmarsch
Preferred title for a part of Robert Schumann's Album für die Jugend

6.14.2.7.1.5 Part of a Larger Part

If:
the part is part of a larger part of a musical work
and
the larger part has a distinctive title
then:
record that distinctive title of the larger part followed by the title and/or designation of the smaller part. Omit the designation of the larger part if it is not distinctive.
However, if an indistinctive designation of the larger part is required to identify the smaller part, record the designation of the larger part preceding the title and/or designation of the smaller part.
Separate the title and/or designation of the larger part from the title and/or designation of the smaller part by a full stop.

Cantiones sacrae. O vos omnes
Preferred title for a part of Hieronymus Praetorius's Opus musicum

Pifa
not Part 1. Pifa
Preferred title for a part of George Frideric Handel's Messiah

Atto 3o. Preludio
Preferred title for a part of Giuseppe Verdi's Traviata

6.14.2.7.2 Two or More Parts

When identifying two or more parts of a musical work, record the preferred titles of the parts. Apply the instructions at **6.14.2.7.1**.

Nr. 5
Preferred title for a part of Johannes Brahms's Ungarische Tänze *in a compilation also including* Nr. 6 *of the same work*

Nr. 6
Preferred title for a part of Johannes Brahms's Ungarische Tänze *in a compilation also including* Nr. 5 *of the same work*

Largo al factotum
Preferred title for a part of Gioacchino Rossini's Il barbiere di Siviglia *in a compilation also including the part* Una voce poco fa

Una voce poco fa
Preferred title for a part of Gioacchino Rossini's Il barbiere di Siviglia *in a compilation also including the part* Largo al factotum

No. 2
Preferred title for a part of Franz Schubert's Impromptus, piano, D. 899 *in a compilation also including* No. 4 *of the same work*

No. 4
Preferred title for a part of Franz Schubert's Impromptus, piano, D. 899 *in a compilation also including* No. 2 *of the same work*

If a composer assembles a group of excerpts from a larger work and calls the group *suite*, record that word as the designation for the part.

Suite, no. 2
Preferred title for a part of Edvard Grieg's Peer Gynt

Alternative

When identifying two or more parts of a musical work, identify the parts collectively. Record the conventional collective title *Selections* as the preferred title for the parts unless the parts form a group called *suite* by the composer. Apply this instruction instead of or in addition to recording the preferred title for each of the parts.

COMPILATIONS OF MUSICAL WORKS

6.14.2.8 Compilations of Musical Works

6.14.2.8.1 Recording the Preferred Title for Compilations of Musical Works

If a compilation of musical works has become known by a title through use in resources embodying that compilation or in reference sources, apply the instructions at **6.2.2.4–6.2.2.5**.

For other compilations, record the preferred title for a compilation of musical works by applying the instructions at **6.14.2.8.2–6.14.2.8.6**, as applicable.

6.14.2.8.2 Complete Works

Record the conventional collective title *Works* for a compilation that consists of, or purports to be, the complete musical works of a composer. Consider complete works to include all works that are complete at the time of publication.

6.14.2.8.3 Complete Works for One Broad Medium

Record one of the following conventional collective titles as the preferred title for a compilation of works that consists of, or purports to be, all the composer's works in one broad medium if the works are of various types.

Chamber music

Choral music

Instrumental music

Keyboard music

Vocal music

If none of these terms is appropriate, record an appropriate specific collective title.

If the works are of a single type, apply the instructions at **6.14.2.8.5**.

6.14.2.8.4 Complete Works for One Specific Medium

Record one of the following conventional collective titles as the preferred title for a compilation of works that consists of, or purports to be, all the composer's works for one specific medium if the works are of various types.

Brass music

Orchestra music

Piano music

Piano music, 4 hands

Piano music, pianos (2)

String quartet music

Violin, piano music

If none of these terms is appropriate, record an appropriate specific collective title.

If the works are of a single type, apply the instructions at **6.14.2.8.5**.

6.14.2.8.5 Complete Works of One Type for One Specific Medium or Various Media

For a compilation that consists of, or purports to be, all the composer's works of one type, record one of the following conventional collective titles.

Concertos

Motion picture music

Musicals

Operas

Polonaises

Quartets

Sonatas

Songs

If none of these terms is appropriate, record an appropriate specific collective title.

6.14.2.8.6 Incomplete Compilations

If:

a compilation corresponds to one of the categories at **6.14.2.8.2–6.14.2.8.5**

and

the compilation is incomplete

then:

identify each of the works in the compilation separately by applying the instructions at **6.14.2.4–6.14.2.7**.

> Renaissance concerto
> Salomon Rossi suite
> Orpheus and Euridice
> *Resource described:* Orchestral works / by Lukas Foss

Alternative

When identifying two or more works in an incomplete compilation, record a conventional collective title as instructed at **6.14.2.8.2–6.14.2.8.5**, as applicable, followed by *Selections*. Apply this instruction instead of or in addition to recording the preferred title for each of the works in the compilation.

Orchestra music. Selections
Resource described: Orchestral works / by Lukas Foss

Symphonies. Selections
Resource described: First, Second, and Third symphonies / Ludwig van Beethoven

6.14.3 Variant Title for a Musical Work

6.14.3.1 Scope

A ***variant title for a musical work*** is a title or form of title by which a musical work is known that differs from the title or form of title chosen as the preferred title for the work.

6.14.3.2 Sources of information

Take variant titles from resources embodying the work and/or from reference sources.

6.14.3.3 General Guidelines on Recording Variant Titles for Musical Works

Record variant titles for musical works by applying the basic instructions at **6.2.1**.

Record a variant title for the work when it is different from the title recorded as the preferred title. Record as a variant title:

a title or form of title under which the work has been issued or cited in reference sources

or

a title resulting from a different transliteration of the title.

Exception

Record a title appearing on a manifestation of the work as a variant title for the work only in the following case:

if the title appearing on the manifestation differs significantly from the preferred title

and

if the work itself might reasonably be searched by that title.

For instructions on recording the title proper and other titles appearing on the manifestation, see **2.3**.

Apply the specific instructions at **6.14.3.4–6.14.3.5**. Also apply instructions in preceding sections of this chapter, as applicable.

6.14.3.4 Recording Alternative Linguistic Forms as Variant Titles for Musical Works

If the title recorded as the preferred title for a musical work has one or more alternative linguistic forms, record them as variant titles for the work.

Different Language Form

Mountain maid
Fille de la montagne
Kind der Berge
Norwegian language form recorded as preferred title: Haugtussa

O Christmas tree
O dannenbom
Oh Christmas tree

Oh tree of fir
German language form recorded as preferred title: O Tannenbaum

Popular Greek melodies
Greek popular melodies
Popular Greek songs
French language form recorded as preferred title: Mélodies populaires grecques

Stücke
English language form recorded as preferred title: Pieces

Etüden
Études
Studies
Polish language form recorded as preferred title: Etiud

Different Script

Золушка
Russian transliterated form recorded as preferred title: Zolushka

フロム·ミー·フローズ·ホワット·ユー·コール·タイム
English language form recorded as preferred title: From me flows what you call time

התקוה
Hebrew transliterated form recorded as preferred title: Hatiḳvah

Different Spelling

Amphitrion
Spelling recorded as preferred title: Amphitryon

Fantasie sonata
Phantasy sonata
Spelling recorded as preferred title: Fantasy sonata

Partsongs
Spelling recorded as preferred title: Part-songs

Different Transliteration

Khovanchtchina
Transliteration recorded as preferred title: Khovanshchina

Hatikva
Hatikvoh
Transliteration recorded as preferred title: Hatiḳvah

6.14.3.5 Recording Other Variant Titles for Musical Works

Record other variant titles and variant forms of the title not covered by **6.14.3.4**.

Songs, airs, duets, and choruses in the masque of King Arthur
Preferred title recorded as: King Arthur

Salzburg sonata
Preferred title recorded as: Sonatas

Forellen-Quintett
Quintette de la truite
Trout quintet
Forellenquintett
Trucha
Forellen-kvintet
Quintette "La truite"
Forelių kvintetas
Grand quintuor
Preferred title recorded as: Quintets

Cinq mélodies populaires grecques
5 mélodies populaires grecques
Preferred title recorded as: Mélodies populaires grecques

Complete organ works
Œuvres complètes pour orgue
Sämtliche Orgelwerke
Preferred title recorded as: Organ music

Complete Takemitsu edition
Takemitsu Tōru zenshū
武満徹全集
Preferred title recorded as: Works

Best of Bach
Preferred title recorded as: Works. Selections

Selected works for piano
Preferred title recorded as: Piano music. Selections

6.15 Medium of Performance

CORE ELEMENT

Medium of performance is a core element when needed to differentiate a musical work from another work with the same title. It may also be a core element when identifying a musical work with a title that is not distinctive.

6.15.1 Basic Instructions on Recording Medium of Performance

6.15.1.1 Scope

Medium of performance is the instrument, instruments, voice, voices, etc., for which a musical work was originally conceived.

6.15.1.2 Sources of Information

Take information on medium of performance from any source.

6.15.1.3 Recording Medium of Performance

Record the medium of performance by applying these instructions, as applicable:

instrumental music intended for one performer to a part (see **6.15.1.4**)

instruments (see **6.15.1.5**)

accompanying ensembles with one performer to a part (see **6.15.1.6**)

instrumental music for orchestra, string orchestra, or band (see **6.15.1.7**) one or more solo instruments and accompanying ensemble (see **6.15.1.8**)

solo voices (see **6.15.1.9**)

choruses (see **6.15.1.10**)

indeterminate medium of performance (see **6.15.1.11**).

Record medium of performance as a separate element, as part of an access point, or as both. For instructions on recording medium of performance as part of the authorized access point, see **6.28.1.9–6.28.1.11**.

horn

voices
piano

piano
clarinet
violoncello

violin
piano

violin
viola
cello

flute
bassoon
continuo

If there is more than one part for a particular instrument or voice, record the number of parts.

flutes (2)
clarinets (2)

viols (5)

violins (2)
viola
cello

Exception

If the term *percussion* is used (see **6.15.1.4**), record the number of players if there is more than one.

percussion (3 players)

Use *continuo* for a thorough bass part whether it is named as *basso*, *basso continuo*, *figured bass*, *thorough bass*, or *continuo*, and whether the individual instrument or instruments of the continuo are specified or not.

For guidelines on recording details about the medium of performance, apply the instructions for medium of performance of musical content at **7.21**.

6.15.1.4 Instrumental Music Intended for One Performer to a Part

For instrumental music intended for one performer to a part, record each instrument by applying the instructions at **6.15.1.5** and **6.15.1.11**.

Exceptions

If there is more than one percussion instrument, and the names of the individual instruments are not specified by the composer in the original title, use *percussion*.

If the medium includes a continuo part, record the name of the part (see **6.15.1.3**).

If the medium includes instruments acting as an accompanying ensemble, record a term for the accompanying ensemble (see **6.15.1.6**).

6.15.1.5 Instruments

When recording names of instruments, use a term in a language preferred by the agency creating the data whenever possible. Use the following list of terms as a guide:

cello *or* violoncello
cor anglais *or* English horn
double bass (*not* bass viol *or* contrabass)
double bassoon *or* contrabassoon
harpsichord (*not* cembalo *or* virginal)
horn (*not* French horn)
kettle drums *or* timpani
piano (*not* fortepiano *or* pianoforte)
viola da gamba (*not* bass viol or gamba)

When alternatives are given, choose a term and use it consistently.

6.15.1.5.1 Number of Hands

For one instrument, specify the number of hands if other than two.

piano, 1 hand
harpsichord, 4 hands
viola, 4 hands

For two or more keyboard or mallet (marimba, vibraphone, xylophone, etc.) instruments, specify the number of hands if other than two per instrument.

pianos (2), 6 hands
pianos (2), 8 hands
marimbas (2), 8 hands
but
organs (2)

6.15.1.5.2 Pitch and Range of Instruments

If considered important for identification and access, record the designation of key in which an instrument is pitched and/or terms indicating the range of an instrument.

clarinet in A
D trumpet

tenor saxophone

alto horn

Optional Omission

Omit the following elements:

a) the designation of the key in which an instrument is pitched

clarinet
not clarinet in A

b) terms indicating a range (e.g., *alto*, *tenor*, *bass*).

recorder
not alto recorder

saxophone
not tenor saxophone

6.15.1.5.3 Alternative Instruments

Record the names of alternative instruments.

viola

Resource described: Sonata for clarinet (or viola) and piano, E flat major, op. 120, no. 2 / Johannes Brahms. *Medium of performance recorded as:* clarinet, viola, piano

6.15.1.5.4 Doubling Instruments

Record the names of doubling instruments.

piccolo

Resource described: Nataraja : for flute (doubling piccolo) and piano / Jonathan Harvey. *Medium of performance recorded as:* flute, piccolo, piano

Optional Omission

Omit doubling instruments.

6.15.1.6 Accompanying Ensembles with One Performer to a Part

For an accompanying ensemble with one performer to a part, record the appropriate term for the instrument or family of instruments followed by the word *ensemble*.

guitar ensemble

string ensemble

percussion ensemble

Record *instrumental ensemble* for an accompanying ensemble with one performer to a part consisting of instruments from two or more families of instruments when a more specific term is not available.

Alternative

For an accompanying ensemble with one performer to a part, record the appropriate term for each instrument of the accompanying ensemble instead of the name of the ensemble.

violins (2)
viola
cello
Resource described: Concerto for flute with string quartet / Jerome Moross

trumpets (2)
horn
trombone
tuba
Resource described: Piano concerto no. 2 In F major for piano and brass quintet / Peter Schickele

6.15.1.7 Instrumental Music for Orchestra, String Orchestra, or Band

For instrumental music intended for orchestra, string orchestra, or band, record an appropriate term from the following list:

orchestra
string orchestra
band

Record *orchestra* for full or reduced orchestra.

Disregard continuo when it is part of an orchestra or string orchestra.

6.15.1.8 One or More Solo Instruments and Accompanying Ensemble

For a work for one or more solo instruments and accompanying ensemble, record:

a) the term or terms for the solo instrument or instruments by applying the instructions at **6.15.1.4–6.15.1.5** and **6.15.1.11**
and
b) the term or terms for the accompanying ensemble by applying the instructions at **6.15.1.6–6.15.1.7**.

violin
orchestra
Resource described: Rhapsody for solo violin and orchestra / Mary Jeanne van Appledorn

piano
orchestra
Resource described: Concierto no. 1 para piano y orquesta : Atlántico / Zulema de la Cruz

piano
woodwind ensemble
Resource described: Concertino for piano and woodwind quintet / by John Diercks

harpsichord
instrumental ensemble
Resource described: Concerto pour clavecin et ensemble instrumental / Jean Françaix

piano
violin
cello

orchestra

Resource described: Konzert für Klavier, Violine, Violoncello und Orchester C-Dur op. 56 : Tripelkonzert / Ludwig van Beethoven

flute
oboe
clarinet
bassoon
orchestra

Resource described: Quadruple concerto : pour flûte, hautbois, clarinette et basson avec accompagnement d'orchestre / Jean Françaix

pianos (2)
string orchestra

Resource described: Divertimento for string orchestra and two pianos / by Ulric Cole

violin
viola
orchestra

Resource described: Sinfonie concertanto in E♭ a violino e viola principale, 2 violini, 2 viole, 2 oboe, 2 corni, violoncello, e basso / di Amadeo Wolfgango Mozart

6.15.1.9 Solo Voices

Record an appropriate term from the following list to identify a type of solo voice:

soprano
mezzo-soprano
alto
tenor
baritone
bass

sopranos (2)
alto
instrumental ensemble

Resource described: Stabat Mater : in G minor : for 2 sopranos, alto, 2 violins & basso continuo / Girolamo Abos ; edited by Alejandro Garri ; assisted by Kent Carlson

soprano
piano

Resource described: Dos canciones para soprano y piano / Federico Ibarra

soprano
accordion

Resource described: Drei Lieder für Sopran und Akkordeon / Horst Lohse ; nach Gedichten von Ingo Cesaro

Record other terms as appropriate.

bass-baritone
countertenor

If no specific voice types or ranges can be ascertained for two or more solo voices of different ranges, record an appropriate term from the following list:

mixed solo voices
men's solo voices
women's solo voices

Record other terms as appropriate.

children's solo voices

For compositions that include solo voices with chorus, record the solo voices, the appropriate terms for the chorus (see **6.15.1.10**), and the accompaniment, if any.

soprano
tenor
mixed voices
orchestra
Resource described: Te Deum : for mixed voices (with soprano and tenor solo) and orchestra / Georges Bizet

6.15.1.10 Choruses

For a choral ensemble, record an appropriate term from the following list:

mixed voices
men's voices
women's voices
unison voices

Record other terms as appropriate.

children's voices

6.15.1.11 Indeterminate Medium of Performance

If the specific medium of performance, or any part of it, is not stated in the resource or other source, record that part of the medium of performance as instructed at **6.15.1.11.1–6.15.1.11.4** (in that order).

6.15.1.11.1 One Family of Instruments, Collective Term, Etc.

If only the family of instruments or voices (see **6.15.1.9**), or a collective term for other media, is indicated by the composer, or is available from any other source, record the family, collective term, etc.

accordion
plucked instrument
violin
Resource described: Trio pour accordéon de concert, violon et instrument à cordes pincées / Alain Abbott

keyboard instrument
Resource described: Three inventions for keyboard / Howard Boatwright

6.15.1.11.2 Range or General Type of Instrument or Voice

If only the range or general type of instrument or voice is indicated by the composer, or is available from any other source, record the range or type.

horn
violin
viola
bass instrument

Resource described: 6 Quartette für Horn, Violine, Viola und Basso, op. 2 / von Leopold Kohl ; Rev., R. Ostermeyer

treble instrument
organ

Resource described: Eight chorale preludes for treble instrument and organ / by Randall Sensmeier

melody instrument
piano

Resource described: Suite für ein Melodieinstrument (Violine, Querflöte, Oboe, Viola, Klarinette (B), Saxophon (B), Trompete (B), Englischhorn (F), Horn (F), Violoncello oder Fagott) und Klavier / Hans-Walter Slembeck

high voice
piano

Resource described: Vocalise, op. 34, no. 14, for high voice and piano / Rachmaninoff

female voice
trombone

Resource described: Merrie English love songs : for woman's voice and trombone / Sharon Davis

voice
marimba

Resource described: Five songs for voice and marimba / Lynn Glassock ; text by Emily Dickinson

6.15.1.11.3 Some Instruments, Etc., Unspecified

If:

some parts of the medium are indicated by the composer, or are available from any other source

and

other parts are unspecified or are indicated as *unspecified* or a similar term

then:

record the individual parts of the medium as instructed at **6.15.1.4–6.15.1.10**.

Also use *unspecified* or a similar term, as appropriate.

unspecified instrument
piano

Resource described: Three carols for piano and solo instrument / David Moore

6.15.1.11.4 Medium Unspecified

If no medium of performance is specified by the composer, and none can be ascertained from any other source, record *unspecified.*

> *Exception*
>
> If there are two or more such works by the same composer, record the number of parts or voices. Use *voices* to indicate both vocal and instrumental parts.
>
> voices (3)
>
> *Resource described:* Canzonets, or, Little short songs to three voyces / published by Thomas Morley

voices (5–6)

Resource described: Canzonets, or, Little short aers to five and sixe voices / by Thomas Morley

voices (4)

Resource described: Fourteen canzonas for four instruments / Claudio Merulo

voices (5–6)

Resource described: Madrigals of 5 and 6 parts, apt for the viols and voices / made & published by Thomas Weelkes

6.16 Numeric Designation of a Musical Work

CORE ELEMENT

Numeric designation is a core element when needed to differentiate a musical work from another work with the same title. It may also be a core element when identifying a musical work with a title that is not distinctive.

6.16.1 Basic Instructions on Recording Numeric Designations of Musical Works

6.16.1.1 Scope

A ***numeric designation of a musical work*** is a serial number, opus number, or thematic index number assigned to a musical work by a composer, publisher, or a musicologist.

6.16.1.2 Sources of Information

Take information on numeric designations of musical works from any source.

6.16.1.3 Recording Numeric Designations of Musical Works

Record as many of the following numeric designations of musical works as can readily be ascertained. Use abbreviations as instructed in appendix B (**B.5.4**). Use inclusive numbering for an aggregate work that is identified by consecutive serial numbers or thematic index numbers in music reference sources and/or thematic indexes.

Record numeric designations of musical works as separate elements, as parts of access points, or as both. For instructions on recording a numeric designation of a musical work as part of the authorized access point, see **6.28.1.9–6.28.1.10**.

6.16.1.3.1 Serial Number

If works with the same title and the same medium of performance are consecutively numbered in music reference sources, record the number.

no. 2

Resource described: String quartet no. 2 / Eleanor Cory. *Preferred title:* Quartets; *medium of performance:* strings

no. 5

Resource described: Fifth symphony for orchestra / by Arnold Bax. *Preferred title:* Symphonies

no. 6-8

Resource described: Violin sonatas op. 30 nos. 1-3 / Beethoven. *Preferred title:* Sonatas; *medium of performance:* violin, piano; *opus number:* op. 30. *Beethoven's violin sonatas no. 6-8 also known as his opus 30, no. 1-3*

If:

different works in a consecutively numbered series have different forms of numeric designation, or different words introducing the number

and

the different forms or words are in the same sources from which the numeric designations for the individual works are taken

then:

select one form of numeric designation and use it for all the works in the series.

> 1st book
>
> *Resource described:* The first set of songs : in four parts / composed by John Dowland ; scored from the first edition, printed in the year 1597, and preceded by a life of the composer by W. Chappell
>
> 2nd book
>
> *Resource described:* Second book of songs (1600) / John Dowland ; edited by Edmund H. Fellows ; revised by Thurston Dart
>
> 1o libro
>
> *Resource described:* Il primo libro de ricercari da cantare : a quattro voci / di Claudio Merulo da Correggio
>
> 3o libro
>
> *Resource described:* Ricercari da cantare : a quattro voci : libro terzo / di Claudio Merulo

6.16.1.3.2 Opus Number

Record the opus number, if any, and the number within the opus, if any.

> op. 114
>
> *Resource described:* Quintett in A für Klavier, Violine, Viola, Violoncello und Kontrabass D 667 (op. post. 114) : Forellen-Quintett = Quintet in A major for piano, violin, viola, violoncello, and double bass : the trout quintet / Franz Schubert ; herausgegeben von Arnold Feil. *Preferred title:* Quintets; *medium of performance:* piano, violin, viola, violoncello, double bass
>
> op. 2, no. 1
>
> *Resource described:* Piano sonata no. 1 in F minor, op. 2, no. 1 / Beethoven. *Preferred title:* Sonatas; *medium of performance:* piano; *serial number:* no. 1
>
> op. 2, no. 2
>
> *Resource described:* Piano sonata no. 2 in A major, op. 2, no. 2 / Beethoven. *Preferred title:* Sonatas; *medium of performance:* piano; *serial number:* no. 2

If:

there is a conflict in opus numbering among works of the same title and medium

or

the overall opus numbering of a composer's works is confused and conflicting

then:

add to the opus number the name of the publisher originally using the number chosen.

Add the publisher's name in parentheses.

> op. 20 (Bland)
>
> *Preferred title for the work by Giuseppe Maria Cambini:* Duets; *medium of performance:* flute, violin
>
> op. 20 (LeDuc)
>
> *Preferred title for the work by Giuseppe Maria Cambini:* Duets; *medium of performance:* flute, violin

6.16.1.3.3 Thematic Index Number

In the case of certain composers, record the number assigned to a work in a recognized thematic index. Precede the number by:

the initial letter or letters of the musicologist's name (e.g., K. 453[1])

or

a generally accepted abbreviation (e.g., BWV 232[2]).

D. 667

Resource described: Quintett in A für Klavier, Violine, Viola, Violoncello und Kontrabass D 667 (op. post. 114) : Forellen-Quintett = Quintet in A major for piano, violin, viola, violoncello, and double bass : the trout quintet / Franz Schubert ; herausgegeben von Arnold Feil. *Preferred title:* Quintets; *medium of performance:* piano, violin, viola, violoncello, double bass

H. III, 37-42

Resource described: 6 string quartets, opus 33, Hoboken III, 37-42 = 6 Streichquartette / Joseph Haydn ; edited by Simon Rowland-Jones ; editorial consultant, David Ledbetter. *Preferred title:* Quartets; *medium of performance:* strings; *opus number:* op. 33

BWV 1046-1051

Resource described: Brandenburg concertos = Les concertos brandebourgeois / J.S. Bach. *Preferred title:* Brandenburgische Konzerte

---

1. Ludwig Köchel, *Chronologisch-thematisches Verzeichnis samtlicher Tonwerke Wolfgang Amadé Mozart s, 8., unveränderte Aufl. (Wiesbaden: Breitkopf & Härtel, 1983, ©1964).*
2. Wolfgang Schmieder, *Thematisch-systematisches Verzeichnis der musikalischen Werke von Johann Sebastian Bach, Bach-Werke-Verzeichnis (BWV). 3., unveränderte Aufl. (Leipzig: Breitkopf & Härtel Musikverlag, 1961, ©1950).*

6.17 Key

CORE ELEMENT

Key is a core element when needed to differentiate a musical work from another work with the same title. It may also be a core element when identifying a musical work with a title that is not distinctive.

6.17.1 Basic Instructions on Recording Key

6.17.1.1 Scope

Key is the set of pitch relationships that establishes the tonal centre, or principal tonal centre, of a musical work. Key is indicated by its pitch name and its mode, when it is major or minor.

6.17.1.2 Sources of Information

Take information on key from any source.

6.17.1.3 Recording Key

Record the key if one or more of the following conditions applies:

a) it is commonly identified in reference sources

b) it appears in the composer's original title or the title proper of the first manifestation

c) it is apparent from the resource described (unless it is known to be transposed in the resource).

Record key as a separate element, as part of an access point, or as both. For instructions on recording key as part of the authorized access point, see **6.28.1.9–6.28.1.10**.

C minor

Resource described: Trio c-Moll Opus 66 für Violine, Violoncello und Klavier / Felix Mendelssohn Bartholdy

D major

Resource described: Symphony no. 93, in D major / Haydn

A major

Resource described: Scherzo in A for pianoforte / Franz Reizenstein

B♭

Resource described: Symphony in B flat for concert band / Paul Hindemith

F♯ minor

Resource described: Sinfonie für Orgel solo fis-Moll, op. 143 = Symphony for organ solo in F sharp minor / Sigfrid Karg-Elert

6.18 Other Distinguishing Characteristic of the Expression of a Musical Work

CORE ELEMENT

Other distinguishing characteristic of the expression is a core element when needed to differentiate an expression of a work from another expression of the same work.

6.18.1 Basic Instructions on Recording Other Distinguishing Characteristics of the Expression of a Musical Work

6.18.1.1 Scope

Other distinguishing characteristic of the expression of a musical work is a characteristic that serves to differentiate an expression of a musical work from another expression of the same work (e.g., an arrangement, sketches, vocal score).

6.18.1.2 Sources of Information

Take information on other distinguishing characteristics of the expression of a musical work from any source.

6.18.1.3 Recording Other Distinguishing Characteristics of the Expression of a Musical Work

Record the other distinguishing characteristics of the expression of a musical work by applying the instructions at **6.18.1.4–6.18.1.6**, as applicable.

Record other distinguishing characteristics of the expression of a musical work as separate elements, as parts of access points, or as both. For instructions on recording other distinguishing characteristics of the expression of a musical work as part of the authorized access point, see **6.28.3**.

6.18.1.4 Arrangements, Transcriptions, Etc.

This instruction applies to an arrangement, transcription, etc. of one or more works of one composer (or of parts of one composer's works) that falls into one or both of these categories:

a) arrangements, transcriptions, versions, settings, etc., in which music for one medium of performance has been rewritten for another

b) simplified versions of previously existing musical works.

If the expression is an arrangement, etc., of a work or part or parts of a work that belongs, broadly speaking, to the category of "serious," "classical," or "art" music, record *arranged.* Apply this instruction also to a transcription by the original composer.

6.18.1.4.1 Arrangements, Etc. in the "Popular" Idiom

If the arrangement, etc., is of a work or of part or parts of a work that belongs, broadly speaking, to the category of music in the "popular" idiom (e.g., rock, jazz), record *arranged* only if the expression is:

either
a) an instrumental work arranged for vocal or choral performance
or
b) a vocal work arranged for instrumental performance.

6.18.1.5 Sketches

If the expression consists of a composer's sketches for one or more musical compositions, record *Sketches.*

6.18.1.6 Vocal and Chorus Scores

If the expression is a vocal score or a chorus score, record *Vocal score*, *Vocal scores*, *Chorus score*, or *Chorus scores*, as applicable.

ADDITIONAL INSTRUCTIONS FOR LEGAL WORKS

6.19 Title of a Legal Work

CORE ELEMENT

Preferred title for the work is a core element. Variant titles for the work are optional.

6.19.1 Basic Instructions on Recording Titles of Legal Works

6.19.1.1 Scope

A ***title of a legal work*** is a word, character, or group of words and/or characters by which a legal work is known.

When identifying legal works, there are two categories of titles:

a) preferred title for a legal work (see **6.19.2**)

b) variant title for a legal work (see **6.19.3**).

6.19.1.2 Sources of Information

Take the title or titles of a legal work from any source.

For additional guidance on sources of information for the preferred title for the work, see **6.19.2.2**.

6.19.1.3 General Guidelines on Recording Titles of Legal Works

When recording a title of a legal work, apply the guidelines on capitalization, numbers, diacritical marks, initial articles, spacing of initials and acronyms, and abbreviations, at **6.2.1**. When those guidelines refer to an appendix, apply the additional instructions in that appendix, as applicable.

6.19.2 Preferred Title for a Legal Work

CORE ELEMENT

6.19.2.1 Scope

The ***preferred title for a legal work*** is the title or form of title chosen to identify the work. It is also the basis for the authorized access point representing that work.

6.19.2.2 Sources of Information

Determine the title to be used as the preferred title for a legal work created after 1500 from resources embodying the work or from reference sources.

Determine the title to be used as the preferred title for a legal work created before 1501 from modern reference sources. If the evidence of modern reference sources is inconclusive, use (in this order of preference):

a) modern editions

b) early editions

c) manuscript copies.

6.19.2.3 Choosing the Preferred Title for a Legal Work

Choose the preferred title for a legal work by applying the instructions at **6.2.2.3–6.2.2.7**.

Exceptions

Laws, etc. For laws, etc., apply the instructions at **6.19.2.5–6.19.2.6**.

Treaties. For treaties, apply the instructions at **6.19.2.7–6.19.2.8**.

RECORDING THE PREFERRED TITLE

6.19.2.4 Recording the Preferred Title for a Legal Work

Record the title chosen as the preferred title for a legal work by applying the basic instructions at **6.2.1**.

Exceptions

Laws, etc. For laws, etc., apply the instructions at **6.19.2.5–6.19.2.6**.

Treaties. For treaties, apply the instructions at **6.19.2.7–6.19.2.8**.

6.19.2.5 Modern Laws, Etc.

Record the preferred title for a law or laws by applying these instructions, as applicable:

compilations of laws, etc. (see **6.19.2.5.1**)
single laws, etc. (see **6.19.2.5.2**).

6.19.2.5.1 Compilations of Laws, Etc.

Record *Laws, etc.* as the preferred title for:

a complete or partial compilation of legislative enactments of a jurisdiction

not

a compilation of laws on a particular subject.

If a compilation of laws on a particular subject has a citation title, record that as the preferred title. Otherwise, apply the instructions at **6.2.2.3–6.2.2.8**.

Labor Code
Resource described: California Labor Code. *Citation title:* Labor Code

Licensing acts
Resource described: Paterson's licensing acts

6.19.2.5.2 Single Laws, Etc.

For a single legislative enactment, record (in this order of preference):

a) the official short title or citation title

b) an unofficial short title or citation title used in legal literature

c) the official title of the enactment

d) any other official designation (e.g., the number, date).

Football (Disorder) Act 2000
Citation title includes date of enactment

Copyright Act 1994
Citation title includes date of enactment

Canada Corporations Act

Downtown Winnipeg Zoning By-law

Act to Direct the Secretary of the Interior to Study the Suitability and Feasibility of Designating the Waco Mammoth Site Area in Waco, Texas, as a Unit of the National Park System, and for Other Purposes

Code de justice administrative

Ley no. 20.744

Legge 27 maggio 1998, n. 165

6.19.2.6 Ancient Laws, Certain Medieval Laws, Customary Laws, Etc.

Record the preferred title by applying the instructions at **6.2.2.4–6.2.2.5**, as applicable, for:

a compilation of ancient, medieval, or customary laws identified by a name

or

a single ancient, medieval, or customary law.

Lex Salica
Resource described: Lex Salica : the ten texts

Code of Hammurabi
Resource described: The oldest code of laws in the world : the code of laws promulgated by Hammurabi, King of Babylon

6.19.2.7 One Treaty

For a treaty between two or more of the following:

national governments
international intergovernmental bodies
the Holy See
jurisdictions now below the national level but retaining treaty-making powers,

record as the preferred title (in this order of preference):

a) the official title of the treaty

b) a short title or citation title used in legal literature

c) any other official designation by which the treaty is known.

Agreement Establishing the World Trade Organization

Treaty of Portsmouth

Resource described: Traité de paix entre le Japon et la Russie. *Short title used in legal literature:* Treaty of Portsmouth

If the treaty is published simultaneously in different languages and the original language cannot be determined, apply the instructions at **6.2.2.4**.

6.19.2.8 Compilations of Treaties

If a compilation of treaties is identified by a collective name, record that name as the preferred title. For a single treaty in the compilation, see **6.19.2.7**.

Treaty of Utrecht

Collective name for a group of treaties signed between 1713 and 1715

For a compilation of treaties not identified by a collective name, apply the instructions at **6.2.2**.

Acordos e convencões internacionais em material de imposto de renda

Canada's tax treaties

6.19.3 Variant Title for a Legal Work

6.19.3.1 Scope

A ***variant title for a legal work*** is a title or form of title by which a legal work is known that differs from the title or form of title chosen as the preferred title for the work.

6.19.3.2 Sources of Information

Take variant titles for a legal work from resources embodying the work and/or from reference sources.

6.19.3.3 General Guidelines on Recording Variant Titles for Legal Works

Record variant titles for legal works by applying the basic instructions at **6.2.1**.

Record a variant title for the work when it is different from the title recorded as the preferred title. Record as a variant title:

a title or form of title under which the work has been issued or cited in reference sources

or

a title resulting from a different transliteration of the title.

Exception

Record a title appearing on a manifestation of the work as a variant title for the work only in the following case:

if the title appearing on the manifestation differs significantly from the preferred title

and

if the work itself might reasonably be searched by that title.

For instructions on recording the title proper and other titles appearing on the manifestation see 2.3.

Apply the specific instructions at **6.19.3.4–6.19.3.6**. Also apply instructions in preceding sections of this chapter, as applicable.

6.19.3.4 Recording Alternative Linguistic Forms as Variant Titles for Legal Works

If the title recorded as the preferred title for a legal work has one or more alternative linguistic forms, record them as variant titles for the work.

Different Language Form

Loi sur les espèces en péril
Preferred title recorded as: Species at Risk Act

Constitution of Japan
Preferred title recorded as: Nihonkoku kenpō

Freden i Utrecht
Friede von Utrecht
Perjanjian Utrecht
Sporazum u Utrehtu
Tractat d'Utrecht
Traités d'Utrecht
Tratado de Utrecht
Trattato di Utrecht
Utrechto sutartis
Vrede van Utrecht
Yutorehito jōyaku
Preferred title recorded as: Treaty of Utrecht

Different Script

Αστικος κωδιξ
Greek transliterated form recorded as preferred title: Astikos kōdix

公司法
Chinese transliterated form recorded as preferred title: Gong si fa

قانون بيمه
Persian transliterated from recorded as preferred title: Qānūn-i bīmah

日本国憲法
Japanese transliterated form recorded as preferred title: Nihonkoku kenpō

Different Spelling

Successful judgement collections in Oklahoma
Preferred title recorded as: Successful judgment collections in Oklahoma

Industrial Coordination Act, 1975
Preferred title recorded as: Industrial Co-ordination Act, 1975

Trademarks Ordinance
Preferred title recorded as: Trade Marks Ordinance

Different Transliteration

Kung ssu fa
Preferred title recorded as: Gong si fa

Nihonkoku kempō
Preferred title recorded as: Nihonkoku kenpō

6.19.3.5 Recording Other Variant Titles for Legal Works

Record other variant titles and variant forms of the title not covered by **6.19.3.4**.

West's Alaska civil procedure
Code of civil procedure
Preferred title recorded as: Alaska civil procedure law

By-law No. 100/2004
By-law of the City of Winnipeg to Control and Regulate the Use of Real Property and Development in Downtown Winnipeg
Preferred title recorded as: Downtown Winnipeg Zoning By-law

Act No. 37 of 1953
Act to Amend the Law Relating to the Property Rights of Spouses, to Orders for Maintenance, to the Guardianship and Custody of Minors, and to Divorce
Preferred title recorded as: Matrimonial Affairs Act 1953

Philippine Anti-Terrorism Law
Anti-Terrorism Law
Preferred title recorded as: Human Security Act of 2007

Native American One Dollar Coin Act
Act to Require the Secretary of the Treasury to Mint and Issue Coins in Commemoration of Native Americans and the Important Contributions Made by Indian Tribes and Individual Native Americans to the Development of the United States and the History of the United States, and for Other Purposes
Public Law 110-82
Preferred title recorded as: Native American $1 Coin Act

StPO
Preferred title recorded as: Strafprozessordnung

L. 27 maggio 1998, n. 165
Preferred title recorded as: Legge 27 maggio 1998, n. 165

Marrakesh Agreement Establishing the World Trade Organization
Preferred title recorded as: Agreement Establishing the World Trade Organization

NAFTA
Tratado Trilateral de Libre Comercio
TTLC
Tratado de Libre Comercio en América del Norte
TLCAN

> Accord de Libre-Échange Nord-Américain
> ALENA
> *Preferred title recorded as:* North American Free Trade Agreement

6.19.3.6 Conventional Collective Titles

When a conventional collective title is used as the preferred title for a compilation of legal works (see **6.19.2.5.1**), record as a variant title:

the title proper of the resource being described

or

the title found in a reference source.

Do not record a variant title if it is the same as, or very similar to, the conventional collective title.

> Acts of the Parliament of the Commonwealth of Australia
> *Preferred title recorded as:* Laws, etc.
>
> Revised ordinances of Newton, Massachusetts, 2001
> *Preferred title recorded as:* Laws, etc.
>
> Bermuda laws online
> *Preferred title recorded as:* Laws, etc.

6.20 Date of a Legal Work

CORE ELEMENT

Date of work is a core element to identify a treaty. Date of work also is a core element when needed to differentiate a legal work from another work with the same title or from the name of a person, family, or corporate body.

6.20.1 Basic Instructions on Recording Date of a Legal Work

6.20.1.1 Scope

Date of a legal work is the earliest date associated with a legal work.

6.20.1.2 Sources of Information

Take information on date of a legal work from any source.

6.20.1.3 Recording Date of a Legal Work

Record dates in terms of the calendar preferred by the agency creating the data. For details on recording dates according to the Christian calendar, see appendix **H**.

Record date of a legal work as a separate element, as part of an access point, or as both. For instructions on recording date of a legal work as part of the authorized access point, see **6.29.1.29–6.29.1.31**.

6.20.2 Date of Promulgation of a Law, Etc.

CORE ELEMENT

Date of work is a core element when needed to differentiate a work from another work with the same title or from the name of a person, family, or corporate body.

6.20.2.1 Scope

Date of promulgation of a law, etc. is the year a law, etc., was promulgated or brought into force.

6.20.2.2 Sources of Information

Take information on date of promulgation of a law, etc., from any source.

6.20.2.3 Recording Date of Promulgation of a Law, Etc.

Record the year in which a law, etc., was promulgated by applying the basic instructions at **6.20.1**.

> 1998
> *Date of promulgation of:* Code pénal : mis à jour au 30 juin 1998 = Fehezandalana famaizana
>
> 2005
> *Date of promulgation of:* Code pénal : mis à jour au 31 mars 2005 = Fehezandalana famaizana

Indicate the source of information by applying the instructions at **5.8.1.3**.

6.20.3 Date of a Treaty

CORE ELEMENT

6.20.3.1 Scope

Date of a treaty is the earliest date a treaty or a protocol to a treaty was adopted by an international intergovernmental body or by an international conference, was opened for signing, was formally signed, was ratified, was proclaimed, etc.

6.20.3.2 Sources of Information

Take information on date of a treaty from any source.

6.20.3.3 Recording Date of a Treaty

For a single treaty, record the date of a treaty or of a protocol to a treaty by applying the basic instructions at 6.20.1. Record the date in the form *[year] [month] [day]*. Record the month in the language and script preferred by the agency creating the data.

> 1978 December 18
> *Date of signing of a treaty between Australia and Papua New Guinea*
>
> 1948 March 25
> *Date of signing of an agreement between Corporación de Fomento de la Producción (Chile) and the World Bank*
>
> 1783 September 3
> *Date of signing of a treaty between France and Great Britain*
>
> 1994 April 15
> *Date of signing of the Agreement Establishing the World Trade Organization*
>
> 1979 December 18
> *Date of adoption of the Convention on the Elimination of All Forms of Discrimination against Women by the U.N. General Assembly*

For a compilation of treaties, record the date or inclusive dates of the treaties. Record the dates for the earliest and latest treaties following the instructions for recording dates of a single treaty, as applicable.

1713–1715
Years of signing of the treaties comprising the Treaty of Utrecht; complete dates of the earliest and latest treaties not known

Indicate the source of information by applying the instructions at **5.8.1.3**.

6.21 Other Distinguishing Characteristic of a Legal Work

CORE ELEMENT

Other distinguishing characteristic of the work is a core element when needed to differentiate a work from another work with the same title or from the name of a person, family, or corporate body.

6.21.1 Basic Instructions on Recording Other Distinguishing Characteristics of Legal Works

6.21.1.1 Scope

Other distinguishing characteristic of a legal work is a characteristic other than form of work, date of work, or place of origin of the work. It serves to differentiate a legal work from another work with the same title or from the name of a person, family, or corporate body.

6.21.1.2 Sources of Information

Take information on other distinguishing characteristics of a legal work from any source.

6.21.1.3 Recording Other Distinguishing Characteristics of Legal Works

For a separately catalogued protocol, amendment, extension, or other agreement ancillary to a treaty, record *Protocols, etc.*

For other legal works, record other distinguishing characteristics of the work by applying the general instructions at **6.6**.

Record other distinguishing characteristics of legal works as separate elements, as parts of access points, or as both. For instructions on recording other distinguishing characteristics of a legal work as part of the authorized access point, see **6.29.1.30–6.29.1.31**.

6.22 Participant in a Treaty

6.22.1 Recording Participant in a Treaty

6.22.1.1 Recording the Relationship Between a Treaty and a Participant

For instructions on recording the relationship between a treaty and a signatory, ratifier, or other participant in the treaty, see **19.3.2.13**.

ADDITIONAL INSTRUCTIONS FOR RELIGIOUS WORKS AND EXPRESSIONS

6.23 Title of a Religious Work

CORE ELEMENT

Preferred title for the work is a core element. Variant titles for the work are optional.

6.23.1 Basic Instructions on Recording Titles of Religious Works

6.23.1.1 Scope

A ***title of a religious work*** is a word, character, or group of words and/or characters by which a religious work is known.

When identifying religious works, there are two categories of titles:

a) preferred title for a religious work (see **6.23.2**)

b) variant title for a religious work (see **6.23.3**).

6.23.1.2 Sources of Information

Take the title or titles of a religious work from any source.

For additional guidance on sources of information for the preferred title for the work, see **6.23.2.2**.

6.23.1.3 General Guidelines on Recording Titles of Religious Works

When recording a title of a religious work, apply the guidelines on capitalization, numbers, diacritical marks, initial articles, spacing of initials and acronyms, and abbreviations, at **6.2.1**. When those guidelines refer to an appendix, apply the additional instructions in that appendix, as applicable.

6.23.2 Preferred Title for a Religious Work

CORE ELEMENT

6.23.2.1 Scope

The ***preferred title for a religious work*** is the title or form of title chosen to identify the work. It is also the basis for the authorized access point representing that work.

6.23.2.2 Sources of Information

Determine the title to be used as the preferred title for a religious work. Apply the instructions applicable to the type of religious work at **6.23.2.5–6.23.2.8**.

For other types of religious works, apply the general guidelines at **6.2.2.2**.

6.23.2.3 Choosing the Preferred Title

Choose the preferred title for a religious work by applying these instructions:

sacred scriptures (see **6.23.2.5**)
apocryphal books (see **6.23.2.6**)
theological creeds, confessions of faith, etc. (see **6.23.2.7**)
liturgical works (see **6.23.2.8**).

For other types of religious works, apply the general guidelines at **6.2.2.3–6.2.2.7**.

6.23.2.4 Recording the Preferred Title

Record the title chosen as the preferred title for a religious work by applying the basic instructions at **6.2.1**.

For parts of individual sacred scriptures, record the preferred title by applying these instructions:

parts of the Bible (see **6.23.2.9**)
parts of the Talmud (see **6.23.2.10**)
parts of the Mishnah and Tosefta (see **6.23.2.11**)
parts of compilations of midrashim (see **6.23.2.12**)
parts of Buddhist scriptures (see **6.23.2.13**)
parts of the Vedas (see **6.23.2.14**)
parts of the Aranyakas, Brahmanas, and Upanishads (see **6.23.2.15**)
parts of the Jaina Āgama (see **6.23.2.16**)
parts of the Avesta (see **6.23.2.17**)
parts of the Qur'an (see **6.23.2.18**)
parts of the other sacred scriptures (see **6.23.2.19**).

For parts of liturgical works, record the preferred title by applying the instructions at **6.23.2.20**.

CHOOSING THE PREFERRED TITLE

6.23.2.5 Sacred Scriptures

Choose as the preferred title for a sacred scripture a title from a reference source that deals with the religious group or groups to which the scripture belongs. The reference source should be in a language preferred by the agency creating the data. If no such source is available, use general reference sources.

Avesta

Bible

Holy Piby

Kitāb al-aqdas

Qur'an

Talmud

Tripiṭaka

6.23.2.6 Apocryphal Books

An apocryphal book is one that is not included in the Catholic canon nor in the Protestant Apocrypha. Choose as the preferred title for an apocryphal book the title commonly found in sources in a language preferred by the agency creating the data.

Book of Jubilees

Epistola Apostolorum

Gospel according to the Hebrews

For compilations of apocryphal books, apply the instructions at **6.2.2**.

6.23.2.7 Theological Creeds, Confessions of Faith, Etc.

For a theological creed, confession of faith, etc., accepted by one or more denominational bodies, choose as a preferred title a well-established title in a language preferred by the agency creating the data. If there is no such title, use a title in the original language.

Augsburg Confession

Westminster Confession of Faith

Apostles' Creed

Nicene Creed

Ani ma'amin

Shema

Shahada

6.23.2.8 Liturgical Works

Choose as the preferred title for a liturgical work a well-established title. Choose a title in a language preferred by the agency creating the data if:

there is a title in that language

and

the preferred name of the corporate body sanctioning the liturgical work is in the same language.

Book of common prayer

Resource described: The book of common prayer, and administration of the sacraments and other rites and ceremonies of the church, according to the use of the Church of England

Exceptions

Early Catholic liturgical works. If a Catholic liturgical work compiled before the Council of Trent (1545–1563) has a close counterpart in a Tridentine work, use the Tridentine title.

Missal

Resource described: Missale ad vsum insignis Ecclesie Sarum 1527

If such a work has no close counterpart among Tridentine liturgical works, or in case of doubt, use the title by which the work is identified in reference sources.

Ordo Romanus primus

Resource described: Ordo Romanus primus. *An early work. Not the same as the later* Ordo divini officii

Recent Catholic liturgical works. Titles of Tridentine texts are not applicable to those post-Vatican II texts that vary in language and content. Where such variations exist, use the individual title of the resource being described as the preferred title.

Liturgy of the hours for the Order of the Holy Cross

Resource described: The liturgy of the hours for the Order of the Holy Cross. — Onamia, Minnesota : Crosier Monastery, 1982

Proper of The liturgy of the hours of the Order of the Brothers of the Blessed Virgin Mary of Mount Carmel

Resource described: Proper of The liturgy of the hours of the Order of the Brothers of the Blessed Virgin Mary of Mount Carmel. — Rome : Institutum Carmelitanum, 1987

Jewish liturgical works. For a Jewish liturgical work, choose the title found in the *Encyclopaedia Judaica* as the preferred title.

Amidah

Haggadah

Maḥzor

If:

there is no well-established title in a language preferred by the agency creating the data

or

the preferred name of the corporate body is not in a language preferred by the agency

then:

choose a brief title in the language of the liturgy.

For further guidance on titles of liturgical works of the Latin and Eastern rites of the Christian church, consult the following reference sources:

Donald Attwater, *A Catholic Dictionary,* 3rd ed. (New York: Macmillan, 1958).

Fernand Cabrol, *Dictionnaire d'archéologie chrétienne et de liturgie* (Paris: Letouzey et Ané, 1907–1953).

International Federation of Library Associations and Institutions, Working Group on Uniform Headings of Liturgical Works, *List of Uniform Titles for Liturgical Works of the Latin Rites of the Catholic Church,* 2nd ed., rev. (London: IFLA International Office for UBC, 1981).

Oliver L. Kapsner, *A Manual of Cataloguing Practice for Catholic Author and Title Entries: Being Supplementary Aids to the A.L.A. and Vatican Library Cataloging Rules* (Washington: Catholic University of American Press, 1953).

New Catholic Encyclopedia, prepared by an editorial staff at the Catholic University of America (New York: McGraw-Hill, 1967–1979).

Euchologion
Resource described: Euchologion to mega periechon tas tōn epta mystēriōn akolouthias. *Name of corporate body:* Orthodox Eastern Church

Handbok
Resource described: Den svenska kyrkohandboken. *Name of corporate body:* Svenska kyrkan

Slūzhēbnik
Resource described: Služebnik. *Name of corporate body:* Srpska pravoslavna crkva; *text in Church Slavic*

RECORDING PREFERRED TITLES FOR PARTS OF SACRED SCRIPTURES

6.23.2.9 Parts of the Bible

Record the preferred title for parts of the Bible by applying the instructions at **6.23.2.9.1–6.23.2.9.7**, as applicable.

6.23.2.9.1 Testaments

For the Old Testament, record *Old Testament* as a subdivision of the preferred title for the Bible.

For the New Testament, record *New Testament* as a subdivision of the preferred title for the Bible.

6.23.2.9.2 Books

For books of the Catholic or Protestant canon, record the brief citation form of the Authorized Version as a subdivision of the preferred title for the Bible.

Bible. Ezra

Bible. Revelation

If the book is one of a numbered sequence of the same name, record its number after the name as an ordinal numeral. Use a comma to separate the name and the number.

Bible. Corinthians, 1st

Bible. Samuel, 2nd

If:
the resource being described is part of a book
and
it is not a single selection known by its own title

then:

add the chapter (in roman numerals) and verse (in arabic numerals).

Use inclusive numbering if appropriate. Use commas to separate the name of the book, the number of the chapter, and the number of the verse or verses.

> Bible. Psalms, VIII
>
> Bible. Corinthians, 1st, XIII, 12
>
> Bible. Ecclesiastes, III, 1–8
>
> Bible. Hosea, IV–XIV
>
> Bible. Genesis, XI, 26–XX, 18

If the part is a single selection known by its own title, apply the instructions at **6.23.2.9.5**.

6.23.2.9.3 Groups of Books

For the following groups of books, record the appropriate name from the list as a subdivision of the preferred title for the Bible.

TABLE 6.3

GROUPS OF BOOKS	NAME RECORDED
Old Testament	
1–2 Chronicles	Chronicles
Song of Solomon, Ruth, Lamentations, Ecclesiastes, Esther	Five Scrolls
Joshua, Judges, 1–2 Samuel, 1–2 Kings	Former Prophets
Ruth, Chronicles, Ezra, Nehemiah, Esther, Job, Psalms, Proverbs, Ecclesiastes, Song of Solomon, Lamentations, Daniel	Hagiographa
Genesis, Exodus, Leviticus, Numbers, Deuteronomy, Joshua, Judges	Heptateuch
Genesis, Exodus, Leviticus, Numbers, Deuteronomy, Joshua	Hexateuch
Joshua, Judges, Ruth, 1–2 Samuel, 1–2 Kings, Chronicles, Ezra, Nehemiah, Esther	Historical Books
1–2 Kings	Kings
Hosea, Joel, Amos, Obadiah, Jonah, Micah, Nahum, Habakkuk, Zephaniah, Haggai, Zechariah, Malachi	Minor Prophets
Genesis, Exodus, Leviticus, Numbers, Deuteronomy	Pentateuch
Isaiah, Jeremiah, Lamentations, Ezekiel, Daniel, Hosea, Joel, Amos, Obadiah, Jonah, Micah, Nahum, Habakkuk, Zephaniah, Haggai, Zechariah, Malachi	Prophets
Joshua, Judges, 1–2 Samuel, 1–2 Kings, Isaiah, Jeremiah, Ezekiel, Minor Prophets	Prophets (Neviim)
1–2 Samuel	Samuel
New Testament	

GROUPS OF BOOKS	NAME RECORDED
General Epistles of James, Peter, John, Jude	Catholic Epistles
1–2 Corinthians	Corinthians
All or miscellaneous Epistles	Epistles
1–3 John	Epistles of John
Romans, 1–2 Corinthians, Galatians, Ephesians, Philippians, Colossians, 1–2 Thessalonians, 1–2 Timothy, Titus, Philemon	Epistles of Paul
Matthew, Mark, Luke, John	Gospels
1–2 Timothy, Titus	Pastoral Epistles
1–2 Peter	Peter
1–2 Thessalonians	Thessalonians
1–2 Timothy	Timothy

Bible. Pentateuch

For other groups of books, apply these instructions, as applicable:

two or more complete selections from the Bible (see **6.23.2.9.6**)

other selections from the Bible (see **6.23.2.9.7**).

6.23.2.9.4 Apocrypha

Record *Apocrypha* as a subdivision of the preferred title for the Bible for the compilation known as the Apocrypha (1–2 Esdras, Tobit, Judith, Rest of Esther, Wisdom of Solomon, Ecclesiasticus, Baruch, History of Susanna, Song of the Three Children, Bel and the Dragon, Prayer of Manasses, 1–2 Maccabees).

Do not treat an edition of the Bible lacking these books as being incomplete.

Bible. Apocrypha

For an individual book use the name of the book as a further subdivision.

Bible. Apocrypha. Song of the Three Children

Bible. Apocrypha. Esdras, 1st

For apocryphal books, see **6.23.2.6**.

6.23.2.9.5 Single Selections

If a single selection is commonly identified by its own title (rather than its designation as part of the Bible), record that directly as the preferred title.

Lord's prayer

Ten commandments

Miserere

Variant titles. Record as a variant title (see **6.23.3.5**) the title of the selection formulated as a part of the Bible (see **6.23.2.9.2**).

Record the title of any other single selection by applying the instructions at **6.23.2.9.2**.

> Bible. Psalms, XXIII

6.23.2.9.6 Two or More Complete Selections from the Bible

If:

the resource being described consists of two or more selections (including whole books)

and

the selections are encompassed precisely by two preferred titles for parts of the Bible as specified at **6.23.2.9.2**, **6.23.2.9.3**, **6.23.2.9.4**, or **6.23.2.9.5**

then:

identify each of the selections separately.

> Bible. Gospels
> Bible. Acts
> *Resource described:* Il Vangelo e gli Atti degli apostoli

6.23.2.9.7 Other Selections from the Bible

For other selections (including miscellaneous extracts) use the most specific title that is appropriate for the selections, followed by the conventional collective title *Selections*.

Record the specific title for the part or parts by applying these instructions, as applicable:

- Testaments (see **6.23.2.9.1**)
- books (see **6.23.2.9.2**)
- groups of books (see **6.23.2.9.3**)
- Apocrypha (see **6.23.2.9.4**)
- single selections (see **6.23.2.9.5**)
- two or more complete selections from the Bible (see **6.23.2.9.6**).

If a specific title for the part is not applicable, record *Bible*, followed by the conventional collective title *Selections*.

> Bible. Selections
> *Resource described:* Memorable passages from the Bible (Authorized Version) / selected and edited by Fred Newton Scott
>
> Bible. New Testament. Selections
> *Resource described:* The records and letters of the apostolic age : the New Testament Acts, Epistles, and Revelation in the version of 1881 / arranged for historical study by Ernest De Witt Burton
>
> Bible. Gospels. Selections
> *Resource described:* The message of Jesus Christ : the tradition of the early Christian communities / restored and translated into German by Martin Dibelius ; translated into English by Frederick C. Grant

6.23.2.10 Parts of the Talmud

Record the preferred title for parts of the Talmud by applying these instructions, as applicable:

orders, tractates, and treatises (see **6.23.2.10.1**)

minor tractates (see **6.23.2.10.2**)

selections from the Talmud (see **6.23.2.10.3**).

6.23.2.10.1 Orders, Tractates, and Treatises

Record the form of title found in the *Encyclopaedia Judaica* for a particular order (*seder*) or a tractate or treatise (*masekhet*) of the Talmud. Record it as a subdivision of the preferred title for the Talmud or Talmud Yerushalmi, as appropriate.

Talmud. Ḥagigah

Resource described: A translation of the treatise Chagigah from the Babylonian Talmud / with introduction, notes, glossary, and indices by A.W. Streane

Talmud Yerushalmi. Bava meẓia

Resource described: Masekhet Bava metsiʻa min Talmud Yerushalmi : ʻim perush Netivot Yerushalayim / ḥubar me-iti Yiśraʾel Ḥayim Daikhes

6.23.2.10.2 Minor Tractates

For separately published editions of the minor tractates, record *Minor tractates* as a subdivision of the preferred title for the Talmud.

Talmud. Minor tractates

Resource described: Shevaʻ masekhtot ḳeṭanot / hutsʾu ʻa.y. Mikhaʾel Higer

If the resource consists of a single tractate, record the title of the tractate as a further subdivision.

Talmud. Minor tractates. Semaḥot

Resource described: Der talmudische Tractat Ebel rabbathi, oder, S'machoth : nach Handschriften und Parallelstellen / bearbeitet, übersetzt und mit erläuternden Anmerkungen versehen von Moritz Klotz

6.23.2.10.3 Selections from the Talmud

If the resource being described consists of selections, use the preferred title for the Talmud, followed by the conventional collective title *Selections*.

Talmud. Selections

Resource described: The Babylonian Talmud in selection / edited and translated from the original Hebrew and Aramaic by Leo Auerbach

Talmud Yerushalmi. Selections

Resource described: Der Jerusalemer Talmud : sieben ausgewälte Kapitel / übersetzt, kommentiert und eingeleitet von Hans-Jürgen Becker

6.23.2.11 Parts of the Mishnah and Tosefta

Record the form of title found in the *Encyclopaedia Judaica* for a particular order or tractate of the Mishnah or Tosefta. Record it as a subdivision of the preferred title for the Mishnah or Tosefta, as appropriate.

Mishnah. Avot
Resource described: Pirke Aboth = Sayings of the Fathers / edited, with translations and commentaries, by Isaac Unterman

6.23.2.12 Midrashim

Record the preferred title for midrashim by applying these instructions, as applicable:

anonymous midrashim (see **6.23.2.12.1**)
compilations (see **6.23.2.12.2**)
separately published components (see **6.23.2.12.3**).

6.23.2.12.1 Anonymous Midrashim

For an anonymous midrash, record the form of title found in the *Encyclopaedia Judaica* as the preferred title.

Mekhilta of Rabbi Ishmael
Tanna de-vei Eliyahu

6.23.2.12.2 Compilations of Midrashim

Record *Midrash ha-gadol*, *Midrash rabbah*, or *Sifrei* as the preferred titles for those midrashim.

For other compilations of midrashim, apply the instructions at **6.2.2**.

6.23.2.12.3 Separately Published Components

For a separately published component of the *Midrash ha-gadol*, *Midrash rabbah*, or *Sifrei*, record the name of the book of the Bible with which it deals. Record the name of the book of the Bible as a subdivision of the preferred title for the midrashim. Record the name in a language preferred by the agency creating the data.

Midrash ha-gadol. Numbers
Midrash rabbah. Ruth
Sifrei. Deuteronomy

6.23.2.13 Parts of Buddhist Scriptures

Record the preferred title for parts of Buddhist scriptures by applying these instructions, as applicable:

parts of the Pali canon (see **6.23.2.13.1**)
parts of the Sanskrit canon (see **6.23.2.13.2**).

6.23.2.13.1 Parts of the Pali Canon

Record the title of a component division of the Pali canon (*Abhidhammapiṭaka*, *Suttapiṭaka*, *Vinayapiṭaka*) as a subdivision of the preferred title for the Tipiṭaka.

Tipiṭaka. Abhidhammapiṭaka

For a separately published part of one of these component divisions, record the title of the part. Record it as a subdivision of the preferred title for the appropriate Piṭaka or the appropriate division.

Tipiṭaka. Abhidhammapiṭaka. Dhātukathā

Tipiṭaka. Suttapiṭaka. Khuddakanikāya. Jātaka

Tipiṭaka. Vinayapiṭaka. Khandhaka. Cullavagga

6.23.2.13.2 Parts of the Sanskrit Canon

Record the title of a component division of the Sanskrit canon (*Abhidharmapiṭaka*, *Sūtrapiṭaka*, *Vinayapiṭaka*) as a subdivision of the preferred title for the Tripiṭaka.

Tripiṭaka. Abhidharmapiṭaka

For a separately published part of one of these component divisions, record the title of the part. Record it as a subdivision of the preferred title for the appropriate Piṭaka or the appropriate division.

Tripiṭaka. Sūtrapiṭaka. Tantra

Tripiṭaka. Vinayapiṭaka. Pratimokṣasūtra

6.23.2.14 Parts of the Vedas

For one of the four standard compilations of Vedas (*Atharvaveda*, *Ṛgveda*, *Sāmaveda*, *Yajurveda*), record the title of the compilation. Record it as a subdivision of the preferred title for the Vedas.

Vedas. Atharvaveda

Vedas. Sāmaveda

6.23.2.15 Parts of the Aranyakas, Brahmanas, and Upanishads

For a part of the Aranyakas, Brahmanas, or Upanishads, record the title of the part. Record it as a subdivision of the preferred title for the appropriate larger compilation.

Aranyakas. Aitareyāraṇyaka

Brahmanas. Gopathabrāhmaṇa

Upanishads. Chāndogyopaniṣad

6.23.2.16 Parts of the Jaina Āgama

For one of the six component compilations of the Jain canon (*Aṅga*, *Upāṅga*, *Prakīrṇaka*, *Cheda*, *Mūla*, and *Cūlikā*), record the title of the component. Record it as a subdivision of the preferred title for the Jaina Āgama.

Jaina Āgama. Aṅga

For a separately titled part of a component compilation, record the title of the part as a subdivision of the preferred title for the component compilation.

Jaina Āgama. Aṅga. Ācārāṅga

6.23.2.17 Parts of the Avesta

For a main component part or a group of parts of the Avesta, record the title by which it is identified. Record the title of the part or parts as a subdivision of the preferred title for the Avesta. Record the title in a language preferred by the agency creating the data.

Avesta. Yasna

Avesta. Khordah Avesta

For an individually titled part of one of the main components, record the title of the part as a subdivision of the preferred title for the main component.

Avesta. Yasna. Gathas

6.23.2.18 Parts of the Qur'an

Record the preferred title for parts of the Qur'an by applying these instructions, as applicable:

chapters, parts, etc. (see **6.23.2.18.1**)

verses (see **6.23.2.18.2**).

6.23.2.18.1 Chapters, Parts, Etc.

For a chapter (*sūrah*), for one of the thirty parts (*juz'*), or for a named grouping of selections of the Qur'an, record the title of the chapter, etc. Record it as a subdivision of the preferred title for the Qur'an. Precede the title of a chapter by *Sūrat*. Precede the title of a part by *Juz'*.

Qur'an. Sūrat al-Baqarah

Qur'an. Juz' ʻAmma

Qur'an. Muʻawwidhatān

Variant titles. Record a form of the title using *Sūrah* or *Juz'* followed by the appropriate roman numeral or numerals as a variant title (see **6.23.3.3**).

Variant titles. Record the title of an established grouping of selections as a variant title (see **6.23.3.3**).

6.23.2.18.2 Verses

For a verse of a chapter, add the numeral of the verse following the title of the *sūrah*. Use a comma to separate the title and the number.

Qur'an. Sūrat al-Baqarah, 255

Variant titles. Record as variant titles (see **6.23.3.3**):

the title of the verse

and

the title of the verse as a subdivision of the preferred title for the Qur'an.

6.23.2.19 Parts of Other Sacred Scriptures

For a part of a sacred scripture not covered by **6.23.2.9–6.23.2.18**, record the title of the part. Record it as a subdivision of the preferred title for the scripture as a whole.

> Book of Mormon. Jacob
>
> Daswen̲ Pādshāh kā Granth. Caubīsa avatāra
>
> Course in Miracles. Workbook for Students
>
> Pearl of Great Price. Book of Abraham
>
> Urantia Book. Central and Superuniverses

For an individually titled part of one of the main components, record the title of the part as a subdivision of the preferred title for the main component.

> Daswen̲ Pādshāh kā Granth. Caubīsa avatāra. Kr̥shṇāvatāra

If a single selection is commonly identified by its own title rather than its designation as part of the larger sacred scripture, record that title directly.

> Allegory of Zenos
> **not**
> Book of Mormon. Jacob, V

RECORDING PREFERRED TITLES FOR PARTS OF LITURGICAL WORKS

6.23.2.20 Parts of Liturgical Works

Record the preferred title for a part or parts of a liturgical work by applying these instructions, as applicable:

general guidelines (see **6.23.2.20.1**)
Offices and Masses (see **6.23.2.20.2**)
numbered plainsong settings (see **6.23.2.20.3**).

6.23.2.20.1 General Guidelines

If the resource being described contains a specific liturgical observance, group of observances, or group of other texts extracted from a larger liturgical work, record a well-established title for the observance, etc., as the preferred title. Record the title in a language preferred by the agency creating the data. If there is no such title, record a brief title in the language of the liturgy.

> Liturgy of St. John Chrysostom
>
> Rite of election
>
> Ordo paenitentiae
>
> Neʻilah

Variant titles. Record the title as a subdivision of the preferred title for the larger work (see **6.23.3.3**).

6.23.2.20.2 Offices and Masses

Record *Office* or *Mass*, as appropriate, followed by a brief identification of the day or occasion, as the preferred title for an Office or for a proper of the Mass for a particular day. If the day is a saint's day, add only the saint's name in direct order and in the language of the preferred name for the saint. Use a comma to separate the title and the saint's name.

> Office, Assumption of the Blessed Virgin Mary
>
> Mass, Sainte Thérèse

6.23.2.20.3 Numbered Plainsong Settings

Record *Mass*, followed by its number in the Gradual, as the preferred title for a numbered plainsong setting of the Ordinary of the Mass.

> Mass XVI

6.23.3 Variant Title for a Religious Work

6.23.3.1 Scope

A ***variant title for a religious work*** is a title or form of title by which a religious work is known that differs from the title or form of title chosen as the preferred title for the work.

6.23.3.2 Sources of Information

Take variant titles from resources embodying the work and/or from reference sources.

6.23.3.3 General Guidelines on Recording Variant Titles for Religious Works

Record variant titles for religious works by applying the basic instructions at **6.2.1**.

Record a variant title for the work when it is different from the title recorded as the preferred title. Record as a variant title:

a title or form of title under which the work has been issued or cited in reference sources

or

a title resulting from a different transliteration of the title.

Exception

Record a title appearing on a manifestation of the work as a variant title for the work only in the following case:

if the title appearing on the manifestation differs significantly from the preferred title

and

if the work itself might reasonably be searched by that title.

For instructions on recording the title proper and other titles appearing on the manifestation see **2.3**.

Apply the specific instructions at **6.23.3.4–6.23.3.5**. Also apply instructions in preceding sections of this chapter, as applicable.

6.23.3.4 Recording Alternative Linguistic Forms as Variant Titles for Religious Works

If the title recorded as the preferred title for a religious work has one or more alternative linguistic forms, record them as variant titles for the work.

> **Different Language Form**
>
> Kitáb-i-aqdas
>
> *Arabic language form recorded as preferred title:* Kitāb al-aqdas

Jerusalem Talmud
Jerusalemische Talmud
Talmud de Jérusalem
Hebrew language form recorded as preferred title: Talmud Yerushalmi

Phrawēt
Khamphī Phrawēt
English language form recorded as preferred title: Vedas

Apostolisches Glaubensbekenntnis
Symbole des apôtres
Symbolum Apostolicum
English language form recorded as preferred title: Apostles' Creed

Bible. Deuteronomium
Bible. Devarim
English language form recorded a preferred title: Bible. Deuteronomy

Different Script

كتاب الأقدس
كتاب اقدس
כתאב אלאקדס
Китаб-и-Агдас
Arabic transliterated form recorded as preferred title: Kitāb al-aqdas

قرآن
English language form recorded as preferred title: Qur'an

Библия
Біблія
Αγία Γραφή
Βίβλος
ბიბლია
성서
聖書
ਬਾਈਬਲ
بائبل
คัมภีร์ไบเบิล
English language form recorded as preferred title: Bible

Different Spelling

Bible. Ezechiel
Preferred title recorded as: Bible. Ezekiel

Hagadah
Preferred title recorded as: Haggadah

Different Transliteration

Koran
Coran
Ḳurʾān
Qorān
Quräan

Qur"on
Xuraan
Preferred title recorded as: Qur'an

Tosefta. Bava ḳama
Tosefta. Baba qamma
Preferred title recorded as: Tosefta. Bava kamma

Bible. Chamesh megilloth
Preferred title recorded as: Bible. Five scrolls. *Preferred transliteration also recorded as a variant title:* Bible. Ḥamesh megilot

6.23.3.5 Recording Other Variant Titles for Religious Works

Record other variant titles and variant forms of the title not covered by **6.23.3.2–6.23.3.4**.

Shemaʻ Yiśra'el
Preferred title recorded as: Shema

Christian Creed
Preferred title recorded as: Apostles' Creed

Lord is my shepherd
Shepherd Psalm
Preferred title recorded as: Bible. Psalms, XXIII

Bible. Torah
Bible. Five Books of Moses
Preferred title recorded as: Bible. Pentateuch

Bible. 5 Scrolls
Preferred title recorded as: Bible. Five Scrolls

Book of Mormon. Fourth Nephi
Book of Mormon. Fourth Book of Nephi
Book of Mormon. Book of Nephi, 4th
Preferred title recorded as: Book of Mormon. Nephi, 4th

Qur'an. Sūrah XLIX
Preferred title recorded as: Qur'an. Sūrat al-Ḥujurāt

Āyat al-Kursī
Qur'an. Āyat al-Kursī
Preferred title recorded as: Qur'an. Sūrat al-Baqarah, 255

6.24 Date of Expression of a Religious Work

CORE ELEMENT

Date of expression is a core element when needed to differentiate one expression of a religious work from another.

6.24.1 Basic Instructions on Recording Date of Expression of a Religious Work

6.24.1.1 Scope

Date of expression of a religious work is the earliest date associated with an expression of a religious work. The date of the earliest manifestation embodying the expression may be treated as the date of expression.

6.24.1.2 Sources of Information

Take information on date of expression of a religious work from any source.

6.24.1.3 Recording Date of Expression of a Religious Work

For the Bible and parts of the Bible, record the date of expression by applying the instructions at **6.24.1.4**.

For other religious works and parts of those works, record the date of expression by applying the general instructions at **6.10**.

Record date of expression of a religious work as a separate element, as part of an access point, or as both. For instructions on recording date of expression as part of the authorized access point, see **6.30.3**.

6.24.1.4 The Bible and Parts of the Bible

Record the year of publication of the resource.

1959

1848

1964?

Resource described: The Old and New Testaments of the Holy Bible. — Revised Standard Version. — New York : Nelson, [1964?]

Alternative

If the resource is a facsimile reproduction, identify the original expression and the facsimile separately. Record the year of publication appropriate for each one.

1534
2002

Resource described: Biblia, das ist, Die gantze Heilige Schrifft deudsch / Mart. Luth. ; begnadet mit kürfurstlicher zu sachsen Freiheit. — Köln : Taschen, ©2002. *Facsimile of a 1534 publication*

If the resource was published over more than one year, record the earlier or earliest year.

1883

Resource described: La Sagrada Biblia / traducida de la Vulgata latina al español, aclarado el sentido de algunos lugares con la luz que dan los textos originales hebreo y griego, é ilustrada con varias notas sacadas de los santos padres y expositores sagrados, por d. Félix Torres Amat. — Barcelona : Montaner y Simon, 1883–1884

6.25 Other Distinguishing Characteristic of the Expression of a Religious Work

CORE ELEMENT

Other distinguishing characteristic of the expression is a core element when needed to differentiate an expression of the Bible or the Vedas, or an expression of a liturgical work from another expression of the same work.

ADDITIONAL INSTRUCTIONS FOR RELIGIOUS WORKS

6.25.1 Basic Instructions on Recording Other Distinguishing Characteristics of the Expression of a Religious Work

6.25.1.1 Scope

Other distinguishing characteristic of the expression of a religious work is a characteristic other than content type, language of expression, or date of expression. It serves to differentiate an expression of a religious work from another expression of the same work.

6.25.1.2 Sources of Information

Take information on other distinguishing characteristics of the expression of a religious work from any source.

6.25.1.3 Recording Other Distinguishing Characteristics of the Expression of a Religious Work

For the Bible and parts of the Bible, record the version by applying the instructions at **6.25.1.4**.

For other religious works and parts of those works, record other distinguishing characteristics of the expression by applying the general instructions at **6.12**.

Record other distinguishing characteristics of religious works as separate elements, as parts of access points, or as both. For instructions on recording other distinguishing characteristics of a religious work as part of the authorized access point, see **6.30.3**.

6.25.1.4 The Bible and Parts of the Bible

Record a brief form of the name of the version.[3] If the resource is in three or more languages, do not record the version.

> Vulgate
>
> Authorized

If the version is identified by the name of the translator, use a short form of the translator's name. If there are two translators, hyphenate their names. If there are more than two, use the name of the first followed by *and others.*

> Lamsa
>
> Ælfric
>
> Smith-Goodspeed
>
> Gordon and others
>
> *An English translation of the* Old Testament *by Alexander R. Gordon, Theophile J. Meek, J.M. Powis Smith, Leroy Waterman*

Record *Douai* for Rheims-Douai-Challoner versions of the whole Bible. Record *Confraternity* for Confraternity-Douai-Challoner versions of the whole Bible.

> Douai
> *Resource described:* The Holy Bible / translated from the Latin Vulgate being the edition published at Rheims, A.D. 1582 and at Douay, 1609 ; as revised and corrected in 1750, according to the Clementine edition of the Scriptures, by Richard Challoner
>
> Confraternity
> *Resource described:* The Holy Bible. *Confraternity text (Genesis to Ruth, Psalms, New Testament), Douay-Challoner text (remaining books of the Old Testament)*

For an expression of the Bible or parts of the Bible:

If:

the expression is in the original language
the version is unknown
the text has been altered[4]
the version cannot be identified by name or translator
more than two versions are involved

then:

record other distinguishing characteristics of the expression in this order of preference:

a) the name of the manuscript or its repository designation (see **6.2.2.7**) if the resource is a manuscript, or a reproduction, transcription, edition, or translation of a manuscript

> Codex Sinaiticus
> *Resource described:* Bibliorum Codex Sinaiticus Petropolitanus

b) the name of the person who has altered the text if the altered text has no name of its own

> Smith
> *Resource described:* The Holy Scriptures : containing the Old and New Testaments : an inspired version of the Authorized Version / by Joseph Smith, Junior

c) a special name or phrase used in the preferred source of information to identify the text.

> Anchor Bible
> *Resource described:* The Anchor Bible
>
> Numerical Bible
> *Resource described:* The Numerical Bible : being a revised translation of the Holy Scriptures with expository notes

If none of the conditions for recording the version applies, do not record this element.

---

3. Here, *version* is used in its narrow sense of a translation. The version from which another version is made is ignored.
4. Do not treat a harmony of different passages of the Bible as an altered text.

ADDITIONAL INSTRUCTIONS FOR OFFICIAL COMMUNICATIONS

6.26 Title of an Official Communication

CORE ELEMENT

Preferred title for the work is a core element. Variant titles for the work are optional.

6.26.1 Basic Instructions on Recording Titles of Official Communications

6.26.1.1 Scope

A ***title of an official communication*** is a word, character, or group of words and/or characters by which an official communication is known.

When identifying official communications, there are two categories of titles of the work:

a) preferred title for an official communication (see **6.26.2**)

b) variant title for an official communication (see **6.26.3**).

6.26.1.2 Sources of Information

Take the title or titles of an official communication from any source.

For additional guidance on sources of information for the preferred title for the work, see **6.26.2.2**.

6.26.1.3 General Guidelines on Recording Titles of Official Communications

When recording a title of an official communication, apply the guidelines on capitalization, numbers, diacritical marks, initial articles, spacing of initials and acronyms, and abbreviations, at **6.2.1**. When those guidelines refer to an appendix, apply the additional instructions in that appendix, as applicable.

6.26.2 Preferred Title for an Official Communication

CORE ELEMENT

6.26.2.1 Scope

The ***preferred title for an official communication*** is the title or form of title chosen to identify the work. It is also the basis for the authorized access point representing that work.

6.26.2.2 Sources of Information

Determine the title to be used as the preferred title for an official communication by applying the instructions applicable to the type of communication at **6.26.2.5–6.26.2.6**.

For other types of official communications, apply the general guidelines at **6.2.2.2**.

6.26.2.3 Choosing the Preferred Title for an Official Communication

Choose the preferred title for an official communication by applying the instructions at **6.2.2.3–6.2.2.7**.

> *Exceptions*
>
> ***Official communications of the pope.*** For official communications of the pope, apply the instructions at 6.26.2.5.
>
> ***Official communications of the Roman Curia.*** For official communications of the Roman Curia, apply the instructions at **6.26.2.6**.

6.26.2.4 Recording the Preferred Title for an Official Communication

Record the title chosen as the preferred title for an official communication. Apply the basic instructions on recording titles of works at **6.2.1**.

6.26.2.5 Official Communications of the Pope

If the pope, as an official (see **6.31.1.2**), is the creator of the individual work, choose the short title by which the work is generally known and cited. Choose the title in the original language (usually Latin). The short title is generally the first word or words of the text.

> Populorum progressio
>
> Redemptor hominis

6.26.2.6 Official Communications of the Roman Curia

If a communication of one of the tribunals, congregations, or offices of the Roman Curia is known by a short title, choose it as the preferred title for the work.

> Communionis notio

6.26.3 Variant Title for an Official Communication

6.26.3.1 Scope

A ***variant title for an official communication*** is a title or form of title by which an official communication is known that differs from the title or form of title chosen as the preferred title for the work.

6.26.3.2 Sources of Information

Take variant titles for an official communication from resources embodying the work and/or from reference sources.

6.26.3.3 General Guidelines on Recording Variant Titles for Official Communications

Record variant titles for official communications by applying the basic instructions at **6.2.1**.

Record a variant title for the work when it is different from the title recorded as the preferred title. Record as a variant title:

a title or form of title under which the work has been issued or cited in reference sources

or

a title resulting from a different transliteration of the title.

Exception

Record a title appearing on a manifestation of the work as a variant title for the work only in the following case:

if the title appearing on the manifestation differs significantly from the preferred title

and

if the work itself might reasonably be searched by that title.

For instructions on recording the title proper and other titles appearing on the manifestation see **2.3**.

Apply the additional specific instructions at **6.26.3.4–6.26.3.5**, as applicable. Also apply instructions in preceding sections of this chapter, as applicable.

6.26.3.4 Recording Alternative Linguistic Forms as Variant Titles for Official Communications

If the title recorded as the preferred title for an official communication has one or more alternative linguistic forms, record them as a variant titles for the work.

Different Language Form

Coordination of foreign commercial loan management
Indonesian language form recorded as preferred title: Koordinasi pengelolaan pinjaman komersial luar negeri

A imagen y semejanza de Dios
English language form recorded as preferred title: In God's image

Different Script

עיצאפיצנאמע ןופ עיצאמאלקארפ
English language form recorded as preferred title: Emancipation Proclamation

開港港則
Japanese transliterated form recorded as preferred title: Kaikō kōsoku

Different Spelling

Handfestning
Preferred title recorded as: Håndfæstning

Pastoris eterni
Preferred title recorded as: Pastoris aeterni

Different Transliteration

Chiang tsung tʻung Ching-kuo hsien sheng tui kuo min ta hui chih tzʻu hui chi
Preferred title recorded as: Jiang zong tong Jingguo xian sheng dui guo min da hui zhi ci hui ji

6.26.3.5 Recording Other Variant Titles for Official Communications

Record other variant titles and variant forms of the title not covered by **6.26.3.4**.

Golden speech of Queen Elizabeth to her last Parliament, November 30, anno Domini 1601
Her maiesties most princelie answere deliuered by her selfe at White-hall on the last day of Nouember 1601
Queene Elizabeth's speech to her last Parliament
Preferred title recorded as: Golden speech

Kim Yŏng-sam Taetʻongnyŏng yŏnsŏl munjip
金泳三大統領演說文集
Collective title recorded as preferred title: Speeches

National drug control strategy
Preferred title recorded as: Reclaiming our communities from drugs and violence

Decretum Nicolai Papae de electione Romani Pontificis
Papal election decree
Preferred title recorded as: In nomine Domini

Bulla Pastoris aeterni
Preferred title recorded as: Pastoris aeterni

ACCESS POINTS REPRESENTING WORKS AND EXPRESSIONS

6.27 Constructing Access Points to Represent Works and Expressions

6.27.1 Authorized Access Point Representing a Work

6.27.1.1 General Guidelines on Constructing Authorized Access Points Representing Works

For an original work or a new work based on a previously existing work, construct the authorized access point representing the work by applying the instructions at **6.27.1.2–6.27.1.8**.

For instructions on constructing access points representing special types of works, see:

musical works (**6.28.1**)
legal works (**6.29.1**)
religious works (**6.30.1**)
official communications (**6.31.1**).

Make the additions specified at **6.27.1.9** if they are needed to distinguish the access point representing the work from an access point representing a different work or from an access point representing a person, family, or corporate body.

For a part or parts of a work, see **6.27.2**.

For new expressions of an existing work (e.g., abridgements, translations), see **6.27.3**.

For instructions relating to creators of works, see **19.2**.

6.27.1.2 Works Created by One Person, Family, or Corporate Body

If one person, family, or corporate body is responsible for creating the work (see **19.2.1.1**), construct the authorized access point representing the work by combining (in this order):

a) the authorized access point representing that person (see **9.19.1**), family (see **10.11.1**), or corporate body (see **11.13.1**), as applicable

b) the preferred title for the work (see **6.2.2**).

Hemingway, Ernest, 1899–1961. Sun also rises

Cassatt, Mary, 1844–1926. Children playing on the beach

John Paul II, Pope, 1920–2005. Speeches

Saigyō, 1118–1190. Works

Swift, Jonathan, 1667–1745. Tale of a tub
Originally published anonymously but known to be by Jonathan Swift

Goodman, Alice. Nixon in China
The libretto for John Adams's opera Nixon in China

Axel-Lute, Paul. Same-sex marriage
A bibliography compiled by Paul Axel-Lute

Ebert, Roger. Roger Ebert's movie yearbook
An annual compilation of Ebert's film reviews and interviews

Barner (Family). Barner family newsletter

Eakin (Family : New Castle County, Del.). Eakin family papers, 1781–1828

Western Cape Housing Development Board. Annual report

Presbyterian Church (U.S.A.). Book of order

American Bar Association. Section of Intellectual Property Law. Membership directory

Hamline University. Biennial catalogue of Hamline University

Canada. Parliament. House of Commons. Standing Committee on the Status of Women. Minutes of proceedings

Annual Workshop on Sea Turtle Biology and Conservation. Proceedings of the ... Annual Workshop on Sea Turtle Biology and Conservation

Antarctic Walk Environmental Research Expedition (1991–1993). Scientific results from the Antarctic Walk Environmental Research Expedition, 1991–1993

Coldplay (Musical group). Parachutes

Rand McNally and Company. Historical atlas of the world

American Geographical Society of New York. Antarctic map folio series

For works of uncertain attribution, see **6.27.1.8**.

6.27.1.3 Collaborative Works

If two or more persons, families, or corporate bodies are collaboratively responsible for creating the work (see **19.2.1.1**), construct the authorized access point representing the work by combining (in this order):

a) the authorized access point representing the person (see **9.19.1**), family (see **10.11.1**), or corporate body (see **11.13.1**) with principal responsibility

b) the preferred title for the work (see **6.2.2**).

Peterson, Megan. Environmental law reform in Queensland

Resource described: Environmental law reform in Queensland / compiled and written by Megan Peterson ; with the assistance of Adrian Jeffreys, Roslyn Macdonald, Tony Woodyatt, Jo Bragg, David Yarrow, and Douglas Fisher

Bartholomew, Gail. Index to The Maui news

Resource described: The index to The Maui news / compiled and edited by Gail Bartholomew with the assistance of Judy Lindstrom

Kaufman, Moisés. Laramie project

Resource described: The Laramie project / by Moisés Kaufman and the members of Tectonic Theatre Project

Porter, Douglas R. Making smart growth work

Resource described: Making smart growth work / principal author, Douglas R. Porter ; contributing authors, Robert T. Dunphy, David Salvesen

Bishop, Henry R. (Henry Rowley), 1786–1855. Faustus

Resource described: Faustus : a musical romance / composed by T. Cooke, Charles E. Horn, and Henry R. Bishop. *Bishop's name is given typographic prominence, appearing in all uppercase letters and in a larger and different typeface from that of the others*

British American Tobacco Company. British American Tobacco Company records

Resource described: British American Tobacco Company records. *An archival collection that includes corporate records of Cameron and Cameron, D.B. Tennant and Company, David Dunlop, Export Leaf Tobacco Company, and T.C. Williams Company, all of which were companies acquired by British American Tobacco Company*

Alternative

Construct the authorized access point representing the work by combining (in this order):

a) the authorized access points for all creators named either in resources embodying the work or in reference sources; include them in the order in which they are named in those sources; apply the guidelines and instructions at **9.19.1** for persons, **10.11.1** for families, or **11.13.1** for corporate bodies, as applicable

b) the preferred title for the work (see **6.2.2**).

Gumbley, Warren, 1962– ; Johns, Dilys; Law, Garry. Management of wetland archaeological sites in New Zealand
Resource described: Management of wetland archaeological sites in New Zealand / Warren Gumbley, Dilys Johns, and Garry Law

Exceptions

Corporate bodies as creators. A corporate body is considered the creator for certain categories of works (see **19.2.1.1.1**). If one or more corporate bodies and one or more persons or families are collaboratively responsible for creating a work that falls into one or more of the categories at **19.2.1.1.1**, construct the authorized access point representing the work by combining (in this order):

a) the authorized access point representing the corporate body with principal responsibility for the work (see **11.13.1**)

b) the preferred title for the work (see **6.2.2**).

California Academy of Sciences. Catalog of the asteroid type-specimens and Fisher voucher specimens at the California Academy of Sciences
Resource described: Catalog of the asteroid type-specimens and Fisher voucher specimens at the California Academy of Sciences / by Chet Chaffee and Barbara Weitbrecht. — San Francisco : California Academy of Sciences, [1984]

Moving image works. For motion pictures, videos, video games, etc., construct the authorized access point representing the work by using the preferred title for the work (see **6.2.2**).

Gunner palace
Resource described: Gunner palace / Palm Pictures presents a Nomados film ; produced, written, and directed by Michael Tucker and Petra Epperlein

Musical works. For collaborations between a composer and a lyricist, librettist, choreographer, etc., apply the instructions at **6.28.1.2–6.28.1.4**.

If two or more persons, families, or corporate bodies are represented as having principal responsibility for the work, construct the authorized access point representing the work by combining (in this order):

a) the authorized access point representing the first-named of those persons, families, or corporate bodies

b) the preferred title for the work (see **6.2.2**).

Cordell, H. Ken. Footprints on the land

Resource described: Footprints on the land : an assessment of demographic trends and the future of natural lands in the United States / H. Ken Cordell, Christine Overdevest, principal authors

Wallace, Robert. Spycraft

Resource described: Spycraft : the secret history of the CIA's spytechs from communism to Al-Qaeda / Robert Wallace and H. Keith Melton ; with Henry R. Schlesinger

Beyard, Michael D. Developing retail entertainment destinations

Resource described: Developing retail entertainment destinations / principal authors, Michael D. Beyard, Raymond E. Braun, Herbert McLaughlin, Patrick L. Phillips, Michael S. Rubin ; contributing authors, Andre Bald, Steven Fader, Oliver Jerschow, Terry Lassar, David Mulvihill, David Takesuye

Jenkins, Carol. Cultures and contexts matter

Resource described: Cultures and contexts matter : understanding and preventing HIV in the Pacific. — "The principal authors of this book were Carol Jenkins, PhD, and Holly Buchanan-Aruwafu, PhD"—Acknowledgments

If principal responsibility for the work is not indicated, construct the authorized access point representing the work by combining (in this order):

a) the authorized access point representing the first-named person, family, or corporate body

b) the preferred title for the work (see **6.2.2**).

Tracey, John Paul. Managing bird damage to fruit and other horticultural crops

Resource described: Managing bird damage to fruit and other horticultural crops / John Tracey, Mary Bomford, Quentin Hart, Glen Saunders, Ron Sinclair

Collins, Jean, 1947– . Directory of fisheries and aquaculture information resources in Africa

Resource described: Directory of fisheries and aquaculture information resources in Africa = Répertoire des sources d'information sur la pêche et l'aquaculture en Afrique / compiled by Jean Collins and Fodé Karim Kaba

Goto, Yoshihiro. Listing of living Mollusca

Resource described: A listing of living Mollusca / assembled by Yoshihiro Goto, Guido T. Poppe

Sami, David. International travel map, Cuba, scale 1:1,000,000

Resource described: An international travel map, Cuba, scale 1:1,000,000 / cartography by David Sami, Chandra Ali, and Olga Martychina

Cage, John. Double music

Resource described: Double music : percussion quartet / John Cage and Lou Harrison. *Composed jointly by Cage and Harrison, each writing two of the four parts*

Nils-Bertil Dahlander Quartet. Jazz smorgasbord

Resource described: Jazz smorgasbord / Nils-Bertil Dahlander Quartet and the Paul Hindberg Quintet. *Joint performances of pop standards by the two jazz groups*

Canadian Botanical Association. Directory of the Canadian Botanical Association & Canadian Society of Plant Physiologists

Resource described: Directory of the Canadian Botanical Association & Canadian Society of Plant Physiologists

International Boreal Forest Research Association. Annual Meeting (2nd : 1992 : Anchorage, Alaska; Fairbanks, Alaska). Proceedings of the Second and Third Annual Meetings of the International Boreal Forest Research Association

Resource described: Proceedings of the Second and Third Annual Meetings of the International Boreal Forest Research Association : September 11–18, 1992, Anchorage and Fairbanks, Alaska, USA, September 26–October 2, 1993, Biri, Norway and Umeå, Sweden / Sheila Andrus, technical coordinator ; Rebecca Nisley, managing editor

Pekar, Harvey. Quitter

Resource described: The quitter / Harvey Pekar, writer ; Dean Haspiel, artist ; Lee Loughridge, gray tones ; Pat Brosseau, letters. *A graphic novel*

Thompson, Tim, 1942– . Puget Sound

Resource described: Puget Sound : sea between the mountains / photography by Tim Thompson ; text by Eric Scigliano

Tudor, Antony, 1909–1987. Soirée musicale

Resource described: Soirée musicale / choreography by Antony Tudor ; suite of movements from Gioachino Rossini, arranged by Benjamin Britten ; notated by Ann Hutchinson Guest. *Choreography for a ballet, notated in Labanotation*

If there is no consistency in the order in which the persons, families, or corporate bodies responsible for the work are named either in resources embodying the work or in reference sources, construct the authorized access point representing the work by combining (in this order):

a) the authorized access point representing the person (see **9.19.1**), family (see **10.11.1**), or corporate body (see **11.13.1**) who is named first in the first resource received

b) the preferred title for the work (see **6.2.2**).

6.27.1.4 Compilations of Works by Different Persons, Families, or Corporate Bodies

If the work is a compilation of works by different persons, families, or corporate bodies, construct the authorized access point representing the work by using the preferred title for the compilation (see **6.2.2**).

Anthologie de la poésie baroque française

Resource described: Anthologie de la poésie baroque française / textes choisis et présentés par Jean Rousset

Exploring the Olympic Mountains

Resource described: Exploring the Olympic Mountains : accounts of the earliest expeditions, 1878–1890 / compiled by Carsten Lien

Music in the classic period

Resource described: Music in the classic period : essays in honor of Barry S. Brook / [edited by] Allan W. Atlas

Tutti i libretti di Bellini

Resource described: Tutti i libretti di Bellini / a cura di Olimpio Cescatti ; con una prefazione di Marzio Pieri. *Librettos for Bellini operas by various librettists*

Treaties and alliances of the world

Resource described: Treaties and alliances of the world / [compiled by] N.J. Rengger with John Campbell

Lesbian history sourcebook

Resource described: The lesbian history sourcebook : love and sex between women in Britain from 1780 to 1970 / [compiled by] Alison Oram and Annmarie Turnbull

U.S. Marines in Iraq, 2003

Resource described: U.S. Marines in Iraq, 2003 : anthology and annotated bibliography / compiled by Christopher M. Kennedy, Wanda J. Renfrow, Evelyn A. Englander, and Nathan S. Lowrey. *An anthology of personal narratives by various authors, originally published in other resources*

Best of Broadway

Resource described: The best of Broadway. *A set of five CDs with selections from original cast recordings of various musicals by various composers*

If the compilation lacks a collective title, construct separate access points for each of the works in the compilation.

Baden, Conrad. Symphonies, no. 6

First work in a compilation without a collective title also containing Symphony no. 3 *by Hallvard Johnsen and* Symphony no. 2 *by Bjarne Brustad*

Johnsen, Hallvard. Symphonies, no. 3, op. 26

Second work in the same compilation

Brustad, Bjarne. Symphonies, no. 2

Third work in the same compilation

Alternative

Construct an authorized access point representing the compilation by using a devised title (see **2.3.2.11**). Construct this access point instead of, or in addition to, access points for each of the works in the compilation.

Three Norwegian symphonies

6.27.1.5 Adaptations and Revisions

If:

one person, family, or corporate body is responsible for an adaptation or revision of a previously existing work that substantially changes the nature and content of that work

and

the adaptation or revision is presented as the work of that person, family, or body

then:

construct the authorized access point representing the new work by combining (in this order):

a) the authorized access point representing the person (see **9.19.1**), family (see **10.11.1**), or corporate body (see **11.13.1**) responsible for the adaptation or revision, as applicable

b) the preferred title for the adaptation or revision (see **6.2.2**).

Gray, Patsey. J.R.R. Tolkien's The hobbit

A dramatization by Gray of Tolkien's novel

Vande Velde, Vivian. Tales from the Brothers Grimm and the Sisters Weird

A parody by Vande Velde of some of Grimm's fairy tales

Sartain, John, 1808–1897. Artist's dream

An engraving by Sartain based on an original painting by George H. Comegys

James, W. Martin. Historical dictionary of Angola

A new edition by James based on Susan H. Broadhead's work with the same title

Exceptions

Adaptations and revisions of compilations of works by different persons, families, or corporate bodies. If the work is an adaptation or revision of a compilation of works by different persons, families, or corporate bodies, apply the instructions at **6.27.1.4**.

> North American mammals
> *Resource described:* North American mammals. *A Web adaptation of:* The Smithsonian book of North American mammals / edited by Don E. Wilson and Sue Ruff; *and of:* Mammals of North America / Roland W. Kays and Don E. Wilson

Adaptations and revisions of works of uncertain or unknown origin. If the work is an adaptation or revision of a work of uncertain or unknown origin, apply the instructions at **6.27.1.8**.

If more than one person, family, or corporate body is responsible for the adaptation or revision, apply the instructions on collaborative works at **6.27.1.3**.

> Abrams, Anthony. Dead man on campus
> *Resource described:* Dead man on campus / a novelization by Tony Abrams and Adam Broder

If the work is presented simply as an edition of the previously existing work, treat it as an expression of that work. Use the authorized access point representing the previously existing work. If it is considered important to identify the particular expression, construct an authorized access point representing the expression as instructed at **6.27.3**.

> Carroll, Bradley W. Introduction to modern astrophysics
> *Authorized access point representing the first edition of a work by Bradley W. Carroll and Dale A. Ostlie*
>
> Carroll, Bradley W. Introduction to modern astrophysics
> *Authorized access point representing the second edition of the work by the same authors*

For additional instructions on authorized access points representing adaptations of musical works, see **6.28.1.5–6.28.1.6**.

6.27.1.6 Commentary, Annotations, Illustrative Content, Etc., Added to a Previously Existing Work

If:

the work consists of a previously existing work with added commentary, annotations, illustrative content, etc.

and

it is presented as the work of the person, family, or corporate body responsible for the commentary, etc.

then:

construct the authorized access point representing the work by combining (in this order):

a) the authorized access point representing the person (see **9.19.1**), family (see **10.11.1**), or corporate body (see **11.13.1**) responsible for the commentary, etc., as applicable

b) the preferred title for the commentary, etc. (see **6.2.2**).

Akram, Malik M. Comprehensive and exhaustive commentary on the Transfer of Property Act, 1882
A commentary by Akram that includes the text of the law and its amendments

If more than one person is responsible for the added commentary, etc., apply the instructions on collaborative works at **6.27.1.3**.

If the work is presented simply as an edition of the previously existing work, treat it as an expression of that work. Use the authorized access point representing the previously existing work. If it is considered important to identify the particular expression, construct an authorized access point representing the expression as instructed at **6.27.3**.

Plato. Gorgias
Resource described: Gorgias : a revised text / Plato ; with introduction and commentary by E.R. Dodds

Joyce, James, 1882–1941. Dubliners
Resource described: James Joyce's Dubliners : an illustrated edition with annotations / [edited by] John Wyse Jackson & Bernard McGinley

Laozi. Dao de jing. English
Resource described: The Tao te ching : a new translation with commentary / Ellen M. Chen

6.27.1.7 Different Identities for an Individual Responsible for a Work

If:

an individual responsible for a work has more than one identity (see **9.2.2.8**)

and

there is no consistency in how that individual is identified on resources embodying the work

then:

construct the authorized access point representing the work by combining (in this order):

a) the authorized access point representing the identity most frequently used on resources embodying the work (see **9.19.1**)

b) the preferred title for the work (see **6.2.2**).

Cunningham, E. V., 1914–2003. Sylvia
not Fast, Howard, 1914–2003. Sylvia
The author's novel Sylvia *was originally published under the pseudonym E.V. Cunningham. On some resources embodying the work the author is identified by his real name, Howard Fast; the identity most frequently used on resources embodying the work is E.V. Cunningham*

If the identity used most frequently cannot be readily determined, construct the authorized access point representing the work by combining (in this order):

a) the authorized access point representing the identity appearing in the most recent resource embodying the work

b) the preferred title for the work (see **6.2.2**).

6.27.1.8 Works of Uncertain or Unknown Origin

If the work has been attributed to one or more persons, families, or corporate bodies, but there is uncertainty as to the probable person, family, or body responsible, construct the authorized access point representing the work by using the preferred title for the work (see **6.2.2**).

Law scrutiny
Resource described: The law scrutiny, or, Attornies' guide. *Variously attributed to Andrew Carmichael, William Norcott, and others*

If reference sources indicate that one person, family, or corporate body is probably responsible for creating the work, construct the authorized access point representing the work by combining (in this order):

a) the authorized access point representing that person (see **9.19.1**), family (see **10.11.1**), or corporate body (see **11.13.1**)

b) the preferred title for the work (see **6.27.1.2**).

If:
the person, family, or corporate body responsible for the work is unknown
or
the work originates from an unnamed group
then:
construct the authorized access point representing the work by using the preferred title for the work (see **6.2.2**).

Log-cabin lady
Resource described: The log-cabin lady : an anonymous autobiography. *Person responsible unknown*

Memorial to Congress, against the tariff law of 1828
Resource described: A memorial to Congress, against the tariff law of 1828 / by citizens of Boston

Mysterious bottle of old hock
Resource described: The mysterious bottle of old hock : an ancient legend / introduction by Franz J. Potter. *An anonymous adaptation of E.T.A. Hoffmann's* Die Elixiere des Teufels

Summer night
Resource described: Summer night. *An anonymous lithograph of a painting by Albert Moore*

Unknown Memphis family photo collection
Unpublished collection in the Mississippi Valley Collection of the University of Memphis. Title devised by cataloguing agency

Yankee Doodle
Resource described: Yankee Doodle / arranged with variations for the piano. *Variations for piano on the patriotic song; name of the composer of the adaptation unknown*

ADDITIONS TO ACCESS POINTS REPRESENTING WORKS

6.27.1.9 Additions to Access Points Representing Works

Make additions to access points if needed to distinguish the access point for a work:

from one that is the same or similar but represents a different work

or

from one that represents a person, family, corporate body, or place.

Add one or more of the following elements, as appropriate:

a) the form of work (see **6.3**)

b) the date of the work (see **6.4**)

c) the place of origin of the work (see **6.5**)

and/or

d) another distinguishing characteristic of the work (see **6.6**).

Advocate (Boise, Idaho)

Advocate (Nairobi, Kenya)

Blue book contractors register (New York-New Jersey-Connecticut edition)

Blue book contractors register (Southern California edition)

Bulletin (Geological Survey (South Africa))

Bulletin (New York State Museum : 1945)

Bulletin (New York State Museum : 1976)

Bulletin (New Zealand. Ministry of Education. Research and Statistics Division)

Charlemagne (Play)

Charlemagne (Tapestry)

Dublin magazine (1762)

Dublin magazine (1965)

Genesis (Anglo-Saxon poem)

Genesis (Middle High German poem)

Genesis (Old Saxon poem)

Last judgement (Chester play)

Last judgement (York play)

Nutcracker (Choreographic work)

NuTCRACKER (Computer file)

Ocean's eleven (Motion picture : 1960)

Ocean's eleven (Motion picture : 2001)

Othello (Television program : 1963 : Canadian Broadcasting Corporation)

Othello (Television program : 1963 : WOR-TV (Television station : New York, N.Y.))

I, Claudius (Television programme)
Term added by an agency following British spelling

Guillaume (Chanson de geste)
To distinguish the access point for the work from the access point for the 13th century person known as Guillaume

Scottish History Society (Series)
To distinguish the access point for the work from the access point for the corporate body of the same name

Connecticut Commission on Children. Annual report (1999)

Connecticut Commission on Children. Annual report (2005)

Eyck, Jan van, 1390–1440. Saint Francis receiving the stigmata (Galleria sabauda (Turin, Italy))

Eyck, Jan van, 1390–1440. Saint Francis receiving the stigmata (Philadelphia Museum of Art)

For instructions on additions to access points representing special types of works, see:

musical works (**6.28.1.9–6.28.1.11**)

legal works (**6.29.1.29–6.29.1.31**).

6.27.2 Authorized Access Point Representing a Part or Parts of a Work

6.27.2.1 General Guidelines on Constructing Authorized Access Points Representing Parts of Works

Construct the authorized access point representing a part or parts of a work by applying the instructions at **6.27.2.2–6.27.2.3**, as applicable.

> *Exceptions*
>
> *Parts of musical works.* For a part or parts of a musical work, apply instead the instructions at **6.28.2**.
>
> *Parts of religious works.* For a part or parts of a religious work, apply instead the instructions at **6.30.2**.

6.27.2.2 One Part

Construct the authorized access point representing a part of a work by combining (in this order):

a) the authorized access point representing the person (see **9.19.1**), family (see **10.11.1**), or corporate body (see **11.13.1**), responsible for the part (see **6.27.1.1–6.27.1.8**, as applicable)

b) the preferred title for the part (see **6.2.2.9**).

Tolkien, J. R. R. (John Ronald Reuel), 1892–1973. Two towers
Authorized access point for a part of Tolkien's The lord of the rings

Proust, Marcel, 1871–1922. Du côté de chez Swann
Authorized access point for a part of Proust's À la recherche du temps perdu

Raven, Simon, 1927–2001. Come like shadows
Authorized access point for a part of Raven's Alms for oblivion

> *Exceptions*
>
> *Non-distinctive titles.* If the part is identified only by a general term (with or without a number), construct the authorized access point representing the part by combining (in this order):
>
> a) the authorized access point representing the work as a whole
>
> b) the preferred title for the part (see **6.2.2.9**).
>
> Goethe, Johann Wolfgang von, 1749–1832. Faust. 1. Theil
>
> Homer. Iliad. Book 1
>
> Duellman, William Edward, 1930– . Amphibian species of the world. Additions and corrections
>
> Manet, Édouard, 1832–1883. Luncheon on the grass. Detail
>
> *Serials and integrating resources.* If the part is a section of, or supplement to, a serial or an integrating resource, whether the title of the section or supplement is distinctive or not, construct the authorized access point representing the part by combining (in this order):
>
> a) the authorized access point representing the work as a whole
>
> b) the preferred title for the section or supplement (see **6.2.2.9.1**).

Acta Universitatis Upsaliensis. Studia musicologica Upsaliensia

Department of State publication. East Asian and Pacific series

Annual report on carcinogens. Executive summary

Colorado. Judicial Branch. Annual report. Statistics and charts

Raffles bulletin of zoology. Supplement

Emergency health series. A

Annale van die Uniwersiteit van Stellenbosch. Reeks B

Bulletin analytique. 2e partie, Sciences biologiques, industries alimentaires, agriculture

Television programs, radio programs, etc. If the part is a season, episode, excerpt, etc., of a television program, radio program, etc., whether the title of the part is distinctive or not, construct the authorized access point representing the part by combining (in this order):

a) the authorized access point representing the work as a whole

b) the preferred title for the part (see **6.2.2.9.1**).

Simpsons (Television program). King of the hill

Buffy, the vampire slayer (Television program). Season 6

Jack Benny program (Radio program). 1946-03-10

If the part is a work for which the instructions at **6.27.1.3–6.27.1.8** specify the use of the preferred title as the authorized access point representing the work, use the preferred title for the part as the authorized access point representing the part. Apply the exceptions in **6.27.2.2**, if applicable.

Sindbad the sailor
Authorized access point for a part of The Arabian nights

Last judgement (Chester play)
Authorized access point for a part of The Chester plays

but

Encyclopedia of philosophy. Supplement
Resource described: Encyclopedia of philosophy. Supplement / Donald M. Borchert, editor in chief. *Authorized access point for the work as a whole:* Encyclopedia of philosophy

6.27.2.3 Two or More Parts

If:

two or more parts of a work are consecutively numbered

and

each is identified only by a general term and a number

then:

construct the authorized access point by combining (in this order):

a) the authorized access point representing the work as a whole (see **6.27.1**)

b) the preferred title for the sequence of parts (see **6.2.2.9.2**).

Homer. Iliad. Book 1–6

Resource described: The first six books of Homer's Iliad / with English notes, critical and explanatory, a metrical index, and Homeric glossary by Charles Anthon

Rollin, Henri, 1885–1955. Apocalypse de notre temps. Chapitre 6–7

Resource described: Une mystification mondiale : précédé de Le faux et son usage, par Gérard Berréby / Henri Rollin. *Originally published as chapters 6–7 of Rollin's* L'apocalypse de notre temps

When identifying two or more parts that are unnumbered or non-consecutively numbered, construct authorized access points for each of the parts. Apply the instructions at **6.27.2.2**.

Dante Alighieri, 1265–1321. Purgatorio
Dante Alighieri, 1265–1321. Paradiso

Resource described: Il Purgatorio ; Paradiso / di Dante Alighieri ; colle figure di G. Doré

Homer. Iliad. Book 1
Homer. Iliad. Book 6
Homer. Iliad. Book 20
Homer. Iliad. Book 24

Resource described: Homer's Iliad, books I, VI, XX, and XXIV / with a copious vocabulary for the use of schools and colleges, by James Fergusson

Alternative

When identifying two or more parts of a work that are unnumbered or non-consecutively numbered, identify the parts collectively. Construct the authorized access point representing the parts by combining (in this order):

a) the authorized access point representing the work as a whole (see **6.27.1**)

b) the conventional collective title *Selections* (see **6.2.2.9.2 alternative**).

Homer. Iliad. Selections

Resource described: Homer's Iliad, books I, VI, XX, and XXIV / with a copious vocabulary for the use of schools and colleges, by James Fergusson

Gibbon, Edward, 1737–1794. History of the decline and fall of the Roman Empire. Selections

Resource described: Selections from The decline and fall of the Roman Empire / Edward Gibbon ; edited with introduction and notes by J.W. Saunders

Gilbert, W. S. (William Schwenck), 1836–1911. Librettos. Selections

Resource described: Gilbert without Sullivan / libretti by W.S. Gilbert ; illustrations by Leonard Lubin. *Librettos for four of Gilbert and Sullivan's fourteen operas*

Simpsons (Television program). Selections

Resource described: The Simpsons gone wild / Twentieth Century Fox Television. *A compilation of four party-themed episodes of the television program The Simpsons originally broadcast between 1990 and 2001*

6.27.3 Authorized Access Point Representing an Expression

Construct an access point representing a particular expression of a work or a part or parts of a work by combining (in this order):

a) the authorized access point representing the work (see **6.27.1**) or the part or parts of a work (see **6.27.2**)

b) one or more terms from the following list:

i. the content type (see **6.9**)

ii. the date of the expression (see **6.10**)

iii. the language of the expression (see **6.11**)
and/or

iv. another distinguishing characteristic of the expression (see **6.12**).

Goncourt, Edmond de, 1822–1896. Frères Zemganno. English

Resource described: The Zemganno brothers / by Edmond de Goncourt. *An English translation of a French novel*

Pushkin, Aleksandr Sergeevich, 1799–1837. Evgeniĭ Onegin. English (Beck)

Resource described: Eugene Onegin / Alexander Pushkin ; translator, Tom Beck

Kolloidnyĭ zhurnal. English

Resource described: Colloid journal of the Russian Academy of Sciences. *An English translation of a Russian serial*

Piave, Francesco Maria, 1810–1876. Ernani. Spanish

Resource described: Ernani : drama lírico en cuatro actos / de F. Piave ; música de G. Verdi ; versión castellana de M. Capdepón. *A Spanish translation of Piave's libretto*

Brunhoff, Jean de, 1899–1937. Babar en famille. English. Spoken word

Resource described: Babar and his children. *An audio recording of an English translation of the children's story*

Wilde, Oscar, 1854–1900. Works. 2000

Resource described: The complete works of Oscar Wilde / general editors, Russell Jackson and Ian Small. — Oxford ; New York : Oxford University Press, 2000– . *Other expressions of Wilde's complete works have been published in other years*

Shakespeare, William, 1564–1616. Works. 2003. Yale University Press

Resource described: The annotated Shakespeare. — New Haven : Yale University Press, ©2003–. *An expression of Shakespeare's complete works; another expression with title* Nelson Thornes Shakespeare *also began in 2003*

Langland, William, 1330?–1400? Piers Plowman (C-text)

Resource described: Piers Plowman / by William Langland ; an edition of the C-text by Derek Pearsall. *Langland's work* Piers Plowman *exists in different versions designated as* A-text, B-text, C-text, *etc.*

Nutcracker (Choreographic work : Baryshnikov)

Resource described: The nutcracker. *A recording of a performance of the American Ballet Theatre and Mikhail Baryshnikov production of the ballet* The nutcracker; *choreography by Baryshnikov*

Hugo, Victor, 1802-1885. Notre-Dame de Paris. Spoken word (Dussollier)

Resource described: Notre-Dame de Paris / Victor Hugo. *An audio recording of the novel narrated by André Dussollier; other audio recordings by different narrators have been made*

6.27.4 Variant Access Point Representing a Work or Expression

6.27.4.1 General Guidelines on Constructing Variant Access Points Representing Works

Use a variant title for the work (see **6.2.3**) as the basis for a variant access point.

Nibelunge Nôt
Authorized access point for the work: Nibelungenlied

If the authorized access point for the work has been constructed by using the authorized access point representing a person, family, or corporate body followed by the preferred title for the work (see **6.27.1.2–6.27.1.8**), construct a variant access point by combining (in this order):

a) the authorized access point representing that person (see **9.19.1**), family (see **10.11.1**), or corporate body (see **11.13.1**)

b) the variant title for the work.

Dickens, Charles, 1812–1870. The posthumous papers of the Pickwick Club
Authorized access point for the work: Dickens, Charles, 1812–1870. The Pickwick papers

Solzhenit͡syn, Aleksandr Isaevich, 1918–2008. Один день Ивана Денисовича
Authorized access point for the work: Solzhenit͡syn, Aleksandr Isaevich, 1918–2008. Odin denʹ Ivana Denisovicha

Make additions to the variant access point, if considered important for identification. Apply the instructions at **6.27.1.9**, as applicable.

Roland (Poem)
Authorized access point for the work: Chanson de Roland; *variant title for the work is identical to the access point for a person known only by the given name Roland and to the preferred title for other works*

Science series (Boston, Mass.)
Authorized access point for the work: Beacon science series; *variant title for the work is identical to the preferred title for other works and to the variant title for still other works*

Science series (Cypress, Calif.)
Authorized access point for the work: Schwartz, David M. Science series; *preferred title for the work is identical to the preferred title for other works and to the variant title for still other works*

Afrique et développement (Éditions Karthala)
Authorized access point for the work: Collection Afrique et développement; *variant title for the work is identical to the preferred title for another work*

OC (Television program)
Orange County (Television program)
Authorized access point for the work: O.C. (Television program)

Frankenstein (Motion picture : 1994)
Authorized access point for the work: Mary Shelley's Frankenstein (Motion picture)

Apply these additional instructions, as applicable:

librettos, lyrics, or other texts for musical works (see **6.27.4.2**)

part or parts of a work (see **6.27.4.3**)

compilations of works (see **6.27.4.4**).

Construct additional variant access points if considered important for access.

Aristotle. Liber de causis

Authorized access point for the work: Liber de causis. *An anonymous work attributed in medieval times to Aristotle*

Fox, Michael W., 1937– . Dr. Michael Fox animal series

Authorized access point for the work: Dr. Michael Fox animal series. *A series of video recordings on animal care featuring Fox*

California Academy of Sciences. Occasional papers of the California Academy of Sciences

Authorized access point for the work: Occasional papers of the California Academy of Sciences

Massachusetts. Bureau of Statistics of Labor. Labor bulletin
Massachusetts. Bureau of Statistics. Labor bulletin
Massachusetts. Department of Labor and Industries. Division of Statistics. Labor bulletin

Authorized access point for the work: Labor bulletin (Boston, Mass.). *Issuing body varies*

Fast, Howard, 1914–2003. Sylvia

Authorized access point for the work: Cunningham, E. V., 1914–2003. Sylvia. *Novel originally published under the pseudonym E.V. Cunningham; author's real name, Howard Fast, appears on some resources embodying the work, but the identity most frequently used is Cunningham*

Jeanne-Claude, 1935– . Wrapped Reichstag

Authorized access point for the work: Christo, 1935– . Wrapped Reichstag. *A work of art created jointly by Christo and Jeanne-Claude. Variant access point considered important for subject access*

Management series (Chicago, Ill.)

Authorized access point for the work: Management series (Ann Arbor, Mich.). *Place of publication of series changed from Ann Arbor to Chicago*

Mysliteli Rossii (Saint Petersburg, Russia)

Authorized access point for the work: Mysliteli Rossii (Leningrad, R.S.F.S.R.). *Name of place of publication of series changed from Leningrad to Saint Petersburg and separate authorized access points for the place names have been established*

The giant animals series

Authorized access point for the work: Johnston, Marianne. The giant animals series. *Variant access point using the preferred title for the work on its own*

The posthumous papers of the Pickwick Club

Authorized access point for the work: Dickens, Charles, 1812-1870. The Pickwick papers. *Variant access point using the variant title for the work on its own*

For variant access points for expressions of works, apply additional instructions at **6.27.4.5**.

6.27.4.2 Variant Access Point Representing One or More Librettos, Lyrics, or Other Texts for Musical Works

Construct a variant access point representing one or more librettos, lyrics, or other texts that have been used in specific musical works by combining (in this order):

a) the authorized access point representing the composer of the musical work or musical works (see **9.19.1** for persons, **10.11.1** for families, or **11.13.1** for corporate bodies, as applicable)

b) the preferred title for the musical work or musical works (see **6.14.2**)

c) the term *Libretto*, *Librettos*, *Lyrics*, *Text*, or *Texts*, as appropriate

d) another distinguishing term, if needed.

Adams, John, 1947– . Nixon in China. Libretto
Authorized access point for the work: Goodman, Alice. Nixon in China

Verdi, Giuseppe, 1813–1901. Ernani. Libretto. Spanish
Authorized access point for the expression: Piave, Francesco Maria, 1810–1876. Ernani. Spanish

Bellini, Vincenzo, 1801–1835. Operas. Librettos
Authorized access point for the compilation: Tutti i libretti di Bellini

Sullivan, Arthur, 1842–1900. Operas. Selections. Librettos
Authorized access point for the compilation: Gilbert, W. S. (William Schwenck), 1836–1911. Librettos. Selections

John, Elton. Songs. Selections. Lyrics
Authorized access point for the compilation: Taupin, Bernie. Lyrics. Selections

Do not apply this instruction in cases where the composer of the musical work or musical works is the same person, family, or corporate body as the author of the text.

6.27.4.3 Variant Access Point Representing a Part of a Work

If:
the title of the part of a work is distinctive
and
the authorized access point for the part has been constructed by using the authorized access point representing a person, family, or corporate body followed by the preferred title for the work as a whole, followed by the preferred title for the part
then:
construct a variant access point representing the part by combining (in this order):

a) the authorized access point representing that person, family, or corporate body

b) the preferred title for the part.

Williams, Kim, 1966– . Penguins
Authorized access point for the part of the work: Williams, Kim, 1966– . Young explorer series. Penguins

Colorado. Judicial Branch. Statistics and charts
Authorized access point for the part of the work: Colorado. Judicial Branch. Annual report. Statistics and charts

If:
the authorized access point for the part has been constructed by using the authorized access point representing a person, family, or corporate body followed directly by the preferred title for the part
and
the authorized access point for the part does not use the preferred title for the work as a whole
then:
construct a variant access point representing the part by combining (in this order):

a) the authorized access point representing that person, family, or corporate body

b) the preferred title for the work as a whole

c) the preferred title for the part.

Tolkien, J. R. R. (John Ronald Reuel), 1892–1973. Lord of the rings. Two towers
Authorized access point for the part of the work: Tolkien, J. R. R. (John Ronald Reuel), 1892–1973. Two towers

Proust, Marcel, 1871–1922. À la recherche du temps perdu. Du côté de chez Swann
Authorized access point for the part of the work: Proust, Marcel, 1871–1922. Du côté de chez Swann

Raven, Simon, 1927–2001. Alms for oblivion. Come like shadows
Authorized access point for the part of the work: Raven, Simon, 1927–2001. Come like shadows

If:

the title of the part of a work is distinctive

and

the authorized access point for the part has been constructed by using the preferred title for the work as a whole, followed by the preferred title for the part

then:

construct a variant access point by using the preferred title for the part on its own.

Studia musicologica Upsaliensia
Authorized access point for the part of the work: Acta Universitatis Upsaliensis. Studia musicologica Upsaliensia

If the authorized access point for the part has been constructed by using the title of the part on its own, construct a variant access point by combining (in this order):

a) the preferred title for the work as a whole

b) the preferred title for the part.

Arabian nights. Sindbad the sailor
Authorized access point for the part of the work: Sindbad the sailor

Chester plays. Last judgement
Authorized access point for the part of the work: Last judgement (Chester play)

Make additions to the variant access point, if considered important for identification. Apply the instructions at 6.27.1.9, as applicable.

Electrical engineering series (Stockholm, Sweden)
Authorized access point for the part of the work: Acta polytechnica Scandinavica. Electrical engineering series.
Title of the part is identical to the preferred title for another work

King of the hill (Television program : Episode of The Simpsons)
Authorized access point for the part of the work: Simpsons (Television program). King of the hill

King of the hill (Television program : Episode of Cheers)
Authorized access point for the part of the work: Cheers (Television program). King of the hill

Construct additional variant access points if considered important for access.

6.27.4.4 Variant Access Point Representing a Compilation of Works

If:

the authorized access point representing a compilation of works by one person, family, or corporate body has been constructed by using the authorized access point representing that person, family, or corporate body followed by a conventional collective title (see **6.2.2.10**)

and

the title proper (excluding any alternative title) of the resource being described or the title found in a reference source is not the same as, nor very similar to, the collective title

then:

construct a variant access point representing the compilation by combining (in this order):

a) the authorized access point representing the person (see **9.19.1**), family (see **10.11.1**), or corporate body (see **11.13.1**)

b) the title proper of the resource being described or the title found in a reference source.

> Andersen, H. C. (Hans Christian), 1805–1875. Eventyr
> *Title proper of the resource being described. Authorized access point recorded as:* Andersen, H. C. (Hans Christian), 1805–1875. Tales
>
> Andersen, H. C. (Hans Christian), 1805–1875. Samlede eventyr og historier
> *Title proper of the resource being described. Authorized access point recorded as:* Andersen, H. C. (Hans Christian), 1805–1875. Tales

Make additions to the variant access point, if considered important for identification. Apply the instructions at **6.27.1.9**, as applicable.

> Dante Alighieri, 1265–1321. Tutte le opere di Dante (1966)
> *Title proper of the resource being described. Authorized access point recorded as:* Dante Alighieri, 1265–1321. Works (1966)

Construct additional variant access points if considered important for access.

6.27.4.5 Variant Access Point Representing an Expression

Construct a variant access point representing an expression, if appropriate, by combining (in this order):

a) the authorized access point representing the work

b) a variant of an addition used in constructing the authorized access point representing the expression (see **6.27.3**).

> Theodore bar Konai, 8th century–9th century. Liber scholiorum (Ourmia version)
> *Authorized access point for the expression:* Theodore bar Konai, 8th century–9th century. Liber scholiorum (Urmiah version)
>
> Blade runner (Motion picture : 2007 version)
> Blade runner (Motion picture : 25th anniversary edition)
> Blade runner (Motion picture : Definitive version)
> *Authorized access point for the expression:* Blade runner (Motion picture : Final cut)

If:

a variant title for a work is associated with a particular expression of the work

and

the authorized access point representing the expression has been constructed by using the authorized access point representing a person, family, or corporate body followed by the preferred title for the work and one or more additions identifying the expression

then:

construct a variant access point representing the expression by combining (in this order):

a) the authorized access point representing the person (see **9.19.1**), family (see **10.11.1**), or corporate body (see **11.13.1**)

b) the variant title associated with that expression.

> Munro, Alice, 1931– . Pigeliv & kvindeliv
> *Authorized access point for the expression:* Munro, Alice, 1931– . Lives of girls and women. Danish
>
> Yamada, Taichi, 1934– . Leto s chuzhimi
> Yamada, Taichi, 1934– . Лето с чужими
> *Authorized access point for the expression:* Yamada, Taichi, 1934– . Ijintachi to no natsu. Russian

Make additions to the variant access point, if considered important for identification. Apply the instructions at **6.27.1.9**, as applicable.

> Akhmatova, Anna Andreevna, 1889–1966. Selected poems (1969)
> *Authorized access point for the expression:* Akhmatova, Anna Andreevna, 1889–1966. Works. Selections. English (1969). *Poems translated by Richard McKane*
>
> Akhmatova, Anna Andreevna, 1889–1966. Selected poems (1976)
> *Authorized access point for the expression:* Akhmatova, Anna Andreevna, 1889–1966. Works. Selections. English (1976). *Poems translated by Walter Arndt, Robin Kemball, and Carl R. Proffer*

Construct additional variant access points if considered important for access.

6.28 Constructing Access Points to Represent Musical Works and Expressions

6.28.1 Authorized Access Point Representing a Musical Work

6.28.1.1 General Guidelines on Constructing Authorized Access Points Representing Musical Works

Apply the instructions at **6.28.1.2–6.28.1.8** when constructing the authorized access point representing one of the following types of musical works:

a) musical works with lyrics, libretto, text, etc. (see **6.28.1.2**)

b) pasticcios, ballad operas, etc. (see **6.28.1.3**)

c) works composed for choreographic movement (see **6.28.1.4**)

d) adaptations of musical works (see **6.28.1.5**)

e) operas and other dramatic works with new text and title (see **6.28.1.6**)

f) cadenzas (see **6.28.1.7**)

g) musical scores and incidental music for dramatic works, etc. (see **6.28.1.8**).

For music that is officially prescribed as part of a liturgy, see **6.30.1.5–6.30.1.7**.

For other types of musical works, see **6.27.1**.

For librettos, lyrics, and other texts for musical works, see **6.27.1**.

Make additions to the authorized access point by applying the instructions at **6.28.1.9–6.28.1.11**, as applicable.

For a part or parts of a musical work, see **6.28.2**.

For new expressions of an existing work (e.g., musical arrangements, works with added accompaniment), apply the instructions on constructing authorized access points representing musical expressions at **6.28.3**.

6.28.1.2 Musical Works with Lyrics, Libretto, Text, Etc.

For a musical work that includes words in the form of lyrics, a libretto, text, etc. (e.g., a song, opera, musical comedy), construct the authorized access point representing the work by combining (in this order):

a) the authorized access point representing the composer of the music (see **9.19.1** for persons, **10.11.1** for families, or **11.13.1** for corporate bodies, as applicable)

b) the preferred title for the work (see **6.14.2**).

Viardot-García, Pauline, 1821–1910. Filles de Cadix
Authorized access point for: Les filles de Cadix / poésie de Alfred de Musset ; musique de Pauline Viardot

Krieger, Henry. Dreamgirls
Authorized access point for: Dreamgirls / music by Henry Krieger ; book and lyrics by Tom Eyen

6.28.1.3 Pasticcios, Ballad Operas, Etc.

For pasticcios, ballad operas, etc., and excerpts from such works, apply the instructions at **6.28.1.3.1–6.28.1.3.4** as applicable.

6.28.1.3.1 Original Composition

If the music of a pasticcio was especially composed for it, construct the authorized access point representing the work by combining (in this order):

a) the authorized access point representing the composer who is named first either in resources embodying the work or in reference sources (see **9.19.1** for persons, **10.11.1** for families, or **11.13.1** for corporate bodies, as applicable)

b) the preferred title for the work (see **6.14.2**).

Amadei, Filippo, flourished 1690–1730. Muzio Scaevola
Authorized access point for: The most favourite songs in the opera of Muzio Scaevola / composed by three famous masters. *The composers are Amadei, Bononcini, and Handel*

6.28.1.3.2 Previously Existing Compositions

If the music of a pasticcio, ballad opera, etc., consists of previously existing ballads, songs, arias, etc., by various composers, construct the authorized access point by using the preferred title for the work (see **6.14.2**) on its own.

Beggar's opera
Authorized access point for: The beggar's opera / written by John Gay ; the overture composed and the songs arranged by John Christopher Pepusch. *A vocal score*

6.28.1.3.3 Compilation of Excerpts

If the work is a compilation of musical excerpts from a pasticcio, ballad opera, etc., use the authorized access point representing the work from which the excerpts were taken.

Beggar's wedding

Authorized access point for: Songs in the opera call'd The beggar's wedding, as it is perform'd at the theatres

6.28.1.3.4 Single Excerpt

If the work is a single excerpt from a pasticcio, etc., construct the access point representing the work by combining (in this order):

a) the authorized access point representing the composer of the excerpt (see **9.19.1** for persons, **10.11.1** for families, or **11.13.1** for corporate bodies, as applicable)

b) the preferred title for the excerpt (see **6.14.2**).

Handel, George Frideric, 1685–1759. Ma come amar?

Authorized access point for: Ma come amar? : duetto nel Muzio Scaevola del sigr Handel. *The other composers of the pasticcio are Amadei and Bononcini*

If the composer of the excerpt is unknown, use the preferred title for the excerpt as the authorized access point representing the work.

O what pain it is to part!

A song from The beggar's opera; *composer unknown*

6.28.1.4 Musical Works Composed for Choreographic Movement

For a musical work composed for choreographic movement, such as a ballet or pantomime, construct the authorized access point representing the work by combining (in this order):

a) the authorized access point representing the composer of the music (see **9.19.1** for persons, **10.11.1** for families, or **11.13.1** for corporate bodies, as applicable)

b) the preferred title for the work (see **6.14.2**).

Copland, Aaron, 1900–1990. Hear ye! Hear ye!

Authorized access point for: Hear ye! Hear ye! : ballet in one act / music by Aaron Copland ; scenario by Ruth Page and Nicolas Remisoff ; settings and costumes by Nicolas Remisoff ; "choreography" by Ruth Page

Delibes, Léo, 1836–1891. Coppélia

Authorized access point for: Coppélia, ou, La fille aux yeux d'émail : ballet en 2 actes et 3 tableaux / de Ch. Nuitter et Saint-Léon ; musique de Léo Delibes

Hahn, Reynaldo, 1875–1947. Fête chez Thérèse

Authorized access point for: La fête chez Thérèse : ballet-pantomime / scénario de Catulle Mendès ; musique de Reynaldo Hahn

6.28.1.5 Adaptations of Musical Works

6.28.1.5.1 Categories of Adaptations of Musical Works

Apply the instructions at **6.28.1.5.2** for an adaptation that falls into one or more of the following categories:

a) arrangements described as freely transcribed, based on, etc., and other arrangements incorporating new material

b) paraphrases of various works or of the general style of another composer

c) arrangements in which the harmony or musical style of the original has been changed

d) performances of musical works involving substantial creative responsibility for adaptation, improvisation, etc., on the part of the performer or performers

e) any other distinct alteration of another musical work.

6.28.1.5.2 Construction of Authorized Access Points for Adaptations of Musical Works

Construct the authorized access point representing the adaptation by combining (in this order):

a) the authorized access point representing the adapter of the music (see **9.19.1** for persons, **10.11.1** for families, or **11.13.1** for corporate bodies, as applicable)

b) the preferred title for the adaptation (see **6.14.2**).

Tausig, Carl, 1841–1871. Nouvelles soirées de Vienne
Authorized access point for: Nouvelles soirées de Vienne : valses-caprices d'après J. Strauss / Ch. Tausig

Rachmaninoff, Sergei, 1873–1943. Rapsodie sur un thème de Paganini
Authorized access point for: Rapsodie sur un thème de Paganini : pour piano et orchestre, op. 43 / S. Rachmaninoff

Wuorinen, Charles. Magic art
Authorized access point for: The magic art : an instrumental masque drawn from works of Henry Purcell, 1977–1978 : in two acts / Charles Wuorinen

Marshall, Wayne. Organ improvisations
Authorized access point for: Organ improvisations / Wayne Marshall. *Improvisations performed by Marshall on songs by George Gershwin, Billy Strayhorn, Jule Styne, Vincent Youmans, and Leonard Bernstein*

Hogan, Moses. Didn't my Lord deliver Daniel?
Authorized access point for: Didn't my Lord deliver Daniel? / traditional spiritual arranged for SATB div. a cappella by Moses Hogan. *Incorporates new material resulting in a new work*

If two or more composers have collaborated in the adaptation, apply the instructions at **6.27.1.3**.

If the composer of the adaptation is unknown or uncertain, apply the instructions at **6.27.1.8**.

In case of doubt about whether a work is an arrangement, etc., or an adaptation, treat it as an arrangement, etc. (see **6.28.3.2**).

6.28.1.6 Operas and Other Dramatic Works with New Text and Title

If:
the text, plot, setting, or other verbal element of a musical work is adapted or if a new text is supplied
and
the title has changed
then:
construct the authorized access point representing the work by combining (in this order):

a) the authorized access point representing the original work

b) the title of the adaptation, enclosed in parentheses.

Strauss, Johann, 1825–1899. Fledermaus
Authorized access point representing the original work

Strauss, Johann, 1825–1899. Fledermaus (Champagne sec)

Strauss, Johann, 1825–1899. Fledermaus (Gay Rosalinda)

Strauss, Johann, 1825–1899. Fledermaus (Rosalinda)

Mozart, Wolfgang Amadeus, 1756–1791. Così fan tutte
Authorized access point representing the original work

Mozart, Wolfgang Amadeus, 1756–1791. Così fan tutte (Dame Kobold)
Authorized access point for: Die Dame Kobold (Così fan tutte) / bearbeitet von Carl Scheidemantel. *Scheidemantel substituted an entirely new libretto based on the play by Calderón de la Barca*

6.28.1.7 Cadenzas

For a cadenza, construct the authorized access point representing the work by combining (in this order):

a) the authorized access point representing the composer of the cadenza (see **9.19.1** for persons, **10.11.1** for families, or **11.13.1** for corporate bodies, as applicable)

b) the preferred title for the cadenza (see **6.14.2**).

Previn, André, 1929– . Cadenza to Mozart's Piano concerto in C minor, KV. 491, 1st movement
Authorized access point for: Cadenza to Mozart's Piano concerto in C minor, KV. 491, 1st movement / André Previn

Barrère, Georges, 1876–1944. Cadenzas for the Flute concerto in G major (K. 313) by Mozart
Authorized access point for: Cadenzas for the Flute concerto in G major (K. 313) by Mozart / Georges Barrère

Schumann, Clara, 1819–1896. Cadenzen zu Beethoven's Clavier-Concerten
Authorized access point for: Cadenzen zu Beethoven's Clavier-Concerten / componirt von Clara Schumann

If the cadenza does not have its own title, devise a title by applying the instructions at **2.3.2.11**.

6.28.1.8 Music and Incidental Music for Dramatic Works, Etc.

For music or incidental music composed for a dramatic work, film, etc., construct the authorized access point representing the work by combining (in this order):

a) the authorized access point representing the composer of the music (see **9.19.1** for persons, **10.11.1** for families, or **11.13.1** for corporate bodies, as applicable)

b) the preferred title for the work (see **6.14.2**).

Beethoven, Ludwig van, 1770–1827. Egmont
Authorized access point for: Musik zu Goethes Trauerspiel Egmont : op. 84 / Ludwig van Beethoven. *A musical score*

Finzi, Gerald, 1901–1956. Love's labours lost
Authorized access point for: Love's labours lost : complete incidental music / Gerald Finzi ; edited by Jeremy Dale Roberts. *A musical score for incidental music for Shakespeare's play*

Steiner, Max, 1888–1971. King Kong
Authorized access point for: King Kong : the complete 1933 film score / Steiner. *An audio recording*

North, Alex. Good morning, Vietnam
Authorized access point for: Good morning, Vietnam / music, Alex North. *A musical score*

ADDITIONS TO ACCESS POINTS REPRESENTING MUSICAL WORKS

6.28.1.9 Additions to Access Points Representing Musical Works with Titles That Are Not Distinctive

Make additions to access points if the preferred title for the work (see **6.14.2**) consists solely of the name of a type, or of two or more types, of composition. Add the following elements (in this order), as applicable:

a) medium of performance (see **6.28.1.9.1**)

b) numeric designation (see **6.28.1.9.2**)

c) key (see **6.28.1.9.3**).

Enesco, Georges, 1881–1955. Sonatas, violin, piano, no. 2, op. 6, F minor

If medium of performance, numeric designation, and key are not sufficient or are not available to distinguish the access point from one that is the same or similar but represents a different work or represents a person, family, corporate body, or place, apply the instructions at **6.28.1.9.4**.

6.28.1.9.1 Medium of Performance

Add the medium of performance (see **6.15**) as applicable, in this order:

a) voices

b) keyboard instrument if there is more than one non-keyboard instrument

c) the other instruments in score order

d) continuo.

For a work for solo instrument or instruments and accompanying ensemble, add the terms for the solo instrument or instruments followed by the term for the accompanying ensemble.

Exceptions

a) Do not add the medium of performance if one or more of the following conditions apply:

i. the medium is implied by the title

Peeters, Flor, 1903–1986. Chorale preludes, op. 69
Implied medium: organ

Poulenc, Francis, 1899–1963. Mass, G major
Implied medium: voices, with or without accompaniment

Martinů, Bohuslav, 1890–1959. Overture
Implied medium: orchestra

Mitchell, Joni. Songs
Implied medium: solo voice or voices with accompaniment for keyboard stringed instrument or, if in a "popular" idiom, solo voice or voices with instrumental and/or vocal accompaniment

Strauss, Richard, 1864–1949. Lieder, op. 10
Implied medium: solo voice or voices with accompaniment for keyboard stringed instrument or, if in a "popular" idiom, solo voice or voices with instrumental and/or vocal accompaniment

Kodály, Zoltán, 1882–1967. Symphony
Implied medium: orchestra

If, however, the medium of performance is not the one implied by the title, add the medium.

Widor, Charles Marie, 1844–1937. Symphonies, organ

Rapf, Kurt. Requiem, organ, horns (4), trumpets (4), trombones (3), tuba, percussion

Raff, Joachim, 1822–1882. Sinfonietta, flutes (2), oboes (2), clarinets (2), bassoons (2), horns (2), op. 188, F major

Goehr, Alexander, 1932–. Songs, clarinet, viola accompaniment

ii. the work consists of a set of compositions for different media, or is one of a series of works with the same title but for different media

Fontana, Giovanni Battista, died 1630. Sonatas (1641)
Six sonatas for 1 violin, three for 2 violins, three for violin and bassoon, five for 2 violins and bassoon, and one for 3 violins, all with continuo

Leonarda, Isabella, 1620–1704. Sonatas, op. 16
Eleven sonatas for 2 violins and continuo and one for violin and continuo

Monteverdi, Claudio, 1567–1643. Madrigals, book 1
For 5 voices

Monteverdi, Claudio, 1567–1643. Madrigals, book 7
For 1–6 voices and instruments

Persichetti, Vincent, 1915–1987. Serenades, no. 14
For solo oboe

Persichetti, Vincent, 1915–1987. Serenades, no. 15
For harpsichord

iii. the medium was not indicated by the composer

iv. the medium of performance cannot be recorded succinctly and other elements are more useful for identifying the work (e.g., thematic index number or opus number, see **6.16**).

Mozart, Wolfgang Amadeus, 1756–1791. Divertimenti, K. 251, D major

b) If there is more than one part for a particular instrument or voice, do not add the number of parts if the number is implicit in the preferred title.

Boccherini, Luigi, 1743–1805. Duets, violins, G. 58, A major

Atterberg, Kurt, 1887–1974. Quartets, violins, viola, cello, no. 2, op. 11

Rosetti, Antonio, approximately 1750–1792. Quartets, clarinets, horns, M. B17, E♭ major

but

White, Ian, 1955–. Quintets, euphoniums (3), tubas (2)

Aladov, N. (Nikolaĭ), 1890–1972. Scherzo, flutes (2), clarinets (2)

Lawes, William, 1602–1645. Suites, viols (4), no. 1, C minor

c) Do not add the number of players for percussion.

Glanville-Hicks, Peggy. Sonatas, piano, percussion
For piano and 4 percussionists

d) Omit the designation of the key in which an instrument is pitched or terms indicating a range (e.g., *alto*, *tenor*, *bass*).

Goehr, Alexander, 1932–. Fantasias, clarinet, piano, op. 3
For clarinet in A and piano

Debussy, Claude, 1862–1918. Rhapsodies, saxophone, orchestra
For alto saxophone and orchestra

e) Omit alternative or doubling instruments.

Hoffmeister, Franz Anton, 1754–1812. Sonatas, flute, piano, op. 12
For flute (or violin) and piano

Holliger, Heinz. Trio, oboe, viola, harp
For oboe (doubling on English horn), viola, and harp

f) For an accompanying ensemble with one performer to a part, record the appropriate term for the ensemble (see **6.15.1.6**) rather than the individual instruments.

Baker, David, 1931–. Sonatas, violin, string ensemble
For jazz violin and string quartet

g) Omit solo voices if the medium includes a chorus.

Hailstork, Adolphus C. Spirituals, mixed voices, orchestra
For 2 solo sopranos, S.A.T.B. chorus, and orchestra

h) *If:*

the work is not in a "popular" idiom

and

the preferred title for the work consists solely of the name of a type, or of two or more types, of composition for solo voice (e.g., *Lieder*, *Mélodie*, *Songs*)

and

the voice is accompanied by anything other than a keyboard stringed instrument alone

then:

add the medium of performance using the name of the accompanying instrument(s) or ensemble, followed by the word *accompaniment*.

If such a work is not accompanied, use *unaccompanied*.

Sor, Fernando, 1778–1839. Songs, guitar accompaniment
For voice and guitar

Hamel, Micha. Lieder, percussion accompaniment
For voice and percussion

Bennett, Sharon. Vocalises, unaccompanied
For unaccompanied voice

Goehr, Alexander, 1932–. Songs, clarinet, viola accompaniment
For voice, clarinet, and viola

Alternative

Apply the individual exceptions according to the policy of the agency creating the data.

6.28.1.9.2 Numeric Designation

Add a numeric designation (see **6.16**).

6.28.1.9.3 Key

Add the key (see **6.17**).

6.28.1.9.4 Additions for Access Points When Medium of Perfomance, Etc. Insufficient, or Not Available

If:

the titles are not distinctive

and

the medium of performance, numeric designation, and key are not sufficient, or are not available, to distinguish between them

then:
add one of the following elements (in this order of preference):

a) the year of completion of composition (see **6.4**)

b) the year of original publication (see **6.4**)

c) any other identifying element, such as place of composition (see **6.5**), or the name of the first publisher (see **6.6**).

Delius, Frederick, 1862–1934. Pieces, piano (1890)

Delius, Frederick, 1862–1934. Pieces, piano (1923)

Krebs, Johann Ludwig, 1713–1780. Trios, flutes, continuo (Nuremberg, Germany)

Geminiani, Francesco, 1687–1762. Solos, flute, continuo (Bland)

Philidor, Pierre Danican, 1681–1731. Suites, op. 1 (Foucault)

Agnesi, Maria Teresa, 1720–1795. Sonatas, harpsichord, G major (Badische Landesbibliothek Karlsruhe)

Agnesi, Maria Teresa, 1720–1795. Sonatas, harpsichord, G major (Biblioteca estense)

Gervasio, Giovanni Battista, approximately 1725–approximately 1785. Sonatas, mandolin, continuo, D major (Bibliothèque nationale de France L 2768)

Gervasio, Giovanni Battista, approximately 1725–approximately 1785. Sonatas, mandolin, continuo, D major (Bibliothèque nationale de France Ms. 2082)

6.28.1.10 Additions to Access Points Representing Musical Works with Distinctive Titles

Make additions to access points if needed to distinguish the access point from one that is the same or similar but represents a different work or represents a person, family, corporate body, or place. Add one of the following elements, as appropriate:

a) the medium of performance (see **6.28.1.9.1**)
or
b) another distinguishing characteristic of the work (see **6.6**).

Use the same type of addition for each of the access points for different musical works with identical titles.

Debussy, Claude, 1862–1918. Images, orchestra

Debussy, Claude, 1862–1918. Images, piano
not Debussy, Claude, 1862–1918. Images (Piano work)

Granados, Enrique, 1867–1916. Goyescas (Opera)

Granados, Enrique, 1867–1916. Goyescas (Piano work)
not Granados, Enrique, 1867–1916. Goyescas, piano

6.28.1.10.1 Additions to Resolve Conflict

If the additions at **6.28.1.10** do not resolve the conflict, add one or more of the following:

a) a numeric designation (see **6.28.1.9.2**)

b) key (see **6.28.1.9.3**)

c) the year of completion of composition (see **6.4**)

d) the year of original publication (see **6.4**)
and/or

e) any other identifying element, such as place of composition (see **6.5**), or the name of the first publisher (see **6.6**).

Bach, Johann Sebastian, 1685–1750. Was Gott tut, das ist wohlgetan (Chorale prelude)

Bach, Johann Sebastian, 1685–1750. Was Gott tut, das ist wohlgetan (Cantata), BWV 98

Bach, Johann Sebastian, 1685–1750. Was Gott tut, das ist wohlgetan (Cantata), BWV 99

6.28.1.11 Additions to Access Points Representing Compilations of Musical Works

For a compilation containing works of one type, add the medium of performance to the access point, unless the medium is the same as the one implied by the title or unless the works are for various media. Record the conventional title *Selections* following the medium, as applicable.

Chopin, Frédéric, 1810–1849. Polonaises, piano

Haydn, Joseph, 1732–1809. Quartets, strings

Grieg, Edvard, 1843–1907. Sonatas, violin, piano

Scriabin, Aleksandr Nikolayevich, 1872–1915. Sonatas, piano. Selections

but

Beethoven, Ludwig van, 1770–1827. Symphonies. Selections
Implied medium: orchestra

Leclerc, Félix. Songs
Implied medium: solo voice or voices with instrumental and/or vocal accompaniment

Poulenc, Francis, 1899–1963. Concertos. Selections
For various media

6.28.2 Authorized Access Point Representing a Part or Parts of a Musical Work

6.28.2.1 General Guidelines

Construct the authorized access point representing a part or parts of a musical work by applying the instructions at **6.28.2.2–6.28.2.4**, as applicable.

6.28.2.2 One Part

Construct the authorized access point representing a part of a musical work by combining (in this order):

a) the authorized access point representing the work as a whole (see **6.28.1**)

b) the preferred title for the part (see **6.14.2.7.1**).

Brahms, Johannes, 1833–1897. Ungarische Tänze. Nr. 5

Verdi, Giuseppe, 1813–1901. Aïda. Celeste Aïda

Larson, Jonathan. Rent. Seasons of love

Beethoven, Ludwig van, 1770–1827. Symphonies, no. 1, op. 21, C major. Andante cantabile con moto

Mozart, Wolfgang Amadeus, 1756–1791. Così fan tutte. Come scoglio

Vivaldi, Antonio, 1678–1741. Estro armonico. N. 8

Schumann, Robert, 1810–1856. Album für die Jugend. Nr. 30

Schumann, Robert, 1810–1856. Album für die Jugend. Nr. 2, Soldatenmarsch

Praetorius, Hieronymus, 1560–1629. Opus musicum. Cantiones sacrae. O vos omnes

Handel, George Frideric, 1685–1759. Messiah. Pifa

Verdi, Giuseppe, 1813–1901. Traviata. Atto 3o. Preludio

6.28.2.3 Two or More Parts

When identifying two or more parts of a musical work, construct authorized access points for each of the parts. Apply the instructions at **6.28.2.2**.

Brahms, Johannes, 1833–1897. Ungarische Tänze. Nr. 5

Brahms, Johannes, 1833–1897. Ungarische Tänze. Nr. 6

Rossini, Gioacchino, 1792–1868. Il barbiere di Siviglia. Largo al factotum

Rossini, Gioacchino, 1792–1868. Il barbiere di Siviglia. Una voce poco fa

Schubert, Franz, 1797–1828. Impromptus, piano, D. 899. No. 2

Schubert, Franz, 1797–1828. Impromptus, piano, D. 899. No. 4

Exception

If the parts form a group called *suite* by the composer, construct the authorized access point representing the suite by combining (in this order):

a) the authorized access point representing the work as a whole (see **6.28.1**)

b) the term *Suite* (see **6.14.2.7.2**).

Sibelius, Jean, 1865-1957. Karelia. Suite

Alternative

When identifying two or more parts of a musical work, identify the parts collectively. Construct the authorized access point representing the parts by combining (in this order):

a) the authorized access point representing the work as a whole (see **6.28.1**)

b) the conventional collective title *Selections* (see **6.14.2.7.2 alternative**).

Brahms, Johannes, 1833–1897. Ungarische Tänze. Selections
Resource described: Ungarische Tänze : Nr. 5/6, für Klavier zu vier Händen / Johannes Brahms. *A score*

Wagner, Richard, 1813–1883. Die Meistersinger von Nürnberg. Selections
Resource described: Die Meistersinger von Nürnberg : Auszüge / Richard Wagner. *An audio recording of excerpts from Wagner's opera*

Rodgers, Richard, 1902–1979. The king and I. Selections

Resource described: Rodgers & Hammerstein's The king and I : selected highlights / music by Richard Rodgers ; book and lyrics by Oscar Hammerstein II. *An audio recording*

Paganini, Nicolò, 1782–1840. Caprices, violin, M.S. 25. Selections

Resource described: Trois caprices pour violon seul / N. Paganini. *A score of the ninth, thirteenth, and seventeenth caprices; the complete work consists of twenty-four parts*

Apply this instruction instead of or in addition to constructing authorized access points for each of the parts. Do not apply to parts that form a group called *suite* by the composer.

6.28.2.4 Two or More Unnumbered Parts Designated by the Same General Term

If:

a part of a musical work is designated by the same general term as other parts

and

the part is unnumbered

then:

add to the access point representing the part one or more of the identifying elements covered in the instructions at **6.28.1.9–6.28.1.11**. Add as many as are necessary to distinguish the part.

Cima, Giovanni Paolo, flourished 1598–1622. Concerti ecclesiastici. Sonata, violin, cornett, violone, trombone, continuo

Cima, Giovanni Paolo, flourished 1598–1622. Concerti ecclesiastici. Sonata, cornett, violin, continuo

If such additions are not appropriate, determine the number of the part in the set and add it.

Milán, Luis, 16th century. Maestro. Pavana (No. 23)

Milán, Luis, 16th century. Maestro. Pavana (No. 24)

Milán, Luis, 16th century. Maestro. Fantasia del primero tono (No. 1)

Milán, Luis, 16th century. Maestro. Fantasia del primero tono (No. 4)

6.28.3 Authorized Access Point Representing a Musical Expression

6.28.3.1 General Guidelines on Constructing Authorized Access Points Representing Musical Expressions

Apply the instructions at **6.28.3.2–6.28.3.6** when constructing the authorized access point representing one of the following types of musical expression:

a) arrangements, transcriptions, etc. (see **6.28.3.2**)

b) added accompaniments, etc. (see **6.28.3.3**)

c) sketches (see **6.28.3.4**)

d) vocal and chorus scores (see **6.28.3.5**)

e) translations (see **6.28.3.6**).

For other types of musical expressions, construct the authorized access point by applying the instructions at **6.27.3**.

6.28.3.2 Arrangements, Transcriptions, Etc.

The instructions at **6.28.3.2.1–6.28.3.2.2** apply to an arrangement, transcription, etc., of one or more works of one composer (or of parts of one composer's works) if the arrangement, transcription, etc., falls into one or more of the following categories:

a) arrangements, transcriptions, versions, settings, etc., in which music for one medium of performance has been rewritten for another

b) simplified versions of previously existing musical works.

6.28.3.2.1 Arrangements of "Classical," Etc. Music

For an arrangement, etc., of a work or part or parts of a work that belong, broadly speaking, to the category of "serious," "classical," or "art" music, construct the authorized access point by combining (in this order).

a) the authorized access point representing the original work (see **6.28.1**) or part or parts of the work (see **6.28.2**), as applicable

b) the term *arranged.*

Apply this instruction also to a transcription by the original composer.

Berlioz, Hector, 1803–1869. Corsaire; arranged

Resource described: The corsaire : overture for concert band / transcribed by Gunther Schuller. *Transcription of a Berlioz overture composed originally for orchestra*

Respighi, Ottorino, 1879–1936. Uccelli; arranged

Resource described: The birds / Respighi. *Arranged for Japanese instruments by H. Okano*

Schubert, Franz, 1797–1828. Octet, clarinet, horn, bassoon, violins, viola, violoncello, double bass, D. 803, F major; arranged

Resource described: Grosses Octet für zwei Violinen, Viola, Violoncello, Contrabass, Horn, Fagott und Clarinette, op. 166 / componirt von Franz Schubert ; Arrangement für das Pianoforte zu vier Händen bearbeitet von S. Leithner. *Arranged for piano, four hands*

Ravel, Maurice, 1875–1937. Pavane pour une infante défunte; arranged

Resource described: Pavane pour une infante défunte : pour petit orchestre / Maurice Ravel. *Originally for piano; transcription by the composer*

Satie, Erik, 1866–1925. Piano music. Selections; arranged

Resource described: Pièces pour guitare / Erik Satie. *Selected piano works by Satie transcribed for guitar*

6.28.3.2.2 Arrangements of "Popular" Music

For an arrangement, etc., of a work or part or parts of a work that belong, broadly speaking, to the category of music in the "popular" idiom (e.g., rock, jazz), use the authorized access point representing the original work (see **6.28.1**) or part or parts of the work (see **6.28.2**), as applicable. Add *arranged* only if the resource being described is:

either

a) an instrumental work arranged for vocal or choral performance

or

b) a vocal work arranged for instrumental performance.

MacDermot, Galt. Hair; arranged

Resource described: Hair '72 : the American tribal love-rock musical / [lyrics] by James Rado, Gerome Ragni ; [music by] Galt MacDermot ; concert band arranged by Len Goldstyne. *Vocal music arranged for band*

Townshend, Pete. Songs. Selections; arranged

Resource described: Who's serious : symphonic music of the Who. *Selected rock songs by Townshend arranged for orchestra*

Brubeck, Dave. Blue rondo à la Turk; arranged

Resource described: Blue rondo à la Turk : SSAATTBB a cappella / music, Dave Brubeck ; arr. Ward Swingle. *Originally written for jazz quartet; arranged for unaccompanied mixed chorus*

John, Elton. Candle in the wind; arranged

Resource described: Candle in the wind / music by Elton John ; words by Bernie Taupin ; arranged by Michael Sweeney. *Song arranged for jazz ensemble*

but

Carmichael, Hoagy, 1899–1981. Songs. Selections

Resource described: Hoagy Carmichael : a choral portrait : for S.A.B. voices and piano with optional guitar, bass, drums, and vibraphone / music by Hoagy Carmichael ; arranged by Robert Sterling. *Selected songs by Carmichael arranged for accompanied choral performance*

Brubeck, Dave. Blue rondo à la Turk

Resource described: Blue rondo à la Turk / Dave Brubeck ; arranged for string quartet by Jeremy Cohen. *Originally written for jazz quartet*

Deep river

Authorized access point for: Deep river / transcription by Hugo Frey. *An arrangement for voice and piano of the spiritual*

6.28.3.3 Added Accompaniments, Etc.

If an instrumental accompaniment or additional parts have been added to a work or part or parts of a work, use the authorized access point representing the original work (see **6.28.1**) or part or parts of the work (see **6.28.2**), as applicable.

Bach, Johann Sebastian, 1685–1750. Sonaten und Partiten, violin, BWV 1001–1006

Authorized access point for: Sechs Sonaten für Violine solo / von Joh. Seb. Bach ; herausgegeben von J. Hellmesberger ; Klavierbegleitung von Robert Schumann. *Solo violin sonatas by Bach with added piano accompaniment by Schumann*

6.28.3.4 Sketches

For a work or part or parts of a work consisting of a composer's sketches, construct the authorized access point by combining (in this order):

a) the authorized access point representing the completed work

b) the term *Sketches*.

Szymanowski, Karol, 1882–1937. Harnasie (Sketches)

Beethoven, Ludwig van, 1770–1827. Quartets, strings, no. 1–6, op. 18 (Sketches)

Gillis, Don, 1912–1978. Quartets, strings, no. 6. Passacaglia (Sketches)

Moore, Douglas, 1893–1969. Works. Selections (Sketches)

6.28.3.5 Vocal and Chorus Scores

For a vocal or chorus score, construct the authorized access point by combining (in this order):

a) the authorized access point representing the work (see **6.28.1**) or part or parts of the work (see **6.28.2**)

b) one of the following terms, as applicable:
Vocal score
Vocal scores
Chorus score
Chorus scores.

Handel, George Frideric, 1685–1759. Messiah. Vocal score

Sullivan, Arthur, 1842–1900. Mikado. Chorus score

Wagner, Richard, 1813–1883. Operas. Vocal scores

6.28.3.6 Translations

If:
the text of a vocal work (or part or parts of a vocal work) is a translation
or
the texts of all the works in a compilation are translations
then:
construct the authorized access point by adding the name of the language to the authorized access point representing the work, part or parts, or compilation, as applicable. Record the name of the language by applying the instructions at **6.11**.

Bizet, Georges, 1838–1875. Carmen. German
Resource described: Carmen : Oper in 4 Akten / Bizet ; deutsche Übersetzung, D. Louis

Schönberg, Claude-Michel. Misérables. Danish
Resource described: Les misérables / musical af Alan Boubil og Claude-Michel Schönberg ; tekst, Herbert Kretzmer ; oversættelse, Niels Brunse. *An audio recording of the musical, sung in Danish; Schönberg is the composer*

If the resource described contains expressions of the work in more than one language, create access points for each of the language expressions.

Handel, George Frideric, 1685–1759. Messiah. Vocal score. German
Handel, George Frideric, 1685–1759. Messiah. Vocal score. English
Resource described: Der Messias : Oratorium = The Messiah : sacred oratorio / von G.F. Händel ; Klavierauszug mit deutschem und englischem Text ; nach W.A. Mozart's Bearbeitung ; neu revidiert von Josef Reiter

Brel, Jacques. Ne me quitte pas. English
Brel, Jacques. Ne me quitte pas. French
Resource described: If you go away = Ne me quitte pas / music and French lyric by Jacques Brel ; English lyric by Rod McKuen

Schumann, Robert, 1810–1856. Songs. French
Schumann, Robert, 1810–1856. Songs. German
Resource described: Collection complète des mélodies pour chant avec accompagnement de piano / de Robert Schumann ; traduction française et texte original

6.28.4 Variant Access Point Representing a Musical Work or Expression

6.28.4.1 General Guidelines on Constructing Variant Access Points Representing Musical Works

Use a variant title for the work (see **6.14.3**) as the basis for a variant access point.

> Om arme
> Ome arme
> Omme arme
> *Authorized access point for the work:* Homme armé
>
> Coming for to carry me home
> *Authorized access point for the work:* Swing low, sweet chariot
>
> God save the Queen
> My country, 'tis of thee
> *Authorized access point for the work:* God save the King

If the authorized access point for a work has been constructed by using the authorized access point representing a person, family, or corporate body followed by the preferred title for the work (see **6.28.1.1–6.28.1.8**), construct a variant access point by combining (in this order):

a) the authorized access point representing that person (see **9.19.1**), family (see **10.11.1**), or corporate body (see **11.13.1**)

b) the variant title for the work.

> Grieg, Edvard, 1843–1907. Mountain maid
> Grieg, Edvard, 1843–1907. Fille de la montagne
> Grieg, Edvard, 1843–1907. Kind der Berge
> *Authorized access point for the work:* Grieg, Edvard, 1843–1907. Haugtussa
>
> Rossini, Gioacchino, 1792–1868. Almaviva
> *Authorized access point for the work:* Rossini, Gioacchino, 1792–1868. Barbiere di Siviglia
>
> Strauss, Johann, 1825–1899. Pink champagne
> *Authorized access point for the work:* Strauss, Johann, 1825–1899. Fledermaus (Pink champagne)

Make additions to the variant access point, if considered important for identification. Apply the instructions at **6.28.1.9–6.28.1.11**, as applicable.

> America (Song)
> *Authorized access point for the work:* God save the King
>
> Rubinstein, Anton, 1829–1894. Etüden, piano, op. 23
> Rubinstein, Anton, 1829–1894. Studies, piano, op. 23
> *Authorized access point for the work:* Rubinstein, Anton, 1829–1894. Études, piano, op. 23
>
> Lœillet, Jacques, 1685–1748. Quintet, recorders, flutes, continuo, B minor
> *Authorized access point for the work:* Lœillet, Jacques, 1685–1748. Sonatas, recorders (2), flutes (2), continuo, B minor
>
> Gluck, Christoph Willibald, Ritter von, 1714–1787. Orpheus und Eurydike (1762)
> *Authorized access point for the work:* Gluck, Christoph Willibald, Ritter von, 1714–1787. Orfeo ed Euridice

Gluck, Christoph Willibald, Ritter von, 1714–1787. Orpheus und Eurydike (1774)
Authorized access point for the work: Gluck, Christoph Willibald, Ritter von, 1714–1787. Orphée et Eurydice

Schubert, Franz, 1797–1828. Forelle (Quintet)
Authorized access point for the work: Schubert, Franz, 1797–1828. Quintets, piano, violin, viola, violoncello, double bass, D. 667, A major. *Variant title for this work is identical to the preferred title for a song by Schubert*

Respighi, Ottorino, 1879–1936. Ancient airs and dances (Orchestral work)
Authorized access point for the work: Respighi, Ottorino, 1879–1936. Antiche arie e danze per liuto, no. 1–3. *Variant title for this work is identical to a variant title for a piano work by Respighi*

Apply these additional instructions, as applicable:

cadenzas (see **6.28.4.2**)
part of a musical work (see **6.28.4.3**)
compilations of musical works (see **6.28.4.4**).

Construct additional variant access points if considered important for access.

Schubert, Franz, 1797–1828. Quintets, piano, violin, viola, violoncello, double bass, op. 114, A major
Authorized access point for the work: Schubert, Franz, 1797–1828. Quintets, piano, violin, viola, violoncello, double bass, D. 667, A major. *Work has two different numeric designations; designation not used in the authorized access point used in a variant access point*

Lœillet, Jacques, 1685–1748. Sonatas, flutes (4), continuo, B minor
Authorized access point for the work: Lœillet, Jacques, 1685–1748. Sonatas, recorders (2), flutes (2), continuo, B minor

Bach, Johann Sebastian, 1685–1750. Bist du bei mir
Authorized access point for the work: Stölzel, Gottfried Heinrich, 1690–1749. Bist du bei mir. *For many years attributed to Bach*

For variant access points for expressions of musical works, apply additional instructions at **6.28.4.5**.

6.28.4.2 Variant Access Point Representing One or More Cadenzas

Construct a variant access point representing one or more cadenzas written to be performed as part of one or more specific musical works by combining (in this order):

a) the authorized access point representing the composer of the musical work or musical works for which the cadenza or cadenzas were written (see **9.19.1** for persons, **10.11.1** for families, or **11.13.1** for corporate bodies, as applicable)

b) the preferred title for the musical work or musical works for which the cadenza or cadenzas were written (see **6.14.2**)

c) the preferred title for the movement of the musical work for which the cadenza or cadenzas were written, when appropriate (see **6.14.2.7**)

d) the term *Cadenza* or *Cadenzas*

e) another distinguishing term, if needed.

Mozart, Wolfgang Amadeus, 1756–1791. Concertos, piano, orchestra, K. 491, C minor. Allegro. Cadenza (Previn)

Authorized access point for the work: Previn, André, 1929– . Cadenza to Mozart's Piano concerto in C minor, KV. 491, 1st movement

Haydn, Joseph, 1732–1809. Concertos, harpsichord, orchestra, H. XVIII, 11, D major. Cadenzas (Badura-Skoda)

Authorized access point for the work: Badura-Skoda, Paul. Kadenzen zum Klavierkonzert in D-dur (Hoboken XVIII: 11) von Joseph Haydn

Mozart, Wolfgang Amadeus, 1756–1791. Sonatas, piano, K. 333, B♭ major. Allegretto grazioso. Cadenzas (Landowska)

Authorized access point for the work: Landowska, Wanda. Cadenzas for the Piano sonata in B-flat major, K. 333, third movement, by W.A. Mozart

Beethoven, Ludwig van, 1770–1827. Concertos, piano, orchestra, no. 3–4. Cadenzas (Schumann)

Authorized access point for the work: Schumann, Clara, 1819–1896. Cadenzen zu Beethoven's Clavier-Concerten

6.28.4.3 Variant Access Point Representing a Part of a Musical Work

If:

the title of the part of a musical work is distinctive

and

the authorized access point representing the part has been constructed by using the authorized access point representing a person, family, or corporate body followed by the preferred title for the work as a whole, followed in turn by the preferred title for the part

then:

construct a variant access point representing the part by combining (in this order):

a) the authorized access point representing that person, family, or corporate body

b) the preferred title for the part.

Verdi, Giuseppe, 1813–1901. Celeste Aïda

Authorized access point for the part of the work: Verdi, Giuseppe, 1813–1901. Aïda. Celeste Aïda

Larson, Jonathan. Seasons of love

Authorized access point for the part of the work: Larson, Jonathan. Rent. Seasons of love

Schumann, Robert, 1810–1856. Soldatenmarsch

Authorized access point for the part of the work: Schumann, Robert, 1810–1856. Album für die Jugend. Nr. 2, Soldatenmarsch

Beach, H. H. A., Mrs., 1867–1944. Graduale

Authorized access point for the part of the work: Beach, H. H. A., Mrs., 1867–1944. Mass, op. 5, E♭ major. Graduale

If:

the title of the part of a work is distinctive

and

the authorized access point representing the part has been constructed by using the preferred title for the work as a whole, followed by the preferred title for the part

then:

construct a variant access point by using the preferred title for the part on its own.

Ecce Rex Darius
Authorized access point for the part of the work: Danielis ludus. Ecce Rex Darius

Make additions to the variant access point, if considered important for identification. Apply the instructions at **6.28.1.9–6.28.1.11**, as applicable.

Sanctus (Messe de Tournai)
Authorized access point for the part of the work: Messe de Tournai. Sanctus. *Addition to access point made to distinguish it from access points representing other works and parts of works with the same preferred title*

Bacon, Ernst, 1898–1990. Last invocation (Song)
Authorized access point for the part of the work: Bacon, Ernst, 1898–1990. Songs at parting. Last invocation. *Title of the part is identical to the preferred title for a requiem by Bacon*

Rodgers, Richard, 1902–1979. I married an angel (Song)
Authorized access point for the part of the work: Rodgers, Richard, 1902–1979. I married an angel. I married an angel. *A song from a musical with the same title; addition to access point made to distinguish it from the authorized access point representing the whole work*

Barber, Samuel, 1910–1981. Adagios, string quartet
Authorized access point for the part of the work: Barber, Samuel, 1910–1981. Quartets, strings, no. 1, op. 11, B minor. Adagio

Busoni, Ferruccio, 1866–1924. Dances, piano, op. 9, no. 5, D major
Authorized access point for the part of the work: Busoni, Ferruccio, 1866–1924. Festa di villaggio. Danza

Construct additional variant access points if considered important for access.

Bellini, Vincenzo, 1801–1835. Puritani. Ouverture
Bellini, Vincenzo, 1801–1835. Puritani. Overture
Bellini, Vincenzo, 1801–1835. Puritani. Preludio
Bellini, Vincenzo, 1801–1835. Puritani. Sinfonia
Authorized access point for the part of the work: Bellini, Vincenzo, 1801–1835. Puritani. Atto 1. Introduzione

Arensky, Anton Stepanovich, 1861–1906. Trios, piano, strings, no. 1, op. 32, D minor. Allegro non troppo
Authorized access point for the part of the work: Arensky, Anton Stepanovich, 1861–1906. Trios, piano, strings, no. 1, op. 32, D minor. Finale

Wagner, Richard, 1813–1883. Adagio, clarinet, string orchestra, D♭ major
Authorized access point for the part of the work: Baermann, Heinrich, 1784–1847. Quintets, clarinet, violins, viola, violoncello, op. 23, E♭ major. Adagio. *Formerly attributed to Richard Wagner as a separate work*

6.28.4.4 Variant Access Point Representing a Compilation of Musical Works

If:

the authorized access point representing a compilation of musical works by one person, family, or corporate body has been constructed using the authorized access point representing that person, family, or corporate body followed by a conventional collective title (see **6.14.2.8**)

and

the title proper (excluding any alternative title) of the resource being described or the title found in a reference source is not the same as, nor very similar to, the collective title

then:

construct a variant access point representing the compilation combining (in this order):

a) the authorized access point representing the person (see **9.19.1**), family (see **10.11.1**), or corporate body (see **11.13.1**)

b) the title proper of the resource being described or the title found in a reference source.

Vierne, Louis, 1870–1937. Complete organ works
Vierne, Louis, 1870–1937. Œuvres complètes pour orgue
Vierne, Louis, 1870–1937. Sämtliche Orgelwerke
Authorized access point for the compilation: Vierne, Louis, 1870–1937. Organ music

Takemitsu, Tōru. Complete Takemitsu edition
Takemitsu, Tōru. Takemitsu Tōru zenshū
Takemitsu, Tōru. 武満徹全集
Authorized access point for the compilation: Takemitsu, Tōru. Works

Bach, Johann Sebastian, 1685–1750. Best of Bach
Authorized access point for the compilation: Bach, Johann Sebastian, 1685–1750. Works. Selections

Bartók, Béla, 1881–1945. Selected works for piano
Authorized access point for the compilation: Bartók, Béla, 1881–1945. Piano music. Selections

Make additions to the variant access point, if considered important for identification. Apply the instructions at **6.28.1.9–6.28.1.11**, as applicable.

Beethoven, Ludwig van, 1770–1827. Ludwig van Beethoven's Werke (1862)
Authorized access point for the compilation: Beethoven, Ludwig van, 1770–1827. Works (1862)

Beethoven, Ludwig van, 1770–1827. Ludwig van Beethoven's Werke (1949)
Authorized access point for the compilation: Beethoven, Ludwig van, 1770–1827. Works (1949)

Glazunov, Aleksandr Konstantinovich, 1865–1936. Orchestral works (Naxos)
Authorized access point for the compilation: Glazunov, Aleksandr Konstantinovich, 1865–1936. Orchestra music (Naxos)

Hindemith, Paul, 1895–1963. Pieces, double bass
Hindemith, Paul, 1895–1963. Stücke, double bass
Authorized access point for the compilation: Hindemith, Paul, 1895–1963. Double bass music

Construct additional variant access points if considered important for access.

Cimarosa, Domenico, 1749–1801. Sonatas, harpsichord
Cimarosa, Domenico, 1749–1801. Sonatas, piano
Authorized access point for the compilation: Cimarosa, Domenico, 1749–1801. Sonatas, keyboard instrument

6.28.4.5 Variant Access Point Representing a Musical Expression

If a variant title for a musical work is associated with a particular expression of the work, use that variant title to construct the variant access point representing that expression.

Fanfare and National anthem
Authorized access point for the expression: God save the King; arranged

If:

a variant title for a musical work is associated with a particular expression of the work

and

the authorized access point representing the expression has been constructed by using the authorized access point representing a person, family or corporate body followed by the preferred title for the work and one or more additions identifying the expression

then:

construct a variant access point representing the expression by combining (in this order):

a) the authorized access point representing the person, family or corporate body

b) the variant title associated with that expression.

> Poulenc, Francis, 1899–1963. Carmelites
> *Authorized access point for the expression:* Poulenc, Francis, 1899–1963. Dialogues des Carmélites. English
>
> Tower, Joan, 1938– . Celebration fanfare
> *Authorized access point for the expression:* Tower, Joan, 1938– . Stepping stones. Love and celebration; arranged
>
> Nyman, Michael. Film music for solo piano
> *Authorized access point for the expression:* Nyman, Michael. Motion picture music. Selections; arranged
>
> Strauss, Richard, 1864–1949. Skizzen zu Intermezzo
> *Authorized access point for the expression:* Strauss, Richard, 1864–1949. Intermezzo (Sketches)

Make additions to the variant access point, if considered important for identification. Apply the instructions at **6.28.1.9–6.28.1.11**, as applicable.

> Shostakovich, Dmitriĭ Dmitrievich, 1906–1975. Chamber symphony, op. 83a
> Shostakovich, Dmitriĭ Dmitrievich, 1906–1975. Kammersinfonie, op. 83a
> *Authorized access point for the expression:* Shostakovich, Dmitriĭ Dmitrievich, 1906–1975. Quartets, strings, no. 4, op. 83, D major; arranged
>
> Henselt, Adolf von, 1814–1889. Berceuse, flute, piano, G♭ major
> *Authorized access point for the expression:* Henselt, Adolf von, 1814–1889. Wiegenlied; arranged
>
> Barber, Samuel, 1910–1981. Adagios, string orchestra
> Barber, Samuel, 1910–1981. Adagios, orchestra
> *Authorized access point for the expression:* Barber, Samuel, 1910–1981. Quartets, strings, no. 1, op. 11, B minor. Adagio; arranged
>
> Copland, Aaron, 1900–1990. House on the hill (Sketches)
> *Authorized access point for the expression:* Copland, Aaron, 1900–1990. Choruses (1925). House on the hill (Sketches)
>
> Sullivan, Arthur, 1842–1900. I have a song to sing, O! (Collection)
> *Authorized access point for the expression:* Sullivan, Arthur, 1842–1900. Operas. Selections. Vocal scores.
> *Variant title for the expression is identical to the title of a song from Sullivan's opera* The Yeomen of the Guard

Construct additional variant access points if considered important for access.

6.29 Constructing Access Points to Represent Legal Works and Expressions

6.29.1 Authorized Access Point Representing a Legal Work

6.29.1.1 General Guidelines on Constructing Authorized Access Points Representing Legal Works

6.29.1.1.1 Laws, Etc.

Apply the instructions at **6.29.1.2–6.29.1.28** when constructing the authorized access point representing one of the following types of legal works:

a) laws, etc. (see **6.29.1.2–6.29.1.6**)

b) administrative regulations, etc., that are not laws (see **6.29.1.7–6.29.1.9**)

c) court rules (see **6.29.1.10–6.29.1.12**)

d) constitutions, charters, etc., of intergovernmental and non-jurisdictional bodies (see **6.29.1.13–6.29.1.14**)

e) treaties (see **6.29.1.15–6.29.1.17**)

f) law reports, citations, digests, etc. (see **6.29.1.18–6.29.1.20**)

g) court proceedings, etc. (see **6.29.1.21–6.29.1.28**).

6.29.1.1.2 Categories Excluded from Laws, Etc.

Apply the instructions at **6.29.1.2–6.29.1.6** to:

a) legislative enactments and decrees of political jurisdictions (including fundamental laws such as constitutions, charters, etc.)

b) decrees of a chief executive having the force of law (all hereinafter referred to as laws).

For administrative regulations that are not laws, see **6.29.1.7–6.29.1.9**.

For court rules, see **6.29.1.10–6.29.1.12**.

For treaties, see **6.29.1.15–6.29.1.17**.

6.29.1.1.3 Annotated Editions of Laws and Commentaries

For annotated editions of laws and commentaries, see **6.27.1.6**.

6.29.1.1.4 Other Types of Legal Works

For other types of legal works, apply the general guidelines and instructions at **6.27.1**.

6.29.1.1.5 Additions to the Authorized Access Point

Make additions to the authorized access point by applying the instructions at **6.29.1.29–6.29.1.31**, as applicable.

LAWS, ETC.

6.29.1.2 Laws Governing One Jurisdiction

For laws governing one jurisdiction, construct the authorized access point representing the work by combining (in this order):

a) the authorized access point representing the jurisdiction governed by the laws (see **11.13.1**)

b) the preferred title for the law or laws (see **6.19.2**).

Canada. Canada Corporations Act
Authorized access point for: Canada Corporations Act : chap. 53, R.S.C. 1952, as amended

Catawba Indian Nation. Constitution and By-laws of the Catawba Indian Tribe of South Carolina
Authorized access point for: Constitution and By-laws of the Catawba Indian Tribe of South Carolina

Austria. Arbeitszeitgesetz
Authorized access point for: Arbeitszeitgesetz (AZG) : Bundesgesetz vom 11. Dezember 1969

Richmond (Va.). Building code of the city of Richmond, Virginia
Authorized access point for: Building code of the city of Richmond, Virginia

California. Labor Code
Authorized access point for: California Labor Code. *Citation title:* Labor Code

United States. Constitution of the United States
Authorized access point for: The Constitution of the United States

Kosovo (Republic). Kushtetuta e Republikës së Kosovës
Authorized access point for: Kushtetuta e Republikës së Kosovës

Colima (Mexico : State). Constitución Política del Estado Libre y Soberano de Colima
Authorized access point for: Constitución Política del Estado Libre y Soberano de Colima

Alaska. Constitution of the State of Alaska
Authorized access point for: The Constitution of the State of Alaska

Canada. Constitution Act, 1982
Authorized access point for: The Constitution Act, 1982

Los Angeles County (Calif.). Charter of the County of Los Angeles
Authorized access point for: Charter of the County of Los Angeles

Australia. Laws, etc.
Authorized access point for: Acts of the Parliament of the Commonwealth of Australia

United States. Laws, etc.
Authorized access point for: United States code

6.29.1.3 Laws Governing More Than One Jurisdiction

For a compilation of laws governing more than one jurisdiction, apply the instructions at **6.27.1.4**.

Narcotic laws of Mexico and the United States of America
Authorized access point for: The narcotic laws of Mexico and the United States of America. *Cover title:* Drugs and the law : compilation of laws on narcotics and dangerous drugs from the United States of America, the United States of Mexico, the state of California, and the state of Baja California

6.29.1.4 Administrative Regulations, Etc., That Are Laws

In certain jurisdictions, administrative regulations, rules, etc., are treated as laws (as is the case in the United Kingdom and Canada). For administrative regulations, etc., from such jurisdictions, construct the authorized access point by applying the instructions appropriate for the regulations as laws (see **6.29.1.2** and **6.29.1.3**).

Canada. Queen's regulations and orders for the Canadian Forces (1994 revision)
Authorized access point for: The Queen's regulations and orders for the Canadian Forces (1994 revision) : issued under the authority of the National Defence Act = Ordonnances et règlements royaux applicables aux Forces canadiennes (révision de 1994) : publiés en vertu de l'autorité conférée par la Loi sur la défense nationale

New Brunswick. Laws, etc.
Authorized access point for: Regulations of New Brunswick

If a law or laws are published together with the regulations, etc., made pursuant to the law or laws, construct the authorized access point representing the work by applying the instructions appropriate for the law or laws (see **6.29.1.2** or **6.29.1.3**, as applicable).

New Brunswick. Laws, etc.
Authorized access point for: N.B. acts and regulations

6.29.1.5 Bills and Drafts of Legislation

For legislative bills, construct the authorized access point representing the work by combining (in this order):

a) the authorized access point representing the appropriate legislative body (see **11.13.1**)

b) the preferred title for the legislative bill (see **6.19.2**).

Australia. Parliament. House of Representatives. Second Corporate Law Simplification Bill
Authorized access point for: Second Corporate Law Simplification Bill : second draft

United States. Congress (70th, 1st session : 1927–1928). Senate. Bill to designate a building site for the National Conservatory of Music of America, and for other purposes
Authorized access point for: A bill to designate a building site for the National Conservatory of Music of America, and for other purposes : 70th Congress, 1st session, S.2170

South Africa. Parliament (1994–). National Assembly. Electronic Communications and Transactions Bill
Authorized access point for: Electronic Communications and Transactions Bill / Republic of South Africa. — "As introduced in the National Assembly as a section 75 Bill"

For other drafts of legislation, apply the general guidelines and instructions at **6.27.1**.

Williston, Samuel, 1861–1963. Draft of an act relating to the sale of goods
Authorized access point for: Draft of an act relating to the sale of goods / by Samuel Williston

Ontario. Ministry of Housing. Local Planning Policy Branch. Planning act
Authorized access point for: The planning act : a draft for public comment. *Issued by the Ontario Ministry of Housing, Local Planning Policy Branch*

6.29.1.6 Ancient Laws, Certain Medieval Laws, Customary Laws, Etc.

For the laws of ancient jurisdictions; laws of non-western jurisdictions before the adoption of legislative institutions based on western models; and customary laws, tribal laws, etc., use as the authorized access point (in this order of preference):

a) the title by which the law or early compilation of laws is known (see **6.19.2.6**)

b) the title proper (excluding any alternative title) of the resource containing the laws, etc.

Lex Salica
Authorized access point for: Lex Salica : the ten texts with the glosses and the Lex Emendata

Institutiones
Authorized access point for: Imperatoris Iustiniani Institutionum libri quattuor / with introductions, commentary, and excursus by J.B. Moyle

Code of Hammurabi
Authorized access point for: The oldest code of laws in the world : the code of laws promulgated by Hammurabi, King of Babylon

Russkai͡a Pravda
Authorized access point for: Pravda Russkai͡a / pod red. B.D. Grekova. *Laws known by the title Russkai͡a Pravda*

Fontes iuris Romani antejustiniani
Authorized access point for: Fontes iuris Romani antejustiniani / in usum scholarum ediderunt S. Riccobono, J. Baviera, C. Ferrini, J. Furlani et V. Arangio-Ruiz juris antecessores

ADMINISTRATIVE REGULATIONS, ETC., THAT ARE NOT LAWS

6.29.1.7 Administrative Regulations, Etc., Promulgated by Government Agencies, Etc., That Are Not Laws

In certain jurisdictions, administrative regulations, rules, etc., are promulgated by government agencies or agents under authority granted by one or more laws (as is the case in the United States). For administrative regulations, etc., from such jurisdictions, construct the authorized access point representing the work by combining (in this order):

a) the authorized access point representing the agency or agent (see **11.13.1**)

b) the preferred title for the regulations, etc. (see **6.19.2**).

Illinois. Department of Public Health. Rules and regulations for recreational areas
Authorized access point for: Rules and regulations for recreational areas : prescribed under the Recreational Area Licensing Act, chapter 111 1/2, paragraphs 761–792 inclusive. *Promulgated by the Illinois Department of Public Health*

6.29.1.8 Laws and Derived Regulations, Etc., Issued Together

If a law or laws are issued together with the regulations, etc., derived from the law or laws, use the authorized access point appropriate for whichever appears first in the preferred source of information of the resource being described.

United States. Department of Labor. Regulations and principal statutes applicable to contractors and subcontractors on public building and public work and on building and work financed in whole or in part by loans or grants from the United States
Authorized access point for: Regulations and principal statutes applicable to contractors and subcontractors on public building and public work and on building and work financed in whole or in part by loans or grants from the United States / United States Department of Labor. *Includes several statutes, in whole and in part*

Germany (West). Gewerbesteuergesetz
Authorized access point for: Gewerbesteuer-Veranlagung 1966 : Gewerbesteuergesetz und Gewerbesteuer-Durchführungsverordnung mit Gewerbesteuer-Richtlinien .... *Regulations and guidelines included were promulgated by the Bundesministerium der Finanzen of West Germany*

If only the law or laws are mentioned in the title proper, use the authorized access point appropriate for the law or laws.

If only the regulations are mentioned in the title proper, use the authorized access point appropriate for the regulations.

If the evidence of the preferred source of information is ambiguous or insufficient, use the authorized access point appropriate for the law or laws.

Alternative

If a law or laws are issued together with the regulations, etc., derived from the law or laws, use the authorized access point appropriate to the law or laws. Use this access point regardless of whether the law or laws or the regulations, etc., appear first in the preferred source of information of the resource being described.

6.29.1.9 Compilations of Administrative Regulations, Etc.

For compilations of regulations, etc., promulgated by government agencies, etc., apply the instructions at **6.27.1.4**.

COURT RULES

6.29.1.10 Rules Governing a Single Court

For court rules governing a single court (regardless of their official nature, e.g., laws, administrative regulations), construct the authorized access point representing the work by combining (in this order):

a) the authorized access point representing the court (see **11.13.1**)

b) the preferred title for the rules (see **6.19.2**).

United States. Tax Court. Rules of practice and procedure of the United States Tax Court
Authorized access point for: Rules of practice and procedure of the United States Tax Court

Zimbabwe. Supreme Court. Rules of the Supreme Court of Zimbabwe
Authorized access point for: Rules of the Supreme Court of Zimbabwe

Ontario. Superior Court of Justice. Ontario Superior Court practice
Authorized access point for: Ontario Superior Court practice

6.29.1.11 Compilations of Rules Governing More Than One Court of a Single Jurisdiction

For a compilation of rules governing more than one court of a single jurisdiction but enacted as laws of that jurisdiction, apply the instructions at **6.29.1.2**.

For all other compilations of court rules governing more than one court of a single jurisdiction, construct the authorized access point by combining (in this order):

a) the authorized access point representing the agency or agent promulgating them (see **11.13.1**)

b) the preferred title for the rules (see **6.19.2**).

Peru. Reglamentos de tribunales, de jueces de paz y comercio
Authorized access point for: Reglamentos de tribunales, de jueces de paz y comercio

6.29.1.12 Other Compilations of Court Rules

For a compilation of court rules that are the laws of more than one jurisdiction, or that are promulgated by more than one agency or agent, apply the instructions at **6.27.1.4**.

West's California rules of court, 1975, state and federal
Authorized access point for: West's California rules of court, 1975, state and federal : with amendments received for January 1, 1975. — St. Paul, Minn. : West Publishing Co. *The rules apply to numerous state and federal courts in California; the state rules are promulgated by the California Judicial Council*

CONSTITUTIONS, CHARTERS, ETC., OF INTERNATIONAL INTERGOVERNMENTAL AND NON-JURISDICTIONAL BODIES

6.29.1.13 Constitutions, Charters, Etc., of International Intergovernmental Bodies

For the constitution, charter, etc., of an international intergovernmental body, construct the authorized access point representing the work by combining (in this order):

a) the authorized access point representing that body (see **11.13.1**)

b) the preferred title for the constitution, etc. (see **6.19.2**).

United Nations. Charter of the United Nations
Authorized access point for: Charter of the United Nations

For amendments to such a document, use the same authorized access point as the one used for the document.

6.29.1.14 Constitutions, Charters, Etc., of Non-jurisdictional Bodies

For a constitution, charter, etc., that is enacted by a jurisdiction but that applies to a body that is not a jurisdiction, construct the authorized access point by applying the instructions appropriate for the type of document (e.g., if the document is a law, apply the instructions at **6.29.1.2**).

Maryland. Charter of the Franklin Bank of Baltimore
Authorized access point for: Charter of the Franklin Bank of Baltimore. *An act of the Maryland legislature*

For amendments to such a document, use the same authorized access point as the one used for the document.

TREATIES, INTERNATIONAL AGREEMENTS, ETC.

6.29.1.15 Treaties

For a treaty, construct the authorized access point representing the work by using the preferred title for the treaty (see **6.19.2.7**).

Treaties between National Governments

Security Treaty between Australia, New Zealand, and the United States of America

The Antarctic Treaty

Treaty for the Prohibition of Nuclear Weapons in Latin America

Schengen Agreement

Agreement Establishing the World Trade Organization

Tratado del Río de la Plata y su Frente Marítimo

Pax Nicephori

Treaties Involving International Intergovernmental Bodies

Agreement between the United Nations and the Food and Agriculture Organisation of the United Nations and the United Kingdom as Administering Power of the Territories of Cyrenaica and Tripolitania Regarding Technical Assistance for Cyrenaica and Tripolitania

Development Credit Agreement (Santa Cruz Water Supply and Sewerage Project) between Republic of Bolivia and International Development Association

Loan Agreement (Agricultural Machinery Project) between Corporación de Fomento de la Producción and International Bank for Reconstruction and Development

Project Agreement (Anhui Hefei Urban Environment Improvement Project) between Asian Development Bank and Anhui Provincial Government, Hefei Municipal Government

Agreement between the United Nations and the World Intellectual Property Organization

Treaties Contracted by the Holy See

Das Konkordat zwischen dem Heiligen Stuhle und dem Freistaate Baden

Concordat of Worms

Treaties Involving Governments below the National Level

Convention between the Government of the United States of America and the Government of the British Virgin Islands for the Avoidance of Double Taxation and the Prevention of Fiscal Evasion with Respect to Taxes on Income

Resource described: Tax convention with the British Virgin Islands : message from the President of the United States transmitting the Convention between the Government of the United States of America and the Government of the British Virgin Islands for the Avoidance of Double Taxation and the Prevention of Fiscal Evasion with Respect to Taxes on Income, together with a related note from the government of the British Virgin Islands, signed at Washington on February 18, 1981

Make additions to the authorized access point by applying the instructions at **6.29.1.30.1**.

6.29.1.16 Protocols, Amendments, Etc.

For a separately issued protocol, amendment, extension, or other agreement ancillary to a treaty, construct the authorized access point by combining (in this order):

a) the authorized access point representing the treaty (see **6.29.1.15**)

b) the elements specified at **6.29.1.30.3**, as applicable.

Treat a general revision of a treaty as a new work.

6.29.1.17 Compilations of Treaties

For a compilation of treaties that has become known by a collective name, construct the authorized access point by combining (in this order):

a) the collective name for the compilation

b) the elements specified at **6.29.1.30.2**, as applicable.

Treaty of Utrecht (1713–1715)
Collective name for the compilation of treaties

For other compilations, apply the instructions at **6.27.1.4**.

United States agreements with the Republic of Korea

EU treaties
Resource described: EU treaties : consolidated versions with the amendments introduced by the Treaty of Lisbon / Prof. Dr. iur. Andreas Kellerhals, Dr. iur. Tobias Baumgartner (Ed.)

Treaties and other international agreements of the United States of America, 1776–1949
Resource described: Treaties and other international agreements of the United States of America, 1776–1949 / compiled under the direction of Charles I. Bevans

Tratados ratificados pelo Brasil
Resource described: Tratados ratificados pelo Brasil / Arnaldo Süssekind. *A compilation of Brazil's treaties*

Acordos e convenções internacionais em matéria de imposto de renda
Resource described: Acordos e convenções internacionais em matéria de imposto de renda : coletânea de edições da Resenha tributária, seções 1.1 e 1.4 : acompanham sumário e índice alfabético-remissivo

LAW REPORTS, CITATIONS, DIGESTS, ETC.

6.29.1.18 Reports of One Court

For law reports of one court, apply these instructions, as applicable:

reports ascribed to a reporter or reporters by name (see **6.29.1.18.1**)
reports not ascribed to a reporter or reporters by name (see **6.29.1.18.2**).

6.29.1.18.1 Reports Ascribed to a Reporter or Reporters by Name

If the reports are ascribed to a reporter or reporters by name, construct the authorized access point by combining (in this order):

a) the authorized access point representing the reporter (or first named reporter) (see **9.19.1**)

b) the preferred title for the reports (see **6.19.2**).

Manning, James, 1781-1866. Common bench reports
Authorized access point for: Common bench reports : cases argued and determined in the Court of Common Pleas / [reported] by James Manning, T.C. Granger, and John Scott

6.29.1.18.2 Reports Not Ascribed to a Reporter or Reporters by Name

If the reports are not ascribed to a reporter or reporters by name, construct the authorized access point by combining (in this order):

a) the authorized access point representing the court (see **11.13.1**)

b) the preferred title for the reports (see **6.19.2**).

Canada. Federal Court. Canada Federal Court reports
Authorized access point for: Canada Federal Court reports / editor, Florence Rosenfeld

Arizona. Court of Appeals. Reports of cases argued and determined in the Court of Appeals of the State of Arizona
Authorized access point for: Report of cases argued and determined in the Court of Appeals of Arizona ...

Germany. Bundesverfassungsgericht. Entscheidungen des Bundesverfassungsgerichts
Authorized access point for: Entscheidungen des Bundesverfassungsgerichts

Nigeria. Supreme Court. Monthly judgments of the Supreme Court of Nigeria
Authorized access point for: Monthly judgments of the Supreme Court of Nigeria

6.29.1.19 Reports of More Than One Court

For law reports of more than one court, apply these instructions, as applicable:

one reporter or collaborating reporters responsible for the reports (see **6.29.1.19.1**)

one reporter or collaborating reporters not responsible for all the reports (see **6.29.1.19.2**).

6.29.1.19.1 One Reporter or Collaborating Reporters Responsible for the Reports

If one reporter is responsible for the reports of all the cases reported, construct the authorized access point by combining (in this order):

a) the authorized access point representing the reporter (see **9.19.1**)

b) the preferred title for the reports (see **6.19.2**).

Freeman, Richard, 1645 or 1646–1710. Reports of cases argued and determined in the Courts of King's Bench and Common Pleas, from 1670 to 1704
Authorized access point for: Reports of cases argued and determined in the Courts of King's Bench and Common Pleas, from 1670 to 1704 / by Richard Freeman

If there are two or more collaborating reporters responsible for the reports of all the cases reported, apply the instructions at **6.27.1.3**.

Bosanquet, John Bernard, 1773–1847. Reports of cases argued and determined in the Courts of Common Pleas, and Exchequer Chamber, and in the House of Lords
Authorized access point for: Reports of cases argued and determined in the Courts of Common Pleas, and Exchequer Chamber, and in the House of Lords / by John Bernard Bosanquet and Christopher Puller

6.29.1.19.2 One Reporter or Collaborating Reporters Not Responsible for All the Reports

If the reporter or collaborating reporters are not responsible for all the reports, use the preferred title as the authorized access point.

If no reporter is named in the preferred source of information of the resource being described, use the preferred title as the authorized access point.

Australian law reports
Authorized access point for: Australian law reports : being reports of judgments of the High Court of Australia and the Judicial Committee of the Privy Council and of state supreme courts exercising federal jurisdiction, other federal courts and tribunals, together with selected cases from the Supreme Court of the Northern Territory and reports of the Supreme Court of the Australian Capital Territory (authorized by the judges) / editor, Robert Hayes.
The report for each case signed by its reporter

6.29.1.20 Citations, Digests, Etc.

If the person responsible for citations to, or digests or indexes of, court reports is prominently named in the resource being described, construct the authorized access point representing the work by combining (in this order):

a) the authorized access point representing that person (see **9.19.1**)

b) the preferred title for the citations, etc. (see **6.19.2**).

Phillips, Richard H. (Richard Henry), 1890–1971. Connecticut digest, 1785 to date
Authorized access point for: Connecticut digest, 1785 to date : Kirby to volume 129 inclusive with current cumulative pocket parts / by Richard H. Phillips

Michie, A. Hewson (Addinell Hewson), born 1897. Michie's digest of Virginia and West Virginia reports
Authorized access point for: Michie's digest of Virginia and West Virginia reports ... / under the editorial supervision of A. Hewson Michie

Otherwise, use the preferred title on its own as the authorized access point representing the work.

Commonwealth digest
Authorized access point for: Commonwealth digest : digest of cases argued and determined in the Commonwealth Trial Court, Commonwealth Superior Court (after May 1989), District Court of the Northern Mariana Islands, Trial and Appellate Divisions. — Saipan, Northern Mariana Islands : Law Revision Commission.
Publisher acts in an editorial capacity

COURT PROCEEDINGS, ETC.

6.29.1.21 Criminal Proceedings and Appeals

For the official proceedings and records of criminal trials, impeachments, courts-martial, etc., and the proceedings of appeals in these types of cases, construct the authorized access point by combining (in this order):

a) the authorized access point representing the person or body prosecuted (see **9.19.1** for persons or **11.13.1** for corporate bodies, as applicable)

b) the preferred title for the proceedings, etc. (see **6.19.2**).

Riel, Louis, 1844–1885. Queen vs. Louis Riel
Authorized access point for: The Queen vs. Louis Riel, accused and convicted of the crime of high treason : report of trial at Regina ...

Alley, Leavitt. Report of the trial of Leavitt Alley, indicted for the murder of Abijah Ellis, in the Supreme Judicial Court of Massachusetts

Authorized access point for: Report of the trial of Leavitt Alley, indicted for the murder of Abijah Ellis, in the Supreme Judicial Court of Massachusetts / reported by Franklin Fiske Heard

Hull, William, 1753–1825. Report of the trial of Brig. General William Hull, commanding the North-Western Army of the United States, by a court martial held at Albany on Monday, 3rd January, 1814, and succeeding days

Authorized access point for: Report of the trial of Brig. General William Hull, commanding the North-Western Army of the United States, by a court martial held at Albany on Monday, 3rd January, 1814, and succeeding days / taken by Lieut. Col. Forbes

Meteor (Ship). Report of the case of the steamship Meteor, libelled for alleged violation of the Neutrality Act

Authorized access point for: Report of the case of the steamship Meteor, libelled for alleged violation of the Neutrality Act / edited by F.V. Balch

6.29.1.21.1 Proceedings and Appeals Involving More Than One Defendant

If more than one person or body is prosecuted, construct the authorized access point representing the work by combining (in this order):

a) the authorized access point representing the first defendant, etc., named in the preferred source of information (see **9.19.1** for persons or **11.13.1** for corporate bodies, as applicable)

b) the preferred title for the proceedings, etc. (see **6.19.2**).

6.29.1.22 Civil and Other Noncriminal Proceedings and Appeals

For the official proceedings and records of civil and other noncriminal proceedings (including election cases), and the proceedings of appeals in these types of cases, construct the authorized access point representing the work by combining (in this order):

a) the authorized access point representing the person or body bringing the action (see **9.19.1** for persons or **11.13.1** for corporate bodies, as applicable)

b) the preferred title for the proceedings, etc. (see **6.19.2**).

Brooks, William, 1803–1863. Case of William Brooks versus Ezekiel Byam and others, in equity, in the Circuit Court of the United States, for the First Circuit-District of Massachusetts

Authorized access point for: The case of William Brooks versus Ezekiel Byam and others, in equity, in the Circuit Court of the United States, for the First Circuit-District of Massachusetts

Smith, John A. Contested election case of John A. Smith, contestant, v. Edwin Y. Webb, contestee, from the Ninth Congressional District of North Carolina, before Committee on Elections No. 2

Authorized access point for: Contested election case of John A. Smith, contestant, v. Edwin Y. Webb, contestee, from the Ninth Congressional District of North Carolina, before Committee on Elections No. 2

Goodwin Film and Camera Company. Goodwin Film and Camera Company, complainant, vs. Eastman Kodak Company, defendant

Authorized access point for: The Goodwin Film and Camera Company, complainant, vs. Eastman Kodak Company, defendant. *Case heard before the United States Circuit Court, Western District of New York*

Goodwin Film and Camera Company. Goodwin Film and Camera Company, complainant-appellee, vs. Eastman Kodak Company, defendant-appellant

Authorized access point for: The Goodwin Film and Camera Company, complainant-appellee, vs. Eastman Kodak Company, defendant-appellant : transcript of record. *Appeal heard before the United States Circuit Court of Appeals for the Second Circuit*

6.29.1.22.1 Actions Brought by More Than One Person or Body

If more than one person or body brings the action, construct the authorized access point representing the work by combining (in this order):

a) the authorized access point representing the first plaintiff, etc., named in the preferred source of information (see **9.19.1** for persons or **11.13.1** for corporate bodies, as applicable)

b) the preferred title for the proceedings, etc. (see **6.19.2**).

6.29.1.23 Indictments

For an indictment, apply the instructions at **6.29.1.21**.

Duane, William, 1760–1835. Copy of an indictment (No. 1) in the Circuit Court of the United States in and for the Pennsylvania District of the Middle Circuit

Authorized access point for: Copy of an indictment (No. 1) in the Circuit Court of the United States in and for the Pennsylvania District of the Middle Circuit. *Indictment of William Duane*

6.29.1.24 Charges to Juries

For a charge to a jury, construct the authorized access point representing the work by combining (in this order):

a) the authorized access point representing the court (see **11.13.1**)

b) the preferred title for the charge (see **6.19.2**).

United States. Circuit Court (Middle Circuit). Charge of Judge Paterson to the jury in the case of Vanhorne's lessee against Dorrance

Authorized access point for: The charge of Judge Paterson to the jury in the case of Vanhorne's lessee against Dorrance : tried at a Circuit Court for the United States, held at Philadelphia, April term, 1795. *The lessee is not named*

6.29.1.25 Judicial Decisions

For a judgment or other case decision by a court, construct the authorized access point representing the work by combining (in this order):

a) the authorized access point representing the court (see **11.13.1**)

b) the preferred title for the decision (see **6.19.2**).

United States. Supreme Court. Freedom of the press
Authorized access point for: Freedom of the press : opinion of the Supreme Court of the United States in the case of Alice Lee Grosjean, supervisor of public accounts for the state of Louisiana, appellant, v. American Press Company, Inc., et al.

6.29.1.26 Judicial Opinions

For an opinion of a judge, construct the authorized access point representing the work by combining (in this order):

a) the authorized access point representing the judge (see **9.19.1**)

b) the preferred title for the opinion (see **6.19.2**).

Sutliff, Milton, 1806–1879. Dissenting opinion of Hon. Milton Sutliff, one of the judges
Authorized access point for: Dissenting opinion of Hon. Milton Sutliff, one of the judges : ex parte Simeon Bushnell : ex parte Charles Langston : on habeas corpus. — At head of title: Supreme Court of Ohio

6.29.1.27 Records of One Party

For court records of one party, apply these instructions, as applicable:

brief, plea, etc. (see **6.29.1.27.1**)
courtroom argument (see **6.29.1.27.2**).

6.29.1.27.1 Brief, Plea, Etc.

For a brief, plea, or other formal record of one party to a case, construct the authorized access point by combining (in this order):

a) the authorized access point representing that party (see **9.19.1** for persons or **11.13.1** for corporate bodies, as applicable)

b) the preferred title for the brief, etc. (see **6.19.2**).

Morewood, George B. George B. Morewood, John R. Morewood, Frederic R. Routh, respondents, appellants versus Lorenzo N. Enequist, libellant, appellee
Authorized access point for: George B. Morewood, John R. Morewood, Frederic R. Routh, respondents, appellants versus Lorenzo N. Enequist, libellant, appellee : brief for appellants on admiralty jurisdiction / Robert Dodge, attorney for appellants. — At head of title: Supreme Court of the United States, no. 132

6.29.1.27.2 Courtroom Argument

For a courtroom argument presented by a lawyer, construct the authorized access point by combining (in this order):

a) the authorized access point representing the lawyer (see **9.19.1**)

b) the preferred title for the argument, etc. (see **6.19.2**).

Gowen, Franklin B. (Franklin Benjamin), 1836–1889. Argument of Franklin B. Gowen, Esq., of counsel for the Commonwealth, in the case of the Commonwealth vs. Thomas Munley

Authorized access point for: Argument of Franklin B. Gowen, Esq., of counsel for the Commonwealth in the case of the Commonwealth vs. Thomas Munley : indicted in the Court of Oyer and Terminer of Schuylkill County, Pa., for the murder of Thomas Sanger, a mining boss, at Raven Run, on September 1st, 1875 / stenographically reported by R.A. West

6.29.1.28 Compilations of Proceedings, Etc.

For a compilation of the official proceedings or records of trials, apply the instructions at **6.27.1.4**.

ADDITIONS TO ACCESS POINTS REPRESENTING LEGAL WORKS

6.29.1.29 Additions to Access Points Representing Laws, Etc.

If the access point representing a law, etc. (constructed according to the instructions at **6.29.1.2–6.29.1.6**) is the same as or similar to an access point representing a different law, etc., add the year of promulgation (see **6.20.2**).

Madagascar. Code pénal (1998)

Madagascar. Code pénal (2005)

Zimbabwe. Constitution of Zimbabwe (1994)

Zimbabwe. Constitution of Zimbabwe (2007)

6.29.1.30 Additions to Access Points Representing Treaties

For treaties, apply these instructions, as applicable:

single treaties (see **6.29.1.30.1**)
compilations of treaties (see **6.29.1.30.2**)
protocols, etc. (see **6.29.1.30.3**).

6.29.1.30.1 Single Treaties

For a single treaty, add the date of the treaty (see **6.20.3**).

Tratado del Río de la Plata y su Frente Marítimo (1973 November 19)

Signed by Argentina and Uruguay on 19 November 1973

Treaty between Australia and the Independent State of Papua New Guinea Concerning Sovereignty and Maritime Boundaries in the Area between the Two Countries, Including the Area Known as Torres Strait, and Related Matters (1978 December 18)

Resource described: Treaty between Australia and the Independent State of Papua New Guinea concerning Sovereignty and Maritime Boundaries in the Area between the Two Countries, Including the Area Known as Torres Strait, and Related Matters : Sydney, 18 December 1978, entry into force, 15 February 1985

Concordat of Worms (1122 September 23)

Agreed to by Pope Callistus II and the Holy Roman Emperor Henry IV on 23 September 1122

Das Konkordat zwischen dem Heiligen Stuhle und dem Freistaate Baden (1932 October 12)

Resource described: Das Konkordat zwischen dem Heiligen Stuhle und dem Freistaate Baden vom 12. Oktober 1932

International Convention for the High Seas Fisheries of the North Pacific Ocean (1952 May 9)

Resource described: International Convention for the High Seas Fisheries of the North Pacific Ocean with a protocol relating thereto : message from the President of the United States transmitting an International

Convention for the High Seas Fisheries of the North Pacific Ocean, together with a protocol relating thereto, signed at Tokyo, May 9, 1952, on behalf of the United States, Canada, and Japan

Agreement Establishing the World Trade Organization (1994 April 15)

Resource described: Uruguay Round of Multilateral Trade Negotiations / General Agreement on Tariffs and Trade. — Spine title: Final texts of the GATT Uruguay Round agreements including the Agreement Establishing the World Trade Organization as signed on April 15, 1994, Marrakesh, Morocco

6.29.1.30.2 Compilations of Treaties

If the access point representing a compilation of treaties is constructed by using the collective name for the treaties (see **6.19.2.8**), add the date or inclusive dates of the treaties (see **6.20.3**).

Treaty of Utrecht (1713–1715)

Treaties of Nijmegen (1678–1679)

6.29.1.30.3 Protocols, Etc.

For a separately described protocol, amendment, extension, or other agreement ancillary to a treaty, combine (in this order):

a) the authorized access point representing the treaty

b) the term *Protocols, etc.*

c) the date of the protocol, etc. (see **6.20.3**).

Convention for the Avoidance of Double Taxation and the Prevention of Fiscal Evasion with Respect to Taxes on Income (1993 June 1). Protocols, etc. (2005 November 11)

Resource described: Protocol between Ireland and the Portuguese Republic Amending the Convention for the Avoidance of Double Taxation and the Prevention of Fiscal Evasion with Respect to Taxes on Income and its Protocol, signed at Dublin on 1st June, 1993 : done at Lisbon on 11th November, 2005

International Convention for the High Seas Fisheries of the North Pacific Ocean (1952 May 9). Protocols, etc. (1978 April 25)

Resource described: Protocol Amending the International Convention for the High Seas Fisheries of the North Pacific Ocean

Agreement between the Member States of the European Coal and Steel Community and the Kingdom of Morocco (1976 April 27). Protocols, etc. (1982 March 11–1991 June 26)

Resource described: Protocols to the EEC-Morocco Cooperation Agreement and other basic texts

6.29.1.31 Additions to Access Points Representing Other Legal Works

If:

the access point represents a type of legal work not covered by **6.29.1.29** or **6.29.1.30**

and

the access point is the same as or similar to an access point representing a different work

then:

make additions to the authorized access point by applying the instructions at **6.27.1.9**.

Judicial Council of California criminal jury instructions (Matthew Bender (Firm))

Judicial Council of California criminal jury instructions (West (Firm))

6.29.2 Authorized Access Point Representing an Expression of a Legal Work

Construct an access point representing a particular expression of a legal work by combining (in this order):

a) the authorized access point representing the legal work (see **6.29.1**)

b) an appropriate element as instructed at **6.27.3**.

Kosovo (Republic). Kushtetuta e Republikës së Kosovës. English

Córdoba (Spain). Fuero (Latin version)

6.29.3 Variant Access Point Representing a Legal Work or Expression

6.29.3.1 General Guidelines on Constructing Variant Access Points Representing Legal Works

Use a variant title for the work (see **6.19.3**) as the basis for a variant access point.

Codes legum
Fori judicum
Forum iudicum
Forum judicum
Fuero juzgo
Lex Visigothorum
Lex Wisigothorum
Liber Gothorum
Liber iudiciorum
Liber iudicum
Liber judicum
Authorized access point for the work: Liber judiciorum

If the authorized access point for the work has been constructed by using the authorized access point representing a person or corporate body followed by the preferred title for the work (see **6.29.1.2**–**6.29.1.28**), construct a variant access point by combining (in this order):

a) the authorized access point representing that person or corporate body

b) the variant title for the work.

Australia. Constitution Act
Authorized access point for the work: Australia. Commonwealth of Australia Constitution Act

Canada. Federal Court. Recueil des arrêts de la Cour fédérale du Canada
Authorized access point for the work: Canada. Federal Court. Canada Federal Court reports

Apply these additional instructions, as applicable:

laws, etc. (see **6.29.3.2**)

treaties (see **6.29.3.3**).

Construct additional variant access points if considered important for access.

Hammurabi, King of Babylonia. Code of Hammurabi

Authorized access point for the work: Code of Hammurabi

Recceswinth, King of the Visigoths, died 672. Liber judiciorum

Authorized access point for the work: Liber judiciorum. *Promulgated in 654 by Recceswinth, Visigothic king of Spain*

Rome. Lex agraria

Authorized access point for the work: Lex agraria

Reports of rules adopted by the Supreme Court of the State of Kansas

Authorized access point for the work: Kansas. Supreme Court. Reports of rules adopted by the Supreme Court of the State of Kansas

Federal Capital Territory (Nigeria). High Court. Abuja law reports
Nigeria. Court of Appeal. Abuja law reports
Nigeria. Supreme Court. Abuja law reports
Abuja Law Reporting Committee. Abuja law reports

Authorized access point for the work: Abuja law reports. *Selected judgments of the High Court of the Federal Capital Territory, the Court of Appeal, and the Supreme Court, prepared by the Abuja Law Reporting Committee*

For variant access points for expressions of legal works, apply additional instructions at **6.29.3.4**.

6.29.3.2 Variant Access Points Representing Laws, Etc.

Construct variant access points representing laws, etc., by applying the general guidelines at **6.29.3.1**.

Add the year of promulgation of a law, etc. (see **6.20.2**) to the variant access point, if considered important for identification.

Madagascar. Fehezandalana famaizana (1998)

Authorized access point for the work: Madagascar. Code pénal (1998)

Madagascar. Fehezandalana famaizana (2005)

Authorized access point for the work: Madagascar. Code pénal (2005)

6.29.3.3 Variant Access Points Representing Treaties

If a title for the treaty was not used as the preferred title, use the title as the basis for a variant access point. Add the date of the treaty (see **6.20.3**).

Protocol Amending the International Convention for the High Seas Fisheries of the North Pacific Ocean (1978 April 25)

Resource described: Protocol Amending the International Convention for the High Seas Fisheries of the North Pacific Ocean : message from the President of the United States transmitting the Protocol Amending the International Convention for the High Seas Fisheries of the North Pacific Ocean, together with related agreed minutes and two memoranda of understanding, signed at Tokyo, April 25, 1978. *Authorized access point for the work:* International Convention for the High Seas Fisheries of the North Pacific Ocean (1952 May 9). Protocols, etc. (1978 April 25)

For a bilateral treaty between two or more of the following:

national governments

international intergovernmental bodies

the Holy See

jurisdictions now below the national level but retaining treaty-making powers

or

between one such body and another corporate body,

construct additional variant access points by combining (in this order):

a) the authorized access point representing a participant

b) the title of the treaty.

Construct such variant access points using the authorized access point for each of the participants.

Make additions to the variant access points, if considered important for identification, by applying the instructions at **6.29.1.30**.

World Intellectual Property Organization. Agreement between the United Nations and the World Intellectual Property Organization (1975 January 21)
United Nations. Agreement between the United Nations and the World Intellectual Property Organization (1975 January 21)
Authorized access point for the work: Agreement between the United Nations and the World Intellectual Property Organization (1975 January 21)

Portugal. Convention for the Avoidance of Double Taxation and the Prevention of Fiscal Evasion with Respect to Taxes on Income (1993 June 1). Protocols, etc. (2005 November 11)
Ireland. Convention for the Avoidance of Double Taxation and the Prevention of Fiscal Evasion with Respect to Taxes on Income (1993 June 1). Protocols, etc. (2005 November 11)
Authorized access point for the work: Convention for the Avoidance of Double Taxation and the Prevention of Fiscal Evasion with Respect to Taxes on Income (1993 June 1). Protocols, etc. (2005 November 11)

For a compilation of bilateral treaties, construct variant access points by combining (in this order):

a) the authorized access point representing a participant

b) the preferred title of the compilation.

Construct such variant access points using the authorized access point for each of the participants.

France. Accords passés entre la France et l'Algérie de juillet 1962 au 31 décembre 1963
Algeria. Accords passés entre la France et l'Algérie de juillet 1962 au 31 décembre 1963
Resource described: Accords passés entre la France et l'Algérie de juillet 1962 au 31 décembre 1963

For a compilation of treaties between one participant and two or more other participants, construct a variant access point by combining (in this order):

a) the authorized access point representing a participant

b) the preferred title of the compilation.

Construct such variant access points using the authorized access point for each of the participants if considered important for access.

United States. Treaties and other international agreements of the United States of America, 1776–1949

Resource described: Treaties and other international agreements of the United States of America, 1776–1949 / compiled under the direction of Charles I. Bevans

Construct additional variant access points for the participants in a multilateral treaty if considered important for access.

6.29.3.4 Variant Access Point Representing an Expression of a Legal Work

Construct a variant access point representing an expression of a legal work, if appropriate, by combining (in this order):

a) the authorized access point representing the legal work

b) a variant of an addition used in constructing the authorized access point representing the expression (see **6.29.2**).

Córdoba (Spain). Fuero (1241 April 8)

Authorized access point for the expression: Córdoba (Spain). Fuero (Latin version)

If:

a variant title for a legal work is associated with a particular expression of the work

and

the authorized access point representing the expression has been constructed by using the authorized access point representing a person, family, or corporate body followed by the preferred title for the work and one or more additions identifying the expression

then:

construct a variant access point representing the expression by combining in this order:

a) the authorized access point representing the person (see **9.19.1**), family (see **10.11.1**), or corporate body (see **11.13.1**)

b) the variant title associated with that expression.

Kosovo (Republic). Constitution of the Republic of Kosovo

Authorized access point for the expression: Kosovo (Republic). Kushtetuta e Republikës së Kosovës. English

Lapage, Joseph, 1837 or 1838–1877. Bekännelse och afrättning af vedhuggare-demonen, Joseph Lapage

Authorized access point for the expression: Lapage, Joseph, 1837 or 1838–1877. Trial of Joseph LaPage the French monster, for the murder of the beautiful school girl, Miss Josie Langmaid. Swedish

Make additions to the variant access point, if considered important for identification. Apply the instructions at **6.27.1.9**, as applicable.

Abkommen zur Errichtung der Welthandelsorganisation (1994 April 15)

Authorized access point for the expression: Agreement Establishing the World Trade Organization (1994 April 15). German

Treaty of Peace, Friendship, and Boundaries between the Republics of Bolivia and Paraguay (1938 July 21)
Authorized access point for the expression: Tratado de Paz, Amistad y Límites (1938 July 21). English

Construct additional variant access points if considered important for access.

ADDITIONAL INSTRUCTIONS FOR RELIGIOUS WORKS

6.30 Constructing Access Points to Represent Religious Works and Expressions

6.30.1 Authorized Access Point Representing a Religious Work

6.30.1.1 General Guidelines on Constructing Authorized Access Points Representing Religious Works

Apply the instructions at **6.30.1.2–6.30.1.7** when constructing the authorized access point representing one of the following types of religious works:

a) sacred scriptures (see **6.30.1.2–6.30.1.3**)

b) theological creeds, confessions of faith, etc. (see **6.30.1.4**)

c) liturgical works (see **6.30.1.5–6.30.1.7**).

For other types of religious works, construct the authorized access point by applying the general guidelines and instructions at **6.27.1**.

SACRED SCRIPTURES

6.30.1.2 Works Accepted as Sacred Scripture

For a work that is accepted as sacred scripture by a religious group, construct the authorized access point representing the work by using the preferred title for the work (see **6.23.2**).

Book of Mormon
Authorized access point representing the work for: The Book of Mormon : an account written by the hand of Mormon upon plates taken from the plates of Nephi / translated by Joseph Smith, Jun.

Qur'an
Authorized access point representing the work for: al-Qurʼān al-karīm

Ādi-Granth
Authorized access point representing the work for: Śrī Guru Granth Sāhib : with complete index / prepared by Winand M. Callewaert

Exception

In some cases, reference sources that deal with the religious group to which the sacred work belongs (e.g., works of the Baha'i Faith) attribute a work accepted as sacred scripture to a single person. When this occurs, construct the authorized access point representing the work by combining (in this order):

a) the authorized access point representing the person responsible for creating the work (see **9.19.1**)

b) the preferred title for the work (see **6.23.2**).

Bahá'u'lláh, 1817–1892. Kitāb al-aqdas

Authorized access point representing the work for: Kitāb al-aqdas / ta'līf Mirzā Ḥusayn 'Alī al-ma'rūf bi-Bahā' Allāh ; ma'a muqaddimah li-nāshirihi Khaddūrī Ilyās 'Ināyat

Hubbard, L. Ron (La Fayette Ron), 1911–1986. Introduction to Scientology Ethics

Authorized access point representing the work for: Introduction to Scientology Ethics / L. Ron Hubbard

Rogers, Robert Athlyi. Holy Piby

Authorized access point representing the work for: The Holy Piby / Robert Athlyi Rogers

Moon, Sun Myung. Wŏlli haesŏl

Authorized access point representing the work for: Wŏlli haesŏl. *Written by Sun Myung Moon*

6.30.1.3 Harmonies of Scriptural Passages

For a harmony of passages from different parts of scripture, use the authorized access point representing those scriptural passages collectively (see **6.30.1.2**).

Bible. Gospels

Authorized access point representing the work for: The life of Our Lord / compiled from the Gospels of the four Evangelists and presented in the very words of the Scriptures as one continuous narrative by Reginald G. Ponsonby ; with a preface by Sir Wilfred Grenfell

For harmonies accompanied by commentary, apply the instructions at **6.27.1.6**.

THEOLOGICAL CREEDS, CONFESSIONS OF FAITH, ETC.

6.30.1.4 General Instructions on Theological Creeds, Confessions of Faith, Etc.

For a theological creed, confession of faith, etc., construct the authorized access point representing the work by using the preferred title (see **6.23.2**).

Nicene Creed

Authorized access point representing the work for: I believe : the Nicene Creed / illustrated by Pauline Baynes

Augsburg Confession

Authorized access point representing the work for: Confessio, oder, Bekantnis des Glaubens etlicher Fürsten und Stedte vberantwortet keiserlicher Maiestat auff dem Reichstag gehalten zu Augsburgk, anno 1530

LITURGICAL WORKS

6.30.1.5 General Instructions on Liturgical Works

6.30.1.5.1 Types of Liturgical Works

Apply the instructions at **6.30.1.5.3** for the following types of works:

a) officially sanctioned or traditionally accepted texts of religious observance

b) books of obligatory prayers to be offered at stated times (including the Liturgy of the hours, Divine office, etc.)

c) calendars and manuals of performance of religious observances

d) compilations of readings from a sacred scripture intended for use in religious services

e) prayer books known as "books of hours."

For liturgical works of the Orthodox Eastern Church, apply the instructions at **6.30.1.6**.

For Jewish liturgical works, apply the instructions at **6.30.1.7**.

For a single passage from a sacred scripture used in religious services, apply the instructions for works accepted as sacred scripture (see **6.30.1.2**).

6.30.1.5.2 Categories Excluded from Types of Liturgical Works

Apply the general guidelines and instructions at **6.27.1**, as applicable, for the following categories:

a) works intended for private devotions (other than "books of hours")

b) compilations of hymns

c) proposals for orders of worship not officially approved

d) unofficial manuals

e) programs of religious services

f) lectionaries without scriptural texts.

6.30.1.5.3 Construction of Authorized Access Points for Liturgical Works

For a liturgical work falling into one or more of the categories listed at **6.30.1.5.1**, construct the authorized access point representing the work by combining (in this order):

a) the authorized access point representing the church or denominational body to which it pertains (see **11.13.1**)

b) the preferred title for the liturgical work (see **6.23.2**).

Episcopal Church. Book of common prayer

Authorized access point representing the work for: The book of common prayer, and administration of the sacraments and other rites and ceremonies of the church, according to the use of the Protestant Episcopal Church in the United States of America ; together with the Psalter or Psalms of David

Church of England. Book of common prayer

Authorized access point representing the work for: The book of common prayer, and administration of the sacraments and other rites and ceremonies of the church, according to the use of the Church of England

Church of England. The communion in Coventry Cathedral

Authorized access point representing the work for: The communion in Coventry Cathedral. *A liturgical work*

United Lutheran Church in America. Common service book of the Lutheran Church

Authorized access point representing the work for: Common service book of the Lutheran Church / authorized by the United Lutheran Church in America

Catholic Church. Missal

Authorized access point representing the work for: Missale Romanum ex decreto sacrosancti Concilii Tridentini restitutum / S. Pii V Pontificis Maximi jussu editum aliorum Pontificum cura recognitum, a Pio X reformatum et Benedicti XV auctoritate vulgatum. *A Tridentine liturgical work*

Catholic Church. Missale Romanum

Authorized access point representing the work for: Missale Romanum : ex decreto Sacrosancti Oecumenici Concilii Vaticani II instauratum / auctoritate Pauli PP. VI promulgatum. *A post-Vatican II liturgical work*

Church of England. Calendar, lectionary, and collects

Authorized access point representing the work for: Calendar, lectionary, and collects : Sundays, principal feasts, and other principal holy days. — London : Church House Publishing, 2001. — (Common worship : services and prayers for the Church of England)

Episcopal Church. Burial of the dead

Authorized access point representing the work for: Burial rites : according to the use of the Episcopal Church

Catholic Church. Liber usualis

Authorized access point representing the work for: The liber usualis : with introduction and rubrics in English / edited by the Benedictines of Solesmes

Catholic Church. The restored Holy Week liturgy

Authorized access point representing the work for: The restored Holy Week liturgy : practical arrangement of the prescribed music for the average church choir / by Carlo Rossini

Catholic Church. Diurnal

Authorized access point representing the work for: Horae diurnae Breviarii Romani ex decreto sacrosancti Concilii Tridentini restituti

Make additions to the access point, if considered important for identification. Apply the instructions at **6.27.1.9**, as applicable.

6.30.1.6 Liturgical Works of the Orthodox Eastern Church

Apply the general instructions at **6.30.1.5** if:

the liturgical work was published for the use of a national Orthodox Church or another autocephalous body within the Orthodox Eastern Church

and

the work is in the original language of the liturgy.

Srpska pravoslavna crkva. Srbljak

Authorized access point representing the work for: Srbljak : sluzbe, kanoni, akatisti / priredio Đorđe Trifunović ; preveo Dimitrije Bogdanović

For any other Orthodox liturgical work, construct the authorized access point representing the work by combining (in this order):

a) the authorized access point representing the church as a whole (see **11.13.1**)

b) the preferred title for the liturgical work (see **6.23.2**).

Orthodox Eastern Church. Octoechos

Authorized access point representing the work for: The Great Octoechos

Orthodox Eastern Church. Menaion

Authorized access point representing the work for: The Menaion of the Orthodox Church : collected services, together with selected Akathist hymns / translated by Isaac E. Lambertsen

Orthodox Eastern Church. Horologion

Authorized access point representing the work for: The great Horologion, or, Book of hours / translated from the Greek by the Holy Transfiguration Monastery

Make additions to the access point, if considered important for identification. Apply the instructions at **6.27.1.9**, as applicable.

6.30.1.7 Jewish Liturgical Works

For a Jewish liturgical work, construct the authorized access point representing the work by using the preferred title for the work (see **6.23.2**).

Haggadah

Authorized access point representing the work for: Hagadah shel Pesaḥ / ʻarikhah, Beno Rotenberg ; mavo, Mikhaʼel Avi-Yonah ; ʻitsuv, Ḥayim Ron

Hallel

Authorized access point representing the work included in: Hallel = הלל: song of praise and thanksgiving : halachah, history, hashkafah, and commentary / by Moshe Bamberger

Make additions to the access point, if considered important for identification. Apply the instructions at **6.27.1.9**, as applicable.

Amidah (Jewish prayer)

Authorized access point representing the work included in: Pathway to prayer : a translation and explanation of the Shemoneh esray= קונטרס עבודת התפלה /Mayer Birnbaum

6.30.2 Authorized Access Point Representing a Part or Parts of a Religious Work

6.30.2.1 General Guidelines

Apply the instructions at **6.30.2.2–6.30.2.3** when constructing the authorized access point representing a part or parts of one of the following types of religious works:

a) sacred scriptures (see **6.30.2.2**)

b) liturgical works (see **6.30.2.3**).

For a part or parts of other types of religious works, apply the general guidelines and instructions at **6.27.2**.

6.30.2.2 Part or Parts of a Sacred Scripture

Construct the authorized access point representing a part or parts of a sacred scripture by using the preferred title for the part or parts (see **6.23.2.9–6.23.2.19**).

Bible. Ezra

Bible. Pentateuch

Bible. Psalms, XXIII

Bible. Psalms, CXX–CXXXIV

Bible. Luke, XIV, 26

Ten commandments

Talmud. Minor tractates

Mishnah. Avot

Vedas. Atharvaveda

Qur'an. Sūrat al-Baqarah

Tipiṭaka. Suttapiṭaka. Dīghanikāya. Mahāsudassanasutta

Exception

In some cases, the authorized access point representing the scripture as a whole has been constructed by using the authorized access point representing the person responsible for creating the work followed by the preferred title for the work (see the exception at **6.30.1.2**). When this occurs, construct the authorized access point representing a part or parts of the work by combining (in this order):

a) the authorized access point representing the person responsible for creating the work

b) the preferred title for the work as a whole

c) the preferred title for the part or parts.

Rogers, Robert Athlyi. Holy Piby. Second Book of Athlyi Called Aggregation
Authorized access point for: The Holy Piby. The Second Book of Athlyi Called Aggregation. *Written by Robert Athlyi Rogers*

When identifying two or more parts that are unnumbered or non-consecutively numbered, construct authorized access points for each of the parts.

Bible. Psalms, VIII
Bible. Psalms, XLVI
Bible. Psalms, C
Resource described: Three Psalms. *Contains the Eighth, Forty-sixth, and One hundredth Psalm*

Qur'an. Sūrat Ibrāhīm
Qur'an. Sūrat al-Ḥajj
Qur'an. Sūrat al-Ṣāffāt
Resource described: Selections from surahs Ibrahim, al-Hajj, as-Saffat : tajweed recitation of the Holy Qur'an. *An audio recording of recitations of Qur'an sūrahs XIV, XXII, and XXXVII*

Alternative

When identifying two or more parts of a work that are unnumbered or non-consecutively numbered, identify the parts collectively. Construct the authorized access point representing the parts by combining (in this order):

a) the authorized access point representing the work as a whole (see **6.27.1** and **6.23.2.9.7**)

b) the conventional collective title *Selections*.

Qur'an. Selections
Resource described: Call to prayer and readings from the Koran. *An audio recording of the Call to prayer followed by the recitation of various sūrahs in classical Arabic*

6.30.2.3 Part or Parts of a Liturgical Work

For a part or parts of a liturgical work falling into one or more of the categories listed at **6.30.1.5**, construct the authorized access point by combining (in this order):

a) the authorized access point representing the church or denominational body to which it pertains (see **11.13.1**)

b) the preferred title for the part (see **6.23.2.20**).

Catholic Church. Rite of election
Authorized access point for a part of the Rite of Christian initiation of adults

Make additions to the access point, if considered important for identification. Apply the instructions at **6.27.1.9**, as applicable.

Episcopal Church. Lectionary (1979)
Authorized access point for a part of the Book of common prayer of 1979

6.30.3 Authorized Access Point Representing an Expression of a Religious Work

6.30.3.1 General Guidelines on Constructing Authorized Access Points Representing Expressions of Religious Works

Construct the authorized access point representing a particular expression of a religious work or of part of a religious work by combining (in this order):

a) the authorized access point representing the work (see **6.30.1**) or the part or parts (see **6.30.2**)

b) one or more of the elements specified at **6.30.3.2–6.30.3.5**, as applicable.

For expressions of religious works not covered by the instructions at **6.30.3.2–6.30.3.5**, apply the general instructions at **6.27.3**, as applicable.

6.30.3.2 Authorized Access Point Representing an Expression of the Bible

Construct the authorized access point representing a particular expression of the Bible or of part of the Bible by combining (in this order):

a) the authorized access point representing the work (see **6.30.1**) or the part (see **6.30.2**)

b) one or more of the following elements, as applicable:

  i. the language of the expression (see **6.11**)

  ii. other distinguishing characteristic of the expression (see **6.25**)

  iii. the date of the expression (see **6.24**).

Bible. English

Bible. New Testament. English

Bible. Revelation. English

Bible. Latin. Vulgate

Bible. Corinthians. English. Authorized

Bible. English. Smith-Goodspeed

Bible. English. Douai
Resource described: The Holy Bible / translated from the Latin Vulgate being the edition published at Rheims, A.D. 1582 and at Douay, 1609 ; as revised and corrected in 1750, according to the Clementine edition of the Scriptures, by Richard Challoner

Bible. Greek. Codex Sinaiticus

Resource described: Bibliorum Codex Sinaiticus Petropolitanus

Bible. French. Martin. 1835

Bible. Gospels. English. Revised Standard. 1975

Resource described: The horizontal line synopsis of the Gospels / Reuben J. Swanson. — First edition. — Dillsboro, North Carolina : Western North Carolina Press, Inc., ©1975. — "The Bible text in this publication is from the Revised Standard Version of the Bible"—Title page verso. *A biblical harmony*

Bible. Old Testament. Ethiopic. 1923

Bible. Psalms. Afrikaans. Oberholzer and others. 2005

Resource described: Afrikaanse Bybel vir Dowes : Psalms. — Eerste uitgawe. — Kaapstad : Bybelgenootskap van Suid-Afrika, 2005. *Translated by J.P. Oberholzer, H.J.B. Combrink, H.C. van Zyl, D.F. Tolmie, C.H.J. van der Merwe, R.P. Hough, and E. Roux*

If the resource described contains more than one language expression of the work, create authorized access points for each of the expressions.

Bible. Latin
Bible. French

Resource described: La sainte Bible : texte latin et traduction française

Bible. Kikuyu
Bible. English

Resource described: The Bible in English and Kikuyu

If the resource described contains more than one version of the work, create authorized access points for each of the versions.

Bible. English. Authorized
Bible. English. Revised

Resource described: Johnson's worker's Bible : self-pronouncing edition of the Holy Scriptures arranged especially for workers, ministers, students, showing a new and simple combination of the Authorized and Revised versions of the Old and New Testaments

Alternative

If:

the resource is a facsimile reproduction

and

the date of the manifestation is being treated as the date of expression (see **6.24.1.1**)

then:

construct one authorized access point representing the expression using the year of publication of the original, and a second authorized access point using the date of the facsimile.

Bible. German. Luther. 1534
Bible. German. Luther. 2002

Resource described: Biblia, das ist, Die gantze Heilige Schrifft deudsch / Mart. Luth. ; begnadet mit kürfurstlicher zu sachsen Freiheit. — Köln : Taschen, ©2002. *Facsimile of a 1534 edition*

6.30.3.3 Authorized Access Point Representing an Expression of the Talmud, Mishnah and Tosefta, or Midrashim

Construct the authorized access point representing a translation of the Talmud, Mishnah and Tosefta, or midrashim by combining (in this order):

a) the authorized access point representing the work (see **6.30.1**) or part of the work(see **6.30.2**), as applicable
and
b) the name of the language or languages (see **6.11**).

Talmud Yerushalmi. French
Resource described: Le Talmud de Jérusalem / traduit pour la première fois en français par Moïse Schwab

Exception

If the resource consists of the original text and a translation, do not add the name of the language. Create a second access point using the name of the language of the translation as an addition.

Talmud
Talmud. English
Resource described: New edition of the Babylonian Talmud, English translation / original text edited, formulated, and punctuated by Michael L. Rodkinson

Tosefta. Beẓah
Tosefta. Beẓah. German
Resource described: Der Tosefta-Traktat Jom Tob / Einleitung, Text, Übersetzung, und Erklärung von Michael Kern

6.30.3.4 Authorized Access Point Representing an Expression of the Vedas

If the resource being described is a particular version of one of the four standard compilations of Vedas, construct the authorized access point representing the expression by combining (in this order):

a) the authorized access point representing the compilation

b) the name of the version in parentheses.

Vedas. Sāmaveda (Kauthumasaṃhitā)

6.30.3.5 Authorized Access Point Representing a Variant or Special Text of a Liturgical Work

If the resource being described contains an authorized or traditional variant or special text of a liturgical work, construct the authorized access point by combining (in this order):

a) the authorized access point representing the work

b) one of the following terms (in this order of preference):

i. the name of a special rite (e.g., a Latin rite other than the Roman rite for Catholic works; a rite other than the unmodified Ashkenazic rite for Jewish works)

Catholic Church. Breviary (Ambrosian)
Resource described: Breviarium Ambrosianum

Haggadah (Sephardic)
Resource described: Hagadah shel Pesaḥ : nusaḥ Sefaradi

ii. the name of the place (e.g., country, diocese) or institution (e.g., monastery) in which the variant is authorized or traditional; if necessary, add both elements, with the institution preceding the place

Catholic Church. Ordo divini officii (Diocese of Trier)
Resource described: Directorium Diocesis Treverensis, seu, Ordo divini officii recitandi missaeque celebrandae

Catholic Church. Officia propria (Ireland)
Resource described: Officia propria sanctorum insulae Hiberniae

Catholic Church. Missal (St. Augustine's Abbey, Canterbury, England)
Resource described: The missal of St. Augustine's Abbey, Canterbury

Seder Haḳafot (Spinḳa)
Resource described: Seder Haḳafot li-Shemini ʻAtseret ṿe-Śimḥat Torah / asher nahag Maran Baʻal Imre Yosef mi-Spinḳa

iii. the name of the religious order for which the variant is authorized or traditional.

Catholic Church. Breviary (Benedictine)
Resource described: Brevarium monasticum

Catholic Church. Missal (Dominican)
Resource described: Missale Dominicanum

If the additions listed in this instruction are insufficient to identify the variant text, add an additional term (e.g., the name of the editor).

Haggadah (Reform : Cantor)
Resource described: The egalitarian Hagada / by Aviva Cantor

Haggadah (Reform : Seligmann)
Resource described: Hagada : Liturgie für die häusliche Feier der Sederabende / in deutscher Sprache neu bearbeitet von C. Seligmann

Catholic Church. Liber ordinarius (Abbaye de Saint-Denis : 1234)
Resource described: The first Ordinary of the Royal Abbey of St.-Denis in France : Paris, Bibliothèque Mazarine 526 / [edited by] Edward B. Foley. *Another* Liber ordinarius *for the same abbey dates to 1254–1259*

Catholic Church. Breviary (Ambrosian : Archdiocese of Milan)
Resource described: Prima dies nona fit iani scorpius hora .... *An Ambrosian breviary for the Archdiocese of Milan*

For post-Vatican II liturgical texts that vary in language and content, use the individual title of the resource being described as the preferred title. Add a term to distinguish between different texts that have the same title.

Catholic Church. Liturgy of the hours (Philippines)
Resource described: The liturgy of the hours. — Manila, Philippines : Missionary Benedictine Sisters, St. Scholastica's Priory, [1979?]. — "The text of the Liturgy of the Hours has been approved for use in the Philippines by the Catholic Bishops' Conference in January 1975"

Catholic Church. Liturgy of the hours (Servite)
Resource described: The liturgy of the hours : proper of the Order of Servants of the Blessed Virgin Mary

Catholic Church. Liturgy of the hours for the Order of the Holy Cross
Resource described: The liturgy of the hours for the Order of the Holy Cross

Catholic Church. Proper of The liturgy of the hours of the Order of the Brothers of the Blessed Virgin Mary of Mount Carmel
Resource described: Proper of The liturgy of the hours of the Order of the Brothers of the Blessed Virgin Mary of Mount Carmel

6.30.4 Authorized Access Point Representing a Manuscript or Manuscript Reproduction of a Religious Work

Construct the authorized access point representing a particular manuscript, or a reproduction of a particular manuscript by combining (in this order):

a) the authorized access point representing the work

b) the term *Manuscript*

c) one of the following terms (in this order of preference):

i. a brief form of the name of a particular owner if that is how the manuscript is identified

Catholic Church. Psalter (Manuscript Queen Mary)

ii. any other name by which the manuscript is identified

Catholic Church. Book of hours (Manuscript Rohan)

iii. a brief form of the name of the repository followed by the repository's designation.

Catholic Church. Missal (Manuscript Biblioteca apostolica vaticana. Borgh. cinese 409)

6.30.5 Variant Access Point Representing a Religious Work or Expression

6.30.5.1 General Guidelines on Constructing Variant Access Points Representing Religious Works

Use a variant title for the work (see **6.23.3**) as the basis for a variant access point.

> Avesto
> *Authorized access point for the work:* Avesta
>
> Koran
> Qorān
> Xuraan
> قرآن
> *Authorized access point for the work:* Qur'an

If the authorized access point for the work is constructed by using the authorized access point representing a person or corporate body followed by the preferred title for the work (see **6.30.1.2–6.30.1.7**), construct a variant access point by combining (in this order):

a) the authorized access point representing that person or corporate body

b) the variant title for the work.

> Rogers, Robert Athlyi. Blackman's Bible
> *Authorized access point for the work:* Rogers, Robert Athlyi. Holy Piby
>
> Catholic Church. Day hours
> Catholic Church. Diurnale
> Catholic Church. Horae diurnae Breviarii Romani
> *Authorized access point for the work:* Catholic Church. Diurnal

Make additions to the variant access point, if considered important for identification. Apply the instructions at **6.27.1.9**, as applicable.

> Concordia (Lutheran creed)
> *Authorized access point for the work:* Konkordienbuch. *Variant title is identical to the preferred title for other works*
>
> Catholic Church. Sacramentary (1970)
> *Authorized access point for the work:* Catholic Church. Missale Romanum (1970)
>
> Episcopal Church. Book of common prayer (1979). Holy Eucharist
> Episcopal Church. Eucharist (Section of Book of common prayer of 1979)
> *Authorized access point for the work:* Episcopal Church. Holy Eucharist

Apply the additional instructions at **6.30.5.2**, as applicable, to a part of a religious work.

Construct additional variant access points if considered important for access.

> Hawatamkʻ
> *Authorized access point for the work:* Armenian Church. Hawatamkʻ

Athanasius, Saint, Patriarch of Alexandria, died 373. Athanasian Creed

Authorized access point for the work: Athanasian Creed. *Traditionally attributed to Saint Athanasius of Alexandria, but scholars now generally agree that he was not the author*

Westminster Assembly (1643–1652). Westminster Confession of Faith
Westminster Assembly (1643–1652). Westminster Confession
Westminster Assembly (1643–1652). Confession of Faith

Authorized access point for the work: Westminster Confession of Faith. *Drawn up in 1646 by the Westminster Assembly*

For variant access points for expressions of religious works, apply additional instructions at **6.30.5.3**.

6.30.5.2 Variant Access Point Representing a Part of a Religious Work

If:

the title of the part of a religious work is distinctive

and

the authorized access point representing the part has been constructed by using the authorized access point representing a person or corporate body followed by the preferred title for the work as a whole, followed in turn by the preferred title for the part

then:

construct a variant access point representing the part by combining (in this order):

a) the authorized access point representing that person or corporate body

b) the preferred title for the part.

Hubbard, L. Ron (La Fayette Ron), 1911–1986. Ethics Codes

Authorized access point for the part of the work: Hubbard, L. Ron (La Fayette Ron), 1911–1986. Introduction to Scientology Ethics. Ethics Codes

Rogers, Robert Athlyi. Second Book of Athlyi Called Aggregation
Rogers, Robert Athlyi. Aggregation

Authorized access point for the part of the work: Rogers, Robert Athlyi. Holy Piby. Second Book of Athlyi Called Aggregation

If:

the title of the part of a religious work is distinctive

and

the authorized access point representing the part has been constructed using the preferred title for the work as a whole, followed by the preferred title for the part (see **6.23.2.9–6.23.2.19**)

then:

construct a variant access point by using the preferred title for the part on its own.

Old Testament

Authorized access point for the part of the work: Bible. Old Testament

Ṛgveda

Authorized access point for the part of the work: Vedas. Ṛgveda

Brahmajālasutta

Authorized access point for the part of the work: Tipiṭaka. Suttapiṭaka. Dīghanikāya. Brahmajālasutta

If the authorized access point representing the part has been constructed by using the preferred title for the part on its own, construct a variant access point by combining (in this order):

a) the preferred title for the work as a whole

b) the preferred title for the part.

Siddur. Shema
Authorized access point for the part of the work: Shema

Bible. Exodus, XX, 2–17
Bible. Deuteronomy, V, 6–21
Bible. Ten commandments
Bible. Decalogue
Authorized access point for the part of the work: Ten commandments

Make additions to the variant access point, if considered important for identification. Apply the instructions at **6.27.1.9**, as applicable.

John (Book of the Bible)
Authorized access point for the part of the work: Bible. John

Construct additional variant access points if considered important for access.

Isaiah (Biblical prophet). Book of Isaiah
Authorized access point for the part of the work: Bible. Isaiah. *Traditionally attributed to the 8th century B.C. Judean prophet Isaiah*

6.30.5.3 Variant Access Point Representing an Expression of a Religious Work

Construct a variant access point representing an expression of a religious work, if appropriate, by combining (in this order):

a) the authorized access point representing the religious work

b) a variant of an addition used in constructing the authorized access point representing the expression (see **6.30.3–6.30.4**).

Bible. English. King James Version
Authorized access point for the expression: Bible. English. Authorized

Bible. New Testament. Spanish. Nueva Versión Internacional. 1985
Authorized access point for the expression: Bible. New Testament. Spanish. New International. 1985

Bible. Psalms. Hebrew. Psalms scroll
Bible. Psalms. Hebrew. Great Psalms scroll
Bible. Psalms. Hebrew. Elizabeth Hay Bechtel Psalms scroll
Authorized access point for the expression: Bible. Psalms. Hebrew. Dead Sea Psalms scroll

Catholic Church. Breviary (Benedictine : Hyde Abbey)
Authorized access point for the expression: Catholic Church. Breviary (Hyde Abbey)

Catholic Church. Book of hours (Manuscript Bibliothèque nationale de France. Latin 9471)
Authorized access point for the expression: Catholic Church. Book of hours (Manuscript Rohan)

Talmud. 1990
Talmud. English. 1990
Authorized access point for the expression: Talmud (Schottenstein edition)

If:
a variant title for a religious work is associated with a particular expression of the work
and
the authorized access point representing the expression has been constructed by using the authorized access point representing a person, family or corporate body followed by the preferred title for the work and one or more additions identifying the expression
then:
construct a variant access point representing the expression by combining (in this order):

a) the authorized access point representing the person (see **9.19.1**), family (see **10.11.1**), or corporate body (see **11.13.1**)

b) the variant title associated with that expression.

Bahá'u'lláh, 1817–1892. Qitapi akdas
Bahá'u'lláh, 1817–1892. Libri më i shenjtë
Authorized access point for the expression: Bahá'u'lláh, 1817–1892. Kitāb al-aqdas. Albanian

Orthodox Eastern Church. Kitāb, al-sawāʻī al-kabīr
Authorized access point for the expression: Orthodox Eastern Church. Horologion. Arabic

Catholic Church. Breviarium Ambrosianum
Authorized access point for the expression: Catholic Church. Breviary (Ambrosian)

Make additions to the variant access point, if considered important for identification. Apply the instructions at **6.27.1.9**, as applicable.

Catholic Church. Breviarium Ambrosianum (Archdiocese of Milan)
Authorized access point for the expression: Catholic Church. Breviary (Ambrosian : Archdiocese of Milan)

Construct additional variant access points if considered important for access.

Nicänische Glaubensbekenntnis
Authorized access point for the expression: Nicene Creed. German

Ko te Paipera Tapu
Paipera Tapu
Holy Bible in Maori
Authorized access point for the expression: Bible. Maori. 1990

Jerusalemer Talmud in deutscher Übersetzung
Authorized access point for the expression: Talmud Yerushalmi. German. 1975

Egalitarian Hagada
Authorized access point for the expression: Haggadah (Reform : Cantor)

Tripiṭaka Koreana
Koryŏ Taejanggyŏng

Koryŏ-dae-jang-kyŏng
Authorized access point for the expression: Da zang jing (Koryŏ version)

6.31 Constructing Access Points to Represent Official Communications

6.31.1 Authorized Access Point Representing an Official Communication

6.31.1.1 General Guidelines on Constructing Authorized Access Points Representing Official Communications

Apply the instructions at **6.31.1.2–6.31.1.5** when constructing the authorized access point representing one of the following types of official communications:

a) official communications by heads of state, heads of government, ruling executive bodies, heads of international bodies, or governors of dependent or occupied territories (e.g., a message to a legislature, a proclamation, an executive order other than one covered by **6.29.1.2–6.29.1.5**)

b) official communications from a pope, patriarch, bishop, etc. (e.g., an order, decree, pastoral letter, bull, encyclical, constitution, an official message to a council, synod, etc.).

Make additions to the authorized access point, as required. Apply the instructions at **6.27.1.9**, **6.27.2**, and **6.27.3**, as applicable.

A person who holds office may also create or contribute to other types of works. For these other types of works, construct the authorized access point by applying the general guidelines and instructions at **6.27.1**.

6.31.1.2 Communications of a Single Official

For an official communication falling into one of the categories listed at **6.31.1.1**, construct the authorized access point representing the work by combining (in this order):

a) the authorized access point representing the official (see **11.13.1**)

b) the preferred title for the work (see **6.26.2**).

Canada. Sovereign (1952– : Elizabeth II). Speech by Her Majesty the Queen in reply to the Prime Minister, Parliament Hill, Ottawa, Wednesday, September 26, 1984
Authorized access point for: Speech by Her Majesty the Queen in reply to the Prime Minister, Parliament Hill, Ottawa, Wednesday, September 26, 1984

Louisiana. Governor (1988–1992 : Roemer). Governor's action agenda for fighting crime in Orleans Parish
Authorized access point for: Governor's action agenda for fighting crime in Orleans Parish : Governor Roemer's response to the New Orleans Crime Summit report

Catholic Church. Pope (1978–2005 : John Paul II). Redemptor hominis
Authorized access point for: Litterae encyclicae Redemptor hominis ad venerabiles fratres in episcopatu, ad sacerdotes et religiosas familias, ad ecclesiae filios et filias necnon ad universos bonae voluntatis homines pontificali eius ministerio ineunte / Ioannis Pauli PP. II, summi pontificis

Catholic Church. Archdiocese of St. Paul and Minneapolis. Archbishop (1995–2008 : Flynn). Pastoral letter on marriage and the family
Authorized access point for: A pastoral letter on marriage and the family / Archbishop Harry J. Flynn, Archdiocese of Saint Paul and Minneapolis, February 8, 1998

Augustinians. Prior General (1357–1358 : Gregory, of Rimini). Registrum generalatus

Authorized access point for: Gregorii de Arimino O.S.A. Registrum generalatus, 1357–1358 / quod edendum curavit Albericus De Meijer

Catholic Church. Pope (1559–1565 : Pius IV). Bulla Collegii Militum (1560 March 13)

Authorized access point for: Bulla Collegii Militum qui pii, de numero participantium, nuncupantur : qua amplissimis & honorifice tissimis priuiiegiis donantur : per S.D.N.D. Pium papam IIII in Alma Vrbe nuperrimè erecti instituti, securisq prouentibus & emolumentis dotati. *Date of work added to the access point to distinguish it from other works with the same preferred title issued in the same year*

6.31.1.3 Letters of Transmittal, Etc.

For a communication that merely accompanies and transmits a document, construct the authorized access point representing the work by combining (in this order):

a) the authorized access point representing the corporate body responsible for the document that it accompanies (see **11.13.1**)

b) the preferred title for the letter of transmittal, etc. (see **6.26.2**).

United States. War Department. Message from the President of the United States, transmitting a report of the Secretary of War, relative to murders committed by the Indians in the state of Tennessee

Authorized access point for: Message from the President of the United States, transmitting a report of the Secretary of War, relative to murders committed by the Indians in the state of Tennessee. *Message of President Madison*

6.31.1.4 Compilations of Official Communications of More Than One Holder of an Office

If:

a compilation consists of official communications by more than one holder of an office

and

that office is one of those listed at **6.31.1.1**

then:

construct the authorized access point representing the work by combining (in this order):

a) the authorized access point representing the office (see **11.2.2.18** or **11.2.2.26**, as applicable)

b) the preferred title for the work (see **6.26.2**).

United States. President. Economic report of the President transmitted to the Congress

Authorized access point for: Economic report of the President transmitted to the Congress. *An annual*

Nebraska. Governor. Biennial message of Gov. ... to the ... session of the Legislature of Nebraska

Authorized access point for: Biennial message of Gov. ... to the ... session of the Legislature of Nebraska

Catholic Church. Pope. Bulls

Authorized access point for: Papal bulls from France : from Biblioteca apostolica vaticana. *Microfilm reproduction of twelve manuscript bulls*

Catholic Church. Pope. Encyclicals

Authorized access point for: Litterae encyclicae

Catholic Church. Pope. Bulls

Authorized access point for: Bullae diuersorum pontificum incipiente a Ioanne XXII vsq ad Sanctiss. D.N.D. Paulum Papam III

6.31.1.5 Compilations of Official Communications and Other Works

For a compilation consisting of official communications and other works by more than one holder of an office, construct the authorized access point for the work by applying the instructions at **6.27.1.4**.

England is here

Authorized access point for: England is here : a selection from the speeches and writings of the prime ministers of England from Sir Robert Walpole to the Rt. Hon. Winston Spencer Churchill / edited and with an introduction by W.L. Hanchant

Papal documents on figured music from the 14th to the 20th century and examples for demonstration

Authorized access point for: Papal documents on figured music from the 14th to the 20th century and examples for demonstration / compiled by Paul M. Ferretti

Presidential documents

Authorized access point for: Presidential documents : the speeches, proclamations, and policies that have shaped the nation from Washington to Clinton / edited by J.F. Watts, Fred L. Israel

6.31.2 Authorized Access Point Representing an Expression of an Official Communication

Construct an access point representing a particular expression of an official communication by combining (in this order):

a) the authorized access point representing the work (see **6.31.1**)

b) an appropriate term or date as instructed at **6.27.3**.

Canada. Prime Minister (1896–1911 : Laurier). Reciprocal trade with the United States. French

Resource described: La réciprocité entre le Canada et les États-Unis : discours de Sir Wilfrid Laurier prononcé à la Chambre des communes, le 7 mars, 1911

Catholic Church. Pope (1978–2005 : John Paul II). Sollicitudo rei socialis. Spanish

Resource described: La preocupación por la cuestión social / Juan Pablo II

United States. President (1861–1865 : Lincoln). Speeches. Japanese

Resource described: Rinkān enzetsushū / Takagi Yasaka, Saitō Hikaru yaku

Catholic Church. Pope. Encyclicals. English

Resource described: The papal encyclicals / [compiled by] Claudia Carlen. *A five-volume set of papal encyclicals from 1740–1981*

Catholic Church. Pope. Bulls. Italian

Resource described: Gli anni santi attraverso le bolle / a cura di Rino Fisichella. *A compilation of all papal bulls proclaiming jubilee years issued from February 22, 1300 to November 29, 1998*

Mexico. President. Informe de gobierno (1989). French

Resource described: Rapport de gouvernement. — México, D.F. : Presidencia de la República, Dirección General de Comunicación Social. *An annual report*

6.31.3 Variant Access Point Representing an Official Communication

6.31.3.1 General Guidelines on Constructing Variant Access Points Representing Official Communications

Use a variant title for the work (see **6.26.3**) as the basis for a variant access point.

> America's commitment to children and families
> *Preferred title recorded as:* Culture of caring

If the authorized access point for the work has been constructed by using the authorized access point representing an official, an office, or a corporate body followed by the preferred title for the work (see **6.31.1.2–6.31.1.4**), construct a variant access point by combining (in this order):

a) the authorized access point representing that official, office, or corporate body

b) a variant title for the work.

> United States. President (1993–2001 : Clinton). Reclaiming our communities from drugs and violence
> *Authorized access point recorded as:* United States. President (1993–2001 : Clinton). National drug control strategy

Construct additional variant access points if considered important for access.

> Humanae vitae
> *Authorized access point for the work:* Catholic Church. Pope (1963–1978 : Paul VI). Humanae vitae
>
> Lateran Council (1059). Papal election decree
> *Authorized access point for the work:* Catholic Church. Pope (1058 or 1059–1061 : Nicholas II). In nomine Domini. *Promulgated by Nicholas II but may be viewed as a decree of the Lateran Council of 1059*

For variant access points for expressions of official communications, apply additional instructions at **6.31.3.2**.

6.31.3.2 Variant Access Point Representing an Expression of an Official Communication

Construct a variant access point representing an expression of an official communication, if appropriate, by combining (in this order):

a) the authorized access point representing the work

b) a variant of an addition used in constructing the authorized access point representing the expression (see **6.27.3**).

> Catholic Church. Pope (1978–2005 : John Paul II). Vita consecrata. English (Simplified version)
> Catholic Church. Pope (1978–2005 : John Paul II). Vita consecrata. English (Institute on Religious Life)
> *Authorized access point for the expression:* Catholic Church. Pope (1978–2005 : John Paul II). Vita consecrata. English (2004)

If:

a variant title for an official communication is associated with a particular expression of the work

and

the authorized access point representing the expression has been constructed by using the authorized access point representing the official followed by the preferred title for the work and one or more additions identifying the expression

then:

construct a variant access point representing the expression by combining (in this order):

a) the authorized access point representing the official

b) the variant title associated with that expression.

> Catholic Church. Pope (1978–2005 : John Paul II). Preocupación por la cuestión social
> *Authorized access point for the expression:* Catholic Church. Pope (1978–2005 : John Paul II). Sollicitudo rei socialis. Spanish
>
> United States. President (1861–1865 : Lincoln). Rinkān enzetsushū
> *Authorized access point for the expression:* United States. President (1861–1865 : Lincoln). Speeches. Japanese
>
> Catholic Church. Pope. Papal encyclicals
> *Authorized access point for the expression:* Catholic Church. Pope. Encyclicals. English

Make additions to the variant access point, if considered important for identification. Apply the instructions at **6.27.1.9**.

> Catholic Church. Pope. Tutte le encicliche dei sommi pontefici (1940)
> *Authorized access point for the expression:* Catholic Church. Pope. Encyclicals. Italian (1940)
>
> Catholic Church. Pope. Tutte le encicliche dei sommi pontefici (1959)
> *Authorized access point for the expression:* Catholic Church. Pope. Encyclicals. Italian (1959)
>
> Catholic Church. Pope. Tutte le encicliche dei sommi pontefici (1964)
> *Authorized access point for the expression:* Catholic Church. Pope. Encyclicals. Italian (1964)

7

DESCRIBING CONTENT

7.0 Purpose and Scope

This chapter provides general guidelines and instructions on recording the attributes of works and expressions that are associated with the intellectual or artistic content of a resource. These attributes are recorded using the elements covered in this chapter.

The elements in chapter 7 are typically used to select a resource that meets the user's needs in terms of its content (e.g., nature of the content, intended audience, language).

Not all of the elements covered in this chapter will be applicable to the description of a particular work or expression. For those elements that are applicable, the description of the resource should include at least those that are identified as core elements (see **5.3**).

For guidelines on recording the subject of a work, see chapter **23** (General Guidelines on Recording the Subject of a Work). [To be added in a later release]

7.1 General Guidelines on Describing Content

7.1.1 Sources of Information

Take information about the content from the resource itself. In many cases, information is also taken from sources outside the resource.

For further guidance on sources of information for describing content, see the specific instruction for each element in this chapter.

ATTRIBUTES OF THE WORK

7.2 Nature of the Content

7.2.1 Basic Instructions on Recording the Nature of the Content

7.2.1.1 Scope

The ***nature of the content*** is the specific character of the primary content of a resource (e.g., legal articles, interim report).

7.2.1.2 Sources of Information

Take information on the nature of the content from any source.

7.2.1.3 Recording the Nature of the Content

Record the nature of the content if considered important for identification or selection.

> Field recording of birdsong
>
> Cross-cultural survey
>
> Combined time series analysis and graph plotting system
>
> Spreadsheet, with word processing and graphic capabilities
>
> Singspiel in two acts

7.3 Coverage of the Content

7.3.1 Basic Instructions on Recording the Coverage of the Content

7.3.1.1 Scope

The *coverage of the content* is the chronological or geographic coverage of the content of a resource.

7.3.1.2 Sources of Information

Take information on the coverage of the content from any source.

7.3.1.3 Recording the Coverage of the Content

Record the coverage of the content if considered important for identification or selection.

Based on 1981 statistics

Shows all of western Europe and some of eastern Europe

7.4 Coordinates of Cartographic Content

7.4.1 Basic Instructions on Recording Coordinates of Cartographic Content

7.4.1.1 Scope

Coordinates of cartographic content is a mathematical system for identifying the area covered by the cartographic content of a resource.

Coordinates are expressed either by means of longitude and latitude on the surface of planets or by the angles of right ascension and declination for celestial cartographic content.

7.4.1.2 Sources of Information

Take information on the coordinates of cartographic content from any source within the resource.

If information on the coordinates of cartographic content is not provided within the resource, take the information from any source.

7.4.1.3 Recording Coordinates

For terrestrial cartographic content, record the coordinates

either

a) by recording longitude and latitude (see **7.4.2**)

or

b) by recording strings of coordinate pairs (see **7.4.3**).

For celestial cartographic content, record the right ascension and declination (see **7.4.4**).

7.4.2 Longitude and Latitude

7.4.2.1 Scope

Longitude and latitude is a system for identifying the area covered by the cartographic content of a resource. This system uses the longitude of the westernmost and easternmost boundaries and the latitude of the northernmost and southernmost boundaries.

Longitude is the distance of a point on a planet or satellite measured east and west from a reference meridian.

Latitude is the distance of a point on a planet or satellite measured north and south from the equator.

7.4.2.2 Sources of Information

Take information on longitude and latitude from any source within the resource.

If information on longitude and latitude is not provided within the resource, take the information from any source.

7.4.2.3 Recording Longitude and Latitude

For terrestrial cartographic content, record the coordinates in the following order:

westernmost extent of area covered (longitude)
easternmost extent of area covered (longitude)
northernmost extent of area covered (latitude)
southernmost extent of area covered (latitude).

Record the coordinates for longitude and latitude as sexagesimal coordinates, using degrees (°), minutes (′), and seconds (″). For longitude, use the Greenwich prime meridian as the reference meridian.

Precede each coordinate by W, E, N, or S, as appropriate.

Separate the west and east coordinates with a hyphen and the north and south coordinates with a hyphen. Do not use a space before or after the hyphen. Separate the set of longitude coordinates from the set of latitude coordinates by using a diagonal slash, with no space before or after the slash.

> E 79°–E 86°/N 20°–N 12°
>
> E 15°00′00″–E 17°30′45″/N 1°30′12″–S 2°30′35″
>
> W 74°50′–W 74°40′/N 45°5′–N 45°00′

Alternative

Record the coordinates for longitude and latitude as decimal degrees. Coordinates for locations east of Greenwich and north of the equator are expressed as positive numbers and may be preceded by a plus sign. Coordinates for locations west of Greenwich and south of the equator are expressed as negative numbers and are preceded by a minus sign. Do not include the plus or minus sign, but precede each coordinate by W, E, N, or S, as appropriate.

Separate the west and east coordinates with a hyphen and the north and south coordinates with a hyphen. Do not use a space before or after the hyphen. Separate the set of longitude coordinates from the set of latitude coordinates by using a diagonal slash, with no space before or after the slash.

> W 95.15°–W 74.35°/N 56.85°–N 41.73°

Optional Addition

Record other meridians appearing on the resource as other details of cartographic content (see 7.27).

7.4.3 Strings of Coordinate Pairs

7.4.3.1 Scope

Strings of coordinate pairs is a system for identifying the precise area covered by the cartographic content of a resource using coordinates for each vertex of a polygon.

Use strings of coordinate pairs for an indication of geographic coverage that is more precise than longitude and latitude coordinates.

7.4.3.2 Sources of Information

Take information on strings of coordinate pairs from any source within the resource.

If information on the strings of coordinate pairs is not provided within the resource, take the information from any source.

7.4.3.3 Recording Strings of Coordinate Pairs

Describe each closed polygon by using a string of coordinate pairs, in which each pair represents a vertex of the polygon.

List coordinate pairs in clockwise order, starting with the most southeastern vertex of the polygon. In each coordinate pair, record longitude, followed by latitude. Record the coordinates as degrees, minutes, and seconds, as appropriate to the size of the area being described.

Separate longitude from latitude in any one pair with a diagonal slash, and separate coordinate pairs within a string with space, semicolon, space.

Polygons have non-intersecting boundaries. The first and last coordinate pairs are the same.

> W 114°/N 32° ; W 117°/N 33° ; W 121°/N 35° ; W 125°/N 43° ; W 120°/N 42° ; W 120°/N 39° ; W 115°/N 34° ; W 114°/N 32°

If an area or areas within a given polygon are excluded, list the coordinate pairs for any excluded area in counterclockwise order.

> W 115°40′/N 33°15′ ; W 115°35′/N 33°20′ ; W 115°55′/N 33°32′; W 116°5′/N 33°32′ ; W 116°10′/N 33°30′ ; W 115°50′/N33°20′ ; W 115°40′/N 33°15′

7.4.4 Right Ascension and Declination

7.4.4.1 Scope

Right ascension and declination is a system for identifying the location of a celestial object in the sky covered by the cartographic content of a resource using the angles of right ascension and declination.

Right ascension is the angular distance measured eastward on the equator from the vernal equinox to the hour circle through a celestial body, from 0 to 24 hours.

Declination is the angular distance to a body on the celestial sphere measured north or south through 90° from the celestial equator along the hour circle of the body.

7.4.4.2 Sources of Information

Take information on right ascension and declination from any source within the resource.

If information on the right ascension and declination is not provided within the resource, take the information from any source.

7.4.4.3 Recording Right Ascension and Declination

For celestial cartographic content, record as coordinates:

a) the right ascension of the content, or the right ascensions of the western and eastern limits of its collective coverage
and
b) the declination of the centre of the content, or the northern and southern limits of its collective coverage.

For the right ascension, use the term *Right ascension,* followed by the hours and, when necessary, minutes and seconds of the twenty-four-hour clock. Abbreviate terms for units of time as instructed in appendix B (**B.5.8**).

For the declination, use the term *Declination,* followed by the degrees (°) and, when necessary, minutes (′) and seconds (″). Use a plus sign (+) for the northern celestial hemisphere and a minus sign (-) for the southern celestial hemisphere.

Separate right ascensions from declinations by using a diagonal slash, with no space before or after the slash.

> Right ascension 16 hr. 30 min. to 19 hr. 30 min./Declination -16° to -49°
>
> Right ascension 16 hr./Declination -23°
>
> Right ascension 2 hr./Declination +30°

If there are two right ascensions, record both separated by *to.* If there are two declinations, record both separated by *to.*

> Right ascension 2 hr. 00 min. to 2 hr. 30 min./Declination -30° to -45°

If the cartographic content is centered on a pole, record the declination limit.

> Centered at South Pole/Declination limit -60°

For an atlas or collection of celestial cartographic content arranged in declination zones, record the declination limits of each zone. Omit the statement of right ascension. If the zones are numerous, record the declination limits of the first few zones followed by the mark of omission (...) and the declination limit of the last zone.

> Zones +90° to +81°, +81° to +63°, +63° to +45°
>
> Zones +90° to +81°, +81° to +63°, ... -81° to -90°

When recording right ascension and declination, record equinox (see **7.5**) and, if applicable, epoch (see 7.6).

7.5 Equinox

7.5.1 Basic Instructions on Recording Equinox

7.5.1.1 Scope

Equinox is one of two points of intersection of the ecliptic and the celestial equator, occupied by the sun when its declination is 0°.

7.5.1.2 Sources of Information

Take information on the equinox from any source within the resource.

7.5.1.3 Recording Equinox

When coordinates are recorded for celestial cartographic content, record also the statement of equinox. Record the equinox as a year.

> 1950

7.6 Epoch

7.6.1 Basic Instructions on Recording Epoch

7.6.1.1 Scope

Epoch is an arbitrary moment in time to which measurements of position for a body or orientation for an orbit are referred.

7.6.1.2 Sources of Information

Take information on the epoch from any source within the resource.

7.6.1.3 Recording Epoch

When recording equinox for celestial cartographic content, record also a statement of the epoch when it is known to differ from the equinox.

1948.5
Equinox recorded as: 1950

7.7 Intended Audience

7.7.1 Basic Instructions on Recording the Intended Audience

7.7.1.1 Scope

Intended audience is the class of user for which the content of a resource is intended, or for whom the content is considered suitable. The class of user is defined by age group (e.g., children, young adults, adults), educational level (e.g., primary, secondary), type of disability, or another categorization.

7.7.1.2 Sources of Information

Take information on the intended audience for the content from any source.

7.7.1.3 Recording the Intended Audience

Record the intended audience for the content if the information is stated on the resource or is readily available from another source. Provide this information if considered important for identification or selection (e.g., if the resource is designed for use by persons with disabilities).

For children aged 7–9

Intended audience: Clinical students and postgraduate house officers

For remedial reading programs

Recommended for mature audiences

BBFC: 18

MPAA rating: PG-13

FSK ab 12 freigegeben

7.8 System of Organization

7.8.1 Basic Instructions on Recording the System of Organization

7.8.1.1 Scope

A *system of organization* is a system of arranging materials in an archival resource or a collection.

7.8.1.2 Sources of Information

Take information on the system of organization from any source.

7.8.1.3 Recording the System of Organization

Record information about the organization of component files or items in an archival resource or a collection.

> Organized in 5 series: 1. Subject files concerning refugee issues, 1978–1997. 2. Project Ngoc organizational files, 1987–1997. 3. Visual and audiovisual materials, 1985–1997. 4. Artwork, 1987–1997. 5. Newspaper clippings, 1980–1998
>
> This subseries is arranged alphabetically by the geographic location of the photograph and then by the item number assigned by the photographer

7.9 Dissertation or Thesis Information

7.9.1 Basic Instructions on Recording Dissertation or Thesis Information

7.9.1.1 Scope

Dissertation or thesis information is information about a work presented as part of the formal requirements for an academic degree.

Dissertation or thesis information includes information about the academic degree for which the work was presented, the granting institution or faculty, and the year the degree was granted.

7.9.1.2 Sources of Information

Take dissertation or thesis information from any source.

7.9.1.3 Recording Dissertation or Thesis Information

Treat the work being described as a dissertation or thesis presented as part of the requirements for an academic degree if it contains a statement declaring that it is a dissertation or thesis. Record the following information:

a) the degree for which the author was a candidate (see **7.9.2**)

b) the name of the institution or faculty to which the thesis was presented (see **7.9.3**)

c) the year in which the degree was granted (see **7.9.4**).

7.9.2 Academic Degree

7.9.2.1 Scope

An ***academic degree*** is a rank conferred as a guarantee of academic proficiency.

7.9.2.2 Sources of Information

Take information on the academic degree from any source.

7.9.2.3 Recording Academic Degree

Record a brief statement of the degree for which the author was a candidate.

> Ph.D.
>
> M.A.
>
> M.Arch.
>
> doctoral

7.9.3 Granting Institution or Faculty

7.9.3.1 Scope

A *granting institution or faculty* is an institution or faculty conferring an academic degree on a candidate.

7.9.3.2 Sources of Information

Take information on the granting institution or faculty from any source.

7.9.3.3 Recording Granting Institution or Faculty

Record the name of the granting institution or faculty.

University of Toronto

University College, London

McGill University

Freie Universität, Berlin

7.9.4 Year Degree Granted

7.9.4.1 Scope

Year degree granted is the calendar year in which a granting institution or faculty conferred an academic degree on a candidate.

7.9.4.2 Sources of Information

Take information on the year the degree was granted from any source.

7.9.4.3 Recording the Year the Degree Was Granted

Record the year in which the degree was granted. Apply the general guidelines on recording numbers expressed as numerals or as words at **1.8**.

2004

1969

1999

1973

ATTRIBUTES OF THE EXPRESSION

7.10 Summarization of the Content

7.10.1 Basic Instructions on Summarizing the Content

7.10.1.1 Scope

A *summarization of the content* is an abstract, summary, synopsis, etc., of the content of a resource.

For instructions on recording contents as whole-part relationships, see chapter **25**.

7.10.1.2 Sources of Information

Take information to be used in summarizing the content from any source.

7.10.1.3 Summarizing the Content

Provide a brief objective summary of the content of the resource if:

a) this information is considered important for identification or selection (e.g., for audiovisual resources or for resources designed for use by persons with disabilities)
and

b) sufficient information is not recorded in another part of the description.

Pictures the highlights of the play Julius Caesar using photographs of an actual production

Episodes from the novel, read by Ed Begley

A brief historical account up to the introduction of wave mechanics

Companion site for the PBS broadcast of the 2001 concert performance of Stephen Sondheim's musical Sweeney Todd with the San Francisco Symphony. It includes background information on: the title character, conditions in 18th century London, and barber-surgeons. Also included are a history of dramatizations of the demon barber legend and culinary recipes

Episodes from the novels, Dune, Children of Dune, Dune messiah, read by the author and connected with new material

Uses the children's tale of Goldilocks and the three bears in a program of Spanish language instruction

Toy medical kit designed to prepare children for hospital and medical procedures

Minutes, membership and dues records, journals, daybooks, forms, circulars, and correspondence from a carpenters' union local in St. Paul, Minnesota. Correspondence and minutes contain data on the union's formation, internal affairs, assessments and benefits, social functions, organizing activities, relations with other local and national unions, and political participation. There is also information on St. Paul labor issues, hiring practices, boycotts, strikes, and employers' attitudes toward unions. Present also are minutes (1914–1923) of Millmen's Local Number 1868, which affiliated with the carpenters in 1923

Letter presented by 21 Oneida Indians, signed with their marks, requesting that Jasper Parrish pay them the amount they are owed for serving in the War of 1812. They state that they are aware that he received the money three months previously and they are anxious to settle the account

7.11 Place and Date of Capture

7.11.1 Basic Instructions on Recording Place and Date of Capture

7.11.1.1 Scope

Place and date of capture are the place and date associated with the capture (i.e., recording, filming, etc.) of the content of a resource.

7.11.1.2 Sources of Information

Take information on the place and date of capture from any source.

7.11.1.3 Recording Place and Date of Capture

For the place of capture, see 7.11.2.

For the date of capture, see 7.11.3.

7.11.2 Place of Capture

7.11.2.1 Scope

Place of capture is the place associated with the capture (i.e., recording, filming, etc.) of the content of a resource.

7.11.2.2 Sources of Information

Take information on the place of capture from any source.

7.11.2.3 Recording Place of Capture

Record the place of capture by naming:

a) the specific studio, concert hall, etc., if applicable and readily ascertainable
and
b) the city, etc.

Paradise Studios, Sydney

Coolidge Auditorium, Library of Congress, Washington, D.C.

7.11.3 Date of Capture

7.11.3.1 Scope

Date of capture is a date or range of dates associated with the capture (i.e., recording, filming, etc.) of the content of a resource.

7.11.3.2 Sources of Information

Take information on the date of capture from any source.

7.11.3.3 Recording Date of Capture

Record the date of capture by giving the year, month, day, and time, as applicable.

1997 April 22–23

2002 September 13

7.12 Language of the Content

7.12.1 Basic Instructions on Recording Language of the Content

7.12.1.1 Scope

Language of the content is a language used to express the content of a resource.

For instructions on recording language of expression, see **6.11**.

For instructions on recording programming language, see **3.20**.

7.12.1.2 Sources of Information

Take information on the language of the content from any source.

7.12.1.3 Recording Language of the Content

Record details of the language or languages used to express the content of the resource if considered important for identification or selection.

Commentary in English

Italian and English words; includes principal melodies

Latin text; parallel English translation

Place names in Italian

Legend in English and Afrikaans

Some items in English; some in French

English with typewritten French translation

Latin with English marginalia

Latin words; words also printed as text at the end of each motet

French words; English translations on pages v–xxii

Sung in French

French dialogue; English subtitles

Dubbed into English

Captions in Spanish

Audiotape in Spanish and English

Collection is predominantly in Vietnamese; materials in English are indicated at the file level

Poems in the dialect of Genoa (Liguria), with Italian version

Contributions in German, French, English, Spanish, and Italian

In Polish; tables of contents and summaries in Polish, Russian, and English

7.13 Form of Notation

7.13.1 Basic Instructions on Recording Form of Notation

7.13.1.1 Scope

Form of notation is a set of characters and/or symbols used to express the content of a resource.

7.13.1.2 Sources of Information

Take information on the form of notation from any source.

7.13.1.3 Recording Form of Notation

Record the following information, as applicable to the content of the resource:

a) the script used to express the language content (see **7.13.2**)

b) the form of musical notation used to express the musical content (see **7.13.3**)

c) the form of tactile notation used to express the content (see **7.13.4**)

d) the form of notated movement used to express the content (see **7.13.5**).

7.13.2 Script

7.13.2.1 Scope

Script is a set of characters and/or symbols used to express the written language content of a resource.

7.13.2.2 Sources of Information

Take information on the script from any source.

7.13.2.3 Recording Scripts

Record the script or scripts used to express the language content of the resource using one or more of the terms from ISO 15924 (http://www.unicode.org/iso15924/codelists.html).

Devanagari

Glagolitic

Armenian
Cyrillic
Resource written in both scripts

If none of the terms listed is appropriate or sufficiently specific, record details of the script (see **7.13.2.4**).

7.13.2.4 Details of Scripts

Record details of the script or scripts used to express the language content of the resource if considered important for identification or selection.

Container inserts written in English, French, and Inuktitut (both syllabic and Latin script)

Kazakh, Uighur (Cyrillic), and Chagatai (Cyrillic and Arabic script)

Sanskrit (Latin and Devanagari) and English

7.13.3 Form of Musical Notation

7.13.3.1 Scope

Form of musical notation is a set of characters and/or symbols used to express the musical content of a resource.

For instructions on recording tactile forms of musical notation, see **7.13.4**.

For instructions on recording the encoding format, etc., for digitally encoded musical notation, see **3.19**.

7.13.3.2 Sources of Information

Take information on the form of musical notation from any source.

7.13.3.3 Recording Form of Musical Notation

Record the form of musical notation used to express the musical content of the resource using one or more appropriate terms from the following list:

graphic notation
letter notation
mensural notation
neumatic notation
number notation
solmization
staff notation
tablature
tonic sol-fa

If more than one term applies to a single form of musical notation used in the resource, record the most specific term.

If none of the terms in the list is appropriate or sufficiently specific, record details of the form of musical notation (see **7.13.3.4**).

7.13.3.4 Details of Form of Musical Notation

Record details of the form of musical notation used to express the musical content of the resource if considered important for identification or selection.

Second book in mensural notation

In part, graphic notation

Lute tablature and staff notation on facing pages

Melody in both staff and tonic sol-fa notation

Shape-note notation

In Sundanese cipher notation

Includes chord symbols

7.13.4 Form of Tactile Notation

7.13.4.1 Scope

Form of tactile notation is a set of characters and/or symbols used to express the content of a resource in a form that can be perceived through touch.

7.13.4.2 Sources of Information

Take information on the form of tactile notation from any source.

7.13.4.3 Recording Form of Tactile Notation

If the content of the resource is expressed in a tactile form, record the form of tactile notation using one or more appropriate terms from the following list:

braille code
computing braille code
mathematics braille code
Moon code
music braille code
tactile graphic
tactile musical notation

braille code

Form of tactile notation for a resource with text in braille

If none of the terms in the list is appropriate or sufficiently specific, record details of the form of tactile notation (see **7.13.4.4**).

7.13.4.4 Details of Form of Tactile Notation

If a form of tactile notation uses contractions and the level of contraction is known, record the level of contraction according to national practice. Add the level of contraction, in parentheses, following the term for the form of tactile notation.

braille code (uncontracted)

Form of tactile notation for a resource in grade 1 braille described by an agency in the United States

braille code (grade 1)

Form of tactile notation for a resource in grade 1 braille (uncontracted) described by an agency in the United Kingdom

Moon code (grade 2)
Form of tactile notation for a resource in grade 2 Moon (contracted) described by an agency in the United Kingdom

Record other details of the form of tactile notation used to express the content of the resource if considered important for identification or selection.

English Braille (grade 3)
Form of tactile notation for a resource described by an agency in the United Kingdom

Chess code

Nemeth code

Contains alternate leaves of print and braille

Contains print, braille, and tactile images

Contains braille and tactile images

Tactile lines for country boundaries, solid dots for capitals

Key to symbols in grade 2 braille
Form of tactile notation for a resource described by an agency in the United Kingdom

Tactile diagrams, legends in grade 2 English Braille
Form of tactile notation for a resource described by an agency in the United Kingdom

Labels in grade 1 French Braille
Form of tactile notation for a resource described by an agency in the United Kingdom

7.13.5 Form of Notated Movement

7.13.5.1 Scope

Form of notated movement is a set of characters and/or symbols used to express the movement content of a resource.

7.13.5.2 Sources of Information

Take information on the form of notated movement from any source.

7.13.5.3 Recording Form of Notated Movement

Record the form of notated movement used to express the movement content of the resource using one or more appropriate terms from the following list:

action stroke dance notation
Beauchamp-Feuillet notation
Benesh movement notation
DanceWriting
Eshkol-Wachman movement notation
game play notation
Kinetography Laban
Labanotation
Stepanov dance notation

If none of the terms in the list is appropriate or sufficiently specific, record details of the form of notated movement (see **7.13.5.4**).

7.13.5.4 Details of Form of Notated Movement

Record details of the form of notated movement used to express the content of the resource if considered important for identification or selection.

> Partly reconstructed from a video of the first performance

7.14 Accessibility Content

7.14.1 Basic Instructions on Recording Accessibility Content

7.14.1.1 Scope

Accessibility content is content that assists those with a sensory impairment in the greater understanding of content which their impairment prevents them fully seeing or hearing.

Accessibility content includes accessible labels, audio description, captioning, image description, sign language, and subtitles.

Accessibility content does not include subtitles in a language different from the spoken content (see **7.12**).

7.14.1.2 Sources of Information

Take information on accessibility content from any source.

7.14.1.3 Recording Accessibility Content

Record information about the accessibility content if the information is evident from the resource or is readily available from another source.

> Closed captioning in German
>
> Includes subtitles
>
> Open signed in American Sign language

7.15 Illustrative Content

7.15.1 Basic Instructions on Recording Illustrative Content

7.15.1.1 Scope

Illustrative content is content designed to illustrate the primary content of a resource.

For instructions on recording the nature of the primary content of a resource, see **7.2**.

7.15.1.2 Sources of Information

Take information on illustrative content from any source.

7.15.1.3 Recording Illustrative Content

If the resource contains illustrative content, record *illustration* or *illustrations,* as appropriate. Tables containing only words and/or numerical data are not considered as illustrative content. Disregard illustrated title pages, etc., and minor illustrations.

> illustrations
> *Resource contains illustrations*

Alternative

Record the type of illustrative content in place of or in addition to the term *illustration* or *illustrations* if considered important for identification or selection. Use one or more appropriate terms from the following list:

charts
coats of arms
facsimiles
forms
genealogical tables
graphs
illuminations
maps
music
photographs
plans
portraits
samples

coats of arms
facsimiles
portraits
Resource contains all three types of illustrative content

If none of the terms in the list is appropriate or sufficiently specific, record details of illustrative content (see **7.15.1.4**).

Optional Addition

Record the number of illustrations if the number can be readily ascertained (e.g., when the illustrations are numbered).

48 illustrations

100 maps

1 form
2 maps
10 photographs
15 plans
Resource contains all four types of illustrations with numbers stated

7.15.1.4 Details of Illustrative Content

Record details of the illustrative content if considered important for identification or selection.

Computer drawings

Map of Australia on endpapers

7.16 Supplementary Content

7.16.1 Basic Instructions on Recording Supplementary Content

7.16.1.1 Scope

Supplementary content is content (e.g., an index, a bibliography, an appendix) designed to supplement the primary content of a resource.

For instructions on recording content that supplements the primary content of a resource as a related work, see chapter **25**.

7.16.1.2 Sources of Information

Take information on supplementary content from any source.

7.16.1.3 Recording Supplementary Content

If the resource contains supplementary content, record the nature of that content (e.g., its type, extent, location within the resource). Provide this information if considered important for identification or selection.

> Includes index
>
> Bibliography: pages 859–910

7.17 Colour Content

7.17.1 Basic Instructions on Recording Colour Content

7.17.1.1 Scope

Colour content is the presence of colour, tone, etc., in the content of a resource.

Colour content is also the specific colours, tones, etc., (including black and white) present in the content of a resource.

For instructions on recording information on hand-coloured items, see **3.21**.

For instructions on recording the broadcast standard used for colour in videos, see **3.18.3**.

7.17.1.2 Sources of Information

Use evidence presented by the resource itself as the basis for recording the presence of colour content in the resource. Take additional evidence from any source.

7.17.1.3 Recording Colour Content

If the content of the resource is in colours other than black and white or shades of grey, record the presence of colour using an appropriate term. Disregard coloured matter outside the actual content of the resource (e.g., the border of a map).

> colour
>
> *Illustrations are in colour*
>
> some color
>
> *10 maps, some of which are in colour*
>
> chiefly colour
>
> *Illustrations, most of which are in colour*

Exceptions

Still images. For resources consisting of or containing still images, apply instead the instructions at 7.17.2.

Moving images. For resources consisting of or containing moving images, apply instead the instructions at 7.17.3.

Three-dimensional forms. For resources consisting of or containing three-dimensional forms, apply instead the instructions at 7.17.4.

Resources designed for persons with visual impairments. For resources designed for persons with visual impairments, apply instead the instructions at 7.17.5.

Record details of colour content as instructed at 7.17.1.4.

7.17.1.4 Details of Colour Content

Record details of the colour content if considered important for identification or selection.

2 maps in colour
Resource containing 4 maps, 2 of which are in colour

Title and headings printed in red
An early printed resource

Displays in red, yellow, and blue

Technicolor

Colourized

7.17.2 Colour of Still Image

7.17.2.1 Scope

Colour of still image is the presence of colour, tone, etc., in a still image or images contained in a resource.

Colour of still image is also the specific colours, tones, etc., (including black and white) present in a still image or images contained in a resource.

7.17.2.2 Sources of Information

Use evidence presented by the resource itself as the basis for recording colour of a still image or images. Take additional evidence from any source.

7.17.2.3 Recording Colour of Still Images

If the still image or images contained in the resource are in black and white or shades of grey, record *black and white*.

Exception

Digital still images. For digital still images in grey scale, record *grey scale*.

If the image or images in black and white are tinted and/or toned, record *tinted, toned*, or *tinted and toned*, as appropriate. Add these terms, in parentheses, following *black and white*.

black and white (tinted)
A photograph in black and white, tinted

If the image or images are in sepia, record *sepia*.

sepia
A photograph in sepia

If the image or images in the resource are in one or two colours, name the colour or colours.

blue and red
An oil painting

If the image or images are in more than two colours, record an appropriate term as instructed at **7.17.1.3**.

color
A set of slides in colour

If the colours are considered important for identification or selection, record details of colour content (see 7.17.1.4).

7.17.3 Colour of Moving Image

7.17.3.1 Scope

Colour of moving image is the presence of colour, tone, etc., in a moving image or images contained in a resource.

Colour of moving image is also the specific colours, tones, etc. (including black and white) present in a moving image or images contained in a resource.

7.17.3.2 Sources of Information

Use evidence presented by the resource itself as the basis for recording colour of moving images. Take additional evidence from any source.

7.17.3.3 Recording Colour of Moving Images

If the moving images contained in the resource are in black and white, record *black and white.*

black and white
A motion picture film in black and white

If the moving images in black and white are tinted and/or toned, specify *tinted*, *toned*, or *tinted and toned*, as appropriate. Add these terms, in parentheses, following *black and white.*

black and white (tinted)
A motion picture film in black and white, tinted

black and white (tinted and toned)
A motion picture film in black and white, tinted and toned

If the moving images are in sepia, record *sepia.*

sepia
A motion picture film in sepia

If the moving images in the resource are in colour, record an appropriate term as instructed at **7.17.1.3**.

If the moving images in the resource are in a combination of colour and black and white, record this information if it can be stated succinctly. If the information cannot be stated succinctly, record this information as details of colour content (see **7.17.1.4**).

color with black and white sequences

black and white with colour introductory sequence

7.17.4 Colour of Three-Dimensional Form

7.17.4.1 Scope

Colour of three-dimensional form is the presence of colour, tone, etc., in a three-dimensional form or forms contained in a resource.

Colour of three-dimensional form is also the specific colours, tones, etc. (including black and white) present in a three-dimensional form or forms contained in a resource.

7.17.4.2 Sources of Information

Use evidence presented by the resource itself as the basis for recording colour of three-dimensional forms. Take additional evidence from any source.

7.17.4.3 Recording Colour of Three-Dimensional Forms

If a three-dimensional form is in black and white, record *black and white.*

If the form is in one or two colours, name the colour or colours.

blue and white
A porcelain bowl in blue and white

If the form is in more than two colours, record an appropriate term as instructed at **7.17.1.3**.

colour
A multicoloured glass paperweight

If the colours are considered important for identification or selection, record details of colour content (see **7.17.1.4**).

7.17.5 Colour Content of Resource Designed for Persons with Visual Impairments

7.17.5.1 Scope

Colour content of resource designed for persons with visual impairments is the presence of colour, tone, etc., in a resource designed for persons with visual impairments.

Colour content of resources designed for persons with visual impairments is also the specific colours, tones, etc. (excluding black and white) present in a resource designed for persons with visual impairments.

7.17.5.2 Sources of Information

Use evidence presented by the resource itself as the basis for recording colour content of resources designed for persons with visual impairments. Take additional evidence from any source.

7.17.5.3 Recording Colour Content of Resources Designed for Persons with Visual Impairments

If the text and background in a resource designed for persons with visual impairments are not black on white, record the colours of the text and background.

> blue text on yellow background

7.18 Sound Content

7.18.1 Basic Instructions on Recording Sound Content

7.18.1.1 Scope

Sound content is the presence of sound in a resource other than one that consists primarily of recorded sound.

7.18.1.2 Sources of Information

Use evidence presented by the resource itself as the basis for recording the sound content of the resource. Take additional evidence from any source.

7.18.1.3 Recording Sound Content

Record *sound* to indicate the presence of sound in a resource that does not consist primarily of recorded sound.

> sound
> *A set of slides with integral sound*
>
> sound
> *A computer chip cartridge with integral sound*

Exception

Moving image resources. For motion pictures and video recordings, record *sound* or *silent* to indicate the presence or absence of a sound track.

> silent
> *A silent motion picture film*

If the sound content is in a separate carrier from the primary content, see also **3.1.4**.

7.19 Aspect Ratio

7.19.1 Basic Instructions on Recording Aspect Ratio

7.19.1.1 Scope

Aspect ratio is the ratio of the width to the height of a moving image.

7.19.1.2 Sources of Information

Use evidence presented by the resource itself (or on any accompanying material or container) as the basis for recording the aspect ratio of a moving image. Take additional evidence from any source.

7.19.1.3 Recording Aspect Ratio

Record the aspect ratio of the resource using one or more terms from the following list, as appropriate:

full screen
wide screen
mixed

Apply the terms listed as follows:

a) Record *full screen* for ratios of less than 1.5:1.

b) Record *wide screen* for ratios of 1.5:1 or greater.

c) Record *mixed* for resources that include multiple aspect ratios within the same work.

In addition, record the numerical ratio in standard format with a denominator of 1, if known.

wide screen (2.35:1)

full screen (1.33:1)

wide screen (1.85:1)
full screen (1.33:1)
Resource includes both versions

Record other information about aspect ratio as details of aspect ratio (see **7.19.1.4**).

7.19.1.4 Details of Aspect Ratio

Record details of the aspect ratio of the original expression when the expression being described is a modification of the original.

Original aspect ratio: 1.85:1

Record the specific method used to achieve the aspect ratio if considered important for identification or selection.

Pan-and-scan

Letterboxed

Anamorphic widescreen

7.20 Format of Notated Music

7.20.1 Basic Instructions on Recording the Format of Notated Music

7.20.1.1 Scope

Format of notated music is the musical or physical layout of the content of a resource that is presented in the form of musical notation.

7.20.1.2 Sources of Information

Take information on the format of notated music from any source within the resource.

7.20.1.3 Recording the Format of Notated Music

If the resource contains notated music, record the musical format using one or more appropriate terms from the following list:

score
condensed score
study score
piano conductor part
violin conductor part
vocal score
piano score
chorus score
part
choir book
table book

If none of the terms in the list is appropriate or sufficiently specific, record details of the format of notated music (see **7.20.1.4**).

7.20.1.4 Details of Format of Notated Music

Record details of the format of notated music if considered important for identification or selection.

7.21 Medium of Performance of Musical Content

7.21.1 Basic Instructions on Recording Medium of Performance of Musical Content

7.21.1.1 Scope

Medium of performance of musical content is the instrument, instruments, voice, voices, etc., used (or intended to be used) for performance of musical content.

For instructions on recording the medium of performance of a musical work, see **6.15**.

7.21.1.2 Sources of Information

Take information on the medium of performance of musical content from any source within the resource.

7.21.1.3 Recording Medium of Performance of Musical Content

Record the details on medium of performance of musical content if considered important for identification or selection. Use abbreviations for voices as instructed in appendix B (**B.5.6**).

For unaccompanied child's voice

Reduction for clarinet and piano

Part for piano only

SA

If the musical content is for solo instruments, record all the instruments.

If the work is for an orchestra, band, etc., do not list the instruments involved.

7.22 Duration

7.22.1 Basic Instructions on Recording Duration

7.22.1.1 Scope

Duration is the playing time, running time, etc., of the content of a resource.

Duration also includes performance time for a resource containing notated music or notated movement (see **7.22.1.4**).

7.22.1.2 Sources of Information

Take information on duration from any source.

7.22.1.3 Playing Time, Running Time, Etc.

If the resource has a playing time, running time, etc., record the time and abbreviate terms for units of time as instructed in appendix B (**B.5.3**). Record the time by applying the following instructions:

a) If the total playing time, running time, etc., is stated on the resource, record the time stated.

40 min.
Playing time of the content of an audiocassette

3 min., 23 sec.
Playing time of the content of a film cartridge

27 min.
Playing time of the content of an online video file

1:30:00
Total playing time of the content of 2 audio discs

75 min.
Playing time of the content of a videocassette

approximately 3 hr.
Playing time as stated of the content of 3 audio discs

b) If the total playing time, running time, etc., is not stated on the resource but is readily ascertainable, record it.

30 min.
Playing time of the content of a videotape reel

c) If the total playing time, running time, etc., is neither stated on the resource nor readily ascertainable, record an approximate time preceded by *approximately*.

approximately 7 min.
Approximate playing time of the content of a piano roll

approximately 90 min.
Approximate total playing time of the content of 2 film reels

d) If the total playing time, running time, etc., cannot be approximated, omit it.

Optional Addition

In some cases, the actual playing time, running time, etc., differs significantly from the time stated on the resource. When this occurs, record the stated playing time followed by *that is* and the actual playing time, running time, etc. Indicate that the information was taken from a source outside the resource itself (see **2.2.4**).

Alternative

If:

the resource consists of more than one unit

and

the units have a stated uniform playing time, running time, etc., or an approximate uniform playing time, running time, etc.

then:

record the playing time, running time, etc., of each unit followed by *each*.

60 min. each

Playing time of the content of each cassette in a set of 31 audiocassettes

approximately 30 min. each

Approximate playing time of the content of each cassette in a set of 11 audiocassettes

approximately 20 min. each

Approximate playing time of the content of each file in an online resource consisting of 3 audio files

7.22.1.4 Performance Time

For notated music and notated movement, if the performance time is stated on the resource, record the time stated.

18 min.

about 1 hr., 10 min.

7.22.1.5 Duration of Individual Parts

When preparing a comprehensive description for a resource consisting of more than one component, record the duration of each component.

17 min.; 23 min.; 9 min.

09:41; 16:00; 24:00

7.22.1.6 Resource Containing Both Sound and/or Moving Images and Text, Still Images, Etc.

For a resource containing sound and/or moving images as well as text, still images, etc., record the duration of the sound and/or moving images as duration.

80 min. of moving images

Duration of moving images on a videodisc also containing 2400 frames of still images

See also **3.22.2.10** for instructions on recording the number of pages of text, frames of still images, etc.

7.23 Performer, Narrator, and/or Presenter

7.23.1 Basic Instructions on Recording Performers, Narrators, and/or Presenters

7.23.1.1 Scope

A ***performer, narrator, and/or presenter*** is a person, family, or corporate body responsible for performing, narrating, and/or presenting a work.

For instructions on recording relationships to persons, families, and corporate bodies associated with a work or expression, see chapters **19** and **20**.

For instructions on recording artistic and/or technical credits, see **7.24**.

7.23.1.2 Sources of Information

Take information on performers, narrators, and/or presenters from any source.

7.23.1.3 Recording Performers, Narrators, and/or Presenters

Record the names of performers, narrators, and/or presenters, if considered important for identification, access, or selection.

For performers of music, indicate the medium in which each performs.

> Genevieve Warner, Lois Hunt, Genevieve Rowe, sopranos; Elizabeth Brown, Virginia Paris, contraltos; Frank Rogier, baritone; Columbia Chamber Orchestra, Lehman Engel, conductor
>
> Backing by Coral Reefer Band
>
> Recordings by Willie Nelson (side 1), Bob Wills and His Texas Playboys (side 2), Asleep at the Wheel (side 3), and Freddy Fender (side 4)
>
> Piano: Joshua Rifkin
>
> Budapest String Quartet (J. Roisman and A. Schneider, violins; B. Kroyt, viola; M. Schneider, cello)
>
> Gerry Mulligan, baritone; Chet Baker, trumpet; Henry Grimes, bass; Dave Bailey, drums
>
> Presenter: Jackie Glanville
>
> Cast: Laurence Harvey, Mia Farrow, Lionel Stander, Harry Andrews
>
> Cast: Gilles Behat (Charles IV), Jean Deschamps (Charles de Valois), Hélène Duc (Mahaut d'Artois)
>
> John Blake, vocals, guitar, speaker; Cora Blake, interviewee; Joseph C. Hickerson, interviewer, collector

7.24 Artistic and/or Technical Credit

7.24.1 Basic Instructions on Recording Artistic and/or Technical Credits

7.24.1.1 Scope

An ***artistic and/or technical credit*** is a listing of persons, families, or corporate bodies making contributions to the artistic and/or technical production of a resource.

For instructions on recording relationships to persons, families, and corporate bodies associated with a work or expression, see chapters **19** and **20**.

For instructions on recording performers, narrators, or presenters, see **7.23**.

7.24.1.2 Sources of Information

Take information on artistic and/or technical credits from any source.

7.24.1.3 Recording Artistic and/or Technical Credits

Record the names of persons, families, or corporate bodies who have contributed to the artistic and/or technical production of a resource if considered important for identification, access, or selection.

Include a statement of function with each name or group of names.

> Producer, Richard Mohr; recording engineer, Lewis Layton
>
> Producers, Gary Usher, Curt Boettcher, Terry Melcher, Bruce Johnston, and Brian Wilson; engineer, Bill Fletcher; container notes, Joe Foster; archiving credit, Gary Usher, Jr.
>
> Producer, Robert Palmer; assistant, Randall Lyon; recording engineer, Bruce Watson; mixers, Robert Norris, Robert Palmer
>
> Editor, Thomas J. Nordberg; music, Nick Urata
>
> Editor, Bernat Vilaplana; music, Javier Navarrete; costume designers, Lala Huete, Rocío Recondo; production designer, Engenio Caballero; special effects supervisor, Reyes Abades; visual effects supervisors, Everett Burrell, Edward Irastorza
>
> Art director, Maria Eugenia Sueiro; editor, Alejandro Brodersohn; music, Cesar Lerner
>
> Music, Joseph Horovitz; editing, Ray Helm; graphic designer, John Tribe
>
> Title music by William Walton; music composed by Geoffrey Burgon; literary consultant, John Wilders; script editor, Alan Shallcross
>
> Edited and special effects by You Oughta Be in Pixels; production design by Paula Dal Santo; director of photography, Luis Molina Robinson; music by Mark Oates
>
> Casting, Angela Heesom; director of photography, Will Gibson; hair and makeup design, Jen Lamphee; special make-up effects, Connelly Make-Up FX Team; costume designer, Nicola Dunn; production designer, Robert Webb; composer, François Tétaz; editor, Jason Ballantine; executive producers, Gary Hamilton, Martin Fabinyi, Simon Hewitt, Michael Gudinski, George Adams; co-producer/executive producer, Matt Hearn
>
> Executive producer, Craig Savage; multimedia producer, Craig Umanoff; editorial director, Clayton DeKorne

7.25 Scale

CORE ELEMENT

Scale is required only for cartographic content.

7.25.1 Basic Instructions on Recording Scale

7.25.1.1 Scope

Scale is the ratio of the dimensions of an image or three-dimensional form contained or embodied in a resource to the dimensions of the thing it represents.

Scale applies to:

still images or three dimensional forms (see **7.25.2**)

cartographic content (see **7.25.3**–**7.25.4**).

Scale can apply to horizontal, vertical, angular, and/or other measurements represented in the resource.

7.25.1.2 Sources of Information

Take information on scale from any source.

7.25.1.3 Recording Scale

Record the scale of the resource as a representative fraction expressed as a ratio.

1:32,500,000

4:1
Model of a human ear four times the actual size

> ***Alternative***
> For content that is not cartographic, record the scale using a term such as *full size*, *life size*, etc., as appropriate.

Record the scale even if it is already recorded as part of the title proper or other title information.

1:800,000
Title proper recorded as: Italy 1:800 000

If the scale statement that appears in the resource is not expressed as a representative fraction, convert the scale statement into a representative fraction.

1:475,200
Scale statement reads: 7.5 miles to 1 inch

If no scale statement is found in the resource, take a scale statement from a source outside the resource. If this scale statement is not expressed as a representative fraction, convert the scale statement into a representative fraction.

1:72
Scale taken from a source outside the resource

If no scale statement is found in the resource or in another source, estimate a representative fraction from a bar scale or a grid. Record *approximately* preceding the estimated representative fraction.

approximately 1:1,200
Estimated scale

If the scale cannot be determined or estimated by the means outlined in this instruction, record *Scale not given.*

> ***Alternative***
> Estimate a scale by comparison with a resource of known scale. Record *approximately* preceding the estimated scale. If the scale cannot be determined by comparison, record *Scale not given.*

If the cartographic content is not drawn to scale, record *Not drawn to scale.*

For digital resources, record the scale if:

a) the resource has a scale statement
or
b) the scale is already recorded as part of the title proper or other title information.

If scale information for a digital resource is not found in a scale statement or as part of the title proper or other title information, record *Scale not given.*

1:250,000
Other title information recorded as: 1:250,000 scale topographic maps of Australia

7.25.1.4 More Than One Scale

If the scale within one image, map, etc., varies and the largest and smallest values are known, record both scales separated by a hyphen. If the values are not known, record *Scale varies.*

1:15,000–1:25,000

If the resource consists of more than one image, map, etc., and the main images, maps, etc., are of more than one scale, record *Scales differ.*

> *Alternative*
>
> Record each scale separately.
>
> 1:50,000
> 1:250,000
>
> 1:7,819,000
> approximately 1:15,000,000

7.25.1.5 Nonlinear Scale

Record a statement of scale for an image, map, etc., with a nonlinear scale only if the information appears on the resource (e.g., celestial charts; some maps of imaginary places). If no scale statement appears on the resource, record *Scale not given.* Do not estimate a scale.

1° per 2 cm

7.25.2 Scale of Still Image or Three-Dimensional Form

7.25.2.1 Scope

Scale of still image or three-dimensional form is the ratio of the dimensions of a still image or three-dimensional form contained or embodied in a resource to the dimensions of the thing it represents.

7.25.2.2 Sources of Information

Take information on the scale of a still image or three-dimensional form from any source.

7.25.2.3 Recording Scale of Still Image or Three-Dimensional Form

Record the scale of the still image or three-dimensional form by applying the basic instructions on recording scale at 7.25.1.

1:100

1:2
Scale statement reads: Half the scale of the original

If the still image or three-dimensional form is not to scale, and this fact is considered important for identification or selection, record *Not drawn to scale.*

7.25.3 Horizontal Scale of Cartographic Content

CORE ELEMENT

7.25.3.1 Scope

Horizontal scale of cartographic content is the ratio of horizontal distances in the cartographic content of a resource to the actual distances they represent.

7.25.3.2 Sources of Information

Take information on the horizontal scale of cartographic content from any source within the resource.

If there is no horizontal scale provided within the resource itself, take the scale of the cartographic content from a source outside the resource.

7.25.3.3 Recording Horizontal Scale of Cartographic Content

Record the horizontal scale of cartographic content by applying the basic instructions on recording scale at 7.25.1.

1:36,000,000

1:63,360
Title proper recorded as: Bartholomew one inch map of the Lake District

1:253,440
Scale statement reads: 1 inch to 4 miles

1:21,600
Scale taken from a source outside the resource

approximately 1:220,000
Estimated scale

1:3,000,000
Scale appears in title: ArcWorld 1:3M

If the cartographic content is not drawn to scale, record *Not drawn to scale.* Do not estimate a scale.

7.25.4 Vertical Scale of Cartographic Content

CORE ELEMENT

7.25.4.1 Scope

Vertical scale of cartographic content is the scale of elevation or vertical dimension of the cartographic content of a resource.

7.25.4.2 Sources of Information

Take information on vertical scale for cartographic content from any source within the resource.

7.25.4.3 Recording Vertical Scale of Cartographic Content

Record the vertical scale in addition to the horizontal scale (see **7.25.3**) when describing a relief model, other three-dimensional cartographic resource, or a two-dimensional cartographic representation of a three-dimensional feature (e.g., block diagram, profile). Indicate that it is the vertical scale.

> Vertical scale 1:96,000
>
> Vertical scale 1:5

7.25.5 Additional Scale Information

7.25.5.1 Scope

Additional scale information is supplemental information about scale such as a statement of comparative measurements or limitation of the scale to particular parts of the content of a resource.

7.25.5.2 Sources of Information

Take additional scale information from any source within the resource.

7.25.5.3 Recording Additional Scale Information

Record additional scale information that appears on the resource. Capitalize words as instructed in appendix A. Use abbreviations or symbols for units of measurement as instructed in appendix B (**B.5.7**) and numerals in place of words (see **1.8.3**).

> 1 in. to 3.95 miles
> 1 cm to 2.5 km
> *Scale recorded as:* 1:250,000

Enclose the additional scale information in quotation marks if:

a) the statement presents unusual information that cannot be verified
or
b) a direct quotation is more precise than a statement in conventional form
or
c) the statement on the resource is in error or contains errors.

> "Along meridians only, 1 inch = 936 statute miles"
> *Scale recorded as:* 1:59,403,960
>
> not "1 inch to the mile"
> *Scale recorded as:* approximately 1:90,000

7.26 Projection of Cartographic Content

7.26.1 Basic Instructions on Recording Projection of Cartographic Content

7.26.1.1 Scope

Projection of cartographic content is the method or system used to represent the surface of the Earth or of a celestial sphere on a plane.

7.26.1.2 Sources of Information

Take information on the projection of cartographic content from any source within the resource.

7.26.1.3 Recording Projection of Cartographic Content

Record the projection of cartographic content if considered important for identification or selection.

conic equidistant projection

Optional Addition

Record phrases about meridians and/or parallels that are associated with the projection statement. Record information about ellipsoids as other details of cartographic content (see **7.27**).

transverse Mercator projection, central meridian 35°13′30″E

azimuthal equidistant projection centered on Nicosia, N 35°10′, E 33°22′

7.27 Other Details of Cartographic Content

7.27.1 Basic Instructions on Recording Other Details of Cartographic Content

7.27.1.1 Scope

Other details of cartographic content include mathematical data and other features of the cartographic content of a resource not recorded in statements of scale, projection, and coordinates.

For instructions on recording technical details of the representation of cartographic content in digital form, see **3.19.8**.

7.27.1.2 Sources of Information

Take information on other details of cartographic content from any source.

7.27.1.3 Recording Other Details of Cartographic Content

Record mathematical data that provides additional information not already recorded in statements of scale, projection, and coordinates.

Scale of original: approximately 1:1,300

Oriented with north to right

Prime meridians: Ferro and Paris

Scale departure graph: "Statute miles, Mercator projection"

Military grid

Clarke 1886 ellipsoid

WGS 84 datum

"Grid 10,000 meter UTM zone 11"

If the information is readily available, record:

the horizontal coordinate system (geographic system or map projection or grid coordinate system)

the name of the geodetic datum

the vertical coordinate system, if applicable (e.g., for digital elevation models).

Enclose each set of projection or ellipsoid parameters in parentheses. Separate the multiple parameters by a space, semicolon, space. Precede the secondary/related reference method by a colon, space.

> Altitude datum name: National Geodetic Vertical Datum of 1929 ; altitude resolution: not given ; units of measurement: feet ; vertical encoding method: explicit elevation coordinate included with horizontal coordinates
>
> Geographic system: coordinates ; longitude resolution: 0.0004 ; latitude resolution: 0.0004 ; unit of measure: decimal degrees
>
> Projection: Lambert conformal conic (standard parallels: 38.3 ; 39.4 ; longitude of central meridian: -77 ; latitude of projection origin: 37.8333 ; false easting: 800000 ; false northing 0)
>
> Horizontal datum name: North American datum of 1927 ; ellipsoid name: Clarke 1866 (semi-major axis: 6378206.4 ; flattening ratio: 294.98)

In cases when the phrase *Scales differ* has been recorded (see **7.25.1.4**), there may be information about the scale of some of the images, maps, etc. If one or more of the scales is readily discernible and can be expressed concisely, record the scale or scales.

> Scale of third and fourth maps: 1:540,000
>
> Predominant scale: 1:250,000

Provide mathematical data not already recorded for remote-sensing images.

> "f5.944, alt. 12,000 ft."
>
> "This image was produced from merging 30-m resolution multispectral data with 15-m resolution panchromatic data collected by Landsat-7"

For celestial cartographic content, record the magnitude of the cartographic content.

> Magnitude: 3.5

Record other features of the cartographic content of the resource that are not recorded elsewhere in the description. Provide this additional information if considered important for identification or selection.

> Maps dissected and pasted onto the sides of 42 wooden blocks to form an educational game
>
> Free ball globe in transparent plastic cradle with graduated horizon circle and "geometer"
>
> "Contour interval 20 feet"
>
> Relief shown by contours, hachures, and spot heights
>
> Relief shown by satellite imagery
>
> "This map is red-light readable"

7.28 Award

7.28.1 Basic Instructions on Recording Information on Awards

7.28.1.1 Scope

An ***award*** is a formal recognition of excellence, etc., given by an award- or prize-granting body, for the content of a resource.

7.28.1.2 Sources of Information

Take information on awards from any source.

7.28.1.3 Recording Information on Awards

Record information on awards if considered important for identification or selection.

> Caldecott Medal, 1996
>
> American Library Association Stonewall Book Award for Nonfiction, 2002
>
> Academy Award: Best Documentary Feature
>
> Academy Award: Best Actress, Diane Keaton; Best Director, Woody Allen; Best Picture; Best Writing, 1978

7.29 Note on Expression

7.29.1 Basic Instructions on Making Notes on Expressions

7.29.1.1 Scope

A ***note on expression*** is an annotation providing additional information about content recorded as an expression attribute.

7.29.1.2 Sources of Information

Take information for notes on expressions from any source.

7.29.1.3 Making Notes on Expression

Make a note on expression by applying the general guidelines on notes at **1.10**.

For notes on changes in content characteristics, see **7.29.2**.

7.29.2 Note on Changes in Content Characteristics

7.29.2.1 Scope

A ***note on changes in content characteristics*** is a note on changes in content characteristics that occur in subsequent issues or parts of a resource issued in successive parts or between iterations of an integrating resource.

7.29.2.2 Sources of Information

Use evidence presented by the resource itself (or on any accompanying material or container) as the basis for making notes on changes in content characteristics of the expression. Take additional evidence from any source.

7.29.2.3 Change in Content Characteristics

Make notes on changes in content characteristics as appropriate to the mode of issuance of the resource:

multipart monographs and serials (see **7.29.2.3.1**)

integrating resources (see **7.29.2.3.2**).

7.29.2.3.1 Multipart Monographs and Serials

Make a note if a content characteristic is changed in a subsequent issue or part of a multipart monograph or serial. Provide this additional information if the change is considered important for identification or selection.

If the changes have been numerous, make a general note instead.

Volumes 1–3 in French, volumes 4–7 in German

Armenian, 1999–2007; Cyrillic, 2008–

Volumes 3–5 lack illustrations

Volumes 1, 4, and 8 lack indexes

7.29.2.3.2 Integrating Resources

Make notes on content characteristics no longer present on the current iteration if the change is considered important for identification or selection.

If the changes have been numerous, make a general note instead.

In French and English, 2002–2009
Website now only in French

8

GENERAL GUIDELINES ON RECORDING ATTRIBUTES OF PERSONS, FAMILIES, AND CORPORATE BODIES

8.0 Scope

This chapter provides background information to support the application of guidelines and instructions in chapters **9–11** on recording attributes of persons, families, and corporate bodies. It includes:

a) an explanation of key terms (see **8.1**)

b) the functional objectives and principles underlying the guidelines and instructions in chapters **9–11** (see **8.2**)

c) the core elements for the identification of persons, families, and corporate bodies (see **8.3**)

d) guidelines on language and script that apply to elements in chapters **9–11** (see **8.4**)

e) general guidelines on recording names (see **8.5**)

f) general guidelines and instructions on constructing authorized access points representing persons, families, and corporate bodies (see **8.6**)

g) general guidelines and instructions on constructing variant access points representing persons, families, and corporate bodies (see **8.7**)

h) instructions on recording elements that provide clarification or justification for the data recorded to identify persons, families, and corporate bodies:

   i. scope of usage for a name identifying a person, family, or corporate body (see **8.8**)

   ii. date of usage for a name identifying a person, family, or corporate body (see **8.9**)

   iii. status of identification to indicate the reliability of data identifying a person, family, or corporate body (see **8.10**)

   iv. undifferentiated name indicator (see **8.11**)

   v. source consulted to cite sources used in determining names and other information identifying a person, family, or corporate body (see **8.12**)

   vi. cataloguer's note to assist in the use or revision of the data (see **8.13**).

8.1 Terminology

8.1.1 Explanation of Key Terms

There are a number of terms used in this chapter and in chapters **9–11** that have meanings specific to their use in RDA. Some of these terms are explained at **8.1.2–8.1.4**.

Terms used as data element names in chapters **9–11** are defined at the beginning of the instructions for the specific element. In addition, all terms used in those chapters with a specific technical meaning are defined in the glossary.

8.1.2 Person, Family, and Corporate Body

The terms *person, family,* and *corporate body* are used as follows:

The term ***person*** refers to an individual or an identity established by an individual (either alone or in collaboration with one or more other individuals).

The term ***family*** refers to two or more persons related by birth, marriage, adoption, civil union, or similar legal status, or who otherwise present themselves as a family.

The term ***corporate body*** refers to an organization or group of persons and/or organizations that is identified by a particular name and that acts, or may act, as a unit.

8.1.3 Name

The terms *name, preferred name,* and *variant name* are used as follows:

The term ***name*** refers to a word, character, or group of words and/or characters by which a person, family, or corporate body is known.

The term ***preferred name*** refers to the name or form of name chosen to identify a person, family, or corporate body. The preferred name is also the basis for the authorized access point representing that person, family, or corporate body.

The term ***variant name*** refers to a name or form of name by which a person, family, or corporate body is known that differs from the name or form of name chosen as the preferred name for that person, family, or corporate body.

8.1.4 Access Point

The terms *access point, authorized access point,* and *variant access point* are used as follows:

The term ***access point*** refers to a name, term, code, etc., representing a specific person, family, or corporate body. Access points include both authorized access points and variant access points.

The term ***authorized access point*** refers to the standardized access point representing an entity. The authorized access point representing a person, family, or corporate body is constructed using the preferred name for the person, family, or corporate body.

The term ***variant access point*** refers to an alternative to the authorized access point representing an entity. A variant access point representing a person, family, or corporate body is constructed using a variant name for that person, family, or corporate body.

8.2 Functional Objectives and Principles

The data recorded to reflect the attributes of a person, family, or corporate body should enable the user to:

a) *find* persons, families, and corporate bodies that correspond to the user's stated search criteria

b) *identify* the person, family, or corporate body represented by the data (i.e., confirm that the person, family, or corporate body represented is the one sought, or distinguish between two or more persons, families, or corporate bodies with the same or similar names)

c) *understand* the relationship between the name used to represent the person, family, or corporate body and another name by which that person, family, or corporate body is known (e.g., a different language form of the name)

d) *understand* why a particular name has been recorded as a preferred or variant name.

To ensure that the data created using RDA meet those functional objectives, the guidelines and instructions in chapters **9–11** were designed according to the following principles:

Differentiation. The data should serve to differentiate the person, family, or corporate body represented from others.

Representation. The name or form of name chosen as the preferred name for a person, family, or corporate body should be:

a) the name or form of name most commonly found in resources associated with that person, family, or corporate body
or
b) a well-accepted name or form of name in a language and script preferred by the agency creating the data.

Other names and other forms of the name should be recorded as variant names:

names found in resources associated with the person, family, or corporate body

names found in reference sources

names that the user might be expected to use when conducting a search.

Language preference. The preferred name for a person, family, or corporate body should be the name or form of name found in resources associated with that person, family, or corporate body in the original language and script of the content. In some cases, the original language and script is not a language and script preferred by the agency creating the data. When this occurs, the preferred name or form of name should be one found in resources associated with that person, family, or corporate body, or in reference sources, in a language and script preferred by the agency.

Common usage or practice. When there is more than one part in the name of a person or family, the part chosen as the first element of the preferred name should reflect the usage or practice in the country and language most closely associated with that person or family.

8.3 Core Elements

When recording data identifying a person, family, or corporate body, include as a minimum the following elements that are applicable and readily ascertainable. Record the elements as separate elements, as parts of the authorized access point representing the person, family, or corporate body, or as both.

Preferred name for the person

Title of the person (a word or phrase indicative of royalty, nobility, ecclesiastical rank or office; a term of address for a person of religious vocation)

Date of birth

Date of death

Other designation associated with the person (for a Christian saint, a spirit, a person named in a sacred scripture or an apocryphal book, a fictitious or legendary person, or a real non-human entity)

Profession or occupation (for a person whose name consists of a phrase or appellation not conveying the idea of a person)

Identifier for the person

Preferred name for the family

Type of family

Date associated with the family

Identifier for the family

Preferred name for the corporate body

Location of conference, etc.

Date of conference, etc.

Associated institution (for conferences, etc., if the institution's name provides better identification than the local place name or if the local place name is unknown or cannot be readily determined)

Number of a conference, etc.

Type of corporate body (for a body whose name does not convey the idea of a corporate body)
Identifier for the corporate body

If the preferred name for the person, family, or corporate body is the same as or similar to a name by which another person, family, or corporate body is known, differentiate them by recording as many of the additional identifying elements as necessary in the following list. Record these elements as separate elements, as parts of the authorized access point representing the person, family, or corporate body, or as both.

Title of the person (another term indicative of rank, honour, or office)
Fuller form of name
Profession or occupation
Period of activity of the person
Other designation associated with the person

Place associated with the family
Prominent member of the family

Location of headquarters
Date of establishment
Date of termination
Period of activity of the corporate body
Associated institution
Other designation associated with the corporate body

Indicate that the name of a person is an undifferentiated name (see **8.11**) if the additional identifying elements to differentiate the name cannot be readily ascertained.

Include additional elements covered in this chapter and in chapters **9–11** according to the policy of the agency creating the data, or according to the judgment of the cataloguer.

8.4 Language and Script

Record names in the language and script in which they appear on the sources from which they are taken.

> *Alternative*
> Record a transliterated form of the name either as a substitute for, or in addition to, the form that appears on the source.

Record other identifying attributes of a person, family, or corporate body in the language and script specified in the applicable instructions in chapters **9–11**.

8.5 General Guidelines on Recording Names

8.5.1 General Guidelines

When recording a name, apply the following general guidelines:

capitalization (see **8.5.2**)
numbers expressed as numerals or as words (see **8.5.3**)
accents and other diacritical marks (see **8.5.4**)
hyphens (see **8.5.5**)
spacing of initials and acronyms (see **8.5.6**)
abbreviations (see **8.5.7**).

When those guidelines refer to an appendix, apply the additional instructions in that appendix, as applicable.

8.5.2 Capitalization

Apply the instructions in appendix A (**A.2**) on the capitalization of names of persons, families, and corporate bodies.

8.5.3 Numbers Expressed as Numerals or as Words

When recording a name, record numbers expressed as numerals or as words in the form in which they appear on the source of information.

> 50 Cent
>
> Vivian One Feather
>
> Thirteenth Avenue Presbyterian Church
>
> 11th Hour Band

For instructions on recording an ordinal numeral as a designation associated with the name of a conference, congress, meeting, etc., see **11.6.1**.

8.5.4 Accents and Other Diacritical Marks

Record accents and other diacritical marks appearing in a name as they appear in the source of information. Add them if it is certain that they are integral to a name but have been omitted in the source from which the name is taken.

> Jacques Lefèvre d'Étaples
>
> Éliphas Lévi
> *Sometimes appears without diacritical marks*

In some cases, the application of the instructions on capitalization in appendix A can result in lower case letters without the accents and other diacritical marks that are standard usage for the language in which the data is recorded. When this occurs, add accents and other diacritical marks according to the standard usage for the language.

8.5.5 Hyphens

Retain a hyphen between given names if the hyphen is used by the person.

> Ann-Marie Ekengren
>
> R.-J. Ahlers

Include hyphens in transliterated names if specified by the transliteration scheme.

> Chʻoe Sin-dŏk
>
> Abutsu-ni
>
> Blo-bzaṅ-rab-gsal

8.5.6 Spacing of Initials and Acronyms

8.5.6.1 Names of Persons or Families

When recording the name of a person or family:

a) if an initial represents a given name or a surname, and the initial is followed by another initial or a name, leave a space after the full stop following the first initial

b) if the name consists entirely or primarily of separate letters, leave a space between the letters (regardless of whether they are followed by full stops or not)

c) if the name includes initials or abbreviations forming part of a title or term of address, leave a space between the initial or abbreviation and a subsequent initial, abbreviation, numeral, or word.

Rowling, J. K.

Franco G. S., José Fernándo

A. Hafiz Anshary A. Z.

A. E. I. O. U.

A. M. do R. A.

Dr. X

Mrs. R. F. D.

Flamanville, Mme de

DJ Q

DJ I. C. O. N.
Initials "DJ" in name are an abbreviated form of the term "Disc jockey"

8.5.6.2 Names of Corporate Bodies

When recording the name of a corporate body:

a) if an initial is followed by another initial, do not leave a space after the full stop, etc., following the first initial

b) if separate letters or initials appear on the source of information without full stops between them, record the letters without spaces between them.

J.A. Folger and Company

Robert A.M. Stern Architects

B.B.C. Symphony Orchestra
Name appears as: B. B. C. Symphony Orchestra

IEEE
Initialism appears as: I E E E

8.5.7 Abbreviations

Apply the instructions in appendix B (**B.2**) on the use of abbreviations in names of persons, families, and corporate bodies.

Fry, Benjamin St. James

Hugh, of St. Victor

De Ste. Croix, Philip
Allegany County Farm Bureau Ass'n
Mt. St. Helens Public Access Task Group
Centro Cultural Prof. Dr. Ramón Melgar
International Mr. Leather, Inc.
Domus Lugdunensis Soc. Jesu
Monicault, Mlle

8.6 Authorized Access Points Representing Persons, Families, and Corporate Bodies

When constructing an authorized access point to represent a person, family, or corporate body, use the preferred name for the person (see **9.2.2**), family (see **10.2.2**), or corporate body (see **11.2.2**) as the basis for the access point.

If two or more persons, families, or corporate bodies have the same or similar names, include one or more additional identifying elements in the access point representing the person, family, or corporate body. Apply the following instructions on making additions, as applicable:

additions to names of persons (see **9.19.1**)
additions to names of families (see **10.11.1**)
additions to names of corporate bodies (see **11.13.1**).

Indicate that the name of a person is an undifferentiated name (see **8.11**) if the additional identifying elements to differentiate the name cannot be readily ascertained.

8.7 Variant Access Points Representing Persons, Families, and Corporate Bodies

When constructing a variant access point to represent a person, family, or corporate body, use a variant name for the person (see **9.2.3**), family (see **10.2.3**), or corporate body (see **11.2.3**) as the basis for the access point.

Make additions to the access point, if considered important for identification. Apply the following instructions on making additions, as applicable:

additions to names of persons (see **9.19.1**)
additions to names of families (see **10.11.1**)
additions to names of corporate bodies (see **11.13.1**).

8.8 Scope of Usage

8.8.1 Basic Instructions on Recording Scope of Usage

8.8.1.1 Scope

Scope of usage is the type or form of work associated with the name chosen as the preferred name for a person, family, or corporate body.

8.8.1.2 Sources of Information

Take information on scope of usage from any source.

8.8.1.3 Recording Scope of Usage

Record information about the scope of usage of the name chosen as the preferred name for the person, family, or corporate body.

Name used in poetry and critical works
Scope of usage of the name C. Day Lewis

Name used in detective novels
Scope of usage of the name Nicholas Blake, *pseudonym of C. Day Lewis*

8.9 Date of Usage

8.9.1 Basic Instructions on Recording Date of Usage

8.9.1.1 Scope

Date of usage is a date or range of dates associated with the use of the name chosen as the preferred name for a person.

8.9.1.2 Sources of Information

Take information on date of usage from any source.

8.9.1.3 Recording Date of Usage

Record information about the date of usage of the name chosen as the preferred name for the person.

1933–2000
Date of usage of the name Howard Fast

1960–1986
Date of usage of the name E.V. Cunningham, *pseudonym of Howard Fast*

8.10 Status of Identification

8.10.1 Basic Instructions on Recording the Status of Identification

8.10.1.1 Scope

The ***status of identification*** is an indication of the level of authentication of the data identifying a person, family, or corporate body.

8.10.1.2 Sources of Information

Take information on the status of identification from any source.

8.10.1.3 Recording the Status of Identification

Record the status of identification using an appropriate term from the following list:

fully established
provisional
preliminary

Apply the terms listed as follows:

a) Record *fully established* if the data is sufficient to fully establish an authorized access point representing the person, family, or corporate body.

b) Record *provisional* if the data is insufficient to establish satisfactorily an authorized access point representing the person, family, or corporate body.

c) Record *preliminary* if the data is taken from the description of a resource when the resource itself is not available.

provisional

8.11 Undifferentiated Name Indicator

8.11.1 Basic Instructions on Recording an Undifferentiated Name Indicator

8.11.1.1 Scope

An ***undifferentiated name indicator*** is a categorization indicating that the core elements recorded are insufficient to differentiate between two or more persons with the same name.

8.11.1.2 Sources of Information

Take information on undifferentiated names from any source.

8.11.1.3 Recording an Undifferentiated Name Indicator

If the core elements recorded are insufficient to differentiate between two or more persons identified by the same name, record *undifferentiated.*

8.12 Source Consulted

8.12.1 Basic Instructions on Recording Sources Consulted

8.12.1.1 Scope

A ***source consulted*** is a resource used in determining the name or other identifying attributes of a person, family, or corporate body.

8.12.1.2 Sources of Information

Take information on sources consulted from any source.

8.12.1.3 Recording Sources Consulted

Cite sources used to determine a preferred or variant name, followed by a brief statement of the information found. Identify the specific location within the source where the information was found.

> Advances in cable-supported bridges, ©2006: back cover (papers presented at the 5th International Cable-Supported Bridge Operators' Conference, held in New York City on August 28–29, 2006)
>
> Rodgers, Sam. Opinions of military personnel on sexual minorities in the military, ©2006: PDF title page (Michael D. Palm Center)
>
> Her Big book of baby names, ©1982, title page: Sandra Buzbee Bailey
>
> Its Annual report, 1960, title page: Raytheon; page 4 of cover: Raytheon Company

When appropriate, indicate the source where the information was found for other identifying attributes of a person (see **9.3–9.18**), a family (see **10.3–10.10**), or a corporate body (see **11.3–11.12**).

> Wallace, W. Stewart. A dictionary of North American authors deceased before 1950, 1951: Smith, Abner Comstock; lawyer; born Randolph, Vt., 1814; died Litchfield, Minn., September 20, 1880
>
> E-mail from author, 10 July 2002 (Alison Charlotte Stewart, born 2 April 1953)
>
> Internet movie database, viewed on October 16, 2007 (Toni Collette; birth name Antonia Collette; born 1 November 1972, Sydney, N.S.W.; Australian actress; resides in Sydney, owns second home in Ireland)

Oxford dictionary of national biography, via WWW, viewed July 22, 2008: Nichols family (per. c.1760–1939), printers and publishers, editors of the Gentleman's magazine, and known especially for their books on local history and antiquarian scholarship, came to prominence in the late eighteenth century with the gifted John Nichols (1745–1826), printer and writer

Michael D. Palm Center home page, viewed March 2, 2007 (Michael D. Palm Center, a new research institute at the University of California, Santa Barbara) about us page (Palm Center, formerly the Center for the Study of Sexual Minorities in the Military; official unit of the Institute for Social, Behavioral, and Economic Research)

Union list of artist names online, viewed on July 28, 2008 (London Stereoscopic Co.; English photography studio and publisher, active 1854–ca. 1900; variants: London Stereoscopic & Photo Co., London Stereoscopic and Photo Co., London Stereoscopic and Photographic Company, London Stereoscopic Company)

Catalogue Bn-Opale plus, via WWW, March 11, 2009. Authorized access point: Colette (1873–1954); variant access points: Willy, Colette (1873–1954); Colette, Gabrielle Sidonie (1873–1954); Colette, Sidonie Gabrielle (1873–1954); nationality: France; language: French; gender: female; roles: author, performer; birth date: 1873–01–28; death date: 1954–08–03

Cite other sources that were consulted but provided no useful information in establishing the preferred name. Record *No information found* following the citation for the source consulted.

Who's who in France, 2006/07 (No information found)

AMICUS database, searched December 5, 2006 (No information found)
Geographical names of Canada website, searched December 5, 2006 (No information found)
GEOnet names server, searched December 5, 2006 (No information found)

8.13 Cataloguer's Note

8.13.1 Basic Instructions on Making Cataloguer's Notes

8.13.1.1 Scope

A ***cataloguer's note*** is an annotation that might be helpful to those using or revising the authorized access point representing a person, family, or corporate body, or creating an authorized access point representing a related person, family, or corporate body.

8.13.1.2 Sources of Information

Take information for use in cataloguer's notes from any source.

8.13.1.3 Making Cataloguer's Notes

Make the following notes, if considered important for clarification or justification:

a) notes on the specific instructions applied in creating the authorized access point

b) notes justifying the choice of preferred name, the form of the access point, etc.

c) notes limiting the use of the access point

d) notes differentiating persons, families, or corporate bodies with similar names.

> French form of given name chosen for authorized access point; works published in U.S. have English form, Isidor
>
> Author prefers that Chinese form of name (Li Zhongqing) be used in access points for resources in Chinese and that English form (James Z. Lee) be used for resources in English
>
> Do not use Luftwaffe in an access point for air force units prior to 1933; use instead "Germany. Heer. Luftstreitkräfte" to cover the period 1910–1920
>
> For resources issued before the latter part of 1950 use Housing Authority of the City of Seattle; for resources issued in late 1950 or after use Seattle Housing Authority
>
> Not to be considered a corporate body. "Museo vaticano" and "Musei vaticani" (Vatican Museum and Vatican Museums) are generic terms which refer to at least nine museums and galleries in Vatican City. Only specific museums, e.g., Museo gregoriano etrusco, should be treated as corporate bodies
>
> This access point is not valid for use as a subject. For works about this place use: Sri Lanka
>
> Not the same as: Imray, James (nr 93026430)
>
> Cannot identify with: Smith, Alan Jay (n 80115098)
>
> Do not confuse with: Council of the European Union; or: Council of Europe
>
> Formerly on undifferentiated name record: n 2007014866

Make any other notes that might be helpful to a cataloguer using or revising the authorized access point, or creating an authorized access point for a related person, family, or corporate body.

> Coded "provisional" because Uzbek form of name unavailable
>
> Coded "provisional" because unable to ascertain whether Trần Trung Phương is a variant name or a separate identity
>
> Different forms of name are regularly appearing on publications issued by this body; treat different forms of name as variant names until proof of a name change

9

IDENTIFYING PERSONS

9.0 Purpose and Scope

This chapter provides general guidelines and instructions on:

a) choosing preferred names for persons (see **9.2.2**)

b) recording preferred and variant names for persons (see **9.2**)

c) recording other identifying attributes of persons (see **9.3–9.18**)

d) constructing authorized access points representing persons (see **9.19.1**)

e) constructing variant access points representing persons (see **9.19.2**).

The chapter provides guidelines on recording names and other identifying attributes as separate elements, as parts of access points, or as both.

The preferred name for the person is used as the basis for the authorized access point. The variant name or names for the person are used as the basis for variant access points. Other identifying attributes of the person may also be included in the access point.

Persons include persons named in sacred scriptures or apocryphal books, fictitious and legendary persons, and real non-human entities.

Appendix **F** includes additional instructions on recording names of persons in the following categories:

names in the Arabic alphabet (see **F.1**)
Burmese and Karen names (see **F.2**)
Chinese names containing a non-Chinese given name (see **F.3**)
Icelandic names (see **F.4**)
Indic names (see **F.5**)
Indonesian names (see **F.6**)
Malay names (see **F.7**)
Roman names (see **F.8**)
Romanian names containing a patronymic (see **F.9**)
Thai names (see **F.10**)
names in various languages that include an article and/or preposition (see **F.11**).

9.1 General Guidelines on Identifying Persons

9.1.1 Sources of Information

Take the name or names of the person from any source.

For additional guidance on sources of information for the preferred name for the person, see **9.2.2.2**.

Take information on other identifying attributes of the person from any source.

9.1.2 Using Access Points to Represent Persons

An authorized access point is one of the techniques used to represent either a person associated with a resource (see **18.4.1**) or a related person (see **30.1**).

When constructing authorized access points representing persons, apply the guidelines at **9.19.1**.

When constructing variant access points representing persons, apply the guidelines at **9.19.2**.

9.2 Name of the Person

CORE ELEMENT

Preferred name for the person is a core element. Variant names for the person are optional.

9.2.1 Basic Instructions on Recording Names of Persons

9.2.1.1 Scope

A ***name of the person*** is a word, character, or group of words and/or characters by which a person is known.

When identifying persons, there are two categories of names:

a) preferred name for the person (see **9.2.2**)

b) variant name for the person (see **9.2.3**).

9.2.1.2 Sources of Information

Take the name or names of the person from any source.

For additional guidance on sources of information for the preferred name for the person, see **9.2.2.2**.

9.2.1.3 General Guidelines on Recording Names of Persons

When recording a name of a person, apply the general guidelines on recording names at **8.5**. When those guidelines refer to an appendix, apply the additional instructions in that appendix, as applicable.

Choose a preferred name for the person by applying the instructions at **9.2.2.3** and **9.2.2.5–9.2.2.7**.

If an individual has more than one identity, choose a preferred name for each identity (see **9.2.2.8**).

Record the name chosen as the preferred name. Apply the instructions at **9.2.2.4** and **9.2.2.9–9.2.2.26**.

Names and forms of the name not chosen as the preferred name may be recorded as variant names (see **9.2.3**).

NAME

9.2.2 Preferred Name for the Person

CORE ELEMENT

9.2.2.1 Scope

The ***preferred name for the person*** is the name or form of name chosen to identify the person. It is also the basis for the authorized access point representing that person.

9.2.2.2 Sources of Information

Determine the preferred name for a person from the following sources (in order of preference):

a) the preferred sources of information (see **2.2.2**) in resources associated with the person

b) other formal statements appearing in resources associated with the person

c) other sources (including reference sources).

When the name of a person appears in more than one language, see additional instructions at **9.2.2.5.2**. When the name is found in a script that is not a preferred script of the agency creating the data, see **9.2.2.5.3**.

9.2.2.3 Choosing the Preferred Name

When choosing the preferred name for the person, generally choose the name by which the person is commonly known. The name chosen can be the person's real name, pseudonym, title of nobility, nickname, initials, or other appellation.

When a person is known by more than one form of the same name, see additional instructions on choosing the preferred name at **9.2.2.5**.

When a person is known by more than one name, see additional instructions on choosing the preferred name at **9.2.2.6–9.2.2.8**.

Caedmon

William Shakespeare

D.W. Griffith
not David Wark Griffith

Tony Blair
not Anthony Charles Lynton Blair

Fats Domino
not Antoine Domino

Capability Brown
not Lancelot Brown

Anatole France
not Jacques-Anatole Thibault

Ouida
not Marie Louise de la Ramée

Ionicus
not Joshua Charles Armitage

H.D.
not Hilda Doolittle

Giorgione
not Giorgio Barbarelli

Fra Angelico
not Giovanni da Fiesole
not Guido da Siena

Maria Helena
not Maria Helena Vaquinhas de Carvalho

Duke of Wellington
not Arthur Wellesley

John Julius Norwich
not Viscount Norwich

Sister Mary Hilary

Sister Mary Joseph Cahill

9.2.2.4 Recording the Preferred Name

Record the name chosen as the preferred name for a person by applying the general guidelines at **8.5**.

If the name consists of several parts, record as the first element that part of the name under which the person would normally be listed in authoritative alphabetic lists in the person's language, country of residence, or country of activity. Record the other part or parts of the name following the first element. Apply the instructions at **9.2.2.9–9.2.2.26**, as applicable.

Exception

If a person's preference is known to be different from normal usage, follow that preference when choosing the part of the name to be recorded as the first element.

See appendix **F** for additional instructions on recording names of persons in the following categories:

names in the Arabic alphabet (see **F.1**)

Burmese and Karen names (see **F.2**)

Chinese names containing a non-Chinese given name (see **F.3**)

Icelandic names (see **F.4**)

Indic names (see **F.5**)

Indonesian names (see **F.6**)

Malay names (see **F.7**)

Roman names (see **F.8**)

Romanian names containing a patronymic (see **F.9**)

Thai names (see **F.10**)

names in various languages that include an article and/or preposition (see **F.11**).

CHOOSING THE PREFERRED NAME

9.2.2.5 Different Forms of the Same Name

If a person is known by more than one form of the same name, choose the preferred name by applying these instructions, as applicable:

fullness (see **9.2.2.5.1**)

language (see **9.2.2.5.2**)

names in a non-preferred script (see **9.2.2.5.3**)

spelling (see **9.2.2.5.4**).

9.2.2.5.1 Fullness

If the forms of a person's name vary in fullness, choose as the preferred name the form most commonly found.

J. Barbey d'Aurevilly

Most common form: J. Barbey d'Aurevilly. *Occasional forms:* Jules Barbey d'Aurevilly; Jules-Amédée Barbey d'Aurevilly. *Rare form:* J.-A. Barbey d'Aurevilly

Morris West

Most common form: Morris West. *Occasional form:* Morris L. West

Juan Valera

Most common form: Juan Valera. *Occasional form:* Juan Valera y Alcalá Galiano

I.C. McIlwaine

Most common form: I.C. McIlwaine. *Occasional forms:* Ia C. McIlwaine; Ia McIlwaine

If no one form predominates, choose the latest form as the preferred name. In case of doubt about which is the latest form, choose the fuller or fullest form.

Variant names. Record the other forms of the name as variant names (see **9.2.3.10**).

9.2.2.5.2 Language

If a person's name has appeared in different language forms in resources associated with the person, choose as the preferred name the form that corresponds to the language of most of the resources.

George Mikes
not György Mikes

Philippe Garigue
not Philip Garigue

Alternative

Choose a well-accepted form of name in a language and script preferred by the agency creating the data.

If the name does not appear in resources associated with the person, or in case of doubt, choose the form most commonly found in reference sources of the person's country of residence or activity.

Hildegard Knef
not Hildegarde Neff

If the form of name chosen is in a script that differs from a preferred script of the agency creating the data, apply the instructions at **9.2.2.5.3**.

Exceptions

Greek or Latin versus other forms. Different forms of the name are sometimes found in reference sources and/or in resources associated with the person. If the name of a person is found in a Greek or Latin form as well as in a form in the person's native or adopted language, choose as the preferred name the form most commonly found in reference sources.

Sixt Birck
not Xystus Betulius

Hugo Grotius
not Hugo de Groot

Philipp Melanchthon
not Philipp Schwarzerd

Friedrich Wilhelm Ritschl
not Fridericus Ritschelius

In case of doubt, choose the Greek or Latin form for persons who were active before, or mostly before, A.D. 1400. For persons active after that date, choose the form in the person's native or adopted language.

Guilelmus Apuliensis
not Guglielmo di Puglia
not Guillaume de Pouille
Active in 12th century

Giovanni da Padova
not Joannes de Padua
Died 1499

Established form in a language preferred by the agency creating the data. If the first element of a person's preferred name consists of a given name and/or a word or phrase associated with the person (see **9.2.2.18**), determine the well-established form or forms of the name in reference sources. If there is a well-established form of the name in a language preferred by the agency creating the data, choose that form of name as the preferred name.[1]

Francis of Assisi
not Francesco d'Assisi

Benedict XVI
not Benedictus XVI

Charles V
not Karl V
not Carlos I
not Charles-Quint

Philip II
not Felipe II

John III Sobieski
not Jan III Sobieski

In case of doubt, choose the form in the person's native or adopted language or the Latin form.

Thérèse de Lisieux
not Theresa of Lisieux

1. For additional instructions on choosing the preferred name for a Roman of classical times, see appendix F (**F.8**).

Variant names. Record the other forms of the name as variant names (see **9.2.3.9**).

9.2.2.5.3 Names Found in a Non-preferred Script

If the name of a person is found in a script that differs from a preferred script of the agency creating the data, transliterate the name according to the scheme chosen by the agency.

Laozi
Name appears in original script as: 老子

Li An
Name appears in original script as: 李安

Jamāl ʻAbd al-Nāṣir
Name appears in original script as: جمال عبد الناصر

Parvez Musharraf
Name appears in original script as: پرویز مشرّف

Yi Sŭng-man
Name appears in original script as: 李承晩

A. Skri͡abin
Name appears in original script as: А. Скрябин

Evgeniĭ Evtushenko
Name appears in original script as: Евгений Евтушенко

Shelomit Kohen-Asif
Name appears in original script as: שלומית כהן־אסיף

If a name is found in more than one non-preferred script, transliterate it according to the scheme for the original language of most of the works.

Muḥammad Riḍā al-Anṣārī al-Qummī
not Muḥammad Riẓā Anṣārī Qumī
Wrote primarily in Arabic but also in Persian

Premacanda
not Prem Cand
Wrote primarily in Hindi but also in Urdu

If the name of a person is found only in a transliterated form in resources associated with the person, choose the transliterated form as the preferred name.

If the name of a person is found in more than one transliterated form in resources associated with the person, choose the form that occurs most frequently.

Variant names. Record the other forms of the transliterated name as variant names (see **9.2.3.9**).

> ***Alternative***
>
> If there is a well-established form of name in reference sources in a language preferred by the agency creating the data, choose that form of name as the preferred name.
>
> If different forms are found in reference sources in a language preferred by the agency creating the data, choose the form that occurs most frequently.
>
> Ang Lee
> *Name appears in original script as:* 李安
>
> Gamal Abdel Nasser
> *Name appears in original script as:* جمال عبد الناصر
>
> Pervez Musharraf
> *Name appears in original script as:* پرویز مشرّف
>
> Syngman Rhee
> *Name appears in original script as:* 李承晩
>
> A. Scriabin
> *Name appears in original script as:* А. Скрябин
>
> Yevgeny Yevtushenko
> *Name appears in original script as:* Евгений Евтушенко
>
> Moshe Dayan
> *Name appears in original script as:* משה דיין
>
> Shlomit Cohen-Assif
> *Name appears in original script as:* שלומית כהן־אסיף

9.2.2.5.4 Spelling

If:

variant spellings of a person's name are found

and

these variations are not the result of different transliterations

then:

choose the form of name found in the first resource received.

For spelling differences resulting from different transliterations, see **9.2.2.5.3**.

Variant names. Record the other spellings of the name as variant names (see **9.2.3.9**).

9.2.2.6 Different Names for the Same Person

If a person is known by more than one name, choose the name by which the person is clearly most commonly known.

If a person has changed his or her name, see **9.2.2.7**.

If a person has more than one identity, see **9.2.2.8**.

Otherwise, choose the preferred name according to the following order of preference:

a) the name that appears most frequently in resources associated with the person

b) the name that appears most frequently in reference sources

c) the latest name.

Variant names. Record the other names by which the person is known as variant names (see **9.2.3**).

9.2.2.7 Change of Name

If a person has changed his or her name, choose the latest name or form of name as the preferred name. Apply the same instruction for a person who has acquired and become known by a title of nobility (see also **9.2.2.17**).

If a person has more than one identity, apply instead the instructions at **9.2.2.8**.

Dorothy B. Hughes
not Dorothy Belle Flanagan
Name used in works before author's marriage

Sister Mary Just
not F.D. David
Name used in works before author entered a religious order

Éloi-Gérard Talbot
not Frère Éloi-Gérard
Name without surname originally used in works

Yosano Akiko
not Hō Akiko
Name used in works before author's marriage

Joan Roughgarden
not Jonathan Roughgarden
Name used in works before author's sex change

Jacqueline Kennedy Onassis
not Jacqueline Bouvier
not Jacqueline Bouvier Kennedy
Names used before marriage and during first marriage

Ford Madox Ford
not Ford Madox Hueffer
Name changed from Hueffer to Ford

Muhammad Ali
not Cassius Clay
Name changed from Cassius Clay to Muhammad Ali

Earl of Longford
not Baron Pakenham
not Francis Aungier Pakenham
Known successively by personal name, title as baron, and title as earl

Exception

If there is reason to believe that an earlier name will persist as the name by which the person is better known, choose that name as the preferred name.

Benjamin Disraeli
not Earl of Beaconsfield
Title acquired late in life; better known by earlier name

Caroline Kennedy
not Caroline Kennedy Schlossberg
Better known by name before marriage

9.2.2.8 Individuals with More Than One Identity

If an individual has more than one identity, choose the name associated with each identity as the preferred name for that identity.

If an individual uses one or more pseudonyms (including joint pseudonyms), consider the individual to have more than one identity.

If an individual uses his or her real name as well as one or more pseudonyms, consider the individual to have more than one identity.

J.I.M. Stewart
Real name used in "serious" novels and critical works

Michael Innes
Pseudonym used by J.I.M. Stewart in detective novels

C. Day Lewis
Real name used in poetic and critical works

Nicholas Blake
Pseudonym used by C. Day Lewis in detective novels

Charles L. Dodgson
Real name used in works on mathematics and logic

Lewis Carroll
Pseudonym used by Charles L. Dodgson in literary works

Molly Keane
Real name used in some works

M.J. Farrell
Pseudonym used by Molly Keane in some works

Denys Watkins-Pitchford
Real name used in some works

BB
Pseudonym used by Denys Watkins-Pitchford in some works

M.W. Ranney
Real name used in most works

Keith Johnson
Pseudonym used by M.W. Ranney in some works

John McDermott
Pseudonym used by M.W. Ranney in some works

John W. Palmer
Pseudonym used by M.W. Ranney in some works

Doris Lessing
Real name used in most works

Jane Somers
Pseudonym used by Doris Lessing in two works

Kingsley Amis
Real name used in most works

Robert Markham
Pseudonym used by Kingsley Amis in one work

William Tanner
Pseudonym used by Kingsley Amis in one work

Howard Fast
Real name used in some works

E.V. Cunningham
Pseudonym used by Howard Fast in some works

Ann Kilborn Cole
Pseudonym used by Claire Wallis Callahan in works on antiques and other nonfiction works

Nancy Hartwell
Pseudonym used by Claire Wallis Callahan in literary works; real name not used

Wade Miller
Wade Miller *is the joint pseudonym of Bill Miller and Bob Wade*

Zizou Corder
Zizou Corder *is the joint pseudonym of Louisa Young and Isabel Adomakoh Young*

Ellery Queen
Ellery Queen *is the joint pseudonym of Frederic Dannay and Manfred B. Lee*

T.W.O.
Initials are the joint pseudonym of Mary C. Hungerford and Virginia C. Young

Exception

If an individual uses only one pseudonym and does not use his or her real name as a creator or contributor, choose the pseudonym as the preferred name. ***Variant names.*** Record the individual's real name as a variant name (see **9.2.3.4**).

John Le Carré
not David John Moore Cornwell

George Orwell
not Eric Arthur Blair

Martin Ross
not Violet Florence Martin

Nevil Shute
not Nevil Shute Norway

Woody Allen
not Allen Stewart Konigsberg

50 Cent
not Curtis Jackson

Futabatei Shimei
not Hasegawa Tatsunosuke

Variant names. Record as a variant name a name that was not chosen as the preferred name for an identity (see **9.2.3**).

If an individual has more than one identity, record the relationships between these separate identities. Apply the instructions in chapter **30** (related persons).

RECORDING NAMES CONTAINING A SURNAME

9.2.2.9 General Guidelines on Recording Names Containing a Surname

The instructions at **9.2.2.9–9.2.2.12** apply to all names containing a surname (or a name that functions as a surname).

For surnames of former members of royal houses, see **9.2.2.13**.

Exceptions

If a person uses a title of nobility rather than a surname in his or her works, apply instead the instructions at **9.2.2.14**.

If a person is listed in reference sources under a title of nobility, apply instead the instructions at **9.2.2.14**.

If both the surname and given names are represented by initials, apply instead the instructions at **9.2.2.21**.

For Thai names containing a surname, apply the instructions at **F.10**.

Record a name containing a surname by applying the general guidelines on recording names at **8.5**.

Record the surname as the first element.

a) If a name consists of a surname preceded by other parts of the name, such as given names, record the surname and follow it by a comma and the parts of the name that precede it.

b) If a name consists of a surname followed by other parts of the name, record the surname and follow it by a comma and the parts of the name that follow it.

c) If the name consists only of a surname, record the surname alone.

Bernhardt, Sarah

Byatt, A. S.

Ching, Francis K. W.

Chiang, Kai-shek
Name: Chiang Kai-shek. *Surname:* Chiang

Molnár, Ferenc
Name: Molnár Ferenc. *Surname:* Molnár

Trịnh, Vân Thanh
Name: Trịnh Vân Thanh. *Surname:* Trịnh

Mantovani

Omit terms of honour and terms of address from any name that includes a surname unless:

a) the name consists only of a surname (see **9.2.2.9.3**)
or
b) the name is of a married person identified only by a partner's name and a term of address (see **9.2.2.9.4**).

Apply the additional instructions at **9.2.2.9.1–9.2.2.9.6**, as applicable.

9.2.2.9.1 Surname Represented by an Initial

If:
a surname is represented by an initial
and
one or more other parts of the name are given in full
then:
record the initial that represents the surname as the first element.

G., Michael

9.2.2.9.2 Part of the Name Treated as a Surname

If:

the name does not contain a surname

and

the name contains a part that identifies the individual and functions as a surname

then:

record the part that functions as a surname as the first element, followed by a comma and the rest of the name.

Hus, Jan

Maḥfūẓ, Ḥusayn ʻAlī

Bāqūrī, ʻAbd al-ʻĀl
not ʻAbd al-ʻĀl al-Bāqūrī

Ali, Muhammad
The American boxer

X, Malcolm

Kurd ʻAlī, Muḥammad

See appendix **F** for additional instructions on names in the Arabic alphabet (**F.1**) and certain Indonesian (**F.6**) and Malay names (**F.7**).

9.2.2.9.3 Persons Known by a Surname Only

If:

the name by which a person is known consists of a surname only

and

the surname is associated with a word or phrase, either in resources that are associated with the person or in reference sources

then:

treat the word or phrase associated with the name as an integral part of the name. Record the surname, followed by a comma and the word or phrase.

Deidier, abbé

Read, Miss

Seuss, Dr.

Nichols, Grandma

Variant names. Record the name in direct order as a variant name (see **9.2.3.10**).

9.2.2.9.4 Married Person Identified Only by a Partner's Name

If a married person is identified only by a partner's name, treat a term of address as an integral part of the name. Record the term of address following the part of the partner's name that is recorded as the last element in that name.

Davis, Maxwell, Mrs.

La Ferrière, Balthasard de, Madame

Strauss, Johann, Frau

Lâm, Thanh Liêm, Bà

Tobi-van der Kop, H., Mevr.

Include a suffix attached to the name of a married woman as part of her name.

Falvy, Zoltánné

Beniczkyné Bajza, Lenke

9.2.2.9.5 Words, Etc., Indicating Relationship Following Surnames

For Portuguese surnames, record *Filho*, *Junior*, *Neto*, *Netto*, or *Sobrinho* as part of the surname.

Castro Sobrinho, Antonio Ribeiro de

Marques Junior, Milton

For languages other than Portuguese, record similar terms (e.g., *Jr.*, *Sr.*, *fils*, *père*) and numbers (e.g., *III*) following the person's given name or names, preceded by a comma.

Saur, Karl-Otto, Jr.

Dumas, Alexandre, père

Hatfield, Frederick C., II

9.2.2.9.6 Saints

Do not include the term *Saint* as part of the name of a canonized person whose name contains a surname. Record the term as a designation associated with the person (see **9.6.1.4**).

More, Thomas

9.2.2.10 Compound Surnames

Treat a surname as a ***compound surname*** if it consists of two or more proper names separated by either a space or a hyphen. Apply also to names that have the appearance of compound surnames. Record the names by applying the general guidelines on recording surnames at **9.2.2.9**.

Take regular or occasional initializing of a part preceding a surname as an indication that the part is not used as part of the surname.

Apply these additional instructions, as applicable:

established usage (see **9.2.2.10.1**)

or

established usage not determined (see **9.2.2.10.2**).

Variant names. Record as variant names forms of the name using other parts of the compound surname as the first element (see **9.2.3.10**).

9.2.2.10.1 Established Usage

Record as the first element the part of the compound surname by which the person prefers to be listed. If this is unknown, record as the first element the part of the name under which the person is listed in reference sources[2] in the person's language or country of residence or activity.

Brindle, Reginald Smith
Family name is Smith Brindle *but author prefers to be listed under Brindle*

Fénelon, François de Salignac de La Mothe-
Listed in French reference sources under Fénelon

Lloyd George, David
Paternal surname: George

Seabra da Silva, José de
Listed in Portuguese reference sources under Seabra da Silva

Stowe, Harriet Beecher
Listed in American reference sources under Stowe

Abril, Nelson Lopez
Name appears on chief source of information as: Nelson Lopez Abril. *Name appears in copyright statement as:* Nelson L. Abril

Szentpál, Mária Sz.
Name appears as: Sz. Szentpál Mária. *Husband's surname:* Szilági

Campbell, Julia Morilla de
Name sometimes appears as: Julia M. de Campbell

---

2. Disregard reference sources that list compound surnames in a uniform style regardless of preference or customary usage.

9.2.2.10.2 Established Usage Not Determined

The preference of the person is sometimes unknown. Also, established usage sometimes cannot be determined in reference sources in the person's language or from the person's country of residence or activity. When this occurs, follow the usage for the person's country of residence as specified in *Names of Persons: National Usages for Entry in Catalogues.*[3]

If the usage for the country of residence or activity of the person is not covered in *Names of Persons: National Usages for Entry in Catalogues*, record the first part of the surname as the first element.

---

3. 4th revised and enlarged edition (München: Saur, 1996).

9.2.2.11 Surnames with Separately Written Prefixes

If a surname has one or more separately written prefixes, apply the general guidelines on recording surnames at **9.2.2.9**.

Apply these additional instructions, as applicable:

articles and prepositions (see **9.2.2.11.1**)

or

other prefixes (see **9.2.2.11.2**).

Variant names. Record as a variant name a form using another part as the first element (see **9.2.3.10**). The first element of the variant name can be another part of the prefix or the part of the name following the prefix.

9.2.2.11.1 Articles and Prepositions

If a surname includes an article or preposition, or a combination of the two, record as the first element the part most commonly used as the first element. Determine common usage by consulting alphabetically arranged lists in the person's language or from the person's country of residence or activity. See appendix **F** for additional guidance on recording such names in the following languages and language groups:

Afrikaans (see **F.11.1**)
Czech and Slovak (see **F.11.2**)
Dutch and Flemish (see **F.11.3**)
English (see **F.11.4**)
French (see **F.11.5**)
German (see **F.11.6**)
Italian (see **F.11.7**)
Portuguese (see **F.11.8**)
Romanian (see **F.11.9**)
Scandinavian (Danish, Norwegian, Swedish) (see **F.11.10**)
Spanish (see **F.11.11**).

The form of name listed in reference sources in the person's language or from the person's country of residence may possibly be in a non-standard form. Nevertheless, record as the first element the part of the name used as the first element in those sources.

If a person has used two or more languages, record the name by applying the instructions for the language of most of that person's works.

In case of doubt, apply the following instructions in this order of preference:

a) apply the instructions for a language preferred by the agency creating the data if that is one of the languages used by the person

b) if the person is known to have changed his or her country of residence, apply the instructions for the language of the person's adopted country

c) apply the instructions for the language of the name.

Variant names. Record as a variant name a form using another part as the first element (see **9.2.3.10**). The first element of the variant name can be another part of the prefix or the part of the name following the prefix.

9.2.2.11.2 Other Prefixes

If the prefix is neither an article, nor a preposition, nor a combination of the two, record the prefix as the first element.

ʻAbd al-Ḥamīd Aḥmad

Abū Zahrah, Muḥammad

Āl Yāsīn, Muḥammad Ḥasan

Ap Gwilym, Owain

Ben Harosh, Mosheh

Fitz Gerald, Gregory

Mac Murchaidh, Ciarán

Ó Faoláin, Dónal

Variant names. Record as a variant name a form using the part of the name following the prefix as the first element (see **9.2.3.10**).

9.2.2.12 Prefixes Hyphenated or Combined with Surnames

Record a name containing a prefix that is hyphenated or combined with a surname by applying the general guidelines on recording surnames at **9.2.2.9**.

If the prefix is regularly or occasionally hyphenated or combined with the surname, record the prefix as the first element.

FitzGerald, Colin

MacDonald, William

Ter-Horst, Joannes Hermannus

Debure, Guillaume

Fon-Lampe, A. A.

Variant names. Record as a variant name a form using the part of the name following the prefix as the first element (see **9.2.3.10**).

9.2.2.13 Surnames of Former Members of Royal Houses

For a member of a royal house no longer identified as royalty (e.g., the house is no longer reigning or the person has lost or renounced the throne), record a name containing a surname (or a name that functions as a surname). Apply the general guidelines on recording surnames at **9.2.2.9**.

For names of royal persons, see **9.2.2.20**.

Record the surname as the first element. If there is no surname, record as the first element the part of the name that is used to identify the person in resources or in reference sources (e.g., name of the house or dynasty, territorial title).

Bernadotte, Folke

Habsburg, Otto von

Paris, Henri

Saxe-Coburg-Gotha, Simeon

Zur Lippe, Rudolf

Record titles that the person still uses by applying the instructions at **9.4.1.5**.

Variant names. Record the earlier name as a variant name (see **9.2.3.7**).

RECORDING NAMES CONTAINING A TITLE OF NOBILITY

9.2.2.14 General Guidelines on Recording Names Containing a Title of Nobility

Record a name containing a title of nobility by applying the general guidelines on recording names at **8.5**. Guidelines on recording names containing a title of nobility also apply to names containing a courtesy title of nobility.

Record the proper name as the first element of the name if the person:

a) uses his or her title rather than surname in resources with which he or she is associated

or

b) is listed under his or her title in reference sources.[4]

Follow the proper name in the title by the personal name in direct order. Exclude unused given names.

Follow the personal name with the term of rank in the language in which it was conferred (see appendix **G**). Precede the personal name and the part of the title denoting rank by commas.

Omit the surname and term of rank if the person does not use a term of rank or a substitute for it.

Abrantès, Laure Junot, duchesse d'

Byron, George Gordon Byron, Baron

Bolingbroke, Henry St. John, Viscount

Caradon, Hugh Foot, Baron

Cavour, Camillo Benso, conte di

Cumberland, William Augustus, Duke of

Dufferin and Ava, Harriot Georgina Blackwood, Marchioness of

Pompadour, Jeanne Antoinette Poisson, marquise de

Willoughby de Broke, John Henry Peyto Verney, Baron

Winchilsea, Anne Kingsmill Finch, Countess of

Corberon, Nicolas de

Name appears as: Nicolas de Corberon, seigneur de Tourvilliers. *Reference sources list name as:* Corberon, Nicolas de

Norwich, John Julius

Name appears as: John Julius Norwich. *Author does not use his title of nobility*

Variant names. Record as a variant name a form using the surname as the first element (see **9.2.3.10**). Do not record it if the proper name in the title is the same as the surname.

9.2.2.14.1 Saints

Do not include the term *Saint* as part of the name of a canonized person known by a title of nobility. Record the term as a designation associated with the person (see **9.6.1.4**).

4. Disregard reference sources that list members of the nobility either all under title or all under surname.

9.2.2.15 Titles in the United Kingdom Peerage That Include a Territorial Designation

Record a name containing a title in the United Kingdom peerage that includes a territorial designation by applying the general guidelines at **9.2.2.14** (recording names containing a title of nobility).

If the territorial designation is an integral part of the title, include it as part of the name.

Moore of Drogheda, Alice Moore, Viscountess

Russell of Liverpool, Edward Frederick Langley Russell, Baron

If it is not an integral part of the title, or if there is doubt that it is, omit it.

Hardinge, Henry Hardinge, Viscount
not Hardinge of Lahore, Henry Hardinge, Viscount

9.2.2.16 Judges of the Scottish Court of Session with a Law Title Beginning with *Lord*

If a judge of the Scottish Court of Session has a law title beginning with *Lord*, apply the general guidelines at **9.2.2.14** (recording names containing a title of nobility).

Kames, Henry Home, Lord

9.2.2.17 Disclaimed and Newly Acquired Titles

If:

a person acquires a title of nobility
or
a person disclaims a title of nobility
or
a person acquires a new title of nobility

then:

choose the preferred name by applying the instructions at **9.2.2.7**. Record the preferred name by applying the instructions at **9.2.2.14–9.2.2.15**, as applicable.

Caradon, Hugh Foot, Baron
Previously Hugh Foot

George-Brown, George Alfred Brown, Baron
Previously George Brown

Grigg, John
Previously Baron Altrincham; *peerage disclaimed*

Hailsham of St. Marylebone, Quintin Hogg, Baron
Originally Quintin Hogg; *became* Viscount Hailsham, *1950; peerage disclaimed, 1963; became* Baron Hailsham of St. Marylebone, *1970*

RECORDING NAMES CONTAINING NEITHER A SURNAME NOR A TITLE OF NOBILITY

9.2.2.18 General Guidelines on Recording Names Containing Neither a Surname nor a Title of Nobility

If:

a person is identified by a name that does not include a surname
and
this person is not identified by a title of nobility

then:

record the name by which the person is identified by applying the general guidelines at **8.5**.

Charles

Nelly

Riverbend

Record as the first element the part of the name under which the person is listed in reference sources. In case of doubt, record the last part of the name as the first element. Apply the instructions at **9.2.2.9.2**.

If a person is commonly associated with a place of origin or domicile, an occupation, or other characteristics (in resources associated with the person or in reference sources), include these words or phrases as an integral part of the name. Precede such words or phrases by a comma.

Paul, the Deacon

Eric, the Red

Salmān, al-Fārisī

Rafa, el Tuerto

Judah, ha-Levi

Chayim, the Priest, of Hebron

Iolo, Goch

Feofan, Grek

Baba, Rabbah

Joannes, Glastoniensis

Alexander, of Aphrodisias

Jeanne, de Flandre

Planudes, Maximus
Listed in reference sources under Planudes

Helena, Maria
Listed in reference sources under Helena

Treat a roman numeral associated with a given name as an integral part of the name (e.g., in the case of some popes, royalty, and ecclesiastics).

Elizabeth I

John Paul II

Maximos IV

Gregory II, of Cyprus

Variant names. Record as variant names, as appropriate:

forms using the associated words or phrases as the first element (see **9.2.3.10**)
other language forms of the name (see **9.2.3.9**)
other names by which the person is known (see **9.2.3.10**).

9.2.2.18.1 Saints

Do not include the term *Saint* as part of the name of a canonized person. Record the term as a designation associated with the person (see **9.6.1.4**).

Joan, of Arc

Paulinus II

9.2.2.19 Names Including a Patronymic

Record a name consisting of one or more given names and a ***patronymic*** by applying the general guidelines at **8.5**.

Record the first given name as the first element. Follow it by the rest of the name in direct order. If the patronymic precedes the first given name, transpose the parts of the name to bring the first given name into first position.

ʾAbé Gubañā
Given name: ʾAbé. *Patronymic:* Gubañā

Solomon Gebre Christos
Given name: Solomon. *Patronymic:* Gebre Christos

Kidāna Māryām Gétāhun
Given names: Kidāna Māryām. *Patronymic:* Gétāhun

Germāčaw Takla Ḥawāryāt
Given name: Germāčaw. *Patronymic:* Takla Ḥawāryāt

Isaac ben Aaron
Given name: Isaac. *Patronymic:* ben Aaron

Shirėndėv, B.
Name appears as: B. Shirėndėv. *Initial of patronymic:* B. *Given name:* Shirėndėv

Moses ben Jacob, of Coucy
Given name: Moses. *Patronymic:* ben Jacob. *Words denoting place:* of Coucy

See appendix **F** for additional instructions on patronymics contained in names in the Arabic alphabet (**F.1**) and in Icelandic (**F.4**) and Romanian names (**F.9**).

Variant names. Record as a variant name a form using the patronymic as the first element (see **9.2.3.10**).

9.2.2.20 Names of Royal Persons

Record names of royal persons by applying the general guidelines at **9.2.2.18** (recording names that contain neither a surname nor a title of nobility).

If the name by which a royal person is known includes the name of a royal house, dynasty, territorial designation, etc., or a surname, record the name in direct order. Record titles by applying the instructions at **9.4.1.4**.

John II Comnenus

Gustav VI Adolf

Louis Bonaparte

Chandragupta Maurya

Eleanor, of Aquitaine

Madhava Rao Sindhia

Ming Taizu

Shuja-ud-Daulah

RECORDING NAMES CONSISTING OF INITIALS, OR SEPARATE LETTERS, OR NUMERALS

9.2.2.21 General Guidelines on Recording Names Consisting of Initials, or Separate Letters, or Numerals

Record a name consisting of initials, or separate letters, or numerals, or consisting primarily of initials by applying the general guidelines at **8.5**.

Record the initials, letters, or numerals in direct order. Include any typographic devices when they appear as part of multi-letter abbreviations of a name, but omit them when they follow single-letter initials. Include any words or phrases associated with the initials, letters, or numerals as an integral part of the name.

H. D.

Q. E. D.

𝔄. 𝔖𝔥.

A. de D.

Th. D. S. A.

Gr. Os.

A! A! A!

A. B. C. D. E.

A G (F)

61648

3-2

20/1631

3PM

FF8282

8Ball

50 Cent

DJ Q

DJ 20/20

A. B—z

A-r Z-h

J. W.
Name appears as: J*** W*********

H., abbé
Name appears as: l'abbé H.

D. S., Master

RECORDING NAMES CONSISTING OF A PHRASE

9.2.2.22 General Guidelines on Recording Names Consisting of a Phrase

If:

a person is commonly identified by:

a) a phrase or appellation that does not contain a given name
or
b) a phrase that consists of a given name or names preceded by words other than a term of address or a title of position or office.

then:

consider this phrase or appellation to be the preferred name for the person. Record the phrase or appellation by applying the general guidelines on recording names at **8.5**. Record the name in direct order.

Dr. X

Mother Hen

Every Other Dad

Sister Friend

Poor Old No. 3

Buckskin Bill

Boy George

Little Richard

Miss Piggy

Happy Harry

Special Ed

D.J. Jazzy Jeff

Variant names. Record as a variant name a form using the given name as the first element followed by the initial word or words (see **9.2.3.10**).

A name consisting of a phrase sometimes has the appearance of a name consisting of a given name or initials, and a surname. When this occurs, record as the first element the word that has the appearance of a surname.

Other, A. N.

Pennypincher, A.

Peeved, I. M.

Nonyme, A.

Variant names. Record as a variant name the name in direct order (see **9.2.3.10**).

9.2.2.23 Phrase Consisting of a Given Name or Given Names Preceded by a Term of Address, Etc.

If a person is commonly identified by a phrase consisting of a given name preceded by a term of address or a title of position or office, consider this phrase to be the preferred name for the person. Record the phrase by applying the general guidelines on recording names at **8.5**.

Record the given name as the first element. Record words or phrases commonly associated with the person (e.g., those denoting place of origin, domicile, occupation, or other characteristics) by applying the instructions at **9.2.2.18**.

Jemima, Aunt

Claire, Tante

Sam, Cousin

Fez, Uncle

Robert, Chef

Vittoria, Signora

Variant names. Record as a variant name the name in direct order (see **9.2.3.10**).

9.2.2.24 Phrase Containing the Name of Another Person

If a person is commonly identified by a phrase that contains the name of another person, consider this phrase to be the preferred name for the person. Record the phrase by applying the general guidelines on recording names at **8.5**.

Record the phrase in direct order.

Pseudo-Brutus

Pseudo-Athanasius

Pseudo-Cotte

Veuve de Balthazar Arnoullet

Mother of Mary Lundie Duncan

Sister of the Late Major-Gen. Bolton

Mr. Latimer's Brother

9.2.2.25 Characterizing Word or Phrase

If a person is commonly identified by a characterizing word or phrase in resources associated with the person and in reference sources, consider this word or phrase to be the preferred name for the person. Record the word or phrase by applying the general guidelines on recording names at **8.5**.

Record the phrase in direct order.

A Physician
Statement of responsibility: by A Physician

A Military Chaplain
Statement of responsibility: by A Military Chaplain

A Teacher of Book-keeping
Statement of responsibility: by A Teacher of Book-keeping

The Daughter of a Wesleyan Minister
Statement of responsibility: by The Daughter of a Wesleyan Minister

Une femme de ménage
Statement of responsibility: par Une femme de ménage

Alternative

Omit an initial article (see appendix C) when recording a characterizing word or phrase.

Physician
Statement of responsibility: by A Physician

Military Chaplain
Statement of responsibility: by A Military Chaplain

Teacher of Book-keeping
Statement of responsibility: by A Teacher of Book-keeping

Daughter of a Wesleyan Minister
Statement of responsibility: by The Daughter of a Wesleyan Minister

Femme de ménage
Statement of responsibility: par Une femme de ménage

Variant names.

If:

a person is commonly identified by a real name or another name (see **9.2.2.6**)

and

a person is also identified by a word or phrase characterizing the person and this word or phrase has appeared in resources associated with the person

then:

record the word or phrase as a variant name (see **9.2.3.10**).

9.2.2.26 Phrase Naming Another Work by the Person

If a person is commonly identified by a phrase naming another work by the person in resources associated with the person and in reference sources, consider this phrase to be the preferred name for the person. Record the phrase by applying the general guidelines on recording names at **8.5**.

Record the phrase in direct order.

The Author of Honesty the best policy
Statement of responsibility: by The Author of Honesty the best policy

The Editor of The young gentleman's book
Statement of responsibility: by The Editor of The young gentleman's book

The Writer of The Lambton worm
Statement of responsibility: by The Writer of The Lambton worm

L'auteur de L'adresse au peuple breton
Statement of responsibility: par L'auteur de L'adresse au peuple breton

Alternative

Omit an initial article (see appendix C) when recording a phrase naming another work by the person.

Author of Honesty the best policy
Statement of responsibility: by The Author of Honesty the best policy

Editor of The young gentleman's book
Statement of responsibility: by The Editor of The young gentleman's book

Writer of The Lambton worm
Statement of responsibility: by The Writer of The Lambton worm

Auteur de L'adresse au peuple breton
Statement of responsibility: par L'auteur de L'adresse au peuple breton

Variant names. Record as a variant name a form using the title of the other work as the first element. Follow the title by a comma and the word or words that precede the title in the phrase (see **9.2.3.10**).

Variant names

If:
a person is commonly identified by a real name or another name (see **9.2.2.6**)
and
a person is also identified by a phrase including the title of another work and this phrase has appeared in resources associated with the person
then:
record the phrase as a variant name (see **9.2.3.10**).

9.2.3 Variant Name for the Person

9.2.3.1 Scope

A ***variant name for the person*** is a name or form of name by which a person is known that differs from the name or form of name chosen as the preferred name.

9.2.3.2 Sources of Information

Take variant names from resources associated with the person and/or from reference sources.

9.2.3.3 General Guidelines on Recording Variant Names for Persons

Record variant names for a person by applying the general guidelines on recording names at **8.5**.

Record a variant name when it is different from the name recorded as the preferred name. Record as a variant name:

a name or form of name used by a person

or

a name or form of name found in reference sources

or

a form of name resulting from a different transliteration of the name.

For persons who have two or more identities, see the instructions on recording relationships between related persons in chapter **30**.

Shaw, Bernie
Form recorded as preferred name: Shaw, Bernard

Sarkisian, Cherilyn
Form recorded as preferred name: Cher

Apply the specific instructions at **9.2.3.4–9.2.3.10**, as applicable. Also apply instructions about recording variant names at **9.2.2.5–9.2.2.26**, as applicable.

9.2.3.4 Real Name

If:

the preferred name or names for an individual are pseudonyms

and

the individual does not use his or her real name as a creator or contributor

and

the individual's real name is known

then:

record the individual's real name as a variant name for each pseudonym.

Cross, Marian Evans
Pseudonym recorded as preferred name: Eliot, George

Dudevant, Amandine-Aurore-Lucile
Pseudonym recorded as preferred name: Sand, George

Munro, Hector Hugh
Pseudonym recorded as preferred name: Saki

Jackson, Curtis
Pseudonym recorded as preferred name: 50 Cent

Callahan, Claire Wallis
Pseudonyms recorded as preferred names: Cole, Ann Kilborn *and* Hartwell, Nancy

9.2.3.5 Secular Name

If the preferred name for a person of religious vocation is the person's name in religion, record the person's secular name as a variant name.

Bojaxhiu, Agnes Gonxha
Name used in religion recorded as preferred name: Teresa, Mother

Samson, Annie Adèle
Name used in religion recorded as preferred name: Cécile-Marie, Sister, F.J.

Ratzinger, Joseph
Name used in religion recorded as preferred name: Benedict XVI

9.2.3.6 Name in Religion

If the preferred name for a person of religious vocation is the person's secular name, record the person's name in religion as a variant name.

Louis
Secular name recorded as preferred name: Merton, Thomas

Leonard
Secular name recorded as preferred name: Bacigalupo, Leonard

Seraphine
Secular name recorded as preferred name: Ireland, Seraphine

9.2.3.7 Earlier Name of Person

If the preferred name for a person is a name used after a change of name, record the person's earlier name or names as variant names.

Rodham, Hillary Diane
Later name recorded as preferred name: Clinton, Hillary Rodham

Kouyoumdjian, Dikran
Later name recorded as preferred name: Arlen, Michael

Foot, Hugh
Later name recorded as preferred name: Caradon, Hugh Foot, Baron

Edward VIII
Later name recorded as preferred name: Windsor, Edward, Duke of

Roughgarden, Jonathan
Later name recorded as preferred name: Roughgarden, Joan

9.2.3.8 Later Name of Person

If the preferred name for a person is a name used before a change of name, record the person's later name or names as variant names.

Nicholls, Charlotte
Earlier name recorded as preferred name: Brontë, Charlotte

Beaconsfield, Benjamin Disraeli, Earl of
Earlier name recorded as preferred name: Disraeli, Benjamin

Schlossberg, Caroline Kennedy
Earlier name recorded as preferred name: Kennedy, Caroline

9.2.3.9 Alternative Linguistic Form of Name

If the name recorded as the preferred name for a person has one or more alternative linguistic forms, record them as variant names.

Different Language Form

Domenico
Dominikus
Dominique
English language form recorded as preferred name: Dominic

Jeanne, d'Arc
English language form recorded as preferred name: Joan, of Arc

Mikes, György

English language form recorded as preferred name: Mikes, George

Ó Maonaigh, Cainneach

English language form recorded as preferred name: Mooney, Canice

Meister der Brugger Chronik von Flandern

English language form recorded as preferred name: Master of the Bruges Chronicle of Flanders

Chemingouaiē, Ernest
Haimingwei, Ouneisite
Haminghwāy, Arnist
Heminguwei, Ānesuto
Hemingvejs, Ernests
Hemingwei, Ŏnesŭt'ŭ
Himinghwāy, Arnist
Khemingueĭ, Ėrnest

English language form recorded as preferred name: Hemingway, Ernest

Benedetto XVI
Benedicto XVI
Benedictum XVI
Benedikt XVI
Benoît XVI
Binidīkt XVI

English language form recorded as preferred name: Benedict XVI

Different Script

Σοφοκλῆς

English language form recorded as preferred name: Sophocles

윤형복

Korean transliterated form recorded as preferred name: Yun, Hyŏng-bok

Чередниченко, Дмитро

Ukrainian transliterated form recorded as preferred name: Cherednychenko, Dmytro

गांधी, इंदिरा

Hindi transliterated form recorded as preferred name: Gandhi, Indira

ヘミングウェイ, アーネスト
헤밍웨이, 어네스트
海明威, 欧内斯特
Хемингуэй, Эрнест
המינגווי, ארנסט
העמינגוועי, ערנעסט
همنغواي، ارنست
همینگوی، ارنست

English language form recorded as preferred name: Hemingway, Ernest

Different Spelling

Ralegh, Walter
Rauleigh, Walter
Rawleigh, Walter
Rawley, Walter

Different spelling recorded as preferred name: Raleigh, Walter

Smyth, Rychard
Smythe, Richard
Different spelling recorded as preferred name: Smith, Richard

Cleary, Joanna
Different spelling recorded as preferred name: Cleary, Johanna

Georgi, Ivonne
Different spelling recorded as preferred name: Georgi, Yvonne

Different Transliteration

Shcharanskiĭ, Anatoliĭ
Sharanski̡, Anaṭoli
Different transliteration recorded as preferred name: Shcharansky, Anatoly

Musharraf, Parvez
Different transliteration recorded as preferred name: Musharraf, Pervez

Teng, Hsiao-pʻing
Different transliteration recorded as preferred name: Deng, Xiaoping

Zipper, Yaacov
Different transliteration recorded as preferred name: Ziper, Yaʻaḳov

9.2.3.10 Other Variant Name

Record other variant names and variant forms of the name not covered by **9.2.3.4–9.2.3.9**, if considered important for identification or access.

Family, Dynastic, Etc., Name of Ruler

Bonaparte, Napoléon
Name as emperor recorded as preferred name: Napoleon I

Bernadotte, Jean-Baptiste-Jules
Name as sovereign recorded as preferred name: Charles XIV John

Stuart, Mary
Name as sovereign recorded as preferred name: Mary

Name as Saint

Edward, the Confessor
Name as sovereign recorded as preferred name: Edward

Constantine
Name as emperor recorded as preferred name: Constantine I

Family Name of Saint

Yepes y Alvarez, Juan de
Name as saint recorded as preferred name: John of the Cross

Soubirous, Marie-Bernarde
Name as saint recorded as preferred name: Bernadette

Pierozzi, Antonio
Name as saint recorded as preferred name: Antoninus

Phrase Used to Name a Person

Bachelor Knight

City Bachelor

South-Carolinian
Real name recorded as preferred name: Simms, William Gilmore

Officer in the Fight
Real name recorded as preferred name: Crysly, James

Author of Memoirs of a fox-hunting man
Real name recorded as preferred name: Sassoon, Siegfried

Editor of The youth's casket
Real name recorded as preferred name: Brayman, James O.

Verfasser der Dramatischen Unterhaltungen
Verfasser des Postzugs
Real name recorded as preferred name: Ayrenhoff, Cornelius von

Widow of Reyner Wolfe
Widowe of Reginalde Wolffe
Real name recorded as preferred name: Wolfe, Joan

Vidua Francisci Regnault
Veuve de François Regnault
Real name recorded as preferred name: Boursette, Madeleine

Difference in Fullness of Name

Valera y Alcalá Galiano, Juan
Form recorded as preferred name: Valera, Juan

Obama, Barack Hussein, II
Form recorded as preferred name: Obama, Barack

Schiller, Johann Christoph Friedrich von
Form recorded as preferred name: Schiller, Friedrich von

Powell, Enoch
Form recorded as preferred name: Powell, J. Enoch

Embleton, G. A.
Form recorded as preferred name: Embleton, Gerry

Mebarak, Shakira
Mebarak R., Shakira
Mebarak Ripoll, Shakira Isabel
Form recorded as preferred name: Shakira

Full Form of Name Consisting of Initials

Worsley, Edward
Initials recorded as preferred name: E. W.

Tardey de Montravel, A. A.
Initials recorded as preferred name: T. D. M.

Different Part of a Compound Surname

Lewis, Daniel Day-
Form recorded as preferred name: Day-Lewis, Daniel

Saint-Hilaire, Étienne Geoffroy
Form recorded as preferred name: Geoffroy Saint-Hilaire, Étienne

Mori, Emilio Cotarelo y
Form recorded as preferred name: Cotarelo y Mori, Emilio

Spang Olsen, Ib
Form recorded as preferred name: Olsen, Ib Spang

Part of Surname Following a Prefix

Polnay, Peter de
Form recorded as preferred name: De Polnay, Peter

Hagen, Christine von
Form recorded as preferred name: Von Hagen, Christine

Annunzio, Gabriele d'
Form recorded as preferred name: D'Annunzio, Gabriele

Fontaine, Jean de la
Form recorded as preferred name: La Fontaine, Jean de

Laan, Ray vander
Form recorded as preferred name: Vander Laan, Ray

Costanzo, Angelo di
Form recorded as preferred name: Di Costanzo, Angelo

Part of Surname Following a Prefix Combined with Surname

Bure, Guillaume de
Form recorded as preferred name: Debure, Guillaume

Witt, Thomas A. de
Form recorded as preferred name: DeWitt, Thomas A.

Meer, Harriet vander
Form recorded as preferred name: VanderMeer, Harriet

Prefix to Surname

Von Hofmannsthal, Hugo
Form recorded as preferred name: Hofmannsthal, Hugo von

Van de Wetering, Janwillem
Form recorded as preferred name: Wetering, Janwillem van de

First Given Name of Person without Surname

Maria Helena
Form recorded as preferred name: Helena, Maria

ʻAlī ibn Muḥammad Abū Ḥayyān al-Tawḥīdī
Form recorded as preferred name: Abū Ḥayyān al-Tawḥīdī, ʻAlī ibn Muḥammad

ʻAbd al-ʻĀl al-Bāqūrī
Form recorded as preferred name: Bāqūrī, ʻAbd al-ʻĀl

Epithet or Byname

Aquinas, Thomas
Form recorded as preferred name: Thomas, Aquinas

Udine, Giovanni da
Form recorded as preferred name: Giovanni, da Udine

Catherine, the Great
Form recorded as preferred name: Catherine II

Edward, the Confessor
Form recorded as preferred name: Edward

Charles, the Lame
Form recorded as preferred name: Charles II

Frederick, Barbarossa
Form recorded as preferred name: Frederick I

Last Part of Name

Barry, Jeanne Bécu, comtesse du
Form recorded as preferred name: Du Barry, Jeanne Bécu, comtesse

Capella, Martianus
Form recorded as preferred name: Martianus Capella

Ḥimyarī, Nashwān ibn Saʻīd
Form recorded as preferred name: Nashwān ibn Saʻīd al-Ḥimyarī

Kyi, Aung San Suu
Form recorded as preferred name: Aung San Suu Kyi

Inverted Form of Initials

D., H.
Form recorded as preferred name: H. D.

D., A. de
Form recorded as preferred name: A. de D.

E., A. B. C. D.
Form recorded as preferred name: A. B. C. D. E.

B—z, A.
Form recorded as preferred name: A. B—z

Direct Form of a Phrase or Appellation

Miss Read
Form recorded as preferred name: Read, Miss

Mister Mydas
Form recorded as preferred name: Mydas, Mister

Mr. Laurence
Form recorded as preferred name: Laurence, Mr.

I. M. Peeved
Form recorded as preferred name: Peeved, I. M.

Inverted Form of an Appellation

George, Boy
Form recorded as preferred name: Boy George

X, Dr.
Form recorded as preferred name: Dr. X

Hen, Mother
Form recorded as preferred name: Mother Hen

Dad, Every Other
Other Dad, Every
Form recorded as preferred name: Every Other Dad

Richard, Little
Form recorded as preferred name: Little Richard

Honorary Titles and Terms of Address

Ū″ Kraṃ
Form recorded as preferred name: Kraṃ, Ū″

Maung, U Aye
U Aye Maung
Form recorded as preferred name: Aye Maung, U

Pandit Anand Koul
Form recorded as preferred name: Koul, Anand

Daw Mi Mi Khaing
Form recorded as preferred name: Mi Mi Khaing

First Word in Title Forming Part of a Phrase

Honesty the best policy, The Author of
Form recorded as preferred name: The Author of Honesty the best policy

The young gentleman's notebook, The Editor of
Form recorded as preferred name: The Editor of The young gentleman's notebook

The Lambton worm, The Writer of
Form recorded as preferred name: The Writer of The Lambton worm

L'adresse au peuple breton, L'auteur de

Form recorded as preferred name: L'auteur de L'adresse au peuple breton

OTHER IDENTIFYING ATTRIBUTES

9.3 Date Associated with the Person

CORE ELEMENT

Date of birth and date of death are core elements. Period of activity of the person is a core element only when needed to distinguish a person from another person with the same name.

9.3.1 Basic Instructions on Recording Dates Associated with Persons

9.3.1.1 Scope

A ***date associated with the person*** is a significant date associated with the history of a person (e.g., date of birth, date of death).

9.3.1.2 Sources of Information

Take information on dates associated with the person from any source.

9.3.1.3 Recording Dates Associated with Persons

Record dates associated with persons by applying these instructions, as applicable:

date of birth (see **9.3.2**)

date of death (see **9.3.3**)

period of activity (see **9.3.4**).

Record dates in terms of the calendar preferred by the agency creating the data. For details on the Christian calendar, see appendix H.

Record dates as separate elements, as parts of access points, or as both. For additional instructions on recording dates as parts of authorized access points, see **9.19.1.3** (date of birth and/or death) or **9.19.1.5** (period of activity of the person and/or profession or occupation).

Record a date associated with a person by giving the year.

Optional Addition

Add the month or month and day in the form *[year] [month] [day]* or *[year] [month]*. Record the month in a language and script preferred by the agency creating the data.

Indicate a probable date by adding a question mark following the year.

1816?

Probable year of birth

If the year is uncertain but known to be either one of two years, record the date in the form *[year] or [year]*.

1666 or 1667

Year of birth uncertain; known to be one of two years

828 or 829

Year of death uncertain; known to be one of two years

If the year can only be approximated, record the date in the form *approximately [year]*.

approximately 931
Approximate year of birth

approximately 680
Approximate year of death

Record a period of activity expressed as a range of dates in the form *[year]–[year]*.

1623–1624
Period of activity

1378–1395
Period of activity

approximately 1479–1499
Period of activity

1687–approximately 1735
Period of activity

Record a period of activity expressed as a range of centuries in the form *[century]–[century]*.

13th century–14th century
Period of activity

1st century B.C.–1st century A.D.
Period of activity

9.3.2 Date of Birth

CORE ELEMENT

9.3.2.1 Scope

Date of birth is the year a person was born.

Date of birth may also include the month or month and day of the person's birth.

9.3.2.2 Sources of Information

Take information on date of birth from any source.

9.3.2.3 Recording Date of Birth

Record the person's date of birth by applying the basic instructions on recording dates associated with persons at **9.3.1**.

1974

361 B.C.

1552?
Probable year of birth

1647 or 1648
Year of birth uncertain; known to be one of two years

approximately 1003
Approximate year of birth

9.3.3 Date of Death

CORE ELEMENT

9.3.3.1 Scope

Date of death is the year a person died.

Date of death may also include the month or month and day of the person's death.

9.3.3.2 Sources of Information

Take information on date of death from any source.

9.3.3.3 Recording Date of Death

Record the date of death of a deceased person by applying the basic instructions on recording dates associated with persons at **9.3.1**.

2000

289 B.C.

14 A.D.
Year of death of person whose year of birth is recorded as 63 B.C.

1874?
Probable year of death

1742 or 1743
Year of death uncertain; known to be one of two years

approximately 1880
Approximate year of death

9.3.4 Period of Activity of the Person

CORE ELEMENT

Period of activity of the person is a core element when needed to distinguish a person from another person with the same name.

9.3.4.1 Scope

Period of activity of the person is a date or range of dates indicative of the period in which a person was active in his or her primary field of endeavour.

9.3.4.2 Sources of Information

Take information on period of activity of the person from any source.

9.3.4.3 Recording Period of Activity of the Person

If a person's date of birth and date of death are both unknown, record a date or range of dates indicative of the person's period of activity. Apply the basic instructions on recording dates associated with persons at **9.3.1**.

1705

1687–1709

1682–1723?

11 B.C.–12 A.D.

approximately 1400

approximately 494 B.C.–approximately 467 B.C.

1688–approximately 1712

jin shi 1499
Date at which a Chinese literary degree was conferred

If it is not possible to establish specific years of activity, record the century or centuries in which the person was active.

19th century

13th century–14th century

7th century B.C.

1st century B.C.–1st century A.D.

9.4 Title of the Person

CORE ELEMENT

Title of the person is a core element when it is a word or phrase indicative of royalty, nobility, or ecclesiastical rank or office, or a term of address for a person of religious vocation. Any other term indicative of rank, honour, or office is a core element when needed to distinguish a person from another person with the same name.

9.4.1 Basic Instructions on Recording Titles of Persons

9.4.1.1 Scope

Title of the person is a word or phrase indicative of royalty, nobility, or ecclesiastical rank or office, a term of address for a person of religious vocation, or another term indicative of rank, honour, or office.

Title of the person excludes terms of address that simply indicate gender or marital status (e.g., Mr., Mrs.).

9.4.1.2 Sources of Information

Take information on the title of the person from any source.

9.4.1.3 Recording Titles of Persons

Record the title of the person by applying the instructions at **9.4.1.4–9.4.1.8**, as applicable.

Record titles as separate elements, as parts of access points, or as both. For additional instructions on recording a title as part of the authorized access point, see **9.19.1.2**.

9.4.1.4 Titles of Royalty

Record titles of royalty by applying these instructions, as applicable:

person with the highest royal status within a state, etc. (see **9.4.1.4.1**)

consorts of royal persons (see **9.4.1.4.2**)

children and grandchildren of royal persons (see **9.4.1.4.3**).

9.4.1.4.1 Person with the Highest Royal Status within a State, Etc.

For the person with the highest royal status within a state or people[5], record the person's title and the name of the state or people. Record both in a language preferred by the agency creating the data if there are satisfactory equivalents in that language.

King of the Franks

Queen of Great Britain

Queen of England

Holy Roman Emperor

King of Iraq

King of Sweden

Emperor of Mexico

Empress of Russia

Emperor of the East

Duke of Burgundy

Grand Duke of Luxembourg

Sultan of the Turks

Shah of Iran

Negus of Ethiopia

Nawab Wazir of Oudh

---

5. Persons with highest status are kings and queens, emperors and empresses, and persons with other titles that indicate such a status within a state or people (grand-dukes, grand-duchesses, princes, princesses, etc.). Rank is the only determining factor in applying these instructions. The degree of authority or power is not a factor.

9.4.1.4.2 Consorts of Royal Persons

For a consort (spouse) of a person with the highest royal status within a state or people, record his or her title followed by *consort of* and the preferred name for the royal person and his or her title (see **9.4.1.4.1**). Record the title of the consort in a language preferred by the agency creating the data if there is a satisfactory equivalent in that language.

Prince, consort of Beatrix, Queen of the Netherlands

Queen, consort of Louis XIII, King of France

King, consort of Maria II, Queen of Portugal

Empress, consort of Akihito, Emperor of Japan

Grand Duchess, consort of Ludwig III, Grand Duke of Hesse-Darmstadt

9.4.1.4.3 Children and Grandchildren of Royal Persons

For a child or grandchild of a person with the highest royal status within a state or people, record the title of the child or grandchild. Record the title in a language preferred by the agency creating the data if there is a satisfactory equivalent in that language.

Prince of Asturias

Infanta of Spain

Duke of York

Crown Princess of Sweden

If the child or grandchild is known only as *Prince* or *Princess* or a similar title, without a territorial designation, record that title. Follow it by:

a) another title associated with the name
or
b) *daughter of*, *son of*, *granddaughter of*, or *grandson of* the preferred name for the parent or grandparent and his or her title (see **9.4.1.4.1**).

Record the title in a language preferred by the agency creating the data if there is a satisfactory equivalent in that language.

Princess, Countess of Snowdon

Prince, Duke of York

Princess, daughter of Juliana, Queen of the Netherlands

Prince, son of Muḥammad V, King of Morocco

Princess, granddaughter of Chulalongkorn, King of Siam

Grand Duke, grandson of Alexander II, Emperor of Russia

Czarevitch, son of Peter I, Emperor of Russia

Infante, son of Jaime II, King of Aragon

9.4.1.5 Titles of Nobility

For a nobleman or noblewoman whose title has not been recorded as the first element in the preferred name (see **9.2.2.14–9.2.2.15**), record the title of nobility in the language in which it was conferred.

marchese
Preferred name recorded as: Dragonetti, Giacinto

graaf van Oostervant
Preferred name recorded as: Borselen, Frank van

comte
Preferred name recorded as: Anglès, Jules-Jean-Baptiste

duc
Preferred name recorded as: Astraudo, Amédée

gróf
Preferred name recorded as: Andrássy, Gyula

9.4.1.6 Popes

Record *Pope* as the title of a pope.

Record *Antipope* as the title of an antipope.

9.4.1.7 Bishops, Etc.

Record the title for a bishop, cardinal, archbishop, metropolitan, abbot, abbess, or other high ecclesiastical official whose given name is recorded as the first element in the preferred name. Record the title in a language preferred by the agency creating the data if there is a satisfactory equivalent in that language. If the person has more than one title, give the one of highest rank.

Record *Archbishop* for all archbishops other than cardinals.

Record *Bishop* for all bishops other than cardinals.

Record *Chorepiscopus* for persons so designated.

Record *Cardinal* for cardinal-bishops, cardinal-priests, and cardinal-deacons.

Add to the title of a diocesan bishop, archbishop, or patriarch the name of that person's latest diocese, archdiocese, or patriarchate. Add the name of the place in a language preferred by the agency creating the data if there is a form in that language.

> Cardinal
>
> Patriarch of Jerusalem
>
> Archbishop of Athens and All Greece
>
> Metropolitan of Moscow
>
> Abbot of Ford
>
> Abbess of Quedlinburg
>
> Chorepiscopus of Trier
>
> Bishop of Limoges
>
> Ecumenical Patriarch of Constantinople

For the name of an ecclesiastical prince of the Holy Roman Empire, record *Prince-Bishop*, *Prince-Archbishop*, *Archbishop and Elector*, etc., as appropriate. Add the name of the ecclesiastical jurisdiction. Also add *Cardinal*, if appropriate.

> Prince-Bishop of Montenegro
>
> Archbishop and Elector of Cologne
>
> Archbishop and Elector of Mainz, Cardinal

9.4.1.8 Other Persons of Religious Vocation

If:

a person of religious vocation is not covered by the instructions at **9.4.1.6** (popes) or **9.4.1.7** (bishops)

and

the person's given name is recorded as the first element in the preferred name

then:

record the title, term of address, etc., in the language in which the title, etc., was conferred or in the language used in the country in which the person resides. If there is more than one such term, use the one that is most often associated with the name or the one that is considered to be more important.

Use spellings found in dictionaries in a language preferred by the agency creating the data. If a title, term of address, etc., has become an integral part of the name, treat it as such.

For Thai names in religion, see also appendix **F.10.1.4**.

Thera

Rabbi

Mullah

fra

Sayadaw

père

Bhikshu

Mother

Swami

Ashin

Ustaz

Imam

fray

If:
a person regularly uses initials and/or abbreviations that indicate membership in a Christian religious order
or
these initials and/or abbreviations appear regularly in resources associated with the person
then:
add the initials and/or abbreviations to the person's title.

Brother, F.S.C.

Father, O.F.M. Cap.

Sister, O.S.B.

sœur, O.P.

padre, O.C.D.

9.4.1.9 Other Term of Rank, Honour, or Office

Record other titles of the person indicative of rank, honour, or office if the terms appear with the name. Record the term in the language in which it was conferred or in the language used in the country in which the person resides.

Captain

Reverend

Sir

9.5 Fuller Form of Name

CORE ELEMENT

A fuller form of name is a core element when needed to distinguish a person from another person with the same name.

9.5.1 Basic Instructions on Recording Fuller Forms of Names

9.5.1.1 Scope

A ***fuller form of name*** is the full form of:

a) a part of a name represented only by an initial or abbreviation in the form chosen as the preferred name,
or
b) a part of the name not included in the form chosen as the preferred name.

9.5.1.2 Sources of Information

Take information on fuller forms of names from any source.

9.5.1.3 Recording Fuller Forms of Names

If:
a fuller form of a person's name is known
and
the preferred name (see **9.2.2**) does not include all of that fuller form[6]
then:
record, as appropriate:

a) the fuller form of all the inverted part of the name (given names, etc.)
and/or
b) the fuller form of the part of the name recorded as the first element of the name (surname, etc.).

Record fuller forms of names as separate elements, as parts of access points, or as both. For additional instructions on recording a fuller form of the name as part of the authorized access point, see **9.19.1.4**.

Nancy Elizabeth
Preferred name recorded as: Smith, Nancy E.

Nancy Ellen
Preferred name recorded as: Smith, Nancy E.

Alva William
Preferred name recorded as: Johnson, A. W.

Anthony W.
Preferred name recorded as: Johnson, A. W.

John Dudley
Preferred name recorded as: Williams, John

Phillip John
Preferred name recorded as: Williams, John

Barbara A.
Preferred name recorded as: Johnson, Barbara

Barbara E.
Preferred name recorded as: Johnson, Barbara

Annie Liddon
Preferred name recorded as: King, Mrs.

Frances Elizabeth
Preferred name recorded as: King, Mrs.

Henry Dawbeny
Preferred name recorded as: H. D.

Hilda Doolittle
Preferred name recorded as: H. D.

Rodríguez Larralde
Preferred name recorded as: Rodríguez L., Oswaldo

Manuel Guillermo Rodríguez Valbuena
Preferred name recorded as: Rodríguez V., Manuel G.

Johann Thomas
Preferred name recorded as: Ahrens, Joh. Thom.

Variant names. Record the name in its fuller form as a variant name, when appropriate (see **9.2.3.10**).

---

6. The most common instances occur when the preferred name contains initials and the spelled out form is known. Less common instances occur when known given names, surnames, or initials are not chosen as part of the preferred name.

9.6 Other Designation Associated with the Person

CORE ELEMENT

Other designation associated with the person is a core element for a Christian saint, a spirit, a person named in a sacred scripture or an apocryphal book, a fictitious or legendary person, or a real non-human entity. For other persons, other designation associated with the person is a core element when needed to distinguish a person from another person with the same name.

9.6.1 Basic Instructions on Recording Other Designations Associated with Persons

9.6.1.1 Scope

Other designation associated with the person is a term other than a title that is associated with a person's name.

9.6.1.2 Sources of Information

Take information on other designations associated with the person from any source.

9.6.1.3 Recording Other Designations Associated with Persons

Record other designations associated with the person by applying these instructions, as applicable:

saints (see **9.6.1.4**)
spirits (see **9.6.1.5**)
persons named in sacred scriptures or apocryphal books (see **9.6.1.6**)
fictitious and legendary persons (see **9.6.1.7**)
non-human entities (see **9.6.1.8**)
other designation (see **9.6.1.9**).

Record other designations associated with the person as separate elements, as parts of access points, or as both. For additional instructions on recording a designation as part of the authorized access point, see **9.19.1.2**.

9.6.1.4 Saints

For a Christian saint, record *Saint.*

9.6.1.5 Spirits

For a spirit, record *Spirit.*

9.6.1.6 Persons Named in Sacred Scriptures or Apocryphal Books

For a person named in a sacred scripture or an apocryphal book, record an appropriate designation.

Angel

Biblical figure

Demon

Talmudic figure

9.6.1.7 Fictitious and Legendary Persons

For a fictitious or legendary person, record *Fictitious character*, *Legendary character*, or another appropriate designation.

Greek deity

Mythical animal

Vampire

9.6.1.8 Real Non-human Entities

For a real non-human entity, record a designation for type, species, or breed.

Chimpanzee

Portuguese water dog

Whale

9.6.1.9 Other Designation

Record an appropriate designation if none of the following attributes are sufficient or appropriate for distinguishing between two or more persons with the same name:

date of birth or date of death (see **9.3**)
fuller form of name (see **9.5**)
period of activity (see **9.3**)
profession or occupation (see **9.16**)
term of rank, honour, or office (see **9.4.1.9**).

Record the designation in a language preferred by the agency creating the data.

Brother of Andrew Lang

Cree Indian

Ship captain's wife

Wife of Gautama Buddha

9.7 Gender

9.7.1 Basic Instructions on Recording Gender

9.7.1.1 Scope

Gender is the gender with which a person identifies.

9.7.1.2 Sources of Information

Take information on gender from any source.

9.7.1.3 Recording Gender

Record the gender of the person using an appropriate term from the following list:

female
male
not known

If none of the terms listed is appropriate or sufficiently specific, record an appropriate term or phrase.

Record gender as a separate element. Gender is not recorded as part of an access point.

intersex
transsexual woman

Indicate the source of information by applying the instructions at **8.12.1.3**.

9.8 Place of Birth

9.8.1 Basic Instructions on Recording Place of Birth

9.8.1.1 Scope

Place of birth is the town, city, province, state, and/or country in which a person was born.

9.8.1.2 Sources of Information

Take information on place of birth from any source.

9.8.1.3 Recording Place of Birth

Record the place (town, city, province, state, and/or country) in which the person was born. Record the place name as instructed in chapter **16**. Abbreviate the names of countries, states, provinces, territories, etc., as instructed in appendix B (**B.11**), as applicable.

Record the place of birth as a separate element. Place of birth is not recorded as part of an access point.

N.Z.
Place of birth of filmmaker Peter Jackson

Radzymin, Poland
Place of birth of author Isaac Bashevis Singer

Newark, N.J.
Place of birth of sculptor Chakaia Booker

Indicate the source of information by applying the instructions at **8.12.1.3**.

9.9 Place of Death

9.9.1 Basic Instructions on Recording Place of Death

9.9.1.1 Scope

Place of death is the town, city, province, state, and/or country in which a person died.

9.9.1.2 Sources of Information

Take information on place of death from any source.

9.9.1.3 Recording Place of Death

Record the place (town, city, province, state, and/or country) in which the person died. Record the place name as instructed in chapter **16**. Abbreviate the names of countries, states, provinces, territories, etc., as instructed in appendix B (**B.11**), as applicable.

Record the place of death as a separate element. Place of death is not recorded as part of an access point.

Surfside, Fla.
Place of death of author Isaac Bashevis Singer

Paris, France
Place of death of actor Tony D'Amario

Indicate the source of information by applying the instructions at **8.12.1.3**.

9.10 Country Associated with the Person

9.10.1 Basic Instructions on Recording Countries Associated with the Person

9.10.1.1 Scope

A ***country associated with the person*** is a country with which a person is identified.

9.10.1.2 Sources of Information

Take information on country or countries associated with the person from any source.

9.10.1.3 Recording Country Associated with the Person

Record the country or countries associated with the person. Record the name of the country as instructed in chapter **16**. Abbreviate the names of countries as instructed in appendix B (**B.11**), as applicable.

Record a country associated with the person as a separate element. Country associated with the person is not recorded as part of an access point.

Canada
Country associated with the author Michael Ondaatje, who was born in Sri Lanka in 1943, moved to England in 1954, and emigrated to Canada in 1962

Russia
France
U.S.
Countries associated with the composer Igor Stravinksy

Indicate the source of information by applying the instructions at **8.12.1.3**.

9.11 Place of Residence, Etc.

9.11.1 Basic Instructions on Recording Places of Residence, Etc.

9.11.1.1 Scope

Place of residence, etc., is a town, city, province, state, and/or country in which a person resides or has resided, or another significant place associated with the person other than place of birth, place of death, or residence (e.g., a place where a person has worked or studied).

9.11.1.2 Sources of Information

Take information on place or places of residence, etc., from any source.

9.11.1.3 Recording Places of Residence, Etc.

Record the place or places (town, city, province, state, and/or country) in which the person resides or has resided, or other significant place associated with the person. Record the place name as instructed in chapter **16**. Abbreviate the names of countries, states, provinces, territories, etc., as instructed in appendix B (**B.11**), as applicable.

Record a place of residence, etc., as a separate element. Place of residence, etc., is not recorded as part of an access point.

Jackson, Miss.
Place of residence, etc., of author Eudora Welty

Oak Park, Ill.
Toronto, Ont.
Chicago, Ill.
Paris, France
Key West, Fla.
Cuba
Ketchum, Idaho
Places of residence, etc., of author Ernest Hemingway

Indicate the source of information by applying the instructions at **8.12.1.3**.

9.12 Address of the Person

9.12.1 Basic Instructions on Recording Addresses of the Person

9.12.1.1 Scope

Address of the person is the address of a person's place of residence, business, or employer and/or an e-mail or Internet address.

9.12.1.2 Sources of Information

Take information on the address or addresses of the person from any source.

9.12.1.3 Recording the Addresses of the Person

Record the address of the person's place of residence, business, or employer, and/or an e-mail or Internet address.

Record an address as a separate element. Address is not recorded as part of an access point.

Box 1216, Barrière, B.C., Canada V0E 1E0
Postal address of J. Richard Arthur

stimmins@doc.govt.nz
E-mail address of Susan M. Timmins

http://www.rodneysharman.com
Web address of Rodney Sharman

Indicate the source of information by applying the instructions at **8.12.1.3**.

9.13 Affiliation

9.13.1 Basic Instructions on Recording Affiliations

9.13.1.1 Scope

An ***affiliation*** is a group with which a person is affiliated or has been affiliated through employment, membership, cultural identity, etc.

9.13.1.2 Sources of Information

Take information on affiliation or affiliations from any source.

9.13.1.3 Recording Affiliations

Record the names of groups with which the person is affiliated or has been affiliated through employment, membership, cultural identity, etc. Record the preferred name for the group (see **11.2.2**).

Record an affiliation as a separate element. Affiliation is not recorded as part of an access point.

New York State College of Agriculture. Department of Entomology
Affiliation of Ann E. Hajek

Istituto nazionale di economia agraria
Affiliation of Carla Abitabile

Furies Collective
Center for Women's Global Leadership
International Council on Human Rights Policy
Affiliations of Charlotte Bunch

Indicate the source of information by applying the instructions at **8.12.1.3**.

9.14 Language of the Person

9.14.1 Basic Instructions on Recording Languages of the Person

9.14.1.1 Scope

Language of the person is a language a person uses when writing for publication, broadcasting, etc.

9.14.1.2 Sources of Information

Take information on the language or languages of the person from any source.

9.14.1.3 Recording the Languages of the Person

Record the language or languages the person uses when writing for publication, broadcasting, etc. Use an appropriate term or terms in a language preferred by the agency creating the data. Select terms from a standard list of names of languages, if available.

Record a language used by the person as a separate element. Language is not recorded as part of an access point.

Icelandic
Language used by the author Halldór Laxness

Russian

English
Languages used by the author Vladimir Nabokov

Indicate the source of information by applying the instructions at **8.12.1.3**.

9.15 Field of Activity of the Person

9.15.1 Basic Instructions on Recording the Fields of Activity of the Person

9.15.1.1 Scope

Field of activity of the person is a field of endeavour, area of expertise, etc., in which a person is engaged or was engaged.

9.15.1.2 Sources of Information

Take information on the field or fields of activity of the person from any source.

9.15.1.3 Recording the Fields of Activity of the Person

Record the field or fields of endeavour, area or areas of expertise, etc., in which the person is engaged or was engaged by recording a term indicating the field.

Record a field of activity as a separate element. Field of activity is not recorded as part of an access point.

Poetry
Preferred name recorded as: Thomas

Stamp collecting
Preferred name recorded as: Lang, Peter

Quiltmaking
Preferred name recorded as: Bilyeu, Michele

Fiction writing
Music criticism
Preferred name recorded as: Haldeman, Philip

Criminology
Preferreed name recorded as: Johnson, Holly

Mathematics
Preferred name recorded as: Thompson, Abigail

Political science
Preferred name recorded as: Tremblay, Manon

Indicate the source of information by applying the instructions at **8.12.1.3**.

9.16 Profession or Occupation

CORE ELEMENT

Profession or occupation is a core element for a person whose name consists of a phrase or appellation not conveying the idea of a person. For other persons, profession or occupation is a core element when needed to distinguish a person from another person with the same name.

9.16.1 Basic Instructions on Recording Professions or Occupations

9.16.1.1 Scope

Profession or occupation is a person's vocation or avocation.

9.16.1.2 Sources of Information

Take information on the profession or occupation of the person from any source.

9.16.1.3 Recording Professions or Occupations

Record the profession or occupation by recording a term indicating the class of persons engaged in the profession or occupation.

Record professions or occupations as separate elements, as parts of access points, or as both. For additional instructions on recording a profession or occupation as part of the authorized access point, see **9.19.1.5**.

Notary
Preferred name recorded as: Johannes

Writer
Preferred name recorded as: River

Poet
Preferred name recorded as: Blue

Rapper
Preferred name recorded as: PSK-13

Disc jockey
Preferred name recorded as: D:Fuse

Musician
Preferred name recorded as: Big Hand

Composer
Preferred name recorded as: Butler, Jean

Tax collector
Preferred name recorded as: Hall, Daniel

Veterinarian
Preferred name recorded as: Orr, Marjorie

Architect
Preferred name recorded as: Hadid, Zaha

Author
Folklorist
Anthropologist
Preferred name recorded as: Hurston, Zora Neale

Indicate the source of information by applying the instructions at **8.12.1.3**.

9.17 Biographical Information

9.17.1 Basic Instructions on Recording Biographical Information

9.17.1.1 Scope

Biographical information is information about the life or history of a person.

9.17.1.2 Sources of Information

Take biographical information from any source.

9.17.1.3 Recording Biographical Information

Record information about the life or history of the person.

Record biographical information as a separate element. Biographical information is not recorded as part of an access point.

> James Sakamoto was born in Seattle in 1903 and graduated from Franklin High School in 1920. He was the founder and publisher of the Japanese-American courier, an English-language newspaper in Seattle (1928–1942), which ceased publication when the Japanese population was removed from the city during World War II. He also helped to found the Japanese American Citizens' League in 1930 and served as its second national president from 1936–1938. Sakamoto spent four months as chief supervisor at the Camp Harmony Assembly Center in Puyallup, Wash., before being incarcerated at Minidoka Relocation Center in Hunt, Idaho, for three years. He returned to Seattle in July, 1945, with his wife and family. Sakamoto worked for the Society of St. Vincent de Paul until his death in 1955
> *Biographical information about James Y. Sakamoto*

As appropriate, incorporate information associated with specific identifying elements (see **9.3–9.16**) into a biographical information element.

> Alice Ann Munro (née Laidlaw) is a Canadian short-story writer and three-time winner of Canada's Governor General Award for English-language fiction. She was born 10 July 1931 in Wingham, Ontario. Married to James Munro in 1951, Alice Munro lived in Vancouver and Victoria, B.C. until her divorce in 1972, when she returned to Ontario to accept the position as Writer-in-Residence at University of Western Ontario. In 1980, Munro held the position of Writer-in-Residence at both University of British Columbia and University of Queensland. She currently lives in Clinton, Ontario. Additional biographical information may be found at http://en.wikipedia.org/wiki/Alice_Munro
> *Biographical information about Alice Munro*

Indicate the source of information by applying the instructions at **8.12.1.3**.

9.18 Identifier for the Person

CORE ELEMENT

9.18.1 Basic Instructions on Recording Identifiers for Persons

9.18.1.1 Scope

An *identifier for the person* is a character string uniquely associated with a person, or with a surrogate for a person (e.g., an authority record). The identifier serves to differentiate that person from other persons.

9.18.1.2 Sources of Information

Take information on identifiers for the person from any source.

9.18.1.3 Recording Identifiers for Persons

Record an identifier for the person. Precede the identifier with the name or an identification of the agency, etc., responsible for assigning the identifier, if readily ascertainable.

> Library of Congress control number: nb2001032740
> *Identifier for Fahimul Quadir*
>
> Library and Archives Canada control number: 1010H0671
> *Identifier for Fahimul Quadir*
>
> Union List of Artist Names ID: 500014816
> *Identifier for Zelda Sayre Fitzgerald*
>
> AMG Artist ID: P 510210
> *AMG Data Solutions identifier for Norah Jones*
>
> Oxford Biography Index Number: 101031126
> *Identifier for Anna Freud*

ACCESS POINTS REPRESENTING PERSONS

9.19 Constructing Access Points to Represent Persons

9.19.1 Authorized Access Point Representing a Person

9.19.1.1 General Guidelines on Constructing Authorized Access Points to Represent Persons

When constructing an authorized access point to represent a person, use the preferred name for the person (see **9.2.2**) as the basis for the authorized access point.

> Fitzgerald, Ella
> *Preferred name for the person:* Ella Fitzgerald
>
> Masson-Vincourt, Marie-Paule
> *Preferred name for the person:* Marie-Paule Masson-Vincourt
>
> Bolingbroke, Henry St. John, Viscount
> *Preferred name for the person:* Henry St. John, Viscount Bolingbroke
>
> Leonardo, da Vinci
> *Preferred name for the person:* Leonardo da Vinci
>
> C. G. A. v. Z.
> *Preferred name for the person:* C.G.A.v.Z.
>
> Buckskin Bill
> *Preferred name for the person:* Buckskin Bill

Make additions to the name as instructed at **9.19.1.2–9.19.1.7**, as applicable.

> Carlos, Prince of Asturias
>
> Clement I, Pope
>
> More, Thomas, Saint
>
> Luke, Saint (Spirit)

Smith, John, 1978–

Smith, John, 1832–1911

Allen, Richard (Richard H.)

Allen, Richard (Richard Ian Gordon)

Person whose name consists of a phrase or appellation not conveying the idea of a person. When constructing an authorized access point for a person whose name consists of a phrase or appellation not conveying the idea of a person, apply the following instructions even if not needed to distinguish access points representing different persons with the same name. Add after the name:

a) a term indicating profession or occupation (see **9.16**) for human entities
or
b) a term indicating fictitious or legendary character (see **9.6.1.7**)
or
c) a term indicating type, species or breed for real non-human entities (see **9.6.1.8**).

Stone Mountain (Writer)

Big Hand (Musician)

PSK-13 (Rapper)

G-8 (Fictitious character)

Battleship (Race horse)

Splash (Dog)

Wolverine (Fictitious character)
not Wolverine (Soldier)
Authorized access point for a comic book superhero. He becomes a soldier in the Canadian military in the comic books

Rin-Tin-Tin (Dog)
not Rin-Tin-Tin (Actor)
Authorized access point for a dog that appeared in several motion pictures

but

Obama, Bo
Preferred name for the dog contains a surname and a given name

Kent, Clark
Preferred name for the fictitious character contains a surname and a given name

Wonder Woman
Preferred name for the comic book superhero conveys the idea of a person

Mr. Ed
Preferred name for the fictitious talking horse conveys the idea of a person

Frosty, the Snowman
Preferred name for the fictitious character consists of a given name and characterizing phrase

Make the additions specified at **9.19.1.2–9.19.1.7** if they are needed to distinguish access points representing different persons with the same name.

Optional Addition

Make the additions specified at **9.19.1.2–9.19.1.7** even if they are not needed to distinguish access points representing different persons with the same name.

If no suitable addition is available, use the same access point for all persons with the same name. Use an undifferentiated name indicator (see **8.11**) to indicate that the name is undifferentiated.

Müller, Heinrich
Author of: 80 Fotos und eine kurze Einführung in die Lage, Geschichte und Sehenswürdigkeiten der Stadt Giessen

Müller, Heinrich
Co-author of: An architecture for vision based human computer interaction

Müller, Heinrich
Author of: Der Diebstahl im Urheberrecht

Müller, Heinrich
Author of: Die Fussballregeln und ihre richtige Auslegung

Müller, Heinrich
Author of: Lehrbuch der speziellen Chirurgie für Tierärzte und Studierende. 15. Auflage, neubearbeitet

Müller, Heinrich
Author of: Die Repser Burg

ADDITIONS TO ACCESS POINTS REPRESENTING PERSONS

9.19.1.2 Title or Other Designation Associated with the Person

Add to the name one or more of the following elements, as instructed at **9.19.1.2.1–9.19.1.2.6**, as applicable:

a) a title of royalty (see **9.19.1.2.1**)

b) a title of nobility (see **9.19.1.2.2**)

c) a title of religious rank (see **9.19.1.2.3**)

d) the term *Saint* (see **9.19.1.2.4**)

e) the term *Spirit* (see **9.19.1.2.5**)

f) an other designation associated with the person (see **9.19.1.2.6**).

The term *Spirit* is always added as the last element in the authorized access point.

Make the additions listed in a)–d) and f) before adding dates of birth and/or death or period of activity.

When adding multiple other designations associated with a person, enclose each term in a set of parentheses.

9.19.1.2.1 Title of Royalty

Add a title of royalty (see **9.4.1.4**) even if it is not needed to distinguish access points representing different persons with the same name. Add the title of royalty after the preferred name.

Anne, Queen of Great Britain

Carlos, Prince of Asturias

Gustav I Vasa, King of Sweden

Isabella, of Parma, consort of Joseph II, Holy Roman Emperor

9.19.1.2.2 Title of Nobility

If the title of nobility (see **9.4.1.5**) or part of the title commonly appears with the name in resources associated with the person or in reference sources, add the title to the name. In this context, disregard reference sources dealing with the nobility. In case of doubt, add the title. Add the title of nobility even if it is not needed to distinguish access points representing different persons with the same name.

Borselen, Frank van, graaf van Oostervant

Anglès, Jules-Jean-Baptiste, comte

Add the title after the preferred name unless applying **9.19.1.4** (fuller form of name). When applying **9.19.1.4**, add the title after the fuller form of name.

Puymaigre, Th. de, (Théodore), comte

9.19.1.2.3 Title of Religious Rank

Popes . Add the title *Pope* or *Antipope* (see **9.4.1.6**) after the preferred name.

Pius XII, Pope

Hippolytus, Antipope

Bishops, etc., and other persons of religious vocation. For bishops, etc. (see **9.4.1.7**) and other persons of religious vocation (see **9.4.1.8**),

If:

the given name is recorded as the first element in the preferred name

and

the title or part of the title commonly appears with the name in resources associated with the person or in reference sources

then:

add the title, even if it is not needed to distinguish access points representing different persons with the same name. In case of doubt, add the title.

Dositheos, Patriarch of Jerusalem

Ruricius I, Bishop of Limoges

Alexander, Bishop of Alexandria, Saint

but

Augustine, of Canterbury, Saint

Title "Archbishop" not commonly used in resources associated with the person or in reference sources

Augustine, of Hippo, Saint

Title "Bishop" not commonly used in resources associated with the person or in reference sources

Teresa, of Avila, Saint
Title "madre" not commonly used in resources associated with the person or in reference sources

Add the title after the preferred name unless applying **9.19.1.4** (fuller form of name). When applying **9.19.1.4**, add the title after the fuller form of name.

M. Alicia (Mary Alicia), Sister, S.C.N.
Title, including initials representing a Christian religious order, added after fuller form of name

9.19.1.2.4 Saint

Add the term *Saint* (see **9.6.1.4**) to the preferred name unless the access point represents a pope or an emperor, empress, king, or queen. Add the term after the fuller form of name (see **9.19.1.4**) and title of nobility (see **9.19.1.2.2**) or title of religious rank (see **9.19.1.2.3**), as applicable.

Arundel, Philip Howard, Earl of, Saint

Manyanet, José (Manyanet I Vives), Saint
"Saint" added after fuller form of name

Boniface IV, Pope
not Boniface IV, Pope, Saint

Vladimir, King of Dalmatia
not Vladimir, King of Dalmatia, Saint

9.19.1.2.5 Spirit

Construct the authorized acess point for the spirit of a person by combining (in this order):

a) the authorized access point for the person

b) the term *Spirit* (see **9.6.1.5**).

Garland, Judy (Spirit)

Blount, Harry, 1880–1913 (Spirit)

Elijah (Biblical prophet) (Spirit)

9.19.1.2.6 Other Designation Associated with the Person

Add one or more or of the following types of terms if needed to distinguish one access point from another:

a) a term indicating a person named in a sacred scripture or an apocryphal book (see **9.6.1.6**)

b) the term *Fictitious character*, *Legendary character*, or another appropriate designation (see **9.6.1.7**)

c) a term indicating type, species, or breed (see **9.6.1.8**).

Adam (Biblical figure)

Adam (Fictitious character from Napoli)

Adam (Fictitious character from Shakespeare)

Henrietta (Cat)

Henrietta (Fictitious character)

Palamedes (Arthurian legendary character)

Palamedes (Greek mythological character)

Add the term after the fuller form of name (see **9.19.1.4**), title of royalty (see **9.19.1.2.1**), title of nobility (see **9.19.1.2.2**), title of religious rank (see **9.19.1.2.3**), or the term *Saint* (see **9.19.1.2.4**), as applicable.

Caulfield, Holden (Holden Morrisey) (Fictitious character)

Mary Theresa, Sister (Fictitious character)

For instructions on adding the term *Saint* to the authorized access point, see **9.19.1.2.4**.

For instructions on adding the term *Spirit* to the authorized access point, see **9.19.1.2.5**.

Optional Addition

Add one of the types of terms listed in **9.6.1.6–9.6.1.8** even if there is no need to distinguish one access point from another.

Obama, Bo (Portuguese water dog)

Lear, King of England (Fictitious character)

Joan, Pope (Fictitious character)

Leibowitz, Isaac Edward, Saint (Fictitious character)

Hygieia (Greek deity)

9.19.1.3 Date of Birth and/or Death

Add the date of birth (see **9.3.2**) and/or date of death (see **9.3.3**) if needed to distinguish one access point from another. Record the year alone.

Smith, John, 1978–

Smith, John, 1718–1791

Smith, John, born 1787

Smith, John, died 1773

Add the month or month and day if needed to distinguish one access point from another.

Smith, John, 1936 May 5–

Smith, John, 1936 December 17–

Optional Addition

Add the date of birth and/or death even if there is no need to distinguish between access points.

Hemingway, Ernest, 1899–1961

Gregory IV, Pope, died 844

Arundel, Philip Howard, Earl of, Saint, 1557–1595

9.19.1.4 Fuller Form of Name

Add a fuller form of the person's name (see **9.5**) if needed to distinguish one access point from another. Make this addition when the person's date of birth or date of death is not available (see **9.19.1.3**).

Johnson, A. W. (Alva William)

Johnson, A. W. (Anthony W.)

Johnson, Carol (Carol Sue)

Johnson, Carol (Carol W.)

S. W. (Simon Wilson)

S. W. (Susanna Warren)

Optional Addition

Add a fuller form of name even if there is no need to distinguish between access points. Add the fuller form of name before the date of birth and/or death.

Lawrence, D. H. (David Herbert)

T. N. I. Fatimah (Teh Nachiar Iskandar Fatimah)

González R., Luis (González Rodríguez)

González E., José I. (José Ignacio González Escobar)

Brandt, Joh. C. Fr. (Johann Carl Friedrich)

Carey-Hobson, Mrs. (Mary Ann)

Eliot, T. S. (Thomas Stearns), 1888–1965

A. Manap A. Malik (Abdul Manap Abdul Malik), 1946–

9.19.1.5 Period of Activity of the Person and/or Profession or Occupation

Add the period of activity of the person (see **9.3.4**) or profession or occupation (see **9.16**) if needed to distinguish one access point from another. Make this addition when the following elements are not available:

date of birth and/or death (see **9.19.1.3**)

or

fuller form of name (see **9.19.1.4**).

Addition of a Period of Activity

Smith, John, flourished 1705

Smith, John, active 1719–1758

Xu, Zhen, active 1377

Xu, Zhen, jin shi 1523

Allen, Charles, 17th century

Allen, Charles, 18th century–19th century

Addition of a Profession or Occupation

Johannes (Notary)

A. K. (Musician)

Chris (Rapper)

Hancock, Mary (Architect)

Butler, Jean (Composer)

Hall, Daniel (Tax collector)

Orr, Marjorie (Veterinarian)

Watt, James (Gardener)

Brown, Carol (Flutist)

Optional Addition

Add the period of activity of the person and/or profession or occupation in any order even if there is no need to distinguish between access points.

Balʿamī Abū ʿAlī Muḥammad ibn Muḥammad, flourished 946–973

Aelfgifu, Queen, consort of Edwy, King of England, flourished 956

Callistratus, of Aphidna, flourished 377 B.C.–361 B.C.

Adam II, Abbot of Dore, flourished 1216–1226

Cai, Shangxiang, jin shi 1761

Zacharias (Notary), active 1232–1274

9.19.1.6 Other Term of Rank, Honour, or Office

Add a term indicative of rank, honour, or office if the term appears with the name (see **9.4.1.9**) if it is needed to distinguish one access point from another. Make this addition when the following elements are not available:

date of birth and/or death (see **9.19.1.3**)

fuller form of name (see **9.19.1.4**)

or

period of activity of the person and/or profession or occupation (see **9.19.1.5**).

Wood, John, Captain

"Captain," a term indicative of rank, added to distinguish the authorized access point from another

Optional Addition

Add a term indicative of rank, honour, or office even if there is no need to distinguish between access points.

> Appleby, Robert, Sir
> *"Sir," a term of honour for a knight, added to help identify the person*

9.19.1.7 Other Designation

If none of the additions at **9.19.1.2–9.19.1.6** is sufficient or appropriate for distinguishing between the access points for two or more persons, add an appropriate designation (see **9.6.1.9**).

> Nichols, Chris (Of the North Oxford Association)
> Lang, John (Brother of Andrew Lang)
> Budd, Henry (Cree Indian)
> Yaśodharā (Wife of Gautama Buddha)
> Independent Burgess (Of Nottingham)

9.19.2 Variant Access Point Representing a Person

9.19.2.1 General Guidelines on Constructing Variant Access Points to Represent Persons

When constructing a variant access point to represent a person, use a variant name for the person (see **9.2.3**) as the basis for the access point.

> Jackson, Curtis
> *Form recorded as authorized access point:* 50 Cent (Musician)
>
> Rodham, Hillary Diane
> *Form recorded as authorized access point:* Clinton, Hillary Rodham
>
> Roughgarden, Jonathan
> *Form recorded as authorized access point:* Roughgarden, Joan
>
> Terencio
> Terencjusz
> Terenz
> Terenzio
> Ṭerenṭyus
> טרנטיוס
> *English language form recorded as preferred name:* Terence
>
> Tsʻao, Pai
> 曹白
> *Form recorded as authorized access point:* Cao, Bai
>
> Pettersen, Kristin Y.
> *Form recorded as authorized access point:* Pettersen, K. Y. (Kristin Y.)
>
> Balzo, Giulio del
> *Form recorded as authorized access point:* Del Balzo, Giulio
>
> Khayyam, Omar
> Omar Chajjam

Chajjam, Omar
Ömer Hayyam
Hayyam, Ömer
Омар Хайам
Хайам, Омар
عمر خيام
عمر الخيام
Form recorded as authorized access point: Omar Khayyam

Wendy, Sister
Form of name recorded as authorized access point: Beckett, Wendy

Dr. Seuss
Form recorded as authorized access point: Seuss, Dr.

Make additions to the name, if considered important for identification. Apply the instructions at **9.19.1.2–9.19.1.7**, as applicable.

Hermione Marie-Gabrielle, Princess of Urach, 1932–1989
Form recorded as authorized access point: Guinness, Mariga, 1932–1989

Poisson, Jeanne Antoinette, marquise de Pompadour, 1721–1764
Pompadour, Madame de (Jeanne Antoinette Poisson), 1721–1764
Form recorded as authorized access point: Pompadour, Jeanne Antoinette Poisson, marquise de, 1721–1764

De Guise, Henri, duc, 1614–1664
Henri, duc de Guise, 1614–1664
Henri, de Lorraine, 1614–1664
Lorraine, Henri de, duc de Guise, 1614–1664
Guyse, Henri, duc de, 1614–1664
Henry II, Duke of Guise, 1614–1664
Henry II, de Lorraine, 1614–1664
Form recorded as authorized access point: Guise, Henri, duc de, 1614–1664

Constantine, Saint, died 337
Константин, Великий, died 337
Konstantin, Velikiĭ, died 337
Κωνσταντίνος, ο Μέγας, died 337
Kōnstantinos, ho Megas, died 337
Form recorded as authorized access point: Constantine I, Emperor of Rome, died 337

Edward, the Martyr, Saint, 962?–978
Form recorded as authorized access point: Edward, King of England, 962?–978

Lewis, Bishop of Saint Asaph, 1741–1802
Form recorded as authorized access point: Bagot, Lewis, 1741–1802

Sanat Kumara (Spirit)
Form recorded as authorized access point: Beloved Sanat Kumara (Spirit)

Oyster (Poet)
Form recorded as authorized access point: Boyes, W. W. (William Watson), 1835–1915

Synthetic Realm (Musician)
System F (Musician)
Form recorded as authorized access point: Corsten, Ferry

Morris, Michael, 1907–1979
Morrison, Duke, 1907–1979
Morrison, Marion Michael, 1907–1979

Wayne, Duke, 1907–1979
Form recorded as authorized access point: Wayne, John, 1907–1979

Mills, Jack, 1918–
Form recorded as authorized access point: Mills, J. (Jack), 1918–

Ross, Ken, 1916–2008
Form recorded as authorized access point: Ross, T. K. (Thomas Kenneth)

Hayward, Bill, 1941–2008
Form recorded as authorized access point: Hayward, William (William L.)

Johnson, Alan (Alan S.)
Form recorded as authorized access point: Johnson, A. S. (Alan S.)

Johnson, Ben (R. Benjamin)
Form recorded as authorized access point: Johnson, R. Benjamin

Jackson, C. (Curtis)
Fifty Cent (Musician)
Form recorded as authorized access point: 50 Cent (Musician)

Dixon, Anthony, flourished 1790-1802
Form recorded as authorized access point: Dixon, A. (Anthony), flourished 1790–1802

Xu, Jing'an, jin shi 1523
許珍, jin shi 1523
Form recorded as authorized access point: Xu, Zhen, jin shi 1523

Brown, Charlie (Composer)
Form recorded as authorized access point: Brown, Charley

Frazer, John (Architect)
Frazier, John (Architect)
Form recorded as authorized access point: Fraser, John (Architect)

White Plume (Indian Chief)
Form recorded as authorized access point: Pocatello, Chief

Ēsaias (Biblical prophet)
Yeshaʻyahu (Biblical prophet)
Ἡσαΐας (Biblical prophet)
ישעיהו (Biblical prophet)
Form recorded as authorized access point: Isaiah (Biblical prophet)

10

IDENTIFYING FAMILIES

10.0 Purpose and Scope

This chapter provides general guidelines and instructions on:

a) choosing preferred names for families (see **10.2.2**)

b) recording preferred and variant names for families (see **10.2**)

c) recording other identifying attributes of families (see **10.3–10.10**)

d) constructing authorized access points representing families (see **10.11.1**)

e) constructing variant access points representing families (see **10.11.2**).

The chapter provides guidelines on recording names and other identifying attributes as separate elements, as parts of access points, or as both.

The preferred name for the family is used as the basis for the authorized access point. The variant name or names for the family are used as the basis for variant access points. Other identifying attributes of the family may also be included in the access point.

10.1 General Guidelines on Identifying Families

10.1.1 Sources of Information

Take the name or names of the family from any source.

For additional guidance on sources of information for the preferred name for the family, see **10.2.2.2**.

Take information on other identifying attributes of the family from any source.

10.1.2 Using Access Points to Represent Families

An authorized access point is one of the techniques used to represent either a family associated with a resource (see **18.4.1.2**) or a related family (see **31.1**).

When constructing authorized access points representing families, apply the guidelines at **10.11.1**.

When constructing variant access points representing families, apply the guidelines at **10.11.2**.

10.2 Name of the Family

CORE ELEMENT

Preferred name for the family is a core element. Variant names for the family are optional.

10.2.1 Basic Instructions on Recording Names of Families

10.2.1.1 Scope

A ***name of the family*** is a word, character, or group of words and/or characters by which a family is known.

When identifying families, there are two categories of names:

a) preferred name for the family (see **10.2.2**)

b) variant name for the family (see **10.2.3**).

10.2.1.2 Sources of Information

Take the name or names of the family from any source.

For additional guidance on sources of information for the preferred name for the family, see **10.2.2.2**.

10.2.1.3 General Guidelines on Recording Names of Families

When recording a name of a family, apply the general guidelines on recording names at **8.5**. When those guidelines refer to an appendix, apply the additional instructions in that appendix, as applicable.

Choose a preferred name for the family by applying the instructions at **10.2.2.3** and **10.2.2.5–10.2.2.6**.

If a family changes its name, choose a new preferred name for use with resources associated with that new name (see **10.2.2.7**). Choose the earlier name as the preferred name for use with resources associated with the earlier name.

Record the name chosen as the preferred name. Apply the instructions at **10.2.2.4** and **10.2.2.8–10.2.2.9**.

Names and forms of the name not chosen as the preferred name may be recorded as variant names (see **10.2.3**).

10.2.2 Preferred Name for the Family

CORE ELEMENT

10.2.2.1 Scope

The ***preferred name for the family*** is the name or form of name chosen to identify the family. It is also the basis for the authorized access point representing that family.

10.2.2.2 Sources of Information

Determine the preferred name for a family from the following sources (in order of preference):

a) the preferred sources of information (see **2.2.2**) in resources associated with the family

b) other formal statements appearing in resources associated with the family

c) other sources (including reference sources).

10.2.2.3 Choosing the Preferred Name

When choosing the preferred name for the family, generally choose the name by which the family is commonly known. The name chosen can be the surname (or equivalent) used by members of the family, the name of a royal house or dynasty, or the name of a clan, etc.

When a family is known by more than one form of the same name, see additional instructions on choosing the preferred name at **10.2.2.5**.

When a family is known by more than one name, see additional instructions on choosing the preferred name at **10.2.2.6–10.2.2.7**.

Taylor

Charron-Lecore

La Ville de Férolles

Goublaye de Ménorval y Rodríguez Quirós

Van den Bergh

Abū ʻUyaynah al-Muhallabī

Mac Fhionnghaile

Windsor

Winchilsea

Pahlavi

Nguyễn

10.2.2.4 Recording the Preferred Name

Record the name chosen as the preferred name for a family by applying the general guidelines at **8.5**.

If the name consists of several parts, record as the first element that part of the name under which the family would normally be listed in authoritative alphabetic lists in its language, country of residence, or country of activity. Record the other part or parts of the name following the first element. Apply the instructions at **10.2.2.8** (surnames) and **10.2.2.9** (names of royal houses, dynasties, clans, etc.), as applicable.

NAME

Exception

If a family's preference is known to be different from normal usage, follow that preference when choosing the part of the name to be recorded as the first element.

CHOOSING THE PREFERRED NAME

10.2.2.5 Different Forms of the Same Name

If a family is known by more than one form of the same name, apply the same instructions used for the name of a person. Choose the preferred name by applying these instructions, as applicable:

fullness (see **9.2.2.5.1**)

language (see **9.2.2.5.2**)

names found in a non-preferred script (see **9.2.2.5.3**)

spelling (see **9.2.2.5.4**).

10.2.2.6 Different Names for the Same Family

If a family is known by more than one name, choose the name by which the family is most commonly known, if there is one.

If the family has changed its name, apply instead the instructions at **10.2.2.7**.

Otherwise, choose one name according to the following order of preference:

a) the name that appears most frequently in resources associated with the family

b) the name that appears most frequently in reference sources.

Variant names. Record other names by which the family is known as variant names (see **10.2.3**).

10.2.2.7 Change of Name

If the name of a family has changed (including changes from one language to another), choose the earlier name as the preferred name for use with resources associated with the earlier name. Choose the later name as the preferred name for use with resources associated with the later name.

Yan

Family changed its surname from De La Resurección *to* Yan *in 1849*

For instructions on recording relationships between the earlier and later names of the family, see chapter **31** (related families).

RECORDING THE PREFERRED NAME

10.2.2.8 Surnames

If the name chosen as the preferred name consists of a surname, or a name that functions as a surname, record that name as the family name. Apply the same instructions on recording surnames that are used for the surnames of persons (see **9.2.2.9**).

Giroux

Wu

Pérez-López y López-Silvero

Apply the same additional instructions on recording surnames that are used for the surnames of persons, as applicable:

compound surnames (see **9.2.2.10**)
surnames with separately written prefixes (see **9.2.2.11**)
prefixes hyphenated or combined with surnames (see **9.2.2.12**).

10.2.2.9 Names of Royal Houses, Dynasties, Clans, Etc.

If the name chosen as the preferred name consists of the name of a royal house, a dynasty, a clan, etc., record that name as the family name. Apply the general guidelines on recording names at **8.5**.

Windsor

Romanov

ʻAdil Shahi

10.2.3 Variant Name for the Family

10.2.3.1 Scope

A ***variant name for the family*** is a name or form of name by which a family is known that differs from the name or form of name chosen as the preferred name.

10.2.3.2 Sources of Information

Take variant names from resources associated with the family and/or from reference sources.

10.2.3.3 General Guidelines on Recording Variant Names for Families

Record variant names for a family by applying the general guidelines on recording names at **8.5**.

Record a variant name when it is different from the name recorded as the preferred name. Record as a variant name:

a name or form of name used by a family

or

a name or form of name found in reference sources

or

a form of name resulting from a different transliteration of the name.

For families who have changed their name, see the instructions on recording relationships between related families in chapter **31**.

Record as a variant name a form using a different part of the name as the first element if the name might reasonably be searched by that part.

Apply the specific instructions at **10.2.3.4–10.2.3.6**, as applicable. Also apply instructions about recording variant names at **10.2.2.5–10.2.2.6** and **10.2.2.8** (and at the parts of chapter 9 to which those instructions refer).

10.2.3.4 Alternative Linguistic Form of Name

If the name recorded as the preferred name for a family has one or more alternative linguistic forms, record them as variant names.

Different Language Form

Accorsi
Latin form recorded as preferred name: Accursius

Leĭë
Lejė
Loĭe
Lully
French form recorded as preferred name: Lœillet

Different Script

李
Chinese transliterated form recorded as preferred name: Li

Σημίτης
Greek transliterated form recorded as preferred name: Sēmitēs

Романов
English language form recorded as preferred name: Romanov

ويندسور
וינדזור
English language form recorded as preferred name: Windsor

Different Spelling

Di Pietro
Different spelling recorded as preferred name: DiPietro

Caragher
Caraher
Carraher
Different spelling recorded as preferred name: Carragher

Different Transliteration

Āgāśe
Different transliteration recorded as preferred name: Agashe

Simitis
Different transliteration recorded as preferred name: Sēmitēs

Romanof
Romanoff
Different transliteration recorded as preferred name: Romanov

10.2.3.5 Hereditary Title

If a family has a hereditary title associated with its name (see **10.7**), record this title as a variant name. Record the proper name in the title as the first element, followed by a comma and the term of rank in the plural.

Chandos, Dukes of

Ericeira, condes da

10.2.3.6 Other Variant Name

Record other variant names and variant forms of the name not covered by **10.2.3.4–10.2.3.5**, if considered important for identification or access.

St. Pierre
Form recorded as preferred name: Saint Pierre

Von Schilling
Form recorded as preferred name: Schilling

Broglie
Form recorded as preferred name: De Broglie

Kangarid
Sallarid
Form recorded as preferred name: Musafirid

Sevunas
Yadavas
Form recorded as preferred name: Yadava

OTHER IDENTIFYING ATTRIBUTES

10.3 Type of Family

CORE ELEMENT

10.3.1 Basic Instructions on Recording Type of Family

10.3.1.1 Scope

Type of family is a categorization or generic descriptor for the type of family.

10.3.1.2 Sources of Information

Take information on type of family from any source.

10.3.1.3 Recording Type of Family

Record the type of family using an appropriate term (e.g., *Family*, *Clan*, *Royal house*, *Dynasty*).

Record type of family as a separate element, as part of an access point, or as both. For additional instructions on recording type of family as part of the authorized access point, see **10.11.1.2**.

Family

Royal house

10.4 Date Associated with the Family

CORE ELEMENT

10.4.1 Basic Instructions on Recording Dates Associated with Families

10.4.1.1 Scope

A *date associated with the family* is a significant date associated with the history of a family.

10.4.1.2 Sources of Information

Take information on dates associated with the family from any source.

10.4.1.3 Recording Dates Associated with the Family

Record dates associated with the family by applying the same instructions used for dates associated with a person (see **9.3**).

Record dates as separate elements, as parts of access points, or as both. For additional instructions on recording a date as part of the authorized access point, see **10.11.1.3**.

> 1529–1739
>
> 1802–1945
>
> 202 B.C.–220 A.D.
>
> 4th century–9th century

Indicate the source of information by applying the instructions at **8.12.1.3**.

10.5 Place Associated with the Family

CORE ELEMENT

A place associated with the family is a core element when needed to distinguish a family from another family with the same name.

10.5.1 Basic Instructions on Recording Places Associated with Families

10.5.1.1 Scope

A *place associated with the family* is a place where a family resides or has resided or has some connection.

10.5.1.2 Sources of Information

Take information on places associated with the family from any source.

10.5.1.3 Recording Places Associated with the Family

Record the place or places (e.g., town, city, province, state, and/or country) in which the family resides or has resided or has some connection. Record the place name as instructed in chapter **16**. Abbreviate the names of countries, states, provinces, territories, etc., as instructed in appendix B (**B.11**), as applicable.

Record places associated with the family as separate elements, as parts of access points, or as both. For additional instructions on recording a place as part of the authorized access point, see **10.11.1.4**.

> Philippines
>
> Sydney, N.S.W.
>
> Armagh, Northern Ireland

Jamestown, Wash.

Québec
Minn.
Wis.

Indicate the source of information by applying the instructions at **8.12.1.3**.

10.6 Prominent Member of the Family

CORE ELEMENT

The name of a prominent member of the family is a core element when needed to distinguish a family from another family with the same name.

10.6.1 Basic Instructions on Recording Prominent Members of the Family

10.6.1.1 Scope

A ***prominent member of the family*** is a well-known individual who is a member of a family.

10.6.1.2 Sources of Information

Take information on prominent members of the family from any source.

10.6.1.3 Recording Prominent Members of the Family

Record the name of a prominent member or members of the family. Record the name in the form used for the authorized access point representing the person (see **9.19.1**).

Record prominent members of the family as separate elements, as parts of access points, or as both. For additional instructions on recording a prominent member of the family as part of the authorized access point, see **10.11.1.5**.

Peale, Charles Willson, 1741–1827
Preferred name for family recorded as: Peale

Peale, Norman Vincent, 1898–1993
Preferred name for family recorded as: Peale

Denny, Arthur Armstrong, 1822–1899
Preferred name for family recorded as: Denny

Denny, Anthony, 1501–1549
Preferred name for family recorded as: Denny

Indicate the source of information by applying the instructions at **8.12.1.3**.

10.7 Hereditary Title

10.7.1 Basic Instructions on Recording Hereditary Titles

10.7.1.1 Scope

A ***hereditary title*** is a title of nobility, etc., associated with a family.

10.7.1.2 Sources of Information

Take information on hereditary titles from any source.

10.7.1.3 Recording Hereditary Titles

Record a hereditary title associated with the family. Record the title in direct order in the plural form.

Record hereditary titles as separate elements, as variant names, or as both. For instructions on recording hereditary titles as variant names, see **10.2.3.5**.

> Earls of Shrewsbury
>
> ducs d'Orléans
>
> Countesses of Mar
>
> Viscounts Falkland
>
> condes de Lemos
>
> Dukes of Chandos
>
> Marquesses of Cholmondeley

Indicate the source of information by applying the instructions at **8.12.1.3**.

10.8 Language of the Family

10.8.1 Basic Instructions on Recording Languages of the Family

10.8.1.1 Scope

Language of the family is a language a family uses in its communications.

10.8.1.2 Sources of Information

Take information on the language or languages of the family from any source.

10.8.1.3 Recording the Languages of the Family

Record the language or languages the family uses in its communications. Use an appropriate term or terms in a language preferred by the agency creating the data. Select terms from a standard list of names of languages, if available.

Record a language used by the family as a separate element. Language is not recorded as part of an access point.

> English
> *Language used by the Baroni family of Natchez, Mississippi*
>
> Spanish
> English
> *Languages used by the Burgess family of Guatemala*

Indicate the source of information by applying the instructions at **8.12.1.3**.

10.9 Family History

10.9.1 Basic Instructions on Recording Family History

10.9.1.1 Scope

Family history is biographical information about the family and its members.

10.9.1.2 Sources of Information

Take information on family history from any source.

10.9.1.3 Recording Family History

Record biographical information about the family and/or its members.

Record family history as a separate element. Family history is not recorded as part of an access point.

> Austrian leatherworkers and bookbinders, active 19th–20th centuries
>
> Italian rulers, bankers, merchants, collectors, and patrons of the arts, active in Florence particularly from 15th through mid-18th centuries
>
> Samuel James, his wife Anna Maria (Foxwell) James, and their sons left Cornwall, England, for America in 1842, having emigrated more for political reasons than because of economic hardship. The James family first lived in Wisconsin, but in 1850–1851, they journeyed by wagon train to Oregon. In 1852 they settled at Grand Mound Prairie (later known as Jamestown) on the Chehalis River in Washington, where they prospered for some years. Samuel James and his sons established new homesteads in what is now known as James Rock on Grays Harbor, Washington, in 1859. Samuel James died in 1866 and Anna Maria James died in 1879. Their descendents continued to live in and around Jamestown, Washington
>
> The Chola dynasty (Tamil: சோழர் குலம்) was a Tamil dynasty that ruled primarily in southern India until the 13th century. The dynasty originated in the fertile valley of the Kaveri River. Karikala Chola was the most famous among the early Chola kings, while Rajaraja Chola, Rajendra Chola, and Kulothunga Chola I were notable emperors of the medieval Cholas. The Cholas were at the height of their power during the tenth, eleventh, and twelfth centuries. The Chola territories stretched from the islands of the Maldives in the south to as far north as the banks of the Godavari River in Andhra Pradesh. The power of the Cholas declined around the 12th century with the rise of the Pandyas and the Hoysala, eventually coming to an end towards the end of the 13th century

As appropriate, incorporate information associated with specific identifying elements (see **10.3–10.8**) into a family history element.

> James Brydges, 1st Duke of Chandos (1673–1744), was a British statesman and patron of the arts. His only surviving son, Henry Brydges, 2nd Duke of Chandos (1708–1771), inherited the dukedom and some of his father's posts. James Brydges, 3rd Duke of Chandos (1732–1789), son of Henry Brydges, was a Whig politician and courtier. The 3rd Duke had no male heirs, and at his death the dukedom became extinct. His daughter Anna Eliza married Richard Grenville, later the 1st Duke of Buckingham and Chandos

Indicate the source of information by applying the instructions at **8.12.1.3**.

10.10 Identifier for the Family

CORE ELEMENT

10.10.1 Basic Instructions on Recording Identifiers for Families

10.10.1.1 Scope

An *identifier for the family* is a character string uniquely associated with a family, or with a surrogate for a family (e.g., an authority record). The identifier serves to differentiate that family from other families.

10.10.1.2 Sources of Information

Take information on identifiers for the family from any source.

10.10.1.3 Recording Identifiers for Families

Record an identifier for the family. Precede the identifier with the name or an identification of the agency, etc., responsible for assigning the identifier, if readily ascertainable.

Libraries Australia control number: 000035401429
Identifier for the Adey family of Sydney, N.S.W.

ACCESS POINTS REPRESENTING FAMILIES

10.11 Constructing Access Points to Represent Families

10.11.1 Authorized Access Point Representing a Family

10.11.1.1 General Guidelines on Constructing Authorized Access Points to Represent Families

When constructing an authorized access point to represent a family, use the preferred name for the family (see **10.2.2**) as the basis for the authorized access point.

De Generes

Romanov

Saxe–Coburg–Gotha

Make additions to the name as instructed at **10.11.1.2–10.11.1.5**, in that order, as applicable.

Make the additions specified at **10.11.1.2–10.11.1.3** even if they are not needed to distinguish access points representing different families with the same name.

Make the additions specified at **10.11.1.4–10.11.1.5** if they are needed to distinguish access points representing different families with the same name.

Nayak (Dynasty : 1529–1739 : Madurai, India)

ADDITIONS TO ACCESS POINTS REPRESENTING FAMILIES

10.11.1.2 Type of Family

Add the type of family (see **10.3**), in parentheses, following the preferred name.

Branson (Family)

Donald (Clan)

Bourbon (Royal house)

10.11.1.3 Date Associated with the Family

Add a date or dates associated with the family (see **10.4**).

Nguyễn (Dynasty : 1558–1775)

Nguyễn (Dynasty : 1802–1945)

Pahlavi (Dynasty : 1925–1979)

10.11.1.4 Place Associated with the Family

Add the name of a place associated with the family (see **10.5**), if needed to distinguish one access point from another.

Yan (Family : Philippines)

Yan (Family : China)

James (Family : Jamestown, Wash.)

James (Family : Summerton, S.C.)

> *Optional Addition*
>
> Add the name of a place associated with the family if the addition assists in the identification of the family.
>
> Alzúa Gómez (Family : Michoacán de Ocampo, Mexico)

10.11.1.5 Prominent Member of the Family

Add the name of a prominent member of the family (see **10.6**) if needed to distinguish one access point from another. Make this addition when a place associated with the family is not available (see **10.11.1.4**).

Peale (Family : Peale, Charles Willson, 1741–1827)

Peale (Family : Peale, Norman Vincent, 1898–1993)

> *Optional Addition*
>
> Add the name of a prominent member of the family if the addition assists in the identification of the family.
>
> Medici (Royal house : Medici, Lorenzo de', 1449–1492)

10.11.2 Variant Access Point Representing a Family

10.11.2.1 General Guidelines on Constructing Variant Access Points to Represent Families

When constructing a variant access point to represent a family, use a variant name for the family (see **10.2.3**) as the basis for a variant access point.

Generes
Form recorded as preferred name: De Generes

Add the type of family (see **10.3**), in parentheses, following the variant name.

St. Amand (Family)
Form recorded as authorized access point: Saint Amand (Family)

Romanof (Dynasty)
Romanoff (Dynasty)
Романов (Dynasty)
Form recorded as authorized access point: Romanov (Dynasty)

Make other additions to the name, if considered important for identification. Apply the instructions at **10.11.1.3–10.11.1.5** in that order, as applicable.

St. Georges (Family : Fla.)

St-Georges (Family : Québec)

Nayak (Dynasty : 1739–1815 : Sri Lanka)
Form recorded as authorized access point: Nāyakkar (Dynasty : 1739–1815). *Variant name is the same as the preferred name for another family*

11

IDENTIFYING CORPORATE BODIES

11.0 Purpose and Scope

This chapter provides general guidelines and instructions on:

a) choosing preferred names for corporate bodies (see **11.2.2**)

b) recording preferred and variant names for corporate bodies (see **11.2**)

c) recording other identifying attributes of corporate bodies (see **11.3–11.12**)

d) constructing authorized access points representing corporate bodies (see **11.13.1**)

e) constructing variant access points representing corporate bodies (see **11.13.2**).

The chapter provides guidelines on recording names and other identifying attributes as separate elements, as parts of access points, or as both.

The preferred name for the corporate body is used as the basis for the authorized access point. The variant name or names for the corporate body are used as the basis for variant access points. Other identifying attributes of the corporate body may also be included in the access point.

A body is considered to be a corporate body only if it is identified by a particular name and if it acts, or may act, as a unit. A particular name consists of words that are a specific appellation rather than a general description.

Typical examples of corporate bodies are associations, institutions, business firms, nonprofit enterprises, governments, government agencies, projects and programs, religious bodies, local church groups identified by the name of the church, and conferences.

Ad hoc events (e.g., athletic contests, exhibitions, expeditions, fairs, and festivals) and vessels (e.g., ships and spacecraft) are considered to be corporate bodies.

11.1 General Guidelines on Identifying Corporate Bodies

11.1.1 Sources of Information

Take the name or names of the corporate body from any source.

For additional guidance on sources of information for the preferred name for the corporate body, see **11.2.2.2**.

Take information on other identifying attributes of the corporate body from any source.

11.1.2 Using Access Points to Represent Corporate Bodies

An authorized access point is one of the techniques used to represent either a corporate body associated with a resource (see **18.4.1**) or a related corporate body (see **32.1**).

When constructing authorized access points representing corporate bodies, apply the guidelines at **11.13.1**.

When constructing variant access points representing corporate bodies, apply the guidelines at **11.13.2**.

11.2 Name of the Corporate Body

CORE ELEMENT

Preferred name for the corporate body is a core element. Variant names for the corporate body are optional.

11.2.1 Basic Instructions on Recording Names of Corporate Bodies

11.2.1.1 Scope

A ***name of the corporate body*** is a word, character, or group of words and/or characters by which a corporate body is known.

When identifying corporate bodies, there are two categories of names:

a) preferred name for the corporate body (see **11.2.2**)

b) variant name for the corporate body (see **11.2.3**).

11.2.1.2 Sources of Information

Take the name or names of the corporate body from any source.

For additional guidance on sources of information for the preferred name for the corporate body, see **11.2.2.2**.

11.2.1.3 General Guidelines on Recording Names of Corporate Bodies

When recording a name of a corporate body, apply the general guidelines on recording names at **8.5**. When those guidelines refer to an appendix, apply the additional instructions in that appendix, as applicable.

Choose a preferred name for the corporate body by applying the instructions at **11.2.2.3** and **11.2.2.5**.

If a body changes its name, choose a new preferred name for use with resources associated with that name (see **11.2.2.6**).

Record the name chosen as the preferred name. Apply the instructions at **11.2.2.4** and **11.2.2.7–11.2.2.29**.

Names and forms of the name not chosen as the preferred name may be recorded as variant names (see **11.2.3**).

NAME

11.2.2 Preferred Name for the Corporate Body

CORE ELEMENT

11.2.2.1 Scope

The ***preferred name for the corporate body*** is the name or form of name chosen to identify the corporate body. It is also the basis for the authorized access point representing that body.

11.2.2.2 Sources of Information

Determine the preferred name for a corporate body from the following sources (in order of preference):

a) the preferred sources of information (see **2.2.2**) in resources associated with the corporate body

b) other formal statements appearing in resources associated with the corporate body

c) other sources (including reference sources).

11.2.2.3 Choosing the Preferred Name

When choosing a preferred name for the corporate body, choose the name by which the corporate body is commonly identified.

When a corporate body is known by more than one form of the same name, see additional instructions on choosing the preferred name at **11.2.2.5**.

When a corporate body changes its name, see the instructions at **11.2.2.6**.

31st December Women's Movement
5 Browns
924 Gilman Street Project
Breitkopf & Härtel
British Museum
Brown Palace Hotel
Carnegie Library of Pittsburgh
Cambridge Anthropological Expedition to Torres Straits
Chama cha Tanzania cha Kutoa Msaada wa Kisheria
Chartered Insurance Institute
Colin Buchanan and Partners
École de cuisine La Varenne
Glasgow Prestwick International Airport
Leicester Chamber of Commerce
Light Fantastic Players
Partridge Family
Radio Society of Great Britain
Reial Acadèmia Catalana de Belles Arts de Sant Jordi
St. Barbara-Bürgerspital
Symposium on World Tuna Fisheries
United States Catholic Conference
University of Adelaide
Voltamp Electric Mfg. Co.

11.2.2.4 Recording the Preferred Name

Record the name chosen as the preferred name for a corporate body by applying the general guidelines at **8.5**.

Record the name of a corporate body as it appears in resources associated with the body. If the name does not appear in resources associated with the body, or in case of doubt, record it in the form most commonly found in reference sources. Apply the instructions at **11.2.2.7–11.2.2.12**, as applicable.

For instructions on recording the names of subordinate and related bodies, see **11.2.2.13–11.2.2.29**.

CHOOSING THE PREFERRED NAME

11.2.2.5 Different Forms of the Same Name

This general instruction applies to the name of a corporate body that appears in different forms in resources associated with this body.

When appropriate, also apply these special instructions:

spelling (see **11.2.2.5.1**)
language (see **11.2.2.5.2**)

international bodies (see **11.2.2.5.3**)

conventional name (see **11.2.2.5.4**).

If variant forms of the name are found in resources associated with the body, choose the name that appears in the preferred sources of information (see **2.2.2**).

Variant forms do not include changes of name, i.e., names that the body has abandoned in the past or adopted for the future. For a change of name, see **11.2.2.6**.

If variant forms of the name appear in the preferred source of information, choose the form of the name that is presented formally. If no form is presented formally, or if all the forms are presented formally, choose the most commonly found form of the name.

If there is no most commonly found form of the name, choose a brief form of the name. The brief form may be an initialism or an acronym. The brief form must be sufficiently specific to differentiate the body from others with the same or similar brief names.

AFL-CIO
not American Federation of Labor and Congress of Industrial Organizations

American Philosophical Society
not American Philosophical Society, Held at Philadelphia, for Promoting Useful Knowledge

Euratom
not European Atomic Energy Community

Zhongguo di zhi ke xue yuan
not Zhongguo di zhi ke xue yan jiu yuan

Maryknoll Sisters
not Congregation of the Maryknoll Sisters of St. Dominic

EuroSSC
not European Conference on Smart Sensing and Context

If there is no brief form of the name that is specific enough to differentiate two or more bodies with the same or similar names, prefer a form found in reference sources over the official form.

Metropolitan Applied Research Center
Official name. Brief form sometimes used by the center, MARC Corporation, is the same as the name of another body located in New York

Variant names. Record other forms of the name as variant names (see **11.2.3**).

11.2.2.5.1 Spelling

If variant spellings of the name appear in resources associated with the body, choose the form found in the first resource received.

African Centre for Fertilizer Development
not African Center for Fertilizer Development
Resource received first has spelling "Centre"; resource received second has spelling "Center"

Variant names. Record the other spellings of the name as variant names (see **11.2.3.6**).

11.2.2.5.2 Language

If a corporate body's name has appeared in different languages, choose as the preferred name the form in the official language of the body.

Comité français de la danse
not French Committee of the Dance

Alternative

Choose a form in a language preferred by the agency creating the data.

Japan Productivity Center
not Nihon Seisansei Honbu

Union of Chambers of Commerce, Industry, and Commodity Exchanges of Turkey
not Türkiye Ticaret Odaları, Sanayi Odaları ve Ticaret Borsaları Birliği

If there is more than one official language and one of these is a language preferred by the agency creating the data, choose that form as the preferred name.

Canadian Committee on Cataloguing
not Comité canadien de catalogage

If:

the body has more than one official language

and

a language preferred by the agency creating the data is not one of the official languages of the body, or, the official language of the body is not known

then:

choose as the preferred name the form of name in the language used predominantly in resources associated with the body.

Schweizerische Nationalbibliothek
not Biblioteca nazionale svizzera
not Bibliothèque nationale suisse
German is the language used predominantly by the body in its publications

In case of doubt, choose the form that is presented first in the first resource received.

Variant names. Record forms of the name in other languages as variant names (see **11.2.3.6**).

11.2.2.5.3 International Bodies

If the name of an international body appears in resources associated with it in a language preferred by the agency creating the data, choose that form as the preferred name. In other cases, apply the instructions at **11.2.2.5.2**.

League of Arab States
not Union des états arabes
not Jāmiʻat al-Duwal al-ʻArabīyah

European Economic Community
not Communauté économique européenne
not Europese Economische Gemeenschap
[etc.]

International Federation of Library Associations and Institutions
not Fédération internationale des associations de bibliothécaires et des bibliothèques
not Internationaler Verband der Bibliothekarischen Vereine und Institutionen
not Mezhdunarodnai͡a federat͡sii͡a bibliotechnykh assot͡siat͡siĭ i uchrezhdeniĭ
[*etc.*]

Nordic Society for Radiation Protection
not Nordiska sällskapet för strålskydd
not Nordisk selskab for strålebeskyttelse
[*etc.*]

Societas Heraldica Scandinavica
not Heraldisk selskab
not Heraldinen seura
not Skjaldfrædafélagid
not Heraldisk selskap
not Heraldiska sällskapet
Official name is Latin; name appears in Danish, Finnish, Icelandic, Norwegian, and Swedish

Variant names. Record forms of the name in other languages as variant names (see **11.2.3.6**).

11.2.2.5.4 Conventional Name

A ***conventional name*** is a name, other than the real or official name, by which a corporate body has come to be known. If a body is frequently identified by a conventional name in reference sources in its own language, choose this conventional name as the preferred name.

York Minster
not Metropolitan Church of St. Peter, York

Museo del Prado
not Museo Nacional de Pintura y Escultura
not Museo Nacional del Prado
not Real Museo de Pinturas y Esculturas

Exceptions

Ancient and international bodies. [1] If the name of a body of ancient origin or of one that is international in character has become well established in a form in a language preferred by the agency creating the data, choose that form as the preferred name.

Assyrian Church of the East

Benedictines

Cluniacs

Coptic Church

Council of Nicaea

Franciscans

Knights of Malta

Paris Peace Conference

Poor Clares

Royal and Select Masters

Royal Arch Masons

Synod of the Oak

Vatican Council

Yalta Conference

Autocephalous patriarchates, archdioceses, etc. Record the name of an ancient autocephalous patriarchate, archdiocese, etc., of the Eastern Church using the name of the place by which it is identified. Add, in parentheses, a word or phrase indicating the type of ecclesiastical jurisdiction.

Antioch (Orthodox patriarchate)

Constantinople (Ecumenical patriarchate)

Cyprus (Archdiocese)

Jerusalem (Orthodox patriarchate)

Religious orders and societies. Choose the best-known form of the name in a language preferred by the agency creating the data, if possible. In case of doubt, follow this order of preference:

a) the conventional name by which its members are known in a language preferred by the agency

b) the form of name in a language preferred by the agency and used by units of the order or society located in countries where that language is spoken

c) the name of the order or society in the language of the country of its origin.

Franciscans
not Friars Minor
not Minorites
not Ordo Fratrum Minorum
[*etc.*]

Jesuits
not Compañía de Jesús
not Societas Iesu
not Society of Jesus
[*etc.*]

Ordo Templi Orientis
not Order of Oriental Templars
not Hermetic Brotherhood of Light
not O.T.O.
not OTO
not Order of the Temple of the East
[*etc.*]

Best-known form of name is in Latin; no predominant conventional name in a language preferred by the agency.

Brothers of Our Lady of Mercy

Community of the Resurrection

Dominican Nuns of the Second Order of Perpetual Adoration
not Dominicans. Second Order

Dominican Sisters of the Perpetual Rosary

Sisters of Providence of the Immaculate Conception
not Soeurs de la Providence et de l'Immaculée Conception

Third Order Regular of St. Francis
not Franciscans. Third Order Regular

Third Order Secular of St. Francis
not Franciscans. Third Order Secular

International Society for Krishna Consciousness
not Hare Krishna Society

Suore collegine della Sacra Famiglia

Zgromadzenie Sióstr Urszulanek Serca Jezusa Konającego

Governments. The conventional name of a government is the name of the area over which the government exercises jurisdiction. This can be a country, province, state, county, municipality, etc. See chapter **16** for instructions on choosing and recording the names of places.

France
not République française

Serbia
not Narodna Republika Srbija
not Republika Srbija
[etc.]

Virginia
not Commonwealth of Virginia

Nottinghamshire (England)
not County of Nottinghamshire (England)

Castle Rock (Colo.)
not Town of Castle Rock (Colo.)

If the official name of the government is in common use, choose it as the preferred name.

Greater Anchorage Area Borough (Alaska)

Region Sjælland (Denmark)

Seminole Nation of Oklahoma

Conferences, congresses, meetings, etc. If different forms of a conference's name appear in the preferred source of information, choose a form of the name that includes the name (or abbreviation of the name) of the associated body.

FAO Technical Meeting on Coffee Production and Protection

Do not apply this instruction for a conference that is recorded as subordinate to the name of a body associated with the conference (e.g., the annual meeting of an association). Apply instead the instructions at **11.2.2.14.6**.

If a conference has both a specific name of its own and a more general name as one of a series of conferences, choose the specific name as the preferred name.

Northwest Conference on the Role of Nuclear Energy (1969 : Portland, Or.)
not Governor's Conference on Conservation (2nd : 1969 : Portland, Or.)

Symposium on Protein Metabolism (1953 : University of Toronto)
not Nutrition Symposium (1953 : University of Toronto)

Symposium on the Role of Some of the Newer Vitamins in Human Metabolism and Nutrition (1955 : Vanderbilt University School of Medicine)
not Nutrition Symposium (1955 : Vanderbilt University School of Medicine)

Symposium on Endocrines and Nutrition (1956 : University of Michigan Medical School)
not Nutrition Symposium (1956 : University of Michigan Medical School)

Joint EMBS-BMES Conference
not IEEE Engineering in Medicine and Biology Society. Conference
not Biomedical Engineering Society. Fall Meeting

Local places of worship. The name of a local place of worship is the name of a church, cathedral, monastery, convent, abbey, temple, mosque, synagogue, etc. If this name appears in different forms in the preferred source of information of resources associated with the body, choose the predominant form. If there is no predominant form, follow this order of preference:

a) a form of name containing the name of any person, object, place, or event to which the local church, etc., is dedicated or after which it is named

All Saints Church

Chapelle Saint-Louis

Church of the Holy Sepulchre

Duomo di Santa Maria in Colle

Jāmiʿ ʿAmr ibn al-ʿĀṣ

Monastère de la Visitation

St. Paul's Cathedral

Stephen Wise Free Synagogue

b) a form of name beginning with a word or phrase descriptive of a type of local church, etc.

Abtei Reichenau

Great Synagogue

Jüdische Reformgemeinde zu Berlin

Monasterio de Rueda

Parish Church of Botley

Unitarian Universalist Church

c) a form of name beginning with the name of the place in which the local church, etc., is situated.

Bushwick Avenue German Presbyterian Church

Island Grove United Methodist Church

Kataragama Mosque and Shrine

Kölner Dom

Oak Park Temple

Vilniaus Didžioji sinagoga

Winchester Cathedral

Variant names. Record other forms of the name as variant names (see **11.2.3**).

---

1. Examples of ancient or international bodies: religious bodies, fraternal and knightly orders, church councils, and diplomatic conferences. If a diplomatic conference has no formal name and has not yet acquired a conventional name, choose the name found most commonly in periodical articles and newspaper accounts in a language preferred by the agency creating the data. If another name becomes established later, change the preferred name to that name.

11.2.2.6 Change of Name

If the name of a corporate body has changed (including changes from one language to another), choose the earlier name as the preferred name for use with resources associated with the earlier name. Choose the later name as the preferred name for use with resources associated with the later name.

Pennsylvania State University
Earlier name: Pennsylvania State College

National Tuberculosis Association
Earlier name: National Association for the Study and Prevention of Tuberculosis

For instructions on recording relationships between the earlier and later names of the body, see chapter **32** (related corporate bodies).

RECORDING THE PREFERRED NAME

11.2.2.7 Names Consisting of or Containing Initials

If the name of a corporate body consists of or contains initials, omit or include full stops and other marks of punctuation according to the most commonly found usage of the body. In case of doubt, omit the full stops, etc.

For instructions on spacing of initials and acronyms, see **8.5.6**.

Aslib

Delegación Nacional de Sindicatos de F.E.T. y de las J.O.N.S.

H. Lee Moffitt International Symposium on Cancer Biology and Therapeutics

IUCN/SSC Polar Bear Specialist Group

L.I.F.E. Choir

Projet Assistance aux entreprises d'état B.I.T./PNUD

USDLA

W.H. Coverdale Collection of Canadiana

11.2.2.8 Initial Articles

When recording the preferred name of a corporate body, include an initial article, if present.

The Library Association

Der Wehrbeauftragte

Alternative

Omit an initial article (see appendix C) unless the name is to be accessed under the article (e.g., a corporate name that begins with an article that is the first part of the name of a person or place).

Amis de la terre du Morvan
not Les Amis de la terre du Morvan

Library Association
not The Library Association

Danske Præsteforening
not Den Danske Præsteforening

but

El Niño Task Force

Le Corbusier Sketchbook Publication Committee

Los Angeles Philharmonic Orchestra

11.2.2.9 Citations of Honours

Omit a phrase citing an honour or order awarded to the body.

Moskovskai͡a gosudarstvennai͡a konservatorii͡a im. P.I. Chaĭkovskogo
not Moskovskai͡a gosudarstvennai͡a dvazhdy ordena Lenina konservatorii͡a imeni P.I. Chaĭkovskogo

Gosudarstvennyĭ akademicheskiĭ teatr imeni Mossoveta
not Gosudarstvennyĭ ordena Lenina i ordena Trudovogo Krasnogo Znameni akademicheskiĭ teatr imeni Mossoveta

Royal Ulster Constabulary
not Royal Ulster Constabulary GC
not Royal Ulster Constabulary George Cross

11.2.2.10 Terms Indicating Incorporation and Certain Other Terms

Omit the following terms unless they are an integral part of the name or are needed to make it clear that the name is that of a corporate body:

a) an adjectival term or abbreviation indicating incorporation (e.g., *Incorporated, E.V., Ltd.*)

b) a term indicating state ownership of a corporate body

c) a word or phrase, abbreviated or in full, indicating the type of incorporated entity (e.g., *Aktiebolaget, Gesellschaft mit beschränkter Haftung, Kabushiki Kaisha, Società per azione*).

American Cancer Society
not American Cancer Society, Inc.

Automobiltechnische Gesellschaft
not Automobiltechnische Gesellschaft E.V.

Daiwa Ginkō
not Daiwa Ginkō Kabushiki Kaisha

Samsŏng Chŏnja
not Samsŏng Chŏnja Chusik Hoesa

Kraftfahrzeugwerk "Ernst Grube" Werdau
not VEB Kraftfahrzeugwerk "Ernst Grube" Werdau

Compañía Internacional de Mapas
not Compañía Internacional de Mapas S.A.

Zhongguo yin hang
not Zhongguo yin hang gu fen you xian gong si

but
Films Incorporated

Nature Photographers Ltd.

Halifax plc

Shenzhen zheng quan xin xi you xian gong si

Gay Men's Health Crisis, Inc.

Nihon Genshiryoku Hatsuden Kabushiki Kaisha

Howard Ricketts Limited

Winwin Consult Sdn. Bhd.

Best Practices, LLC

If:
a term indicating incorporation, etc., is needed to make it clear that the name is that of a corporate body
and
the term occurs at the beginning of the name
then:
transpose the term to the end of the name.

Aerotransport, Aktiebolaget
not Aktiebolaget Aerotransport

Forstprojektierung Potsdam, VEB
not VEB Forstprojektierung Potsdam

If the name of a corporate body in an Asian language includes an initial word or phrase indicating the private character of the body (e.g., *Shiritsu, Si li*), omit this initial word or phrase. Do not omit it if it is an integral part of the name.

Dong hai da xue
not Si li Dong hai da xue

but

Shiritsu Daigaku Toshokan Kyōkai

Omit abbreviations occurring before the name of a ship (e.g., *U.S.S., H.M.S.*).

Arizona (Battleship)
not U.S.S. Arizona

Swift (Sloop of war)
not H.M.S. Swift

11.2.2.11 Number or Year of Convocation of a Conference, Etc.

Omit from the name of a conference, etc., indications of its number, or year or years of convocation, etc. Apply this instruction to the name of a congress, meeting, exhibition, fair, festival, etc., and to the name of a conference, etc., treated as a subordinate body (see **11.2.2.14.6**).

Conference on Co-ordination of Galactic Research
not Second Conference on Co-ordination of Galactic Research

Calcutta Film Festival
not 4th Calcutta Film Festival

Expedição Brasileira à Antártica
not 1a. Expedição Brasileira à Antártica

Biennial Symposium on Active Control of Vibration and Noise
not Sixth Biennial Symposium on Active Control of Vibration and Noise

Symposium on Some Mathematical Questions in Biology
not 1992 Symposium on Some Mathematical Questions in Biology

Schweizerische Grönland-Expedition
not Schweizerische Grönland-Expedition 1912/13

Polyurethanes Expo
not Polyurethanes Expo '99

San Francisco Art Association. Annual Drawing and Print Exhibition
not San Francisco Art Association. Twenty-second Annual Drawing and Print Exhibition

11.2.2.12 Names Found in a Non-preferred Script

If the name of the body is found in a script that differs from a preferred script of the agency creating the data, transliterate the name according to the scheme chosen by the agency.

Zhongguo wen zi gai ge wei yuan hui
Name appears in original script as: 中國文字改革委員会

Institut mirovoĭ literatury imeni A.M. Gor'kogo
Name appears in original script as: Институт мировой литературы имени А.М. Горького

Matsushita Denki Sangyō
Name appears in original script as: 松下電器産業

Agudah ha-geʼografit ha-Yiśreʼelit
Name appears in original script as: אגודה הגיאוגרפית הישראלית

Alternative

If:

the name of the body is in a script that differs from a preferred script of the agency creating the data

and

a transliterated form appears in resources associated with the body

then:

use the transliterated form. In some cases, there is more than one transliterated form. If one of the forms matches the agency's transliteration of the name (i.e., the form transliterated using the transliteration scheme chosen by the agency[2]), use that form.

Zhongshan daxue
not Zhongshan da xue

Nippon Tōki Kabushiki Kaisha
not Nihon Tōki Kabushiki Kaisha

Himalaya Seva Sangh
not Himālaya Sevā Saṅgha

2. This alternative instruction can be applied selectively language by language.

Variant names. Record the other forms of the transliterated name as variant names (see **11.2.3.6**).

RECORDING NAMES OF SUBORDINATE AND RELATED BODIES

11.2.2.13 General Guidelines on Recording Names of Subordinate and Related Bodies

Record the name of a subordinate body or a related body by applying the basic instructions at **11.2.2.4**, unless its name belongs to one or more of the types listed at **11.2.2.14**.

Canadian National Railways

Association of College and Research Libraries

BBC Symphony Orchestra

Bodleian Library

NWT Geographic Names Program

Provinciale Bibliotheek Centrale voor Noord-Brabant

Harvard Law School

Informit

Consejo Superior de Investigaciones Científicas

Australia Post

Variant names. Record as a variant name the name of the body in the form of a subdivision of the authorized access point representing the higher body (see **11.2.3.7**).

11.2.2.14 Subordinate and Related Bodies Recorded Subordinately

This instruction applies to subordinate or related bodies.

If a body's name belongs to one or more of the types listed at **11.2.2.14.1–11.2.2.14.6** or if it is a type of body listed at **11.2.2.14.7–11.2.2.14.18**, record the name of the subordinate or related body as a subdivision of the higher or related body. Record it in the form of a subdivision of the authorized access point representing the higher or related body. Make it a direct or indirect subdivision applying the instructions at **11.2.2.15**.

Omit from the subdivision the name (or abbreviation of the name) of the higher or related body in noun form unless the omission would result in a name that does not make sense.

Stanford University. Archives
not Stanford University. Stanford University Archives
Name: Stanford University Archives

British Broadcasting Corporation. Political Research Unit
not British Broadcasting Corporation. BBC Political Research Unit
Name: BBC Political Research Unit

Canada. Department of Consumer and Corporate Affairs
not Canada. Canada Department of Consumer and Corporate Affairs
Name: Canada Department of Consumer and Corporate Affairs

but

American Library Association. Activities Committee on New Directions for ALA
not American Library Association. Activities Committee on New Directions
Name: Activities Committee on New Directions for ALA

Canada. Corporations Canada
not Canada. Corporations
Name: Corporations Canada. *A major executive agency of Canada. The name of the higher body is retained because the omission would result in a name that does not make sense*

In case of doubt about whether the corporate body is subordinate or whether it falls within the scope of a specific instruction, record the name of the body directly.

Human Resources Center
Name: Human Resources Center

Governor's Fellowship Program (Ind.)
not Indiana. Governor's Fellowship Program
Name: Governor's Fellowship Program

Musées de l'État (Luxembourg)
not Luxembourg. Musées de l'État
Name: Musées de l'État

National Health Institute (N.Z.)
not New Zealand. National Health Institute
Name: National Health Institute

Research & Advisory Services
Name: Research & Advisory Services

National Portrait Gallery (Australia)
not Australia. National Portrait Gallery
Name: National Portrait Gallery

11.2.2.14.1 Body Whose Name Implies It Is Part of Another

Apply the instructions at **11.2.2.14** to a name containing a term that by definition implies that the body is part of another (e.g., *Department*, *Division*, *Section*, *Branch*).

Bangalore University. Department of Botany
Name: Department of Botany

British Broadcasting Corporation. Finance Division
Name: Finance Division

Oregon. Bridge Engineering Section
Name: Bridge Engineering Section

Hamburg (Germany). Abteilung Landwirtschaft und Gartenbau
Name: Abteilung Landwirtschaft und Gartenbau

Koninklijk Instituut voor de Tropen. Afdeling Anthropologie
Name: Afdeling Anthropologie

Costa Rica. Departamento de Medicina Preventiva
Name: Departamento de Medicina Preventiva

Società italiana di psicologia. Divisione di psicologia clinica
Name: Divisione di psicologia clinica

Zhongguo yi qi yi biao xue hui. Jing mi ji xie fen hui
Name: Zhongguo yi qi yi biao xue hui jing mi ji xie fen hui

Kent (England). Land Use and Transport Policy Unit
Name: Land Use and Transport Policy Unit

11.2.2.14.2 Body Whose Name Implies Administrative Subordination

Apply the instructions at **11.2.2.14** to a name containing a term that normally implies administrative subordination (e.g., *Committee*, *Commission*). Apply only if the name of the higher body is required for the identification of the subordinate body.

Vienna (Austria). Statistisches Amt
Name: Statistisches Amt

Côte d'Ivoire. Agence d'études et de promotion de l'emploi
Name: Agence d'études et de promotion de l'emploi

Fundación Terram. Dirección de Estudios
Name: Dirección de Estudios

Institut sénégalais de recherches agricoles. Bureau d'analyses macroéconomiques
Name: Bureau d'analyses macro-économiques

International Council for the Exploration of the Sea. Marine Chemistry Working Group
Name: Marine Chemistry Working Group

International Dairy Congress (22nd : 1986 : The Hague, Netherlands). Organizing Committee
Name: Organizing Committee

Valencia (Spain). Servicio de Investigación Arqueológica Municipal
Name: Servicio de Investigación Arqueológica Municipal

National Audubon Society. Advisory Panel on the Spotted Owl
Name: Advisory Panel on the Spotted Owl

Japan. Kishōchō
Name: Kishōchō

Canada. Royal Commission on Banking and Finance
Name: Royal Commission on Banking and Finance

Minas Gerais (Brazil). Secretaria de Indústria, Comércio e Turismo
Name: Secretaria de Indústria, Comércio e Turismo

but

ACS Office of Statistical Services
Name: ACS Office of Statistical Services

U.S. Census Bureau
Name: U.S. Census Bureau

Royal Commission on Education in Ontario
Name: Royal Commission on Education in Ontario

Honolulu Committee on Aging
Name: Honolulu Committee on Aging

National Commission on United Methodist Higher Education
Name: National Commission on United Methodist Higher Education

UW-Madison Campus Planning Committee
Name: UW-Madison Campus Planning Committee

11.2.2.14.3 Body Whose Name Is General in Nature or Simply Indicates a Geographic, Chronological, or Numbered or Lettered Subdivision of a Parent Body

Apply the instructions at **11.2.2.14** to a name that is general in nature (e.g., contains neither distinctive proper nouns or adjectives, nor subject words) or that simply indicates a geographic, chronological, or numbered or lettered subdivision of a parent body.

American Dental Association. Research Institute
Name: Research Institute

Niger. Commissariat général au développement. Centre de documentation
Name: Centre de documentation

Jean and Alexander Heard Library. Friends of the Library
Name: Friends of the Library

United States. National Labor Relations Board. Library
Name: Library

Malaysia. Customs and Excise Department. Sabah Region
Name: Sabah Region

Canadian Jewish Congress. Central Region
Name: Central Region

Dartmouth College. Class of 1957
Name: Class of 1957

Knights of Labor. District Assembly No. 3
Name: District Assembly No. 3

11.2.2.14.4 Body Whose Name Does Not Convey the Idea of a Corporate Body and Does Not Contain the Name of the Higher Body

Apply the instructions at **11.2.2.14** to a name that does not convey the idea of a corporate body and does not contain the name of the higher body.

British Library. Science, Technology, and Business
Name: Science, Technology, and Business

CBS Inc. Economics and Research
Name: Economics and Research

Canada. Citizenship and Immigration Canada. Human Resources
Name: Human Resources

Illinois. Bureau of Employment Security. Research & Analysis
Name: Research & Analysis

but

BC Fisheries
not British Columbia. BC Fisheries
Name: BC Fisheries

California Records & Information Management
not California. Records & Information Management
not California. Department of General Services. Records & Information Management
Name: California Records & Information Management

11.2.2.14.5 University Faculty, School, College, Institute, Laboratory, Etc., with Name That Simply Indicates a Particular Field of Study

Apply the instructions at **11.2.2.14** to the name of a university faculty, school, college, institute, laboratory, etc., that simply indicates a particular field of study.

École polytechnique fédérale de Lausanne. Laboratoire d'experimentation architecturale
Name: Laboratoire d'experimentation architecturale

Københavns universitet. Ægyptologisk institut
Name: Ægyptologisk institut

Princeton University. Bureau of Urban Research
Name: Bureau of Urban Research

St. Patrick's College (Dublin, Ireland). Educational Research Centre
Name: Educational Research Centre

Syracuse University. College of Medicine
Name: College of Medicine

Universidad Autónoma de Nuevo León. Facultad de Ciencias Forestales
Name: Facultad de Ciencias Forestales

but

Australian Centre for Child Protection
not University of South Australia. Australian Centre for Child Protection
Name: Australian Centre for Child Protection

Harvard Law School
not Harvard University. Harvard Law School
not Harvard University. Law School
Name: Harvard Law School

John F. Kennedy School of Government
not Harvard University. John F. Kennedy School of Government
Name: John F. Kennedy School of Government

McGill Institute for the Study of Canada
not McGill University. Institute for the Study of Canada
not McGill University. McGill Institute for the Study of Canada
Name: McGill Institute for the Study of Canada

11.2.2.14.6 Non-Governmental Body with Name That Includes the Entire Name of the Higher or Related Body

Apply the instructions at **11.2.2.14** to a name of a non-governmental body with a name that includes the entire name of the higher or related body.

Distinguish cases in which the subordinate body's name includes the names of higher bodies from cases in which the names of higher bodies appear only in association with the subordinate body's name.

American Legion. Auxiliary
Name: American Legion Auxiliary

Auburn University. Agricultural Experiment Station
Name: Agricultural Experiment Station of Auburn University

Dunedin Botanic Garden. Friends
Name: Friends of the Dunedin Botanic Garden

International Whaling Commission. Annual Meeting
Name: Annual Meeting of the International Whaling Commission

United Methodist Church (U.S.). General Conference
Name: General Conference of the United Methodist Church

Brock University. Philosophical Society
Name: Brock University Philosophical Society

University of Vermont. Choral Union
Name: University of Vermont Choral Union

St. John's College (University of Oxford). Library
Name: St. John's College Library

but

BBC Symphony Orchestra
not British Broadcasting Corporation. Symphony Orchestra
Name: BBC Symphony Orchestra

Friends of the Corcoran
not Corcoran Gallery of Art. Friends
Name: Friends of the Corcoran

Utah Museum of Fine Arts
not University of Utah. Museum of Fine Arts
Name: Utah Museum of Fine Arts

CU-Boulder Alumni Association
not University of Colorado, Boulder. Alumni Association
Name: CU-Boulder Alumni Association

11.2.2.14.7 Ministry or Similar Major Executive Agency

Apply the instructions at **11.2.2.14** to a government body that is a ministry or similar major executive agency (i.e., one that has no other agency above it) as defined by official publications of the government in question.

Vanuatu. Ministry of Internal Affairs and Social Services

Madagascar. Ministère de la jeunesse et des sports

Japan. Kankyōshō

Brunei. Kementerian Perindustrian dan Sumber-Sumber Utama

United States. National Aeronautics and Space Administration

11.2.2.14.8 Government Official or a Religious Official

Apply the instructions at **11.2.2.14** to a government official (see also **11.2.2.18**) or a religious official (see also **11.2.2.26**).

11.2.2.14.9 Legislative Body

Apply the instructions at **11.2.2.14** to a legislative body (see also **11.2.2.19**).

11.2.2.14.10 Constitutional Convention

Apply the instructions at **11.2.2.14** to a constitutional convention (see also **11.2.2.20**).

11.2.2.14.11 Court

Apply the instructions at **11.2.2.14** to a court (see also **11.2.2.21**).

11.2.2.14.12 Principal Service of the Armed Forces of a Government

Apply the instructions at **11.2.2.14** to a principal service of the armed forces of a government (see also **11.2.2.22**).

11.2.2.14.13 Embassy, Consulate, Etc.

Apply the instructions at **11.2.2.14** to an embassy, consulate, etc. (see also **11.2.2.23**).

11.2.2.14.14 Delegation to an International or Intergovernmental Body

Apply the instructions at **11.2.2.14** to a delegation to an international or intergovernmental body (see also **11.2.2.24**).

11.2.2.14.15 Council, Etc., of a Single Religious Body

Apply the instructions at **11.2.2.14** to a council, etc., of a single religious body (see also **11.2.2.25**).

11.2.2.14.16 Religious Province, Diocese, Synod, Etc.

Apply the instructions at **11.2.2.14** to a religious province, diocese, synod, etc. (see also **11.2.2.27**).

11.2.2.14.17 Central Administrative Organ of the Catholic Church

Apply the instructions at **11.2.2.14** to a central administrative organ of the Catholic Church (see also **11.2.2.28**).

11.2.2.14.18 Papal Diplomatic Mission, Etc.

Apply the instructions at **11.2.2.14** to a papal diplomatic mission, etc. (see also **11.2.2.29**).

11.2.2.15 Direct or Indirect Subdivision

Unless instructed otherwise at **11.2.2.16–11.2.2.29**, record the name of a body belonging to one or more of the types listed at **11.2.2.14** as a subdivision of the authorized access point representing the lowest organizational unit in the hierarchy that is recorded directly under its own name.

Omit intervening units in the hierarchy, unless the name of the subordinate or related body has been, or is likely to be, used by another body recorded as a subdivision of the authorized access point representing the same higher or related body. In that case, interpose the name of the lowest unit in the hierarchy that will distinguish between the bodies.

Public Library Association. Audiovisual Committee

Hierarchy: American Library Association - Public Library Association - Audiovisual Committee

France. Commission centrale des marchés

Hierarchy: France - Ministère de l'économie et des finances - Commission centrale des marchés

University of Texas at Austin. Petroleum Extension Service

Hierarchy: University of Texas at Austin - Division of Continuing Education - Petroleum Extension Service

El Salvador. Servicio de Parques Nacionales y Vida Silvestre

Hierarchy: El Salvador - Ministerio de Agricultura y Ganaderia - Dirección General de Recursos Naturales Renovables - Servicio de Parques Nacionales y Vida Silvestre

but

American Library Association. Reference and Adult Services Division. History Section. Bibliography and Indexes Committee

Hierarchy: American Library Association - Reference and Adult Services Division - History Section - Bibliography and Indexes Committee. *Intervening units are not omitted because the name seems likely to be used by another body in the organization*

California. Department of Corrections. Research Division

Hierarchy: California - Health and Welfare Agency - Department of Corrections - Research Division. *Other California departments have units called Research Division*

France. Ministère de la jeunesse, des sports et des loisirs. Division des études et de la statistique

Hierarchy: France - Ministère de la jeunesse, des sports et des loisirs - Direction de l'administration - Division des études et de la statistique

Variant names. Record other forms of direct or indirect subdivision as variant names (see **11.2.3.7**).

11.2.2.16 Joint Committees, Commissions, Etc.

Record the name of a body made up of representatives of two or more other bodies by applying the general instructions at **11.2.2.4**.

For legislative committees, see **11.2.2.19.2**.

Joint Committee on Court Calendar Congestion

A joint committee of the Association of the Bar of the City of New York and the Columbia Project for Effective Justice

Canadian Committee on MARC

A joint committee of Asted, the Canadian Library Association, Library and Archives Canada, A-G Canada, and the Bureau of Canadian Archivists

Omit the names of the parent bodies in these cases:

a) when the names of the parent bodies occur within or at the end of the name
and
b) when the name of the joint unit is distinctive without them.

Joint Committee on Insulator Standards

Name: Joint Committee on Insulator Standards of the Edison Electric Institute and the National Electrical Manufacturers Association

but

Joint Committee of the American Library Association and the Rural Sociological Society

If the names of the parent bodies are recorded as subdivisions of a common higher body, record the name of the joint unit as a subordinate body of the common higher body. Apply the general guidelines at **11.2.2.13**.

American Library Association. Joint Committee to Compile a List of International Subscription Agents

A joint committee of the Acquisitions and Serials sections of the American Library Association's Resources and Technical Services Division

11.2.2.17 Conventionalized Names for State and Local Units of United States Political Parties

Record the name of a state or local unit of a political party in the United States as a subdivision of the party. Record it in the form of a subdivision of the authorized access point representing the party. Omit from the name of the unit any indication of the name of the party or the state or locality.

Democratic Party (Mo.). State Committee

Name: Missouri Democratic State Committee

Republican Party (Ohio). State Executive Committee

Name: Ohio Republican State Executive Committee

Republican Party (La.). Convention

Name: Convention of the Republican Party of Louisiana

11.2.2.18 Government Officials

Record the names of government officials by applying these instructions, as applicable:

heads of state, heads of government, etc. (see **11.2.2.18.1**)

ruling executive bodies (see **11.2.2.18.2**)

heads of international intergovernmental bodies (see **11.2.2.18.3**)
governors of dependent or occupied territories (see **11.2.2.18.4**)
other officials (see **11.2.2.18.5**).

11.2.2.18.1 Heads of State, Heads of Government, Etc.

Record the title of a sovereign, president, other head of state, governor, head of government, or chief executive who is acting in an official capacity (see **6.31.1**), as a subdivision of the jurisdiction. Record the title in the form of a subdivision of the authorized access point representing the jurisdiction. Record the title in a language preferred by the agency creating the data (unless there is no equivalent term in that language).

Indonesia. President
not Indonesia. Presiden

Chiapas (Mexico). Governor
not Chiapas (Mexico). Gobernador

Swaziland. Prime Minister

Managua (Nicaragua). Mayor
not Managua (Nicaragua). Alcalde

King County (Wash.). Executive

Japan. Prime Minister
not Japan. Naikaku Sōri Daijin

Thailand. Prime Minister
not Thailand. Nāyok Ratthamontrī

If the official being identified is a specific incumbent of the office, add, in parentheses (in this order):

a) the inclusive years of the reign or incumbency

b) the name of the person in a brief form, in the language of the preferred name for that person.

Separate the years of the reign or incumbency from the name of the person using a space, colon, space.

Portugal. President (1996–2006 : Sampaio)

New Jersey. Governor (2002–2004 : McGreevey)

Iran. Shah (1941–1979 : Mohammed Reza Pahlavi)

Brunei. Sultan (1967– : Hassanal Bolkiah Mu'izzaddin Waddaulah)

Papal States. Sovereign (1800–1823 : Pius VII)

British Columbia. Premier (2000–2001 : Dosanjh)

Central African Republic. Prime Minister (2001–2003 : Ziguele)

Germany. Chancellor (1990–1998 : Kohl)

Germany. Chancellor (2005– : Merkel)

Israel. Prime Minister (1999–2001 : Barak)

New Zealand. Prime Minister (2008– : Key)

Seattle (Wash.). Mayor (1978–1990 : Royer)

If the title varies with the gender of the incumbent, use a general term (e.g., *Sovereign* rather than *King* or *Queen*).

Scotland. Sovereign (1649–1685 : Charles II)

Scotland. Sovereign (1542–1567 : Mary)

Spain. Sovereign (1833–1868 : Isabella II)

Spain. Sovereign (1975– : Juan Carlos I)

Spain. Sovereign (1479–1504 : Ferdinand V and Isabella I)

If there are two or more non-consecutive periods of incumbency for the same incumbent, record each period as a separate preferred name.

United States. President (1885–1889 : Cleveland)

United States. President (1893–1897 : Cleveland)

Canada. Prime Minister (1867–1873 : Macdonald)

Canada. Prime Minister (1878–1891 : Macdonald)

Record the relationships between the office and the person by applying the instructions in chapters **30** (related persons) and **32** (related corporate bodies).

11.2.2.18.2 Ruling Executive Bodies

Record the name of a ruling executive body (e.g., a military junta), that is acting in an official capacity (see **6.31.1**), as a subdivision of the jurisdiction. Record the name in the form of a subdivision of the authorized access point representing the jurisdiction. Record the name in the official language of the jurisdiction.

Argentina. Junta Militar

Somalia. Golaha Sare ee Kacaanka

Thailand. Khana Patiwat

Ghana. Armed Forces Revolutionary Council

If there is more than one official language in the jurisdiction, apply the instructions at **11.2.2.5.2**.

If necessary for identification, add, in parentheses, the inclusive years of the ruling executive body.

Chile. Junta de Gobierno (1813)

Chile. Junta de Gobierno (1973-1990)

11.2.2.18.3 Heads of International Intergovernmental Bodies

Record the title of a head of an international, intergovernmental organization, who is acting in an official capacity (see **6.31.1**), as a subdivision of the organization. Record the title in the form of a subdivision of the authorized access point representing the organization. Record the title of the official in the language of the preferred name for the organization.

Asociación Latinoamericana de Integración. Secretaría General

European Commission. President

If the official being identified is a specific incumbent of the office, add, in parentheses (in this order):

a) the inclusive years of the incumbency

b) the name of the person in a brief form, in the language of the preferred name for that person.

Separate the years of the incumbency from the name of the person using a space, colon, space.

United Nations. Secretary-General (1997–2006 : Annan)

European Commission. President (2004– : Barroso)

Record the relationships between the office and the person by applying the instructions in chapters **30** (related persons) and **32** (related corporate bodies).

11.2.2.18.4 Governors of Dependent or Occupied Territories

Record the title of a governor of a dependent territory (e.g., a colony, protectorate) or of an occupied territory (see **11.7.1.5**), who is acting in an official capacity (see **6.31.1**), as a subdivision of the territory. Record the title in the form of a subdivision of the authorized access point representing the colony, territory, etc. Record the title of the governor in the language of the governing power.

Hong Kong. Governor

French Polynesia. Gouverneur

Macau. Governador

Bechuanaland Protectorate. Prime Minister

France (Territory under German occupation, 1940–1944). Militärbefehlshaber in Frankreich

Norway (Territory under German occupation, 1940–1945). Reichskommissar für die Besetzten Norwegischen Gebiete

Germany (Territory under Allied occupation, 1945–1955 : U.S. Zone). Military Governor

Michigan (British military government, 1812–1813). Governor

If there is more than one official language in the jurisdiction of the governing power, apply the instructions at **11.2.2.5.2**.

If the official being identified is a specific incumbent of the office, add, in parentheses (in this order):

a) the inclusive years of the incumbency

b) the name of the person in a brief form, in the language of the preferred name for that person.

Separate the years of the incumbency from the name of the person using a space, colon, space.

Macau. Governador (1951–1956 : Esparteiro)

11.2.2.18.5 Other Officials

For any official not covered by **11.2.2.18.1–11.2.2.18.4**, use the preferred name for the ministry or agency that the official represents.

Northern Ireland. Audit Office
not Northern Ireland. Comptroller and Auditor General

United States. Public Health Service. Office of the Surgeon General
not United States. Surgeon General (Public Health Service)

An official is sometimes not part of a ministry, etc., or is part of a ministry, etc., that is identified only by the title of the official. When this occurs, record the title of the official in the form of a subdivision of the authorized access point representing the jurisdiction.

Scotland. Queen's and Lord Treasurer's Remembrancer

North Carolina. State Geologist

Alberta. Superintendent of Insurance

Northern Ireland. Commissioner for Complaints

Australia. Director of National Parks

South Africa. Minister of Public Health

Bahamas. Minister of Transport

11.2.2.19 Legislative Bodies

Record the names of legislative bodies by applying these instructions, as applicable:

legislatures (see **11.2.2.19.1**)
legislative committees and subordinate units (see **11.2.2.19.2**)
successive legislatures (see **11.2.2.19.3**).

11.2.2.19.1 Legislatures

Record the name of a legislature as a subdivision of the jurisdiction for which it legislates. Record the name in the form of a subdivision of the authorized access point representing the jurisdiction.

Iceland. Alþingi

Idaho. Legislature

If a legislature has more than one chamber, treat each chamber as a separate corporate body. Record the name of each chamber as a subdivision of the legislature. Record the name in the form of a subdivision of the authorized access point representing the legislature.

Lesotho. Parliament. National Assembly

Lesotho. Parliament. Senate

Switzerland. Bundesversammlung. Nationalrat

Switzerland. Bundesversammlung. Ständerat

Variant names. Record the name of the chamber in the form of a direct subdivision of the authorized access point representing the jurisdiction (see **11.2.3.7**).

11.2.2.19.2 Legislative Committees and Subordinate Units

Record the name of a committee or other subordinate unit of the legislature as a subdivision of the legislature or of the particular chamber, as appropriate. Record the name in the form of a subdivision of the authorized access point representing the legislature or the particular chamber.

Australia. Parliament. Joint Committee on Foreign Affairs and Defence

Australia. Parliament. Sub-committee on Industrial Support for Defence Needs and Allied Matters
not Australia. Parliament. Joint Committee on Foreign Affairs and Defence. Sub-committee on Industrial Support for Defence Needs and Allied Matters

Australia. Parliament. House of Representatives. Standing Committee on Aboriginal and Torres Strait Islander Affairs

Australia. Parliament. Senate. Legal and Constitutional References Committee

Exception

Record the name of a legislative subcommittee of the United States Congress as a subdivision of the committee to which it is subordinate. Record the name in the form of a subdivision of the authorized access point representing the higher committee.

United States. Congress. Senate. Committee on Foreign Relations. Subcommittee on African Affairs
not United States. Congress. Senate. Subcommittee on African Affairs

11.2.2.19.3 Successive Legislatures

If successive legislatures are numbered consecutively, add, in parentheses, the ordinal numeral and the inclusive years for the particular legislature or one of its chambers.

Separate the ordinal number from the inclusive years using a space, colon, space.

United States. Congress (107th : 2001–2002)

United States. Congress (107th : 2001–2002). Senate

If:

successive legislatures are numbered consecutively

and

sessions of the legislature are numbered

then:

add, in parentheses (in this order): the number of the legislature, the session and its number, the inclusive years of the session.

Separate the ordinal number of the legislature from the session number using a comma, and separate the session number from its inclusive years using a space, colon, space.

United States. Congress (107th, 1st session : 2001)

United States. Congress (107th, 1st session : 2001). Senate

11.2.2.20 Constitutional Conventions

Record the name of a constitutional convention as a subdivision of the government that convened it. Record the name in the form of a subdivision of the authorized access point representing the government. Add the inclusive years in which it was held, in parentheses.

Germany. Nationalversammlung (1919–1920)

Portugal. Assembleia Constituinte (1975)

If:
there are different forms of the name for a constitutional convention
and
English is the official language of the jurisdiction that convened the convention
then:
record *Constitutional Convention* as a subdivision of the jurisdiction.

New Hampshire. Constitutional Convention (1781–1783)
not New Hampshire. Convention for Framing a New Constitution or Form of Government (1781–1783)

New Hampshire. Constitutional Convention (1902)

New Hampshire. Constitutional Convention (1984)
not New Hampshire. Convention to Revise the Constitution (1984)

If English is not an official language of the jurisdiction, apply the instructions at **11.2.2.5.2**.

11.2.2.21 Courts

Record the names of courts by applying these instructions, as applicable:

civil and criminal courts (see **11.2.2.21.1**)

ad hoc military courts (see **11.2.2.21.2**).

11.2.2.21.1 Civil and Criminal Courts

Record the name of a civil or criminal court as a subdivision of the jurisdiction whose authority it exercises. Record the name in the form of a subdivision of the authorized access point representing the jurisdiction.

Vermont. Court of Chancery

Brazil. Supremo Tribunal de Justiça

Omit the name (or abbreviation of the name) of the place in which the court sits or the area which it serves. If the name of the place or the area served is required to distinguish a court from others of the same name, add the conventional name of the place in parentheses.

Canada. Supreme Court
Name: Supreme Court of Canada

France. Cour d'appel (Grenoble)
Name: Cour d'appel de Grenoble

France. Cour d'appel (Lyon)
Name: Cour d'appel de Lyon

India. High Court (Himachal Pradesh, India)
Name: High Court of Himachal Pradesh

India. High Court (Karnataka, India)
Name: High Court of Karnataka

Italy. Corte di appello (Rome)
Name: Corte di appello di Roma

Italy. Corte di appello (Trieste)
Name: Corte di appello di Trieste

United States. Court of Appeals (2nd Circuit)
Name: United States Court of Appeals for the Second Circuit

United States. Court of Appeals (District of Columbia Circuit)
Name: United States Court of Appeals for the District of Columbia Circuit

United States. District Court (Delaware)
Name: United States District Court for the District of Delaware

United States. District Court (Illinois : Northern District : Eastern Division)
Name: United States District Court for the Eastern Division of the Northern District of Illinois

California. Municipal Court (Los Angeles Judicial District)
Name: Municipal Court, Los Angeles Judicial District

California. Superior Court (San Bernardino County)
Name: Superior Court of the State of California in and for San Bernardino County

11.2.2.21.2 Ad Hoc Military Courts

Record the name of an ad hoc military court (e.g., court-martial, court of inquiry) as a subdivision of the particular military service (see **11.2.2.22**). Record the name in the form of a subdivision of the authorized access point representing the military service. Add, in parentheses, the surname of the defendant and the year of the trial. Separate the surname of the defendant from the year of the trial using a space, colon, space.

Massachusetts. Militia. Court-martial (Watson : 1810)

United States. Army. Court of Inquiry (Reno : 1879)

11.2.2.22 Armed Forces

Record the names of armed forces by applying these instructions, as applicable:

armed forces at the national level (see **11.2.2.22.1**)

armed forces below the national level (see **11.2.2.22.2**).

11.2.2.22.1 Armed Forces at the National Level

Record the name of a principal service of the armed forces of a national government as a subdivision of the government. Record the name in the form of a subdivision of the authorized access point representing the government. Omit the name (or abbreviation of the name) of the government in noun form unless the omission results in objectionable distortion.

Australia. Royal Australian Air Force

Canada. Canadian Armed Forces

United States. Marine Corps

Argentina. Ejército

Romania. Marina

Record the name of a component branch, command district, or military unit, large or small, as a subdivision of the principal service of which it is a part. Record the name in the form of a direct subdivision of the authorized access point representing the principal service.

Canada. Canadian Armed Forces. Snowbirds

Canada. Canadian Army. Nova Scotia Highland Brigade

Canada. Royal Canadian Navy. Sick Berth and Medical Assistant Branch

Canada. Royal Canadian Air Force. Women's Division

Russia (Federation). Russkai͡a Armii͡a. Gvardeĭskai͡a raketnai͡a Glukhovskai͡a divizii͡a

United States. Army. Corps of Engineers

United States. Army. District of Kanawha

United States. Army. Special Forces

If the component branch, etc., is identified by a number, follow the style of numbering found in the name (spelled out, roman numerals, or arabic numerals). Place the numbering after the name, preceded by a comma.

United States. Army. Infantry Division, 27th

United States. Navy. Fleet, 6th

United States. Army Air Forces. Air Force, First

United States. Marine Corps. Amphibious Corps, V

United States. Army. Engineer Combat Battalion, 1st

United States. Army. Volunteer Cavalry, 1st

United States. Navy. Torpedo Squadron, 35

Confederate States of America. Army. Tennessee Infantry Regiment, 41st

Canada. Canadian Army. French-Canadian Battalion, 22nd

France. Armée. Régiment de dragons, 26e

Germany. Heer. Panzerdivision, 11

Germany. Heer. Armeekorps, XIII

Germany. Luftwaffe. Fallschirmjägerdivision, 9

Germany. Kriegsmarine. Unterseebootsflottille, 7

Soviet Union. Raboche-Krestʹi͡anskai͡a Krasnai͡a Armii͡a. Vozdushnai͡a armii͡a, 5

If the name of a component branch, etc., begins with the name, or an indication of the name, of the principal service, record it as a subdivision of the government. Record the name in the form of a direct subdivision of the authorized access point representing the government.

United States. Army Broadcasting Service
Name: Army Broadcasting Service

United States. Naval Air Ferry Service
Name: Naval Air Ferry Service

Australia. Australian Army Psychology Corps
Name: Australian Army Psychology Corps

If the name of a component branch, etc., contains, but does not begin with, the name (or an indication of the name) of the principal service, record it as a subdivision of the principal service. Record the name in the form of a direct subdivision of the authorized access point representing the principal service. Omit the name (or indication of the name) of the principal service from the name of the component branch unless the omission results in an objectionable distortion.

South Africa. Army. Service Corps
not South Africa. Army. Army Service Corps
not South Africa. Army. South African Army Service Corps
Name: South African Army Service Corps

but

Canada. Canadian Army. Royal Canadian Army Medical Corps
not Canada. Canadian Army. Medical Corps
Name: Royal Canadian Army Medical Corps

11.2.2.22.2 Armed Forces below the National Level

Record the name of an armed force of a government below the national level as a subdivision of that government. Record the name in the form of a direct subdivision of the access point representing the government.

New York (State). Militia

New York (State). National Guard

Record the name of a component branch of an armed force of a government below the national level as a subdivision of the force. Record the name in the form of a subdivision of the authorized access point representing the force. Apply the instructions for armed forces at the national level (see **11.2.2.22.1**).

New York (State). Militia. Regiment, 71st
Name: 71st Regiment, N.Y.S.M.

Arkansas. National Guard. Coast Artillery, 206th

If a component branch, etc., of a force below the national level has been absorbed into a national military force, record it as a subdivision of the national force (see **11.2.2.22.1**).

United States. Army. New York Volunteers, 122nd

United States. Army. Regiment, California U.S. Volunteer Infantry, 1st

11.2.2.23 Embassies, Consulates, Etc.

Record the name of an embassy, consulate, legation, or other continuing office that represents one country in another as a subdivision of the country represented. Record the name in the form of a subdivision of the authorized access point for the country represented, in the language of the country represented (see **11.2.2.5.2**). Omit the name of the country represented from the name of the embassy, etc.

For an embassy or legation, add the name of the country to which it is accredited, in parentheses.

Canada. Embassy (Belgium)

Germany. Gesandtschaft (Chile)

India. High Commission (Trinidad and Tobago)

Serbia. Poslanstvo (Romania)

United States. Legation (Sweden)

For a consulate or other local office, add the name of the city in which it is located before the name of the country to which it is accredited. Separate the name of the city from the name of the country using a comma. Record the name of the country and the city as instructed in chapter **16**.

France. Consulat (Buenos Aires, Argentina)

Japan. Sōryōjikan (Portland, Or.)

Netherlands. Consulaat-Generaal (Cape Town, South Africa)

United States. Consulate (Port Louis, Mauritius)

11.2.2.24 Delegations to International and Intergovernmental Bodies

Record the name of a delegation, commission, etc., that represents a country in an international or intergovernmental body, conference, undertaking, etc., as a subdivision of the country represented. Record the name in the form of a subdivision of the authorized access point for the country represented, in the language of the country represented (see **11.2.2.5.2**). Omit from the name of the delegation, etc., the name (or abbreviation of the name) of the government when it is in noun form, unless the omission results in an objectionable distortion.

If the name of the delegation, etc., is uncertain, record *Delegation* [*Mission*, etc.], or equivalent terms in the language of the country represented.

If it is necessary to distinguish the delegation, etc., from others of the same name, add the name of the international or intergovernmental body, conference, undertaking, etc., to which the delegation, etc., is accredited. Add the name in parentheses, in the form and language of the preferred name for that body.

Mexico. Delegación (Inter-American Conference for the Maintenance of Peace (1936 : Buenos Aires, Argentina))

India. Delegation (International Labour Conference)

United States. Delegation (International Monetary Conference (1892 : Brussels, Belgium))

United States. Mission to the United Nations

If it is uncertain that a delegation represents the government of a country, record it under its own name.

Delegation of the Parliament of Zimbabwe to Botswana, Namibia, and Zambia

RECORDING NAMES OF RELIGIOUS BODIES AND OFFICIALS

11.2.2.25 Councils, Etc., of a Single Religious Body

Record the name of a council, etc., of the clergy and/or membership of a single religious body as a subdivision of the religious body. Record the name in the form of a subdivision of the authorized access point representing the religious body, whether the council, etc., functions at the international, national, regional, provincial, state or local level.

Catholic Church. Antilles Episcopal Conference

Catholic Church. Bishops' Conference of Bangladesh

Catholic Church. International Council for Catechesis

Central Conference of American Rabbis. Social Justice Commission

Mennonite Church. Lancaster Conference

United Methodist Church (U.S.). Northern Illinois Conference

If the name is given in more than one language, use the language form presented first in the first resource received.

Catholic Church. Canadian Conference of Catholic Bishops
not Catholic Church. Conférence des évèques catholiques du Canada

Form of name presented first in first resource received: Canadian Conference of Catholic Bishops. *Form presented second in same resource:* Conférence des évèques catholiques du Canada

Catholic Church. Plenary Council of Baltimore
not Catholic Church. Concilium Plenarium Baltimorensis

Form of name presented in resource received first: Third Plenary Council of Baltimore. *Form presented in resource received later:* Concilii Plenarii Baltimorensis Tertii

Catholic Church. Concilium Plenarium Americae Latinae
not Catholic Church. Concilio Plenario de la América Latina
not Catholic Church. Concilio Plenario de América Latina
not Catholic Church. Concílio Plenário da América Latina
not Catholic Church. Concilio Plenario dell'America Latina

Form of name presented in first resource received: Concilium Plenarium Americae Latinae. *Forms presented in resources received later:* Concilio Plenario de la América Latina; Concilio Plenario de América Latina; Concílio Plenário da América Latina; Concilio Plenario dell'America Latina

If a council, etc., is subordinate to a particular district of the religious body, record it as a subdivision of that district (see **11.2.2.27**). Record the name in the form of a subdivision of the authorized access point representing the district. If the name appears in more than one language, record the name in the official language of the district.

Catholic Church. Province of Baltimore. Provincial Council

Church of England. Diocese of Exeter. Synod

Catholic Church. Province of Mexico City. Concilio Provincial

If there is more than one official language in the jurisdiction, apply the instructions at **11.2.2.5.2**.

Variant names. Record other language forms of the name as variant names (see **11.2.3.6**).

11.2.2.26 Religious Officials

Record the names of religious officials by applying the following instructions, as applicable:

bishops, rabbis, mullahs, patriarchs, etc. (see **11.2.2.26.1**)

popes (see **11.2.2.26.2**).

11.2.2.26.1 Bishops, Rabbis, Mullahs, Patriarchs, Etc.

Record the title of a religious official (e.g., bishop, abbot, rabbi, moderator, mullah, patriarch), who is acting in an official capacity (see **6.31.1**), as a subdivision of the religious jurisdiction. Record the name in the form of a subdivision of the authorized access point representing the religious jurisdiction (see **11.2.2.27**).

Church of England. Diocese of Winchester. Bishop

Franciscans. Minister General

United Hebrew Congregations of the Commonwealth. Chief Rabbi

United Presbyterian Church in the U.S.A. General Assembly. Moderator

If the official being identified is a specific incumbent of the office, add, in parentheses (in this order):

a) the inclusive years of the incumbency

b) the name of the person in a brief form, in the language of the preferred name for that person.

Separate the years of the incumbency from the name of the person using a space, colon, space.

Catholic Church. Archdiocese of St. Paul and Minneapolis. Archbishop (1995–2008 : Flynn)

United Hebrew Congregations of the Commonwealth. Chief Rabbi (1991– : Sacks)

Franciscans. Minister General (1947–1952 : Perantoni)

Dominicans. Master General (1756–1777 : Boxadors)

Catholic Church. Diocese of Winchester. Bishop (1282–1304 : John, of Pontoise)

Record the relationships between the office and the person by applying the instructions in chapters **30** (related persons) and **32** (related corporate bodies).

11.2.2.26.2 Popes

Record the title of a pope who is acting in an official capacity (see **6.31.1**) as a subdivision of the Catholic Church. Record the title in the form of a subdivision of the authorized access point representing the Catholic Church. Record the title in a language preferred by the agency creating the data.

Catholic Church. Pope

If the official being identified is a specific incumbent of the office, add, in parentheses (in this order):

a) the inclusive years of the reign

b) the pontifical name of the incumbent (see **9.2.2.18**).

Separate the years of the reign from the pontifical name using a space, colon, space.

Catholic Church. Pope (1878–1903 : Leo XIII)
Catholic Church. Pope (1978–2005 : John Paul II)
Catholic Church. Pope (2013– : Francis)

Record the relationships between the office and the person by applying the instructions in chapters **30** (related persons) and **32** (related corporate bodies).

11.2.2.27 Religious Provinces, Dioceses, Synods, Etc.

Record the name of a province, diocese, synod, or other subordinate unit of a religious body with jurisdiction over a geographic area as a subdivision of the religious body. Record the name in the form of a subdivision of the authorized access point representing the religious body.

Church of England. Diocese of Ely

Lutheran Church in America. Florida Synod

Evangelische Kirche der Altpreussischen Union. Kirchenprovinz Sachsen

Church of England. Archdeaconry of Surrey

Nederlandse Hervormde Kerk. Classis Rotterdam

Episcopal Church. Diocese of Central New York

Russkai͡a pravoslavnai͡a t͡serkov′. Moskovskai͡a patriarkhii͡a

Svenska kyrkan. Göteborgs stift

Church in Wales. Deanery of Kidwelly

Exceptions

Record the name of a Catholic patriarchate, diocese, province, etc., as a subdivision of the Catholic Church. Record the name in the form of a subdivision of the authorized access point representing the Catholic Church. Record the name in a language preferred by the agency creating the data.

Catholic Church. Archdiocese of Santo Domingo

Catholic Church. Diocese of Würzburg

Catholic Church. Deanery of Legnica

Catholic Church. Patriarchate of Cilicia

Catholic Church. Province of Nicaragua

Catholic Church. Ukrainian Catholic Archeparchy of Philadelphia

Catholic Church. Vicariate Apostolic of Chaco Paraguayo

Do not apply this instruction to an ecclesiastical principality of the Holy Roman Empire when it has the same name as a Catholic diocese and is ruled by the same bishop. This type of ecclesiastical principality is often called *Bistum*.

Würzburg
Name of ecclesiastical principality: Würzburg. *Also called:* Bistum Würzburg; Hochstift Würzburg

Bremen
Name of ecclesiastical principality: Erzstift Bremen

11.2.2.28 Central Administrative Organs of the Catholic Church (Roman Curia)

Record the name of a congregation, tribunal, or other central administrative organ of the Catholic Church (i.e., one that is part of the Roman Curia) as a subdivision of the Catholic Church. Record the name in the form of a subdivision of the authorized access point representing the Catholic Church. Record the Latin form of the name of the congregation, etc. Omit any form of the word *sacer* when it is the first word of the name.

Catholic Church. Congregatio Sacrorum Rituum

Catholic Church. Congregatio de Propaganda Fide

Catholic Church. Signatura Gratiae

Catholic Church. Rota Romana
not Catholic Church. Sacra Rota Romana
not Catholic Church. Sac. Rota Romana

11.2.2.29 Papal Diplomatic Missions, Etc.

Record the name of a diplomatic mission from the pope to a secular power as a subdivision of the Catholic Church. Record the name in the form of a subdivision of the authorized access point representing the Catholic Church, and use the term *Apostolic Nunciature* or *Apostolic Internunciature*, as appropriate. Add the name of the government to which the mission is accredited, in parentheses.

Catholic Church. Apostolic Internunciature (China)

Catholic Church. Apostolic Nunciature (Ethiopia)

Catholic Church. Apostolic Nunciature (Flanders, Belgium)

Record the name of a nondiplomatic apostolic delegation as a subdivision of the Catholic Church. Record the name in the form of a subdivision of the authorized access point representing the Catholic Church, and use the term *Apostolic Delegation*. Add the name of the country, region, or other location in which the delegation functions, in parentheses.

Catholic Church. Apostolic Delegation (Malta)

Catholic Church. Apostolic Delegation (Loreto, Italy)

Catholic Church. Apostolic Delegation (West Africa)

Record the name of an emissary of the pope acting in an official capacity (other than a nuncio, internuncio, or apostolic delegate) as a subdivision of the Catholic Church. Record the name in the form of a subdivision of the authorized access point representing the Catholic Church. Record the title of the emissary in a language preferred by the agency creating the data. If there is no term in that language, use the Latin term. Add the name of the country, region, or other location in which the emissary functions, in parentheses.

Catholic Church. Legate (France)

If the country, region, or other location in which the emissary functions cannot be ascertained, add the name of the emissary in brief form.

Catholic Church. Commissary Apostolic (Robertus Castellensis)

11.2.3 Variant Name for the Corporate Body

11.2.3.1 Scope

A ***variant name for the corporate body*** is a name or form of name by which a corporate body is known that differs from the name or form of name chosen as the preferred name.

11.2.3.2 Sources of Information

Take variant names for a corporate body from resources associated with the corporate body and/or from reference sources.

11.2.3.3 General Guidelines on Recording Variant Names for Corporate Bodies

Record variant names for a corporate body by applying the general guidelines on recording names at **8.5**.

Record a variant name when it is different from the name recorded as the preferred name. Record as a variant name:

a name or form of name used by the corporate body

or

a name or form of name found in reference sources

or

a form of name resulting from a different transliteration of the name.

For corporate bodies that have changed their name, see the instructions on recording relationships between related corporate bodies in chapter **32**.

Record as a variant name a direct form of the name if the preferred name is recorded as a subdivision of a higher or related body. Record only if the name might reasonably be searched in that variant form.

Record as a variant name the name as a subdivision of a higher or related body if the preferred name is recorded in direct form. Record only if the name might reasonably be searched in that variant form.

Apply the specific instructions at **11.2.3.4–11.2.3.7**, as applicable. Also apply instructions about recording variant names at **11.2.2.5–11.2.2.29**, as applicable.

11.2.3.4 Expanded Name

If the preferred name for the corporate body consists of or includes an acronym, initialism, or an abbreviated form of name, record the expanded form of the name as a variant name.

United States Distance Learning Association
Initialism recorded as preferred name: USDLA

Guyana Agricultural and General Workers' Union
Initialism recorded as preferred name: G.A.W.U.

European Atomic Energy Community
Acronym recorded as preferred name: Euratom

International Business Machines Canada
Initialism recorded as preferred name: IBM Canada

United Kingdom Advocacy Network
Initialism recorded as preferred name: U.K. Advocacy Network

Alabama A and M University
Alabama Agricultural and Mechanical University
Abbreviated form recorded in preferred name: Alabama A & M University

European Conference on Smart Sensing and Context
Initialism recorded as preferred name: EuroSSC

If:
the preferred name begins with an abbreviation or contains an abbreviation
and
abbreviations are accessed differently from words written in full
then:
record the expanded form of the name as a variant name. Expand abbreviations into words written in full using the language of the preferred name as the language for words written in full.

Sankt Annen-Museum
Form beginning with an abbreviation recorded as preferred name: St. Annen-Museum

International Arab Aluminum Conference
Form beginning with an abbreviation recorded as preferred name: Int'l Arab Aluminum Conference

Abbey of Saint Peter and Saint Paul
Form containing an abbreviation recorded as preferred name: Abbey of St. Peter and St. Paul

Mount Tamalpais and Muir Woods Railroad Company
Form beginning with and containing an abbreviation recorded as preferred name: Mt. Tamalpais and Muir Woods Railroad Co.

11.2.3.5 Acronym / Initialism / Abbreviated Form

If the preferred name for the corporate body is a full form of the name, record an acronym, initialism, or abbreviated form of the name as a variant name.

EEC
Full form recorded as preferred name: European Economic Community

IBM

I.B.M.

Full form recorded as preferred name: International Business Machines Corporation

Gospel Faith Mission Int'l

Full form recorded as preferred name: Gospel Faith Mission International

If the preferred name consists of an acronym or initialism, it is recorded with or without full stops according to the instructions at **11.2.2.7**. If the presence or absence of full stops affects access, record the form not chosen as the preferred name as a variant name.

U.N.E.S.C.O.

Form recorded as preferred name: Unesco

TOE

Form recorded as preferred name: T.O.E.

If an acronym or initialism is recorded as a variant name and the presence or absence of full stops affects access, record the acronym or initialism both with full stops and without full stops.

NATO
N.A.T.O.

Full form recorded as preferred name: North Atlantic Treaty Organization

IUSSI
I.U.S.S.I.
UIEIS
U.I.E.I.S.

Full form recorded as preferred name: International Union for the Study of Social Insects

11.2.3.6 Alternative Linguistic Form of Name

If the name recorded as the preferred name for a corporate body has one or more alternative linguistic forms, record them as variant names.

Different Language Form

Croce rossa svizzera
Croix-Rouge suisse

German language form recorded as preferred name: Schweizerisches Rotes Kreuz

Chiang Mai University
Chiangmai University
Đại học tổng hợp Chiang Mai

Thai transliterated form recorded as preferred name: Mahāwitthayālai Chīang Mai

Hēnōmena Ethnē
Kokusai Rengō
Naciones Unidas
Nations Unies
Nazioni Unite
Organizace spojených národů
Perserikatan Bangsa-Bangsa
Sahaprachāchāt

Sāzmān-i Milal-i Muttafiq
Sjuninejal Konob'laq
English language form recorded as preferred name: United Nations

Qatar. Embassy (U.S.)
Arabic language form recorded as preferred name: Qatar. Safārah (U.S.)

Estonian National Symphony Orchestra
Estonian State Symphony Orchestra
Nationaal Symfonieorkest van Estland
Orchestre symphonique national d'Estonie
Staatliches Sinfonieorchester Estland
Staatliches Symphonieorchester Estland
Estonian language form recorded as preferred name: Eesti Riiklik Sümfooniaorkester

Different Script

Македонска Православна Црква
Macedonian transliterated form recorded as preferred name: Makedonska pravoslavna crkva

มหาวิทยาลัยเชียงใหม่
Thai transliterated form recorded as preferred name: Mahāwitthayālai Chīang Mai

中央研究院
Chinese transliterated form recorded as preferred name: Zhong yang yan jiu yuan

موزهملیایران
Persian transliterated form recorded as preferred name: Mūzih-i Millī-i Īrān

日本弁護士連合会. 公害対策環境保全委員会
Japanese transliterated form recorded as preferred name: Nihon Bengoshi Rengōkai. Kōgai Taisaku Kankyō Hozen Iinkai

Οργανισμός Ηνωμένων Εθνών
Організація Об'єднаних Націй
Уједињене нације
Միավորված Ազգերի Կազմակերպություն
สหประชาชาติ
ஐக்கிய நாடுகள் அவை
أمم المتحدة
سازمان ملل متحد
אומות המאוחדות
联合国
聯合國
국제연합
国際連合
English language form recorded as preferred name: United Nations

Different Spelling

Organization for Economic Cooperation and Development
Different spelling recorded as preferred name: Organisation for Economic Co-operation and Development

International Color Vision Society
Different spelling recorded as preferred name: International Colour Vision Society

Different Transliteration

Akademija nauk SSSR

Different transliteration recorded as preferred name: Akademii͡a nauk SSSR

Hsin hua tʻung hsün she

Different transliteration recorded as preferred name: Xin hua tong xun she

If:

the name recorded as the preferred name begins with a number expressed as a numeral or contains a number expressed as a numeral

and

numbers expressed as words are accessed differently from numbers expressed as numerals

then:

record the form with the number expressed as a word as a variant name.

Five Browns

Form beginning with a number expressed as a numeral recorded as preferred name: 5 Browns

Dvidešimt septynių Knygos mėgėjų draugija

Form beginning with a number expressed as a numeral recorded as preferred name: XXVII Knygos mėgėjų draugija

Group of Seventy-seven

Form containing a number expressed as a numeral recorded as preferred name: Group of 77

September Eleventh Fund

Form containing a number expressed as an ordinal number recorded as preferred name: September 11th Fund

If:

the name recorded as the preferred name begins with a number expressed as a word or contains a number expressed as a word

and

numbers expressed as words are accessed differently from numbers expressed as numerals

then:

record the form with the number expressed as a numeral as a variant name.

4 Corners Interpretive Center

Form beginning with a number expressed as a word recorded as preferred name: Four Corners Interpretive Center

11.2.3.7 Other Variant Name

Record other variant names and variant forms of the name not covered by **11.2.3.4–11.2.3.6**, if considered important for identification or access.

Different Name

Common Market

Name recorded as preferred name: European Economic Community

Friars Minor
Gray Friars

Minorites
Order of Friars Minor
Name recorded as preferred name: Franciscans

Corps of Discovery Expedition
Name recorded as preferred name: Lewis and Clark Expedition

Museo Nacional de Pintura y Escultura
Museo Nacional del Prado
Real Museo de Pinturas y Esculturas
Name recorded as preferred name: Museo del Prado

General Name of a Conference, Etc.

Governor's Conference on Conservation
Specific name recorded as preferred name: Northwest Conference on the Role of Nuclear Energy

Nutrition Symposium
Specific name recorded as preferred name: Symposium on Protein Metabolism

Nutrition Symposium
Specific name recorded as preferred name: Symposium on the Role of Some of the Newer Vitamins in Human Metabolism and Nutrition

Nutrition Symposium
Specific name recorded as preferred name: Symposium on Endocrines and Nutrition

IEEE Engineering in Medicine and Biology Society. Conference
Biomedical Engineering Society. Fall Meeting
Specific name recorded as preferred name: Joint EMBS-BMES Conference

Name as Subdivision of Authorized Access Point for a Higher or Related Body

American Library Association. American Association of School Librarians
Form recorded as preferred name: American Association of School Librarians

University of Oxford. Bodleian Library
Form recorded as preferred name: Bodleian Library

London School of Economics and Political Science. British Library of Political and Economic Science
Form recorded as preferred name: British Library of Political and Economic Science

University of London. London School of Economics and Political Science
Form recorded as preferred name: London School of Economics and Political Science

Tasmania. State Library
Form recorded as preferred name: State Library of Tasmania

United States. Tennessee Valley Authority
Form recorded as preferred name: Tennessee Valley Authority

Snohomish County (Wash.). Office of Community Planning
Form recorded as preferred name: Snohomish County Office of Community Planning

Newport (Ky.). High School
Form recorded as preferred name: Newport High School

Name as Subdivision of Authorized Access Point for Immediately Superior Body

American Library Association. Resources and Technical Services Division. Cataloging and Classification Section

Form recorded as preferred name: American Library Association. Cataloging and Classification Section

United States. Department of Agriculture. Economic Research Service. National Economy and History Branch. Agricultural and Rural History Section

Form recorded as preferred name: United States. Agricultural and Rural History Section

Name as Direct Subdivision of Authorized Access Point for a Higher-Level Body

Lesotho. National Assembly

Form recorded as preferred name: Lesotho. Parliament. National Assembly

Name of a Subordinate Body Whose Name Does Not Suggest Subordination Recorded Directly

Burdette Tomlin Memorial Hospital Auxiliary

Form recorded as preferred name: Burdette Tomlin Memorial Hospital. Auxiliary

Friends of the Ellen Clarke Bertrand Library

Form recorded as preferred name: Ellen Clarke Bertrand Library. Friends

Other Variants (Including Shorter, Fuller, and Inverted Forms)

William Hayes Fogg Art Museum

Shorter form recorded as preferred name: Fogg Art Museum

Alabama Agricultural and Mechanical University

Shorter form recorded as preferred name: Alabama A & M University

Roman Catholic Church

Shorter form recorded as preferred name: Catholic Church

European Conference on Smart Sensing and Context

Brief form recorded as preferred name: EuroSSC

M.E. Kolagbodi Memorial Foundation
Kolagbodi Memorial Foundation

Fuller form recorded as preferred name: Dr. M.E. Kolagbodi Memorial Foundation

United States. State Department

Other form recorded as preferred name: United States. Department of State

Canada. Canadian Armed Forces. Air Demonstration Squadron, 431 Snowbirds

Other form recorded as preferred name: Canada. Canadian Armed Forces. Snowbirds

Aktiebolaget Aerotransport

Inverted form recorded as preferred name: Aerotransport, Aktiebolaget

VEB Forstprojektierung Potsdam

Inverted form recorded as preferred name: Forstprojektierung Potsdam, VEB

International Conference on Low-cost Planetary Missions, IAA
Conference on Low-cost Planetary Missions, IAA International

Uninverted form recorded as preferred name: IAA International Conference on Low-cost Planetary Missions

Academia de Bellas Artes de San Fernando, Real
Uninverted form recorded as preferred name: Real Academia de Bellas Artes de San Fernando

Australia. Environment and Water Resources, Department of the
Uninverted form recorded as preferred name: Australia. Department of the Environment and Water Resources

27 Knygos mėgėjų draugija
Form beginning with a number expressed as a roman numeral recorded as preferred name: XXVII Knygos mėgėjų draugija

Arkansas. Office of Title 20 Services
Form containing a number expressed as a roman numeral recorded as preferred name: Arkansas. Office of Title XX Services

OTHER IDENTIFYING ATTRIBUTES

11.3 Place Associated with the Corporate Body

CORE ELEMENT

*Place associated with the corporate body is a core element for conferences, etc. (see **11.3.2**). For other corporate bodies, place associated with the corporate body is a core element when needed to distinguish a corporate body from another corporate body with the same name.*

11.3.1 Basic Instructions on Recording Places Associated with Corporate Bodies

11.3.1.1 Scope

A ***place associated with the corporate body*** is a significant location associated with a corporate body (e.g., location of a conference, etc., location of the headquarters of an organization).

11.3.1.2 Sources of Information

Take information on places associated with the corporate body from any source.

11.3.1.3 General Guidelines

Record places associated with the corporate body by applying these instructions, as applicable:

location of conference, etc. (see **11.3.2**)
location of headquarters (see **11.3.3**).

See chapter **16** for instructions on choosing and recording place names. Abbreviate the names of countries, states, provinces, territories, etc., as instructed in appendix **B** (**B.11**), as applicable.

Record places associated with the corporate body as separate elements, as parts of access points, or as both. For additional instructions on recording a place as part of the authorized access point, see **11.13.1.3**.

11.3.2 Location of Conference, Etc.

CORE ELEMENT

11.3.2.1 Scope

A ***location of conference, etc.***, is a local place in which a conference, congress, meeting, exhibition, fair, festival, etc., was held.

11.3.2.2 Sources of Information

Take information on the location of conference, etc., from any source.

11.3.2.3 Recording Location of Conference, Etc.

Record the name of the local place in which the conference, etc., was held by applying the basic instructions at **11.3.1**.

If the conference was held in more than one place, record the names of each of the places in which it was held.

Columbia Falls, Me.
Preferred name for the conference recorded as: Clambake Conference on the Nature and Source of Human Error

Moscow, Russia
Preferred name for the conference recorded as: Mezhdunarodnyĭ simpozium "Global'noe rasselenie gominid"

Vancouver, B.C.
Preferred name for the event recorded as: Olympic Winter Games

Orlando, Fla.
Preferred name for the exposition recorded as: Polyurethanes Expo

Salzburg, Austria
Preferred name for the event recorded as: Salzburger Festspiele

Malling, England
Dundee, Scotland
Preferred name for the conference recorded as: Symposium on Breeding and Machine Harvesting of Rubus and Ribes

Tehran, Iran
Iṣfahān, Iran
Shīrāz, Iran
Preferred name for the conference recorded as: International Congress of Iranian Art and Archaeology

Exceptions

Record the name of an associated institution (see **11.5**) instead of the local place name if:

the name of the associated institution provides better identification

or

the local place name is not known

or

the local place name cannot be readily determined.

Record *Online* for a conference that was held online.

11.3.3 Location of Headquarters

CORE ELEMENT

Location of the headquarters is a core element when needed to distinguish a corporate body from another corporate body with the same name.

11.3.3.1 Scope

A ***location of headquarters*** is a country, state, province, etc., or local place in which an organization has its headquarters.

Alternatively, location of headquarters can be used to record the geographic area (state, province, city, etc.) in which a corporate body carries out its activities.

11.3.3.2 Sources of Information

Take information on location of headquarters from any source.

11.3.3.3 Recording Location of Headquarters

If a body has a character that is national, state, provincial, etc., record the name of the country, state, province, etc., in which it is located. Apply the basic instructions on recording places associated with corporate bodies at **11.3.1**.

Ill.
Preferred name recorded as: Republican Party

Mont.
Preferred name recorded as: Republican Party

Chile
Preferred name recorded as: Sociedad Nacional de Agricultura

Peru
Preferred name recorded as: Sociedad Nacional de Agricultura

Australia
Preferred name recorded as: National Measurement Laboratory

U.S.
Preferred name recorded as: National Measurement Laboratory

Ariz.
Preferred name recorded as: Governor's Conference on Aging

Fla.
Preferred name recorded as: Governor's Conference on Aging

B.C.
Preferred name recorded as: Provincial Intermediate Teacher's Association

Wales
Preferred name recorded as: National Entrepreneurship Observatory

Exception

If the name of a country, state, province, etc., in which a body is located does not provide sufficient identification or is inappropriate, record the local place name (e.g., in the case of national, state, provincial, etc., universities of the same name serving the same country, state, province, etc.).

For other bodies, record the name of the local place that is commonly associated with the name of the body, whether it is a jurisdiction or not.

Newport, Ky.
Preferred name recorded as: Newport High School

Newport, R.I.
Preferred name recorded as: Newport High School

Newport, Wash.
Preferred name recorded as: Newport High School

Washington County, Ind.
Preferred name recorded as: Washington County Historical Society

Washington County, N.Y.
Preferred name recorded as: Washington County Historical Society

Hope, England
Preferred name recorded as: St. Peter's Church

Limpsfield, England
Preferred name recorded as: St. Peter's Church

Stourton, Wiltshire, England
Preferred name recorded as: St. Peter's Church

Florence, Italy
Preferred name recorded as: Grand Hotel

Mackinac Island, Mich.
Preferred name recorded as: Grand Hotel

Stockholm, Sweden
Preferred name recorded as: Grand Hôtel

Chittenden County, Vt.
Preferred name recorded as: Project HOME

Ingleside, N.S.W.
Preferred name recorded as: Baha'i House of Worship

Toronto, Ont.
Preferred name recorded as: Beth Tikvah Synagogue

Abberley, England
Preferred name recorded as: St. Mary

Cape May County, N.J.
Preferred name recorded as: First Baptist Church

Duisburg, Germany
Essen, North Rhine-Westphalia, Germany
Preferred name recorded as: Universität Duisburg-Essen. *Corporate body has headquarters in two locations*

Kathmandu, Nepal
Preferred name recorded as: Bhadrakāli

Iṣfahān, Iran
Preferred name recorded as: Masjid-i Jumʻah

La Paz, Bolivia
Preferred name recorded as: Basílica de San Francisco

Havana, Cuba
Preferred name recorded as: CMQ

Brisbane, Qld.
Preferred name recorded as: Radio 4EBFM

Prague, Czech Republic
Preferred name recorded as: Televize Nova

If more precise identification is necessary, add the name of a particular area within the local place. Add it before the name of the local place.

Georgetown, Washington, D.C.
Preferred name recorded as: St. John's Church

Lafayette Square, Washington, D.C.
Preferred name recorded as: St. John's Church

11.3.3.4 Change of Name of Jurisdiction or Locality

If the name of the local jurisdiction or geographic locality changes during the lifetime of the body, record the latest name in use during the lifetime of the body.

> Harare, Zimbabwe
> **not** Salisbury, Zimbabwe
> *Preferred name recorded as:* School of Social Work. *School established in 1968. Place name changed from Salisbury to Harare in 1982*
>
> **but**
>
> Kristiania, Norway
> *Preferred name recorded as:* Skulpturmuseet. *Founded 1882, closed 1902. Corporate body ceased to exist before Kristiania became Oslo in 1925*

Optional Addition

Record earlier names of the local jurisdiction or geographic locality if considered important for identification.

11.4 Date Associated with the Corporate Body

CORE ELEMENT

Date associated with the corporate body is a core element for a conference, etc. (see ***11.4.2****). For other corporate bodies, date associated with the corporate body is a core element when needed to distinguish a corporate body from another corporate body with the same name.*

11.4.1 Basic Instructions on Recording Dates Associated with Corporate Bodies

11.4.1.1 Scope

A ***date associated with the corporate body*** is a significant date associated with the history of a corporate body, such as date of establishment, date of termination, or its period of activity. For a conference, it is the date or range of dates on which a conference, etc., was held.

11.4.1.2 Sources of Information

Take information on dates associated with the corporate body from any source.

11.4.1.3 General Guidelines

Record dates associated with the corporate body by applying these instructions, as applicable:

- date of conference (see **11.4.2**)
- date of establishment (see **11.4.3**)
- date of termination (see **11.4.4**)
- period of activity (see **11.4.5**).

Record dates in terms of the calendar preferred by the agency creating the data. For details on recording dates according to the Christian calendar, see appendix H.

Record dates as separate elements, as parts of access points, or as both. For additional instructions on recording dates as parts of authorized access points, see **11.13.1.5**.

Record a date associated with a corporate body by giving the year or range of years.

> *Exception*
>
> For instructions on recording dates for two or more conferences, etc., with the same name held in the same year, see **11.4.2.3**.

If the year can only be approximated, record the date in the form *approximately [year]*.

Record a period of activity expressed as a range of years in the form *[year]–[year]*.

Record a period of activity expressed as a range of centuries in the form *[century]–[century]*.

11.4.2 Date of Conference, Etc.

CORE ELEMENT

11.4.2.1 Scope

A ***date of conference, etc.***, is the date or range of dates on which a conference, congress, meeting, exhibition, fair, festival, etc., was held.

11.4.2.2 Sources of Information

Take information on the date of a conference, etc., from any source.

11.4.2.3 Recording Date of Conference, Etc.

Record the year or years in which the conference, etc., was held by applying the basic instructions at **11.4.1**. Record a range of two or more years in the form *[year]–[year]*.

> 1995
>
> *Preferred name recorded as:* International Conference on Georgian Psalmody
>
> 2010
>
> *Preferred name recorded as:* Olympic Winter Games
>
> 1911–1912
>
> *Preferred name recorded as:* Deutsche Antarktische Expedition

Record specific dates if necessary to distinguish between two or more conferences, etc., with the same name held in the same year. Record the date in the form *[year] [month] [day]*. Record the month in the language and script preferred by the agency creating the data.

> 1978 February 13–15
>
> *Preferred name recorded as:* Federal-Provincial Conference of First Ministers
>
> 1978 November 27–29
>
> *Preferred name recorded as:* Federal-Provincial Conference of First Ministers

11.4.3 Date of Establishment

CORE ELEMENT

Date of establishment is a core element when needed to distinguish a corporate body from another corporate body with the same name.

11.4.3.1 Scope

A ***date of establishment*** is the date on which a corporate body was established or founded.

11.4.3.2 Sources of Information

Take information on the date of establishment from any source.

11.4.3.3 Recording Date of Establishment

Record the date of the establishment of the corporate body by applying the basic instructions at **11.4.1**.

1868
Preferred name recorded as: Gesellschaft für Musikforschung

1946
Preferred name recorded as: Gesellschaft für Musikforschung

1977
Preferred name recorded as: Double Image

1989
Preferred name recorded as: Double Image

If two or more governments claim jurisdiction over the same area (e.g., as with occupying powers and insurgent governments), record the year of establishment of the government, as appropriate.

1940
Preferred name recorded as: France. *Access point represents the territory under German occupation from 1940 to 1944*

1945
Preferred name recorded as: Germany. *Access point represents the territory under Allied occupation from 1945 to 1955*

1958
Preferred name recorded as: Algeria. *Access point represents the provisional government that was in power from 1958 to 1962*

11.4.4 Date of Termination

CORE ELEMENT

Date of termination is a core element when needed to distinguish a corporate body from another corporate body with the same name.

11.4.4.1 Scope

A ***date of termination*** is the date on which a corporate body was terminated or dissolved.

11.4.4.2 Sources of Information

Take information on the date of termination from any source.

11.4.4.3 Recording Date of Termination

Record the date of termination of the corporate body by applying the basic instructions at **11.4.1**.

1906
Preferred name recorded as: Gesellschaft für Musikforschung

If two or more governments claim jurisdiction over the same area (e.g., as with occupying powers and insurgent governments), record the year of termination of the government, as appropriate.

1944

Preferred name recorded as: France. *Access point represents the territory under German occupation from 1940 to 1944*

1955

Preferred name recorded as: Germany. *Access point represents the territory under Allied occupation from 1945 to 1955*

1962

Preferred name recorded as: Algeria. *Access point represents the provisional government that was in power from 1958 to 1962*

11.4.5 Period of Activity of the Corporate Body

CORE ELEMENT

Period of activity of the corporate body is a core element when needed to distinguish a corporate body from another corporate body with the same name.

11.4.5.1 Scope

Period of activity of the corporate body is a date or range of dates indicative of the period in which a corporate body was active.

11.4.5.2 Sources of Information

Take information on period of activity of the corporate body from any source.

11.4.5.3 Recording Period of Activity of the Corporate Body

If a corporate body's date of establishment and date of termination are both unknown, record a date or range of dates indicative of the corporate body's period of activity. Apply the basic instructions on recording dates associated with corporate bodies at **11.4.1**.

1810–1818

approximately 1700

If it is not possible to establish specific years of activity, record the century or centuries in which the corporate body was active.

19th century

16th century–17th century

11.5 Associated Institution

CORE ELEMENT

Associated institution is a core element for conferences, etc., if the institution's name provides better identification than the local place name or if the local place name is unknown or cannot be readily determined. Associated institution is a core element for other corporate bodies if the institution's name provides better identification than the local place name or if the local place name is unknown or cannot be readily determined, and it is needed to distinguish the corporate body from another corporate body with the same name.

11.5.1 Basic Instructions on Recording Associated Institutions

11.5.1.1 Scope

An ***associated institution*** is an institution commonly associated with a corporate body.

11.5.1.2 Sources of Information

Take information on associated institutions from any source.

11.5.1.3 Recording Associated Institutions

Record the name of an associated institution by using the preferred name for the institution (see **11.2.2**).

Record associated institutions as separate elements, as parts of access points, or as both. For additional instructions on recording an associated institution as part of the authorized access point, see **11.13.1.4**.

University of Cincinnati
Preferred name recorded as: B'nai B'rith Hillel Federation Jewish Student Center.

University of Maryland, College Park
Preferred name recorded as: B'nai B'rith Hillel-Federation Jewish Student Center.

Akademii͡a nauk SSSR. Karelʹskiĭ nauchnyĭ t͡sentr
Preferred name recorded as: Institut geologii.

Akademii͡a nauk SSSR. Komi nauchnyĭ t͡sentr
Preferred name recorded as: Institut geologii.

Practising Law Institute
Preferred name recorded as: Annual Computer Law Institute. *A series of conferences associated with the Practising Law Institute*

University of Southern California. Law Center
Preferred name recorded as: Annual Computer Law Institute. *A different series of conferences associated with the University of Southern California Law Center*

American Museum of Natural History
Preferred name recorded as: Center for Biodiversity and Conservation.

Cornell University
Preferred name recorded as: Delta Tau Delta Fraternity. Beta Omicron Chapter.

University of Michigan. School of Dentistry
Preferred name for the conference recorded as: Symposium on Herpes, Hepatitis, and AIDS. *Name of associated institution appears on resource being described as:* University of Michigan School of Dentistry. *Preferred name recorded as:* University of Michigan. School of Dentistry

11.6 Number of a Conference, Etc.

CORE ELEMENT

11.6.1 Basic Instructions on Recording Number of a Conference, Etc.

11.6.1.1 Scope

A ***number of a conference, etc.***, is a designation of the sequencing of a conference, etc., within a series of conferences, etc.

1st
Preferred name recorded as: International Conference on Georgian Psalmody

> 48th
> *Preferred name recorded as:* International Whaling Commission. Annual Meeting

11.6.1.2 Sources of Information

Take information on the number of a conference, etc., from any source.

11.6.1.3 Recording Number of a Conference, Etc.

If a conference, etc., is stated or inferred to be one of a series of numbered meetings of the same name, record the number of the conference. Record it as an ordinal numeral in the form preferred by the agency creating the data.

Record numbers of conferences as separate elements, as parts of access points, or as both. For additional instructions on recording the number of a conference as part of the authorized access point, see **11.13.1.8**.

11.7 Other Designation Associated with the Corporate Body

CORE ELEMENT

Type of corporate body is a core element for a body with a name that does not convey the idea of a corporate body. For other corporate bodies, other designation associated with the corporate body is a core element when needed to distinguish a corporate body from another corporate body with the same name.

11.7.1 Basic Instructions on Recording Other Designations Associated with Corporate Bodies

11.7.1.1 Scope

Other designation associated with the corporate body is:

a) a word, phrase, or abbreviation that indicates incorporation or legal status of a corporate body
or
b) any term that differentiates the body from other corporate bodies, persons, etc.

11.7.1.2 Sources of Information

Take information on other designations associated with the corporate body from any source.

11.7.1.3 Recording Other Designations Associated with Corporate Bodies

Record other designations associated with the corporate body by applying these instructions, as applicable:

type of corporate body (see **11.7.1.4**)
type of jurisdiction (see **11.7.1.5**)
other designation (see **11.7.1.6**).

Record other designations as separate elements, as parts of access points, or as both. For additional instructions on recording a designation as part of the authorized access point, see **11.13.1.6–11.13.1.7**.

11.7.1.4 Type of Corporate Body

Record the type of corporate body in a language preferred by the agency creating the data. If there is no equivalent term for the type of corporate body in a language preferred by the agency, or in case of doubt, record the type of corporate body in the official language of the corporate body.

> Spacecraft
> *Preferred name recorded as:* Apollo 11

Sloop
Preferred name recorded as: Rachel Ann

Program
Preferred name recorded as: Health of the Public. *Designation recorded by an agency following American spelling*

Programme
Preferred name recorded as: Security at Work. *Designation recorded by an agency following British spelling*

Fraternal order
Preferred name recorded as: Elks

Firm
Preferred name recorded as: Johann Traeg

Organisation
Preferred name recorded as: Gingerbread. *Designation recorded by an agency following British spelling*

Organization
Preferred name recorded as: Environmental Defense. *Designation recorded by an agency following American spelling*

Musical group
Preferred name recorded as: Red Hot Chili Peppers

Church
Preferred name recorded as: St. Mary

Radio station
Preferred name recorded as: CMQ

Radio station
Preferred name recorded as: KBS Kyōto

Television station
Preferred name recorded as: KUON

11.7.1.5 Type of Jurisdiction

For a government, record the type of jurisdiction in a language preferred by the agency creating the data. If there is no equivalent term for the type of jurisdiction in a language preferred by the agency, or in case of doubt, record it in the official language of the jurisdiction.

County
Preferred name recorded as: Cork (Ireland)

Landkreis
Preferred name recorded as: Darmstadt (Germany)

Regierungsbezirk
Preferred name recorded as: Darmstadt (Germany)

Province
Preferred name recorded as: Guadalajara (Spain)

Powiat
Preferred name recorded as: Lublin (Poland)

Voivodeship
Preferred name recorded as: Lublin (Poland)

State
Preferred name recorded as: New York

Federation
Preferred name recorded as: Russia

Judeţ
Preferred name recorded as: Tulcea (Romania)

Duchy
Preferred name recorded as: Westphalia

Kingdom
Preferred name recorded as: Westphalia

Ecclesiastical principality
Preferred name recorded as: Würzburg

City
Preferred name recorded as: York (England)

Village
Preferred name recorded as: Fangfoss (England)

If the type of jurisdiction does not provide sufficient identification, record a suitable word or phrase designation as instructed at **11.7.1.6**.

If two or more governments claim jurisdiction over the same area (e.g., as with occupying powers and insurgent governments), record suitable designations to distinguish one from the other. Apply the instructions at **11.7.1.6**, as appropriate.

11.7.1.6 Other Designation

Record a suitable designation if none of the following attributes are sufficient or appropriate for distinguishing between two or more corporate bodies with the same name:

place associated with the corporate body (see **11.3**)
date associated with the corporate body (see **11.4**)
associated institution (see **11.5**)
type of corporate body (see **11.7.1.4**)
type of jurisdiction (see **11.7.1.5**).

Record the designation in a language preferred by the agency creating the data.

Holiness
Preferred name recorded as: Church of God

Seventh Day
Preferred name recorded as: Church of God

Cricket
Preferred name recorded as: World Cup

Soccer
Preferred name recorded as: World Cup. *Designation recorded by an agency in the United States*

Brazzaville
Preferred name recorded as: Congo

Democratic Republic
Preferred name recorded as: Congo

North
Preferred name recorded as: Korea

South
Preferred name recorded as: Korea

BB-50
Preferred name recorded as: Indiana. *Type of corporate body recorded as:* Battleship

BB-58
Preferred name recorded as: Indiana. *Type of corporate body recorded as:* Battleship

If two or more governments claim jurisdiction over the same area (e.g., as with occupying powers and insurgent governments), record suitable designations to distinguish one from the other.

British military government
Preferred name recorded as: Michigan. *Designation for the military government that was in power from 1812 to 1813*

Provisional government
Preferred name recorded as: Algeria. *Designation for the provisional government that was in power from 1958 to 1962*

Territory under Allied occupation
Preferred name recorded as: Germany. *Designation for the territory under Allied occupation from 1945 to 1955*

Territory under German occupation
Preferred name recorded as: France. *Designation for the territory under German occupation from 1940 to 1944*

11.8 Language of the Corporate Body

11.8.1 Basic Instructions on Recording Languages of the Corporate Body

11.8.1.1 Scope

Language of the corporate body is a language a corporate body uses in its communications.

11.8.1.2 Sources of Information

Take information on the language or languages of the corporate body from any source.

11.8.1.3 Recording the Languages of the Corporate Body

Record the language or languages the body uses in its communications. Use an appropriate term or terms in a language preferred by the agency creating the data. Select terms from a standard list of names of languages, if available.

Record a language used by the corporate body as a separate element. Language is not recorded as part of the access point.

Russian
Language used by the corporate body Institut geologii

English
French
Languages used by the corporate body Canadian Standards Association

Indicate the source of information by applying the instructions at **8.12.1.3**.

11.9 Address of the Corporate Body

11.9.1 Basic Instructions on Recording Addresses of a Corporate Body

11.9.1.1 Scope

Address of the corporate body is the address of a corporate body's headquarters or offices, or an e-mail or Internet address for the body.

11.9.1.2 Sources of Information

Take information on the address or addresses of the corporate body from any source.

11.9.1.3 Recording the Addresses of the Corporate Body

Record the address of the corporate body's place of business and/or an e-mail or Internet address for the body.

Record an address as a separate element. Address is not recorded as part of the access point.

119 Spadina Avenue, Suite 600, Toronto, ON M5V 2L1 Canada
Postal address of Community Legal Education Ontario

cleo@cleo.on.ca
E-mail address of Community Legal Education Ontario

http://www.cleo.on.ca/
Web address of Community Legal Education Ontario

Indicate the source of information by applying the instructions at **8.12.1.3**.

11.10 Field of Activity of the Corporate Body

11.10.1 Basic Instructions on Recording Fields of Activity of the Corporate Body

11.10.1.1 Scope

Field of activity of the corporate body is a field of business in which a corporate body is engaged and/or the body's area of competence, responsibility, jurisdiction, etc.

11.10.1.2 Sources of Information

Take information on the field or fields of activity of the corporate body from any source.

11.10.1.3 Recording the Fields of Activity of the Corporate Body

Record the field or fields of activity of the corporate body.

Record a field of activity of the corporate body as a separate element. Field of activity is not recorded as part of the access point.

The North Atlantic Treaty Organization (NATO) is a political and military alliance of 26 countries from North America and Europe committed to fulfilling the goals of the North Atlantic Treaty signed on 4 April 1949

Note describing the field of activity of the North Atlantic Treaty Organization

CSA Group consists of 3 divisions: Canadian Standards Association, which develops and aids in the application of standards; CSA International, which provides testing and certification services; and Quality Management Institute (QMI), which delivers management system registration and training services

Note describing the fields of activity of CSA Group and its subordinate bodies, Canadian Standards Association, CSA International, and Quality Management Institute

Indicate the source of information by applying the instructions at **8.12.1.3**.

11.11 Corporate History

11.11.1 Basic Instructions on Recording Corporate History

11.11.1.1 Scope

Corporate history is historical information about the corporate body.

11.11.1.2 Sources of Information

Take information on corporate history from any source.

11.11.1.3 Recording Corporate History

Record historical information about the corporate body.

Record corporate history as a separate element. Corporate history is not recorded as part of an access point.

Established 28 January (8 February) 1724 in Saint Petersburg by decree of Peter I; opened in 1725. According to regulation of 1747 officially called Imperatorskaâ akademiâ nauk i khudozhestv; 1803–1855 called Imperatorskaâ akademiâ nauk; 1836–1917 officially named Imperatorskaâ Sankt-Peterburgskaâ akademiâ nauk. From 1724 to 1917 conventional name was Peterburgskaâ akademiâ nauk. Name changed May 1917 to Rossiĭskaâ akademiâ nauk. Renamed Akademiâ nauk SSSR June 1925

Corporate history for Akademiâ nauk SSSR

The Salem Female Academy was originally founded in 1772 and chartered as Salem Female Academy and College in 1866. In 1907 name was changed to Salem Academy and College, and in 1912, the institution was separated into Salem College and Salem Academy

Corporate history for Salem College

As appropriate, incorporate information associated with specific identifying elements (see **11.3–11.10**) into a corporate history element.

The company was incorporated in 1911 as the Computing-Tabulating-Recording Corporation. It adopted the current name in 1924. The company headquarters are located at 1 New Orchard Road, Armonk, NY 10504-1722 United States. A more detailed history of the company may be found at http://www-03.ibm.com/ibm/history/history/history_intro.html

Corporate history for International Business Machines Corporation

Indicate the source of information by applying the instructions at **8.12.1.3**.

11.12 Identifier for the Corporate Body

CORE ELEMENT

11.12.1 Basic Instructions on Recording Identifiers for Corporate Bodies

11.12.1.1 Scope

An ***identifier for the corporate body*** is a character string uniquely associated with a corporate body, or with a surrogate for a corporate body (e.g., an authority record). The identifier serves to differentiate that corporate body from other corporate bodies.

11.12.1.2 Sources of Information

Take information on identifiers for corporate bodies from any source.

11.12.1.3 Recording Identifiers for Corporate Bodies

Record an identifier for the corporate body. Precede the identifier with the name or an identification of the agency, etc., responsible for assigning the identifier, if readily ascertainable.

Library of Congress control number: no 88000581
Identifier for American Academy of Actuaries

Library and Archives Canada control number: 0067B4875
Identifier for American Academy of Actuaries

Union List of Artist Names ID: 5000033242
Identifier for Barton Myers Associates, Architects & Planners

AMG Artist ID: P 435023
AMG Data Solutions identifier for Coldplay

11.13 Constructing Access Points to Represent Corporate Bodies

11.13.1 Authorized Access Point Representing a Corporate Body

11.13.1.1 General Guidelines on Constructing Authorized Access Points to Represent Corporate Bodies

When constructing an authorized access point to represent a corporate body, use the preferred name for the corporate body (see **11.2.2**) as the basis for the authorized access point.

Museum of American Folk Art

Royal Aeronautical Society

World Methodist Conference

Eurovision Song Contest

E. Azalia Hackley Memorial Collection

Unesco

Society of St. John the Evangelist

Synagogue de la place des Vosges

Boundary Commission for England

Centro Universitário Belas Artes de São Paulo

National Association of Insurance Commissioners. Securities Valuation Office

California Home Economics Association. Orange District

University of London. School of Pharmacy

American Library Association. Resources and Technical Services Division. Board of Directors

Jean Piaget Society. Annual Meeting

Italy. Ministero del bilancio e della programmazione economica

Catholic Church. Diocese of Newport and Menevia

Make additions to the name as instructed at **11.13.1.2–11.13.1.8**, in that order, as applicable.

Elks (Fraternal order)

National Gallery of Art (Nigeria)

National Gallery of Art (U.S.)

Fusion (Organization : Brighton, England)

Fusion (Organization : Chichester, England)

Center for the Study of Man (Smithsonian Institution)

Blackfoot Mining and Milling Company (1885–1905)

Elizabeth (Schooner : 1846–1855)

Georgia (Republic)

Bagua (Peru : Province)

New England Invitational Tournament (Hockey)

National and Household Food Security Workshop (2003 : Lusaka, Zambia)

European Society for Neurochemistry. Meeting (11th : 1996 : Groningen, Netherlands)

Jornadas de Estudios Históricos (Salamanca, Spain)

Jornadas de Estudios Históricos (Universidad del País Vasco)

Exception

If two or more governments claim jurisdiction over the same area (e.g., occupying powers and insurgent governments), add a designation to the access point for the jurisdiction to distinguish between the two. Add the designation (see **11.13.1.7**) before the date or dates associated with the government (see **11.13.1.5**).

Belgium (Territory under German occupation, 1914–1918)

China (Provisional government, 1937–1940)

China (Reformed government, 1938–1940)

Make the additions specified at **11.13.1.2** if the preferred name for the body does not convey the idea of a corporate body.

Make the additions specified at **11.13.1.2–11.13.1.7** if they are needed to distinguish access points representing different corporate bodies with the same name.

Make the additions at **11.13.1.8** for the access point representing a conference, as appropriate.

ADDITIONS TO ACCESS POINTS REPRESENTING CORPORATE BODIES

11.13.1.2 Type of Corporate Body

Add a term designating the type of corporate body (see **11.7.1.4**), if needed to distinguish one access point from another (i.e., when two or more bodies have the same name or names so similar that they may be confused). Also add such a term if the preferred name for the body does not convey the idea of a corporate body.

Apollo 11 (Spacecraft)

Beanpot (Hockey tournament)

Gingerbread (Organisation)

Designation added by an agency following British spelling conventions

Health of the Public (Program)

Designation added by an agency following American spelling conventions

Johann Traeg (Firm)

KBS Kyōto (Radio station)

Merced de Quito (Monastery)

Niagara (Passenger ship)

Niagara (Whaling ship)

Rachel Ann (Sloop)

Red Hot Chili Peppers (Musical group)

11.13.1.3 Place Associated with the Body

Add the name of a place associated with the corporate body if needed to distinguish one access point from another (i.e., when two or more bodies have the same name or names so similar that they may be confused).

Add the name of the country, state, province, etc., or the name of a local place with which the body is associated (see **11.3.3**).

For instructions on using the name of an associated institution instead of the local place name, see **11.13.1.4**.

Country, State, Province, Etc.

Republican Party (Ill.)

Republican Party (Mont.)

Sociedad Nacional de Agricultura (Chile)

Sociedad Nacional de Agricultura (Peru)

National Measurement Laboratory (Australia)

National Measurement Laboratory (U.S.)

Governor's Conference on Aging (Ariz.)

Governor's Conference on Aging (Fla.)

Local Place

Newport High School (Newport, Ky.)

Newport High School (Newport, R.I.)

Newport High School (Newport, Wash.)

Washington County Historical Society (Washington County, Ind.)

Washington County Historical Society (Washington County, N.Y.)

Grand Hotel (Florence, Italy)

Grand Hotel (Mackinac Island, Mich.)

Grand Hôtel (Stockholm, Sweden)

Dominique's (Restaurant : New Orleans, La.)

Dominique's (Restaurant : Washington, D.C.)

St. Peter's Church (Hope, England)

St. Peter's Church (Limpsfield, England)

St. Peter's Church (Stourton, Wiltshire, England)

St. John's Church (Georgetown, Washington, D.C.)

St. John's Church (Lafayette Square, Washington, D.C.)

Optional Addition

Add the name of the place associated with the body if the addition assists in the identification of the body.

Provincial Intermediate Teachers' Association (B.C.)
No conflict

National Entrepreneurship Observatory (Wales)
No conflict

Project HOME (Chittenden County, Vt.)
No conflict

Bushcare (Program : Australia)
No conflict

If:
a chapter, branch, etc., is recorded as a subdivision of a higher body (see **11.2.2.14**)
and
it carries out the activities of the higher body in a particular locality
and
the name of the locality is not already part of the name of the chapter, branch, etc.
then:
add the name of the locality.

Knights Templar (Masonic order). Grand Commandery (Ohio)

Knights Templar (Masonic order). DeWitt Clinton Commandery No. 1 (Virginia City, Nev.)

but

Knights Templar (Masonic order). Boston Encampment
not Knights Templar (Masonic order). Boston Encampment (Boston, Mass.)

If the preferred name for a local church, temple, mosque, etc., does not clearly indicate the place in which it is located, add the name of the place or the local ecclesiastical jurisdiction (e.g., parish).

Baha'i House of Worship (Ingleside, N.S.W.)

Beth Tikvah Synagogue (Toronto, Ont.)

St. Mary (Church : Abberley, England)

First Baptist Church (Cape May County, N.J.)

St. James' Church (Gleninagh Heights, Galway, Ireland)

Bhadrakāli (Temple : Kathmandu, Nepal)

Masjid-i Jumʻah (Iṣfahān, Iran)

Basílica de San Francisco (La Paz, Bolivia)

but

Grande synagogue de Bruxelles

London Central Mosque

Mesa Arizona Temple

Montreal South Methodist Church

Abingdon Abbey

Cattedrale di Palermo

If the preferred name for a radio or television station consists solely or mainly of its call letters, add the name of the place in which the station is located.

KUON (Television station : Lincoln, Neb.)

Radio 4EBFM (Brisbane, Qld.)

If the preferred name for a radio or television station does not include the name of the local place as an integral part of its name, add the name of the local place. If the preferred name includes the name of the local place, do not add the name of the place.

Rádio Moçambique (Maputo, Mozambique)

but

KBS Kyōto (Radio station)

TV Tacoma

If the name of the place associated with the body changes during the lifetime of the body, record the latest name in use during the lifetime of the body (see **11.3.3.4**).

If the following elements provide better identification than the name of the local place, use one of these elements instead of the name of the local place:

the name of an associated institution (see **11.13.1.4**)

a date or dates associated with the body (see **11.13.1.5**)

other designation (see **11.13.1.7**).

For instructions on adding a place name to the preferred name for a conference, etc., see **11.13.1.8**.

11.13.1.4 Associated Institution

Add the name of an associated institution if needed to distinguish one access point from another (i.e., when two or more corporate bodies have the same name or have names so similar that they may be confused).

Add the name of an associated institution if the institution's name is commonly associated with the name of the corporate body (see **11.5**). Prefer this addition instead of the local place name (see **11.13.1.3**).

B'nai B'rith Hillel Federation Jewish Student Center (University of Cincinnati)
not B'nai B'rith Hillel Federation Jewish Student Center (Cincinnati, Ohio)

B'nai B'rith Hillel-Federation Jewish Student Center (University of Maryland, College Park)
not B'nai B'rith Hillel-Federation Jewish Student Center (College Park, Md.)

Institut geologii (Akademii͡a nauk SSSR. Karelʹskiĭ nauchnyĭ t͡sentr)

Institut geologii (Akademii͡a nauk SSSR. Komi nauchnyĭ t͡sentr)

Annual Computer Law Institute (Practising Law Institute)

Annual Computer Law Institute (University of Southern California. Law Center)

Optional Addition

Add the name of an institution associated with the body if the addition assists in the identification of the body.

Center for Biodiversity and Conservation (American Museum of Natural History)
No conflict

Delta Tau Delta Fraternity. Beta Omicron Chapter (Cornell University)
No conflict

11.13.1.5 Date Associated with the Body

Add a date or dates associated with the body (see **11.4.3–11.4.5**) if needed to distinguish one access point from another when the following elements are not available:

place (see **11.13.1.3**)

associated institution (see **11.13.1.4**).

Gesellschaft für Musikforschung (1868–1906)

Gesellschaft für Musikforschung (1946–)

South Dakota. Department of Public Safety (1973–1984)

South Dakota. Department of Public Safety (2003–)

Double Image (Musical group : 1977–)

Double Image (Musical group : 1989–)

Double Image (Musical group : 1997–)

Mary (Sloop : 1752)

Mary (Sloop : 1846–1855)

Harrison & Leigh (–2007)

Harrison & Leigh (active 1810–1818)

Period of activity added because date of establishment and date of termination are unknown

Optional Addition

Add a date or dates associated with the body if the addition assists in the identification of the body.

If two or more governments claim jurisdiction over the same area (e.g., occupying powers and insurgent governments), add a designation to the access point for the jurisdiction to distinguish between the two. Add the designation (see **11.13.1.7**) before the date or dates associated with the government.

Dutch East Indies (Territory under Japanese occupation, 1942–1945)

Korea (Provisional government, 1919–1945)

For instructions on adding a date or dates to the preferred name for a conference, etc., see **11.13.1.8**.

11.13.1.6 Type of Jurisdiction

Add the type of jurisdiction (see **11.7.1.5**) if needed to distinguish one access point from another (i.e., when two or more corporate bodies have the same name or have names so similar that they may be confused). Add the term to the name of a government other than a city or a town.

Cork (Ireland)

Cork (Ireland : County)

Darmstadt (Germany)

Darmstadt (Germany : Landkreis)

Darmstadt (Germany : Regierungsbezirk)

Guadalajara (Spain)

Guadalajara (Spain : Province)

Lublin (Poland)

Lublin (Poland : Powiat)

Lublin (Poland : Voivodeship)

New York (N.Y.)

New York (State)

Tulcea (Romania)

Tulcea (Romania : Județ)

Westphalia (Duchy)

Westphalia (Kingdom)

Würzburg (Germany)

Würzburg (Ecclesiastical principality)

11.13.1.7 Other Designation Associated with the Body

If none of the additions at **11.13.1.2–11.13.1.6** is sufficient or appropriate for distinguishing between the access points for two or more bodies, add a suitable designation (see **11.7.1.6**).

Church of God (Holiness)

Church of God (Seventh Day)

Congo (Brazzaville)

Congo (Democratic Republic)

Indiana (Battleship : BB-50)

Indiana (Battleship : BB-58)

Korea (North)

Korea (South)

World Cup (Cricket)

World Cup (Soccer)
Designation added by an agency in the United States

Optional Addition

Add such a designation if the addition assists in the understanding of the nature or purpose of the body.

World Series (Baseball)

HSBC World Match Play Championship (Golf tournament)

Oxford University International (Chess tournament)

Rucker Tournament (Basketball)

Bunker Hill (Aircraft carrier : CV-17)
No conflict with other aircraft carriers

Bunker Hill (Cruiser : CG-52)
No conflict with other cruisers

If a designation is required to distinguish between the access points for two or more bodies with the same name and associated with the same place, add the designation following the place name.

All Hallows (Church : London, England : Bread Street)

All Hallows (Church : London, England : Honey Lane)

All Hallows (Church : London, England : London Wall)

If two or more governments claim jurisdiction over the same area (e.g., occupying powers and insurgent governments), add a designation to the access point to distinguish between the two. Add the designation before the date or dates associated with the government (see **11.13.1.5**).

Algeria (Provisional government, 1958–1962)

France (Territory under German occupation, 1940–1944)

Germany (Territory under Allied occupation, 1945–1955)

Michigan (British military government, 1812–1813)

11.13.1.8 Number, Date, and Location of a Conference, Etc.

11.13.1.8.1 Access Point for a Single Instance of a Conference, Etc.

Apply this instruction to a one-time conference, etc., or a single instance of a series of conferences. Apply this instruction also to a conference recorded subordinately (see **11.2.2.14.6**).

Add the following elements to the name of a conference, etc., if applicable and readily ascertainable. Add them in this order:

a) the number of the conference, etc. (see **11.6**)

b) the date of the conference, etc. (see **11.4.2**)

c) the location of the conference, etc. (see **11.3.2**)

Clambake Conference on the Nature and Source of Human Error (1st : 1980 : Columbia Falls, Me.)

Governor's Conference on Aging (Fla.) (3rd : 1992 : Tallahassee, Fla.)

Mezhdunarodnyĭ simpozium "Global′noe rasselenie gominid" (1993 : Moscow, Russia)
No applicable number

Australian Bioethics Association. National Conference (6th : 1998 : Hobart, Tas.)

Federal-Provincial Conference of First Ministers (1978 November 27–29 : Ottawa, Ont.)
No applicable number; specific dates added to distinguish between another conference with the same name held in the same year

Gapapaiwa Writers' Workshop (1st : 1993)
Location of workshop not readily ascertainable

Olympic Winter Games (21st : 2010 : Vancouver, B.C.)

Inter-American Music Festival (12th : 1981 : Washington, D.C.)

Auckland Art Fair (2009 : Auckland, N.Z.)
Number of fair not readily ascertainable

Polyurethanes Expo (1999 : Orlando, Fla.)
No applicable number

EuroSSC (2006 : Enschede, Netherlands)
No applicable number

Deutsche Antarktische Expedition (1911–1912)
No applicable number or local place

Archbold Expedition to New Guinea (7th : 1964)
No applicable local place

Exceptions

Add the name of the associated institution instead of the local place name if:

the name of an associated institution (see **11.5**) provides better identification than the local place name

or

the local place name is not known or cannot be readily determined.

International Conference on Georgian Psalmody (2nd : 1997 : Colchester Institute)

Marine Awareness Workshop for Beqa Lagoon (1996 : Pacific Harbour International Hotel)
No applicable number

Society for the Study of Economic Inequality. Meeting (1st : 2005 : Universitat de les Illes Balears)

Symposium on Herpes, Hepatitis, and AIDS (1983 : University of Michigan. School of Dentistry)
No applicable number

International Conference "Linguistics by the End of the XXth Century— Achievements and Perspectives" (1995 : Moskovskiĭ gosudarstvennyĭ universitet im. M.V. Lomonosova)
No applicable number

Seminário a Situação Económica de Moçambique e os Possíveis Cenários para o seu Desenvolvimento (1994 : Universidade Eduardo Mondlane. Faculdade de Economia)
No applicable number

U.S. Open (Golf tournament) (1989 : Oak Hill Country Club)
Number of tournament not readily ascertainable

If the conference, etc., was held online, record *Online* as the location.

Electronic Conference on Land Use and Land Cover Change in Europe (1997 : Online)
No applicable number

If the sessions of a conference, etc., were held in two or more locations, add each of the place names.

Symposium on Breeding and Machine Harvesting of Rubus and Ribes (1976 : East Malling, England; Dundee, Scotland)
No applicable number

Conference on the Appalachian Frontier (1985 : James Madison University; Mary Baldwin College)
No applicable number

International Congress of Iranian Art and Archaeology (5th : 1968 : Tehran, Iran; Iṣfahān, Iran; Shīrāz, Iran)

Danish-Swedish Analysis Seminar (1995 : Copenhagen, Denmark; Lund, Sweden; Paris, France)
No applicable number

Adolescent Medicine Symposium (1984–1985 : Yale University. School of Medicine; St. Joseph Hospital; Dartmouth Medical School; Maine Medical Center; University of Massachusetts Medical Center/Worcester)
No applicable number

11.13.1.8.2 Access Point for a Series of Conferences, Etc.

If the access point represents a series of conferences, etc., do not add the number, date, or location of the conferences, etc.

Blue Ridge Folklife Festival
Access point for its annual program book described as a serial

Salzburger Festspiele
Access point for an audio recording of music performed at the 1956-1965 festivals

Intermountain West Student Philosophy Conference
Access point for its website

Annual Symposium on Sea Turtle Biology and Conservation
Access point for its proceedings described as a serial

If additions are required to distinguish two or more series of conferences, etc., with the same name or a name so similar that they may be confused, apply the instructions at **11.13.1.2–11.13.1.7**, as applicable.

11.13.2 Variant Access Point Representing a Corporate Body

11.13.2.1 General Guidelines on Constructing Variant Access Points to Represent Corporate Bodies

When constructing a variant access point to represent a corporate body, use a variant name for the corporate body (see **11.2.3**) as the basis for a variant access point.

Hertfordshire Technical Information Service
Form recorded as authorized access point: Hertis

Uffizi Gallery
Authorized access point recorded as: Galleria degli Uffizi

HMS Beagle
H.M.S. Beagle
Form recorded as authorized access point: Beagle (Ship)

Concours Eurovision de la chanson
Eurovisie Songfestival
Eurovision laulukilpailu
Festival de la Canción de Eurovisión
Festival Eurovisão da Canção
Gran premio Eurovisione della canzone europea
Grand Prix Eurovision de la chanson
Konkurs pesni Eŭrabachanne
Konkurs pesni "Evrovidenie"
Pesma Evrovizije
Söngvakeppni evrópskra sjónvarpsstöðva
Конкурс песні Еўрабачанне
Конкурс песни «Евровидение»

Песма Евровизије
Form recorded as authorized access point: Eurovision Song Contest

Black Friars
Friars Preachers
Order of Preachers
Ordo Praedicatorum
Form recorded as authorized access point: Dominicans

London School of Economics and Political Science. British Library of Political and Economic Science
BLPES
Form recorded as authorized access point: British Library of Political and Economic Science

King County (Wash.). Cultural Development Authority
Form recorded as authorized access point: Cultural Development Authority of King County

Newport (Ky.). High School
Form recorded as authorized access point: Newport High School (Newport, Ky.)

Koryŏ Taehakkyo. Legal Association
Legal Association of Korea University
高麗大學校. 法律學會
Form recorded as authorized access point: Koryŏ Taehakkyo. Pŏmnyul Hakhoe

Yale University. ITSMed. Media Services. Video Production
Form recorded as authorized access point: Yale University. ITSMed. Video Production

West Virginia Agricultural College
West Virginia. Agricultural College
Form recorded as authorized access point: Agricultural College of West Virginia

Conference on Georgian Psalmody, International
Form recorded as authorized access point: International Conference on Georgian Psalmody

Exhibition of Contemporary American Painting, Biennial
Corcoran Biennial Exhibition of American Painting
Corcoran Gallery of Art. Biennial Exhibition of Contemporary American Painting
Form recorded as authorized access point: Biennial Exhibition of Contemporary American Painting

New South Wales. Environment and Climate Change, Department of
DECC
Form recorded as authorized access point: New South Wales. Department of Environment and Climate Change

Make additions to the name, if considered important for identification. Apply the instructions at **11.13.1.2–11.13.1.8**, as applicable.

Addition to a Name Not Conveying the Idea of a Corporate Body

Apollo Eleven (Spacecraft)
Apollo XI (Spacecraft)
Form recorded as authorized access point: Apollo 11 (Spacecraft)

Eroṿizyon (Contest)
Eurovisió (Contest)
Evrovizija (Contest)
Евровизија (Contest)
Form recorded as authorized access point: Eurovision Song Contest

Place Associated with the Body

Royal Academy of Music (Denmark)

Form recorded as authorized access point: Jydske musikkonservatorium

Royal Academy of Music (France)

Form recorded as authorized access point: Opéra de Paris

Royal Academy of Music (Sweden)

Form recorded as authorized access point: Kungl. Musikaliska akademien (Sweden)

Smith and Son (Dublin, Ireland)

Form recorded as authorized access point: Smith & Son (Dublin, Ireland)

Smith and Son (Houma, La.)

Form recorded as authorized access point: T. Baker Smith and Son

Joe's (Restaurant : Miami, Fla.)

Form recorded as authorized access point: Joe's Stone Crab Restaurant

Associated Institution

Digital Library Project (American Museum of Natural History)

Form recorded as authorized access point: AMNH Digital Library Project

Ripley Center (Smithsonian Institution)

Form recorded as authorized access point: S. Dillon Ripley Center (Smithsonian Institution)

Date Associated with the Body

Universidad de Puerto Rico (1903–1966)

Form recorded as authorized access point: University of Puerto Rico (1903–1966)

Alexander (Ship : 1805–1851)

Form recorded as authorized access point: Ann Alexander (Ship)

Type of Jurisdiction

Budyšin (Germany : Landkreis)

Form recorded as authorized access point: Bautzen (Germany : Landkreis)

Géorgie (Republic)
Gjeorgjia (Republic)
Gruusia (Republic)
Gruzija (Republic)
Gu̇rzhīstan (Republic)
Jorjia (Republic)
Sakʻartʻvelo (Republic)
Xeorxia (Republic)
Γεωργία (Republic)
Грузија (Republic)
Гуржістан (Republic)
საქართველო (Republic)

Form recorded as authorized access point: Georgia (Republic)

Other Designation Associated with the Body

Beanpot Tournament (Hockey)
Form recorded as authorized access point: Beanpot (Hockey tournament)

All Souls Church (Washington, D.C. : Episcopal)
Form recorded as authorized access point: All Souls Memorial Episcopal Church (Washington, D.C.)

Church of All Hallows (London, England : Bread Street)
Form recorded as authorized access point: All Hallows (Church : London, England : Bread Street)

Congo (People's Republic)
Kongo (Brazzaville)
République du Congo (Brazzaville)
Republic of Congo (Brazzaville)
Republic of the Congo (Brazzaville)
Form recorded as authorized access point: Congo (Brazzaville)

USS Indiana (BB-58)
Form recorded as authorized access point: Indiana (Battleship : BB-58)

Number, Date, and Location of a Conference, Etc.

Corps of Discovery (1804–1806)
Corps of Discovery Expedition (1804–1806)
Lewis & Clark Expedition (1804–1806)
Meriwether Lewis and William Clark Expedition (1804–1806)
Form recorded as authorized access point: Lewis and Clark Expedition (1804–1806)

Conférence internationale de mécanique des sols (1982 : Mexico City, Mexico)
Conferencia Internacional de Mecánica de Suelos (1982 : Mexico City, Mexico)
Form recorded as authorized access point: International Conference of Soil Mechanics (1982 : Mexico City, Mexico)

12

GENERAL GUIDELINES ON RECORDING ATTRIBUTES OF CONCEPTS, OBJECTS, EVENTS, AND PLACES

[To be developed after the initial release of RDA]

13

IDENTIFYING CONCEPTS

[To be developed after the initial release of RDA]

14

IDENTIFYING OBJECTS

[To be developed after the initial release of RDA]

15

IDENTIFYING EVENTS

[To be developed after the initial release of RDA]

16

IDENTIFYING PLACES

16.0 Purpose and Scope

This chapter provides general guidelines and instructions on:

a) choosing preferred names for places (see **16.2.2**)

b) recording preferred and variant names for places (see **16.2**)

c) recording other identifying attributes of places (see **16.3**).

The names of places are commonly used in the following ways:

as the names of governments (see **11.2.2.5.4**) and communities that are not governments

as additions to titles of works (see **6.5**)

as additions to the names of corporate bodies to distinguish between bodies with the same name (see **11.13.1.3**)

as additions to conference names (see **11.13.1.8**)

in recording places associated with a person (see **9.8–9.11**), family (see **10.5**), or corporate body (see **11.3**).

The instructions in chapter **16** do not cover using names of places to indicate a subject relationship or geographic coverage. Such instructions will be developed after the initial release of RDA.

16.1 General Guidelines on Identifying Places

16.1.1 Sources of Information

Take the name or names of the place from any source.

For additional guidance on sources of information for the preferred name for the place, see **16.2.2.2**.

Take information on other identifying attributes of the place from any source.

16.1.2 Using Access Points to Identify Places

[To be added in a later release]

16.2 Name of the Place

16.2.1 Basic Instructions on Recording Names of Places

16.2.1.1 Scope

A ***name of the place*** is a word, character, or group of words and/or characters by which a place is known.

When identifying places, there are two categories of names:

a) preferred name for the place (see **16.2.2**)

b) variant name for the place (see **16.2.3**).

16.2.1.2 Sources of Information

Take the name or names of the place from any source.

For additional guidance on sources of information for the preferred name for the place, see **16.2.2.2**.

16.2.1.3 General Guidelines on Recording Names of Places

Record the name of a place in the form found in the source from which the name is taken, unless the instructions at **16.2.2.8–16.2.2.13** indicate otherwise.

16.2.2 Preferred Name for the Place

16.2.2.1 Scope

The ***preferred name for the place*** is the name or form of name chosen to identify a place.

The preferred name for the place is also used:

a) as the conventional name of a government, etc.

b) as an addition to the name of a family, a corporate body, a conference, etc., or a work

c) to record a place associated with a person, family, or corporate body.

16.2.2.2 Sources of Information

Determine the preferred name for a place from (in order of preference):

a) gazetteers and other reference sources in a language preferred by the agency creating the data

b) gazetteers and other reference sources issued in the jurisdiction in which the place is located in the official language or languages of that jurisdiction.

16.2.2.3 Choosing the Preferred Name

Choose as the preferred name of a place (in this order):

a) the form of the name in the language preferred by the agency creating the data, if there is one in general use

b) the form of the name in the official language of the jurisdiction in which the place is located.

When a place is known by more than one form of the same name, see additional instructions on choosing the preferred name at **16.2.2.6**.

When the name of a place changes, see the instructions at **16.2.2.7**.

16.2.2.4 Recording the Preferred Name

Record as the preferred name of a place the form most commonly found in gazetteers or other reference sources. If an instruction at **16.2.2.8–16.2.2.14** indicates otherwise, apply the specific instruction instead.

When recording the preferred name of a place, include an initial article if present.

The Dalles

Los Angeles

El Centro

Le Mans

al-Ghardaqah

Y Bala

The Hague

Alternative

Omit an initial article (see appendix **C**) unless the name is to be accessed under the article.

Dalles
not The Dalles

Ghardaqah
not al-Ghardaqah

Bala
not Y Bala

Hague
not The Hague

but

La Ronge

Los Angeles

Record as part of the name of a place (other than a country or a state, etc., listed at **16.2.2.9.1**, **16.2.2.10**, or **16.2.2.11**) the name of the larger place in which it is located or the larger jurisdiction to which it belongs (see **16.2.2.9–16.2.2.14**).

When the place name is being used as the conventional name for a government (see **11.2.2.5.4**), enclose the name of the larger place in parentheses.

Budapest (Hungary)

Precede the name of the larger place by a comma when the place name is used in the following elements:

the location of a conference, etc., (see **11.3.2**)
the location of the headquarters of a corporate body (see **11.3.3**)
the place of origin of a work (see **6.5**)
a place associated with a person (see **9.8–9.11**), family (see **10.5**), or corporate body (see **11.3**).

Budapest, Hungary
Place name recorded as the location of the corporate body with the preferred name: Rumbach Utcai Zsinagóga

16.2.2.5 Names Found in a Non-preferred Script

If the name of the place is found in a script that differs from a preferred script of the agency creating the data, transliterate the name according to the scheme chosen by the agency.

ʿAqabah
Arabic script name عقبة *transliterated according to the* ALA-LC Romanization Tables

Alternative

If:

the name of the place is in a script that differs from a preferred script of the agency creating the data

and

a transliterated form is found in reference sources

then:
use the transliterated form. If there is more than one transliterated form, use the form that matches the agency's transliteration of the name (i.e., the form transliterated using the transliteration scheme chosen by the agency).

Tétouan
not Tiṭwān
Transliterated form of Arabic script name تطوان *that appears in reference sources*

Variant names. Record other forms of the transliterated names as variant names (see **16.2.3.6**).

CHOOSING THE PREFERRED NAME

16.2.2.6 Different Language Forms of the Same Name

If:
there is a form of the name of a place in a language preferred by the agency creating the data
and
that form is in general use
then:
choose that form as the preferred name. Determine the form from gazetteers and other reference sources published in that language.

Austria
not Österreich

Copenhagen
not København

Florence
not Firenze

Ghent
not Gent
not Gand

If:
the form of name for a place is found in a language preferred by the agency creating the data
and
that form of the name is the name of the government that has jurisdiction over the place
then:
choose that form.

Soviet Union
not Sovetskiĭ Soi͡uz
not Russia
Name of government having jurisdiction over the place between 1923 and 1991

If there is no form in general use in a language preferred by the agency creating the data, choose the form in the official language of the jurisdiction in which the place is located.

Buenos Aires

Horlivka

Tallinn

Livorno
not Leghorn
English form no longer in general use

If:

there is no form in general use in a language preferred by the agency creating the data

and

the jurisdiction has more than one official language

then:

choose the form most commonly found in sources in a language preferred by the agency.

Louvain
not Leuven

Helsinki
not Helsingfors

16.2.2.7 Change of Name

When the name of the place changes, see the appropriate instruction in chapter **10** or **11** to determine which name or names to use:

a) the instructions on government names (see **11.2.2.5.4**) (e.g., use *Nyasaland* or *Malawi*, as appropriate)
or
b) the instructions on additions to family names (see **10.11.1.4**), corporate names (see **11.13.1.3**), and conference names (see **11.13.1.8**) (e.g., use *Leopoldville* or *Kinshasa*, as appropriate)
or
c) other relevant instructions in chapter **11**.

RECORDING THE PREFERRED NAME

16.2.2.8 Place Names for Jurisdictions

Record the preferred place name for a jurisdiction by applying these instructions, as applicable:

place names that include a term indicating type of jurisdiction (see **16.2.2.8.1**)

place names that require a term indicating type of jurisdiction (see **16.2.2.8.2**).

16.2.2.8.1 Place Names That Include a Term Indicating Type of Jurisdiction

If:

the first part of a place name is a term indicating a type of jurisdiction

and

the place is commonly listed under another part of its name in lists published in the language of the country in which it is located

then:

omit the term indicating the type of jurisdiction.

Kerry (Ireland)
not County Kerry (Ireland)

Ostholstein (Germany)
not Kreis Ostholstein (Germany)

In all other cases, include the term indicating the type of jurisdiction.

Città di Castello (Italy)

Ciudad Juárez (Mexico)

District of Columbia

Distrito Federal (Brazil)

Mexico City (Mexico)

16.2.2.8.2 Place Names That Require a Term Indicating Type of Jurisdiction

If:
the place name is not the name for a city or town
and
the place name does not include a term indicating a type of jurisdiction
and
the place name is being used as the conventional name for a government
then:
add the type of jurisdiction by applying the instructions at **11.7.1.5**.

16.2.2.9 Places in Australia, Canada, the United States, the former U.S.S.R., or the former Yugoslavia

For a place in Australia, Canada, the United States, or a country that was a constituent republic of the former U.S.S.R. or of the former Yugoslavia, apply these instructions, as appropriate:

states, provinces, territories, etc. (see **16.2.2.9.1**)

places in a state, province, territory, etc. (see **16.2.2.9.2**).

16.2.2.9.1 States, Provinces, Territories, Etc.

For a state, province, territory, etc., of Australia, Canada, the United States, or a country that was a constituent republic of the former U.S.S.R. or of the former Yugoslavia, do not record the name of the larger jurisdiction as part of the preferred name.

Northern Territory

Prince Edward Island

Oregon

District of Columbia

Guam

Puerto Rico

Azerbaijan S.S.R.

Slovenia

Dakota Territory

16.2.2.9.2 Places in a State, Province, Territory, Etc.

If the place is in a state, province, territory, etc., of one of the countries listed at **16.2.2.9.1**, record the name of the state, etc., in which it is located as part of the preferred name.

Record the preferred name for the place by applying the instructions at **16.2.2.4**. Abbreviate the name of the larger place as instructed in appendix B (**B.2**), as applicable.

Darwin (N.T.)

Jasper (Alta.)

Clayoquot Land District (B.C.)

Cook County (Ill.)

Alexandria (Va.)

Latah Soil and Water Conservation District (Idaho)

Washington (D.C.)

San Juan (P.R.)

Kiev (Ukraine)

Split (Croatia)

16.2.2.10 England, Northern Ireland, Scotland, and Wales

Do not record the name of the larger jurisdiction (e.g., United Kingdom or Great Britain) as part of the preferred names of England, Northern Ireland, Scotland, and Wales.

England

Northern Ireland

Record the preferred name for a place in England, Northern Ireland, Scotland, or Wales by applying the instructions at **16.2.2.10.1**, as applicable.

16.2.2.10.1 Places in England, Northern Ireland, Scotland, and Wales

If a place is located in England, Northern Ireland, Scotland, or Wales, record *England*, *Northern Ireland*, *Scotland*, or *Wales*, as appropriate, as part of the preferred name by applying the instructions at **16.2.2.4**.

Dorset (England)

Bangor (Northern Ireland)

Dumfries and Galloway (Scotland)

Powys (Wales)

16.2.2.11 Overseas Territories, Dependencies, Etc.

Do not record the name of the larger jurisdiction as part of the preferred name of an overseas territory, dependency, etc.

Greenland

Isle of Man

Guadeloupe

French Guiana

For an overseas territory of the United States (e.g., Guam, Puerto Rico), see **16.2.2.9.1**.

For jurisdictional islands, etc., that are not overseas territories, dependencies, etc., (e.g., Sicily, Corsica, Japan), see **16.2.2.4** or **16.2.2.12**, as applicable.

Record the preferred name for a place in an overseas territory, dependency, etc., as instructed at **16.2.2.11.1**.

16.2.2.11.1 Places in Overseas Territories, Dependencies, Etc.

If the place is in an overseas territory, dependency, etc., record the name of the overseas territory, dependency, etc., in which it is located as part of the preferred name of the place by applying the instructions at **16.2.2.4**.

Papeete (French Polynesia)

Ramsey (Isle of Man)

Saint-Denis (Réunion)

16.2.2.12 Places in Other Jurisdictions

Record the name of the country in which a place is located as part of the preferred name for the place if that place is in a jurisdiction not covered by the following:

places in Australia, Canada, the United States, the former U.S.S.R., or the former Yugoslavia (see **16.2.2.9**)

places in England, Northern Ireland, Scotland, and Wales (see **16.2.2.10.1**)

places in overseas territories, dependencies, etc. (see **16.2.2.11.1**).

Abbreviate the name of the country as instructed in Appendix B (**B.2**), as applicable.

Formosa (Argentina)

Maputo (Mozambique)

Lucca (Italy)

Queenstown-Lakes District (N.Z.)

Madras (India)

Palawan (Philippines)

Region Sjælland (Denmark)

Paris (France)

Urlingford (Ireland)

Far North Province (Cameroon)

Perak (Malaysia)

Sarawak (Malaysia)

Ipoh (Malaysia)

Georgetown (Malaysia)

Alternative

Record the name of a state, province, or highest-level administrative division preceding the name of the country.

Aba Zangzu Qiangzu Zizhizhou (Sichuan Sheng, China)

Ipoh (Perak, Malaysia)

Georgetown (Pulau Pinang, Malaysia)

Urlingford (Kilkenny, Ireland)

Wiesbaden (Hesse, Germany)

16.2.2.13 Places with the Same Name

If the inclusion of the name of the larger place or jurisdiction (see **16.2.2.9–16.2.2.12**) is insufficient to distinguish between two or more places with the same name, include as part of the preferred name a word or phrase commonly used to distinguish them.

Alhama de Almería (Spain)

Short form of name: Alhama. *Fuller form of name recorded to distinguish the place from other places with the same name*

Alhama de Granada (Spain)

Short form of name: Alhama. *Fuller form of name recorded to distinguish the place from other places with the same name*

If there is no commonly used word or phrase to distinguish between places in the same larger place or jurisdiction, record the name of an intermediate place between the name of the place being identified and the larger place or jurisdiction.

Friedberg (Bavaria, Germany)

Friedberg (Hesse, Germany)

Tarbert (Argyll and Bute, Scotland)

Tarbert (Western Isles, Scotland)

Farnham (Dorset, England)

Farnham (Essex, England)

Oakdale (Stearns County, Minn.)

Oakdale (Washington County, Minn.)

Qianxi Xian (Guizhou Sheng, China)

Qianxi Xian (Hebei Sheng, China)

16.2.2.14 Places within Cities, Etc.

For the name of a place within a city, etc., record as part of the preferred name for the place:

a) the name of the city, etc.
and
b) the larger place within which the city, etc., is located (see **16.2.2.9–16.2.2.13**).

Hyde Park (Chicago, Ill.)

Chelsea (London, England)

Tamaki (Auckland, N.Z.)

Las Condes (Santiago, Chile)

Cabbagetown (Toronto, Ont.)

Quartier latin (Paris, France)

Minato-ku (Tokyo, Japan)

Art Deco Historic District (Miami Beach, Fla.)

Dongcheng Qu (Beijing, China)

16.2.3 Variant Name for the Place

16.2.3.1 Scope

A ***variant name for the place*** is a name or form of name by which a place is known that differs from the name or form of the name chosen as the preferred name.

16.2.3.2 Sources of Information

Take variant names from any source.

16.2.3.3 General Guidelines on Recording Variant Names for Places

Record a variant name for a place when it is significantly different from the name recorded as the preferred name for the place. Record as a variant name:

a name or form of name found in reference sources

or

a form of name resulting from a different transliteration of the name.

Apply the specific instructions at **16.2.3.4–16.2.3.8**, as applicable. Also apply the instruction about recording variant names at **16.2.2.5**, as applicable.

16.2.3.4 Initial Articles

If the name chosen as the preferred name of the place includes an initial article, record the name without the article as a variant name.

Dalles (Or.)
Preferred form of name recorded as: The Dalles (Or.)

If an initial article present in the name of the place has been omitted from the preferred name of the place, record the name with the initial article as a variant name.

The Dalles (Or.)
Preferred form of name recorded as: Dalles (Or.)

16.2.3.5 Expanded Name

If the preferred name for the place is an initialism or an abbreviated or shortened form of name, record the expanded form of the name as a variant name.

Saint John's (N.L.)
Abbreviated form recorded as preferred name: St. John's (N.L.)

Armenian Soviet Socialist Republic
Abbreviated form recorded as preferred name: Armenian S.S.R.

If:
the preferred name begins with an abbreviated word or contains an abbreviated word in a position that it affects access
and
abbreviations are accessed differently from words written in full
then:
record the expanded form of the name as a variant name. Expand abbreviations into words written in full using the language of the preferred name as the language for words written in full.

Sankt Veit im Pongau (Austria)
Abbreviated form recorded as preferred name: St. Veit im Pongau (Austria)

Thorpe Saint Andrew (England)
Abbreviated form recorded as preferred name: Thorpe St. Andrew (England)

16.2.3.6 Initialism / Abbreviated Form

If the preferred name for the place is a full form of the name, record an initialism or abbreviated form of the name as a variant name.

P.E.I.
Full form recorded as preferred name: Prince Edward Island

So. Daytona (Fla.)
Full form recorded as preferred name: South Daytona (Fla.)

Mt. Morgan (Qld.)
Full form recorded as preferred name: Mount Morgan (Qld.)

SOMA (San Francisco, Calif.)
Full form recorded as preferred name: South of Market (San Francisco, Calif.)

Lo Do (Denver, Colo.)
LoDo (Denver, Colo.)
Full form recorded as preferred name: Lower Downtown (Denver, Colo.)

If the preferred name consists of an initialism, record it with or without full stops according to the way it appears in the sources of information (see **16.2.2.2**). If the presence or absence of full stops affects access, record the form not chosen as the preferred name as a variant name.

RAF Kenley (England)
Preferred form recorded as initials with full stops: R.A.F. Kenley (England)

If an initialism is recorded as a variant name, and the presence or absence of full stops affects access, record the initialism both with full stops and without full stops.

US
USA
U.S.
U.S.A.
Full form recorded as preferred name: United States

16.2.3.7 Alternative Linguistic Form of Name

If the name recorded as the preferred name for a place has one or more alternative linguistic forms, record them as variant names.

Different Language Form

Danmark
English language form recorded as preferred name: Denmark

Grussia
Sak'art'velo
Xeorxia
English language form recorded as preferred name: Georgia

Albaanje
Albanie
Albanija
Albánsko
Arbinishia
Arnavutluk
Arubania
Elbanya
Shkiperiya
Shqipëria
English language form recorded as preferred name: Albania

Aix-la-Chapelle (Germany)
Aken (Germany)
Akwizgran (Germany)
Aquisgrão (Germany)
Cáchy (Germany)
Oche (Germany)
German language form recorded as preferred name: Aachen (Germany)

Latin Quarter (Paris, France)
French language form recorded as preferred name: Quartier latin (Paris, France)

Different Script

Србија
English language form recorded as preferred name: Serbia

日本
English language form recorded as preferred name: Japan

საქართველო
English language form recorded as preferred name: Georgia

ᓄᓇᕗᑦ
English language form recorded as preferred name: Nunavut

Москва (Russia)
Μόσχα (Russia)
English language form recorded as preferred name: Moscow (Russia)

تطوان (Morocco)
French transliterated form recorded as preferred name: Tétouan (Morocco)

אשדוד (Israel)
Hebrew transliterated form recorded as preferred name: Ashdod (Israel)

Αλβανία
Албанија
Албания
Албанія
אלבניה
ألبانيا
آلبانی
阿尔巴尼亚
アルバニア
알바니아
अल्बानिया
আলবেনিয়া
அல்பேனியா
แอลเบเนีย
English language form recorded as preferred name: Albania

Different Spelling

Rumania
Different spelling recorded as preferred name: Romania

Allapatah (Miami, Fla.)
Different spelling recorded as preferred name: Allapattah (Miami, Fla.)

Different Transliteration

Aqaba
Akaba
Different transliteration recorded as preferred name: ʻAqabah

Tiṭwān (Morocco)
Different transliteration recorded as preferred name: Tétouan (Morocco)

Halandri (Athens, Greece)
Khalandri (Athens, Greece)
Different transliteration recorded as preferred name: Chalandri (Athens, Greece)

Other Alternative Linguistic Form

Melinheli (Wales)
Preferred form of name recorded as: Y Felinheli (Wales)

If:

the name recorded as the preferred name begins with a number expressed as a numeral or contains a number expressed as a numeral

and

numbers expressed as words are accessed differently from numbers expressed as numerals

then:

record the form with the number expressed as a word as a variant name.

Zweiter Bezirk (Vienna, Austria)

Preferred name begins with an ordinal number expressed as a numeral: 2. Bezirk (Vienna, Austria)

Tredicesima Circoscrizione (Perugia, Italy)

Preferred name begins with a number expressed as a roman numeral: XIII Circoscrizione (Perugia, Italy)

Quận tám (Ho Chi Minh City, Vietnam)

Preferred name contains a number expressed as a numeral: Quận 8 (Ho Chi Minh City, Vietnam)

East Seventh Avenue Historic District (Denver, Colo.)

Preferred name contains a number expressed as an ordinal numeral: East 7th Avenue Historic District (Denver, Colo.)

Pio Doze (Brazil)

Preferred name contains a number expressed as a roman numeral: Pio XII (Brazil)

If:

the name recorded as the preferred name begins with a number expressed as a word or contains a number expressed as a word

and

numbers expressed as words are accessed differently from numbers expressed as numerals

then:

record the form with the number expressed as an arabic numeral as a variant name.

9th Ward (New Orleans, La.)

Preferred name begins with an ordinal number expressed as a word: Ninth Ward (New Orleans, La.)

District 6 (Cape Town, South Africa)

Preferred name contains a number expressed as a word: District Six (Cape Town, South Africa)

16.2.3.8 Other Variant Name

Record other variant names and variant forms of the name not covered by **16.2.3.4–16.2.3.7**, if considered important for identification or access.

Different Name

People's Republic of Albania
People's Socialist Republic of Albania
Republic of Albania
República d'Albània
Republika e Shqipërisë
Republika Popullore e Shqipërisë
Republika Popullore Socialiste e Shqipërisë

Name recorded as preferred name: Albania

Pio 12 (Brazil)

Name recorded as preferred name: Pio XII (Brazil)

13. Circoscrizione (Perugia, Italy)

Name recorded as preferred name: XIII Circoscrizione (Perugia, Italy)

Region 7 (Guyana)
Region Seven (Guyana)
Name recorded as preferred name: Cuyuni-Mazaruni Region (Guyana)

Little Dominican Republic (Miami, Fla.)
Name recorded as preferred name: Allapattah (Miami, Fla.)

Camden Town (London, England)
London Borough of Camden (England)
Name recorded as preferred name: Camden (London, England)

Name of Place within a City, etc., as Subdivision of Authorized Access Point for the City, Etc.

Toronto (Ont.). Cabbagetown
Name recorded as preferred name: Cabbagetown (Toronto, Ont.)

Paris (France). Quartier latin
Paris (France). Latin Quarter
Name recorded as preferred name: Quartier latin (Paris, France)

OTHER IDENTIFYING ATTRIBUTES

16.3 Identifier for the Place

[To be added in a later release]

ACCESS POINTS REPRESENTING PLACES

16.4 Constructing Access Points to Represent Places

For the construction of access points using place names as conventional names for governments, see **11.13.1.1**.

16.4.1 Authorized Access Point for the Place

[To be added in a later release]

16.4.2 Variant Access Point for the Place

[To be added in a later release]

17

GENERAL GUIDELINES ON RECORDING PRIMARY RELATIONSHIPS

17.0 Purpose and Scope

Primary relationships are the relationships between a work, expression, manifestation, and item that are inherent in the FRBR definitions of those entities:

a) the relationship between a work and an expression through which that work is realized and the reciprocal relationship from the expression to the work

b) the relationship between an expression of a work and a manifestation that embodies that expression and the reciprocal relationship from the manifestation to the expression

c) the relationship between a manifestation and an item that exemplifies that manifestation and the reciprocal relationship from the item to the manifestation.

For practical purposes, it is possible to declare a relationship and its reciprocal between a work and a manifestation with an implied expression. In such cases, the expression is understood to exist, but is not identified explicitly.

This chapter provides both the general guidelines and specific instructions on recording primary relationships. It includes:

a) an explanation of key terms (see **17.1**)

b) the functional objectives and principles underlying the guidelines and instructions on recording the primary relationships (see **17.2**)

c) the core elements required to meet the functional objectives (see **17.3**)

d) instructions on recording the primary relationships by using identifiers, authorized access points, and composite descriptions (see **17.4–17.12**).[1]

---

1. Some encoding standards may not have a design that is suitable for recording the primary relationships. In these cases, primary relationships are not explicitly recorded though they may be inferred from other data elements in composite descriptions.

17.1 Terminology

17.1.1 Explanation of Key Terms

There are a number of terms used in this chapter that have meanings specific to their use in RDA. Some of these terms are explained at **17.1.2–17.1.3**.

Terms used as data element names in this chapter are defined at the beginning of the instructions for the specific element. In addition, all terms used in this chapter with a specific technical meaning are defined in the glossary.

17.1.2 Work, Expression, Manifestation, and Item

The terms *work, expression, manifestation,* and *item* are used as follows:

The term ***work*** refers to a distinct intellectual or artistic creation (i.e., the intellectual or artistic content).

The term ***expression*** refers to the intellectual or artistic realization of a work in the form of alpha-numeric, musical or choreographic notation, sound, image, object, movement, etc., or any combination of such forms.

The term ***manifestation*** refers to the physical embodiment of an expression of a work.

The term ***item*** refers to a single exemplar or instance of a manifestation.

Each of these terms, depending on what is being described, can refer to individual entities, aggregates, or components of these entities (e.g., the term *work* can refer to an individual work, an aggregate work, or a component of a work).

17.1.3 Access Point

The terms *access point* and *authorized access point* are used as follows:

The term ***access point*** refers to a name, term, code, etc., representing a specific work or expression.

The term ***authorized access point*** refers to the standardized access point representing an entity.

The authorized access point representing a work or expression is constructed by combining (in this order):

a) the authorized access point representing a person, family, or corporate body responsible for the work, if appropriate

b) the preferred title for the work

c) other elements as instructed at **6.27–6.31**.

17.2 Functional Objectives and Principles

The data recorded to reflect primary relationships should enable the user to:

a) *find* all resources that embody a particular work or a particular expression

b) *find* all items that exemplify a particular manifestation.

To ensure that the data created using RDA meet those functional objectives, the data should reflect the primary relationships.

17.3 Core Elements

When recording primary relationships between a work, expression, manifestation, and item, include as a minimum the work manifested. If there is more than one expression of the work, record the expression manifested.

If more than one work is embodied in the manifestation, only the predominant or first-named work manifested is required.

If more than one expression is embodied in the manifestation, only the predominant or first-named expression manifested is required.

17.4 Recording Primary Relationships

17.4.1 Scope

Primary relationships are the relationships between a work, expression, manifestation, and item that are inherent in the FRBR definitions of those entities:

a) the relationship between a work and an expression through which that work is realized

b) the relationship between an expression of a work and a manifestation that embodies that expression

c) the relationship between a manifestation and an item that exemplifies that manifestation.

The relationship between a work and a manifestation that embodies that work may also be recorded without explicitly identifying the expression through which the work is realized:

manifestation of work (see **17.7**)

work manifested (see **17.8**).

17.4.2 Techniques Used to Record Primary Relationships

Record primary relationships by using one or more of these techniques, as applicable:

a) identifier for the work, expression, manifestation, or item (see **17.4.2.1**)

b) authorized access point representing the work or expression (see **17.4.2.2**)

c) composite description (see **17.4.2.3**).

17.4.2.1 Identifier for the Work, Expression, Manifestation, or Item

Provide an identifier for the work, expression, manifestation, or item, by applying the following instructions, as applicable:

a) identifiers for works (see **6.8**)

b) identifiers for expressions (see **6.13**)

c) identifiers for manifestations (see **2.15**)

d) identifiers for items (see **2.19**).

ISWC: T-072.106.546-8
International Standard Musical Work Code for Cole Porter's I love Paris

VA 1-403-863 U.S. Copyright Office
Copyright registration number for State highway map of Minnesota

http://larvatusprodeo.net
URI for the blog Larvatus prodeo

ISBN 978-1-59688-083-2
ISBN for a large print manifestation of Joseph Conrad's The secret agent

17.4.2.2 Authorized Access Point Representing the Work or Expression

Provide an authorized access point representing the work or expression by applying the following instructions, as applicable:

a) an authorized access point representing a work (see **6.27.1–6.27.2**)

United States. Constitution of the United States

b) an authorized access point representing an expression (see **6.27.3**).

United States. Constitution of the United States. Lao

17.4.2.3 Composite Description

Provide a composite description that combines one or more elements identifying the work and/or expression embodied in a manifestation with the description of that manifestation.

Beethoven, Ludwig van, 1770–1827. Sonatas, violin, piano, no. 2, op. 12, no. 2, A major. Allegro piacèvole; arranged
Divertimento, op. 12, no. 2 / L. van Beethoven ; transcribed for woodwind by George J. Trinkaus. — New York : M. Witmark & Sons, ©1933. — Arranged for flute, oboe, clarinet, horn, and bassoon

Medium of performance of musical content—an attribute of the expression—combined with the description of the manifestation

17.5 Expression of Work

17.5.1 Basic Instructions on Recording an Expression of a Work

17.5.1.1 Scope

An ***expression of work*** is a realization of a work in the form of alpha-numeric, musical or choreographic notation, sound, image, object, movement, etc., or any combination of such forms.

17.5.1.2 Sources of Information

Take information on the relationship between a work and an expression of that work from any source.

17.5.1.3 Recording an Expression of a Work

Record an expression of a work by applying the general guidelines on recording primary relationships at 17.4.

Identifier for the Expression

Library and Archives Canada control number: 1011A7775E

Identifier for Slovak translations of Margaret Atwood's The handmaid's tale

Library of Congress control number: n 80008554

Identifier for English translations of Edmond de Goncourt's Les frères Zemganno

Library of Congress control number: no2008127532

Identifier for the Final cut *version of the motion picture* Blade runner

Authorized Access Point Representing the Expression

Qur'an. Spoken word

Authorized access point representing the expression, constructed by adding the content type of the expression to the authorized access point representing the work

United States. Constitution of the United States. Lao

Authorized access point representing the expression, constructed by adding the language of the expression to the authorized access point representing the work

Composite Description

Mercadante, Saverio, 1795–1870. Concertos, clarinet, orchestra, op. 101, B♭ major; arranged
Concerto in si bemolle minore per clarinetto e orchestra da camera / Saverio Mercadente ; revisione di Giovanni Carli Ballola. — Milano : Editioni Suvini Zerboni, ©1975. — Originally for clarinet and chamber orchestra; this version a reduction for clarinet and piano

Medium of performance of musical content of expression combined with the description of the manifestation

17.6 Work Expressed

17.6.1 Basic Instructions on Recording the Work Expressed

17.6.1.1 Scope

The ***work expressed*** is the work realized through an expression.

17.6.1.2 Sources of Information

Take information on the relationship between an expression and the work realized through that expression from any source.

17.6.1.3 Recording the Work Expressed

Record the work expressed by applying the general guidelines on recording primary relationships at **17.4**.

> **Identifier for the Work**
>
> ISWC: T-010.190.038-2
>
> *International Standard Musical Work Code for Mozart's* Eine kleine Nachtmusik
>
> Library of Congress control number: n 80008555
>
> *Identifier for Edmond de Goncourt's* Les frères Zemganno

> **Authorized Access Point Representing the Work**
>
> Qur'an
>
> United States. Constitution of the United States
>
> Mozart, Wolfgang Amadeus, 1756–1791. Kleine Nachtmusik
>
> Straits times (Kuala Lumpur, Malaysia)

> **Composite Description**
>
> The three evangelists / Fred Vargas ; translated from the French by Siân Reynolds. — London : Vintage Books, 2006. — Translation of: Debout les morts
>
> *Original title of the work combined with the description of the manifestation*

17.7 Manifestation of Work

17.7.1 Basic Instructions on Recording a Manifestation of a Work

17.7.1.1 Scope

A ***manifestation of work*** is a physical embodiment of an expression of a work.

17.7.1.2 Sources of Information

Take information on the relationship between a work and a manifestation of that work from any source.

17.7.1.3 Recording a Manifestation of a Work

Record a manifestation of a work by applying the general guidelines on recording primary relationships at 17.4.

> **Identifier for the Manifestation**
>
> ISSN 1440-0960
>
> *ISSN for the online manifestation of* Australasian journal of dermatology

ISBN 978-1-59688-083-2
ISBN for a large print edition of Joseph Conrad's The secret agent

Roadshow Entertainment: 1034539
Publisher number for a DVD manifestation of the 2001 motion picture Ocean's eleven

http://larvatusprodeo.net
URI for the blog Larvatus prodeo

Composite Description

Babylon and golden city : representations of London in Black and Asian British novels since the 1990s / Susanne Cuevas. — Heidelberg : Universitätsverlag Winter, [2008], ©2008. — Thesis (doctoral)—Technische Universität Dresden, 2007
Dissertation information about the work combined with the description of the manifestation

Mongol Khans and their legacy / produced by the Cartographic Division, National Geographic Society ; John F. Shupe, chief cartographer. — Scale 1:18,500,000 ; orthographic projection (E 0°—E 180°/N 90°—N 0°). — Washington, D.C. : National Geographic Society, [1996], ©1996. — Shows all of Asia: west to Mediterranean Sea, east to Japan, north to Arctic Ocean, and south to Java
Scale, projection, coordinates, and coverage of the content combined with the description of the manifestation

17.8 Work Manifested

CORE ELEMENT

If more than one work is embodied in the manifestation, only the predominant or first-named work manifested is required.

17.8.1 Basic Instructions on Recording a Work Manifested

17.8.1.1 Scope

A ***work manifested*** is a work embodied in a manifestation.

17.8.1.2 Sources of Information

Take information on the relationship between a manifestation and a work embodied in that manifestation from any source.

17.8.1.3 Recording a Work Manifested

Record a work manifested by applying the general guidelines on recording primary relationships at **17.4**.

Identifier for the Work

Library of Congress control number: n 80025571
Identifier for Joseph Conrad's The secret agent

Authorized Access Point Representing the Work

Larvatus prodeo

Écho (Louiseville, Québec)

Ocean's eleven (Motion picture : 2001)

Conrad, Joseph, 1857–1924. Secret agent

Schumann, Clara, 1819–1896. Scherzos, piano, no. 1, op. 10, D minor

Composite Description

Gabriella's Book of fire / Venero Armanno. — New York : Hyperion, 2000. — Original title: Firehead

Original title of the work combined with the description of the manifestation

17.9 Manifestation of Expression

17.9.1 Basic Instructions on Recording a Manifestation of an Expression

17.9.1.1 Scope

A ***manifestation of expression*** is a physical embodiment of an expression.

17.9.1.2 Sources of Information

Take information on the relationship between an expression and a manifestation of that expression from any source.

17.9.1.3 Recording a Manifestation of an Expression

Record a manifestation of an expression by applying the general guidelines on recording primary relationships at **17.4**.

Identifier for the Manifestation

ISBN 99918-42-25-X

ISBN for a manifestation of a Faroese translation of Shakespeare's Julius Caesar

ISMN M-006-52070-1

ISMN for a printed manifestation of an expression of Mozart's Eine kleine Nachtmusik *for string quartet*

ISBN 1-85549-961-4

ISBN for a manifestation of a spoken word recording of Dickens's Bleak House

VCI Entertainment: 8202

Publisher number for a DVD manifestation of the motion picture Uccello dalle piume di cristallo, *dubbed into English from the original Italian*

Library and Archives Canada control number: 910025029

Identifier for the 1989 manifestation of the German translation of Alice Munro's Who do you think you are?

Composite Description

My cousin, my husband : clans and kinship in Mediterranean societies / Germaine Tillion ; translated from the French by Quintin Hoare. — London : Saqi Books, 2007. — Translation of: Le harem et les cousins. Paris : Éditions du Seuil, 1966. This translation first published as The republic of cousins

Variant title associated with the expression combined with the description of the manifestation

17.10 Expression Manifested

CORE ELEMENT

Expression manifested is a core element if there is more than one expression of the work manifested. If more than one expression is embodied in the manifestation, only the predominant or first-named expression manifested is required.

17.10.1 Basic Instructions on Recording an Expression Manifested

17.10.1.1 Scope

An ***expression manifested*** is an expression embodied in a manifestation.

17.10.1.2 Sources of Information

Take information on the relationship between a manifestation and an expression embodied in that manifestation from any source.

17.10.1.3 Recording an Expression Manifested

Record an expression manifested by applying the general guidelines on recording primary relationships at 17.4.

Identifier for the Expression

Library of Congress control number: n 2001092139

Identifier for Faroese translations of Shakespeare's Julius Caesar

Library of Congress control number: no2008110036

Identifier for the B-text *version of William Langland's* Piers Plowman

Authorized Access Point Representing the Expression

Dickens, Charles, 1812–1870. Bleak house. Spoken word

Authorized access point representing the expression, constructed by adding the content type of the expression to the authorized access point representing the work

Blade runner (Motion picture : Final cut)

Authorized access point representing the expression, constructed by adding another distinguishing characteristic of the expression to the authorized access point representing the work

Bacewicz, Grażyna. Sonatas, violin, no. 2; arranged

Authorized access point representing the musical expression, constructed by adding the term arranged *to the authorized access point representing the original work*

Composite Description

Keep swingin' / Julian Priester. — Berkeley, CA : Riverside, [1995]. — Place of capture: Reeves Sound Studios, New York City. — Date of capture: January 11, 1960. — Riverside: OJCCD-1863-2

Place and date of capture of the expression combined with the description of the manifestation

Het officie van Antonius Eremita : critische uitgave volgens Ms. Leeuwarden 6168hs / door een team van candidaten in de muziekwetenschap ; ingeleid door H. Wagenaar-Nolthenius en J. Smits van Waesberge. — Plainsong notation. — Utrecht : Instituut voor Muziekwetenschap der Rijksuniversiteit, 1975. — (Scripta musicologica Ultrajectina ; 5). — Text in Latin; commentary in Dutch; summary in English

Language of the content and form of notation of the expression combined with the description of the manifestation

17.11 Exemplar of Manifestation

17.11.1 Basic Instructions on Recording an Exemplar of the Manifestation

17.11.1.1 Scope

An ***exemplar of manifestation*** is a single exemplar or instance of a manifestation.

17.11.1.2 Sources of Information

Take information on the relationship between a manifestation and an exemplar of that manifestation from any source.

17.11.1.3 Recording an Exemplar of a Manifestation

Record an exemplar of a manifestation by applying the general guidelines on recording primary relationships at 17.4.

Identifier for the Item

YK.2001.a.5815

British Library shelf mark for its copy of Michael Clarke's The concise Oxford dictionary of art terms

E887.C55 A3 2003 c.2

Washington State University Libraries call number for its second copy of the 2003 Simon & Schuster printed manifestation of Hillary Clinton's Living history

Score M452.M69 K.525 1964

Griffith University Library call number for its copy of the 1964 manifestation of an expression of Mozart's Eine kleine Nachtmusik *for string quartet*

P780 QS M939 KLE

Monash University Library call number for its copy of the 2002 manifestation of the same expression of Mozart's Eine kleine Nachtmusik *for string quartet*

I86831380

University of Washington Libraries integrated library system item record number for a copy of a DVD manifestation of the final cut expression of the motion picture Blade runner

39352069538890

University of Washington Libraries barcode number for the same copy of a DVD manifestation of the final cut expression of the motion picture Blade runner

Composite Description

Noah and the waters / C. Day Lewis. — London : Published by Leonard & Virginia Woolf at the Hogarth Press, 1936. — Limited edition of 100 numbered copies, signed by the author. Library's copy is no. 80

Marks/inscriptions on the item combined with the description of the manifestation

17.12 Manifestation Exemplified

17.12.1 Basic Instructions on Recording the Manifestation Exemplified

17.12.1.1 Scope

The ***manifestation exemplified*** is the manifestation exemplified by an item.

17.12.1.2 Sources of Information

Take information on the relationship between an item and the manifestation exemplified by that item from any source.

17.12.1.3 Recording the Manifestation Exemplified

Record the manifestation exemplified by applying the general guidelines on recording primary relationships at **17.4**.

Identifier for the Manifestation

British national bibliography number: GBA1-Z5901

Identifier for the 2001 print manifestation of Michael Clarke's The concise Oxford dictionary of art terms

Libraries Australia system control number: 000013619137

Identifier for the 1997 braille manifestation of an expression of the score of Robert Schumann's Carnaval

ISBN 978-0-8416-5457-0

ISBN for the large print manifestation of Chicagoland seven county 2007 street atlas

Composite Description

History of the Indian tribes of North America : with biographical sketches and anecdotes of the principal chiefs / embellished with one hundred and twenty portraits, from the Indian Gallery in the Department of War, at Washington ; by Thomas L. M'Kenney and James Hall. — Philadelphia : Edward C. Biddle, 1836–1844. — Library's copy once belonged to Charles Dickens and has his personal bookplate and a label that reads: “From the Library of Charles Dickens, Gadshill Place, June 1870.”

Description of the manifestation combined with custodial history

18

GENERAL GUIDELINES ON RECORDING RELATIONSHIPS TO PERSONS, FAMILIES, AND CORPORATE BODIES ASSOCIATED WITH A RESOURCE

18.0 Scope

This chapter provides background information to support the application of guidelines and instructions in chapters **19–22** on recording relationships to persons, families, and corporate bodies associated with a resource. It includes:

a) an explanation of key terms (see **18.1**)

b) the functional objectives and principles underlying the guidelines and instructions in chapters **19–22** (see **18.2**)

c) the core elements for recording relationships to persons, families, and corporate bodies (see **18.3**)

d) the use of identifiers and authorized access points to record those relationships (see **18.4**)

e) the use of relationship designators to indicate the specific function performed by the person, family, or corporate body in relation to the resource (see **18.5**)

f) the use of notes to provide additional information about relationships (see **18.6**).

18.1 Terminology

18.1.1 Explanation of Key Terms

There are a number of terms used in this chapter and in chapters **19–22** that have meanings specific to their use in RDA. Some of these terms are explained at **18.1.2–18.1.6**.

Terms used as data element names in chapters **19–22** are defined at the beginning of the instructions for the specific element. In addition, all terms used in those chapters with a specific technical meaning are defined in the glossary.

18.1.2 Person, Family, and Corporate Body

The terms *person, family,* and *corporate body* are used as follows:

The term ***person*** refers to an individual or an identity established by an individual (either alone or in collaboration with one or more other individuals).

The term ***family*** refers to two or more persons related by birth, marriage, adoption, civil union, or similar legal status, or who otherwise present themselves as a family.

The term ***corporate body*** refers to an organization or group of persons and/or organizations that is identified by a particular name and that acts, or may act, as a unit.

18.1.3 Resource

The term ***resource*** is used in chapters **19–22** to refer to a work, expression, manifestation, or item (see **18.1.4**).

The term *resource*, depending on what is being described, can refer to:

a) an individual entity (e.g., a single videodisc)
or
b) an aggregate of entities (e.g., three sheet maps)
or
c) a component of an entity (e.g., a single slide issued as part of a set of twenty, an article in an issue of a scholarly journal).

The term *resource* can refer either to a tangible entity (e.g., an audiocassette) or to an intangible entity (e.g., a website).

18.1.4 Work, Expression, Manifestation, and Item

The terms *work, expression, manifestation,* and *item* are used as follows:

The term ***work*** refers to a distinct intellectual or artistic creation (i.e., the intellectual or artistic content).

The term ***expression*** refers to the intellectual or artistic realization of a work in the form of alpha-numeric, musical or choreographic notation, sound, image, object, movement, etc., or any combination of such forms.

The term ***manifestation*** refers to the physical embodiment of an expression of a work.

The term ***item*** refers to a single exemplar or instance of a manifestation.

Each of these terms, depending on what is being described, can refer to individual entities, aggregates, or components of these entities (e.g., the term *work* can refer to an individual work, an aggregate work, or a component of a work).

18.1.5 Access Point

The terms *access point* and *authorized access point* are used as follows:

The term ***access point*** refers to a name, term, code, etc., representing a specific person, family, or corporate body.

The term ***authorized access point*** refers to the standardized access point representing an entity. The authorized access point representing a person, family, or corporate body is constructed by using the preferred name for the person, family, or corporate body.

18.1.6 Relationship Designator

The term ***relationship designator*** refers to a designator that indicates the nature of the relationship between a resource and a person, family, or corporate body associated with that resource.

A relationship designator is recorded with the authorized access point and/or identifier representing the associated person, family, or corporate body.

18.2 Functional Objectives and Principles

The data recorded to reflect relationships to persons, families, and corporate bodies associated with a resource should enable the user to *find* all resources associated with a particular person, family, or corporate body.

To ensure that the data created using RDA meet that functional objective, the data should reflect all significant relationships between a resource and persons, families, and corporate bodies associated with that resource.

18.3 Core Elements

When recording relationships between a resource and persons, families, and corporate bodies associated with that resource, include as a minimum the following elements that are applicable and readily ascertainable.

Creator (if more than one, only the creator having principal responsibility named first in resources embodying the work or in reference sources is required; if principal responsibility is not indicated, only the first-named creator is required)

Other person, family, or corporate body associated with a work (if the access point representing that person, family, or corporate body is used to construct the authorized access point representing the work)

18.4 Recording Relationships to Persons, Families, and Corporate Bodies Associated with a Resource

18.4.1 Recording Relationships to Persons, Families, and Corporate Bodies Associated with the Resource

Record the relationship between the resource and a person, family, or corporate body associated with that resource by using one or both of these techniques:

a) identifier (see **18.4.1.1**)
and/or
b) authorized access point (see **18.4.1.2**).

Record a relationship designator to indicate the specific function performed by a person, family, or corporate body in relation to the resource (see **18.5**).

Record the appropriate relationship designator with the identifier and/or the authorized access point representing that person, family, or corporate body.

18.4.1.1 Identifier for the Person, Family, or Corporate Body

Provide an identifier for the person, family, or corporate body by applying the appropriate instructions:

identifier for the person (see **9.18**)
identifier for the family (see **10.10**)
identifier for the corporate body (see **11.12**).

> Library and Archives Canada control number: 0062A7592E
> *Identifier for Canadian Lesbian and Gay History Network, the issuing body of* Canadian Lesbian and Gay History Network newsletter

18.4.1.2 Authorized Access Point Representing the Person, Family, or Corporate Body

Provide an authorized access point representing the person, family, or corporate body, by applying the appropriate instructions:

authorized access point representing a person (see **9.19.1**)
authorized access point representing a family (see **10.11.1**)
authorized access point representing a corporate body (see **11.13.1**).

> Canadian Lesbian and Gay History Network
> *Authorized access point representing the issuing body of* Canadian Lesbian and Gay History Network newsletter

18.4.2 Change in Responsibility

When changes in responsibility occur between parts of a multipart monograph, between issues or parts of a serial, or between iterations of an integrating resource, provide additional access points as appropriate to the mode of issuance of the resource:

multipart monographs (see **18.4.2.1**)
serials (see **18.4.2.2**)
integrating resources (see **18.4.2.3**).

When a change in responsibility affects the identification of the work and requires the construction of an authorized access point representing a new work, see **6.1.3**.

18.4.2.1 Multipart Monographs

Provide additional access points for any persons, families, or corporate bodies associated with a subsequent part of a multipart monograph (see **19.1**, **20.1**, and **21.1**) if:

there is a change in responsibility between the parts of a multipart monograph

and

the change is considered important for access.

18.4.2.2 Serials

Provide additional access points for any persons, families, or corporate bodies associated with a subsequent issue or part of a serial (see **19.1**, **20.1**, and **21.1**) if:

there is a change in responsibility between the issues or parts of a serial that does not require a new description (see **1.6.2**)

and

the change is considered important for access.

18.4.2.3 Integrating Resources

Provide access points for any persons, families, or corporate bodies associated with the current iteration of an integrating resource (see **19.1**, **20.1**, and **21.1**) if:

there is a change in responsibility between iterations of an integrating resource

and

the change is considered important for access.

Retain access points for any persons, families, or bodies previously responsible if considered important for access.

18.5 Relationship Designator

18.5.1 Basic Instructions on Recording Relationship Designators

18.5.1.1 Scope

A ***relationship designator*** is a designator that indicates the nature of the relationship between a resource and a person, family, or corporate body associated with that resource. A relationship designator is recorded with the authorized access point and/or identifier representing the associated person, family, or corporate body.

The defined scope of a relationship element provides a general indication of the relationship between a resource and a person, family, or corporate body associated with the resource (e.g., creator, owner). Relationship designators provide more specific information about the nature of the relationship (e.g., author, donor).

18.5.1.2 Sources of Information

Take information on the nature of the relationship between a resource and a person, family, or corporate body associated with that resource from any source.

18.5.1.3 Recording Relationship Designators

Record one or more appropriate terms from the list in appendix I to indicate the specific function performed by the person, family, or corporate body in relation to the resource. Record the designator with an identifier and/or authorized access point representing that person, family, or corporate body.

author

Relationship designator recorded in conjunction with the authorized access point representing Alice Munro as the author of Lives of girls and women

film producer
film director
actor
composer (expression)

Relationship designators recorded in conjunction with the authorized access point representing Clint Eastwood as producer, director, actor, and composer for Million dollar baby

enacting jurisdiction

Relationship designator recorded in conjunction with the authorized access point representing Hong Kong, China as the jurisdiction enacting and governed by its Disability Discrimination Ordinance

cartographer

Relationship designator recorded in conjunction with an identifier representing Multi Mapping Ltd. as the cartographer of International travel map of Syria, scale 1:850,000

printer

Relationship designator recorded in conjunction with an identifier representing William Caxton as the manufacturer of Here begynneth the table of the rubryshys of the boke of the fayt of armes and of chyualrye, *a manifestation of an English expression of Christine de Pisan's* Livre des faits d'armes et de chevalerie

issuing body

Relationship designator recorded in conjunction with an identifier representing the Canadian Lesbian and Gay History Network as the issuing body of Canadian Lesbian and Gay History Network newsletter

composer
conductor

Relationship designators recorded in conjunction with an identifier and the authorized access point representing Victoria Bond as the composer and conductor of an audio recording of a performance of The frog prince

If none of the terms listed in appendix I is appropriate or sufficiently specific, use another concise term to indicate the nature of the relationship.

18.6 Note on Persons, Families, and Corporate Bodies Associated with a Resource

If the relationship to a person, family, or corporate body associated with a resource requires explanation (e.g., in a case where an attribution of authorship is dubious), make one or more of the following types of notes, as applicable:

a) note on statement of responsibility (see **2.17.3**)

b) note on edition statement (see **2.17.4**)

c) note on production statement (see **2.17.6**)

d) note on publication statement (see **2.17.7**)

e) note on distribution statement (see **2.17.8**)

f) note on manufacture statement (see **2.17.9**)

g) cataloguer's note (see **5.9**).

19

PERSONS, FAMILIES, AND CORPORATE BODIES ASSOCIATED WITH A WORK

19.0 Purpose and Scope

This chapter provides general guidelines and instructions on recording relationships to persons, families, and corporate bodies associated with a work (i.e., creators and others).

19.1 General Guidelines on Recording Persons, Families, and Corporate Bodies Associated with a Work

19.1.1 Sources of Information

Take information on persons, families, and corporate bodies associated with a work from statements appearing on the preferred sources of information (see **2.2.2**) in resources embodying the work.

If those statements are ambiguous or insufficient, use the following sources of information, in order of preference:

a) other statements appearing prominently in the resources

b) information appearing only in the content of the resources (e.g., the text of a book, the sound content of an audio recording)

c) other sources.

For instructions on recording changes in responsibility for multipart monographs, serials, and integrating resources, see **18.4.2**.

19.1.2 Recording Persons, Families, and Corporate Bodies Associated with a Work

Record the persons, families, and corporate bodies associated with the work by applying the following instructions, as applicable:

creator (see **19.2**)

other person, family, or corporate body associated with a work (see **19.3**).

If:

the resource being described is an aggregate resource containing two or more works

and

each of the works is associated with different persons, families, or corporate bodies

then:

record the persons, families, and corporate bodies associated with each of the works (see **19.2–19.3**).

19.2 Creator

CORE ELEMENT

If there is more than one creator responsible for the work, only the creator having principal responsibility named first in resources embodying the work or in reference sources is required.

If principal responsibility is not indicated, only the first-named creator is required.

19.2.1 Basic Instructions on Recording Creators

19.2.1.1 Scope

A *creator* is a person, family, or corporate body responsible for the creation of a work.

Creators include persons, families, or corporate bodies jointly responsible for the creation of a work. There are two types of joint responsibility:

a) creators who perform the same role (e.g., as in a collaboration between two writers)

b) creators who perform different roles (e.g., as in a collaboration between a composer and a lyricist).

In some cases, the selection, arrangement, editing, etc., of content for a compilation effectively results in the creation of a new work. When this occurs, the person, family, or corporate body responsible for compiling the aggregate work may be considered to be the creator of the compilation.

In some cases, the modification of a previously existing work substantially changes the nature or content of the original and results in a new work. When this occurs, the person, family, or corporate body responsible for modifying the previously existing work is considered to be the creator of the new work.

For instructions on recording relationships to persons, families, or corporate bodies contributing to a particular expression of a work (e.g., editors, translators), see **20.2.1**.

For corporate bodies functioning solely as producers, publishers, or, manufacturers, see **21.2–21.5**.

19.2.1.1.1 Corporate Bodies Considered to Be Creators

Corporate bodies are considered to be creators when they are responsible for originating, issuing, or causing to be issued, works that fall into one or more of the following categories:

a) works of an administrative nature dealing with any of the following aspects of the body itself:

  i. its internal policies, procedures, finances, and/or operations
  or
  ii. its officers, staff, and/or membership (e.g., directories)
  or
  iii. its resources (e.g., catalogues, inventories)

b) works that record the collective thought of the body (e.g., reports of commissions, committees; official statements of position on external policies, standards)

c) works that record hearings conducted by legislative, judicial, governmental, and other corporate bodies

d) works that report the collective activity of

  i. a conference (e.g., proceedings, collected papers)
  or
  ii. an expedition (e.g., results of exploration, investigation)
  or
  iii. an event (e.g., an exhibition, fair, festival) falling within the definition of a corporate body (see **18.1.2**)

  provided that the conference, expedition, or event is named in the resource being described

e) works that result from the collective activity of a performing group as a whole where the responsibility of the group goes beyond that of mere performance, execution, etc.

f) cartographic works originating with a corporate body other than a body that is merely responsible for their publication or distribution

g) legal works of the following types:

   i. laws of a political jurisdiction

   ii. decrees of a head of state, chief executive, or ruling executive body

   iii. bills and drafts of legislation

   iv. administrative regulations, etc.

   v. constitutions, charters, etc.

   vi. court rules

   vii. charges to juries, indictments, court proceedings, and court decisions

h) named individual works of art by two or more artists acting as a corporate body.

19.2.1.1.2 Government and Religious Officials Considered to Be Creators

Government and religious officials are considered to be creators when they are responsible for the following types of official communications:

a) official communications by heads of state, heads of government, heads of dependent or occupied territories, or heads of international bodies (e.g., messages to legislatures, proclamations, executive orders)

b) official communications from popes, patriarchs, bishops, etc. (e.g., orders, decrees, pastoral letters, bulls, encyclicals; official messages to councils, synods).

19.2.1.1.3 Persons or Families Considered to be Creators of Serials

A person or family is considered to be the creator of a serial if it is responsible for the serial as a whole, not an individual issue or a few issues.

Indications that a person or family may be considered responsible for the serial as a whole include the following:

a) the name or part of the name of the person is in the title proper

b) the person or family is the publisher of the serial

c) content consists of personal opinions, etc.

d) lack of another person, another family, or a corporate body involved with the serial.

Stone, I. F. (Isidor Feinstein), 1907-1989
Authorized access point representing the creator for: I.F. Stone's weekly. *Stone was also the publisher*

Bolles, Richard Nelson
Authorized access point representing the creator for: What color is your parachute? *An annual publication of Bolles' career advice*

Lehrer, Jonah
Authorized access point representing the creator for: Frontal cortex. *A blog*

If different issues of the serial are likely to be created by different persons or families, do not consider a person or family to be the creator.

If it is likely that the serial would continue without that person's or family's responsibility for the serial, do not consider the person or family to be the creator. In case of doubt, do not consider the person or family to be the creator.

19.2.1.2 Sources of Information

Take information on creators from the sources specified at **19.1.1**.

19.2.1.3 Recording Creators

Record a creator by applying the general guidelines on recording relationships to persons, families, and corporate bodies associated with a resource (see **18.4**).

One Person Responsible for the Creation of the Work

Hemingway, Ernest, 1899–1961

Authorized access point representing the creator for: The sun also rises / by Ernest Hemingway

Riverbend

Authorized access point representing the creator for: Baghdad burning : girl blog from Iraq... let's talk war, politics, and occupation / Riverbend. *A blog*

Kermit, the Frog

Authorized access point representing the creator for: Before you leap : a frog's-eye view of life's greatest lessons / by Kermit the Frog

Ebert, Roger

Authorized access point representing the creator for: Roger Ebert's movie yearbook. *An annual compilation of Ebert's film reviews and interviews*

Andrews, Emery E., 1894–1976

Authorized access point representing the creator for: Emery E. Andrews papers, 1925–1969 (bulk 1942–1947). *An archival collection*

Axel-Lute, Paul

Authorized access point representing the creator for: Same-sex marriage : a selective bibliography of the legal literature / compiled by Paul Axel-Lute

Goodman, Alice

Nixon in China : an opera in three acts / music by John Adams ; libretto by Alice Goodman. *A separately published libretto for the opera composed by Adams*

John Paul II, Pope, 1920–2005

Authorized access point representing the creator for: The role of the Christian in the world / Pope John Paul II. *Not an official communication*

Ford, E. B.

Authorized access point representing the creator for: British butterflies / by E.B. Ford ; with 16 colour plates by Paxton Chadwick

Lindemans, Micha F.

Authorized access point representing the creator for: Encyclopedia mythica. — "Micha F. Lindemans, founder, main contributor, editor & webmaster"—Information page. *A website*

Sutliff, Milton, 1806–1879

Authorized access point representing the creator for: Dissenting opinion of Hon. Milton Sutliff, one of the judges : ex parte Simeon Bushnell : ex parte Charles Langston : on habeas corpus. — At head of title: Supreme Court of Ohio

Blunden, Edmund, 1896–1974

Authorized access point representing the creator for: De bello Germanico : a fragment of trench history / written in 1918 by the Author of Undertones of war. *Author of* Undertones of war *known to be Edmund Blunden*

Gemmell, Nikki

Authorized access point representing the creator for: The bride stripped bare : a novel / Anonymous ; with an afterword by the author. *Work known to be by Nikki Gemmell*

Miller, Wade

Authorized access point representing the creator for: Deadly weapon / Wade Miller. *Wade Miller is an alternate identity established jointly by Bill Miller and Bob Wade*

Rogers, Robert Bruce, 1907–

Authorized access point representing the creator for: Toccata Manhatta / designed, animated, and filmed by R.B. Rogers. *An animated short film*

Friedlander, Martin

Authorized access point representing the creator for: Stemming vision loss with stem cells / Martin Friedlander. *Online streaming video file of a lecture authored and presented by Friedlander*

Brahms, Johannes, 1833–1897

Authorized access point representing the creator for: Symphony no. 4, E minor, for orchestra, op. 98 / by Johannes Brahms. *A score*

Beethoven, Ludwig van, 1770–1827

Authorized access point representing the creator for: Divertimento, op. 12, no. 2 / L. van Beethoven ; transcribed for woodwind by George J. Trinkaus

Weber, Carl Maria von, 1786–1826

Authorized access point representing the creator for: Aufforderung zum Tanz : Rondo brillant für das Pianoforte, op. 65 / by Carl Maria von Weber ; arranged for orchestra by Hector Berlioz

Ornes, Rafael V.

Authorized access point representing the creator for: Choral public domain library. *A wiki providing access to free sheet music, created and managed by Ornes, with many additional contributors*

Hines, Earl, 1903–1983

Authorized access point representing the creator for: The indispensable Earl Hines. *A selection of recordings by the jazz pianist, with various accompanying musicians*

Winehouse, Amy

Authorized access point representing the creator for: Back to black / Amy Winehouse. *Songs by Winehouse and other composers, performed by Winehouse and accompanying musicians*

Barrère, Georges, 1876–1944

Authorized access point representing the creator for: Cadenzas for the Flute concerto in G major (K. 313) by Mozart / Georges Barrère

Cassatt, Mary, 1844–1926

Authorized access point representing the creator for: Children playing on the beach / Mary Cassatt. *A photomechanical reproduction*

Leonardo, da Vinci, 1452–1519

Authorized access point representing the creator for: Leonardo da Vinci (1452–1519) : an introductory survey. *A set of 41 slides*

Bewick, Thomas, 1753–1828

Authorized access point representing the creator for: Thomas Bewick : ten working drawing reproductions : shown with impressions of the corresponding engravings. *Pairs of plates mounted in 10 numbered folders in a portfolio within a case*

Popple, Henry, died 1743

Authorized access point representing the creator for: Map of the British Empire in America with the French and Spanish settlements adjacent thereto / by Henry Popple

Blaeu, Joan, 1596–1673

Authorized access point representing the creator for: Blaeu's The grand atlas of the 17th century world / introduction, captions, and selection of maps by John Goss ; foreword by Peter Clark. *Facsimile of selected maps from Blaeu's 1662* Atlas maior

Physician

Authorized access point representing the creator for: Shall we teach cruelty as an art? / by a Physician. *Real name of person responsible is unknown*

Author of Honesty the best policy

Authorized access point representing the creator for: Plain facts / by the Author of Honesty the best policy. *Real name of author of* Honesty the best policy *is unknown*

One Family Responsible for the Creation of the Work

Eakin (Family : New Castle County, Del.)

Authorized access point representing the creator for: Eakin family papers, 1781–1828. *An archival collection*

Romanov (Dynasty)

Authorized access point representing the creator for: Romanov collection, 1894–1935 (bulk 1907–1918). *An archival collection*

Austen (Family : Austen, Jane, 1775–1817)

Authorized access point representing the creator for: Austen papers, 1704–1856 / edited by R.A. Austen-Leigh. *A published collection of family papers*

Barner (Family)

Authorized access point representing the creator for: The Barner family newsletter. — Harrisburg, Pa. : Barner Family

Adey (Family : Sydney, N.S.W.)

Authorized access point representing the creator for: Fresh from the garden : recipes from Darling Mills / the Adey Family. *A cookbook by the family that owns and operates the Darling Mills Restaurant*

Two or More Persons, Families, or Corporate Bodies Responsible for the Creation of the Work Performing the Same Role

Gumbley, Warren, 1962–
Johns, Dilys
Law, Garry

Authorized access points representing the creators for: Management of wetland archaeological sites in New Zealand / Warren Gumbley, Dilys Johns, and Garry Law

Zim, Herbert S. (Herbert Spencer), 1909–1994
Gabrielson, Ira Noel, 1889–1977

Authorized access points representing the creators for: Birds : a guide to the most familiar American birds / by Herbert S. Zim and Ira N. Gabrielson ; illustrated by James Gordon Irving

Hamill, Dorothy
Amelon, Deborah

Authorized access points representing the creators for: A skating life / Dorothy Hamill with Deborah Amelon

Tracey, John Paul
Bomford, Mary
Hart, Quentin
Saunders, Glen
Sinclair, Ron

Authorized access points representing the creators for: Managing bird damage to fruit and other horticultural crops / John Tracey, Mary Bomford, Quentin Hart, Glen Saunders, Ron Sinclair

Jepson, Willis Linn, 1867–1946
Dempster, Lauramay T., 1905–1997

Authorized access points representing the creators for: A flora of California / by Willis Linn Jepson. *Volume 4, part 2 authored by Dempster; all other parts by Jepson*

Adams, Phillip
Newell, Patrice, 1956–

Authorized access points representing the creators for: The Penguin book of jokes from cyberspace / collected by Phillip Adams and Patrice Newell

Amadei, Filippo, flourished 1690–1730
Bononcini, Antonio Maria, 1677–1726
Handel, George Frideric, 1685–1759

Authorized access points representing the creators for: The most favourite songs in the opera of Muzio Scaevola / compos'd by three famous masters. *The composers are Amadei, Bononcini, and Handel*

Kaufman, Moisés
Tectonic Theater Project

Authorized access points representing the creators for: The Laramie project / by Moisés Kaufman and the members of Tectonic Theater Project. *The script of a play*

Beyard, Michael D.
Braun, Raymond E.
McLaughlin, Herbert
Phillips, Patrick L.
Rubin, Michael S.
Bald, Andre
Fader, Steven, 1951–
Jerschow, Oliver
Lassar, Terry J.
Mulvihill, David A.
Takesuye, David

Authorized access points representing the creators for: Developing retail entertainment destinations / principal authors, Michael D. Beyard, Raymond E. Braun, Herbert McLaughlin, Patrick L. Phillips, Michael S. Rubin ; contributing authors, Andre Bald, Steven Fader, Oliver Jerschow, Terry Lassar, David Mulvihill, David Takesuye

Asher, Robert E., 1910–
Kotschnig, Walter M. (Walter Maria), born 1901
Brown, William Adams, Jr., 1894–1957

Authorized access points representing the creators for: The United Nations and economic and social co-operation / by Robert E. Asher, Walter M. Kotschnig, William Adams Brown, Jr., and associates

Harrison, Benjamin, 1833–1901
Blaine, James Gillespie, 1830–1893

Authorized access points representing the creators for: The correspondence between Benjamin Harrison and James G. Blaine, 1882–1893

Darrow, Clarence, 1857–1938
Holmes, John Haynes, 1879–1964

Authorized access points representing the creators for: Debate, subject, resolved that the United States continue the policy of prohibition as defined in the Eighteenth Amendment / Clarence Darrow, negative, versus John Haynes Holmes, affirmative ; introduction by Royal S. Copeland

Savage, George A., 1844–1920
Pulsipher, Catherine Savage

Authorized access points representing the creators for: George A. Savage and Catherine Savage Pulsipher papers, 1916–1963. *An archival collection*

Short (Family : Ohio)
Harrison (Family : Ohio)
Symmes (Family : Symmes, John Cleves, 1742–1814)

Authorized access points representing the creators for: Short-Harrison-Symmes family papers, 1760–1878 (bulk 1800–1860). *An archival collection*

Victoria and Albert Museum
Peabody Essex Museum
Jaffer, Amin

Authorized access points representing the creators for: Furniture from British India and Ceylon : a catalogue of the collections in the Victoria and Albert Museum and the Peabody Essex Museum / Amin Jaffer ; assisted in Salem by Karina Corrigan and with a contribution by Robin D. Jones ; photographs by Mike Kitcatt, Markham Sexton and Jeffrey Dykes. — Salem, Massachusetts : Peabody Essex Museum. *The corporate bodies are considered creators*

Two or More Persons, Families, or Corporate Bodies Responsible for the Creation of the Work Performing Different Roles

Shinozaki, Mamoru, 1908–1991
Lim, Yoon Lin

Authorized access points representing the creators for: My wartime experiences in Singapore / Mamoru Shinozaki ; interviewed by Lim Yoon Lin

Boetticher, Budd, 1916–2001
Bogdanovich, Peter, 1939–
Fuller, Samuel,1912–1997
Penn, Arthur, 1922–
Polonsky, Abraham
Sherman, Eric
Rubin, Martin, 1947–

Authorized access points representing the creators for: The director's event : interviews with five American film-makers : Budd Boetticher, Peter Bogdanovich, Samuel Fuller, Arthur Penn, Abraham Polonsky / by Eric Sherman and Martin Rubin

Aaron, Hank, 1934–
Bisher, Furman

Authorized access points representing the creators for: "Aaron, r.f." / by Henry Aaron as told to Furman Bisher

Snoopy, Dr.
Schulz, Charles M. (Charles Monroe), 1922–2000

Authorized access points representing the creators for: Dr. Snoopy's advice to pet owners / by Dr. Snoopy ; illustrations by Charles M. Schulz

Pekar, Harvey
Haspiel, Dean
Loughridge, Lee
Brosseau, Pat

Authorized access points representing the creators for: The quitter / Harvey Pekar, writer ; Dean Haspiel, artist ; Lee Loughridge, gray tones ; Pat Brosseau, letters. *A graphic novel*

Schurtzfleisch, Konrad Samuel, 1641–1708
Küpfender, Gottfried

Authorized access points representing the creators for: Principium Mosellae Ausonii, ad disputandum publice propositum / praeside Conrado Samuele Schurzfleischio ; respondente M. Godefrido Kupfender

Lloyd Webber, Andrew, 1948–
Hart, Charles, 1961–
Stilgoe, Richard

Authorized access points representing the creators for: The phantom of the Opera / music by Andrew Lloyd Webber ; lyrics by Charles Hart ; additional lyrics by Richard Stilgoe

Schumann, Robert, 1810–1856
Rückert, Friedrich, 1788–1866

Authorized access points representing the creators for: Dedication = Widmung : op. 25, no. 1 / Robert Schumann ; original poem by Friedrich Rückert

Gay, John, 1685–1732
Pepusch, John Cristopher,1667–1752

Authorized access points representing the creators for: The beggar's opera / written by John Gay ; the overture composed and the songs arranged by John Christopher Pepusch. *A score*

Still, William Grant, 1895–1978
Forsythe, Harold Bruce

Authorized access points representing the creators for: The sorcerer : fantastic scene for pantominists and dancers / music by William Grant Still ; scenario by Bruce Forsythe

Nuitter, Charles, 1828–1899
Saint-Léon, Arthur, 1821–1870

Delibes, Léo, 1836–1891

Authorized access points representing the creators for: Coppélia, ou, La fille aux yeux d'émail : ballet en 2 actes et 3 tableaux / de Ch. Nuitter et Saint-Léon ; musique de Léo Delibes

Bailey, David, 1938–
Evans, Peter, 1933–

Authorized access points representing the creators for: Goodbye baby & amen : a saraband for the sixties / David Bailey & Peter Evans. *Photographs by Bailey, text by Evans*

Simkin, Tom
Tilling, Robert I.
Vogt, Peter R. (Peter Richard), 1939–
Kirby, Stephen H.
Kimberly, Paul
Stewart, David B. (David Benjamin), 1928–
Stettner, Will R.

Authorized access points representing the creators for: This dynamic planet : world map of volcanoes, earthquakes, impact craters, and plate tectonics / by Tom Simkin, Robert I. Tilling, Peter R. Vogt, Stephen H. Kirby, Paul Kimberly, and David B. Stewart ; cartography and design by Will R. Stettner, with contributions by Antonio Villaseñor, and edited by Katharine S. Schindler ; U.S. Department of the Interior, U.S. Geological Survey ; prepared in cooperation with the Smithsonian Institution and the U.S. Naval Research Laboratory

Persons, Families, or Corporate Bodies Responsible for Creating a New Work Based on a Previously Existing Work

Gray, Patsey

Authorized access point representing the creator for: J.R.R. Tolkien's The hobbit / dramatized by Patricia Gray

Rusch, Kristine Kathryn
Smith, Dean Wesley

Authorized access points representing the creators for: X-men : a novelization / by Kristine Kathryn Rusch and Dean Wesley Smith ; based on the movie written by Christopher McQuarrie and Ed Solomon

Bell, Florence

Authorized access point representing the creator for: Great expectations / Charles Dickens ; retold by Florence Bell

Vande Velde, Vivian

Authorized access point representing the creator for: Tales from the Brothers Grimm and the Sisters Weird / Vivian Vande Velde. *A parody of some Grimm's fairy tales*

Smith, Wade C. (Wade Cothran), 1869 or 1870–1960

Authorized access point representing the creator for: Pilgrim's progress : John Bunyan's story rewritten for young people / by Wade C. Smith ; read by Betty Panosian. *Two audio cassettes*

Heuston, R. F. V.

Authorized access point representing the creator for: Salmond on the law of torts. — 17th edition / by R.F.V. Heuston

Heuston, R. F. V.
Chambers, R. S.

Authorized access points representing the creators for: Salmond and Heuston on the law of torts. — 18th edition / by R.F.V. Heuston and R.S. Chambers

Dutch, Robert A.

Authorized access point representing the creator for: Roget's Thesaurus of English words and phrases. — New edition / completely revised and modernized by Robert A. Dutch

Marshall, Wayne

Authorized access point representing the creator for: Organ improvisations / Wayne Marshall. *Improvisations performed by Marshall on songs by George Gershwin, Billy Strayhorn, Jule Styne, Vincent Youmans, and Leonard Bernstein*

Elling, Kurt
Hobgood, Laurence
Amster, Rob
Raynor, Michael

Authorized access points representing the creators for: Live in Chicago / Kurt Elling. — Kurt Elling, vocals; Laurence Hobgood, piano; Rob Amster, bass; Michael Raynor, drums, percussion. *Jazz performances of songs by various composers*

Tausig, Carl, 1841–1871

Authorized access point representing the creator for: Nouvelles soirées de Vienne : valses-caprices d'après J. Strauss / Ch. Tausig

Wuorinen, Charles

Authorized access point representing the creator for: The magic art : an instrumental masque drawn from works of Henry Purcell, 1977–1978 : in two acts / Charles Wuorinen

Sartain, John, 1808–1897

Authorized access point representing the creator for: The artist's dream / painted by Geo. H. Comegys ; engraved by J. Sartain

Works of an Administrative Nature

Kiowa Indian Tribe of Oklahoma

Authorized access point representing the creator for: Annual report / Kiowa Tribe of Oklahoma

Maine

Authorized access point representing the creator for: Maine.gov : official Web site of the state of Maine

Asiatic Society of Bangladesh

Authorized access point representing the creator for: The constitution of the Asiatic Society of Bangladesh

Multi-State Teacher Education Project

Authorized access point representing the creator for: M-STEP today : interim report of project activities. — Baltimore : Multi-State Teacher Education Project

Bon Homme Richard (Ship)

Authorized access point representing the creator for: The log of the Bon Homme Richard / with introduction by Louis F. Middlebrook

American Bar Association. Section of Intellectual Property Law

Authorized access point representing the creator for: Membership directory / American Bar Association, Section of Intellectual Property Law

Canadian Botanical Association
Canadian Society of Plant Physiologists

Authorized access points representing the creators for: Directory of the Canadian Botanical Association & Canadian Society of Plant Physiologists

First National Bank of Chicago

Authorized access point representing the creator for: The art collection of the First National Bank of Chicago. — Chicago : First National Bank of Chicago. *Catalogue of the collection*

University of Michigan. Library

Authorized access point representing the creator for: Microforms relating to African Americans at the University of Michigan Libraries / compiled by Charles G. Ransom. — [Ann Arbor, Michigan] : University Library. *An updating Web site*

Asahel Curtis Photo Co.

Authorized access point representing the creator for: Asahel Curtis Photo Co. photographs, 1853–1941. *A collection of photographs*

Northern Pacific Railway Company

Authorized access point representing the creator for: Northern Pacific Railway Company records, 1864–1957. *An archival collection*

British American Tobacco Company
Cameron and Cameron
D.B. Tennant and Company
David Dunlop (Firm)
Export Leaf Tobacco Company
T.C. Williams Company

Authorized access points representing the creators for: British American Tobacco Company records. *An archival collection that includes corporate records of Cameron and Cameron, D.B. Tennant and Company, David Dunlop, Export Leaf Tobacco Company, and T.C. Williams Company, all of which were companies acquired by British American Tobacco Company*

Works Recording the Collective Thought of the Body

Zambia

Authorized access point representing the creator for: The national conservation strategy for Zambia / prepared by the Government of the Republic of Zambia with assistance from the Conservation for Development Centre of the International Union for Conservation of Nature and Natural Resources (IUCN)

Victoria. Parliament. Drugs and Crime Prevention Committee

Authorized access point representing the creator for: Inquiry into misuse/abuse of benzodiazepines and other forms of pharmaceutical drugs : interim report / Parliament of Victoria, Drugs and Crime Prevention Committee

United States. Bureau of Customs

Authorized access point representing the creator for: Draft of proposed Navigation Act of 1967 / United States Bureau of Customs

Seattle Public Utilities

Authorized access point representing the creator for: Drinking water quality : a report to the community. — Seattle, WA : Seattle Public Utilities

Parti québécois

Authorized access point representing the creator for: Restons forts : plate-forme électorale 2003 / Parti québécois

American National Standards Institute
National Information Standards Organization

Authorized access points representing the creators for: American national standard for permanence of paper for publications and documents in libraries and archives / approved October 26, 1992 by the American National Standards Institute ; developed by the National Information Standards Organization

American Academy of Arts and Sciences. Committee on International Security Studies. Middle East Program

Authorized access point representing the creator for: Transition to Palestinian self-government : practical steps toward Israeli-Palestinian peace : report of a study group of the Middle East Program, Committee on International Security Studies, American Academy of Arts and Sciences / Ann Mosely Lesch, principal author. *The study group is unnamed*

Works Recording Hearings Conducted by Legislative, Judicial, Governmental, and Other Bodies

Australia. Parliament. House of Representatives. Standing Committee on Legal and Constitutional Affairs

Authorized access point representing the creator for: Inquiry into equal opportunity and equal status for Australian women : public hearings 24–25 July 1990 / House of Representatives Standing Committee on Legal and Constitutional Affairs

United States. Congress. Senate. Committee on Homeland Security and Governmental Affairs

Authorized access point representing the creator for: Ensuring full implementation of the 9/11 Commission's recommendations : hearing before the Committee on Homeland Security and Governmental Affairs, United States Senate, One Hundred Tenth Congress, first session, January 7, 2007

New York (State). Insurance Department

Authorized access point representing the creator for: Welfare and pension fund public hearing : held at New York County Lawyers Association, 14 Vesey Street, New York, New York / New York State Insurance Department. *Cover title:* Official report of proceedings before the New York State Insurance Department : in the matter of, public hearing, welfare and pension fund

Joint Federal-Provincial Panel on Uranium Mining Developments in Northern Saskatchewan (Canada)

Authorized access point representing the creator for: Transcript of the public hearings held by the Joint Federal-Provincial Panel on Uranium Mining Developments in Northern Saskatchewan for the McArthur River and Cigar Lake projects held at Community Hall, Pinehouse, Saskatchewan, October 7, 1996

United States Sentencing Commission

Authorized access point representing the creator for: Transcripts of proceedings of the public hearings of the United States Sentencing Commission : November 16–17, 2004 and February 15–16, 2005

Chicago (Ill.). Mayor's Advisory Commission on Latino Affairs

Authorized access point representing the creator for: Transcript of the Commission on Latino Affairs hearing on the proposed 1992 World's Fair

American Bar Association. Standing Committee on Legal Aid and Indigent Defendants

Authorized access point representing the creator for: Gideon undone : the crisis in indigent defense spending : transcript of a hearing on the crisis in indigent defense funding held during the Annual Conference of the National Legal Aid and Defender Association, November 1982 / John Thomas Moran, editor. *Hearing conducted by the Standing Committee on Legal Aid and Indigent Defendants of the American Bar Association*

New York (State). Legislature. Senate. Select Task Force on Court Reorganization
New York (State). Legislature. Assembly. Standing Committee on the Judiciary

Authorized access points representing the creators for: Transcript of the minutes of a hearing of the Senate Task Force on Court Reorganization and the Assembly Judiciary Committee, held at the Queens County Bar Association, Jamaica, N.Y., on November 19, 1976

Works Reporting the Collective Activity of a Conference, Expedition, or Event

Annual Workshop on Sea Turtle Biology and Conservation

Authorized access point representing the creator for: Proceedings of the ... Annual Workshop on Sea Turtle Biology and Conservation

Janus Conference on Research Library Collections (2005 : Cornell University. Library)

Authorized access point representing the creator for: Janus Conference on Research Library Collections : managing the shifting ground between writers and readers : October 9–11, 2005, Cornell University Library. *Conference proceedings. On two DVD videodiscs; second disc is a hybrid DVD containing data files*

Army Materials Technology Conference (2nd : 1973 : Hyannis, Mass.)

Authorized access point representing the creator for: Ceramics for high-performance applications : proceedings of the Second Army Materials Technology Conference, held at Hyannis, Massachusetts, November 13–16, 1973 / sponsored by Army Materials and Mechanics Research Center ; editors, John J. Burke, Alvin E. Gorum, R. Nathan Katz

Association for Computational Linguistics. Annual Meeting (45th : 2007 : Prague, Czech Republic)

Authorized access point representing the creator for: ACL 2007 : proceedings of the 45th Annual Meeting of the Association for Computational Linguistics, June 23–30, 2007, Prague, Czech Republic

International Organization for Masoretic Studies. International Congress (9th : 1989 : Jerusalem; Louvain, Belgium; Anaheim, Calif.)

Authorized access point representing the creator for: Proceedings of the Ninth Congress of the International Organization for Masoretic Studies, 1989 / edited by Aron Dotan. *Conference held: Jerusalem, August 16; Louvain, Belgium, August 27; Anaheim, California, November 20*

Asia-Pacific Conference on Communications (10th : 2004 : Qing hua da xue)
International Symposium on Multi-Dimensional Mobile Communications (5th: 2004: Qing hua da xue)

Authorized access points representing the creators for: APCC/MDMC '04 : the 2004 joint conference of the 10th Asia-Pacific Conference on Communications and the 5th International Symposium on Multi-Dimensional Mobile Communications proceedings : August 29–September 1, 2004, Tsinghua University, Beijing, China / editors, Ke Gong, Zhisheng Niu, Pingyi Fan, Jian Yang

Council of Trent (1545–1563)

Authorized access point representing the creator for: The canons and decrees of the Council of Trent : celebrated under Paul III, Julius III, and Pius IV, Bishops of Rome / faithfully translated into English

Antarctic Walk Environmental Research Expedition (1991–1993)

Authorized access point representing the creator for: Scientific results from the Antarctic Walk Environmental Research Expedition, 1991–1993 / edited by K. Yoshikawa, K. Harada, S. Ishimaru

Miss America Pageant

Authorized access point representing the creator for: Miss America Pageant programs, 1957–1985. *An archival collection*

Eurovision Song Contest (48th : 2003 : Rīga, Latvia)

Authorized access point representing the creator for: Eurovision Song Contest, Riga 2003 : the official album of the Eurovision Song Contest 2003, including all the songs of all participating countries. *An audio recording*

Salzburger Festspiele (1996 : Salzburg, Austria)

Authorized access point representing the creator for: Salzburger Festspiele 20. Juli–31. August 1996. — "Offizielles Programm"—Cover

Biennale di Venezia (35th : 1970: Venice, Italy)

Authorized access point representing the creator for: Catalogo della 35a Esposizione biennale internazionale d'arte, Venezia

Works Resulting from the Collective Activity of a Performing Group

Living Theatre (New York, N.Y.)

Authorized access point representing the creator for: Paradise now / collective creation of the Living Theatre ; written down by Judith Malina and Julian Beck. *Written record of a play created by the group*

Coldplay (Musical group)

Authorized access point representing the creator for: Parachutes / Coldplay. *Songs written by Coldplay and performed by them*

Red Hot Chili Peppers (Musical group)

Authorized access point representing the creator for: Stadium arcadium / Red Hot Chili Peppers ; music transcriptions by Pete Billman and David Stocker. *Songs composed by the rock group Red Hot Chili Peppers*

Nils-Bertil Dahlander Quartet
Paul Hindberg Quintet

Authorized access points representing the creators for: Jazz smorgasbord / Nils-Bertil Dahlander Quartet and the Paul Hindberg Quintet. *Joint performances of pop standards by the two jazz groups*

Cartographic Works Originating with a Corporate Body Responsible for More Than Just Publication or Distribution

Ordnance Survey of Ireland

Authorized access point representing the creator for: Cork city street map and index : scale 1:15,000 / Ordnance Survey of Ireland

Kansas Geological Survey

Authorized access point representing the creator for: Geothermal map of North America / North American map editors, David D. Blackwell and Maria C. Richards ; map production by the Kansas Geological Survey

Australia. Department of the Environment and Heritage

Authorized access point representing the creator for: Major vegetation groups in Australia ; Native vegetation in Australia / produced by Australian Government Department of the Environment and Heritage, January 2006. *Two maps on one sheet*

Pittsburgh (Pa.). GIS Division

Authorized access point representing the creator for: City of Pittsburgh : ESRI shapefiles complete / GIS Division, City of Pittsburgh. *A CD-ROM*

United States Exploring Expedition (1838–1842)

Authorized access point representing the creator for: Map of the Oregon Territory / by the U.S. Ex. Ex., Charles Wilkes, Esqr., Commander, 1841

East View Cartographic, Inc.

Authorized access point representing the creator for: Digital aeronautical flight information file / East View Cartographic. *A DVD-ROM*

Oxford University Press. Cartographic Department

Authorized access point representing the creator for: The new Oxford atlas for Pakistan / all maps drawn by the Cartographic Unit, Oxford University Press ; editorial adviser, Fazle Karim Khan

National Geographic Society (U.S.). Cartographic Division

Authorized access point representing the creator for: National Geographic globe / produced by the Cartographic Division, National Geographic Society ; John F. Shupe, chief cartographer

Laws of a Political Jurisdiction

Canada

Authorized access point representing the enacting jurisdiction for: Canada Corporations Act : chap. 53, R.S.C. 1952, as amended

United States

Authorized access point representing the enacting jurisdiction for: An Act to Assist in the Conservation of Marine Turtles and the Nesting Habitats of Marine Turtles in Foreign Countries

Vancouver (B.C.)

Authorized access points representing the enacting jurisdiction for: 2010 Winter Games Sign Designation and Relaxation By-law No. 9697 / City of Vancouver, British Columbia

Richmond (Va.)

Authorized access point representing the enacting jurisdiction for: Building code of the city of Richmond, Virginia

Tulalip Tribes of the Tulalip Reservation, Washington

Authorized access point representing the enacting jurisdiction for: Tulalip ordinances & codes / Tulalip Tribes

Bermuda Islands

Authorized access point representing the enacting jurisdiction for: Bermuda laws online

Maryland

Authorized access point representing the enacting jurisdiction for: Code of the public local laws of Worcester County : article 24 of the Code of public local laws of Maryland : comprising all the local laws of the state of

Maryland in force in Worcester County to and inclusive of the Acts of the General Assembly of 1961 / edited by Carl N. Everstine

Catawba Indian Nation

Authorized access point representing the enacting jurisdiction for: Constitution and By-laws of the Catawba Indian Tribe of South Carolina

Bern (Switzerland : Canton)

Authorized access point representing the enacting jurisdiction for: Bernische Systematische Gesetzessammlung : BSG

United States
Mexico
California
Baja California (Mexico : State)

Authorized access points representing the enacting jurisdictions for: The narcotic laws of Mexico and the United States of America. — Cover title: Drugs and the law : compilation of laws on narcotics and dangerous drugs from the United States of America, the United States of Mexico, the state of California, and the state of Baja California

Decrees of a Head of State, Chief Executive, or Ruling Executive Body

Kazakhstan. President (1991– : Nazarbaev)

Authorized access point representing the head of state for: Decrees of the President of the Kazakh Republic, valid as a law

Indonesia. President (2004– : Yudhoyono)

Authorized access point representing the head of state for: Peraturan presiden nomor 73 tahun 2005. *Presidential regulation on government budget of Indonesia for fiscal year 2006*

Peru. Junta Militar de Gobierno (1948–1956)

Authorized access point representing the ruling executive body for: Decretos-leyes de la Junta Militar de Gobierno. *Decrees, published in 1949, of the ruling executive body of Peru*

Bills and Drafts of Legislation

Australia. Parliament. House of Representatives

Authorized access point representing the legislative body for: Second Corporate Law Simplification Bill : second draft

United States. Congress (107th, 1st session : 2001). Senate

Authorized access point representing the legislative body for: S. 1216 in the Senate of the United States : a bill making appropriations for the Departments of Veterans Affairs and Housing and Urban Development, and for sundry independent agencies, boards, commissions, corporations, and offices for the fiscal year ending September 30, 2002, and for other purposes

Administrative Regulations, Etc.

Canada

Authorized access point representing the enacting jurisdiction for: The Queen's regulations and orders for the Canadian Forces (1994 revision) : issued under the authority of the National Defence Act = Ordonnances et règlements royaux applicables aux Forces canadiennes (révision de 1994) : publiés en vertu de l'autorité conférée par la Loi sur la défense nationale

Saskatchewan

Authorized access point representing the enacting jurisdiction for: The regulations of Saskatchewan

Canada. Governor General

Authorized access point representing the promulgating agent for: Regulations under the Destructive Insect and Pest Act as they apply to the importation of plants and plant products / Department of Agriculture. *Promulgated by the Governor in Council*

Illinois. Department of Public Health

Authorized access point representing the promulgating agency for: Rules and regulations for recreational areas : prescribed under the Recreational Area Licensing Act, chapter 111 1/2, paragraphs 761–792 inclusive. *Promulgated by the Illinois Department of Public Health*

Constitutions, Charters, Etc.

United States

Authorized access point representing the enacting jurisdiction for: The Constitution of the United States

Kosovo (Republic)

Authorized access point representing the enacting jurisdiction for: Kushtetuta e Republikës së Kosovës

Georgia

Authorized access point representing the enacting jurisdiction for: Charter of Columbus Savings Bank, incorporated by special act of Legislature of the state of Georgia, December 24, 1888

Colima (Mexico : State)

Authorized access point representing the enacting jurisdiction for: Constitución política del estado libre y soberano de Colima

Los Angeles County (Calif.)

Authorized access point representing the enacting jurisdiction for: Charter of the County of Los Angeles

Montréal (Québec)

Authorized access point representing the enacting jurisdiction for: Charte montréalaise des droits et responsabilités

United Nations

Authorized access point representing the international intergovernmental body governed for: Charter of the United Nations

Universal Postal Union

Authorized access point representing the international intergovernmental body governed for: Constitution, general regulations : resolutions and decisions, rules of procedure, legal status of the UPU : with commentary by the International Bureau of the UPU / Universal Postal Union

Court Rules

India

Authorized access point representing the enacting jurisdiction for: Code of civil procedure, 1908 (5 of 1908), as modified up to the 1st May 1977

Oregon. Council on Court Procedures

Authorized access point representing the promulgating agency for: Oregon rules of civil procedure / promulgated by Council on Court Procedures

Palau. Supreme Court

Authorized access point representing the promulgating agency for: Rules and regulations of the Land Court / promulgated by the Palau Supreme Court, pursuant to RPPL no. 4-43 section 16

Charges to Juries, Indictments, Court Proceedings, and Court Decisions

United States. Circuit Court (Middle Circuit)

Authorized access point representing the court for: The charge of Judge Paterson to the jury, in the case of Vanhorne's lessee against Dorrance : tried at a Circuit Court for the United States, held at Philadelphia, April term, 1795 : wherein the controverted title to the Wyoming lands, between the claimants under Pennsylvania and Connecticut, received a decision. *The lessee is not named*

International Tribunal for the Prosecution of Persons Responsible for Serious Violations of International Humanitarian Law Committed in the Territory of the Former Yugoslavia since 1991

Authorized access point representing the court for: Indictment, Rajic ("Stupni Do"), 23 August 1995

Wisconsin. Circuit Court (Marinette County)

Authorized access point representing the court for: Indictment record book, 1889-1897. *Copies of indictments filed by attorneys with the Circuit Court charging the defendant with a criminal violation of the statutes; an archival collection*

United States. District Court (New York : Eastern District)

Authorized access point representing the court for: Transcript of trial proceedings in the case of United States of America v. Mario Biaggi and Meade Esposito : in the United States District Court for the Eastern District of New York : Crim. no. 87–151 and related materials

Massachusetts. Supreme Judicial Court

Authorized access point representing the court for: Report of the trial of Leavitt Alley, indicted for the murder of Abijah Ellis, in the Supreme Judicial Court of Massachusetts / reported by Franklin Fiske Heard

California. Supreme Court

Authorized access point representing the court for: Reports of cases determined in the Supreme Court of the state of California, October 23, 1969, to January 30, 1970 / Robert E. Formichi, reporter of decisions

Canada. Federal Court

Authorized access point representing the court for: Canada Federal Court reports / editor, Florence Rosenfeld

United States. Supreme Court

Authorized access point representing the court for: Freedom of the press : opinion of the Supreme Court of the United States in the case of Alice Lee Grosjean, supervisor of public accounts for the state of Louisiana, appellant, v. American Press Company, Inc., et al.

European Court of Human Rights

Authorized access point representing the court for: Case of Foti and others, 4/1981/43/68–71 : judgment

Individual Works of Art by Two or More Artists Acting as a Corporate Body

Critical Art Ensemble

Authorized access point representing the creator for: Molecular invasion

Seekers of Lice

Authorized access point representing the creator for: Quandries

Pierre et Gilles

Authorized access point representing the creator for: Maison de poupée

General Idea

Authorized access point representing the creator for: No mean feet

Official Communications

United States. President (1993–2001 : Clinton)
Clinton, Bill, 1946–

Authorized access points representing the official and the person issuing the communication for: Additional steps with the continuing human rights and humanitarian crisis in Kosovo : message from the President of the United States transmitting a report on developments concerning the national emergency with regards to Kosovo as described and declared in Executive Order 13088 of June 9, 1998, pursuant to 50 U.S.C. 1703(c). *An official communication of President Bill Clinton*

France. Sovereign (1774–1792 : Louis XVI)
Louis XVI, King of France, 1754–1793

Authorized access points representing the official and the person issuing the communication for: Proclamation du roi, pour la conservation des forêts & bois: du 3 novembre 1789. *An official communication of King Louis XVI*

Virginia. Governor (2002–2006 : Warner)
Warner, Mark R. (Mark Robert)

Authorized access points representing the official and the person issuing the communication for: Declaration of a state of emergency for central Virginia due to significant flooding caused by Tropical Depression Gaston. *An executive order of Governor Mark Warner*

New York (N.Y.). Mayor (1933–1945 : La Guardia)
La Guardia, Fiorello H. (Fiorello Henry), 1882–1947

Authorized access points representing the official and the person issuing the communication for: New York City at war : emergency services : report / by F.H. La Guardia, mayor. *An official communication*

Hong Kong. Governor (1992–1997 : Patten)
Patten, Chris, 1944–

Authorized access points representing the official and the person issuing the communication for: Hong Kong : today's success, tomorrow's challenges : address by the Governor, the Right Honourable Christopher Patten at the opening of the 1993/1994 session of the Legislative Council, 6 October, 1993. *An official communication*

Catholic Church. Pope (1939–1958 : Pius XII)
Pius XII, Pope, 1876–1958

Authorized access points representing the official and the person issuing the communication for: Fulgens Corona : on the Marian Year and the dogma of the Immaculate Conception / encyclical letter of Pius XII. *An official communication*

Franciscans. Minister General (1947–1952 : Perantoni)
Perantoni, Pacifico M. (Pacifico Maria), 1895–1982

Authorized access points representing the official and the person issuing the communication for: Our vocation as children of Saint Francis : being the encyclical letter Divina Providentia of the Most Rev. Fr. General Pacific M. Perantoni, O.F.M. *An official communication*

United Hebrew Congregations of the British Empire. Chief Rabbi (1913–1946 : Hertz)
Hertz, Joseph H. (Joseph Herman), 1872–1946

Authorized access points representing the official and the person issuing the communication for: Civilian morale: grave warning : and the Chief Rabbi's Passover letter / by the Chief Rabbi. *An official communication of Joseph H. Hertz, Chief Rabbi of the United Hebrew Congregations of the British Empire*

Catholic Church. Archdiocese of St. Paul and Minneapolis. Archbishop (1995–2008 : Flynn)
Flynn, Harry J. (Harry Joseph), 1933–

Authorized access points representing the official and the person issuing the communication for: In God's image : a pastoral letter on racism = A imagen y semejanza de Dios : carta pastoral acerca del racismo / Harry J. Flynn. *A pastoral letter from the Archbishop of St. Paul and Minneapolis*

United States. President

Authorized access point representing the officials issuing the communications for: Economic report of the President transmitted to the Congress. *Annual official communication; compilation of more than one holder of the office*

Catholic Church. Pope

Authorized access point representing the officials issuing the communications for: Tutte le encicliche dei sommi pontefici / raccolte e annotate da Eucardio Momigliano. *Compilation of official communications of more than one holder of the office*

Baltimore (Md.). Mayor

Authorized access point representing the officials issuing the communications for: Annual report from the Mayor to the people of Baltimore. *An official communication; compilation of more than one holder of the office*

Brunei. Jabatan Mufti Kerajaan

Authorized access point representing the officials issuing the communications for: Fatwa mufti kerajaan. *A serially issued compilation of official communications of the State Mufti of Brunei*

Catholic Church. Pope

Authorized access point representing the officials issuing the communications for: Papal thought on the state : excerpts from encyclicals and other writings of recent popes / edited by Gerard F. Yates. *Includes official communications and other works*

United States. President

Authorized access point representing the officials issuing the communications for: A compilation of the messages and papers of the Presidents, 1789-1902 / by James D. Richardson. *Includes official communications and other works*

19.3 Other Person, Family, or Corporate Body Associated with a Work

CORE ELEMENT

*Other person, family, or corporate body associated with a work is a core element if the access point representing that person, family, or corporate body is used to construct the authorized access point representing the work (see **6.27–6.31**).*

19.3.1 Basic Instructions on Recording Other Persons, Families, and Corporate Bodies Associated with a Work

19.3.1.1 Scope

Other person, family, or corporate body associated with a work is a person, family, or corporate body associated with a work in a relationship other than that of creator.

Other persons, families, or corporate bodies associated with a work include:

persons, etc., to whom correspondence is addressed

persons, etc., honoured by a festschrift

directors, cinematographers, etc.

sponsoring bodies

production companies, etc.

institutions, etc., hosting an exhibition or event, etc.

For guidance on recording relationships to persons, families, and corporate bodies who are the subject of a work, see chapter **23**. [To be added in a later release]

19.3.1.2 Sources of Information

Take information on other persons, families, and corporate bodies associated with a work from the sources specified at **19.1.1**.

19.3.1.3 Recording Other Persons, Families, and Corporate Bodies Associated with a Work

Record other persons, families, and corporate bodies associated with the work if considered important for access. Apply the general guidelines at **18.4**.

Macmillan, Alexander, 1818–1896
Ellis, Frederick Startridge, 1830–1901

Authorized access points representing the addressees for: The Rossetti-Macmillan letters : some 133 unpublished letters written to Alexander Macmillan, F.S. Ellis, and others, by Dante Gabriel, Christina, and William Michael Rossetti, 1861–1889 / edited, with an introduction and notes, by Lona Mosk Packer

Brook, Barry S.

Authorized access point representing the honouree for: Music in the classic period : essays in honor of Barry S. Brook / [edited by] Allan W. Atlas

Lot, Ferdinand, 1866–1952

Authorized access point representing the dedicatee for: Mélanges d'histoire du Moyen Âge / offerts à Ferdinand Lot par ses amis et ses élèves

American Geological Institute

Authorized access point representing the corporate body associated with the work for: Dictionary of mining, mineral, and related terms / compiled by the American Geological Institute.

Canadian Wildlife Service. Migratory Birds Conservation Division

Authorized access point representing the corporate body associated with the work for: Directory of Canadian ornithologists = Répertoire des ornithologistes canadiens. — Gatineau, QC : Environment Canada, [2000]- — "Compiled by the Migratory Birds Conservation Division of the Canadian Wildlife Service, with assistance from the Society of Canadian Ornithologists"—English home page. *A website*

Travel Industry Association of America. Research Department

Authorized access point representing the corporate body associated with the work for: Japan travel view / prepared by the Research Department of the Travel Industry Association of America

Daughters of St. Paul

Authorized access point representing the corporate body associated with the work for: The Bible for young readers / written and illustrated by the Daughters of St. Paul. *A retelling of Bible stories*

Canon Law Society of America

Authorized access point representing the sponsoring body for: The Code of Canon Law : a text and commentary / commissioned by the Canon Law Society of America ; edited by James A. Coriden, Thomas J. Green, Donald E. Heintschel

Cleveland Museum of Art

Authorized access point representing the host institution for: Fifty years of modern art, 1916–1966 / Edward B. Henning. — Cleveland, Ohio : Cleveland Museum of Art. *A catalogue of an exhibition held at the museum*

United Nations. Secretariat

Authorized access point representing the registering body for: Treaty series : treaties and international agreements registered or filed and recorded with the Secretariat of the United Nations

Salzburger Festspiele

Authorized access point representing the host institution for: Die Salzburger Liederabende, 1956–1965 / Dietrich Fischer-Dieskau, Gerald Moore. *Songs by various composers performed by Fischer-Dieskau, baritone, and Moore, piano, recorded live at the 1956–1965 Salzburg Festivals*

European Monitoring Centre on Racism and Xenophobia

Authorized access point representing the sponsoring body for: Policing racist crime and violence : a comparative analysis / prepared by Robin Oakley on behalf of the EUMC

Illinois. Institute for Environmental Quality

Authorized access point representing the sponsoring body for: Hydrogen sulfide health effects and recommended air quality standard / prepared for the Illinois Institute for Environmental Quality by the Environmental Health Resource Center

Army Materials and Mechanics Research Center (U.S.)

Authorized access point representing the sponsoring body for: Ceramics for high-performance applications : proceedings of the Second Army Materials Technology Conference, held at Hyannis, Massachusetts, November 13–16, 1973 / sponsored by Army Materials and Mechanics Research Center ; editors, John J. Burke, Alvin E. Gorum, R. Nathan Katz

Stanwood Chamber of Commerce
Camano Island Chamber of Commerce

Authorized access points representing the sponsoring bodies for: Stanwood area and Camano Island street map. — Sedro-Woolley, Washington : Published by Sizemore Enterprises in conjunction with the Stanwood & Camano Island Chambers of Commerce

ABC News Productions

Authorized access point representing the production company for: Gay rights, marriage, and the Supreme Court / ABC News Productions

Lee, Ang, 1954–
McMurtry, Larry
Ossana, Diana
Schamus, James, 1959–
Prieto, Rodrigo
Focus Features
River Road Entertainment (Firm)

Authorized access points representing the other persons and corporate bodies associated with the work for: Brokeback Mountain / Focus Features and River Road Entertainment ; directed by Ang Lee ; screenplay by Larry McMurtry & Diana Ossana ; producers, Diana Ossana, James Schamus. — Credits: Director of photography, Rodrigo Prieto ; art director, Laura Ballinger ; edited, Geraldine Peroni, Dylan Tichenor ; music, Gustavo Santaolalla ; costume designer, Marit Allen ; production designer, Judy Becker. *The particular access points recorded reflect choices made by the agency creating the data.*

Agonito, Joseph
Onondaga Community College. Radio/Television Department

Authorized access points representing the other persons and corporate bodies associated with the work for: Womanpriest : Betty Bone Schiess, Episcopal priest / produced & directed by Joseph Agonito. — "Produced under the auspices of the Radio and Television Department at Onondaga Community College, chairperson, Catherine Hawkins"

Vilniaus Universitetas. Tarptautinių santykių ir politikos mokslų institutas

Authorized access point representing the corporate body associated with the work for: Lithuania under German occupation, 1941–1945 : despatches from US Legation in Stockholm / compiled and edited by Thomas Remeikis. — Vilnius : Vilnius University Press. — At head of title: Institute of International Relations and Political Science, Vilnius University

West (Firm)

Authorized access point representing the corporate body associated with the work for: American law reports. ALR 6th, Annotations and cases. — [Eagan, Minnesota] : Thomson/West. *Publisher has significant responsibility for the creation of the work*

California Academy of Sciences

Authorized access point representing the issuing body for: Occasional papers of the California Academy of Sciences

Gandhi-King Society

Authorized access point representing the issuing body for: The acorn. *Published by the Philosophy Department of Eastern Illinois University (1986–1990) and the Philosophy Department of St. Bonaventure University (1990–); issued by the Gandhi-King Society*

American Association of Zoological Parks and Aquariums
American Zoo and Aquarium Association

Authorized access points representing the issuing bodies for: Zoological parks and aquariums in the Americas. *Volumes for 1978–79 to 1993–94 issued by American Association of Zoological Parks and Aquariums; volumes for 1994–95 to 1996–97 issued by American Zoo and Aquarium Association*

Società italiana di gastroenterologia
Associazione italiana per lo studio del fegato

Authorized access points representing the issuing bodies for: Digestive and liver disease : official journal of the Italian Society of Gastroenterology and the Italian Association for the Study of the Liver

19.3.2 Other Person, Family, or Corporate Body Associated with Legal Works

CORE ELEMENT

Other person, family, or corporate body associated with a work is a core element if the access point representing that person, family, or corporate body is used to construct the authorized access point representing the work (see **6.29** *).*

19.3.2.1 Application

The instructions at **19.3.2.2–19.3.2.5** apply to:

a) legislative enactments and decrees of political jurisdictions (including fundamental laws such as constitutions, charters, etc.)

b) decrees of a chief executive having the force of law

c) administrative regulations

d) court rules

e) constitutions, charters, etc., of other bodies that are not jurisdictions.

The instructions at **19.3.2.6–19.3.2.13** apply to:

a) law reports for a trial court, appeals court, tribunal, etc.

b) law reports covering two or more courts

c) citations to, and digests and indexes of, court reports

d) criminal proceedings and appeals

e) civil and other non-criminal proceedings and appeals

f) indictments

g) charges to juries

h) judicial decisions

i) judicial opinions

j) records of one party

k) treaties.

For other types of legal works, apply the basic instructions on recording other persons, families, and corporate bodies associated with a work (see **19.3.1**).

19.3.2.2 Jurisdiction Governed by a Law, Regulation, Etc.

If the jurisdiction governed by a law, regulation, etc., is not the jurisdiction that enacted it, record the jurisdiction or jurisdictions governed. Apply the basic instructions on recording other persons, families, and corporate bodies associated with a work at **19.3.1**.

Worcester County (Md.)

Authorized access point representing the jurisdiction governed for: Code of the public local laws of Worcester County : article 24 of the Code of public local laws of Maryland : comprising all the local laws of the state of Maryland in force in Worcester County to and inclusive of the Acts of the General Assembly of 1961 / edited by Carl N. Everstine

19.3.2.3 Issuing Agency or Agent

Record a non-legislative corporate body responsible for issuing a law. Apply the basic instructions on recording other persons, families, and corporate bodies associated with a work at **19.3.1**.

> North Dakota. Department of Public Instruction
> *Authorized access point representing the issuing agency for:* North Dakota century school code / issued by the Department of Public Instruction ; Wayne G. Sanstead, state superintendent

If a regulation, etc., is issued by an agency or agent other than the promulgating agency or agent, record the issuing agency or agent. Apply the basic instructions on recording other persons, families, and corporate bodies associated with a work at **19.3.1**.

> Virginia. Department of Labor and Industry
> *Authorized access point representing the issuing agency for:* Virginia occupational safety and health standards for general industry (29 CFR part 1910) / as adopted by the Safety and Health Codes Commission of the Commonwealth of Virginia ; issued by the Department of Labor and Industry
>
> Canada. Department of Agriculture
> *Authorized access point representing the issuing agency for:* Regulations under the Destructive Insect and Pest Act as they apply to the importation of plants and plant products / Department of Agriculture. *Promulgated by the Governor in Council*

19.3.2.4 Court Governed by Rules

For court rules (regardless of their official nature, e.g., laws, administrative regulations), record the court governed by the rules. Apply the basic instructions on recording other persons, families, and corporate bodies associated with a work at **19.3.1**.

> United States. Tax Court
> *Authorized access point representing the court governed for:* Rules of practice and procedure of United States Tax Court
>
> Palau. Land Court
> *Authorized access point representing the court governed for:* Rules and regulations of the Land Court / promulgated by the Palau Supreme Court, pursuant to RPPL no. 4-43 section 16

19.3.2.5 Body Governed by a Constitution, Etc.

For a constitution, charter, etc., that is enacted by a jurisdiction but governs a body that is not a jurisdiction, record the body governed. Apply the basic instructions on recording other persons, families, and corporate bodies associated with a work at **19.3.1**.

> Columbus Savings Bank (Columbus, Ga.)
> *Authorized access point representing the body governed by a constitution, etc., for:* Charter of Columbus Savings Bank, incorporated by special act of Legislature of the state of Georgia, December 24, 1888

19.3.2.6 Person or Corporate Body Prosecuted in a Criminal Trial, Etc.

For the official proceedings and records of criminal trials, impeachments, courts-martial, etc., and the proceedings of appeals in these types of cases, record the person, persons, body, or bodies prosecuted. Apply the basic instructions on recording other persons, families, and corporate bodies associated with a work at **19.3.1**.

Alley, Leavitt

Authorized access point representing the defendant for: Report of the trial of Leavitt Alley, indicted for the murder of Abijah Ellis, in the Supreme Judicial Court of Massachusetts / reported by Franklin Fiske Heard

Hull, William, 1753–1825

Authorized access point representing the defendant for: Report of the trial of Brig. General William Hull, commanding the North-Western Army of the United States, by a court martial held at Albany on Monday, 3rd January, 1814, and succeeding days / taken by Lieut. Col. Forbes

Meteor (Ship)

Authorized access point representing the defendant for: Report of the case of the steamship Meteor, libelled for alleged violation of the Neutrality Act / edited by F.V. Balch

American Tobacco Company

Authorized access point representing the defendant for: United States of America, et al., plaintiff, vs. the American Tobacco Company, et al., defendants : criminal no. 6670: transcripts of proceedings, Lexington, Kentucky, May 5–Dec. 11, 1941. — At head of title: In the District Court of the United States, Eastern District of Kentucky (at Lexington)

Williams, Harrison A.

Authorized access point representing the defendant for: Trial proceedings (trial transcript excerpts and tape recording transcripts) in the case of the United States of America v. Harrison A. Williams, Jr., et al. in the United States District Court for the Eastern District of New York, crim no. 80 CR-00575 / prepared for the use of the Select Committee on Ethics, United States Senate, 97th Congress, first session

For a charge to a jury, record the person, persons, body, or bodies prosecuted.

Latrimouille, Hilaire

Authorized access point representing the defendant for: The charge to the jury and the sentence by Judge Theodoric R. Westbrook in the case of Hilaire Latrimouille / reported by James M. Ruso, court stenographer

Warner Bros.
Paramount Pictures, Inc.
RKO Radio Pictures, Inc.

Authorized access points representing the defendants for: Charge to the jury by Hon. George H. Moore, judge of the United States District Court in St. Louis, in the case of United of America States of America vs. Warner Bros. Pictures, Inc., et al., delivered November 11, 1935. *Defendants include: Warner, Paramount, and R.K.O. distributing companies*

For a judgement or other decision of a court in a case, record the person, persons, body or bodies prosecuted.

Danforth, Stephen

Authorized access point representing the defendant for: Stephen Danforth, petitioner v. Minnesota : on writ of certiorari to the Supreme Court of Minnesota: opinion of the court. — At head of title: Supreme Court of the United States

For an opinion of a judge, record the person, persons, body or bodies prosecuted.

Milligan, Lambdin P.

Authorized access point representing the defendant for: The dissenting opinion in the Milligan case. *Written by Chief Justice Salmon P. Chase; concerns the case of Lambdin P. Milligan argued and determined in the United States Supreme Court*

Tadić, Dušan
Authorized access point representing the defendant for: Prosecutor v. Dusko Tadic a/k/a "Dule" : separate and dissenting opinion of Judge McDonald regarding the applicability of Article 2 of the statute

19.3.2.7 Person or Corporate Body Indicted

For an indictment, record the person, persons, body, or bodies indicted. Apply the basic instructions on recording other persons, families, and corporate bodies associated with a work at **19.3.1**.

Duane, William, 1760–1835
Authorized access point representing the person indicted for: Copy of an indictment (No. 1) in the Circuit Court of the United States in and for the Pennsylvania District of the Middle Circuit. *Indictment of William Duane*

Rajic, Ivica
Authorized access point representing the person indicted for: Indictment, Rajic ("Stupni Do"), 23 August 1995. *Indictment in the International Criminal Tribunal for the Former Yugoslavia*

19.3.2.8 Person or Corporate Body Bringing the Action in Noncriminal Proceedings

For the official proceedings and records of civil and other noncriminal proceedings (including election cases), and the proceedings of appeals in these types of cases, record the person, persons, body, or bodies bringing the action. Apply the basic instructions on recording other persons, families, and corporate bodies associated with a work at **19.3.1**.

Brooks, William, 1803–1863
Authorized access point representing the plaintiff for: The case of William Brooks versus Ezekiel Byam and others, in equity, in the Circuit Court of the United States, for the First Circuit–District of Massachusetts

Goodwin Film and Camera Company
Authorized access point representing the plaintiff for: The Goodwin Film and Camera Company, complainant, vs. Eastman Kodak Company, defendant. *Case heard before the United States Circuit Court, Western District of New York*

Goodwin Film and Camera Company
Authorized access point representing the plaintiff for: The Goodwin Film and Camera Company, complainant-appellee, vs. Eastman Kodak Company, defendant-appellant : transcript of record. *Appeal heard before the United States Circuit Court of Appeals for the Second Circuit*

For a charge to a jury, record the person, persons, body, or bodies bringing the action.

Dalton, Benjamin Franklin
Authorized access point representing the plaintiff for: Judge Merrick's charge to the jury, in the Dalton divorce case

Granville (Family)
Authorized access point representing the plaintiffs for: The charge of Judge Potter to the jury in the suit of the devisees of the Earl Granville against Josiah Collins in the Circuit Court of the United States, December term, 1805 as it appeared in the Raleigh register, Jan. 20 & 27, 1806

For a judgement or other decision of a court in a case, record the person, persons, body, or bodies bringing the action.

Steel, Helen, 1965–
Morris, David, 1954–

Authorized access points representing the plaintiffs for: Helen Marie Steel and David Morris, appellants, v. McDonald's Corporation and McDonald's Restaurants Ltd., respondents: judgment (as approved by the Court) / handed down transcript of Smith Bernal Reporting Limited. — At head of title: In the Supreme Court of Judicature, in the Court of Appeal (Civil Division), on appeal from the Queen's Bench Division (the Hon. Mr. Justice Bell), before Lord Justice Pill, Lord Justice May, Mr. Justice Keene

For an opinion of a judge, record the person, persons, body, or bodies bringing the action.

Goodyear, Charles, 1800–1860

Authorized access point representing the plaintiff for: Opinion of Judge Pitman in the case of Charles Goodyear et al. vs. Bourn, Brown et al. : in the Circuit Court of the United States, Rhode Island District, November term, 1856. — "A bill in equity has been filed in this court in the name of Charles Goodyear and others against George O. Bourn, Wm. W. Brown and Edwin M. Chaffee, charging them with a violation of a patent granted to Charles Goodyear"—Page 3

Little, Edwin C.
Scoville, Oliver

Authorized access points representing the plaintiffs for: Opinion of the Hon. Alfred Conkling, District Judge of the United States for the Northern District of New York, sitting in the Circuit Court of the United States : upon the question of copyright in manuscripts, in the case of Little and company against Hall, Goulds, and Banks, respecting the fourth volume of Comstock's reports. — "Edwin C. Little & Oliver Scoville vs. Levi W. Hall, Anthony Gould, William Gould, David Banks and David Banks, Jr."—Page 3

19.3.2.9 Person or Corporate Body on the Opposing Side in Noncriminal Proceedings

A person or body on the opposing side is the party against whom the action is brought.

For the official proceedings and records of civil and other noncriminal proceedings (including election cases), and the proceedings of appeals in these types of cases, record the person, persons, body, or bodies on the opposing side. Apply the basic instructions on recording other persons, families, and corporate bodies associated with a work at **19.3.1**.

Webb, E. Y. (Edwin Yates), 1872–1955

Authorized access point representing the defendant for: Contested election case of John A. Smith, contestant, v. Edwin Y. Webb, contestee, from the Ninth Congressional District of North Carolina, before Committee on Elections No. 2

For a charge to a jury, record the person, persons, body, or bodies on the opposing side.

Dalton, Helen Maria, born 1837

Authorized access point representing the defendant for: Judge Merrick's charge to the jury, in the Dalton divorce case

Collins, Josiah

Authorized access point representing the defendant for: The charge of Judge Potter to the jury in the suit of the devisees of the Earl Granville against Josiah Collins in the Circuit Court of the United States, December term, 1805 as it appeared in the Raleigh register, Jan. 20 & 27, 1806

For a judgement or other decision of a court in a case, record the person, persons, body, or bodies on the opposing side.

McDonald's Corporation
McDonald's Restaurants Ltd.

Authorized access points representing the defendants for: Helen Marie Steel and David Morris, appellants, v. McDonald's Corporation and McDonald's Restaurants Ltd., respondents: judgment (as approved by the Court) / handed down transcript of Smith Bernal Reporting Limited. — At head of title: In the Supreme Court of Judicature, in the Court of Appeal (Civil Division), on appeal from the Queen's Bench Division (the Hon. Mr. Justice Bell), before Lord Justice Pill, Lord Justice May, Mr. Justice Keene

For an opinion of a judge, record the person, persons, body, or bodies on the opposing side.

Bourn, George Osborn, 1809–1859
Brown, Wm. W. (William W.)
Chaffee, Edwin M.

Authorized access points representing the defendants for: Opinion of Judge Pitman in the case of Charles Goodyear et al. vs. Bourn, Brown et al. : in the Circuit Court of the United States, Rhode Island District, November term, 1856. — "A bill in equity has been filed in this court in the name of Charles Goodyear and others against George O. Bourn, Wm. W. Brown and Edwin M. Chaffee, charging them with a violation of a patent granted to Charles Goodyear"—Page 3

Hall, Levi W.
Gould, Anthony, 1802?–1858
Gould, William, 1772–1846
Banks, David, 1786–1871
Banks, David, Jr.

Authorized access points representing the defendants for: Opinion of the Hon. Alfred Conkling, District Judge of the United States for the Northern District of New York, sitting in the Circuit Court of the United States : upon the question of copyright in manuscripts, in the case of Little and company against Hall, Goulds, and Banks, respecting the fourth volume of Comstock's reports. — "Edwin C. Little & Oliver Scoville vs. Levi W. Hall, Anthony Gould, William Gould, David Banks and David Banks, Jr."—Page 3

19.3.2.10 Judge

For a charge to a jury, record the judge delivering the charge. Apply the basic instructions on recording other persons, families, and corporate bodies associated with a work at **19.3.1**.

Westbrook, Theodoric R., died 1885

Authorized access point representing the judge delivering the charge for: The charge to the jury and the sentence by Judge Theodoric R. Westbrook in the case of Hilaire Latrimouille / reported by James M. Ruso, court stenographer

Sprague, Peleg, 1756–1800

Authorized access point representing the judge delivering the charge for: William Johnson vs. James E. Root : suit for violation of the plaintiff's patent for sewing machines, by sale of a machine containing his feeding mechanism : charge of Hon. Peleg Sprague, district judge, to the jury / phonographic report by James M. Pomeroy. — At head of title: Circuit Court of the United States, District of Massachusetts

Potter, Henry, 1766–1857

Authorized access point representing the judge delivering the charge for: The charge of Judge Potter to the jury in the suit of the devisees of the Earl Granville against Josiah Collins in the Circuit Court of the United States, December term, 1805 as it appeared in the Raleigh register, Jan. 20 & 27, 1806

19.3.2.11 Parties to a Case

For a brief, plea, or other formal record of one party to a case, record the parties to the case. Apply the basic instructions on recording other persons, families, and corporate bodies associated with a work at **19.3.1**.

Morewood, George B.
Morewood, John Rowland, 1821–1903
Routh, Frederic R.
Enequist, Lorenzo N.
Authorized access points representing the parties to the case for: George B. Morewood, John R. Morewood, Frederic R. Routh, respondents, appellants versus Lorenzo N. Enequist, libellant, appellee : brief for appellants on admiralty jurisdiction / Robert Dodge, attorney for appellants. — At head of title: Supreme Court of the United States, no. 132

For a courtroom argument presented by a lawyer, record the party represented. Do not apply this instruction for cases prosecuted by the jurisdiction.

Stanford, Leland, 1824–1893
Authorized access point representing the defendant represented by the courtroom argument for: In the Superior Court of the county of Sonoma, state of California, Ellen M. Colton, plaintiff, vs. Leland Stanford et al., defendants : argument of Mr. Cohen on behalf of the defendants

19.3.2.12 Lawyer Representing a Party

For a brief, plea, or other formal record of one party to a case, record the lawyer representing the party. Apply the basic instructions on recording other persons, families, and corporate bodies associated with a work at **19.3.1**.

Belli, Melvin M., 1907–1996
Authorized access point for the lawyer submitting the brief for: Jack Ruby, appellant vs. the state of Texas, appellee : amicus curiae brief for Jack Ruby, defendant and appellant / Melvin M. Belli, Sr. — At head of title: In the Court of Criminal Appeals of the state of Texas

For a courtroom argument presented by a lawyer, record the lawyer.

Gowen, Franklin B. (Franklin Benjamin), 1836–1889
Authorized access point representing the lawyer for: Argument of Franklin B. Gowen, Esq., of counsel for the Commonwealth in the case of the Commonwealth vs. Thomas Munley, indicted in the Court of Oyer and Terminer of Schuylkill County, Pa., for the murder of Thomas Sanger, a mining boss, at Raven Run, on September 1st, 1875 / stenographically reported by R.A. West

Cohen, Alfred A. (Alfred Andrew), 1829–1887
Authorized access point representing the lawyer for: In the Superior Court of the county of Sonoma, state of California, Ellen M. Colton, plaintiff, vs. Leland Stanford et al., defendants : argument of Mr. Cohen on behalf of the defendants

19.3.2.13 Participants in a Treaty

For a treaty, record the governments or other corporate bodies participating in the treaty as signatories, ratifiers, etc. Apply the basic instructions on recording other persons, families, and corporate bodies associated with a work at **19.3.1**.

Great Britain
France
Spain

Portugal

Authorized access points representing the participants in a treaty for: The Definitive Treaty of Peace and Friendship between His Britannick Majesty, the Most Christian King, and the King of Spain : concluded at Paris, the 10th day of February, 1763 : to which the King of Portugal acceded on the same day. *The participants are Great Britain, France, Spain, and Portugal*

Iceland
World Bank

Authorized access points representing the participants in a treaty for: Guarantee agreement, Second Agricultural Project, between Republic of Iceland and International Bank for Reconstruction and Development

United Nations
International Civil Aviation Organization

Authorized access points representing the participants in a treaty for: Agreement between the United Nations and the International Civil Aviation Organization

Asian Development Bank
North-West Frontier Province (Pakistan)

Authorized access points representing the participants in a treaty for: Project Agreement (Forestry Sector Project) between Asian Development Bank and North-West Frontier Province

World Bank
Corporación de Fomento de la Producción (Chile)
Compañía Manufacturera de Papeles y Cartones

Authorized access points representing the participants in a treaty for: Loan Agreement, (Paper and Pulp Project) between International Bank for Reconstruction and Development and Corporación de Fomento de la Producción and Compañía Manufacturera de Papeles y Cartones

19.3.3 Other Person, Family, or Corporate Body Associated with a Religious Work

CORE ELEMENT

*Other person, family, or corporate body associated with a work is a core element if the access point representing that person, family, or corporate body is used to construct the authorized access point representing the work (see **6.30**).*

19.3.3.1 Application

The instructions at **19.3.3.2** apply to theological creeds, confessions of faith, etc., accepted by one or more denominational bodies.

The instructions at **19.3.3.3–19.3.3.4** apply to:

a) officially sanctioned or traditionally accepted texts of religious observance

b) books containing obligatory prayers used at stated times (including the Liturgy of the hours, Divine office, etc.)

c) calendars and manuals for the performance of religious observances

d) readings from sacred scripture intended for use in a religious service

e) prayer books known as “books of hours.”

For works in the following categories, apply the basic instructions on recording creators at **19.2**:

a) works intended for private devotions (other than “books of hours”)

b) compilations of hymns for congregations and choirs

c) proposals for orders of worship that are not officially approved

d) unofficial manuals

e) programs of religious services

f) lectionaries without scriptural texts.

For other types of religious works, apply the basic instructions on recording other persons, families, and corporate bodies associated with a work at **19.3.1**.

19.3.3.2 Denominational Body Associated with a Creed, Etc.

For a theological creed, confession of faith, etc., accepted by one or more denominational body, record the denominational body or bodies. Apply the basic instructions on recording other persons, families, and corporate bodies associated with a work at **19.3.1**.

Orthodox Presbyterian Church

Authorized access point representing the denominational body associated with a confession of faith and catechisms for: The confession of faith and catechisms : the Westminster Confession of Faith and catechisms as adopted by the Orthodox Presbyterian Church : with proof texts

General Conference Mennonite Church
Mennonite Church

Authorized access points representing the denominational bodies associated with a confession of faith for: Confession of Faith in a Mennonite Perspective. *Adopted at the delegate sessions of the General Conference Mennonite Church and the Mennonite Church, meeting at Wichita, Kansas, July 25–30, 1995*

Catholic Church

Authorized access point representing the denominational body associated with a catechism for: Catechism of the Catholic Church: revised in accordance with the official Latin text promulgated by Pope John Paul II

19.3.3.3 Church or Denominational Body Associated with a Liturgical Work

For a liturgical work, record the church or denominational body associated with it. Apply the basic instructions on recording other persons, families, and corporate bodies associated with a work at **19.3.1**.

United Methodist Church (U.S.)

Authorized access point representing the church associated with the work for: The United Methodist book of worship

Church of England

Authorized access point representing the church associated with the work for: The book of common prayer and administration of the sacraments and other rites and ceremonies of the church, according to the use of the Church of England

Central Conference of American Rabbis

Authorized access point representing the denominational body associated with the work for: A Passover Haggadah : the new Union Haggadah / prepared by the Central Conference of American Rabbis ; edited by Herbert Bronstein ; drawings by Leonard Baskin

Catholic Church

Authorized access point representing the church associated with the work for: Horae diurnae Breviarii Romani ex decreto sacrosancti Concilii Tridentini restituti

Rabbinical Council of America

Authorized access point representing the denominational body associated with the work for: The ArtScroll Rabbinical Council of America Sabbath and festival Siddur = סדור בית רנוב : שבת, שלוש רגלים / a new translation and anthologized commentary by Nosson Scherman ; co-edited by Meir Zlotowitz ; designed by Sheah Brander

United Lutheran Church in America

Authorized access point representing the church associated with the work for: Common service book of the Lutheran church / authorized by the United Lutheran Church in America

Church of England

Authorized access point representing the church associated with the work for: The coronation service of Her Majesty Queen Elizabeth II

Catholic Church

Authorized access point representing the church associated with the work for: Epistles and Gospels for Sundays and holy days / prepared, with the addition of brief exegetical notes, by the Catholic Biblical Association of America

Episcopal Church

Authorized access point representing the church associated with the work for: Proper lessons for the Sundays and holy days throughout the year. — Caption title: Lessons of the Protestant Episcopal Church

Catholic Church

Authorized access point representing the church associated with the work for: The liber usualis : with introduction and rubrics in English / edited by the Benedictines of Solesmes

Catholic Church

Authorized access point representing the church associated with the work for: The restored Holy Week liturgy : practical arrangement of the prescribed music for the average church choir / by Carlo Rossini

Orthodox Eastern Church

Authorized access point representing the church associated with the work for: The Menaion / translated from Greek by the Holy Transfiguration Monastery

Orthodoxos Ekklēsia tēs Hellados

Authorized access point representing the church associated with the work for: The Gospel lectionary : the Evangelion of the Greek Orthodox Church according to the King James Version, emended and arranged for the liturgical year

Catholic Church

Authorized access point representing the church associated with the work for: Sacramentary for celebrations proper to the Society of Jesus / edited by Martin D. O'Keefe

Church of England

Authorized access point representing the church associated with the work for: The communion in Coventry Cathedral. *A liturgical work*

19.3.3.4 Body within a Church, Etc., Associated with a Liturgical Work

If the work is associated with a particular body within the church (e.g., a diocese, cathedral, monastery, religious order), record that body. Apply the basic instructions on recording other persons, families, and corporate bodies associated with a work at **19.3.1**.

Jesuits

Authorized access point representing the particular body associated with the work for: Sacramentary for celebrations proper to the Society of Jesus / edited by Martin D. O'Keefe

Cyprus (Archdiocese)

Authorized access point representing the particular body associated with the work for: Hēmerologion Ekklēsias Kyprou : typikē diataxis Hierōn Akolouthiōn, 1997. *A liturgical calendar*

Catholic Church. Maronite Patriarchate of Antioch (Syria)

Authorized access point representing the particular body associated with the work for: Official text of the divine liturgy according to the Maronite Antiochene Church / translated by the Maronite Seminary and revised by the Maronite Chancery Office

United Hebrew Congregations of the Commonwealth

Authorized access point representing the particular body associated with the work for: The authorised daily prayer book of the United Hebrew Congregations of the Commonwealth / original translation by Simeon Singer ; with a new translation and commentary by Sir Jonathan Sacks

Coventry Cathedral

Authorized access point representing the particular body associated with the work for: The communion in Coventry Cathedral. *A liturgical work*

Temple Emanuel (Grand Rapids, Mich.)

Authorized access point representing the particular body associated with the work for: Temple Emanuel High Holy Day prayer book / Albert M. Lewis, editor

20

PERSONS, FAMILIES, AND CORPORATE BODIES ASSOCIATED WITH AN EXPRESSION

20.0 Purpose and Scope

This chapter provides general guidelines and instructions on recording relationships to persons, families, and corporate bodies associated with an expression (e.g., editors, translators, illustrators, performers).

20.1 General Guidelines on Recording Persons, Families, and Corporate Bodies Associated with an Expression

20.1.1 Sources of Information

Take information on persons, families, and corporate bodies associated with an expression from statements appearing on the preferred sources of information (see **2.2.2**) in resources embodying the expression.

If those statements are ambiguous or insufficient, use the following sources of information, in order of preference:

a) other statements appearing prominently in the resources

b) information appearing only in the content of the resources (e.g., the text of a book, the sound content of an audio recording)

c) other sources.

For instructions on recording changes in responsibility for multipart monographs, serials, and integrating resources, see **18.4.2**.

20.1.2 Recording Persons, Families, and Corporate Bodies Associated with an Expression

Record the persons, families, and corporate bodies associated with the expression as instructed at **20.2**.

If:

the resource being described is an aggregate resource containing two or more expressions

and

each of the expressions is associated with different persons, families, or corporate bodies

then:

record the persons, families, and corporate bodies associated with each of the expressions (see **20.2**).

20.2 Contributor

20.2.1 Basic Instructions on Recording Contributors

20.2.1.1 Scope

A ***contributor*** is a person, family, or corporate body contributing to an expression.

Contributors include editors, translators, arrangers of music, performers, etc.

For instructions on recording relationships to persons, families, or corporate bodies responsible for compilations of data, information, etc., that result in new works, see **19.2.1**.

In some cases, an expression consists of a primary work accompanied by commentary, etc., illustrations, additional musical parts, etc. When this occurs, the writers of commentary, etc., illustrators, composers of additional parts, etc., are considered to be contributors.

20.2.1.2 Sources of Information

Take information on contributors from the sources specified at **20.1.1**.

20.2.1.3 Recording Contributors

Record a contributor by applying the general guidelines on recording relationships to persons, families, and corporate bodies associated with a resource (see **18.4**).

Editor, Compiler, Etc.

Borchardt, Julian, 1868–1932

Authorized access point representing the editor for: The people's Marx : abridged popular edition of the three volumes of Capital / edited by Julian Borchardt ; translated by Stephen L. Trask

Blackwell, David D.
Richards, Maria C.

Authorized access points representing the editors for: Geothermal map of North America / North American map editors, David D. Blackwell and Maria C. Richards ; map production by the Kansas Geological Survey

Goss, Charles Mayo, born 1899

Authorized access point representing the editor for: Anatomy of the human body / by Henry Gray. — 25th edition / edited by Charles Mayo Goss

Committee on Women's Studies in Asia

Authorized access point representing the editor for: Changing lives : life stories of Asian pioneers in women's studies / edited by the Committee on Women's Studies in Asia ; foreword by Florence Howe

Arneil, Barbara
Deveaux, Monique
Dhamoon, Rita, 1970–
Eisenberg, Avigail I., 1962–

Authorized access points representing the editors for: Sexual justice/cultural justice : critical perspectives in political theory and practice / edited by Barbara Arneil, Monique Deveaux, Rita Dhamoon and Avigail Eisenberg

Jonas, Wayne B.

Authorized access point representing the editor for: Mosby's dictionary of complementary and alternative medicine / editorial consultant, Wayne B. Jonas

Atlas, Allan W.

Authorized access point representing the editor for: Music in the classic period : essays in honor of Barry S. Brook / [edited by] Allan W. Atlas

Payne, Claire
Bowker, James M.
Reed, Patrick C.

Authorized access points representing the editors of compilation for: The economic value of wilderness : proceedings of the conference, Jackson, Wyoming, May 8–11, 1991 / compilers, Claire Payne, J.M. Bowker, Patrick C. Reed

Dionne, René, 1929–

Authorized access point representing the editor of compilation for: Anthologie de la littérature franco-ontarienne des origines à nos jours / [compilé par] René Dionne

Rousset, Jean

Authorized access point representing the editor of compilation for: Anthologie de la poésie baroque française / textes choisis et présentés par Jean Rousset

Perigault de Ortíz, Tilsia

Authorized access point representing the editor of compilation for: Colección de rimas infantiles / [seleccionada por] Tilsia Perigault

Richardson, James D. (James Daniel), 1843–1914

Authorized access point representing the editor of compilation for: A compilation of the messages and papers of the Presidents, 1789–1902 / by James D. Richardson

Momigliano, Eucardio, born 1888

Authorized access point representing the editor of compilation for: Tutte le encicliche dei sommi pontefici / raccolte e annotate da Eucardio Momigliano

Harmonizer

Stevens, William Arnold, 1839–1910
Burton, Ernest DeWitt, 1856–1925

Authorized access points representing the harmonizers for: A harmony of the Gospels for historical study : an analytical synopsis of the four Gospels / by Wm. Arnold Stevens and Ernest DeWitt Burton

Swanson, Reuben J.

Authorized access point representing the harmonizer for: The horizontal line synopsis of the Gospels / Reuben J. Swanson

Ponsonby, Reginald G. (Reginald Gordon)

Authorized access point representing the harmonizer for: The life of Our Lord / compiled from the Gospels of the four Evangelists and presented in the very words of the Scriptures as one continuous narrative by Reginald G. Ponsonby ; with a preface by Sir Wilfred Grenfell

Writer of Added Commentary, Etc.

Whiston, Robert

Authorized access point representing the writer of added commentary for: Demosthenes : with an English commentary / by Robert Whiston

Bellinger, Carl-Hermann, 1935–

Authorized access point representing the writer of added commentary for: Wohnungsbindungsgesetz : Textausgabe mit Verwaltungsvorschriften des Landes Nordrhein-Westfalen und Kommentar / von Carl-Hermann Bellinger

Burian, Peter, 1943–

Authorized access point representing the writer of added commentary for: Ion / Euripides ; translated by W.S. Di Piero ; introduction, notes, and commentary by Peter Burian

Cobb, Margaret G.

Authorized access point representing the writer of added commentary for: Debussy's letters to Inghelbrecht : the story of a musical friendship / annotated by Margaret G. Cobb ; translations by Richard Miller

Feaster, Patrick, 1971–
Giovannoni, David

Authorized access points representing the writers of added commentary for: Actionable offenses : indecent phonograph recordings from the 1890s. — Program, historical, and biographical notes, with discographical information and bibliographical references, and transcripts of the performances, all in English, by Patrick Feaster and David Giovannoni (58 pages : illustrations (some coloured), portraits) inserted in container. *A compact disc compilation of bawdy and scurrilous comedy routines and recitations recorded between 1892 and 1900*

Lambourne, Nigel, 1919–

Authorized access point representing the writer of added commentary for: Renoir : paintings, drawings, lithographs, and etchings / selected and introduced by Nigel Lambourne

Bayes, Walter (Walter John), 1869–1956

Authorized access point representing the writer of added commentary for: The landscapes of George Frederick Watts. *Author of commentary, Walter Bayes, named in contents list*

Wynberg, Simon, 1955–

Authorized access point representing the writer of added commentary for: Concert works for guitar / Giulio Regondi ; in reprints of the first editions with historical notes and a commentary by Simon Wynberg. *A score*

Del Mar, Jonathan

Authorized access point representing the writer of added commentary for: Concerto for violoncello and orchestra in E minor, op. 85 : Royal College of Music London MS 402 / Edward Elgar ; introduction by Jonathan Del Mar ; foreword by Steven Isserlis. *A manuscript score facsimile*

Composer of Added Accompaniment, Etc.

Kelley, Daniel

Authorized access point representing the composer of additional music for: Syrinx : for flute and piano : flute solo / Claude Debussy ; with piano accompaniment by Daniel Kelley

Pilati, Mario, 1903–1938

Authorized access point representing the composer of additional music for: Caprices, op. 1 / Paganini ; with piano accompaniment by Mario Pilati

Schumann, Robert, 1810–1856

Authorized access point representing the composer of additional music for: Sechs Sonaten für Violine solo / von Joh. Seb. Bach ; herausgegeben von J. Hellmesberger ; Klavierbegleitung von Robert Schumann

Abramson, Robert M.

Authorized access point representing the composer of incidental music for: The Countess Cathleen / by W.B. Yeats ; incidental music composed by Robert M. Abramson. *An audio recording of a performance of the play*

Illustrator

Irving, James Gordon

Authorized access point representing the illustrator for: Birds : a guide to the most familiar American birds / by Herbert S. Zim and Ira N. Gabrielson ; illustrated by James Gordon Irving

Dulac, Edmund, 1882–1953

Authorized access point representing the illustrator for: Stories from the Arabian nights / retold by Laurence Housman ; with drawings by Edmund Dulac

Bishop, Nic, 1955–

Authorized access point representing the illustrator for: Red-eyed tree frog / story by Joy Cowley ; illustrated with photographs by Nic Bishop

Chadwick, Paxton

Authorized access point representing the illustrator for: British butterflies / by E.B. Ford ; with 16 colour plates by Paxton Chadwick

Weir, Harrison, 1824–1906
Greenaway, John, 1816–1890

Authorized access points representing the illustrators for: Three hundred and fifty Aesop's fables / literally translated from the Greek by Geo. Fyler Townsend ; with one hundred and fourteen illustrations, designed by Harrison Wier, and engraved by J. Greenaway

Nature Photographers Ltd.

Authorized access point representing the illustrator for: Field guide to the trees of Britain, Europe, and North America / Andrew Cleave ; photographs by Nature Photographers Ltd.

Translator

Edmonds, Rosemary

Authorized access point representing the translator for: Fathers and sons / Ivan Turgenev ; translated by Rosemary Edmonds

Kapari, Jaana, 1955–

Authorized access point representing the translator for: Harry Potter ja Azkabanin vanki / J.K. Rowling ; suomentanut Jaana Kapari

Heaney, Seamus, 1939–

Authorized access point representing the translator for: Beowulf : a new verse translation / Seamus Heaney

Cruse, Mark
Hoogenboom, Hilde

Authorized access points representing the translators for: The memoirs of Catherine the Great / a new translation by Mark Cruse and Hilde Hoogenboom

Buddhist Text Translation Society

Authorized access point representing the translator for: Relatos sobre la vida del venerable maestro Hsuan Hua / compilado por la Bhikṣuṇī Heng Yin ; traducido al español por la Sociedad de Traducción de Textos Budistas

Lauzières, Achille de
Louis, D.

Authorized access points representing the translators for: Carmen : opéra en 4 actes / de Henri Meilhac et Ludovic Halévy ; musique de Georges Bizet ; traduction italienne de A. de Lauzières ; traduction allemande de D. Louis. *A vocal score*

Brunse, Niels

Authorized access points representing the translator for: Les misérables / musical af Alan Boubil og Claude-Michel Schönberg ; tekst, Herbert Kretzmer ; oversættelse, Niels Brunse. *An audio recording of the musical, performed in Danish translation from the original French*

Taverner, Richard, 1505?–1575
Jacobs, Henry Eyster, 1844–1932

Authorized access points representing the translator and editor for: The Augsburg Confession / translated from the Latin, in 1536, by Richard Taverner ; with variations of the English translations, directly or indirectly dependent thereon ; edited for the use of the Joint Committee of the General Council, the General Synod, and the United Synod of the South, charged with the preparation of a revised translation, by Henry E. Jacobs

Arranger, Transcriber, Etc., of Music

Price, Florence, 1887–1953

Authorized access point representing the arranger of music for: Peter go ring dem bells : Negro spiritual / arranged by Florence B. Price

Trinkaus, George J., 1878–1960

Authorized access point representing the arranger of music for: Divertimento, op. 12, no. 2 / L. van Beethoven ; transcribed for woodwind by George J. Trinkaus

Berlioz, Hector, 1803–1869

Authorized access point representing the arranger of music for: Aufforderung zum Tanz : Rondo brillant für das Pianoforte, op. 65 / by Carl Maria von Weber ; arranged for orchestra by Hector Berlioz

Performer

Baez, Joan

Authorized access point representing the performer for: Any day now : Bob Dylan's songs / sung by Joan Baez

Ruiz, Adrian, 1937–

Authorized access point representing the performer for: Adrian Ruiz plays Niels Gade and Christian Sinding

Dion, Céline
Anastacia, 1968–
Cher, 1946–

Shakira
Dixie Chicks (Musical group)
Nicks, Stevie

Authorized access points representing the performers for: Divas Las Vegas : a concert to benefit the VH1 Save the Music Foundation. *Songs by various composers performed by Celine Dion, Anastacia, Cher, Shakira, Dixie Chicks, and Stevie Nicks*

Chieftains

Authorized access point representing the performer for: Bonaparte's retreat. *Folk tunes and songs by various composers performed by the band The Chieftains*

Blind Boys of Alabama

Authorized access point representing the performer for: If I had a hammer / Blind Boys of Alabama. *Traditional soul gospel music performed by the group The Blind Boys of Alabama*

St. Paul Chamber Orchestra
Davies, Dennis Russell

Authorized access points representing the performers for: Sinfonia in G minor, op. 6, no. 6 / Johann Christian Bach. Symphony in G / Michael Haydn. Cassation in D, K. 62a / Wolfgang Amadeus Mozart. *All performed by the Saint Paul Chamber Orchestra, conducted by Dennis Russell Davies*

Kubelík, Rafael, 1914–1996
Chicago Symphony Orchestra
Dorati, Antal
Minneapolis Symphony Orchestra

Authorized access points representing the performers for: Concerto grosso no. 1 : for string orchestra with piano obbligato / Bloch. Spirituals : for string choir and orchestra / Gould. *First work performed by Rafael Kubelík conducting the Chicago Symphony Orchestra. Second work performed by Antal Dorati conducting the Minneapolis Symphony Orchestra*

Mikulaš, Peter, 1954–
Slovenská filharmónia. Zbor
Symfonický orchester Čs. rozhlasu v Bratislave
Slovák, Ladislav, 1919–1999

Authorized access points representing the performers for: Symphony no. 13 : "Babi Yar" / Shostakovich. *Performed by Peter Mikulaš, bass; Slovak Philharmonic Chorus; Czecho-Slovak Radio Symphony Orchestra (Bratislava); Ladislav Slovák, conductor*

Edmonton Symphony Orchestra
Mayer, Uri, 1946–

Authorized access points representing the performers for: Orchestral suites of the British Isles. *Works by various composers performed by the Edmonton Symphony Orchestra, conducted by Uri Mayer*

Thigpen, Lynne

Authorized access point representing the performer for: The bluest eye / by Toni Morrison. *An audiobook narrated by Lynne Thigpen*

Sarandon, Susan, 1946–

Authorized access point representing the performer for: Dying to be thin / a Nova production by Twin Cities Public Television, Inc. for WGBH/Boston ; written, produced, and directed by Larkin McPhee. — Narrator, Susan Sarandon

Koppel, Ted, 1940 February 8–

Authorized access point representing the performer for: Gay rights, marriage, and the Supreme Court / ABC News Productions. — Hosted by Ted Koppel

Kermit, the Frog
Whitmire, Steve, 1959–

Authorized access points representing the performers for: One frog can make a difference : Kermit's guide to life in the '90s / by Kermit the Frog, as told to Robert P. Riger ; read by Kermit the Frog ; sound effects by Tom Keith. *An audiobook; voice of Kermit the Frog by Steve Whitmire*

Streep, Meryl
Chieftains

Authorized access points representing the performers for: Meryl Streep reads The tailor of Gloucester / written by Beatrix Potter ; music by the Chieftains

Ledger, Heath, 1979–2008
Gyllenhaal, Jake, 1980–
Cardellini, Linda, 1975–
Faris, Anna, 1976–
Hathaway, Anne, 1982–
Williams, Michelle, 1980–
Quaid, Randy, 1953–

Authorized access points representing the performers for: Brokeback Mountain / Focus Features and River Road Entertainment ; directed by Ang Lee ; screenplay by Larry McMurtry & Diana Ossana ; producers, Diana Ossana, James Schamus. — Cast: Heath Ledger, Jake Gyllenhaal, Linda Cardellini, Anna Faris, Anne Hathaway, Michelle Williams, Randy Quaid. *The particular access points recorded reflect choices made by the agency creating the data*

Court Reporter

Manning, James, 1803–1896
Granger, Thomas Colpitts, died 1852
Scott, John, 1803–1896

Authorized access points representing the court reporters for: Common bench reports : cases argued and determined in the Court of Common Pleas / [reported] by James Manning, T.C. Granger, and John Scott. *Cited as Manning, Granger & Scott*

Bosanquet, John Bernard, 1773–1847
Puller, Christopher, 1774–1824

Authorized access points representing the court reporters for: Reports of cases argued and determined in the Courts of Common Pleas, and Exchequer Chamber, and in the House of Lords / by John Bernard Bosanquet and Christopher Puller

Ruso, James M.

Authorized access point representing the court reporter for: The charge to the jury and the sentence by Judge Theodoric R. Westbrook in the case of Hilaire Latrimouille / reported by James M. Ruso, court stenographer

Pomeroy, James M. (James Morgarum), 1836–1887

Authorized access point representing the court reporter for: William Johnson vs. James E. Root : suit for violation of the plaintiff's patent for sewing machines, by sale of a machine containing his feeding mechanism : charge of Hon. Peleg Sprague, district judge, to the jury / phonographic report by James M. Pomeroy. — At head of title: Circuit Court of the United States, District of Massachusetts

Compiler of Laws

Lumley, W. G. (William Golden), 1802–1878
Lumley, Edmund

Authorized access points representing the editors of compilation for: The public health acts / annotated by William Golden Lumley and Edmund Lumley

Compiler of Regulations, Etc.

National Insurance Law Service

Authorized access point representing the editor of compilation for: Michigan related regulations / compiled by National Insurance Law Service

Shoemaker, Alan H.
Vehrs, Kristin L.

Authorized access points representing the editors of compilation for: AAZPA manual of federal wildlife regulations. — Contents: v. 1. Protected species / compiled by Alan H. Shoemaker — v. 2. Laws and regulations / compiled by Kristin L. Vehrs

Compiler of Treaties

Bevans, Charles I. (Charles Irving), 1908–1986

Authorized access point representing the editor of compilation for: Treaties and other international agreements of the United States of America, 1776–1949 / compiled under the direction of Charles I. Bevans

Rengger, N. J. (Nicholas J.)
Campbell, John (John R. E.)

Authorized access points representing the editors of compilation for: Treaties and alliances of the world / [compiled by] N.J. Rengger with John Campbell

Compiler of Court Rules

West Publishing Company

Authorized access point representing the editor of compilation for: West's California rules of court, 1975, state and federal : with amendments received for January 1, 1975. — St. Paul, Minnesota : West Publishing Co. *The rules apply to numerous state and federal courts in California; the state rules are promulgated by the California Judicial Council*

Compiler of Court Reports, Etc.

Hayes, Robert A. (Robert Alexander), 1942–

Authorized access point representing the editor of compilation for: Australian law reports : being reports of judgments of the High Court of Australia and the Judicial Committee of the Privy Council and of state supreme courts exercising federal jurisdiction, other federal courts and tribunals, together with selected cases from the Supreme Court of the Northern Territory and reports of the Supreme Court of the Australian Capital Territory (authorized by the judges) / editor, Robert Hayes. *The report for each case signed by its reporter*

Phillips, Richard H. (Richard Henry), 1890–1971

Authorized access point representing the editor of compilation for: Connecticut digest, 1785 to date : Kirby to volume 129 inclusive ... / by Richard H. Phillips

Michie, A. Hewson (Addinell Hewson), born 1897

Authorized access point representing the editor of compilation for: Michie's digest of Virginia and West Virginia reports : being a complete encyclopedia and digest of all the Virginia and West Virginia case law up to and including volume 151 Virginia reports and volume 105 West Virginia reports : also federal cases decided pursuant to and including volume 22F (2d) / under the editorial supervision of A. Hewson Michie

Other Contributor

Albanese, Denise
Haselkom, Anne M.
Gross, Janet S. (Janet Sussman), 1944–
Pauley, Caren A. (Caren Altchek)

Authorized access points representing the other contributors for: The instruction of a Christen woman / Juan Luis Vives ; coordinating editors, Virginia Walcott Beauchamp, Elizabeth H. Hageman, and Margaret Mikesell ; contributing editors, Sheila Ffolliott and Betty S. Travitsky ; other contributors, Denise Albanese, Anne M. Haselkorn, Janet S. Gross, and Caren A. Pauley

Feistner, Kelly
Halverson, Janet
Yunag, Lori
Matheson, Greg
Dee, David
Delinski, George
Warren, Alden

Authorized access points representing the other contributors for: South Florida Everglades : satellite image map / U.S. Department of the Interior, U.S. Geological Survey ; authors: John W. Jones, Jean-Claude Thomas and Gregory B. Desmond ; other contributors: Kelly Feistner, Janet Halverson, Lori Yunag, Greg Matheson, David Dee, George Delinski, Alden Warren

Russotto, Ellen

Authorized access point representing the other contributor for: Esteban Vicente / by Elizabeth Frank ; chronology and appendices by Ellen Russotto

Daugherty, Ruth A.

Authorized access point representing the other contributor for: John Wesley : holiness of heart & life / Charles Yrigoyen, Jr. ; with study guide by Ruth A. Daugherty

Isserlis, Steven, 1958–

Authorized access point representing the other contributor for: Concerto for violoncello and orchestra in E minor, op. 85 : Royal College of Music London MS 402 / Edward Elgar ; introduction by Jonathan Del Mar ; foreword by Steven Isserlis. *A facsimile of a manuscript score*

United States. Embassy (Greece). Foreign Commercial Service
United States. Embassy (Greece). Economic Section

Authorized access point representing the other contributors for: Marketing in Greece / prepared by Ann Corro ; with contributions by the Foreign Commercial Service and the Economic Section of U.S. Embassy, Athens

Society of Canadian Ornithologists

Authorized access point representing the other contributor for: Directory of Canadian ornithologists = Répertoire des ornithologistes canadiens. — Gatineau, QC : Environment Canada, [2000]– — "Compiled by the Migratory Birds Conservation Division of the Canadian Wildlife Service of Environment Canada, with assistance from the Society of Canadian Ornithologists"—English home page. *A website*

Ballinger, Laura
Peroni, Geraldine
Tichenor, Dylan
Santaolalla, Gustavo
Allen, Marit
Becker, Judy

Authorized access points representing the other contributors for: Brokeback Mountain / Focus Features and River Road Entertainment ; directed by Ang Lee ; screenplay by Larry McMurtry & Diana Ossana ; producers, Diana Ossana, James Schamus. — Credits: Director of photography, Rodrigo Prieto ; art director, Laura Ballinger ; editors, Geraldine Peroni, Dylan Tichenor ; music, Gustavo Santaolalla ; costume designer, Marit Allen ; production designer, Judy Becker. *The particular access points recorded reflect choices made by the agency creating the data*

21

PERSONS, FAMILIES, AND CORPORATE BODIES ASSOCIATED WITH A MANIFESTATION

21.0 Purpose and Scope

This chapter provides general guidelines and instructions on recording relationships to persons, families, and corporate bodies associated with a manifestation (e.g., producers, publishers, distributors, manufacturers).

21.1 General Guidelines on Recording Persons, Families, and Corporate Bodies Associated with a Manifestation

21.1.1 Sources of Information

Take information on persons, families, and corporate bodies associated with a manifestation from statements appearing on the preferred source of information (see **2.2.2**) in the resource being described.

If those statements are ambiguous or insufficient, use the following sources of information, in order of preference:

a) other statements appearing prominently in the resource

b) information appearing only in the content of the resource (e.g., the text of a book, the sound content of an audio recording)

c) other sources.

For instructions on recording changes in responsibility for multipart monographs, serials, and integrating resources, see **18.4.2**.

21.1.2 Recording Persons, Families, and Corporate Bodies Associated with a Manifestation

Record the persons, families, and corporate bodies associated with the manifestation by applying the following instructions, as applicable:

producer of an unpublished resource (see **21.2**)
publisher (see **21.3**)
distributor (see **21.4**)
manufacturer (see **21.5**)
other person, family, or corporate body associated with a manifestation (see **21.6**).

If:

the resource being described is an aggregate resource containing two or more manifestations

and

each of the manifestations is associated with different persons, families, or corporate bodies

then:

record the persons, families, and corporate bodies associated with each of the manifestations (see **21.2–21.6**).

21.2 Producer of an Unpublished Resource

21.2.1 Basic Instructions on Recording Producers of Unpublished Resources

21.2.1.1 Scope

A ***producer of an unpublished resource*** is a person, family, or corporate body responsible for inscribing, fabricating, constructing, etc., a resource in an unpublished form.

21.2.1.2 Sources of Information

Take information on producers of unpublished resources from the sources specified at **21.1.1**.

21.2.1.3 Recording Producers of Unpublished Resources

Record a producer of an unpublished resource, if considered important for access. Apply the general guidelines on recording relationships to persons, families, and corporate bodies associated with a resource (see **18.4**).

Hitchman, Robert

Authorized access point representing the producer for: Vessels on the Northwest coast between Alaska and California--1543–1811 / J. Neilson Barry. — [Place of production not identified] : Robert Hitchman, 1952. — Typewritten carbon, "copied from Doctor Barry's typescript by Robert Hitchman, April 27, 1952"

Middleton, R. Hunter (Robert Hunter), 1898–1985

Authorized access point representing the producer for: The large water spaniel. — [United States?] : R. Hunter Middleton, [between 1960 and 1969?]. — 1 print : wood engraving, black and white ; 5 x 8 cm, on sheet 11 x 15 cm. *A modern print made by R. Hunter Middleton from a white line wood engraving by Thomas Bewick (1753–1828)*

Edison, Thomas A. (Thomas Alva), 1847–1931

Authorized access point representing the producer for: Annabella / produced by Thomas A. Edison. — [United States?] : Thomas A. Edison, 1897. *An early motion picture*

Grainger, Percy, 1882–1961
Cross, Burnett

Authorized access points representing the producers for: Sliding pipe free music invention / Percy Grainger, Burnett Cross. — [Place of production not identified] : Percy Grainger : Burnett Cross, 1946. *An experimental musical instrument*

Weequahic High School (Newark, N.J.)

Authorized access points representing the producer for: Bookends made with bricks from the house in which Stephen Crane was born / prepared by industrial arts students in Weequahic High School, Newark, New Jersey. — [Newark, New Jersey?] : Industrial Arts Students in Weequahic High School, [1940?]. — "These bookends were constructed from bricks taken from the house in which Stephen Crane was born, 14 Mulberry Place, Newark, N.J., at its demolition in October, 1940"—Inscription

21.3 Publisher

21.3.1 Basic Instructions on Recording Publishers

21.3.1.1 Scope

A ***publisher*** is a person, family, or corporate body responsible for publishing, releasing, or issuing a resource.

21.3.1.2 Sources of Information

Take information on publishers from the sources specified at **21.1.1**.

21.3.1.3 Recording Publishers

Record a publisher, if considered important for access. Apply the general guidelines on recording relationships to persons, families, and corporate bodies associated with a resource (see **18.4**).

Northern Prairie Wildlife Research Center

Authorized access point representing the publisher for: Tiger beetles of the United States / coordinated by W. Wyatt Hoback and John J. Riggins. — Jamestown, ND : Northern Prairie Wildlife Research Center, [2001]– . *An updating website*

American Association of Petroleum Geologists

Authorized access point representing the publisher for: Geothermal map of North America / North American map editors, David D. Blackwell and Maria C. Richards ; map production by the Kansas Geological Survey. — Tulsa, OK : American Association of Petroleum Geologists, 2004. *A wall map*

Sizemore Enterprises

Authorized access point representing the publisher for: Stanwood area and Camano Island street map. — Sedro-Woolley, Washington : Published by Sizemore Enterprises in conjunction with the Stanwood & Camano Island Chambers of Commerce, [2003]

Chard, Thomas, died 1624

Authorized access point representing the publisher for: A very fruitfull exposition of the commaundements by way of questions and answeres for greater plainnesse : together with an application of euery one to the soule and conscience of man : profitable for all, and especially for them that (beeing not otherwise furnished) are yet desirous both to see themselues and to deliuer to others some larger speech of euerie point that is but briefely named in the shorter catechismes / by Geruase Babington ; whereunto is newely annexed a table, conteyning the principall matters in this booke. — At London : Printed by Henrie Midleton for Thomas Charde, 1586

Kelmscott Press

Authorized access point representing the publisher for: The poetical works of Percy Bysshe Shelley. — Hammersmith : Kelmscott Press, 1895

Farmhouse Press

Authorized access point representing the publisher for: A train / Jim Koss. — Seattle : Farmhouse Press, [1996]. *A one-of-a-kind artist's book*

Women's Studio Workshop
Paradise Press

Authorized access points representing the publishers for: The Queen of Wands : a paper sculpture / Susan E. King. — Rosendale, NY : Women's Studio Workshop ; Santa Monica, CA : Paradise Press, [1993] (Rochester, New York : Printed offset by Paul Muhly at Visual Studies Workshop Press, [date of manufacture not identified]). *A paper construction issued in a plastic envelope with two cards that have publication information and instructions for operating*

Milton Bradley Company

Authorized access point representing the publisher for: Scrabble crossword game. — Deluxe edition. — Springfield, MA : Milton Bradley Company, [1989] *A board game*

Currier & Ives

Authorized access point representing the publisher for: Woodcock shooting / from nature and on stone by F.F. Palmer ; lith. of N. Currier N.Y. — New York : Currier & Ives, [1852] *A lithograph*

Australian National Parks and Wildlife Service

Authorized access point representing the publisher for: Australian macropods. — Canberra, ACT : Produced by Australian National Parks and Wildlife Service, [1985]. *Set of four posters; the Service is the publisher*

21.4 Distributor

21.4.1 Basic Instructions on Recording Distributors

21.4.1.1 Scope

A ***distributor*** is a person, family, or corporate body responsible for distributing a resource.

21.4.1.2 Sources of Information

Take information on distributors from the sources specified at **21.1.1**.

21.4.1.3 Recording Distributors

Record a distributor, if considered important for access. Apply the general guidelines on recording relationships to persons, families, and corporate bodies associated with a resource (see **18.4**).

Genius Entertainment

Authorized access point representing the distributor for: This film is not yet rated / IFC presents in association with Netflix and BBC ; a Chain Camera production ; produced by Eddie Schmidt ; directed by Kirby Dick. — [United States?] : [publisher not identified], [2007] ; Santa Monica, CA : Distributed by Genius Entertainment, [2007]. *A motion picture released on DVD*

Health Edco, Inc.

Authorized access point representing the distributor for: Detailed ear model. — [Hamburg, Germany] : 3B Scientific, 2000 ; Waco, TX : Distributed by Health Edco, [date of distribution not identified]. *An anatomical model*

Murray the Map Man (Firm)

Authorized access point representing the distributor for: Street map of Everett & vicinity. — San Francisco, CA : North American Maps, [1978] ; Belmont, CA : Murray the Map Man [distributor], [date of distribution not identified]

21.5 Manufacturer

21.5.1 Basic Instructions on Recording Manufacturers

21.5.1.1 Scope

A ***manufacturer*** is a person, family, or corporate body responsible for printing, duplicating, casting, etc., a resource in a published form.

21.5.1.2 Sources of Information

Take information on manufacturers from the sources specified at **21.1.1**.

21.5.1.3 Recording Manufacturers

Record a manufacturer, if considered important for access. Apply the general guidelines on recording relationships to persons, families, and corporate bodies associated with a resource (see **18.4**).

Columbia Music Video (Firm)

Authorized access point representing the manufacturer for: The blues, a musical journey / Vulcan Productions and Road Movies Production in association with Cappa Productions & Jigsaw Productions ; series producer, Alex Gibney. — New York : Sony Music Entertainment, [2003] ([Place of manufacture not identified] : Manufactured by Columbia Music Video, [date of manufacture not identified]). *A set of seven DVDs*

Middleton, Henry, died 1587

Authorized access point representing the printer for: A very fruitfull exposition of the commaundements by way of questions and answeres for greater plainnesse : together with an application of euery one to the soule and conscience of man : profitable for all, and especially for them that (beeing not otherwise furnished) are yet desirous both to see themselues and to deliuer to others some larger speech of euerie point that is but briefely named in the shorter catechismes / by Geruase Babington ; whereunto is newely annexed a table, conteyning the principall matters in this booke. — At London : Printed by Henrie Midleton for Thomas Charde, 1586

Worde, Wynkyn de, died 1534?

Authorized access point representing the printer for: Here begynneth the lyf of Saint Katherin of Senis the Blessid Virgin. — [Place of publication not identified] : [publisher not identified], [date of publication not identified] (Emprynted at Westemynster : By Wynkyn de Worde, [1492?])

Grabhorn Press

Authorized access point representing the printer for: San Francisco, old & new / written by Marion Brown and pictured by Jean Williamson. — [Place of publication not identified] : [publisher not identified], [date of publication not identified] (San Francisco : Printed by the Grabhorn Press, 1939)

Muhly, Paul
Visual Studies Workshop. Press

Authorized access points representing the printers for: The Queen of Wands : a paper sculpture / Susan E. King. — Rosendale, NY : Women's Studio Workshop ; Santa Monica, CA : Paradise Press, [1993] (Rochester, New York : Printed offset by Paul Muhly at Visual Studies Workshop Press, [date of manufacture not identified]). *A paper construction issued in a plastic envelope with two cards that have publication information and instructions for operating*

Heliotype Printing Co.

Authorized access point representing the printer for: Central Virginia / from the map prepared by authority of the Hon. Secretary of War ; under the direction of A.A. Humphreys, Chief of Engineers, U.S.A. ; by N. Michler, Major of Engineers. — [United States] : [publisher not identified], [1870s?] (Boston : Heliotype Printing Co., [date of manufacture not identified])

21.6 Other Person, Family, or Corporate Body Associated with a Manifestation

21.6.1 Basic Instructions on Recording Other Persons, Families, and Corporate Bodies Associated with a Manifestation

21.6.1.1 Scope

Other person, family, or corporate body associated with a manifestation is a person, family, or corporate body other than a producer, publisher, distributor, or manufacturer associated with a manifestation.

Other persons, families, or corporate bodies associated with a manifestation include book designers, platemakers, etc.

21.6.1.2 Sources of Information

Take information on other persons, families, and corporate bodies associated with a manifestation from the sources specified at **21.1.1**.

21.6.1.3 Recording Other Persons, Families, and Corporate Bodies Associated with a Manifestation

Record other persons, families, and corporate bodies associated with the manifestation, if considered important for access. Apply the general guidelines on recording relationships to persons, families, and corporate bodies associated with a resource (see **18.4**).

Vignelli, Massimo

Authorized access point representing the book designer for: The architecture of Ulrich Franzen : selected works / text by Peter Blake ; foreword by George Weissman ; project descriptions by Ulrich Franzen ; book design by Massimo Vignelli. — Basel ; Boston : Birkhäuser, 1999

Currier, Nathaniel, 1813–1888

Authorized access point representing the lithographer for: Woodcock shooting / from nature and on stone by F.F. Palmer ; lith. of N. Currier N.Y. — New York : Currier & Ives, [1852]. *A lithograph*

Thompson, Edmund, 1897–1974
Hawthorne House (Firm)
Meridien Gravure Company

Authorized access points representing the other persons and corporate bodies associated with the manifestation for: Specimens of printing types / by John Baskerville ; in facsimile with a bibliographical note by Paul Alcorn. — Connecticut : The Columbiad Club, 1939. — "Of one hundred copies issued, seventy are offered for sale ... The collotype plates are by the Meridien Gravure Company, typography by Edmund Thompson at Hawthorne House"

American Printing House for the Blind (Louisville, Ky.)
Authorized access point representing the braille embosser for: Red book on work incentives : a summary guide to social security and supplemental security income work incentives for people with disabilities / developed by Social Security Administration, Office of Disability, Office of Supplemental Security Income. — [Baltimore, Maryland?] : Social Security Administration, 1998. — "Embossed by American Printing House for the Blind, Louisville, Kentucky"

22

PERSONS, FAMILIES, AND CORPORATE BODIES ASSOCIATED WITH AN ITEM

22.0 Purpose and Scope

This chapter provides general guidelines and instructions on recording relationships to persons, families, and corporate bodies associated with an item (e.g., owners, custodians).

22.1 General Guidelines on Recording Persons, Families, and Corporate Bodies Associated with an Item

22.1.1 Sources of Information

Take information on persons, families, and corporate bodies associated with an item from any source.

22.1.2 Recording Persons, Families, and Corporate Bodies Associated with an Item

Record the persons, families, and corporate bodies associated with the item by applying the following instructions, as applicable:

owner (see **22.2**)

custodian (see **22.3**)

other person, family, or corporate body associated with an item (see **22.4**).

If:

the resource being described is an aggregate resource containing two or more items

and

each of the items is associated with different persons, families, or corporate bodies

then:

record the persons, families, and corporate bodies associated with each of the items (see **22.2–22.4**).

22.2 Owner

22.2.1 Basic Instructions on Recording Owners

22.2.1.1 Scope

An ***owner*** is a person, family, or corporate body having legal possession of an item.

22.2.1.2 Sources of Information

Take information on owners from the sources specified at **22.1.1**.

22.2.1.3 Recording Owners

Record an owner, if considered important for access. Apply the general guidelines on recording relationships to persons, families, and corporate bodies associated with a resource (see **18.4**).

> Ebenezer Reformed Church (Holland, Mich.)
>
> *Authorized access point representing the depositor for:* Ebenezer Reformed Church records, 1867–1979. — [Holland, Michigan] : Ebenezer Reformed Church, 1867–1979. — Ownership retained by Ebenezer Reformed Church. Joint Archives of Holland serves as custodian. *An archival collection*

Dickens, Charles, 1812–1870

Authorized access point representing the former owner for: History of the Indian tribes of North America : with biographical sketches and anecdotes of the principal chiefs / embellished with one hundred and twenty portraits, from the Indian Gallery in the Department of War, at Washington ; by Thomas L. M'Kenney and James Hall. — Philadelphia : Edward C. Biddle, 1836–1844. — Library's copy once belonged to Charles Dickens and has his personal bookplate and a label that reads: "From the Library of Charles Dickens, Gadshill Place, June 1870." *A three-volume set of books*

Roethke, Theodore, 1908–1963

Authorized access point representing the former owner for: Friday's child / by Wilfred Watson. — London : Faber and Faber, 1955. — This copy belonged to Theodore Roethke and is signed by him on the title page. Roethke has also made a correction to the text on the inside front dust jacket

Grolier Club. Library

Authorized access point representing the former owner for: The other house / by Henry James. — London : William Heinemann, 1896. — This copy once in the Grolier Club Library and has their bookplate

Kissinger, Henry, 1923–

Authorized access point representing the donor for: Palatinatvs Bavariæ. — [Amsterdam] : Apud Ioannem Ianssonium, [between 1660 and 1669?]. — Donated by Henry Kissinger, former Secretary of State. Mr. Kissinger received the map as a gift from the Federal Republic of Germany

22.3 Custodian

22.3.1 Basic Instructions on Recording Custodians

22.3.1.1 Scope

A ***custodian*** is a person, family, or corporate body having legal custody of an item.

22.3.1.2 Sources of Information

Take information on custodians from the sources specified at **22.1.1**.

22.3.1.3 Recording Custodians

Record a custodian, if considered important for access. Apply the general guidelines on recording relationships to persons, families, and corporate bodies associated with a resource (see **18.4**).

Owens, Virginia Ronzio

Authorized access point representing the former custodian for: Gilpin tram, Black Hawk, iron mill. — [Place of production not identified] : [producer not identified], [1898]. *A photoprint, originally collected by Richard A. Ronzio and maintained by Virginia Ronzio Owens, estate trustee. Purchased by Jefferson County Public Library, September, 1996*

Joint Archives of Holland

Authorized access point representing the custodian for: Ebenezer Reformed Church records, 1867–1979. — [Holland, Michigan] : Ebenezer Reformed Church, 1867–1979. — Ownership retained by Ebenezer Reformed Church. Joint Archives of Holland serves as custodian. *An archival collection*

22.4 Other Person, Family, or Corporate Body Associated with an Item

22.4.1 Basic Instructions on Recording Other Persons, Families, and Corporate Bodies Associated with an Item

22.4.1.1 Scope

Other person, family, or corporate body associated with an item is a person, family, or corporate body other than an owner or custodian associated with an item.

Other persons, families, or corporate bodies associated with an item include curators, binders, restorationists, etc.

22.4.1.2 Sources of Information

Take information on other persons, families, and corporate bodies associated with an item from the sources specified at **22.1.1**.

22.4.1.3 Recording Other Persons, Families, and Corporate Bodies Associated with an Item

Record other persons, families, and corporate bodies associated with the item, if considered important for access. Apply the general guidelines on recording relationships to persons, families, and corporate bodies associated with a resource (see **18.4**).

Brock, David

Authorized access point representing the binder for: I dream Atget / Susan E. King. — Los Angeles : Paradise Press, 1997. — "Letterpress printed in an edition of seventeen. The paper is Stonehenge, the type is Greeting Monotone. The photographs are Polaroid transfers printed on silk by the artist. The binding is by David Brock in San Diego"—Colophon

Kreger, David J.

Authorized access point representing the collector for: Berlin Wall portion. — [Berlin, Germany] : [producer not identified], [1961?] — Collected by S.Sgt. David J. Kreger at Karl Marx Strasse and Duppel (block W8) during summer 1990

Reitz, Ralph B.

Authorized access point representing the collector for: 100 botanical specimens from Meadville and vicinity / collected and presented to Allegheny College, by Ralph B. Reitz. — [Pennsylvania] : Ralph B. Reitz, [1889]. *One hundred specimens collected from 1887 to 1889, mounted in a scrapbook*

Bakken, Dick, 1941–

Authorized access point representing the dedicatee of item for: The Buddha uproar : poems / by John Tagliabue ; with illustrations by Jacqueline McFarland. — San Francisco : Kayak Press, [1967?]. — One of 1,000 copies printed by George Hitchcock at the Kayak Press. This copy is inscribed by the author and is a presentation copy to poet Dick Bakken

Chapple, Stanley, 1900–1987

Authorized access point representing the dedicatee of item for: The martyred : an opera in two acts and 10 scenes / music and libretto by James Wade (1965–1967) ; Korean version by David Yousun Lee ; based on the novel by Richard E. Kim and the drama by Kim Ki-pal ; special lyrics for Italian song by Valerio Anselmo. — [Seattle, Washington] : J. Wade, ©1968. — Composer's autograph presentation copy to Stanley Chapple. *A vocal score*

Santen, Dirck Jansz van, 1637 or 1638–1708

Authorized access point representing the illuminator for: Helvetiæ, Rhetiæ & Valesiæ cum omnibus finitimis regionibus tabula, vulgo Schweitzerland. — Amstelodami : Apud Joannem Janssonium, [1649]. — Illuminated in gold and watercolor by Dirck Jansz van Santen. *A map*

Ryan, Nolan, 1947–

Authorized access point representing the autographer for: Baseball autographed by Nolan Ryan. — [Place of manufacture not identified] : [manufacturer not identified], [date of manufacture not identified]. — Baseball autographed by Nolan Ryan in black ink. Awarded to the Cornette Library as first place winners in the First Annual Chili Challenge held at the West Texas A & M University Baseball Complex on April 13, 1996

23

GENERAL GUIDELINES ON RECORDING THE SUBJECT OF A WORK

[To be developed after the initial release of RDA]

24

GENERAL GUIDELINES ON RECORDING RELATIONSHIPS BETWEEN WORKS, EXPRESSIONS, MANIFESTATIONS, AND ITEMS

24.0 Scope

This chapter provides background information to support the application of guidelines and instructions in chapters **25–28** on recording relationships between works, expressions, manifestations, or items. It includes:

a) an explanation of key terms (see **24.1**)

b) the functional objectives and principles underlying the guidelines and instructions in chapters **25–28** (see **24.2**)

c) the core elements for recording relationships between works, expressions, manifestations, and items (see **24.3**)

d) the use of identifiers, authorized access points, and/or descriptions to record those relationships (see **24.4**)

e) the use of relationship designators to indicate the specific nature of the relationship (see **24.5**)

f) instructions on recording the numbering of a part or parts within a larger work (see **24.6**)

g) instructions on recording elements that provide clarification or justification for the data recorded about relationships:

   i. source consulted to cite sources used in determining the relationships between works, expressions, manifestations, or items (see **24.7**)

   ii. cataloguer's note to assist in the use or revision of the relationship data (see **24.8**).

24.1 Terminology

24.1.1 Explanation of Key Terms

There are a number of terms used in this chapter and in chapters **25–28** that have meanings specific to their use in RDA. Some of these terms are explained at **24.1.2–24.1.5**.

Terms used as data element names in chapters **25–28** are defined at the beginning of the instructions for the specific element. In addition, all terms used in those chapters with a specific technical meaning are defined in the glossary.

24.1.2 Work, Expression, Manifestation, and Item

The terms *work, expression, manifestation,* and *item* are used as follows:

The term ***work*** refers to a distinct intellectual or artistic creation (i.e., the intellectual or artistic content).

The term ***expression*** refers to the intellectual or artistic realization of a work in the form of alpha-numeric, musical, or choreographic notation, sound, image, object, movement, etc., or any combination of such forms.

The term ***manifestation*** refers to the physical embodiment of an expression of a work.

The term *item* refers to a single exemplar or instance of a manifestation.

Each of these terms, depending on what is being described, can refer to individual entities, aggregates, or components of these entities (e.g., the term *work* can refer to an individual work, an aggregate work, or a component of a work).

24.1.3 Related Work, Expression, Manifestation, and Item

The terms *related work, related expression, related manifestation,* and *related item* are used as follows:

The term ***related work*** is a work, represented by an identifier, an authorized access point, or a description, that is related to the work being described (e.g., an adaptation, commentary, supplement, sequel, part of a larger work).

The term ***related expression*** is an expression, represented by an identifier, an authorized access point, or a description, that is related to the expression being described (e.g., a revised version, a translation).

The term ***related manifestation*** is a manifestation, represented by an identifier or a description, that is related to the manifestation being described (e.g., a manifestation in a different format).

The term ***related item*** is an item, represented by an identifier or a description, that is related to the item being described (e.g., an item used as the basis for a microform reproduction).

24.1.4 Access Point

The terms *access point* and *authorized access point* are used as follows:

The term ***access point*** refers to a name, term, code, etc., representing a specific work or expression.

The term ***authorized access point*** refers to the standardized access point representing an entity.

The authorized access point representing a work or expression is constructed by combining (in this order):

a) the authorized access point representing a person, family, or corporate body responsible for the work, if appropriate

b) the preferred title for the work

c) other elements as instructed at **6.27–6.31**.

24.1.5 Relationship Designator

The term ***relationship designator*** refers to a designator that indicates the nature of the relationship between works, expressions, manifestations, or items. A relationship designator is recorded with the authorized access point, identifier, and/or description representing the related work, expression, manifestation, or item.

24.2 Functional Objectives and Principles

The data recorded to reflect relationships between works, expressions, manifestations, and items should enable the user to:

a) *find* works, expressions, manifestations, and items that are related to those represented by the data retrieved in response to the user's search

b) *understand* the relationship between two or more works, expressions, manifestations, or items.

To ensure that the data created using RDA meet those functional objectives, the data should reflect all significant bibliographic relationships between related works, expressions, manifestations, and items.

24.3 Core Elements

The recording of relationships between related works, expressions, manifestations, and items is not required. For the primary relationships, see **17.3**.

24.4 Recording Relationships between Works, Expressions, Manifestations, and Items

Record the relationship between a work, expression, manifestation, or item and a related work, expression, manifestation, or item by using one or more of these techniques, as applicable:

a) identifier for the related work, expression, manifestation, or item (see **24.4.1**)

b) authorized access point representing the related work or expression (see **24.4.2**)
and/or

c) description of the related work, expression, manifestation, or item (see **24.4.3**).

Record an appropriate relationship designator to specify the nature of the relationship (see **24.5**).

Record the numbering of a part within a larger work (see **24.6**) if applicable and if considered important for identification or access.

For guidelines on using the authorized access point representing a related work or expression to generate a *see also* reference, see appendix E (**E.1.3.3**).

24.4.1 Identifier for the Related Work, Expression, Manifestation, or Item

Provide an identifier for the related work, expression, manifestation, or item, by applying the appropriate instructions:

identifier for the work (see **6.8**)

identifier for the expression (see **6.13**)

identifier for the manifestation (see **2.15**)

identifier for the item (see **2.19**).

University of Western Australia law review = ISSN 0042-0328
ISSN provided in conjunction with the key title for a related resource

ISBN 978-1-74146-163-3
ISBN for a related manifestation

urn-3:RAD.ARCH:15009
Resource identifier for a related resource

24.4.2 Authorized Access Point Representing the Related Work or Expression

Provide an authorized access point representing the related work or expression, by applying the appropriate instructions:

authorized access point representing a work or part of a work (see **6.27.1–6.27.2**)

authorized access point representing an expression (see **6.27.3**).

Shakespeare, William, 1564–1616. Taming of the shrew

TEIC quarterly seismological bulletin

Connecticut Commission on Children. Annual report (2005)

Goncourt, Edmond de, 1822–1896. Frères Zemganno. English

24.4.3 Description of the Related Work, Expression, Manifestation, or Item

Provide a description of the related work, expression, manifestation, or item by using either a structured or an unstructured description, as appropriate:

a structured description (i.e., a full or partial description of the related resource using the same data that would be recorded in RDA elements for a description of that related resource). Present the data in the order specified by a recognized display standard (e.g., ISBD presentation (see appendix **D.1**)).

an unstructured description (i.e., a full or partial description of the related resource written as a sentence or paragraph).

Structured Description

Reprint of: Venice / by Cecil Roth. — Philadelphia : The Jewish Publication Society of America, 1930. — (Jewish communities series)

Verse adaptation: Harshacarita gāthā : mahākāvya / Śarada Miśra. — 1. saṃskaraṇa. — Śahaḍola : Racanā Prakāśana, [2000]

Supplement: Forbes ASAP. — New York, NY : Forbes, 1992–2001. — Absorbed by: Forbes, September 2001

Filmed with: Russkie skazki Vostochnoĭ Sibiri / sbornik Aleksandra Gurevicha. — Irkutsk : Ogiz, 1939

Facsimile of: 2nd edition, revised. — London : Routledge, 1877
Partial description of the related resource

Unstructured Description

Reprint of the revised and updated edition published in 1971 by Farrar, Straus & Giroux

Original letters in the collection of the Watkinson Library, Trinity College, Hartford, Connecticut

Related materials providing visual documentation of racially segregated facilities may be found in the following collections in this repository: Birmingfind Project Photographs and Common Bonds Project Photographs

Filmed with three other titles

Activities are based on the book How the brain learns, by David A. Sousa, 3rd edition, 2006

Motion picture films and sound and video recordings transferred to Library of Congress Motion Picture, Broadcasting and Recorded Sound Division

Continues in part: Journal de physique; and replaces the supplement to Journal de physique called: Revue de physique appliquée

24.5 Relationship Designator

24.5.1 Basic Instructions on Recording Relationship Designators

24.5.1.1 Scope

A ***relationship designator*** refers to a designator that indicates the nature of the relationship between works, expressions, manifestations, or items. A relationship designator is recorded with the authorized access point, identifier, and/or description representing the related work, expression, manifestation, or item.

The defined scope of a relationship element provides a general indication of the relationship between works, expressions, manifestations, or items (e.g., related work, related item). Relationship designators provide more specific information about the nature of the relationship (e.g., parody of, facsimile of).

24.5.1.2 Sources of Information

Take information on the nature of the relationship between related works, expressions, manifestations, or items from any source.

24.5.1.3 Recording Relationship Designators

Record an appropriate term from the list in appendix **J** to indicate the specific nature of the relationship between related works, expressions, manifestations, or items.

continued by

Resource described: Annual law review / University of Western Australia. *Relationship designator recorded in conjunction with an identifier for* University of Western Australia law review, *the successor to* Annual law review

motion picture adaptation of

Resource described: 10 things I hate about you / Touchstone Pictures presents a Mad Chance/Jaret Entertainment production ; produced by Andrew Lazar ; written by Karen McCullah Lutz & Kirsten Smith ; directed by Gil Junger. *Relationship designator recorded in conjunction with the authorized access point representing Shakespeare's* The taming of the shrew

augmented by

Resource described: Die slavischen und Slavica betreffenden Drucke der Wiener Mechitharisten : ein Beitrag zur Wiener Druck-und zur österreichischen Kulturgeschichte / Günther Wytrzens. — Wien : Verlag der Österreichischen Akademie der Wissenschaften,1985. *Relationship designator recorded in conjunction with a structured description of the related work:* Addenda und Corrigenda zum Buch "Die Slavica der Wiener Mechitharisten-Druckerei" / Günther Wytrzens, Ashot Hovakimian. — Wien : Verlag der Österreichischen Akademie der Wissenschaften, 2001

If none of the terms listed in appendix **J** is appropriate or sufficiently specific, use another concise term indicating the nature of the relationship.

When using an unstructured description, include information about the nature of the relationship as part of the unstructured description.

Based on the author's dissertation (doctoral—University of Helsinki, 2002)

Accompanying disc (Hataklit: CD 9415) includes selections set to music by Gideon Koren and performed by The Brothers and the Sisters

Includes an abridgement of the original text, an adaptation into vernacular English, and discussions of Shakespearean English, character analysis, and performance and production

24.6 Numbering of Part

24.6.1 Basic Instructions on Recording Numbering of Parts

24.6.1.1 Scope

Numbering of part is a designation of the sequencing of a part or parts within a larger work.

Numbering of part may include:

a) a numeral, a letter, any other character, or a combination of these (with or without a caption (volume, number, etc.))
   and/or
b) a chronological designation.

24.6.1.2 Sources of Information

Take information on numbering of parts from any source.

24.6.1.3 Recording Numbering of Parts

Record the numbering of a part or parts as it appears on the source of information. Apply the general guidelines on numbers expressed as numerals or as words at **1.8**. Abbreviate terms used as part of the numbering as instructed in appendix B (**B.5.5**).

> 1
> *Numbering of part within the work:* Central Institute of Indian Languages. CIIL linguistic atlas series
>
> t. 15
> *Numbering of part within the work:* Mémoires de la Société archéologique de Montpellier
>
> AW14
> *Numbering of part within the work:* ArtWorld video series
>
> new series, no. 21
> *Numbering of part within the work:* Synopses of the British fauna
>
> řada D, sv. 7
> *Numbering of part within the work:* Janáček, Leoš, 1854–1928. Works (1978)
>
> 1980, Heft 7/8
> *Numbering of part within the work:* Aus Theorie und Praxis des Films
>
> dai 8-gō
> *Numbering of part within the work:* Kankyōhō Seisaku Gakkai shi
>
> 13 September 1993
> *Numbering of part within the work:* International Court of Justice. Reports of judgments, advisory opinions, and orders
>
> v. 3–5, 11–12
> *Numbering of parts within the work:* Sources and studies for the history of the Americas

24.7 Source Consulted

24.7.1 Basic Instructions on Recording Sources Consulted

24.7.1.1 Scope

A ***source consulted*** is a resource used in determining the relationship between works, expressions, manifestations, or items.

24.7.1.2 Sources of Information

Take information on sources consulted from any source.

24.7.1.3 Recording Sources Consulted

Cite sources used to determine a relationship, followed by a brief statement of the information found.

> Internet movie database, viewed on June 10, 2008 (10 things I hate about you: adaptation of the classic Shakespeare play "The taming of the shrew," set in a modern day high school)
>
> Schoenberg, Arnold. Gurrelieder, ℗1995: booklet, page 7 (The libretto is based on the Gurresange (1868) by Jens Peter Jacobsen; it was translated by Robert Franz Arnold, and set by Schoenberg with some alterations)

Preventing illness among people with coronary heart disease, ©1996, series title page: The prevention & intervention in the community series; formerly The prevention in human services series

ISSN portal, viewed January 13, 2006: Australasian studies in history and philosophy of science, ISSN 0929-6425; continued by Studies in history and philosophy of science (Dordrecht), ISSN 1871-7381

24.8 Cataloguer's Note

24.8.1 Basic Instructions on Making Cataloguer's Notes

24.8.1.1 Scope

A ***cataloguer's note*** is an annotation that might be helpful to those using or revising the relationship data, or creating an authorized access point representing a related work or expression.

24.8.1.2 Sources of Information

Take information for use in cataloguer's notes from any source.

24.8.1.3 Making Cataloguer's Notes

Make any notes that might be helpful to a cataloguer using or revising the relationship data, or creating an authorized access point for a related work or expression.

The words "Vocal works," "Orchestral works," etc., appearing on the container are considered an aid to retail store presentation and not a subseries

Make room for daddy changed its title to The Danny Thomas show for seasons 5–11. Reference sources continue the season numbering of the earlier title, rather than starting back at one

Originally suite for piano, 4 hands; orchestrated by the composer; later new music added by the composer for ballet version

Title fluctuates between Geological Survey professional paper and U.S. Geological Survey professional paper but as of 1300 is more consistently given in latter form; 1299 chosen as cut-off in consultation with U.S. Department of the Interior Library

Cannot determine which Molodai͡a gvardii͡a published in Moscow is related

May be related to: GUM (Series). Storia e documenti. (Title appeared in both forms in 1995)

Possibly related to: Cmd. R.Z. (n 42007388); and to: Cmd. R. ZR. (n 42007389)

Not related to: Technical report series (Tennessee Valley Authority)

Does not appear to be related to the American traveler series published by Renaissance House in Frederick, Colorado

Unable to determine if related to Lippincott's educational guides

25

RELATED WORKS

25.0 Purpose and Scope

This chapter provides general guidelines and instructions on recording relationships between works.

25.1 Related Work

25.1.1 Basic Instructions on Recording Relationships to Related Works

25.1.1.1 Scope

A ***related work*** is a work, represented by an identifier, an authorized access point, or a description, that is related to the work being described (e.g., an adaptation, commentary, supplement, sequel, part of a larger work).

25.1.1.2 Sources of Information

Take information on related works from any source.

25.1.1.3 Recording Relationships to Related Works

Record a relationship to a related work by applying the general guidelines at **24.4**.

Identifier for the Related Work

Paraphrase of: ISWC T-010.304.108-2

Resource described: Triumph : for concert band (1992) / Michael Tippett. — "A paraphrase on music from The mask of time"

Reviewed in: http://www.mrqe.com/lookup?Capote+(2005)

Resource described: Capote / A-Line Pictures/Cooper's Town Productions/Infinity Media production ; produced by Caroline Baron, Michael Ohoven, William Vince ; screenplay by Dan Futterman ; directed by Bennett Miller. *A motion picture. Related work represented in the manifestation identified by the resource identifier*

Finding aid: http://bibpurl.oclc.org/web/14192

Resource described: Andrews, Emery E., 1894–1976. Emery E. Andrews papers, 1925–1969. *Archival collection of papers and related materials. Related work represented in the manifestation identified by the resource identifier*

Supplement: Supplément historique et littéraire de Recherches et débats = ISSN 1273-9901

Resource described: Recherches et débats du Centre catholique des intellectuels français. *Related work represented in the manifestation identified by key title and ISSN*

Supplement to: Novum Testamentum = ISSN 0048-1009

Resource described: Supplements to Novum Testamentum. *Irregular; the augmented work, Novum Testamentum, is quarterly. Related work represented in the manifestation identified by key title and ISSN*

Complemented by: Health technology trends = ISSN 1041-6072

Resource described: Health technology forecast. *An annual; the complemented work is monthly. Related work represented in the manifestation identified by key title and ISSN*

Continues: Arctic & Antarctic regions = ISSN 1043-7479

Resource described: PolarInfo. *An online resource that indexes materials published between 1996 and June 2004; the preceding CD-ROM publication covers materials published between 1972 and 1995. Related work represented in the manifestation identified by key title and ISSN*

Continued by: Tropical ecology = ISSN 0564-3295

Resource described: Bulletin of the International Society for Tropical Ecology. *A semiannual published in 1960; the succeeding semiannual work began in 1961. Related work represented in the manifestation identified by key title and ISSN*

Authorized Access Point Representing the Related Work

Parody of: Tolkien, J. R. R. (John Ronald Reuel), 1892–1973. Lord of the rings

Resource described: Bored of the rings : a parody of J.R.R. Tolkien's The lord of the rings / by Henry N. Beard and Douglas C. Kenney of The Harvard lampoon

Musical variations based on: Mozart, Wolfgang Amadeus, 1756–1791. Don Giovanni. Là ci darem la mano

Resource described: Variationen über Là ci darem la mano : für das Pianoforte mit Begleitung des Orchesters / von Friedrich Chopin. *Based on an aria from Mozart's* Don Giovanni

Libretto based on: Michener, James A. (James Albert), 1907–1997. Tales of the South Pacific

Resource described: South Pacific : a musical play / music by Richard Rodgers ; lyrics by Oscar Hammerstein II ; book by Oscar Hammerstein II and Joshua Logan. *A vocal score; libretto based on James A. Michener's* Tales of the South Pacific

Adaptation of: Healy, G. P. A. (George Peter Alexander), 1813–1894. Abraham Lincoln

Resource described: Abraham Lincoln / Edward V. Bremer. *Portrait of Lincoln, after a painting by G.P.A. Healy*

Remake of: Psycho (Motion picture : 1960)

Resource described: Psycho / Universal Pictures and Imagine Entertainment ; screenplay, Joseph Stefano ; produced by Brian Grazer, Gus Van Sant ; directed by Gus Van Sant. *A shot-for-shot 1998 remake of the 1960 Alfred Hitchcock film*

Motion picture adaptation of: Jonas, George, 1935– . Vengeance

Resource described: Munich / Universal Pictures and Dreamworks Pictures present an Amblin Entertainment-Kennedy/Marshall-Barry Mendel production in association with Alliance Atlantis Communications ; produced by Kathleen Kennedy, Barry Mendel, Steven Spielberg, Colin Wilson ; screenplay by Tony Kushner and Eric Roth ; directed by Steven Spielberg. *Motion picture based on the book* Vengeance *by George Jonas*

Based on: Star trek, Deep Space Nine (Television program)

Resource described: The fallen. *Computer game based on the television series* Star trek, Deep Space Nine

Dramatized as: Gilsenan, Nancy. Judith Guest's Ordinary people

Resource described: Ordinary people / Judith Guest. *A novel*

Screenplay for the motion picture: Hiroshima mon amour (Motion picture)

Resource described: Hiroshima mon amour : scénario et dialogues / Marguerite Duras ; réalisation, Alain Resnais. *A screenplay*

Analysis of: Mozart, Wolfgang Amadeus,1756–1791. Quartets, strings, K. 465, C major

Resource described: Microsoft multimedia Mozart : the Dissonant quartet : an illustrated, interactive musical exploration. *A CD-ROM*

Description of: Swan lake (Choreographic work)

Resource described: Swan lake / Ann Nugent. *A synopsis and history of the ballet*

Commentary in: Tingey, Robert J. Commentary on Schematic geological map of Antarctica, scale 1:10,000,000

Resource described: Schematic geological map of Antarctica : 1991 / Australian Geological Survey Organisation ; compiled by R.J. Tingey. *A map*

Guide: Guide to the microfilm edition of Papers of the NAACP

Resource described: National Association for the Advancement of Colored People. Papers of the NAACP. *Microfilm version of manuscript and typescript originals*

Supplement to: Journal of clinical psychology

Resource described: Archives of the behavioral sciences. *An irregular monographic series; issued as a supplement to the serial,* Journal of clinical psychology

Subseries of: Agriculture handbook (United States. Department of Agriculture)

Resource described: Forest management chemicals. *An annual subseries of the main series,* Agriculture handbook

Contained in: Diptera site

Resource described: The biosystematic database of world Diptera. *A web-based catalogue of scientific names, part of the larger website,* The Diptera site

Contained in: Farquharson, Mary U. Mary U. Farquharson papers, 1875–1982

Resource described: Mary Farquharson papers relating to the incarceration of Japanese Americans during World War II, 1942–1945. *An archival collection; forms part of a larger collection of Farquharson's papers*

In series: Central Institute of Indian Languages. CIIL linguistic atlas series

Resource described: India literacy atlas. *An atlas issued as part of the* CIIL linguistic atlas series

Contains: Davis, Jack, 1917–2000. Dreamers
Contains: Johnson, Eva. Murras
Contains: Walley, Richard. Coordah
Contains: Maza, Bob, 1939–2000. Keepers

Resource described: Plays from Black Australia / Jack Davis, Eva Johnson, Richard Walley, Bob Maza ; with an introduction by Justine Saunders. *An anthology of four plays*

Contains: Bax, Arnold, 1883–1953. Sketches. Dance of wild Irravel
Contains: Bax, Arnold, 1883–1953. Paean; arranged
Contains: Bax, Arnold, 1883–1953. Symphonies, no. 3

Resource described: Dance of wild Irravel ; Paean ; Symphony no. 3 / Sir Arnold Bax. *An audio CD containing performances of three works by Bax*

Contains: Wizard of Oz (Motion picture : 1910)
Contains: Magic cloak of Oz
Contains: His majesty, the Scarecrow of Oz
Contains: Wizard of Oz (Motion picture : 1925)
Contains: Wizard of Oz (Motion picture : 1933)
Contains: Wizard of Oz (Motion picture : 1939)

Resource described: The Wizard of Oz / a Metro-Goldwyn-Mayer picture ; produced by Loew's Incorporated ; screen play by Noel Langley, Florence Ryerson and Edgar Allan Woolf ; produced by Mervyn LeRoy ; directed by Victor Fleming. — Three-disc collector's edition. *A three-disc DVD set of the 1939 motion picture that also includes earlier short and feature-length motion pictures based on the same characters*

Libretto for: Adams, John, 1947– . Nixon in China

Resource described: Nixon in China : an opera in three acts / music by John Adams ; libretto by Alice Goodman. *A separately published libretto*

Index: Cumulative book index

Resource described: The United States catalog. *Supplemented by annual cumulations of* Cumulative book index

Augmented by: Roche, Don. Microsoft Access 2000 bible quick start

Resource described: Microsoft Access 2000 bible / Cary N. Prague and Michael R. Irwin. *Accompanied by* Microsoft Access 2000 bible quick start, *by Don Roche*

Guide to: Fischer, Louis, 1924– . Teachers and the law

Resource described: Instructor's manual to accompany Teachers and the law, fourth edition, Louis Fischer, David Schimmel, Cynthia Kelly / prepared by Max E. Pierson. *An instructor's manual for a textbook*

Index to: Colloquium on the Law of Outer Space. Proceedings

Resource described: Space law : a bibliography : cumulative index of the proceedings of colloquiums of the International Institute of Space Law, 1958–1994 / prepared in cooperation with the International Institute of Space Law (IISL). — New York : United Nations, 1996. *A cumulative index to the Colloquium's* Proceedings

Cadenza composed for: Mozart, Wolfgang Amadeus, 1756–1791. Concertos, flute, orchestra, K. 313, G major

Resource described: Cadenzas for the Flute concerto in G major (K. 313) by Mozart / Georges Barrère. *Flute cadenzas by Barrère for Mozart's concerto*

Incidental music for: Goethe, Johann Wolfgang von, 1749–1832. Egmont

Resource described: Musik zu Goethes Trauerspiel Egmont : op. 84 / Ludwig van Beethoven. *A musical score of Beethoven's incidental music to Goethe's tragedy,* Egmont

Illustrations for: Dante Alighieri, 1265–1321. Divina commedia

Resource described: The Doré illustrations for Dante's Divine comedy : 136 plates / by Gustave Doré. *Reproductions of Doré's wood engravings depicting scenes from Dante's work*

Contains: WONCA news

Resource described: Family practice. *A quarterly periodical that includes a section with title:* WONCA news, *which is published for the World Organization of National Colleges, Academies, and Academic Associations of General Practitioners/Family Physicians*

Continues: Jane's intelligence review pointer

Resource described: Pointer. *A monthly periodical succeeding* Jane's intelligence review pointer

Continues in part: Journal of youth services in libraries

Resource described: Young adult library services. *A quarterly periodical that continues in part the* Journal of youth services in libraries

Continues: Top of the news
Split into: Children & libraries
Split into: Young adult library services

Resource described: Journal of youth services in libraries. *A quarterly periodical that succeeded* Top of the news, *and then later split into* Children & libraries *and* Young adult library services

Separated from: International authors' and writers' who's who

Resource described: International who's who in poetry and poets' encyclopaedia. *Separated from* International authors' and writers' who's who *in 1993/1994*

Absorbed: Curriculum report (Reston, Va.)

Resource described: The high school magazine. *Absorbed the bimonthly* Curriculum report

Motion picture adaptation of: Boulle, Pierre, 1912–1994. Planète des singes
Remade as: Planet of the apes (Motion picture : 2001)

Resource described: Planet of the apes / Apjac Productions and Twentieth Century-Fox presents an Arthur P. Jacobs production ; producer, Arthur P. Jacobs ; director, Franklin Schaffner ; screenplay, Michael Wilson, Rod Serling. *A motion picture adaptation of Pierre Boulle's book* La planète des singes*; the film was remade in 2001*

Sequel to: Planet of the apes (Motion picture : 1968)

Resource described: Beneath the planet of the apes. *Sequel to the 1968 motion picture* Planet of the apes

Continued by: British journal of animal behaviour

Resource described: Bulletin of animal behaviour. *An irregularly issued periodical continued by the quarterly* The British journal of animal behaviour

Absorbed by: Bobbin (Columbia, S.C. : 1987)

Resource described: Apparel industry magazine. *A monthly periodical absorbed in 2001 by the magazine* Bobbin

Sequel: Harris, Edwin. John Jasper's gatehouse

Resource described: The mystery of Edwin Drood / Charles Dickens. *Harris's work is a sequel to Dickens's unfinished last novel*

Prequel to: Exorcist (Motion picture)

Resource described: Dominion : prequel to The exorcist / James G. Robinson presents a Morgan Creek production ; a film by Paul Schrader ; produced by James G. Robinson ; written by William Wisher and Caleb Carr ; directed by Paul Schrader. *A prequel to the 1973 motion picture* The exorcist

Structured Description of the Related Work

Described in: Virginia Woolf : a list of manuscripts. — London : Spencer, 1986

Described in: Sibelius, Symphony no. 5 / James Hepokoski. — Cambridge ; New York : Cambridge University Press, 1993. — (Cambridge music handbooks)

Resource described: Symphony no. 5 in E-flat major, op. 82 / Jean Sibelius. *A score*

Contained in: Acadia early music facsimile archive / Gordon J. Callon (editor). — http://ace.acadiau.ca/score/archive/facsim.htm

Resource described: Louis Moreau Gottschalk / site designed by Michelle E. Keddy. *A website that includes a biography of Gottschalk, a facsimile reproduction of the 1881 Lippincott edition of his journal, and links to other*

sites of interest to Gottschalk scholars. The site is part of the website Acadia early music facsimile archive. *Resource identifier provided in conjunction with a partial description of the related work*

Contains: 'Til death do us plots / by Julianne Bernstein — Class act / by Michael Elkin — Where's your stuff? / by Daniel Brenner — Foot peddler / by Vivian Green — Smoke / by Louis Greenstein — Single Jewish female / by Julianne Bernstein — In spite of everything / by Hindi Brooks — Ger (the convert) / by Leslie B. Gold and Louis Greenstein — Golden opportunity / by Julianne Bernstein — Interview with a scapegoat / by Louis Greenstein

Resource described: Voices from Ariel : ten-minute plays reflecting the Jewish experience : a collection of ten short plays / compiled and edited by Julianne Bernstein and Deborah Baer Mozes. *An anthology of ten-minute plays*

Contains: The woman voter : official organ of the League of Women Voters

Resource described: The woman's journal. *A periodical published 1917–1931; issues for 1922–1931 include* The woman voter

Guide: The Jane Addams papers : a comprehensive guide / Mary Lynn McCree Bryan, editor ; Nancy Slote, associate editor ; Maree de Angury, assistant to the editor

Resource described: Addams, Jane, 1860–1935. The Jane Addams papers, 1860–1960 / Mary Lynn McCree Bryan, editor. *82 microfilm reels of Addams's papers*

Augmented by: A manual on perspective / by Marcel Sedletzky

Resource described: Marcel Sedletzky : architect and teacher / by Bill Staggs. *A critical analysis with accompanying CD-ROM containing Sedletzky's* A manual on perspective

Supplement to: Flammulated, boreal, and great gray owls in the United States : a technical conservation assessment / Gregory D. Hayward, technical editor ; Jon Verner, co-technical editor. — Fort Collins, CO : U.S. Department of Agriculture, Forest Service, Rocky Mountain Forest and Range Experiment Station, 1994. — (USDA Forest Service general technical report RM ; 253)

Resource described: Boreal owl locations and distribution of associated vegetative ecosystems in the United States, 1993. — At head of title: Map 2a (addendum to map 2). *A separately issued map that supplements the second of three maps issued with the book* Flammulated, boreal, and great gray owls in the United States

Supersedes: The action plan for Australian birds / by Stephen Garnett. — Canberra : Australian National Parks and Wildlife Service, 1992

Resource described: The action plan for Australian birds, 2000 / by Stephen T. Garnett and Gabriel M. Crowley. — Canberra, ACT : Environment Australia ; [Hawthorn East, Victoria] : Birds Australia, 2000

Sequel: Scarlett : the sequel to Margaret Mitchell's Gone with the wind / by Alexandra Ripley. — New York, NY : Warner Books, 1991

Resource described: Gone with the wind / by Margaret Mitchell. *A sequel to Mitchell's novel,* Scarlett, *by Alexandra Ripley, was published in 1991*

Unstructured Description of the Related Work

Author's adaptation of his Russian text

Inspired by themes from the music of George Butterworth

A shot-for-shot remake of the 1960 Alfred Hitchcock film of the same name

Resource described: Psycho / Universal Pictures and Imagine Entertainment ; screenplay, Joseph Stefano ; produced by Brian Grazer, Gus Van Sant ; directed by Gus Van Sant

"An exegesis of Mark 11:15:19"

Resource described: God's order vs. the Jewish/Roman social order / by Douglas Cunningham

A collection of material about the play Der gute Mensch von Sezuan; includes several versions of selected scenes from the play

Resource described: Brechts "Guter Mensch von Sezuan" / herausgegeben von Jan Knopf

"As described in: The proposed water quality standards for surface waters of the State of Washington, Chapter 173-201A"—Cover

Resource described: Waters requiring supplemental spawning and incubation protection for salmonid species / prepared by Sabrina Payne. — Revised November 2006

Reviews available on the composer's website

Links to reviews, blogs, and news are available from the Movie review query engine website

Also contains two short prose pieces dated 1937

Contains letters to Mrs. Wells and Gabrielle Gissing

Includes "Travel connections" map of air, rail, bus, and ferry routes, insets of "Ryukyu Islands, 1:2,000,000" and "Okinawa, 1:1,000,000," and 5 city map insets showing places of interest: Sapporo — Kyōto — Tōkyō — Ōsaka — Kōbe

Resource described: Japan. — London : Published by Collins, an imprint of HarperCollins Publishers, [2001]. *A tourist map*

Includes: Bibliography of Northwest materials

Kept up to date between editions by annual supplements

Resource described: Public library catalog / edited by Paula B. Entin and Juliette Yaakov

Accompanied by annual supplements covering: periodicals and series; maps and atlases; and: music, 1982–

Resource described: Bibliographie de Belgique

One issue each year includes: AMWA annual freelance directory

Includes separately paged newsletter: PPO perspectives

Finding aid available in the repository and online

"This cumulative index covers the Quarterly newsletter numbers 1 to 17 (1966–1972), Occasional paper numbers 1 and 2 (1969 & 1970), Garden history volumes 1 to 27 (1972–1999), and Newsletter numbers 1 to 57 (1981–1999)"

Resource described: The Garden History Society cumulative index to the Quarterly newsletters, Garden history, Newsletters & the Occasional papers, 1966–1999

Volumes for 2001–2005 complemented by: Physicians' desk reference companion guide; 2006– by: PDR guide to drug interactions, side effects, and indications

Resource described: Physicians' desk reference for ophthalmic medicines

Mounted on a wooden stand to form a pair with: Bale's new celestial globe. 1845

Merger of: British abstracts. B I, Chemical engineering, fuels, metallurgy, applied electrochemistry, and industrial inorganic chemistry; and: British abstracts. B II, Industrial organic chemistry

Resource described: Journal of applied chemistry

"Updated and expanded version of an original publication by the Great Lakes Planetarium Association, ©1983 and 1999"

Resource described: Tips for excellent planetarium scriptwriting / contributing editor, Steve Tidey

A later state of the map first published in 1715 and later in 1745. This state has the additions of "King's roads" and an advertisement for Overton's large map of the British Isles, dated 1746

Sequel to both the Alien and Predator films

Resource described: AVP : Alien vs. Predator / Twentieth Century Fox presents a Davis Entertainment Company/ Brandywine production ; produced by Gordon Carroll, John Davis, David Giler, Walter Hill, Thierry Potok ; screenplay, Paul W.S. Anderson ; director, Paul W.S. Anderson

Merged with: International legal perspectives, to form: Lewis & Clark law review

Resource described: Journal of small and emerging business law

Split into: Children & libraries; and: Young adult library services
Resource described: Journal of youth services in libraries

Continued by unnumbered monographic series with same title
Resource described: Progress in molecular and subcellular biology

Absorbed in 2002 by: Reference & user services quarterly
Resource described: RUSA update / Reference and User Services Association, a division of the American Library Association. *A quarterly periodical absorbed by* Reference & user services quarterly *in 2002*

Continued in part by: Medical humanities, which split off in June 2000 and assumed volume numbering beginning with volume 26
Resource described: Journal of medical ethics

25.2 Explanation of Relationship

25.2.1 Basic Instructions on Recording Explanations of Relationships

25.2.1.1 Scope

An ***explanation of relationship*** is information elaborating on or clarifying the relationship between related works.

25.2.1.2 Sources of Information

Take information explaining a relationship from any source.

25.2.1.3 Recording Explanations of Relationships

Record an explanation of the relationship between related works if considered important for identification or clarification.

Proust, Marcel, 1871–1922. À la recherche du temps perdu
For the separately published parts of this work, see
Proust, Marcel, 1871–1922. Du côté de chez Swann
Proust, Marcel, 1871–1922. À l'ombre des jeunes filles en fleurs
Proust, Marcel, 1871–1922. Côté de Guermantes
Proust, Marcel, 1871–1922. Sodome et Gomorrhe
Proust, Marcel, 1871–1922. Prisonnière
Proust, Marcel, 1871–1922. Albertine disparue
Proust, Marcel, 1871–1922. Temps retrouvé

For guidelines on presenting an explanation of a relationship as part of an explanatory reference, see appendix E (**E.1.3.4**).

26

RELATED EXPRESSIONS

26.0 Purpose and Scope

This chapter provides general guidelines and instructions on recording relationships between expressions.

26.1 Related Expression

26.1.1 Basic Instructions on Recording Relationships to Related Expressions

26.1.1.1 Scope

A ***related expression*** is an expression, represented by an identifier, an authorized access point, or a description, that is related to the expression being described (e.g., a revised version, a translation).

26.1.1.2 Sources of Information

Take information on related expressions from any source.

26.1.1.3 Recording Relationships to Related Expressions

Record a relationship to a related expression by applying the general guidelines at **24.4**.

Identifier for the Related Expression

Translated as: http://bibpurl.oclc.org/web/14222

Resource described: After Amsterdam : sexual orientation and the European Union : a guide / ILGA-Europe. *Related expressions represented in the manifestation identified by a resource identifier for French, German, Hungarian, Lithuanian, and Spanish translations*

Revised as: Library of Congress control number: no2008127546

Identifier for the 1992 director's cut version of the 1982 motion picture Blade runner

Abridged as: Library of Congress control number: no 91002344

Identifier for the English abridged version of Charles Alexandre de Calonne's Requête au roi

Continued by: Izvestiya. Mathematics = ISSN 1064-5632

Resource described: Mathematics of the USSR. Izvestija. *Related expression represented in the manifestation identified by key title and ISSN*

Authorized Access Point Representing the Related Expression

Revision of: Roget, Peter Mark, 1779–1869. Thesaurus of English words and phrases

Resource described: Roget's Thesaurus of English words and phrases. — New edition / completely revised and modernized by Robert A. Dutch

Expanded version of: Saw, Swee-Hock, 1931– . Population control for zero growth in Singapore

Resource described: Population policies and programmes in Singapore / Saw Swee-Hock

Translation of: Simenon, Georges, 1903–1989. Long cours

Resource described: The long exile / Georges Simenon ; translated from the French by Eileen Ellenbogen

Libretto for: Weill, Kurt, 1900–1950. Die Dreigroschenoper. English

Resource described: The threepenny opera / Bertolt Brecht ; translated by Ralph Manheim and John Willett ; with commentary and notes by Non and Nick Worrall

Revised as: Bauer, Michael D. Linux server security

Resource described: Building secure servers with Linux / Michael D. Bauer

Supplement: Adweek agency directory (Midwestern edition)
Resource described: Adweek. — Midwest edition

Continued by: Izvestii͡a Rossiĭskoĭ Akademii nauk. Serii͡a matematicheskai͡a. English
Resource described: Mathematics of the USSR. Izvestija

Structured Description of the Related Expression

Revision of: Biology of fishes / Carl E. Bond. — Second edition. — Fort Worth : Saunders College Publishing, [1996]
Resource described: Bond's Biology of fishes / Michael Barton. — Third edition — Belmont, CA : Thomson, [2007]

Abridged as: The concise Oxford companion to Irish literature / edited by Robert Welch
Resource described: The Oxford companion to Irish literature / edited by Robert Welch ; assistant editor, Bruce Stewart

Unstructured Description of the Related Expression

Revised and shortened version of the author's thesis (Ph.D.)—Yale University, 1982

Revised edition of Lectures chantées, originally published in 1968

The English edition of a Spanish publication, which is also issued in French, German, and Arabic editions

Recast in bronze from artist's plaster original of 1903

Shorter version of the 1969 motion picture of the same name
Resource described: Walt Whitman's Civil War / Churchill Films ; produced by Magus Films ; produced and directed by Frederic Goodich ; written by Neal Ruben

Issued also in Portuguese as: Air & space power journal em portugues; and in Spanish as: Air & space power journal español
Resource described: Air & space power journal

Also issued in other regional editions: Eastern edition; Midwest edition; New England edition; Southwest edition; and Western edition
Resource described: Adweek. — Southeast edition

Also available in a 45 min. abridged version
Resource described: Inside America's military academies / presented courtesy of the USAA Educational Foundation ; written and directed by Dan Jackson. — Unabridged version

"This concordance is based on Paul de Woestijne's edition of Priscian's Periegesis"—Preface

26.2 Explanation of Relationship

26.2.1 Basic Instructions on Recording Explanations of Relationships

26.2.1.1 Scope

An ***explanation of relationship*** is information elaborating on or clarifying the relationship between related expressions.

26.2.1.2 Sources of Information

Take information explaining a relationship from any source.

26.2.1.3 Recording Explanations of Relationships

Record an explanation of the relationship between related expressions if considered important for identification or clarification.

> Illustrated directory of modern Soviet weapons
> For the separately published parts revised for this compilation, *see*
> Gunston, Bill. Illustrated guide to the modern Soviet Air Force
> Illustrated guide to weapons of the modern Soviet ground forces
> Jordan, John. Illustrated guide to the modern Soviet Navy

For guidelines on presenting an explanation of a relationship as part of an explanatory reference, see appendix E (**E.1.3.4**).

27

RELATED MANIFESTATIONS

27.0 Purpose and Scope

This chapter provides general guidelines and instructions on recording relationships between manifestations.

27.1 Related Manifestation

27.1.1 Basic Instructions on Recording Relationships to Related Manifestations

27.1.1.1 Scope

A ***related manifestation*** is a manifestation, represented by an identifier or a description, that is related to the manifestation being described (e.g., a manifestation in a different format).

27.1.1.2 Sources of Information

Take information on related manifestations from any source.

27.1.1.3 Recording Relationships to Related Manifestations

Record a relationship to a related manifestation by applying the general guidelines at **24.4**.

Identifier for the Related Manifestation

Also issued as: ISBN 978-0-06128-533-2

Resource described: Michael Tolliver lives / Armistead Maupin. — New York : HarperCollins, 2007. *ISBN provided for equivalent manifestation in large print*

Also issued as: Walt Disney Studios Home Entertainment: 5568103

Resource described: Enchanted / Walt Disney Pictures presents a Barry Sonnenfeld/Josephson Entertainment Production ; Andalasia Productions ; produced by Barry Josephson and Barry Sonnenfeld ; written by Bill Kelly ; directed by Kevin Lima. — Walt Disney Studios Home Entertainment: 52391. *Publisher number provided for equivalent manifestation on Blu-ray Disc*

Review of: Docurama: NVG-9830

Identifier for the subject of a DVD review

Reviewed in: SICI 0003-0716(200903/04)72:2>170:MS3<2.0.TX;2-K

Resource described: Symphony no. 3 / Mahler. — London, UK : LSO Live, [2008]. — London Symphony Orchestra ; Valery Gergiev, conductor ; Anna Larsson, alto ; Tiffin Boys' Choir ; Ladies of the London Symphony Chorus. *Serial Item and Contribution Identifier for an audio recording review appearing in* American record guide

Also issued as: Euscorpius (Online) = ISSN 1536-9307

Resource described: Euscorpius : occasional publications in scorpiology. — Huntington, WV : Marshall University, [2001]-. — computer discs ; 12 cm. *A serial issued on CD-ROM. ISSN provided in conjunction with the key title of the equivalent online manifestation*

Inserted in: Canadian theatre review = ISSN 0315-0836

Resource described: The Canadian newsletter / ITI. *A quarterly periodical published as an insert in* Canadian theatre review. *ISSN provided in conjunction with the key title of the related manifestation*

Special issue of: ISSN 0024-4937

Resource described: Granites and migmatites : their temporal, spatial and causal relationships / edited by Carlo Dietl, Friedrich Finger. — Amsterdam : Elsevier, 2008. *A special issue of the journal* Lithos

Special issue of: Art and AsiaPacific = ISSN 1039-3625

Resource described: Art AsiaPacific almanac. — New York : Art AsiaPacific, [2006]-. — Annual special issue of Art and AsiaPacific. *ISSN provided in conjunction with the key title of the related manifestation*

Electronic reproduction: http://hdl.handle.net/2246/4473

Resource described: Adaptive branching of the kangaroo family in relation to habitat / by H.C. Raven and William K. Gregory. — New York City : The American Museum of Natural History, [1946]. — (American Museum novitates ; no. 1309)

Mirror site: http://muse.uq.edu.au/

Resource described: Project MUSE : scholarly journals online. — Baltimore, MD : Johns Hopkins University Press in collaboration with the Milton S. Eisenhower Library, [1995]-. — http://muse.jhu.edu/

Reprint of: ISBN 0-80-523932-4

Resource described: Mountain time : a Yellowstone memoir / Paul Schullery. — Albuquerque : University of New Mexico Press, 2008. — "Reprinted from the original 1984 edition by Nick Lyons/Schocken" — Title page verso

Issued with: ISBN 978-0-7575-4388-3

Resource described: An introduction to the aquatic insects of North America / edited by R.W. Merritt, K.W. Cummins, M.B. Berg. — 4th edition. — Dubuque, Iowa : Kendall/Hunt Publishing Company, [2008]. *ISBN provided for accompanying manifestation:* Interactive key to the aquatic insect orders of North America / R.W. Holzenthal, A.L. Prather, S.A. Marshall

Contains: ISBN 978-1-86969-287-2
Contains: ISBN 978-1-86969-288-9
Contains: ISBN 978-1-86969-289-6
Contains: ISBN 1-86969-282-9

Resource described: Ka mau te wehi! : an introduction to Te Reo Māori. — Wellington, New Zealand : Published for the Ministry of Education by CWA New Media, 2007. *Kit containing 1 teacher's guide, 2 DVDs, and 1 audio CD*

Structured Description of the Related Manifestation

Reprint of: Venice / by Cecil Roth. — Philadelphia : The Jewish Publication Society of America, 1930. — (Jewish communities series)

Resource described: History of the Jews in Venice / Cecil Roth. — New York : Schocken Books, 1975

Contained in: Understanding our environment / NSTA. — Arlington, VA : National Science Teachers Association, [1995]

Resource described: The Earth's fractured surface ; Living on the edge : [West Coast of U.S.] / produced by the Cartographic Division, National Geographic Society ; John F. Shupe, chief cartographer. — Washington, D.C. : National Geographic Society, 1995. *Two maps on one sheet*

Contains: Map of area with highlighted street. — NYDA.1933.010.00130
Contains: View of Mill Brooks Houses from one of the houses, 89/05. — NYDA.1993.010.00131
Contains: View SE from Mill Brook House on rooftop on Cypress Ave. between 136th St. and 137th St., 93/05. — NYDA.1933.010.00132
Contains: View N from 136th St. rooftop of area between Bruckner Expressway and Cypress Ave., 93/06. — NYDA.1933.010.00133
Contains: View E from rooftop of garden bounded by Bruckner Expressway, 136th St. and 135th St., 93/06. — NYDA.1933.010.00134

Resource described: 136th Street, southeastern section of the Bronx. *Set of 11 slides*

Contains: v. 1. Status, distribution, and taxonomy (xvii, 848 pages : 1 map) — v. 2. Field guide (xvii, 740 pages, 96 leaves of plates : illustrations (some coloured), maps (1 coloured))

Resource described: The birds of Ecuador / by Robert S. Ridgely and Paul J. Greenfield ; with the collaboration of Mark B. Robbins and Paul Coopmans ; in association with the Academy of Natural Sciences. — Ithaca, NY : Comstock Publishing, 2001. *A two-volume set*

Filmed with: The Jewish faith : its spiritual consolation, moral guidance, and immortal hope : with a brief notice of the reasons for many of its ordinances and prohibitions : a series of letters answering the inquiries of youth / by Grace Aguilar. — London : Richard Groombridge and Sons, 1846

Resource described: Catalogue sommaire des manuscrits indiens, indo-chinois & malayo-polynésiens / par A. Cabaton. — Paris : Ernest Leroux éditeur, 1912

Facsimile of: A classification and subject index for cataloguing and arranging the books and pamphlets of a library. — Amherst, Mass. : Melvil Dewey, 1876 (Hartford, Conn. : Printed by the Case, Lockwood & Brainard Company, [1876])

Resource described: Dewey decimal classification : centennial 1876–1976. — [Lake Placid?, New York] : Forest Press Division, Lake Placid Education Foundation, [1976]

Electronic reproduction: Boulder, Colorado : NetLibrary, 2007. — Available via World Wide Web. Access may be limited to NetLibrary affiliated libraries. — http://www.netLibrary.com/urlapi.asp?action=summary&v=1&bookid=186297

Partial description of the equivalent manifestation

Reproduced as: Lacey, WA : OCLC Preservation Service Center on behalf of University of Washington Libraries, 2005. — 1 microfilm reel ; 10 cm, 35 mm. — On reel with other titles

Partial description of the equivalent manifestation

Also issued as: Large print edition. — Thorndike, Maine : Center Point Publishing, [2005]

Partial description of the equivalent manifestation

Facsimile of: 2nd edition, revised. — London : Routledge, 1877

Partial description of the equivalent manifestation

Electronic reproduction of: New York : Bettini Phonograph Laboratory, [1898?]. — 1 audio cylinder (2 min., 33 sec.) : analog, 125 rpm, mono ; 2 1/4 x 4 in. — Originally for voice with orchestra. — Title announced at beginning of recording. — Acoustic recording

Partial description of the equivalent manifestation

Contained in: The New Yorker. — Volume 73, number 31 (October 13, 1997)

Resource described: Brokeback Mountain / by Annie Proulx. — pages 74–80, 82–85

Unstructured Description of the Related Manifestation

Also issued electronically via World Wide Web in PDF format

Electronic reproduction of thesis is available through the Theses Canada portal website

Issued also as Super Audio CD

Issued also in Blu-ray Disc format

Reprinted from chapters 1–9 of: Atlas of virtual colonoscopy / Abraham H. Dachman, editor

Annual special issue of Art and AsiaPacific

"Shōwa Sensō zen'ikizu" inserted in volume 2

Offprint from: Indiana Slavic studies, v. 9, 1998

Available also as streaming video in both Windows Media and RealPlayer formats on the Frontline website

Articles reprinted from various journals

Compilation of essays, interviews, and discussions previously published in the webzine Library juice between 1998 and 2005

Also issued as a set of wall charts

Available also through the Library of Congress website as a raster image

Numerous mirror sites available

Includes petition to the King from the citizens of London, 1783, in scroll form

The reporter contains binders: Current developments; Monographs; State solid waste — Land use; Federal laws; Federal regulations; State water laws; State air laws; Mining; Decisions (later published in bound volumes as Environment reporter. Cases)

Filmed with five other titles

Reports for 2000/01 and 2001/02 issued together

"Lịch sử chiến tranh : đính chính" (53 pages ; 20 cm) inserted in pocket

Disc 1 includes feature length commentary by the director, Julia Stiles, and cinematographer, and theatrical trailer; disc 2 includes comprehensive analysis of key basketball scenes, deleted scenes with commentary, and the restored 1922 film: Othello (80 min.) / National Film Museum Incorporated ; Ben Blumenthal presents ; directed by Dimitri Buchowetzki

Resource described: "O" / a Chickie the Cop production in association with Daniel Fried Productions and Rhulen Entertainment ; a film by Tim Blake Nelson ; producers, Eric Gitter, Daniel L. Fried, Anthony Rhulen ; screenplay writer, Brad Kaaya ; director, Tim Blake Nelson. — Deluxe edition. — [United States] : Trimark Home Video : Lions Gate Home Entertainment, [2002]. *Two videodiscs*

Shots: LS through heat haze of jet landing towards camera (20 ft.). CU front view of jet as it taxis towards camera (40 ft.). CU fuselage turning right to left through picture (30 ft.). CU braking parachute as it is discarded (52 ft.). CU nose and engines (57 ft.)

28

RELATED ITEMS

28.0 Purpose and Scope

This chapter provides general guidelines and instructions on recording relationships between items.

28.1 Related Item

28.1.1 Basic Instructions on Recording Relationships to Related Items

28.1.1.1 Scope

A ***related item*** is an item, represented by an identifier or a description, that is related to the item being described (e.g., an item used as the basis for a microform reproduction).

28.1.1.2 Sources of Information

Take information on related items from any source.

28.1.1.3 Recording Relationships to Related Items

Record a relationship to a related item by applying the general guidelines at **24.4**.

Identifier for the Related Item

Facsimile of: Bodleian Library: MS. Junius 11
Accession number provided for related item

Reproduction of: ADM 55/40
Piece number provided for related item held by The National Archives, Kew

Structured Description of the Related Item

Bound with: Report of the Committee on the District of Columbia in relation to the city of Washington : read in Senate, February 2, 1835. — [Washington] : [publisher not identified], [1835] (City of Washington : Printed at the Globe Office, 1835)
Resource described: Memorial of the Committee of the Corporation of Washington : relating to the pecuniary claims of said corporation on the general government, &c. — [Washington] : [publisher not identified], [1835] (Washington : Blair & Rives, [1835]). *Library of Congress copy*

Unstructured Description of the Related Item

Reproduction of original from Harvard Law School Library

Library's copy bound with 11 other songs

Electronic reproduction of more than 9,000 notarial protocols registered in the books of the notaries Joseph Manuel Albarez de Aragón (1701–1743) and Joseph Alvarez (1780–1821)

Library's copy has separately published index bound with each volume

Electronic reproduction of the copy in the National Wetlands Research Center Library

Original letters in the collection of the Watkinson Library, Trinity College, Hartford, Connecticut

29

GENERAL GUIDELINES ON RECORDING RELATIONSHIPS BETWEEN PERSONS, FAMILIES, AND CORPORATE BODIES

29.0 Scope

This chapter provides background information to support the application of guidelines and instructions in chapters **30–32** on recording relationships between a person, family, or corporate body and related persons, families, and corporate bodies. It includes:

a) an explanation of key terms (see **29.1**)

b) the functional objectives and principles underlying the guidelines and instructions in chapters **30–32** (see **29.2**)

c) the core elements for recording relationships between persons, families, and corporate bodies (see **29.3**)

d) the use of identifiers and/or authorized access points to record those relationships (see **29.4**)

e) the use of relationship designators to indicate the specific nature of the relationship (see **29.5**)

f) instructions on recording elements that provide clarification or justification for the data recorded about relationships:

  i. source consulted to cite sources used in determining the relationships between persons, families, or corporate bodies (see **29.6**)

  ii. cataloguer's note to assist in the use or revision of the relationship data (see **29.7**).

29.1 Terminology

29.1.1 Explanation of Key Terms

There are a number of terms used in this chapter and in chapters **30–32** that have meanings specific to their use in RDA. Some of these terms are explained at **29.1.2–29.1.5**.

Terms used as data element names in chapters **30–32** are defined at the beginning of the instructions for the specific element. In addition, all terms used in those chapters with a specific technical meaning are defined in the glossary.

29.1.2 Person, Family, and Corporate Body

The terms *person*, *family*, and *corporate body* are used as follows:

The term ***person*** refers to an individual or an identity established by an individual (either alone or in collaboration with one or more other individuals).

The term ***family*** refers to two or more persons related by birth, marriage, adoption, civil union, or similar legal status, or who otherwise present themselves as a family.

The term ***corporate body*** refers to an organization or group of persons and/or organizations that is identified by a particular name and that acts, or may act, as a unit.

29.1.3 Related Person, Family, and Corporate Body

The terms *related person*, *related family*, and *related corporate body* are used as follows:

The term ***related person*** refers to a person who is associated with the person, family, or corporate body being identified (e.g., a collaborator, a member of a family, a founder of a corporate body). Related persons include separate identities established by an individual (either alone or in collaboration with one or more other individuals).

The term ***related family*** refers to a family that is associated with the person, family, or corporate body being identified (e.g., a person's family, a family that owns the controlling interest in a corporate body).

The term ***related corporate body*** refers to a corporate body that is associated with the person, family, or corporate body being identified (e.g., a musical group to which a person belongs, a subsidiary company). Related corporate bodies include corporate bodies that precede or succeed the corporate body being identified as the result of a change of name.

29.1.4 Access Point

The terms *access point* and *authorized access point* are used as follows:

The term ***access point*** refers to a name, term, code, etc., representing a specific person, family, or corporate body.

The term ***authorized access point*** refers to the standardized access point representing an entity. The authorized access point representing a person, family, or corporate body is constructed using the preferred name for the person, family, or corporate body.

29.1.5 Relationship Designator

The term ***relationship designator*** refers to a designator that indicates the nature of the relationship between persons, families, or corporate bodies. A relationship designator is recorded with the authorized access point and/or identifier representing the related person, family, or corporate body.

29.2 Functional Objectives and Principles

The data recorded to reflect relationships between persons, families, and corporate bodies should enable the user to:

a) *find* persons, families, or corporate bodies that are related to the person, family, or corporate body represented by the data retrieved in response to the user's search

b) *understand* the relationship between two or more persons, families, or corporate bodies.

To ensure that the data created using RDA meet those functional objectives, the data should reflect all significant bibliographic relationships between related persons, families, and corporate bodies.

29.3 Core Elements

The recording of relationships between persons, families, and corporate bodies is not required.

29.4 Recording Relationships between Persons, Families, and Corporate Bodies

Record the relationship between a person, family, or corporate body, and a related person, family, or corporate body by using one or both of these techniques:

a) identifier (see **29.4.1**)
and/or
b) authorized access point (see **29.4.2**).

Record an appropriate relationship designator to specify the nature of the relationship (see **29.5**).

For guidelines on using the authorized access point representing a related person, family, or corporate body to generate a *see also* reference, see Appendix E (**E.1.3.3**).

29.4.1 Identifier for the Related Person, Family, or Corporate Body

Provide an identifier for the related person, family, or corporate body, by applying the applying the appropriate instructions:

identifier for the person (see **9.18**)
identifier for the family (see **10.10**)
identifier for the corporate body (see **11.12**).

Library and Archives Canada control number: 1007F6454
Identifier for Nicholas Blake, alternate identity of C. Day Lewis

Library of Congress control number: n 79065003
Identifier for I.M. Pei, founder of the architectural firm I.M. Pei & Partners

Union List of Artist Names ID: 500114961
Identifier for Medici family, descendants of Lorenzo de' Medici

Library of Congress control number: nr 95008045
Identifier for Newport Jazz Festival, the successor to the American Jazz Festival

29.4.2 Authorized Access Point Representing the Related Person, Family, or Corporate Body

Provide an authorized access point representing the related person, family, or corporate body, by applying the applying the appropriate instructions:

authorized access point representing a person (see **9.19.1**)
authorized access point representing a family (see **10.11.1**)
authorized access point representing a corporate body (see **11.13.1**).

Blake, Nicholas, 1904–1972
Authorized access point representing the alternate identity as a mystery writer of the poet C. Day Lewis

Pei, I. M., 1917–
Authorized access point representing the founder of the architectural firm I.M. Pei & Partners

Medici (Royal house : Medici, Lorenzo de', 1449–1492)
Authorized access point representing the descendants of Lorenzo de' Medici

Newport Jazz Festival
Authorized access point representing the successor to the American Jazz Festival

29.5 Relationship Designator

29.5.1 Basic Instructions on Recording Relationship Designators

29.5.1.1 Scope

A ***relationship designator*** refers to a designator that indicates the nature of the relationship between persons, families, or corporate bodies. A relationship designator is recorded with the authorized access point and/or identifier representing the related person, family, or corporate body.

The defined scope of a relationship element provides a general indication of the relationship between persons, families, or corporate bodies (e.g., related person, related corporate body). Relationship designators provide more specific information about the nature of the relationship (e.g., alternate identity, predecessor).

29.5.1.2 Sources of Information

Take information on the nature of the relationship between related persons, families, or corporate bodies from any source.

29.5.1.3 Recording Relationship Designators

Record an appropriate term from the list in appendix K to indicate the specific nature of the relationship between related persons, families, or corporate bodies.

alternate identity

Relationship designator recorded in conjunction with an identifier for Nicholas Blake, pseudonym of C. Day Lewis

real identity

Relationship designator recorded in conjunction with an identifier for C. Day Lewis

successor

Relationship designator recorded in conjunction with the authorized access point representing Newport Jazz Festival, the successor to the American Jazz Festival

predecessor

Relationship designator recorded in conjunction with the authorized access point representing American Jazz Festival, the predecessor of the Newport Jazz Festival

If none of the terms listed in appendix K is appropriate or sufficiently specific, use another concise term indicating the nature of the relationship.

29.6 Source Consulted

29.6.1 Basic Instructions on Recording Sources Consulted

29.6.1.1 Scope

A ***source consulted*** is a resource used in determining the relationship between persons, families, or corporate bodies.

29.6.1.2 Sources of Information

Take information on sources consulted from any source.

29.6.1.3 Recording Sources Consulted

Cite sources used to determine a relationship, followed by a brief statement of the information found.

Somerville, Wilson. A history of the Department of Anesthesiology, 1942–1997, ©1998: title page (Wake Forest University School of Medicine) page 79 (name changed from Bowman Gray School of Medicine to Wake Forest University School of Medicine in 1997)

Familia de Yan desde 1719 Pagsanjaniaguna, ©2005 page 47: family changed its surname "De La Resurección" to "Yan" in 1849; lived in Pagsanjan, Philippines

Wikipedia, viewed December 2, 2007 (Howard Fast; Howard Melvin Fast (11 November 1914, New York City–12 March 2003, Old Greenwich, Connecticut) was a Jewish American novelist and television writer, who wrote also under the pen names E.V. Cunningham and Walter Ericson)

29.7 Cataloguer's Note

29.7.1 Basic Instructions on Making Cataloguer's Notes

29.7.1.1 Scope

A ***cataloguer's note*** is an annotation that might be helpful to those using or revising the relationship data, or creating an authorized access point representing a related person, family, or corporate body.

29.7.1.2 Sources of Information

Take information for use in cataloguer's notes from any source.

29.7.1.3 Making Cataloguer's Notes

Make any notes that might be helpful to a cataloguer using or revising the relationship data, or creating an authorized access point for a related person, family, or corporate body.

> Pseudonyms of Robert Silverberg not found on published works: Ivor Jorgenson; Walter Drummond; David Osborne
>
> King has written seven novels under the pseudonym Richard Bachman and one short story under the pseudonym John Swithen
>
> Relationship between Count Basie Big Band and Count Basie Orchestra uncertain
>
> Relationship between Robert Shaw Festival Chorus and Robert Shaw Festival Singers unknown
>
> Access point Nationalgalerie (Germany : West) valid for 1949–1991. Resources by and about the museum after the German reunification can be found under the access point: Neue Nationalgalerie (Germany)
>
> Census Office is valid name for U.S. censuses up to and including the twelfth (1900); the thirteenth census (1910) and those subsequent were conducted by the Bureau of the Census
>
> Access point valid for period from 1958 (when established) to March 23, 1972 (when name changed to Defense Advanced Research Projects Agency); also valid from March 15, 1993 to March 11, 1996, when body resumed earlier name
>
> Access point valid from March 23, 1972 (name changed from Advanced Research Projects Agency) to March 15, 1993 when body resumed earlier name, and also valid after March 11, 1996
>
> Do not use Luftwaffe in access points for German air force units prior to 1933; use instead "Germany. Heer. Luftstreitkräfte" to cover the period 1910–1920
>
> Byron Company was established in 1888 in New York City by Joseph Byron, a photographer who had just emigrated from the United Kingdom in that same year. Previously, he had worked for Byron Company, a firm started by his grandfather in Nottingham-on-Trent, England, in 1844. The exact connection between the English and American firms is unknown

30

RELATED PERSONS

30.0 Purpose and Scope

This chapter provides general guidelines and instructions on recording relationships between a person, family, or corporate body and related persons.

30.1 Related Person

30.1.1 Basic Instructions on Recording Relationships to a Related Person

30.1.1.1 Scope

A ***related person*** is a person who is associated with the person, family, or corporate body being identified (e.g., a collaborator, a member of a family, a founder of a corporate body).

Related persons include separate identities established by an individual (either alone or in collaboration with one or more other individuals).

The relationship to the related person is recorded by using an authorized access point and/or identifier representing the related person.

30.1.1.2 Sources of Information

Take information on related persons from any source.

30.1.1.3 Recording Relationships to a Related Person

Record a relationship to a related person by applying the general guidelines at **29.4**.

Identifier for the Related Person

Library of Congress control number: n 79056546
Identifier for Lewis Carroll, the alternate identity established by Charles Lutwidge Dodgson for his literary works

Union List of Artist Names ID: 500017044
Identifier for Titian Ramsay Peale, family member of the Peale family

Library of Congress control number: n 50035608
Identifier for Miles Davis, founder of the Miles Davis Quintet

Library and Archives Canada control number: 1013B3788E
Identifier for Paul Martin, the incumbent of the office of Prime Minister of Canada, 2003–2006

Authorized Access Point Representing the Related Person

Innes, Michael, 1906–1994
Authorized access point representing the alternate identity established by J.I.M. Stewart for his detective novels

Carroll, Lewis, 1832–1898
Authorized access point representing the alternate identity established by Charles Lutwidge Dodgson for his literary works

Dannay, Frederic, 1905–1982
Lee, Manfred B. (Manfred Bennington), 1905–1971
Authorized access points representing the real identities of the individuals who also wrote under the joint pseudonym Ellery Queen

Brutus, Marcus Junius, 85 B.C.?–42 B.C.
Authorized access point representing the person whose name forms part of the appellation for an unknown person identified as Pseudo-Brutus

Peale, Titian Ramsay, 1799–1885
Authorized access point representing a family member of the Peale family

Davis, Miles
Authorized access point representing the founder of the Miles Davis Quintet

Bono, Sonny
Cher, 1946–
Authorized access points representing the group members of the musical group Sonny & Cher

Martin, Paul, 1938–
Authorized access point representing the incumbent of the office of Prime Minister of Canada, 2003–2006

30.2 Explanation of Relationship

30.2.1 Basic Instructions on Recording Explanations of Relationships

30.2.1.1 Scope

An ***explanation of relationship*** is information elaborating on or clarifying the relationship to a related person.

30.2.1.2 Sources of Information

Take information explaining a relationship from any source.

30.2.1.3 Recording Explanations of Relationships

Record an explanation of the relationship to a related person if considered important for identification or clarification.

Greek letters by the person identified as Pseudo-Brutus were erroneously attributed to Marcus Junius Brutus

Real name: Ngô Thế Thái; pseudonym: Thanh Nam

Author wrote picture books under the pseudonym Will, and young adult fiction and a thesis under the name William Lipkind

American architectural firm McKim, Mead & White was formed in 1879 by Charles Follen McKim (1847–1909), William Rutherford Mead (1846–1928), and Stanford White (1853–1906)

For works of this author written under other names, see: Carr, Philippa, 1906–1993; Ford, Elbur, 1906–1993; Holt, Victoria, 1906–1993; Kellow, Kathleen, 1906–1993; Tate, Ellalice, 1906–1993

For guidelines on presenting an explanation of a relationship as part of an explanatory reference, see appendix E (**E.1.3.4**).

31

RELATED FAMILIES

31.0 Purpose and Scope

This chapter provides general guidelines and instructions on recording relationships between a person, family, or corporate body and related families.

31.1 Related Family

31.1.1 Basic Instructions on Recording Relationships to a Related Family

31.1.1.1 Scope

A ***related family*** is a family that is associated with the person, family, or corporate body being identified (e.g., a person's family, a family that owns the controlling interest in a corporate body).

The relationship to the related family is recorded by using an authorized access point and/or identifier representing the related family.

31.1.1.2 Sources of Information

Take information on related families from any source.

31.1.1.3 Recording Relationships to a Related Family

Record a relationship to a related family by applying the general guidelines at **29.4**.

Identifier for the Related Family

Libraries Australia control number: 000035401429

Identifier for the Adey family of Sydney, N.S.W., founding family of the Darling Mills Restaurant

Union List of Artist Names ID: 500092478

Identifier for Duchamp family, a French family of artists whose members include Marcel Duchamp, Suzanne Duchamp, Raymond Duchamp-Villon, and Jacques Villon

Authorized Access Point Representing the Related Family

Adey (Family : Sydney, N.S.W.)

Authorized access point representing the founding family of the Darling Mills Restaurant

Duchamp (Family : France)

Authorized access point representing the family whose members include Marcel Duchamp, Suzanne Duchamp, Raymond Duchamp-Villon, and Jacques Villon

Romanov (Dynasty)

Authorized access point representing the descendants of Peter I, Emperor of Russia

Chola (Dynasty : 850–1279)

Authorized access point representing the descendants of Kulottunga I, Chola King

Wettin (Royal house)

Authorized access point representing the progenitor family of the House of Windsor

McMahon (Family : McMahon, Vince)

Authorized access point representing the founding family of World Wrestling Entertainment, Inc.

31.2 Explanation of Relationship

31.2.1 Basic Instructions on Recording Explanations of Relationships

31.2.1.1 Scope

An ***explanation of relationship*** is information elaborating on or clarifying the relationship to a related family.

31.2.1.2 Sources of Information

Take information explaining a relationship from any source.

31.2.1.3 Recording Explanations of Relationships

Record an explanation of the relationship to a related family if considered important for identification or clarification.

> Pierre Samuel du Pont de Nemours was the progenitor of the du Pont family of Delaware
>
> Charles-Pierre Coustou, a member of the Coustou family of French artists, was architect to King Louis XIV
>
> Marcel Duchamp was the last surviving member of the Duchamp family of artists
>
> As of November 2007, the McMahon family holds approximately 70% of World Wrestling Entertainment, Inc.'s economic interest and 96% of all voting power in the company

For guidelines on presenting an explanation of a relationship as part of an explanatory reference, see appendix E (**E.1.3.4**).

32

RELATED CORPORATE BODIES

32.0 Purpose and Scope

This chapter provides general guidelines and instructions on recording relationships between a person, family, or corporate body and related corporate bodies.

32.1 Related Corporate Body

32.1.1 Basic Instructions on Recording Relationships to a Related Corporate Body

32.1.1.1 Scope

A ***related corporate body*** is a corporate body that is associated with the person, family, or corporate body being identified (e.g., a musical group to which a person belongs, a subsidiary company).

Related corporate bodies include corporate bodies that precede or succeed the corporate body being identified as the result of a change of name.

The relationship to the related corporate body is recorded by using an authorized access point and/or identifier representing the related corporate body.

32.1.1.2 Sources of Information

Take information on related corporate bodies from any source.

32.1.1.3 Recording Relationships to a Related Corporate Body

Record a relationship to a related corporate body by applying the general guidelines at **29.4**.

Identifier for the Related Corporate Body

Library and Archives Canada control number: 1009J7378E
Identifier for CSA Group, the hierarchical superior of Quality Management Institute, CSA International, and Canadian Standards Association

Library of Congress control number: n 85375529
Identifier for College of Surgeons of Australasia, the predecessor to Royal Australasian College of Surgeons

Library of Congress control number: n 85375527
Identifier for Royal Australasian College of Surgeons, the successor to College of Surgeons of Australasia

Union List of Artist Names ID: 500033103
Identifier for I.M. Pei & Partners, the architectural firm founded by I.M. Pei

Library of Congress control number: no2007001419
Identifier for Miles Davis Quartet, the musical group founded by Miles Davis

Library of Congress control number: no 96050543
Identifier for Heinz Family Foundation, the sponsored organization of the Heinz family of Pittsburgh, Pennsylvania

Authorized Access Point Representing the Related Corporate Body

Canadian Standards Association
CSA International

Quality Management Institute
Authorized access points representing the hierarchical subordinates of CSA Group

College of Surgeons of Australasia
Authorized access point representing the predecessor to Royal Australasian College of Surgeons

Royal Australasian College of Surgeons
Authorized access point representing the successor to College of Surgeons of Australasia

Miles Davis Quartet
Authorized access point representing the musical group founded by Miles Davis

Heinz Family Foundation
Authorized access point representing the sponsored organization of the Heinz family of Pittsburgh, Pennsylvania

Lewis and Clark Expedition (1804–1806)
Authorized access point representing the expedition related to its group members, Meriwether Lewis and William Clark

Canada. Prime Minister (2003–2006 : Martin)
Authorized access point representing the government official related to its incumbent Paul Martin

32.2 Explanation of Relationship

32.2.1 Basic Instructions on Recording Explanations of Relationships

32.2.1.1 Scope

An ***explanation of relationship*** is information elaborating on or clarifying the relationship to a related corporate body.

32.2.1.2 Sources of Information

Take information explaining a relationship from any source.

32.2.1.3 Recording Explanations of Relationships

Record an explanation of the relationship to a related corporate body if considered important for identification or clarification.

The National Library of Canada and the National Archives of Canada merged in 2003 to form Library and Archives Canada

The American-Asian Educational Exchange was founded in 1957. In 1962 the name was changed to American Afro-Asian Educational Exchange. In 1967 the name American-Asian Educational Exchange was resumed

William Nicholson and his brother-in-law, James Pryde, adopted the pseudonym Beggarstaff Brothers while collaborating in the 1890s as poster artists

As per the family genealogy committee, the official form of the surname of all of the American descendants of Pierre Samuel du Pont de Nemours is "du Pont" with a space. Some, but not all, institutions founded by family members have since changed the spelling to “duPont” or “DuPont”

For guidelines on presenting an explanation of a relationship as part of an explanatory reference, see appendix E (**E.1.3.4**).

33

GENERAL GUIDELINES ON RECORDING RELATIONSHIPS BETWEEN CONCEPTS, OBJECTS, EVENTS, AND PLACES

[To be developed after the initial release of RDA]

34

RELATED CONCEPTS

[To be developed after the initial release of RDA]

35

RELATED OBJECTS

[To be developed after the initial release of RDA]

36

RELATED EVENTS

[To be developed after the initial release of RDA]

37

RELATED PLACES

[To be developed after the initial release of RDA]

A

CAPITALIZATION

A.0 Scope

This appendix provides guidelines on capitalization for English and a selected number of other languages. The guidelines apply when transcribing or recording specified elements.

When instructed to capitalize in this appendix, the first letter of a word is recorded with a capital letter.

A.1 General Guideline

Unless instructed otherwise at **A.2–A.9**, capitalize words according to the guidelines for the language involved. Record in lower case any words not covered by the guidelines in this appendix.

See **A.10–A.55** for information that applies to the languages included in this appendix. For other languages, consult style manuals that apply to that language.

> *Alternative*
>
> When recording the attributes of a manifestation or item (see chapters **1–4**), the agency creating the data can choose to establish in-house guidelines for capitalization or to choose a published style manual, etc., as its preferred guide (see the alternative at **1.10.2**). When this occurs, use those guidelines or that style manual instead of appendix **A**.

A.2 Names of Persons, Families, Corporate Bodies, and Places

A.2.1 General Guideline

In general, capitalize the first word of each name. Capitalize other words by applying the guidelines at **A.10–A.55**, as applicable to the language involved.

For names with unusual capitalization, follow the capitalization of the commonly known form.

Alexander, of Aphrodisias

De la Mare, Walter

Musset, Alfred de

Cavour, Camillo Benso, conte di

Third Order Regular of St. Francis

Société de chimie physique

Ontario. High Court of Justice

El Greco Society

eBay (Firm)

netViz Corporation

hHead (Musical group)

doctorjob.com

lang, k. d.

A.2.2 Names Beginning with Arabic or Hebrew Articles

If:

a transliterated name begins with the Arabic article *al* in any of its various orthographic forms (e.g., *al, el, es*)

or

a transliterated name begins with the Hebrew article *ha* (*he*)

then:

do not capitalize it, whether it is written separately or hyphenated with the following word.

al-Jumhūrīyah al-Islāmīyah al-Mūrītānīyah

A.2.3 Words or Phrases Characterizing Persons

Capitalize a word, or the substantive words in a phrase characterizing a person and used as a name (see **9.2.2.25–9.2.2.26**) as applicable to the language involved.

Capitalize proper names contained in such a phrase by applying the guidelines at **A.10–A.55**, as applicable to the language involved.

Capitalize a quoted title within a personal name as instructed at **A.4**.

A Physician

Lady of Quality

Citizen of Albany

Une femme de ménage

Author of Early impressions

A.2.4 Other Terms Associated with Names of Persons

If:

a title and other term is treated as an integral part of the name of a person (see **9.2.2.9–9.2.2.26**)

or

a title and other term is associated with the name (see **9.4**)

then:

capitalize the title or term by applying the guidelines at **A.10–A.55**, as applicable to the language involved.

Moses, Grandma

Deidier, abbé

Alfonso XIII, King of Spain

John, Abbot of Ford

Capitalize the first word and any proper names in:

a) other designations associated with a person (see **9.6**)

b) a field of activity (see **9.15**)

c) an occupation or profession (see **9.16**).

Joan, of Arc, Saint, 1412-1431

Butler, Jean (Composer)

A.2.5 Initialisms and Acronyms

For an initialism or acronym used by a corporate body, capitalize the letters according to the predominant usage of the body.

AFL-CIO

Unesco

A.2.6 Other Terms Associated with Names of Families and Corporate Bodies

Capitalize the first word of the term used for the type of family (see **10.3**) or for a designation associated with a corporate body (see **11.7**).

Capitalize other words by applying the guidelines at **A.10–A.55**, as applicable to the language involved.

Bounty (Ship)

Knights Templar (Masonic order)

Regional Conference on Mental Measurement of the Blind (1st : 1951 : Perkins Institution)

A.3 Titles of Works

A.3.1 General Guideline

Capitalize the title of a work as instructed at **A.4.**

Hard times

Short stories

De bello Gallico

A.3.2 Other Terms Associated with Titles of Works

Capitalize the first word of each term. Capitalize other words in the term by applying the guidelines at **A.10–A.55**, as applicable to the language involved.

Seven sages of Rome (Southern version)

Guillaume (Chanson de geste)

Genesis (Middle High German poem)

Goyescas (Opera)

Exceptions

Music. Do not capitalize words or abbreviations used for medium of performance (see **6.15**) or for numeric designation of a musical work (see **6.16**), unless the word is, or the abbreviation stands for, a proper name. For thematic index numbers (see **6.16**), follow the capitalization practice used in the thematic index.

Trios, piano, strings, no. 2, op. 66, C minor

Sonatas, piano, K. 457, C minor

Suites, ondes Martenot, piano, op. 120c

Series. Do not capitalize words or abbreviations used for numbering of a part (see **24.6**) unless the word or abbreviation is capitalized in the language involved (see **A.10**–**A.55**).

v. 18

Heft 4

no. 7

pt. 1

ABA 16

A.4 Titles of Manifestations

A.4.1 General Guidelines

Capitalize the first word or the abbreviation of the first word in a title, or in a title of a part, section, or supplement (see **2.3.1.7**). Capitalize other words within titles by applying the guidelines at **A.10**–**A.55**, as applicable to the language involved.

The big book of stories from many lands

The 1919/1920 Breasted Expedition to the Far East

Les misérables

IV informe de gobierno

Eileen Ford's a more beautiful you in 21 days

Journal of polymer science

Sechs Partiten für Flöte

Still life with bottle and grapes

Harry Potter and the Order of the Phoenix

Strassenkarte der Schweiz = Carte routière de la Suisse = Carta stradale della Svizzera = Road map of Switzerland

The greenwood tree : newsletter of the Somerset and Dorset Family History Society

Quo vadis? : a narrative from the time of Nero

King Henry the Eighth ; and, The tempest

An interpretation of The ring and the book

Selections from the Idylls of the king

… / by the Author of Memoirs of a fox-hunting man

A dictionary of American English on historical principles

Les cahiers du cinéma

The anatomical record

Faust. Part one

Advanced calculus. Student handbook

Journal of biosocial science. Supplement

Acta Universitatis Carolinae. Philologica

Progress in nuclear energy. Series 2, Reactors

Exceptions

Other title information. In general, do not capitalize the first word or the abbreviation of the first word in other title information (see **2.3.4**). Capitalize the first word or abbreviation if:

it is one that should be capitalized according to the guidelines at **A.10–A.55**

or

it is capitalized in appendix **B**.

Arabic and Hebrew articles. If a transliterated title begins with the Arabic article *al* in any of its various orthographic forms (e.g., *al*, *el*, *es*), do not capitalize it. If a transliterated title begins with the Hebrew article *ha* (*he*), do not capitalize it. Apply this instruction whether the article is written separately or hyphenated with the word that follows it.

ha-Milon he-hadash

Unusual capitalization. For titles with unusual capitalization, follow the capitalization of the title as found on the source of information.

eBay bargain shopping for dummies

SympoTIC '06

RoMoCo '02

eWell being

e-Commerce security

iTV games and gambling

re:Organize

robgray.com

www.jurisdiction.com

www.advertising

A.4.2 Titles Preceded by Punctuation Indicating Incompleteness

Do not capitalize the first word of a title if it is preceded by punctuation indicating that the beginning of the phrase from which the title was derived has been omitted.

… and master of none

A.4.3 Titles of Works That Have Merged or Been Absorbed

When one work absorbs or merges with another, the title of the absorbed or merged work is sometimes incorporated with the title of the work that absorbed or merged with it. When this occurs, do not capitalize the first word of the incorporated title unless capitalization is required for another reason according to the guidelines at **A.10–A.55**, as applicable to the language involved.

> Farm chemicals and crop life
> **not** Farm chemicals and Crop life

A.5 Edition Statement

Capitalize the first word or abbreviation of the first word in a designation of edition (see **2.5.2**). Capitalize other words in an edition statement by applying the guidelines at **A.10–A.55**, as applicable to the language involved.

A.6 Numbering of Serials

Capitalize the first word or abbreviation of the first word of the numeric and/or alphabetic designation of the first issue or part of a sequence of numbering (see **2.6.2**). If that element is lacking, capitalize the first word or abbreviation of the first word of the chronological designation of the first issue or part of the sequence (see **2.6.3**).

> Vol. 1, no. 1
>
> Number 1
>
> Juin 2007

A.7 Numbering within Series and Subseries

Do not capitalize a term that is part of the numbering within a series (see **2.12.9**) or subseries (see **2.12.17**) unless capitalization is required according to the guidelines at **A.10–A.55**. Capitalize other words and alphabetic devices according to the usage on the resource.

> Band 33
>
> group 4
>
> no. 16
>
> program 1
>
> volume 14
>
> NSRDS-NBS 5

A.8 Notes

Capitalize the first word or abbreviation of a word in a note (see note on manifestation or item (**2.20**, **3.22**) or cataloguer's note (**5.9**, **8.13**, **24.8**, and **29.7**)).

If a note consists of more than one sentence, capitalize the first word of each subsequent sentence.

Capitalize a title as instructed at **A.4**. Capitalize other words as instructed at **A.10–A.55**, as applicable to the language involved.

A.9 Details of Elements

Capitalize the first word or abbreviation of a word when recording details of an element (e.g., **7.13.2.4**). Capitalize other words as instructed at **A.10–A.55**, as applicable to the language involved.

ENGLISH LANGUAGE

A.10 General Guideline for English Language Capitalization

The guidelines for English-language capitalization basically follow those of *The Chicago Manual of Style*. When guidelines differ, they have been modified to conform to the requirements of bibliographic records and long-standing cataloguing practice.

When instructed to capitalize a name or term, capitalize each separate word or initial except articles, prepositions, and conjunctions. Apply this guideline to the name of a person, corporate body, or place, or to a title of nobility, term of honour, appellation, epithet, etc. However, for a place name, capitalize an article that forms an accepted part of the name according to gazetteers.

Capitalize a plural generic term when it is used with distinctive nouns as part of two or more proper names. Do not capitalize a generic term that is not part of a proper name.

Saints Constantine and Helen

Secretaries of Defense and State

Lakes Erie and Ontario

Illinois and Chicago Rivers

but

Authorized and Revised versions

Term "versions" follows the brief forms of name of two different versions of the Bible

Three Brothers and Middle Knob mountains

Term "mountains" is a descriptive noun. Neither place contains the word "mountain" as part of its name

ENGLISH LANGUAGE

A.11 Personal Names

A.11.1 General Guideline

Capitalize the name of a person (including initials).

D.H. Lawrence

H.D.

John the Baptist

Benjamin Franklin

C. Day-Lewis

A.11.2 Names with Prefixes

If a name includes a prefix from a language other than English (e.g., *de, des, la, l', della, von, von der*), follow the person's use of capitalization for the prefix. In case of doubt, capitalize it.

Daphne du Maurier; du Maurier

Eva Le Gallienne; Le Gallienne

Mark Van Doren; Van Doren

Mazo de la Roche; de la Roche

A.11.3 Titles Preceding the Name

Capitalize any title or term of honour or address that immediately precedes a personal name.

Dame Judi Dench

Field Marshal Sir Michael Carver

Gen. Fred C. Weyand

Grandma Moses

John Henry Cardinal Newman

Mrs. Humphry Ward

Pope Paul VI

President Carter

Prime Minister Pierre Trudeau

Queen Elizabeth II

Rabbi Stephen Wise

Senator Hubert H. Humphrey

Sir Gordon Richards

Sister Mary Joseph

A.11.4 Ordinal Numbers Following Names of Sovereigns and Popes

Capitalize an ordinal number expressed as a word or words used after the name of a sovereign or pope to denote order of succession.

King George the Sixth

John the Twenty-third

A.11.5 Titles Following a Name or Used Alone in Place of a Name

A.11.5.1 Royalty, Nobility, Baronets

Capitalize a title of royalty or nobility.

Elizabeth II, Queen of the United Kingdom; the Queen

Charles, Prince of Wales; the Prince of Wales; the Prince

Frank Pakenham, Earl of Longford; the Earl of Longford; the Earl

Do not capitalize *bart.*

Sir Thomas Beecham, bart.
A baronet is not a member of the nobility

A.11.5.2 Religious Titles

Capitalize a religious title.

His Holiness Paul VI, Pope; the Pope

Most Rev. and Rt. Hon. Frederick Donald Coggan, Archbishop of Canterbury; the Archbishop of Canterbury

the Reverend Michael O'Sullivan, Pastor of Saint Peter's Church; the Pastor

the Dalai Lama

A.11.5.3 Civil and Military Titles

Do not capitalize a civil or military title.[1]

Jimmy Carter, president of the United States; the president of the United States; the president

James Callaghan, prime minister; the prime minister

the Hon. Walter Stewart Owen, lieutenant-governor of British Columbia; the lieutenant-governor of British Columbia; the lieutenant-governor

Warren Earl Burger, chief justice of the United States; the chief justice of the United States; the chief justice

Gen. Bernard A. Rogers, chief of staff, U.S. Army; the general

James F. Calvert, rear admiral, USN

Hubert H. Humphrey, senator from Minnesota, the senator from Minnesota; the senator

Kingman Brewster, ambassador to the United Kingdom; the ambassador to the United Kingdom; the ambassador

---

1. Capitalize words such as *president*, *prime minister*, and *governor* as instructed in **A.16.2** when they refer to the office rather than a particular person occupying the office.

A.11.5.4 Professional and Academic Titles

Capitalize the title of a named professorship. In general, do not capitalize other professional and academic titles.

W. Carson Ryan, Kenan Professor of Education (*but* the professor)

Robert Paul Bergman, associate professor of fine arts; the professor

R.F. Bennett, president of the Ford Motor Company of Canada; the president

Olga Porotnikoff, secretary, IFLA Committee on Cataloguing

A.11.6 Certain Other Terms Following Names

Capitalize the name or abbreviation of an academic degree, honour, religious order, etc.

C.D. Needham, Fellow of the Library Association

R.C. Strong, Ph.D., F.S.A.

Father Joseph Anthony Barrett, S.J.

Ralph Damian Goggens, Order of Preachers

Capitalize *esquire, junior,* or *senior* (and their abbreviations) in a name.

John Mytton, Esq.

John D. Rockefeller, Jr.

A.11.7 Terms of Honour and Respect

Capitalize a term of honour or respect.

Her Majesty

His Royal Highness

His Holiness

Your Excellency

Your Grace

Your Honour

A.11.8 Epithets

Capitalize an epithet occurring with, or used in place of, a personal name.

the Iron Chancellor

Old Hickory

Bonnie Prince Charlie

Elroy “Crazy Legs” Hirsch

Jerome H. (Dizzy) Dean

Abraham Lincoln, the Great Emancipator

A.11.9 Personifications

Capitalize a personification.

A dialogue between Death and a beautiful lady

Let Fame sound the trumpet

A.12 Names of Peoples, Etc.

Capitalize the name of a people, race, tribe, or ethnic or linguistic group.

Africans

Celts

Germans

Hottentots

Mongols

Polynesians

Scandinavians

Slavs

Teutons

Yoruba

Capitalize an adjective derived from such a name.

African

Scandinavian

Capitalize the name of a language.

English

Estonian

A.13 Place Names

A.13.1 Geographic Features, Regions, Etc.

Capitalize the name of a geographic feature, region, etc. Do not capitalize a descriptive adjective not part of an accepted name.

Arctic Circle

Arctic Ocean

Asia; Asian continent

Atlantic; South Atlantic (*but* southern Atlantic)

Central America; central European (*but* Central Europe *when referring to the geopolitical region*)

Cheviot Hills

the Continent (i.e., Europe); continental Europe; the European continent; Continental customs

East; the Orient; Far East(ern); Near East(ern); Middle East(ern); Eastern customs; oriental (adjective); eastern Europe (*but* Eastern Europe *when referring to the geopolitical region*); the East (U.S.)

Great Lakes

Great Slave Lake

Isthmus of Suez

Mississippi Delta

North Temperate Zone

Sea of Marmara

South America; South American continent

Southeast Asia; southern Asia

Strait of Dover

Tropic of Capricorn (*but* the tropics)

the West, Far West, Middle West, Midwest (U.S.) (*but* western, far western, midwestern)

A.13.2 Political Divisions

Capitalize the name of a political division (e.g., a country, state, province, city). Capitalize a word such as *empire*, *kingdom*, *state*, *country*, and *city* following a proper name if it is a commonly accepted part of the name. Do not capitalize such a word when used alone to indicate a political division.

Austrian Empire (*but* the empire)

Eleventh Congressional District (*but* the congressional district)

New York City (*but* the city of New York)

Simcoe County (*but* the county)

Sixth Precinct (*but* the precinct)

Washington State (*but* the state of Washington)

A.13.3 Popular Names

Capitalize a popular name of a place, or the name of a legendary place.

Atlantis

Bay Area

Benelux

the Channel (English Channel)

City of Brotherly Love

Erin

Eternal City

Latin Quarter

Middle Earth

New World

Old World

the Nutmeg State

Old Dominion

Panhandle

the Potteries

South Seas

the Village

West End

A.14 Names of Structures, Streets, Etc.

Capitalize the name of a building, monument, or other structure, and the name of a road or street.

Capitalize a plural generic term when it is used with distinctive nouns as part of two or more proper names. Do not capitalize a generic term that is not part of a proper name.

For the capitalization of names of buildings in which religious bodies meet, apply the guidelines at **A.16.5**.

the Capitol

Central Park (*but* the park)

Cleopatra's Needle

Drury Lane Theatre (*but* the theatre)

Forty-Second Street

Hoover Dam (*but* the dam)

Iroquois Lock

Jacques Cartier Bridge (*but* the bridge)

Oxford Circus (*but* the circus)

Pyramid of the Sun (*but* the pyramid)

Royal Air Force Memorial

Fifty-Seventh and Fifty-Fifth Streets

A.15 Derivatives of Proper Names

Do not capitalize a word derived from a personal or place name when it is used with a specialized meaning.

angstrom unit

arabic numerals

bikini

bourbon whiskey

burnt sienna

cologne

diesel engine

hamburger

italicize

malapropism

melba toast

nile green

raglan sleeves

roman type

timothy grass

vernier telescope

A.16 Names of Corporate Bodies

A.16.1 International Organizations and Alliances

Capitalize the name of an international organization or alliance.

Central Treaty Organization

Common Market

Hanseatic League; Hansa

Holy Alliance

International Monetary Fund

Little Entente

Organization of African Unity

Triple Alliance, 1882

United Nations; United Nations Security Council; Security Council (*but* the council)

World Health Organization

A.16.2 Government Bodies

Capitalize the full name of a legislative or judicial body; administrative department, bureau, or office; armed force (or component part of an armed force). If there is an accepted shortened form of name for any of these corporate bodies, capitalize the shortened form.

Do not capitalize other incomplete designations (except abbreviations) or adjectives derived from such a name.

Agency for International Development

Atlantic Fleet

Canadian Armed Forces

Canadian Citizenship Branch

Central Office of Information

Circuit Court of the United States; the federal Circuit Court

Commission on Post-Secondary Education in Ontario

Congress; the Ninety-fifth Congress (*but* congressional)

Court of Appeals of the State of Colorado

Department of State; State Department

District Court for the Southern District of New York (*but* district court)

Division of Education for the Disadvantaged

Domestic Council Committee on Illegal Aliens

First Army; the First

First Infantry Division

House of Commons

House of Representatives; the House (*but* the lower house of Congress)

Juvenile and Domestic Relations Court (*but* juvenile court; domestic relations court)
Middlesex Regiment; the Diehards (*but* the regiment)
Ministry of Agriculture, Fisheries, and Food
Parliament (*but* parliamentary)
Peace Corps
President of the United States (i.e., the office)
Prime Minister (i.e., the office)
Queen's Bench Division of the High Court of Justice
Royal Air Force
Royal Gloucestershire Hussars
Twenty-first Regiment of U.S. Infantry
United States Court of Appeals for the Second Circuit (*but* court of appeals)
United States Navy

A.16.3 Political Parties

Capitalize the name of a political party and of its members.

Communist Party of Great Britain; Communist(s)
Democratic Party; Democrat(s)
Liberal Party; Liberal(s)
Nazi Party; Nazi(s)

A.16.4 Political and Economic Systems

Do not capitalize the name of a political or economic system or school of thought or its proponents unless derived from proper nouns. In general, do not capitalize names of political groups other than parties.

anarchism
capitalism
egalitarianism
farm bloc
fascism
independent(s)
mercantilism
monarchism
mugwumps
nationalism
right wing
socialist bloc

but

Benthamism

Marxism

Thatcherism

A.16.5 Other Corporate Bodies

Capitalize the name of an institution, association, conference, company, religious denomination or order, local church, etc. (see **A.17.4** for the names of religions), or of a department or division.

Do not capitalize an article preceding the name, even when it is part of the official name.

Do not capitalize a generic word (e.g., *society*, *company*, *conference*) when used alone or with an article.

Capitalize a noun, noun phrase, adjective, or adjectival phrase derived from the name of the body that refers to a member or members of the body.

Abbey of Mont Saint-Michel

American Library Association

the Board of Regents of the University of California

Boy Scouts of America; a Boy Scout; a Scout

Canadian National Railways

Christian Brothers

Church of England

Church of the Redeemer

Conference, 1980 Advances in Reactor Physics and Shielding

Congregation Anshe Mizrach

Fifty-second Annual Meeting of the American Historical Association

First Baptist Church

Garrick Club

General Council of the United Church of Canada

General Foods Corporation

Green Bay Packers; the Packers (*but* the team)

Independent Order of Odd Fellows; IOOF; an Odd Fellow

Iowa Falls High School

League of Women Voters

Midwest Baptist Conference

Mosque of Sidi Okba

National Bank of New Zealand, Ltd.

National Dance Theatre Company of Jamaica

Order of Preachers

Presbyterian Church in Canada

Printed Circuit World Expo '81 West

Reference Section of the Canadian Library Association

Second Vatican Council; Vatican II

Society of Jesus; Jesuits; a Jesuit; Jesuitical

Special Session on Ordered Fields and Real Algebraic Geometry

Synod of Whitby

Temple Israel

Textile Workers Union of America (*but* the union)

Toronto Symphony Orchestra

Young Men's Christian Association

A.17 Religious Names and Terms

A.17.1 Deities

Capitalize the name of a deity and any term referring to the Christian Trinity.

Adonai

Allah

the Almighty

Astarte

Brahma

Christ

the Father

the First Cause

Hera

Holy Ghost

Holy Spirit

Jehovah

King of Kings

Lamb of God

Mars

Messiah (Jesus Christ)

Minerva

the Omnipotent

Prince of Peace

Providence

Son of God

Son of Man

the Supreme Being
Vishnu
the Word
Yahweh
Zeus

Do not capitalize a pronoun referring to the name of a deity unless capitalization is necessary to avoid ambiguity.

God as I understand him
The appearance of Christ after his resurrection
but
God gives man what He wills
Trust Him who doeth all things well

Do not capitalize words derived from the names of deities.

God's fatherhood, kingship, omnipotence
Jesus' sonship
godlike
messianic hope
christological
but
Christ-like

A.17.2 Names of Satan

Capitalize a word specifically denoting Satan.

the Devil
His Satanic Majesty
Lord of the Flies
Lucifer
but
a devil; the devils
devilled eggs
the devil's advocate

A.17.3 Revered Persons

Capitalize an appellation of a revered person such as a prophet, guru, saint, or other religious leader.

the Apostle to the Gentiles
the Baptist
the Beloved Apostle
the Blessed Virgin
Buddha
the Fathers (*but* church fathers)
the Mahatma
Mother of God
Our Lady
Panchen Lama
the Prophet (i.e., *Mohammed*)
the Twelve
the Virgin (i.e., *Mary*)

A.17.4 Religions

Capitalize the name of a religion, sect, or specific religious movement. Also capitalize a name describing its members and any adjective derived from such a name.

For the names of denominations, orders, local churches, etc., apply the guidelines at **A.16.5**.

Anglicanism; an Anglican; Anglican communion
Arianism; Arian heresy
Buddhism; a Buddhist; Buddhist ideas
Catholicism; a Catholic
Christian Science; a Christian Scientist
Dissenter
Islam; Islamic; Muslim
Judaism; Orthodox Judaism; Reform Judaism; an Orthodox Jew
Lutheranism; a Lutheran
Protestantism; a Protestant
Shinto
Theosophy; Theosophist
Vedanta
Zen; Zen Buddhism
Zoroastrianism

A.17.5 Religious Events and Concepts

Capitalize the name of a major Biblical or religious event or concept.

Armageddon

the Assumption of the Virgin

the Captivity (Babylonian)

the Crucifixion

the Enlightenment (Buddhism)

the Hegira

Judgment Day

the Last Supper

Redemption

the Second Advent

A.17.6 Creeds and Confessions

Capitalize the name of a creed or confession.

Augsburg Confession

Nicene Creed

the Thirty-nine Articles

A.17.7 The Eucharist

Capitalize a term referring to the Eucharist.

Communion

the Divine Liturgy

Holy Communion

the Lord's Supper

the Mass

A.17.8 Sacred Scriptures

Capitalize the title of a sacred scripture, one of its divisions, a group of books, or an individual book.

Holy Bible

Holy Scriptures

Sacred Scriptures

New Testament

Old Testament

New Covenant

Gospels

Acts of the Apostles

Apocalypse of John

Epistles of Paul

Apocrypha

Five Scrolls

Historical Books

Minor Prophets

Pentateuch

History of Susanna

Song of Songs

Koran

Qur'an

Zend-Avesta

Talmud Yerushalmi

Capitalize *book* when it refers to the entire Bible; otherwise, do not capitalize it.

the Book

but

the book of Proverbs

the book of the Prophet Isaiah

the second book of Kings

A.17.9 Special Selections from the Bible

Capitalize the first word of the name of a special selection from the Bible if it is commonly referred to by its specific name.

the Beatitudes

the Decalogue

the Lord's prayer

the Miserere

the Nunc dimittis

the Shema

the Sermon on the mount

the Ten commandments

A.17.10 Versions of the Bible

Capitalize the name of a version of the Bible (see **6.25.1.4**).

Authorized Version
Confraternity Version
Jerusalem Bible
New American Standard Bible
New English Bible
Septuagint
Vulgate

A.18 Names of Documents

Capitalize the formal, or conventional, name of a document such as a charter, constitution, legislative act, pact, plan, statement of policy, or treaty.

Do not capitalize a generic word (e.g., *constitution*) when used alone or with an article.

Articles of Confederation
Atlantic Charter
Bill of Rights
British North America Act
Civil Rights Act of 1964
Constitution of Virginia (*but* the constitution)
Declaration of Independence
Fourteenth Amendment (U.S. Constitution)
Magna Charta
Marshall Plan (*but* the plan
Reform Bill
Third Five Year Plan (India)
Treaty of Versailles (*but* the treaty)
Universal Copyright Convention (*but* the convention)

In case of doubt whether the title of a document is its formal or conventional name, capitalize the title according to other guidelines in this appendix.

An act to amend the constitution and to prohibit taxes on property ...

A.19 Names of Historical and Cultural Events and Periods

Capitalize the name of an historical or cultural event and of a major historical or cultural period.

Age of Discovery
Battle of Dunkirk

Boxer Rebellion
Dark Ages
Elizabethan Age
French Revolution
Grand National Steeplechase
Norman Conquest
Operation Deep Freeze
Reformation
Second Battle of the Marne
Second World War
Siege of Leningrad
Thirty Years' War

A.20 Decorations, Medals, Etc.

Capitalize the name of a particular decoration, medal, or award.

Bronze Star Medal
Congressional Medal of Honor
Iron Cross
Victoria Cross

A.21 Names of Calendar Divisions

Capitalize the name of a month of the year or day of the week.

January
Monday

Do not capitalize the name of a season.

winter

A.22 Names of Holidays

Capitalize the name of a secular or religious holiday and of a religious season.

Advent
Boxing Day
Christmas Day
Epiphany

Feast of the Annunciation

Fourth of July

Lent

Ramadan

Saint Patrick's Day

Thanksgiving

A.23 Scientific Names of Plants and Animals

Capitalize the Latin name of a phylum, class, order, family, or genus, and names of intermediate groupings (e.g., subclasses).

Do not capitalize the name of a species or subspecies even if it is derived from a proper name.

Do not capitalize English derivatives of scientific names.

Arthropoda (*phylum*)

Insecta (*class*)

but

arthropod (*from* Arthropoda)

A.24 Geologic Terms

Capitalize the distinctive word(s) in the name of a geologic era, period, etc.

Do not capitalize words such as *era* and *period* and modifiers such as *early*, *middle*, or *late* when used only descriptively.

Eocene epoch

Jurassic period

Lower Triassic period

Mesozoic period

the early Miocene

the late Eocene

A.25 Astronomical Terms

Capitalize the name of a planet, satellite, star, constellation, asteroid, etc.

Do not capitalize the words *sun* and *moon*.

Capitalize *Earth* when it is used to refer to the planet.

Alpha Centauri

Canis Major

Little Dipper

Mercury

the Milky Way

North Star

A.26 Soil Names

Capitalize the name of a soil classification.

Alpine Meadow

Chernozem

Half Bog

Prairie

A.27 Trade Names

Capitalize a trade name, variety name, or market grade. Do not capitalize a common noun following such a name.

Choice lamb (*market grade*)

Formica (*trade name*)

Orlon (*trade name*)

Polaroid film (*trade name*)

Red Radiance rose (*variety*)

Yellow Stained cotton (*market grade*)

A.28 Single and Multiple Letters Used as Words or Parts of Compounds

Capitalize the pronoun *I* and the interjection *O* (*Oh*).

Capitalize a letter that refers to a letter of the alphabet.

A major

H-bomb

U-boat

vitamin B

X-ray

Y is for yellow

For corporate names with compound terms, apply the guidelines at **A.2.1**.

For titles beginning with a compound term, apply the guidelines at **A.4.1**.

If a compound term appears elsewhere in the resource with a single letter or multiple letters capitalized, follow the capitalization as found.

A.29 Hyphenated Compounds

If the guidelines require the capitalization of a hyphenated compound, capitalize the first part. Capitalize the second, etc., part if it is a noun or a proper adjective or if it has the same force as the first part.

Twentieth-Century

Basket-Maker

Blue-Black

Secretary-Treasurer

Do not capitalize the second part if it modifies the first part or if the two parts constitute a single word.

French-speaking

Twenty-five

Co-ordinate

A.30 Hyphenated Prefixes

If a prefix is joined by a hyphen to a capitalized word, do not capitalize the prefix unless other guidelines require its capitalization.

ex-President Roosevelt

pre-Cambrian

trans-Siberian

un-American

OTHER LANGUAGES

A.31 General Guideline on Capitalization for Languages Other Than English

For languages other than English, apply the guidelines for the capitalization of English at **A.10–A.30** unless a guideline at **A.33–A.55** instructs otherwise. The guidelines at **A.33–A.55** are arranged by language, in alphabetical order according to the English name of the language.

If the agency creating the data has chosen a transliteration scheme for a language and the scheme provides guidelines on capitalization, follow those guidelines.

A.32 Capitalization of Transliterated Names and Titles

Capitalize words in transliterated names and titles as instructed at **A.31**. If the language has no system of capitalization, capitalize the first word of a title or a sentence and the first word of the name of a corporate body. Capitalize proper names according to English usage.

A.33 Bosnian

A.33.1 Proper Names and Their Derivatives

Do not capitalize names of peoples and races: *bijelac; crnac; semit.*

Do not capitalize proper adjectives: *bosanski.*

Do not capitalize names of religions and their adherents: *islam; musliman.*

A.33.2 Names of Regions, Localities, and Geographic Features, Including Streets, Parks, Etc.

Capitalize the first word and proper nouns: *Bihaćki okrug; Mostarska opština; Ulica bosanska; Ulica Bosanske Srebrne; Opština Bosanski Brod.*

A.33.3 Names of Administrative Division of Countries

Capitalize the first word and proper nouns in the names of administrative divisions of countries: *Bosansko-podrinjski kanton; Srednjobosanski kanton, Općina Bihać.*

A.33.4 Names of Corporate Bodies

Capitalize the first word and proper nouns in the names of corporate bodies: *Udruženje izdavača i knjižara Bosne i Hercegovine; Republički zavod za zaštitu spomenika; Pozorište lutaka Sarajevo.*

A.33.5 Titles of Persons

Do not capitalize titles of persons: *sultan Mehmed; magistar Imamović; direktor Kovačević.* However, capitalize *sveti* when it appears in the name of a holiday (see **A.33.8**).

A.33.6 Personal Pronouns

Do not capitalize *ja.*

Capitalize the pronouns of formal address: *Ti, Tvoj, Ti; Vi, Vam, Vas, Vaš.*

A.33.7 Names of Calendar Divisions

Do not capitalize names of days of the week and of months.

A.33.8 Names of Historic Events, Holidays, Etc.

Capitalize the first word and proper nouns in the names of historic periods and events: *Bronzano doba; Isa-begova vakufnama; Ustanak Desidijata pod Batonom; Prvi svjetski rat.*

Capitalize the first word and proper nouns in the names of holidays: *Kurban bajram; Božić; Ramazanski bajram; Sveti Petar, Međunarodni praznik rada.*

A.34 Bulgarian

A.34.1 Proper Names and Their Derivatives

Do not capitalize names of peoples, races, and residents of specific localities: българин; софиянец; семит.

Do not capitalize names of religions and their adherents: будизъм; християнство; лютеранец.

Do not capitalize proper adjectives: софийски улици.

A.34.2 Names of Regions, Localities, and Geographic Features, Including Streets, Parks, Etc.

Capitalize the first word unless it is a common noun. Capitalize other words only if they are proper nouns: Орлово гнездо; Бряг на слоновата кост; Стара Загора; Охридско езеро; село Белица; Червеният площад; ул. Шипка.

A.34.3 Names of Countries and Administrative Divisions

Capitalize the first word and proper nouns in names of countries and administrative subdivisions: Обединена арабска република; Народна република България; Софийска област; Министерство на селскостопанското производство.

A.34.4 Names of Corporate Bodies

Capitalize only the first word and proper nouns in the names of corporate bodies: Българска комунистическа партия; Организация на обединените народи; Държвна библиотаека "Васил Коларв"; Български червен кръст.

A.34.5 Titles of Persons

Capitalize свети and titles of royalty, high government officials, and high ecclesiastical officials if they are followed by a name: Министър Даскалов; Свети Климент.

Capitalize any title occurring in conjunction with the name of a well-known personage: Отец Паисий; Хаджи Димитър; Бачо Киро.

In general, do not capitalize other titles: министър; крал; отец; професор; отец Борис.

A.34.6 Personal Pronouns

Do not capitalize аз.

Capitalize Вие (Вий), Ви, Вас, and Вам when used in formal address.

A.34.7 Names of Calendar Divisions

Do not capitalize the names of days of the week and of months.

A.34.8 Names of Historic Events, Etc.

Capitalize the first word and proper nouns in the names of historic events, etc.: Първата световна война; Великата октомврийска социалистическа революция; Възраждането; Битката при Косово поле.

A.35 Croatian

A.35.1 Proper Names and Their Derivatives

Do not capitalize names of peoples and races: *bijelac; crnac; semit.*

Do not capitalize proper adjectives: *hrvatski.*

Do not capitalize names of religions and their adherents: *katoličanstvo; katolik.*

A.35.2 Names of Regions, Localities, and Geographic Features, Including Streets, Parks, Etc.

Capitalize only the first word and proper nouns: *Slavonski Brod; Hrvatsko zagorje; Gundulićeva ulica; Trg bana Josipa Jelačića.*

A.35.3 Names of Administrative Division of Countries

Capitalize the first word and proper nouns in the names of administrative divisions of countries: *Splitsko-dalmatinska županija; Istarska županija; Primorsko-goranska županija; Zadarska županija; Grad Zagreb.*

A.35.4 Names of Corporate Bodies

Capitalize only the first word and proper nouns in the names of corporate bodies: *Turistička zajednica grada Splita; Filozofski fakultet u Zagrebu; Savez samostalnih sindikata Hrvatske.*

A.35.5 Titles of Persons

Do not capitalize titles of persons: *kralj Tomislav; profesor Jurić; sveti Stjepan.* However, capitalize *sveti* when it appears in the name of a holiday (see **A.35.8**).

A.35.6 Personal Pronouns

Do not capitalize *ja.*

Capitalize the pronouns of formal address: *Ti, Tvoj, Ti; Vi, Vam, Vas, Vaš.*

A.35.7 Names of Calendar Divisions

Do not capitalize names of days of the week and of months.

A.35.8 Names of Historic Events, Holidays, Etc.

Capitalize the first word and proper nouns in the names of historic periods and events: *Srednji vijek; Seljačka buna; Krbavska bitka; Bitka na Mohačkom polju.*

Capitalize the first word and proper nouns in the names of holidays: *Sveti Petar; Tri kralja; Dan domovinske zahvalnosti.*

A.36 Czech (Bohemian)

A.36.1 Proper Names and Their Derivatives

For geographic names consisting of a distinctive word and a generic word, capitalize only the distinctive word: *Tichý oceán*.

For the names of streets, capitalize the first word and any other word that is a derivative of a proper name: *U invalidovny*; *Na růžku*; *Na Smetance*.

A.36.2 Names of Corporate Bodies

In general, capitalize only the first word in names of corporate bodies: *Československá republika*; *Česká akademie věd a umění*; *Bratří čeští*; *Milosrdní bratří*.

Do not capitalize names of branches of schools, conservatories, universities, ministries, and departments of government: *ministerstvo školství*; *závodní rada*.

A.36.3 Titles of Persons

Do not capitalize titles of persons: *doktor*; *král*; *ministr*; *svatý*.

A.36.4 Personal Pronouns

Do not capitalize *já*.

Capitalize the pronouns of formal address: *Ty, Tvůj, Tobě*; *Vy, Vám*; *Vás, Váš*.

A.36.5 Names of Calendar Divisions

Do not capitalize the names of days of the week and of months.

A.37 Danish

Apply the guidelines for Scandinavian languages at **A.49**.

A.38 Dutch

A.38.1 Single Letter as the First Word

Capitalize the first word of a sentence if it is the interjection *O*, the pronoun *U*, or a letter referring to a letter of the alphabet (e.g., *A is een aapje*).

Do not capitalize any other single letter that is the first word of a sentence or the first word of a proper name. Capitalize the next word: *'s Avonds is het koud*; *'k Weet niet wat hij zegt*; *'s Gravenhage*.

A.38.2 Prefixes in Personal Names

Capitalize the prefixes *de*, *ten*, *van*, if not preceded by the Christian name.

A.38.3 Personal Pronouns

Do not capitalize *ik*.

In general, capitalize *U*, *Uw*, and *Gij* in personal correspondence.

A.38.4 Names of Calendar Divisions

Do not capitalize the names of days of the week and of months.

A.39 Finnish

A.39.1 Names of Corporate Bodies

Capitalize only the first word and proper nouns in names of state and local government agencies, courts, and church bodies: *Erillinen komppania Kontula*; *Helsingin kaupunginkirjasto*; *Kauppa- ja teollisuusministeriö*; *Kirkon ulkomaanasiain toimikunta*; *Korkein oikeus*; *Suomen Unesco-toimikunta*.

In general, capitalize only the first word and proper nouns in names of scientific and economic institutions of the state: *Kansallismuseon esihistoriallinen osasto*; *Geodeettinen laitos*; *Helsingin yliopisto*. Exceptions: *Suomen Akatemia*; *Suomen Pankki*.

For the names of other institutions, societies, and firms, follow the usage of the body. If the usage is not known, capitalize all words.

A.39.2 Names of Buildings

Capitalize proper nouns in the names of buildings: *Kuopion kaupungintalo*; *Helsingin kulttuuritalo*.

A.40 French

A.40.1 Proper Names and Their Derivatives

Do not capitalize names of members of religious groups, sects, religious orders, political and other organizations, names of religions, and names of languages: *les jésuites*; *les démocrates*; *le bouddhisme*; *l'anglais* (the English language).

Do not capitalize adjectives derived from names of members of religious groups, sects, religious orders, political and other organizations, names of religions, names of languages, geographic names, and adjectives indicating nationality: *la religion catholique*; *la région alpine*; *le peuple français*.

Capitalize nouns indicating nationality: *les Français*.

Do not capitalize a common noun used as a generic word in a geographic name: *la mer du Nord*; *l'île aux Oiseaux*.

A.40.2 Names of Corporate Bodies

In general, capitalize the first word, any adjectives preceding the first noun, the first noun, and all proper nouns in the names of corporate bodies: *Société de chimie physique*; *Grand Orchestre symphonique de la R.T.B*; *Église réformée de France*. Notable exceptions: *Société des Nations*; *Nations Unies*.

Capitalize the nouns and adjectives in hyphenated corporate names: *le Théâtre-Français*.

A.40.3 Prefixes in Names of Persons

Capitalize prefixes consisting of an article or a contraction of an article and a preposition: *La Fontaine*; *Du Cange*.

A.40.4 Titles of Persons

Do not capitalize titles indicating rank or office: *le roi*; *le ministre*; *le pape Léon X*.

Capitalize titles of address and titles of respectful address or reference: *Monsieur*; *Mme de Lafayette*; *Son Éminence*; *Sa Majesté le roi de France*.

Do not capitalize *saint* (*sainte*, etc.) when it refers exclusively to a person; otherwise capitalize it: *saint Thomas More*; but *la cathédrale Saint-Lambert*; *l'été de la Saint-Martin*.

A.40.5 Personal Pronouns

Do not capitalize a personal pronoun.

A.40.6 Names of Calendar Divisions

Do not capitalize the names of days of the week and of months.

A.40.7 Miscellaneous

Do not capitalize *rue* and its synonyms: *rue de la Nation*; *avenue de l'Opéra*.

Do not capitalize *église* when it indicates a building: *l'église Notre-Dame*. Capitalize it when it refers to the church as an institution.

Capitalize *état* when it refers to the nation: *le Conseil d'État*.

A.41 German

A.41.1 Nouns

Capitalize all nouns and words used as nouns: *das Buch*; *das Geben*; *die Armen*; *das intime Du* (reference to the word *du*); *Not tun*; *ausser Acht lassen*; *aufs Neue*; *fürs Erste*; *im Voraus*; *die Übrigen*; *heute Mittag*; *im Grossen und Ganzen*; *das Hundert*; *das Tausend* (but *hundert* or *tausend* when used as cardinal numbers; see **A.41.4**).

A.41.2 Proper Names and Their Derivatives

In general, do not capitalize proper adjectives: *die deutsche Sprache.*

Capitalize adjectives that consist of a personal name followed by an apostrophe and the ending *–sche* (including its inflected forms): *die Darwin'sche Evolutionstheorie*; *das Wackernagel'sche Gesetz*; *die Goethe'schen Dramen.* Do not capitalize other adjectives containing a personal name: *die platonische Liebe*; *eine kafkaeske Stimmung.*

Capitalize indeclinable adjectives derived from geographic names: *Schweizer Ware*; *die Zürcher Bürger.*

Capitalize adjectives, pronouns, and numerals used as parts of a name or title: *Alexander der Grosse*; *das Schweizerische Konsulat*; *Seine Excellenz*; *Friedrich der Zweite*; *Bund der Technischen Angestellten und Beamten*; *der Erste der Klasse* (expressing rank). See also **A.41.4**.

A.41.3 Pronouns

Do not capitalize *ich.*

Capitalize *Sie* and *Ihr* and their inflected forms when used in formal address.

A.41.4 Miscellaneous

Do not capitalize the following:

a) pronouns (see also **A.41.3**): *jemand*, *ein jeder*, *der eine . . . der andere*, *die beiden*, *die meisten*

b) cardinal numbers under one million: *hundert, tausend, an die zwanzig, wir zwei, alle drei, bis drei zählen*

c) adverbs: *mittags, anfangs, morgen, montags*

d) verbal phrases: *preisgeben, teilhaben, wundernehmen, zuteil werden, zumute sein* (but *zu Mute sein*), *schuld sein* (words such as *schuld* or *leid* are considered to be adjectives when used in conjunction with the verbs *sein*, *werden*, or *bleiben*)

e) adjectives modifying nouns that are implied if the noun has been expressed elsewhere in the same sentence: *Hier ist die beste Arbeit, dort die schlechteste*

f) fractions, when they directly precede a noun or a cardinal number: *ein viertel Kilogramm* (but *um ein Viertel vor acht*).

A.42 Hungarian

A.42.1 Proper Names and Their Derivatives

Do not capitalize nouns indicating nationality: *az oroszok.*

Do not capitalize adjectives derived from proper names: *budapesti.*

A.42.2 Titles of Persons

Capitalize titles used in direct address: *Felséges Uram.*

Do not capitalize titles of nobility, including titles that consist of an adjectival term derived from a place of origin, etc.: *gróf Teleki Pál*; *körmendi Frim Jakab.*

A.42.3 Personal Pronouns

Do not capitalize *én*.

Capitalize pronouns used in formal address: *Maga*.

A.42.4 Names of Calendar Divisions

Do not capitalize the names of days of the week and of months.

A.43 Italian

A.43.1 Proper Names and Their Derivatives

Do not capitalize names of members of religious groups, sects, religious orders, political and other organizations, names of religions, and names of languages: *i protestanti*; *i benedettini*; *un democratico*; *il buddhismo*; *il francese* (the French language).

Do not capitalize adjectives derived from names of members of religious groups, sects, religious orders, political and other organizations, names of religions, names of languages, geographic and personal names, and adjectives indicating nationality: *la religione cattolica*; *la flora alpina*; *il popolo italiano*; *iconografia dantesca*.

Capitalize nouns indicating nationality: *gl'Italiani*.

A.43.2 Names of Corporate Bodies

In general, capitalize only the first word, proper nouns, religious terms, and the word following an adjective denoting royal or pontifical privilege in the names of corporate bodies: *Istituto nazionale di fisica nucleare*; *Accademia nazionale de Santa Cecilia*; *Università cattolica del Sacro Cuore*; *Pontificio Seminario francese*; *Chiesa evangelica italiana*. Notable exceptions: *Società delle Nazioni*; *Nazioni Unite*; *Croce Rossa*.

A.43.3 Titles of Persons

Do not capitalize titles of persons except for ceremonial titles consisting of a possessive pronoun and a noun expressing an abstract quality: *signora*; *il signor Donati*; *il duca d'Aosta*; *Umberto I, re d'Italia*; but *Sua Santità*; *Sua Altezza Reale il principe Umberto*; *le LL. MM. il re e la regina*.

Do not capitalize *san* (*santo*, etc.) when referring exclusively to a person; capitalize it when it is abbreviated and when it is an integral part of the name of a place, a building, etc.: *san Francesco d'Assisi*; but *S. Girolamo*; *Castel Sant'Angelo*.

A.43.4 Personal Pronouns

Do not capitalize *io*.

Capitalize the pronouns of formal address: *Ella*; *Lei*; *Loro*.

A.43.5 Names of Calendar Divisions

Do not capitalize the names of days of the week and of months.

A.43.6 Names of Centuries

Capitalize the proper names of centuries: *il Cinquecento*; *il Seicento*; but *il sedicesimo secolo*.

A.43.7 Miscellaneous

Do not capitalize *via* and its synonyms: *via Vittorio Veneto*; *corso Umberto I*.

Do not capitalize *chiesa* when it indicates a building: *la chiesa di S. Maria degli Angeli*. Capitalize it when it refers to the church as an institution.

Capitalize *stato* when it refers to the nation: *Consiglio di Stato*.

A.44 Latin

Apply the guidelines for English at **A.10–A.30**.

A.45 Norwegian

Apply the guidelines for Scandinavian languages at **A.49**.

A.46 Polish

A.46.1 Proper Names and Their Derivatives

Do not capitalize names of residents of cities and towns: *warszawianin.*

Do not capitalize adjectives derived from proper names: *mickiewiczowski.*

Do not capitalize names of religions and their adherents and names of members of religious orders: *katolicyzm*; *katolik*; *mahometanin*; *jezuici.*

Capitalize each part of a compound geographic name. If the distinctive word in the compound name is in the nominative case and can stand alone, capitalize only the distinctive word: *Morze Bałtyckie*; but *jezioro Narocz.*

Do not capitalize geographic names applied to wines, dances, etc.: *tokaj*; *krakowiak.*

Do not capitalize names of administrative districts and geographic adjectives: *województwo poznańskie*; *diecezja łomżyńska.*

A.46.2 Names of Corporate Bodies

Capitalize all words except conjunctions and prepositions in the names of corporate bodies: *Towarzystwo Naukowe w Toruniu*; *Ewangelicko-Augsburski Kościół.*

A.46.3 Titles of Persons

Do not capitalize titles of persons except in direct address: *papież*; *król*; *święty.*

A.46.4 Personal Pronouns

Do not capitalize *ja.*

Capitalize the pronouns of formal address: *Ty, Tobie, Twój; On, Ona, Jego, Jej, Jemu*; *Wy, Wam, Was.*

A.46.5 Names of Calendar Divisions

Do not capitalize the names of days of the week and of months.

A.46.6 Names of Historic Events, Etc.

Do not capitalize names of historic events and wars: *pokój wersalski*; *wojna siedmioletnia.*

A.47 Portuguese

A.47.1 Derivatives of Proper Names

Do not capitalize derivatives of proper names: *os homens alemães*; *os franceses.*

A.47.2 Titles of Persons

Capitalize names of positions or posts of dignitaries and titles of persons: *o Arcebispo de Braga*; *o Duque de Caxias*; *o Presidente da República*; *Senhor Professor.*

A.47.3 Personal Pronouns

Do not capitalize *eu.*

A.47.4 Religious Terms

Capitalize *igreja* when referring to the church as an institution.

A.47.5 Names of Calendar Divisions

Do not capitalize the names of days of the week and of months.

A.48 Russian

A.48.1 Proper Names and Their Derivatives

Do not capitalize prefixes, prepositions, and conjunctions forming part of a proper name, except when they are connected to the following part of the name by a hyphen: фон Клаузевиц; ван Бетховен; Ван-Гог.

Do not capitalize names of peoples, races, and residents of specific localities: араб; таджик; москвичи.

Do not capitalize the names of religions and their adherents: католицизм; католик.

Do not capitalize proper nouns that are parts of adverbs: по-пушкински.

A.48.2 Names of Regions, Localities, and Geographic Features, Including Streets, Parks, Etc.

Do not capitalize a common noun forming part of a geographic name: мыс Горн; остров Рудолъфа; канал Москва-Волга.

Capitalize a common noun forming an integral part of a name: Кривой Рог; Белая Церковъ; Богемский Лес.

Capitalize the common noun if it is a foreign word that has not become a part of the Russian language: Рю-де-ла-Пе (Рю—meaning street, Пе—meaning peace); Сыр-Дарья (Дарья—meaning river).

Do not capitalize the title or rank of the person in whose honour a place is named: остров королевы Виктории; мыс капитана Джеральда.

Do not capitalize adjectives derived from geographic names: московские улицы.

Do not capitalize geographic names applied to wines, species of animals, birds, etc.: мадера; херес; сенбернар.

A.48.3 Names of Countries and Administrative Divisions

Capitalize the first word in the commonly accepted names of groups of countries: Балканские страны.

Capitalize unofficial but commonly accepted names of countries, cities, and territorial divisions: Советский Союз; Страна Советов; Приуралье; Белокаменная (for Moscow).

Capitalize administrative divisions of the USSR as follows:

a) Capitalize every word in the names of republics and autonomous republics: Башкирская Автономная Советская Социалистическая Республика.

b) Capitalize only the first word in the names of provinces, autonomous provinces, territories, regions, and village soviets: Алма-Атинская область; Приморский край; Коми-Пермяцкий национальный округ; Егоршинский район; Краснинский сельсозет.

c) Capitalize every word in the names of the highest Soviet and non-Russian governmental units and Communist Party organizations except those in parentheses and партия: Верховный Совет СССР (also of the Union republics and autonomous republics); Совет Союза, Совет Национальностей; Всесоюзная Коммунистическая партия (большевнков); Рейхстаг; Конгресс США; Правительствующий Сенат.

d) Capitalize only the first word and proper nouns in the names of other governmental units: Государственная плановая комиссия СССР; Народный комиссариат иностранных дел; Военный совет Закавказского военного округа.

e) Do not capitalize the names of bureaus when used in the plural and when used in a general sense: советы народных комиссаров; народный комиссариат.

f) Capitalize Совет in Совет депутатов трудящихся : Загорский районный Совет депутатов трудящихся.

A.48.4 Names of Corporate Bodies

Capitalize only the first word and proper nouns in names of corporate bodies: Академия наук СССР; Книжная палата; Профессиональный союз работников высшей школы и научных учреждений; Дом книги.

If part of the name of a corporate body is in quotation marks, capitalize only the first word and proper nouns within the quotation marks: завод "Фрезер"; совхоз "Путъ к социализму."

If a corporate body is also known by a part of its name, capitalize the first word of the part when it appears in conjunction with the full name: Государственный ордена Ленина академический Большой театр (Большой театр).

Do not capitalize the following words in the names of congresses, conferences, etc.: съезд; конференция; сессия; пленум.

Do not capitalize совет when used to refer to the council of a society or institution.

A.48.5 Titles of Persons

Capitalize the titles of the highest government officials: Председатель Совета Народных Комиссаров; Маршал Советского Союза.

A.48.6 Pronouns

Do not capitalize я.

Capitalize pronouns of formal address: Вы; Вам; Вас.

A.48.7 Names of Calendar Divisions

Do not capitalize the names of days of the week and of months.

A.48.8 Names of Historic Events, Etc.

Capitalize the first word, the distinctive word, and proper nouns in the names of historic periods and events: Великая Октябрьская социалистическая революция; Возрождение; Третья республика; Парижская коммуна; Кровавое воскресенье; Ленский расстрел; Бородинский бой.

Do not capitalize the names of the five-year plans: третья сталинская пятилетка; but соревнование имени Третьей Сталинской Пятилетки.

Do not capitalize война in the names of wars: Франко-Прусская война; Русско-Японская война; Великая Отечественная война; Отечественная война.

A.49 Scandinavian Languages

A.49.1 Derivatives of Proper Names

Do not capitalize adjectives derived from proper names: *europeisk*; *københavnsk*; *luthersk*; *svensk*.

A.49.2 Names of Corporate Bodies

In general, capitalize the first word and the word following an adjective indicating royal privilege in the names of corporate bodies. Capitalize other words, such as proper nouns, according to the appropriate guideline: *Kungl. Biblioteket*; *Ministeriet for kulturelle anliggender*; *Selskabet for dansk skolehistorie*.

A.49.3 Compound Names

In general, capitalize only the first word of a compound name, other than a compound personal name: *Förenta staterna*; *Kronborg slot*; *Norske kirke*.

A.49.4 Titles of Persons

In general, do not capitalize titles of persons: *fru Larsen*; *kong Haakon VII*; *Gustav, prins av Vasa*.

A.49.5 Personal Pronouns

A.49.5.1 Danish

Do not capitalize *jeg*. Capitalize *De*; *Dem*; *Deres*. Capitalize the familiar form *I* (you) to distinguish it from *i* (in).

A.49.5.2 Norwegian

Do not capitalize *jeg*. Capitalize *De*; *Dem*; *Deres*; *Dykk*; *Dykkar*.

A.49.5.3 Swedish

Do not capitalize *jag*. Capitalize *Ni*, *Eder*, and *Er* in correspondence.

A.49.6 Names of Calendar Divisions

Do not capitalize the names of days of the week, of months, and of holidays: *jul*; *nyår*.

A.50 Serbian

A.50.1 Proper Names and Their Derivatives

Do not capitalize names of peoples and races: *belac*; *crnac*; *semit*.

Do not capitalize proper adjectives: *srpski*.

Do not capitalize names of religions and their adherents: *pravoslavstvo; pravoslavac*.

A.50.2 Names of Regions, Localities, and Geographic Features, Including Streets, Parks, Etc.

Capitalize only the first word and proper nouns: *Velika Morava*; *Beogradska ulica*; *Trg Nikole Tesle*; *Fruška gora*.

A.50.3 Names of Administrative Divisions of Countries

Do not capitalize names of administrative divisions of countries: *Sremski okrug*; *Grad Beograd*; *Grad Niš*; *Zapadno-bački okrug*.

A.50.4 Names of Corporate Bodies

Capitalize only the first word and proper nouns in the names of corporate bodies: *Matica srpska*; *Vojvođanska banka*; *Beogradsko dramsko pozorište*; *Narodna biblioteka Srbije*; *Muzej Nikole Tesle*.

A.50.5 Titles of Persons

Do not capitalize titles of persons: *car Dušan*; *kralj Milutin*; *ministar*; *sveti Petar*. However, capitalize *sveti* when it appears in the name of a holiday (see **A.50.8**).

A.50.6 Personal Pronouns

Do not capitalize *ja*.

Capitalize the pronouns of formal address: *Ti, Tvoj, Ti; Vi, Vam, Vas, Vaš*.

A.50.7 Names of Calendar Divisions

Do not capitalize names of days of the week and of months.

A.50.8 Names of Historic Events, Holidays, Etc.

Capitalize proper nouns in the names of historic periods and events: *Kameno doba; Boj na Kosovu*; *Prvi srpski ustanak*; *Kolubarska bitka*; *Bitka na Ivankovcu*.

Capitalize the first word and proper nouns in the names of holidays: *Sveti Sava*; *Veliki četvrtak*.

A.51 Slovak

Apply the guidelines for Czech at **A.36**.

A.52 Slovenian

A.52.1 Proper Names and Their Derivatives

Do not capitalize names of peoples and races: *arijec*; *semit*; *črnec*.

Capitalize only the distinctive words in the names of nationalities that consist of more than one word: *severni Korejec*; *zahodni Nemec*.

Do not capitalize proper adjectives: *slovenski jezik*.

Do not capitalize the names of religions and their adherents: *katolicizem*; *katoličan*.

A.52.2 Names of Regions, Localities, and Geographic Features, Including Streets, Parks, Etc.

Capitalize only the first word and proper nouns of regions, etc.: *Ziljska dolina*; *Novo mesto*; *Škofja Loka*; *Daljni vzhod*; *Otok kraljice Viktorije*; *Rtič dobrega upanja*; *Ulica stare pravde*.

A.52.3 Names of Countries and Administrative Divisions

Capitalize the first word and proper nouns in the names of countries and administrative subdivisions: *Federativna socialistična republika Jugoslavija*; *Združene države Amerike*.

A.52.4 Names of Corporate Bodies

Capitalize the first word and proper nouns in the names of corporate bodies: *Društvo slovenskih književnikov*; *Državna založba Slovenije*.

A.52.5 Titles of Persons

Do not capitalize titles of persons: *predsednik*; *sekretar*; *doktor*; *maršal Tito*; *kralj Matjaž*; *sveti Peter*. However, capitalize *sveti* when it appears in the name of a holiday (see **A.52.8**).

A.52.6 Personal Pronouns

Do not capitalize *jaz*.

Capitalize the pronouns of formal address: *Ti, Tebe, Tebi, s Teboj*; *Vidva, Vidve, Vaju, Vama*; *Vi, Vas, Vam, z Vami*.

A.52.7 Names of Calendar Divisions

Do not capitalize the names of days of the week and of months.

A.52.8 Names of Historic Events, Holidays, Etc.

Capitalize the first word and proper nouns in the names of historic events, holidays, etc.: *Ledena doba*; *Renesansa*; *Francoska revolucija*; *Boj na Mišaru*; *Prva srbska vstaja*; *Božič*; *Velika noč*; *Sveti Peter*.

A.53 Spanish

A.53.1 Derivatives of Proper Names

Do not capitalize derivatives of proper names: *las mujeres colombianas*.

Do not capitalize adjectives used substantively: *los franceses*.

A.53.2 Titles of Persons

Capitalize titles of honour and address only when they are abbreviated: *señor, Sr.*; *doctor, Dr.*; *general, Gral.*

Capitalize *Su Excelencia, Su Majestad,* etc., when used alone, whether written out or abbreviated. Do not capitalize these words when they are used with a name or another title: *su majestad Juan Carlos*; *su majestad el Rey*.

A.53.3 Personal Pronouns

Do not capitalize *yo*.

Capitalize the pronouns of formal address: *Vd., Vds.* (*Ud., Uds.*).

A.53.4 Religious Terms

Capitalize *iglesia* when it refers to the church as an institution.

A.53.5 Names of Calendar Divisions

Do not capitalize the names of days of the week and of months.

A.53.6 Questions within a Sentence

In general, do not capitalize the first word of a question occurring within a sentence: *Cuando viene la noche ¿cómo se puede ver?*

A.54 Swedish

Apply the guidelines for Scandinavian languages at **A.49**.

A.55 Ukrainian

Apply the guidelines for Russian at **A.48**.

B

ABBREVIATIONS AND SYMBOLS

B.0 Scope

This appendix provides instructions on the use of abbreviations when recording specified elements and on using symbols instead of abbreviations, when appropriate. It includes lists of abbreviations in English and a selected number of other languages.

B.1 General Guideline

Use the abbreviations and symbols listed at **B.7**–**B.11** as instructed at **B.2**–**B.6**.

> *Alternative*
>
> When recording the attributes of a manifestation or item (see chapters **1**–**4**), follow appropriate international standards on the use of abbreviations or of symbols for units of measurement. However, the agency creating the data can choose to establish in-house guidelines for abbreviations or symbols for units of measurement, or choose a published style manual, etc., as its preferred guide (see the alternative at **1.10.2**). When this occurs, use those guidelines or that style manual instead of appendix **B**.

B.2 Names of Persons, Families, Corporate Bodies, and Places

For the names of persons, families, corporate bodies, and places, use only the following abbreviations:

a) those that are integral parts of the name (e.g., "Wm.") if the person, family, corporate body, or place uses the abbreviation

b) certain names of larger places (see **B.11**) recorded as part of the name of another place (see **16.2.2.9** and **16.2.2.11**).

B.3 Titles of Works

For titles of works, use only the following abbreviations:

a) those that are integral parts of the title

b) *etc.* in the title *Laws, etc.* (see **6.19.2.5**).

B.4 Transcribed Elements

For transcribed elements, use only those abbreviations found in the sources of information for the element.

If supplying all or part of a transcribed element, generally do not abbreviate words.

B.5 Other Elements

B.5.1 Dimensions

When recording dimensions (see **3.5**), use symbols or abbreviations in the list at **B.7** that apply to units of measurement.

Metric symbols are not abbreviations and are not followed by a full stop.

B.5.2 Extent of Storage Space

When recording extent of storage space in non-metric units of measurement (see **3.4.1.11.2**), use symbols or abbreviations in the list at **B.7** that apply to units of measurement.

Metric symbols are not abbreviations and are not followed by a full stop.

B.5.3 Duration

When recording duration (see **7.22**), use symbols or abbreviations in the list at **B.7** that apply to units of time.

B.5.4 Numeric Designation of a Musical Work

When recording the numeric designation of a musical work (see **6.16**), use appropriate abbreviations from the lists at **B.7–B.10**.

B.5.5 Numbering of Part

When recording the numbering of a part (see **24.6**), use appropriate abbreviations from the lists at **B.7–B.10**.

B.5.6 Medium of Performance of Musical Content

When recording two or more voices as medium of performance of musical content (see **7.21**), use appropriate abbreviations from the list at **B.7** (e.g., "SA" for "soprano" and "alto").

B.5.7 Additional Scale Information

When recording additional scale information (see **7.25.5**), use symbols or abbreviations in the list at **B.7** that apply to units of measurement.

Metric symbols are not abbreviations and are not followed by a full stop.

B.5.8 Right Ascension

When recording right ascension (see **7.4.4**), use abbreviations in the list at **B.7** that apply to units of time.

B.5.9 Date

Use the abbreviations *A.D.* and *B.C.* when recording a date in the Christian calendar for dates associated with:

a person (see **9.3**)
a family (see **10.4**)
a corporate body (see **11.4**)
a work (see **6.4**)
an expression (see **6.10**).

B.5.10 Other Distinguishing Characteristic of a Legal Work

Use *etc.* in the term *Protocols, etc.* (see **6.21.1.3**).

B.5.11 Other Elements

Generally do not abbreviate words in elements except those covered at **B.5.1** and **B.5.3–B.5.9**.

Do not abbreviate words quoted in notes.

Generally do not abbreviate words recorded as part of details of an element.

B.6 Corresponding Words in Another Language

Use an abbreviation for the corresponding word in another language if the abbreviation commonly used in that language has the same spelling as one in appendix **B**. In case of doubt, do not use the abbreviation.

B.7 Latin Alphabet Abbreviations

TERM	ABBREVIATION
alto	A[1]
Anno Domini	A.D.
Band	Bd.

TERM	ABBREVIATION
band	bd.
Bände	Bde.
baritone	Bar[1]
bass	B[1]
Before Christ	B.C.
bind	bd.
book	bk.
broj	br.
číslo	čís.
djilid	djil.
et cetera	etc.[2]
foot, feet	ft.
frames per second	fps
hour, -s	hr.
inch, -es	in.
inches per second	ips
jilid	jil.
kniha	kn.
knjiga	knj.
kötet	köt.
mezzo-soprano	Mz[1]
minute, -s	min.
nombor	no.
nomor	no.
number, -s	no.
numer	nr.
numero (Finnish)	n:o
numéro, -s (French)	n^{o}, n^{os}
numero (Italian)	n.
número (Spanish)	no.
Nummer	Nr.
nummer	nr.
opus	op.

TERM	ABBREVIATION
part, -s	pt., pts.[3]
partie, -s	part.[3]
revolutions per minute	rpm
ročník	roč.
rocznik	rocz.
second, -s	sec.
sešit	seš.
soprano	S[1]
številka	št.
svazek	sv.
szám	sz.
tenor	T[1]
tome	t.
tomo	t.
volume, -s (English)	v.
volume, -s (French)	vol.
volume (Italian)	vol.
vuosikerta	vuosik.
zväzok	zv.
zvezek	zv.

1. Use only when recording details of medium of performance of musical content to indicate voice range of vocal works when two or more voices are given.
2. Use only in the title *Laws, etc.* and in the term *Protocols, etc.*
3. Do not use when recording the extent of notated music.

B.8 Cyrillic Alphabet Abbreviations

TERM	ABBREVIATION
выпуск	вып.
год	г.
головний	гол.
дополненный	доп.
заглавие	загл.

TERM	ABBREVIATION
књига	књ.
книга	кн.
отделение	отд-ние
рік	р.
том	т.
часть	ч.

B.9 Greek Alphabet Abbreviations

TERM	ABBREVIATION
ἀριθμός	ἀρ.
μέρος	μέρ.
τεῦχος	τεῦχ.
τόμος	τ.

B.10 Hebrew and Yiddish Abbreviations

TERM	ABBREVIATION
באנד	בד.
גליון	גל'
חוברת	חוב'
טייל	טל.
יארגאנג	יארג.
מספר	מס'
נומער	נומ.

B.11 Names of Certain Countries, States, Provinces, Territories, Etc.

Use the abbreviations in **table B.1** for the names of certain countries and for the names of states, provinces, territories, etc., of Australia, Canada, and the United States when the names are recorded:

a) as part of the name of a place located in that state, province, territory, etc. (see **16.2.2.9**) or other jurisdiction (see **16.2.2.11**)

b) as the name or part of the name of a place associated with a person (see **9.8–9.11**), family (see **10.5**), or corporate body (see **11.3**).

Do not abbreviate the name of a city or town even if it has the same name as a state, etc., listed in **table B.1** (e.g., *Washington, D.C.* not *Wash., D.C.*). Do not abbreviate any place name that is not in the list.

TABLE B.1

NAME	ABBREVIATION
Alabama	Ala.
Alberta	Alta.
Arizona	Ariz.
Arkansas	Ark.
Australian Capital Territory	A.C.T.
British Columbia	B.C.
California	Calif.
Colorado	Colo.
Connecticut	Conn.
Delaware	Del.
District of Columbia	D.C.
Florida	Fla.
Georgia	Ga.
Illinois	Ill.
Indiana	Ind.
Kansas	Kan.
Kentucky	Ky.
Louisiana	La.
Maine	Me.
Manitoba	Man.
Maryland	Md.
Massachusetts	Mass.
Michigan	Mich.
Minnesota	Minn.
Mississippi	Miss.
Missouri	Mo.
Montana	Mont.
Nebraska	Neb.
Nevada	Nev.
New Brunswick	N.B.

NAME	ABBREVIATION
New Hampshire	N.H.
New Jersey	N.J.
New Mexico	N.M.
New South Wales	N.S.W.
New York	N.Y.
New Zealand	N.Z.
Newfoundland	Nfld.
Newfoundland and Labrador	N.L.
North Carolina	N.C.
North Dakota	N.D.
Northern Territory	N.T.
Northwest Territories	N.W.T.
Nova Scotia	N.S.
Oklahoma	Okla.
Ontario	Ont.
Oregon	Or.
Pennsylvania	Pa.
Prince Edward Island	P.E.I.
Puerto Rico	P.R.
Queensland	Qld.
Rhode Island	R.I.
Russian Soviet Federated Socialist Republic	R.S.F.S.R
Saskatchewan	Sask.
South Australia	S.A.
South Carolina	S.C.
South Dakota	S.D.
Tasmania	Tas.
Tennessee	Tenn.
Territory of Hawaii	T.H.
Texas	Tex.
Union of Soviet Socialist Republics	U.S.S.R.
United Kingdom	U.K.
United States	U.S.

NAME	ABBREVIATION
Vermont	Vt.
Victoria	Vic.
Virginia	Va.
Washington	Wash.
West Virginia	W. Va.
Western Australia	W.A.
Wisconsin	Wis.
Wyoming	Wyo.

C

INITIAL ARTICLES

C.0 Scope

This appendix lists initial articles that are to be omitted when applying the alternative instructions to record titles for works and names of persons, corporate bodies, and places. The list includes initial articles in a selected number of languages.

C.1 General Instructions

Omit the articles listed at **C.2** and **C.3** as instructed in the alternative instructions for:

titles of works (see **6.2.1.7**)

characterizing word or phrase used as the name of a person (see **9.2.2.25**)

phrase naming another work by the person (see **9.2.2.26**)

names of corporate bodies (see **11.2.2.8**)

names of places (see **16.2.2.4**).

For the languages included in the lists at **C.2** and **C.3**, all the definite and indefinite articles to be omitted are in those lists.

Generally consider that the articles identified for a language also apply to a dialect of that language.

For languages not included in the lists in **C.2** and **C.3**, consult reference sources to determine if the language uses definite and/or indefinite articles and to identify those definite and/or indefinite articles.

C.2 Articles Listed by Language

An asterisk (*) after an article indicates that the same form is also used in other contexts (e.g., the cardinal numeral one, a demonstrative pronoun). For those words, take care to determine the meaning before omitting the word.

LANGUAGE	ARTICLES
Afrikaans	die, `n
Albanian	një
Ancient Greek	[See separate list of Ancient Greek articles below]
Arabic	ال al-, el-
Baluchi	al-
Basque	bat*
Brahui	al-
Breton	al, an, ar, eul*, eun*, eur*, ul*, un*, ur*
Catalan	el, els, en*, l’, la, les, un*, una*
Danish	de, den, det, en*, et*
Dutch	de, een*, eene*, het, ’n, ’t

LANGUAGE	ARTICLES
English	a, an, d', de, the, ye
Esperanto	la
Fijian	a, e dua na, e na dua, na
French	l', la, le, les, un*, une*
Galician	a, as, o*, unha
German	das, dem, den, der, des, die, ein*, eine*, einem, einen, einer, eines
Hawaiian	he, ka, ke, na, o*
Hebrew	ה ha-, he-
Hungarian	a, az [not if used as "az az" (that) or "ez az" (this)], egy*
Icelandic	hin, hina, hinar, hinir, hinn, hinna, hinnar, hinni, hins, hinu, hinum, hið, 'r
Irish	an, an t-, an t [only in certain situations], na, na h-, na h [only in certain situations]
Italian	gl', gli, i, il, l', la, le, lo*, un', un*, una*, uno*
Malagasy	ny
Maltese	il-, l-
Maori	he, ngā, te
Modern Greek	[See separate list for Modern Greek articles below]
Neapolitan	'o
Niuean	a, e, e taha, ha, ko e
Norwegian	de, dei, den, det, e, ei*, ein*, eit*, en*, et*
Occitan	il, l', la, las, le, les, lh, lhi, li, lis, lo*, los, lou, lu, un*, una*, uno*, uns, us
Old Provençal	ih', l', la, las, le, les, lh, lhi, li, lis, lo*, los, lou, lu, un*, una*, uno*, uns, us
Panjabi (Perso-Arabic script)	ال- al-
Persian	ال- al-
Portuguese	a, as, o*, os, um*, uma*
Rarotongan	ngā, te
Romanian	o*, un*
Samoan	le, ʻo le, ʻo lo, ʻo se, se
Scots	a, an, ane

LANGUAGE	ARTICLES
Scottish Gaelic	a', am, an, an t-, na, na h-
Shetland dialect	da
Spanish	el, la, las, lo*, los, un*, una*
Swedish	de, den, det, en*, ett*
Tagalog	ang, ang mga, ang m̃g̃a, mga, m̃g̃a ["mga" or "m̃g̃a may be spelled as "manga" or "m̃ãa"]
Tahitian	e, e tahi, hui, ma, maa, mau, na, o, pue, tau, te, te hoe
Tokelau	he, ko na, ko te, nā, ni, o, te
Tonga (Tonga Islands)	e, ha, he, ko e, ko ha, koe
Turkish	al-
Urdu	ال- al-
Walloon	des, ein*, enne, l', les, li
Western Frisian	de, 'e, in, it, 'n, 't
Western Panjabi	ال- al-
Welsh	y, yr
Yiddish	א, אן, דעם, דער, די, דיא, דאס, איין, איינע a, an, dem, der, di, die, dos, eyn*, eyne*
Ancient Greek	hai–αἱ hē–ἡ ho–ὁ hoi–oi ta–τά tain–ταῖν tais–ταῖς tas–τάς tē–τῃ tēn–τήν tēs–τῆς to–τό tō–τῳ, τώ [dative masculine/neuter singular form and nominative/accusative dual form, respectively] toin–τοῖν tois–τοῖς ton–τόν tōn–τῶν tou–τοῦ
Modern Greek	ē — η (monotonic) ena* — ένα (monotonic) enan* — έναν (monotonic) enas* — ένας (monotonic) enos* — ενός (monotonic) hai — αἱ (polytonic only)

LANGUAGE	ARTICLES
	hē — ἡ (polytonic) heis* — εἷς (polytonic only) hen* — ἕν (polytonic only) hena* — ἕνα (polytonic) henan* — ἕναν (polytonic) henas* — ἕνας (polytonic) henos* — ἑνός (polytonic) ho — ὁ (polytonic) hoi — οἱ (polytonic) mia* — μια (monotonic), μιά (polytonic) mian* — μιαν (monotonic), μιάν (polytonic) mias* — μιας (monotonic), μιᾶς (polytonic) o — ο (monotonic) oi — οι (monotonic) ta — τα (monotonic), τά (polytonic) tē — τη (monotonic), τή (polytonic) tēs — της (monotonic), τῆς (polytonic) tis — τις (monotonic), τίς (polytonic) to — το (monotonic), τό (polytonic) ton — τον (monotonic), τόν (polytonic) tōn — των (monotonic), τῶν (polytonic) tou — του (monotonic), τοῦ (polytonic) tous — τους (monotonic), τούς (polytonic)

C.3 Articles Listed by Word or Words

An asterisk (*) after an article indicates that the same form is also used in other contexts (e.g., the cardinal numeral one, a demonstrative pronoun). For those words, take care to determine the meaning before omitting the word.

ARTICLE	LANGUAGES
a	English, Fijian, Galician, Hungarian, Niuean, Portuguese, Scots, Yiddish
a'	Scottish Gaelic
al	Breton
al-	Arabic, Baluchi, Brahui, Panjabi (Perso-Arabic script), Persian, Turkish, Urdu
am	Scottish Gaelic
an	Breton, English, Irish, Scots, Scottish Gaelic, Yiddish
an t-	Irish, Scottish Gaelic
an t [only in certain situations]	Irish
ane	Scots
ang	Tagalog
ang mga ["mga" may be spelled as "manga"]	Tagalog
ang m͠ga ["mga" may be spelled as man͠ga]	Tagalog

ARTICLE	LANGUAGES
ar	Breton
as	Galician, Portuguese
az — not if used as "az az" (that) or "ez az" (this)	Hungarian
bat*	Basque
d'	English
da	Shetland dialect
das	German
de	Danish, Dutch, English, Western Frisian, Norwegian, Swedish
dei	Norwegian
dem	German, Yiddish
den	Danish, German, Norwegian, Swedish
der	German, Yiddish
des	German, Walloon
det	Danish, Norwegian, Swedish
di	Yiddish
die	Afrikaans, German, Yiddish
dos	Yiddish
e	Niuean, Norwegian, Tahitian, Tonga (Tonga Islands)
'e	Western Frisian
e dua na	Fijian
e na dua	Fijian
e taha	Niuean
e tahi	Tahitian
een*	Dutch
eene*	Dutch
egy*	Hungarian
ei*	Norwegian
ein*	German, Norwegian, Walloon
eine*	German
einem	German
einen	German
einer	German

ARTICLE	LANGUAGES
eines	German
eit*	Norwegian
el	Catalan, Spanish
el-	Arabic
els	Catalan
en*	Catalan, Danish, Norwegian, Swedish
enne	Walloon
et*	Danish, Norwegian
ett*	Swedish
eul*	Breton
eun*	Breton
eur*	Breton
eyn*	Yiddish
eyne*	Yiddish
gl'	Italian
gli	Italian
ha	Niuean, Tonga (Tonga Islands)
ha-	Hebrew
he	Hawaiian, Maori, Tokelau, Tonga (Tonga Islands)
hai	Ancient Greek, Modern Greek
he-	Hebrew
hē	Ancient Greek, Modern Greek
heis*	Modern Greek
hen*	Modern Greek
hena*	Modern Greek
henan*	Modern Greek
henas*	Modern Greek
henos*	Modern Greek
het	Dutch
hin	Icelandic
hina	Icelandic
hinar	Icelandic
hinir	Icelandic

ARTICLE	LANGUAGES
hinn	Icelandic
hinna	Icelandic
hinnar	Icelandic
hinni	Icelandic
hins	Icelandic
hinu	Icelandic
hinum	Icelandic
hið	Icelandic
ho	Ancient Greek, Modern Greek
hoi	Ancient Greek, Modern Greek
hui	Tahitian
i	Italian
ih'	Old Provençal
il	Italian, Occitan, Old Provençal
il-	Maltese
in	Western Frisian
it	Western Frisian
ka	Hawaiian
ke	Hawaiian
ko e	Niuean, Tonga (Tonga Islands)
ko ha	Tonga (Tonga Islands)
ko na	Tokelau
ko te	Tokelau
koe	Tonga (Tonga Islands)
l'	Catalan, French, Italian, Provençal/Occitan, Walloon
l-	Maltese
la	Catalan, Esperanto, French, Italian, Occitan, Old Provençal, Spanish
las	Occitan, Old Provençal, Spanish
le	French, Italian, Occitan, Old Provençal, Samoan
les	Catalan, French, Occitan, Old Provençal, Walloon
lh	Occitan, Old Provençal
lhi	Occitan, Old Provençal

ARTICLE	LANGUAGES
li	Occitan, Old Provençal, Walloon
lis	Occitan, Old Provençal
lo*	Italian, Occitan, Old Provençal, Spanish
los	Occitan, Old Provençal, Spanish
lou	Occitan, Old Provençal
lu	Occitan, Old Provençal
ma	Tahitian
maa	Tahitian
mau	Tahitian
mga [may be spelled as "manga"]	Tagalog
m͠ga [may be spelled as "man͠ga"]	Tagalog
mia*	Modern Greek
mian*	Modern Greek
mias*	Modern Greek
’n	Afrikaans, Dutch, Western Frisian
na	Fijian, Hawaiian, Irish, Scottish Gaelic, Tahitian
nā	Tokelau
na h-	Irish, Scottish Gaelic
na h [only in certain situations]	Irish
ngā	Maori, Rarotongan
ni	Tokelau
një	Albanian
ny	Malagasy
o	Tahitian, Tokelau
’o	Neapolitan
o*	Galician, Hawaiian, Portuguese, Romanian
‘o le	Samoan
‘o lo	Samoan
‘o se	Samoan
os	Portuguese
pue	Tahitian
’r	Icelandic
se	Samoan

ARTICLE	LANGUAGES
't	Dutch, Western Frisian
ta	Ancient Greek, Modern Greek
tain	Ancient Greek
tais	Ancient Greek
tas	Ancient Greek
tau	Tahitian
te	Maori, Rarotongan, Tahitian, Tokelau
tē	Ancient Greek, Modern Greek
te hoe	Tahitian
tēn	Ancient Greek, Modern Greek
tēs	Ancient Greek, Modern Greek
the	English
tis	Modern Greek
to	Ancient Greek, Modern Greek
tō	Ancient Greek
toin	Ancient Greek
tois	Ancient Greek
ton	Ancient Greek, Modern Greek
tōn	Ancient Greek, Modern Greek
tou	Ancient Greek, Modern Greek
tous	Modern Greek
ul*	Breton
um*	Portuguese
uma*	Portuguese
un'	Italian
un*	Breton, Catalan, French, Italian, Occitan, Old Provençal, Romanian, Spanish
una*	Catalan, Italian, Occitan, Old Provençal, Spanish
une*	French
unha	Galician
uno*	Italian, Occitan, Old Provençal
uns	Occitan, Old Provençal
ur*	Breton

ARTICLE	LANGUAGES
us	Occitan, Old Provençal
y	Welsh
ye	English
yr	Welsh

D

RECORD SYNTAXES FOR DESCRIPTIVE DATA

D.0 Scope

This appendix provides mappings of the RDA elements used to describe a resource to metadata schemes for presenting or encoding resource description data. The appendix includes:

guidelines on the presentation of data according to ISBD specifications (see **D.1**)

a mapping of the variable fields and subfields defined in the *MARC 21 format for bibliographic data* to the corresponding elements in RDA (see **D.2**).

D.1 ISBD Presentation

D.1.1 Order of Elements

The following table sets out the areas of description and order of elements within each area as specified in the preliminary consolidated edition of the *International Standard Bibliographic Description (ISBD)*.[1]

The table will be updated in a later release to conform with the consolidated edition of the *International Standard Bibliographic Description (ISBD)* published in 2011.[2]

An "M" in parentheses following the ISBD element name indicates that the element is mandatory in the consolidated edition of the ISBD. Certain notes are also mandatory in the ISBD (for details see section 7 of the consolidated edition).

The center column of the table shows the punctuation that precedes or encloses each ISBD element.

The corresponding RDA elements are identified in the right-hand column.

ISBD AREA/ELEMENT	PUNCTUATION	RDA ELEMENT
1. Title and Statement of Responsibility Area		
1.1. Title proper (M)		**2.3.2 Title Proper**
1.2. General material designation [3]	[ ]	**3.2 Media Type**
		6.9 Content Type
1.3. Parallel title	=	**2.3.3 Parallel Title Proper**
1.4. Other title information	:	**2.3.4 Other Title Information**
1.5. Statements of responsibility		
First statement (M)	/	**2.4.2 Statement of Responsibility Relating to Title Proper**
Subsequent statement	;	**2.4.2 Statement of Responsibility Relating to Title Proper**
2. Edition Area		
2.1. Edition statement (M)		**2.5.2 Designation of Edition**
2.2. Parallel edition statement	=	**2.5.3 Parallel Designation of Edition**

ISBD AREA/ELEMENT	PUNCTUATION	RDA ELEMENT
2.3. Statements of responsibility relating to the edition		
First statement (M)	/	2.5.4 Statement of Responsibility Relating to the Edition
Subsequent statement	;	2.5.4 Statement of Responsibility Relating to the Edition
2.4. Additional edition statement (M)	,	2.5.6 Designation of a Named Revision of an Edition
2.5. Statements of responsibility following an additional edition statement		
First statement (M)	/	2.5.8 Statement of Responsibility Relating to a Named Revision of an Edition
Subsequent statement	;	2.5.8 Statement of Responsibility Relating to a Named Revision of an Edition
3. Material or Type of Resource Specific Area		
3.1. Mathematical data (Cartographic resources) (M)		
3.1.1. Statement of scale		7.25.3 Horizontal Scale of Cartographic Content
		7.25.4 Vertical Scale of Cartographic Content
		7.25.5 Additional Scale Information
3.1.2. Statement of projection	;	7.26 Projection of Cartographic Content
3.1.3. Statement of coordinates and equinox	(	7.4.2 Longitude and Latitude
		7.4.3 Strings of Coordinate Pairs
		7.4.4 Right Ascension and Declination
	;)	7.5 Equinox
		7.6 Epoch
3.2. Music format statement (Notated music) (M)		
3.2.1. Music format statement		2.5.2 Designation of Edition
3.2.2. Parallel music format statement	=	2.5.3 Parallel Designation of Edition
3.3. Numbering (Serials) (M)		
		2.6.2 Numeric and/or Alphabetic Designation of First Issue or Part of Sequence
	( )	2.6.3 Chronological Designation of First Issue or Part of Sequence

ISBD AREA/ELEMENT	PUNCTUATION	RDA ELEMENT
		2.6.4 Numeric and/or Alphabetic Designation of Last Issue or Part of Sequence
	( )	2.6.5 Chronological Designation of Last Issue or Part of Sequence
		2.6.6 Alternative Numeric and/or Alphabetic Designation of First Issue or Part of Sequence
	( )	2.6.7 Alternative Chronological Designation of First Issue or Part of Sequence
		2.6.8 Alternative Numeric and/or Alphabetic Designation of Last Issue or Part of Sequence
	( )	2.6.9 Alternative Chronological Designation of Last Issue or Part of Sequence
4. Publication, Production, Distribution, Etc., Area		
4.1. Place of publication, production, and/or distribution		
First place (M)		2.7.2 Place of Production
		2.8.2 Place of Publication
		2.9.2 Place of Distribution
Subsequent place	;	2.7.2 Place of Production
		2.8.2 Place of Publication
		2.9.2 Place of Distribution
4.2. Name of publisher, producer, and/or distributor (M)	:	2.7.4 Producer's Name
		2.8.4 Publisher's Name
		2.9.4 Distributor's Name
4.3. Statement of function of distributor	[ ]	2.9.4 Distributor's Name
4.4. Date of publication, production, and/or distribution (M)	,	2.7.6 Date of Production
		2.8.6 Date of Publication
		2.9.6 Date of Distribution
		2.11 Copyright Date
4.5. Place of printing, manufacture, or engraving	(	2.10.2 Place of Manufacture
4.6. Name of printer, manufacturer, or engraver	:	2.10.4 Manufacturer's Name
4.7. Date of printing or manufacture	,)	2.10.6 Date of Manufacture
5. Physical Description Area		

ISBD AREA/ELEMENT	PUNCTUATION	RDA ELEMENT
5.1. Specific material designation and extent (M)		3.4 Extent
5.2. Other physical details	:	3.6 Base Material
		3.7 Applied Material
		7.15 Illustrative Content
		7.17 Colour Content
		3.15 Reduction Ratio
		7.18 Sound Content
		3.16 Sound Characteristic
		3.11 Layout
		3.9 Production Method
5.3. Dimensions	;	3.5 Dimensions
Format (for older monographic resources)		3.12 Book Format
5.4. Accompanying material statement	+	27.1 Related Manifestation
6. Series Area		
6.1. Title proper of series, subseries, or multipart monographic resource (M)		2.12.2 Title Proper of Series
		2.12.10 Title Proper of Subseries
6.2. Parallel title of series, subseries, or multipart monographic resource	=	2.12.3 Parallel Title Proper of Series
		2.12.11 Parallel Title Proper of Subseries
6.3. Other title information of series, subseries, or multipart monographic resource	:	2.12.4 Other Title Information of Series
		2.12.12 Other Title Information of Subseries
6.4. Statements of responsibility relating to the series, subseries or multipart monographic resource		
First statement	/	2.12.6 Statement of Responsibility Relating to Series
		2.12.14 Statement of Responsibility Relating to Subseries
Subsequent statement	;	2.12.6 Statement of Responsibility Relating to Series
		2.12.14 Statement of Responsibility Relating to Subseries

ISBD AREA/ELEMENT	PUNCTUATION	RDA ELEMENT
6.5. International Standard Serial Number of series or subseries (M)	,	2.12.8 ISSN of Series
		2.12.16 ISSN of Subseries
6.6. Numbering within series, subseries, or multipart monographic resource	;	2.12.9 Numbering within Series
		2.12.17 Numbering within Subseries
7. Note Area		
		25.1 Related Work [published description]
		2.14 Frequency
		2.17.12 Note on Frequency
		3.20 Equipment or System Requirement
		26.1 Related Expression [translation of]
		2.17.2 Note on Title
		2.3.6 Variant Title
		7.2 Nature of the Content
		7.3 Coverage of the Content
		7.11 Place and Date of Capture
		7.21 Medium of Performance of Musical Content
		7.12 Language of the Content
		7.16 Supplementary Content
		2.17.3 Note on Statement of Responsibility
		7.23 Performer, Narrator, and/or Presenter
		7.24 Artistic and/or Technical Credit
		2.17.4 Note on Edition Statement
		25.1 Related Work
		26.1 Related Expression
		27.1 Related Manifestation
		7.27 Other Details of Cartographic Content
		2.17.5 Note on Numbering of Serials
		2.17.6 Note on Production Statement
		2.17.7 Note on Publication Statement
		2.17.8 Note on Distribution Statement
		2.17.9 Note on Manufacture Statement

ISBD AREA/ELEMENT	PUNCTUATION	RDA ELEMENT
		2.17.10 Note on Copyright Date
		3.21.2 Note on Extent of Manifestation
		3.6 Base Material
		3.7 Applied Material
		3.8 Mount
		3.9 Production Method
		3.10 Generation
		3.11 Layout
		7.17 Colour Content
		3.12 Book Format
		3.13 Font Size
		3.14 Polarity
		3.15 Reduction Ratio
		3.16 Sound Characteristic
		7.19 Aspect Ratio
		3.17 Projection Characteristic of Motion Picture Film
		3.18 Video Characteristic
		3.19 Digital File Characteristic
		3.21.3 Note on Dimensions of Manifestation
		3.21.4 Note on Changes in Carrier Characteristics
		7.15 Illustrative Content
		2.17.11 Note on Series Statement
		7.16 Supplementary Content
		2.15 Identifier for the Manifestation
		2.17.13 Note on Issue, Part, or Iteration Used as Basis for Identification of the Resource
		7.22 Duration
		7.13.3 Form of Musical Notation
		7.10 Summarization of the Content
		4.4. Restrictions on Access
		4.5. Restrictions on Use
		7.7 Intended Audience

ISBD AREA/ELEMENT	PUNCTUATION	RDA ELEMENT
		3.22.2 Note on Extent of Item
		3.22 Note on Item-Specific Carrier Characteristic
		3.22.3 Note on Dimensions of Item
		2.18 Custodial History of Item
		2.19 Immediate Source of Acquisition of Item
8. Resource Identifier and Terms of Availability Area		
8.1. Resource identifier (M)		**2.15 Identifier for the Manifestation**
Fingerprint (for older monographic resources)		**2.15 Identifier for the Manifestation**
8.2. Key title (for continuing resources)	=	**2.3.9 Key Title**
8.3. Terms of availability and/or price	:	**4.2 Terms of Availability**
8.4. Qualifications	( )	**2.15 Identifier for the Manifestation**
		4.2 Terms of Availability

1. *International Standard Bibliographic Description (ISBD).* Preliminary consolidated edition. München: K.G. Saur, 2007.
2. *ISBD : International standard bibliographic description* / recommended by the ISBD Review Group ; approved by the Standing Committee of the IFLA Cataloguing Section. — Consolidated ed. — Berlin ; München : De Gruyter Saur, 2011. — xvii, 284 p. ; 25 cm. — (IFLA series on bibliographic control ; vol. 44). — ISBN 978-3-11-026379-4.
3. In the consolidated edition of the ISBD published in 2011, the general material designation is replaced by Area 0 Content Form and Media Type.

D.1.2 ISBD Punctuation

D.1.2.1 General Instructions

Precede each area, other than the first area, or each occurrence of a note or standard number, etc., area, by a full stop, space, dash, space (. —) unless the area begins a new paragraph.

Precede or enclose each occurrence of an element within an area with standard punctuation as prescribed in **D.1.2.2–D.1.2.9**. If the element is the first element present in an area, omit any preceding punctuation prescribed for that element.

Precede each mark of prescribed punctuation by a space and follow it by a space, except for the comma, full stop, and opening and closing parentheses and square brackets. The comma, full stop, and closing parenthesis and square bracket are not preceded by a space; the opening parenthesis and square bracket are not followed by a space.

Omit any area or element that does not apply to the resource being described; also omit its prescribed preceding or enclosing punctuation. Do not indicate the omission of an area or element by the mark of omission.

When adjacent elements within one area are to be enclosed in square brackets, enclose each in its own set of square brackets.

> [London] : [Phipps], [1870]

When an element ends with an abbreviation followed by a full stop or ends with the mark of omission and the punctuation following that element either is or begins with a full stop, include the full stop that constitutes or begins the prescribed punctuation.

> 3rd ed.. —
> **not**
> 3rd ed. —

When punctuation occurring within or at the end of an element is retained, give it with normal spacing. Prescribed punctuation is always added, even though double punctuation may result.

> Quo vadis? : a narrative from the time of Nero

When in an area or an element the same information appears in two or more languages and/or scripts, the following provisions apply.

a) When one element is recorded in two or more languages and/or scripts, the information in each language and/or script after the first is preceded by an equals sign.

b) When, in a single area, two or more elements are recorded in two or more languages and/or scripts, the elements in each language and/or script are given together with the appropriate preceding punctuation for each element. The whole group of elements for the first language and/or script recorded is preceded by punctuation appropriate to the first element and each group after the first is preceded by an equals sign.

c) When a single statement (e.g., a statement of responsibility) is recorded partly in one language and/or script and partly in two or more languages and/or scripts, the several linguistic forms are transcribed together. Equals signs or other punctuation symbols are used as appropriate.

D.1.2.2 Title and Statement of Responsibility Area

Precede the title of a section or supplement (see **2.3.1.7**) by a full stop, unless the title of the section, etc., is preceded by an enumeration or alphabetic designation, in which case precede the enumeration or alphabetic designation by a full stop and precede the title by a comma.

Enclose the general material designation in square brackets.[4]

Precede each parallel title by an equals sign.

Precede each unit of other title information by a colon.

Precede the first statement of responsibility by a diagonal slash.

Precede each subsequent statement of responsibility by a semicolon.

When using a comprehensive description for a resource that lacks a collective title (see **2.3.2.9**), the following provisions apply.

a) Separate the titles proper of the parts by semicolons if the parts are all by the same person(s) or emanate from the same body (bodies), even if the titles are linked by a connecting word or phrase. Follow the title proper of each part by its parallel title(s) (preceded by an equals sign) and other title information (preceded by a colon).

Clock symphony : no. 101 ; Surprise symphony : no. 94 / Haydn

Lord Macaulay's essays ; and, Lays of ancient Rome

b) If the parts are by different persons or families, or corporate bodies, or in case of doubt, separate the groups of data about each part with a full stop. The title proper of each part is followed by its parallel title(s) (preceded by an equals sign), other title information (preceded by a colon), and statement(s) of responsibility (preceded by a diagonal slash or by a semicolon, as appropriate).

Saudades do Brasil : suite de danses pour orchestre / Darius Milhaud. Symphonie concertante pour trompette et orchestre / Henry Barraud

Le prince / Machiavel. Suivi de L'anti-Machiavel de Frédéric II
Title page reads: Machiavel. Le prince, suivi de L'anti-Machiavel de Frédéric II

---

4. In the consolidated edition of the ISBD published in 2011, the general material designation is replaced by Area 0 Content Form and Media Type.

D.1.2.3 Edition Area

Precede this area by a full stop, space, dash, space.

Precede a statement relating to a named revision of an edition by a comma.

Precede the first statement of responsibility following an edition statement by a diagonal slash.

Precede each subsequent statement of responsibility by a semicolon.

D.1.2.4 Material or Type of Resource Specific Area

Precede or enclose each occurrence of an element of an area with standard punctuation as instructed at D.1.2.4.1–D.1.2.4.3, as applicable.

D.1.2.4.1 Mathematical Data (Cartographic Resources)

Precede this area, or each occurrence of this area, by a full stop, space, dash, space.

Precede the projection statement by a semicolon.

Enclose the statement of coordinates and equinox in one pair of parentheses.

If both coordinates and equinox are recorded, precede the statement of equinox by a semicolon.

Precede the statement of epoch by a comma.

D.1.2.4.2 Music Format Statement (Notated Music)

Precede this area, or each occurrence of this area, by a full stop, space, dash, space.

Precede each parallel music format statement by a space, equals sign, space.

D.1.2.4.3 Numbering (Serials)

Precede this area, or each occurrence of this area, by a full stop, space, dash, space.

Follow the numbering of the first issue or part of a serial by a hyphen.

Precede the numbering by a hyphen when only the numbering of the last issue or part of a serial is given.

Enclose a date following a numeric and/or alphabetic designation in parentheses.

Precede an alternative numbering system by an equals sign when more than one system of designation is used.

Precede a new sequence of numbering by a semicolon.

D.1.2.5 Publication, Production, Distribution, Etc., Area

Precede this area by a full stop, space, dash, space.

Precede a second or subsequently named place of publication, production and/or distribution by a semicolon.

Precede the name of a publisher, producer and/or distributor by a colon.

Enclose a supplied statement of function of a distributor in square brackets.

Precede the date of publication, production and/or distribution by a comma.

Precede the date of publication, production and/or distribution in a different calendar by an equals sign when giving a date appearing on the resource in more than one calendar.

Enclose the details of manufacture (place, name, date) in parentheses.

Precede the name of a manufacturer by a colon.

Precede the date of manufacture by a comma.

Precede the date of manufacture in a different calendar by an equals sign when giving a date appearing on the resource in more than one calendar.

D.1.2.6 Physical Description Area

Precede this area by a full stop, space, dash, space or start a new paragraph.

Precede other physical details (i.e., other than extent or dimensions) by a colon.

Precede dimensions by a semicolon.

Precede each statement of accompanying material by a plus sign.

Enclose extent, other physical details, and dimensions of accompanying material in parentheses.

D.1.2.7 Series Area

Precede this area by a full stop, space, dash, space.

Enclose each series statement or each multipart monographic resource statement (see **2.12.1.5**) in parentheses.

Precede each parallel title by an equals sign.

Precede other title information by a colon.

Precede the first statement of responsibility by a diagonal slash.

Precede each subsequent statement of responsibility by a semicolon.

Precede the ISSN of a series or sub-series by a comma.

Precede the numbering within a series or sub-series or multipart monographic resource by a semicolon.

D.1.2.8 Note Area

Precede each note by a full stop, space, dash, space, or start a new paragraph for each.

D.1.2.9 Resource Identifier and Terms of Availability Area

Precede this area by a full stop, space, dash, space, or start a new paragraph.

Precede each repetition of this area by a full stop, space, dash, space.

Precede a key-title by an equals sign.

Precede terms of availability by a colon.

Enclose a qualification to the standard number or terms of availability in parentheses.

D.1.3 Multilevel Description

D.1.3.1 Definition

A multilevel description is a form of presentation of descriptive data based on the division of descriptive information into two or more levels. The first level contains information common to the whole or main resource. The second and subsequent levels contain information about the individual part.

D.1.3.2 Presentation of a Multilevel Description

When describing both the larger resource and its parts using a multilevel description (see **1.5.4**), divide the descriptive information into two or more levels. Record at the first level only information about the resource as a whole or the main resource. Record at the second level information about the part or parts being described. If information at the second level describes a group of parts, record information about the individual part at a third level. Make the levels distinct by layout and/or other means.

When all the parts are received, complete any element left open.

D.2 MARC 21 Format for Bibliographic Data

D.2.1 Mapping of MARC 21 Bibliographic to RDA

See the RDA mappings on the Tools tab of the RDA Toolkit (**MARC Bibliographic to RDA Mapping**) for mappings between RDA and the *MARC 21 format for bibliographic data*. Obsolete fields and subfields, control fields (00X), and control subfields ($0-$8) have been excluded.

E

RECORD SYNTAXES FOR ACCESS POINT CONTROL

E.0 Scope

This appendix provides mappings of RDA data elements used to describe an entity associated with a resource to metadata schemes for presenting or encoding access point and authority data. The appendix includes:

guidelines on the presentation of data derived from AACR2 rules and examples (see **E.1**)

a mapping of the variable fields and subfields defined in the *MARC 21 format for authority data* to the corresponding elements in RDA (see **E.2**).

E.1 Presentation

E.1.1 Presentation of Access Points

The following table lists the elements that are used in AACR2 headings and references for persons and corporate bodies and in uniform titles and title references.

The center column of the table shows the punctuation that precedes or encloses each element as specified in the rules and/or illustrated in examples.

The right-hand column lists the corresponding RDA elements.

AACR2 ACCESS POINT ELEMENTS	PUNCTUATION	RDA ELEMENT
Headings for persons		
Name		**9.2.2 Preferred Name for the Person**
Additions		
Titles of nobility	,	**9.4 Title of the Person**
Saints	,	**9.6 Other Designation Associated with the Person**
Spirits	()	**9.6 Other Designation Associated with the Person**
Royalty	,	**9.4 Title of the Person**
Popes	,	**9.4 Title of the Person**
Bishops	,	**9.4 Title of the Person**
Other persons of religious vocation	,	**9.4 Title of the Person**
Other term of rank, honour, or office	,	**9.4 Title of the Person**
Dates	,	**9.3 Date Associated with the Person**
Fuller forms	()	**9.5 Fuller Form of Name**
Distinguishing terms	()	**9.16 Profession or Occupation**

AACR2 ACCESS POINT ELEMENTS	PUNCTUATION	RDA ELEMENT
		9.6.1.6 Persons Named in Sacred Scriptures or Apocryphal Books
		9.6.1.7 Fictitious and Legendary Persons
		9.6.1.8 Real Non-human Entities
		9.6.1.9 Other Designation
Headings for corporate bodies		
Name		11.2.2 Preferred Name for the Corporate Body
Subheading	.	11.2.2 Preferred Name for the Corporate Body
Additions		
Names not conveying the idea of a corporate body	()	11.7 Other Designation Associated with the Corporate Body
Names of countries, states, provinces, etc.	()	11.3.3 Location of Headquarters
Local place names	()	11.3.3 Location of Headquarters
Institutions	()	11.5 Associated Institution
Years	()	11.4.3 Date of Establishment
		11.4.4 Date of Termination
Other additions	()	11.7 Other Designation Associated with the Corporate Body
Additions to names of governments		
Type of jurisdiction	()	11.7 Other Designation Associated with the Corporate Body
Distinguishing word or phrase	:	11.7 Other Designation Associated with the Corporate Body
Additions to names of conferences, etc.		
Number	()	11.6 Number of a Conference, Etc.
Date	:	11.4.2 Date of Conference, Etc.
Location	:	11.3.2 Location of Conference, Etc.
		11.5 Associated Institution
Additions to names of exhibitions, etc.		
Number	()	11.6 Number of a Conference, Etc.
Date	:	11.4.2 Date of Conference, Etc.
Location	:	11.3.2 Location of Conference, Etc.
		11.5 Associated Institution

AACR2 ACCESS POINT ELEMENTS	PUNCTUATION	RDA ELEMENT
Uniform titles		
Uniform title		6.2.2 Preferred Title for the Work
Designation and/or title for part of a work	.	6.2.2 Preferred Title for the Work
Additions to uniform titles		
Conflict resolution	()	6.3 Form of Work
		6.4 Date of Work
		6.5 Place of Origin of the Work
		6.6 Other Distinguishing Characteristic of the Work
Language	.	6.11 Language of Expression
General material designation	.	6.9 Content Type
Selections	.	6.2.2 Preferred Title for the Work
		6.12 Other Distinguishing Characteristic of the Expression
Additions to uniform titles for laws, etc.		
Year of promulgation	()	6.4 Date of Work
Additions to uniform titles for treaties		
Year of signing	()	6.4 Date of Work
Date of signing	,	6.4 Date of Work
Additions to uniform titles for sacred scriptures		
Language	.	6.11 Language of Expression
Version	.	6.12 Other Distinguishing Characteristic of the Expression
Alternative to version	.	6.12 Other Distinguishing Characteristic of the Expression
Year	.	6.10 Date of Expression
Additions to uniform titles for music		
Medium of performance	,	6.15 Medium of Performance
Number of parts or players	()	6.15 Medium of Performance
Number of hands	,	6.15 Medium of Performance
Numeric identifying elements	,	6.16 Numeric Designation of a Musical Work
Key for music	,	6.17 Key
Other identifying elements	()	6.4 Date of Work

AACR2 ACCESS POINT ELEMENTS	PUNCTUATION	RDA ELEMENT
		6.5 Place of Origin of the Work
		6.6 Other Distinguishing Characteristic of the Work
Sketches	()	6.12 Other Distinguishing Characteristic of the Expression
Arrangements	;	6.12 Other Distinguishing Characteristic of the Expression
Vocal and chorus scores	.	6.12 Other Distinguishing Characteristic of the Expression
Librettos and song texts	.	6.12 Other Distinguishing Characteristic of the Expression
Language	.	6.11 Language of Expression
See references from variant names for persons		
Variant name		9.2.3 Variant Name for the Person
Additions		
Titles of nobility	,	9.4 Title of the Person
Saints	,	9.6 Other Designation Associated with the Person
Spirits	()	9.6 Other Designation Associated with the Person
Royalty	,	9.4 Title of the Person
Popes	,	9.4 Title of the Person
Bishops	,	9.4 Title of the Person
Other persons of religious vocation	,	9.4 Title of the Person
Other term of rank, honour, or office	,	9.4 Title of the Person
Dates	,	9.3 Date Associated with the Person
Fuller forms	()	9.5 Fuller Form of Name
Distinguishing terms	()	9.16 Profession or Occupation
		9.6.1.6 Persons Named in Sacred Scriptures or Apocryphal Books
		9.6.1.7 Fictitious and Legendary Persons
		9.6.1.8 Real Non-human Entities
		9.6.1.9 Other Designation
See references from variant names for corporate bodies		
Variant name		11.2.3 Variant Name for the Corporate Body

AACR2 ACCESS POINT ELEMENTS	PUNCTUATION	RDA ELEMENT
Subheading	.	11.2.3 Variant Name for the Corporate Body
Additions		
Names not conveying the idea of a corporate body	()	11.7 Other Designation Associated with the Corporate Body
Names of countries, states, provinces, etc.	()	11.3.3 Location of Headquarters
Local place names	()	11.3.3 Location of Headquarters
Institutions	()	11.5 Associated Institution
Years	()	11.4.3 Date of Establishment
		11.4.4 Date of Termination
Other additions	()	11.7 Other Designation Associated with the Corporate Body
Additions to names of governments		
Type of jurisdiction	()	11.7 Other Designation Associated with the Corporate Body
Distinguishing word or phrase	:	11.7 Other Designation Associated with the Corporate Body
Additions to names of conferences, etc.		
Number	()	11.6 Number of a Conference, Etc.
Date	:	11.4.2 Date of Conference, Etc.
Location	:	11.3.2 Location of Conference, Etc.
		11.5 Associated Institution
Additions to names of exhibitions, etc.		
Number	()	11.6 Number of a Conference, Etc.
Date	:	11.4.2 Date of Conference, Etc.
Location	:	11.3.2 Location of Conference, Etc.
		11.5 Associated Institution
See references from variant titles for works		
Variant title		6.2.3 Variant Title for the Work
Designation and/or title for part of a work	.	6.2.3 Variant Title for the Work
Additions to uniform titles		
Conflict resolution	()	6.3 Form of Work

AACR2 ACCESS POINT ELEMENTS	PUNCTUATION	RDA ELEMENT
		6.4 Date of Work
		6.5 Place of Origin of the Work
		6.6 Other Distinguishing Characteristic of the Work
Language	.	6.11 Language of Expression
General material designation	.	6.9 Content Type
Selections	.	6.12 Other Distinguishing Characteristic of the Expression
Additions to uniform titles for laws, etc.		
Year of promulgation	()	6.4 Date of Work
Additions to uniform titles for treaties		
Year of signing	()	6.4 Date of Work
Date of signing	,	6.4 Date of Work
Additions to uniform titles for sacred scriptures		
Language	.	6.11 Language of Expression
Version	.	6.12 Other Distinguishing Characteristic of the Expression
Alternative to version	.	6.12 Other Distinguishing Characteristic of the Expression
Year	.	6.10 Date of Expression
Additions to uniform titles for music		
Medium of performance	,	6.15 Medium of Performance
Numeric identifying elements	,	6.16 Numeric Designation of a Musical Work
Key for music	,	6.17 Key
Other identifying elements	()	6.4 Date of Work
		6.5 Place of Origin of the Work
		6.6 Other Distinguishing Characteristic of the Work
Sketches	()	6.12 Other Distinguishing Characteristic of the Expression
Arrangements	;	6.12 Other Distinguishing Characteristic of the Expression
Vocal and chorus scores	.	6.12 Other Distinguishing Characteristic of the Expression
Librettos and song texts	.	6.12 Other Distinguishing Characteristic of the Expression

AACR2 ACCESS POINT ELEMENTS	PUNCTUATION	RDA ELEMENT
Language	.	6.11 Language of Expression
See also references from names for related persons		
Name		9.2.2 Preferred Name for the Person
Additions		
Titles of nobility	,	9.4 Title of the Person
Saints	,	9.6 Other Designation Associated with the Person
Spirits	()	9.6 Other Designation Associated with the Person
Royalty	,	9.4 Title of the Person
Popes	,	9.4 Title of the Person
Bishops	,	9.4 Title of the Person
Other persons of religious vocation	,	9.4 Title of the Person
Other term of rank, honour, or office	,	9.4 Title of the Person
Dates	,	9.3 Date Associated with the Person
Fuller forms	()	9.5 Fuller Form of Name
Distinguishing terms	()	9.16 Profession or Occupation
		9.6.1.6 Persons Named in Sacred Scriptures or Apocryphal Books
		9.6.1.7 Fictitious and Legendary Persons
		9.6.1.8 Real Non-human Entities
		9.6.1.9 Other Designation
See also references from names for related corporate bodies		
Name		11.2.2 Preferred Name for the Corporate Body
Subheading	.	11.2.2 Preferred Name for the Corporate Body
Additions		
Names not conveying the idea of a corporate body	()	11.7 Other Designation Associated with the Corporate Body
Names of countries, states, provinces, etc.	()	11.3.3 Location of Headquarters
Local place names	()	11.3.3 Location of Headquarters
Institutions	()	11.5 Associated Institution
Years	()	11.4.3 Date of Establishment

AACR2 ACCESS POINT ELEMENTS	PUNCTUATION	RDA ELEMENT
		11.4.4 Date of Termination
Other additions	()	11.7 Other Designation Associated with the Corporate Body
Additions to names of governments		
Type of jurisdiction	()	11.7 Other Designation Associated with the Corporate Body
Distinguishing word or phrase	:	11.7 Other Designation Associated with the Corporate Body
Additions to names of conferences, etc.		
Number	()	11.6 Number of a Conference, Etc.
Date	:	11.4.2 Date of Conference, Etc.
Location	:	11.3.2 Location of Conference, Etc.
		11.5 Associated Institution
Additions to names of exhibitions, etc.		
Number	()	11.6 Number of a Conference, Etc.
Date	:	11.4.2 Date of Conference, Etc.
Location	:	11.3.2 Location of Conference, Etc.
		11.5 Associated Institution
See also references from uniform titles for related works		
Uniform title		6.2.2 Preferred Title for the Work
Designation and/or title for part of a work	.	6.2.2 Preferred Title for the Work
Additions to uniform titles		
Conflict resolution	()	6.3 Form of Work
		6.4 Date of Work
		6.5 Place of Origin of the Work
		6.6 Other Distinguishing Characteristic of the Work
Language	.	6.11 Language of Expression
General material designation	.	6.9 Content Type
Selections	.	6.12 Other Distinguishing Characteristic of the Expression
Additions to uniform titles for laws, etc.		
Year of promulgation	()	6.4 Date of Work

AACR2 ACCESS POINT ELEMENTS	PUNCTUATION	RDA ELEMENT
Additions to uniform titles for treaties		
Year of signing	()	6.4 Date of Work
Date of signing	,	6.4 Date of Work
Additions to uniform titles for sacred scriptures		
Language	.	6.11 Language of Expression
Version	.	6.12 Other Distinguishing Characteristic of the Expression
Alternative to version	.	6.12 Other Distinguishing Characteristic of the Expression
Year	.	6.10 Date of Expression
Additions to uniform titles for music		
Medium of performance	,	6.15 Medium of Performance
Numeric identifying elements	,	6.16 Numeric Designation of a Musical Work
Key for music	,	6.17 Key
Other identifying elements	()	6.4 Date of Work
		6.5 Place of Origin of the Work
		6.6 Other Distinguishing Characteristic of the Work
Sketches	()	6.12 Other Distinguishing Characteristic of the Expression
Arrangements	;	6.12 Other Distinguishing Characteristic of the Expression
Vocal and chorus scores	.	6.12 Other Distinguishing Characteristic of the Expression
Librettos and song texts	.	6.12 Other Distinguishing Characteristic of the Expression
Language	.	6.11 Language of Expression

E.1.2 Punctuation of Access Points

E.1.2.1 General

The instructions at E.1.2.2–E.1.2.5 reflect the punctuation for access points derived from AACR2 rules and examples. These instructions cover the punctuation that precedes or encloses additions to names and titles in access points representing persons, corporate bodies, and works.

Punctuation that is internal to an element is specified in the instructions addressing that element.

E.1.2.2 Access Points Representing Persons

Precede a title of nobility by a comma and a space.

Precede the term *Saint* by a comma and a space.

Enclose the term *Spirit* in parentheses.

Precede a title of royalty or religious rank, or a term of address for a person of religious vocation, or other term indicative of rank, honour, or office by a comma and a space.

Precede a date or range of dates by a comma and a space.

Separate a date of birth and a date of death by a hyphen. If a date of birth is not followed by a date of death, follow the date of birth with a hyphen or precede that date by the word *born*. If a date of death is not preceded by a date of birth, precede the date of death by a hyphen or by the word *died*.

Precede a single year used as a date for the period of activity of the person by a word such as *active* or *flourished*.

Enclose a fuller form of name in parentheses.

Enclose a profession or occupation in parentheses.

Enclose a designation for a person named in a sacred scripture or an apocryphal book in parentheses.

Enclose a designation for a fictitious or legendary person in parentheses.

Enclose a designation for a real non-human entity in parentheses.

Enclose other designation in parentheses.

E.1.2.3 Access Points Representing Families

Enclose additions to the name of a family in a single set of parentheses, separating each addition by a space, colon, space.

E.1.2.4 Access Points Representing Corporate Bodies

Precede a subheading by a full stop and a space.

Enclose a term indicating the type of corporate body in parentheses.

Enclose the name of a country, state, province, etc., in parentheses.

Enclose a local place name in parentheses.

Enclose the name of an institution in parentheses.

Enclose a date or dates associated with the body in parentheses.

Enclose a general designation in parentheses.

Enclose a term indicating the type of jurisdiction in parentheses.

Enclose a distinguishing word or phrase in parentheses.

Separate a term indicating the type of corporate body and a date, a place name, or a distinguishing word or phrase by a space, colon, space.

Separate a term indicating the type of jurisdiction and a distinguishing word or phrase by a space, colon, space.

Separate a term used to distinguish one government from another claiming jurisdiction over the same area and the date or dates associated with that government by a comma and a space.

Enclose the number, date, and location of a conference, etc., in parentheses. Separate the number, date, and location by a space, colon, space. Separate multiple locations by a semicolon.

Enclose the number, date, and location of an exhibition, etc., in parentheses. Separate the number, date, and location by a space, colon, space. Separate multiple locations by a semicolon.

E.1.2.5 Access Points Representing Works and Expressions

Apply the instructions at **E.1.2.2–E.1.2.4** for the punctuation of the portion of the access point that represents the person, family, or corporate body, as applicable, when the access point representing a work is constructed by combining (in this order):

a) an access point representing a person, family, or corporate body

b) a preferred or variant title for the work.

Precede a designation and/or title for part of a work by a full stop and a space.

Enclose a word, phrase, date, or other designation used for conflict resolution in parentheses.

Separate a word, phrase, date, or other designation used for conflict resolution from another word, phrase, date, or other designation also used for conflict resolution by a space, colon, space.

Precede the name of a language by a full stop and a space.

Precede the content type by a full stop and a space.

Enclose the year of promulgation of a law, etc., in parentheses.

Enclose the date of a treaty in parentheses.

Precede the name of the language of a sacred scripture by a full stop and a space.

Precede the conventional collective title *Selections* by a full stop and a space.

Precede the name of the version of a sacred scripture by a full stop and a space.

Precede an alternative designation for the version of a sacred scripture by a full stop and a space.

Precede the year of publication of a sacred scripture by a full stop and a space.

Precede medium of performance by a comma and a space.

Enclose the number of parts or players in parentheses.

Precede the number of hands by a comma and a space.

Precede a numeric identifying element for music by a comma and a space.

Precede key for music by a comma and a space.

Precede other identifying elements for music by a comma and a space.

Enclose a descriptive word or phrase for music in parentheses.

Enclose the term *Sketches* in parentheses.

Precede the term *arranged* by a semicolon and a space.

Precede the terms *Vocal score* and *Chorus score* by a full stop and a space.

Precede the terms *Libretto* and *Text* by a full stop and a space.

Precede the name of the language of a vocal musical work by a full stop and a space.

E.1.3 Presentation of References

E.1.3.1 General

The guidelines at E.1.3.2–E.1.3.4 reflect the presentation of *see*, *see also*, and explanatory references as illustrated in examples in AACR2.

E.1.3.2 *See* References to Authorized Access Points Representing Persons, Families, Corporate Bodies, and Works

Present a *see* reference from a variant access point representing a person, family, corporate body, or work to the authorized access point representing that person, family, corporate body, or work as illustrated in the following examples:

Thascius Caecilius Cyprianus, Saint, Bishop of Carthage
see
Cyprian, Saint, Bishop of Carthage

Beethoven, Ludwig van, 1770–1827. Moonlight sonata
see
Beethoven, Ludwig van, 1770–1827. Sonatas, piano, no. 14, op. 27, no. 2, C# minor

Alternatives

For a *see* reference from a variant access point to two or more authorized access points representing different persons, families, corporate bodies, or works, present one *see* reference. List all the authorized access points representing persons, families, corporate bodies, or works to which reference is being made.

Mahfouz, Nagib
see
Maḥfūẓ, Najīb, 1882–1974
Maḥfūẓ, Najīb, 1911–2006

ABM
see
Academia Brasileira de Música
Associação Bahiana de Medicina
Associação Brasileira de Metais
Association des amis de la Bibliothèque et du Musée des beaux-arts de Tours

Bava kamma
see
Mishnah. Bava kamma
Talmud. Bava kamma
Talmud Yerushalmi. Bava kamma
Tosafot. Bava kamma
Tosefta. Bava kamma

If a *see* reference from a variant access point does not provide adequate guidance to the user of the catalogue, present an explanatory reference with more explicit guidance (see **E.1.3.4**).

E.1.3.3 *See also* References to Authorized Access Points Representing Related Persons, Families, Corporate Bodies, and Works

Present a *see also* reference from the authorized access point as illustrated in the following examples:

Canadian Figure Skating Association
see also
Skate Canada

Klage
see also
Nibelungenlied

Catholic Church. Breviary
see also
Catholic Church. Liturgy of the hours

When using a relationship designator with an authorized access point, present the *see also* reference by combining (in this order):

a) the relationship designator, followed by a colon, space

b) the authorized access point for the related person, family, corporate body, or work.

Library and Archives Canada
see also
Predecessor: National Archives of Canada
Predecessor: National Library of Canada

Union of American Republics
see also
Predecessor: International Union of American Republics
Successor: Organization of American States

Alternatives

For a *see also* reference from the authorized access point representing a person, family, corporate body, or work to two or more authorized access points representing different related persons, families, corporate bodies, or works, present one *see also* reference. List all the authorized access points for related persons, families, corporate bodies, or works to which reference is being made.

Pennsylvania. Department of Public Welfare
see also
Pennsylvania. Department of Public Assistance
Pennsylvania. Department of Welfare

Nongame Bird and Mammal Program report
see also
Nongame Bird and Mammal Section report
Bird and Mammal Conservation Program report

If a *see also* reference to the authorized access point representing a related person, family, corporate body, or work does not provide adequate guidance to the user of the catalogue, present an explanatory reference with more explicit guidance (see **E.1.3.4**).

E.1.3.4 Explanatory References

Present an explanatory reference as illustrated in the following examples:

Gustaf Adolf, King of Sweden
Kings of Sweden with this name are listed in a single sequence of all the kings of Sweden with the first name Gustaf, e.g.,
Gustaf I Vasa, King of Sweden, 1496–1560
Gustaf II Adolf, King of Sweden, 1594–1632
Gustaf III, King of Sweden, 1746–1792
Gustav IV Adolf, King of Sweden, 1778–1837
Present a similar reference under Gustaf Vasa, King of Sweden

Plaidy, Jean, 1906–1993
For works of this author written under other names, *see*
Carr, Philippa, 1906–1993
Ford, Elbur, 1906–1993
Holt, Victoria, 1906–1993
Kellow, Kathleen, 1906–1993

Tate, Ellalice, 1906–1993
etc., as required

Carr, Philippa, 1906–1993
For works of this author written under other names, *see*
Ford, Elbur, 1906–1993
Holt, Victoria, 1906–1993
Kellow, Kathleen, 1906–1993
Plaidy, Jean, 1906–1993
Tate, Ellalice, 1906–1993
etc., as required
Present similar references under the other names

or alternatively

Carr, Philippa, 1906–1993
Works by this author are listed under the name used in the item. For a list of other names used by this author, *search also under* Plaidy, Jean, 1906–1993.
Present the same reference under each of the other names

American-Asian Educational Exchange
The American-Asian Educational Exchange was founded in 1957. In 1962 the name was changed to American Afro-Asian Educational Exchange. In 1967 the name American-Asian Educational Exchange was resumed.
Works of this body are listed under the name used at the time of publication.
Present the same reference under American Afro-Asian Educational Exchange

Pentateuch
For the Pentateuch as a whole, *see* Bible. Pentateuch. For an individual book of the Pentateuch, *see* the name of the book as a subdivision of Bible (e.g., Bible. Genesis).

Proust, Marcel, 1871–1922. À la recherche du temps perdu
For the separately published parts of this work, *see*
Proust, Marcel, 1871–1922. Du côté de chez Swann
Proust, Marcel, 1871–1922. À l'ombre des jeunes filles en fleurs
Proust, Marcel, 1871–1922. Côté de Guermantes
Proust, Marcel, 1871–1922. Sodome et Gomorrhe
Proust, Marcel, 1871–1922. Prisonnière
Proust, Marcel, 1871–1922. Albertine disparue
Proust, Marcel, 1871–1922. Temps retrouvé

E.2 MARC 21 Format for Authority Data

E.2.1 Mapping of MARC 21 Authorities to RDA

See the RDA mappings on the Tools tab of the RDA Toolkit (**MARC Authority to RDA Mapping**) for mappings between RDA and the *MARC 21 format for authority data*. Obsolete fields and subfields, control fields (00X), and control subfields ($0-$8) have been excluded.

F

ADDITIONAL INSTRUCTIONS ON NAMES OF PERSONS

F.0 Scope

This appendix supplements the general guidelines and instructions in chapter **9**. It provides instructions on choosing and recording names of persons in the following specific categories:

Names in the Arabic alphabet (see **F.1**)
Burmese and Karen names (see **F.2**)
Chinese names containing a non-Chinese given name (see **F.3**)
Icelandic names (see **F.4**)
Indic names (see **F.5**)
Indonesian names (see **F.6**)
Malay names (see **F.7**)
Roman names (see **F.8**)
Romanian names containing a patronymic (see **F.9**)
Thai names (see **F.10**)

For more detailed treatment of names in other national contexts, see the IFLA UBCIM Programme's survey of personal names.[1]

If a surname includes an article and/or preposition, practices for determining the first element of the name differ depending on the language. This appendix summarizes those practices for surnames in a selected number of languages (see **F.11**).

---

1. IFLA Universal Bibliographic Control and International MARC Programme, *Names of Persons: National Usages for Entry in Catalogues,* 4th rev. and enlarged edition (München: K.G. Saur, 1996).

F.1 Names in the Arabic Alphabet

F.1.1 Additional Instructions on Names in the Arabic Alphabet

F.1.1.1 Application

The instructions at **F.1** apply only to names that:

a) are originally written in the Arabic alphabet (regardless of their origin)
and
b) do not contain a surname or a name performing the function of a surname.

In case of doubt, assume that a name of a person active in the twentieth century includes a surname (see **9.2.2.9–9.2.2.13**). Assume that names of persons active in previous centuries do not include a surname.

To determine the preferred name, apply the following instructions:

a) choose the first element for the preferred name (see **F.1.1.2**)

b) determine the essential parts of the name to be included in the preferred name (see **F.1.1.3**)

c) determine the order of the essential parts of the name (see **F.1.1.4**).

For further guidance on the treatment of names written in the Arabic alphabet, consult the following major reference sources (note that transliteration practices in these sources differ):

Franz Babinger, *Die Geschichtsschreiber der Osmanen und ihre Werke,* mit einem Anhang, Osmanische Zeitrechnungen von Joachim Mayr (Leipzig: Harrassowitz, 1927).

Carl Brockelmann, *Geschichte der arabischen Litteratur,* 2. den Supplementbänden angepasste Aufl. (Leiden: E.J. Brill, 1943–1949). — 1.-3. Supplementband: Leiden: E.J. Brill, 1937–1942.

Leone Caetani, *Onomasticon Arabicum, ossia, Repertorio alfabetico dei nomi di persona e di luogo contenuti nelle principali opere storiche, biografiche e geografiche, stampate e manoscritte, relative all'Islām,* compilato per cura di Leone Caetani e Giuseppe Gabrieli (Roma: Casa editrice italiana, 1915).

The Encyclopaedia of Islām: A Dictionary of the Geography, Ethnography, and Biography of the Muhammadan Peoples, prepared by a number of leading orientalists, edited by M. Th. Houtsma [et al.] (Leyden: E.J. Brill, 1913–1934). — Supplement: Leiden: E.J. Brill, 1938.

The Encyclopaedia of Islam, prepared by a number of leading orientalists, new ed., edited by an editorial committee consisting of H.A.R. Gibb [et al.] (Leiden: E.J. Brill, 1960–2002). — Supplement: Leiden: E.J. Brill, 1980–2004.

İslâm ansiklopedisi: İslâm âlemi coğrafya, etnoğrafya ve biyografya lûgati, Beynelmilel Akademiler Birliğinin yardımı ve tanınmış müsteşriklerin iştiraki ile neşredenler, M. Th. Houtsma [et al.] (İstanbul: Maarif Matbaası, 1940–1943; İstanbul: Millî Eğitim Basımevi, 1945–1952; İstanbul: Maarif Basımevi, 1954–1960; İstanbul: Millî Eğitim Basımevi, 1960–1988).

Philologiae Turcicae Fundamenta, iussu et auctoritate Unionis Universae Studiosorum Rerum Orientalium, auxilio et opera Unitarum Nationum Educationis Scientiae Culturae Ordinis, una cum praestantibus Turcologis, ediderunt Jean Deny [et al.] (Aquis Mattiacis: Steiner, 1959–).

Fuat Sezgin, *Geschichte des arabischen Schrifttums* (Leiden: E.J. Brill, 1967–1984; Frankfurt am Main: Institut für Geschichte der Arabisch-Islamischen Wissenschaften an der Johann Wolfgang Goethe-Universität, 2000–). — Gesamtindices zu Band I-IX: Frankfurt am Main: Institut für Geschichte der Arabisch-Islamischen Wissenschaften an der Johann Wolfgang Goethe-Universität, 1995.

C.A. Storey, *Persian Literature: A Bio-bibliographical Survey* (London: Luzac & Co., 1927–1971; Leiden: E.J. Brill, 1977–).

F.1.1.2 First Element

For a name made up of a number of parts, record the part or combination of parts by which the person is best known as the first element of the preferred name. Determine this from reference sources. When there is insufficient evidence available, record the first part of the name as the first element.

Variant names. Record other forms of the name as variant names by applying the following instructions, as applicable:

a) record a form of name using another part as the first element if the name might reasonably be searched by that part

b) record a form of name resulting from a different transliteration, if considered important for identification or access (see **9.2.3.9**).

F.1.1.3 Essential Parts of the Name

Determine the essential parts of the name to be included in the preferred name.

If the first element is not the given name (ism), include the given name unless it is not customarily used in the name by which the person is known.

If the first element is not a patronymic derived from the name of the father, include the patronymic unless it is not customarily used in the name by which by the person is known. For names in the Arabic alphabet, a patronymic is a name usually following the given name and compounded with *ibn.*

Include an additional name, descriptive epithet, or term of honour that is treated as part of the name if it assists in identifying the individual.

Generally omit other parts of the name, particularly patronymics derived from anyone other than the father.

F.1.1.4 Order of Parts

When the parts of the name have been determined (see **F.1.1.3**), determine the order of the parts. Record first the best-known part or combination of parts. Record the other parts in the following order: khiṭāb, kunyah, ism, patronymic, any other name.

Insert a comma after the first element unless it is the first part of the name.

Khiṭāb (honorific compound of which the last part is typically *al-Dīn*)

Rashīd al-Dīn Ṭabīb

Ṣadr al-Dīn al-Qūnawī, Muḥammad ibn Isḥāq

Kunyah (typically a compound with *Abū* or *Umm* as the first word)

Abū al-Barakāt Hibat Allāh ibn ʻAlī

Abū Ḥayyān al-Tawḥīdī, ʻAlī ibn Muḥammad

Abū Hurayrah

Umm Kulthūm

Ism (given name)

ʻAlī ibn Abī Ṭālib, Caliph

Bashshār ibn Burd

Mālik ibn Anas

Nashwān ibn Saʻīd al-Ḥimyarī

Muḥammad Ismāʻīl Pānīpatī

Nādirah K̲h̲ātūn

Patronymic (typically a compound with *Ibn* or *Bin* (son of) or *Bint* (daughter of) as the first word)

Ibn Hishām, ʻAbd al-Malik

Ibn Ḥazm, ʻAlī ibn Aḥmad

Ibn Sanāʼ al-Mulk, Hibat Allāh ibn Jaʻfar

Ibn al-Muʻtazz, ʻAbd Allāh

Ibn al-Muqaffaʻ

Bin Mālik, Aḥmad

Bint Ṭalāl, Basmah

Bint al-Ḥasan, Khadījah

Other Names: *Laqab* (descriptive epithet)

Jāḥiẓ

Abū Shāmah, ʻAbd al-Raḥmān ibn Ismāʻīl

Kātib al-Iṣfahānī, ʻImād al-Dīn Muḥammad ibn Muḥammad

Qāḍī al-Fāḍil, ʻAbd al-Raḥīm ibn ʻAlī

Other Names: *Nisbah* (proper adjective ending in *ī*, indicating origin, residence, or other circumstances)

Bukhārī, Muḥammad ibn Ismāʻīl

Māzandarānī, ʻAbd Allāh ibn Muḥammad

ʻAbbāsī, ʻAlī Aḥmad

Hilālī, Muḥammad Khān Mīr

Other Names: *Takhalluṣ* (pen name)

Qāʼānī, Ḥabīb Allāh Shīrāzī

ʻIbrat, Ẓafar Ḥasan

Ghalib, Mirza Asadullah Khan

F.2 Burmese and Karen Names

F.2.1 Additional Instructions on Burmese and Karen Names

F.2.1.1 First Element

For a Burmese or Karen name that includes a Western given name preceding the vernacular name(s), record the vernacular name(s) as the first element. Transpose the Western name to the end.

Aung Din, Margaret
Name: Margaret Aung Din

F.2.1.2 Term of Address, Etc.

Treat the term of address that usually accompanies a Burmese or Karen name as an integral part of the name. If the name of the same person is found with different terms of address, use the term of highest honour. Distinguish terms of address from the same words used as names.

Ba U, U

Tin Tin Myint, Daw

Lha, Lū thu Ū″

Ba Han, Maung

Record any other distinguishing terms generally associated with the name (see **9.6**).

F.3 Chinese Names Containing a Non-Chinese Given Name

F.3.1 Additional Instructions on Chinese Names Containing a Non-Chinese Given Name

If:

a name of Chinese origin contains a non-Chinese given name
and
the name is found in the order [*non-Chinese given name*] [*surname*] [*Chinese given names*]
then:
record the name as [*surname*], [*non-Chinese given name*] [*Chinese given names*].
Record all other names by applying the instructions at **9.2.2.9**.

Loh, Philip Fook Seng
Name appears as: Philip Loh Fook Seng

F.4 Icelandic Names

F.4.1 Additional Instructions on Icelandic Names

For Icelandic names, record names in this order:

a) the first given name

b) other given names (if present)

c) the patronymic

d) the family name, in direct order.

If a phrase naming a place follows the given name(s), patronymic, or family name, treat it as an integral part of the name.

Svava Jakobsdóttir
Given name: Svava
Patronymic: Jakobsdóttir

Halldór Laxness
Given name: Halldór
Family name: Laxness

Bjarni Benediktsson frá Hofteigi
Given name: Bjarni
Patronymic: Benediktsson
Words denoting place: frá Hofteigi

Jóhannes úr Kötlum
Given name: Jóhannes
Words denoting place: úr Kötlum

Variant names. Record as variant names both a form using the patronymic as the first element and a form using the family name as the first element (see **9.2.3.10**).

F.5 Indic Names

F.5.1 Additional Instructions on Indic Names

F.5.1.1 Early Names

For an Indic name of a person who was active before the middle of the nineteenth century, record the first part of the personal name as the first element.

Generally ignore honorifics and religious terms of address that precede the name (e.g., *Shri (Sri)*, *Swami*, *Acharya*, *Muni*, *Bhikkhu*). However, include a title (e.g., *Shri (Sri)*, *Swami*, *Sastri*, *Acharya*, *Bhatta*,

Saraswati, *Muni*, *Gani*) as an integral part of the name if it usually appears with the name in reference sources.

Do not include the suffix *-ji* (or *-jee*) sometimes added to the personal element of the name.

Kālidāsa

Pāṇini

Kārttikeyasvāmin

Śaṅkarācārya

Śrīharṣa

Śrīdharasvāmin

but

Rāmānuja

Sometimes appears as: Rāmānujācārya

For the name of an ancient or medieval Sanskrit author or an author (usually Jain) of a Prakrit text, record the Sanskrit form of the name as the preferred name.

Āryabhaṭa

Aśvaghoṣa

Bhaṭṭojī Dīkṣita

Karṇapūra

For the name of a Buddhist author of a Pali text, record the Pali form of the name as the preferred name.

Dhammakitti

Ñāṇamoli, Bhikkhu

Variant names. Record as a variant name a form of the name that is significantly different from the form recorded as the preferred name (see **9.2.3.10**).

F.5.1.2 Modern Names

For an Indic name of a person who was active after the middle of the nineteenth century, record as the first element of the preferred name the surname or the name that the person is known to have used as a surname. If there is no surname, record the last name as the first element. See also the exceptions for Kannada, Malayalam, Tamil, and Telugu names, Sikh names, and religious names.

Dutt, Romesh Chunder

Krishna Menon, V. K.

Singh, Indrajit

For Sikh names ending in Singh, see the following exception for Sikh names

Das Gupta, Hemendra Nath

Shastri, Lal Bahadur

Sastri (Shastri) is sometimes used as a surname, sometimes as a religious title, sometimes as an appendage to a personal name, and sometimes as a reinforcement to another surname.

Exceptions

Kannada, Malayalam, Tamil, and Telugu names. If a name in one of these languages does not contain a surname or a name known to have been used by the person as a surname, record the given name as the first element of the preferred name. Given names in these languages are normally preceded by a place name, occasionally preceded by the father's given name and sometimes followed by a caste name.

Kiruṣṇa Ayyaṅkār, Tiṭṭai
Given name: Kiruṣṇa
Caste name: Ayyaṅkār
Place name: Tiṭṭai

Sankaran Nair, C.
Given name: Sankaran
Caste name: Nair
House name: C. (Chettur)

Ranganathan, S. R.
Given name: Ranganathan
Initials of place name and of father's given name: S. R. (Shiyali Ramamrita)

Radhakrishnan, S.
Given name: Radhakrishnan
Initial of place name: S. (Sarvepalli)

Sikh names. For the Sikh name of a person who does not use *Singh* or *Kaur* as a surname, record the first of his or her names (the given name) as the first element of the preferred name.

Surjit Kaur

Khushwant Singh

Religious names. For a modern person of religious vocation (Hindu, Buddhist, or Jain), record the religious name as the first element of the preferred name, followed by a comma and the religious title.

Chinmayananda, Swami

Ramana, Maharshi

Puṇyavijaya, Muni

Sangharakshita, Bhikshu

Variant names. Record as a variant name a form of the name that is significantly different from the form recorded as the preferred name (see **9.2.3.10**).

F.6 Indonesian Names

F.6.1 Additional Instructions on Indonesian Names

F.6.1.1 Scope

The instructions at **F.6** apply to Indonesian names of Arabic, Chinese, Dutch, Indic, Javanese, Malayan, Sumatran, or other origin.

F.6.1.2 First Element

For an Indonesian name consisting of more than one part, record the last part as the first element unless instructed otherwise at **F.6.1.3**–**F.6.1.6**).

Hatta, Mohammad
Compound given name

Salim, Emil
Given name and surname

Purbatjaraka, Purnadi
Given name and father's name

Nasution, Amir Hamzah
Given name and clan name

Andika, Nyoman
Balinese name containing a part indicating seniority of children

Djelantik, I Gusti Ketut
Balinese name

Hanafie, Sitti Hawang
Married woman's name; last part may be the husband's or the father's name

Variant names. Record the name in direct order as a variant name unless the first part is a European name (see **9.2.3.10**).

F.6.1.3 First Part of the Name Recorded as the First Element

Record the first part of the name as the first element for the following categories of names:

a) a name consisting of a given name followed by a part indicating filial relationship (e.g., *bin, binti, ibni*) and the father's name

b) a name that can be written either as one word or as separate words and that begins with one of the following elements: *Adi*, *Budi (Boedi)*, *Joko (Djoko)*, *Karta*, *Kusuma (Koesoema)*, *Mangku (Mangkoe)*, *Noto*, *Prawira*, *Pura (Poera)*, *Sastra*, *Sri*, *Surya (Soerya, Surja, Suria)*, and *Tri* (if the name of a particular person sometimes appears as one word and sometimes as separate words, use the one-word form)

c) a name containing an initial or abbreviation as the last element.

Rohani binti Abdul Rahim

Budi Agustono

Djokomudjirahardjo

Sri Mulyono

Suman Hs.

Variant names. Record as a variant name a form using the last part of the name as the first element. If the last part is an initial, also record as a variant name a form using the next to the last part of the name as the first element (see **9.2.3.10**).

F.6.1.4 Names Consisting of Given Name(s) and *Adat* Title

Record as the first element the part of the name introduced by one or more of the following terms: *gelar* (sometimes abbreviated as *gl.* or *glr.*), *Daeng, Datuk,* or *Sutan.*

Palindih, Rustam Sutan

Matutu, Mustamin Daeng

Radjo Endah, Sjamsuddin Sutan

Variant names. Record the name in direct order as a variant name (see **9.2.3.10**).

F.6.1.5 Names Containing Place Names

For a name consisting of personal names followed by a place name, record the part preceding the place name as the first element. Treat the place name as an integral part of the name.

Abubakar Aceh

Daud Beureuh, Muhammad

F.6.1.6 Names of Chinese Origin

For a name of Chinese origin that follows the normal Chinese order (surname first), record the first part of the name as the first element.

Lim, Yauw Tjin
Name appears as: Lim Yauw Tjin

Oei, Hong Djien
Name appears as: Oei Hong Djien

Variant names. Record as a variant name a form using the last element of the name as the first element.

F.6.1.7 Titles

Record titles and honorific words[2] as instructed at **9.4.1.5**.

Poerbatjaraka, Raden Mas Ngabei

Distinguish words used as titles from the same words adopted by a person as elements of his or her name. When in doubt, treat the words as a title.

Djuanda, H.
Name and title hadji Djuanda *appears as:* Dr. H. Djuanda

Variant names. Record as a variant name the direct form of the title and the name (even when the title is not recorded as a title of the person) (see **9.2.3.10**).

---

2. See appendix **G** for a list of Indonesian titles and honorific words.

F.7 Malay Names

F.7.1 Additional Instructions on Malay Names

F.7.1.1 Scope

The instructions at **F.7** apply to Malay names of persons living in Malaysia, Singapore, or Brunei, including names of Arabic origin beginning with the element *al-*.

Also apply the instructions to names from other ethnic groups native to Malaysia such as Ibans, Kedazans, etc.

For names of persons from an ethnic group of non-Malay origin (e.g., Indian, Chinese) who live in Malaysia, Singapore, or Brunei, apply the instructions for the language of the name.

F.7.1.2 General Guidelines

Record as the first element the first part of a Malay name unless it is known that the person treats another part of the name as a surname. In that case, record the surname as the first element.

A. Samad Said

Rejab F. I.

Shahnon Ahmad

H. M. Dahlan

but

Merican, Zahara
Surname: Merican

Variant names. Record variant names by applying the following instructions, as applicable:

a) If the first part of the name is recorded as the first element, record as a variant name a form using the last part of the name as the first element (see **9.2.3.10**).

b) If the surname is recorded as the first element, record as a variant name a form using the first part of the name as the first element (see **9.2.3.10**).

F.7.1.3 Filial Indicators

Omit the following words or abbreviations that indicate filial relationship, unless consistently used by the person:

anak (a., ak, *or* ak.)–child of

bin (b.)–son of

binte (bte.)–daughter of

binti (bt.)–daughter of

ibni–son of (royalty)

Adibah Amin
Sometimes appears as: Khalidah Adibah binti Haji Amin

but

Abdullah Sanusi bin Ahmad
Person consistently uses the word bin *as part of name*

If the filial relationship is shown beyond one generation, include only the first unless more are required to distinguish between names that are otherwise identical.

Ali bin Ahmad
Name appears as: Ali bin Ahmad bin Hussein

Variant names. Record as a variant name a form of the name that is significantly different from the form recorded as the preferred name (see **9.2.3.10**).

F.7.1.4 Titles

Record titles of honour, rank, or position[3] that are commonly associated with the name by applying the instructions at **9.4**.

Abdul Majid bin Zainuddin, Haji

Hamzah Sendut, Tan Sri Datuk

Variant names. Record as a variant name the direct form of the title folowed by the name (see **9.2.3.10**).

3. See appendix **G** for a list of Iban titles of honour, etc.

F.8 Roman Names

F.8.1 Additional Instructions on Roman Names

For a Roman of classical times, choose as the preferred name a well-established form of the name in a language preferred by the agency creating the data. Determine a well-established form in references sources in that preferred language.

Horace
not Quintus Horatius Flaccus

Pliny, the Elder
not C. Plinius Secundus

For a Roman active before, or mostly before, A.D. 476, record as the first element the part of the name under which the person is most commonly listed in reference sources.

Caesar, Julius

Messalina, Valeria

Messalla Corvinus, Marcus Valerius

Antoninus Pius

In case of doubt, record the name in direct order.

Martianus Capella

Variant names. Record as a variant name a form using a different part of the name as the first element if the name might reasonably be searched by that part.

F.9 Romanian Names Containing a Patronymic

F.9.1 Additional Instructions on Romanian Names Containing a Patronymic

If a name of a person whose language is Romanian contains a patronymic with the suffix *ade*, record that patronymic as the first element.

Heliade Rădulescu, Ion

F.10 Thai Names

F.10.1 Additional Instructions on Thai Names

F.10.1.1 General Guidelines

Record the first part of a Thai name as the first element. Omit a term of address (e.g., *Khun*, *Nāi*, *Nāng*, *Nāngsāo*) unless it is a title of nobility. In case of doubt, include it.

Dhanit Yupho

Prayut Sitthiphan

S. Kanlayanarat

Kǭ. Khaosūanlūang

Variant names. Record as a variant name a form using the last part of the name (normally a surname) as the first element.[4]

---

4. Surnames became a legal requirement for most persons in 1915.

F.10.1.2 Royalty

Record the title of a king or queen of Thailand (and of a consort of a king or queen) by applying the instructions at **9.4.1.4**.

Bhumibol Adulyadej, King of Thailand

Chulalongkorn, King of Siam

Ramphaiphannī, Queen, consort of Prajadhipok, King of Siam

Thapthim, Chaochommanda, consort of Chulalongkorn, King of Siam

For the name of a person of royal descent, record as the first element the first part of the name, or latest name, that he or she uses.

Record *Prince* or *Princess* for those of the ranks *Čhaofā* and *Phra'ong Čhao*. Record *M.C.*, *M.R.*, and *M.L.* for *Mǭm Čhao*, *Mǭm Rātchawong*, and *Mǭm Lūang*, respectively. If the person also has a *krom* rank, do not add it.

Damrongrāchānuphāp, Prince

Seni Pramoj, M.R.

Variant names. Record as variant names any earlier names of the person, including associated ranks and titles (see **9.2.3.7**).

F.10.1.3 Nobility (Khunnāng)

For a name containing a title of nobility, record that title in the vernacular (*rātchathinanām*) as the first element. If a person has more than one title, use the latest. Add the given name, when ascertainable, in parentheses. Add the vernacular rank (*yot bandāsak*) associated with the title.

Prachākitčhakǭnračhak (Chǣm), Phrayā

Bǭrommamahāsīsuriyawong (Chūang), Somdet Čhaophrayā

Rāmrākhop (Fư̄a), Čhaophrayā

Variant names. Record as variant names forms using the given name, the surname, and any earlier titles of the person (see **9.2.3.10**).

For the name of the wife of a man with a title of nobility, record her own name as the first element. Follow it by the husband's title and the wife's conferred rank, if any.

Sangīam Phrasadetsurēnthrāthibǭdī, Thānphūying

F.10.1.4 Buddhist Monastics, Ecclesiastics, and Patriarchs

Record the name of a Buddhist monastic, ecclesiastic, or patriarch as instructed at **F.10.1.4.1–F.10.1.4.3**, as applicable.

F.10.1.4.1 Monastics

For the name of a Buddhist monastic, record the Pali name in religion as the first element unless the monastic is better known by the given name. Follow a Pali name in religion by a comma and *Phikkhu*.

If the monastic is better known by the given name, record the given name as the first element followed by a comma and the rank (*samanasak*) *Phra Mahā* or *Phra Khrū*.

Thammasārō, Phikkhu

Variant names. If the given name is recorded as the first element, record as a variant name a form using the Pali name in religion as the first element.

F.10.1.4.2 Ecclesiastics

For the name of a Buddhist ecclesiastic, record the latest title as the first element. Record the given name in parentheses following the title. Also record any word indicating rank.

Phra Thammathatsanāthọ̄n (Thọ̄ngsuk)

Variant names. Record as variant names forms using the distinctive word in the title, the given name, and the surname as the first element (see **9.2.3.10**).

F.10.1.4.3 Supreme Patriarchs

For the name of a supreme patriarch who is a commoner, record the given name as the first element. Follow the given name by a comma and *Supreme Patriarch*.

Plot, Supreme Patriarch

Variant names. Record as variant names forms using the surname (see **9.2.3.10**) as the first element. Also record as variant names any earlier names or titles by which the person is identified (see **9.2.3.7**).

For the name of a supreme patriarch of royal descent, record the conferred name as the first element. Follow the conferred name by a comma and the secular and ecclesiastical titles in that order.

Wachirayānawong, Prince, Supreme Patriarch

Variant names. Record as variant names any earlier names or titles by which the person is identified (see **9.2.3.7**).

F.11 Recording Surnames That Include an Article and/or Preposition

F.11.1 Afrikaans

Record the prefix as the first element.

De Wet, Reza

Du Toit, Stefanus Jacobus

Van der Post, C. W. H.

Von Breitenbach, Friedrich

F.11.2 Czech and Slovak

If the surname consists of a place name in the genitive case preceded by *z*, record the part following the prefix as the first element.

Žerotína, Karel z

F.11.3 Dutch and Flemish

If the surname is Dutch and the prefix is *ver*, record the prefix as the first element. Otherwise, record the part following the prefix as the first element.

Aa, Pieter van der

Beeck, Jan op de

Beijerse, Jolande uit

Braak, Menno ter

Brink, Jan ten

Driessche, André van

Duurstede, Wijk bij

Hertog, Gerard Cornelis den

Hoff, J. H. van 't

Reve, Gerard Kornelis van het

Wijngaert, Frank van den

Winter, Adriaan de

Ver Boven, Daisy

For the name of a Netherlander whose surname is not Dutch, record the part following the prefix as the first element.

For the name of a Belgian whose surname is not Dutch, apply the instructions for the language of the name.

Faille, J.-B. de la
Netherlander

Long, Isaäc le
Netherlander

Du Jardin, Thomas
Belgian who wrote in Dutch; French name

F.11.4 English

Record the prefix as the first element.

À Beckett, Gilbert Abbott

D'Anvers, Knightley

De Morgan, Augustus

De la Mare, Walter

Du Maurier, Daphne

Le Gallienne, Richard

Van Buren, Martin

Van der Post, Laurens

Von Braun, Wernher

F.11.5 French

If the prefix consists of an article or of a contraction of an article and a preposition, record the prefix as the first element.

Le Rouge, Gustave

La Bruyère, René

Du Méril, Édélestand

Des Granges, Charles-Marc

For other French names, record the part of the name following the preposition as the first element.

Aubigné, Agrippa d'

Musset, Alfred de

La Fontaine, Jean de

F.11.6 German

If the name is German and the prefix consists of an article or a contraction of an article and a preposition, record the prefix as the first element.

Am Acher, Paul

Aus'm Weerth, Ernst

Vom Ende, Erich A.

Zum Busch, J. P.

Zur Linde, Otto

If the name is Dutch and the prefix consists of an article or a contraction of an article and a preposition, record the prefix as the first element.

De Boor, Hans Otto
Name of Dutch origin

Ten Cate, Maria
Name of Dutch origin

For other German and Dutch names, record the part of the name following the prefix as the first element.

Goethe, Johann Wolfgang von

Mayenberg, Wilhelm Anton Wolfgang von und zu

Mühll, Peter von der

For names that are neither German nor Dutch, apply the instructions for the language of the name.

Du Bois-Reymond, Emil Heinrich

Le Fort, Gertrud

F.11.7 Italian

For modern names, record the prefix as the first element.

A Prato, Giovanni
D'Arienzo, Nicola
Da Ponte, Lorenzo
De Amicis, Vincenzo
Del Lungo, Isidoro
Della Volpaia, Eufrosino
Di Costanzo, Angelo
Li Gotti, Ettore
Lo Sapio, Francesco Paolo

For medieval and early modern names, consult reference sources to determine if a prefix is part of a name. If a preposition is sometimes omitted from the name, record the part following the preposition as the first element. For names of this period, *de*, *de'*, *degli*, *dei*, and *de li* are rarely part of the surname.

Alberti, Antonio degli
Anghiera, Pietro Martire d'
Medici, Lorenzo de'

If an Italian title of nobility is used as the first element in a name (see **9.2.2.14–9.2.2.17**), and the title includes a preposition, do not use the preposition as a prefix in the first element.

F.11.8 Portuguese

Record the part of the name following the prefix as the first element.

Canedo, Eneida Vieira da Silva Ostria de
Fonseca, Martinho da
Santos, João Antonio Correia dos

F.11.9 Romanian

If the prefix is *de*, record the part of the name following the prefix as the first element. Otherwise, record the prefix as the first element.

A Mariei, Vasile
Hurmuzaki, Eudoxiu de

F.11.10 Scandinavian (Danish, Norwegian, Swedish)

Record the part of the name following the prefix as the first element if the prefix is of Scandinavian, German, or Dutch origin (except for the Dutch *de*).

If the prefix is the Dutch *de* or is of another origin, record the prefix as the first element.

Hällström, Gunnar af

Linné, Carl von

De Geer, Gerard

De la Gardie, Jakob

La Cour, Jørgen Karl

F.11.11 Spanish

If the prefix consists of an article only, record the article as the first element.

El Bravo, Pancho

La Torre Lagares, Elidio

Las Heras, José María

For all other Spanish names, record the part following the prefix as the first element.

Figueroa, Francisco de

Casas, Bartolomé de las

Río, Antonio del

G

TITLES OF NOBILITY, TERMS OF RANK, ETC.

France

The terms of rank in France are:

MASCULINE	FEMININE
duc	duchesse
marquis	marquise
comte	comtesse
vicomte	vicomtesse
baron	baronne
chevalier	
écuyer	

The following titles may be used by individuals claiming royal status:

MASCULINE	FEMININE
prince	princesse

Iban

Iban titles are:

Titles of Honour

Tuai Serang
Tuai Kayau
Kepala Manok Sabong
Manok Sabong
Kepala Pugu Menoa
Tuai Menoa
Orang Kaya
Orang Kaya Panglima
Orang Kaya Pemanca
Orang Kaya Temenggong
Patinggi
Temenggong

Radin
Pateh

Titles of Office

Penghulu Dalam
Pengarah
Penghulu
Mandal
Tuai rumah

Religious Titles

Kepala Lemambang
Saut Lemambang
Lemambang
Manang Bali
Manang Mansau
Manang Mengeris

Indonesia

The following list of Indonesian titles and honorific words is incomplete as only some of the more commonly used titles are listed. A few variant spellings are also noted.

adipati
anak agung (or agoeng) gde
anak agung (or agoeng) istri
andi
aria (arja, arya, arjo, aryo, ardjueh, arjueh)
datuk (datoek, dato, datok)
desak
dewa gde (or gede)
gusti aju (gusti ayu, goesti ajoe)
gusti gde (goesti gede)
hadji (haji)
ide (ida)
ide aju (ide ayu, ide ajoe)
ide bagus (ide bagoes)
imam
marah
mas
ngabei (ngabehi, ngabeui)
nganten
pangeran
pedanda
raden
raden adjeng (or ajeng)
raden aju (or ayu)
raden aria (or arya)

raden mas
raden nganten
raden pandji (or panji)
raden roro
radja (raja)
ratu (ratoe, ratoh)
sidi
siti
sultan (soeltan)
susuhunan (soesoehoenan)
sutan (soetan)
tengku (tungku, teuku, teungku)
tjokorde (cokorde)
tjokorde (or cokorde) gde
tjokorde (or cokorde) istri
tubagus (or toebagoes)
tumenggung (toemenggoeng)
tunku (toenkoe)

Gelar, meaning "titled," often precedes an Indonesian title. The following terms of address are not considered to be part of the title:

bung (boeng)—brother, when used as a term of respect
empu (mpu)—mister
engku (ungku)—mister
entjik (encik che, entje, inche, the)—mister or mistress
ibu (boe, bu, iboe)—mother, when used as a term of respect
njonja (yonya)—mistress
nona—miss
pak (pa')—father, when used as a term of respect
tuan (toean)—mister
wan—mister

United Kingdom

The terms of rank in the United Kingdom peerage are:

MASCULINE	FEMININE
duke	duchess
marquess (marquis)	marchioness
earl	countess
viscount	viscountess
baron	baroness

The heir of a British peer above the rank of baron usually takes the next to highest title of the peer during the peer's lifetime.

H

DATES IN THE CHRISTIAN CALENDAR

H.0 Scope

This appendix provides information on recording dates in the Christian calendar.

H.1 B.C. and A.D. Dates

Use the abbreviation *B.C.* for dates in the pre-Christian era. Place the abbreviation at the end of a date or each date in a span in that era.

14th century B.C.
Period of activity associated with Queen Nefertiti of Egypt

flourished 377 B.C.–361 B.C.
Period of activity associated with Callistratus, of Aphidna

71 B.C.
Date of death of Spartacus

approximately 495 B.C.
429 B.C.
Approximate date of birth and date of death of Pericles

Use the abbreviation *A.D.* only when the dates span both eras.

63 B.C.
14 A.D.
Dates of birth and death of Augustus, Emperor of Rome

43 B.C.
17 A.D. or 18 A.D.
Date of birth and uncertain date of death of Ovid

approximately 4 B.C.
65 A.D.
Approximate date of birth and date of death of Seneca

I

RELATIONSHIP DESIGNATORS: RELATIONSHIPS BETWEEN A RESOURCE AND PERSONS, FAMILIES, AND CORPORATE BODIES ASSOCIATED WITH THE RESOURCE

I.0 Scope

This appendix provides general guidelines on using relationship designators to specify the relationship between a resource and a person, family, or corporate body associated with that resource, and lists relationship designators used for that purpose.

I.1 General Guidelines on Using Relationship Designators

The defined scope of a relationship element provides a general indication of the relationship between a resource and a person, family, or corporate body associated with the resource (e.g., creator, owner). If the relationship element is considered sufficient for the purposes of the agency creating the data, do not use a relationship designator to indicate the specific nature of the relationship.

Relationship designators provide more specific information about the nature of the relationship (e.g., author, donor).

Use relationship designators at the level of specificity that is considered appropriate for the purposes of the agency creating the data. For example, the relationship between a screenplay and the screenwriter responsible for the work can be recorded using either the specific relationship designator *screenwriter* or the more general relationship designator *author*.

If none of the terms listed in this appendix is appropriate or sufficiently specific, use another concise term to indicate the nature of the relationship.

I.2 Relationship Designators for Persons, Families, and Corporate Bodies Associated with a Work

I.2.1 Relationship Designators for Creators

Record an appropriate term from the following list with the authorized access point or identifier for a creator of a work (see **19.2**). Apply the general guidelines on using relationship designators at **I.1**.

architect A person, family, or corporate body responsible for creating an architectural design, including a pictorial representation intended to show how a building, etc., will look when completed.

landscape architect An architect responsible for creating landscape works.

artist A person, family, or corporate body responsible for creating a work by conceiving, and often implementing, an original graphic design, drawing, painting, etc.

sculptor An artist responsible for creating a three-dimensional work by modeling, carving, or similar technique.

author A person, family, or corporate body responsible for creating a work that is primarily textual in content, regardless of media type (e.g., printed text, spoken word, electronic text, tactile text) or genre (e.g., poems, novels, screenplays, blogs). Use also for persons, etc., creating a new work by paraphrasing, rewriting, or adapting works by another creator if the modification has substantially changed the nature and content of the original or changed the medium of expression.

librettist An author of the words of an opera or other musical stage work, or an oratorio. For an author of the words of just the songs from a musical, see *lyricist*.

lyricist An author of the words of a popular song, including a song or songs from a musical. For an author of just the dialogue from a musical, see *librettist*.

screenwriter An author of a screenplay, script, or scene.

cartographer A person, family, or corporate body responsible for creating a map, atlas, globe, or other cartographic work.

choreographer A person, family, or corporate body responsible for creating a work of movement.

compiler A person, family, or corporate body responsible for creating a new work (e.g., a bibliography, a directory) by selecting, arranging, aggregating, and editing data, information, etc. For a compiler as a contributor, see *editor of compilation* at **I.3.1**.

composer A person, family, or corporate body responsible for creating a musical work. Use also for persons, etc., adapting another musical work to form a distinct alteration (e.g., free transcription), paraphrasing a work or creating a work in the general style of another composer, or creating a work that is based on the music of another composer (e.g., variations on a theme).

designer A person, family, or corporate body responsible for creating a design for an object.

enacting jurisdiction A jurisdiction enacting a law, regulation, constitution, court rule, etc.

filmmaker A person, family, or corporate body responsible for creating an independent or personal film. A filmmaker is individually responsible for the conception and execution of all aspects of the film.

interviewee A person, family, or corporate body responsible for creating a work by responding to an interviewer, usually a reporter, pollster, or some other information gathering agent.

interviewer A person, family, or corporate body responsible for creating a work by acting as an interviewer, reporter, pollster, or some other information gathering agent.

inventor A person, family, or corporate body responsible for creating a new device or process.

photographer A person, family, or corporate body responsible for creating a photographic work.

praeses A person who is the faculty moderator of an academic disputation, normally proposing a thesis and participating in the ensuing disputation.

programmer A person, family, or corporate body responsible for creating a computer program.

respondent A candidate for a degree who defends or opposes a thesis provided by the praeses in an academic disputation.

I.2.2 Relationship Designators for Other Persons, Families, or Corporate Bodies Associated with a Work

Record an appropriate term from the following list with the authorized access point or identifier for an other person, family, or corporate body associated with a work (see **19.3**). Apply the general guidelines on using relationship designators at **I.1**.

addressee A person, family, or corporate body to whom a work or part of a work is addressed.

appellant A person or corporate body who appeals a lower court's decision.

appellee A person or corporate body against whom an appeal is taken.

consultant A person, family, or corporate body who provides consultation services, and often makes recommendations, for another person, family or corporate body that is represented as the creator of a work.

court governed A court governed by court rules, regardless of their official nature (e.g., laws, administrative regulations).

dedicatee A person, family, or corporate body to whom a work is dedicated.

dedicator A person, family, or corporate body by whom a work is dedicated.

defendant A person or corporate body who is accused in a criminal proceeding or sued in a civil proceeding.

degree granting institution A corporate body granting an academic degree.

degree supervisor A person overseeing a higher-level academic degree.

director A person, family, or corporate body responsible for the general management and supervision of a filmed performance, a radio or television program, etc.

film director A director responsible for the general management and supervision of a filmed performance.

radio director A director responsible for the general management and supervision of a radio program.

television director A director responsible for the general management and supervision of a television program.

director of photography A person, family, or corporate body that captures images, either electronically or on film or video stock, and often selects and arranges the lighting. The director of photography for a movie is also called the chief cinematographer. Use this designation also for videographers.

honouree A person, family, or corporate body honoured by a work (e.g., the honouree of a festschrift).

host institution A corporate body hosting the event, exhibit, conference, etc., which gave rise to a work, but having little or no responsibility for the content of the work.

issuing body A person, family or corporate body issuing a work, such as an official organ of the body.

judge A person who hears and decides on legal matters in court.

jurisdiction governed A jurisdiction governed by a law, regulation, etc., that was enacted by another jurisdiction.

medium A person held to be a channel of communication between the earthly world and a world of spirits.

organizer A person, family, or corporate body organizing the exhibit, event, conference, etc., which gave rise to a work.

participant in a treaty A government, international intergovernmental body, or other corporate body that has signed, ratified, or acceded to a treaty.

plaintiff A person or corporate body who brings a suit in a civil proceeding.

producer A person, family, or corporate body responsible for most of the business aspects of a production for screen, audio recording, television, webcast, etc. The producer is generally responsible for fund raising, managing the production, hiring key personnel, arranging for distributors, etc.

film producer A producer responsible for most of the business aspects of a film.

radio producer A producer responsible for most of the business aspects of a radio program.

television producer A producer responsible for most of the business aspects of a television program.

production company A corporate body that is responsible for financial, technical, and organizational management of a production for stage, screen, audio recording, television, webcast, etc.

sponsoring body A person, family, or corporate body sponsoring some aspect of a work, e.g., funding research, sponsoring an event.

I.3 Relationship Designators for Persons, Families, and Corporate Bodies Associated with an Expression

I.3.1 Relationship Designators for Contributors

Record an appropriate term from the following list with the authorized access point or identifier for a contributor to an expression (see **20.2**). Apply the general guidelines on using relationship designators at **I.1**.

abridger A person, family, or corporate body contributing to an expression of a work by shortening or condensing the original work but leaving the nature and content of the original work substantially unchanged. For substantial modifications that result in the creation of a new work, see *author* at **I.2.1**.

animator A person, family, or corporate body contributing to an expression of a moving image work or computer program by giving apparent movement to inanimate objects or drawings. For the creator of the drawings that are animated, see *artist* at **I.2.1**.

arranger of music A person, family, or corporate body contributing to an expression of a musical work by rewriting the composition for a medium of performance different from that for which the work was originally intended. An arranger of music may also modify the work for the same medium of performance, etc., keeping the musical substance of the original composition essentially unchanged. For extensive modification that effectively results in the creation of a new musical work, see *composer* at **I.2.1**.

art director A person, family, or corporate body contributing to an expression of a work by overseeing the artists and craftspeople who build the sets for moving image productions.

cartographer (expression) A person, family, or corporate body contributing to an expression of a work by providing additional cartography, or by modifying the previous cartography.

choreographer (expression) A person, family, or corporate body contributing to an expression of a work by providing additional choreography, or by modifying the previous choreography.

composer (expression) A person, family, or corporate body contributing to an expression by adding music to a work that originally lacked it, by composing new music to substitute for the original music, or by composing new music to supplement the existing music.

costume designer A person, family, or corporate body contributing to an expression of a work by designing the costumes for a moving image production or for a musical or dramatic presentation or entertainment.

court reporter A person, family, or corporate body contributing to an expression of a work by preparing a court's opinions for publication.

draftsman A person, family, or corporate body contributing to an expression of a work by an architect, inventor, etc., by making detailed plans or drawings for buildings, ships, aircraft, machines, objects, etc.

editor A person, family, or corporate body contributing to an expression of a work by revising or clarifying the content, or by selecting and putting together works, or parts of works, by one or more creators. Contributions may include adding an introduction, notes, or other critical matter, or preparing the expression of a work for production, publication, or distribution. For major revisions, adaptations, etc., that substantially change the nature and content of the original work, resulting in a new work, see *author* at **I.2.1**.

editor of moving image work A person, family, or corporate body responsible for assembling, arranging, and trimming film, video, or other moving image formats, including both visual and audio aspects.

illustrator A person, family, or corporate body contributing to an expression of a work by supplementing the primary content with drawings, diagrams, photographs, etc. If the work is primarily the artistic content created by the person, family, or corporate body, see *artist* and *photographer* at **I.2.1**.

interviewee (expression) A person, family, or corporate body contributing to an expression of a work by responding to an interviewer, usually a reporter, pollster, or some other information gathering agent.

interviewer (expression) A person, family, or corporate body contributing to an expression of a work by acting as an interviewer, reporter, pollster, or some other information gathering agent.

minute taker A person, family, or corporate body responsible for recording the minutes of a meeting.

musical director A person, family, or corporate body contributing to an expression of a work by coordinating the activities of the composer, the sound editor, and sound mixers for a moving image production or for a musical or dramatic presentation or entertainment.

performer A person, family, or corporate body contributing to an expression of a work by performing music, acting, dancing, speaking, etc., often in a musical or dramatic presentation, etc.

actor A performer contributing to an expression of a work by acting as a cast member or player in a musical or dramatic presentation, etc.

voice actor An actor contributing to an expression of a work by providing the voice for characters in radio and audio productions and for animated characters in moving image works, as well as by providing voice-overs in radio and television commercials, dubbed resources, etc.

commentator A performer contributing to an expression of a work by providing interpretation, analysis, or a discussion of the subject matter on a recording, film, or other audiovisual medium.

conductor A performer contributing to an expression of a musical work by leading a performing group (orchestra, chorus, opera, etc.) in a musical or dramatic presentation, etc.

dancer A performer contributing to an expression of a work by dancing in a musical, dramatic, etc., presentation.

host A performer contributing to an expression of a work by leading a program (often broadcast) that includes other guests, performers, etc. (e.g., talk show host).

instrumentalist A performer contributing to an expression of a work by playing a musical instrument.

moderator A performer contributing to an expression of a work by leading a program (often broadcast) where topics are discussed, usually with participation of experts in fields related to the discussion.

narrator A performer contributing to an expression of a work by reading or speaking in order to give an account of an act, occurrence, course of events, etc.

on-screen presenter A performer contributing to an expression of a work by appearing on screen to provide contextual or background information. An on-screen presenter may appear in nonfiction moving image materials or in introductions to fiction moving image materials. Use when another term (e.g., *narrator, host*) is either not applicable or not desired.

panelist A performer contributing to an expression of a work by participating in a program (often broadcast) where topics are discussed, usually with participation of experts in fields related to the discussion.

puppeteer A performer contributing to an expression of a work by manipulating, controlling, or directing puppets or marionettes in a moving image production or a musical or dramatic presentation or entertainment.

singer A performer contributing to an expression of a work by using his/her/their voice, with or without instrumental accompaniment, to produce music. A singer's performance may or may not include actual words.

speaker A performer contributing to an expression of a work by speaking words, such as a lecture, speech, etc.

storyteller A performer contributing to an expression of a work by relaying a creator's original story with dramatic or theatrical interpretation.

teacher A performer contributing to an expression of a work by giving instruction or providing a demonstration.

presenter A person, family, or corporate body mentioned in an "X presents" credit for moving image materials and who is probably associated with production, finance, or distribution in some way.

production designer A person, family, or corporate body responsible for designing the overall visual appearance of a moving image production.

recording engineer A person, family, or corporate body contributing to an expression of a work by supervising the technical aspects of a sound or video recording session.

recordist A person, family, or corporate body contributing to an expression of a work by using a recording device to capture sound and/or video during a recording session, including field recordings of natural sounds, folkloric events, music, etc.

stage director A person, family, or corporate body contributing to an expression of a stage work through the general management and supervision of a performance.

surveyor A person, family, or corporate body contributing to an expression of a cartographic work by providing measurements or dimensional relationships for the geographic area represented.

transcriber A person, family, or corporate body contributing to an expression of a work by changing it from one system of notation to another. For a work transcribed for a different instrument or performing group, see *arranger of music* at **I.3.1**.

translator A person, family, or corporate body contributing to an expression of a work by expressing the original text of the work in a language different from that of the original work. A translator may also translate a text from an older form of a language into the modern form.

writer of supplementary textual content A person, family, or corporate body contributing to an expression of a work by providing supplementary textual content (e.g., an introduction, a preface) to the original work.

writer of added commentary A person, family, or corporate body contributing to an expression of a work by providing an interpretation or critical explanation of the original work.

writer of added text A person, family, or corporate body contributing to an expression of a primarily non-textual work by providing text for the non-textual work (e.g., writing captions for photographs, descriptions of maps).

writer of added lyrics A writer of words added to an expression of a musical work. For lyric writing in collaboration with a composer to form an original work, see *lyricist* at **I.2.1**.

writer of afterword A person, family, or corporate body contributing to an expression of a work by providing an afterword to the original work.

writer of introduction A person, family, or corporate body contributing to an expression of a work by providing an introduction to the original work.

writer of postface A person, family, or corporate body contributing to an expression of a work by providing a postface to the original work.

writer of preface A person, family, or corporate body contributing to an expression of a work by providing a preface to the original work.

I.4 Relationship Designators for Persons, Families, and Corporate Bodies Associated with a Manifestation

I.4.1 Relationship Designators for Manufacturers

Record an appropriate term from the following list with the authorized access point or identifier for a manufacturer of a manifestation (see **21.5**). Apply the general guidelines on using relationship designators at **I.1**.

book designer A person, family, or corporate body involved in manufacturing a manifestation by being responsible for the entire graphic design of a book, including arrangement of type and illustration, choice of materials, and process used.

braille embosser A person, family, or corporate body involved in manufacturing a manifestation by embossing Braille cells using a stylus, special embossing printer, or other device.

caster A person, family, or corporate body involved in manufacturing a manifestation by pouring a liquid or molten substance into a mold and leaving it to solidify to take the shape of the mold.

collotyper A person, family, or corporate body involved in manufacturing a manifestation of photographic prints from film or other colloid that has ink-receptive and ink-repellent surfaces.

engraver A person, family, or corporate body involved in manufacturing a manifestation by cutting letters, figures, etc., on a surface such as a wooden or metal plate used for printing.

etcher A person, family, or corporate body involved in manufacturing a manifestation by subjecting metal, glass, or some other surface used for printing, to acid or another corrosive substance.

lithographer A person, family, or corporate body involved in manufacturing a manifestation by preparing a stone or plate for lithographic printing, including a graphic artist creating a design directly on the surface from which printing will be done.

platemaker A person, family, or corporate body involved in manufacturing a manifestation by preparing plates used in the production of printed images and/or text.

printer A person, family, or corporate body involved in manufacturing a manifestation of printed text, notated music, etc., from type or plates, such as a book, newspaper, magazine, broadside, score, etc.

printmaker A person, family, or corporate body involved in manufacturing a manifestation by making a relief, intaglio, or planographic printing surface.

I.4.2 Relationship Designators for Publishers

Record an appropriate term from the following list with the authorized access point or identifier for a publisher of a manifestation (see **21.3**). Apply the general guidelines on using relationship designators at **I.1**.

broadcaster A person, family, or corporate body involved in broadcasting a manifestation to an audience via radio, television, webcast, etc.

I.4.3 Relationship Designators for Distributors

Record an appropriate term from the following list with the authorized access point or identifier for a distributor of a manifestation (see **21.4**). Apply the general guidelines on using relationship designators at **I.1**.

film distributor A person, family, or corporate body involved in distributing a moving image manifestation to theatres or other distribution channels.

I.5 Relationship Designators for Persons, Families, and Corporate Bodies Associated with an Item

I.5.1 Relationship Designators for Owners

Record an appropriate term from the following list with the authorized access point or identifier for an owner of an item (see **22.2**). Apply the general guidelines on using relationship designators at **I.1**.

current owner A person, family, or corporate body currently having legal possession of an item.

depositor A current owner of an item who deposited the item into the custody of another person, family, or corporate body, while still retaining ownership.

former owner A person, family, or corporate body formerly having legal possession of an item.

donor A former owner of an item who donated that item to another owner.

seller A former owner of an item who sold that item to another owner.

I.5.2 Relationship Designators for Other Persons, Families, or Corporate Bodies Associated with an Item

Record an appropriate term from the following list with the authorized access point or identifier for an other person, family, or corporate body associated with an item (see **22.4**). Apply the general guidelines on using relationship designators at **I.1**.

annotator A person who makes manuscript annotations on an item.

autographer A person whose manuscript signature appears on an item.

binder A person who binds an item.

curator A person, family, or corporate body conceiving, aggregating, and/or organizing an exhibition, collection, or other item.

> *collection registrar* A curator who lists or inventories the items in an aggregate work such as a collection of items or works.
>
> *collector* A curator who brings together items from various sources that are then arranged, described, and cataloged as a collection.

dedicatee (item) A person, family, or corporate body to whom an item is dedicated.

honouree (item) A person, family, or corporate body honoured by an item, e.g., a person to whom a copy is presented.

illuminator A person providing decoration to a specific item using precious metals or color, often with elaborate designs and motifs.

inscriber A person who has written a statement of dedication or gift on an item.

restorationist A person, family, or corporate body responsible for the set of technical, editorial, and intellectual procedures aimed at compensating for the degradation of an item by bringing it back to a state as close as possible to its original condition.

J

RELATIONSHIP DESIGNATORS: RELATIONSHIPS BETWEEN WORKS, EXPRESSIONS, MANIFESTATIONS, AND ITEMS

J.0 Scope

This appendix provides general guidelines on using relationship designators to specify relationships between works, expressions, manifestations, and items, and lists relationship designators used for that purpose.

J.1 General Guidelines on Using Relationship Designators

The defined scope of a relationship element provides a general indication of the nature of the relationship between works, expressions, manifestations, or items (e.g., related work, related item). If the relationship element is considered sufficient for the purposes of the agency creating the data, do not use a relationship designator to indicate the specific nature of the relationship.

Relationship designators provide more specific information about the nature of the relationship (e.g., parody of, facsimile of).

Use relationship designators at the level of specificity that is considered appropriate for the purposes of the agency creating the data. For example, the relationship between an adaptation and the work on which it is based can be recorded using either the specific relationship designator *adaptation of (work)* or the more general relationship designator *based on (work).*

If none of the terms listed in this appendix is appropriate or sufficiently specific, use another concise term to indicate the nature of the relationship.

J.2 Relationship Designators for Related Works

J.2.1 Related Work Relationships

Record an appropriate term from the lists at **J.2.2–J.2.6** with the identifier, authorized access point, or structured description of the related work (see **25.1**). Apply the general guidelines on using relationship designators at **J.1**.

J.2.2 Derivative Work Relationships

based on (work) A work used as the source for a derivative work. *Reciprocal relationship:* derivative (work)

abridgement of (work) A work that has been abridged, i.e., shortened without changing the general meaning or manner of presentation of the source work. *Reciprocal relationship:* abridged as (work)

abstract of (work) A work that has been abstracted, i.e., abbreviated in a brief, objective manner. *Reciprocal relationship:* abstract (work)

abstracts for (work) A work whose contents have been abstracted by an abstracting and indexing service. *Reciprocal relationship:* abstracted in (work)

adaptation of (work) A work that has been modified for a purpose, use, or medium other than that for which it was originally intended. *Reciprocal relationship:* adapted as (work)

dramatization of (work) A work that has been adapted as a drama. *Reciprocal relationship:* dramatized as (work)

motion picture adaptation of (work) A work that has been adapted as a motion picture. *Reciprocal relationship:* adapted as motion picture (work) *musical theatre adaptation of (work)* A work that has been adapted as a musical theatre work. *Reciprocal relationship:* adapted as musical theatre (work)

novelization of (work) A work that has been adapted as a novel. *Reciprocal relationship:* novelization (work)

opera adaptation of (work) A work that has been adapted as opera. *Reciprocal relationship:* adapted as opera (work)

radio adaptation of (work) A work that has been adapted as a radio program. *Reciprocal relationship:* adapted as radio program (work)

radio script based on (work) A work that has been adapted as the script for a radio program. *Reciprocal relationship:* adapted as radio script (work)

screenplay based on (work) A work that has been adapted as the screenplay for a motion picture, television program, or video. *Reciprocal relationship:* adapted as screenplay (work)

motion picture screenplay based on (work) A work that has been adapted as the screenplay for a motion picture. *Reciprocal relationship:* adapted as motion picture screenplay (work)

television screenplay based on (work) A work that has been adapted as the screenplay for a television program. *Reciprocal relationship:* adapted as television screenplay (work)

video screenplay based on (work) A work that has been adapted as the screenplay for a video. *Reciprocal relationship:* adapted as video screenplay (work)

television adaptation of (work) A work that has been adapted as a television program. *Reciprocal relationship:* adapted as television program (work)

verse adaptation of (work) A work that has been adapted as a literary composition in verse form. *Reciprocal relationship:* verse adaptation (work)

video adaptation of (work) A work that has been adapted for video. *Reciprocal relationship:* adapted as video (work)

choreography for (work) A work used as the basis for a derivative work consisting of dance. *Reciprocal relationship:* choreography (work)

digest of (work) A work that has been digested, i.e., systematically and comprehensively condensed. *Reciprocal relationship:* digest (work)

expanded version of (work) A work used as the basis for a derivative work that enlarges upon the content of the source work. *Reciprocal relationship:* expanded as (work)

free translation of (work) A work that has been translated freely, preserving the spirit of the original, but not its linguistic details. *Reciprocal relationship:* freely translated as (work)

imitation of (work) A work whose style or content is copied in a derivative work. *Reciprocal relationship:* imitated as (work)

parody of (work) A work whose style or content is imitated for comic effect. *Reciprocal relationship:* parodied as (work)

indexing for (work) A work whose contents have been indexed by an abstracting and indexing service. *Reciprocal relationship:* indexed in (work)

libretto based on (work) A work used as the basis for the text of an opera or other work for the musical stage, or an oratorio. *Reciprocal relationship:* basis for libretto (work)

musical setting of (work) A work that provides the text for a non-dramatic musical work, other than an oratorio. *Reciprocal relationship:* musical setting (work)

musical variations based on (work) A musical work from which melodic, thematic, or harmonic material is taken to form a discrete theme, which is repeated one or more times with subsequent modifications. *Reciprocal relationship:* musical variations (work)

paraphrase of (work) A work used as the basis for a paraphrase, i.e., a restating of the content of the source work in a different form. *Reciprocal relationship:* paraphrased as (work)

remake of (work) A work used as the basis for a new motion picture, radio program, television program, or video. *Reciprocal relationship:* remade as (work)

summary of (work) A work used as the basis for a brief recapitulation of its content. *Reciprocal relationship:* summary (work)

derivative (work) A work that is a modification of a source work. *Reciprocal relationship:* based on (work)

abridged as (work) A work that shortens the source work without changing the general meaning or manner of presentation. *Reciprocal relationship:* abridgement of (work)

abstract (work) A work that abbreviates the source work in a brief, objective manner. *Reciprocal relationship:* abstract of (work)

abstracted in (work) A work (an abstracting and indexing service) that abstracts the contents of a source work. *Reciprocal relationship:* abstracts for (work)

adapted as (work) A work that modifies the source work for a purpose, use, or medium other than that for which it was originally intended. *Reciprocal relationship:* adaptation of (work)

adapted as motion picture (work) A motion picture based on the source work. *Reciprocal relationship:* motion picture adaptation of (work)

adapted as musical theatre (work) A musical theatre work based on the source work. *Reciprocal relationship:* musical theatre adaptation of (work)

adapted as opera (work) An opera based on the source work. *Reciprocal relationship:* opera adaptation of (work)

adapted as radio program (work) A radio program based on the source work. *Reciprocal relationship:* radio adaptation of (work)

adapted as radio script (work) A work consisting of the script for a radio program, based on the source work. *Reciprocal relationship:* radio script based on (work)

adapted as screenplay (work) A work consisting of the screenplay for a motion picture, television program, or video, based on the source work. *Reciprocal relationship:* screenplay based on (work)

adapted as motion picture screenplay (work) A work consisting of the screenplay for a motion picture, based on the source work. *Reciprocal relationship:* motion picture screenplay based on (work)

adapted as television screenplay (work) A work consisting of the screenplay for a television program, based on the source work. *Reciprocal relationship:* television screenplay based on (work)

adapted as video screenplay (work) A work consisting of the screenplay for a video, based on the source work. *Reciprocal relationship:* video screenplay based on (work)

adapted as television program (work) A television program based on the source work. *Reciprocal relationship:* television adaptation of (work)

adapted as video (work) A video based on the source work. *Reciprocal relationship:* video adaptation of (work)

dramatized as (work) A dramatic work adapted from the source work. *Reciprocal relationship:* dramatization of (work)

novelization (work) A novel adapted from the source work. *Reciprocal relationship:* novelization of (work)

verse adaptation (work) A literary composition in verse form adapted from the source work. *Reciprocal relationship:* verse adaptation of (work)

basis for libretto (work) A work that consists of the text of an opera or other work for the musical stage, or an oratorio, based on the source work. *Reciprocal relationship:* libretto based on (work)

choreography (work) A work consisting of dance based on the source work. *Reciprocal relationship:* choreography for (work)

digest (work) A work that systematically and comprehensively condenses the source work. *Reciprocal relationship:* digest of (work)

expanded as (work) A work that enlarges upon the content of the source work. *Reciprocal relationship:* expanded version of (work)

freely translated as (work) A work created by freely translating the source work into another language, preserving the spirit of the original, but not its linguistic details. *Reciprocal relationship:* free translation of (work)

imitated as (work) A work that copies the style or content of the source work. *Reciprocal relationship:* imitation of (work)

parodied as (work) A work that imitates the style or content of the source work for comic effect. *Reciprocal relationship:* parody of (work)

indexed in (work) A work (an abstracting and indexing service) that indexes the contents of the source work. *Reciprocal relationship:* indexing for (work)

musical setting (work) A non-dramatic musical work, other than an oratorio, that uses the text of the source work. *Reciprocal relationship:* musical setting of (work)

musical variations (work) A musical work in which melodic, thematic, or harmonic material is taken from the source work to form a discrete theme, which is repeated one or more times with subsequent modifications. *Reciprocal relationship:* musical variations based on (work)

paraphrased as (work) A work that restates the content of the source work in a different form. *Reciprocal relationship:* paraphrase of (work)

remade as (work) A new motion picture, radio program, television program, or video based on an earlier work. *Reciprocal relationship:* remake of (work)

summary (work) A work that consists of a brief recapitulation of the content of the source work. *Reciprocal relationship:* summary of (work)

J.2.3 Descriptive Work Relationships

described in (work) A work that describes a described work. *Reciprocal relationship:* description of (work)

analysed in (work) A work that examines the source work to identify its components and their relations. *Reciprocal relationship:* analysis of (work)

commentary in (work) A work that contains a set of explanatory or critical notes on the described work. *Reciprocal relationship:* commentary on (work)

critiqued in (work) A work that contains a critical evaluation of the described work. *Reciprocal relationship:* critique of (work)

evaluated in (work) A work that examines or judges the described work. *Reciprocal relationship:* evaluation of (work)

reviewed in (work) A work that contains a brief evaluation of the described work. *Reciprocal relationship:* review of (work)

description of (work) A work described by a describing work. *Reciprocal relationship:* described in (work)

analysis of (work) A work that has been examined to identify its components and their relations. *Reciprocal relationship:* analysed in (work)

commentary on (work) A work used as the basis for a set of explanatory or critical notes. *Reciprocal relationship:* commentary in (work)

critique of (work) A work used as the basis for a critical evaluation. *Reciprocal relationship:* critiqued in (work)

evaluation of (work) A work that is examined or judged. *Reciprocal relationship:* evaluated in (work)

review of (work) A work used as the basis for a brief evaluation. *Reciprocal relationship:* reviewed in (work)

J.2.4 Whole-Part Work Relationships

contained in (work) A larger work of which the work is a discrete component. *Reciprocal relationship:* container of (work)

in series A work in which the part has been issued; the title of the larger work appears on the part. *Reciprocal relationship:* series container of

subseries of A work in which the part consistently appears; the title of the larger work appears on all issues or parts of the subseries. *Reciprocal relationship:* subseries

container of (work) A work that is a discrete component of a larger work. *Reciprocal relationship:* contained in (work)

series container of A work that has been issued as part of a series. *Reciprocal relationship:* in series

subseries A serial or multipart work that consistently appears in a larger work; the title of the larger work appears on all issues or parts of the subseries. *Reciprocal relationship:* subseries of

J.2.5 Accompanying Work Relationships

augmentation of (work) A work whose content is added to by another work. *Reciprocal relationship:* augmented by (work)

addenda to (work) A work to which is added brief additional material, less extensive than a supplement, but essential to the completeness of the content of the work; it is usually added at the end of the work, but is sometimes issued separately. *Reciprocal relationship:* addenda (work)

appendix to (work) A work that is augmented by another work that consists of material that is not essential to the completeness of the content, such as a list of references, statistical tables, and explanatory matter; the augmenting work can either come at the end of the content, or be issued separately. *Reciprocal relationship:* appendix (work)

cadenza composed for (work) A musical work such as a concerto for which an ornamental passage for a soloist has been composed, either by the same or a different composer. *Reciprocal relationship:* cadenza (work)

catalogue of (work) A work used as the basis for a catalogue, i.e., a complete enumeration of items arranged systematically. *Reciprocal relationship:* catalogue (work)

concordance to (work) A work used as the basis for a concordance, i.e. an index of all the words in the predominant work. *Reciprocal relationship:* concordance (work)

errata to (work) A work that is augmented by a list of errors in the predominant work, discovered after publication, with their corrections. *Reciprocal relationship:* errata (work)

finding aid for (work) An archival collection that is described in a finding aid, i.e., a guide to the organization, arrangement, and contents of the collection. *Reciprocal relationship:* finding aid (work)

guide to (work) A work that is augmented by another work consisting of material to help the user of the predominant work, such as notes, learning and study aids, exercises, problems, questions and answers, instructor or student materials, etc. *Reciprocal relationship:* guide (work)

illustrations for (work) A work that is augmented by pictorial content designed to explain or decorate it. *Reciprocal relationship:* illustrations (work)

index to (work) A work used as the basis for an index, i.e., a systematic, alphabetical guide to the contents of the predominant work, usually keyed to page numbers or other reference codes. *Reciprocal relationship:* index (work)

supplement to (work) A work that is updated or otherwise complemented by the augmenting work. *Reciprocal relationship:* supplement (work)

augmented by (work) A work that adds to the content of a predominant work. *Reciprocal relationship:* augmentation of (work).

addenda (work) A work that consists of brief additional material, less extensive than a supplement, but essential to the completeness of the text of the predominant work; it is usually added at the end of the content, but is sometimes issued separately. *Reciprocal relationship:* addenda to (work)

appendix (work) A work that forms an augmenting part of another work which is not essential to the completeness of the content, such as a list of references, statistical tables, and explanatory matter; it can either be material which comes at the end of the content of the predominant work, or be issued separately. *Reciprocal relationship:* appendix to (work)

cadenza (work) A musical work consisting of an ornamental passage for a soloist, added to a musical work such as a concerto, either by the same or a different composer. *Reciprocal relationship:* cadenza composed for (work)

catalogue (work) A work that consists of a complete enumeration of items arranged systematically. *Reciprocal relationship:* catalogue of (work)

concordance (work) A work that consists of an index of all the words in the predominant work. *Reciprocal relationship:* concordance to (work)

errata (work) A work consisting of errors discovered after the publication of the predominant work, with their corrections. *Reciprocal relationship:* errata to (work)

finding aid (work) A work that provides a guide to the organization, arrangement, and contents of an archival collection. *Reciprocal relationship:* finding aid for (work)

guide (work) A work that guides a user through the use of the predominant work, using notes, learning and study aids, exercises, problems, questions and answers, instructor or student materials, etc. *Reciprocal relationship:* guide to (work)

illustrations (work) A work consisting of pictorial content designed to explain or decorate the augmented work. *Reciprocal relationship:* illustrations for (work)

index (work) A work that provides a systematic, alphabetical guide to the contents of the predominant work, usually keyed to page numbers or other reference codes. *Reciprocal relationship:* index to (work)

supplement (work) A work that updates or otherwise complements the predominant work. *Reciprocal relationship:* supplement to (work)

complemented by (work) A work paired with another work without either work being considered to predominate. *Reciprocal relationship:* complemented by (work)

libretto (work) A work that provides the text of an opera or other work for the musical stage, or an oratorio. *Reciprocal relationship:* libretto for (work)

libretto for (work) A musical work such as an opera or other work for the musical stage, or an oratorio, that uses the text of the related work as a libretto. *Reciprocal relationship:* libretto (work)

music (work) A musical work that is used in a motion picture, play, television program, etc. *Reciprocal relationship:* music for (work)

incidental music (work) A musical work that provides the incidental music for a play or other spoken work for the stage. *Reciprocal relationship:* incidental music for (work)

motion picture music (work) A musical work that is used in a motion picture. *Reciprocal relationship:* music for motion picture (work) *radio program music (work)* A musical work that is used in a radio program. *Reciprocal relationship:* music for radio program (work)

television program music (work) A musical work that is used in a television program. *Reciprocal relationship:* music for television program (work)

video music (work) A musical work that is used in a video. *Reciprocal relationship:* music for video (work)

music for (work) A work such as a motion picture, play, television program, etc., that uses the musical work. *Reciprocal relationship:* music (work)

incidental music for (work) A work such as a play or other spoken work for the stage that uses the musical work as incidental music. *Reciprocal relationship:* incidental music (work)

music for motion picture (work) A work that uses the musical work in a motion picture. *Reciprocal relationship:* motion picture music (work)

music for radio program (work) A work that uses the musical work in a radio program. *Reciprocal relationship:* radio program music (work)

music for television program (work) A work that uses the musical work in a television program. *Reciprocal relationship:* television program music (work)

music for video (work) A work that uses the musical work in a video. *Reciprocal relationship:* video music (work)

radio script (work) A work that provides the text for a radio program. *Reciprocal relationship:* script for radio program (work)

screenplay (work) A work that provides the text for a motion picture, television program or video. *Reciprocal relationship:* screenplay for (work)

motion picture screenplay (work) A work that provides the text for a motion picture. *Reciprocal relationship:* screenplay for motion picture (work)

television screenplay (work) A work that provides the text for a television program. *Reciprocal relationship:* screenplay for television program (work)

video screenplay (work) A work that provides the text for a video. *Reciprocal relationship:* screenplay for video (work)

screenplay for (work) A work such as a motion picture, television program, or video, that uses the text of the work as a screenplay. *Reciprocal relationship:* screenplay (work)

screenplay for motion picture (work) A work that uses the text as a screenplay for a motion picture. *Reciprocal relationship:* motion picture screenplay (work)

screenplay for television program (work) A work that uses the text as a screenplay for a television program. *Reciprocal relationship:* television screenplay (work)

screenplay for video (work) A work that uses the text as a screenplay for a video. *Reciprocal relationship:* video screenplay (work)

script for radio program (work) A work that uses the text as the script for a radio program. *Reciprocal relationship:* radio script (work)

J.2.6 Sequential Work Relationships

preceded by (work) A work that precedes (e.g., is earlier in time or before in a narrative) the succeeding work. For sequentially numbered works with revised content, see **J.2.2** (derivative works). *Reciprocal relationship:* succeeded by (work)

absorption in part of (work) The work that has been partially incorporated into another work. *Reciprocal relationship:* absorbed in part by (work)

absorption of (work) The work that has been incorporated into another work. *Reciprocal relationship:* absorbed by (work)

continuation in part of (work) A work that split into two or more separate works with new titles. Apply generally to serials. *Reciprocal relationship:* split into (work)

continuation of (work) The work that is continued by the content of a later work. Apply generally to serials. *Reciprocal relationship:* continued by (work)

merger of (work) One of two or more works which came together to form a new work. *Reciprocal relationship:* merged to form (work)

prequel A work that extends the narrative of an earlier work backwards in time. *Reciprocal relationship:* prequel to

replacement in part of (work) An earlier work whose content has been partially replaced by a later work, usually because the later work contains updated or new information that makes the earlier work obsolete. Apply generally to single-part units, multipart monographs, and integrating resources. *Reciprocal relationship:* replaced in part by (work)

replacement of (work) An earlier work whose content has been replaced by a later work, usually because the later work contains updated or new information that makes the earlier work obsolete. Apply generally to single-part units, multipart monographs, and integrating resources. *Reciprocal relationship:* replaced by (work)

separated from (work) A work that spun off a part of its content to form a new work. *Reciprocal relationship:* continued in part by (work)

sequel to The work whose narrative is continued by the later work. *Reciprocal relationship:* sequel

succeeded by (work) A work that succeeds (e.g., later in time or after in a narrative) the preceding work. For sequentially numbered works with revised content, see **J.2.2** (derivative works). *Reciprocal relationship:* preceded by (work)

absorbed by (work) A work that incorporates another work. *Reciprocal relationship:* absorption of (work)

absorbed in part by (work) A work that incorporates part of the content of another work. *Reciprocal relationship:* absorption in part of (work)

continued by (work) A work whose content continues an earlier work. Apply generally to serials. *Reciprocal relationship:* continuation of (work)

continued in part by (work) A work part of whose content separated from an earlier work to form a new work. Apply generally to serials. *Reciprocal relationship:* separated from (work)

merged to form (work) One of two or more works that come together to form a new work. *Reciprocal relationship:* merger of (work)

prequel to A work whose narrative is extended backwards in time by the later work. *Reciprocal relationship:* prequel

replaced by (work) A later work used in place of an earlier work, usually because the later work contains updated or new information that makes the earlier work obsolete. Apply generally to single-part units, multipart monographs, and integrating resources. *Reciprocal relationship:* replacement of (work)

replaced in part by (work) A later work used in part in place of an earlier work, usually because the later work contains updated or new information that makes part of the earlier work obsolete. Apply generally to single-part units, multipart monographs, and integrating resources. *Reciprocal relationship:* replacement in part of (work)

sequel A later work that continues the narrative of an earlier work. *Reciprocal relationship:* sequel to

split into (work) One of two or more works resulting from the division of an earlier work into separate works. *Reciprocal relationship:* continuation in part of (work)

J.3 Relationship Designators for Related Expressions

J.3.1 Related Expression Relationships

Record an appropriate term from the lists at **J.3.2–J.3.6** with the identifier, authorized access point, or structured description of the related expression (see **26.1**). Apply the general guidelines on using relationship designators at **J.1**.

Use relationship designators for related expressions only when specifying the relationship to a particular expression of a work, e.g., a particular edition.

J.3.2 Derivative Expression Relationships

based on (expression) An expression used as the basis for a derivative expression. *Reciprocal relationship:* derivative (expression)

abridgement of (expression) An expression of a work that has been abridged, i.e., shortened without changing the general meaning or manner of presentation of the source work. *Reciprocal relationship:* abridged as (expression)

abstract of (expression) An expression of a work that has been abstracted, i.e., abbreviated in a brief, objective manner. *Reciprocal relationship:* abstract (expression)

abstracts for (expression) An expression of a work whose contents have been abstracted by an abstracting and indexing service. *Reciprocal relationship:* abstracted in (expression)

adaptation of (expression) An expression of a work that modifies the source expression for a purpose, use, or medium other than that for which it was originally intended. *Reciprocal relationship:* adapted as (expression)

dramatization of (expression) An expression of a work that has been adapted as a drama. *Reciprocal relationship:* dramatized as (expression)

motion picture adaptation of (expression) An expression of a work that has been adapted as a motion picture. *Reciprocal relationship:* adapted as motion picture (expression)

musical theatre adaptation of (expression) An expression of a work that has been adapted as a musical theatre work. *Reciprocal relationship:* adapted as musical theatre (expression)

novelization of (expression) An expression of a work that has been adapted as a novel. *Reciprocal relationship:* novelization (expression)

opera adaptation of (expression) An expression of a work that has been adapted as an opera. *Reciprocal relationship:* adapted as opera (expression)

radio adaptation of (expression) An expression of a work that has been adapted as a radio program. *Reciprocal relationship:* adapted as radio program (expression)

radio script based on (expression) An expression of a work that has been adapted as the script for a radio program. *Reciprocal relationship:* adapted as radio script (expression) *screenplay based on (expression)* An expression of a work that has been adapted as the screenplay for a motion picture, television program, or video. *Reciprocal relationship:* adapted as screenplay (expression)

motion picture screenplay based on (expression) An expression of a work that has been adapted as the screenplay for a motion picture. *Reciprocal relationship:* adapted as motion picture screenplay (expression)

television screenplay based on (expression) An expression of a work that has been adapted as the screenplay for a television program. *Reciprocal relationship:* adapted as television screenplay (expression)

video screenplay based on (expression) An expression of a work that has been adapted as the screenplay for a video. *Reciprocal relationship:* adapted as video screenplay (expression)

television adaptation of (expression) An expression of a work that has been adapted as a television program. *Reciprocal relationship:* adapted as television program (expression)

verse adaptation of (expression) An expression of a work that has been adapted as a literary composition in verse form. *Reciprocal relationship:* verse adaptation (expression)

video adaptation of (expression) An expression of a work that has been adapted for video. *Reciprocal relationship:* adapted as video (expression)

choreography for (expression) An expression of a work used as the basis for a derivative work consisting of dance. *Reciprocal relationship:* choreography (expression)

digest of (expression) An expression of a work that has been digested, i.e., systematically and comprehensively condensed. *Reciprocal relationship:* digest (expression)

expanded version of (expression) An expression of a work used as the basis for a derivative work that enlarges upon the content of the source work. *Reciprocal relationship:* expanded as (expression)

free translation of (expression) An expression of a work that has been translated freely, preserving the spirit of the original, but not its linguistic details. *Reciprocal relationship:* freely translated as (expression)

imitation of (expression) An expression of a work whose style or content is copied in a derivative work. *Reciprocal relationship:* imitated as (expression)

parody of (expression) An expression of a work whose style or content is imitated for comic effect. *Reciprocal relationship:* parodied as (expression)

indexing for (expression) An expression of a work whose contents have been indexed by an abstracting and indexing service. *Reciprocal relationship:* indexed in (expression)

libretto based on (expression) An expression of a work used as the basis for the text of an opera or other work for the musical stage, or an oratorio. *Reciprocal relationship:* basis for libretto (expression)

musical arrangement of An expression of a work that has been rewritten for a medium of performance different from that for which the work was originally intended. *Reciprocal relationship:* musical arrangement

musical setting of (expression) An expression of a work that provides the text for a non-dramatic musical work, other than an oratorio. *Reciprocal relationship:* musical setting (expression)

musical variations based on (expression) An expression of a musical work from which melodic, thematic, or harmonic material is taken to form a discrete theme, which is repeated one or more times with subsequent modifications. *Reciprocal relationship:* musical variations (expression)

paraphrase of (expression) An expression of a work used as the basis for a paraphrase, i.e., a restating of the content of the source work in a different form. *Reciprocal relationship:* paraphrased as (expression)

remake of (expression) An expression of a work used as the basis for a new motion picture, radio program, television program, or video. *Reciprocal relationship:* remade as (expression)

revision of An expression of a work used as the basis for an updated, corrected, or expanded version. *Reciprocal relationship:* revised as

summary of (expression) An expression of a work used as the basis for a brief recapitulation of its content. *Reciprocal relationship:* summary (expression)

translation of An expression of a work that has been translated, i.e., the text expressed in a language different from that of the original work. *Reciprocal relationship:* translated as

dubbed version of An expression of a moving image work in which the spoken dialogue has been translated into a language different from that of the original work. *Reciprocal relationship*: dubbed version

derivative (expression) An expression that is a modification of a source expression. *Reciprocal relationship:* based on (expression)

abridged as (expression) An expression of a work that shortens the source expression without changing the general meaning or manner of presentation. *Reciprocal relationship:* abridgement of (expression)

abstract (expression) An expression of a work that abbreviates the source expression in a brief, objective manner. *Reciprocal relationship:* abstract of (expression)

abstracted in (expression) An expression of a work (an abstracting and indexing service) that abstracts the contents of a source expression. *Reciprocal relationship:* abstracts for (expression)

adapted as (expression) An expression of a work that modifies the source expression for a purpose, use, or medium other than that for which it was originally intended. *Reciprocal relationship:* adaptation of (expression)

adapted as motion picture (expression) A motion picture based on the source expression. *Reciprocal relationship:* motion picture adaptation of (expression)

adapted as musical theatre (expression) An expression of a musical theatre work based on the source expression. *Reciprocal relationship:* musical theatre adaptation of (expression)

adapted as opera (expression) An expression of an opera based on the source expression. *Reciprocal relationship:* opera adaptation of (expression)

adapted as radio program (expression) A radio program based on the source expression. *Reciprocal relationship:* radio adaptation of (expression)

adapted as radio script (expression) An expression of a work consisting of the script for a radio program, based on the source work. *Reciprocal relationship:* radio script based on (expression)

adapted as screenplay (expression) An expression of a work consisting of the screenplay for a motion picture, television program, or video, based on the source work. *Reciprocal relationship:* screenplay based on (expression)

adapted as motion picture screenplay (expression) An expression of a work consisting of the screenplay for a motion picture, based on the source work. *Reciprocal relationship:* motion picture screenplay based on (expression)

adapted as television screenplay (expression) An expression of a work consisting of the screenplay for a television program, based on the source work. *Reciprocal relationship:* television screenplay based on (expression)

adapted as video screenplay (expression) An expression of a work consisting of the screenplay for a video, based on the source work. *Reciprocal relationship:* video screenplay based on (expression) *adapted as television program (expression)* A television program based on the source expression. *Reciprocal relationship:* television adaptation of (expression)

adapted as video (expression) A video based on the source expression. *Reciprocal relationship:* video adaptation of (expression)

dramatized as (expression) An expression of a dramatic work adapted from the source expression. *Reciprocal relationship:* dramatization of (expression)

novelization (expression) An expression of a novel adapted from the source expression. *Reciprocal relationship:* novelization of (expression)

verse adaptation (expression) An expression of a literary composition in verse form adapted from the source expression. *Reciprocal relationship:* verse adaptation of (expression)

basis for libretto (expression) An expression of a work that consists of the text of an opera or other work for the musical stage, or an oratorio, based on the source work. *Reciprocal relationship:* libretto based on (expression)

choreography (expression) An expression of a work consisting of dance based on the source work. *Reciprocal relationship:* choreography for (expression)

digest (expression) An expression of a work that systematically, comprehensively condenses the source expression. *Reciprocal relationship:* digest of (expression)

expanded as (expression) An expression of a work that enlarges upon the content of the source work. *Reciprocal relationship:* expanded version of (expression)

freely translated as (expression) An expression of a work that freely translates the text into another language, preserving the spirit of the original, but not its linguistic details. *Reciprocal relationship:* free translation of (expression)

imitated as (expression) An expression of a work that copies the style or content of the source work. *Reciprocal relationship:* imitation of (expression)

parodied as (expression) An expression of a work that imitates the style or content of the source work for comic effect. *Reciprocal relationship:* parody of (expression)

indexed in (expression) An expression of a work (an abstracting and indexing service) that indexes the contents of a source expression. *Reciprocal relationship:* indexing for (expression)

musical arrangement An expression of a work that rewrites the source expression for a medium of performance different from that for which the work was originally intended. *Reciprocal relationship:* musical arrangement of

musical setting (expression) An expression of a non-dramatic musical work, other than an oratorio, that uses the text of the source work. *Reciprocal relationship:* musical setting of (expression)

musical variations (expression) An expression of a musical work in which melodic, thematic, or harmonic material is taken from the source work to form a discrete theme, which is repeated one or more times with subsequent modifications. *Reciprocal relationship:* musical variations based on (expression)

paraphrased as (expression) An expression of a work that restates the content of the source work in a different form. *Reciprocal relationship:* paraphrase of (expression)

remade as (expression) An expression of a new motion picture, radio program, television program, or video based on an earlier work. *Reciprocal relationship:* remake of (expression)

revised as An expression of a work that has been updated, corrected, or expanded. *Reciprocal relationship:* revision of

summary (expression) An expression of a work that consists of a brief recapitulation of the content of the source expression. *Reciprocal relationship:* summary of (expression)

translated as An expression of a work that translates the text of the source expression into a language different from that of the original work. *Reciprocal relationship:* translation of

dubbed version An expression of a moving image work that translates the spoken dialogue of the original work into a different language. *Reciprocal relationship:* dubbed version of

J.3.3 Descriptive Expression Relationships

described in (expression) An expression of a work that describes an expression. *Reciprocal relationship:* description of (expression)

analysed in (expression) An expression of a work that examines the source expression to identify its components and their relations. *Reciprocal relationship:* analysis of (expression)

commentary in (expression) An expression of a work that contains a set of explanatory or critical notes on the described expression. *Reciprocal relationship:* commentary on (expression)

critiqued in (expression) An expression of a work that contains a critical evaluation of the described expression. *Reciprocal relationship:* critique of (expression)

evaluated in (expression) An expression of a work that examines or judges the described expression. *Reciprocal relationship:* evaluation of (expression)

reviewed in (expression) An expression of a work that contains a brief evaluation of the described expression. *Reciprocal relationship:* review of (expression)

description of (expression) An expression described by an expression of a describing work. *Reciprocal relationship:* described in (expression)

analysis of (expression) An expression of a work that has been examined to identify its components and their relations. *Reciprocal relationship:* analysed in (expression)

commentary on (expression) An expression of a work used as the basis for a set of explanatory or critical notes. *Reciprocal relationship:* commentary in (expression)

critique of (expression) An expression of a work used as the basis for a critical evaluation. *Reciprocal relationship:* critiqued in (expression)

evaluation of (expression) An expression of a work that is examined or judged. *Reciprocal relationship:* evaluated in (expression)

review of (expression) An expression of a work used as the basis for a brief evaluation. *Reciprocal relationship:* reviewed in (expression)

J.3.4 Whole-Part Expression Relationships

contained in (expression) An expression of a larger work of which the expression is a discrete component. *Reciprocal relationship:* container of (expression)

container of (expression) An expression of a work that is a discrete component of a larger expression. *Reciprocal relationship:* contained in (expression)

J.3.5 Accompanying Expression Relationships

augmentation of (expression) An expression of a work whose content is added to by another expression. *Reciprocal relationship:* augmented by (expression)

addenda to (expression) An expression of a work to which is added brief additional material, less extensive than a supplement, but essential to the completeness of the content of the work; it is usually added at the end of the content but is sometimes issued separately from it. *Reciprocal relationship:* addenda (expression)

appendix to (expression) An expression of a predominant work that is augmented by another work that consists of material that is not essential to the completeness of the content, such as a list of references, statistical tables, and explanatory matter; the augmenting work can either come at the end of the content, or be issued separately. *Reciprocal relationship:* appendix (expression)

cadenza composed for (expression) An expression of a musical work such as a concerto for which an ornamental passage for a soloist has been composed, either by the same or a different composer. *Reciprocal relationship:* cadenza (expression)

catalogue of (expression) An expression of a work used as the basis for a catalogue, i.e., a complete enumeration of items arranged systematically. *Reciprocal relationship:* catalogue (expression)

concordance to (expression) An expression of a work used as the basis for a concordance, i.e., an index of all the words in the predominant expression. *Reciprocal relationship:* concordance (expression)

errata to (expression) An expression of a work that is augmented by a list of errors in the predominant work, discovered after publication, with their corrections. *Reciprocal relationship:* errata (expression)

finding aid for (expression) An expression of an archival collection that is described in a finding aid, i.e., a guide to the organization, arrangement, and contents of the collection. *Reciprocal relationship:* finding aid (expression)

guide to (expression) An expression of a work that is augmented by another work consisting of material to help the user of the predominant work, such as notes, learning and study aids, exercises, problems, questions and answers, instructor or student materials, etc. *Reciprocal relationship:* guide (expression)

illustrations for (expression) An expression of a work that is augmented by pictorial content designed to explain or decorate it. *Reciprocal relationship:* illustrations (expression)

index to (expression) An expression of a work used as the basis for an index, i.e., a systematic, alphabetical guide to the contents of the predominant expression, usually keyed to page numbers or other reference codes. *Reciprocal relationship:* index (expression)

supplement to (expression) An expression of a work that is updated or otherwise complemented by the augmenting expression. *Reciprocal relationship:* supplement (expression)

augmented by (expression) An expression of a work that adds to the content of a predominant expression. *Reciprocal relationship:* augmentation of (expression)

addenda (expression) An expression of a work that consists of brief additional material, less extensive than a supplement, but essential to the completeness of the text of the predominant work; it is usually added at the end of the content, but is sometimes issued separately. *Reciprocal relationship:* addenda to (expression)

appendix (expression) An expression of a work that forms an augmenting part of another work which is not essential to the completeness of the content, such as a list of references, statistical tables, and explanatory matter; it can be material which either comes at the end of the content of the predominant work, or is issued separately. *Reciprocal relationship:* appendix to (expression)

cadenza (expression) An expression of a musical work consisting of an ornamental passage for a soloist, added to a musical work such as a concerto, either by the same or a different composer. *Reciprocal relationship:* cadenza composed for (expression)

catalogue (expression) An expression of a work that consists of a complete enumeration of items arranged systematically. *Reciprocal relationship:* catalogue of (expression)

concordance (expression) An expression of a work that consists of an index of all the words in the predominant expression. *Reciprocal relationship:* concordance to (expression)

errata (expression) An expression of a work consisting of errors discovered after the publication of the predominant work, with their corrections. *Reciprocal relationship:* errata to (expression)

finding aid (expression) An expression of a work that provides a guide to the organization, arrangement, and contents of an archival collection. *Reciprocal relationship:* finding aid for (expression)

guide (expression) An expression of a work that guides a user through the use of the predominant work, using notes, learning and study aids, exercises, problems, questions and answers, instructor or student materials, etc. *Reciprocal relationship:* guide to (expression)

illustrations (expression) An expression of a work consisting of pictorial content designed to explain or decorate the augmented expression. *Reciprocal relationship:* illustrations for (expression)

index (expression) An expression of a work that provides a systematic, alphabetical guide to the contents of the predominant expression, usually keyed to page numbers or other reference codes. *Reciprocal relationship:* index to (expression)

supplement (expression) An expression of a work that updates or otherwise complements the predominant expression. *Reciprocal relationship:* supplement to (expression)

complemented by (expression) An expression of a work paired with another expression without either expression being considered to predominate. *Reciprocal relationship:* complemented by (expression)

libretto (expression) An expression of a work that provides the text of an opera or other work for the musical stage, or an oratorio. *Reciprocal relationship:* libretto for (expression)

libretto for (expression) An expression of a musical work such as an opera or other work for the musical stage, or an oratorio, that uses the text of the related work. *Reciprocal relationship:* libretto (expression)

music (expression) An expression of a musical work that is used in a motion picture, play, television program, etc. *Reciprocal relationship:* music for (expression)

incidental music (expression) An expression of a musical work that provides the incidental music for a play or other spoken work for the stage. *Reciprocal relationship:* incidental music for (expression)

motion picture music (expression) An expression of a musical work that is used in a motion picture. *Reciprocal relationship:* music for motion picture (expression)

radio program music (expression) An expression of a musical work that is used in a radio program. *Reciprocal relationship:* music for radio program (expression)

television program music (expression) An expression of a musical work that is used in a television program. *Reciprocal relationship*: music for television program (expression)

video music (expression) An expression of a musical work that is used in a video. *Reciprocal relationship:* music for video (expression)

music for (expression) An expression of a work such as a motion picture, play, television program, etc., that uses the musical work. *Reciprocal relationship:* music (expression)

incidental music for (expression) An expression of a work such as a play or other spoken work for the stage that uses the musical work as incidental music. *Reciprocal relationship:* incidental music (expression)

music for motion picture (expression) An expression of a work that uses the musical work in a motion picture. *Reciprocal relationship:* motion picture music (expression)

music for radio program (expression) An expression of a work that uses the musical work in a radio program. *Reciprocal relationship:* radio program music (expression)

music for television program (expression) An expression of a work that uses the musical work in a television program. *Reciprocal relationship:* television program music (expression)

music for video (expression) An expression of a work that uses the musical work in a video. *Reciprocal relationship:* video music (expression)

radio script (expression) An expression of a work that provides the text for a radio program. *Reciprocal relationship:* script for radio program (expression)

screenplay (expression) An expression of a work that provides the text for a motion picture, television program or video. *Reciprocal relationship:* screenplay for (expression)

motion picture screenplay (expression) An expression of a work that provides the text for a motion picture. *Reciprocal relationship:* screenplay for motion picture (expression)

television screenplay (expression) An expression of a work that provides the text for a television program. *Reciprocal relationship:* screenplay for television program (expression)

video screenplay (expression) An expression of a work that provides the text for a video. *Reciprocal relationship:* screenplay for video (expression)

screenplay for (expression) An expression of a work such as a motion picture, television program, or video, that uses the text of the work as a screenplay. *Reciprocal relationship:* screenplay (expression)

screenplay for motion picture (expression) An expression of a work that uses the text as a screenplay for a motion picture. *Reciprocal relationship:* motion picture screenplay (expression)

screenplay for television program (expression) An expression of a work that uses the text as a screenplay for a television program. *Reciprocal relationship:* television screenplay (expression)

screenplay for video (expression) An expression of a work that uses the text as a screenplay for a video. *Reciprocal relationship:* video screenplay (expression)

script for radio program (expression) An expression of a work that uses the text of the source work as the script for a radio program. *Reciprocal relationship:* radio script (expression)

J.3.6 Sequential Expression Relationships

preceded by (expression) An expression of a work that precedes (e.g., is earlier in time or before in narrative) the succeeding expression. For sequentially numbered works with revised content, see **J.3.2** (derivative expressions). *Reciprocal relationship:* succeeded by (expression)

absorption in part of (expression) An expression of a work that has been partially incorporated into another entity. *Reciprocal relationship:* absorbed in part by (expression)

absorption of (expression) An expression of a work that has been incorporated into another entity. *Reciprocal relationship:* absorbed by (expression)

continuation in part of (expression) An expression of a work that split into two or more separate expressions with new titles. Apply generally to serials. *Reciprocal relationship:* split into (expression)

continuation of (expression) An expression of a work that is continued by the content of an expression of a later work. Apply generally to serials. *Reciprocal relationship:* continued by (expression)

merger of (expression) An expression of one of two or more works which came together to form a new expression. *Reciprocal relationship:* merged to form (expression)

replacement in part of (expression) An expression of an earlier work whose content has been partially replaced by a later expression, usually because the later work contains updated or new information that makes the earlier expression obsolete. Apply generally to single-part units, multipart monographs, and integrating resources. *Reciprocal relationship:* replaced in part by (expression)

replacement of (expression) An expression of an earlier work whose content has been replaced by a later expression, usually because the later work contains updated or new information that makes the earlier expression obsolete. Apply generally to single-part units, multipart monographs, and integrating resources. *Reciprocal relationship:* replaced by (expression)

separated from (expression) An expression of a work that spun off a part of its content to form a new expression. *Reciprocal relationship:* continued in part by (expression)

succeeded by (expression) An expression of a work that succeeds (e.g., later in time or after in a narrative) the preceding expression. For sequentially numbered expressions with revised content, see **J.3.2** (derivative expressions). *Reciprocal relationship:* preceded by (expression)

absorbed by (expression) An expression of a work that incorporates another entity. *Reciprocal relationship:* absorption of (expression)

absorbed in part by (expression) An expression of a work that incorporates part of the content of another entity. *Reciprocal relationship:* absorption in part of (expression)

continued by (expression) An expression of a work whose content continues an expression of an earlier work. Apply generally to serials. *Reciprocal relationship:* continuation of (expression)

continued in part by (expression) An expression of a work part of whose content separated from an earlier expression to form a new expression. Apply generally to serials. *Reciprocal relationship:* separated from (expression)

merged to form (expression) One of two or more expressions of works that come together to form a new expression. *Reciprocal relationship:* merger of (expression)

replaced by (expression) An expression of a later work used in place of the earlier expression, usually because the later work contains updated or new information that makes the earlier expression obsolete. Apply generally to single-part units, multipart monographs, and integrating resources. *Reciprocal relationship:* replacement of (expression)

replaced in part by (expression) An expression of a later work used in part in place of the earlier expression, usually because the later work contains updated or new information that makes part of the earlier expression obsolete. Apply generally to single-part units, multipart monographs, and integrating resources. *Reciprocal relationship:* replacement in part of (expression)

split into (expression) An expression of one of two or more works resulting from the division of an earlier expression into separate expressions. *Reciprocal relationship:* continuation in part of (expression)

J.4 Relationship Designators for Related Manifestations

J.4.1 Related Manifestation Relationships

Record an appropriate term from the lists at **J.4.2**–**J.4.5** with the identifier or structured description of the related manifestation (see **27.1**). Apply the general guidelines on using relationship designators at **J.1**.

J.4.2 Equivalent Manifestation Relationships

equivalent (manifestation) A manifestation embodying the same expression of a work. *Reciprocal relationship:* equivalent (manifestation)

also issued as A manifestation issued in a different format embodying the same expression of a work as the resource being described. *Reciprocal relationship:* also issued as

mirror site A manifestation of a website that is an exact copy, used to reduce network traffic or improve the availability of the original site. *Reciprocal relationship:* mirror site

reproduced as A manifestation that reproduces another manifestation embodying the same expression of a work. *Reciprocal relationship:* reproduction of (manifestation)

digital transfer A manifestation resulting from the transfer of a resource from one digital format to another. *Reciprocal relationship:* digital transfer of (manifestation)

electronic reproduction A digital manifestation resulting from the reproduction of an analog manifestation. *Reciprocal relationship:* electronic reproduction of (manifestation)

facsimile A manifestation that exactly reproduces another manifestation embodying the same expression of a work. *Reciprocal relationship:* facsimile of (manifestation)

preservation facsimile A manifestation consisting of an exact reproduction on preservation-quality media, such as acid-free permanent or archival paper. *Reciprocal relationship:* preservation facsimile of (manifestation)

reprinted as A manifestation that reissues the same expression of the work as the printed resource being described. *Reciprocal relationship:* reprint of (manifestation)

reproduction of (manifestation) A manifestation used as the basis for a reproduction. *Reciprocal relationship:* reproduced as

digital transfer of (manifestation) A manifestation transferred from one digital format to another. *Reciprocal relationship:* digital transfer

electronic reproduction of (manifestation) An analog manifestation used as the basis for an electronic reproduction. *Reciprocal relationship:* electronic reproduction

facsimile of (manifestation) A manifestation used as the basis for an exact reproduction. *Reciprocal relationship:* facsimile

preservation facsimile of (manifestation) A manifestation used as the basis for an exact reproduction on preservation-quality media, such as acid-free permanent or archival paper. *Reciprocal relationship:* preservation facsimile

reprint of (manifestation) A printed manifestation that is used as the basis for a reissue with the same content as the resource being described. *Reciprocal relationship:* reprinted as

J.4.3 Descriptive Manifestation Relationships

description of (manifestation) A manifestation described by a describing work.

analysis of (manifestation) A manifestation that has been examined to identify its components and their relations.

commentary on (manifestation) A manifestation used as the basis for a set of explanatory or critical notes.

critique of (manifestation) A manifestation used as the basis for a critical evaluation.

evaluation of (manifestation) A manifestation that is examined or judged.

review of (manifestation) A manifestation used as the basis for a brief evaluation.

J.4.4 Whole-Part Manifestation Relationships

contained in (manifestation) A larger manifestation of which the manifestation is a discrete component. *Reciprocal relationship:* container of (manifestation)

facsimile contained in A larger manifestation of which a part is a discrete component that exactly reproduces another manifestation embodying the same expression of a work. *Reciprocal relationship:* facsimile container of

inserted in A manifestation into which material has been inserted that is not an integral part of the publication. *Reciprocal relationship:* insert

special issue of A serial or newspaper containing a single issue or a supplementary section devoted to a special subject, with or without serial numbering, such as an anniversary number of a periodical or newspaper. *Reciprocal relationship:* special issue

container of (manifestation) A manifestation that is a discrete component of a larger manifestation. *Reciprocal relationship:* contained in (manifestation)

facsimile container of A manifestation used as the basis for an exact reproduction that is a discrete component of a larger manifestation. *Reciprocal relationship:* facsimile contained in

insert A manifestation consisting of separately issued material that is not an integral part of the larger manifestation into which it has been inserted. *Reciprocal relationship:* inserted in

special issue A manifestation that consists of a single issue or a supplementary section of a serial or newspaper devoted to a special subject. *Reciprocal relationship:* special issue of

J.4.5 Accompanying Manifestation Relationships

accompanied by (manifestation) A manifestation issued with another manifestation, without any relationship to its content. *Reciprocal relationship:* accompanied by (manifestation)

issued with A manifestation that is issued on the same carrier as the manifestation being described. *Reciprocal relationship:* issued with

filmed with (manifestation) A manifestation that is issued on the same microform with the manifestation being described. *Reciprocal relationship:* filmed with (manifestation)

on disc with (manifestation) A manifestation that is issued on the same disc with the manifestation being described. *Reciprocal relationship:* on disc with (manifestation)

J.5 Relationship Designators for Related Items

J.5.1 Related Item Relationships

Record an appropriate term from the lists at **J.5.2–J.5.5** with the identifier or structured description of the related item (see **28.1**). Apply the general guidelines on using relationship designators at **J.1**.

Use relationship designators for related items only when specifying the relationship to a particular copy of a manifestation.

J.5.2 Equivalent Item Relationships

equivalent (item) An item embodying the same expression of a work. *Reciprocal relationship:* equivalent (item)

reproduction of (item) An item used as the basis for a reproduction.

digital transfer of (item) An item transferred from one digital format to another.

electronic reproduction of (item) An analog item used as the basis for an electronic reproduction.

facsimile of (item) An item used as the basis for an exact reproduction.

preservation facsimile of (item) An item used as the basis for an exact reproduction on preservation-quality media, such as acid-free permanent or archival paper.

reprint of (item) An item that is used as the basis for a reprint with the same content as the resource being described.

J.5.3 Descriptive Item Relationships

description of (item) An item described by a describing work.

analysis of (item) An item that has been examined to identify its components and their relations.

commentary on (item) An item used as the basis for a set of explanatory or critical notes.

critique of (item) An item used as the basis for a critical evaluation.

evaluation of (item) An item that is examined or judged.

review of (item) An item used as the basis for a brief evaluation.

J.5.4 Whole-Part Item Relationships

contained in (item) A larger item of which the item is a discrete component. *Reciprocal relationship:* container of (item)

container of (item) An item that is a discrete component of a larger item. *Reciprocal relationship:* contained in (item)

J.5.5 Accompanying Item Relationships

accompanied by (item) An item brought together with another item after being issued. *Reciprocal relationship:* accompanied by (item)

bound with An item that has been bound within the same binding as the item being described. *Reciprocal relationship:* bound with

filmed with (item) An item that is contained on the same microform with the item being described. *Reciprocal relationship:* filmed with (item)

on disc with (item) An item that is contained on the same disc with the item being described. *Reciprocal relationship:* on disc with (item)

K

RELATIONSHIP DESIGNATORS: RELATIONSHIPS BETWEEN PERSONS, FAMILIES, AND CORPORATE BODIES

K.0 Scope

This appendix provides general guidelines on using relationship designators to specify relationships between persons, families, and corporate bodies, and lists relationship designators used for that purpose.

The relationship designators in this appendix are provisional. They will be reviewed and revised as necessary.

K.1 General Guidelines on Using Relationship Designators

The defined scope of a relationship element provides a general indication of the relationship between persons, families, and corporate bodies (e.g., related person, related corporate body). If the relationship element is considered sufficient for the purposes of the agency creating the data, do not use a relationship designator to indicate the specific nature of the relationship.

Relationship designators provide more specific information about the nature of the relationship (e.g. alternate identity, predecessor).

Use relationship designators at the level of specificity that is considered appropriate for the purposes of the agency creating the data. For example, the relationship between a person and the family descended from that person can be recorded using either the specific relationship designator *progenitor* or the more general relationship designator *family member*.

If none of the terms listed in this appendix is appropriate or sufficiently specific, use another concise term to indicate the nature of the relationship.

K.2 Relationship Designators for Related Persons

K.2.1 Relationship Designators to Relate Persons to Other Persons

Record an appropriate term from the following list with the authorized access point or identifier for a related person (see **30.1**). Apply the general guidelines on using relationship designators at **K.1**.

alternate identity A pseudonymous or other identity assumed by the person.

real identity A real person who assumes the alternate identity.

K.2.2 Relationship Designators to Relate Persons to Families

Record an appropriate term from the following list with the authorized access point or identifier for a related person (see **30.1**). Apply the general guidelines on using relationship designators at **K.1**.

family member A person who is a member of the family.

progenitor A person from whom the family is descended.

K.2.3 Relationship Designators to Relate Persons to Corporate Bodies

Record an appropriate term from the following list with the authorized access point or identifier for a related person (see **30.1**). Apply the general guidelines on using relationship designators at **K.1**.

employee A person employed by the corporate body.

founder A person who founded the corporate body.

incumbent A person holding an office in the corporate body.

member A person who is a member of the corporate body.

sponsor A person sponsoring the corporate body.

K.3 Relationship Designators for Related Families

K.3.1 Relationship Designators to Relate Families to Persons

Record an appropriate term from the following list with the authorized access point or identifier for a related family (see **31.1**). Apply the general guidelines on using relationship designators at **K.1**.

descendants A family descended from the particular person.

family A family to which the person belongs.

K.3.2 Relationship Designators to Relate Families to Other Families

Record an appropriate term from the following list with the authorized access point or identifier for a related family (see **31.1**). Apply the general guidelines on using relationship designators at **K.1**.

descendant family A family descended from the other family.

K.3.3 Relationship Designators to Relate Families to Corporate Bodies

Record an appropriate term from the following list with the authorized access point or identifier for a related family (see **31.1**). Apply the general guidelines on using relationship designators at **K.1**.

founding family A family that founded the corporate body.

sponsoring family A family that sponsors the corporate body.

K.4 Relationship Designators for Related Corporate Bodies

K.4.1 Relationship Designators to Relate Corporate Bodies to Persons

Record an appropriate term from the following list with the authorized access point or identifier for a related corporate body (see **32.1**). Apply the general guidelines on using relationship designators at **K.1**.

employer A corporate body that employs the person.
corporate body A corporate body of which the person is a member.
founded corporate body An organization that the person founded.
officiated corporate body A corporate body in which the person holds an office.

K.4.2 Relationship Designators to Relate Corporate Bodies to Families

Record an appropriate term from the following list with the authorized access point or identifier for a related corporate body (see **32.1**). Apply the general guidelines on using relationship designators at **K.1**.

founded corporate body An organization that the family founded.

sponsored corporate body An organization that the family sponsors.

K.4.3 Relationship Designators to Relate Corporate Bodies to Other Corporate Bodies

Record an appropriate term from the following list with the authorized access point or identifier for a related corporate body (see **32.1**). Apply the general guidelines on using relationship designators at **K.1**.

component of a merger A corporate body that formed the other corporate body by merging with one or more other corporate bodies.

corporate member A corporate body that is a member of the other corporate body

founded corporate body A corporate body that the other corporate body founded.

founding corporate body A corporate body that founded the other corporate body.

hierarchical subordinate A corporate body that is subordinate to the other corporate body.

hierarchical superior A corporate body that is hierarchically superior to the other corporate body.

membership corporate body A corporate body formed from the membership of other corporate bodies.

mergee A corporate body that merged with the other corporate body to form a third.

predecessor A corporate body that precedes the other corporate body.

predecessor of split A corporate body that split or divided into the other corporate body.

product of merger A corporate body that resulted from a merger of two or more other corporate bodies.

product of split A corporate body that resulted from a split or division of the other corporate body.

sponsored corporate body A corporate body that is sponsored by the other corporate body.

sponsoring corporate body A corporate body that sponsors the other corporate body.

successor A corporate body that succeeds or follows the other corporate body.

L

RELATIONSHIP DESIGNATORS: RELATIONSHIPS BETWEEN CONCEPTS, OBJECTS, EVENTS, AND PLACES

[To be developed after the initial release of RDA]

GLOSSARY

A-B

4to	Quarto; a book format consisting of one or more leaves that are 1/4 of the whole sheet.
8vo	Octavo; a book format consisting of one or more leaves that are 1/8 of the whole sheet.
12mo	Duodecimo or twelvemo; a book format consisting of one or more leaves that are 1/12 of the whole sheet.
16mo	Decimo-sexto, sexto-decimo, or sixteenmo; a book format consisting of one or more leaves that are 1/16 of the whole sheet.
24mo	Vigesimo-quarto or twenty-fourmo; a book format consisting of one or more leaves that are 1/24 of the whole sheet.
32mo	Trigesimo-secundo or thirty-twomo; a book format consisting of one or more leaves that are 1/32 of the whole sheet.
48mo	Forty-eightmo; a book format consisting of one or more leaves that are 1/48 of the whole sheet.
64mo	Sixty-fourmo; a book format consisting of one or more leaves that are 1/64 of the whole sheet.
Abbreviated Title	A title that has been abbreviated for purposes of indexing or identification.
Academic Degree	A rank conferred as a guarantee of academic proficiency.
Access Point	A name, term, code, etc., representing a specific entity. *see also* **Authorized Access Point** *see also* **Variant Access Point**
Accessibility Content	Content that assists those with a sensory impairment in the greater understanding of content which their impairment prevents them fully seeing or hearing.
Accessible Labels	Accessible tactile language text that is attached to a tactile image, map or diagram.
Acrylic Paint	Applied material consisting of pigments or dyes bound in an emulsion of acrylic resin.

Action Stroke Dance Notation
A form of notated movement using abstract symbols to represent body and limb positions and movements. It is recorded on separate vertical staffs representing the arms, legs, and trunk.

Activity Card
A unit of extent of still image that is a card printed with words, numerals, and/or pictures to be used by an individual or a group as a basis for performing a specific activity. Usually issued in sets.
see also **Game**

Adaptation
1. A new derivative work created by revision of a previously existing work that substantially changes the nature and content of that work.
2. In the case of a musical work, a derivative work described as freely transcribed, based on, etc.; a revision incorporating new material; a paraphrase of various works by, or in the general style of, another composer; revisions in which the harmony or musical style of the original has been changed; performances involving substantial creative responsibility for adaptation, improvisation, etc., on the part of the performer or performers; or any other distinct alteration of another musical work.

For changes that result in a new expression of the same work,
see **Arrangement**

Added Title Page
A title page preceding or following the title page chosen as the preferred source of information. It may be more general (e.g., a series title page), or equally general (e.g., a title page in another language).
see also **Series Title Page**
see also **Title Page**

Additional Scale Information
Supplemental information about scale such as a statement of comparative measurements or limitation of the scale to particular parts of the content of a resource.

Address of the Corporate Body
The address of a corporate body's headquarters or offices, or an e-mail or Internet address for the body.

Address of the Person
The address of a person's place of residence, business, or employer, and/or an e-mail or Internet address.

Affiliation
A group with which a person is affiliated or has been affiliated through employment, membership, cultural identity, etc.

Alternative Chronological Designation of First Issue or Part of Sequence
A second or subsequent system of numbering presented in the form of a date (e.g., a year; year and month; month, day, and year) on the first issue or part of a sequence of numbering for a serial.

Alternative Chronological Designation of Last Issue or Part of Sequence
A second or subsequent system of numbering presented in the form of a date (e.g., a year; year and month; month, day, and year) on the last issue or part of a sequence of numbering for a serial.

Alternative Numeric and/or Alphabetic Designation of First Issue or Part of Sequence	A second or subsequent system of numbering presented in numeric and/or alphabetic form on the first issue or part of a sequence of numbering for a serial.
Alternative Numeric and/or Alphabetic Designation of Last Issue or Part of Sequence	A second or subsequent system of numbering presented in numeric and/or alphabetic form on the last issue or part of a sequence of numbering for a serial.
Alternative Title	The second part of a title proper that consists of two parts (each of which has the form of an independent title), joined by a word such as "or" or its equivalent in another language.
Analog	A type of recording in which the content is stored as continuous variable quantities in or on the media.
Analytical Description	A description that describes a part of a larger resource (e.g., a single volume of a three-volume biography, a single map forming part of a map series).
Annual	Frequency for a resource issued or updated once every year.
Aperture Card	A card with one or more rectangular openings or apertures holding frames of microfilm.
Applied Material	A physical or chemical substance applied to a base material of a resource.
Archival Resource	A document or documents organically created, accumulated, and/or used by a person, family, or corporate body in the course of the conduct of affairs and preserved because of their continuing value. This resource may be an aggregation of documents or it may be a discrete item. It may also be a collection acquired and assembled by an archival repository, individual, or other institution, that does not share a common provenance or origin but that reflects some common characteristic, for example, a particular subject, theme, or form.
Arrangement	An expression of a musical work resulting from (a) a change in the medium of performance, or (b) a simplification or other modification of the work, with or without a change in medium of performance. For changes that result in a new work, *see* **Adaptation (2)**
Artistic and/or Technical Credit	A listing of persons, families, or corporate bodies making contributions to the artistic and/or technical production of a resource.
Aspect Ratio	The ratio of the width to the height of a moving image.
Associated Institution	An institution commonly associated with a corporate body.

Atlas	A unit of extent of cartographic resource that is a volume of maps or other cartographic content with or without descriptive text.
Audio	Media used to store recorded sound, designed for use with a playback device such as a turntable, audiocassette player, CD player, or MP3 player. Includes media used to store digitally encoded as well as analog sound.
Audio Cartridge	A cartridge containing an audio tape.
Audio Cylinder	A roller-shaped object on which sound waves are incised or indented in a continuous circular groove. Includes wax cylinders, wire cylinders, etc.
Audio Description	Narrative text, read out loud by a human being or by voice synthesis, that succinctly explains visual details not apparent from the audio element of the resource. Also known as: audio narration, video description, descriptive video, audio captioning.
Audio Disc	A disc on which sound waves, recorded as modulations, pulses, etc., are incised or indented in a continuous spiral groove.
Audio File	A file type for storing electronically recorded audio content.
Audio Recording	A recording on which sound vibrations have been registered by mechanical or electrical means so that the sound may be reproduced.
Audio Roll	A roll of paper on which musical notes are represented by perforations, designed to mechanically reproduce the music when used in a player piano, player organ, etc. Includes piano rolls, etc.
Audiocassette	A cassette containing an audio tape.
Audiotape	A length of magetic tape on which are recorded electrical signals that can be converted to sound using audio playback equipment.
Audiotape Reel	An open reel holding a length of audio tape to be used with reel-to-reel audio equipment.
Authorized Access Point	The standardized access point representing an entity.
Award	A formal recognition of excellence, etc., given by an award- or prize-granting body, for the content of a resource.
Base Material	The underlying physical material of a resource.

Base Material for Microfilm, Microfiche, Photographic Film, and Motion Picture Film	The underlying physical material of a microfilm, microfiche, photographic film, or motion picture film resource.
Beauchamp-Feuillet Notation	A form of notated movement using abstract symbols to represent movements of the feet during an associated passage of music. It is recorded on a track drawing that traces the path of the dancer across the floor.
Benesh Movement Notation	A form of notated movement using abstract symbols to represent body and limb positions as seen from the back. It is recorded on a five-line horizontal staff that represents the body.
Biennial	Frequency for a resource issued or updated once every two years.
Bimonthly	Frequency for a resource issued or updated once every two months.
Binding	An outer cover affixed to a gathering of one or more sheets.
Biographical Information	Information about the life or history of a person.
Biweekly	Frequency for a resource issued or updated once every two weeks. Used for: Fortnightly.
Blueline	A production method consisting of prints made on light-sensitized surfaces that produce blue images on neutral backgrounds. For white images on blue backgrounds, *see* **Blueprint**
Blueprint	A production method consisting of a photographic process using iron salts and producing an image in Prussian blue. Blueprints are reproductive prints of architectural plans, maps, mechanical drawings, and other technical drawings, characterized by having white images on blue backgrounds. For blue images on white backgrounds, *see* **Blueline**
Book Format	The result of folding a printed sheet to form a gathering of leaves (e.g., a sheet folded once to form a folio, twice to form a quarto, three times to form an octavo, etc.).
Braille Code	A form of tactile notation for text using embossed characters formed by raised dots in six-dot cells.
Brass Music	Conventional collective title for a compilation of all brass music of a composer.

Bristol Board	A base material consisting of a high-grade white cardboard, supercalendered with China clay or made by pasting together sheets of heavy ledger paper.
Broadcast Standard	A system used to format a video resource for television broadcast.

C

Canvas	A base material consisting of a closely woven textile made in various weights, usually of flax, hemp, jute, or cotton, used as a support for oil painting; or a loosely woven, lattice-like mesh, usually of flax, hemp, jute, or cotton, used as a needlepoint foundation.
Caption Title	A title given at the beginning of the first page of the text or, for notated music, at the top of the first page.
Captioning	Text representing speech and other audible information that is displayed on screen in the written language of the audio element of the resource. Usually found as "closed captions" which are encoded and must be decoded (switched on) to be made visible. There are also "open captions" which are always visible and cannot be turned off. Excludes subtitles in a language different from the spoken content.
Carbon Copy	A production method for manuscript that uses an intermediate sheet of paper coated with carbon to create copies at the same time as the original.
Card	A small sheet of opaque material.
Cardboard	A base material consisting of a type of stiff pasteboard that is thicker than 0.006 inches, typically consisting of good-quality chemical pulp or rag pasteboard, and varying greatly in type and stability.
Carrier	A physical medium in which data, sound, images, etc., are stored. For certain types of resources, the carrier may consist of a storage medium (e.g., tape, film) sometimes encased in a plastic, metal, etc., housing (e.g., cassette, cartridge) that is an integral part of the resource. *see also* **Container** *see also* **Media** *see also* **Storage Medium**
Carrier Type	A categorization reflecting the format of the storage medium and housing of a carrier in combination with the type of intermediation device required to view, play, run, etc., the content of a resource.
Cartographic Content	Content that represents the whole or part of the Earth, any celestial body, or imaginary place at any scale.

Cartographic Dataset	Cartographic content expressed through a digitally encoded dataset intended to be processed by a computer. For cartographic data intended to be perceived in the form of an image or three-dimensional form, *see* **Cartographic Image** *see* **Cartographic Moving Image** *see* **Cartographic Tactile Image** *see* **Cartographic Tactile Three-Dimensional Form** *see* **Cartographic Three-Dimensional Form**
Cartographic Image	Cartographic content expressed through line, shape, shading, etc., intended to be perceived visually as a still image or images in two dimensions. Includes maps, views, atlases, remote-sensing images, etc.
Cartographic Moving Image	Cartographic content expressed through images intended to be perceived as moving, in two dimensions. Includes satellite images of the Earth or other celestial bodies in motion.
Cartographic Tactile Image	Cartographic content expressed through line, shape, and/or other forms, intended to be perceived through touch as a still image in two dimensions.
Cartographic Tactile Three-Dimensional Form	Cartographic content expressed through a form or forms intended to be perceived through touch as a three-dimensional form or forms.
Cartographic Three-Dimensional Form	Cartographic content expressed through a form or forms intended to be perceived visually in three dimensions. Includes globes, relief models, etc.
Case	A unit of extent consisting of a box containing bound or unbound resources.
Cataloguer's Note	An annotation that might be helpful to those using or revising the relationship data, or creating an authorized access point representing a related entity.
Centre Track	A track configuration in which the audio track is located in the centre of a separate film roll.
Ceramic	Base material consisting of a nonmetallic mineral, such as clay, fired at a high temperature to form a hard, brittle, heat- and corrosion-resistant material.
Chalk	Applied material consisting of fine-grained limestone, or a soft, earthy form of calcium carbonate; used chiefly in putty, crayons, paint, rubber products, linoleum, and as a pigment and abrasive.

Chamber Music	Conventional collective title for a compilation of all chamber music of a composer.
Charcoal	Applied material consisting of the dark grey residue consisting of carbon, and any remaining ash, obtained by removing water and other volatile constituents from animal and plant substances.
Chart	1. A two-dimensional representation of data in graphic or tabular form (e.g., a wall chart). 2. A map designed primarily for navigation through water, air, or space.
Choir Book	A large music book made to be placed on a stand in front of a choir. Each part is notated separately, usually in the configuration that presents, when the book is open, the soprano and tenor parts on the verso of a leaf, and the alto and bass parts on the recto of the next leaf.
Choral Music	Conventional collective title for a compilation of all choral music of a composer, including compilations of various types of works originally for one choral medium, with or without accompaniment.
Choreographic Content	*see* Notated Movement
Chorus Score	A score of a work for solo voices and chorus showing only the parts for chorus, at least in those portions of the work in which the chorus sings, with the instrumental accompaniment either arranged for keyboard(s) or other chordal instrument(s) or omitted. *see also* Vocal Score
Chronological Designation of First Issue or Part of Sequence	Numbering presented in the form of a date (e.g., a year; year and month; month, day, and year) on the first issue or part of a sequence of numbering for a serial.
Chronological Designation of Last Issue or Part of Sequence	Numbering presented in the form of a date (e.g., a year; year and month; month, day, and year) on the last issue or part of a sequence of numbering for a serial.
Citation Title of a Legal Work	A title of a legal work used for the citation of the work either in the text of the work or in legal literature.
Close Score	*see* Condensed Score
Coarse Groove	Groove characteristic for an analog disc with a groove width typically around 40 grooves per cm (100 grooves per inch). Coarse groove is generally found in early acoustic and electric recordings mostly on shellac carriers.

Coat of Arms	An illustrative content that includes the full display of armorial bearings: the escutcheon plus its adjuncts (helm, crest, mantling, motto, supporters).
Coin	A unit of extent of three-dimensional form consisting of a piece of metal stamped by government authority for use as money.
Collage	A unit of extent of still image consisting of a work in two dimensions or very low relief that were made by affixing paper, fabrics, photographs, or other materials onto a flat surface.
Collection	A group of resources assembled by a person, family or corporate body from a variety of sources.
Collective Title	A title proper that is an inclusive title for a resource containing several separately titled component parts. A collective title may be supplied by the publisher, etc., or devised by a cataloger.
Collotype	A production method consisting of a type of photolithography in which the printing plate is prepared using a bichromate process. Unhardened gelatin areas hold water and thus resist greasy ink; hardened areas accept ink and hold it in the characteristic wormlike pattern of cracks.
Colour Content	The presence of colour, tone, etc., in the content of a resource. Colour content is also the specific colours, tones, etc., (including black and white) present in the content of a resource.
Colour Content of Resource Designed for Persons with Visual Impairments	The presence of colour, tone, etc., in a resource designed for persons with visual impairments. Colour content of resources designed for persons with visual impairments is also the specific colours, tones, etc., (excluding black and white) present in a resource designed for persons with visual impairments.
Colour of Moving Image	The presence of colour, tone, etc., in a moving image or images contained in a resource. Colour of moving image is also the specific colours, tones, etc., (including black and white) present in a moving image or images contained in a resource.
Colour of Still Image	The presence of colour, tone, etc., in a still image or images contained in a resource. Colour of still image is also the specific colours, tones, etc., (including black and white) present in a still image or images contained in a resource.
Colour of Three-Dimensional Form	The presence of colour, tone, etc., in a three-dimensional form or forms contained in a resource. Colour of three-dimensional form is also the specific colours, tones, etc., (including black and white) present in a three-dimensional form or forms contained in a resource.

Column	A unit of extent of text consisting of one of two or more vertical sections of text appearing on the same page or leaf.
Component Part	A discrete unit of intellectual content within a larger resource.
Composite Description	A description that combines one or more elements identifying a work and/or expression embodied in a manifestation with a description of the manifestation.
Compound Surname	A surname consisting of two or more proper names, sometimes connected by a hyphen, or conjunction, and/or preposition.
Comprehensive Description	A description that describes the resource as a whole (e.g., a map, a periodical, a collection of posters assembled by a library, a kit consisting of a filmstrip, an audiotape, and a teacher's manual).
Computer	Media used to store electronic files, designed for use with a computer. Includes media that are accessed remotely through file servers as well as direct-access media such as computer tapes and discs.
Computer Card	A card containing digitally encoded data designed for use with a computer.
Computer Chip Cartridge	A cartridge containing a miniaturized electronic circuit on a small wafer of semiconductor silicon.
Computer Dataset	Content expressed through a digitally encoded dataset intended to be processed by a computer. Includes numeric data, environmental data, etc., used by applications software to calculate averages, correlations, etc., or to produce models, etc., but not normally displayed in its raw form. For data intended to be perceived visually in the form of notation, image, or three-dimensional form, *see* **Notated Movement** *see* **Notated Music** *see* **Still Image** *see* **Text** *see* **Three-Dimensional Form** *see* **Three-Dimensional Moving Image** *see* **Two-Dimensional Moving Image** For data intended to be perceived in an audible form, *see* **Performed Music** *see* **Sounds** *see* **Spoken Word** For cartographic data, *see* **Cartographic Dataset**
Computer Disc	A disc containing digitally encoded data, magnetically or optically recorded.

Computer Disc Cartridge	A cartridge containing one or more computer discs.
Computer File	*see* **Digital Resource**
Computer Program	Content expressed through digitally encoded instructions intended to be processed and performed by a computer. Includes operating systems, applications software, etc.
Computer Tape	A length of magnetic tape on which are recorded digitally encoded data designed to be processed by a computer.
Computer Tape Cartridge	A cartridge containing a computer tape.
Computer Tape Cassette	A cassette containing a computer tape.
Computer Tape Reel	An open reel holding a length of computer tape to be used with a computer tape drive.
Computing Braille Code	A form of tactile notation for computer related materials which enables the representation of symbols and ASCII code. Also called Computer Braille code.
Concertos	Conventional collective title for a compilation of all concertos of a composer.
Condensed Score	A score in which the number of staves is reduced to two or a few, generally organized by instrumental sections or vocal parts, and often with cues for individual parts. Used for: Close score, Reduced score, Short score.
Conference	1. A meeting of individuals or representatives of various bodies for the purpose of discussing and/or acting on topics of common interest. 2. A meeting of representatives of a corporate body that constitutes its legislative or governing body.
Configuration of Playback Channels	The number of sound channels used to make a recording (e.g., one channel for a monophonic recording, two channels for a stereophonic recording).
Contact Information	Information about an organization, etc., from which a resource may be obtained.
Container	Housing that is physically separable from the resource being housed (e.g., a box for a disc or videocassette, a sleeve for a videodisc). *see also* **Carrier**

Content Type	A categorization reflecting the fundamental form of communication in which the content is expressed and the human sense through which it is intended to be perceived. For content expressed in the form of an image or images, content type also reflects the number of spatial dimensions in which the content is intended to be perceived and the perceived presence or absence of movement.
Contributor	A person, family, or corporate body contributing to an expression. Contributors include editors, translators, arrangers of music, performers, etc.
Conventional Collective Title	A title used as the preferred title for a compilation containing two or more works by one person, family, or corporate body, or two or more parts of a work (e.g., Works, Poems, Selections).
Conventional Name	A name, other than the real or official name, by which a corporate body has come to be known.
Coordinates of Cartographic Content	A mathematical system for identifying the area covered by the cartographic content of a resource. Coordinates may be expressed by means of longitude and latitude on the surface of planets or by the angles of right ascension and declination for celestial charts.
Copyright Date	A date associated with a claim of protection under copyright or a similar regime.
Corporate Body	An organization or group of persons and/or organizations that is identified by a particular name and that acts, or may act, as a unit.
Corporate History	Historical information about the corporate body.
Correspondence	Conventional collective title for compilations of all correspondence of a person, family, or corporate body.
Country Associated with the Person	A country with which a person is identified.
Cover	The outer protective material attached to a volume, consisting of both sides of the front and back panels and the spine to which they are joined.
Coverage of the Content	The chronological or geographic coverage of the content of a resource.
Creator	A person, family, or corporate body responsible for the creation of a work.
Custodial History of Item	A record of previous ownership or custodianship of an item.

Custodian	A person, family, or corporate body having legal custody of an item.

D-F

Daguerreotype	A production method consisting of exposure in a camera of a silver-coated copper plate that is subsequently developed, usually using mercury vapour, and fixed with salt to create a positive image.
Daily	Frequency for a resource issued or updated once every day, usually exclusive of non-working days.
DanceWriting	A form of notated movement using figurative and abstract symbols to represent body and limb positions and movements. It is recorded on a five-line horizontal staff that represents the body.
Data Type	The direct reference method (i.e., the system of objects) used to represent geospatial information in an electronic resource (e.g., raster, vector, point).
Dataset	Factual information presented in a structured form.
Date Associated with the Corporate Body	A significant date associated with the history of a corporate body, such as date of establishment, date of termination, or its period of activity. For a conference, it is the date or range of dates on which a conference, etc., was held.
Date Associated with the Family	A significant date associated with the history of a family.
Date Associated with the Person	A significant date associated with the history of a person (e.g., date of birth, date of death).
Date of a Treaty	The earliest date a treaty or a protocol to a treaty was adopted by an international intergovernmental body or by an international conference, was opened for signing, was formally signed, was ratified, was proclaimed, etc.
Date of Birth	The year a person was born. Date of birth may also include the month or month and day of the person's birth.
Date of Capture	A date or range of dates associated with the capture (i.e., recording, filming, etc.) of the content of a resource.
Date of Conference, Etc.	The date or range of dates on which a conference, congress, meeting, exhibition, fair, festival, etc., was held.
Date of Death	The year a person died. Date of death may also include the month or month and day of the person's death.

Date of Distribution	A date associated with the distribution of a resource in a published form.
Date of Establishment	The date on which a corporate body was established or founded.
Date of Expression	The earliest date associated with an expression.
Date of Manufacture	A date associated with the printing, duplicating, casting, etc., of a resource in a published form.
Date of Production	A date associated with the inscription, fabrication, construction, etc., of a resource in an unpublished form.
Date of Promulgation of a Law, Etc.	The year a law, etc., was promulgated or brought into force.
Date of Publication	A date associated with the publication, release, or issuing of a resource.
Date of Termination	The date on which a corporate body was terminated or dissolved.
Date of Usage	A date or range of dates associated with the use of the name chosen as the preferred name for a person.
Date of Work	The earliest date associated with a work.
Decimo-sexto	*see* **16mo**
Declination	The angular distance to a body on the celestial sphere measured north or south through 90° from the celestial equator along the hour circle of the body.
Derivative Master	A generation of digital resource that is derived from the master. *see also* **Master**
Description	A set of data recording and identifying an entity.
Designation of a Named Revision of an Edition	A word, character or group of words and/or characters, identifying a particular revision of a named edition.
Designation of Edition	A word, character or group of words and/or characters, identifying the edition to which a resource belongs.

Devised Title A title proper created by an agency preparing a description of a resource that bears no title itself and has no title associated with it that can be found in other sources (e.g., accompanying material, a published description of the resource, a reference source).

Diagram A unit of extent of cartographic resource that is a geographic representation of numeric data, or of the course or results of an action or process. The term is sometimes also applied to maps characterized by much simplified, or schematic, representation.

Diazo An emulsion on microfilm and microfiche consisting of one or more light-sensitive layers of diazonium salts in a polyester or acetate base that react with dye couplers when processed to produce azo dye images.

Digital A type of recording in which the content is continuously sampled and a sequence of discrete binary values is stored to represent the amplitude of each sample in the waveform.

Digital File Characteristic A technical specification relating to the digital encoding of text, image, audio, video, and other types of data in a resource.

Digital Representation of Cartographic Content A set of technical details relating to the encoding of geospatial information in a cartographic resource.

Digital Resource A resource (data and/or program(s)) encoded for manipulation by a computerized device. The resource may require the use of a peripheral device directly connected to a computerized device (e.g., a CD-ROM drive), an application program (e.g., a media player, an image viewer), and/or a connection to a computer network (e.g., the Internet).

Dimensions The measurements of the carrier or carriers and/or the container of a resource.

Dimensions of Map, Etc. The measurements of the face of a map, etc.

Dimensions of Still Image The measurements of the pictorial area of a still image.

Diorama A unit of extent of three-dimensional form consisting of a three-dimensional representation of a scene created by placing objects, figures, etc., in front of a two-dimensional painted background.

Disc Master Generation designation for an audio recording comprising a negative metal copy of a recording cut (typically) onto a laquer-coated disc by means of a disc lathe; the laquer original is destroyed in the process. The term master can also apply to the lacquer original if it has not been used to create a metal "father".

Dissertation or Thesis Information	Information about a work presented as part of the formal requirements for an academic degree.
Distinctive Title	In the context of musical works, a title that is not just a form or musical genre, a tempo indication, a number of performers, or a type of liturgical text.
Distribution Statement	A statement identifying the place or places of distribution, distributor or distributors, and date or dates of distribution of a resource in a published form.
Distributor	A person, family, or corporate body responsible for distributing a resource.
Distributor's Name	The name of a person, family, or corporate body responsible for distributing a resource in a published form.
Double Leaf	A leaf of double size with a fold at the fore edge or at the top edge of the resource.
Drawing	A unit of extent of still image consisting of a visual work produced by drawing, which is the application of lines on a surface, often paper, by using a pencil, pen, chalk, or some other tracing instrument to focus on the delineation of form rather than the application of colour. This term is often defined broadly to refer to computer-generated images as well.
Duodecimo	*see* **12mo**
Duration	The playing time, running time, etc., of the content of a resource. Duration also includes performance time for a resource containing notated music or notated movement.
Dye	Applied material consisting of a coloured substance dissolved or suspended in a liquid that can be absorbed by the base material.
Earlier Title Proper	A title proper appearing on an earlier iteration of an integrating resource that differs from that on the current iteration.
Early Printed Resources	Materials manufactured before the advent of machine printing in approximately 1825-1830.
Edge Track	A track configuration in which the audio track is located near the edge of a film roll.
Edition Statement	A statement identifying the edition to which a resource belongs.

Electronic Flash Card	*see* **Flash Card**
Element	A word, character, or group of words and/or characters representing a distinct unit of bibliographic information.
Embossed	A production method for tactile resources using either a metal or plastic sheet as a master or embossing equipment (often in combination with a computer and specialized software) to produce braille and Moon copies. Use for "plate copy" or "press braille" or braille generated using Braillo equipment. Also use for "dotty Moon" (where the Moon characters are embossed as lines of dots), including use of Tiger Embosser equipment.
Emulsion on Microfilm and Microfiche	A suspension of light-sensitive chemicals used as a coating on a microfilm or microfiche (e.g., silver halide).
Encoded Bitrate	The speed at which streaming audio, video, etc., is designed to play.
Encoding Format	A schema, standard, etc., used to encode the digital content of a resource.
Engraving	A production method consisting of creating marks on the surface of a hard material, such as metal or glass, by incising with a sharp tool. In printing, the intaglio process in which the design is incised into a printing plate, usually a flat copper plate, with the aid of a graver or burin that is held in the palm of the hand and pushed against the copper to cut lines comprising V-shaped grooves. The plate is then inked up, wiped so that ink is retained in the grooves and then forced out under the pressure of the printing process to create lines on the paper. The technique was first developed in the early 15th century in Germany. Historically, "engraving" has sometimes been used incorrectly to refer to all printmaking processes, particularly any process employing printing plates.
Epoch	An arbitrary moment in time to which measurements of position for a body or orientation for an orbit are referred.
Equinox	One of two points of intersection of the ecliptic and the celestial equator, occupied by the sun when its declination is 0°.
Equipment or System Requirement	The equipment or system required for use, playback, etc., of an analog, digital, etc., resource.
Eshkol-Wachman Movement Notation	A form of notated movement using a spherical coordinate system to denote body and limb positions. It is recorded on a grid that represents the body.
Essays	Conventional collective title for compilations of all essays by a person.

Etching	Production method consisting of an intaglio process in which the design is worked into an acid-resistant substance coating the metal printing plate; the plate is then exposed to acid, which etches the plate where the metal is exposed, to create lines and dark areas. For designs incised directly into a copper plate using a burin or graver, *see* **Engraving**
Exemplar of Manifestation	A single exemplar or instance of a manifestation.
Exhibit	A unit of extent of three-dimensional form consisting of objects on display, along with the display environment (cases, labels, etc.).
Explanation of Relationship	Information elaborating on or clarifying the relationship between related entities.
Explanatory Reference	An elaborated *see* or *see also* reference that explains the circumstances under which the authorized access points involved should be consulted.
Expression	The intellectual or artistic realization of a work in the form of alpha-numeric, musical or choreographic notation, sound, image, object, movement, etc., or any combination of such forms.
Expression Manifested	An expression embodied in a manifestation.
Expression of Work	A realization of a work in the form of alpha-numeric, musical or choreographic notation, sound, image, object, movement, etc., or any combination of such forms.
Extent	The number and type of units and/or subunits making up a resource.
Extent of Cartographic Resource	The number and type of units and/or subunits making up a cartographic resource.
Extent of Notated Music	The number and type of units and/or subunits making up a resource consisting of notated music, with or without accompanying text and/or illustrations.
Extent of Still Image	The number and type of units and/or subunits making up a resource consisting of one or more still images.
Extent of Text	The number and type of units and/or subunits making up a resource consisting of text, with or without accompanying illustrations.
Extent of Three-Dimensional Form	The number and type of units and/or subunits making up a resource consisting of one or more three-dimensional forms.

Extra Large Print	*see* **Giant Print**
Facsimile	1. A reproduction simulating the physical appearance of the original in addition to reproducing its content exactly. 2. An illustrative content consisting of an exact copy of an original, usually in the same dimensions as the original, especially of books, documents, prints, and drawings. Today often reproduced photographically or digitally; in the past, reproduced by engraving or other printmaking process.
Family	Two or more persons related by birth, marriage, adoption, civil union, or similar legal status, or who otherwise present themselves as a family.
Family History	Biographical information about the family and its members.
Female	The gender designation for woman or girl.
Field of Activity of the Corporate Body	A field of business in which a corporate body is engaged and/or the body's area of competence, responsibility, jurisdiction, etc.
Field of Activity of the Person	A field of endeavour, area of expertise, etc., in which a person is engaged or was engaged.
File Size	The number of bytes in a digital file.
File Type	A general type of data content encoded in a computer file.
Film Cartridge	A cartridge containing a motion picture film.
Film Cassette	A cassette containing a motion picture film.
Film Reel	An open reel holding a motion picture film to be used with a motion picture film projector.
Film Roll	A wound length of film.
Filmslip	A short strip of film, usually in rigid format rather than rolled.
Filmstrip	A roll of film, with or without recorded sound, containing a succession of images intended for projection one at a time.
Filmstrip Cartridge	A cartridge containing a filmstrip.
Finding Aid	A descriptive tool providing access to a resource.

Fine	Groove characteristic for an analog cylinder with a groove pitch in the range of 60-64 turns per cm (150 or 160 turns per inch) for 6 1/8 inch dictation format cylinders, or 200 TPI for "4 minute" cylinders.
First Generation	Generation designation for a microform resource comprising the original camera film on which the picture of the document was taken. Also known as the first-generation master or preservation master.
Flash Card	A unit of extent of still image consisting of a card (or digital representation of a card) carrying words, numerals, pictures, etc., designed for rapid display as an aid to learning.
Flipchart	A hinging device holding two or more sheets designed for use on an easel.
Folio	A book format consisting of one or more leaves that are 1/2 of the whole sheet.
Font Size	The size of the type used to represent the characters and symbols in a resource.
Form	An illustrative content consisting of labeled areas for recording structured data to be input by specified persons for specific purposes, usually accompanied by prompts and guidance.
Form of Musical Notation	A set of characters and/or symbols used to express the musical content of a resource.
Form of Notated Movement	A set of characters and/or symbols used to express the movement content of a resource.
Form of Notation	A set of characters and/or symbols used to express the content of a resource.
Form of Tactile Notation	A set of characters and/or symbols used to express the content of a resource in a form that can be perceived through touch.
Form of Work	A class or genre to which a work belongs.
Formally Presented	Appearing in isolation, as opposed to appearing embedded in text, and in a prominent location.
Format of Notated Music	The musical or physical layout of the content of a resource that is presented in the form of musical notation.
Fortnightly	*see* **Biweekly**

Forty-eightmo	*see* **48mo**
Frequency	The intervals at which the issues or parts of a serial or the updates to an integrating resource are issued.
Full Score	*see* **Score**
Full Screen	Aspect ratio for a moving image resource of less than 1.5:1.
Fuller Form of Name	The full form of a part of a name represented only by an initial or abbreviation in the form chosen as the preferred name, or a part of the name not included in the form chosen as the preferred name.
Fully Established	Status of identification for an authorized access point when the data is complete.

G-L

Game	A unit of extent of three-dimensional form consisting of a set of objects designed for manipulation according to prescribed or implicit rules for education, entertainment, or therapy. *see also* **Activity Card** *see also* **Toy**
Game Play Notation	A form of notated movement recording tactical movements during the course of a game, such as chess.
Gathering	One or more pairs of leaves — made up of a folded sheet, a fraction of a folded sheet, or several folded sheets tucked inside one another — that together form a distinctive unit for binding purposes.
Gender	The gender with which a person identifies.
Genealogical Table	An illustrative content consisting of a table or diagram representing the lineage of a person or family.
Generation	The relationship between an original carrier and the carrier of a reproduction made from the original (e.g., a first generation camera master, a second generation printing master).
Generation of Audio Recording	The relationship between an original audio carrier and the carrier of a reproduction made from the original (e.g., a tape duplication master, a test pressing).
Generation of Digital Resource	The relationship between an original carrier of a digital resource and the carrier of a reproduction made from the original (e.g., a derivative master).

Generation of Microform	The relationship between an original microform carrier and the carrier of a reproduction made from the original (e.g., a printing master).
Generation of Motion Picture Film	The relationship between an original carrier of a motion picture film resource and the carrier of a reproduction made from the original (e.g., a reference print).
Generation of Videotape	The relationship between an original carrier of a videotape resource and the carrier of a reproduction made from the original (e.g., a show copy).
Giant Print	A font size that is very large, designed to aid readers who experience difficulty reading large print. Used for: Extra large print, Super large print.
Glass	A base material consisting of silicon dioxide (silica) fused with a basic oxide; generally transparent but often translucent or opaque.
Globe	A unit of extent of cartographic resource that is a depiction of the Earth or other celestial body (real or imaginary) on the surface of a sphere.
Gouache	Applied material consisting of pigment and a binding agent, and sometimes added inert materials, to form an opaque, coloured, water-soluble paint. Includes poster paints. The term originally referred to oil applied on top of tempera painting.
Government	The totality of corporate bodies (executive, legislative, and judicial) exercising the powers of a jurisdiction.
Granting Institution or Faculty	An institution or faculty conferring an academic degree on a candidate.
Graph	An illustrative content consisting of a diagram showing relative quantitative and qualitative aspects of a data set.
Graphic Notation	A form of musical notation that uses various suggestive lines, symbols, colour, etc., to prompt or guide the performers. It is used for music that is indeterminate in pitch, duration, temperament, etc., and also to depict electronic music in which no performer is involved.
Graphite	Applied material consisting of a naturally occurring allotrope of carbon which is opaque, soft, greasy to the touch, and iron black to steel gray in color. It is used in the form of powder, sticks, or in pencils.
Groove Characteristic	The groove width of an analog disc or the groove pitch of an analog cylinder.

Hardboard	A base material consisting of any firm, dense, rigid board, often manufactured from fiber consolidated under heat and pressure in a hot press.
Harmony	1. In the context of the Bible, an arrangement of passages of the Bible on the same topic into parallel columns so that similarities and differences may be compared readily. 2. An interweaving of such passages into a continuous text.
Hereditary Title	A title of nobility, etc., associated with a family.
Hierarchical Description	A description that combines a comprehensive description of the whole resource with analytical descriptions of one or more of its parts.
High Reduction	A reduction ratio between 31× and 60× for a microform resource.
History of the Work	Information about the history of a work.
Holograph	A manuscript handwritten by the person(s) responsible for the work(s) contained therein.
Horizontal Scale of Cartographic Content	The ratio of horizontal distances in the cartographic content of a resource to the actual distances they represent.
Hot Spot	*see* Swell Paper
Icon	A unit of extent of still image consisting of an image that portrays a sacred entity and that is itself regarded as sacred. Most commonly comprising tempera on panel, but it may be in any two-dimensional or relief medium, including fresco.
Identifier for the Corporate Body	A character string uniquely associated with a corporate body, or with a surrogate for a corporate body (e.g., an authority record). The identifier serves to differentiate that corporate body from other corporate bodies.
Identifier for the Expression	A character string uniquely associated with an expression, or with a surrogate for an expression (e.g., an authority record). The identifier serves to differentiate that expression from other expressions.
Identifier for the Family	A character string uniquely associated with a family, or with a surrogate for a family (e.g., an authority record). The identifier serves to differentiate that family from other families.
Identifier for the Item	A character string associated with an item that serves to differentiate that item from other items.

Identifier for the Manifestation	A character string associated with a manifestation that serves to differentiate that manifestation from other manifestations.
Identifier for the Person	A character string uniquely associated with a person, or with a surrogate for a person (e.g., an authority record). The identifier serves to differentiate that person from other persons.
Identifier for the Work	A character string uniquely associated with a work, or with a surrogate for a work (e.g., an authority record). The identifier serves to differentiate that work from other works.
Illumination	An illustrative content consisting of adornments, including miniature scenes and portraits, in one or more colours and applied by hand to a resource using paint, ink, or metal foil.
Illustration	An illustrative content consisting of a still image.
Illustration Board	A base material consisting of laminated paper board that has paper layers glued to its surface; used commonly as temporary artists' supports.
Illustrative Content	Content designed to illustrate the primary content of a resource.
Image Description	Descriptive audio or tactile language text that is attached to, or supplied with, a tactile image, map or diagram.
Image File	A file type for storing electronically recorded content representing still images.
Immediate Source of Acquisition of Item	The source from which the agency directly acquired an item and the circumstances under which it was received.
Ink	Applied material consisting of pigments or dyes contained in a liquid or paste that can be applied with a pen or stylus.
Instrumental Music	Conventional collective title for a compilation of all instrumental music of a composer.
Integrating Resource	A resource that is added to or changed by means of updates that do not remain discrete but are integrated into the whole (e.g., a loose-leaf manual that is updated by means of replacement pages, a website that is updated continuously).

Intended Audience	The class of user for which the content of a resource is intended, or for whom the content is considered suitable. The class of user is defined by age group (e.g., children, young adults, adults), educational level (e.g., primary, secondary), type of disability, or another categorization.
International Intergovernmental Body	An international body created by intergovernmental action.
Irregular	Frequency for a resource issued with no consistent interval between issues.
ISSN of Series	The identifier assigned to a series by an ISSN registration agency.
ISSN of Subseries	The identifier assigned to a subseries by an ISSN registration agency.
Issue	One of the successive parts of a serial. *see also* **Part**
Item	A single exemplar or instance of a manifestation.
Iteration	An instance of an integrating resource, either as first released or after it has been updated.
Ivory	A base material consisting of the dentine forming the bulk of the teeth and tusks of animals such as elephants, walruses, and narwhals.
Jacket	The detachable, protective wrapping of a volume, issued as part of the resource by a publisher, etc. Also known as a book jacket or a dust jacket. For the sleeve that houses a disc, *see* **Container**
Jigsaw Puzzle	A unit of extent of three-dimensional form consisting of a picture usually on pasteboard or wood, which has been cut into interlocking shapes intended to be re-assembled.
Jumbo Braille	A font size of braille text where the individual cells are expanded to give wider spacing between standard size dots or between dots larger than standard size.
Key	The set of pitch relationships that establishes the tonal centre, or principal tonal centre, of a musical work. Key is indicated by its pitch name and its mode, when it is major or minor.
Key Title	The unique name assigned to a resource by an ISSN registration agency.

Keyboard Music	Conventional collective title for a compilation of all keyboard music of a composer.
Kinetography Laban	A form of notated movement using abstract symbols to represent movement of the body and limbs as seen from the back. It is recorded on a vertical three-line staff that represents the body. Similar to Labanotation.
Labanotation	A form of notated movement using abstract symbols to represent movement of the body and limbs as seen from the back. It is recorded on a vertical three-line staff that represents the body. Similar to Kinetography Laban.
Language of Expression	A language in which a work is expressed.
Language of the Content	A language used to express the content of a resource.
Language of the Corporate Body	A language a corporate body uses in its communications.
Language of the Family	A language a family uses in its communications.
Language of the Person	A language a person uses when writing for publication, broadcasting, etc.
Large Print	A font size designed to aid readers who experience difficulty reading regular print.
Later Title Proper	A title proper appearing on a later issue or part of a multipart monograph or serial that differs from that on the first or earliest issue or part.
Latitude	The distance of a point on a planet or satellite measured north and south from the equator.
Layout	The arrangement of text, images, tactile notation, etc., in a resource.
Leaf	A unit of extent consisting of a single bound or fastened sheet as a subunit of a volume; each leaf consists of two pages, one on each side, either or both of which may be blank.
Leather	A base material consisting of the skin or hide of an animal that has been tanned to render it resistant to putrefaction and relatively soft and flexible when dry.
Letter Notation	Musical notation that uses the letters of the alphabet to designate pitches.

Libretto	The words of an opera or other musical stage work, or an oratorio. For the words of just the songs from a musical, *see* **Lyrics**
Location of Conference, Etc.	A local place in which a conference, congress, meeting, exhibition, fair, festival, etc., was held.
Location of Headquarters	A country, state, province, etc., or local place in which an organization has its headquarters.
Logical Unit	A constituent of an intangible resource, such as a digital file.
Longitude	The distance of a point on a planet or satellite measured east and west from a reference meridian.
Longitude and Latitude	A system for identifying the area covered by the cartographic content of a resource using longitude of the westernmost and easternmost boundaries and latitude of the northernmost and southernmost boundaries.
Low Reduction	A reduction ratio less than 16× for a microform resource.
Lyrics	The words of a popular song, including a song or songs from a musical. For just the dialogue from a musical, *see* **Libretto**

M-O

Magnetic	Recording medium that relies on pole reversal in a ferromagnetic medium, typically ferromagnetic oxide particles bound to a continuous flexible surface (tape) or a rigid platter (disc).
Magneto-optical	Recording medium that uses a combination of laser heating with a varying magnetic field to write data to a disc. The Sony MiniDisc is the most prominent format.
Main Series	A series that contains one or more subseries.
Male	The gender designation for man or boy.
Manifestation	The physical embodiment of an expression of a work.
Manifestation Exemplified	The manifestation exemplified by an item.
Manifestation of Expression	A physical embodiment of an expression.

Manifestation of Work
A physical embodiment of an expression of a work.

Manufacture Statement
A statement identifying the place or places of manufacture, manufacturer or manufacturers, and date or dates of manufacture of a resource in a published form.

Manufacturer
A person, family, or corporate body responsible for printing, duplicating, casting, etc., a resource in a published form.

Manufacturer's Name
The name of a person, family, or corporate body responsible for printing, duplicating, casting, etc., a resource in a published form.

Manuscript
1. In general, a text, musical score, map, etc., inscribed or written entirely by hand, or the handwritten or typescript copy of a creator's work.
2. In the context of production method for manuscripts, any handwritten manuscript which is not a holograph.

Map
A unit of extent of cartographic resource that is a representation, normally to scale and on a two-dimensional medium, of a selection of material or abstract features on, or in relation to, the surface of Earth, another celestial body, or an imaginary place.
see also **Cartographic Image**
see also **Chart**

Map Section
see **Section (2)**

Map Series
A number of related but physically separate and bibliographically distinct cartographic units intended to form a single group. For bibliographic treatment, the group is collectively identified by any commonly occurring unifying characteristic or combination of characteristics including a common designation (e.g., collective title, number, or a combination of both); sheet identification system (including successive or chronological numbering systems); scale; publisher; cartographic specifications; uniform format; etc.

Master
A generation of digital resource that is created from the process of digitization at the highest resolution and often used to make derivative copies.
see also **Original**

Master Tape
Generation designation for an audio recording comprising the original recorded version of a tape from which copies can be made.

Mathematics Braille Code
A form of tactile notation used to transcribe mathematical and scientific information.

Medal	A unit of extent of three-dimensional form consisting of a small piece of metal, bearing a relief design on one or both sides and having a commemorative purpose; not used as a medium of exchange.
Media	The means used to convey information or artistic content. *see also* **Carrier**
Media Type	A categorization reflecting the general type of intermediation device required to view, play, run, etc., the content of a resource.
Medium of Performance	The instrument, instruments, voice, voices, etc., for which a musical work was originally conceived.
Medium of Performance of Musical Content	The instrument, instruments, voice, voices, etc., used (or intended to be used) for performance of musical content.
Mensural Notation	A system of notating duration, beginning around 1260 and continuing through about 1600, employing four principal note-values and associated rests: long, breve, semibreve, and minim.
Metal	A base material consisting of a substance typified by being a good conductor of electricity and heat, opaque with a characteristic lustre, fusible, and usually malleable or ductile.
Microcapsule Paper	*see* **Swell Paper**
Microfiche	A sheet of film bearing a number of microimages in a two-dimensional array.
Microfiche Cassette	A cassette containing uncut microfiches.
Microfilm	A film bearing a number of microimages in linear array.
Microfilm Cartridge	A cartridge containing a microfilm.
Microfilm Cassette	A cassette containing a microfilm.
Microfilm Reel	An open reel holding a microfilm, to be threaded into a microfilm reader.
Microfilm Roll	A wound length of microfilm.
Microfilm Slip	A short strip of microfilm cut from a roll.

Microform	Media used to store reduced-size images not readable to the human eye, designed for use with a device such as a microfilm or microfiche reader. Includes both transparent and opaque micrographic media.
Microgroove	Groove characteristic for an analog disc with a groove width typically in the range 120 to 160 or more per cm (300 to 400 or more grooves per inch), generally pressed into vinyl and in use post 1945.
Microopaque	A card or sheet of opaque material bearing a number of microimages in a two-dimensional array.
Microscope Slide	A small sheet of transparent material (with or without a protective mount) bearing a minute object designed for use with a device such as a microscope.
Microscopic	Media used to store minute objects, designed for use with a device such as a microscope to reveal details invisible to the naked eye.
Miniature Score	*see* **Study Score**
Minolta Paper	*see* **Swell Paper**
Mixed	Aspect ratio for a moving image resource that includes multiple aspect ratios within the same resource.
Mixed Generation	Generation designation for a microform resource comprising a combination of generations of film, for which it is not possible to assign more precise terms.
Mixed Materials	Applied material consisting of multiple materials known to have been applied, but not all can be readily identified.
Mixed Polarity	A polarity in which colours and tones used for images are a mixture of those seen with the human eye and those opposite what the human eye would see.
Mock-up	A unit of extent of three-dimensional form consisting of a physical representation of a device or process that may be modified for training or analysis to emphasize a particular part or function.
Mode of Issuance	A categorization reflecting whether a resource is issued in one or more parts, the way it is updated, and its intended termination.

Model	1. A unit of extent of three-dimensional form consisting of a physical representation of a real or imagined object usually on a smaller scale. 2. A unit of extent of cartographic resource that is a three-dimensional representation of the whole or part of the Earth or any celestial body (real or imaginary) at any scale. *see also* **Toy**
Monograph	A resource that is complete in one part or intended to be completed within a finite number of parts.
Monthly	Frequency for a resource issued or updated once every month.
Moon Code	A form of tactile notation based on simplified letter forms.
Mother	Generation designation for an audio recording comprising a positive metal copy of a disc master used to create one or more stampers.
Motion Picture Music	Conventional collective title for a compilation of all motion picture music of a composer.
Mount	The physical material used for the support or backing to which the base material of a resource has been attached.
Multilevel Description	In an ISBD display, a multilevel description is a form of presentation of descriptive data based on the division of descriptive information into two or more levels. The first level contains information common to the whole or main resource. The second and subsequent levels contain information about the individual part.
Multipart Monograph	A resource issued in two or more parts (either simultaneously or successively) that is complete or intended to be completed within a finite number of parts (e.g., a dictionary in two volumes, three audiocassettes issued as a set).
Music	An illustrative content consisting of musical notation.
Music Braille Code	A form of tactile notation for music using braille cells.
Musicals	Conventional collective title for a compilation of all musicals of a composer.
Name	A word, character, or group of words and/or characters by which a person, family, or corporate body is known.
Name of the Corporate Body	A word, character, or group of words and/or characters by which a corporate body is known.

Name of the Family	A word, character, or group of words and/or characters by which a family is known.
Name of the Person	A word, character, or group of words and/or characters by which a person is known.
Name of the Place	A word, character, or group of words and/or characters by which a place is known.
Nature of the Content	The specific character of the primary content of a resource (e.g., legal articles, interim report).
Neat Line	A line marking the outer edge of a map or chart, separating its detail from any border or margin.
Negative	A polarity in which colours and tones used for images are opposite those seen with the human eye.
Neumatic Notation	A system of musical notation using neumes, i.e., graphic signs that represent essentially the movement in pitch of a melody.
Normal Reduction	A reduction ratio between 16× and 30× for a microform resource.
Not Drawn to Scale	Scale designation for a still image or three-dimensional form that is not to scale.
Not Known (Gender)	The gender designation when specific gender is unknown.
Notated Movement	Content expressed through a form of notation for movement intended to be perceived visually. Includes all forms of movement notation other than those intended to be perceived through touch. *see also* **Tactile Notated Movement**
Notated Music	Content expressed through a form of musical notation intended to be perceived visually. Includes all forms of musical notation other than those intended to be perceived through touch. *see also* **Tactile Notated Music**
Note on Carrier	A note providing information on attributes of the carrier or carriers of the manifestation.
Note on Changes in Carrier Characteristics	A note on changes in the characteristics of the carrier that occur in subsequent issues or parts of a resource issued in successive parts or between iterations of an integrating resource.

Note on Changes in Content Characteristics	A note on changes in content characteristics is a note on changes in content characteristics that occur in subsequent issues or parts of a resource issued in successive parts or between iterations of an integrating resource.
Note on Copyright Date	A note providing information on copyright dates not recorded as part of the copyright date element.
Note on Dimensions of Item	A note providing information on the dimensions of the specific item being described that is not recorded as part of the dimensions element.
Note on Dimensions of Manifestation	A note providing information on the dimensions of a manifestation that is not recorded as part of the dimensions element.
Note on Distribution Statement	A note providing details on place of distribution, distributor, or date of distribution, or information on changes in the place of distribution, distributor, or distributor's name.
Note on Edition Statement	A note providing information on the source of an edition statement, on edition statements relating to issues, parts, etc., on changes in edition statements, or other information relating to an edition statement.
Note on Expression	An annotation providing additional information about content recorded as an expression attribute.
Note on Extent of Item	A note providing information on the extent of the specific item being described that is not recorded as part of the extent element.
Note on Extent of Manifestation	A note providing information on the extent of a manifestation that is not recorded as part of the extent element.
Note on Frequency	A note providing details on the currency of the contents, on the frequency of release of issues or parts of a serial or the frequency of updates to an integrating resource, or on changes in frequency.
Note on Issue, Part, or Iteration Used as the Basis for Identification of the Resource	A note identifying the issue or part of a multipart monograph or serial, or the iteration of an integrating resource that has been used as the basis for the identification of a resource.
Note on Item	A note providing information on attributes of the item.
Note on Item-Specific Carrier Characteristic	A note providing additional information about carrier characteristics that are specific to the item being described and are assumed not to apply to other items exemplifying the same manifestation.
Note on Manifestation	A note providing information on attributes of the manifestation.

Note on Manufacture Statement	A note providing details on place of manufacture, manufacturer, or date of manufacture, or information on changes in the place of manufacture, manufacturer, or manufacturer's name.
Note on Numbering of Serials	A note providing information on the numbering of the first and/or last issue or part, on complex or irregular numbering (including numbering errors), or on the period covered by a volume, issue, part, etc.
Note on Production Statement	A note providing details on place of production, producer, or date of production, or information on changes in the place of production, producer, or producer's name.
Note on Publication Statement	A note providing details on place of publication, publisher, or date of publication, information on changes in the place of publication, publisher, or publisher's name, or on suspension of publication.
Note on Series Statement	A note providing information on complex series statements, incorrect numbering within series, or changes in series statements.
Note on Statement of Responsibility	A note providing information on a person, family, or corporate body not named in a statement of responsibility to whom responsibility for the intellectual or artistic content of the resource has been attributed, on variant forms of names appearing in the resource, on changes in statements of responsibility, or on other details relating to a statement of responsibility.
Note on Title	A note providing information on the source from which a title was taken, the date the title was viewed, variations in titles, inaccuracies, deletions, etc., or other information relating to a title.
Novels	Conventional collective title for compilations of all novels by a person, family, or corporate body.
Number Notation	A system of musical notation conveying pitch by use of numbers, assigned to the notes of a scale, the keys of a keyboard, the finger positions or frets of a string instrument, or to the holes or valves of a wind instrument.
Number of a Conference, Etc.	A designation of the sequencing of a conference, etc., within a series of conferences, etc.
Number of Objects	A count of the number of point or vector objects present in a geospatial resource.
Numbering of Part	A designation of the sequencing of a part or parts within a larger work. Numbering of part may include a numeral, a letter, any other character, or the combination of these with or without an accompanying caption (*volume, number*, etc.) and/or a chronological designation.

Numbering of Serials	The identification of each of the issues or parts of a serial. Numbering of serials may include a numeral, a letter, any other character, or the combination of these with or without an accompanying caption (*volume, number*, etc.) and/or a chronological designation.
Numbering within Series	A designation of the sequencing of a part or parts within a series. Numbering within series may include a numeral, a letter, any other character, or the combination of these with or without an accompanying caption (*volume, number,* etc.) and/or a chronological designation.
Numbering within Subseries	A designation of the sequencing of a part or parts within a subseries. Numbering within subseries may include a numeral, a letter, any other character, or the combination of these with or without an accompanying caption (*volume, number*, etc.) and/or a chronological designation.
Numeric and/or Alphabetic Designation of First Issue or Part of Sequence	Numbering presented in numeric and/or alphabetic form on the first issue or part of a sequence of numbering for a serial.
Numeric and/or Alphabetic Designation of Last Issue or Part of Sequence	Numbering presented in numeric and/or alphabetic form on the last issue or part of a sequence of numbering for a serial.
Numeric Designation of a Musical Work	A serial number, opus number, or thematic index number assigned to a musical work by a composer, publisher, or a musicologist.
Object	A three-dimensional artefact (or a replica of an artefact) or a naturally-occurring object.
Object Type	The specific type of point, raster, and/or vector objects used to represent geospatial information in an electronic resource.
Octavo	*see* **8vo**
Oil Paint	Applied material consisting of particles of pigment suspended in a drying oil, commonly linseed oil.
Online Resource	A digital resource accessed by means of hardware and software connections to a communications network.
Operas	Conventional collective title for a compilation of all operas of a composer.
Optical	Recording medium for recording binary encoded data in a transparent medium with a reflective backing. A laser is used to read the changes in reflectivity as a binary data stream.

Orchestra Music	Conventional collective title for a compilation of all orchestra music of a composer.
Original	A generation of digital resource that is the first of a resource created digitally.
Other Designation Associated with the Corporate Body	A word, phrase, or abbreviation indicating incorporation or legal status of a corporate body, or any term serving to differentiate the body from other corporate bodies, persons, etc.
Other Designation Associated with the Person	A term other than a title that is associated with a person's name.
Other Details of Cartographic Content	Mathematical data and other features of the cartographic content of a resource not recorded in statements of scale, projection, and coordinates.
Other Distinguishing Characteristic of the Expression	A characteristic other than content type, language of expression, or date of expression. It serves to differentiate an expression from another expression of the same work.
Other Distinguishing Characteristic of the Work	A characteristic other than form of work, date of work, or place of origin of the work. It serves to differentiate a work from another work with the same title or from the name of a person, family, or corporate body.
Other Person, Family, or Corporate Body Associated with a Manifestation	A person, family, or corporate body other than a producer, publisher, distributor or manufacturer associated with a manifestation. Includes book designers, platemakers, etc.
Other Person, Family, or Corporate Body Associated with a Work	A person, family, or corporate body associated with a work other than as a creator. Includes persons, etc., to whom correspondence is addressed, persons, etc., honoured by a festschrift, directors, cinematographers, sponsoring bodies, production companies, institutions, etc., hosting an exhibition or event, etc.
Other Person, Family, or Corporate Body Associated with an Item	A person, family, or corporate body other than an owner or custodian associated with an item. Includes curators, binders, restorationists, etc.
Other Title Information	Information that appears in conjunction with, and is subordinate to, the title proper of a resource.
Other Title Information of Series	Information that appears in conjunction with, and is subordinate to, the title proper of a series.
Other Title Information of Subseries	Information that appears in conjunction with, and is subordinate to, the title proper of a subseries.

Overhead Projectural	*see* Overhead Transparency
Overhead Transparency	A sheet of transparent material (with or without a protective mount) bearing an image designed for use with an overhead projector.
Owner	A person, family, or corporate body having legal possession of an item.

P

Page	A unit of extent consisting of a single side of a leaf.
Painting	A unit of extent of still image consisting of an item in which images are formed primarily by the direct application of pigments suspended in a medium, arranged in masses of color onto a generally two-dimensional surface.
Paper	A base material consisting of thin matter or felted sheets or webs of animal, plant, mineral, or synthetic fibres formed and dried from a suspension in water.
Parallel Designation of a Named Revision of an Edition	A designation of a named revision of an edition in a language and/or script that differs from that recorded in the designation of a named revision of an edition element.
Parallel Designation of Edition	A designation of edition in a language and/or script that differs from that recorded in the designation of edition element.
Parallel Distributor's Name	A distributor's name in a language and/or script that differs from that recorded in the distributor's name element.
Parallel Manufacturer's Name	A manufacturer's name in a language and/or script that differs from that recorded in the manufacturer's name element.
Parallel Other Title Information	Other title information in a language and/or script that differs from that recorded in the other title information element.
Parallel Other Title Information of Series	Other title information of a series in a language and/or script that differs from that recorded in the other title information of series element.
Parallel Other Title Information of Subseries	Other title information of a subseries in a language and/or script that differs from that recorded in the other title information of subseries element.
Parallel Place of Distribution	A place of distribution in a language and/or script that differs from that recorded in the place of distribution element.

Parallel Place of Manufacture	A place of manufacture in a language and/or script that differs from that recorded in the place of manufacture element.
Parallel Place of Production	A place of production in a language and/or script that differs from that recorded in the place of production element.
Parallel Place of Publication	A place of publication in a language and/or script that differs from that recorded in the place of publication element.
Parallel Producer's Name	A producer's name in a language and/or script that differs from that recorded in the producer's name element.
Parallel Publisher's Name	A publisher's name in a language and/or script that differs from that recorded in the publisher's name element.
Parallel Statement of Responsibility Relating to a Named Revision of an Edition	A statement of responsibility relating to a named revision of an edition in a language and/or script that differs from that recorded in the statement of responsibility relating to a named revision of an edition element.
Parallel Statement of Responsibility Relating to Series	A statement of responsibility relating to series in a language and/or script that differs from that recorded in the statement of responsibility relating to series element.
Parallel Statement of Responsibility Relating to Subseries	A statement of responsibility relating to subseries in a language and/or script that differs from that recorded in the statement of responsibility relating to subseries element.
Parallel Statement of Responsibility Relating to the Edition	A statement of responsibility relating to the edition in a language and/or script that differs from that recorded in the statement of responsibility relating to the edition element.
Parallel Statement of Responsibility Relating to Title Proper	A statement of responsibility relating to title proper in a language and/or script that differs from that recorded in the statement of responsibility relating to title proper element.
Parallel Title Proper	The title proper in another language and/or script.
Parallel Title Proper of Series	The title proper of a series in another language and/or script.
Parallel Title Proper of Subseries	The title proper of a subseries in another language and/or script.
Parchment	A base material consisting of calf, sheep, or goat skin which has been prepared to produce a thin, strong, translucent or opaque substance for writing, bookbinding, or other uses. *see also* **Vellum**

Part	1. One of the units into which a resource has been divided by the publisher, manufacturer, etc.. It is distinguished from a fascicle by being a formal component unit rather than a temporary division of a resource. *see also* **Issue** 2. In the context of notated music, a component consisting of the music for the use of one or more, but not all, performers.
Pastel	Applied material consisting of pigment mixed with a binder, usually in the form of a stick.
Patronymic	A name derived from the given name of a father.
Performed Music	Content expressed through music in an audible form. Includes recorded performances of music, computer-generated music, etc.
Performer, Narrator, and/or Presenter	A person, family, or corporate body responsible for performing, narrating, and/or presenting a work.
Period of Activity of the Corporate Body	A date or range of dates indicative of the period in which a corporate body was active.
Period of Activity of the Person	A date or range of dates indicative of the period in which a person was active in his or her primary field of endeavour.
Person	An individual or an identity established by an individual (either alone or in collaboration with one or more other individuals).
Photocopy	A production method consisting of a macroform photoreproduction produced directly on opaque material by radiant energy through contact or projection.
Photoengraving	A production method using a photomechanical process to prepare chemically etched printing plates.
Photogravure	A production method consisting of an intaglio method in which the metal printing plate is prepared using a bichromate process, leaving a gelatin resist of varying thickness. The plate is etched to form cells of varying depth able to hold different amounts of ink.
Physical Carrier	*see* **Carrier**
Physical Unit	A constituent of a tangible resource, such as a volume, audiocassette, or film reel.

Piano Conductor Part	A performance part for a piano performer in an ensemble, with cues for the other instruments that enable the performer of that part also to conduct.
Piano Music	Conventional collective title for a compilation of all piano music of a composer.
Piano Music, 4 Hands	Conventional collective title for a compilation of all four-hand piano music of a composer.
Piano Music, Pianos (2)	Conventional collective title for a compilation of all two-piano music of a composer.
Piano Score	A reduction of an instrumental work or a vocal work with instruments to a version for piano. May include the words of a vocal work.
Picture	A unit of extent of still image consisting of two-dimensional representations.
Place	A location identified by a name.
Place and Date of Capture	The place and date associated with the capture (i.e., recording, filming, etc.) of the content of a resource.
Place Associated with the Corporate Body	A significant location associated with a corporate body (e.g., location of a conference, etc., location of the headquarters of an organization).
Place Associated with the Family	A place where a family resides or has resided or has some connection.
Place of Birth	The town, city, province, state, and/or country in which a person was born.
Place of Capture	The place associated with the capture (i.e., recording, filming, etc.) of the content of a resource.
Place of Death	The town, city, province, state, and/or country in which a person died.
Place of Distribution	A place associated with the distribution of a resource in a published form.
Place of Manufacture	A place associated with the printing, duplicating, casting, etc., of a resource in a published form.
Place of Origin of the Work	The country or other territorial jurisdiction from which a work originated.

Place of Production
A place associated with the inscription, fabrication, construction, etc., of a resource in an unpublished form.

Place of Publication
A place associated with the publication, release, or issuing of a resource.

Place of Residence, Etc.
A town, city, province, state, and/or country in which a person resides or has resided, or another significant place associated with the person other than place of birth, place of death, or residence (e.g., a place where a person has worked or studied).

Plan (Cartography)
see **Map**

Plaster
1. An applied material consisting of a powder prepared from calcium sulphate dihydrate (gypsum) or calcium carbonate and mixed with water and sometimes a filler to form a paste that liberates heat and then hardens.
2. A base material consisting of a powder prepared from calcium sulphate dihydrate (gypsum) or calcium carbonate and mixed with water and sometimes a filler to form a paste that liberates heat and then hardens.

Plastic
A base material consisting of synthetic or semi-synthetic organic polymers of high molecular weight that are moldable.

Plate
A leaf containing illustrative content, with or without explanatory text, that does not form part of either the preliminary or the main sequence of pages or leaves.

Plate Number for Music
A numbering designation assigned to a resource by a music publisher. The number is usually printed at the bottom of each page, and sometimes also appears on the title page.
see also **Publisher's Number for Music**

Playing Speed
The speed at which an audio carrier must be operated to produce the sound intended.

Plays
Conventional collective title for compilations of all plays by a person, family, or corporate body.

Poems
Conventional collective title for compilations of all poems by a person, family, or corporate body.

Polarity
The relationship of the colours and tones in an image to the colours and tones of the object reproduced (e.g., positive, negative).

Polonaises
Conventional collective title for a compilation of all polonaises of a composer.

Porcelain	A base material consisting of a refractory white clay (kaolin) and a feldspathic rock that is heated to form a ceramic material.
Portfolio	A unit of extent that is a container for holding loose materials (e.g., paintings, drawings, papers, unbound sections of a book, and similar materials) usually consisting of two covers joined together at the back.
Portrait	An illustrative content consisting of a representation of an individual or group of persons or animals that is intended to capture a known or supposed likeness, especially the face of the individual.
Positive	A polarity in which colours and tones used for images are the same as those seen with the human eye.
Postcard	A unit of extent of still image consisting of a card on which a message may be written or printed for mailing without an envelope.
Poster	A unit of extent of still image consisting of a notice, usually decorative or pictorial, intended to be posted to advertise, promote, or publicize an activity, cause, product, or service; also, a decorative, mass-produced print intended for hanging.
Preferred Citation	A citation for a resource in the form preferred by a creator, publisher, custodian, indexing or abstracting service, etc.
Preferred Name	The name or form of name chosen as the basis for the authorized access point representing an entity.
Preferred Name for the Corporate Body	The name or form of name chosen to identify the corporate body. It is also the basis for the authorized access point representing that body.
Preferred Name for the Family	The name or form of name chosen to identify the family. It is also the basis for the authorized access point representing that family.
Preferred Name for the Person	The name or form of name chosen to identify the person. It is also the basis for the authorized access point representing that person.
Preferred Name for the Place	The name or form of name chosen to identify a place.
Preferred Title for the Work	The title or form of title chosen to identify the work. The preferred title is also the basis for the authorized access point representing that work.
Preliminary	Status of identification for an authorized access point when the data is taken from a description without the resource described in hand.

Presentation Format	The format used in the production of a projected image (e.g., Cinerama, IMAX).
Primary Relationships	The relationships between a work, expression, manifestation, and item that are inherent in the FRBR definitions of those entities: a. the relationship between a work and an expression through which that work is realized b. the relationship between an expression of a work and a manifestation that embodies that expression c. the relationship between a manifestation and an item that exemplifies that manifestation.
Print	A unit of extent of still image consisting of a pictorial work produced by transferring an image by means of a matrix such as a plate, block, or screen, using any of various printing processes.
Printing Master	Generation designation for a microform resource used to produce subsequent generations of microforms. Also known as copying master, intermediate, dupe neg, or sub-master.
Printout	Text, images or other data from a computer file printed as output on paper, or some other printing surface, by a peripheral device (a printer).
Producer of an Unpublished Resource	A person, family, or corporate body responsible for inscribing, fabricating, constructing, etc., a resource in an unpublished form.
Producer's Name	The name of a person, family, or corporate body responsible for inscribing, fabricating, constructing, etc., a resource in an unpublished form.
Production Method	The process used to produce a resource.
Production Method for Manuscript	The process used to produce an original manuscript or a copy.
Production Method for Tactile Resource	The process used to produce a tactile resource (e.g., embossing, thermoform).
Production Statement	A statement identifying the place or places of production, producer or producers, and date or dates of production of a resource in an unpublished form.
Profession or Occupation	A person's vocation or avocation.

Profile	A unit of extent of cartographic resource that is a scale representation of the intersection of a vertical surface (which may or may not be a plane) with the surface of the ground, or of the intersection of such a vertical surface with that of a conceptual three-dimensional model representing phenomena having a continuous distribution (e.g., rainfall).
Program File	A file type for storing electronically recorded programs consisting of organized lists of instructions to be executed by computer software.
Projected	Media used to store moving or still images, designed for use with a projection device such as a motion picture film projector, slide projector, or overhead projector. Includes media designed to project both two-dimensional and three-dimensional images.
Projection Characteristic of Motion Picture Film	A technical specification relating to the projection of a motion picture film.
Projection of Cartographic Content	The method or system used to represent the surface of the Earth or of a celestial sphere on a plane.
Projection Speed	The speed at which a projected carrier must be operated to produce the moving image intended.
Prominent Member of the Family	A well-known individual who is a member of a family.
Prose Works	Conventional collective title for compilations of all prose works by a person, family, or corporate body.
Protocol	A treaty amending and supplementing another treaty.
Provisional	Status of identification for an access point when the data is insufficient to establish an authorized access point representing the entity.
Pseudonym	A name used by a person (either alone or in collaboration with others) that is not the person's real name.
Publication Statement	A statement identifying the place or places of publication, publisher or publishers, and date or dates of publication of a resource.
Publisher	A person, family, or corporate body responsible for publishing, releasing, or issuing a resource.
Publisher's Name	The name of a person, family, or corporate body responsible for publishing, releasing, or issuing a resource.

Publisher's Number for Music — A numbering designation assigned to a resource by a music publisher, appearing normally only on the title page, the cover, and/or the first page of music.
see also **Plate Number for Music**

Q-R

Quarterly — Frequency for a resource issued or updated once every three months.

Quartets — Conventional collective title for a compilation of all quartets of a composer.

Quarto — *see* **4to**

Radiograph — A unit of extent of still image consisting of a photograph produced by the passage of radiation, such as X rays, gamma rays, or neutrons, through a visually opaque object.

Recording Medium — The type of medium used to record sound on an audio carrier (e.g., magnetic, optical).

Reduced Score — *see* **Condensed Score**

Reduction Ratio — The size of a micro-image in relation to the original from which it was produced.

Reference — A direction from one access point to another.

Reference Source — Any source from which authoritative information may be obtained, including authority files, reference works, etc.

Regional Encoding — A code identifying the region of the world for which a videodisc has been encoded and preventing the disc from being played on a player sold in a different region.

Related Corporate Body — A corporate body that is associated with the person, family, or corporate body being identified (e.g., a musical group to which a person belongs, a subsidiary company). Related corporate bodies include corporate bodies that precede or succeed the corporate body being identified as the result of a change of name.

Related Expression — An expression, represented by an identifier, an authorized access point, or a description, that is related to the expression being described (e.g., a revised version, a translation).

Related Family	A family that is associated with the person, family, or corporate body being identified (e.g., a person's family, a family that owns the controlling interest in a corporate body).
Related Item	An item, represented by an identifier or a description, that is related to the item being described (e.g., an item used as the basis for a microform reproduction).
Related Manifestation	A manifestation, represented by an identifier or a description, that is related to the manifestation being described (e.g., a manifestation in a different format).
Related Person	A person who is associated with the person, family, or corporate body being identified (e.g., a collaborator, a member of a family, a founder of a corporate body). Related persons include separate identities established by an individual (either alone or in collaboration with one or more other individuals).
Related Resource	A different resource (e.g., a separately issued supplement) that is related to the resource being described.
Related Work	A work, represented by an identifier, an authorized access point, or a description, that is related to the work being described (e.g., an adaptation, commentary, supplement, sequel, part of a larger work).
Relationship Designator	A designator that indicates the nature of the relationship between entities represented by authorized access points, descriptions, and/or identifiers.
Remote-Sensing Image	A unit of extent of cartographic resource that is a pictorial product of any remote-sensing instrument that detects and measures reflected and/or emitted electromagnetic radiation from a distance and reflected underwater sound waves in the case of sonar.
Reproduction	An exact copy of the content of a resource made by mechanical or electronic means.
Resolution	The clarity or fineness of detail in a digital image, expressed by the measurement of the image in pixels, etc.
Resource	A work, expression, manifestation or item. The term includes not only an individual entity but also aggregates and components of such entities (e.g., three sheet maps, a single slide issued as part of a set of twenty, an article in an issue of a scholarly journal). It may refer to a tangible entity (e.g., an audiocassette) or an intangible entity (e.g., a website).
Restrictions on Access	Limitations placed on access to a resource.

Restrictions on Use	Limitations placed on uses such as reproduction, publication, exhibition, etc.
Right Ascension	The angular distance measured eastward on the equator from the vernal equinox to the hour circle through a celestial body, from 0 to 24 hours.
Right Ascension and Declination	A system for identifying the location of a celestial object in the sky covered by the cartographic content of a resource using the angles of right ascension and declination.
Roll	A wound length of material (paper, film, tape, etc.).
Running Title	A title, or abbreviated title, that is repeated at the head or foot of each page or leaf.

S

Sample	An illustrative content consisting of an individual unit, segment, or small quantity taken as evidence of the quality or character of the entire group or lot.
Scale	The ratio of the dimensions of an image or three-dimensional form contained or embodied in a resource to the dimensions of the thing it represents.
Scale Differs	Scale designation for a resource consisting of more than one image, map, etc., with different scales.
Scale Not Given	Scale designation for a resource when no scale can be determined.
Scale of Still Image or Three-Dimensional Form	The ratio of the dimensions of a still image or three-dimensional form contained or embodied in a resource to the dimensions of the thing it represents.
Scale Varies	Scale designation for a resource whose scale is variable across the resource, when the range of values cannot be determined.
Scope of Usage	The type or form of work associated with the name chosen as the preferred name for a person, family, or corporate body.

Score — Graphical, symbolic, or word-based musical notation representing the sounds of all the parts of an ensemble or a work for solo performer or electronic media. Do not confuse with Part.
see also Choir Book
see also Chorus Score
see also Condensed Score
see also Part (2)
see also Piano Conductor Part
see also Piano Score
see also Study Score
see also Table Book
see also Violin Conductor Part
see also Vocal Score

Script — A set of characters and/or symbols used to express the written language content of a resource.

Sculpture — A unit of extent of three-dimensional form consisting of physical representations, usually of art, in which images and forms are produced in relief, in intaglio, or in the round. The term refers particularly to art created by carving or engraving a hard material, by molding or casting a malleable material (which usually then hardens), or by assembling parts to create a three-dimensional object.

Section

1. A separately issued part of a resource, usually representing a particular subject category within the larger resource and identified by a designation that may be a topic, or an alphabetic or numeric designation, or a combination of these.
2. A unit of extent of cartographic resource that is a scale representation of a vertical surface (commonly a plane) displaying both the profile where it intersects the surface of a celestial body, or some conceptual model, and the underlying structures along the plane of intersection (e.g., a geological section).

Semiannual — Frequency for a resource issued or updated twice every year.

Semimonthly — Frequency for a resource issued or updated twice every month.

Semiweekly — Frequency for a resource issued or updated twice every week.

Serial — A resource issued in successive parts, usually having numbering, that has no predetermined conclusion (e.g., a periodical, a monographic series, a newspaper). Includes resources that exhibit characteristics of serials, such as successive issues, numbering, and frequency, but whose duration is limited (e.g., newsletters of events) and reproductions of serials.

Series	1. A group of separate resources related to one another by the fact that each resource bears, in addition to its own title proper, a collective title applying to the group as a whole. The individual resources may or may not be numbered. 2. A separately numbered sequence of volumes or issues within a series or serial (e.g., *Notes and queries*, 1st series, 2nd series, etc.).
Series Statement	A statement identifying a series to which a resource belongs and the numbering of the resource within the series. A series statement may also include information identifying one or more subseries to which the resource being described belongs.
Series Title Page	An added title page bearing the series title proper and usually, though not necessarily, other information about the series (e.g., statement of responsibility, numeric designation, data relating to publication, title of the resource within the series).
Service Copy	Generation designation for a microform resource made from another microform that is intended primarily for use. Also known as a reference or use copy.
Sexto-decimo	*see* **16mo**
Sheet	A unit of extent consisting of a single flat loose piece of paper or similar material.
Shellac	A base material consisting of lac, a resinous substance excreted by the female lac insect, that can be dissolved in ethyl alcohol to form a liquid that can be applied with a brush.
Short Score	*see* **Condensed Score**
Short Stories	Conventional collective title for compilations of all short stories by a person, family, or corporate body.
Short Title of a Legal Work	A title of a legal work that is given either in the text of the work or in legal literature and that succinctly names the work and often reflects how it is popularly known.
Sign Language	In the context of accessibility content, a sign language version of the dialogue of the resource that is displayed on the screen.
Silent	Sound content for a motion picture or video recording that does not contain a sound track.

Silver Halide	An emulsion on microfilm and microfiche consisting of a light-sensitive compound of silver and a halogen (chlorine, bromine, iodine or fluorine) suspended in a colloidal medium, usually gelatin.
Single Unit	A resource that is issued either as a single physical unit (e.g., as a single-volume monograph) or, in the case of an intangible resource, as a single logical unit (e.g., as a PDF file mounted on the web).
Sixteenmo	*see* **16mo**
Sixty-fourmo	*see* **64mo**
Skin	A base material consisting of the integument of animals, such as sheep, goats, or calves, separated from the body and variously processed to remove hair, dry, tan, or otherwise dress. *see also* **Leather** *see also* **Parchment**
Slide	A small sheet of transparent material (usually in a protective mount) bearing an image designed for use with a slide projector or viewer. For slides designed to be used with a microscope, *see* **Microscope Slide**
Solid Dot	A production method for tactile resources in which solid plastic dots are heat sealed onto the surface of thin but strong paper.
Solmization	The designation of pitches by means of conventional syllables rather than letter names.
Sonatas	Conventional collective title for a compilation of all sonatas of a composer.
Songs	Conventional collective title for a compilation of all songs of a composer.
Sound	Sound content for a resource that contains sound, other than one that consists primarily of recorded sound.
Sound Characteristic	A technical specification relating to the encoding of sound in a resource.
Sound Content	The presence of sound in a resource other than one that consists primarily of recorded sound.
Sound Disc	*see* **Audio Disc**
Sound Recording	*see* **Audio Recording**

Sounds	Content other than language or music, expressed in an audible form. Includes natural sounds, artificially produced sounds, etc.
Sound-Track Reel	An open reel holding a length of film on which sound is recorded.
Source Consulted	A resource used in determining the name, title, or other identifying attributes of an entity, or in determining the relationship between entities.
Source of Information	The source of data from which a description (or portion thereof) is prepared.
Special Playback Characteristic	An equalization system, noise reduction system, etc., used in making an audio recording.
Specimen	A unit of extent of three-dimensional form consisting of an individual unit or sample chosen to represent a larger population or aggregation.
Speeches	Conventional collective title for compilations of all speeches by a person, family, or corporate body.
Spoken Word	Content expressed through language in an audible form. Includes recorded readings, recitations, speeches, interviews, oral histories, etc., computer-generated speech, etc.
Staff Notation	A system of musical notation in wide use for Western art music, conveying pitch and duration using a staff of multiple parallel lines (in 15th- to 21st-century music, usually five lines) often in combination with other staves.
Stamper	Generation designation for an audio recording comprising a hard metal negative copy of a disc master that can be mounted within a press and used to impress the groove pattern in a production run of discs.
Standard	Groove characteristic for an analog cylinder with a groove pitch of 40 turns per cm (100 turns per inch).
Statement of Responsibility	A statement relating to the identification and/or function of any persons, families, or corporate bodies responsible for the creation of, or contributing to the realization of, the intellectual or artistic content of a resource.
Statement of Responsibility Relating to a Named Revision of an Edition	A statement relating to the identification of any persons, families, or corporate bodies responsible for a named revision of an edition.

Statement of Responsibility Relating to Series	A statement relating to the identification of any persons, families, or corporate bodies responsible for a series.
Statement of Responsibility Relating to Subseries	A statement relating to the identification of any persons, families, or corporate bodies responsible for a subseries.
Statement of Responsibility Relating to the Edition	A statement relating to the identification of any persons, families, or corporate bodies responsible for the edition being described but not to all editions.
Statement of Responsibility Relating to Title Proper	A statement associated with the title proper of a resource that relates to the identification and/or function of any persons, families, or corporate bodies responsible for the creation of, or contributing to the realization of, the intellectual or artistic content of the resource.
Status of Identification	An indication of the level of authentication of the data identifying an entity.
Stepanov Dance Notation	A form of notated movement for dance using musical notation to represent movements by single parts of the body. It is recorded on a horizontal nine-line staff that represents the body.
Stereograph Card	A card bearing stereographic images.
Stereograph Disc	A disc with openings around the perimeter holding pairs of still images designed for use with a stereograph viewer.
Stereograph Reel	*see* **Stereograph Disc**
Stereographic	Media used to store pairs of still images, designed for use with a device such as a stereoscope or stereograph viewer to give the effect of three dimensions.
Still Image	Content expressed through line, shape, shading, etc., intended to be perceived visually in two dimensions. Includes drawings, paintings, diagrams, photographic images (stills), etc. For cartographic content intended to be perceived as a two-dimensional image, *see also* **Cartographic image** For images intended to be perceived through touch, *see also* **Tactile image**
Stone	A base material consisting of rock in its naturally occurring shape or that has been cut, shaped, crushed, or otherwise formed.
Storage Medium	A physical material or substance on which information or artistic content is stored. *see also* **Carrier**

String Quartet Music	Conventional collective title for a compilation of all string quartet music of a composer.
Strings of Coordinate Pairs	A system for identifying the precise area covered by the cartographic content of a resource using coordinates for each vertex of a polygon.
Structured Description	A full or partial description of a resource using the same structure (i.e., the same order of elements) that is used for the resource being described.
Study Score	A score issued in a musical image of reduced size, not primarily intended for use in performance. A descriptive phrase such as "Study score", "Miniature score", "Taschenpartitur", "Partition de poche", etc., usually appears on the resource.
Subordinate Body	A corporate body that forms an integral part of a larger body in relation to which it holds an inferior hierarchical rank.
Subseries	A series within a series (i.e., a series that always appears in conjunction with another, usually more comprehensive, series of which it forms a section). Its title may or may not be dependent on the title of the main series.
Subunit	A physical or logical subdivision of a unit (e.g., a page of a volume, a frame of a microfiche, a record in a digital file).
Summarization of the Content	An abstract, summary, synopsis, etc., of the content of a resource.
Super Large Print	*see* **Giant Print**
Supplementary Content	Content (e.g., an index, a bibliography, an appendix) designed to supplement the primary content of a resource.
Supplied Title	*see* **Devised Title**
Surname	Any name used as a family name (other than those used as family names by Romans of classical times).
Swell Paper	A production method for tactile resources in which an image is printed on a special type of paper with embedded microcapsules of alcohol which burst when exposed to heat to make the surface of the paper swell up. Used for tactile graphics and for embossing text in Moon characters (linear Moon). Also known as: Minolta paper (brand name), microcapsule paper, hot spot.
Synthetic	A base material created by processing man-made materials, usually as a substitute for a natural material.

System of Organization	A system of arranging materials in an archival resource or a collection.

T-U

Tablature	Any notational system from 1300 or later that uses letters, numerals, or other signs as an alternative to conventional staff notation.
Table Book	A music book made to be placed on a table and displayed in such a way that the performers can read their parts while seated or standing across or around the table. Each part is notated separately, usually in a configuration that presents, when the book is open, different parts in inverted and/or perpendicular positions.
Tactile Graphic	A form of tactile notation using a raised version of a print graphic.
Tactile Image	Content expressed through line, shape, and/or other forms, intended to be perceived through touch as a still image in two dimensions.
Tactile Musical Notation	A form of tactile notation for music.
Tactile Notated Movement	Content expressed through a form of notation for movement intended to be perceived through touch.
Tactile Notated Music	Content expressed through a form of musical notation intended to be perceived through touch. Includes braille music and other tactile forms of musical notation.
Tactile Text	Content expressed through a form of notation for language intended to be perceived through touch. Includes braille text and other tactile forms of language notation.
Tactile Three-Dimensional Form	Content expressed through a form or forms intended to be perceived through touch as a three-dimensional form or forms.
Tape Configuration	The number of tracks on an audiotape.
Tape Duplication Master	Generation designation for an audio recording comprising a tape copy (usually a first generation copy of the master) used for creating multiple copies of the content (e.g., for compact cassettes).
Technical Drawing	A unit of extent of still image consisting of a cross section, detail, diagram, elevation, perspective, plan, working plan, etc., made for use in an engineering or other technical context.

Tempera	Applied material consisting of coloured pigment mixed with a water-soluble binder medium, usually a glutinous material such as egg yolk or some other size, to form a permanent fast-drying painting medium.
Terms of Availability	The conditions under which the publisher, distributor, etc., will normally supply a resource or the price of a resource.
Test Pressing	Generation designation for an audio recording comprising one of a short run of pressings used to check for any flaws before running a full pressing. The term is ambiguous because it is also used to refer to initial pressing sent out to reviewers, DJs, etc.
Text	1. Content expressed through a form of notation for language intended to be perceived visually. Includes all forms of language notation other than those intended to be perceived through touch. *see also* **Tactile Text** 2. The words of a musical work other than an opera or other musical stage work, oratorio, or popular song. For just the dialogue from a musical, *see* **Libretto** For the words of just the songs from a musical, *see* **Lyrics**
Text File	A file type for storing electronically recorded textual content.
Textile	A base material produced by weaving, felting, knotting, twining, or otherwise processing natural or synthetic fibers so that they cohere. Excludes fibreboard, paper, papier-mâché, and papyrus.
Thematic Index	A list of a composer's works, usually arranged in chronological order or by categories, with the theme given for each composition or for each section of large compositions.
Thermoform	A production method for tactile resources in which a collage master is covered with a sheet of plastic, which is heated and vacuumed to generate a copy of a model or diagram. Also known as: vacuum form.
Thirty-twomo	*see* **32mo**
Three-Dimensional Form	Content expressed through a form or forms intended to be perceived visually in three dimensions. Includes sculptures, models, naturally occurring objects and specimens, holograms, etc. For cartographic content intended to be perceived as a three-dimensional form, *see also* **Cartographic Three-Dimensional Form** For three-dimensional forms intended to be perceived through touch, *see also* **Tactile Three-Dimensional Form**

Three-Dimensional Moving Image	Content expressed through images intended to be perceived as moving, in three dimensions. Includes 3-D motion pictures (using live action and/or animation), 3-D video games, etc. Three-dimensional moving images may or may not be accompanied by sound.
Three Times a Month	Frequency for a resource issued or updated three times every month.
Three Times a Week	Frequency for a resource issued or updated three times every week.
Three Times a Year	Frequency for a resource issued or updated three times every year.
Title	A word, character, or group of words and/or characters that names a resource or a work contained in it. *see also* **Abbreviated Title** *see also* **Alternative Title** *see also* **Caption Title** *see also* **Devised Title** *see also* **Parallel Title Proper** *see also* **Running Title** *see also* **Title Proper**
Title Frame	One or more frames, usually found at the beginning of a resource produced on film (motion picture, filmstrip, etc.) containing identifying textual information which is not part of the subject content of the resource and which is used as the source of information in creating the description.
Title of the Person	A word or phrase indicative of royalty, nobility, or ecclesiastical rank or office, a term of address for a person of religious vocation, or another term indicative of rank, honour, or office.
Title of the Work	A word, character, or group of words and/or characters by which a work is known.
Title Page	A page at the beginning of a resource bearing the title proper and usually, though not necessarily, the statement of responsibility and the data relating to publication. If this information is given on facing pages or pages on successive leaves, with or without repetition, treat these pages collectively as the title page.
Title Proper	The chief name of a resource (i.e., the title normally used when citing the resource).
Title Proper of Series	The chief name of a series (i.e., the title normally used when citing the series)
Title Proper of Subseries	The chief name of a subseries (i.e., the title normally used when citing the subseries)

Title Screen	A display of data about a digital resource that includes the title proper and usually, though not necessarily, the statement of responsibility and the data relating to publication.
Tonic Sol-Fa	A system of musical notation that replaces staff notation with sol-fa syllables or their initials.
Toy	A unit of exit of three-dimensional form consisting of an object designed for education, entertainment, or stimulation through play. *see also* **Game** *see also* **Model**
Track Configuration	The configuration of the audio track on a sound-track film (e.g., centre track).
Transcript	1. A copy of an original, usually made by hand or typewritten (e.g., a legal document, an official record). 2. The written record of words spoken in a speech, interview, broadcast or audio recording.
Transparency	*see* **Overhead Transparency**
Treaty	An international agreement concluded between states or international organizations in written form and governed by international law. May be designated by various other terms such as agreement, concordat, convention, charter, declaration, exchange of notes, memorandum of understanding, modus vivendi, or protocol.
Triennial	Frequency for a resource issued or updated once every three years.
Trigesimo-secundo	*see* **32mo**
Twelvemo	*see* **12mo**
Twenty-fourmo	*see* **24mo**
Two-Dimensional Moving Image	Content expressed through images intended to be perceived as moving, in two dimensions. Includes motion pictures (using live action and/or animation), film and video recordings of performances, events, etc., video games, etc., other than those intended to be perceived in three dimensions. *see also* **Three-Dimensional Moving Image** Moving images may or may not be accompanied by sound. For cartographic content intended to be perceived as a two-dimensional moving image, *see also* **Cartographic Moving Image**

Type of Composition	A form, a genre, or a generic term used frequently by different composers (e.g., capriccio, concerto, intermezzo, Magnificat, mass, movement, muziek, nocturne, requiem, Stück, symphony, suite, Te Deum, trio sonata).
Type of Family	A categorization or generic descriptor for the type of family.
Type of Recording	The method used to encode audio content for playback (e.g., analog or digital).
Typescript	A creator's original typewritten copy of a work or a typewritten copy of the original commissioned by a creator or publisher, as opposed to a manuscript written by hand.
Ultra High Reduction	A reduction ratio over 90× for a microform resource.
Undifferentiated Name Indicator	A categorization indicating that the core elements recorded are insufficient to differentiate between two or more persons with the same name.
Uniform Resource Locator	The address of a remote access resource.
Unit	A physical or logical constituent of a resource (e.g., a volume, audiocassette, film reel, a map, a digital file).
Unmediated	Media used to store content designed to be perceived directly through one or more of the human senses without the aid of an intermediating device. Includes media containing visual and/or tactile content produced using processes such as printing, engraving, lithography, etc., embossing, texturing, etc., or by means of handwriting, drawing, painting, etc. Also includes media used to convey three-dimensional forms such as sculptures, models, etc.
Unnumbered Column	A unit of extent consisting of a column having no sequential designation. *see* **Column**
Unnumbered Leaf	A unit of extent consisting of a leaf having no sequential designation. *see* **Leaf**
Unnumbered Page	A unit of extent consisting of a page having no sequential designation. *see* **Page**
Unstructured Description	A full or partial description of a resource written as a sentence or paragraph.

Updating Loose-Leaf	An integrating resource that consists of one or more base volumes updated by separate pages that are inserted, removed, and/or substituted.

V-Z

Vacuum Form	*see* **Thermoform**
Variant Access Point	An alternative to the authorized access point representing an entity.
Variant Name	A name or form of name by which a person, family, or corporate body is known that differs from the name or form of name chosen as the preferred name for that person, family, or corporate body.
Variant Name for the Corporate Body	A name or form of name by which a corporate body is known that differs from the name or form of name chosen as the preferred name.
Variant Name for the Family	A name or form of name by which a family is known that differs from the name or form of name chosen as the preferred name.
Variant Name for the Person	A name or form of name by which a person is known that differs from the name or form of name chosen as the preferred name.
Variant Name for the Place	A name or form of name by which a place is known that differs from the name or form of name chosen as the preferred name.
Variant Title	A title associated with a resource that differs from a title recorded as the title proper, a parallel title proper, other title information, parallel other title information, earlier title proper, later title proper, key title, or abbreviated title.
Variant Title for the Work	A title or form of title by which a work is known that differs from the title or form of title chosen as the preferred title for the work.
Vellum	A base material consisting of fine-quality calf or lamb parchment. *see also* **Parchment**
Version	*see* **Other Distinguishing Characteristic of the Expression**
Vertical Scale of Cartographic Content	The scale of elevation or vertical dimension of the cartographic content of a resource.
Very High Reduction	A reduction ratio between 61× and 90× for a microform resource.

Vesicular	An emulsion on microfilm and microfiche consisting of one or more light-sensitive layers of diazonium salts in a polyester thermoplastic base that decompose on exposure to produce nitrogen bubbles (vesicles) that form the latent image, which becomes visible and fixed when heated and allowed to cool. Vesicular images are commonly blue or beige in color. They do not appear to have much contrast (very high density) until projected in a microform reader.
Video	Media used to store moving or still images, designed for use with a playback device such as a videocassette player or DVD player. Includes media used to store digitally encoded as well as analog images.
Video Cartridge	A cartridge containing a video tape.
Video Characteristic	A technical specification relating to the encoding of video images in a resource.
Video Format	A standard, etc., used to encode the analog video content of a resource.
Video Tape	A length of magnetic tape on which are recorded electrical signals that can be converted to images using video playback equipment.
Videocassette	A cassette containing a video tape.
Videodisc	A disc on which video signals, with or without sound, are recorded.
Videotape Reel	An open reel holding a video tape for use with reel-to-reel video equipment.
View	A unit of extent of cartographic resource that is a perspective representation of the landscape in which detail is shown as if projected on an oblique plane (e.g., a bird's-eye view, panorama, panoramic drawing, worm's-eye view).
Vigesimo-quarto	*see* **24mo**
Vinyl	A base material consisting of a polymer or copolymer derived from a vinyl (ethenyl) group, typically vinyl chloride.
Violin Conductor Part	A performance part for a violin performer in an ensemble, with cues for the other instruments that enable the performer of that part also to conduct.
Violin, Piano Music	Conventional collective title for a compilation of all violin and piano music of a composer.

Vocabulary Encoding Scheme	A named structured list of representations of controlled values for elements (e.g., internal RDA lists of terms or their corresponding value vocabularies with assigned URIs in the RDA Registry, ISO code lists, standard terminologies).
Vocal Music	Conventional collective title for a compilation of all vocal music of a composer, including compilations of various types of works originally for one solo voice or one combination of solo voices, with or without accompaniment.
Vocal Score	A score showing all vocal parts, with the instrumental accompaniment either arranged for keyboard(s) or other chordal instrument(s) or omitted. *see also* Chorus Score
Volume	One or more sheets bound or fastened together to form a single unit.
Volume (Loose-Leaf)	A unit of extent consisting of one or more sheets bound or fastened together to form a single unit in such a way that individual sheets can be easily removed or replaced, and new sheets added.
Wall Chart	A unit of extent of still image consisting of a tabular or graphic representation of data appropriate for display on a wall.
Watercolor	*see* Watercolour
Watercolour	Applied material consisting of coloured pigment suspended in water to form a transparent painting medium.
Wax	A base material consisting of a chemical compound from an animal, plant, mineral, or synthetic source that is malleable near ambient temperatures, slightly greasy to the touch, with a low melting point, and usually translucent, water-repellant, and soluble in organic solvents.
Weekly	Frequency for a resource issued or updated once every week.
White Print	A production method consisting of copies made by light-sensitive processes, often the diazo process, usually of line drawings, in which black or coloured lines appear on a white background.
Wide Screen	Aspect ratio for a moving image resource of 1.5:1 or greater.
Wood	A base material consisting of the principal tissue of trees and similar plants.

Work	A distinct intellectual or artistic creation (i.e., the intellectual or artistic content).
Work Expressed	The work realized through an expression.
Work Manifested	A work embodied in a manifestation.
Year Degree Granted	The calendar year in which a granting institution or faculty conferred an academic degree on a candidate.

INDEX

This index covers the instructions and appendices for *Resource Description and Access*. The locators for the instructions are the rule numbers. Because the locators are arranged hierarchically, index entry terms with shorter (higher) locators can be assumed to include all the instructions under it. For example, "Extent of Text, **3.4.5**" covers the range of rules from **3.4.5.1–3.4.5.22**. Some of the instructions with their examples may run for several pages, e.g., **6.27.1.3** (Collaborative Works). Remember to read the entire instruction before applying it.

Appendices **D** (Record Syntaxes for Descriptive Data) and **E** (Record Syntaxes for Access Point Control) are not indexed in detail. In general, examples are not indexed, but there are see or see also references for instructions **19.2.1.3** (creators) and **20.2.1.3** (contributors) from the classes of persons. For example:

Administrative regulations
 compilers
 See examples under **20.2.1.3** [Recording Contributors]

Users who are comfortable with RDA terminology can use the index to refresh their memory on a specific instruction. Terms from AACR2 *(Anglo-American Cataloguing Rules)* are also included in the index with appropriate *see* references. For example:

General material designation
 See **Carrier type**; **Content type**; **Media type**

Words and phrases enclosed in square brackets are explanatory glosses which clarify or distinguish index terms with different meanings. For example:

Subtitles [moving images]
 accessibility content, **7.14**
 in language different from spoken content, **7.12**
Subtitles [texts]
 See **Other title information**

Words enclosed in parentheses—(work), (expression), (manifestation), and (item)—are part of the element name for relationship designators.

The relationship designators for related works in appendix **J** are indexed with their reciprocal relationships, for example, based on (work)/derivative work.

The index is alphabetized word-by-word, with numerals preceding letters. Numbers, symbols, and punctuation marks at the beginning of index entries are filed as if spelled out. They are also filed at the beginning of the alphabet, before the A's. Hyphens and other punctuation, as well as prepositions preceding subentries, are ignored in filing. Thus "reel-to-reel" is filed as if spelled "reeltoreel."

Abbreviations used in the index:

App.	Appendix
n	Footnote
[rd]	relationship designator
WEMI	Work, expression, manifestation, or item
PFC	Person, Family, or Corporate body

A

B

C

D

M

N

O

P

Q

R

S

U

V

W

Y

Z

CPSIA information can be obtained at www.ICGtesting.com
Printed in the USA
LVOW09s1321280914
406158LV00003BA/3/P

9 780838 912935